Dewey Decimal Classification and Relative Index

Dewey Decimal Classification and Relative Index

Devised by Melvil Dewey

EDITION 21

Edited by
Joan S. Mitchell, Editor
Julianne Beall, Assistant Editor
Winton E. Matthews, Jr., Assistant Editor
Gregory R. New, Assistant Editor

VOLUME 4

Relative Index ■ Manual

FOREST PRESS
A Division of
OCLC Online Computer Library Center, Inc.
ALBANY, NEW YORK
1996

Library of Congress Cataloging-in-Publication Data
Dewey, Melvil, 1851-1931.
Dewey decimal classification and relative index / devised by Melvil Dewey. -- Ed. 21 / edited by Joan S. Mitchell, Julianne Beall, Winton E. Matthews, Jr., Gregory R. New.
p. cm.
Contents: v. 1. Introduction. Tables --v. 2-3. Schedules --v. 4. Relative index. Manual.
ISBN 0-910608-50-4 (set : alk. paper)
1. Classification, Dewey decimal. I. Mitchell, Joan S. II. Beall, Julianne, 1946- . III. Matthews, Winton, E. IV. New, Gregory R. V. Forest Press. VI. Title.
Z696.D52 1996 96-7393
025.4'31--dc20 CIP

The paper used in this publication meets the requirements of ANSI/NISO Z39.48-1992 (Permanence of Paper).

ISBN: (set) 0-910608-50-4; v. 1 0-910608-51-2; v. 2 0-910608-52-0;
v. 3 0-910608-53-9; v. 4 0-910608-54-7

Recycled paper

Contents

Volume 1

Publisher's Foreword xi
Preface by the Decimal Classification Editorial Policy Committee xiii
Acknowledgments xvii
New Features in Edition 21 xix
Introduction to the Dewey Decimal Classification xxxi
  About the Introduction xxxi
  Classification: What It Is and What It Does xxxi
  History and Current Use of the Dewey Decimal Classification xxxi
  Overview of the Dewey Decimal Classification xxxii
    Conceptual Framework xxxii
    Notation xxxiii
    Principle of Hierarchy xxxiii
  Classifying with the DDC xxxiv
    Determining the Subject of a Work xxxv
    Determining the Discipline of a Work xxxv
    More Than One Subject in the Same Discipline xxxvi
    More Than One Discipline xxxvii
    Table of Last Resort xxxviii
  How DDC 21 Is Arranged xxxviii
  Key Features of the Schedules and Tables xxxix
    Summaries xxxix
    Entries xxxix
    Notes xli
  Number Building xlv
  Citation and Preference Order xlix
    Citation Order xlix
    Preference Order xlix
  The Manual l
    Arrangement and Format of the Manual li
  The Relative Index li
    Arrangement and Format of the Relative Index lii
    Interdisciplinary Numbers liii
    Terms Included in the Relative Index liii
    Terms Not Included in the Relative Index liv

Options liv
Close and Broad Classification lv
Selected Bibliography lvi
Glossary lvii
Index to the Introduction and Glossary lxvii
Publishing History of the Dewey Decimal Classification lxix
Tables 1
Use of the Tables 2
Table 1. Standard Subdivisions 3
Table 2. Geographic Areas, Historical Periods, Persons 34
Table 3. Subdivisions for the Arts, for Individual Literatures, for Specific Literary Forms 405
Table 3-A. Subdivisions for Works by or about Individual Authors 406
Table 3-B. Subdivisions for Works by or about More than One Author 411
Table 3-C. Notation to Be Added Where Instructed in Table 3-B, 700.4, 791.4, 808-809 428
Table 4. Subdivisions of Individual Languages and Language Families 437
Table 5. Racial, Ethnic, National Groups 444
Table 6. Languages 464
Table 7. Groups of Persons 490
Relocations and Reductions 517
Relocations 517
Reductions 526
Comparative Tables 530
Eastern Europe Russia 530
Public administration 532
Education 540
Life sciences 545
General topics in biology 546
Microorganisms, fungi, algae 556
Plants 557
Animals 563
Paleontology 570
Equivalence Tables 573
Eastern Europe Russia 573
Public administration 576
Education 586

Paleontology 597
Life sciences 601
Plants 606
Animals 616
Reused Numbers 625

Volume 2

Summaries ix
Schedules 1
Use of the Schedules 2
000 Generalities 3
100 Philosophy, paranormal phenomena, psychology 91
200 Religion 153
300 Social sciences 314
400 Language 861
500 Natural sciences and mathematics 899

Volume 3

Schedules 1
Use of the Schedules 2
600 Technology (Applied sciences) 3
700 The arts Fine and decorative arts 511
800 Literature (Belles-lettres) and rhetoric 737
900 Geography, history, and auxiliary disciplines 801

Volume 4

Relative Index 1
Use of the Relative Index 2
Abbreviations Used in the Index 3
A-Z 5
Manual 901
Use of the Manual 902
Notes on Table Numbers 903
Notes on Schedule Numbers 959
Appendix: Policies and Procedures of the Library of Congress Decimal Classification Division 1205

Relative Index

Use of the Relative Index

Full instructions on the use of the Relative Index are found in section 11 of the Introduction to the Dewey Decimal Classification in volume 1.

Alphabetizing is word by word. A hyphenated word is filed as two words. Initialisms and acronyms are entered without punctuation and are filed as if spelled as one word. Entries beginning with the same word or phrase are arranged as follows:

Term
Term. Subheading
Term (Parenthetical qualifier)
Term, inverted term qualifier
Term as part of phrase

The first class number displayed in an index entry (the unindented term) is the number for interdisciplinary works. If the term also appears in the tables, the table numbers are listed next, followed by subentries arranged in alphabetical order. See-also references or see-Manual references come at the end of the alphabet of subentries or under the subentry to which the reference applies. See-Manual references follow see-also references under the same term.

Digits are printed in groups of three for ease in reading and copying. The spaces are not part of the numbers, and the groups are not related to the segmentation shown in DDC numbers on Library of Congress cataloging records.

Abbreviations Used in the Index

T1	Table 1	Standard Subdivisions
T2	Table 2	Geographic Areas, Historical Periods, Persons
T3	Table 3	Subdivisions for the Arts, for Individual Literatures, for Specific Literary Forms
T3A	Table 3-A	Subdivisions for Works by or about Individual Authors
T3B	Table 3-B	Subdivisions for Works by or about More than One Author
T3C	Table 3-C	Notation to Be Added Where Instructed in Table 3-B, 700.4, 791.4, 808-809
T4	Table 4	Subdivisions of Individual Languages and Language Families
T5	Table 5	Racial, Ethnic, National Groups
T6	Table 6	Languages
T7	Table 7	Groups of Persons

A.C.T.	Australian Capital Territory
Ala.	Alabama
Alta.	Alberta
Ariz.	Arizona
Ark.	Arkansas
B.C.	Before Christ
	British Columbia
Calif.	California
Colo.	Colorado
Conn.	Connecticut
D.C.	District of Columbia
Del.	Delaware
Dept.	Department
Fla.	Florida
Ga.	Georgia
Ill.	Illinois
Inc.	Incorporated
Ind.	Indiana
Kan.	Kansas
Ky.	Kentucky
La.	Louisiana
Man.	Manitoba
Mass.	Massachusetts
Md.	Maryland
Me.	Maine
Mich.	Michigan
Minn.	Minnesota
Miss.	Mississippi
Mo.	Missouri
Mont.	Montana
N.B.	New Brunswick
N.C.	North Carolina
N.D.	North Dakota
N.H.	New Hampshire
N.J.	New Jersey
N.M.	New Mexico
N.S.	Nova Scotia
N.S.W.	New South Wales
N.T.	Northern Territory
N.W.T.	Northwest Territories
N.Y.	New York
N.Z.	New Zealand
Neb.	Nebraska
Nev.	Nevada
Okla.	Oklahoma
Ont.	Ontario
Or.	Oregon
P.E.I.	Prince Edward Island
P.R.	Puerto Rico
Pa.	Pennsylvania
Qld.	Queensland
R.I.	Rhode Island
S. Aust.	South Australia
S.C.	South Carolina
S.D.	South Dakota
Sask.	Saskatchewan
Tas.	Tasmania
Tenn.	Tennessee
Tex.	Texas
U.S.	United States of America
V.I.	Virgin Islands
Va.	Virginia
Vic.	Victoria
Vt.	Vermont
W.A.	Western Australia
W. Va.	West Virginia
Wash.	Washington
Wis.	Wisconsin
Wyo.	Wyoming
Yukon	Yukon Territory

100 Mile House (B.C.) T2—711 75

A

A level examination 378.166 2
Aachen (Germany) T2—435 511
A'ālī al-Nīl (Sudan) T2—629 3
Aardvark 599.31
Aardwolf 599.743
Aargau (Switzerland) T2—494 56
Aarhus amt (Denmark) T2—489 5
Abaca
  botany 584.39
  fiber crop 633.571
Abacus 513.028 4
Abalones 641.394
  cooking 641.694
  fishing and culture 639.483 2
  food 641.394
  zoology 594.32
Abandoned children 305.906 945
  T1—086 945
  social group 305.906 945
  social services 362.73
Abaza language 499.962
  T6—999 62
Abazin language 499.962
  T6—999 62
Abbeville County (S.C.) T2—757 35
Abbeys
  architecture 726.7
  church history 271
  religious significance of buildings 246.97
Abbotsford (B.C.) T2—711 37
Abbott, J. J. C. (John Jospeh Caldwell), Sir
  Canadian history 971.055
Abbreviated longhand 653.2
Abbreviation dictionaries 413.1
  specific languages T4—31
  specific subject T1—014 8
Abbreviations 411
  specific languages T4—11
  specific subject T1—014 8
Abdias (Biblical book) 224.91
Abdomen 573.997
  biology 573.997
  human anatomy 611.95
  human physiology 612.95
  regional medicine 617.55
  surgery 617.550 59
Abdominal hernia
  regional medicine 617.559
  surgery 617.559 059
Abdominal muscles
  human anatomy 611.736
  see also Musculoskeletal system
Abdominal pregnancy
  obstetrics 618.31
Abduction 364.154
  law 345.025 4
Abdul Rahman, Tunku, Putra Al-Haj
  Malaysian history 959.505 1
Abdul Razak bin Dato' Hussein, Tun Haji
  Malaysian history 959.505 2
Abel (Biblical person)
  Bible stories 222.110 950 5
Abel Tasman National Park (N.Z.) T2—937 7
Abelian categories 512.55
Abelian groups 512.2
Aberconwy (Wales : Borough) T2—429 27
Aberdeen (Scotland) T2—412 35
Aberdeen (South Africa : District) T2—687 15
Aberdeen Angus cattle 636.223
Aberdeenshire (Scotland) T2—412 32
Aberration
  astronomy 522.9
Abhidhammapiṭaka 294.382 4
Abhidharmapiṭaka 294.382 4
Abia State (Nigeria) T2—669 45
Abidjan (Ivory Coast) T2—666 8
Ability grouping in education 371.254
Ability testing 153.93
  education 371.262
  personnel selection 658.311 25
Abitibi (Quebec : Regional County Municipality) T2—714 13
Abitibi, Lake (Ont. and Quebec) T2—713 142
Abitibi-Ouest (Quebec : Regional County Municipality) T2—714 13
Abitibi-Témiscamingue (Quebec : Administrative region) T2—714 13
Abitibi-Témiscamingue Region (Quebec) T2—714 13
Abitibi Territory (Quebec) T2—714 115
Abkhaz (Georgia) T2—475 8

Abkhaz language 499.962 3
T6—999 623
Abkhaz literature 899.962 3
Abkhaziîa (Georgia) T2—475 8
Abkhazo-Adyghian languages 499.962
T6—999 62
Ablation of snow 551.578 464
Ablutions
  Islam 297.38
ABM (Missiles) 358.174 82
  engineering 623.451 94
  military equipment 358.174 82
Abnaki Indians T5—973
Abnormal psychology 616.89
  see also Mental illness
Abnormalities
  human teratology 616.043
  physical anthropology 599.949
Abodah Zarah 296.123 4
  Babylonian Talmud 296.125 4
  Mishnah 296.123 4
  Palestinian Talmud 296.124 4
Abolition of slavery 326.8
  political science 326.8
  sociology 306.362
  United States history 973.711 4
Abolitionists (Antislavery activists) 326.809 2
Abominable snowman 001.944
Aborigines 306.08
  legal status 346.013
    constitutional law 342.087 2
    private law 346.013
  social group 306.08
Abortifacients
  pharmacodynamics 615.766
Abortion 363.46
  criminology 364.185
    criminal law 345.028 5
  demographic effect 304.667
  ethics 179.76
    religion 291.569 76
      Buddhism 294.356 976
      Christianity 241.697 6
      Hinduism 294.548 697 6
      Islam 297.569 76
      Judaism 296.369 76
  law 342.084
    legal right of fetuses 342.085
    legal right of women 342.087 8
    medical law 344.041 92
  pharmacodynamics 615.766
  social problem 363.46
    law 344.054 6
Abortion (continued)
  social theology 291.178 366 67
    Christianity 261.836 667
    Judaism 296.38
  surgery 618.88
Aboth 296.123 47
Abra (Philippines) T2—599 1
Abrading tools 621.92
Abraham (Patriarch)
  Bible 222.110 92
  Islam 297.246 3
Abrasions
  medicine 617.13
Abrasives
  mineral resources 553.65
Abreaction
  psychology 154.2
Abruzzi (Italy) T2—457 1
Absaroka Range (Mont. and Wyo.) T2—787 4
Absentee ownership
  land economics 333.4
Absentee voting 324.65
  law 342.075
Absenteeism 331.259 8
  labor economics 331.259 8
  personnel management 658.314
    public administration 352.66
  sociology 306.361
Absinthe 641.255
  commercial processing 663.55
Absolute (Philosophy) 111.6
Absolute monarchy 321.6
Absolute rights 323.01
Absolute temperature 536.5
Absolution (Christian rite) 234.166
  public worship 265.64
  theology 234.166
Absorbency
  skin 573.5
    human physiology 612.791
    see also Skin
Absorber oil 665.538 4
Absorption 541.33
  chemical engineering 660.284 23
  chemistry 541.33
  gaseous-state physics 530.435
  nutrition
    human physiology 612.38
    see also Digestive system
Absorption of heat 536.3
Absorption of light 535.326
  meteorology 551.566

Absorption of sound
  physics 534.208
Abstinence 178
  ethics 178
  religious practice 291.447
    Buddhism 294.344 47
    Christianity 248.47
    Hinduism 294.544 7
Abstract algebra 512.02
Abstract data types 005.73
Abstract expressionism 709.040 52
  painting 759.065 2
  sculpture 735.230 452
Abstract harmonic analysis 515.785
Abstract spaces 516.1
Abstract thought 153.24
  philosophy 128.3
  psychology 153.24
Abstracting techniques
  information science 025.402 8
  rhetoric 808.062
Abstractionism 709.040 52
  painting 759.065 2
  sculpture 735.230 452
Abstracts of title 346.043 8
Abū Dā'ūd Sulaymān ibn al-Ash'ath al-Sijistānī
  Hadith 297.124 2
Abu Dhabi (United Arab Emirates : Emirate) T2—535 7
Abū Ẓaby (United Arab Emirates : Emirate) T2—535 7
Abuja (Federal Capital Territory, Nigeria) T2—669 68
Abuse of power
  civil rights issue 323.49
  law 345.023 2
  public administration 353.46
Abused children 305.906 945
  T1—086 945
  pediatrics 618.928 582 23
  social group 305.906 945
  social theology 291.178 327 1
    Christianity 261.832 71
  social welfare 362.76
  see also Child abuse
Abutments 721.3
  architecture 721.3
  construction 690.13
  structural engineering 624.16
Abydos (Egypt : Extinct city) T2—32
Abyssal zone
  biology 578.779
Abyssal zone (continued)
  ecology 577.79
Abyssinia T2—63
Abyssinian cat 636.826
Abyssinians T5—928
Acacias 583.748
  forestry 634.973 748
  ornamental arboriculture 635.977 374 8
Academic costume 378.28
Academic degrees 378.2
Academic dissertations 378.242
Academic freedom 371.104
  higher education 378.121
  law 344.078
Academic high schools 373.241
  see also Secondary education
Academic libraries 027.7
  administration 025.197 7
  collection development 025.218 77
  use studies 025.587 7
Academic placement 371.264
  see Manual at 371.262 vs. 371.264
Academic prognosis 371.264
  see Manual at 371.262 vs. 371.264
Academic status 371.104
  higher education 378.121
Academic year 371.23
  law 344.079 2
Academicians
  occupational group T7—090 1
Academies (Organizations) 060
Acadia 971.601
  T2—716
Acadia National Park (Me.) T2—741 45
Acadia Parish (La.) T2—763 56
Acadians T5—41
Acadians in Canada T5—114
  expulsion of 971.018 7
Acanthaceae 583.95
Acanthocephala 592.33
  paleozoology 562.33
Acanthodii 567.2
Acanthopterygii 597.64
  paleozoology 567.64
Acanthuses 635.933 95
  botany 583.95
  floriculture 635.933 95
Acari 595.42
Acarida 595.42
Acariformes 595.42
Acarina 595.42

Acarnania (Greece) T2—495 18
  ancient T2—383
Acceleration
  classical mechanics 531.112
  human biophysics 612.014 414
Acceleration of particles 539.73
Accelerator effect
    (Macroeconomics) 339.41
Accelerometers
  aircraft 629.135 2
Accent (Linguistics) 414.6
  specific languages T4—16
Accent (Poetry) 808.1
Acceptances (Commercial
    paper) 332.77
  exchange medium 332.55
  law 346.096
Access control (Computers) 005.8
  management 658.478
Access points (Cataloging) 025.322
Access roads 388.13
  see also Roads
Access to airports 387.736 2
Accessories (Clothing) 391.44
  care 646.6
  commercial technology 687.19
  customs 391.44
  home economics 646.3
  home sewing 646.48
  see also Clothing
Accident insurance 368.384
  government-sponsored 368.42
  industrial casualty 368.7
  law 346.086 384
    social insurance 344.022
  see also Insurance
Accident investigation 363.106 5
  technology 620.86
  see Manual at 363.1065 vs.
    620.86
Accidents 363.1
  personal safety 613.69
  psychology 155.936
  social services 363.1
    law 344.047
    public administration 353.9
  tort law 346.032 2
  see also Safety
Accidents (Philosophy) 111.1
Accipitridae 598.94
Acclimation
  health 613.1
Acclimatization
  animals 591.42
Acclimatization (continued)
  biology 578.42
  plants 581.42
Accomack County (Va.) T2—755 16
Accommodation
  disorders of eye
    incidence 614.599 7
    optometry 617.755
    see also Eyes
Accompaniment
  musical technique 781.47
  see Manual at 781.47
Accomplices 364.3
  see also Offenders
Accordions 788.86
  instrument 788.861 9
  music 788.86
  see also Woodwind
    instruments
Account security
  credit management 658.88
Accountability
  Christian doctrines 233.4
  ethics 170
  executive management 658.402
  military administration 355.685
  public administration 352.35
  public education 379.158
  teachers 371.144
Accountants 657.092
  occupational group T7—657
Accounting 657
  home economics 640.42
  law 346.063
    corporation law 346.066 48
    public administration 343.034
  malpractice 346.063 1
  management policy 658.151 1
  see Manual at 657 vs.
    658.1511, 658.1512
Accounts payable 657.74
  accounting 657.74
  financial management 658.152 6
Accounts receivable 657.72
  accounting 657.72
  financial management 658.152 44
Accra (Ghana) T2—667
Accreditation 352.84
  education 379.158
  public administration 352.84
  see also Licensing
Accreditation of prior learning 371.264
Acculturation 303.482

Accumulators
  hydraulic 621.254
Accuracy drills and tests
  shorthand 653.15
  typing 652.307
Aceraceae 583.78
Acetabularia 579.836
Acetals 668.423
Acetates 668.423
Acetobacter 579.33
Acetylene 547.413
  chemical engineering 661.814
  gas technology 665.85
Achaea (Greece) T2—495 27
  ancient T2—387
Achaia (Greece) T2—495 27
  ancient T2—387
Achievement tests 371.262
  secondary education 373.126 2
  teacher-prepared tests 371.271
Acid-base imbalances
  medicine 616.399 2
  see also Digestive system
Acid mine drainage 363.738 4
  environmental protection 363.738 4
  preventive technology 622.5
  water pollution engineering 628.168 32
Acid pollution
  ecology 577.275 2
Acid precipitation 363.738 6
  see also Acid rain
Acid rain 363.738 6
  international law 341.762 3
  law 344.046 336
  meteorology 551.577 1
  pollution technology 628.532
  social welfare 363.738 6
  weather forecasting 551.647 71
  see also Pollution
Acid rock 781.66
Acid-soil conditioners 631.821
  chemical engineering 668.64
Acidification
  ecology 577.275 2
Acidity
  soil science 631.42
Acidosis
  medicine 616.399 2
  see also Digestive system
Acids 546.24
  aromatic chemistry 547.637
  chemical engineering 661.2
  chemistry 546.24
  human toxicology 615.921
Acids (continued)
  organic chemistry 547.037
    applied 661.86
  see also Chemicals
Acidulous salts 546.342
  chemical engineering 661.4
Acinonyx 599.759
Acipenseriformes 597.42
  paleozoology 567.42
Acne
  medicine 616.53
  see also Skin
Acochlidacea 594.34
Acoela (Platyhelminthes) 592.42
Acoli (African people) T5—965
Acoli language 496.5
  T6—965
Aconcagua (Chile) T2—832 4
Aconcagua (Chile : Region) T2—832 4
Aconites 583.34
Acorns
  coffee substitute
    commercial processing 663.97
Acoustical communications engineering 621.382 8
Acoustical engineering 620.2
Acoustical engineers 620.209 2
  occupational group T7—620 2
Acoustical insulation
  buildings 693.834
Acoustical pattern recognition 006.45
  engineering 621.399
Acoustical properties
  materials science 620.112 94
Acoustical prospecting 622.159 2
Acoustics 534
  architectural design 729.29
  engineering 620.2
  see also Sound
Acousto-optical communications engineering 621.382 8
Acquired immune deficiency syndrome 362.196 979 2
  medicine 616.979 2
  social services 362.196 979 2
  see also AIDS (Disease)
Acquired immunity 571.96
  humans 616.079
Acquisition of corporations 338.83
  see also Mergers
Acquisition of real property 333.33
  economics 333.33
    private ownership 333.33

Acquisition of real property
economics (continued)
public ownership 333.13
law 346.043 62
private ownership 346.043 62
public ownership 343.025 2
Acquisition of territory 325.32
international law 341.42
law 342.041 2
Acquisitions (Libraries) 025.2
Acquisitions (Museums) 069.51
Acrasia 579.52
Acre (Brazil) T2—811 2
Acreage allotments 338.18
law 343.076 1
Acrididae
agricultural pests 632.726
Acrobatics 796.47
circuses 791.34
sports 796.47
see also Sports
Acrobats 796.470 92
circus group T7—791 3
circuses 791.340 92
sports 796.470 92
sports group T7—796 4
Acromegaly
medicine 616.47
see also Endocrine system
Acronym dictionaries 413.1
specific languages T4—31
specific subject T1—014 8
Acronyms 411
specific languages T4—11
specific subject T1—014 8
Acrostics 793.73
Acrothoracica 595.35
Acrylic painting 751.426
Acrylics 668.423 2
textiles 677.474 2
see also Textiles
Acrylonitrile rubber 678.72
Act
philosophical anthropology 128.4
ACT (College testing program) 378.166 2
Act of Union, 1840 971.039
ACTH (Hormone)
pharmacology 615.363
production
human physiology 612.492
see also Endocrine system
Acting 792.028
motion pictures 791.430 28
radio 791.440 28
Acting (continued)
stage 792.028
television 791.450 28
Actinide series 669.292
chemistry 546.42
metallurgy 669.292
see also Chemicals; Metals
Actinium
chemistry 546.421
metallurgy 669.292 1
see also Chemicals; Metals
Actinomycetales 579.37
Actinomycetes 579.37
see Manual at 579.37
Actinopoda 579.45
Actinopterygii 597
see also Fishes
Actinotherapy
medicine 615.842
Action
philosophical anthropology 128.4
psychology 150
Action games
indoor 793.4
Action toys 790.133
manufacturing technology 688.728
see also Toys
Activated carbon 662.93
water treatment 628.166
Activated sludge process 628.354
Activation analysis 543.088 2
Activity therapy
medicine 615.851 5
Acton (Quebec : Regional
County Municipality) T2—714 525
Actors 792.028 092
motion picture 791.430 280 92
occupational group T7—791 4
occupational group T7—792
radio 791.440 280 92
occupational group T7—791 4
stage 792.028 092
occupational group T7—792
television 791.450 280 92
occupational group T7—791 4
see Manual at 791.092
Actresses 792.028 092
see also Actors
Acts of the Apostles 226.6
pseudepigrapha 229.925
Actual grace 234.1
Actuarial science 368.01
Acuity (Visual perception)
psychology 152.142 2

Acupressure
  therapeutics 615.822
Acupuncture
  therapeutics 615.892
Acylation 547.21
  chemical engineering 660.284 41
Ad Dakhla (Western
    Sahara) T2—648
Ada County (Idaho) T2—796 28
Adages 398.9
Adair County (Iowa) T2—777 73
Adair County (Ky.) T2—769 675
Adair County (Mo.) T2—778 264
Adair County (Okla.) T2—766 89
Adam
  Bible stories 222.110 950 5
  Islam 297.246
Adamawa-Eastern languages 496.361
  T6—963 61
Adamawa languages 496.361
  T6—963 61
Adamawa State (Nigeria) T2—669 88
Adamawa-Ubangi languages 496.361
  T6—963 61
Adams, John
  United States history 973.44
Adams, John Quincy
  United States history 973.55
Adams County (Colo.) T2—788 81
Adams County (Idaho) T2—796 26
Adams County (Ill.) T2—773 44
Adams County (Ind.) T2—772 73
Adams County (Iowa) T2—777 76
Adams County (Miss.) T2—762 26
Adams County (N.D.) T2—784 89
Adams County (Neb.) T2—782 397
Adams County (Ohio) T2—771 86
Adams County (Pa.) T2—748 42
Adams County (Wash.) T2—797 34
Adams County (Wis.) T2—775 56
Adams Lake (B.C.) T2—711 72
Adams River (B.C.) T2—711 75
Adana İli (Turkey) T2—564
Adangme (African people) T5—963 37
Adangme language 496.337
  T6—963 37
Adaptability
  psychology 155.24
    children 155.418 24
    late adulthood 155.672
    situational influences 155.9
Adaptation (Biology) 578.4
  animals 591.4
  plants 581.4
Adaptive control systems
  automation engineering 629.836
Addax 599.645
Added-value tax 336.271 4
Adder's-tongues (Ferns) 587.33
Addiction 362.29
  customs 394.14
  devotional literature 291.432
    Christianity 242.4
  medicine 616.86
  pastoral theology 291.61
    Christianity 259.429
  personal health 613.8
  religious guidance 291.442
    Christianity 248.862 9
  social theology 291.178 322 9
    Christianity 261.832 29
  social welfare 362.29
  see also Substance abuse
Addictive drugs
  pharmacodynamics 615.78
Addicts T1—087 4
Addis Ababa (Ethiopia) T2—633
Addison County (Vt.) T2—743 5
Addison's disease
  medicine 616.45
  see also Endocrine system
Addition 512.92
  algebra 512.92
  arithmetic 513.211
Addition (Chemical reaction) 541.393
  organic chemistry 547.2
    applied 660.284 4
Additive processes
  color photography 778.65
Additive properties 512.73
Addo Elephant National
    Park (South Africa) T2—687 5
Addresses 080
Addressing machines
  office use 651.759
Adelaide (S. Aust.) T2—942 31
Adelaide (South Africa :
    District) T2—687 5
Aden T2—533 5
Aden, Gulf of 551.467 32
  T2—165 32
Adenomas
  medicine 616.993
  see also Diseases (Human)
Adenophorea 592.57
Adenosine triphosphate 572.475
Adenoviridae 579.244 3
Adephaga 595.762

Adhesion 541.33
  chemical engineering 660.293
Adhesiveness
  materials science 620.112 92
Adhesives 668.3
  building materials 691.99
  manufacturing technology 668.3
  materials science 620.199
  structural engineering 624.189 9
Adi Granth 294.682
Adipose tissues 571.57
  human histology 611.018 2
Adirondack Mountains
    (N.Y.) T2—747 5
Adiyaman İli (Turkey) T2—565
Adjectivals 415
  specific languages T4—5
Adjectives 415
  specific languages T4—5
Adjudication 347.07
  competitions T1—079
  criminal law 345.07
  international law 341.55
Adjustment (Insurance) 368.014
Adjustment (Psychology) 155.24
  children 155.418 24
  late adulthood 155.672
Adlerian psychology 150.195 3
Administration 658
  T1—068
  see Manual at 658 and
    T1—068
Administration of estates 346.056
Administration of justice 347
  crimes against 364.134
  law 345.023 4
Administration régionale
    Kativik (Quebec) T2—714 111
Administrative agencies 351
  description and duties 351
  government publications
    bibliographies 011.534
  law 342.064
  organization and structure 352.29
    see Manual at 352.29
  see Manual at 352–354
Administrative areas
  area planning 711.551
Administrative assistants
  office management 651.3
Administrative courts 342.066 4
Administrative discretion 342.066 4
Administrative law 342.06
  see Manual at 342.06
Administrative personnel
  office management 651.3
Administrative procedure
  law 342.066
Administrative regulations
    (Compilations) 348.025
Administrative reports T1—06
  public administration 351.05
Administrative responsibility 658.402
  military services 355.685
  public administration 352.35
Administrative revenues
  public finance 336.16
Administrators (Public officials) 352.3
  occupational group T7—35
  see also Public administrators
Admirals 359.009 2
  role and function 359.331
Admiralty courts 347.04
Admiralty Islands (Papua
    New Guinea) T2—958 1
Admiralty law 343.096
  international law 341.756 6
Admissibility of evidence 347.062
  criminal law 345.062
Admission tests 371.262
  higher education 378.166 2
Admission to schools 371.21
  higher education 378.161
Admission to the bar 344.017 613 4
Adobe
  architectural construction 721.044 22
  building construction 693.22
Adolescence 305.235
  human physiology 612.661
  literature 808.803 54
    history and criticism 809.933 54
    specific literatures T3B—080 354
      history and criticism T3B—093 54
  psychology 155.5
  social aspects 305.235
Adolescent development 305.235 5
  psychology 155.5
  sociology 305.235 5
Adolescent literature 808.899 283
  history and criticism 809.892 83
  specific literatures T3B—080 928 3
    history and criticism T3B—099 283
Adolescent medicine 616.008 35
Adolescent psychiatry 616.890 083 5
Adolescent psychology 155.5
Adolescent
    psychopathology 616.890 083 5

Adolescents 305.235
T1—083 5
T7—055
  arts 700.452 055
T3C—352 055
  etiquette 395.123
  government programs 353.536 5
  health 613.043 3
  home care 649.125
  journalism for 070.483 3
  labor economics 331.347
    law 344.013 47
  legal status 346.013 5
    constitutional law 342.087
    private law 346.013 5
  libraries for 027.626
  literature 808.803 520 55
    history and criticism 809.933 520 55
    specific literatures T3B—080 352 055
      history and criticism T3B—093 520 55
  physical fitness 613.704 3
  physiology 612.661
  psychology 155.5
  publications for
    bibliographies 011.625
    reviews 028.165
  reading
    library science 028.535
  religion 200.835
    Christianity 270.083 5
      devotional literature 242.63
      guides to Christian life 248.83
      pastoral care of 259.23
      religious education 268.433
      social theology 261.834 235
    guides to life 291.440 835
    Judaism 296.083 5
      guides to life 296.708 35
      religious education 296.680 835
    social theology 291.178 342 35
  sex hygiene 613.951
  social aspects 305.235
  social welfare 362.708 3
    law 344.032 708 3
    public administration 353.536 5
    see Manual at 362.7083
Adopted children 306.874
T1—085 4
T7—044 1
  family relationships 306.874
  home care 649.145
  psychology 155.445
  social welfare 362.829 8
Adoption 362.734
  criminology 364.18
    criminal law 345.028
  law 346.017 8
  social welfare 362.734
Adoptive parents 306.874
T1—085
T7—043 1
Adoration of magi 232.923
Adoration of shepherds 232.922
ADP (Computing) 004
Adrar (Algeria : Province) T2—657
Adrenal glands 573.46
  biology 573.46
  human anatomy 611.45
  human physiology 612.45
  medicine 616.45
  surgery 617.461
  see also Endocrine system
Adrenal hormones 573.464
  human physiology 612.45
  pharmacology 615.364
  see also Endocrine system
Adrenalin
  chemistry 547.734 5
Adrenocorticotrophic hormone
  pharmacology 615.363
  production
    human physiology 612.492
  see also Endocrine system
Adrianople (Turkey :
    Province) T2—496 1
Adriatic Sea 551.462 5
T2—163 85
Adsorbent carbons 662.93
Adsorbent charcoals 662.93
Adsorption 541.33
  chemical engineering 660.284 235
  chemistry 541.33
  gaseous-state physics 530.435
  semiconductors 537.622 6
Adsorption chromatography 543.089 2
Adult baptism 234.161 3
  public worship 265.13
  theology 234.161 3
Adult child abuse victims
  medicine 616.858 223 9
  social theology 291.178 327 3
    Christianity 261.832 73
  social welfare 362.764
Adult child sexual abuse victims
  medicine 616.858 369
  social theology 291.178 327 3
    Christianity 261.832 73

Adult child sexual abuse victims (continued)	
social welfare	362.764
Adult children of alcoholics	
medicine	616.861 9
social welfare	362.292 4
Adult children of substance abusers	
medicine	616.869
social welfare	362.291 4
Adult easy literature	
rhetoric	808.067
Adult education	374
	T1—071 5
law	344.074
public administrative support	353.84
public support	379.114
law	344.076 85
university extension	378.175
Adultery	306.736
criminology	364.153
criminal law	345.025 3
ethics	176
see also Sexual relations—ethics	
social theology	291.178 357 36
Christianity	261.835 736
sociology	306.736
Adulthood	305.24
psychology	155.6
social aspects	305.24
Adults	305.24
	T7—056
criminal offenders	364.37
education	374
see also Adult education	
health	613.043 4
journalism for	070.483 4
physical fitness	613.704 4
psychology	155.6
recreation	790.192
indoor	793.019 2
outdoor	796
religion	200
Christianity	230
guides to Christian life	248.84
religious education	268.434
social theology	261.834 24
social aspects	305.24
social theology	291.178 342 4
Adur (England)	T2—422 69
Advaita (Philosophy)	181.482
Advanced placement (Education)	371.264
Advent	263.912
devotional literature	242.332
music	781.722
sermons	252.612
Advent Christian Church	286.73
see also Adventists	
Adventists	286.7
biography	286.709 2
church government	262.067
parishes	254.067
church law	262.986 7
doctrines	230.67
catechisms and creeds	238.67
guides to Christian life	248.486 7
missions	266.67
moral theology	241.046 7
public worship	264.067
religious associations	267.186 7
religious education	268.867
religious group	T7—267
seminaries	230.073 67
theology	230.67
Adventure	904
specific places	930–990
Adventure fiction	808.838 7
history and criticism	809.387
specific literatures	T3B—308 7
individual authors	T3A—3
Adventure games	793.93
see Manual at 793.932 vs. 794.822	
Adverbials	415
specific languages	T4—5
Adverbs	415
specific languages	T4—5
Adversary system	347
Adverse drug reactions	
pharmacodynamics	615.704
Advertisements	380.102 94
	T1—029 4
illustration	741.67
see Manual at 383–388: Offers for sale vs. Economic aspects	
Advertisers	659.109 2
occupational group	T7—659
Advertising	659.1
illustration	741.67
law	343.082
medical ethics	174.26
see Manual at 658.8, T1—0688 vs. 659	
Advertising agencies	659.112 5
Advertising campaigns	659.113

Advertising cards
  illustration 741.685
Advertising departments 659.112 2
Advice to readers
  journalism 070.444
Advisory bodies
  public administration 352.743
Advocacy
  law 347.052
Adygea (Russia) T2—475 2
Adyghe language 499.962 5
  T6—999 625
Adyghe literature 899.962 5
Adzhar (Georgia) T2—475 8
Adzharii͡a (Georgia) T2—475 8
Aegadian Islands T2—458 24
Aegean architecture 722.61
Aegean Islands (Greece and Turkey) 949.58
  T2—495 8
  ancient 939.1
  T2—391
Aegean Islands (Greece : Periphereia) T2—495 8
Aegean Sea 551.462 8
  T2—163 88
Aeolian instruments 786.69
  chamber music 785.669
  construction 786.691 923
    by hand 786.691 923
    by machine 681.866 9
  see Manual at 784–788
Aeolian Islands (Italy) T2—458 11
Aepyornithiformes 568.5
Aequian language 479.7
  T6—797
Aeration
  sewage treatment 628.35
  water supply treatment 628.165
Aerial photography 778.35
  military engineering 623.72
Aerial railways 385.6
  engineering 625.5
  transportation services 385.6
  see also Railroad transportation
Aerial surveying 526.982
Aerial warfare 358.4
  see also Air warfare
Aerobatics 797.54
  see also Sports
Aerobic dancing 613.715
Aerobic exercise 613.71
Aerobic-macroaerophilic gram-negative bacteria 579.323
Aerobic respiration 573.2
Aerodynamic load 624.175
  aeronautics 629.132 35
Aerodynamics 533.62
  aeronautics 629.132 3
  engineering 620.107 4
  space flight 629.415 1
Aeroelasticity
  aeronautics 629.132 362
Aeromechanics 533.6
  aeronautics 629.132 3
  engineering 620.107
Aeronautical engineers 629.130 092
  occupational group T7—629 1
Aeronautics 629.13
  law 343.097
Aerophones 788
  see also Wind instruments
Aerosols 541.345 15
  chemical engineering 660.294 515
  colloid chemistry 541.345 15
  meteorology 551.511 3
Aerospace engineering 629.1
  military 623.66
Aerospace engineers 629.109 2
  occupational group T7—629 1
Aerospace medicine 616.980 21
Aerospace photography 778.35
Aerospace physiology
  humans 612.014 4
Aerostatics 533.61
  aeronautics 629.132 2
  engineering 620.107 3
Aerotherapy
  medicine 615.836
Aesthetics 111.85
  arts 701.17
  literature 801.93
  music 781.17
  philosophy 111.85
Aestivation 571.786
Aeta (Philippine people) T5—991 1
Aetolia (Greece) T2—383
Aetolia and Acarnania (Greece) T2—495 18
Afan (Wales) T2—429 85
Afar (African people) T5—935
Afar language 493.5
  T6—935
AFDC (Social welfare) 362.713
Affection
  psychology 152.41

Affective disorders 362.25
  psychiatry 616.852 7
  social welfare 362.25
  see also Mental illness
Affects
  psychology 152.4
Affenpinscher 636.76
Affine geometry 516.4
Affinity (Law) 346.015
Affirmative action
  education 379.26
  employment 331.133
    see also Equal employment opportunity
  government programs 353.53
  law 342.087
    constitutional law 342.087
    labor law 344.011 33
Affixes (Grammar) 415
  specific languages T4—5
Afforestation 333.751 52
  law 346.046 751 52
  resource economics 333.751 52
  silviculture 634.956
Afghan hound 636.753 3
Afghan language 491.593
  T6—915 93
Afghan literature 891.593
Afghan rugs
  arts 746.758 1
  see also Rugs
Afghanistan 958.1
  T2—581
Afghans T5—915 93
Afghans (Coverlets) 643.53
  arts 746.430 437
  home sewing 646.21
  household equipment 643.53
AFL (Labor) 331.883 209 73
AFL-CIO 331.880 973
Aflatoxins
  human toxicology 615.952 956 57
Africa 960
  T2—6
Africa, Black T2—67
Africa, Central 967
  T2—67
Africa, East 967.6
  T2—676
Africa, North 961
  T2—61
  ancient 939.7
  T2—397
Africa, Southern 968
  T2—68
Africa, Sub-Saharan 967
  T2—67
Africa, West 966
  T2—66
African American cooking 641.592 960 73
African American Methodist churches 287.8
  see also Methodist Church
African Americans 973.049 607 3
  T5—960 73
  civilization 973.049 607 3
  education 371.829 960 73
  military troops
    World War II 940.540 3
  social aspects 305.896 073
  see Manual at T5—96073
African bush pig 599.633
African elephant 599.674
  big game hunting 799.276 74
  conservation technology 639.979 674
  resource economics 333.959 674
African independent churches 289.93
  see also Christian denominations
African languages 496
  T6—96
African lilies 584.33
African literature 808.899 6
  history and criticism 809.896
  in African languages 896
African Methodist Episcopal Church 287.83
  see also Methodist Church
African Methodist Episcopal Zion Church 287.83
  see also Methodist Church
African mole rat 599.359
African religions 299.6
African sleeping sickness
  incidence 614.533
  medicine 616.936 3
  see also Communicable diseases (Human)
African violets 635.933 95
  botany 583.95
  floriculture 635.933 95
Africans T5—96
Afrihili (Artificial language) 499.99
  T6—999 9
Afrikaans language 439.36
  T6—393 6
Afrikaans literature 839.36

Afrikaners T5—393 6
Afro-Americans 973.049 607 3
T5—960 73
see also African Americans
Afro-Asian bloc T2—171 65
Afro-Asiatic languages 492
T6—92
non-Semitic 493
T6—93
Afro-Asiatic literatures 892
non-Semitic 893
Afro-Cuban jazz 781.657
Afrohili (Artificial language) 499.99
T6—999 9
After-dinner speeches
literature 808.851
history and criticism 809.51
specific literatures T3B—501
individual authors T3A—5
rhetoric 808.51
Afterimages
psychology 152.148
Afyon İli (Turkey) T2—562
Afyonkarahisar (Turkey : İli) T2—562
Agadir (Morocco : Province) T2—646
Agapes (Christian rites) 265.9
Agaricaceae 579.6
Agaricales 579.6
Agates 553.87
see also Semiprecious stones
Agavaceae 584.352
Agaves 584.352
fiber crop 633.577
Age characteristics
physical anthropology 599.937
Age discrimination in employment 331.398
law 344.013 98
Age groups 305.2
T1—083–084
T7—05
Age-hardening metals 671.36
Aged abuse 362.6
criminology 364.155 5
criminal law 345.025 55
social welfare 362.6
Aged persons 305.26
T1—084 6
see also Older persons
Agency law 346.029
Agent Orange
human toxicology 615.951 37
Aggadah 296.19
Midrash 296.142
Talmud 296.127 6
Aggeus (Biblical book) 224.97
Aggregates (Materials) 553.62
economic geology 553.62
materials science 620.191
mining 622.362
Aggression 302.54
law of war 341.62
psychology 155.232
drives 153.8
emotions 152.47
personality trait 155.232
social psychology 302.54
Agin Buri͡at (Russia : Okrug) T2—575
Agin Buri͡atskiĭ avtonomnyĭ okrug (Russia) T2—575
Aging 571.878
biology 571.878
human physiology 612.67
literature 808.803 54
history and criticism 809.933 54
specific literatures T3B—080 354
history and criticism T3B—093 54
psychology of late adulthood 155.67
Aging alcoholic beverages 663.17
Agnatha 597.2
paleozoology 567.2
Agnosticism 211.7
Christian polemics 239.7
philosophy 149.72
philosophy of religion 211.7
Agnostics 211.709 2
religious group T7—291
Agnus Dei 264.36
music 782.323 2
Agoraphobia
medicine 616.852 25
see also Mental illness
Agostinho Neto, António
Angolan history 967.304 1
Agoutis 599.359
Agrammatism
medicine 616.855 2
see also Communicative disorders
Agranulocytosis
medicine 616.154
see also Cardiovascular system

Agraphia
  medicine 616.855 3
  see also Communicative disorders
Agreement (Grammar) 415
  specific languages T4—5
Ağri İli (Turkey) T2—566 2
Agricultural areas T2—173 4
  area planning 711.554
Agricultural assistance
  international law 341.759 2
  law 343.076
  production economics 338.18
Agricultural banks 332.31
Agricultural chemicals 631.8
  engineering 668.6
  public safety 363.179 2
    see also Hazardous materials
  use 631.8
Agricultural civilization 909
Agricultural commodities 338.17
  investment economics 332.644 1
  public administration 354.59
Agricultural communities 307.72
Agricultural cooperative credit associations 334.2
Agricultural cooperatives 334.683
Agricultural credit 332.71
  law 346.073
  production economics 338.18
Agricultural ecology 577.55
Agricultural economics 338.1
Agricultural engineering 630
Agricultural enterprises 338.763
Agricultural equipment 631.3
  manufacturing technology 681.763
Agricultural experiment stations 630.724
Agricultural extension 630.715
Agricultural genetics 631.523 3
Agricultural industries 338.1
  accounting 657.863
  economics 338.1
  public administration 354.5
Agricultural insurance 368.096
  crop 368.121
  livestock liability 368.56
  see also Insurance
Agricultural lands 333.76
  biology 578.755
  ecology 577.55
  economics 333.76
    sale and rental 333.335
Agricultural law 343.076
Agricultural libraries 026.63
Agricultural life
  civilization 909
Agricultural machinery 631.3
  manufacturing technology 681.763
  shortages
    economics 338.14
Agricultural marketing 380.141
  public administration 354.59
Agricultural meteorology 630.251 5
Agricultural pests 632.6
  see Manual at 632.2–632.8
Agricultural pollution 577.273
Agricultural price supports
  economics 338.18
  public administration 354.528 5
Agricultural productivity 338.16
Agricultural products 338.17
  commerce 380.141
  economics 338.17
  military resources 355.245
Agricultural schools 630.71
Agricultural sociology 306.349
Agricultural structures 631.2
  architecture 728.92
  construction 690.892
  see also Farm buildings
Agricultural wastes 363.728 8
  animal feed 636.085 56
  animal husbandry 636.083 8
  sanitary engineering 628.746
  social services 363.728 8
  water pollution engineering 628.168 4
  see also Waste control
Agricultural workers 630.92
  economics 331.763
  occupational group T7—63
  social class 305.563
  sociology 306.364
Agriculture 630
  applied science 630
  economics 338.1
  enterprises 338.763
  law 343.076
  public administration 354.5
Agriculture and state 338.18
Agriculturists 630.92
  occupational group T7—63
Agrigento (Italy : Province) T2—458 22
Agroforestry 634.99
Agromyzidae 595.774
Agronomy 630
Agrosteae 584.9

Agrostis 633.23
  botany 584.9
  forage crop 633.23
Aguadilla (P.R. : District) T2—729 54
Aguascalientes (Mexico : State) T2—724 2
Aharonim 296.180 92
Ahilot 296.123 6
Ahimsa 294.548 697
  Buddhism 294.356 97
  Hinduism 294.548 697
  Jainism 294.456 97
Ahmadiyya movement 297.86
  doctrines 297.204 6
Ahom (India) T5—959 19
Ahuachapán (El Salvador : Dept.) T2—728 411
Ahvenanmaa (Finland) T2—489 73
Aichi-ken (Japan) T2—521 67
Aid to families with dependent children 362.713
AIDS (Disease) 362.196 979 2
  church work with patients 259.419 697 92
  incidence 614.599 392
  law 344.043 697 92
  medicine 616.979 2
  nursing 610.736 99
  pediatrics 618.929 792
  social services 362.196 979 2
  social theology 291.178 321 969792
    Christianity 261.832 196 9792
Aigaio Nēsoi (Greece : Periphereia) T2—495 8
Aiken County (S.C.) T2—757 75
Aikido 796.815 4
  physical fitness 613.714 8
  see also Sports
Ailanthuses 635.977 377
  botany 583.77
  ornamental arboriculture 635.977 377
Ailerons 629.134 33
Ailuropoda 599.789
Ain (France) T2—444 4
Ain Chok-Hay Hassani (Morocco : Prefecture) T2—643
Aïn Defla (Algeria : Province) T2—653
Aïn Temouchent (Algeria : Province) T2—651
Ainu T5—946
Ainu language 494.6
  T6—946
Ainu literature 894.6
Air
  gas technology 665.82
  health 613.19
Air artillery 358.43
Air bags
  automobile 629.276
Air bases 358.417
  military engineering 623.66
  World War I 940.443
  World War II 940.544 3
  see also Air warfare
Air circulation equipment
  buildings 697.932 5
Air-compression engines
  automotive 629.250 7
Air-compression-powered automobiles
  engineering 629.229 4
Air-compression-powered locomotives 385.365
  engineering 625.265
  transportation services 385.365
  see also Rolling stock
Air compression technology 621.51
Air conditioning
  aircraft 629.134 42
  automobile 629.277 2
  buildings 697.93
  health 613.5
  household management 644.5
  library buildings 022.8
  mining 622.42
  museums 069.29
  plant management 658.25
  ships 623.853 7
  vehicles 629.040 289
Air conditioning engineers
  building trades 697.930 92
    occupational group T7—697
Air currents 551.517
  aeronautics 629.132 4
Air-cushion vehicles 388.35
  engineering 629.3
  land 388.35
  military engineering 623.748
  ocean 387.2
  transportation services 388.35
    inland water 386.22
Air engines 621.42
Air force personnel 358.400 92
  occupational group T7—358
  role and function 358.413 3
Air forces 358.4

Air freight 387.744
  airport services 387.736 4
  international law 341.756 78
  law 343.097 8
Air guns 683.4
  art metalwork 739.73
  see also Guns (Small arms)
Air holes
  aeronautics 629.132 327
Air mail 383.144
  see also Postal service
Air masses 551.551 2
Air mechanics 533.6
  aeronautics 629.132 3
  engineering 620.107
Air-mileage indicators 629.135 1
Air motors 621.42
Air national guards 358.413 7
Air operations (Military science) 358.414
Air ordnance 358.418
  engineering 623.746 1
  military equipment 358.418
Air pilots 629.130 92
  occupational group T7—629 1
Air pockets
  aeronautics 629.132 327
Air pollution 363.739 2
  crop damage 632.19
  ecology 577.276
  international law 341.762 52
  law 344.046 342
  public administration 354.373 5
  social welfare 363.739 2
  technology 628.53
  toxicology 571.956
  see also Pollution
Air pollution rights 363.739 26
  law 344.046 342
Air-position indicators 629.135 1
Air pressure control
  aircraft 629.134 42
  spacecraft 629.477 5
Air propulsion 621.42
Air pumps 621.69
Air raid shelters 363.35
  civil defense 363.35
  military engineering 623.38
  see also Civil defense
Air raid warning systems 358.414
  civil defense 363.35
    see also Civil defense
  military engineering 623.737
Air raids 358.414
  civil defense 363.35
    see also Civil defense
  World War I 940.442
  World War II 940.544 2
  see also Air warfare
Air resistance
  aeronautics 629.132 34
Air resources 333.92
  economics 333.92
  law 346.046 92
  public administration 354.37
Air rights (National airspace) 341.46
Air rights (Real estate)
  economics 333.3
    law 346.043 2
  sale and rental 333.339
  urban area planning 711.4
  zoning 333.771 7
    law 346.045
Air safety 363.124
  international law 341.756 7
  law 343.097
  public administration 353.988
  social services 363.124
Air-sea interactions 551.524 6
Air seasoning
  lumber 674.382
Air-speed indicators 629.135 2
Air sports 797.5
  see also Sports
Air-supply control
  spacecraft 629.477 5
Air-supported construction 693.98
Air-taxi accidents 363.124 93
  see also Air safety
Air temperatures
  meteorology 551.525
Air terminals 387.736 2
  see also Airports
Air-to-air guided missiles 358.43
  engineering 623.451 91
  military equipment 358.43
Air-to-air missile forces 358.43
Air-to-surface guided missiles 358.428 2
  engineering 623.451 92
  military equipment 358.428 2
Air-to-surface missile forces 358.42
Air-to-underwater guided missiles 358.42
  engineering 623.451 93
  military equipment 358.42
Air-to-underwater missile forces 358.42

Air traffic control 387.740 426
  engineering 629.136 6
  international law 341.756 76
  law 343.097 6
  military engineering 623.666
  transportation services 387.740 426
  see Manual at 629.1366 vs. 387.740426
Air traffic controllers 629.136 609 2
  occupational group T7—629 1
Air transportation 387.7
  engineering 629.13
  international law 341.756 7
  law 343.097
  public administration 354.79
  safety 363.124
    see also Air safety
  transportation services 387.7
Air transportation facilities 387.736 2
  engineering 629.136
  see also Airports
Air transportation insurance 368.093
  inland marine 368.24
  liability 368.576
  see also Insurance
Air transportation police 363.287 6
Air transportation workers 387.709 2
  occupational group T7—387 7
Air warfare 358.4
  Algerian Revolution 965.046 48
  Chaco War 989.207 164 8
  Civil War (Spain) 946.081 48
  Falkland Islands War 997.110 244 8
  Indo-Pakistan War, 1971 954.920 514 8
  Indochinese War 959.704 148
  Iraqi-Iranian Conflict 955.054 248
  Korean War 951.904 248
  Persian Gulf War, 1991 956.704 424 8
  Vietnamese War 959.704 348
  World War I 940.44
  World War II 940.544
Airborne infantry 356.166
Airbrush drawing 741.29
Airbrush painting 751.494
Aircraft 387.73
  engineering 629.133
  international law 341.756 75
  law 343.097 5
  military engineering 623.746
  military equipment 358.418 3
  piloting 629.132 52
  psychological influence 155.965
  sanitation services 363.729 3
    see also Waste control
Aircraft (continued)
  sports 797.5
    see also Sports
  transportation services 387.73
    operation 387.740 44
  see Manual at 629.046 vs. 388
Aircraft accidents 363.124
  see also Air safety
Aircraft carriers 359.948 35
  design 623.812 55
  engineering 623.825 5
  naval equipment 359.948 35
  naval units 359.943 5
Aircraft detection 358.414
  civil defense 363.35
    see also Civil defense
Aircraft engineers 629.130 092
  occupational group T7—629 1
Aircraft failures 363.124 16
  public safety 363.124 16
  wreckage studies 629.132 55
  see also Air safety
Aircraft gunnery 623.555
Aircraft navigators 629.132 510 92
  occupational group T7—629 1
Aircraft noise 363.741
  engineering 629.132 3
  social welfare 363.741
  see also Noise
Aircraft operation
  transportation services 387.740 44
Aircraft racing 797.52
Aire River (England) T2—428 15
Airflow
  aeronautics 629.132 32
Airfoils 629.134 32
Airframes 629.134 31
Airline cooking 641.575
Airline employees 387.709 2
  occupational group T7—387 7
Airlines 387.7
  see also Air transportation
Airplane accidents 363.124
  see also Air safety
Airplane-banner advertising 659.134 4
Airplane hijacking 364.155 2
  international law 341.772
  law 345.025 52
Airplane racing 797.52
  see also Sports
Airplanes 387.733 4
  engineering 629.133 34
  military engineering 623.746
  piloting 629.132 52

Airplanes (continued)
  transportation services 387.733 4
  see also Aircraft
Airport facilities 387.736 2
  see also Airports
Airport police 363.287 6
Airports 387.736
  architecture 725.39
  area planning 711.78
  construction 690.539
  engineering 629.136
  institutional housekeeping 647.963 9
  international law 341.756 77
  law 343.097 7
  military engineering 623.66
  public administration 354.79
  transportation services 387.736
  see also Aircraft
Airships 387.732 4
  engineering 629.133 24
  military engineering 623.743
  piloting 629.132 522
  transportation services 387.732 4
  see also Aircraft
Airspace (Territorial right) 341.46
Airstrips 387.736
  engineering 629.136 12
  military engineering 623.661 2
  transportation services 387.736
  see also Airports
Aisén (Chile : Province) T2—836 22
Aisén del General Carlos Ibáñez del Campo (Chile : Region) T2—836 2
Aisne (France) T2—443 45
Aitkin County (Minn.) T2—776 72
Aitōlia kai Akarnania (Greece) T2—495 18
Aix 598.412
Aix-la-Chapelle (Germany) T2—435 511
Aizoaceae 583.53
'Ajmān (United Arab Emirates : Emirate) T2—535 7
Aka (African people) T5—965
Aka language (Central African Republic) 496.396
  T6—963 96
Akan (African people) T5—963 385
Akan language 496.338 5
  T6—963 385
Akan literature 896.338 5
Akarnania (Greece)
  ancient T2—383
Akbar, Emperor of Hindustan
  Indian history 954.025 4
Akershus fylke (Norway) T2—482 2
Akhenaton, King of Egypt
  Egyptian history 932.014
Akita 636.73
Akita-ken (Japan) T2—521 13
Akkadian language 492.1
  T6—921
Akkadian literature 892.1
Akkadian period 935.01
Akkadians T5—921
Aklan (Philippines) T2—599 5
Aklavik (N.W.T.) T2—719 6
Akoli language 496.5
  T6—965
Akpes language 496.33
  T6—963 3
Akron (Ohio) T2—771 36
Akwa Ibom State (Nigeria) T2—669 43
Akwamu (Kingdom) 966.701 6
  T2—667
Akwe-Shavante language 498.4
  T6—984
Al-Jaza'ir (Algeria : Province) T2—653
Al Mafraq (Jordan : Province) T2—569 597
Alabama 976.1
  T2—761
Alabama, Battle of Kearsarge and, 1864 973.754
Alabama River (Ala.) T2—761 2
Alabaster 553.635
  economic geology 553.635
  mining 622.363 5
Alachua County (Fla.) T2—759 79
Alagoas (Brazil) T2—813 5
Alajuela (Costa Rica : Province) T2—728 65
Alamance County (N.C.) T2—756 58
Alameda County (Calif.) T2—794 65
Alamo, Siege, 1836 976.403
Alamosa County (Colo.) T2—788 36
Åland (Finland) T2—489 73
Åland Islands (Finland) T2—489 73
Alarm systems
  engineering 621.389 28
  fire safety technology 628.922 5
Alaska 979.8
  T2—798
Alaska, Gulf of (Alaska) 551.466 34
  T2—164 34
Alaska Panhandle T2—798 2

Alaska Range (Alaska) T2—798 3
Alaskan Inuit languages 497.12
T6—971 2
Alaskan Inuktitut languages 497.12
T6—971 2
Alaskan Malamute 636.73
Alaskan Pacific seawaters 551.466 34
T2—164 34
Alastrim
incidence 614.521
medicine 616.913
see also Communicable diseases (Human)
Alaudidae 598.825
Alava (Spain) T2—466 5
Alba (Romania : Judeţ) T2—498 4
Albacete (Spain : Province) T2—464 6
Albacore 597.783
Albania 949.65
T2—496 5
ancient 939.8
T2—398
Albania (Ancient kingdom) 939.5
T2—395
Albanian language 491.991
T6—919 91
Albanian literature 891.991
Albanians T5—919 91
Albany (N.Y.) T2—747 43
Albany (South Africa : District) T2—687 5
Albany (W.A.) T2—941 2
Albany County (N.Y.) T2—747 42
Albany County (Wyo.) T2—787 95
Albatrosses 598.42
Albay (Philippines) T2—599 1
Albemarle County (Va.) T2—755 482
Albemarle Sound (N.C.) 551.461 48
T2—163 48
Alberni-Clayoquot (B.C.) T2—711 2
Albert (N.B. : County) T2—715 31
Albert (South Africa : District) T2—687 13
Albert I, King of the Belgians
Belgian history 949.304 1
Albert II, Holy Roman Emperor
German history 943.028
Albert II, King of the Belgians
Belgian history 949.304 4
Albert Falls and Nature Reserve (South Africa) T2—684 75
Alberta 971.23
T2—712 3
Alberton (South Africa : District) T2—682 2
Albigensianism 273.6
denomination 284.4
see also Christian denominations
persecution of 272.3
Albigensians
religious group T7—244
Albinism
medicine 616.55
see also Skin
Albumin glue 668.32
Albumins 572.66
biochemistry 572.66
chemistry 547.752
see also Proteins
Albuminuria
medicine 616.63
see also Urinary system
Albuquerque (N.M.) T2—789 61
Albury (N.S.W.) T2—944 8
Alcedinidae 598.78
Alcelaphinae 599.645
Alces 599.657
Alchemy 540.112
Alcidae 598.33
Alcohol 547.031
see also Alcoholic beverages; Alcohols
Alcohol abuse 362.292
see also Alcoholism
Alcoholic beverages 641.21
commercial processing 663.1
cooking with 641.62
customs 394.13
ethics 178.1
see also Ethical problems
home preparation 641.874
product safety 363.192 9
see also Food—product safety
public control 363.41
law 344.054 1
public administration 353.37
Alcoholics T1—087 4
Alcoholics Anonymous 362.292 86
Alcoholism 362.292
law 344.044 61
medicine 616.861
pastoral theology 291.61
Christianity 259.429 2
personal health 613.81
school problem 371.784

Alcoholism (continued)
  social theology 291.178 322 92
    Christianity 261.832 292
  social welfare 362.292
  see also Substance abuse
Alcohols 547.031
  aromatic chemistry 547.631
  chemical engineering 661.82
  chemistry 547.031
  fuel 662.669 2
    cooking 641.585
  human toxicology 615.951 31
  pharmacodynamics 615.782 8
Alcona County (Mich.) T2—774 79
Alcorn County (Miss.) T2—762 993
Alcyonaria 593.6
Aldabra Island (Seychelles) T2—696
Aldehydes 547.036
  aromatic chemistry 547.636
  chemical engineering 661.85
Alderflies 595.747
Alderney (England) T2—423 43
Alders 583.48
Ale 641.23
  commercial processing 663.42
  cooking with 641.623
  home preparation 641.873
Aleatory composition 781.32
Alekseĭ Mikhaĭlovich, Czar of Russia
  Russian history 947.048
Alemán, Miguel
  Mexican history 972.082 7
Alentejo (Portugal) T2—469 5
Aleppo (Syria : Province) T2—569 13
Alessandri, Jorge
  Chilean history 983.064 4
Alessandria (Italy : Province) T2—451 4
Alethopteris 561.597
Aleut T5—971 9
Aleut language 497.19
  T6—971 9
Aleut literature 897.19
Aleutian Islands (Alaska) T2—798 4
Alexander I, Emperor of Russia
  Russian history 947.072
Alexander II, Emperor of Russia
  Russian history 947.081
Alexander III, Emperor of Russia
  Russian history 947.082
Alexander County (Ill.) T2—773 999
Alexander County (N.C.) T2—756 795
Alexandria (Egypt)
  ancient T2—32
Alexandria (Egypt : Province) T2—621
Alexandria (South Africa : District) T2—687 5
Alexandria (Va.) T2—755 296
Alexandrian philosophy 186.4
Alexis, Czar of Russia
  Russian history 947.048
Alfalfa 633.31
  botany 583.74
  forage crop 633.31
Alfalfa County (Okla.) T2—766 22
Alfonsinos 597.64
Alfonso XII, King of Spain
  Spanish history 946.074
Alfonso XIII, King of Spain
  Spanish history 946.074
Alfred (South Africa : District) T2—684 6
Alfred, King of England
  English history 942.016 4
Alfred the Great, King of England
  English history 942.016 4
Algae 579.8
  paleobotany 561.93
  physiology 571.298
  resource economics 333.953 8
Algal blooms 579.817 6
Algarve (Portugal) T2—469 6
Algebra 512
Algebraic function theory 512.74
Algebraic geometry 516.35
Algebraic groups 512.2
Algebraic K-theory 512.55
Algebraic logic 511.324
Algebraic number theory 512.74
Algebraic operations 512.92
Algebraic progressions 512.93
Algebraic topology 514.2
Algebraic varieties 516.353
Alger County (Mich.) T2—774 932
Algeria 965
  T2—65
Algerians T5—927 65
Algic languages 497.3
  T6—973
Algicides 668.652
  agricultural use 632.95
  chemical engineering 668.652
  pest control technology 628.97

Algiers (Algeria :
Province) T2—653
Algiers, War with United States,
1815 973.53
Algologists 579.809 2
Algology 579.8
Algoma (Ont. : District) T2—713 132
Algonkian era 551.715
geology 551.715
paleontology 560.171 5
Algonkian Indians T5—973
Algonkian languages 497.3
T6—973
Algonquin Provincial Park
(Ont.) T2—713 147
Algorithms 511.8
computer programming 005.1
see Manual at 005.1 vs. 510
Alicante (Spain : Province) T2—467 65
Alice (South Africa :
District) T2—687 92
Alice Springs (N.T.) T2—942 91
Alicyclic compounds 547.5
chemical engineering 661.8
Alien labor 331.62
law 344.016 2
Alien property
international law 341.484
law of war 341.67
Alienated classes 305.568
T1—086 94
Alienation (Law) 346.043 6
Alienation (Social psychology) 302.544
arts 700.453
T3C—353
literature 808.803 53
history and criticism 809.933 53
specific literatures T3B—080 353
history and criticism T3B—093 53
Aliens 323.631
T1—086 91
T7—069 1
international law 341.484
law of war 341.67
labor economics 331.62
labor law 344.016 2
legal status 346.013
constitutional law 342.083
private law 346.013
naturalization 323.623
political status 323.631
social group 305.906 91
Alimony 346.016 6
Aliphatic compounds 547.4
chemical engineering 661.8
Alismales 584.72
Alismatales 584.72
Alismidae 584.7
Aliwal North (South
Africa : District) T2—687 6
Alizarines 667.256
Alkali heath 583.628
Alkali metals 669.725
chemistry 546.38
materials science 620.189 6
metallurgy 669.725
see also Chemicals; Metals
Alkaline-earth metals 669.725
chemistry 546.39
materials science 620.189 6
metallurgy 669.725
see also Chemicals; Metals
Alkaline salts 546.342
chemical engineering 661.4
Alkaline-soil conditioners 631.825
chemical engineering 668.64
Alkalinity
soil science 631.42
Alkalis 546.32
chemical engineering 661.3
human toxicology 615.922
Alkaloidal plants 581.63
agriculture 633.7
botany 581.63
Alkaloids 572.549
biochemistry 572.549
humans 612.015 72
chemistry 547.72
pharmacognosy 615.321
Alkanes 547.411
chemical engineering 661.814
Alkenes 547.412
chemical engineering 661.814
Alkylation 547.21
chemical engineering 660.284 41
Alkynes 547.413
chemical engineering 661.814
All-age schools 371
All-cargo plane services 387.744
All-risk insurance coverage 368.09
All-star games (Baseball) 796.357 648
All-terrain cycling 796.63
see also Sports
All-terrain vehicles 388.34
driving 629.283 042
engineering 629.220 42

All-terrain vehicles (continued)
  military engineering 623.747
  repair 629.287 042
  transportation services 388.34
  see also Automotive vehicles
All-volunteer army 355.223 62
All-year school 371.236
Allah 297.211
Allamakee County (Iowa) T2—777 33
Allegan County (Mich.) T2—774 14
Allegany County (Md.) T2—752 94
Allegany County (N.Y.) T2—747 84
Alleghany County (N.C.) T2—756 832
Alleghany County (Va.) T2—755 816
Allegheny County (Pa.) T2—748 85
Allegheny Mountains T2—748 7
  Pennsylvania T2—748 7
  West Virginia T2—754 8
Allegheny River (Pa. and N.Y.) T2—748 6
Allegiance 323.6
Allegory
  art representation 704.946
  arts 700.415
    T3C—15
  Biblical 220.68
  literature 808.801 5
    history and criticism 809.915
    specific literatures T3B—080 15
      history and criticism T3B—091 5
  paintings 753.6
Allen, Bog of (Ireland) T2—418 5
Allen County (Ind.) T2—772 74
Allen County (Kan.) T2—781 94
Allen County (Ky.) T2—769 732
Allen County (Ohio) T2—771 42
Allen Parish (La.) T2—763 58
Allendale County (S.C.) T2—757 77
Allende Gossens, Salvador
  Chilean history 983.064 6
Allerdale (England : District) T2—427 87
Allergenic plants
  botany 581.657
Allergies (Biology) 571.972
Allergies (Human)
  cooking for 641.563 1
  incidence 614.599 3
  medicine 616.97
  pediatrics 618.929 7
  see also Diseases (Human)
Alliaceae 584.33
  edible bulbs 641.352 6
    cooking 641.652 6
    food 641.352 6
    garden crop 635.26
Alliances 327.116
  international relations 327.116
  military science 355.031
  see also Allies (Military powers)
Allied fire insurance lines 368.12
  see also Insurance
  see Manual at 368.12
Allied forces 355.356
Allier (France : Dept.) T2—445 7
Allies (Military powers) 355.031
  armed forces 355.356
Allies (World War I group) 940.332
Allies (World War II group) 940.533 2
Alligator pears 641.346 53
  see also Avocados
Alligators 597.98
  big game hunting 799.279 8
  conservation technology 639.977 98
  farming 639.398
  resource economics 333.957 98
Alliopteris 561.597
Allocation (Rationing)
  public administration 352.86
Allocation of staff 658.312 8
  public administration 352.66
Allodium 333.323 2
Alloecoela 592.42
Alloiocoela 592.42
Allopathy 610
  therapeutic system 615.531
Allorhythmia
  medicine 616.128
  see also Cardiovascular system
Allosaurus 567.912
Allotheria 569.29
Alloy binary systems
  metallurgy 669.94
Alloys 669
  chemistry 546.3
  materials science 620.16
  metallography 669.95
  metallurgy 669
  ship design 623.818 2
  shipbuilding 623.820 7
  structural engineering 624.182
  see Manual at 669: Alloys

Allspice 641.338 3
  botany 583.765
  see also Spices
Alluvial mining 622.292 7
Alluvium 551.354
Almanacs 030
Almanacs (Ephemerides) 528
Almere (Netherlands) T2—492 2
Almería (Spain : Province) T2—468 1
Almonds 641.345 5
  agriculture 634.55
  botany 583.73
  commercial processing 664.804 55
  cooking 641.645 5
  food 641.345 5
Almsgiving 291.446
  Christianity 248.46
  ethics 177.7
    see also Ethical problems
  Islam 297.54
Almshouses 362.585
  architecture 725.55
Alnwick (England :
    District) T2—428 87
Alodium 333.323 2
Aloe barbadensis
  pharmacology 615.324 32
Aloe vera
  pharmacology 615.324 32
Aloes (Century plants) 584.352
Aloes (Hemp) 584.352
Aloes (Lilies) 584.32
  floriculture 635.934 32
Alopecia
  medicine 616.546
  see also Hair
Alopex 599.776 4
Alouatta 599.855
Alpaca wool textiles 677.32
  see also Textiles
Alpacas 636.296 6
Alpena County (Mich.) T2—774 81
Alpenhorns 788.92
  see also Brass instruments
Alpes de Haute-Provence
    (France) T2—449 5
Alpes-Maritimes (France) T2—449 41
Alpha cellulose 676.4
Alpha decay 539.752 2
Alpha particles 539.723 2
Alphabets 411
  applied linguistics 418
    specific languages T4—81
  decorative arts 745.61
Alphabets (continued)
  printing 686.21
  specific languages T4—11
Alphorns 788.92
  see also Brass instruments
Alpine biology 578.753 8
Alpine County (Calif.) T2—794 43
Alpine ecology 577.538
Alpine gardens 635.952 8
Alpine plants 581.753 8
  floriculture 635.952 8
Alpine skiing 796.935
  see also Sports
Alps T2—494 7
  France T2—449
  Italy T2—451
  Switzerland T2—494 7
Alsace (France) T2—443 83
Alsatian (Dog) 636.737 6
Alsatian dialect 437.944 383
  T6—34
Alstroemeriaceae 584.353
Alta Verapaz (Guatemala) T2—728 151
Altagracia (Dominican
    Republic : Province) T2—729 385
Altai language 494.33
  T6—943 3
Altai Mountains T2—517 3
Altaic languages 494
  T6—94
Altaic literatures 894
Altaĭskiĭ kraĭ (Russia) T2—573
Altar railings 247.1
  architecture 726.529 6
Altar screens 247.1
  architecture 726.529 6
Altars 291.37
  architecture 726.529 1
  Christianity 247.1
Altay (Russia) T2—573
Alterations
  arts 702.874
  clothing 646.408
    commercial 687.044
    home sewing 646.408
Altered states of consciousness 154.4
Alternating current 621.31
Alternating-current machinery 621.313 3
Alternating-current transmission 621.319 13
Alternating manic-depressive
    psychoses
  medicine 616.895
  see also Mental illness
Alternation of generations 571.884

Alternative education 371.04
Alternative energy resources 333.794
  economics 333.794
  engineering 621.042
Alternative higher education 378.03
  see also Higher education
Alternative medicine 610
  health 613
  therapeutics 615.5
Alternative schools 371.04
  elementary education 372.104 24
Alternative technology
  economics 338.927
Altimeters 629.135 2
Altitude sickness
  medicine 616.989 3
  see also Environmental diseases (Human)
Alto Adige (Italy) T2—453 83
Alto Alentejo (Portugal) T2—469 52
Alto horns 788.974
  see also Brass instruments
Alto Paraguay (Paraguay : Dept.) T2—892 27
Alto Paraná (Paraguay) T2—892 132
Alto recorders 788.365
  see also Woodwind instruments
Alto saxophones 788.73
  see also Woodwind instruments
Alto voices
  children's 782.78
    choral and mixed voices 782.78
    single voices 783.78
  men's 782.86
    choral and mixed voices 782.86
    single voices 783.86
  women's 782.68
    choral and mixed voices 782.68
    single voices 783.68
Altos (Guatemala : Province) T2—728 18
Altruism
  ethical systems 171.8
  personality trait 155.232
Alumina 553.67
  economic geology 553.67
  technology 666.72
Aluminum 669.722
  architectural construction 721.044 772 2
  building construction 693.772 2
  building material 691.872 2
  chemical engineering 661.067 3
Aluminum (continued)
  chemistry 546.673
  decorative arts 739.57
  economic geology 553.492 6
  human toxicology 615.925 673
  materials science 620.186
  metallography 669.957 22
  metallurgy 669.722
  metalworking 673.722
  mining 622.349 26
  physical metallurgy 669.967 22
  ship design 623.818 26
  shipbuilding 623.820 7
  structural engineering 624.182 6
  see also Chemicals; Metals
Aluminum lithography 763.23
Aluminum soaps 668.125
Alumni
  social group T7—379
Alunite
  mineralogy 549.755
Alvarez, Luis Echeverría
  Mexican history 972.083 2
Alveolar abscesses
  dentistry 617.632
  see also Dentistry
Älvsborgs län (Sweden) T2—486
Alwa (Kingdom) 962.620 22
Alyn and Deeside (Wales) T2—429 36
Alyssums 635.933 64
  botany 583.64
  floriculture 635.933 64
Alzheimer's disease 362.196 831
  geriatrics 618.976 831
  medicine 616.831
  social services 362.196 831
  see also Nervous system
AM radio stations 384.545 3
  see also Radio stations
AM radio systems 621.384 153
Amaas
  medicine 616.913
  see also Communicable diseases (Human)
Amador County (Calif.) T2—794 42
Amalgamations of corporations 338.83
  see also Mergers
Amalgams
  dentistry 617.675
  see also Dentistry
Amambay (Paraguay) T2—892 137
Amanzimtoti (South Africa) T2—684 55
Amapá (Brazil : State) T2—811 6

Amaranthaceae 583.53
Amaranths 583.53
  botany 583.53
  cooking 641.631
  field crop 633.1
  floriculture 635.933 53
  food 641.331
Amaryllidaceae 584.34
Amaryllises 635.934 34
  botany 584.34
  floriculture 635.934 34
Amasya İli (Turkey) T2—563
Amateur cinematography 778.534 9
Amateur circuses 791.3
Amateur motion pictures 791.433
  see also Motion pictures
Amateur radio 384.54
  communications services 384.54
  engineering 621.384 16
    see Manual at 621.38416 vs. 621.38454
  international law 341.757 7
  law 343.099 45
  public administration 354.75
Amateur sports 796.042
  see also Sports
  see Manual at 796.08 vs. 796.04
Amateur theater 792.022 2
Amateur video recording 778.59
Amateur workshops 684.08
Amateurs
  social group T7—090 9
Amaurotic idiocy
  medicine 616.858 845
  see also Mental retardation
Amazon River T2—811
  Brazil T2—811
  Peru T2—854 4
Amazonas (Brazil) T2—811 3
Amazonas (Colombia : Comisaría) T2—861 7
Amazonas (Peru) T2—854 6
Amazonas (Venezuela : Territory) T2—876 4
Amazónica (Ecuador) T2—866 4
Ambassadors 327.209 2
  occupational group T7—352 2
Amber 553.879
  carving 736.6
  see also Semiprecious stones
Amber Valley (England : Borough) T2—425 16
Ambition
  social psychology 302.54
Amblypygi 595.453 6
Ambulance services 362.188
  armed forces 355.345
  World War I 940.475 3
  World War II 940.547 53
  see also Health services
Ambulances 362.188
  driving 629.283 34
  engineering 629.222 34
  health services 362.188
    see also Health services
  military engineering 623.747 24
  military equipment 355.83
  repair 629.287 234
  sanitation services 363.729 7
    see also Waste control
Ambulatory services 362.12
  see also Health services
Ambush tactics 355.422
Amebiasis
  incidence 614.53
  medicine 616.936
  see also Communicable diseases (Human)
Amebic dysentery
  incidence 614.516
  medicine 616.935 3
  see also Communicable diseases (Human)
Amelia County (Va.) T2—755 634
Amenhetep IV, King of Egypt
  Egyptian history 932.014
Amenhotep, King of Egypt
  Egyptian history 932.014
Amenorrhea
  gynecology 618.172
  see also Female genital system
Amens
  music 782.295
American Arctic seawaters 551.468 7
  T2—163 27
American Baptist Association 286.136
  see also Baptists
American Baptist Churches in the U.S.A. 286.131
  see also Baptists
American Baptist Convention 286.131
  see also Baptists
American bison 599.643
  see also Bison
American black bear 599.785

American buffalo 599.643
see also Bison
American College Testing Program 378.166 2
American elk 599.654 2
big game hunting 799.276 542
American English dialects (U.S.) 427.973
T6—21
American English pronunciation (U.S.) 421.54
American English spelling (U.S.) 421.54
American Evangelical Lutheran Church 284.133 2
see also Lutheran church
American Federation of Labor 331.883 209 73
American Federation of Labor and Congress of Industrial Organizations 331.880 973
American folk music 781.621 3
American folk songs 782.421 621 3
American football 796.332
see also Sports
American football players 796.332 092
American Independent Party 324.273 3
American Indian languages 497
T6—97
South America 498
T6—98
American Indian literatures 897
South America 898
American Indians T5—97
South America T5—98
American Legion 369.186 1
American literature (English) 810
American Lutheran Church 284.131
see also Lutheran church
American-Mexican Border Region T2—721
American Muslim Mission 297.87
American native languages 497
T6—97
South America 498
T6—98
American native literatures 897
South America 898
American native peoples T5—97
military troops
United States Revolutionary War 973.343
War of 1812 973.524 2
World War II 940.540 3
American native peoples (continued)
religion 299.7
North America 299.7
South America 299.8
social aspects 305.897
South America T5—98
see Manual at 970.004
American Nazi Party 324.273 38
American opossums 599.276
American organs 786.55
instrument 786.551 9
music 786.55
see also Keyboard instruments
American Party 324.273 2
American Reformed Church 285.7
see also Reformed Church (American Reformed)
American Revised version Bible 220.520 4
American Revolution, 1775–1783 973.3
American saddlebred horse 636.13
American Samoa 996.13
T2—961 3
American Sign Language 419
American Standard version Bible 220.520 4
American Veterans of World War II, Korea, and Vietnam 369.186 2
American Whig Party 324.273 23
Americans (U.S.) T5—13
Americas T2—7
Americium 546.441
see also Chemicals
Amerind languages 497
T6—97
South America 498
T6—98
Amerind literatures 897
South America 898
Amerindians T5—97
South America T5—98
Amersfoort (South Africa : District) T2—682 7
Ameslan (Sign language) 419
Amethysts 553.87
see also Semiprecious stones
Amhara (African people) T5—928
Amharic language 492.87
T6—928 7
Amharic literature 892.87
Amherst (N.S.) T2—716 11
Amherst County (Va.) T2—755 496

Amherst of Arracan, William Pitt Amherst, Earl
  Indian history 954.031 3
Ami (Taiwan people) T5—992 5
Amiante (Quebec) T2—714 573
Amicicide (Military science) 355.422
Amides 547.042
  chemical engineering 661.894
Amiiformes 597.41
Amin, Idi
  Ugandan history 967.610 42
Amination 547.25
  chemical engineering 660.284 45
Amines 547.042
  biochemistry 572.548
  chemical engineering 661.894
Amino acid sequence 572.633
Amino acids 572.65
  applied nutrition 613.282
  biochemistry 572.65
    humans 612.015 75
  chemistry 547.75
  see also Proteins
Aminoglycosides
  pharmacology 615.329
Amish
  biography 289.709 2
  religious group T7—287
Amish churches 289.73
  see also Mennonite Church
Amish cooking 641.566
Amite County (Miss.) T2—762 24
Amman (Jordan : Province) T2—569 58
Ammeters 621.374 4
Ammonia 546.711 2
  chemical engineering 661.34
Ammonite language 492.6
  T6—926
Ammonium fertilizers 631.841
  chemical engineering 668.624 1
Ammonium hydroxide 546.711 2
  chemical engineering 661.34
Ammonium nitrate fertilizer 631.842
  chemical engineering 668.624 2
Ammonium salts 546.711 24
  chemical engineering 661.5
Ammonoidea 564.53
Ammunition 355.825
  military 355.825
    engineering 623.45
    use 355.825
  small arms engineering
    military 623.451
Ammunition (continued)
  small arms manufacturing
    technology 683.406
Amnesia
  medicine 616.852 32
  see also Mental illness
Amnesty 364.65
  law 345.077
  penology 364.65
Amniocentesis
  obstetrics 618.320 427 5
Amniotic fluid
  human physiology 612.63
  obstetrics 618.34
Amoebas 579.432
Amoebiasis
  incidence 614.53
  medicine 616.936
  see also Communicable diseases (Human)
Amoebic dysentery
  incidence 614.516
  medicine 616.935 3
  see also Communicable diseases (Human)
Amoebida 579.432
Amoraim 296.120 092
Amorites T5—921
Amorphous solids 530.413
Amos (Biblical book) 224.8
Amoy dialect 495.17
  T6—951 7
Ampere-hour meters 621.374 4
Amphetamine abuse 362.299
  medicine 616.864
  personal health 613.84
  social welfare 362.299
  see also Substance abuse
Amphibians 597.8
  art representation 704.943 278
  commercial hunting 639.13
  conservation technology 639.977 8
  drawing 743.676
  farming 639.378
  food 641.396
    cooking 641.696
  paleozoology 567.8
  resource economics 333.957 8
  zoology 597.8
Amphibious air-cushion vehicles
  engineering 629.325
  military engineering 623.748 5
Amphibious operations 355.46
  marine forces 359.964 6

Amphibious planes 387.733 48
  engineering 629.133 348
  transportation services 387.733 48
  see also Aircraft
Amphiboles
  mineralogy 549.66
Amphineura 594.27
Amphipoda 595.378
Amphisbaenia 597.94
Amphissa (Greece) T2—383
Amphitheaters 796.068
  architecture 725.827
Amphoteric salts 546.342
  chemical engineering 661.4
Amplifiers 621.381 535
  electronic circuits 621.381 535
  radio engineering 621.384 12
Amplitude-modulation radio systems 621.384 153
Amplitude modulators
  electronic circuits 621.381 536 2
Amputation of limbs
  surgery 617.580 59
Amsterdam (Netherlands) T2—492 352
Amsterdam Island 969.9
  T2—699
Amulets 133.44
  Islamic popular practices 297.39
  numismatics 737.23
  religious significance 291.37
Amundsen Sea 551.469 4
  T2—167 4
Amur (Russia : Oblast) T2—577
Amur River (China and Russia) T2—577
Amurskaîa oblast´ (Russia) T2—577
Amusement parks 791.068
  architecture 725.76
  area planning 711.558
  landscape architecture 712.5
  recreation 791.068
Amusements 790
  journalism 070.444
  law 344.099
  see also Recreation
  see Manual at 790
AMVETS (Veterans) 369.186 2
Amyl nitrite abuse 362.299
  medicine 616.86
  personal health 613.8
  social welfare 362.299
  see also Substance abuse
Amylases 572.756
  see also Enzymes
Amyloidosis
  medicine 616.399 5
  see also Digestive system
Amyotrophic lateral sclerosis
  medicine 616.83
  see also Nervous system
Anabaptists 284.3
  religious group T7—243
  see also Christian denominations
Anabolism 572.45
  see also Metabolism
Anacardiaceae 583.77
  edible fruits 641.344 4
    cooking 641.644 4
    food 641.344 4
    orchard crops 634.44
Anaerobic bacteria 579.314 9
Anaerobic digestion (Sewage treatment) 628.354
Anaerobic gram-negative rods 579.325
Anaerobic respiration 572.478
Anagrams 793.734
Anahim Lake (B.C.) T2—711 75
Analgesic abuse 362.299
  medicine 616.86
  personal health 613.8
  social welfare 362.299
  see also Substance abuse
Analgesics
  pharmacodynamics 615.783
  see also Nervous system
Analog circuits
  electronics 621.381 5
Analog communications 621.382
Analog computers 004.19
  electronic 004.19
    engineering 621.391 9
  nonelectronic 004.9
  peripherals 004.719
Analog instruments
  technology 681.1
Analog-to-digital converters
  computer engineering 621.398 14
  computer science 004.64
  electronic engineering 621.381 59
Analogy
  logic 169
Analysis (Mathematics) 515
Analysis of covariance 519.538
Analysis of variance 519.538
Analysis situs 514
Analytic curves 516.362
Analytic functions 515.73

Analytic geometry 516.3
Analytic number theory 512.73
Analytic spaces 515.94
Analytic surfaces 516.362
Analytic topology 514.7
Analytic trigonometry 516.34
Analytical accounting 657.48
Analytical bibliography 010.42
Analytical biochemistry 572.36
humans 612.015 85
Analytical chemistry 543
minerals 549.133
organic 547.3
qualitative 544
quantitative 545
see Manual at 543 vs. 544–545
Analytical guides (Music) 780.15
Analytical mechanics 531.015 15
Analytical philosophy 146.4
Anambra State (Nigeria) T2—669 48
Ananda Mahidol, King of Thailand
Thai history 959.304 3
Anaphrodisiacs
pharmacodynamics 615.766
Anapsida 567.92
Anarchism 335.83
economics 335.83
ideal state 321.07
political ideology 320.57
Anarchist communities
economics 335.9
see Manual at 338.7 vs. 335.9
Anarchists 335.830 92
political group T7—335
Anarcho-syndicalism 335.82
economics 335.82
political ideology 320.57
Anarchy 335.83
see also Anarchism
Anas 598.413
Anaspidea 594.37
Anatidae 598.41
Anatolia T2—561
Anatolian languages 491.998
T6—919 98
Anatolikē Makedonia kai Thrakē (Greece) T2—495 7
Anatomic embryology
humans 611.013
Anatomy 571.3
domestic animals 636.089 1
drawing
animals 743.6
humans 743.49
humans 611
see Manual at 599.94 vs. 611; *also at* 612 vs. 611
microorganisms 571.633 29
Anatosaurus 567.914
Anaxagorean philosophy 182.8
Anbār (Iraq) T2—567 4
Ancash (Peru) T2—852 1
Ancestors T1—085 3
T7—043
family relationships 306.874
objects of worship 291.213
Ancestry 929.1
Anchor ice 551.344
Anchorages 387.1
engineering 627.22
see also Ports
Anchors 623.862
Anchovies 641.392
cooking 641.692
food 641.392
zoology 597.45
Ancienne-Lorette (Quebec) T2—714 471
Ancient Arabic Order of the Nobles of the Mystic Shrine for North America 366.16
biography 366.160 92
social group T7—366 1
Ancient architecture 722
Ancient civilization 930
Ancient history 930
T1—090 1
Ancient law 340.53
Ancient philosophy 180
Ancient remedies
therapeutics 615.899
Ancient sculpture 732
Ancient world T2—3
see Manual at T2—3 vs. T2—4–T2—9
Ancona (Italy : Province) T2—456 71
Ancyclostomiasis
incidence 614.555 4
medicine 616.965 4
see also Communicable diseases (Human)
Andalusia (Spain) T2—468
Andalusite
mineralogy 549.62

Andaman and Nicobar Islands T2—548 8
Andaman Sea 551.467 65
  T2—165 65
Andamanese T5—991 1
Andean languages 498.32
  T6—983 2
Anderson County (Kan.) T2—781 672
Anderson County (Ky.) T2—769 463
Anderson County (S.C.) T2—757 25
Anderson County (Tenn.) T2—768 73
Anderson County (Tex.) T2—764 229
Andes T2—8
Andes (Chile : Province) T2—832 42
Andesite 552.23
Andhra language 494.827
  T6—948 27
Andhra literature 894.827
Andhra Pradesh (India) T2—548 4
Andi languages 499.964
  T6—999 64
Andoke language 498
  T6—98
Andoque language 498
  T6—98
Andorra 946.79
  T2—467 9
Andreaeales 588.2
Andrew County (Mo.) T2—778 126
Andrews County (Tex.) T2—764 856
Androgens
  human physiology 612.61
  see also Male genital system
Androgynous behavior
  psychology 155.334
Andropogoneae 584.92
Andropov, I͡U. V. (I͡Uriĭ Vladimirovich)
  Russian history 947.085 4
Andros Island (Bahamas) T2—729 6
Andros Island (Greece) T2—495 85
Androscoggin County (Me.) T2—741 82
Androscoggin River (Me.) T2—741 8
Anecdotes
  literature 808.882
    specific literatures T3B—802
      individual authors T3A—8
Anemia
  medicine 616.152
  see also Cardiovascular system
Anemones 583.34
  floriculture 635.933 34
Anesthesiologists 617.960 92
  law 344.041 2
  occupational group T7—617
Anesthesiology 617.96
Anesthetics
  pharmacodynamics 615.781
Anesthetists 617.960 92
  law 344.041 2
  occupational group T7—617
Aneuploidy 572.877
Aneurysms
  medicine 616.133
  see also Cardiovascular system
Angas language 493.7
  T6—937
Angaston (S. Aust.) T2—942 32
Angelfishes 597.72
  Cichlidae 597.74
  Pomacanthidae 597.72
Angelina County (Tex.) T2—764 173
Angels 291.215
  art representation 704.948 64
  arts T3C—382 912 15
  Christianity 235.3
  Islam 297.215
  Judaism 296.315
  literature 808.803 829 1215
    history and criticism 809.933 829 1215
    specific literatures T3B—080 382 91215
      history and criticism T3B—093 829 1215
Anger 152.47
  ethics 179.8
  psychology 152.47
  see also Vices
Angina pectoris
  medicine 616.122
  see also Cardiovascular system
Angiocardiography
  medicine 616.120 757 2
  see also Cardiovascular system
Angiography
  medicine 616.130 757 2
  see also Cardiovascular system
Angiology 616.13
  see also Cardiovascular system
Angioplasty 617.413
  see also Cardiovascular system

Angiospermae		580
see also Plants		
see Manual at 583–584		
Angle harps		787.94
see also Stringed instruments		
Angle trisection		516.204
Anglerfishes		597.62
Angles		516.15
Anglesey (Wales)	T2—429 21	
Anglican cathedrals		
architecture		726.65
Anglican chant		782.322 3
Anglican Communion		283
church government		262.03
parishes		254.03
church law		262.983
doctrines		230.3
catechisms and creeds		238.3
general councils		262.53
guides to Christian life		248.483
liturgy		264.03
missions		266.3
moral theology		241.043
persecution by Queen Mary		272.6
public worship		264.03
religious associations		267.183
religious education		268.83
religious orders		255.83
church history		271.83
women		255.983
church history		271.983
seminaries		230.073 3
theology		230.3
Anglican sacred music		781.713
public worship		782.322 3
music		782.322 3
religion		264.030 2
Anglicans		
biography		283.092
religious group	T7—23	
Angling		799.12
see also Sports		
Anglo-Boer War, 1880–1881		968.204 6
Anglo-Boer War, 1899–1902		968.048
Anglo-Dutch Wars, 1652–1653		949.204
Anglo-Egyptian Sudan		962.403
	T2—624	
Anglo-Indians	T5—914 11	
Anglo-Irish War, 1919–1921		941.508 21
Anglo-Saxon language		429
	T6—29	
Anglo-Saxon law		340.536 2
Anglo-Saxon literature		829
Anglo-Saxons	T5—2	
Anglo-Spanish War, 1739–1741		946.055
Angola		967.3
	T2—673	
Angolans	T5—967 3	
Angolese	T5—967 3	
Angoni language		496.398
	T6—963 98	
Angora cat		636.83
Angora goat		636.398 5
Angoulême, House of		944.028
Angoumois (France)	T2—446 5	
Angra do Heroísmo (Azores : District)	T2—469 9	
Anguilla		972.973
	T2—729 73	
Anguilla (Eels)		597.432
Anguillidae		597.432
Anguilliformes		597.43
Angular momentum (Nuclear physics)		539.725
Angus (Scotland)	T2—412 6	
Angus cattle		636.223
Anhidrosis		
medicine		616.56
see also Skin		
Anhimidae		598.41
Anhui Sheng (China)	T2—512 25	
Anhwei Province (China)	T2—512 25	
Anhydrite		
mineralogy		549.752
Anhydrous sulfates		
mineralogy		549.752
Animal babies		591.39
domestic animals		636.07
mammals		599.139
Animal behavior		591.5
comparative psychology		156
Animal black		662.93
Animal body disposal		363.78
Animal breeding		636.082
Animal combat sports		791.8
performing arts		791.8
Animal communication		591.59
physiology		573.92
Animal communities		591.782
Animal courtship		591.562
Animal defenses		591.47
Animal-derived drugs		
pharmacology		615.36
Animal-derived poisons		
human toxicology		615.94
Animal diseases		571.91
agricultural economics		338.14
veterinary medicine		636.089 6

Animal ecology 591.7
Animal experimentation 571.107 24
  ethics 179.4
    see also Animals—
      treatment of—ethics
  medicine 619
Animal fats 665.2
  food 641.36
  food technology 664.3
  home cooking 641.66
  industrial technology 665.2
Animal feeding 636.084
Animal feeds 636.085 5
  see also Feeds
Animal fibers 338.476 773
  materials science 620.197
  production economics 338.476 773
  textiles 677.3
    arts 746.043
    see also Textiles
Animal flight 573.798
Animal food 636.085 5
  see also Feeds
Animal ghosts 133.14
Animal glue 668.32
Animal grooming
  agriculture 636.083 3
  zoology 591.563
Animal heat 571.76
Animal hormones 573.44
Animal hospitals 636.083 2
Animal husbandry 636
  equipment manufacturing
      technology 681.763 6
  production economics 338.176
  public administration 354.56
Animal industry 338.176
  law 343.076 6
  public administration 354.56
Animal intelligence 591.513
  comparative psychology 156.39
Animal language 591.59
Animal locomotion 573.79
Animal magnetism 154.72
  parapsychology 133.89
Animal manures
  waste technology 628.746 6
Animal migration 591.568
Animal oils 665.2
  food 641.36
  food technology 664.3
  home cooking 641.66
  industrial technology 665.2
Animal performances 791.8
  circuses 791.32
Animal pest control 363.78
  see also Pest control
Animal pests 591.65
Animal physiology 571.1
  see Manual at 571–575
Animal populations 591.788
Animal psychology 591.5
  comparative psychology 156
Animal racing 798
  see also Sports
Animal rescue 636.083 2
Animal resources 333.954
  law 346.046 954
  public administration 354.349
  see Manual at 338.37 vs.
      333.954
Animal rights
  ethics 179.3
    see also Animals—
      treatment of—ethics
Animal sacrifice 291.34
Animal shelters 636.083 2
Animal sounds 591.594
Animal viruses 579.2
Animal wastes 631.86
  law 344.046 22
  technology 628.746 6
  water pollution engineering 628.168 46
Animal waxes 665.13
Animal weapons 591.47
Animal welfare 636.083 2
  animal husbandry 636.083 2
  law 344.049
Animals 590
  agricultural pests 632.6
  agriculture 636
    production economics 338.176
  art representation 704.943 2
  arts 700.462
    T3C—362
  care and maintenance 636.083
  conservation 333.954 16
    see Manual at
      333.955–333.959 vs.
      639.97
  conservation technology 639.9
  disease carriers 571.986
    medicine 614.43
  drawing 743.6
  folklore 398.245
    history and criticism 398.369

Animals (continued)
  food source 641.306
    agriculture 636.088 3
  growth 571.81
  legendary 398.245 4
    see also Legendary animals
  literature 808.803 62
    history and criticism 809.933 62
    specific literatures T3B—080 362
      history and criticism T3B—093 62
  painting 758.3
  physiology 571.1
    see Manual at 571–575
  religious worship 291.212
  resource economics 333.954
    see Manual at 333.955–333.959 vs. 639.97
  treatment of
    ethics 179.3
      religion 291.569 3
        Buddhism 294.356 93
        Christianity 241.693
        Hinduism 294.548 693
        Judaism 296.369 3
  use in mining 622.65
  zoology 590
  see Manual at 579–590; *also at* 800 vs. 398.245, 590, 636
Animals for specific purposes 636.088
  see Manual at 636.1–636.8 vs. 636.088
Animals in Bible 220.859
Animals in warfare (Tactics) 355.424
Animated cartoons
  cinematography 778.534 7
  drawing 741.58
  motion pictures 791.433
Animism
  comparative religion 291.21
  philosophy 147
Anion separation analysis 544.13
Anis 598.74
Anise 641.338 2
  botany 583.849
  see also Flavorings
Aniseikonia
  incidence 614.599 7
  ophthalmology 617.758
  see also Eyes
Anisophylleaceae 583.76
Anjou (France) T2—441 8
Ankara İli (Turkey) T2—563
Ankles (Human) 612.98
  physiology 612.98
  regional medicine 617.584
  surgery 617.584
  see also Lower extremities (Human)
Anklets (Ornaments) 391.7
  customs 391.7
  making 739.278
  see also Jewelry
Ankole (Kingdom) 967.610 1
  T2—676 1
Ankylosauria 567.915
Ankylosing spondylitis
  medicine 616.73
  see also Musculoskeletal system
Ann Arbor (Mich.) T2—774 35
Anna, Empress of Russia
  Russian history 947.061
Annaba (Algeria : Province) T2—655
Annam-Muong languages 495.92
  T6—959 2
Annam-Muong literatures 895.92
Annam-Muong peoples T5—959 2
Annamese T5—959 2
Annamese language 495.922
  T6—959 22
Annandale and Eskdale (Scotland : District) T2—414 83
Annapolis (Md.) T2—752 56
Annapolis (N.S. : County) T2—716 33
Annatto tree 583.625
Anne (Mother of the Virgin Mary), Saint 232.933
  private prayers to 242.75
Anne, Queen of England
  British history 941.069
  English history 942.069
  Scottish history 941.106 9
Anne Arundel County (Md.) T2—752 55
Annealing glass 666.129
Annealing metals 671.36
Annelida 592.6
  paleozoology 562.6
Annexation 325.32
  city government 320.859
  international law 341.42
  law 342.041 2
  political science 325.32
Annihilation (Nuclear particles) 539.75
Annihilationism 236.23

Anniversaries 394.2
  see also Celebrations
Annobón (Equatorial Guinea) T2—671 86
Annonaceae 583.22
  edible fruits 641.344 1
    cooking 641.644 1
    food 641.344 1
    orchard crops 634.41
Annotations to cases 348.047
Annotations to laws 348.027
Announcements
  etiquette 395.4
Announcing
  radio performances 791.443
  television performances 791.453
Annual publications 050
  T1—05
  see also Annuals (Publications)
Annual wages 331.216 2
  personnel management 658.322 2
Annuals (Plants) 582.12
  floriculture 635.931 2
Annuals (Publications) 050
  T1—05
  almanacs 030
  encyclopedia yearbooks 030
  publishing 070.572
Annuities
  insurance 368.37
    see also Insurance
  personal finance 332.024 01
  tax law 343.064
Annulment 346.016 65
Annunciation to Mary 232.912
Anodynes
  pharmacodynamics 615.783
  see also Nervous system
Anointing of the sick 234.167
  public worship 265.7
  theology 234.167
Anoka County (Minn.) T2—776 65
Anomochloeae 584.9
Anomura 595.387
Anonymous works
  bibliographies 014
Anoplura 595.756
Anorexia nervosa 362.25
  medicine 616.852 62
  social welfare 362.25
  see also Mental illness
Anostraca 595.32
Anoxygenic phototrophic bacteria 579.38
Anschluss
  Austrian history 943.605 22
Anser 598.417 3
Anseriformes 598.41
  paleozoology 568.4
Anserini 598.417
Anson County (N.C.) T2—756 753
Answers
  books of miscellaneous facts 030
  study and teaching T1—076
Ant bear 599.31
Ant lions 595.747
Antacids
  pharmacodynamics 615.73
  see also Digestive system
Antalya İli (Turkey) T2—564
Antananarivo (Madagascar : Province) T2—691
Antarctic regions T2—989
Antarctic waters 551.469
  T2—167
Antarctica T2—989
Antártica Chilena (Chile : Province) T2—836 48
Antbirds 598.822 6
Ante-Nicene church 270.1
Anteaters 599.314
Antelope County (Neb.) T2—782 55
Antelopes 599.64
  big game hunting 799.276 4
  conservation technology 639.979 64
  resource economics 333.959 64
Antennas 621.382 4
  communications engineering 621.382 4
  radar engineering 621.384 83
  radio engineering 621.384 135
  satellite communication 621.382 54
  television engineering 621.388 35
Antenuptial contracts 346.016
Anterior chambers (Eyes)
  human physiology 612.841
  see also Eyes
Anthelmintics
  pharmacodynamics 615.733
Anthems 782.265
  choral and mixed voices 782.526 5
  single voices 783.092 65
Anthers 575.65
Anthocerotidae 588.3

Anthologies 080
  literature 808.8
    specific literatures T3B—08
      see Manual at T3B—08
        and T3B—09:
        Preference order
    see Manual at 808.8
  see Manual at 080; *also at* 080
      vs. 800; *also at* 081–089
Anthozoa 593.6
  paleozoology 563.6
Anthracenes 547.616
  chemical engineering 661.816
Anthracite coal 553.25
  economic geology 553.25
  mining 622.335
  properties 662.622 5
Anthrax (Biology)
  veterinary medicine 636.089 695 6
Anthrax (Human)
  incidence 614.561
  medicine 616.956
  see also Communicable
      diseases (Human)
Anthribidae 595.768
Anthropogenesis 599.938
Anthropoidea 599.8
  see also Primates
Anthropologists 301.092
  occupational group T7—309
Anthropology 301
  philosophical 128
  physical 599.9
  theological 291.22
    Christianity 233
    philosophy of religion 218
    see also Humans—religion
  see Manual at 302–307
Anthropometric design 620.82
Anthropometry 599.94
  see Manual at 599.94 vs. 611
Anthropomorphism
  comparative religion 291.211 2
  philosophy of religion 211
Anthroposophy 299.935
Anthuriums 635.934 64
  botany 584.64
  floriculture 635.934 64
Anti-federalist Party (U.S.) 324.273 26
Anti-Lebanon T2—569 14
Anti-mission Baptists 286.4
  see also Baptists
Anti-Semitism 305.892 4
  political aspects 323.119 24
Anti-Semitism (continued)
  social theology 291.172
    Christianity 261.26
Anti-Trinitarianism 289.1
Anti-union theories 331.880 1
Antiaircraft artillery 358.138 2
  military equipment 358.138 2
Antiaircraft artillery forces 358.13
Antiaircraft defenses 355.422
  see also Air warfare
Antiballistic missiles 358.174 82
  engineering 623.451 94
  military equipment 358.174 82
Antibiotics 615.329
  biochemistry
    humans 612.015 76
  chemistry 547.76
  pharmacology 615.329
Antibodies 571.967
  human immunology 616.079 8
Antibody-dependent immune
    mechanisms 571.968
  humans 616.079 9
Antichrist 236
Anticlines 551.86
Anticoagulants
  pharmacodynamics 615.718
  see also Cardiovascular
      system
Anticommunist international
    leagues 324.13
Anticonvulsants
  pharmacodynamics 615.784
  see also Nervous system
Anticosti Island (Quebec) T2—714 17
Anticyclones (Meteorology) 551.551 4
Antidepressants
  drug therapy 616.852 706 1
  pharmacodynamics 615.78
  see also Mental illness
Antidiuretics
  pharmacodynamics 615.761
  see also Urinary system
Antidotes
  human toxicology 615.908
Antiemetics
  pharmacodynamics 615.73
  see also Digestive system
Antifreeze solutions
  automotive 629.256
Antigen-antibody reactions 571.967 7
  human immunology 616.079 87
Antigen recognition 571.964 6
  human immunology 616.079 5

Antigens 571.964 5
  human immunology 616.079 2
Antigonish (N.S. : County) T2—716 14
Antigua T2—729 74
Antigua and Barbuda 972.974
  T2—729 74
Antiguans T5—969 729 74
Antillean Arawak Indians T5—979
Antilles 972.9
  T2—729
Antilles, Lesser T2—729
Antilocapridae 599.639
Antilopinae 599.646
Antimacassars 645.4
  arts 746.95
  home sewing 646.21
  household management 645.4
Antimatter 530
Antimilitarism 355.021 3
  military science 355.021 3
  sociology 303.66
Antimissile defense forces 358.174
Antimissile missiles 358.174 82
  engineering 623.451 94
  military equipment 358.174 82
Antimission Baptists 286.4
  see also Baptists
Antimonides
  mineralogy 549.32
Antimony 669.75
  chemical engineering 661.071 6
  chemistry 546.716
  economic geology 553.47
  materials science 620.189 5
  metallography 669.957 5
  metallurgy 669.75
  mining 622.347
  physical metallurgy 669.967 5
  see also Chemicals; Metals
Antinomianism 273.6
Antioch (Turkey) T2—564
  ancient 939.43
  T2—394 3
Antione-Labelle (Quebec) T2—714 225
Antioquia (Colombia : Dept.) T2—861 26
Antiparticles 539.72
Antipersonnel devices 623.451 4
Antipodes Islands (N.Z.) T2—939 9
Antiprotons 539.721 23
Antipyretics
  pharmacodynamics 615.75
Antique (Philippines) T2—599 5
Antique furniture 749.1
Antiques 745.1
  see Manual at 745.1
Antiquities 930.1
  international law 341.767 7
  law 344.094
Antisepsis
  obstetrics 618.89
  public health 614.48
  surgery 617.910 1
Antislavery movements 326.8
  see also Abolition of slavery
Antisocial personality disorders
  medicine 616.858 2
  see also Mental illness
Antisocial persons 305.906 92
  T1—086 92
Antispasmodics
  pharmacodynamics 615.784
  see also Nervous system
Antisubmarine reconnaissance (Air warfare) 358.45
Antisubmarine warfare 359.93
  World War I 940.451 6
  World War II 940.545 16
Antitank artillery forces 358.12
Antitoxins
  pharmacology 615.375
Antitrust law 343.072 1
Antitrust policies 338.8
Antitrust violations 364.168
  law 345.026 8
  public administration 353.43
Antofagasta (Chile : Province) T2—831 38
Antofagasta (Chile : Region) T2—831 3
Antonines 255.18
  church history 271.18
Antonym dictionaries 413.1
  specific languages T4—31
  specific subjects T1—03
Antrim (Northern Ireland : Borough) T2—416 12
Antrim (Northern Ireland : County) T2—416 1
Antrim County (Mich.) T2—774 85
Ants 595.796
  control technology 628.965 7
  culture 638.579 6
Antsiranana (Madagascar : Province) T2—691
Antwerp (Belgium) T2—493 222
Antwerp (Belgium : Province) T2—493 22

Anura 597.8
  paleozoology 567.8
Anus
  human anatomy 611.35
  human physiology 612.36
  medicine 616.35
  surgery 617.555
  see also Digestive system
Anvers (Belgium) T2—493 222
Anvil Island (B.C. : Island) T2—711 31
Anvils 682
  blacksmithing 682
  music 786.884 3
    see also Percussion instruments
Anxiety 152.46
Anxiety neuroses
  medicine 616.852 23
  see also Mental illness
Anyi (African people) T5—963 385
Anyi language 496.338 5
  T6—963 385
Anzoátegui (Venezuela : State) T2—875 2
Aomori-ken (Japan) T2—521 12
Aorta
  human anatomy 611.13
  human physiology 612.133
  medicine 616.138
  see also Cardiovascular system
Aortic valve
  human anatomy 611.12
  human physiology 612.17
  medicine 616.125
  see also Cardiovascular system
Aosta (Italy) T2—451 1
Aoudad 599.649
AP ammunition 623.451 8
Apache County (Ariz.) T2—791 37
Apache Indians T5—972
Apache languages 497.2
  T6—972
Apachean languages 497.2
  T6—972
Apalachicola River (Fla.) T2—759 92
Apartheid 305.800 968
  political ideology 320.560 968
Apartment-house districts
  area planning 711.58
Apartment houses 647.92
  architecture 728.314
  construction 690.831 4
Apartment houses (continued)
  household management 647.92
  social provision 363.5
Apartment sales 381.195
  management 658.87
  see also Commerce
Apartments 643.2
  architecture 728.314
  home economics 643.2
Apathy
  social psychology 302.17
Apatites 553.64
  mineralogy 549.72
Apatosaurus 567.913 8
Apennines T2—45
Aperients
  pharmacodynamics 615.732
  see also Digestive system
Apes 599.88
  animal husbandry 636.988
  experimental animals
    medicine 619.98
Aphanites 552.2
Aphasia
  medicine 616.855 2
  special education 371.914 2
  see also Communicative disorders
Aphid flies 595.774
Aphids 595.752
  agricultural pests 632.752
Aphorisms 398.9
Aphrodisiacs
  pharmacodynamics 615.766
Aphyllophorales 579.597
Apiaceae 583.849
Apical meristem 575.485
Apiculture 638.1
Apidae 595.799
APL (Educational credit) 371.264
Aplacophora 594.2
Aplastic anemia
  medicine 616.152
  see also Cardiovascular system
Apnea
  medicine 616.2
  see also Respiratory system
Apocalypse (Biblical book) 228
Apocalypses (Biblical literature) 220.046
  New Testament
    pseudepigrapha 229.94
  Old Testament
    pseudepigrapha 229.913

Apocrita 595.79
Apocrypha (Bible) 229
Apocryphal wisdom literature 229.3
Apocynaceae 583.93
Apoda (Amphibians) 597.82
Apodacea 593.96
Apodemus 599.358 5
Apodi 598.762
Apodidae 598.762
Apodiformes 598.76
  paleozoology 568.7
Apoidea 595.799
Apollo project 629.454
Apologetics 291.2
  Christianity 239
  Islam 297.29
  Judaism 296.35
Aponogetonaceae 584.74
Apoplexy
  medicine 616.81
  see also Nervous system
Apostates
  Christian polemics 239.7
Apostles 225.92
  art representation 704.948 62
  arts T3C—352 204
Apostles' Creed 238.11
Apostleship (Spiritual gift) 234.13
Apostolic Church 270.1
Apostolic succession 262.11
Apostolicity 262.72
Appalachian dulcimers 787.75
  see also Stringed instruments
Appalachian Mountains T2—74
  North Carolina T2—756 8
Appaloosa 636.13
Appanoose County (Iowa) T2—777 89
Apparatus T1—028 4
  teaching aids 371.33
  T1—078
Apparel 391
  see also Clothing
Apparitions 133.1
Apparitions of Mary 232.917
Appeal (Law) 347.08
Appeals of labor grievances 331.889 6
  see also Grievances (Labor)
Appellate courts 347.03
  England 347.420 3
  Scotland 347.411 03
  United States 347.732 4
Appellate procedure 347.08
Appendages 573.998
Appendectomies
  surgery 617.554 5
  see also Digestive system
Appendicitis
  medicine 616.34
  surgery 617.554 5
  see also Digestive system
Appenzell (Switzerland : Canton) T2—494 71
Appenzell Ausser-Rhoden (Switzerland) T2—494 712
Appenzell Inner-Rhoden (Switzerland) T2—494 714
Apperception
  psychology 153.73
Appetite disorders
  medicine 616.852 6
  see also Digestive system; Mental illness
Appetizers 641.812
Apples 641.341 1
  botany 583.73
  commercial processing 664.804 11
  cooking 641.641 1
  food 641.341 1
  orchard crop 634.11
Appleton layers 538.767 4
Application generators 005.13
Application programming 005.1
  see Manual at 005.1–005.2 vs. 005.42
Application programs 005.3
  see Manual at 005.3 vs. 005.43–005.45; *also at* 005.3682 vs. 005.365, 005.3684; *also at* 005.369
Applications for positions 650.14
  job hunting 650.14
  personnel selection 658.311 2
  public administration 352.65
Applied chemistry 660
Applied ethics 170
  see also Ethical problems
Applied linguistics 418
  T1—014
  specific languages T4—8
Applied mathematics 519
Applied mechanics 620.1
Applied numerical analysis 519.4
Applied nutrition 363.8
  see also Nutrition
Applied physics 621
  see Manual at 530 vs. 621

Applied psychology 158
see Manual at 158 vs. 155.2
Applied sciences 600
Applied sociology 360
Appling County (Ga.) T2—758 784
Appliqué
textile arts 746.445
Appointment power (Legislative bodies) 328.345 5
Appomattox County (Va.) T2—755 625
Apportionment (Legislatures) 328.334 5
law 342.053
Appraisal
land economics 333.332
Appreciation
arts 701.1
literature 801
music 781.17
Apprentices T1—071 55
economics 331.55
see also Apprenticeship
Apprenticeship 331.259 22
T1—071 55
economics 331.259 22
union control 331.889 4
education 371.227
secondary level 373.27
personnel management 658.312 4
public administration 354.968
Approach piloting 623.892 9
Appropriate technology
economics 338.927
Approval plans
library acquisitions 025.233
Approximation (Mathematics) 511.4
algebra 512.924
arithmetic 513.24
Apraxia of speech
medicine 616.855 2
see also Communicative disorders
Apricots 641.342 1
botany 583.73
commercial processing 664.804 21
cooking 641.642 1
food 641.342 1
orchard crop 634.21
Aprons 391.44
commercial technology 687.19
leather 685.22
see also Accessories (Clothing)
Apses
Christian church architecture 726.593
Apterous insects 595.756
Apterygiformes 598.54
paleozoology 568.5
Apterygota 595.72
Aptitude tests 153.94
education 371.262
personnel selection 658.311 25
teacher-prepared tests 371.271
see Manual at 153.94
Aptitudes
psychology 153.9
Apulia (Italy) T2—457 5
ancient T2—377
Apure (Venezuela) T2—874 2
Apurímac (Peru) T2—852 94
Aqaba, Gulf of 551.467 33
T2—165 33
'Aqā'id (Islam) 297.2
Aquaculture 639.8
Aquariums 597.073
fish culture 639.34
Aquarius (Zodiac) 133.527 6
Aquaspirillum 579.323
Aquatic animals 591.76
resource economics 333.954 8
Aquatic biological resources 333.952 8
public administration 354.57
Aquatic biology 578.76
see Manual at 578.76–578.77 vs. 551.46
Aquatic birds 598.176
resource economics 333.958 28
Aquatic ecology 577.6
marine environments 577.7
Aquatic exercises 613.716
Aquatic gardens 635.967 4
botany 581.760 73
floriculture 635.967 4
Aquatic plants 581.76
floriculture 635.967 4
Aquatic resources 333.91
Aquatic sports 797
see also Sports
Aquatinting 766.3
Aqueducts
water supply engineering 628.15
Aqueous humor
human anatomy 611.84
human physiology 612.844
see also Eyes
Aqueous solutions 541.342 2
chemical engineering 660.294 22
Aquiculture 639.8

Aquifers 553.79
  artificial recharge 627.56
  hydrology 551.49
  see also Groundwater
Aquifoliaceae 583.85
Aquila, Italy (Province) T2—457 11
Aquila chrysaetos 598.942 3
Aquino, Corazon Cojuangco
  Philippine history 959.904 7
Aquitaine (France) T2—447
Aquitania T2—364
Arab countries T2—174 927
Arab League 341.247 7
Arabesques (Music) 784.189 4
Arabia 953
  T2—53
  ancient 939.49
    T2—394 9
Arabia, Roman T2—394 8
Arabia Deserta 939.47
  T2—394 7
Arabia Felix 939.49
  T2—394 9
Arabia Petraea 939.48
  T2—394 8
Arabian Desert (Egypt) T2—623
Arabian Peninsula 953
  T2—53
Arabian Sea 551.467 37
  T2—165 37
Arabic language 492.7
  T6—927
  Biblical texts 220.46
  Hadith texts 297.124 04
  Koran texts 297.122 4
  printing 686.219 27
Arabic literature 892.7
Arabic philosophy 181.92
Arabs T5—927
Araceae 584.64
Arachnida 595.4
  disease carriers 571.986
    medicine 614.433
  paleozoology 565.4
Arad (Romania : Judeţ) T2—498 4
Araeoscelidia 567.93
Arafura Sea 551.465 75
  T2—164 75
Aragon (Spain) T2—465 5
Aragonite
  mineralogy 549.785
Aragua (Venezuela : State) T2—873 4
Arakhin 296.123 5
  Babylonian Talmud 296.125 5
  Mishnah 296.123 5
Aral Sea (Uzbekistan and Kazakhstan) T2—587
Arales 584.64
Araliaceae 583.84
Aramaeans T5—922
Aramaic languages 492.2
  T6—922
  Biblical texts 220.42
  Midrashic texts 296.140 4
  Talmudic texts 296.120 4
Aramaic literatures 892.2
Arameans T5—922
Aran Islands (Ireland) T2—417 48
Araneae 595.44
Araneida 595.44
Aransas County (Tex.) T2—764 122
Aranyakas 294.592 1
Araona language 498
  T6—98
Arapaho Indians T5—973
Arapahoe County (Colo.) T2—788 82
Ararat (Vic.) T2—945 7
Arauca (Colombia : Intendancy) T2—861 38
Araucanía (Chile) T2—834 6
Araucanian Indians T5—98
Araucanian language 498
  T6—98
Araucariaceae 585.3
Arauco (Chile : Province) T2—834 2
Arawak Indians T5—983 9
  South America T5—983 9
  West Indies T5—979
Arawak language 498.39
  T6—983 9
Arawakan languages 498.39
  T6—983 9
  Middle America 497.9
    T6—979
  South America 498.39
    T6—983 9
Arbitrage 332.645
Arbitration
  international law 341.522
  international relations 327.17
  labor economics 331.891 43
    law 344.018 914 3
    public administration 354.97
  law 347.09
  personnel management 658.315 4
    public administration 352.68

Arborvitaes 585.4
Arboviruses 579.256 2
Arbuckle Mountains
(Okla.) T2—766 5
Arc furnace practice 669.142 4
Arc length
calculus 515.43
integral geometry 516.362
Arc lighting 621.325
see also Lighting
Arc welding 671.521 2
Arcade games 794.822
see Manual at 793.932 vs. 794.822
Arcades 721.41
architecture 721.41
construction 690.141
Arcadia (Greece) T2—495 22
ancient T2—388
Arcellinida 579.43
Arch bridges 388
construction 624.6
see also Bridges
Archaeobacteria 579.321
Archaeoceti 569.5
Archaeocyatha 563.47
Archaeogastropoda 594.32
Archaeologists 930.109 2
occupational group T7—93
Archaeology 930.1
ancient places 931–939
Bible 220.93
law 344.094
modern places 940–990
Archaeopteris 561.597
Archaeornithes 568.22
Archaisms (Linguistics) 417.7
specific languages T4—7
Archbishops 270.092
biography 270.092
specific denominations 280
see Manual at 230–280
ecclesiology 262.12
Archean era 551.712
geology 551.712
paleontology 560.171 2
Arched harps 787.94
see also Stringed instruments
Archeology 930.1
see also Archaeology
Archeozoic era 551.712
geology 551.712
paleontology 560.171 2
Archer County (Tex.) T2—764 543
Archers 799.320 92
sports group T7—799 3
Archery 799.32
see also Sports
Arches (Structural elements) 721.41
architecture 721.41
construction 690.141
structural engineering 624.177 5
concrete 624.183 45
Arches (Structures) 725.96
Arches National Park
(Utah) T2—792 58
Archetype (Psychology)
Jungian system 150.195 4
personality theory 155.264
Archiannelida 592.62
Architarbi 565.4
Architects 720.92
occupational group T7—72
Architectural acoustics
construction 690.2
Architectural decoration 729
see Manual at 729
Architectural design 729
see Manual at 729
Architectural drawing 720.284
Architectural drawings 720.222
Architectural orders 721.36
architecture 721.36
construction 690.13
Architectural schools and styles 720.9
ancient 722
construction details 721
design and decoration 729
Architectural structure 721
Architecture 720
art representation 704.944
arts T3C—357
landscapes 712
literature 808.803 57
history and criticism 809.933 57
specific literatures T3B—080 357
history and criticism T3B—093 57
naval 623.81
painting 758.7
religious significance 291.37
Christianity 246.9
see also Arts—religious significance
see also Arts
Architecture (Computer science)
databases 005.74

Archival materials
  cataloging 025.341 4
  library treatment 025.171 4
  records management 651.56
Archive buildings
  architecture 725.15
Archives 027
  law 344.092
  operations 025
  public administrative support 352.744
  publishing 070.594
  relationships 021
  see also Libraries
  see Manual at 027
Archivists 020.92
  occupational group T7—092
Archosauria 567.9
Archostemata 595.762
Archuleta County (Colo.) T2—788 32
Arcs 516.15
Arctic animals 591.709 113
Arctic Archipelago (N.W.T.) T2—719 5
Arctic Bay (N.W.T.) T2—719 5
Arctic biology 578.091 13
Arctic climate
  health 613.111
Arctic cod 597.632
Arctic cooking 641.591 1
Arctic ecology 577.091 13
Arctic fox 599.776 4
Arctic islands T2—98
Arctic Ocean 551.468
  T2—163 2
  see Manual at T2—163 and T2—164, T2—165
Arctic plants 581.709 113
  floriculture 635.952
Arctocephalinae 599.797 3
Arctocephalus 599.797 38
Ardèche (France) T2—448 2
Ardeidae 598.34
Ardennes T2—493 48
Ardennes (France) T2—443 1
Ardennes, Battle of the, 1944–1945 940.542 143 1
Ards (Northern Ireland) T2—416 54
Area planning 307.12
  arts 711
  community sociology 307.12
  see Manual at 307.12 vs. 711
Area studies 940–990
  collection development 025.29
Area treatment T1—09
Arecales 584.5
  paleobotany 561.45
Arecibo (P.R. : District) T2—729 53
Arecidae 584.5
  paleobotany 561.45
Arena theater 792.022 8
Arenac County (Mich.) T2—774 73
Arenaviridae 579.256
Areolar tissues
  human histology 611.018 2
Arequipa (Peru : Dept.) T2—853 2
Arezzo (Italy : Province) T2—455 9
Arfon (Wales : Borough) T2—429 25
Argenteuil (Quebec : County) T2—714 23
Argenteuil (Quebec : Regional County Municipality) T2—714 23
Argentina 982
  T2—82
Argentine literature 860
Argentine Republic T2—82
Argentineans T5—688 2
Argentines T5—688 2
Argeş (Romania : Judeţ) T2—498 2
Argolis (Greece) T2—495 22
  ancient T2—388
Argon
  chemistry 546.753
  gas technology 665.822
  see also Chemicals
Argonne (France) T2—443 8
Argot 417.2
  specific languages T4—7
Arguloida 595.36
Argument (Logic) 168
Argyll and Bute (Scotland) T2—414 23
Århus amt (Denmark) T2—489 5
Arhynchobdellida 592.66
Ari liturgy 296.450 4
Ariana T2—396
Arianism 273.4
Arica (Chile : Province) T2—831 23
Arid lands 551.415
  T2—154
  biology 578.754
  ecology 577.54
  economics 333.736
  geography 910.915 4
  geomorphology 551.415
  physical geography 910.021 54
Ariège (France) T2—448 8
Aries (Zodiac) 133.526 2

Aristocracy	305.52
	T1—086 21
political system	321.5
Aristolochiales	583.26
Aristotelian philosophy	185
modern	149.91
Arithmetic	513
elementary education	372.72
Arithmetic progressions	513.4
Arizona	979.1
	T2—791
Ark of the Covenant	296.493
Arkadia (Greece)	T2—495 22
ancient	T2—388
Arkansas	976.7
	T2—767
Arkansas County (Ark.)	T2—767 86
Arkansas River	T2—767 3
Arkansas	T2—767 3
Colorado	T2—788 9
Kansas	T2—781
Oklahoma	T2—766 8
Arkhangel′sk (Russia : Oblast)	T2—471 7
Arkhangel′skaîa oblast′ (Russia)	T2—471 7
Arlington County (Va.)	T2—755 295
Arm muscles	
human anatomy	611.737
see also Musculoskeletal system	
Arm techniques	
music	784.193 6
Arm wrestling	796.812
Armada, 1588	942.055
Armadillos	599.312
Armageddon	236.9
Armagh (Northern Ireland : County)	T2—416 6
Armagh (Northern Ireland : District)	T2—416 61
Armatures (Electrical equipment)	
generators	621.316
Armatures (Sculpture)	731.3
Armed forces	355
see also Armed services	
Armed services	355
cooking	641.57
law	343.013
libraries	027.65
life insurance	368.364
see also Insurance	
relation to state	322.5
Armed services (continued)	
reserves	355.37
law	343.012
Armenia (Region)	T2—566 2
ancient	939.55
	T2—395 5
Armenia (Republic)	T2—475 6
Turkey	T2—566 2
Armenia (Republic)	947.56
	T2—475 6
Armenian Church	281.62
see also Eastern churches	
Armenian language	491.992
	T6—919 92
Biblical texts	220.49
Armenian literature	891.992
Armenians	T5—919 92
Armidale (N.S.W.)	T2—944 4
Armies (Military units)	355.31
Armies (National armies)	355.3
Arminians	284.9
religious group	T7—249
see also Christian denominations	
Armistice	327.17
law	341.66
World War I	940.439
Armor (Wearable)	623.441
art metalwork	739.75
Armor-piercing ammunition	623.451 8
Armored animals	591.477
Armored cavalry	358.18
Armored dinosaurs	567.915
Armored forces	358.18
Armored personnel carriers	358.188 3
engineering	623.747 5
military equipment	358.188 3
Armored vehicles	358.188 3
engineering	623.747 5
military equipment	358.188 3
Armored warfare	358.18
Armorial bearings	929.6
Armories	355.75
architecture	725.18
Arms (Human)	612.97
physiology	612.97
regional medicine	617.574
surgery	617.574 059
see also Upper extremities (Human)	
Arms (Military)	355.8
art metalwork	739.7
customs	399
engineering	623.4

Arms (Military) (continued)
  military equipment 355.8
  procurement 355.621 2
  see Manual at 355 vs. 623
Arms (Small firearms) 683.4
  see also Guns (Small arms)
Arms control 327.174
  international politics 327.174
  law 341.733
  military science 355.03
  see also Arms race
Arms race 327.174
  ethics 172.422
  social theology 291.178 732
    Christianity 261.873 2
  see also Arms control
Armstrong (B.C.) T2—711 5
Armstrong County (Pa.) T2—748 88
Armstrong County (Tex.) T2—764 833
Army artillery forces 358.12
Army engineer corps 358.22
Armyworms 595.78
  agricultural pests 633.104 978
Arnhem (Netherlands) T2—492 18
Arnhem Land (N.T.) T2—942 95
Arnold, Benedict
  treason 973.382
Arnsberg (Germany : Regierungsbezirk) T2—435 63
Aromatic compounds 547.6
  chemical engineering 661.8
Aromatic herbs 641.357
  see also Herbs
Aromatic hydrocarbons
  human toxicology 615.951 1
Aromatic teas 641.357
  home preparation 641.877
  see also Herb teas; Tea
Aromatization 547.21
  chemical engineering 660.284 41
Aroostook County (Me.) T2—741 1
Árpád, House of 943.902
Arpeggiones 787.6
  see also Stringed instruments
Arpeggios 781.252
Arraignment 345.072
Arrangement (Music) 781.37
Arrangements (Music) 781.38
  see Manual at 781.382–781.388
Array processing 004.35
  see also Processing modes—computer science
Array processors 004.35
  see also Processing modes—computer science
Arrest 363.232
  law 345.052 7
  police services 363.232
Arrhythmia
  medicine 616.128
  see also Cardiovascular system
Arrondissements 320.83
  see also Counties
Arrow grasses 584.74
Arrow Lakes (B.C.) T2—711 62
Arrowheads (Plants) 584.72
Arrowroot 641.336 8
  botany 584.39
  commercial processing 664.23
  cooking 641.636 8
  food 641.336 8
  starch crop 633.68
Arrows 799.202 85
  see also Bows and arrows
Arrowworms 592.38
Ars antiqua 780.902
Ars nova 780.902
Arsenals 355.7
  architecture 725.18
Arsenates
  mineralogy 549.72
Arsenic 669.75
  chemical engineering 661.071 5
  chemistry 546.715
  economic geology 553.47
  human toxicology 615.925 715
  metallography 669.957 5
  metallurgy 669.75
  mining 622.347
  organic chemistry 547.057 15
    applied 661.895
  physical metallurgy 669.967 5
  see also Chemicals; Metals
Arsenides
  mineralogy 549.32
Ārsī Kifle Hāger (Ethiopia) T2—632
Arson 364.164
  law 345.026 4
Art 700
  investment economics 332.63
  sociology 306.47
  therapeutics 615.851 56
  see also Arts
Art and religion 291.175
  Christianity 261.57

Art and religion (continued)
  Islam 297.267
  Judaism 296.377
Art appreciation 701.1
Art dealers 709.2
  see Manual at 709.2 vs. 380.1457092
Art deco 709.040 12
  sculpture 735.230 412
Art galleries 708
  architecture 727.7
  law 344.093
Art libraries 026.7
Art metalwork 739
Art metalworkers 739.092
  occupational group T7—739
Art museums 708
  architecture 727.7
  institutional housekeeping 647.997
Art music 781.68
  nonwestern 781.69
  western 781.68
Art needlework 746.4
Art nouveau 709.034 9
  architecture 724.6
  decoration 745.444 1
Art paper 676.282 5
Art songs 782.421 68
Art therapy
  medicine 615.851 56
  psychiatry 616.891 656
    see also Mental illness
Arta (Greece) T2—495 3
Arterial occlusive diseases
  medicine 616.13
  see also Cardiovascular system
Arteries 573.185
  biology 573.185
  human anatomy 611.13
  human physiology 612.133
  medicine 616.13
  surgery 617.413
  see also Cardiovascular system
Arteriosclerosis
  medicine 616.136
  see also Cardiovascular system
Artesian wells
  engineering 628.114
  hydrology 551.498
Arthabaska (Quebec : County) T2—714 565
Arthabaska (Quebec : Regional County Municipality) T2—714 565
Arthritis
  medicine 616.722
  see also Musculoskeletal system
Arthrobacter 579.373
Arthrochirotida 563.96
Arthropoda 595
  see also Arthropods
Arthropods 595
  agricultural pests 632.65
  paleozoology 565
  pesticides
    agricultural use 632.951 7
Arthroscopy 617.472 059
  see also Musculoskeletal system
Arthur, Chester Alan
  United States history 973.84
Arthur, King
  English history 942.014
Arthur County (Neb.) T2—782 785
Arthur's Pass National Park (N.Z.) T2—938 1
Artibonite (Haiti : Dept.) T2—729 446
Artichokes 641.353 2
  botany 583.99
  commercial processing 664.805 32
  cooking 641.653 2
  food 641.353 2
  garden crop 635.32
Articles (Grammar) 415
  specific languages T4—5
Articles of Confederation, 1781
  United States history 973.318
Articulata 593.92
  paleozoology 563.92
Articulatae 587.2
Articulation (Education) 371.21
Articulation disorders
  medicine 616.855
  see also Communicative disorders
Articulations
  human anatomy 611.72
  human physiology 612.75
  see also Musculoskeletal system
Artificial arms
  medicine 617.574
Artificial environments
  health 613.5

Artificial flies (Fishing)
  angling 799.124
  making 688.791 24
Artificial flower arrangements 745.92
Artificial flowers
  handicrafts 745.594 3
Artificial gems 666.88
Artificial harbors 387.1
  hydraulic engineering 627.2
  military engineering 623.64
  see also Ports
Artificial heart
  surgery 617.412 059 2
  see also Cardiovascular system
Artificial insemination
  animal husbandry 636.082 45
  ethics 176
    religion 291.566
      Christianity 241.66
    see also Reproduction—ethics
  family law 346.017
  gynecology 618.178
  health 613.94
Artificial intelligence 006.3
  T1—028 563
  engineering 621.399
  see Manual at 153 vs. 006.3: Cognitive science
Artificial islands 627.98
Artificial languages 499.99
  T6—999 9
Artificial legs
  medicine 617.58
Artificial-light gardening 635.048 3
  floriculture 635.982 6
Artificial-light photography 778.72
Artificial limbs
  manufacturing technology 681.761
  medicine 617.58
Artificial minerals 666.86
Artificial modification of weather 551.68
Artificial organs
  plastic surgery 617.95
Artificial radioactivity
  physics 539.753
Artificial recharge (Groundwater) 627.56
Artificial respiration
  medicine 617.180 6
Artificial road surfaces 625.8
Artificial satellites
  engineering 629.46
  flight 629.434
  telecommunications 384.51
    see also Satellite communication
  weather reporting 551.635 4
Artificial stone 666.89
  architectural construction 721.044 4
  building construction 693.4
  building materials 691.3
  materials science 620.139
Artificial teeth
  dentistry 617.69
  see also Dentistry
Artificial tissue
  plastic surgery 617.95
Artigas (Uruguay : Dept.) T2—895 36
Artillery 355.821
  art metalwork 739.742
  engineering 623.41
  military equipment 355.821
Artillery ballistics 623.51
Artillery installations 355.73
Artillery projectiles 623.451 3
Artiodactyla 599.63
  paleozoology 569.63
Artisans 609.2
  labor economics 331.794
  occupational group T7—6
  see also Handicrafters
Artistic études 784.189 49
Artistic lettering 745.61
Artistic principles 700.1
Artistic themes
  arts 700.457
  T3C—357
  folklore 398.27
    history and criticism 398.357
  literature 808.803 57
    history and criticism 809.933 57
    specific literatures T3B—080 357
      history and criticism T3B—093 57
Artists 700.92
  labor economics 331.761 7
  occupational group T7—7
  see Manual at 700.92
Artists' books 700
  fine arts 702.81
Artists' marks 702.78
  T1—027 8
Artists' sketches
  criminal investigation 363.258
Artois (France) T2—442 7

Arts 700
  decorative 745
  elementary education 372.5
  influence on crime 364.254
  law 344.097
  public administrative support 353.77
  religious significance 291.37
    Buddhism 294.343 7
    Christianity 246
    Hinduism 294.537
    Islam 297.3
    Judaism 296.46
  sociology 306.47
  study and teaching 700.7
  see Manual at 700
Arts and crafts 745
  sociology 306.489
Arts and religion 291.175
  Christianity 261.57
  Islam 297.267
  Judaism 296.377
Artvin İli (Turkey) T2—566 2
Aruba T2—729 86
Arums 584.64
Arun (England : District) T2—422 67
Arunāchal Pradesh (India) T2—541 63
Arundineae 584.9
Arundinelleae 584.9
Arusha Region (Tanzania) T2—678 26
Arvicola 599.354
Arya-Samaj 294.556 3
Aryan languages
    (Indo-European) 410
  T6—1
Aryan languages (Indo-Iranian) 491.1
  T6—911
Asante (Empire) 966.701 8
Asante (Kingdom) T2—667
Asbestos 553.672
  building material 691.95
  economic geology 553.672
  human toxicology 615.925 392 24
  materials science 620.195
  mining 622.367 2
  pollution 363.738 4
    law 344.046 335
    see also Pollution
  public safety 363.179 1
    see also Hazardous
        materials
  technology 666.72
  textiles 677.51
    see also Textiles
Asbestos paper 676.289
Asbestosis
  medicine 616.244
  workers' compensation law 344.021 8
  see also Respiratory system
Ascariasis
  incidence 614.555 4
  medicine 616.965 4
  see also Communicable
      diseases (Human)
Ascension Island (Atlantic
    Ocean) T2—973
Ascension of Jesus Christ 232.97
Ascension of Mary 232.914
Ascension Parish (La.) T2—763 19
Ascensiontide 263.93
  devotional literature 242.36
  music 781.728
  sermons 252.63
Ascent to Heaven of Muḥammad 297.633
Asceticism 291.447
  Buddhism 294.344 47
  Christianity 248.47
  Hinduism 294.544 7
  Islam 297.576
    Sufi 297.446
  Judaism 296.7
Aschaffenburg (Germany) T2—433 31
Aschelminthes 592.5
  paleozoology 562.5
Ascidiacea 596.2
Asclepiadaceae 583.93
Ascobolus 579.578
Ascoli Piceno (Italy :
    Province) T2—456 75
Ascomycetes 579.56
Ascomycotina 579.56
Ascophyllum 579.888
Ascothoracica 595.35
ASEAN 341.247 3
  public administration 352.115 9
Asepsis
  obstetrics 618.89
  public health 614.48
  surgery 617.910 1
Asexual reproduction 571.89
  microorganisms 571.842 9
  plants 575.49
Asexuality 306.762
Ash trays
  automobile 629.277
  manufacturing 688.4
Ash Wednesday 263.925
  devotional literature 242.35
  sermons 252.625

Ashante language 496.338 5
T6—963 385
Ashanti 966.701 8
Ashanti (African people) T5—963 385
Ashanti (Kingdom) T2—667
Ashburton District (N.Z.) T2—938 6
Ashe County (N.C.) T2—756 835
Asheninca Campa language 498.39
T6—983 9
Ashes (Trees) 583.87
forestry 634.973 87
Asheville (N.C.) T2—756 88
Ashfield (England) T2—425 25
Ashford (England : Borough) T2—422 392
Ashkenazic liturgy 296.45
Ashland County (Ohio) T2—771 29
Ashland County (Wis.) T2—775 21
Ashley County (Ark.) T2—767 83
Ashoka, King of Magadha
Indian history 934.045
Ashtabula County (Ohio) T2—771 34
Ashur (Extinct city) T2—35
'Āshūrā' 297.36
Asia 950
T2—5
Asia, Central 958
T2—58
Asia, Southeastern 959
T2—59
Asia Minor 956.1
T2—561
ancient 939.2
T2—392
Asian Americans T5—950 73
education 371.829 950 73
Asian Arctic seawaters 551.468 5
T2—163 25
Asian international organizations 341.247
Asians T5—95
Asiatic cholera
incidence 614.514
medicine 616.932
see Manual at 616.932 vs. 616.33
see also Communicable diseases (Human)
Asiatic elephant 599.676
Asilidae 595.773
'Āṣimah (Jordan : Province) T2—569 58
ASL (Sign language) 419
Asmara (Eritrea) T2—635
Āsmera (Eritrea) T2—635
Asocial persons 305.568
T1—086 92
Aśoka, King of Magadha
Indian history 934.045
Asotin County (Wash.) T2—797 42
Asparagaceae 584.355
Asparagus 641.353 1
botany 584.355
commercial processing 664.805 31
cooking 641.653 1
food 641.353 1
garden crop 635.31
Aspect (Grammar) 415
specific languages T4—5
Aspects (Astrology) 133.530 44
Aspens 583.65
Aspergillus 579.565 7
Asphalt 553.27
building materials 691.96
economic geology 553.27
materials science 620.196
mining 622.337
petroleum product 665.538 8
processing 665.4
Asphalt concrete 666.893
road engineering 625.85
Asphalt pavements 625.85
Asphyxia
medicine 617.18
Asphyxiating gases
human toxicology 615.91
Aspidobothria 592.4
Aspidochirotacea 593.96
Aspidocotylea 592.4
Aspidogastrea 592.48
Aspirin 615.313 7
Assam (India) T2—541 62
Assamese T5—914 5
Assamese language 491.451
T6—914 51
Assamese literature 891.451
Assassination 364.152 4
law 345.025 24
Assateague Island (Md. and Va.) T2—752 21
Assault and battery 364.155 5
law 345.025 55
criminal law 345.025 55
torts 346.033
Assaying
metallurgy 669.92
Assemblage
arts 702.814

Assemblers (Computer programs) 005.456
Assemblies (Legislative bodies) 328
Assemblies of God 289.94
see also Christian denominations
Assembling machines 670.427
Assembling products 670.42
factory engineering 670.42
production management 658.533
Assembly languages 005.136
Assembly-line processes 670.42
production management 658.533
technology 670.42
Assertiveness training
applied psychology 158.2
Asses 636.18
animal husbandry 636.18
zoology 599.665
Assessment tests
education 371.262
Assimilation (Physiology)
humans 612.39
see also Metabolism
Assimilation (Sociology) 303.482
Assiniboine River (Sask. and Man.) T2—712 73
Assistant teachers 371.141 24
Assisted suicide
criminology 364.152 3
law 345.025 23
ethics 179.7
see also Right to die—ethics
medical ethics 174.24
Associate-degree nurses 610.730 92
role and function 610.730 692
see also Nurses
Association 302.3
Association analysis 519.537
Association football 796.334
electronic games 794.863 34
see also Sports
Association of ideas
psychology 153.22
Association of South East Asian Nations 341.247 3
public administration 352.115 9
Associationism
psychological system 150.194 4
Associations 060
fraternal organizations 366
see also Organizations
Associations for religious work 291.65
Christianity 267
Judaism 296.67
Associative algebras 512.24
Associative learning
psychology 153.152 6
Associative memory 004.5
Associative processing 004.35
see also Processing modes—computer science
Associative processors 004.35
engineering 621.391
see also Processing modes—computer science
Assumption of Mary 232.914
Assumption Parish (La.) T2—763 43
Assurance 368
see also Insurance
Assyria 935.03
T2—35
Mesopotamian history 935.03
Palestinian history 933.03
Assyrian dialect 492.17
T6—921
Assyrian literature 892.1
Assyrians T5—921
Assyro-Babylonian language 492.1
T6—921
Assyro-Babylonian literature 892.1
Astatine 546.735
Asterales 583.99
Asteridae 583.9
Asterinales 579.564
Asteroidea 593.93
Asteroids 523.44
T2—992 4
astrology 133.539 8
Asterozoa 593.93
paleozoology 563.93
Asters 635.933 99
botany 583.99
floriculture 635.933 99
Asthenic reactions
medicine 616.852 8
see also Mental illness
Asthma
medicine 616.238
pediatrics 618.922 38
see also Respiratory system
Asti (Italy : Province) T2—451 5
Astigmatism
optometry 617.755
Astrakhan (Russia : Oblast) T2—474 8

Astrakhanskaîa oblastʹ (Russia) T2—474 8
Astral projection 133.95
Astrapotheria 569.62
Astrobiology 576.839
Astrodomes 796.068
  architecture 725.827
Astrolabes 522.4
Astrolatry 291.212
Astrologers 133.509 2
  occupational group T7—13
Astrology 133.5
  natural 520
Astrology and religion 291.175
  Christianity 261.513
Astromechanics
  engineering 629.411
Astrometry 522
Astronautical engineering 629.47
  military 623.69
Astronautical engineers 629.409 2
  occupational group T7—629 4
Astronautics 629.4
Astronauts 629.450 092
  occupational group T7—629 4
  selection and training 629.450 7
Astronavigation 527
Astronomers 520.92
  occupational group T7—521
Astronomical almanacs 528
Astronomical geography 525
Astronomical instruments 522.2
Astronomical interpretation
  Bible 220.68
Astronomical observatories 522.1
  architecture 727.552
Astronomy 520
  see Manual at 520 vs. 523.1, 523.112, 523.8
Astronomy and religion 291.175
  Christianity 261.55
  philosophy of religion 215.2
Astrophotography 522.63
Astrophysics 523.01
Asturias (Spain) T2—461 9
Asua language 496.5
  T6—965
Asunción (Paraguay) T2—892 121
Aswān (Egypt : Province) T2—623
Asylum 323.631
  international law 341.488
  law 342.083
Asymptotic curves 516.362
Asynchronous machinery 621.313 6
Asynchronous transfer mode
  communications engineering 621.382 16
  computer communications 004.66
    engineering 621.398 1
Asyūṭ (Egypt : Province) T2—622
Atacama (Chile : Region) T2—831 4
Atamasco lilies 584.34
Atascosa County (Tex.) T2—764 443
Atatürk, Kemal
  Turkish history 956.102 4
Atayal (Taiwan people) T5—992 5
Atchison County (Kan.) T2—781 36
Atchison County (Mo.) T2—778 113
Atelinae 599.858
Athabasca, Lake (Sask. and Alta.) T2—712 41
Athabascan languages 497.2
  T6—972
Athabaska River (Alta.) T2—712 32
Athanasian Creed 238.144
Athapascan-Eyak languages 497.2
  T6—972
Athapascan Indians T5—972
Athapascan languages 497.2
  T6—972
Atharvaveda 294.592 15
Atheism 211.8
  Christian polemics 239.7
Atheistic religions 291.14
Atheists 211.809 2
  religious group T7—291
Athelstan, King of England
  English history 942.017 1
Athenian supremacy 938.04
Athens (Ga.) T2—758 18
Athens (Greece) T2—495 12
  ancient T2—385
Athens County (Ohio) T2—771 97
Atheriniformes 597.66
  paleozoology 567.66
Atherosclerosis
  medicine 616.136
  see also Cardiovascular system
Atherton (Qld.) T2—943 6
Athletes 796.092
  health 613.711
  occupational ethics 174.979 6
  physical fitness 613.711
  sports group T7—796
  see Manual at 796: Sports personnel

Athlete's foot
  medicine 616.57
  see also Skin
Athletic club buildings
  architecture 725.85
Athletic fields 796.420 68
  area planning 711.558
Athletic games 796
  see also Sports
Athletic garments 796
  commercial technology 687.16
  customs 391
  home sewing 646.47
  use 796
  see also Clothing
Athletic gloves and mitts
  manufacturing technology 685.43
Athletic injuries
  medicine 617.102 7
Athletic services
  armed forces 355.346
Athletic sports 796
  see also Sports
Athos (Greece) T2—495 65
Atkinson County (Ga.) T2—758 822
Atlanta (Ga.) T2—758 231
Atlanta Campaign, 1864 973.737 1
Atlantic City (N.J.) T2—749 85
Atlantic Coast (Nicaragua) T2—728 53
Atlantic Coastal Plain T2—75
  Maryland T2—752 1
  North Carolina T2—756 1
  South Carolina T2—757 6
  United States T2—75
  Virginia T2—755 1
Atlantic County (N.J.) T2—749 84
Atlantic international
    organizations 341.243
Atlantic Islands 997
  T2—97
Atlantic languages (Africa) 496.32
  T6—963 2
Atlantic Ocean 551.461
  T2—163
  see Manual at T2—163 and
    T2—164, T2—165; *also*
    at T2—163, T2—164,
    T2—165 vs. T2—182
Atlantic Provinces 971.5
  T2—715
Atlantic Region T2—182 1
Atlántico (Colombia :
    Dept.) T2—861 15
Atlántida (Honduras) T2—728 312
Atlantis 001.94
  see also Legendary places
Atlas Mountains T2—64
Atlases 912
  T1—022 3
  cataloging 025.346
  geography 912
  library treatment 025.176
  pictorial T1—022 2
  see Manual at T1—0222 vs.
    T1—0223; *also at* 912 vs.
    T1—0223
Atmosphere 551.5
  T2—161
  meteorology 551.5
  public administration 354.37
Atmosphere-land interactions 551.523
Atmosphere-ocean interactions 551.524 6
Atmosphere-water interactions 551.524
Atmospheric disturbances 551.55
Atmospheric electricity 551.563
Atmospheric entry
  manned space flight 629.458 8
Atmospheric formations 551.551
Atmospheric ionization 538.767
Atmospheric nucleation 551.574 1
Atmospheric optics 551.565
Atmospheric pressure 551.54
Atmospheric radiation
  meteorology 551.527 3
Atmospheric thermodynamics
  space flight 629.415 2
Atoka County (Okla.) T2—766 66
Atolls 551.424
  T2—142
  geography 910.914 2
  geomorphology 551.424
  physical geography 910.021 42
Atomic bomb 355.825 119
  see also Nuclear weapons
Atomic energy 333.792 4
  economics 333.792 4
  law 343.092 5
  physics 539.7
Atomic mass
  chemistry 541.242
Atomic number 541.242
Atomic physics 539.7
  astronomy 523.019 7
Atomic structure 539.14
  chemistry 541.24
Atomic weapons 355.825 119
  see also Nuclear weapons
Atomic weight 541.242

Atomism 146.5
Atoms 539.7
theoretical chemistry 541.24
Atonality 781.267
Atonement 291.22
Christianity 234.5
Islam 297.22
Judaism 296.32
Atonement Day
Judaism 296.432
liturgy 296.453 2
Atonement of Jesus Christ 232.3
Atopic dermatitis
medicine 616.521
see also Skin
ATP (Triphosphate) 572.475
Atrium buildings 720.48
architectural construction 721.042
architecture 720.48
Atrocities
World War I 940.405
World War II 940.540 5
see also Military history
Attaché cases
manufacturing technology 685.51
Attachment (Law) 347.077
private law 346.077
Attack (Military science) 355.4
tactics 355.422
Attack (Music) 781.235
Attack airplanes 358.438 3
engineering 623.746 3
military equipment 358.438 3
Attala County (Miss.) T2—762 644
Attendance officers 371.295
Attention
psychology
learning 153.153 2
perception 153.733
Attention deficit disorder
medicine 616.858 9
pediatrics 618.928 589
see also Nervous system
Attenuators
electronic circuits 621.381 536 2
Attica (Greece) T2—495 12
ancient T2—385
Attics 643.5
Attie language 496.337
T6—963 37
Attikē (Greece) T2—495 12
ancient T2—385
Attitude training
personnel management 658.312 44
executives 658.407 124 4
public administration 352.669
Attitudes 152.4
psychology 152.4
sociology 303.38
Attorney-General (Great Britain) 345.420 1
Attorneys'-general advisory
opinions 348.05
United States 348.735
Attracting birds 639.978
Attraction (Social psychology) 302.13
Attributes of God 212.7
Christianity 231.4
comparative religion 291.211 2
Islam 297.211 2
Judaism 296.311 2
philosophy of religion 212.7
Attributes of the Church 262.72
Attribution (Social psychology) 302.12
Au Sable River (Mich.) T2—774 7
Aube (France) T2—443 31
Auckland (N.Z.) T2—932 4
Auckland, George Eden, Earl of
Indian history 954.031 4
Auckland City (N.Z.) T2—932 4
Auckland Islands (N.Z.) T2—939 9
Auckland Province (N.Z.) T2—931 2
Auckland Region (N.Z.) T2—932
Auction bridge 795.414
Auction catalogs T1—029 4
arts 700.294
exhibitions 700.74
bibliographical materials
alphabetic subject 017.7
classed 017.3
fine arts 702.94
exhibitions 707.4
Auctions 381.17
management 658.84
see also Commerce
Aude (France) T2—448 7
Audience participation programs 791.443
radio 791.443
television performances 791.453
Audiences 302.33
mass media 302.23
Audio input devices
computer science 006.45
engineering 621.399
Audio-lingual language study 418
specific languages T4—83

Audio output devices
  computer science 006.5
    engineering 621.399
Audio systems engineering 621.382 8
  recording and reproduction 621.389 3
Audiologists 617.809 2
  occupational group T7—617 8
Audiology 617.8
  pediatrics 618.920 978 9
  see also Ears
Audiotex 384.646
  see also Telephone
Audiovisual engineering 621.389 7
Audiovisual equipment
  libraries 022.9
  museology 069.32
Audiovisual materials
  art appreciation use 701.1
  bibliographies 011.37
  cataloging 025.347
  Christian religious education 268.635
  instructional use 371.335
  library treatment 025.177
  reviews 028.137
Audiovisual treatment T1—020 8
Auditing 657.45
  accounting 657.45
    government accounts 657.835 045
Auditoriums
  architecture 725.83
Auditory canals
  human physiology 612.851
  otology 617.83
  see also Ears
Auditory memory 153.133
Auditory perception
  psychology 152.15
Auditory tubes
  human physiology 612.854
  otology 617.86
  see also Ears
Audits 657.45
  see also Auditing
Audrain County (Mo.) T2—778 332
Audubon County (Iowa) T2—777 486
Aughrabies National Park (South Africa) T2—687 12
Auglaize County (Ohio) T2—771 43
Augsburg (Germany) T2—433 75
Augsburg, War of the League of, 1688–1697 940.252 5
  North American history 973.25
Augsburg Confession 238.41
Augusan del Norte (Philippines) T2—599 7
Augusan del Sur (Philippines) T2—599 7
Augusta (Ga.) T2—758 64
Augusta (Me.) T2—741 6
Augusta County (Va.) T2—755 916
Augustana Evangelical Lutheran Church 284.133 3
  see also Lutheran church
Augustinians 255.4
  church history 271.4
Auks 598.33
Aunis (France) T2—446 4
Aunts 306.87
  T1—085
  T7—046
Aura
  human physiology 612.014 2
  parapsychology 133.892
Aural nervous system
  human anatomy 611.85
  human diseases
    incidence 614.599 8
    otology 617.886
  human physiology 612.85
  see also Ears
Aurangzeb, Emperor of Hindustan
  Indian history 954.025 8
Aurich (Germany : Landkreis) T2—435 917
Auricles (Ears)
  human anatomy 611.85
  human diseases
    incidence 614.599 8
    otology 617.82
  human physiology 612.851
  see also Ears
Auricles (Heart)
  human anatomy 611.12
  human physiology 612.17
  see also Cardiovascular system
Auriculas 635.933 675
  botany 583.675
  floriculture 635.933 675
Aurora County (S.D.) T2—783 375
Auroras (Geomagnetism) 538.768
Ausdehnungslehre 512.5
Aust-Agder fylke (Norway) T2—483 1
Austin (Tex.) T2—764 31
Austin County (Tex.) T2—764 252

Austral Islands T2—962 2
Australasia T2—9
Australasian possums 599.23
Australia 994
T2—94
Australian aboriginal languages 499.15
T6—991 5
Australian aboriginal literatures 899.15
Australian aborigines T5—991 5
religion 299.921 5
Australian Alps (N.S.W. and Vic.) T2—944
Australian bass 597.73
Australian Capital Territory T2—947
Australian cattle dog 636.737
Australian Country Party 324.294 04
Australian football 796.336
see also Sports
Australian football players 796.336 092
Australian grayling 597.55
Australian Labor Party 324.294 07
Australian languages 499.15
T6—991 5
Australian Liberal Party 324.294 05
Australian literature (English) 820
Australian native peoples T5—991 5
Australian salmon 597.7
culture 639.377
Australian school shark 597.34
Australians T5—24
Australoid race T5—991 5
Australopithicus 569.9
Austria 943.6
T2—436
ancient 936.3
T2—363
Austrian Empire 943.604
T2—436
Austrian school (Economics) 330.157
Austrian Succession, War of the, 1740–1748 940.253 2
North American history 973.26
Austrian winter peas 633.369
botany 583.74
Austrians T5—36
Austro-Hungarian Monarchy 943.604 4
T2—436
Austrian history 943.604 4
Hungarian history 943.904 3
Austro-Prussian War, 1866 943.076
Austroasiatic languages 495.93
T6—959 3
Austroasiatic literatures 895.93
Austronesian languages 499.2
T6—992
Austronesian literatures 899.2
Autarchy (Absolute monarchy) 321.6
Autarchy (Economic self-sufficiency) 338.9
Autauga County (Ala.) T2—761 463
Autecology 577.26
animals 591.7
microorganisms 579.17
plants 581.7
see Manual at 577.26 vs. 579–590
Authenticating
arts 702.88
Author catalogs 025.315
bibliography 018
library science 025.315
Author-title catalogs 025.315
bibliography 018
library science 025.315
Author-title indexing 025.322
Authoritarian government 321.9
Authoritarianism 320.53
Authority 303.36
ethical systems 171.1
Christianity 241.2
religion 291.65
Christianity 262.8
Judaism 296.67
social control 303.36
Authority control (Cataloging) 025.322 2
Authority files (Cataloging) 025.322 2
name and title 025.322 2
subject 025.49
Authorized strikes 331.892 2
see also Strikes (Work stoppages)
Authorized version (Bible) 220.520 3
Authors
relations with publishers 070.52
see Manual at 808.001–808.7 vs. 070.52
Authors (Literature) 809
collected biography 809
specific literatures T3B—09
occupational group T7—8
Authorship of Bible 220.66
Authorship techniques 808.02
Autism
medicine 616.898 2
pediatrics 618.928 982

Autism (continued)
special education 371.94
see also Mental illness
Autobiography 920
T1—092
literary form 809.935 92
specific literatures T3B—094 92
Autocracy (Absolute monarchy) 321.6
Autogiros
engineering 629.133 35
Autograph scores 780
treatises 780.262
Autographs 929.88
Autoharps 787.75
see also Stringed instruments
Autoimmune diseases (Biology) 571.973
Autoimmune diseases (Human)
incidence 614.599 38
medicine 616.978
see also Diseases (Human)
Autoimmunity 571.973
medicine 616.978
Automata 511.3
artificial intelligence 006.3
Automated information systems 025.04
see also Information storage and retrieval systems
Automatic cameras 771.32
Automatic control engineering 629.8
Automatic data collection systems 006
engineering 621.399
Automatic data processing 004
T1—028 5
Automatic movements
psychology 152.32
Automatic piloting
aircraft 629.132 6
Automatic pilots
aircraft 629.135 2
Automatic pistols 683.432 5
see also Pistols
Automatic rifles
military engineering 623.442 4
military equipment 355.824 24
see also Guns (Small arms)
Automatic sprinkler systems
fire technology 628.925 2
Automatic train control
engineering 625.27
Automatic transmissions
automotive engineering 629.244 6
Automatic writing (Spiritualism) 133.932
Automation
agricultural economics 338.161
control engineering 629.8
economics 338.064
manufacturing technology 670.427
mineral industries 338.26
production management 658.514
secondary industries 338.454
social effects 303.483 4
Automation engineers 629.809 2
occupational group T7—629 8
Automation training
personnel management 658.312 43
Automatons 629.8
Automobile accidents 363.125
see also Automobile safety
Automobile bodies 629.26
Automobile cars (Railroad) 385.34
engineering 625.24
see also Rolling stock
Automobile driving 629.283
international law 341.756 86
law 343.094 6
recreation 796.7
Automobile engineers 629.209 2
occupational group T7—629 2
Automobile industry 338.476 292 22
law 343.078 629 222
Automobile insurance 368.092
inland marine 368.232
law 346.086 092
liability 368.572
see also Insurance
Automobile noise 363.741
see also Noise
Automobile parking 388.474
see also Parking facilities
Automobile racers 796.720 92
sports group T7—796 7
Automobile racing 796.72
electronic games 794.867 2
see also Sports
Automobile rallies 796.73
see also Sports
Automobile registration 354.765 284
international law 341.756 84
law 343.094 4
public administration 354.765 284
Automobile safety 363.125
see also Highway safety
Automobile theft 364.162
law 345.026 2

Automobile transportation 388.321
engineering 629.222
international law 341.756 8
law 343.094
public administration 354.765
safety 363.125
see also Highway safety
transportation services 388.321
urban 388.413 21
Automobiles 388.342
engineering 629.222
international law 341.756 84
law 343.094 4
military engineering 623.747 2
production economics 338.476 292 22
repair 629.287 2
sports 796.7
see also Sports
transportation services 388.342
see Manual at 629.046 vs. 388
Automorphic functions 511.33
calculus 515.9
number theory 512.7
Automorphisms
geometry 516.1
topological algebras 512.55
Automotive industry 338.476 292
law 343.078 629 2
Automotive vehicles 388.34
engineering 629.2
international law 341.756 84
law 343.094 4
military engineering 623.747
production economics 338.476 292
public administration 354.765
repair 629.287
safety 363.125
see also Highway safety
safety engineering 629.204 2
sports 796.7
transportation services 388.34
see Manual at 629.046 vs. 388
Autonomic nervous system
human anatomy 611.83
human physiology 612.89
medicine 616.88
see also Nervous system
Autonomous agencies
public administration 352.264
Autonomous Communities (Spain) 321.023
see also States (Members of federations)
Autonomous Republics (Soviet Union) 321.023
see also States (Members of federations)
Autonomy of states 320.15
Autopilots
aircraft 629.135 2
Autopsy
forensic medicine 614.1
medicine 616.075 9
Autumn 508.2
music 781.524 6
see also Seasons
Autumn-flowering plants 581.43
floriculture 635.953
Auvergne (France) T2—445 9
Auxiliaries (Foreign troops) 355.359
Auxiliary party organizations 324.3
Auxiliary power systems
spacecraft 629.474 4
Auxiliary procedures T1—028
see Manual at T1—028
Auxiliary routes
marine 387.523
Auxiliary storage
computer science 004.56
engineering 621.397 6
Auxiliary techniques T1—028
see Manual at T1—028
Auxins
chemistry 547.734 2
Auyuittuq National Park (N.W.T.) T2—719 5
Available light photography 778.76
Avalanches 551.307
snow 551.578 48
Avant-garde arts 700.411
T3C—11
Avant-garde jazz 781.656
Avant-garde literary works 808.887
specific literatures T3B—807
individual authors T3A—8
Avant-garde music 780.904
Avar language 499.964
T6—999 64
Avaric language 499.964
T6—999 64
Avarice 178
moral theology 291.568
see also Vices
Avaro-Andi-Dido languages 499.964
T6—999 64
Ave Maria 242.74
Aveiro (Portugal : District) T2—469 35

Avellino (Italy : Province) T2—457 21
Aveneae 584.9
Average costs 338.514 2
  management 658.155 3
Averaging 519.533
Avery County (N.C.) T2—756 862
Aves 598
  see also Birds
Avesta 295.82
Avestan language 491.52
  T6—915 2
Avestan literature 891.52
Aveyron (France) T2—447 4
Aviaries 598.073
  animal husbandry 636.6
  architecture 728.927
  construction 690.892 7
Aviary birds 636.68
  see also Birds
Aviation 387.7
  see also Air transportation
Aviation fuel 665.538 25
Aviation insurance 368.093
  inland marine 368.24
  liability 368.576
  see also Insurance
Aviation law 343.097
Aviation medicine 616.980 213
Aviation meteorology 629.132 4
Aviation psychology 155.965
Avignon (France) T2—449 22
Avignon (Quebec) T2—714 78
Avila (Spain : Province) T2—463 59
Avila Camacho, Manuel
  Mexican history 972.082 6
Avionics 629.135
  military aircraft 623.746 049
Avitaminosis
  medicine 616.39
  see also Digestive system
Avocados 641.346 53
  agriculture 634.653
  botany 583.23
  commercial processing 664.804 653
  cooking 641.646 53
  food 641.346 53
Avodah Zarah 296.123 4
  Babylonian Talmud 296.125 4
  Mishnah 296.123 4
  Palestinian Talmud 296.124 4
Avon (England) T2—423 9
Avon, River
  (Gloucestershire-Avon,
  England) T2—423 9
Avon River
  (Leicestershire-Gloucestershire,
  England) T2—424 4
Avon River
  (Wiltshire-Dorset,
  England) T2—423 19
Avot 296.123 47
Avoyelles Parish (La.) T2—763 71
Awadhi dialect 491.49
  T6—914 9
Awadhi literature 891.49
Awards 929.81
  T1—079
  armed forces 355.134
    biography 355.134 092
      see Manual at
        355.134092
    see also Military
        commemorations
  research 001.44
Awnings 645.3
  household management 645.3
  manufacturing technology 684
Axes 621.93
  art metalwork 739.72
Axiology 121.8
Axiomatic set theory 511.3
Axioms 160
  mathematical logic 511.3
Axis Powers (World War II
  group) 940.533 4
Axles 621.823
  automotive engineering 629.245
  railroad engineering 625.21
Axons
  human histology 611.018 8
  see also Nervous system
Axum (Kingdom) 963.501
  T2—635
Ayacucho (Peru : Dept.) T2—852 92
Ayatollahs 297.092
  biography 297.092
    specific sects 297.8
  role and function 297.61
  see Manual at 297.092
Aydin İli (Turkey) T2—562
Aye-ayes 599.83
  conservation technology 639.979 83
  resource economics 333.959 83
Ayers Rock (N.T.) T2—942 91
Ayers Rock-Mount Olga
  National Park (N.T.) T2—942 91
Aylesbury Vale (England) T2—425 93
Aylmer (Quebec) T2—714 221

Aymara Indians T5—983 24
Aymara language 498.324
T6—983 24
Aymara literature 898.324
Aymaran languages 498.324
T6—983 24
Ayrshire (Scotland) T2—414 6
Ayrshire cattle 636.225
Aysen (Chile : Province) T2—836 22
Aythya 598.414
Ayub Khan, Mohammad
Pakistani history 954.904 5
Ayurveda 615.53
Ayutthaya (Kingdom) 959.302 3
Az Zarqā' (Jordan :
Province) T2—569 593
Azad Kashmir T2—549 13
Azaleas 635.933 66
botany 583.66
floriculture 635.933 66
Āzarbāyjān-i Bākhtarī
(Iran) T2—554
Āzarbāyjān-i Khāvarī
(Iran) T2—553
Azerbaijan 947.54
T2—475 4
Azerbaijan (Iran) T2—553
Azerbaijan (Region) T2—553
Azerbaijan T2—475 4
Iran T2—553
Azerbaijani T5—943 61
Azerbaijani language 494.361
T6—943 61
Azerbaijani literature 894.361
Azilal (Morocco :
Province) T2—644
Azimuth 526.63
Azlon
textiles 677.472
see also Textiles
Azo compounds 547.043
chemical engineering 661.894
Azo-oxy dyes 667.253
Azo-tetrazo dyes 667.253
Azores T2—469 9
Azospirillum 579.323
Azov, Sea of (Ukraine and
Russia) 551.462 9
T2—163 89
Aztec calendar 529.329 784 52
Aztec language 497.452
T6—974 52
Aztec literature 897.452
Aztec period 972.018
Azteco-Tanoan Indians T5—974 5
Aztecs T5—974 52
Azua (Dominican
Republic : Province) T2—729 372
Azuay (Ecuador) T2—866 24

B

B cells 571.967
human immunology 616.079 8
B-flat horns 788.974
see also Brass instruments
B lymphocytes 571.967
human immunology 616.079 8
Baalbek (Lebanon)
ancient T2—394 4
'Bab el Mandeb 551.467 32
T2—165 32
Baba Batra 296.123 4
Babylonian Talmud 296.125 4
Mishnah 296.123 4
Palestinian Talmud 296.124 4
Baba Kamma 296.123 4
Babylonian Talmud 296.125 4
Mishnah 296.123 4
Palestinian Talmud 296.124 4
Baba Mezia 296.123 4
Babylonian Talmud 296.125 4
Mishnah 296.123 4
Palestinian Talmud 296.124 4
Babanango (South Africa :
District) T2—684 2
Babangida, Ibrahim Badamosi
Nigerian history 966.905 3
Babblers 598.834
Babenberg, House of 943.602 3
Babergh (England :
District) T2—426 48
Babies 305.232
T1—083 2
health 613.043 2
pediatrics 618.92
psychology 155.422
see also Infants
Bābil (Iraq : Province) T2—567 5
Babine language 497.2
T6—972
Babirusa 599.633
Babism 297.92
Babists
biography 297.920 92
religious group T7—297 8
Baboons 599.865

Babouvism (Socialist school)	335.2
Babur, Emperor of Hindustan	
Indian history	954.025 2
Baby animals	591.39
domestic animals	636.07
mammals	599.139
Baby blue-eyes (Plant)	635.933 94
botany	583.94
floriculture	635.933 94
Baby food	641.300 832
commercial preparation	664.62
cooking	641.562 2
feeding	649.3
food	641.300 832
Babylon (Extinct city)	T2—35
Babylonia	935.02
	T2—35
Mesopotamian history	935.02
Palestinian history	933.03
Babylonian dialect	492.17
	T6—921
Babylonian literature	892.1
Babylonian Talmud	296.125
Babylonians	T5—921
Babysitters' handbooks	649.102 48
Baca County (Colo.)	T2—788 99
Bacău (Romania : Județ)	T2—498 1
Baccarat	795.42
Bachelors	305.389 652
	T1—086 52
Bachelor's degree	378.2
Bacillariophyceae	579.85
Bacillary diseases	
incidence	614.512
medicine	616.931
see also Communicable diseases (Human)	
Bacillary dysentery	
incidence	614.516
medicine	616.935 5
see also Communicable diseases (Human)	
Bacillus	579.362
Back (Body part)	
human anatomy	611.9
human physiology	612.9
regional medicine	617.56
surgery	617.560 59
Back muscles	
human anatomy	611.731
see also Musculoskeletal system	
Back play	
American football	796.332 24
rugby	796.333 26
soccer	796.334 25
Backache	
medicine	617.564
Backgammon	795.15
Backhand	
tennis	796.342 23
Backpacking	796.51
equipment technology	688.765 1
Backyards	
biology	578.755 4
ecology	577.554
landscape architecture	712.6
Bacon County (Ga.)	T2—758 787
Bács-Kiskun Megye (Hungary)	T2—439 8
Bacteria	579.3
medical microbiology	616.014
paleontology	561.91
see Manual at 579.3	
Bacteria culture	
biology	571.638 293
Bacteria-enhanced oil recovery	622.338 27
Bacterial blood diseases	
incidence	614.577
medicine	616.94
see also Communicable diseases (Human)	
Bacterial counts	
milk processing	637.127 7
Bacterial diseases (Biology)	571.993
agriculture	632.32
plant crops	632.32
veterinary medicine	636.089 692
Bacterial diseases (Human)	
incidence	614.57
medicine	616.92
see also Communicable diseases (Human)	
Bacterial food poisons	
human toxicology	615.952 93
Bacterial viruses	579.26
Bactericides	668.653
agricultural use	632.953
chemical engineering	668.653
Bacterins	
pharmacology	615.372
Bacteriological examination	
medicine	616.075 81
Bacteriologists	579.309 2
occupational group	T7—579

Bacteriology 579.3
medicine 616.014
Bacteriophages 579.26
Bacteroides 579.325
Bactria T2—396
Baculoviridae 579.243 6
Bad debts
tax law 343.052 36
Badajoz (Spain : Province) T2—462 7
Baden (Germany) T2—434 64
Baden-Württemberg (Germany) T2—434 6
Badenoch and Strathspey (Scotland) T2—411 92
Badgers 599.767
Badges
armed forces 355.134 2
Badlands National Park (S.D.) T2—783 93
Badminton 796.345
see also Sports
Badminton players 796.345 092
sports group T7—796 34
Baetica T2—366
Baffin (N.W.T.) T2—719 5
see Manual at T2—7193–T2—7197
Baffin Bay 551.468 7
T2—163 27
Baffin Island (N.W.T.) T2—719 5
Bafia languages 496.396
T6—963 96
Bag papers 676.287
Bagasse
fuel technology 662.88
plastic technology 668.411
Bagasse pulp 676.14
Bagaza, Jean-Baptiste
Burundi history 967.572 04
Bagēmder (Ethiopia) T2—634
Baggage cars 385.33
engineering 625.23
see also Rolling stock
Baggage insurance 368.2
see also Insurance
Baggage services 388.042
see also Passenger services
Baghdād (Iraq : Province) T2—567 47
Bagheli dialect 491.49
T6—914 9
Bagheli literature 891.49
Bagot (Quebec : County) T2—714 525
Bagpipes 788.49
instrument 788.491 9
music 788.49
see also Woodwind instruments
Bags 688.8
paper 676.33
Baguios (Hurricanes) 551.552
see also Hurricanes
Bahai Faith 297.93
Bahais
biography 297.930 92
religious group T7—297 9
Bahama Islands 972.96
T2—729 6
Bahamas 972.96
T2—729 6
Bahamians T5—969 729 6
Bahasa Indonesia 499.221
T6—992 21
Bahasa Indonesia literature 899.221
Bahasa Kebangsaan 499.28
T6—992 8
Bahasa Malaysia 499.28
T6—992 8
Bahasa Malaysia literature 899.28
Bahasa Melayu 499.28
T6—992 8
Bahāwalpur District (Pakistan) T2—549 16
Bahia (Brazil : State) T2—814 2
Bahía Blanca Estuary (Argentina) 551.464 68
T2—163 68
Bahing-Vayu languages 495.49
T6—954 9
Bahoruco (Dominican Republic : Province) T2—729 326
Baḥr al-Abyaḍ (Sudan : Province) T2—626 4
Bahr al Ahmar (Egypt) T2—623
Baḥr al-Aḥmar (Sudan : Province) T2—625
Baḥr al Ghazāl (Sudan : Region) T2—629 4
Bahrain 953.65
T2—536 5
Bahraini T5—927 536 5
Baikal seal 599.792
Bail (Law) 345.056
Bailey bridges 388
construction 624.37
see also Bridges
Bailey County (Tex.) T2—764 844

Bailments	346.025
Bairnsdale (Vic.)	T2—945 6
Bait-casting	799.126
Bait fishing	799.122
Bait worm culture	639.75
Baixo Alentejo (Portugal)	T2—469 55
Baja California (Mexico)	T2—722
Baja California Norte (Mexico)	T2—722 3
Baja California Sur (Mexico)	T2—722 4
Baja Verapaz (Guatemala)	T2—728 152
Baked goods	641.815
commercial processing	664.752
home preparation	641.815
Baker County (Fla.)	T2—759 13
Baker County (Ga.)	T2—758 967
Baker County (Or.)	T2—795 75
Baker Lake (N.W.T.)	T2—719 4
Bakery goods	
commercial processing	664.752
Bakhtīarī va Chahār Mahāll (Iran : Province)	T2—559 5
Baking	
commercial food preparation	664.02
home cooking	641.71
Baking powder	664.68
Baking soda	
food technology	664.68
Bakongo (Kingdom)	967.320 1
	T2—673 2
Ba'labakk (Lebanon)	
ancient	T2—394 4
Balaena	599.527 6
Balaenidae	599.527
Balaenoptera	599.524
Balaenopteridae	599.524
Balalaikas	787.875
instrument	787.875 19
music	787.875
see also Stringed instruments	
Balance of payments	382.17
international banking	332.152
international commerce	382.17
Balance of power	327.112
Balance of trade	382.17
Balance sheets	657.3
accounting	657.3
financial management	658.151 2
investment analysis	332.632 042
Balancing machinery	621.816
Balanopales	583.43
Balanophoraceae	583.88
Balanopsidales	583.43
Balconies	721.84
architecture	721.84
construction	690.184
Balcony furniture	645.8
see also Outdoor furniture	
Balcony gardening	635.967 1
Bald cypresses	585.5
Bald eagle	598.943
conservation technology	639.978 943
resource economics	333.958 943
Baldachins	
church architecture	726.529 3
Baldness	
medicine	616.546
see also Hair	
Baldwin County (Ala.)	T2—761 21
Baldwin County (Ga.)	T2—758 573
Balē Kifle Hāger (Ethiopia)	T2—632
Bâle-Ville (Switzerland)	T2—494 32
Baleares	T2—467 5
Balearic Islands	T2—467 5
Balearic Sea	551.462 2
	T2—163 82
Baleen whales	599.5
Balfour (South Africa : District)	T2—682 7
Bali Island (Indonesia)	T2—598 6
Bali Sea	551.465 74
	T2—164 74
Balikesir İli (Turkey)	T2—562
Balinese language	499.22
	T6—992 2
Balinese literature	899.22
Baling crops	631.56
equipment manufacturing technology	681.763 1
Balkan Mountains (Bulgaria)	T2—499
Balkan Peninsula	949.6
	T2—496
Balkan States	949.6
	T2—496
Balkan Wars	949.6
Balkar language	494.38
	T6—943 8
Ball bearings	621.822
Ball games	796.3
equipment technology	688.763
indoor	794.7
outdoor	796.3
see also Sports	
Ball lightning	551.563 4
Ballad operas	782.14
music	782.14

Ballad operas (continued)
  stage presentation 792.6
    see also Theater
Ballades (Music) 784.189 6
Ballads
  literature 808.814 4
    history and criticism 809.144
    specific literatures T3B—104 4
      individual authors T3A—1
  music 782.43
Ballarat (Vic.) T2—945 7
Ballard County (Ky.) T2—769 96
Ballast (Railroad) 625.141
Ballet 792.8
  see also Theater
  see Manual at 792.78 vs. 792.8, 793.3
Ballet dancers 792.802 809 2
  occupational group T7—792 8
Ballet music 781.556
Ballet skiing 796.937
  see also Sports
Balletts 782.43
Ballina (N.S.W.) T2—944 3
Ballistic missile forces 358.17
Ballistic missiles 358.171 82
  engineering 623.451 95
  military equipment 358.171 82
Ballistics 531.55
  criminal investigation 363.256 2
  engineering 620.105
  military engineering 623.51
  physics 531.55
Ballistocardiography
  medicine 616.120 754
  see also Cardiovascular system
Balloons
  engineering 629.133 22
  military engineering 623.742
  piloting 629.132 522
  sports 797.51
    see also Sports
  see also Aircraft
Ballots 324.65
Ballroom dancing 793.33
Balls (Dances) 793.38
Balls (Recreational equipment) 796.3
  manufacturing technology 688.763
Ballymena (Northern Ireland : Borough) T2—416 13
Ballymoney (Northern Ireland : District) T2—416 14
Balms 583.77
Balms (Burseraceae) 583.77
Balms (Lamiaceae) 583.96
Balneotherapy
  medicine 615.853
Balochi T5—915 98
Balochi language 491.598
  T6—915 98
Balochi literature 891.598
Balong language 496.396
  T6—963 96
Balqā' (Jordan : Province) T2—569 55
Balsa
  botany 583.68
  forestry 634.973 68
Balsaminaceae 583.79
Balsams (Impatiens) 583.79
Baltic languages 491.9
  T6—919
Baltic literatures 891.9
Baltic Sea 551.461 34
  T2—163 34
Baltic States 947.9
  T2—479
Baltimore (Md.) T2—752 6
Baltimore County (Md.) T2—752 71
Balto-Finnic languages 494.54
  T6—945 4
Balto-Slavic languages 491.8
  T6—918
Balto-Slavic literatures 891.8
Balts (Indo-European people) T5—919
Baluchi T5—915 98
Baluchi language 491.598
  T6—915 98
Baluchi literature 891.598
Baluchistan T2—549 15
  Iran T2—558 3
  Pakistan T2—549 15
Baluchistan (Pakistan) T2—549 15
Balūchistān va Sīstān (Iran) T2—558 3
Balustrades 721.8
  architecture 721.8
  artistic ironwork 739.48
  construction 690.18
Bamako (Mali) T2—662 3
Bambara (African people) T5—963 452
Bambara language 496.345 2
  T6—963 452
Bambara literature 896.345 2
Bamberg (Germany) T2—433 18
Bamberg County (S.C.) T2—757 78
Bamboo pulp 676.14

Bamboos 584.9
  basketwork crop 633.58
  floriculture 635.934 9
  handicrafts 745.51
  textiles 677.54
    see also Textiles
Bambuseae 584.9
Bambute (African people) T5—963 94
Bamileke (African people) T5—963 6
Bamileke languages 496.36
  T6—963 6
Bamun language 496.36
  T6—963 6
Bana (African people) T5—963 6
Bana language 496.36
  T6—963 6
Banach algebras 512.55
Banach groups 512.55
Banach spaces 515.732
Bananas 641.347 72
  botany 584.39
  commercial processing 664.804 772
  cooking 641.647 72
  food 641.347 72
  horticulture 634.772
Banat T2—498 4
  Romania T2—498 4
  Yugoslavia T2—497 1
Banbridge (Northern Ireland : District) T2—416 57
Band leaders 784.092
  occupational group T7—784
Banda (African people) T5—963 61
Banda, H. Kamuzu (Hastings Kamuzu)
  Malawian history 968.970 41
Banda languages 496.361
  T6—963 61
Banda Sea 551.465 74
  T2—164 74
Bandages 677.8
  manufacturing technology 677.8
  surgical use 617.93
Bandera County (Tex.) T2—764 885
Bandi language 496.348
  T6—963 48
Bandicoots 599.26
Bandjoun language 496.36
  T6—963 6
Bandoneons 788.84
  see also Woodwind instruments
Bands 784
  see Manual at 784–788
Bandundu (Zaire) T2—675 116
Banff (Alta.) T2—712 332
Banff and Buchan (Scotland) T2—412 25
Banff National Park (Alta.) T2—712 332
Bangalore torpedoes 623.454 5
Banghāzī (Libya) T2—612
Bangi-Ntumba languages 496.396 8
  T6—963 968
Bangiophycideae 579.89
Bangladesh 954.92
  T2—549 2
Bangladesh people T5—914 126
Bangladeshis T5—914 126
Bangor (Me.) T2—741 3
Bang's disease 636.208 969 57
Bangui (Central African Republic) T2—674 1
Banī Suwayf (Egypt : Province) T2—622
Banjoists 787.880 92
  occupational group T7—787
Banjos 787.88
  instrument 787.881 9
  music 787.88
  see also Stringed instruments
Banjul (Gambia) T2—665 1
Bank accounts 332.175 2
Bank deposit insurance 368.854
  law 346.086 854
  see also Insurance
Bank failures 332.1
Bank for International Settlements 332.155
Bank holding companies 332.16
Bank mergers 332.16
Bank notes 332.404 4
  central banking 332.112
Bank reserves 332.1
  macroeconomic policy 339.53
  requirements 332.113
Bankers 332.109 2
  occupational group T7—332
Banking 332.1
  see also Banks (Finance)
Banking cooperatives 334.2
Banking services 332.17
Bankruptcy 332.75
  credit economics 332.75
  law 346.078
    commercial law 346.078
    public finance 343.037
  public finance 336.368

Banks (Finance) 332.1
accounting 657.833 3
credit regulation
macroeconomic policy 339.53
international law 341.751 1
law 346.082
public administration 354.86
Banks County (Ga.) T2—758 143
Banks Island (N.W.T.) T2—719 6
Banks Peninsula (N.Z.) T2—938 4
Banks Peninsula District (N.Z.) T2—938 4
Banksias 583.89
Bann River (Northern Ireland) T2—416
Banned books 098.1
Banner County (Neb.) T2—782 975
Banners 929.92
armed forces 355.15
Bannock County (Idaho) T2—796 47
Bannockburn, Battle of, 1314 941.102
Banquets 642.4
Bansuris 788.35
see also Woodwind instruments
Bantams 636.587 1
Banteng 599.642 2
Bantoid languages 496.36
T6—963 6
Bantu languages 496.39
T6—963 9
see Manual at T6—9639
Bantu literatures 896.39
Bantu-speaking peoples T5—963 9
Bantustans T2—682 9
Cape of Good Hope T2—687 9
Natal T2—684 9
Orange Free State T2—685 9
Transvaal T2—682 9
Banyan 583.45
Baobabs 583.68
Baoulé (African people) T5—963 385
Baoulé language 496.338 5
T6—963 385
Baptism 234.161
customs 392.12
etiquette 395.24
music 781.582
public worship 265.1
theology 234.161
Baptism in the Holy Spirit 234.13
Baptism of Jesus Christ 232.95
Baptismal fonts 247.1
architecture 726.529 1
Baptismal names 929.44
Baptismal records
genealogy 929.3
Baptist General Conference of America 286.5
see also Baptists
Baptist sacred music 781.716 1
public worship 782.322 61
music 782.322 61
religion 264.060 2
Baptistries
accessory building
architecture 726.4
architecture 726.596
Baptists 286
biography 286.092
church government 262.06
parishes 254.06
church law 262.986
doctrines 230.6
catechisms and creeds 238.6
general councils 262.56
guides to Christian life 248.486
missions 266.6
moral theology 241.046
persecution of 272.8
public worship 264.06
religious associations 267.186
religious education 268.86
religious group T7—261
seminaries 230.073 6
theology 230.6
Bar-code scanners 006.42
computer engineering 621.399
Bar coding 006.42
computer science 006.42
materials management 658.780 285 642
Bar examination 340.076
Bar mitzvah 296.442 4
customs 392.14
etiquette 395.24
liturgy 296.454 24
music 781.583
Baraga County (Mich.) T2—774 973
Barahona (Dominican Republic : Province) T2—729 324
Barai language 499.12
T6—991 2
Baraita 296.126 3
Baranya Megye (Hungary) T2—439 7
Barbadians T5—969 729 81
Barbados 972.981
T2—729 81
Barbary horse 636.11

Barbary States T2—61
Barbecuing 641.76
indoor cooking 641.76
outdoor cooking 641.578 4
Barbels (Fishes) 597.482
sports fishing 799.174 82
Barber County (Kan.) T2—781 82
Barbering 646.724
customs 391.5
Barberries 583.34
botany 583.34
cooking 641.647 4
floriculture 635.933 34
food 641.347 4
horticulture 634.74
Barbers 646.724 092
occupational group T7—646 7
Barbershops
sanitation services 363.729 9
see also Waste control
Barberton (South Africa : District) T2—682 6
Barbets 598.72
Barbeyales 583.43
Barbiturate abuse 362.299
medicine 616.86
personal health 613.8
social welfare 362.299
see also Substance abuse
Barbiturates
pharmacodynamics 615.782
Barbour County (Ala.) T2—761 32
Barbour County (W. Va.) T2—754 59
Barbs (Fishes) 597.482
Barbuda T2—729 74
Barcaldine (Qld.) T2—943 5
Barcelona (Spain : Province) T2—467 2
Barents Sea 551.468 4
T2—163 24
Bargain theory of wages 331.210 1
Barge canals 386.48
engineering 627.138
transportation services 386.48
see also Canals
Bargello 746.442
Barges 386.229
design 623.812 9
engineering 623.829
freight services 386.244
see also Ships
Bari (Italy : Province) T2—457 51
Bari language 496.5
T6—965
Bariatric surgery 617.43
see also Digestive system
Baric languages 495.4
T6—954
Barinas (Venezuela : State) T2—874 3
Barite 553.662
mineralogy 549.752
Baritone voices 782.88
choral and mixed voices 782.88
single voices 783.88
Baritones (Horns)
American 788.975
instrument 788.975 19
music 788.975
see also Brass instruments
British 788.974
see also Brass instruments
Barium 669.725
chemical engineering 661.039 5
chemistry 546.395
economic geology 553.499
metallurgy 669.725
physical metallurgy 669.967 25
see also Chemicals
Bark 581.47
descriptive botany 581.47
forest product 634.985
physiology 575.452
Bark beetles 595.768
Barkerville (B.C.) T2—711 75
Barking and Dagenham (London, England) T2—421 75
Barkley, Lake (Ky. and Tenn.) T2—769 79
Barkly East (South Africa : District) T2—687 6
Barkly West (South Africa : District) T2—687 11
Barley 641.331 6
botany 584.9
cooking 641.631 6
food 641.331 6
food crop 633.16
forage crop 633.256
Barlow, George Hilaro, Sir
Indian history 954.031 2
Barmera (S. Aust.) T2—942 33
Barnabites 255.52
church history 271.52
Barnacles 595.35
paleozoology 565.35
Barnes County (N.D.) T2—784 32
Barnet (London, England) T2—421 87
Barnouic (England) T2—423 49

Barns 631.22
  animal husbandry 636.083 1
  architecture 728.922
  construction 690.892 2
  use 631.22
Barnsley (England) T2—428 25
Barnstable County (Mass.) T2—744 92
Barnwell County (S.C.) T2—757 76
Barometric leveling 526.37
Barometric pressure 551.54
Baroque architecture 724.16
Baroque art 709.032
Baroque decoration 745.443
Baroque music 780.903 2
Baroque painting 759.046
Baroque sculpture 735.21
Barotse kingdoms (Zambian history) 968.940 1
Barracks 355.71
  architecture 725.18
  military housing 355.71
Barracudas 597.7
Barrage balloons
  military engineering 623.744
Barrages
  engineering 627.123
Barramunda 597.39
  culture 639.373 9
  fishing 639.273 9
Barrels 688.8
  wooden 674.82
Barren County (Ky.) T2—769 72
Barrier islands 551.423
  T2—142
  geography 910.914 2
  geomorphology 551.423
  physical geography 910.021 42
Barron County (Wis.) T2—775 18
Barrow County (Ga.) T2—758 195
Barrow-in-Furness (England : District) T2—427 81
Barrow Island National Park (W.A.) T2—941 3
Barrow River (Ireland) T2—418
Barry County (Mich.) T2—774 16
Barry County (Mo.) T2—778 76
Bars (Drinking places) 647.95
  architecture 725.72
  home economics 643.4
  public household management 647.95
Bars (Musical instruments) 786.82
  concussed 786.873
  friction 786.863
    set 786.863
Bars (Musical instruments)
  friction (continued)
    single 786.888
  percussed 786.843
    set 786.843
    single 786.884 3
  plucked 786.85
    set 786.85
    single 786.887
  see also Percussion instruments
Bars (Structural elements) 624.177 4
Bartenders' manuals 641.874
Barter instruments 332.5
Bartholomew County (Ind.) T2—772 24
Barton County (Kan.) T2—781 52
Barton County (Mo.) T2—778 71
Bartow County (Ga.) T2—758 365
Baruch (Bible) 229.5
Baryons 539.721 64
Baryonyx 567.912
Barytons 787.6
  see also Stringed instruments
Bas-Rhin (France) T2—443 835
Bas-Richelieu (Quebec) T2—714 51
Bas-Saint-Laurent-Gaspésie Region (Quebec) T2—714 77
Bas-Zaïre (Zaire) T2—675 114
Basa (Cameroon people) T5—963 96
Basa (Liberian people) T5—963 3
Basa language 496.396
  T6—963 96
Basal body 571.67
Basal ganglia
  medicine 616.83
  see also Nervous system
Basalts 552.26
Basari (Senegal-Guinea people) T5—963 2
Basari (Togo-Ghana people) T5—963 5
Bascule bridges 388
  construction 624.82
  see also Bridges
Base lines (Surveying) 526.33
Base running
  baseball 796.357 27
Base sequences (Nucleotides) 572.863 3
Baseball 796.357
  electronic games 794.863 57
  equipment manufacturing 688.763 57
    gloves and mitts 685.43
  see also Sports

Baseball cards 796.357 075
Baseball players 796.357 092
  sports group T7—796 35
Baseband computer equipment 004.64
  engineering 621.398 1
Baseband local-area networks 004.68
  see also Computer communications
Basel (Switzerland : Canton) T2—494 32
Basel-Stadt (Switzerland) T2—494 32
Baselland (Switzerland) T2—494 33
Basements
  home economics 643.5
Basenji 636.753 6
Bases (Chemicals) 546.32
  chemical engineering 661.3
  see also Chemicals
Bases (Military installations) 355.7
  international law 341.725
  law 343.01
Bashfulness 155.232
Bashkir T2—474 3
Bashkir language 494.38
  T6—943 8
Bashkortostan T2—474 3
Basic Christian communities 250
  ecclesiology 262.26
  see Manual at 260 vs. 251–254, 259
Basic education 370
  adults 374.012
  see also Education
Basic English 428
Basic races T5—03
Basic skills education 370
  see also Education
Basic sulfates
  mineralogy 549.755
Basic training (Military) 355.54
  living conditions 355.129 2
Basidiomycetes 579.59
Basidiomycotina 579.59
Basil 641.357
  botany 583.96
  see also Herbs
Basil III, Czar of Russia
  Russian history 947.042
Basilan (Philippines : Province) T2—599 7
Basilan Island (Philippines) T2—599 7
Basildon (England) T2—426 772
Basilians 255.17
  church history 271.17
Basilicata (Italy) T2—457 7
  ancient T2—377
Basilisks (Mythical animal) 398.245 4
  see also Legendary animals
Basingstoke and Deane (England) T2—422 71
Basket stars 593.94
Basketball 796.323
  electronic games 794.863 23
  see also Sports
Basketball cards 796.323 075
Basketball players 796.323 092
  sports group T7—796 32
Basketry
  handicrafts 746.412
Basketwork plants
  agriculture 633.58
Basommatophora 594.38
Basotho T5—968 85
Basotho-Qwaqwa (South Africa) T2—685 91
Basque language 499.92
  T6—999 2
Basque literature 899.92
Basque Provinces (Spain) T2—466
Basques T5—999 2
Basques (Quebec : Regional County Municipality) T2—714 76
Basṛah (Iraq : Province) T2—567 5
Bass clarinets 788.65
  see also Woodwind instruments
Bass drums 786.95
  see also Percussion instruments
Bass flutes 788.34
  see also Woodwind instruments
Bass recorders 788.367
  see also Woodwind instruments
Bass saxophones 788.75
  see also Woodwind instruments
Bass Strait (Vic. and Tas.) 551.467 76
  T2—165 76
Bass viols 787.65
  see also Stringed instruments
Bass voices 782.89
  choral and mixed voices 782.89
  single voices 783.89
Bassa (Cameroon people) T5—963 96
Bassa (Liberian people) T5—963 3

Bassa language (Cameroon) 496.396
T6—963 96
Bassa language (Liberia) 496.33
T6—963 3
Bassari (Senegal-Guinea people) T5—963 2
Bassari (Togo-Ghana people) T5—963 5
Basse-Normandie (France) T2—442
Basse-taille
ceramic arts 738.4
Basses (Fishes) 597.73
conservation technology 639.977 73
cooking 641.692
culture 639.377 3
food 641.392
resource economics 333.956 73
sports fishing 799.177 3
zoology 597.73
Basses (Stringed instruments) 787.5
instrument 787.519
music 787.5
see also Stringed instruments
Basses-Alpes (France) T2—449 5
Basses-Pyrénées (France) T2—447 9
Basset horns 788.62
Basset hound 636.753 6
Bassetlaw (England : District) T2—425 21
Basslets 597.73
Bassoons 788.58
instrument 788.581 9
music 788.58
see also Woodwind instruments
Basswood
botany 583.68
forestry 634.972 77
lumber 674.142
Bast fibers
textiles 677.1
see also Textiles
Bastille Day 394.263 5
Bastrop County (Tex.) T2—764 32
Basutoland 968.850 2
T2—688 5
Bat flies 595.774
Bat games 796.35
Bat mitzvah 296.443 4
customs 392.14
etiquette 395.24
liturgy 296.454 34
music 781.583
Bataan (Philippines : Province) T2—599 1
Batanes (Philippines) T2—599 1
Batangas (Philippines : Province) T2—599 1
Batavian Republic 949.205
Batch processing 004.3
see also Processing modes—computer science
Batemans Bay (N.S.W.) T2—944 7
Bates County (Mo.) T2—778 43
Batfishes 597.62
Bath (England) T2—423 98
Bath County (Ky.) T2—769 555
Bath County (Va.) T2—755 87
Bathhouses
architecture 725.73
domestic 728.96
public 725.73
construction
domestic 690.896
public 690.573
Bathing 613.41
child training 649.63
customs 391.64
health 613.41
personal care 646.71
therapeutics 615.853
Bathrooms 643.52
home economics 643.52
plumbing 696.182
residential interior decoration 747.78
Bathurst (N.B.) T2—715 12
Bathurst (N.S.W.) T2—944 5
Bathurst (South Africa : District) T2—687 5
Bathurst Inlet (N.W.T.) T2—719 7
Bathyscaphes 387.27
design 623.812 7
engineering 623.827
transportation services 387.27
Bathyspheres 387.27
design 623.812 7
engineering 623.827
transportation services 387.27
Batik 746.662
Bating leather 675.22
Batna (Algeria : Province) T2—655
Batoidei 597.35
paleozoology 567.35
Baton Rouge (La.) T2—763 18
Baton twirling 791.6
Batrachoidiformes 597.62

Bats 599.4
  conservation technology 639.979 4
  paleozoology 569.4
  resource economics 333.959 4
Bats (Baseball)
  manufacturing technology 688.763 57
Batswana (Ethnic group) T5—963 977 5
Batswana (National group) T5—968 83
Battalions (Military units) 355.31
Battered wives 362.829 2
  criminology 364.155 53
    criminal law 345.025 553
  social welfare 362.829 2
  see also Family violence
Batteries (Artillery units) 358.123
Batteries (Electric) 621.312 42
  automotive 629.254 2
Battery (Crime) 364.155 5
  law 345.025 55
    criminal law 345.025 55
    torts 346.033
Batting (Sports)
  baseball 796.357 26
  cricket 796.358 26
Battle games 793.92
Battle tactics 355.42
Battleford (Sask.) T2—712 42
Battlefords (Sask.) T2—712 42
Battles 355.4
  see also Land operations;
      Military history
Battleships 359.835 2
  design 623.812 52
  engineering 623.825 2
  naval equipment 359.835 2
  naval units 359.325 2
Bauchi State (Nigeria) T2—669 82
Baudouin I, King of the Belgians
  Belgian history 949.304 3
Bauxite 553.492 6
  economic geology 553.492 6
  mineralogy 549.53
  mining 622.349 26
Bava Batra 296.123 4
  Babylonian Talmud 296.125 4
  Mishnah 296.123 4
  Palestinian Talmud 296.124 4
Bava Kamma 296.123 4
  Babylonian Talmud 296.125 4
  Mishnah 296.123 4
  Palestinian Talmud 296.124 4
Bava Meẓia 296.123 4
  Babylonian Talmud 296.125 4
  Mishnah 296.123 4
Bava Meẓia (continued)
  Palestinian Talmud 296.124 4
Bavaria (Germany) T2—433
Bavarian Forest (Germany) T2—433 5
Baxter County (Ark.) T2—767 21
Bay County (Fla.) T2—759 95
Bay County (Mich.) T2—774 47
Bay laurel 641.357
  botany 583.23
Bay of Bengal 551.467 64
  T2—165 64
Bay of Biscay (France and
    Spain) 551.461 38
  T2—163 38
Bay of Fundy 551.461 45
  T2—163 45
Bay of Plenty Region
    (N.Z.) T2—934 2
Bay rum tree 583.765
Bayadh (Algeria :
    Province) T2—657
Bayamón (P.R. : District) T2—729 52
Bayberries (Myricaceae) 583.43
Bayberry wax 665.12
Bayern (Germany) T2—433
Bayesian statistical decision
    theory 519.542
Bayfield County (Wis.) T2—775 13
Baylor County (Tex.) T2—764 744
Bayonet practice 355.547
Bayonets 623.441
  art metalwork 739.723
Bayreuth (Germany) T2—433 15
Bays
  international law 341.448
  resource economics 333.916 4
Bazaars 381.18
  architecture 725.21
  management 658.87
  see also Commerce
Bazookamen 356.162
Bazookas 356.162
  engineering 623.442 6
    ammunition 623.455
  military equipment 356.162
Beach activities
  recreation 796.53
Beach erosion 551.36
  engineering 627.58
Beach flies 595.774
Beaches 551.457
  T2—146
  area planning 711.558
  geography 910.914 6

Beaches (continued)
  geomorphology 551.457
  landscape architecture 714
  physical geography 910.021 46
  recreational resources 333.784
  resource economics 333.917
  sanitation services 363.729 2
    see also Waste control
Beacons 387.155
  construction 627.924
  transportation services 387.155
  use in navigation 623.894 4
Beaconsfield (Tas.) T2—946 5
Bead embroidery 746.5
Beadle County (S.D.) T2—783 274
Beads 391.7
  customs 391.7
  handicrafts 745.582
  home sewing 646.19
Beagle 636.753 7
Beak 591.4
  descriptive zoology 591.4
  physiology 573.355
Beak rushes 584.84
Beaked reptiles 597.945
Beaked whales 599.545
Beam warfare 358.39
Beams (Light) 535.5
Beams (Structural elements) 624.177 23
  naval architecture 623.817 723
  structural engineering 624.177 23
    concrete 624.183 423
Beans 641.356 5
  botany 583.74
  commercial processing 664.805 65
  cooking 641.656 5
  field crop 633.3
  food 641.356 5
  garden crop 635.65
Bear Lake County (Idaho) T2—796 44
Beard 646.724
  care 646.724
  customs 391.5
Beard fishes 597.62
Bearded pig 599.633 2
Bearded seal 599.796
Beardworms 592.3
Bearing walls 721.2
  architecture 721.2
  construction 690.12
  see also Walls (Building element)
Bearings 621.822
  clockwork 681.112
  machine engineering 621.822
  railroad engineering 625.21
Béarn (France) T2—447 9
Bears 599.78
  animal husbandry 636.978
  big game hunting 799.277 8
  conservation technology 639.979 78
  predator control technology 636.083 9
    conservation technology 639.966
  resource economics 333.959 78
  zoology 599.78
Bearsden and Milngavie (Scotland : District) T2—414 34
Beasts of burden 636.088 2
Beatification of saints 235.24
Beating metals
  decorative arts 739.14
  sculpture 731.41
Beatitudes 226.93
  Christian moral theology 241.53
Beatrix, Queen of the Netherlands
  Dutch history 949.207 3
Beauce (Quebec) T2—714 71
Beauce-Sartigan (Quebec) T2—714 71
Beaufort County (N.C.) T2—756 186
Beaufort County (S.C.) T2—757 99
Beaufort Sea 551.468 7
  T2—163 27
Beaufort West (South Africa : District) T2—687 15
Beauharnois (Quebec : County) T2—714 32
Beauharnois-Salaberry (Quebec) T2—714 32
Beauport (Quebec) T2—714 471
Beauregard Parish (La.) T2—763 59
Beauticians 646.720 92
Beauty 111.85
  personal
    arts 700.453
      T3C—353
    literature 808.803 53
      history and criticism 809.933 53
      specific literatures T3B—080 353
        history and criticism T3B—093 53
  philosophy 111.85
Beauty shops 646.72
  personal care 646.72
  sanitation services 363.729 9
    see also Waste control

Beaver County (Okla.) T2—766 14
Beaver County (Pa.) T2—748 92
Beaver County (Utah) T2—792 46
Beaverhead County (Mont.) T2—786 69
Beavers 599.37
  conservation technology 639.979 37
  resource economics 333.959 37
  trapping 639.113 7
Bebop 781.655
Bécancour (Quebec : Regional County Municipality) T2—714 55
Béchar (Algeria : Province) T2—657
Bechuanaland 968.830 2
  T2—688 3
Becker County (Minn.) T2—776 84
Beckham County (Okla.) T2—766 43
Becoming
  philosophy 116
Bed and breakfasts 647.94
Bedbugs 595.754
Bedclothing 643.53
  arts 746.97
  commercial technology 684.3
  home sewing 646.21
  household equipment 643.53
Bedford (England : District) T2—425 61
Bedford (South Africa : District) T2—687 5
Bedford (Va.) T2—755 676
Bedford County (Pa.) T2—748 71
Bedford County (Tenn.) T2—768 583
Bedford County (Va.) T2—755 675
Bedfordshire (England) T2—425 6
Bedouins T5—927 2
Bedrooms 643.53
  home economics 643.53
  interior decoration 747.77
Beds (Furniture) 645.4
  manufacturing technology 684.15
  see also Furniture
Bedsores
  medicine 616.545
  see also Skin
Bedspreads 643.53
  arts 746.97
  home sewing 646.21
  household equipment 643.53
Bedwetting
  medicine 616.849
  pediatrics 618.928 49
  see also Nervous system
Bee balms 583.96
Bee County (Tex.) T2—764 117
Bee eaters 598.78
Bee flies 595.773
Bee keeping 638.1
Bee lice 595.774
Bee venom
  human toxicology 615.942
Beeches
  botany 583.46
  forestry 634.972 5
  lumber 674.142
Beechworth (Vic.) T2—945 5
Beef 641.362
  commercial processing
    economics 338.476 649 2
    technology 664.92
  cooking 641.662
  food 641.362
Beef cattle
  agricultural economics 338.176 213
  animal husbandry 636.213
Beefwoods 583.43
Beekeepers 638.109 2
  occupational group T7—638
Beer 641.23
  commercial processing 663.42
  cooking with 641.623
  home preparation 641.873
Bees 595.799
  agriculture 638.1
Beeswax
  apiculture processing 638.17
Beet sugar 641.336 3
  commercial processing 664.123
  food 641.336 3
  see also Sugar
Beet syrup
  commercial processing 664.123
Beetles 595.76
  agricultural pests 632.76
  culture 638.576
  paleozoology 565.76
Beetling textiles 677.028 25
Beets 641.351 1
  botany 583.53
  commercial processing 664.805 11
  cooking 641.651 1
  food 641.351 1
  garden crop 635.11
  sugar crop 633.63
Bega (N.S.W.) T2—944 7
Beggar's lice 583.74
Begheli literature 891.49
Beginner cooking 641.512

Beginners
  social group T7—090 9
Begoniales 583.627
Begonias 635.933 627
  botany 583.627
  floriculture 635.933 627
Behavior
  animals 591.5
  comparative psychology 156
  educational psychology 370.153
  evolutional psychology 155.7
  general psychology 150
  plants 575.9
  social psychology 302
Behavior modification 153.85
  educational psychology 370.153
  home child care 649.64
  teaching methods 371.393
Behavior modification therapy
  psychiatry 616.891 42
  see also Mental illness
Behavior therapy
  psychiatry 616.891 42
  see also Mental illness
Behavioral adaptation
  animals 591.5
Behavioral genetics 155.7
Behavioral pharmacology 615.78
  see also Mental illness
Behavioral sciences 300
  psychology 150
  public administrative support 352.745
Behaviorism 150.194 3
Beheira (Egypt) T2—621
Beijing (China) T2—511 56
Beijing dialect 495.1
  T6—951 1
Being 111
Beira (Portugal : Province) T2—469 3
Beira Alta (Portugal) T2—469 31
Beira Baixa (Portugal) T2—469 33
Beira Litoral (Portugal) T2—469 35
Beirut (Lebanon) T2—569 25
Beja (Portugal : District) T2—469 55
Beja language 493.5
  T6—935
Bejaïa (Algeria : Province) T2—655
Békés Megye (Hungary) T2—439 9
Bekhorot 296.123 5
  Babylonian Talmud 296.125 5
  Mishnah 296.123 5
Bekhterev, Vladimir Mikhailovich
  psychological system 150.194 4
Bektashi 297.48
Bel and the Dragon (Bible) 229.6
Belarus 947.8
  T2—478
Belarusian language 491.799
  T6—917 99
Belarusian literature 891.799
Belarusians T5—917 99
Belau 996.6
  T2—966
Belfast (Northern Ireland) T2—416 7
Belfast (South Africa : District) T2—682 7
Belfort (France : Territory) T2—444 55
Belgian Congo 967.510 24
  T2—675 1
Belgian draft horse 636.15
Belgian hare 636.932 2
Belgian literature
  Flemish 839.31
  French 840
Belgian Malinois 636.737
Belgian Tervuren 636.737
Belgians T5—393 2
Belgica T2—364
Belgium 949.3
  T2—493
  ancient 936.4
  T2—364
Belgorod (Russia : Oblast) T2—473 5
Belgorodskaîa oblast´ (Russia) T2—473 5
Belgrade (Serbia) T2—497 1
Belief
  epistemology 121.6
Belief and doubt
  epistemology 121.6
Belief systems
  social control 303.372
Belize 972.82
  T2—728 2
Belize District (Belize) T2—728 22
Belizeans T5—969 728 2
Belknap County (N.H.) T2—742 45
Bell County (Ky.) T2—769 123
Bell County (Tex.) T2—764 287
Bell-jar gardening
  floriculture 635.985
Bell magpies 598.8
Bell peppers 641.356 43
  see also Sweet peppers
Bell towers
  architecture 725.97
Bella Coola (B.C.) T2—711 1

Bella Coola language 497.9
T6—979
Bella Coola River (B.C.) T2—711 1
Belladonna
botany 583.952
pharmacology 615.323 952
Bellechasse (Quebec : County) T2—714 733
Bellechasse (Quebec : Regional County Municipality) T2—714 733
Bellenden Ker National Park (Qld.) T2—943 6
Belles-lettres 800
history and criticism 809
see Manual at 800
Bellflowers 635.933 98
botany 583.98
floriculture 635.933 98
Belligerency 341.62
Belligerent countries T2—171 82
Bellingshausen Sea 551.469 4
T2—167 4
Bells 786.884 8
instrument 786.884 819
music 786.884 8
see also Percussion instruments
Belluno (Italy : Province) T2—453 7
Bellville (South Africa : District) T2—687 35
Belly dancing 793.3
Belmont County (Ohio) T2—771 93
Beloit (Wis.) T2—775 87
Belorussia 947.8
T2—478
Belorussian language 491.799
T6—917 99
Belorussian literature 891.799
Belorussians T5—917 99
Belt buckles 391.7
customs 391.7
making 739.278
see also Jewelry
Belt conveyors 621.867 5
Beltrami County (Minn.) T2—776 82
Belts
power transmission 621.852
Belts (Clothing) 391.44
commercial technology 687.19
leather 685.22
see also Accessories (Clothing)
Beltways 388.122
see also Roads
Beluga 599.542
Bemba (African people) T5—963 915
Bemba kingdoms (Zambian history) 968.940 1
Bemba language 496.391 5
T6—963 915
Bemba literature 896.391 5
Bembe-Kabwari languages 496.394
T6—963 94
Ben Hill County (Ga.) T2—758 852
Ben Lomond National Park (Tas.) T2—946 4
Ben Msik-Sidi Othmane (Morocco : Prefecture) T2—643
Ben Slimane (Morocco : Province) T2—643
Bena-Kinga languages 496.391
T6—963 91
Benalla (Vic.) T2—945 5
Bench marks 526.32
Bench-scale plants
chemical engineering 660.280 71
Bendel State (Nigeria) T2—669 3
Bendel states (Nigeria) T2—669 3
Bendigo (Vic.) T2—945 4
Bending metals
decorative arts 739.14
sculpture 731.41
Bending tools 621.982
Bendjedid, Chadli
Algerian history 965.053
Bends
medicine 616.989 4
see also Environmental diseases (Human)
Benedictines 255.1
church history 271.1
women 255.97
church history 271.97
Benedictions 291.38
Christianity 264.13
Judaism 296.45
Benedictus 264.36
music 782.323 2
Beneficial animals 591.63
Beneficial microorganisms 579.163
Beneficial organisms 578.63
Beneficial plants 581.63
Beneficiation (Ore dressing) 622.7
Benefit cost analysis 658.155 4
public administration 352.43

Benefit societies		334.7
economics		334.7
insurance		368
see also Insurance		
Benefits (Insurance)		368.014
Benelux countries		949.2
	T2—492	
Benesh choreology		792.82
Benevento (Italy : Province)	T2—457 23	
Benevolence		
ethics		177.7
see also Ethical problems		
Benevolent and Protective Order of Elks		366.5
Benevolent societies		334.7
economics		334.7
insurance		368
see also Insurance		
Benewah County (Idaho)	T2—796 93	
Benga language		496.396
	T6—963 96	
Bengal (India)	T2—541 4	
Bengal, Bay of		551.467 64
	T2—165 64	
Bengal cat		636.822
Bengali	T5—914 4	
Bengali-Assamese languages		491.44
	T6—914 4	
Bengali language		491.44
	T6—914 4	
Bengali literature		891.44
Benghazi (Libya)	T2—612	
Bengo (Angola : Province)	T2—673 2	
Benguela (Angola : Province)	T2—673 4	
Benguet (Philippines : Province)	T2—599 1	
Beni (Bolivia)	T2—844 2	
Beni Mellal (Morocco : Province)	T2—644	
Benign tumors		
medicine		616.993
see also Diseases (Human)		
Benin		966.83
	T2—668 3	
Benin (Kingdom)		966.930 1
	T2—669 3	
Benin (Nigeria)	T2—669 3	
Benin City (Nigeria)	T2—669 32	
Beninese	T5—966 83	
Bennett, Richard Bedford Bennett, 1st Viscount		
Canadian history		971.062 3
Bennett County (S.D.)	T2—783 65	
Bennettitales		561.592
Bennington County (Vt.)	T2—743 8	
Benoni (South Africa : District)	T2—682 2	
Benson County (N.D.)	T2—784 39	
Bent County (Colo.)	T2—788 97	
Bent grasses		633.23
botany		584.9
forage crop		633.23
Benthic biology		
oceans		578.777
Benthic ecology		
oceans		577.77
Bentinck, William Henry Cavendish, Lord		
Indian history		954.031 4
Benton County (Ark.)	T2—767 13	
Benton County (Ind.)	T2—772 972	
Benton County (Iowa)	T2—777 61	
Benton County (Minn.)	T2—776 67	
Benton County (Miss.)	T2—762 89	
Benton County (Mo.)	T2—778 493	
Benton County (Or.)	T2—795 34	
Benton County (Tenn.)	T2—768 33	
Benton County (Wash.)	T2—797 51	
Bentonite		553.61
economic geology		553.61
mining		622.361
Benue-Congo languages		496.36
	T6—963 6	
Benue-Niger languages		496.36
	T6—963 6	
Benue-Plateau State (Nigeria)	T2—669 52	
Benue State (Nigeria)	T2—669 54	
Benzene		547.611
chemical engineering		661.816
fuel		662.669
human toxicology		615.951 1
Benzie County (Mich.)	T2—774 632	
Beowulf		829.3
Berakhot		296.123 1
Babylonian Talmud		296.125 1
Mishnah		296.123 1
Palestinian Talmud		296.124 1
Berber languages		493.3
	T6—933	
Berber literatures		893.3
Berberidaceae		583.34
Berbers	T5—933	

Bereavement
  psychology 155.937
  religion 291.442
    Christianity
      devotional literature 242.4
      pastoral theology 259.6
      personal religion 248.866
      rites 265.85
    devotional literature 291.432
    Judaism
      pastoral theology 296.61
      personal religion 296.7
      rites 296.445
        liturgy 296.454 5
    pastoral theology 291.61
    personal religion 291.442
    rites 291.38
Bereina (New Guinea) T2—954 6
Bergamo (Italy : Province) T2—452 4
Bergen County (N.J.) T2—749 21
Bergius process 662.662 2
Bergsonism 143
Bergville (South Africa : District) T2—684 7
Berhou (England) T2—423 47
Beriberi
  medicine 616.392
  see also Digestive system
Bering Sea 551.465 51
  T2—164 51
Bering Strait 551.465 51
  T2—164 51
Berit milah 296.442 2
  liturgy 296.454 22
Berkeley (Calif.) T2—794 67
Berkeley County (S.C.) T2—757 93
Berkeley County (W. Va.) T2—754 97
Berkelium 546.444
  see also Chemicals
Berks County (Pa.) T2—748 16
Berkshire (England) T2—422 9
Berkshire County (Mass.) T2—744 1
Berkshire Hills (Mass.) T2—744 1
Berlin (Germany) T2—431 55
Berlin (Germany : East) T2—431 552
Berlin (Germany : West) T2—431 554
Berlin, Battle of, 1945 940.542 131 55
Bermuda 972.99
  T2—729 9
Bermuda Islands 972.99
  T2—729 9
Bermuda Triangle 001.94
Bermudians T5—969 729 9
Bern (Switzerland) T2—494 542
Bern (Switzerland : Canton) T2—494 54
Bernalillo County (N.M.) T2—789 61
Bernese Alps T2—494 54
Bernese mountain dog 636.73
Bernier and Dorre Islands National Park (W.A.) T2—941 3
Berri (S. Aust.) T2—942 33
Berrien County (Ga.) T2—758 862
Berrien County (Mich.) T2—774 11
Berries 581.464
  commercial processing 664.804 7
  cooking 641.647
  descriptive botany 581.464
  food 641.347
  horticulture 634.7
  physiology 575.67
Berry (France) T2—445 5
Berry Islands (Bahamas) T2—729 6
Berthier (Quebec : County) T2—714 43
Berthing structures
  engineering 627.32
Bertie County (N.C.) T2—756 163
Berwick-upon-Tweed (England : District) T2—428 89
Berwickshire (Scotland) T2—413 95
Beryciformes 597.64
Beryl
  mineralogy 549.64
Beryllium 669.724
  chemical engineering 661.039 1
  chemistry 546.391
  economic geology 553.492 3
  human toxicology 615.925 391
  materials science 620.189 4
  metallography 669.957 24
  metallurgy 669.724
  metalworking 673.724
  mining 622.349 23
  physical metallurgy 669.967 24
  see also Chemicals; Metals
Bessarabia (Moldova and Ukraine) T2—476
Bessel function 515.53
Bessemer steel 669.142 3
Best books
  bibliographies 011.73
Beta decay 539.752 3
Beta functions 515.52
Beta Israel T5—924
Beta particles 539.721 12
Beta radiation
  biophysics 571.459
    humans 612.014 486

Betatron-synchrotrons 539.735
Betatrons 539.734
Bété language 496.33
T6—963 3
Bethal (South Africa : District) T2—682 7
Bethlehem (South Africa : District) T2—685 1
Bethulie (South Africa : District) T2—685 7
Betrothal 392.4
see also Engagement (Betrothal)
Betsimisaraka (Kingdom) 969.101
T2—691
Betta (Fighting fish) 597.7
culture 639.377
Better business bureaus 381.34
Betting 306.482
see also Gambling—sociology
Betting systems 795.01
Betulales 583.48
Bevel gears 621.833 2
Beverage containers
disposal 363.728 8
see also Waste control
Beverage technologists 663.092
occupational group T7—663
Beverage technology 663
equipment manufacturing technology 681.766 4
Beverages 641.2
commercial processing 663
cooking with 641.62
customs 394.12
health 613.2
home economics 641.2
home preparation 641.87
product safety 363.192 9
see also Food—product safety
Beverley (England : Borough) T2—428 36
Bexar County (Tex.) T2—764 35
Bexley (London, England) T2—421 77
Bezah 296.123 2
Babylonian Talmud 296.125 2
Mishnah 296.123 2
Palestinian Talmud 296.124 2
Bhagavad Gita 294.592 4
Bhakti Yoga 294.543 6
Bharals 599.649
Bhedabheda (Philosophy) 181.484 2
Bhil (Indic people) T5—914 7
Bhili language 491.47
T6—914 7
Bhili literature 891.47
Bhojpuri language 491.454 7
T6—914 54
Bhojpuri literature 891.454
Bhopal (India) T2—543
Bhumibol Adulyadej, King of Thailand
Thai history 959.304 4
Bhutan 954.98
T2—549 8
Bhutanese T5—914 18
Bhutia (Asian people) T5—954
Biafra T2—669 4
Biafran War, 1967–1970 966.905 2
Biała Podlaska (Poland : Voivodeship) T2—438 4
Białystok (Poland : Voivodeship) T2—438 3
Bias bindings 677.76
Biathlon 796.932
see also Sports
Bibb County (Ala.) T2—761 82
Bibb County (Ga.) T2—758 552
Bibionidae 595.772
Bible 220
homiletical use 251
music 782.295
choral and mixed voices 782.529 5
single voices 783.092 95
use in public worship 264.34
see Manual at 220.92
Bible as literature 809.935 22
Bible Christians (Methodist denomination) 287.53
see also Methodist Church
Bible colleges 230.071 1
Bible meditations 242.5
Bible prayers 242.722
Bible stories 220.950 5
Bible study 220.07
Biblical Aramaic language 492.29
T6—922 9
Biblical characters
art representation 704.948 4
arts 700.452 2
T3C—352 2
Biblical events
art representation 704.948 4
arts 700.482 2
T3C—382 2
Biblical Greek language 487.4
T6—87

Biblical moral precepts
  Christianity 241.5
  Judaism 296.36
Biblical theology
  Christianity 230.041
  Judaism 296.3
  see Manual at 220: Biblical theology
Bibliographers 010.92
  occupational group T7—091
Bibliographic analysis 025.3
Bibliographic Classification (Bliss) 025.434
Bibliographic control 025.3
  see Manual at 025.3
Bibliographic description 025.324
Bibliographic headings 025.322
Bibliographic instruction 025.56
Bibliographical centers
  cooperation 021.64
Bibliographies 011
Bibliography 010
Bibliotherapy
  medicine 615.851 6
Bicameral legislatures 328.39
Biche, Lac la (Alta.) T2—712 33
Bichirs 597.42
Bichon frise 636.72
Biculturalism
  sociolinguistics 306.446
Bicycle accidents 363.125 9
  see also Highway safety
Bicycle paths 388.12
  area planning 711.72
  engineering 625.7
  transportation services 388.12
  urban 388.411
Bicycle racing 796.62
  mountain 796.63
  see also Sports
Bicycle touring 796.64
  see also Sports
Bicycle troops (Armed forces) 357.52
Bicycles 388.347 2
  engineering 629.227 2
  law 343.094 4
  repair 629.287 72
  riding 629.284 72
    sports 796.6
  transportation services 388.347 2
Bicycling
  sports 796.6
    see also Sports
Bidding (Games)
  contract bridge 795.415 2
Bié (Angola : Province) T2—673 4
Bielefeld (Germany) T2—435 655
Bielorussian language 491.799
  T6—917 99
Bielorussian literature 891.799
Bielsko (Poland : Voivodeship) T2—438 6
Bielsko-Biała (Poland : Voivodeship) T2—438 6
Biennials (Plants) 582.12
  floriculture 635.931 4
Bienville Parish (La.) T2—763 93
Bifidobacterium 579.373
Biflagellate molds 579.54
Bifurcation theory 515.35
Big bands 784.48
Big bang theory (Cosmogony) 523.18
Big Bend National Park (Tex.) T2—764 932
Big Bend Region (Tex.) T2—764 93
Big Black River (Miss.) T2—762 4
Big brown bats 599.47
Big business 338.644
  economics 338.644
  management 658.023
  personnel management 658.303
Big cats 599.755
Big Cypress Swamp (Fla.) T2—759 44
Big game 599.6
  conservation technology 639.979 6
  resource economics 333.959 6
Big game hunting 799.26
  see also Sports
Big Horn County (Mont.) T2—786 38
Big Horn County (Wyo.) T2—787 33
Big Horn Mountains (Wyo.) T2—787 3
Big Sandy River (Ky. and W. Va.) T2—754 47
  Kentucky T2—769 2
  West Virginia T2—754 47
Big Sioux River (S.D. and Iowa) T2—783 39
  Iowa T2—777 1
  South Dakota T2—783 39
Big Stone County (Minn.) T2—776 432
Bigamy 364.183
  law 345.028 3
Bigfoot 001.944
Bighead carp 597.482

Bighorn sheep 599.649 7
  big game hunting 799.276 497
  conservation technology 639.979 649 7
  resource economics 333.959 649 7
Bignoniaceae 583.95
Bihar (India) T2—541 2
Bihari T5—914 5
Bihari language 491.454
  T6—914 54
Bihari literature 891.454
Bihor (Romania) T2—498 4
Bikeways 388.12
  see also Bicycle paths
Bikini Atoll (Marshall Islands) T2—968 3
Bikkurim 296.123 1
  Mishnah 296.123 1
  Palestinian Talmud 296.124 1
Bilateral trade agreements 382.9
Bilateral treaties 341.1
  texts 341.026 6
Bilbao (Spain) T2—466 3
Bile 573.383 79
  human physiology 612.35
  see also Digestive system
Bile acids
  biochemistry
    humans 612.015 737
  chemistry 547.737
Bile ducts 573.38
  biology 573.38
  human anatomy 611.36
  human physiology 612.35
  medicine 616.365
  surgery 617.556 7
  see also Digestive system
Bilecik İli (Turkey) T2—563
Bilharziasis
  incidence 614.553
  medicine 616.963
  see also Communicable diseases (Human)
Biliary tract 573.38
  biology 573.38
  human anatomy 611.36
  human physiology 612.35
  medicine 616.36
  surgery 617.556
  see also Digestive system
Bilinear forms 512.944
  algebraic geometry 516.35
Bilingual dictionaries T4—32–39
  see Manual at T4—32–T4—39
Bilingual education 370.117 5
  adult level 374.017 5
Bilingual instruction
  elementary education 372.651
Bilingual phrase books T4—834
Bilingual programs
  public administration 353.7
Bilingualism 306.446
  linguistics 404.2
    specific languages T4—042
  sociology 306.446
Bill (Mouth part) 591.4
  descriptive zoology 591.4
  physiology 573.355
Bill collection
  law 346.077
  management 658.88
Billboards 659.134 2
  land use law 346.045
  outdoor advertising 659.134 2
Billfishes 597.78
Billiard players 794.720 92
  sports group T7—794 7
Billiards 794.72
  equipment technology 688.747 2
Billings County (N.D.) T2—784 94
Bills (Legislation) 328.37
  texts 348.01
    United States 348.731
  see Manual at 350 vs. 342–347
Bills of exchange 332.77
  exchange medium 332.55
  law 346.096
Bills of lading
  law 346.025
Biluchi T5—915 98
Biluchi language 491.598
  T6—915 98
Biluchi literature 891.598
Bimetallic monetary standards 332.423
Bimini Islands (Bahamas) T2—729 6
Binary form 781.822 2
  instrumental 784.182 2
Binary numbers 513.52
Binary salts 546.342
  chemical engineering 661.4
Binary stars 523.841
Binary system 513.52
Bingham County (Idaho) T2—796 51
Bingo 795.3
Bingöl İli (Turkey) T2—566 7
Bini (African people) T5—963 3

Bini language 496.33
T6—963 3
Binocular imbalance
ophthalmology 617.762
see also Eyes
Binocular-vision photography 778.4
Binoculars
manufacturing technology 681.412 5
Binomial equations 512.942
algebra 512.942
calculus 515.252
Binuclear family 306.89
Bío Bío (Chile : Province) T2—834 3
Bío Bío (Chile : Region) T2—834 1
Bioactive proteins 572.69
Bioastronautics 571.499
humans 612.014 5
Biobibliographies 012
Biobío (Chile) T2—834 1
Biochemical engineering 660.63
Biochemical evolution 572.38
Biochemical genetics 572.8
humans 611.018 16
see Manual at 572.8; *also at* 576.5 vs. 572.8
Biochemical interactions 572.43
Biochemical qualitative analysis 544.94
Biochemical reactions 572.43
Biochemicals 572
Biochemistry 572
ecology 577.14
humans 612.015
origin of life 576.83
Bioclimatology 577.22
Biodegradation
materials science 620.112 23
Biodiversity 333.95
biology 578.7
conservation 333.951 6
ecology 577
resource economics 333.95
see Manual at 333.7–333.9 vs. 363.1, 363.73, 577
Biodynamics 571.43
humans 612.014 41
Bioelectricity 572.437
electric organs 573.97
humans 612.014 27
Bioelectrochemistry 572.437
Bioenergetics 572.43
ecology 577.13
humans 612.014 21
Bioethics 174.957
religion 291.564 957
Christianity 241.649 57
see also Ethical problems
Biofeedback 152.188
Biogas
technology 665.776
Biogenesis 576.83
Biogeochemical cycles 577.14
Biogeochemical prospecting 622.12
Biogeochemistry 577.14
Biogeography 578.09
animals 591.9
plants 581.9
Biographers 920
occupational group T7—92
Biographical dictionaries T1—092 2
Biography 920
T1—092
literary form 809.935 92
specific literatures T3B—094 92
see Manual at T1—092; *also at* 913–919: Add table: 04: Biography; *also at* 930–990: Biography
Bioinorganic chemistry 572.51
humans 612.015 24
Bioko (Equatorial Guinea) T2—671 86
Biological agents
law 341.735
military engineering 623.459 4
Biological classification 578.012
Biological clocks 571.77
Biological communities 577.82
Biological control of pests
agriculture 632.96
Biological control systems 571.7
human physiology 612.022
see also Endocrine system
Biological determinants
psychology 155.7
evolutional psychology 155.7
individual psychology 155.234
Biological diversity 333.95
see also Biodiversity
Biological instruments
manufacturing technology 681.757
Biological invasions 577.18
Biological oceanography 578.77
Biological parents
law 346.017
social welfare 362.829 8

Biological processes 570
  internal processes 571
  see Manual at 560–590
Biological productivity 577.15
Biological projectiles 623.451 6
Biological resources 333.95
  conservation technology 639.9
  economics 333.95
  law 346.046 95
  public administration 354.349
Biological rhythms 571.77
  human physiology 612.022
Biological sciences 570
  see Manual at 560–590
Biological specimens
  preservation 570.752
Biological transport 571.64
Biological treatment
  sewage 628.35
Biological warfare 358.38
  civil defense 363.35
    see also Civil defense
  ethics 172.42
    see also War—ethics
  weapons engineering 623.451 6
    biological agents 623.459 4
Biological weapons
  disarmament 327.174 5
Biologists 570.92
  occupational group T7—57
Biology 570
  ethical systems 171.7
  specific environments 578.7
    see Manual at 577 vs. 578.7
  see Manual at 560–590; *also at* 570–590
Biology and religion 291.175
  Christianity 261.55
  philosophy of religion 215.7
Bioluminescence 572.435 8
Bioluminescent organs 573.95
Biomagnetism 154.72
Biomass energy 333.953 9
  animals 333.954
  fuel technology 662.88
  plants 333.953 9
  resource economics 333.953 9
Biomechanics 571.43
  humans 612.014 41
  locomotion 573.793 43
    humans 612.76
Biomedical engineering 610.28
Biomedical instrumentation 610.284
Biomes 577
  see Manual at 577.26 vs. 579–590: Autecology
Biometeorology 577.22
Biometrics 570.151 95
Biomineralization 572.51
  animals 573.764 51
Bionics 003.5
Bioparks 578.073
Biophysics 571.4
  humans 612.014
Biopsy
  medicine 616.075 8
Biorhythms 571.77
  human physiology 612.022
Biosociology 304.5
  biological ecology 577.8
  sociology 304.5
  see Manual at 302–307 vs. 156
Biosphere
  resource economics 333.95
Biostatistics 570.151 95
Biosynthesis 572.45
  humans 612.015 4
  see also Metabolism
Biotechnologists 660.609 2
  occupational group T7—66
Biotechnologists (Ergonomists) 620.820 92
  occupational group T7—620 8
Biotechnology 660.6
  food technology 664.024
  law 343.078 660 6
Biotechnology (Ergonomics) 620.82
Biotic communities 577.82
Bipolar disorders
  medicine 616.895
  see also Mental illness
Bipolar memory 004.53
  engineering 621.397 32
Bipolar transistors 621.381 528
Bira (African people) T5—963 94
Bira-Huku languages 496.394
  T6—963 94
Birational transformations
  algebraic geometry 516.35
Birches 583.48
  forestry 634.972 6
Bird attracting 639.978
Bird dogs 636.752
Bird hunting 799.24
Bird lice 595.757
Bird watching 598.072 34
Birdbanding 598.072 32

Birdhouses 636.508 31
  animal husbandry 636.508 31
  architecture 728.927
  construction 690.892 7
Birds 598
  agricultural pests 632.68
  air transportation hazard 363.124 12
  animal husbandry 636.5
  art representation 704.943 28
  commercial hunting 639.12
  conservation technology 639.978
  control technology 628.968
    agriculture 632.68
  disease carriers 571.986
    medicine 614.434
  drawing 743.68
  experimental animals
    medicine 619.5
  paleozoology 568
  resource economics 333.958
  sports hunting 799.24
    see also Sports
  zoology 598
Bird's-eye fabrics 677.615
Bird's-nest fungi 579.599
Birds' nests 598.156 4
Birds of paradise 598.865
Birds of prey 598.9
  conservation technology 639.978 9
  resource economics 333.958 9
Biremes 387.21
  design 623.812 1
  engineering 623.821
  handling 623.882 1
  transportation services 387.21
  see also Ships
Birmingham (Ala.) T2—761 781
Birmingham (England) T2—424 96
Birth
  customs 392.12
    etiquette 395.24
  folklore 398.27
    history and criticism 398.354
  literature 808.803 54
    history and criticism 809.933 54
    specific literatures T3B—080 354
      history and criticism T3B—093 54
  music 781.582
  see also Childbirth
Birth certificates
  public administration 353.59
Birth control 363.96
  demographic effect 304.666
  ethics 176
    religion 291.566
      Buddhism 294.356 6
      Christianity 241.66
      Hinduism 294.548 66
      Islam 297.566
      Judaism 296.366
  health 613.94
  law 344.048
  public administration 353.59
  school programs 371.714
  social services 363.96
  social theology 291.178 366 66
    Christianity 261.836 666
    Judaism 296.38
Birth intervals
  demography 304.63
Birth of Jesus Christ 232.92
Birth order 306.87
  environmental psychology 155.924
  family relationships 306.87
Birthday books
  astrology 133.540 42
Birthday parties
  cooking 641.568
Birthdays
  customs 394.2
  fortune-telling 133.335 4
Birthmarks
  capillary hemangiomas
    medicine 616.993 15
  medicine 616.55
  see also Skin
Births
  demography 304.63
Birthwort 583.26
Bisa-Lamba languages 496.391
  T6—963 91
Bisayan Islands (Philippines) T2—599 5
Biscay (Spain) T2—466 3
Biscay, Bay of (France and Spain) 551.461 38
  T2—163 38
Biscayne Bay (Fla.) 551.461 48
  T2—163 48
Biscayne National Park (Fla.) T2—163 48
Biscuit mixes 664.753
Biscuits (Breads) 641.815
  commercial processing 664.752
  cooking 641.815

Biscuits (Cookies) 641.865 4
commercial processing 664.752 5
home preparation 641.865 4
Bisexuality 306.765
ethics 176
see also Sexual relations—ethics
psychology 155.334
Bisexuals 305.906 63
T1—086 63
Bishops 270.092
biography 270.092
specific denominations 280
see Manual at 230–280
ecclesiology 262.12
Bishops (Chessmen) 794.145
Bishops' thrones 247.1
architecture 726.529 3
Biskra (Algeria : Province) T2—655
Bislama language 427.995 95
T6—217
Bismarck (N.D.) T2—784 77
Bismarck, Otto, Fürst von
German history 943.081
Bismarck Archipelago (Papua New Guinea) 995.8
T2—958
Bismarck Range (Papua New Guinea) T2—956
Bismarck Sea 551.465 76
T2—164 76
Bismuth 669.75
chemical engineering 661.071 8
chemistry 546.718
economic geology 553.47
materials science 620.189 5
metallography 669.957 5
metallurgy 669.75
mining 622.347
physical metallurgy 669.967 5
see also Chemicals; Metals
Bison 599.643
animal husbandry 636.292
commercial hunting 639.116 43
conservation technology 639.979 643
resource economics 333.959 643
subsistence hunting 639.116 43
zoology 599.643
Bissau (Guinea-Bissau) T2—665 7
Bistriţa-Năsăud (Romania) T2—498 4
Bithynia T2—392 5
Biting lice 595.757
Bitlis İli (Turkey) T2—566 7
Bitterns 598.34
Bitterroot Range (Idaho and Mont.) T2—786 8
Idaho T2—796 6
Montana T2—786 8
Bittersweet (Celastraceae) 583.85
Bittersweet (Solanaceae) 583.952
Bitumens 553.27
see also Asphalt
Bituminous coal 553.24
properties 662.622 4
prospecting 622.182 4
see also Coal
Bituminous materials 553.2
building materials 691.96
economic geology 553.2
materials science 620.196
structural engineering 624.189 6
Bituminous pavements 625.85
Bituminous sands 553.283
processing 665.4
see also Tar sands
Bituminous shale 553.283
see also Oil shale
Bivalvia 594.4
fishing and culture 639.4
paleozoology 564.4
resource economics 333.955 4
Bivouac 355.412
military training 355.544
Biwas 787.85
see also Stringed instruments
Bixaceae 583.625
Biya, Paul
Cameroonian history 967.110 4
Bizard Island (Quebec) T2—714 28
Bizerte (Tunisia) T2—611
Blaby (England : District) T2—425 41
Black Africa T2—67
Black Americans 973.049 607 3
T5—960 73
see also African Americans
Black and tan coonhound 636.753 6
Black-and-white television 621.388 02
Black art (Witchcraft) 133.4
Black authors (Literature) 809.889 6
specific literatures T3B—098 96
Black basses 597.738 8
sports fishing 799.177 388
Black bear 599.785
big game hunting 799.277 85
conservation technology 639.979 785
resource economics 333.959 785
Black Belt (Ala.) T2—761 4
Black Country (England) T2—424 9

Black Death	
European history	940.192
incidence	614.573 2
medicine	616.923 2
see also Communicable diseases (Human)	
Black duck	598.413
Black-eyed peas	641.356 592
botany	583.74
commercial processing	664.805 659 2
cooking	641.656 592
field crop	633.33
food	641.356 592
garden crop	635.659 2
Black-eyed Susans	583.99
Black flies	595.772
Black-footed ferret	599.766 29
conservation technology	639.979 766 29
resource economics	333.959 766 29
Black Forest (Germany)	T2—434 6
Black grouse	598.634
Black Hawk County (Iowa)	T2—777 37
Black Hawk War, 1832	973.56
Black Hills (S.D. and Wyo.)	T2—783 9
Black holes (Astronomy)	523.887 5
Black lead	553.26
see also Graphite	
Black-letter calligraphy	745.619 75
Black lung disease	362.196 244
medicine	616.244
social services	362.196 244
workers' compensation law	344.021 8
see also Respiratory system	
Black magic	133.4
Black mangrove	583.96
Black mass	133.422
Black Methodist churches	287.8
see also Methodist Church	
Black mosses	588.2
Black Muslim religion	297.87
Black Muslims	
biography	297.870 92
religious group	T7—297 7
Black pepper	641.338 4
botany	583.25
see also Hot spices	
Black powder	662.26
Black rat	599.352
see also Rats (Rattus)	
Black River (S.C.)	T2—757 8
Black Rock Desert (Nev.)	T2—793 54
Black Sea	551.462 9
	T2—163 89
Black shale	553.283
processing	665.4
see also Oil shale	
Black theology	291.208 996
Christianity	230.089 96
Black vulture (New World)	598.92
Black vulture (Old World)	598.94
Blackall (Qld.)	T2—943 5
Blackberries	641.347 13
botany	583.73
commercial processing	664.804 713
cooking	641.647 13
food	641.347 13
horticulture	634.713
Blackberry lily	635.934 38
botany	584.38
floriculture	635.934 38
Blackbirds (American)	598.874
Blackburn (England)	T2—427 623
Blackdown Hills (England)	T2—423 87
Blackford County (Ind.)	T2—772 68
Blackheads	
medicine	616.53
see also Skin	
Blackjack (Game)	795.423
Blacklands (Tex.)	T2—764 26
Blacklisting (Labor)	331.894
law	344.018 94
Blackmail	364.165
law	345.026 5
Blackouts	
electrical engineering	621.319
military engineering	623.77
Blackpool (Lancashire, England)	T2—427 65
Blacks (United States)	973.049 607 3
	T5—960 73
see also African Americans	
Blacksmithing	682
Blacksmiths	682.092
occupational group	T7—682
Blacktip shark	597.34
Blackwater River (Cavan-Meath, Ireland)	T2—419 5
Blackwood River (W.A.)	T2—941 2
Bladder (Urinary)	573.49
biology	573.49
human anatomy	611.62
human physiology	612.467
medicine	616.62
surgery	617.462
see also Urinary system	
Bladdernuts	583.78

Bladderworts 583.95
Bladen County (N.C.) T2—756 32
Blaenau Gwent (Wales) T2—429 95
Blagoevgrad (Bulgaria : Okrŭg) T2—499 8
Blagoevgradski okrŭg (Bulgaria) T2—499 8
Blaine County (Idaho) T2—796 32
Blaine County (Mont.) T2—786 15
Blaine County (Neb.) T2—782 772
Blaine County (Okla.) T2—766 31
Blair County (Pa.) T2—748 75
Blanco County (Tex.) T2—764 64
Bland County (Va.) T2—755 765
Blanket orders
  library acquisitions 025.233
Blankets 643.53
  arts 746.97
  home sewing 646.21
  household equipment 643.53
  manufacturing technology 677.626
Blantyre (Malawi) T2—689 7
Blasphemy 291.569 5
  criminology 364.188
  ethics 179.5
    see also Ethical problems
  law 345.028 8
Blast-furnace gas 665.772
Blast-furnace practice 669.141 3
Blast injuries
  medicine 617.19
Blast-resistant construction 624.176
  buildings 693.854
Blasting 624.152
  excavation 624.152
  mining 622.23
  underwater engineering 627.74
Blastozoa 563.92
Blastulas 571.865
Blattaria 595.728
Blazers 391
  commercial technology 687.113
  customs 391
  home sewing 646.433
  see also Clothing
Blazonry 929.6
Bleaching
  clothes and related materials 667.14
    home economics 648.1
  oils and gases 665.028 3
Bleckley County (Ga.) T2—758 525
Bledsoe County (Tenn.) T2—768 76
Bleeding
  therapeutics 615.899
Bleeding hearts (Plants) 635.933 35
  botany 583.35
  floriculture 635.933 35
Blekinge län (Sweden) T2—486
Blended waxes 665.19
Blenders
  use in cooking 641.589
Blending oils and gases 665.028 3
Blending petroleum distillates 665.534
Blennies 597.77
Blenoidei 597.77
Blepharitis
  medicine 617.771
  see also Eyes
Blessings 291.38
  Christianity 264.13
  Judaism 296.45
Blida (Algeria : Province) T2—653
Blighted areas
  area planning 711.5
Blimps (Airships) 387.732 7
  engineering 629.133 27
  military engineering 623.743 7
  transportation services 387.732 7
  see also Aircraft
Blind-deaf persons 305.908 161
  T1—087 1
  T7—081 61
  see also Blind persons
Blind persons 305.908 161
  T1—087 1
  T7—081 61
  education 371.911
  library services 027.663
  social group 305.908 161
  social welfare 362.41
Blind play (Chess) 794.17
Blind workers 331.591
Blindman's buff 793.4
Blindness
  incidence 614.599 7
  ophthalmology 617.712
  social welfare 362.41
  see also Eyes
Blinds 645.3
  architecture 721.82
  construction 690.182
  household management 645.3
  manufacturing technology 684
Bliss's Bibliographic Classification 025.434
Blister beetles 595.769
Blitz tactics 355.422

Blizzards 551.555
  social services 363.349 25
Block books 092
Block diagramming
  program design 005.120 28
Block Island (R.I.) T2—745 8
Block printing 761
  textile arts 746.62
Blockades 355.44
  Civil War (United States) 973.75
  international law 341.584
    law of war 341.63
  military operations 355.44
  World War I 940.452
  World War II 940.545 2
  see also Naval operations
Blockbusters (Ammunition) 355.825 17
  engineering 623.451 7
  military equipment 355.825 17
Blocking
  American football 796.332 26
Blocks (Musical instruments) 786.82
  see also Bars (Musical instruments)
Bloemfontein (South Africa : District) T2—685 4
Bloemhof (South Africa : District) T2—682 4
Blood 573.15
  biology 573.15
  human cancer
    medicine 616.994 18
    see also Cancer (Human)
  human histology 611.018 5
  human physiology 612.11
  puerperal diseases
    obstetrics 618.77
  see also Cardiovascular system
Blood analysis
  criminal investigation 363.256 2
  diagnosis
    general disease 616.075 61
Blood banks 362.178 4
  law 344.041 94
  see also Health services
Blood-brain barrier 573.862 1
Blood cells 573.153 6
  human histology 611.018 5
  see also Cardiovascular system
Blood chemistry
  human physiology 612.12
  see also Cardiovascular system
Blood coagulation 573.159
  human physiology 612.115
  medicine 616.157
  see also Cardiovascular system
Blood diseases
  medicine 616.15
  see also Cardiovascular system
Blood-forming system 573.155
  biology 573.155
  geriatrics 618.976 41
  human anatomy 611.41
  human cancer 362.196 994 41
    incidence 614.599 944 1
    medicine 616.994 41
    social services 362.196 994 41
    see also Cancer (Human)
  human diseases 362.196 41
    incidence 614.594 1
    medicine 616.41
    social services 362.196 41
  human physiology 612.41
  pediatrics 618.924 1
  pharmacodynamics 615.718
Blood groups
  human physiology 612.118 25
  see also Cardiovascular system
Blood plasma 573.156
  see also Plasma (Blood)
Blood plasma banks 362.178 4
  see also Health services
Blood platelets 573.159
  human histology 611.018 5
  see also Cardiovascular system
Blood pressure
  human physiology 612.14
  see also Cardiovascular system
Blood River (South Africa) T2—684 1
Blood River, Battle of, 1838 968.404 2
Blood transfusion 362.178 4
  law 344.041 94
  pharmacology 615.39
  social services 362.178 4

Blood types
  human physiology 612.118 25
  see also Cardiovascular system
Blood vessels 573.18
  biology 573.18
  human anatomy 611.13
  human physiology 612.13
  medicine 616.13
  surgery 617.413
  see also Cardiovascular system
Bloodhound 636.753 6
Bloodletting
  therapeutics 615.899
Bloodroot 583.35
Bloodworts 584.354
Blotting paper 676.284 4
Blount County (Ala.) T2—761 72
Blount County (Tenn.) T2—768 885
Blouses 391.2
  commercial technology 687.115
  customs 391.2
  home sewing 646.435
  see also Clothing
Blow flies 595.774
Blowers 621.61
Blowing glass 666.122
  decorative arts 748.202 82
Blown glassware
  decorative arts 748.2
Blowpipes (Chemical apparatus) 542.4
Blowpipes (Weapons)
  sports 799.202 82
Blue and white transfer ware 738.27
Blue catfish 597.492
Blue collar workers 331.79
  T1—086 23
  labor economics 331.79
    labor force 331.119 042
    labor market 331.129 042
  labor unions 331.880 42
  personnel management 658.304 4
    training 658.312 45
  public administration 354.93
  social class 305.562
  see also Laboring classes
Blue Cross and Blue Shield Association 368.382 006 573
  see also Insurance
Blue Earth County (Minn.) T2—776 21
Blue goose 598.417 5
Blue-green algae 579.39
Blue monkeys 599.862
Blue Mountains (N.S.W.) T2—944 5
Blue Mountains (Or. and Wash.) T2—795 7
  Oregon T2—795 7
  Washington T2—797 46
Blue Mountains National Park (N.S.W.) T2—944 5
Blue Nile (Sudan) T2—626 4
Blue Nile River (Ethiopia and Sudan) T2—626 4
Blue Ridge Mountains T2—755
  Georgia T2—758 2
  North Carolina T2—756 8
  South Carolina T2—757 2
  Virginia T2—755
Blue shark 597.34
Blue whale 599.524 8
Blue-winged teal 598.413
Bluebells (Boraginaceae) 635.933 94
  botany 583.94
  floriculture 635.933 94
Bluebells (Campanulaceae) 635.933 98
  botany 583.98
  floriculture 635.933 98
Bluebells (Liliaceae) 635.934 32
  botany 584.32
  floriculture 635.934 32
Blueberries 641.347 37
  botany 583.66
  commercial processing 664.804 737
  cooking 641.647 37
  food 641.347 37
  horticulture 634.737
Bluebirds 598.842
Bluebonnet 583.74
  floriculture 635.933 74
Bluegrass music 781.642
Bluegrass region (Ky.) T2—769 3
Bluegrasses 633.21
  botany 584.9
  forage crop 633.21
Blueprints 604.25
  building construction 692.1
  printing technology 686.42
  technical drawing 604.25
Blues 781.643
  songs 782.421 643
Bluestone 553.53
  economic geology 553.53
  quarrying 622.353
Blyth Valley (England) T2—428 84
Bo tree
  Buddhism 294.343 5
Boaco (Nicaragua : Dept.) T2—728 526

Boadicea, Queen
  English history 936.204
Boar fishes 597.64
Board games 794
  equipment technology 688.74
Board of Governors of the Federal Reserve System (U.S.) 332.110 973
Board of trade buildings
  architecture 725.25
Board zithers 787.74
  see also Stringed instruments
Boarding schools 373.222
Boardinghouses 647.94
  sanitation services 363.729 8
    see also Waste control
Boards of directors
  executive management 658.422
  public administration 352.25
Boards of education 353.822 5
  local public schools 379.153 1
  public administration 353.822 5
Boardsailing 797.33
  see also Sports
Boat lily 584.86
Boat racing 797.14
  see also Sports
Boatbuilding 623.82
Boathouses
  architecture 725.87
Boating 623.88
  seamanship 623.88
  sports 797.1
    see also Sports
Boating safety 363.123
  sports 363.14
    law 344.047 6
  see also Water transportation—safety
Boatmen
  sports 797.109 2
  sports group T7—797 1
  technologists 623.880 92
    occupational group T7—623 8
Boats 387.2
  see also Ships
Bobangi language 496.396 8
  T6—963 968
Bobbin laces 677.653
  arts 746.222
  manufacturing technology 677.653
Bobcat 599.753 6
Bobo (African people) T5—963 5
Bobo-Dioulasso (Burkina Faso) T2—662 5
Bobo language 496.35
  T6—963 5
Bobsledding 796.95
  see also Sports
Bobwhites 598.627 3
  conservation technology 639.978 627 3
  resource economics 333.958 627 3
  sports hunting 799.246 273
Bocas del Toro (Panama : Province) T2—728 712
Bochum (Germany) T2—435 632
Bochum (South Africa : District) T2—682 93
Boden See T2—434 62
  Germany T2—434 62
  Switzerland T2—494 59
Bodish languages 495.4
  T6—954
Bodo languages 495.4
  T6—954
Bodoni type 686.224 7
Body (Human)
  philosophy 128.6
  religion 291.22
    Christianity 233.5
    see also Humans—religion
Body and mind
  philosophy 128.2
  psychology 150
Body and soul 128.1
  religion 291.22
    Christianity 233.5
    Judaism 296.32
    philosophy of religion 218
    see also Humans—religion
Body contours 646.75
  customs 391.62
  grooming 646.75
Body fluid disorders
  medicine 616.399 2
    see Manual at 612.01522 vs. 612.3923, 616.3992
  see also Digestive system
Body language 302.222
  psychology 153.69
  social psychology 302.222
Body measurements
  humans 599.94
Body mechanics
  human physiology 612.76
Body size 591.41

Body temperature	571.76	Bok choy	641.353
humans	612.014 26	cooking	641.653
Body weight	591.41	food	641.353
Bodybuilding	646.75	garden crop	635.3
Bodyguards	363.289	Bokhara rugs	
Bodywork	629.260 288	arts	746.758 7
Boeotia (Greece)	T2—495 15	*see also* Rugs	
ancient	T2—384	Bokmål language	439.82
Boer War, 1880–1881	968.204 6		T6—398 2
Boer War, 1899–1902	968.048	Bokmål literature	839.82
Bog mosses	588.29	Boksburg (South Africa : District)	T2—682 2
Bog myrtle (Buckbean)	583.93	Boland (South Africa)	T2—687 3
Bog myrtle (Sweet gale)	583.43	Bolas	
Bog of Allen (Ireland)	T2—418 5	sports	799.202 82
Bogotá (Colombia)	T2—861 48	Boletaceae	579.6
Bogs		Boletes	579.6
biology	578.768 7	Bolívar (Colombia : Dept.)	T2—861 14
ecology	577.687	Bolívar (Ecuador : Province)	T2—866 16
see also Wetlands		Bolívar (Venezuela : State)	T2—876 3
Bogus wrapping paper	676.287	Bolívar, Simón	
Bohemia (Czech Republic)	T2—437 1	South American history	980.02
Bohemia (Kingdom)	943.702	Bolivar County (Miss.)	T2—762 43
	T2—437	Bolivia	984
Bohemia and Moravia (Protectorate)	943.703 3		T2—84
	T2—437	Bolivia (Game)	795.418
Böhm-Bawerk, Eugen von		Bolivian literature	860
economic school	330.157	Bolivians	T5—688 4
Bohol (Philippines)	T2—599 5	Boll weevil	
Boiler and machinery insurance	368.7	agricultural pest	633.519 768
see also Insurance		Bollinger County (Mo.)	T2—778 94
Boiler-house practice	621.194	Bollworm	
Boiler insurance	368.7	agricultural pest	633.519 78
see also Insurance		Bolobedu (South Africa : District)	T2—682 93
Boiler operations	621.194	Bologna (Italy : Province)	T2—454 1
Boilers		Bolsena (Italy)	T2—456 25
heating buildings	697.07	ancient	T2—376
steam	697.507	Bolshevik International	324.175
ship power plants	623.873	Bolshevik parties	324.217 5
steam engineering	621.183	Bolsover (England : District)	T2—425 15
Boiling		Bolton (Greater Manchester, England)	T2—427 37
home cooking	641.73	Bolts	621.882
Boiling points	536.44	Bolts (Locks)	683.31
Boils		Boltzmann statistics	530.132
medicine	616.523	Bolu İli (Turkey)	T2—563
see also Skin		Bolyai geometry	516.9
Boina (Kingdom)	969.101	Bolzano (Italy : Province)	T2—453 83
	T2—691	Bomb disposal units	
Bois-Francs Region (Quebec)	T2—714 565	armed forces	358.23
Boise (Idaho)	T2—796 28	Bombacaceae	583.68
Boise County (Idaho)	T2—796 74		
Bojutsu	796.86		
see also Sports			

Bombala (N.S.W.) T2—944 7
Bombardment
  military science 355.4
  particle physics 539.73
  solid-state physics 530.416
Bombay (India) T2—547 923
Bombers 358.428 3
  engineering 623.746 3
  military equipment 358.428 3
Bombing forces 358.42
Bombs 623.451
Bombsights 623.46
Bombycillidae 598.852
Bombycoidea 595.78
Bombyliidae 595.773
Bon (Tibetan religion) 299.54
Bon Homme County (S.D.) T2—783 395
Bonaire T2—729 86
Bonaparte River (B.C.) T2—711 72
Bonasa 598.635
Bonaventure (Quebec : County) T2—714 78
Bonaventure (Quebec : Regional County Municipality) T2—714 78
Bond (Employee)
  insurance 368.83
  law 346.086 83
Bond (Law) 345.056
Bond County (Ill.) T2—773 873
Bond paper 676.282 3
Bonded fabrics 677.69
  see also Textiles
Bonding metals 671.58
Bonds (Chemical forces) 541.224
  biochemistry 572.33
Bonds (Securities) 332.632 3
  accounting 657.75
  financial management 658.152 24
    capital procurement 658.152 24
    debt management 658.152 6
  investment economics 332.632 3
  law 346.092 2
    corporate law 346.066 6
    income tax law 343.052 46
  see Manual at 332.632044 vs. 332.6323: Gilt-edged securities; *also at* 332.6322 vs. 332.6323
Bône (Algeria : Dept.) T2—655
Bone carving 736.6
Bone char 662.93
Bone marrow 573.155 6
  biology 573.155 6
  human cancer
    incidence 614.599 947 1
    medicine 616.994
    see also Cancer (Human)
  human diseases
    incidence 614.594 1
    medicine 616.41
  human histology 611.018 4
  human physiology 612.491
  surgery 617.44
  see also Blood-forming system
Bone meal
  use as fertilizer 631.85
Bone tissues
  human histology 611.018 4
  see also Musculoskeletal system
Bones 573.76
  anthropometry 599.947
  biology 573.76
  drawing
    animals 743.6
    humans 743.46
  fractures
    medicine 617.15
  human anatomy 611.71
  human physiology 612.75
  medicine 616.71
  pharmacodynamics 615.771
  surgery 617.471
  see also Musculoskeletal system
Bongo (Mammal) 599.642 3
Bongo, Omar
  Gabonese history 967.210 42
Bongo-Bagirmi languages 496.5
  T6—965
Bongos 786.95
  see also Percussion instruments
Bonin Islands (Japan) T2—528
Bonito 641.392
  cooking 641.692
  food 641.392
  zoology 597.783
Bonn (Germany) T2—435 518
Bonner County (Idaho) T2—796 96
Bonneville County (Idaho) T2—796 53
Bono (Kingdom) 966.701 6
  T2—667
Bonsai 635.977 2

Bonuses	331.216 4
labor economics	331.216 4
personnel management	658.322 5
Bony fishes	597
see also Fishes	
Bony ganoids	597.41
Boobies	598.43
resource economics	333.958 43
Booby traps	623.451 4
Book arts	
technology	686
Book catalogs	025.313
bibliography	017
library science	025.313
Book clubs	070.5
Book illumination	745.67
Book illustration	741.64
Book jacket illustration	741.64
Book lice	595.732
Book numbers (Shelflisting)	025.428
Book of Common Prayer	264.03
Book of Mormon	289.322
Book paper	676.282 4
Book reports	371.302 81
Book restoration	
library science	025.7
Book reviews	028.1
Book scorpions	595.47
Book selection	
library science	025.21
Bookbinders	686.300 92
occupational group	T7—686 3
Bookbinding	686.3
library operations	025.7
notable books	095
Bookcases	
manufacturing technology	684.16
Booking services	
transportation	388.042
see also Passenger services	
Bookkeepers	657.209 2
occupational group	T7—651
Bookkeeping	657.2
Bookmobiles	
plant management	022
public library use	027.4
Bookplates	769.52
bibliography	010.42
Books	002
bibliographies	011
cataloging	025.32
influence on crime	364.254
Books (continued)	
literature	808.803 57
history and criticism	809.933 57
specific literatures	T3B—080 357
history and criticism	T3B—093 57
postal handling	383.124
see also Postal service	
publishing	070.5
sociology	302.232
technology	686
Books and reading	028
Books of Hours	242
Booksellers' catalogs	
alphabetic subject	017.8
classed	017.4
Bookselling	381.450 02
Boolean algebra	511.324
Boomerangs	
sports hunting	799.202 82
sports throwing	796.435
Boone County (Ark.)	T2—767 18
Boone County (Ill.)	T2—773 29
Boone County (Ind.)	T2—772 54
Boone County (Iowa)	T2—777 544
Boone County (Ky.)	T2—769 363
Boone County (Mo.)	T2—778 29
Boone County (Neb.)	T2—782 51
Boone County (W. Va.)	T2—754 39
Booster rockets	629.475
see Manual at 629.046 vs. 621.43	
Boosters (Detonators)	662.4
Boothferry (England : Borough)	T2—428 35
Boothia Peninsula (N.W.T.)	T2—719 7
Bootlace worms	592.32
Bootlegging	364.133
law	345.023 3
Boots	391.413
customs	391.413
manufacturing technology	685.31
see also Clothing	
Bop	781.655
Bophuthatswana (South Africa)	T2—682 94
Boquerón (Paraguay : Dept.)	T2—892 24
Borage	583.94
Boraginaceae	583.94
Borates	553.633
economic geology	553.633
mineralogy	549.735
mining	622.363 3

Borax 553.633
  economic geology 553.633
  mineralogy 549.735
  mining 622.363 3
Bordeaux (France) T2—447 14
Borden, Robert Laird, Sir
  Canadian history 971.061 2
Borden County (Tex.) T2—764 853
Border Country (Scotland) T2—413 7
Border defense 355.45
Border patrols 363.285
Borderline personality disorder
  medicine 616.858 52
  see also Mental illness
Borders (Floriculture) 635.963
Borders Region (Scotland) T2—413 7
Bordj Bou Arréridj
    (Algeria : Province) T2—655
Boreal forests
  biology 578.737
  ecology 577.37
  see also Forest lands
Borers (Insects)
  agricultural pests 634.049 7
Boring
  mining 622.24
Boring tools 621.952
Boris Fyodorovich Godunov,
    Czar of Russia
  Russian history 947.044
Bornean languages 499.22
  T6—992 2
Borneo T2—598 3
  Indonesia T2—598 3
  Malaysia T2—595 3
Borneo languages 499.22
  T6—992 2
Bornholm (Denmark) T2—489 2
Bornholms amt (Denmark) T2—489 2
Borno State (Nigeria) T2—669 85
Bornu (Kingdom) 966.980 1
  T2—669 8
Boron 553.6
  chemical engineering 661.067 1
  chemistry 546.671
  economic geology 553.6
  organic chemistry 547.056 71
    applied 661.895
  see also Chemicals
Boron fuels 662.86
Borrowing 332.041 54
  capital management 658.152 24
  public finance 336.34
    administration 352.45
    see also Public debt
Borsod-Abaúj-Zemplén
    Megye (Hungary) T2—439 9
Borstals 365.42
  see also Correctional
      institutions
Borzoi 636.753 5
Bos 599.642 2
Boshof (South Africa :
    District) T2—685 8
Bosnia and Hercegovina T2—497 42
Bosnian Muslims T5—918 2
Bosons 539.721
Bosporus (Turkey) 551.462 9
  T2—163 89
Bosque County (Tex.) T2—764 518
Bossier Parish (La.) T2—763 97
Boston (England : District) T2—425 37
Boston (Mass.) T2—744 61
Boston ivy 635.933 86
  botany 583.86
  floriculture 635.933 86
Boston Massacre, 1770 973.311 3
Boston Port Bill, 1774 973.311 6
Boston Tea Party, 1773 973.311 5
Boston terrier 636.72
Bostrychoidea 595.763
Bot flies 595.774
Botanic medicine
  therapeutic system 615.53
Botanical drugs
  pharmacology 615.32
Botanical gardens 580.73
  architecture 727.658
  landscape architecture 712.5
Botanical specimens
  preservation 580.752
Botanists 580.92
  occupational group T7—58
Botany 580
Botetourt County (Va.) T2—755 83
Botha, Louis
  South African history 968.052
Botha, P. W. (Pieter Willem)
  South African history 968.063
Bothaville (South Africa :
    District) T2—685 2
Bothnia, Gulf of 551.461 34
  T2—163 34
Botoşani (Romania : Judeţ) T2—498 1

Botshabelo (South Africa : District)	T2—685 6
Botswana	968.83
	T2—688 3
Botswana people	T5—968 83
Bottineau County (N.D.)	T2—784 61
Bottle cutting	
decorative arts	748.202 86
Bottle-nose dolphins	599.533
Bottled water	
commercial processing	663.61
Bottles	688.8
glass	666.192
decorative arts	748.82
technology	666.192
Bottling alcoholic beverages	663.19
Bottom fishing	799.122
Bottoms (Petroleum)	665.538 8
Botulism	
incidence	614.512 5
medicine	616.931 5
see also Communicable diseases (Human)	
Bouaké (Ivory Coast)	T2—666 8
Bouches-du-Rhône (France)	T2—449 1
Boudicca, Queen	
English history	936.204
Bougainville Island (Papua New Guinea)	T2—959 2
Bougainvilleas	635.933 53
botany	583.53
floriculture	635.933 53
Bougie (Algeria : Province)	T2—655
Bouira (Algeria : Province)	T2—653
Boujdour (Morocco : Province)	T2—648
Boulaida (Algeria : Province)	T2—653
Boulder County (Colo.)	T2—788 63
Boulemane (Morocco : Province)	T2—643
Boumerdes (Algeria : Province)	T2—653
Boundaries	320.12
international law	341.42
local government	320.8
political science	320.12
Boundary County (Idaho)	T2—796 98
Boundary layers	532.051
aeronautics	629.132 37
engineering	620.106 4
physics	532.051
space flight	629.415 1
Boundary surveying	526.9
Boundary-value problems	515.35
calculus of finite differences	515.62
differential equations	515.35
Bounty Islands (N.Z.)	T2—939 9
Bounty Mutiny, 1789	996.18
Bourbon	641.252
commercial processing	663.52
Bourbon, House of	944.03
French history	944.03
genealogy	929.74
Spanish history	946.054
Bourbon County (Kan.)	T2—781 97
Bourbon County (Ky.)	T2—769 423
Bourbon Restoration, 1814–1833	946.072
Bourbon Restoration, 1871–1873	946.073
Bourbonnais (France)	T2—445 7
Bourgeoisie	305.55
	T1—086 22
Bourgogne (France)	T2—444
Bourguiba, Habib	
Tunisian history	961.105 1
Bourke (N.S.W.)	T2—944 9
Bournemouth (England)	T2—423 38
Boutonneuse fever	
incidence	614.526 3
medicine	616.922 3
see also Communicable diseases (Human)	
Boutonnieres	745.923
Bouvet Island	T2—971 3
Bouvier des Flandres	636.737
Bovidae	599.64
paleozoology	569.64
Bovinae	599.642
Bovines	599.64
animal husbandry	636.2
Bow harps	787.94
see also Stringed instruments	
Bow River (Alta.)	T2—712 33
Bowed stringed instruments	787
see also Stringed instruments	
Bowell, Mackenzie, Sir	
Canadian history	971.055
Bowen (Qld.)	T2—943 6
Bowen Island (B.C. : Island)	T2—711 33
Bowfins	597.41
Bowhead whale	599.527 6
Bowie County (Tex.)	T2—764 197

Bowing techniques	784.193 69
Bowl games (Football)	796.332 63
Bowland, Forest of	T2—427 685
Bowlers	794.609 2
sports group	T7—794 6
Bowling (Cricket)	796.358 22
Bowling (Game)	794.6
equipment technology	688.746
Bowling alleys	794.6
architecture	725.84
Bowman County (N.D.)	T2—784 92
Bowron Lake Provincial Park (B.C.)	T2—711 75
Bows and arrows	799.202 85
art metalwork	739.73
manufacturing technology	688.792 028 5
military equipment	623.441
shooting game	799.215
sports	799.202 85
target shooting	799.32
Box (Plants)	583.69
floriculture	635.933 69
Box Butte County (Neb.)	T2—782 94
Box Elder County (Utah)	T2—792 42
Box-girder bridges	388
construction	624.4
see also Bridges	
Box lily	584.353
Box lunches	642.4
Boxcars	385.34
engineering	625.24
see also Rolling stock	
Boxer (Dog)	636.73
Boxer Rebellion, 1899–1901	951.035
Boxers (Pugilists)	796.830 92
sports group	T7—796 8
Boxes	688.8
paperboard	676.32
Boxfishes	597.64
Boxing	796.83
law	344.099
see also Sports	
Boxwoods	583.69
floriculture	635.933 69
Boy Scout camps	796.542 2
Boy Scouts	369.43
Boyacá (Colombia)	T2—861 37
Boycott	
international politics	327.117
international law	341.582
labor economics	331.893
law	344.018 93
Boycott (continued)	
restraint of trade	338.604 8
law	343.072 3
Boyd County (Ky.)	T2—769 27
Boyd County (Neb.)	T2—782 723
Boyer Ahmadī-ye Sardīr va Kohkīlūyeh (Iran : Province)	T2—556
Boyle County (Ky.)	T2—769 523
Boyne River (Ireland)	T2—418 22
Boys	305.23
	T1—083
criminal offenders	364.36
education	371.823
health	613.042 32
home care	649.132
journalism for	070.483 26
psychology	155.432
publications for	
bibliographies	011.624 1
recreation	790.194
indoor	793.019 4
outdoor	796.083
sex hygiene	613.953
social aspects	305.23
Boys' clubs	369.42
Boys' societies	369.42
Boysenberries	641.347 18
commercial processing	664.804 718
cooking	641.647 18
food	641.347 18
horticulture	634.718
Bozca Island (Turkey)	T2—562
Bozcaada (Turkey)	T2—562
Brabant (Belgium)	T2—493 3
Bracelets	391.7
customs	391.7
making	739.278
see also Jewelry	
Brachiopoda	594.68
paleozoology	564.68
Brachycera	595.773
Brachycera-Cyclorrhapha	595.774
Brachycera-Orthorrhapha	595.773
Brachyura	595.386
Bracing equipment	
aircraft	629.134 37
Bracken (Ferns)	587.3
Bracken County (Ky.)	T2—769 325
Bracket fungi	579.597
Brackish water	553.72
	T2—169
economic geology	553.72
hydrology	551.48

Bracknell Forest (England : Borough) T2—422 98
Bradford (England : City) T2—428 17
Bradford County (Fla.) T2—759 15
Bradford County (Pa.) T2—748 57
Bradley County (Ark.) T2—767 63
Bradley County (Tenn.) T2—768 873
Bradyodonti 567.3
Bradypodidae 599.313
Braga (Portugal : District) T2—469 12
Bragança (Portugal : District) T2—469 2
Braganza, House of 946.903
Brahma Samaj 294.556 2
Brahmanas 294.592 1
Brahmanism 294.5
Brahmans
  biography 294.509 2
  religious group T7—294 5
Brahmans (Cattle) 636.291
Brahmaputra River T2—549 2
  Bangladesh T2—549 2
  India T2—541 6
Brahui T5—948 3
Brahui language 494.83
  T6—948 3
Brahui literature 894.83
Braided rugs
  arts 746.73
  see also Rugs
Braiding textiles 677.028 2
  arts 746.42
Braids (Hairstyling) 646.724
Braids (Mathematics) 514.224
Braids (Textile trim) 677.76
  arts 746.27
Brăila (Romania : Județ) T2—498 1
Braille 411
  printing 686.282
  specific languages T4—11
Braille publications
  bibliographies 011.63
  cataloging 025.349 2
  library treatment 025.179 2
  publishing 070.579 2
Brain 573.86
  biology 573.86
  human anatomy 611.81
  human diseases
    incidence 614.598
    medicine 616.8
  human physiology 612.82
  surgery 617.481
  see also Nervous system
Brain-damaged persons 305.908 26
  T1—087 4
  education 371.91
  see also Mentally retarded persons
Brain drain 331.127 91
Brain stem
  human anatomy 611.81
  human physiology 612.826
  see also Nervous system
Braintree (England : District) T2—426 715
Brainwashing 153.853
Braising 641.77
Brakes
  automotive engineering 629.246
  railroad engineering 625.25
Brakes (Ferns) 587.3
Brakpan (South Africa : District) T2—682 2
Bran 641.331
  commercial processing 664.720 8
    wheat 664.722 8
  cooking 641.631
  food 641.331
Branch banking 332.16
Branch County (Mich.) T2—774 21
Branch libraries
  architecture 727.84
  public librarianship 027.4
Branch organization accounting 657.99
Branch stores 381.12
  management 658.870 6
  see also Commerce
Branches of government 320.404
  law 342.044
Branching processes 519.234
Branchiopoda 595.32
  paleozoology 565.32
Branchiura 595.36
Brand name products
  sales promotion 658.827
Brand preferences
  marketing management 658.834 3
Brandenburg (Germany) T2—431 5
Brandfort (South Africa : District) T2—685 3
Branding animals 636.081 2
Brandon (Man.) T2—712 73
Brands
  sales promotion 658.827
Brandy 641.253
  commercial processing 663.53
Brant (Ont. : County) T2—713 47

Branta	598.417 8
Brantford (Ont.)	T2—713 47
Brantley County (Ga.)	T2—758 753
Bras d'Or Lake (N.S.)	T2—716 9
Brasília (Brazil)	T2—817 4
Braşov (Romania : Judeţ)	T2—498 4
Brass	669.3
decorative arts	739.52
materials science	620.182
metallography	669.953
metallurgy	669.3
metalworking	673.3
physical metallurgy	669.963
Brass bands	784.9
Brass ensembles	785.9
Brass instruments	788.9
bands and orchestras	784
chamber ensembles	785
mixed	785.2–.5
single type	785.9
construction	788.919 23
by hand	788.919 23
by machine	681.889
solo music	788.9
see Manual at 784–788	
Brassicaceae	583.64
Bratislava (Slovakia)	T2—437 3
Brauer groups	512.2
Braulidae	595.774
Braunschweig (Germany)	T2—435 976
Braunschweig (Germany : Regierungsbezirk)	T2—435 97
Braxton County (W. Va.)	T2—754 66
Brayer painting	751.49
Braziers	
ceramic arts	738.8
heating buildings	697.1
Brazil	981
	T2—81
Brazil nut	641.345 75
agriculture	634.575
botany	583.76
cooking	641.645 75
food	641.345 75
Brazilian literature	869
Brazilian Portuguese dialects	469.798
	T6—69
Brazilian spiderflowers	583.76
Brazilians	T5—698
Brazing	671.56
decorative arts	739.14
sculpture	731.41
Brazoria County (Tex.)	T2—764 137
Brazos County (Tex.)	T2—764 242
Brazos River (Tex.)	T2—764
Brazzaville (Congo)	T2—672 4
Breach of contract	346.022
Bread	641.815
commercial baking	664.752 3
home baking	641.815
Bread-dough handicrafts	745.5
Bread molds (Fungi)	579.53
Breadfruits	641.343 9
botany	583.45
cooking	641.643 9
food	641.343 9
orchard crop	634.39
Break dancing	793.3
Break-even analysis	658.155 4
Breakfast	642
cooking	641.52
customs	394.15
Breakfast foods	
commercial processing	664.756
Breakfast rooms	643.4
Breaking	
materials science	620.112 6
Breaks (Rest periods)	
labor economics	331.257 6
personnel management	658.312 1
Breakwaters	
engineering	627.24
Bream (Abramis)	597.482
sports fishing	799.174 82
Breast	
human anatomy	611.49
medicine	618.19
men	616.49
women	618.19
surgery	618.190 59
women's physiology	612.664
Breast cancer	
incidence	614.599 944 9
medicine	616.994 49
see also Cancer (Human)	
Breast feeding	649.33
child rearing	649.33
health	613.269
human physiology	612.664
see Manual at 649.33 vs. 613.269	
Breast implants	618.190 592
Breathing	573.2
biology	573.2
health	613.192
human physiology	612.2

Breathing (continued)
  musical technique 781.48
    instrumental 784.193 2
  see also Respiratory system
Breathitt County (Ky.) T2—769 19
Brechou (England) T2—423 47
Breckinridge County (Ky.) T2—769 854
Breckland (England : District) T2—426 14
Brecknock (Wales : District) T2—429 56
Breconshire (Wales) T2—429 56
Brecqhou (England) T2—423 47
Bredasdorp (South Africa : District) T2—687 3
Breeder reactors 621.483 4
Breeding
  animal husbandry 636.082
  plant cultivation 631.52
Breeding stock
  plants 631.52
Bremen (Germany) T2—435 2
Bremer County (Iowa) T2—777 34
Bremerhaven (Germany) T2—435 21
Bremsstrahlung 539.722 2
Brent (London, England) T2—421 85
Brentwood (England : District) T2—426 76
Brescia (Italy : Province) T2—452 6
Brėst (Belarus : Voblasts) T2—478 9
Brėstskaı͡a voblastsʹ (Belarus) T2—478 9
Bretagne (France) T2—441
Breton language 491.68
  T6—916 8
Breton literature 891.68
Bretons T5—916 8
Brevard County (Fla.) T2—759 27
Breviaries 264.15
  Roman Catholic 264.020 15
    texts 264.024
Brewed alcoholic beverages 641.23
  commercial processing 663.3
  cooking with 641.62
  home preparation 641.873
Brewed nonalcoholic beverages 641.26
  commercial processing 663.9
  home preparation 641.877
Brewster County (Tex.) T2—764 932
Brexias 583.72
Brezhnev, Leonid Ilʹich
  Russian history 947.085 3
Bri͡anskai͡a oblastʹ (Russia) T2—472 5
Briard (Dog) 636.737
Bribery of officials 364.132 3
  law 345.023 23
  public administration 353.46
Bribery of voters 364.132 4
  law 345.023 24
Brick pavements 625.82
Bricklayers 693.210 92
  occupational group T7—693
Bricks 666.737
  architectural construction 721.044 21
  building construction 693.21
  building materials 691.4
  ceramic arts 738.6
  materials science 620.142
  structural engineering 624.183 6
Bride purchase 392.4
Bridge (Game) 795.415
Bridge circuits 621.374 2
  electronics 621.381 548
Bridge engineers 624.209 2
  occupational group T7—624
Bridge harps 787.98
  see also Stringed instruments
Bridge River (B.C.) T2—711 31
Bridge whist 795.413
Bridges 388
  architecture 725.98
  construction 624.2
  military engineering 623.67
  public administration 354.76
  transportation services 388
    railroads 385.312
    roads 388.132
Bridges (Dentistry) 617.692
  see also Dentistry
Bridgnorth (England : District) T2—424 59
Brie (Cheese) 641.373 53
  cooking 641.673 53
  food 641.373 53
  processing 637.353
Briefcases
  manufacturing technology 685.51
Brigades (Military units) 355.31
Brightness perception
  psychology 152.143
Brighton (England) T2—422 56
Bright's disease
  medicine 616.612
  see also Urinary system

Brill's disease
  incidence 614.526 2
  medicine 616.922 2
  see also Communicable diseases (Human)
Brindisi (Italy : Province) T2—457 54
Brine 553.72
Brine shrimps 595.32
Brining foods 664.028 6
  commercial preservation 664.028 6
  home preservation 641.46
Briquettes 662.6
Brisbane (Qld.) T2—943 1
Brisbane River (Qld.) T2—943 2
Brisbane Waters National Park (N.S.W.) T2—944 2
Briscoe County (Tex.) T2—764 839
Bristles
  animal husbandry 636.088 45
  manufacturing technology 679.6
Bristletails 595.723
Bristling (Fish) 641.392
  cooking 641.692
  food 641.392
  zoology 597.452
Bristol (England) T2—423 93
Bristol (Va.) T2—755 726
Bristol Avon River (England) T2—423 9
Bristol Bay (Alaska) 551.466 34
  T2—164 34
Bristol Bay Borough (Alaska) T2—798 4
Bristol board 676.288
Bristol County (Mass.) T2—744 85
Bristol County (R.I.) T2—745 5
Britain 941
  T2—41
  ancient 936.1
  T2—361
  see Manual at 941
Britain, Battle of, 1940 940.542 11
Britain, Northern 941.1
  T2—411
  ancient 936.11
  T2—361 1
Britain, Southern 942
  T2—42
  ancient 936.2
  T2—362
British Americans T5—13
  see Manual at T5—13 vs. T5—2073, T5—21073
British ancestry T5—2
  see Manual at T5—201–T5—209 vs. T5—2101–T5—2109
British Antarctic Territory T2—989
British Columbia 971.1
  T2—711
British Commonwealth of Nations T2—171 241
British Empire T2—171 241
British Guiana T2—881
British Honduras T2—728 2
British Isles 941
  T2—41
  ancient 936.1
  T2—361
  see Manual at 941
British Kaffraria T2—687 5
British New Guinea 995.402 1
British North America Act, 1867 971.049
British Open (Golf) 796.352 66
British pronunciation 421.55
British Solomon Islands T2—959 3
British Somaliland T2—677 3
British spelling 421.55
British system (Measurement) 530.813
  social aspects 389.15
British Virgin Islands T2—729 725
British western seawaters 551.461 37
  T2—163 37
Britons T5—21
  see Manual at T5—201–T5—209 vs. T5—2101–T5—2109
Brits (South Africa : District) T2—682 3
Britstown (South Africa : District) T2—687 13
Brittany (Dog) 636.752
Brittany (France) T2—441
Brittle stars 593.94
Brittleness
  materials science 620.112 6
Broaching tools 621.954
Broad beans 641.356 51
  cooking 641.656 51
  food 641.356 51
  garden crop 635.651
Broad-gage railroads 385
  see also Railroad transportation
Broad jump 796.432
  see also Sports
Broad River (S.C.) T2—757 4

Broadband computer equipment 004.64
  engineering 621.398 1
Broadband local-area networks 004.68
  see also Computer communications
Broadbills 598.822
Broadcast advertising 659.14
Broadcast media
  journalism 070.19
Broadcast videotex 004.696
  communications services 384.352
  see also Computer communications
Broadcasters 384.540 92
  occupational group T7—384
Broadcasting 384.54
  law 343.099 4
  public administration 354.75
  see Manual at 384.54, 384.55, 384.8 vs. 791.4
Broadcasting channels 384.545 2
  radio 384.545 2
  television 384.552 1
Broadcasting networks 384.540 65
  see also Networks (Communications)
Broadcasting stations 384.545 3
  radio 384.545 3
    see also Radio stations
  television 384.552 2
    see also Television stations
Broadland (England) T2—426 17
Broads, The (England) T2—426 17
Broadsides
  cataloging 025.342
  direct advertising 659.133
  library treatment 025.172
Broadwater County (Mont.) T2—786 664
Brocade 677.616
Brocatelle 677.616
Broccoli 641.353 5
  commercial processing 664.805 35
  cooking 641.653 5
  food 641.353 5
  garden crop 635.35
Broiling 641.76
Broken Hill (N.S.W.) T2—944 9
Broken homes 362.829 4
  social services 362.829 4
  sociology 306.89
  see also Families—social welfare
Brokers (Securities) 332.62
  law 346.092 6
  public administration 354.88
Brokopondo (Surinam : District) T2—883 9
Brome (Quebec : County) T2—714 64
Brome-Missisquoi T2—714 62
Bromegrasses 584.9
Bromeliads 584.85
  floriculture 635.934 85
Bromeliales 584.85
Bromes (Grasses) 584.9
Bromine
  chemical engineering 661.073 3
  chemistry 546.733
  economic geology 553.6
  organic chemistry 547.02
    applied 661.891
  see also Chemicals
Bromley (London, England) T2—421 78
Bromoil process 773.8
Bromsgrove (England : District) T2—424 42
Bronchi
  human anatomy 611.23
  human physiology 612.2
  medicine 616.23
  surgery 617.544
  see also Respiratory system
Bronchial asthma
  medicine 616.238
  see also Respiratory system
Bronchiectasis
  medicine 616.23
  see also Respiratory system
Bronchitis
  medicine 616.234
  see also Respiratory system
Bronchopneumonia
  medicine 616.241
  see also Respiratory system
Bronkhorstspruit (South Africa : District) T2—682 3
Brontosaurus 567.913 8
Bronx (New York, N.Y.) T2—747 275
Bronze 669.3
  decorative arts 739.512
  materials science 620.182
  metallography 669.953
  metallurgy 669.3
  metalworking 673.3
  physical metallurgy 669.963
Bronze Age 930.15

Bronze sculpture
casting 731.456
Brooches 391.7
customs 391.7
making 739.278
see also Jewelry
Brook trout 597.554
sports fishing 799.175 54
Brooke County (W. Va.) T2—754 13
Brookings County (S.D.) T2—783 272
Brooklyn (New York, N.Y.) T2—747 23
Brooks County (Ga.) T2—758 874
Brooks County (Tex.) T2—764 475
Brooks Range (Alaska) T2—798 7
Broome (W.A.) T2—941 4
Broome County (N.Y.) T2—747 75
Broomrapes 583.95
Brooms 679.6
Brothers 306.875
T1—085 5
T7—045
see also Siblings
Brothers (Christian religious orders) 255.092
biography 271.092 02
church history 271.092
Brothers and sisters 306.875 3
psychological influence 155.924
psychology 155.443
Brothers Hospitallers of St. John of God 255.49
church history 271.49
Brotulas 597.63
Broward County (Fla.) T2—759 35
Brown algae 579.88
Brown bear 599.784
conservation technology 639.979 784
resource economics 333.959 784
Brown coal 553.22
economic geology 553.22
mining 622.332
properties 662.622 2
Brown County (Ill.) T2—773 473
Brown County (Ind.) T2—772 253
Brown County (Kan.) T2—781 34
Brown County (Minn.) T2—776 31
Brown County (Neb.) T2—782 736
Brown County (Ohio) T2—771 796
Brown County (S.D.) T2—783 144
Brown County (Tex.) T2—764 548
Brown County (Wis.) T2—775 61
Brown lung disease
medicine 616.244
see also Respiratory system
Brown rat 599.352
see also Rats (Rattus)
Brown Swiss cattle 636.234
Brownian motion 530.475
liquid-state physics 530.425
see Manual at 530.475 vs. 530.12, 531.16
Brownouts 333.793 217
electrical engineering 621.319
Browsing 591.54
animal husbandry 636.084 5
descriptive zoology 591.54
Broxbourne (England) T2—425 87
Broxtowe (England : Borough) T2—425 26
Bruce (Ont. : County) T2—713 21
Brucella 579.33
Brucellosis (Biology)
veterinary medicine 636.208 969 57
Brucellosis (Human)
incidence 614.565
medicine 616.957
see also Communicable diseases (Human)
Bruges (Belgium) T2—493 122
Brugge (Belgium) T2—493 122
Bruises
medicine 617.13
Brule County (S.D.) T2—783 381
Brunch 642
cooking 641.53
customs 394.15
Brundusium (Extinct city) T2—377
Brunei 959.55
T2—595 5
Brunelliaceae 583.72
Bruniaceae 583.72
Brunswick County (N.C.) T2—756 29
Brunswick County (Va.) T2—755 575
Bruny Island (Tas.) T2—946 2
Brush disposal
forestry 634.955
Brush drawing 741.26
Brush-tailed possum 599.232
Brush turkeys 598.64
Brushes 679.6
Brushes (Generator parts) 621.316
Brussels (Belgium) T2—493 32
Brussels griffon 636.76
Brussels sprouts 641.353 6
commercial processing 664.805 36

Brussels sprouts (continued)
  cooking 641.653 6
  food 641.353 6
  garden crop 635.36
Bruttium T2—377
Bryales 588.2
Bryan County (Ga.) T2—758 732
Bryan County (Okla.) T2—766 62
Bryansk (Russia : Oblast) T2—472 5
Bryce Canyon National Park (Utah) T2—792 52
Bryde's whale 599.524
Bryophyta 588
  paleobotany 561.8
  pharmacology 615.322
Bryopodales 579.835
Bryopsida 588.2
Bryozoa 594.67
  paleozoology 564.67
Brythonic languages 491.6
  T6—916
Brythonic literatures 891.6
Bubble memory 004.56
  engineering 621.397 63
Bubbles 530.427 5
  chemical engineering 660.293
  chemistry 541.33
  physics 530.427 5
Bube-Benga languages 496.396
  T6—963 96
Bubonic plague
  incidence 614.573 2
  medicine 616.923 2
  see also Communicable diseases (Human)
Bucconidae 598.72
Bucerotidae 598.78
Buchanan, James
  United States history 973.68
Buchanan County (Iowa) T2—777 382
Buchanan County (Mo.) T2—778 132
Buchanan County (Va.) T2—755 752
Bucharest (Romania) T2—498 2
Bücher, Karl
  economic school 330.154 2
Buckbeans 583.93
Buckeyes 583.78
Buckingham County (Va.) T2—755 623
Buckinghamshire (England) T2—425 9
Buckles 391.7
  customs 391.7
  making 739.278
  see also Jewelry
Bucks County (Pa.) T2—748 21
Buckthorns 583.86
Buckwheat 641.331 2
  botany 583.57
  commercial processing 664.72
  cooking 641.631 2
  food 641.331 2
  food crop 633.12
București (Romania) T2—498 2
Budapest (Hungary) T2—439 12
Buddha 294.363
  art representation 704.948 943 63
  arts 700.482 943 63
  T3C—382 943 63
Buddhism 294.3
  art representation 704.948 943
  arts 700.482 943
  T3C—382 943
  Islamic polemics 297.294
Buddhism and Islam 294.337 2
  Buddhist view 294.337 2
  Islamic view 297.284 3
Buddhist architecture 720.95
Buddhist calendar 529.324 3
  religion 294.343 6
Buddhist education 294.375
Buddhist ethics 294.35
Buddhist holidays 294.343 6
  customs 394.265 43
  see also Holidays
Buddhist monasteries 294.365 7
  architecture 726.784 3
Buddhist philosophy 181.043
Buddhist sculpture 730.95
Buddhist temples and shrines 294.343 5
  architecture 726.143
Buddhists
  biography 294.309 2
  religious group T7—294 3
Buddlejaceae 583.95
Budgerigars 636.686 4
  animal husbandry 636.686 4
  zoology 598.71
Budget deficits 352.48
  macroeconomic policy 339.523
  see also Budgets (Public)
Budget messages 352.48
  specific jurisdictions 352.493–.499
Budget surpluses
  macroeconomic policy 339.523
Budgeting 658.154
  armed forces 355.622 8
  public administration 352.48
  see also Budgets (Public)

Budgets (Business)
  management 658.154
Budgets (Personal) 640.42
Budgets (Public) 352.48
  armed forces 355.622 8
    specific jurisdictions 355.622 9
  law 343.034
  specific international organizations 352.491
  specific jurisdictions 352.493–.499
Buds 581.46
  descriptive botany 581.46
  physiology 575.486
  plant propagation 631.533
Budworms 595.78
  agricultural pests 632.78
Buena Vista (Va.) T2—755 851
Buena Vista County (Iowa) T2—777 18
Buenos Aires (Argentina) T2—821 1
Buenos Aires (Argentina : Province) T2—821 2
Buffalo 599.642
  animal husbandry 636.293
Buffalo (Bison) 599.643
  see also Bison
Buffalo (N.Y.) T2—747 97
Buffalo County (Neb.) T2—782 45
Buffalo County (S.D.) T2—783 31
Buffalo County (Wis.) T2—775 48
Buffalo gnats 595.772
Buffers
  railroad engineering 625.25
Buffing metals 671.72
Buffing tools 621.922
Bufonidae 597.87
Bufonoidea 597.87
Buganda T2—676 1
Buganda (Kingdom) 967.610 1
Bugey (France) T2—444 4
Bugles 788.95
  instrument 788.951 9
  music 788.95
  see also Brass instruments
Bugs (Heteroptera) 595.754
Buḥayrah (Egypt) T2—621
Buḥayrāh (Sudan : Region) T2—629 4
Buhid (Philippine people) T5—992 1
Builders 690.092
  occupational group T7—69
Building
  enterprises 338.769
    restrictive practices 338.826 9
  government control 354.642 8
  production economics 338.476 9
Building (continued)
  technology 690
Building and loan associations 332.32
  law 346.082 32
  public administration 354.86
Building codes 343.078 69
  criminology 364.142
    criminal law 345.024 2
  enforcement 363.233
Building construction services (Armed forces) 358.22
Building cooperatives 334.1
Building engineering services 696
Building industries 338.476 9
  public administration 354.64
Building management 658.2
  public administration 352.56
  see Manual at 658.2 and T1—0682
Building materials 691
  architectural construction 721.044
  construction 691
  synthetic 666.89
Building paper 676.289
Building remodeling 690.24
  home economics 643.7
  see Manual at 690 vs. 643.7
Buildings 720
  architecture 720
  area planning 711.6
  art representation 704.944
  capital procurement 658.152 42
  construction 690
    see Manual at 624 vs. 690
  economics 333.338
  investment economics 332.632 43
  landscape architecture 717
  management 658.2
    public administration 352.56
    see Manual at 658.2 and T1—0682
  planning
    museums 069.22
Built-in furniture 645.4
  decorative arts 749.4
  manufacturing technology 684.16
  see also Furniture
Bujumbura (Burundi) T2—675 72
Buka Island (Papua New Guinea) T2—959 2
Bukhara rugs
  arts 746.758 7
  see also Rugs

Bukhārī, Muḥammad ibn Ismāʻīl
  Hadith 297.124 1
Bukidnon (Philippines) T2—599 7
Bukovina T2—498 4
  Romania T2—498 4
  Ukraine T2—477 9
Bulacan (Philippines) T2—599 1
Bulawayo (Zimbabwe) T2—689 1
Bulbs (Plants) 584.146
  descriptive botany 584.146
  nursery production 631.526
    ornamental plants 635.915 26
  physiology 575.495
  planting 631.532
    ornamental plants 635.915 32
Bulganin, Nikolay
    Aleksandrovich
  Russian history 947.085 2
Bulgaria 949.9
  T2—499
  ancient 939.8
    T2—398
Bulgarian Empire, 680–1014 949.901 3
Bulgarian Empire, 1185–1396 949.901 4
Bulgarian language 491.81
  T6—918 11
Bulgarian literature 891.81
Bulgarian Macedonia T2—499 8
Bulgarian Thrace T2—499 5
Bulgarians T5—918 11
Bulimia
  medicine 616.852 63
  see also Mental illness
Bulk carriers (Ships) 387.245
  engineering 623.824 5
  see also Ships
Bulk mailings 383.124
  see also Postal service
Bulkley-Nechako (B.C.) T2—711 82
Bulkley River (B.C.) T2—711 82
Bull Moose Movement (U.S.) 324.273 27
Bull-roarers 788.29
  see also Wind instruments
Bull shark 597.34
Bull Shoals Lake (Ark. and
    Mo.) T2—767 193
Bull terriers 636.755 9
Bulldog 636.72
Bulldozers 624.152
  engineering 629.225
  repair 629.287 5
Buller District (N.Z.) T2—937 3
Bulletin boards
  instructional use 371.335 6
  management use 658.455
Bulletin boards (Computer) 004.693
  see also Computer
    communications
Bullets
  military engineering 623.455
Bullfighting 791.82
Bullfinches 598.885
Bullheads (Catfishes) 597.492
Bullis fever
  incidence 614.526 6
  medicine 616.922 6
  see also Communicable
    diseases (Human)
Bullitt County (Ky.) T2—769 453
Bullmastiff 636.73
Bulloch County (Ga.) T2—758 766
Bullock County (Ala.) T2—761 483
Bullroarers 788.29
  see also Wind instruments
Bullying
  education 371.58
Bulrushes 584.84
Bulrushes (Cattails) 584.68
Bulrushes (Sedges) 584.84
Bultfontein (South Africa :
    District) T2—685 3
Bulu language 496.396
  T6—963 96
Bumpers
  automobile 629.276
Bunbury (W.A.) T2—941 2
Buncombe County (N.C.) T2—756 88
Bundaberg (Qld.) T2—943 2
Bundling (Customs) 392.4
Bungalows
  architecture 728.373
  construction 690.837 3
Bungee jumping 797.5
  see also Sports
Bunker Hill, Battle of, 1775 973.331 2
Bunker oils 665.538 8
Bunsen burners (Chemical
    apparatus) 542.4
Bunt (Fungi) 579.593
  disease of wheat 633.119 493
Buntings 598.883
Bunun (Taiwan people) T5—992 5
Bunya Mountains National
    Park (Qld.) T2—943 2
Bunyoro (Kingdom) 967.610 1
  T2—676 1

Buoyancy 532.02
  air mechanics 533.61
  gas mechanics 533.12
  liquid mechanics 532.25
Buoys 387.155
  construction 627.924
  navigation aids 623.894 4
  transportation services 387.155
Buprestoidea 595.763
Bur reeds 584.68
Būr Sa'īd (Egypt : Province) T2—621 5
Burbots 597.632
Burdekin River (Qld.) T2—943 6
Burdur İli (Turkey) T2—562
Bureau County (Ill.) T2—773 372
Bureaucracy 302.35
  public administration 352.63
  sociology 302.35
Burgas (Bulgaria : Oblast) T2—499 5
Burgas (Bulgaria : Okrŭg) T2—499 5
Burgaska oblast (Bulgaria) T2—499 5
Burgaski okrŭg (Bulgaria) T2—499 5
Burgenland (Austria) T2—436 15
Burglarproofing
  household security 643.16
Burglary 364.162
  see also Theft
Burglary insurance 368.82
  see also Insurance
Burgos (Spain : Province) T2—463 53
Burgundian language 439.9
  T6—399
Burgundy (France) T2—444
Burhou (England) T2—423 47
Burial insurance 368.366
  see also Insurance
Burial of dead 363.75
  customs 393.1
  see also Undertaking (Mortuary)
Burial of Jesus Christ 232.964
Burial of waste 363.728 5
  technology 628.445 64
  see also Waste control
Buriat language 494.2
  T6—942
Buriātiīa (Russia) T2—575
Burke County (Ga.) T2—758 65
Burke County (N.C.) T2—756 85
Burke County (N.D.) T2—784 72
Burkina Faso 966.25
  T2—662 5
Burkinabe T5—966 25
Burkinans T5—966 25
Burkitt's lymphoma
  incidence 614.599 944 6
  medicine 616.994 46
  see also Cancer (Human)
Burleigh County (N.D.) T2—784 77
Burleson County (Tex.) T2—764 241
Burlesque shows 792.7
  see also Theater
Burlington (Vt.) T2—743 17
Burlington County (N.J.) T2—749 61
Burma 959.1
  T2—591
Burma Campaign, 1944 940.542 5
Burmanniaceae 584.38
Burmese T5—958
Burmese cat 636.824
Burmese language 495.8
  T6—958
Burmese literature 895.8
Burnaby (B.C.) T2—711 33
Burnet County (Tex.) T2—764 63
Burnet-Llano region (Tex.) T2—764 6
Burnett County (Wis.) T2—775 14
Burnie (Tas.) T2—946 5
Burnley (England) T2—427 642
Burnout (Psychology) 158.723
Burns
  crop damage 632.18
  medicine 617.11
Burramyidae 599.23
Burreeds 584.68
Burros 636.182
  animal husbandry 636.182
  conservation technology 639.979 665
  resource economics 333.959 665
  zoology 599.665
Burrowing animals 591.564 8
Burrowing toads 597.86
Burrows 591.564 8
Bursa İli (Turkey) T2—563
Bursae
  human anatomy 611.75
  human physiology 612.75
  medicine 616.76
  surgery 617.475
  see also Musculoskeletal system
Bursaries T1—079
Burseraceae 583.77
Burt County (Neb.) T2—782 243
Burundi 967.572
  T2—675 72
Burundi people T5—967 572

Burundians T5—967 572
Bury (England) T2—427 38
Buryat language 494.2
T6—942
Buryatia (Russia) T2—575
Burying beetles 595.764 2
Bus cooking 641.575
Bus drivers 388.322 092
occupational group T7—388
Bus stops 388.33
urban 388.473
see also Bus transportation
Bus terminals 388.33
architecture 725.38
urban 388.473
see also Bus transportation
Bus transportation 388.322
international law 341.756 882
law 343.094 82
public administration 354.765 3
transportation services 388.322
urban 388.413 22
law 343.098 2
public administration 354.769
Buses 388.342 33
driving 629.283 33
engineering 629.222 33
military engineering 623.747 23
operation 388.322 044
repair 629.287 233
sanitation services 363.729 3
see also Waste control
transportation services 388.342 33
see also Automotive vehicles
Bush, George
United States history 973.928
Bush babies 599.83
Bush clovers 633.364
botany 583.74
forage crop 633.364
Bushbuck 599.642 3
Būshehr (Iran : Province) T2—557 5
Bushman languages 496.1
T6—961
Bushmen (African people) T5—961
Business 650
social theology 291.178 5
Christianity 261.85
Judaism 296.383
see also Commerce
see Manual at 330 vs. 650
Business administration 658
Business arithmetic 650.015 13
Business cards
illustration 741.685
Business crime 364.168
law 345.026 8
Business cycles 338.542
Business districts 307.333
area planning 711.552 2
land economics 333.77
Business enterprises 338.7
economics 338.7
finance 338.604 1
management 658.15
initiation 338.71
economics 338.71
management 658.11
T1—068 1
international law 341.753
law 346.065
location 338.09
economic rationale 338.604 2
economics 338.09
law 346.07
management 658.11
T1—068 1
see also Plant location—management
management 658
relations with government 322.3
social welfare 361.765
valuation 658.15
see Manual at 338.09 vs. 332.67309, 338.6042, 346.07, 658.11, T1—0681, 658.21, T1—0682; *also at* 380: Add table: 09 vs. 065; *also at* 658.04 vs. 658.114, 658.402
Business ethics 174.4
religion 291.564 4
Christianity 241.644
Islam 297.564 4
Judaism 296.364 4
see also Ethical problems
Business etiquette 395.52
Business finance
management 658.15
production economics 338.604 1
Business forecasting 338.544
Business forecasts 338.544 3
Business forms 651.29
Business income tax 336.241 7
public administration 352.44
public finance 336.241 7

Business insurance 368.094
  liability 368.81
  see also Insurance
Business intelligence
  management use 658.47
Business interruption insurance 368.815
  see also Insurance
Business law 346.07
Business liability insurance 368.81
  see also Insurance
Business libraries 027.69
Business logistics
  management 658.5
Business losses
  tax economics 336.241 7
  tax law 343.052 36
Business machines 651.2
  manufacturing technology 681.14
  office services 651.2
Business management 658
  T1—068
  see Manual at 658 and T1—068
Business names 929.97
  law 346.048
Business organizations 338.7
  see also Business enterprises
Business records
  law 346.065
  records management 651.5
Business relationships (Personal) 650.13
Business security
  management 658.47
Business success 650.1
Business tax 336.207
  law 343.068
  public administration 352.44
  public finance 336.207
Business writing 808.066 65
  see Manual at 658.45 vs. 651.7, 808.06665
Businesses 338.7
  see also Business enterprises
Businessmen 338.092
  occupational group T7—338
  see Manual at 338.092
Businessowners insurance 368.094
  see also Insurance
Busing (School desegregation) 379.263
  law 344.079 8
Buskerud fylke (Norway) T2—482 6
Busoga (Kingdom) 967.610 1
  T2—676 1
Bustards 598.32
Busts (Sculpture) 731.74
Butadiene-styrene rubber 678.72
Butane 665.773
Butcher paper 676.287
Butene 665.773
Butler County (Ala.) T2—761 37
Butler County (Iowa) T2—777 29
Butler County (Kan.) T2—781 88
Butler County (Ky.) T2—769 755
Butler County (Mo.) T2—778 93
Butler County (Neb.) T2—782 322
Butler County (Ohio) T2—771 75
Butler County (Pa.) T2—748 91
Butomaceae 584.72
Butte (Mont.) T2—786 68
Butte County (Calif.) T2—794 32
Butte County (Idaho) T2—796 59
Butte County (S.D.) T2—783 43
Butter 641.372
  cooking 641.672
  food 641.372
  processing 637.2
Butter prints and molds
  wood carving 736.4
Buttercups 583.34
Butterfat tests
  milk processing 637.127 6
Butterflies 595.789
  conservation technology 639.975 789
  culture 638.578 9
  resource economics 333.955 7
Butterfly bushes 583.95
Butterfly farming 638.578 9
Butterfly fishes (Freshwater) 597.47
Butterfly fishes (Marine) 597.72
Butterfly flowers 635.933 952
  botany 583.952
  floriculture 635.933 952
Butterfly gardening 638.578 9
Buttermilk 641.372 4
  cooking 641.672 4
  food 641.372 4
  processing 637.24
Butternuts 583.49
Butterworth (South Africa : District) T2—687 91
Buttock muscles
  human anatomy 611.738
  see also Musculoskeletal system

Button accordions 788.863
  instrument 788.863 19
  music 788.863
  see also Woodwind instruments
Button mangrove 583.763
Button quails 598.32
Buttonbushes 635.933 93
  botany 583.93
  floriculture 635.933 93
Buttons 391.45
  commercial technology 687.8
  customs 391.45
  home sewing 646.19
  numismatics 737.24
  see also Clothing
Butts County (Ga.) T2—758 585
Butyrates 668.423
Buxaceae 583.69
Buyers' guides 381.33
  T1—029 6
  see Manual at 338 vs. 060, 381, 382, 670.294, 910, T1—025, T1—0294, T1—0296: 3. Buyers' guides
Buzău (Romania : Judeţ) T2—498 2
Buzzards 598.94
Buzzards (Turkey vulture) 598.92
Buzzards Bay (Mass. : Bay) 551.461 46
  T2—163 46
By-products
  commercial food processing 664.08
  pulp 676.5
Byblidaceae 583.72
Byblos (Lebanon) T2—569 2
  ancient T2—394 4
Bydgoszcz (Poland : Voivodeship) T2—438 2
Byelarus 947.8
  T2—478
Byelorussian language 491.799
  T6—917 99
Byelorussian literature 891.799
Byelorussians T5—917 99
Bylot Island (N.W.T.) T2—719 5
Bypass surgery (Coronary) 617.412
  see also Cardiovascular system
Byrrhoidea 595.763
Byssinosis
  medicine 616.244
  see also Respiratory system
Byzantine architecture 723.2
Byzantine art 709.021 4
  religious significance 246.1
Byzantine decoration 745.442
Byzantine Empire 949.502
  T2—495
  Egyptian history 932.023
Byzantine Greek language 487.3
  T6—87
Byzantine Greek literature 880
Byzantine law 340.54
Byzantine painting 759.021 4
Byzantine rite churches 281.5
  see also Eastern churches
Byzantine sculpture 734.224

C

C* algebras 512.55
Caaguazú (Paraguay : Dept.) T2—892 134
Caazapá (Paraguay : Dept.) T2—892 127
Cabala 296.16
  Jewish mysticism
    experience 296.712
    movement 296.833
  Jewish religious sources 296.16
  occultism 135.47
Cabañas (El Salvador) T2—728 426
Cabaret shows 792.7
  see also Theater
Cabarrus County (N.C.) T2—756 72
Cabbages 641.353 4
  botany 583.64
  commercial processing 664.805 34
  cooking 641.653 4
  food 641.353 4
  garden crop 635.34
Cabell County (W. Va.) T2—754 42
Cabin pressurization
  aircraft 629.134 42
Cabinda (Angola : Province) T2—673 1
Cabinet government 321.804 3
Cabinet-level committees 352.24
Cabinet members 352.293
  occupational group T7—352 1
Cabinet organs 786.55
  instrument 786.551 9
  music 786.55
  see also Keyboard instruments
Cabinet secretariats 352.243
Cabinet secretaries 352.243 229 3
Cabinetmakers 684.104 092

Cabinetmaking 684.104
Cabinets (Furniture)
  decorative arts 749.3
  manufacturing technology 684.16
Cabinets (Government councils) 321.804 3
  public administration 352.24
Cabins 643.1
  architecture 728.73
  home economics 643.1
Cabins (Aircraft) 629.134 45
Cable communication systems 384.6
  see also Telephone
Cable railways 385.6
  engineering 625.5
  transportation services 385.6
  see also Railroad transportation
Cable television 384.555
  engineering 621.388 57
  see also Television
  see Manual at 384.555 vs. 384.5554
Cables (Electrical conductors) 621.319 34
  computer science 004.64
    engineering 621.398 1
Cables (Ropes)
  knotting and splicing 623.888 2
  metal 671.84
  structural engineering 624.177 4
Cabo Delgado (Mozambique) T2—679 8
Cabooses 385.32
  engineering 625.22
  transportation services 385.32
  see also Rolling stock
Cabs 388.342 32
  see also Taxicabs
Cacao 583.68
  agriculture 633.74
  see also Cocoa
Cacao butter 665.354
  see also Cocoa butter
Cáceres (Spain : Province) T2—462 8
Cachapoal (Chile : Province) T2—833 2
Cache County (Utah) T2—792 12
Cache Creek (B.C.) T2—711 72
Cachets (Philately) 769.567
Cactales 583.56
Cacti 583.56
  edible fruits 641.347 75
    cooking 641.647 75
    horticulture 634.775
  floriculture 635.933 56
Cactuses 583.56
  see also Cacti
CAD (Computer-aided design) 620.004 202 85
CAD/CAM (Manufacturing) 670.285
Caddis flies 595.745
Caddo County (Okla.) T2—766 41
Caddo Lake (La. and Tex.) T2—763 99
Caddo Parish (La.) T2—763 99
Caddoan languages 497.9
  T6—979
Cadence (Music) 781.254
Cadenzas 784.186
Cádiz (Spain : Province) T2—468 8
Cadmium 669.56
  chemical engineering 661.066 2
  chemistry 546.662
  human toxicology 615.925 662
  materials science 620.184 6
  metallography 669.955 6
  metallurgy 669.56
  metalworking 673.56
  physical metallurgy 669.965 6
  see also Chemicals
Caecilians 597.82
Caedmon 829.2
Caenagnathiformes 568.5
Caenolestidae 599.27
Caernarvonshire (Wales) T2—429 2
Caesalpiniaceae 583.749
Caesarean section
  obstetrical surgery 618.86
Caesium 669.725
  see also Cesium
Café Filho, João
  Brazilian history 981.062
Cafeteria meal service 642.5
Cafeterias 647.95
  see also Eating places
Caffeine abuse 362.299
  medicine 616.864
  personal health 613.84
  social welfare 362.299
  see also Substance abuse
Cagayan (Philippines) T2—599 1
Cage birds 636.68
  see also Birds
Cages
  animal husbandry 636.083 1
Cages (Elevators)
  mining 622.68
Cagliari (Sardinia : Province) T2—459 1

Cahuapanan languages 498
T6—98
Cahuilla Indians T5—974 5
Cahuilla language 497.45
T6—974 5
CAI (Computer-assisted instruction) 371.334
T1—078 5
adult level 374.26
Cain (Biblical person)
Bible stories 222.110 950 5
Cairngorm Mountains (Scotland) T2—412 4
Cairngorms (Scotland) T2—412 4
Cairns (Qld.) T2—943 6
Cairo (Egypt : Province) T2—621 6
Caisson disease
medicine 616.989 4
see also Environmental diseases (Human)
Caissons 624.157
Caithness (Scotland) T2—411 62
Cajamarca (Peru : Dept.) T2—851 5
Cajun cooking 641.597 63
Cajun French dialect 447.976 3
T6—41
Cajuns T5—410 763
Cakchikel Indians T5—974 15
Cakchikel language 497.415
T6—974 15
Cake decorating 641.865 3
Cake mixes 664.753
Cakes (Pastry) 641.865 3
commercial processing 664.752 5
home preparation 641.865 3
Cakewalks 791.12
music 784.188 7
Cala (South Africa : District) T2—687 91
Calabar (Nigeria) T2—669 44
Calabash tree 635.977 395
botany 583.95
ornamental arboriculture 635.977 395
Calabria (Italy) T2—457 8
ancient T2—377
Caladiums 635.934 64
botany 584.64
floriculture 635.934 64
Calamitales 561.72
Calamopityaceae 561.595
Calanoida 595.34
Călăraşi (Romania : Judeţ) T2—498 2
Calaveras County (Calif.) T2—794 44
Calcarea 593.42
paleozoology 563.4
Calcaronea 593.42
Calcasieu Lake (La.) T2—763 52
Calcasieu Parish (La.) T2—763 54
Calcimining 698.2
Calcinea 593.42
Calcispongiae 593.42
paleozoology 563.4
Calcite
mineralogy 549.782
Calcium 669.725
applied nutrition 613.285
biochemistry 572.516
humans 612.015 24
chemical engineering 661.039 3
chemistry 546.393
metabolism
human physiology 612.392 4
metallurgy 669.725
organic chemistry 547.053 93
applied 661.895
physical metallurgy 669.967 25
see also Chemicals
Calcium soaps 668.125
Calculators 681.145
manufacturing technology 681.145
mathematics 510.284
Calculus 515
Calculus of finite differences 515.62
Calculus of variations 515.64
Calcutta (India) T2—541 47
Caldas (Colombia : Dept.) T2—861 35
Calderdale (England) T2—428 12
Caldwell County (Ky.) T2—769 815
Caldwell County (Mo.) T2—778 185
Caldwell County (N.C.) T2—756 845
Caldwell County (Tex.) T2—764 33
Caldwell Parish (La.) T2—763 76
Caledon (South Africa : District) T2—687 3
Caledon River (Lesotho and South Africa) T2—685 6
Caledonia County (Vt.) T2—743 34
Calendar reform 529.5
Calendars 529.3
chronology 529.3
illustration 741.682
religion 291.36
Christianity 263.9
Islam 297.36
Judaism 296.43

Calendars (Liturgical books) 264
  Anglican 264.031
  Roman Catholic 264.021
Calendering paper 676.234
Calendering rubber 678.27
Calendering textiles 677.028 25
Calgary (Alta.) T2—712 338
Calhoun County (Ala.) T2—761 63
Calhoun County (Ark.) T2—767 64
Calhoun County (Fla.) T2—759 943
Calhoun County (Ga.) T2—758 956
Calhoun County (Ill.) T2—773 853
Calhoun County (Iowa) T2—777 43
Calhoun County (Mich.) T2—774 22
Calhoun County (Miss.) T2—762 81
Calhoun County (S.C.) T2—757 72
Calhoun County (Tex.) T2—764 121
Calhoun County (W. Va.) T2—754 29
Calibration 530.8
  electrical instruments 621.372
Calico bass 597.738
California 979.4
  T2—794
California, Gulf of (Mexico) 551.466 1
  T2—164 1
California, Southern T2—794 9
California halibut 597.69
California laurel 583.23
Californium 546.448
  see also Chemicals
Caligoida 595.34
Caliphate 297.61
Caliphs
  companions of Muḥammad 297.648
  role and function 297.61
Calisthenics 613.714
  child care 649.57
  therapeutics 615.824
Calitzdorp (South Africa : District) T2—687 16
Call 332.645
  multiple forms of investment 332.645
  stocks 332.632 28
Call to Islam 297.74
Calla lilies 635.934 64
  botany 584.64
  floriculture 635.934 64
Callahan County (Tex.) T2—764 726
Callao (Peru : Province) T2—852 6
Callaway County (Mo.) T2—778 335
Caller ID telephone service 384.64
Calles, Plutarco Elías
  Mexican history 972.082 3
Calligraphy 745.61
Calliphoridae 595.774
Callipteris 561.597
Callithricidae 599.84
  paleozoology 569.84
Callorhinus 599.797 3
Callosities
  medicine 616.544
  see also Skin
Calloway County (Ky.) T2—769 92
Caloosahatchee River (Fla.) T2—759 48
Calorie counters 613.23
Calories
  applied nutrition 613.23
Calorimeters
  manufacturing technology 681.2
Calorimetry 536.6
Caltanissetta (Sicily : Province) T2—458 21
Calumet County (Wis.) T2—775 66
Calvados (France) T2—442 2
Calvert County (Md.) T2—752 44
Calvinia (South Africa : District) T2—687 17
Calvinistic Baptists 286.1
  see also Baptists
Calvinistic churches 284.2
  see also Reformed Church
Calvinists
  biography 284.209 2
  religious group T7—242
Calycerales 583.9
Calypso 781.64
CAM (Manufacturing) 670.427
Camagüey (Cuba : Province) T2—729 156
Camarines Norte (Philippines) T2—599 1
Camarines Sur (Philippines) T2—599 1
Camas County (Idaho) T2—796 31
Cambistry 332.45
Cambium 575.488
Cambodia 959.6
  T2—596
Cambodian language 495.932
  T6—959 32
Cambodian literature 895.932
Cambodians T5—959 3
Cambria County (Pa.) T2—748 77
Cambrian Mountains (Wales) T2—429

Cambrian period 551.723
geology 551.723
paleontology 560.172 3
Cambridge (England) T2—426 59
Cambridge (Mass.) T2—744 4
Cambridge Bay (N.W.T.) T2—719 7
Cambridgeshire (England) T2—426 5
Camcorders 384.558
see also Video recorders
Camden (London, England) T2—421 42
Camden (N.S.W.) T2—944 6
Camden County (Ga.) T2—758 746
Camden County (Mo.) T2—778 54
Camden County (N.C.) T2—756 135
Camden County (N.J.) T2—749 87
Camelidae 599.636
Camellias 583.624
floriculture 635.933 624
Camels 636.295
animal husbandry 636.295
zoology 599.636 2
Camel's hair textiles 677.34
see also Textiles
Camelus 599.636 2
Camembert cheese 641.373 53
cooking 641.673 53
food 641.373 53
processing 637.353
Cameos 736.222
Cameras 771.3
manufacturing technology 681.418
television engineering 621.388 34
Camerata 563.92
Cameron County (Pa.) T2—748 66
Cameron County (Tex.) T2—764 495
Cameron Parish (La.) T2—763 52
Cameroon 967.11
T2—671 1
Cameroon people T5—967 11
Cameroonians T5—967 11
Cameroun T2—671 1
Camiguin (Philippines) T2—599 7
Camillians 255.55
church history 271.55
Camouflage (Biology) 578.47
animals 591.472
Camouflage (Military science) 355.41
engineering 623.77
Camp cooking 641.578 2
Camp County (Tex.) T2—764 219
Camp Fire, inc. 369.47
Camp Fire Girls 369.47
Camp health 613.67
Camp meetings
Christian religious practices 269.24
Camp programs 796.5
church work 253.7
Jewish religious work 296.67
Campa Indians T5—983 9
Campa language 498.39
T6—983 9
Campaign buttons
numismatics 737.242
Campaign finance 324.78
law 342.078
Campaign finance offenses 364.132 4
law 345.023 24
Campaign literature 324.23
Campaign pins
numismatics 737.242
Campaign strategy (Elections) 324.72
Campaigns (Military science) 355.4
see also Land operations
Campaigns (Politics) 324.9
elections 324.9
law 342.078
nominations 324.5
specific countries 324.24–.29
techniques 324.7
see Manual at 909, 930–990 vs. 320: Political activities
Campania (Italy) T2—457 2
ancient T2—377
Campanula 583.98
floriculture 635.933 98
Campanulales 583.98
Campbell, Kim
Canadian history 971.064 7
Campbell County (Ky.) T2—769 34
Campbell County (S.D.) T2—783 17
Campbell County (Tenn.) T2—768 72
Campbell County (Va.) T2—755 672
Campbell County (Wyo.) T2—787 12
Campbell Island (N.Z.) T2—939 9
Campbellites 286.6
biography 286.609 2
see also Disciples of Christ
Campbelltown (N.S.W.) T2—944 6
Campeche (Mexico : State) T2—726 4
Camperdown (South Africa : District) T2—684 7
Campers (Vehicles) 388.346
cooking 641.575
engineering 629.226
see also Motor homes
Campfires 796.545

Camphors
  chemistry 547.71
Camping 796.54
  meal service 642.3
  military operations 355.412
  military training 355.544
Camping equipment 796.540 28
  armed forces 355.81
  manufacturing technology 685.53
Campobasso (Italy : Province) T2—457 192
Campus Crusade for Christ 267.61
Campus ministry 259.24
Campus police 363.289
Campus unrest 371.81
Cams 621.838
Canaanite language 492.6
  T6—926
Canaanite literature 892.6
Canaanites T5—926
Canaanitic languages 492.6
  T6—926
Canaanitic literatures 892.6
Canada 971
  T2—71
  see Manual at T2—73 vs. T2—71
Canada, Eastern T2—713
Canada, Western T2—712
Canada goose 598.417 8
Canadian Arctic T2—719
Canadian Arctic Archipelago (N.W.T.) T2—719 5
Canadian County (Okla.) T2—766 39
Canadian football 796.335
  see also Sports
Canadian football players 796.335 092
Canadian language
  English 420.971
    T6—21
  French 440.971
    T6—41
  Inuit 497.12
    T6—971 2
Canadian literature
  English 810
  French 840
  Inuit 897.12
Canadian Pacific seawaters 551.466 33
  T2—164 33
Canadian pronunciation
  English 421.52
  French 441.52
Canadian River (Okla.) T2—766
Canadian River, North (Okla.) T2—766 1
Canadian Rockies (B.C. and Alta.) T2—711
Canadian Shield T2—714
  Canada T2—714
  Manitoba T2—712 72
  Ontario T2—713 1
Canadian spelling
  English 421.52
  French 441.52
Canadians T5—11
Canaigre 633.87
  agriculture 633.87
  botany 583.57
  see also Tannins
Çanakkale İli (Turkey) T2—562
  Asia T2—562
  Europe T2—496 1
Canal Area (Panama) T2—728 75
Canal transportation 386.4
  see also Inland water transportation
Canal Zone T2—728 75
Canalboats
  freight services 386.244
  power-driven 386.224 36
    design 623.812 436
    engineering 623.824 36
    transportation services 386.224 36
  towed 386.229
    design 623.812 9
    engineering 623.829
    transportation services 386.229
  see also Ships
Canalized rivers 386.4
  engineering 627.13
  see also Canals
Canals 386.4
  engineering 627.13
  international law 341.446
  law 343.096 4
  transportation services 386.4
Canapés 641.812
Cañar (Ecuador : Province) T2—866 23
Canarese T5—948 14
Canaries 636.686 25
  animal husbandry 636.686 25
  zoology 598.885
Canary grasses 584.9
Canary Islands 964.9
  T2—649
Canasta 795.418
Canberra (A.C.T.) T2—947 1

Cancellations (Philately) 769.567
Cancer (Biology) 571.978
  veterinary medicine 636.089 699 4
Cancer (Human) 362.196 994
  geriatrics 618.976 994
  incidence 614.599 94
  medicine 616.994
    see Manual at 616.994 vs. 616.992
  nursing 610.736 98
  pediatrics 618.929 94
  social services 362.196 994
    public administration 353.63
  surgery 616.994 059
Cancer (Zodiac) 133.526 5
Candelilla wax 665.12
Candidiasis
  medicine 616.969
  see also Communicable diseases (Human)
Candleberry 583.43
Candleberry wax 665.12
Candler County (Ga.) T2—758 773
Candles 621.323
  handicrafts 745.593 32
  see also Lighting
Candlesticks 621.323
  ceramic arts 738.8
  handicrafts 745.593 3
  see also Lighting
Candlewood 583.628
Candomblé 299.673
Candy 641.853
  commercial processing 664.153
  home preparation 641.853
Candytufts (Plants) 583.64
Cane fruits 641.347 1
  botany 583.73
  cooking 641.647 1
  food 641.347 1
  horticulture 634.71
Cane rat 599.359
Cane sugar 641.336 1
  commercial processing 664.122
  food 641.336 1
  see also Sugar
Cane syrup
  commercial processing 664.122
Cane textiles 677.54
  see also Textiles
Canea (Greece : Nome) T2—495 9
Canella language 498.4
  T6—984
Canelones (Uruguay : Dept.) T2—895 14
Canendiyú (Paraguay) T2—892 133
Canes (Sticks)
  customs 391.44
Caniaspiscau (Quebec : Regional County Municipality) T2—714 115
Canidae 599.77
  paleozoology 569.77
Canine police services 363.232
Canines 636.7
  see also Dogs
Canis 599.772
Çankiri İli (Turkey) T2—563
Cannabaceae 583.45
Cannabis
  pharmacodynamics 615.782 7
Cannabis abuse 362.295
  medicine 616.863 5
  personal health 613.835
  social welfare 362.295
  see also Substance abuse
Cannaceae 584.39
Cannas 635.934 39
  botany 584.39
  floriculture 635.934 39
Canned foods
  cooking 641.612
  product safety 363.192 9
    see also Food—product safety
Cannel coal 553.23
  economic geology 553.23
  properties 662.622 3
Cannibalism
  customs 394.9
Canning, John Charles, Earl
  Indian history 954.031 7
Canning foods 664.028 2
  commercial preservation 664.028 2
  home preservation 641.42
Cannock Chase (England : District) T2—424 67
Cannon County (Tenn.) T2—768 535
Cannons 355.822
  art metalwork 739.742
  engineering 623.42
  military equipment 355.822
Canoe racing 797.14
  see also Sports
Canoeing
  sports 797.122
    see also Sports

Canoes 386.229
  design 623.812 9
  engineering 623.829
  transportation services 386.229
Canoidea 599.76
  paleozoology 569.76
Canon law 262.9
Canon of Bible 220.12
Canonization of saints 235.24
Canons (Music) 784.187 8
Canons regular 255.08
  church history 271.08
  women 255.908
    church history 271.908
Canopies
  church architecture 726.529 3
Cant 417.2
  specific languages T4—7
Cantabria (Spain) T2—463 51
Cantabrian Mountains (Spain) T2—462
Cantal (France) T2—445 92
Cantaloupes 641.356 117
  cooking 641.656 117
  food 641.356 117
  garden crop 635.611 7
Cantatas 782.24
  choral and mixed voices 782.524
  single voices 783.092 4
Canteen cooking 641.577
Canteen meal service 642.5
Canteens
  armed forces 355.341
Canterbury (England : City) T2—422 34
Canterbury Province (N.Z.) T2—938
Canterbury Region (N.Z.) T2—938
Cantharidae 595.764 4
Cantharoidea 595.764 4
Canticle of Canticles 223.9
Canticles 782.295
Cantilever bridges 388
  construction 624.35
  see also Bridges
Cantilever foundations 624.156
Canton (China) T2—512 75
Cantonese dialect 495.17
  T6—951 7
Cantons 320.83
  see also Counties
Cantors (Judaism)
  biography 296.462 092
Cantus firmus 781.828
Canunda National Park (S. Aust.) T2—942 34
Canute I, King of England
  English history 942.018 1
Canvas embroidery 746.442
Canvasback 598.414
Canyon County (Idaho) T2—796 23
Canyonlands National Park (Utah) T2—792 59
Canyons 551.442
  T2—144
  geography 910.914 4
  geomorphology 551.442
  physical geography 910.021 44
Canzonas 784.187 5
Cap-de-la-Madeleine (Quebec) T2—714 455
Cap-Rouge (Quebec) T2—714 471
Cap Vert (Senegal) T2—663
Capacitance meters 621.374 2
Capacitors
  electrical engineering 621.315
  radio engineering 621.384 133
Capacity (Law) 346.013
Cape (South Africa : District) T2—687 355
Cape Breton (N.S. : County) T2—716 95
Cape Breton Highlands National Park (N.S.) T2—716 91
Cape Breton Island (N.S.) T2—716 9
Cape Cod (Mass.) T2—744 92
Cape Cod Bay (Mass.) 551.461 45
  T2—163 45
Cape Dorset (N.W.T.) T2—719 5
Cape Fear River (N.C.) T2—756 2
Cape Girardeau County (Mo.) T2—778 96
Cape Hatteras (N.C.) T2—756 175
Cape Le Grand National Park (W.A.) T2—941 7
Cape May County (N.J.) T2—749 98
Cape of Good Hope (South Africa) 968.7
  T2—687
Cape of Good Hope (South Africa : Cape) T2—687 35
Cape Peninsula (South Africa : Cape) T2—687 35
Cape Range National Park (W.A.) T2—941 3
Cape Town (South Africa) T2—687 355
Cape Verde 966.58
  T2—665 8

Cape Verde Islands T2—665 8
Cape Verdeans T5—966 58
Cape York Peninsula (Qld.) T2—943 8
Capercaillies 598.634
Capers 641.338 2
botany 583.64
see also Flavorings
Capetian dynasty 944.021
genealogy 929.74
Capillaries 573.187
biology 573.187
human anatomy 611.15
human physiology 612.135
medicine 616.148
surgery 617.415
see also Cardiovascular system
Capillarity 541.33
chemical engineering 660.293
physics 530.427
Capillary circulation
human physiology 612.135
see also Cardiovascular system
Capital 332.041
distribution
macroeconomics 339.21
financial economics 332.041
management 658.152
production economics 338.604 1
Capital (B.C.) T2—711 28
Capital accounting 657.76
Capital budgets 658.154
Capital budgets (Public) 352.48
see also Budgets (Public)
Capital cities
area planning 711.45
Capital District (Paraguay) T2—892 121
Capital Federal (Argentina) T2—821 1
Capital flight 332.042
Capital formation 332.041 5
agricultural industries 338.13
economics 332.041 5
financial management 658.152 2
macroeconomics 339.43
mineral industries 338.23
production economics 338.604 1
secondary industries 338.43
Capital gains tax 336.242 4
law 343.052 45
public administration 352.44
public finance 336.242 4
individual income 336.242 4
Capital management 658.152
Capital movements 332.042
Capital punishment 364.66
ethics 179.7
religion 291.569 7
Christianity 241.697
Buddhism 294.356 97
Hinduism 294.548 697
Islam 297.569 7
Judaism 296.369 7
law 345.077 3
penology 364.66
social theology 291.178 336 6
Christianity 261.833 66
Capital sources 332.041 54
financial management 658.152 2
Capital transactions (Balance of payments)
international banking 332.152
international finance 332.042
Capitalism 330.122
economics 330.122
social theology 291.178 5
Christianity 261.85
Judaism 296.383
sociology 306.342
Capitalization (Finance) 658.152
Capitalization (Writing) 411
specific languages T4—11
Capitals (Architecture) 721.3
Capitán Prat (Chile : Province) T2—836 28
Capitol Reef National Park (Utah) T2—792 54
Capitols
architecture 725.11
Capitonidae 598.72
Capiz (Philippines : Province) T2—599 5
Cappadocia (Kingdom) T2—393 4
Cappadocia (Turkey) T2—564
Capparales 583.64
Capparidales 583.64
Capra 599.648
Capreolus 599.659
Capri Island (Italy) T2—457 3
Capricorn (Zodiac) 133.527 5
Caprifoliaceae 583.92
Caprimulgiformes 598.99
paleozoology 568.9
Caprinae 599.647

Capsicums 641.338 4
  botany 583.952
  see also Hot spices; Sweet peppers
Capstans 621.864
Capsule cockpits 629.134 386
Capsules (Pharmaceuticals)
  practical pharmacy 615.43
Captive balloons
  engineering 629.133 22
  military engineering 623.744
Captives (Military) 355.113
  war customs 399
  see also Prisoners of war
Capture (Nuclear particles) 539.75
Capuchins 255.36
  church history 271.36
Capybaras 599.359
Caquetá (Colombia) T2—861 64
Car cards (Advertising) 659.134 4
Car pools 388.413 212
  law 343.098 2
Car sickness
  medicine 616.989 2
  see also Environmental diseases (Human)
Carabidae 595.762
Carabobo (Venezuela : State) T2—873 2
Caracaras 598.96
Caracas (Venezuela) T2—877
Caracciolini 255.56
  church history 271.56
Caradon (England : District) T2—423 74
Carapidae 597.63
Carapodidae 597.63
Caraş-Severin (Romania) T2—498 4
Carassius (Goldfish) 639.374 84
  culture 639.374 84
  zoology 597.484
Caravans (Vehicles) 388.346
  engineering 629.226
  see also Motor homes
Caravels 387.21
  design 623.812 1
  engineering 623.821
  handling 623.882 1
  transportation services 387.21
  see also Ships
Caraway 641.338 3
  botany 583.849
  see also Spices
Carazo (Nicaragua) T2—728 516
Carbines 683.422
  art metalwork 739.744 25
  military engineering 623.442 5
  shooting game 799.213
  sports 799.202 832
  target shooting 799.31
  see also Guns (Small arms); Rifles
Carbohydrases 572.756
  see also Enzymes
Carbohydrate cooking 641.563 8
Carbohydrates 572.56
  applied nutrition 613.283
  biochemistry 572.56
    humans 612.015 78
  chemistry 547.78
  metabolic disorders 571.945 6
    medicine 616.399 8
  metabolism 572.564
    human physiology 612.396
    see also Digestive system
Carbon
  chemical engineering 661.068 1
  chemistry 546.681
  materials science 620.193
  mineralogy 549.27
  organic chemistry 547
    applied 661.8
  see also Chemicals
Carbon black 662.93
Carbon County (Mont.) T2—786 652
Carbon County (Pa.) T2—748 26
Carbon County (Utah) T2—792 566
Carbon County (Wyo.) T2—787 86
Carbon cycle (Biogeochemistry) 577.144
Carbon dioxide 546.681 2
  gas technology 665.89
  therapeutics 615.836
Carbon dioxide removal
  human physiology 612.22
    see also Respiratory system
Carbon dioxide sinks 577.144
Carbon processes
  photographic printing 773.1
Carbonaceous materials 553.2
  economic geology 553.2
  mining 622.33
Carbonate rocks 552.58
Carbonated beverages 641.875
  commercial processing 663.62
  home preparation 641.875
Carbonated water
  commercial processing 663.61

Carbonates
  mineralogy 549.78
Carboniferous period 551.75
  geology 551.75
  paleontology 560.175
Carboxylic acids 547.037
  chemical engineering 661.86
Carbro process 773.1
Carbuncles
  medicine 616.523
  see also Skin
Carbureted-blue gas 665.772
Carburetors 621.437
  automotive 629.253 3
Carcharhinidae 597.34
Carcharodon carcharias 597.33
Carchi (Ecuador) T2—866 11
Carcinogenesis
  medicine 616.994 071
  see also Cancer (Human)
Carcinoma
  medicine 616.994
  see also Cancer (Human)
Card catalogs 025.313
Card games 795.4
Card players 795.409 2
  sports group T7—795
Card readers (Computer) 004.76
  engineering 621.398 6
Card tricks 793.85
Card weaving
  arts 746.14
Cardamom 641.338 3
  botany 584.39
  see also Spices
Cardboard 676.288
Cárdenas, Lázaro
  Mexican history 972.082 5
Cardiac arrest
  medicine 616.123 025
  see also Cardiovascular system
Cardiac asthma
  medicine 616.12
  see also Cardiovascular system
Cardiac muscle tissues
  human histology 611.018 6
Cardiff (Wales) T2—429 87
Cardigans 391
  commercial technology 687.146
  customs 391
  home sewing 646.454
  see also Clothing
Cardinal fishes 597.7
Cardinal sins 241.3
Cardinals (Birds) 598.883
Cardinals (Clergy) 282.092
  biography 282.092
  ecclesiology 262.135
Carding textiles 677.028 21
  arts 746.11
  manufacturing technology 677.028 21
Cardiology 616.12
  pediatrics 618.921 2
  see also Cardiovascular system
Cardiopulmonary diseases
  medicine 616.1
  see also Cardiovascular system
Cardiopulmonary resuscitation
  medicine 616.102 5
  see also Cardiovascular system
Cardiovascular agents
  pharmacodynamics 615.71
  see also Cardiovascular system
Cardiovascular diseases
  medicine 616.1
  see also Cardiovascular system
Cardiovascular organs 573.1
  human physiology 612.1
  see also Cardiovascular system
Cardiovascular system 573.1
  anesthesiology 617.967 41
  biology 573.1
  geriatrics 618.976 1
  human anatomy 611.1
  human cancer 362.196 994 1
    medicine 616.994 1
    social services 362.196 994 1
    see also Cancer (Human)
  human diseases 362.196 1
    incidence 614.591
    medicine 616.1
    social services 362.196 1
  human histology 611.018 91
  human physiology 612.1
  nursing 610.736 91
  pediatrics 618.921
  perinatal medicine 618.326 1
  pharmacodynamics 615.71
  surgery 617.41
  veterinary medicine 636.089 61

Cardoso, Fernando Henrique
  Brazilian history 981.064
Cards
  divination 133.324 2
Cards (Games) 795.4
  manufacturing technology 688.754
Carduelidae 598.885
CARE (Firm) 361.763
Career changes
  business 650.14
  executive management 658.409
Career development 370.113
  business 650.1
  industrial psychology 158.7
  see also Vocational education; Vocational guidance
Career education 370.113
  T1—071
  see also Vocational education
Career guidance 331.702
  T1—023
  see also Vocational guidance
Career opportunities 331.702
  T1—023
  see also Vocational guidance
Caregivers 362.042 5
Cargados Carajos Shoals (Mauritius) T2—698 2
Cargo airplanes
  military engineering 623.746 5
Cargo handling 388.044
  see also Freight services
Cargo-handling equipment 623.867
  port engineering 627.34
  ships 623.867
Cargo insurance 368.2
  see also Insurance
Cargo ships 387.245
  petroleum technology 665.543
  power-driven 387.245
    design 623.812 45
    engineering 623.824 5
  wind-driven 387.224
    design 623.812 24
    engineering 623.822 4
  see also Merchant ships; Ships
Caria T2—392 4
Carib Indians (South America) T5—984
Carib language 498.4
  T6—984
Cariban languages 498.4
  T6—984
Caribbean Area 972.9
  T2—729
Caribbean Islands T2—729
Caribbean Sea 551.463 5
  T2—163 65
Caribbees T2—729
Cariboo (B.C. : Regional District) T2—711 75
Cariboo Mountains (B.C.) T2—711 7
Caribou 599.658
  conservation technology 639.979 658
  resource economics 333.959 658
Caribou County (Idaho) T2—796 45
Caricaceae 583.626
Caricatures 741.5
Caries
  dentistry 617.67
  incidence 614.599 6
  see also Dentistry
Carillons 786.64
  see also Mechanical musical instruments
Caring
  ethics 177.7
    religion 291.567 7
      Christianity 241.4
Carinthia (Austria) T2—436 6
Carleton (N.B. : County) T2—715 52
Carleton (Ont.) T2—713 83
Carlisle (England : District) T2—427 89
Carlisle County (Ky.) T2—769 97
Carlow (Ireland : County) T2—418 82
Carlsbad Caverns National Park (N.M.) T2—789 42
Carlton County (Minn.) T2—776 73
Carmarthen (Wales : District) T2—429 65
Carmarthenshire (Wales) T2—429 65
Carmelite Nuns 255.971
  church history 271.971
Carmelites 255.73
  church history 271.73
  women 255.971
    church history 271.971
Carnallite 553.636
  mineralogy 549.4
Carnarvon (South Africa : District) T2—687 17
Carnarvon National Park (Qld.) T2—943 5
Carnations 635.933 53
  botany 583.53
  floriculture 635.933 53

Carnauba wax 665.12
Carnivals 791.1
  customs 394.25
  performing arts 791.1
Carnivora 599.7
  conservation technology 639.979 7
  paleozoology 569.7
  resource economics 333.959 7
Carnivorous animals 591.53
Carnivorous dinosaurs 567.912
Carnivorous plants 583.75
  Byblidaceae 583.72
  Cephalotaceae 583.72
  floriculture 635.933 75
  Lentibulariaceae 583.95
  Nepenthales 583.75
  physiology 575.99
  Sarraceniaceae 583.36
Carnot cycle 536.71
Caro, Joseph
  Jewish legal codes 296.182
Carob 641.344 6
  botany 583.74
  cooking 641.644 6
  food 641.344 6
  orchard crop 634.46
Carolina (South Africa : District) T2—682 7
Caroline County (Md.) T2—752 31
Caroline County (Va.) T2—755 362
Caroline Islands T2—966
Carolingian calligraphy 745.619 74
Carolingian dynasty 944.014
  French history 944.014
  German history 943.014
  Italian history 945.02
Carols 782.28
  choral and mixed voices 782.528
  single voices 783.092 8
Carotid glands
  human anatomy 611.47
  human physiology 612.492
  see also Endocrine system
Carp 641.392
  cooking 641.692
  culture 639.374 83
  food 641.392
  sports fishing 799.174 83
  zoology 597.483
Carp family 597.482
Carpal tunnel syndrome
  medicine 616.87
  see also Nervous system
Carpals
  human anatomy 611.717
  see also Musculoskeletal system
Carpathian Mountains T2—477 9
Carpathos Island (Greece) T2—495 87
  ancient T2—391 7
Carpels 575.665
Carpenter Lake (B.C.) T2—711 31
Carpenters 694.092
  occupational group T7—694
Carpentry 694
  ship hulls 623.844
Carpeting
  building construction 698.9
Carpetmakers 746.792
  occupational group T7—746
Carpets 645.1
  arts 746.7
  household management 645.1
  interior decoration 747.5
  manufacturing technology 677.643
    nonwoven felts 677.632
Carpetweeds 583.53
Carpio 597.483
Carpoids 563.92
Carranza, Venustiano
  Mexican history 972.082 1
Carrera, Rafael
  Guatemalan history 972.810 44
Carriacou Island 972.984 5
  T2—729 845
Carriage horses 636.14
Carriages 388.341
  manufacturing technology 688.6
Carrick (England : District) T2—423 78
Carrickfergus (Northern Ireland) T2—416 17
Carrier language 497.2
  T6—972
Carrier proteins 572.69
Carrier RNA 572.886
Carriers (Common carriers) 388.041
  law 343.093
  see also Passenger services
Carriers (Pneumatic) 621.54
Carrion beetles 595.764 2
Carrion flowers (Asclepiadaceae) 583.93
Carrion flowers (Smilacaceae) 584.356
Carroll County (Ark.) T2—767 17
Carroll County (Ga.) T2—758 39
Carroll County (Ill.) T2—773 345
Carroll County (Ind.) T2—772 94

Carroll County (Iowa) T2—777 465
Carroll County (Ky.) T2—769 373
Carroll County (Md.) T2—752 77
Carroll County (Miss.) T2—762 633
Carroll County (Mo.) T2—778 225
Carroll County (N.H.) T2—742 42
Carroll County (Ohio) T2—771 67
Carroll County (Tenn.) T2—768 25
Carroll County (Va.) T2—755 714
Carrots 641.351 3
  botany 583.849
  commercial processing 664.805 13
  cooking 641.651 3
  food 641.351 3
  garden crop 635.13
Carrying cases
  cameras 771.38
Cars (Automobiles) 388.342
  driving 629.283
  engineering 629.222
  repair 629.287 2
  transportation services 388.342
  see also Automobiles
Carson City (Nev.) T2—793 57
Carson County (Tex.) T2—764 826
Cartagena (Spain) T2—467 7
Cartago (Costa Rica : Province) T2—728 62
Cartan geometry 516.376
Cartels 338.87
  international 338.88
  see also Combinations (Enterprises)
Carter, James Earl
  United States history 973.926
Carter, Jimmy
  United States history 973.926
Carter County (Ky.) T2—769 28
Carter County (Mo.) T2—778 892
Carter County (Mont.) T2—786 36
Carter County (Okla.) T2—766 58
Carter County (Tenn.) T2—768 984
Carteret County (N.C.) T2—756 197
Carterton District (N.Z.) T2—936 7
Cartesian coordinate system 516.16
Carthage (Extinct city) 939.73
  T2—397 3
Carthaginian architecture 722.32
Carthaginian period 939.73
  Spanish history 936.602
  Tunisian history 939.73
Carthusians 255.71
  church history 271.71
  women 255.97
    church history 271.97
Cartier, Jacques
  Quebec history 971.401 2
Cartilage 573.763 56
  human histology 611.018 3
  see also Musculoskeletal system
Cartilaginous fishes 597.3
Cartilaginous ganoids 597.42
Cartographers 526.092
  occupational group T7—526
Cartographic materials
  cataloging 025.346
  library treatment 025.176
Cartography 526
  military engineering 623.71
  military intelligence service 355.343 2
Cartomancy 133.324 2
Cartons 688.8
  paperboard 676.32
Cartoon fiction 741.5
Cartoons 741.5
  T1—022 2
  drawing 741.5
  humorous 741.5
    T1—020 7
  journalism
    comics 070.444
    editorial 070.442
Cartridge tapes (Computer) 004.56
  engineering 621.397 6
Cartridges (Ammunition) 683.406
  manufacturing technology 683.406
  military engineering 623.455
Carts 388.341
  manufacturing technology 688.6
Cārvāka 181.46
Carver County (Minn.) T2—776 53
Carving 730.028
  architectural decoration 729.5
  decorative arts 736
  sculpture 731.46
Carving (Meats) 642.6
Caryophyllales 583.53
Caryophyllidae 583.5
Casaba melon 641.356 117
  cooking 641.656 117
  food 641.356 117
  garden crop 635.611 7
Casablanca (Morocco) T2—643

Casablanca-Anfa
(Morocco : Prefecture) T2—643
Casamance (Senegal) T2—663
Casanare (Colombia :
Intendancy) T2—861 43
Cascade County (Mont.) T2—786 611
Cascade Mountains (B.C.) T2—711 5
Cascade Range T2—795
British Columbia T2—711 5
California T2—794 2
Oregon T2—795
Washington T2—797 5
Cascades
landscape architecture 714
Case (Grammar) 415
specific languages T4—5
Case grammar (Theory) 415
specific languages T4—5
Case histories
medicine 616.09
Case studies (Historical
research) 001.432
T1—072 2
Casein-derived plastics 668.43
Casein glue 668.32
Casein painting 751.422
Caserta (Italy : Province) T2—457 25
Cases (Law) 348.04
international law 341.026 8
Casework 361.32
Casey County (Ky.) T2—769 66
Cash 332.041 2
accounting 657.72
financial management 658.152 44
Cash balance theory 332.401
Cash flow
financial management 658.152 44
Cash management
financial management 658.152 44
Cash-on-delivery mail 383.184
Cash registers
manufacturing technology 681.14
Cash renting
land economics 333.562
Cashews 641.345 73
agriculture 634.573
botany 583.77
cooking 641.645 73
food 641.345 73
Casino (N.S.W.) T2—944 3
Casinos
architecture 725.76
Casks
wooden 674.82

Caspian Sea T2—475
Commonwealth of
Independent States T2—475
Iran T2—551
Caspian seal 599.792
Casquets (England) T2—423 48
Cass County (Ill.) T2—773 465
Cass County (Ind.) T2—772 86
Cass County (Iowa) T2—777 72
Cass County (Mich.) T2—774 12
Cass County (Minn.) T2—776 86
Cass County (Mo.) T2—778 42
Cass County (N.D.) T2—784 13
Cass County (Neb.) T2—782 272
Cass County (Tex.) T2—764 195
Cassations 784.185
Cassava 641.336 82
botany 583.69
commercial processing 664.23
cooking 641.636 82
food 641.336 82
starch crop 633.682
Casserole dishes 641.821
Cassettes (Computer) 004.56
engineering 621.397 6
Cassettes (Sound) 384
bibliographies 011.38
sound reproduction 621.389 324
see also Sound recordings
Cassettes (Video) 384.558
see also Video recordings
Cassia County (Idaho) T2—796 39
Cassiar Mountains (B.C.
and Yukon) T2—711 85
Cassiterite
mineralogy 549.524
Cassowaries 598.53
Cast glassware
decorative arts 748.2
Cast iron 669.141 3
Cast latex 678.533
Castaneoideae 583.46
Castanets 786.873
see also Percussion
instruments
Caste systems 305.512 2
Castellón (Spain :
Province) T2—467 61
Castelo Branco (Portugal :
District) T2—469 33
Castelo Branco, Humberto de
Alencar
Brazilian history 981.063
Castile (Spain) T2—463

Castilla-La Mancha
(Spain) T2—464
Castilla-León (Spain) T2—462
Castilla y León (Spain) T2—462
Casting
arts 730.028
ceramic arts 738.142
sculpture 731.45
Casting (Fishing) 799.124
Casting glass 666.125
Casting latex 678.527
Casting metals 671.2
arts 730.028
decorative arts 739.14
sculpture 731.456
technology 671.2
Casting plastics 668.412
Casting pottery 666.442
arts 738.142
technology 666.442
Castle Morpeth (England) T2—428 83
Castle Point (England : District) T2—426 792
Castlegar (B.C.) T2—711 62
Castlemaine (Vic.) T2—945 3
Castlereagh (Northern Ireland : District) T2—416 51
Castles
architecture 728.81
domestic 728.81
military 725.18
Castles (Chessmen) 794.143
Castor oil 665.353
Castor-oil plant 583.69
Castoridae 599.37
paleozoology 569.37
Castrato voices 782.86
choral and mixed voices 782.86
single voices 783.86
Castro, Cipriano
Venezuelan history 987.063 12
Castro, Fidel
Cuban history 972.910 64
Castro County (Tex.) T2—764 837
Castroism 335.434 7
economics 335.434 7
political ideology 320.532 309 7291
Casual clothes 391
see also Clothing
Casual workers 331.544
Casualty insurance 368.5
law 346.086 5
see also Insurance
Casuariiformes 598.53
paleozoology 568.5
Casuarinales 583.43
Casuistry
ethical systems 171.6
Caswell County (N.C.) T2—756 575
CAT (Air transportation hazard) 363.124 12
Cat breeds 636.8
see Manual at 636.82–636.83
Cat briers 584.356
Cat family (Felidae) 599.75
CAT scan
medicine 616.075 72
Catabolism 572.48
see also Metabolism
Catahoula Parish (La.) T2—763 74
Catalan language 449.9
T6—499
Catalan literature 849.9
Catalans T5—49
Catalases 572.791
see also Enzymes
Cataloging
library science 025.3
museology 069.52
Cataloging in publication 025.3
Catalogs T1—021 6
postal handling 383.124
see also Postal service
Catalogs (Bibliographic materials) 025.31
bibliography 017
library science 025.31
Catalogs of exhibits 069.52
T1—074
museology 069.52
see Manual at T1—074 vs. T1—0294
Catalonia (Spain) T2—467
Catalpas 635.977 395
botany 583.95
ornamental arboriculture 635.977 395
Cataluña (Spain) T2—467
Catalysis 541.395
chemical engineering 660.299 5
Catalytic cracking 665.533
Catamarca (Argentina : Province) T2—824 5
Catamblyrhynchidae 598.88
Catanduanes Island (Philippines) T2—599 1
Catanduanes Province (Philippines) T2—599 1
Catania (Sicily : Province) T2—458 13

Catanzaro (Italy : Province) T2—457 81
Catapults 623.441
Cataracts
ophthalmology 617.742
see also Eyes
Catarrhini 599.86
paleozoology 569.86
Catastrophes 904
see also Disasters
Catastrophes (Biological evolution) 576.84
Catastrophes (Mathematics) 514.74
Catastrophic health insurance 368.382 8
government-sponsored 368.42
law 344.022
see also Insurance
Catawba County (N.C.) T2—756 785
Catawba River (N.C. and S.C.) T2—757 45
Catbirds 598.844
Catch-as-catch-can wrestling 796.812 3
see also Sports
Catch basins
sewers 628.25
Catchers' mitts
manufacturing technology 685.43
Catching
baseball 796.357 23
Catchword indexing 025.486
Catechetics 268
Catechisms 291.2
Christianity 238
Catechists 268.092
biography 268.092
see Manual at 230–280
role and function 268.3
Catechols 547.633
Catechumenate 265.13
Categorial grammar 415
specific languages T4—5
Categories (Mathematics) 511.3
topological algebras 512.55
Catered meals 642.4
Caterers 642.409 2
occupational group T7—642
Catering 642.4
Caterpillars 595.781 39
culture 638.578 139
Catfishes 597.49
see also Catfishes (Channel catfish)
Catfishes (Channel catfish) 641.392
conservation technology 639.977 492
cooking 641.692
culture 639.374 92
food 641.392
resource economics 333.956 492
sports fishing 799.174 92
zoology 597.492
Catharine, the Great
Russian history 947.063
Catharism 273.6
denomination 284.4
see also Christian denominations
persecution of 272.3
Catharists
religious group T7—244
Cathartics
pharmacodynamics 615.732
see also Digestive system
Cathartidae 598.92
Cathcart (South Africa : District) T2—687 5
Cathedral systems
Christian ecclesiology 262.3
Cathedrals
architecture 726.6
religious significance 246.96
Catherine I, Empress of Russia
Russian history 947.061
Catherine II, Empress of Russia
Russian history 947.063
Cathode-ray tubes 621.381 542 2
television engineering 621.388 32
Catholic Church 282
see also Roman Catholic Church
Catholic epistles 227.9
Catholic regions T2—176 12
Catholic schools 371.071 2
Catholicity 262.72
Cation separation analysis 544.12
Catnip 583.96
Catnip tea 641.357
see also Herb teas
Catoosa County (Ga.) T2—758 326
Catron County (N.M.) T2—789 93
Cats 636.8
animal husbandry 636.8
experimental animals
medicine 619.8
predator control technology 636.083 9
zoology 599.752
Cat's cradles 793.96

Catskill Mountains (N.Y.) T2—747 38
Catsup 641.814
  commercial processing 664.58
  home preparation 641.814
Cattails (Plants) 584.68
Cattaraugus County (N.Y.) T2—747 94
Cattle 636.2
  agricultural economics 338.176 2
  animal husbandry 636.2
  zoology 599.642 2
Cattle cars 385.34
  engineering 625.24
  see also Rolling stock
Cattlemen 636.213 092
CATV systems 384.554 6
  see also Television
Cauca (Colombia : Dept.) T2—861 53
Caucasian languages 499.96
  T6—999 6
Caucasian literatures 899.96
Caucasian race T5—034
Caucasians T5—034
Caucasians (Peoples of the Caucasus) T5—999 6
Caucasic languages 499.96
  T6—999 6
Caucasic literatures 899.96
Caucasoid race T5—034
Caucasus 947.5
  T2—475
  ancient 939.5
  T2—395
Caucasus rugs
  arts 746.759
  see also Rugs
Cauchy integral 515.43
Cauchy problem 515.35
Caucus nomination 324.52
Caucuses (Legislative) 328.36
Caudal anesthesia
  surgery 617.964
Caudata 597.85
Caudofoveata 594.2
Caulerpales 579.835
Cauliflower 641.353 5
  commercial processing 664.805 35
  cooking 641.653 5
  food 641.353 5
  garden crop 635.35
Causation
  philosophy 122
Causative (Linguistics) 415
  specific languages T4—5
Cause
  philosophy 122
Causes of war 355.027
Caustic potash 546.383 22
  chemical engineering 661.332
Caustic soda 546.382 22
  chemical engineering 661.322
Cautín (Chile) T2—834 6
Cavalier County (N.D.) T2—784 37
Cavalry (Horse mounted) 357.1
Cavalry (Mechanized) 357.5
Cavalry forces 357
Cavan (Ireland : County) T2—416 98
Cave dwellers 569.9
Cave fishes 597.62
Caves 551.447
  T2—144
  biology 578.758 4
  ecology 577.584
  exploring 796.525
    see also Sports
  geography 910.914 4
  geomorphology 551.447
  physical geography 910.021 44
  psychological influence 155.964
Cavia 599.359 2
Cavies 599.359 2
Caviidae 599.359 2
Caviomorpha 599.359
Cavitation 532.597
  engineering 620.106 4
Cavite Province (Philippines) T2—599 1
Cavities (Teeth)
  dentistry 617.67
  incidence 614.599 6
  see also Dentistry
Cavity resonators 621.381 332
Cayenne (French Guiana) T2—882
Cayenne pepper 641.338 4
  botany 583.952
  see also Hot spices
Cayley algebra 512.5
Cayman Islands 972.921
  T2—729 21
Cayo District (Belize) T2—728 25
Cayuga County (N.Y.) T2—747 68
Cayuga Lake (N.Y.) T2—747 68
CB radio 384.53
  communications services 384.53
  engineering 621.384 54
CBR warfare 358.3
  law 341.735
CCF (Machine-readable format) 025.316

CD-ROMs
  bibliographies 011.3
  cataloging 025.344
  computer memory 004.565
  engineering 621.397 6
  library treatment 025.174
  publishing 070.579 7
CDs (Compact discs) 384
  see also Sound recordings
Ceará (Brazil : State) T2—813 1
Ceasefires 327.17
  law 341.66
Cebidae 599.85
  paleozoology 569.85
Cebu (Philippines) T2—599 5
Cebu Island (Philippines) T2—599 5
Cebuano language 499.21
  T6—992 1
Cecidomyiidae 595.772
Cecil County (Md.) T2—752 38
Cecum
  human anatomy 611.345
  human physiology 612.33
  surgery 617.554 5
  see also Digestive system
Cedar County (Iowa) T2—777 66
Cedar County (Mo.) T2—778 743
Cedar County (Neb.) T2—782 58
Cedar Mountains (South Africa) T2—687 2
Cedarberg (South Africa) T2—687 2
Cedars 585.2
  forestry 634.975 6
  lumber 674.144
Cefalonia (Greece) T2—495 5
CEGEP (Quebec, Canada) 378.154 3
Ceiling coverings
  household management 645.2
Ceilings 721.7
  architecture 721.7
  construction 690.17
  interior decoration 747.3
Celandines 635.933 35
  botany 583.35
  floriculture 635.933 35
Celastrales 583.85
Celebes (Indonesia) T2—598 4
Celebes Sea 551.465 73
  T2—164 73
Celebrations 394.2
  armed forces 355.16
    see also Military commemorations
  cooking 641.568
Celebrations (continued)
  customs 394.2
  public administrative support 353.77
Celeriac 641.351 28
  cooking 641.651 28
  food 641.351 28
  garden crop 635.128
Celery 641.355 3
  botany 583.849
  commercial processing 664.805 53
  cooking 641.655 3
  food 641.355 3
  garden crop 635.53
Celery root 641.351 28
  see also Celeriac
Celestas 786.83
  instrument 786.831 9
  music 786.83
  see also Percussion instruments
Celestial bodies 520
  folklore 398.26
    history and criticism 398.362
Celestial Church of Christ 289.93
  see also Christian denominations
Celestial mechanics 521
  engineering 629.411
Celestial navigation 527
  nautical 623.89
Celestial reference systems 522.7
Celestines 255.16
  church history 271.16
Celestite
  mineralogy 549.752
Celibacy 306.732
  customs 392.6
  ethics 176
    religion 291.566
      Buddhism 294.356 6
      Christianity 241.66
      Hinduism 294.548 66
  psychology 155.3
  religious practice 291.447
    Buddhism 294.344 47
    Christianity 248.47
      clergy 253.25
    Hinduism 294.544 7
  sociology 306.732
Cell biology 571.6
  humans 611.018 1
Cell chemistry 572
Cell culture 571.638
Cell differentiation 571.835

Cell digestion 572.4
Cell division 571.844
Cell-mediated immunity 571.966
  humans 616.079 7
Cell membranes 571.64
Cell metabolism 572.4
Cell movement 571.67
Cell physiology 571.6
  humans 611.018 1
Cell reproduction 571.84
Cell respiration 572.47
Cell walls 571.68
Cellists 787.409 2
  occupational group T7—787
Cello concertos 784.274
Cellos 787.4
  instrument 787.419
  music 787.4
  see also Stringed instruments
Cells (Biology) 571.6
  humans 611.018 1
Cells (Rooms)
  architecture 726.79
Cellular immunity 571.966
  humans 616.079 7
Cellular pathology 571.936
  humans 611.018 15
Cellular radio 384.53
  engineering 621.384 56
Cellular telephones 384.535
  engineering 621.384 56
Cellulases 572.756
  see also Enzymes
Celluloid 668.44
Cellulose 572.566 82
  biochemistry 572.566 82
  chemistry 547.782
  see also Carbohydrates
Cellulose acetate
  textiles 677.464
    see also Textiles
Cellulose derivatives
  chemical engineering 661.802
Cellulosics 668.44
  textiles 677.46
    see also Textiles
Celtic harps 787.95
  see also Stringed instruments
Celtic languages 491.6
  T6—916
Celtic literatures 891.6
Celtic period 936.401
  English history 936.202
  French history 936.401
Celtic regions 944
  T2—44
  ancient 936.4
  T2—364
Celtic religion 299.16
Celts T5—916
Cement 666.94
  economic geology 553.68
  materials science 620.135
  structural engineering 624.183 3
Cement casting
  sculpture 731.452
Cementum
  dentistry 617.634
  see also Dentistry
Cemeteries 363.75
  landscape architecture 718
  public administration 353.6
  World War I 940.465
  World War II 940.546 5
  see also Military commemorations
Cemetery records
  genealogy 929.5
Cenozoic era 551.78
  geology 551.78
  paleontology 560.178
Censored books 098.1
Censorship 363.31
  law 344.053 1
  libraries 025.213
  social control 303.376
  see Manual at 363.31 vs. 303.376, 791.4
Census
  law 342.08
  public administration 352.75
  statistical reports 310
Census bureaus 352.75
Census records
  genealogy 929.3
Census taking (Birds) 598.072 32
Centaurs
  folklore 398.21
  see also Legendary beings
Center Hill Lake (Tenn.) T2—768 532
Centipedes 595.62
Central (Paraguay) T2—892 122
Central (Scotland) T2—413 1
Central Africa 967
  T2—67
Central African Empire T2—674 1
Central African Federation 968.903

Central African Republic 967.41
T2—674 1
Central African Republic people T5—967 41
Central Africans (National group) T5—967 41
Central America 972.8
T2—728
Central America (Federal Republic : 1823–1840) 972.804
T2—728
  Costa Rican history 972.860 42
  Guatemalan history 972.810 42
  Honduran history 972.830 4
  Nicaraguan history 972.850 42
  Salvadoran history 972.840 42
Central American native languages 497
T6—97
Central American native literatures 897
Central American native peoples T5—97
Central Asia 958
T2—58
  ancient 939.6
T2—396
Central Australia T2—942
Central banks 332.11
Central Black Earth Region (Russia) T2—473 5
Central business district
  community redevelopment 307.342
Central Chernozem Region (Russia) T2—473 5
Central Coast (B.C.) T2—711 1
Central Dravidian languages 494.82
T6—948 2
Central Dravidian literatures 894.82
Central Dravidians T5—948 2
Central Europe 943
T2—43
Central Fraser Valley (B.C.) T2—711 37
Central Greece (Greece) T2—495 15
Central Hawke's Bay District (N.Z.) T2—934 69
Central heating 697.03
Central Intelligence Agency (U.S.) 327.127 3
Central Islands and Santa Isabel Province (Solomon Islands) T2—959 35
Central Italy T2—456
Central Kootenay (B.C.) T2—711 62
Central Lowlands (Scotland) T2—413
Central Macedonia (Greece) T2—495 65
Central nervous system 573.86
  biology 573.86
  human anatomy 611.81
  human physiology 612.82
  medicine 616.8
  see also Nervous system
Central Okanagan (B.C.) T2—711 5
Central Otago District (N.Z.) T2—939 4
Central Pacific Basin 551.465 9
T2—164 9
  see Manual at T2—1644 and T2—1648, T2—1649
Central Pacific islands T2—96
Central Powers (World War I) 940.334
Central processing units 004
  engineering 621.39
Central Province (Kenya) T2—676 26
Central Province (Papua New Guinea) T2—954 6
Central Province (Solomon Islands) T2—959 35
Central Province (Zambia) T2—689 4
Central Region (Scotland) T2—413 1
Central Saanich (B.C.) T2—711 28
Central-Southern Region (China) T2—512
Central stations
  steam engineering 621.19
Central Turkic languages 494.34
T6—943 4
Central Valley (Calif. : Valley) T2—794 5
Centralization
  executive management 658.402
  libraries 021.6
  public administration 352.283
  schools 379.153 5
Centralized databases
  computer science 005.75
Centralized processing 004.3
  see also Processing modes—computer science
Centrarchidae 597.738
Centre (France) T2—445
Centre (Haiti) T2—729 442
Centre County (Pa.) T2—748 53
Centre-de-la-Mauricie (Quebec) T2—714 451

Centrifugal blowers	621.63
Centrifugal casting	
metals	671.254
Centrifugal fans	621.63
Centrifugal force	531.113
fluid mechanics	532.059 5
solid mechanics	531.35
Centrifugal pumps	621.67
hydraulic	621.252
Centrifuging latex	678.522
Centripetal force	531.113
fluid mechanics	532.059 5
solid mechanics	531.35
Centrist parties	324.215
international organizations	324.15
Centrocercus	598.636
Centrolenidae	597.87
Centromeres	571.844
Centropomidae	597.72
Century plants	584.352
Cephalaspidea	594.34
Cephalocarida	595.36
Cephalochordata	596.4
paleozoology	566
Cephalophinae	599.64
Cephalopoda	594.5
paleozoology	564.5
Cephalotaceae	583.72
Cephalotaxaceae	585.3
Cepheids	523.844 25
Ceram Sea	551.465 73
	T2—164 73
Cerambycidae	595.764 8
Ceramic artists	738.092
occupational group	T7—738
Ceramic arts	738
Ceramic engineers	666.092
occupational group	T7—666
Ceramic fillings	
dentistry	617.675
see also Dentistry	
Ceramic inlays	
dentistry	617.675
see also Dentistry	
Ceramic materials	553.61
building materials	691.4
chemical engineering	666
economic geology	553.61
materials science	620.14
mining	622.361
pottery	666.42
arts	738.12
sculpture material	731.2
ship hulls	623.845
Ceramic materials (continued)	
shipbuilding	623.820 7
structural engineering	624.183
Ceramic-to-metal bonding	666.042
Ceramics	
materials science	620.14
see also Ceramic materials	
Ceramics industry	338.476 66
equipment manufacturing technology	681.766 6
Ceratophyllaceae	583.29
Ceratopsia	567.915
Cercidiphyllales	583.43
Cercopithecidae	599.86
paleozoology	569.86
Cercopithecus	599.862
Cereal grains	
commercial processing	664.7
Cereal grasses	584.9
forage crops	633.25
see Manual at 633–635: Cereals versus cereal grasses (633.1 vs. 633.25)	
Cereals	641.331
agriculture	633.1
animal feed	636.086
botany	584.9
commercial processing	664.7
cooking	641.631
food	641.331
forage crops	633.25
see Manual at 633–635: Cereals versus cereal grasses (633.1 vs. 633.25)	
Cereals (Breakfast food)	641.331
commercial processing	664.756
cooking	641.631
food	641.331
Cerebellum	
human anatomy	611.81
human physiology	612.827
see also Nervous system	
Cerebral commissures	
human physiology	612.826
see also Nervous system	
Cerebral hemispheres	
human anatomy	611.81
human physiology	612.825
see also Nervous system	
Cerebral infarction	
medicine	616.81
see also Nervous system	

Cerebral ischemia
medicine 616.81
see also Nervous system
Cerebral palsy
medicine 616.836
see also Nervous system
Cerebral peduncles
human physiology 612.826
see also Nervous system
Cerebral sphingolipidosis
medicine 616.858 845
see also Mental retardation
Cerebrospinal fluid
human physiology 612.804 2
see also Nervous system
Cerebrovascular diseases
medicine 616.81
see also Nervous system
Cerebrum
human anatomy 611.81
human physiology 612.825
see also Nervous system
Ceredigion (Wales : District) T2—429 61
Ceremonial robes 391
commercial technology 687.15
customs 391
see also Clothing
Ceremonials 264.022
Ceremonies 390
armed forces 355.17
customs 390
religion 291.38
see also Rites—religion
Ceres (South Africa : District) T2—687 3
Cerigo Island (Greece) T2—495 2
Cerium
chemistry 546.412
see also Rare earths
Cerium-group metals
economic geology 553.494 3
see also Rare earths
Cerro Gordo County (Iowa) T2—777 25
Cerro Largo (Uruguay) T2—895 23
Certainty
epistemology 121.63
Certhiidae 598.82
Certificates of deposit 332.175 2
Certificates of indebtedness (Government) 332.632 32
investment economics 332.632 32
public finance 336.32
Certification 352.84
see also Licensing
Certitude
epistemology 121.63
Cervical caps
health 613.943 5
see also Birth control
Cervical vertebrae
medicine 616.73
see also Musculoskeletal system
Cervicitis
gynecology 618.142
see also Female genital system
Cervidae 599.65
paleozoology 569.65
Cervix (Uterine)
gynecology 618.14
human anatomy 611.66
human physiology 612.62
surgery 618.145
see also Female genital system
Cervus 599.654
César (Colombia) T2—861 23
Cesarean section
obstetrical surgery 618.86
Cesium 669.725
chemical engineering 661.038 5
chemistry 546.385
metallurgy 669.725
see also Chemicals
Cessnock (N.S.W.) T2—944 2
Cestoda 592.46
Cestode-caused diseases
medicine 616.964
see also Communicable diseases (Human)
Cetacea 599.5
conservation technology 639.979 5
paleozoology 569.5
resource economics 333.959 5
Cetewayo, King of Zululand
Natal history 968.404 5
Ceuta (Spain) T2—642
Cévennes Mountains (France) T2—448
Ceylon T2—549 3
Ceylonese T5—914 13
Chabad Lubavitch Hasidism 296.833 22
Chachalacas 598.64
Chaco (Argentina) T2—823 4
Chaco (Paraguay : Dept.) T2—892 26
Chaco Boreal (Paraguay and Bolivia) T2—892 2

Chaco War, 1933–1935 989.207 16
Chaconnes 781.827
 instrumental 784.182 7
Chad 967.43
 T2—674 3
Chadians T5—967 43
Chadic languages 493.7
 T6—937
Chadic literatures 893.7
Chaetodontidae 597.72
Chaetognatha 592.38
 paleozoology 562.38
Chaetomiales 579.567
Chaetophorales 579.83
Chafers 595.764 9
 agricultural pests 632.764 9
Chaffee County (Colo.) T2—788 47
Chafing dish cooking 641.585
Chaga language 496.395
 T6—963 95
Chagas' disease
 incidence 614.533
 medicine 616.936 3
 see also Communicable diseases (Human)
Chagatai language 494.364
 T6—943 64
Chagga language 496.395
 T6—963 95
Chagos Islands 969.7
 T2—697
Chahār Mahāll va Bakhtīarī (Iran : Province) T2—559 5
Chain banking 332.16
Chain drives 621.859
Chain gangs 365.65
Chain hoists 621.863
Chain indexing 025.482
Chain reactions
 chemical engineering 660.299 3
 chemistry 541.393
 nuclear engineering 621.483 1
 organic chemistry 547.139 3
Chain-stitch fabrics 677.66
 see also Textiles
Chain stores 381.12
 management 658.870 2
 see also Commerce
Chains
 power transmission 621.859
Chair cars 385.33
 engineering 625.23
 see also Rolling stock
Chair lifts 621.868
Chairs 645.4
 decorative arts 749.32
 manufacturing technology 684.13
 outdoor furniture 645.8
  see also Outdoor furniture
 see also Furniture
Chaka, Zulu Chief
 Natal history 968.403 9
Chalatenango (El Salvador : Dept.) T2—728 421
Chalcidice (Greece) T2—495 65
Chalcidoidea 595.79
Chalcids 595.79
Chalcis (Extinct city) T2—384
Chalcocite
 mineralogy 549.32
Chaldean Empire 935.04
 T2—35
Chaldeans (Religious order) 255.18
 church history 271.18
Chaldee (Aramaic) language 492.29
 T6—922 9
Chalk 553.68
 economic geology 553.68
 petrology 552.58
Chalk drawing 741.23
Chalkidikē (Greece) T2—495 65
Challoner Bible 220.520 2
Chamaeidae 598.834
Chamaemyiidae 595.774
Chamber music 785
 see Manual at 784–788
Chamber orchestras 784.3
Chambers County (Ala.) T2—761 56
Chambers County (Tex.) T2—764 143
Chambers of commerce 380.106
 architecture 725.25
 domestic trade 381.06
Chambly (Quebec : County) T2—714 37
Chameleons 597.95
Chamic languages 499.22
 T6—992 2
Chamois 599.647
Chamomiles 583.99
Chamorro language 499.2
 T6—992
Champagne 641.222 4
 commercial processing 663.224
Champagne (France : Province) T2—443
Champagne-Ardenne (France) T2—443

Champaign County (Ill.) T2—773 66
Champaign County (Ohio) T2—771 465
Champlain (Quebec : County) T2—714 455
Champlain (Quebec : Regional County Municipality) T2—714 37
Champlain, Lake T2—747 54
  New York T2—747 54
  Vermont T2—743 1
Champlevé
  ceramic arts 738.4
Ch'an Buddhism 294.392 7
Chañaral (Chile : Province) T2—831 42
Chance
  philosophy 123.3
  probabilities 519.2
Chance composition 781.32
Chancel railings 247.1
  architecture 726.529 6
Chancellors (Prime ministers) 321
  cabinet governments 321.804 3
  occupational group T7—351
  public administration 352.23
Chancels
  architecture 726.593
Chancery Division of the High Court of Justice (Great Britain) 347.420 26
Chancroid
  incidence 614.547
  medicine 616.951 8
  see also Communicable diseases (Human)
Chandeliers
  furniture arts 749.63
Chandīgarh (India) T2—545 52
Chandra Shekhar
  Indian history 954.052
Changamire (Kingdom) 968.910 1
  T2—689 1
Change 116
  executive management 658.406
  philosophy 116
  political science 320.011
  sociology 303.4
Changing voices 782.79
  choral and mixed voices 782.79
  single voices 783.79
Chania (Greece : Nome) T2—495 9
Channel bass 597.725
Channel catfish 641.392
  see also Catfishes (Channel catfish)
Channel Islands (Calif.) T2—794 91
Channel Islands (England) T2—423 4
Channel Islands National Park (Calif.) T2—794 91
Channeling (Spiritualism) 133.91
Channels (Navigation)
  engineering 627.23
Channiformes 597.64
Chansons 782.43
Chants (Music) 782.292
  choral and mixed voices 782.529 2
  single voices 783.092 92
Chanukah 296.435
  liturgy 296.453 5
Chaos
  philosophy 117
Chaotic behavior in systems 003.857
Chaotic systems 003.857
Chaouen (Morocco : Province) T2—642
Chaparral biology 578.738
Chaparral ecology 577.38
Chapbooks 398.5
Chapels
  architecture 726.4
Chaperonage
  customs 392.6
Chaplain services (Military) 355.347
  Algerian Revolution 965.046 7
  Chaco War 989.207 167
  Civil War (Spain) 946.081 7
  Civil War (United States) 973.778
  Falkland Islands War 997.110 247
  Indochinese War 959.704 17
  Korean War 951.904 27
  Mexican War 973.627
  Napoleonic Wars 940.277
  Persian Gulf War, 1991 956.704 427
  South African War 968.048 7
  Spanish-American War 973.897
  United States Revolutionary War 973.37
  Vietnamese War 959.704 37
  War of 1812 973.527
  War of the Pacific 983.061 67
  World War I 940.478
  World War II 940.547 8
Chaplaincy 291.61
  Christianity 253
  Judaism 296.61
Chapping
  medicine 616.58
  see also Skin

Chapter houses
  architecture 726.69
Characidae 597.48
Characiformes 597.48
Characins 597.48
Character 155.2
  child psychology 155.418 2
  influence on crime 364.24
  psychology 155.2
Character disorders
  medicine 616.858
  see also Mental illness
Character education 370.114
Character recognition 006.4
  computer engineering 621.399
Character training
  home child care 649.7
Characters (Fictitious persons) 808.802 7
  history and criticism 809.927
  specific literatures T3B—080 27
    history and criticism T3B—092 7
Characters (Symbols)
  printing 686.21
Charades 793.24
Charadrii 598.33
Charadriiformes 598.33
  paleozoology 568.3
Charales 579.839
Charbon
  incidence 614.561
  medicine 616.956
  see also Communicable diseases (Human)
Charcoal
  chemical engineering 662.74
Charcoal cooking 641.58
Charcoal drawing 741.22
Chard 641.354 2
  cooking 641.654 2
  food 641.354 2
  garden crop 635.42
Charente (France) T2—446 5
Charente-Inférieure (France) T2—446 4
Charente-Maritime (France) T2—446 4
Charente River T2—446 5
Charge of particles (Nuclear physics) 539.725
Chari-Nile languages 496.5
  T6—965
Charismatic gifts 234.13
Charismatic movement 270.82
Charismatic spiritual renewal 269
Charitable donations
  financial management 658.153
  tax law 343.052 32
Charitable trusts 361.763 2
  law 346.064
    income tax law 343.052 668
    tax law 343.066 8
  social welfare 361.763 2
Charities 361.7
  see also Welfare services
Chariton County (Mo.) T2—778 25
Chariton River (Iowa and Mo.) T2—778 2
Charity
  ethics 177.7
    religion 291.567 7
      Christianity 241.4
  see also Virtues
Charles I, King of England
  British history 941.062
  English history 942.062
  Scottish history 941.106 2
Charles I, King of Spain
  Spanish history 946.042
Charles II, King of England
  British history 941.066
  English history 942.066
  Scottish history 941.106 6
Charles II, King of Spain
  Spanish history 946.053
Charles III, King of Spain
  Spanish history 946.057
Charles IV, King of France
  French history 944.024
Charles IV, King of Spain
  Spanish history 946.058
Charles V, Holy Roman Emperor
  German history 943.031
  Spanish history 946.042
Charles V, King of France
  French history 944.025
Charles VI, Holy Roman Emperor
  German history 943.052
Charles VI, King of France
  French history 944.026
Charles VII, Holy Roman Emperor
  German history 943.054
Charles VII, King of France
  French history 944.026
Charles VIII, King of France
  French history 944.027

Charles IX, King of France
  French history 944.029
Charles X, King of France
  French history 944.062
Charles City County (Va.) T2—755 44
Charles County (Md.) T2—752 47
Charles Mix County (S.D.) T2—783 382
Charles River (Mass.) T2—744 4
Charlesbourg (Quebec) T2—714 471
Charleston (S.C.) T2—757 915
Charleston (W. Va.) T2—754 37
Charleston County (S.C.) T2—757 91
Charleville (Qld.) T2—943 4
Charlevoix (Quebec : Regional County Municipality) T2—714 49
Charlevoix County (Mich.) T2—774 86
Charlevoix-Est (Quebec) T2—714 49
Charlevoix-Est (Quebec : Regional County Municipality) T2—714 49
Charlevoix-Ouest (Quebec) T2—714 49
Charlotte (N.B.) T2—715 33
Charlotte (N.C.) T2—756 76
Charlotte County (Fla.) T2—759 49
Charlotte County (Va.) T2—755 65
Charlottesville (Va.) T2—755 481
Charlottetown (P.E.I.) T2—717 5
Charlottetown Conference, 1864 971.049
Charlton County (Ga.) T2—758 752
Charm
  personal living 646.76
Charms (Occultism) 133.44
Charnwood (England) T2—425 47
Charophyceae 579.839
Chars 597.554
Charter services 388.042
  air 387.742 8
  bus 388.322 2
  see also Passenger services
Chartered banks 332.122
Chartered surveyors (United Kingdom)
  economics 333.08
Chartering 352.84
  see also Licensing
Charters 352.84
  administrative law 342.066
  constitutional law 342.02
  private law 346.06
  public administration 352.84
  see also Licensing
Charters Towers (Qld.) T2—943 6
Chartreaux cat 636.82
Charts 912
  aeronautics 629.132 54
  diagrammatic T1—022 3
  geography 912
  pictorial T1—022 2
  see Manual at T1—0222 vs. T1—0223
Chārvāka 181.46
Chase (B.C.) T2—711 72
Chase County (Kan.) T2—781 59
Chase County (Neb.) T2—782 87
Chasing metals
  decorative arts 739.15
Chasms 551.442
  T2—144
  geography 910.914 4
  geomorphology 551.442
  physical geography 910.021 44
Chassis 629.24
Chastity
  ethics 176
    religion 291.566
      Buddhism 294.356 6
      Christianity 241.66
      Hinduism 294.548 66
  religious practice 291.447
    Buddhism 294.344 47
    Christianity 248.47
    Hinduism 294.544 7
Chateau Clique 971.038
Châteauguay (Quebec : County) T2—714 33
Chateaux
  architecture 728.8
Chatham County (Ga.) T2—758 724
Chatham County (N.C.) T2—756 59
Chatham Islands (N.Z.) T2—939 9
Chatsworth (South Africa : District) T2—684 5
Chattahoochee County (Ga.) T2—758 476
Chattahoochee River T2—758
Chattanooga (Tenn.) T2—768 82
Chattel mortgages
  law 346.074
Chattisgarhi dialect 491.49
  T6—914 9
Chattisgarhi literature 891.49
Chattooga County (Ga.) T2—758 344
Chaudière River (Quebec) T2—714 71
Chaunceys Line Reserve National Park (S. Aust.) T2—942 32
Chausey Islands (England) T2—423 48

Chautauqua County (Kan.) T2—781 918
Chautauqua County (N.Y.) T2—747 95
Chaves County (N.M.) T2—789 43
Chayahuita language 498
T6—98
Cheat River (W. Va. and Pa.) T2—754 8
Cheatham County (Tenn.) T2—768 462
Cheating 179.8
see also Vices
Cheboygan County (Mich.) T2—774 87
Chebyshev polynomials 515.55
Chechen T5—999 641
Chechen language 499.964 1
T6—999 641
Checheno-Ingushetia (Russia) T2—475 2
Chechnia (Russia) T2—475 2
Chechnya (Russia) T2—475 2
Checkered beetles 595.763
Checkers 794.2
Checking accounts 332.175 2
Checklists T1—021 6
Checkoff (Union dues) 331.889 6
Checks 332.76
law 346.096
Checks and balances 320.404
public administration 352.88
Cheddar cheese 641.373 54
cooking 641.673 54
food 641.373 54
processing 637.354
Cheeks 591.4
descriptive zoology 591.4
human anatomy 611.318
human physiology 612.31
physiology 573.355
see also Digestive system
Cheerfulness 179.9
see also Virtues
Cheerleading 791.64
Cheese 641.373
cooking 641.673
food 641.373
processing 637.3
Cheese foods 641.373 58
cooking 641.673 58
food 641.373 58
processing 637.358
Cheese pies 641.824
Cheetah 599.759
animal husbandry 636.89
Cheilostomata 594.676
Chekiang Province (China) T2—512 42
Chelan County (Wash.) T2—797 59
Chelates 547.590 442 42
Cheliabinskaia oblast´ (Russia) T2—474 3
Chelicerata 595.4
paleozoology 565.4
Cheliff (Algeria : Province) T2—653
Chełm (Poland : Voivodeship) T2—438 4
Chelmsford (England : Borough) T2—426 752
Chelmsford, Frederic John Napier Thesiger, Viscount
Indian history 954.035 7
Chelonia 597.92
paleozoology 567.92
Cheltenham (England) T2—424 16
Chelyabinsk (Russia : Oblast) T2—474 3
Chemical analysis 543
see also Analytical chemistry
Chemical bonds 541.224
Chemical communication 573.929
Chemical compounds 546
engineering 660
Chemical contraceptives
health 613.943 2
pharmacodynamics 615.766
see also Birth control
Chemical crystallography 548.3
Chemical diagnosis
medicine 616.075 6
Chemical engineering 660
Chemical engineers 660.092
occupational group T7—66
Chemical equilibrium 541.392
Chemical fire extinction 628.925 4
Chemical forces (Armed services) 358.34
Chemical industries 338.476 6
technology 660
Chemical instruments 542
manufacturing technology 681.754
Chemical laboratories 542.1
Chemical lasers 621.366 4
Chemical metallurgy 669.9
Chemical mineralogy 549.13
Chemical mutagens 576.542
Chemical pollution 363.738
Chemical preservation
food 664.028 6
home economics 641.46
lumber 674.386
Chemical projectiles 623.451 6

Chemical propulsion 621.435
aircraft 629.134 353
spacecraft 629.475 2
Chemical reactions 541.39
biochemistry 572.43
Chemical reactors 660.283 2
Chemical senses 573.877
human physiology 612.86
Chemical sensory perception
psychology 152.16
Chemical technologists 660.092
occupational group T7—66
Chemical technology 660
Chemical treatment
water supply engineering 628.166
Chemical warfare 358.34
civil defense 363.35
see also Civil defense
Chemical waste disposal 363.728 8
see also Waste control
Chemical wastes
water pollution engineering 628.168 36
Chemical weapons 358.348 2
disarmament 327.174 5
engineering 623.445
law 341.735
military equipment 358.348 2
Chemicals 540
hazardous materials 363.179
see also Hazardous materials
photography 771.5
product safety 363.19
law 344.042 4
see also Product safety
Chemiculture 631.585
Chemiluminescence 541.35
chemical engineering 660.295
Chemisorption 541.33
chemical engineering 660.293
Chemistry 540
applied 660
information systems 025.065 4
see Manual at 530 vs. 500.2; *also at* 530 vs. 540
Chemistry of interfaces 541.33
Chemists 540.92
occupational group T7—541
Chemnitz (Germany) T2—432 162
Chemolithotrophic bacteria 579.32
Chemotaxonomy 578.012
Chemotherapy
medicine 615.58
Chemung County (N.Y.) T2—747 78
Chen 598.417 5
Chenango County (N.Y.) T2—747 73
Chenille 677.617
Chenopodiaceae 583.53
Chepang (Nepalese people) T5—95
Chepang language 495.49
T6—954 9
Cheques 332.76
law 346.096
Cher (France) T2—445 52
Cheremis T5—945 6
Cheremis language 494.56
T6—945 6
Cherimoya 583.22
Cherkas´ka oblast´ (Ukraine) T2—477 6
Cherkasy (Ukraine : Oblast) T2—477 6
Chernenko, K. U. (Konstantin Ustinovich)
Russian history 947.085 4
Chernihiv (Ukraine : Oblast) T2—477 6
Chernihivs´ka oblast´ (Ukraine) T2—477 6
Chernivets´ka oblast´ (Ukraine) T2—477 9
Chernivtsy (Ukraine : Oblast) T2—477 9
Cherokee County (Ala.) T2—761 65
Cherokee County (Ga.) T2—758 253
Cherokee County (Iowa) T2—777 17
Cherokee County (Kan.) T2—781 99
Cherokee County (N.C.) T2—756 99
Cherokee County (Okla.) T2—766 88
Cherokee County (S.C.) T2—757 42
Cherokee County (Tex.) T2—764 183
Cherokee Indians T5—975 5
Cherokee language 497.55
T6—975 5
Cherokee literature 897.55
Cherries 641.342 3
botany 583.73
commercial processing 664.804 23
cooking 641.642 3
food 641.342 3
orchard crop 634.23
ornamental arboriculture 635.977 373
Cherry County (Neb.) T2—782 732
Cherubim and Seraphim Church 289.93
see also Christian denominations
Cherwell (England : District) T2—425 73

Chesapeake (Va.) T2—755 523
Chesapeake Bay (Md. and Va.) 551.461 47
T2—163 47
Chesapeake Bay Region
(Md. and Va.) T2—755 18
Cheshire (England) T2—427 1
Cheshire County (N.H.) T2—742 9
Cheshire swine 636.484
Chess 794.1
equipment technology 688.741
Chess players 794.109 2
sports group T7—794 1
Chessmen 794.1
manufacturing technology 688.741
Chest
human anatomy 611.94
human physiology 612.94
regional medicine 617.54
surgery 617.540 59
Chest bones
human anatomy 611.712
human physiology 612.75
see also Musculoskeletal system
Chest muscles
human anatomy 611.735
see also Musculoskeletal system
Chester (England : City) T2—427 14
Chester County (Pa.) T2—748 13
Chester County (S.C.) T2—757 47
Chester County (Tenn.) T2—768 265
Chester-le-Street
(England : District) T2—428 69
Chester River (Md.) T2—752 34
Chester White swine 636.484
Chesterfield (England :
Borough) T2—425 12
Chesterfield County (S.C.) T2—757 63
Chesterfield County (Va.) T2—755 594
Chesterfield Inlet (N.W.T.) T2—719 4
Chestnut bean 641.356 57
see also Chick-peas
Chestnuts 583.46
cooking 641.645 3
food 641.345 3
forestry 634.972 4
lumber 674.142
nut crop 634.53
Chests (Furniture) 645.4
manufacturing technology 684.16
see also Furniture
Cheviot Hills (England) T2—428 8
Chevrotains 599.63
Chewa (African people) T5—963 918
Chewa language 496.391 8
T6—963 918
Chewa literature 896.391 8
Chewing
animal physiology 573.35
descriptive zoology 591.53
human physiology 612.311
see also Digestive system
Chewing gum 641.338
commercial processing 664.6
food 641.338
Chewing lice 595.757
Cheyenne (Wyo.) T2—787 19
Cheyenne County (Colo.) T2—788 92
Cheyenne County (Kan.) T2—781 112
Cheyenne County (Neb.) T2—782 96
Cheyenne Indians T5—973
Chhattisgarhi dialect 491.49
T6—914 9
Chhattisgarhi literature 891.49
Chi-square test 519.56
Chiapas (Mexico) T2—727 5
Chiaroscuro 701.8
Chiba-ken (Japan) T2—521 37
Chibcha Indians T5—982
Chibchan languages 498.2
T6—982
North America 497.8
T6—978
Chibougamau (Quebec) T2—714 115
Chibougamau Wildlife
Reserve (Quebec) T2—714 14
Chicago (Ill.) T2—773 11
Chicago breakdown 781.653
Chicago school of economics 330.15
Chicanos T5—687 207 3
Chich 641.356 57
see also Chick-peas
Chichester (England :
District) T2—422 62
Chichewa language 496.391 8
T6—963 918
Chichewa literature 896.391 8
Chick-peas 641.356 57
botany 583.74
commercial processing 664.805 657
cooking 641.656 57
food 641.356 57
garden crop 635.657
Chickadees 598.824
Chickamauga Lake (Tenn.) T2—768 82
Chickarees 599.363
Chickasaw County (Iowa) T2—777 315

Chickasaw County (Miss.)	T2—762 942
Chickasaw Indians	T5—973
Chicken (Meat)	641.365
agricultural economics	338.176 513
commercial processing	
economics	338.476 649 3
technology	664.93
cooking	641.665
food	641.365
home preservation	641.493
Chicken pox	
incidence	614.525
medicine	616.914
pediatrics	618.929 14
see also Communicable diseases (Human)	
Chickens	636.5
agricultural economics	338.176 5
animal husbandry	636.5
zoology	598.625
Chicory (Beverage)	641.337 8
agriculture	633.78
botany	583.99
commercial processing	663.97
cooking with	641.637 8
food	641.337 8
home preparation	641.877
Chicory (Salad green)	641.355 4
agriculture	635.54
botany	583.99
commercial processing	664.805 54
cooking	641.655 4
food	641.355 4
Chicot County (Ark.)	T2—767 84
Chicoutimi (Quebec : County)	T2—714 16
Chicozapotes	583.674
see also Sapotaceae	
Chief executives	
executive management	658.42
law	342.062
public administration	352.23
Chiefs of staff	
executive management	658.42
public administration	352.237 229 3
Chieti (Italy : Province)	T2—457 13
Chiga (African people)	T5—963 956
Chiga language	496.395 6
	T6—963 956
Chiggers	595.42
Chihuahua (Dog)	636.76
Chihuahua (Mexico : State)	T2—721 6
Chilako River (B.C.)	T2—711 82
Chilblains	
medicine	616.58
see also Skin	
Chilcotin River (B.C.)	T2—711 75
Child abuse	362.76
criminology	364.155 54
criminal law	345.025 554
family relationships	306.874
medicine	616.858 223
social theology	291.178 327 1
Christianity	261.832 71
social welfare	362.76
law	344.032 76
Child care	649.1
Child care services	362.7
see also Children—social welfare	
Child cooks	641.512 3
Child custody	346.017 3
Child development	305.231
physiology	612.65
psychology	155.4
sociology	305.231
Child labor	331.31
law	344.013 1
Child molesting	364.153 6
law	345.025 36
medicine	616.858 36
Child neglect	362.76
see also Child abuse	
Child-parent relations	306.874
see also Parent-child relations	
Child prostitution	306.745
see also Prostitution	
Child protection	362.76
see also Child abuse	
Child psychology	155.4
Child rearing	649.1
customs	392.13
personal religion	291.441
Christianity	248.845
Judaism	296.74
Child study	305.23
physiology	612.65
psychology	155.4
sociology	305.23
Child support	346.017 2
Child training	649.6
Childbed fever	
obstetrics	618.74
Childbirth	618.4
human physiology	612.63
music	781.582
obstetrics	618.4

Childbirth (continued)
  preparation
    obstetrics 618.24
  psychology 155.646 3
Childhood 305.23
  psychology 155.4
  sociology 305.23
Childhood of Jesus Christ 232.927
Childlessness 306.87
Children 305.23
  T1—083
  T7—054
  art representation 704.942 5
  arts 700.452 054
    T3C—352 054
  civil rights 323.352
  cooking for 641.562 2
  drawing 743.45
  etiquette 395.122
  government programs 353.536
  grooming 646.704 6
  health 613.043 2
    home care 649.4
  institutional buildings
    architecture 725.57
  journalism for 070.483 2
  labor economics 331.31
    law 344.013 1
  legal status 346.013 5
    constitutional law 342.087
    private law 346.013 5
  literature 808.803 520 54
    history and criticism 809.933 520 54
    specific literatures T3B—080 352 054
      history and criticism T3B—093 520 54
  painting 757.5
  physical fitness 613.704 2
  psychology 155.4
  publications for
    bibliographies 011.62
    reviews 028.162
  reading
    library science 028.534
  recreation 790.192 2
    indoor 793.019 22
    outdoor 796.083
  relation to government 323.352
  religion 200.83
    Christianity 270.083
      devotional literature 242.62
      guides to Christian life 248.82
      pastoral care of 259.22
      prayer books 242.82
      religious education 268.432
Children
  religion
    Christianity (continued)
      social theology 261.834 23
    guides to life 291.440 83
    Judaism 296.083
      guides to life 296.708 3
      religious education 296.680 83
    social theology 291.178 342 3
  sex hygiene 613.951
  social aspects 305.23
  social welfare 362.7
    law 344.032 7
    public administration 353.536
    see Manual at 362.7083
  socialization 303.32
  treatment of
    ethics 179.2
      see also Ethical problems
  World War I 940.316 1
  World War II 940.531 61
Children (Progeny) 306.874
  T1—085 4
  T7—044 1
Children of alcoholics
  pediatrics 618.928 619
  social welfare 362.292 3
Children of minorities
  home care 649.157
  psychology 155.457
Children of prisoners 362.829 5
Children of substance abusers
  pediatrics 618.928 69
  social welfare 362.291 3
Children's books
  bibliographies 011.62
  illustration 741.642
  literature 808.899 282
    see also Children's literature
  publishing 070.508 3
Children's church 264.008 3
Children's clothing 391.3
  child rearing 649.4
  commercial technology 687.083
  customs 391.3
  home economics 646.36
  home sewing 646.406
  see also Clothing
Children's diseases 362.198 92
  medicine 618.92
  social welfare 362.198 92
Children's Hearings (Scotland) 345.411 08

Children's homes 362.732
  see also Children—social welfare
Children's hospitals 362.198 92
  see also Health care facilities; Health services
Children's libraries 027.625
  administration 025.197 625
  collection development 025.218 762 5
  use studies 025.587 625
Children's literature 808.899 282
  history and criticism 809.892 82
  rhetoric 808.068
  specific literatures T3B—080 928 2
    history and criticism T3B—099 282
Children's parties 793.21
Children's songs 782.420 83
Children's theater 792.022 6
Children's voices 782.7
  choral and mixed voices 782.7
  single voices 783.7
Childress County (Tex.) T2—764 754
Chile 983
  T2—83
Chile saltpeter 553.64
  economic geology 553.64
  mineralogy 549.732
Chilean cedar 585.4
Chilean literature 860
Chileans T5—688 3
Chili 641.823
Chili peppers 641.338 4
  see also Hot spices
Chilko River (B.C.) T2—711 75
Chilled dishes
  cooking 641.79
Chilliwack (B.C.) T2—711 37
Chiloé (Chile) T2—835 6
Chilopoda 595.62
Chiltern (England) T2—425 97
Chiltern Hill (England) T2—425
Chilterns (England) T2—425
Chilton County (Ala.) T2—761 81
Chimaeriformes 597.38
Chimaltenango (Guatemala : Dept.) T2—728 161
Chimborazo (Ecuador) T2—866 17
Chimbu Province (Papua New Guinea) T2—956 7
Chimeras (Fishes) 597.38
Chimes 786.848
  see also Percussion instruments
Chimneys 721.5
  architecture 721.5
  buildings 697.8
  steam furnaces 621.183
Chimpanzees 599.885
Chin dynasty 931.04
Ch'in dynasty 931.04
China 951
  T2—51
  ancient 931
    T2—31
China (Republic : 1949–) 951.249 05
  T2—512 49
China cabinets 645.4
  manufacturing technology 684.16
  see also Furniture
China fir 585.5
China grass plant 583.45
Chinaberry tree 635.977 377
  botany 583.77
  ornamental arboriculture 635.977 377
Chinandega (Nicaragua : Dept.) T2—728 511
Chinch bugs
  agricultural pests 633.104 975 4
  zoology 595.754
Chinchillas 636.935 93
  animal husbandry 636.935 93
  zoology 599.359 3
Chinchillidae 599.359 3
Chincoteague pony 636.16
Chinese T5—951
Chinese artichoke 641.352
  agriculture 635.2
  botany 583.96
  cooking 641.652
  food 641.352
Chinese calendar 529.329 51
  religion 299.51
Chinese calligraphy 745.619 951
Chinese chess 794.18
Chinese communism 335.434 5
  economics 335.434 5
  political ideology 320.532 309 51
Chinese crested (Dog) 636.76
Chinese evergreen 635.934 64
  botany 584.64
  floriculture 635.934 64
Chinese flower arrangements 745.922 51
Chinese gooseberry 641.344
  see also Kiwi (Fruit)
Chinese ink painting 751.425 1
Chinese language 495.1
  T6—951

Chinese literature		895.1
Chinese opera		782.109 51
Chinese religions		299.51
Chinese rugs		
arts		746.751
see also Rugs		
Chinese Shar-Pei		636.72
Chinese water chestnut		584.84
Chinese wood oil		665.333
Ch'ing dynasty		951.03
Chinook Indians	T5—974 1	
Chinook language		497.41
	T6—974 1	
Chinooks (Winds)		551.518 5
Chinquapins		583.46
Ch'ins		787.75
see also Stringed instruments		
Chinyanja (African people)	T5—963 918	
Chinyanja language		496.391 8
	T6—963 918	
Chios (Greece)	T2—495 82	
Chios Island (Greece)	T2—495 82	
ancient	T2—391 3	
Chip boards		676.183
Chipaya language		498
	T6—98	
Chipewyan Indians	T5—972	
Chipewyan language		497.2
	T6—972	
Chipmunks		599.364
animal husbandry		636.936 4
Chipped soaps		668.124
Chippewa County (Mich.)	T2—774 91	
Chippewa County (Minn.)	T2—776 39	
Chippewa County (Wis.)	T2—775 44	
Chippewa Indians	T5—973	
Chippewa language		497.3
	T6—973	
Chippewa literature		897.3
Chippewa River (Wis.)	T2—775 4	
Chipping		
golf		796.352 34
Chiquimula (Guatemala : Dept.)	T2—728 141	
Chiriguano Indians	T5—983 82	
Chiriquí (Panama : Province)	T2—728 711	
Chirognomy		133.6
Chiromancy		133.6
Chironomidae		595.772
Chiropody		617.585
Chiropractic		
therapeutic system		615.534
see Manual at 615.534		
Chiroptera		599.4
paleozoology		569.4
Chisago County (Minn.)	T2—776 61	
Chiseling		730.028
decorative arts		736
sculpture		731.46
Chita (Russia : Oblast)	T2—575	
Chital		599.65
Chitarrones		787.82
see also Stringed instruments		
Chitin		573.774
chemistry		547.782
see also Carbohydrates		
Chitinskaîa oblast′ (Russia)	T2—575	
Chitons		594.27
Chitrāl District (Pakistan)	T2—549 122	
Chittagong (Bangladesh : Division)	T2—549 23	
Chittenden County (Vt.)	T2—743 17	
Chivalry		394.7
literature		808.803 53
history and criticism		809.933 53
specific literatures	T3B—080 353	
history and criticism	T3B—093 53	
Chives		641.352 6
botany		584.33
cooking		641.652 6
food		641.352 6
garden crop		635.26
Chkalov (Russia : Oblast)	T2—474 3	
Chlamydia infections		
medicine		616.92
see also Communicable diseases (Human)		
Chlamydias		579.327
Chlamydomonadaceae		579.832
Chlef (Algeria : Province)	T2—653	
Chloranthaceae		583.23
Chlordane		
human toxicology		615.951 2
Chlorideae		584.9
Chlorination		
water supply treatment		628.166 2
Chlorine		553.95
chemical engineering		661.073 2
chemistry		546.732
economic geology		553.95
human toxicology		615.91
organic chemistry		547.02
applied		661.891
see also Chemicals		
Chlorite		
mineralogy		549.67
Chlorococcales		579.833

Chloromonadophyta 579.82
Chlorophyceae 579.83
Chlorophylls 572.46
  chemical engineering 661.894
  organic chemistry 547.593
Chlorophyta 579.83
Chloroplastic DNA 572.869
Chloroplasts 571.659 2
Chloroprene rubber 678.72
Chlorpromazine
  pharmacodynamics 615.788 2
  see also Mental illness
Choapa (Chile : Province) T2—832 38
Chocó (Colombia) T2—861 27
Chocolate 641.337 4
  beverage
    commercial processing 663.92
  commercial processing 664.5
  cooking with 641.637 4
  food 641.337 4
Choctaw County (Ala.) T2—761 395
Choctaw County (Miss.) T2—762 694
Choctaw County (Okla.) T2—766 63
Choctaw Indians T5—973
Choctaw language 497.3
  T6—973
Choice
  mathematics 511.65
  psychology 153.83
Choice of entry (Cataloging) 025.322
Choice of vocation 331.702
  T1—023
  see also Vocational guidance
Choir lofts
  architecture 726.593
Choir stalls 247.1
  architecture 726.529 3
Choirs 782.5
Chokeberries 583.73
Chokwe (African people) T5—963 99
Chokwe language 496.399
  T6—963 99
Chokwe-Luchazi languages 496.399
  T6—963 99
Chol Indians T5—974 15
Chol language 497.415
  T6—974 15
Cholera
  incidence 614.514
  medicine 616.932
    see Manual at 616.932 vs. 616.33
  see also Communicable diseases (Human)
Cholesterol 572.579 5
  applied nutrition 613.284
  biochemistry 572.579 5
  chemistry 547.731
Cholic acids
  chemistry 547.737
Choluteca (Honduras : Dept.) T2—728 351
Chondrichthyes 597.3
  paleozoology 567.3
Chondrophora 593.55
Chondrostei 597.42
  paleozoology 567.42
Chongqing Shi (China) T2—513 8
Chontales (Nicaragua) T2—728 527
Chopi (African people) T5—963 97
Chopi languages 496.397
  T6—963 97
Choptank River (Del. and Md.) T2—752 31
Choral music 782.5
Choral recitations
  literature 808.855
    history and criticism 809.55
    specific literatures T3B—505
      individual authors T3A—5
Choral speaking 808.55
  elementary education 372.676
  literature 808.855
    history and criticism 809.55
  music 782.96
  rhetoric 808.55
Chorale preludes 784.189 92
  musical form 784.189 92
  organ music 786.518 992
Chorales 782.27
  instrumental form 784.189 925
Chordata 596
  see also Vertebrates
Chordophones 787
  see also Stringed instruments
Chords (Music) 781.252
Chorea
  medicine 616.851
  see also Nervous system
Choreographers 792.820 92
  occupational group T7—792 8
Choreography 792.82
  musical plays 792.62
Choreology 792.82
Chorionic villus biopsy
  obstetrics 618.320 427 5
Chorley (England) T2—427 615

Choroids
  human physiology 612.842
  ophthalmology 617.72
  see also Eyes
Chosen people (Judaism) 296.311 72
Chou dynasty 931.03
Chouteau County (Mont.) T2—786 293
Chow chow 636.72
Chowan County (N.C.) T2—756 147
Chowan River (N.C.) T2—756 15
Chrétien, Jean
  Canadian history 971.064 8
Christchurch (England : Borough) T2—423 39
Christchurch (N.Z.) T2—938 3
Christchurch City (N.Z.) T2—938 3
Christening 265.1
  customs 392.12
  music 781.582
Christian and Missionary Alliance 289.9
  see also Christian denominations
Christian art 704.948 2
  religious significance 246
Christian Brothers 255.78
  church history 271.78
Christian calendars 529.4
  religion 263.9
Christian church 260
  history 270
  local 250
  specific denominations 280
  see Manual at 260 vs. 251–254, 259
Christian Church (Disciples of Christ) 286.63
  see also Disciples of Christ
Christian County (Ill.) T2—773 81
Christian County (Ky.) T2—769 78
Christian County (Mo.) T2—778 792
Christian democratic parties 324.218 2
  international organizations 324.182
Christian denominations 280
  T1—088 204
  church government 262.01–.09
    parishes 254.01–.09
  church law 262.98
  doctrines 230.1–.9
    catechisms and creeds 238.1–.9
  general councils 262.51–.59
  guides to Christian life 248.48
  missions 266.1–.9
  moral theology 241.04
Christian denominations (continued)
  public worship 264.01–.09
  religious associations 267.18
  religious education 268.8
  religious group T7—204
  religious orders 255
    church history 271
    women's 255.9
  seminaries 230.073
  theology 230.1–.9
  see Manual at T1—0882 and 200; *also at* 283–289
Christian doctrine 230
Christian education 268
  see Manual at 268 vs. 230.071
Christian ethics 241
Christian holidays 263.9
  customs 394.266
  devotional literature 242.3
  sermons 252.6
  see also Holidays
Christian initiation 265.1
Christian leadership 262.1
  local church 253
Christian life 248.4
Christian-Marxist dialogue
  Christian theology 261.21
Christian Methodist Episcopal Church 287.83
  see also Methodist Church
Christian names 929.44
Christian philosophy 190
Christian Reformed Church 285.731
  see also Reformed Church (American Reformed)
Christian regions T2—176 1
Christian sacred music 781.71
  public worship 782.32
    music 782.32
      choral and mixed voices 782.532
      single voices 783.093 2
    religion 264.2
  religious symbolism 246.75
Christian schools (General education) 371.071
Christian Science 289.5
  see also Christian denominations
Christian Scientists
  biography 289.509 2
  religious group T7—285

Christian socialism 335.7
economics 335.7
political ideology 320.531 2
Christiana (South Africa : District) T2—682 4
Christianity 230
art representation 704.948 2
religious significance 246
arts 700.482 3
T3C—382 3
religious significance 246
Islamic polemics 297.293
literature 808.803 823
history and criticism 809.933 823
specific literatures T3B—080 382 3
history and criticism T3B—093 823
Christianity and anti-Semitism 261.26
Christianity and atheism 261.21
Christianity and culture 261
Christianity and Islam 261.27
Christian view 261.27
Islamic view 297.283
Christianity and Judaism 261.26
Christian view 261.26
Jewish view 296.396
Christianity and occultism 261.513
Christianity and other religions 261.2
Christianity and politics 261.7
Christianity and secular disciplines 261.5
see Manual at 261.5; *also at* 261.5 vs. 231–239
Christianity in public schools 379.28
Christians 270.092
religious group T7—204
specific denominations 280
see Manual at 280: Biography
see Manual at 230–280
Christmas 263.915
arts 700.434
T3C—334
customs 394.266 3
devotional literature 242.335
literature 808.803 34
history and criticism 809.933 34
specific literatures T3B—080 334
history and criticism T3B—093 34
sermons 252.615
Christmas cards 394.266 3
customs 394.266 3
handicrafts 745.594 12
Christmas carols 782.281 723
Christmas cooking 641.568
Christmas decorations 394.266 3
customs 394.266 3
handicrafts 745.594 12
Christmas Island (Indian Ocean) T2—948
Christmas Island (Kiribati) T2—964
Christmas music 781.723
Christmas ornaments 394.266 3
customs 394.266 3
making 688.726
handicrafts 745.594 12
technology 688.726
Christmas roses 635.933 34
botany 583.34
floriculture 635.933 34
Christmas seals (Prints) 769.57
Christmas story 232.92
Christmas trees
ornamental arboriculture 635.977 5
Christology 232
see Manual at 232
Chromates
mineralogy 549.752
Chromatids 571.844
Chromatin 572.87
Chromatographic analysis 543.089
qualitative 544.92
quantitative 545.89
Chrome brick 666.72
Chromite
mineralogy 549.526
Chromium 669.734
chemical engineering 661.053 2
chemistry 546.532
decorative arts 739.58
economic geology 553.464 3
materials science 620.189 34
metallography 669.957 34
metallurgy 669.734
metalworking 673.734
mining 622.346 43
organic chemistry 547.055 32
applied 661.895
physical metallurgy 669.967 34
see also Chemicals; Metals
Chromium group
chemical engineering 661.053
chemistry 546.53
Chromolithography 764.2
Chromoproteins 572.68
biochemistry 572.68
chemistry 547.754
see also Proteins

Chromosomal DNA 572.86
  humans 611.018 16
Chromosome mapping 572.863 3
  humans 611.018 16
Chromosomes 572.87
  humans 611.018 16
  see Manual at 572.8
Chromosphere of sun 523.75
Chronic diseases
  medicine 616.044
  see also Diseases (Human)
Chronic fatigue syndrome
  medicine 616.047 8
  see also Diseases (Human)
Chronic obstructive pulmonary disease
  medicine 616.24
  see also Respiratory system
Chronic pain
  symptomatology 616.047 2
Chronicles 900
  see also History
Chronicles (Biblical books) 222.6
Chronobiology 571.77
Chronographs
  astronomy 522.5
  technology 681.118
Chronologies 902.02
  T1—020 2
Chronologists 529.092
Chronology 529
Chronometers
  astronomy 522.5
  technology 681.118
Chronoscopes
  technology 681.118
Chroococcales 579.39
Chrysanthemums 635.933 99
  botany 583.99
  floriculture 635.933 99
Chrysobalanaceae 583.73
Chrysocloridae 599.335
Chrysocolla
  mineralogy 549.64
Chrysomelidae 595.764 8
Chrysomeloidea 595.764 8
Chrysophyceae 579.86
Chrysophyta 579.86
Chubs 597.482
  sports fishing 799.174 82
Chūbu Region (Japan) T2—521 6
Chubut (Argentina) T2—827 4
Chuckchee Sea 551.468 5
  T2—163 25
Chucks 621.992
Chūgoku Region (Japan) T2—521 9
Chukchi (Russia : Okrug) T2—577
Chukchi-Kamchatkan languages 494.6
  T6—946
Chukchi Sea 551.468 5
  T2—163 25
Chukotskiĭ avtonomnyĭ okrug (Russia) T2—577
Chulalongkorn, King of Siam
  Thai history 959.303 5
Chulupí language 498
  T6—98
Chumashan Indians T5—975 7
Ch'ung-ch'ing shih (China) T2—513 8
Chungking (China) T2—513 8
Chuquisaca (Bolivia) T2—842 4
Church 260
  ecclesiology 262
  history 270
    specific denominations 280
  local 250
Church and state 322.1
  social theology 291.177
    Christianity 261.7
  see also Politics and religion
  see Manual at 322.1 vs. 261.7, 291.177
Church authority 262.8
Church buildings
  architecture 726.5
  institutional housekeeping 647.985
  landscape architecture 712.7
  management 254.7
  religious significance 246.9
Church calendar 263.9
  chronology 529.44
Church camps 796.542 2
Church controversies 262.8
  local church 250
  specific denominations 280
Church etiquette 395.53
Church fathers 270
  biography 270.092
  religious group T7—211
Church finance 262.006 81
  local church 254.8
Church furniture 247.1
Church government 262
  local church 254
Church group work 253.7
Church growth
  local church 254.5
  missionary work 266

Church history 270
  specific denominations 280
Church holidays 263.9
  customs 394.266
  devotional literature 242.3
  sermons 252.6
  see also Holidays
Church in public education 379.28
Church law 262.9
Church membership
  local church 254.5
Church modes 781.263
Church music 781.71
Church of Christ, Scientist 289.5
  see also Christian denominations
Church of England 283.42
  church government 262.034 2
    parishes 254.034 2
  church law 262.983 42
  doctrines 230.3
    catechisms and creeds 238.3
  guides to Christian life 248.483
  liturgy 264.03
  missions 266.3
  moral theology 241.043
  persecution by Queen Mary 272.6
  religious associations 267.183 42
  religious education 268.834 2
  religious orders 255.83
    church history 271.83
    women 255.983
      church history 271.983
  seminaries 230.073 342
  theology 230.3
Church of God General Conference 286.73
  see also Adventists
Church of God in Christ, Mennonites 289.73
  see also Mennonite Church
Church of Jesus Christ of Latter-Day Saints 289.332
  see also Mormon Church
Church of North India 287.95
  see also Christian denominations
Church of Scotland 285.233
  see also Presbyterian Church
Church of South India 287.94
  see also Christian denominations
Church of the Brethren 286.5
  see also Baptists
Church of the Nazarene 287.99
  religious group T7—27
  see also Christian denominations
Church of the New Jerusalem 289.4
  see also Christian denominations
Church organization 262
Church polity 262
Church presses
  publishing 070.594
Church-related colleges and universities 378.071
  see also Higher education
Church renewal 262.001 7
Church schools (General education) 371.071
  libraries 027.83
Church services 264
  flower arrangements 745.926
  music 782.32
Church Slavic language 491.817 01
  T6—918 17
Church Slavic literature 891.81
Church Slavonic language 491.817 01
  T6—918 17
Church Slavonic literature 891.81
Church suppers 642.4
Church welfare work 361.75
Church work with disabled persons 259.44
Church work with families 259.1
Church work with juvenile delinquents 259.5
Church work with the aged 259.3
Church work with the sick 259.4
Church work with young adults 259.25
Church work with youth 259.23
Church year 263.9
  chronology 529.44
  devotional literature 242.3
  music 781.72
  sermon preparation 251.6
  sermons 252.6
Church youth groups 259.23
Churches of Christ 286.63
  see also Disciples of Christ
Churches of Christ in Christian Union 289.9
  see also Christian denominations
Churches of God 289.9
  see also Christian denominations

Churchill (Man.) T2—712 71
Churchill County (Nev.) T2—793 52
Churchill River (Sask. and Man.) T2—712 71
Chūsei period 952.02
Chutes-de-la-Chaudière (Quebec) T2—714 59
Chutney 641.814
  commercial processing 664.58
  home preparation 641.814
Chuvash language 494.315
  T6—943 15
Chuvash literature 894.315
Chuvashes T5—945 6
Chuvashia (Russia) T2—474 6
Chyromyiidae 595.774
Chytridiomycetes 579.53
CIA (Intelligence agency) 327.127 3
Cibola County (N.M.) T2—789 91
Cicadas 595.752
Cicewâ language 496.391 8
  T6—963 918
Cicewâ literature 896.391 8
Cichlidae 597.74
  culture 639.377 4
Cicindelidae 595.762
Ciconiidae 598.34
Ciconiiformes 598.34
  paleozoology 568.3
Cider 641.341 1
  commercial processing 663.63
  cooking with 641.641 1
  fermented 641.229
    commercial processing 663.2
  food 641.341 1
Ciechanów (Poland : Voivodeship) T2—438 4
Ciego de Avila (Cuba : Province) T2—729 153
Cienfuegos (Cuba : Province) T2—729 143
Cigar flower 583.76
Cigarette holders 688.4
Cigarettes 679.73
Cigars 679.72
Cilia 571.67
Ciliary bodies
  human physiology 612.842
  ophthalmology 617.72
  see also Eyes
Ciliatea 579.49
Ciliates 579.49
Cilicia T2—393 5
Ciliophora 579.49
CIM (Manufacturing) 670.285
Cimarron County (Okla.) T2—766 132
Cimbaloms 787.74
  see also Stringed instruments
Cinchonas 583.93
  medicinal crops 633.883 93
Cincinnati (Ohio) T2—771 78
Cinclidae 598.832
Cinder blocks 666.894
  building construction 693.4
  building materials 691.3
  manufacturing technology 666.894
  materials science 620.139
  structural engineering 624.183 2
Cinema 791.43
  see also Motion pictures
Cinemas
  architecture 725.823
Cinematography 778.53
  see Manual at 791.43, 791.45 vs. 778.5
Cinemax 384.555 4
  see also Television
Cinnabar
  mineralogy 549.32
Cinnamon 641.338 3
  botany 583.23
  see also Spices
Cinque Ports (England) T2—422 352
Cinquefoils 583.73
CIO (Labor) 331.883 309 73
CIP (Cataloging) 025.3
Ciphers (Cryptography) 652.8
  computer science 005.82
Circadian rhythms 571.77
Circassian languages 499.962 4
  T6—999 624
Circassians T5—999 624
Circle geometry 516.184
Circle-squaring 516.204
Circles 516.15
Circuit breakers 621.317
Circuit courts 347.02
Circuit switching 621.381 537
  communications engineering 621.382 16
  computer communications 004.66
    engineering 621.398 1
Circuits 621.319 2
  computer engineering 621.395
  electronics 621.381 5
  microwave electronics 621.381 32
  radio engineering 621.384 12

Circular buildings 720.48
  architectural construction 721.042
  architecture 720.48
Circular manic-depressive
    psychoses
  medicine 616.895
  see also Mental illness
Circulars
  direct advertising 659.133
  postal handling 383.124
    see also Postal service
Circulation (Biology) 573.1
  animals 573.1
  brain 573.862 1
    human physiology 612.824
    see also Nervous system
  human physiology 612.1
  plants 575.7
  see also Cardiovascular
      system
Circulation (Meteorology) 551.517
Circulation services
  library science 025.6
  museology 069.13
Circulation theory (Economics) 332.401
Circulatory fluids 573.15
  biology 573.15
  human physiology 612.1
  plants 575.75
  see also Cardiovascular
      system
Circulatory organs
  human anatomy 611.1
  human physiology 612.1
Circulatory system 573.1
  animals 573.1
  plants 575.7
  see also Cardiovascular
      system
Circumcision 392.1
  customs 392.1
  female
    gynecology 618.16
  Jewish rites 296.442 2
    liturgy 296.454 22
  male
    surgery 617.463
  music 781.582
Circumcision of Jesus Christ 232.92
Circumstantial evidence 347.064
  criminal investigation 363.25
  criminal law 345.064
  law 347.064
Circumterrestrial flights
  manned 629.454
  unmanned 629.435 2
Circus animals 791.32
  animal husbandry 636.088 8
Circus performers 791.309 2
  occupational group T7—791 3
Circuses 791.3
Cire perdue casting
  metals 671.255
Cirques (Geologic landforms) 551.315
Cirrhosis
  medicine 616.362 4
  see also Digestive system
Cirripedia 595.35
  paleozoology 565.35
CISC (Computer science) 004.3
  see also Processing modes—
      computer science
Ciskei (South Africa) T2—687 92
Cistaceae 583.625
Cistercians 255.12
  church history 271.12
  women 255.97
    church history 271.97
Citation indexing 025.48
Citations
  armed forces 355.134
    see also Military
        commemorations
Citators to cases 348.047
  United States 348.734 7
Citators to laws 348.027
  United States 348.732 7
Citharinidae 597.48
Cities 307.76
   T2—173 2
  arts T3C—321 732
  government 320.85
  influence on precipitation 551.577 5
  literature 808.803 217 32
    history and criticism 809.933 217 32
    specific literatures T3B—080 321 732
      history and criticism T3B—093 217 32
  psychological influence 155.942
  public administration 352.16
    control by higher
        jurisdictions 353.336
    see Manual at 351.3–351.9
        vs. 352.13–352.19
  public administrative support 352.793
  social services to residents 361.917 32
    public administration 353.533 3

Cities (continued)
  sociology 307.76
  see Manual at T2—4–T2—9: Cities, towns, villages; *also at* T2—41 and T2—42; *also at* T2—93
Citizen participation 323.042
  crime prevention 364.43
  election campaigns 324.72
  social welfare 361.25
Citizens advice bureaus 361.06
Citizens and state 323
  see also Civil rights
Citizens band radio 384.53
  communications services 384.53
  engineering 621.384 54
    see Manual at 621.38416 vs. 621.38454
  see also Radiotelephony
Citizenship 323.6
  elementary education 372.832
  ethics 172.1
    see also Political ethics
  international law 341.482
  law 342.083
  political science 323.6
  public administration 353.48
  social theology 291.177
    Christianity 261.7
    Judaism 296.382
Citric acid cycle 572.475
Citronella 584.92
Citrons 641.343 31
  cooking 641.643 31
  food 641.343 31
  orchard crop 634.331
Citrus County (Fla.) T2—759 72
Citrus fruits 641.343 04
  botany 583.77
  commercial processing 664.804 304
  cooking 641.643 04
  food 641.343 04
  orchard crop 634.304
Citterns 787.85
  see also Stringed instruments
City churches 250.917 32
  administration 254.22
  pastoral theology 253.091 732
City colleges 378.052
  see also Higher education
City core
  community redevelopment 307.342
City directories 910.25
City gas 665.772
City government 320.85
City government buildings
  architecture 725.13
City-manager government 320.854
City managers
  public administration 352.232 16
City noise 363.741
  technology 620.23
  see also Noise
City planners 711.409 2
  occupational group T7—309
City planning 307.121 6
  civic art 711.4
  law 346.045
  public administration 354.353
City schools 371.009 173 2
City-states 321.06
City traffic 388.41
  law 343.098 2
City warfare 355.426
Cityscapes
  drawing 743.84
  fine arts 704.944
  painting 758.7
Ciudad da La Habana (Cuba) T2—729 123
Ciudad Real (Spain : Province) T2—464 5
Civets 599.742
Civic action of armed forces 355.34
Civic art 711
  see Manual at 307.12 vs. 711
Civic centers 307.33
  architecture 725.1
  area planning 711.551
  community sociology 307.33
Civics 320.4
  elementary education 372.832
Civil actions 347.053
Civil commotion insurance 368.125
  see also Insurance
Civil defense 363.35
  international law 341.72
  law 344.053 5
  public administration 353.95
Civil disobedience 303.61
  ethics 172.1
    religion 291.562 1
      Christianity 241.621
      Buddhism 294.356 21
      Hinduism 294.548 621
      Judaism 296.362 1
  law 342.085 4
  political action 322.4

Civil disobedience (continued)
  social conflict 303.61
  social theology 291.177
    Christianity 261.7
    Judaism 296.382
Civil disorder 303.62
  social conflict 303.62
  social services 363.349 7
Civil Division of Court of Appeal (Great Britain) 347.420 35
Civil engineering 624
  see Manual at 624 vs. 624.1; *also at* 624 vs. 690
Civil engineers 624.092
  occupational group T7—624
Civil law (Legal system) 340.56
  see Manual at 340.56 vs. 342–347
Civil liberties 323
  see also Civil rights
Civil-military relations 322.5
Civil procedure 347.05
  public administration 353.44
Civil rights 323
  government programs 353.48
  international law 341.481
  law 342.085
  legal theory 340.112
  political science 323
  social theology 291.177
    Buddhism 294.337 7
    Christianity 261.7
    Hinduism 294.517 7
    Islam 297.272
    Judaism 296.382
  social welfare 361.614
Civil rights leaders 323.092
Civil rights violations 364.132 2
  law 345.023 22
  public administration 353.46
Civil rights workers 323.092
  occupational group T7—323
Civil service (Merit system) 352.63
  law 342.068
Civil service (Nonmilitary government agencies) 351
Civil service examinations 351.076
  T1—076
Civil service pensions 331.252 913 51
  public administration 353.549
Civil service workers 352.63
  see also Government workers
Civil supremacy over the military 322.5
Civil war 355.021 8
  ethics 172.1
  international law 341.68
  social conflict 303.64
  social theology 291.177
    Buddhism 294.337 7
    Christianity 261.7
    Hinduism 294.517 7
    Judaism 296.382 7
Civil War (England), 1642–1649 942.062
Civil War (Spain), 1936–1939 946.081
Civil War (United States), 1861–1865 973.7
Civilian workers 331.79
  armed forces 355.23
    management 355.619
  labor economics 331.79
    labor force 331.119 042
    labor market 331.129 042
Civilization 909
  arts 700.458
    T3C—358
    specific places 700.42
      T3C—32
  Bible 220.95
  elementary education 372.89
  history 909
    ancient 930
    specific places 930–990
    see also History
  literature 808.803 58
    history and criticism 809.933 58
    specific literatures T3B—080 358
      history and criticism T3B—093 58
    specific places 808.803 2
      history and criticism 809.933 2
      specific literatures T3B—080 32
        history and criticism T3B—093 2
  painting 758.99
  sociology 306
  see Manual at 305 vs. 306, 909, 930–990; *also at* 909, 930–990 vs. 910
Clackamas County (Or.) T2—795 41
Clackmannan (Scotland : District) T2—413 15
Cladding
  buildings 698
  nuclear engineering 621.483 35
Cladding metals 671.73
Cladistic analysis 578.012
Cladocera 595.32

Cladocopa 595.33
paleozoology 565.33
Cladoselachii 567.3
Claiborne County (Miss.) T2—762 285
Claiborne County (Tenn.) T2—768 944
Claiborne Parish (La.) T2—763 94
Claiming
library acquisitions 025.236
Claims (Customer)
marketing management 658.812
Claims (Insurance) 368.014
Claims adjustment
insurance 368.014
Claims against government
public administration 352.885
Claims courts 347.04
Clairaudience 133.85
Clairvoyance 133.84
Clairvoyants 133.840 92
occupational group T7—13
Clallam County (Wash.) T2—797 99
Clam shrimps 595.32
Clamming 639.44
sports 799.254 4
Clamps 621.992
Clams 594.4
conservation technology 639.974 4
cooking 641.694
fishing 639.44
food 641.394
commercial processing 664.94
resource economics 333.955 44
sports clamming 799.254 4
zoology 594.4
Clandestine publications
bibliographies 011.56
Clanwilliam (South Africa : District) T2—687 2
Clare (Ireland) T2—419 3
Clare (S. Aust.) T2—942 32
Clare County (Mich.) T2—774 71
Clarendon County (S.C.) T2—757 81
Claricipitales 579.567
Clarinet concertos 784.286 2
Clarinetists 788.620 92
occupational group T7—788
Clarinets 788.62
instrument 788.621 9
music 788.62
see also Woodwind instruments
Clarion County (Pa.) T2—748 69
Clark, Charles Joseph
Canadian history 971.064 5
Clark, Joe
Canadian history 971.064 5
Clark County (Ark.) T2—767 49
Clark County (Idaho) T2—796 57
Clark County (Ill.) T2—773 71
Clark County (Ind.) T2—772 185
Clark County (Kan.) T2—781 77
Clark County (Ky.) T2—769 54
Clark County (Mo.) T2—778 343
Clark County (Nev.) T2—793 13
Clark County (Ohio) T2—771 49
Clark County (S.D.) T2—783 22
Clark County (Wash.) T2—797 86
Clark County (Wis.) T2—775 28
Clarke County (Ala.) T2—761 245
Clarke County (Ga.) T2—758 18
Clarke County (Iowa) T2—777 856
Clarke County (Miss.) T2—762 673
Clarke County (Va.) T2—755 98
Clarkias 635.933 76
botany 583.76
floriculture 635.933 76
Class actions 347.053
Class groups (Mathematics) 512.74
Class numbers 512.74
Class schedules 371.242
Class size (Education) 371.251
Class struggle 305.5
influence on crime 364.256
Marxian theory 335.411
theory of union role 331.880 1
Classed catalogs
bibliography 017
library science 025.315
Classes (Education) 371.25
museum services 069.15
Classical Arabic language 492.7
T6—927
Classical Arabic literature 892.7
Classical architecture 722.8
Classical conditioning 153.152 6
Classical economics 330.153
Classical education
secondary level 373.242
Classical geometry 516.02
Classical Greek language 480
T6—81
Classical Greek literature 880
Classical high schools 373.242
see also Secondary education
Classical languages (Greek and Latin) 480
T6—8

Classical literatures (Greek and Latin) 880
Classical mechanics 531
see Manual at 530.12 vs. 531
Classical music 781.68
Classical physics 530
theory 530.14
Classical religion 292
temples and shrines
architecture 726.12
Classical revival 709.034 1
Classical revival architecture 724.2
Classical revival decoration 745.444 1
Classical revival painting 759.051
Classical revival sculpture 735.22
Classical statistical mechanics 530.132
Classical typology (Psychology) 155.262
Classicism
arts 700.414 2
T3C—142
literature 808.801 42
history and criticism 809.914 2
specific literatures T3B—080 142
history and criticism T3B—091 42
music 780.903 3
Classification 001.012
T1—012
information science 025.42
knowledge 001.012
Classified catalogs
bibliography 017
library science 025.315
Classroom discipline 371.102 4
Classroom management 371.102 4
Classroom reading programs
elementary education 372.427
Classroom techniques 371.3
Classrooms 371.621
Clatsop County (Or.) T2—795 46
Clauses (Grammar) 415
specific languages T4—5
Claves 786.872
see also Percussion instruments
Clavichords 786.3
instrument 786.319
music 786.3
see also Keyboard instruments
Clavicles
human anatomy 611.717
see also Musculoskeletal system
Clawless otters 599.769
Claws 591.47
descriptive zoology 591.47
physiology 573.59
Clay 553.61
building materials 691.4
economic geology 553.61
materials science 620.191
mineralogy 549.6
mining 622.361
petrology 552.5
pottery 666.42
arts 738.12
technology 666.42
sculpture material 731.2
Clay County (Ala.) T2—761 58
Clay County (Ark.) T2—767 995
Clay County (Fla.) T2—759 16
Clay County (Ga.) T2—758 927
Clay County (Ill.) T2—773 795
Clay County (Ind.) T2—772 44
Clay County (Iowa) T2—777 153
Clay County (Kan.) T2—781 275
Clay County (Ky.) T2—769 145
Clay County (Minn.) T2—776 92
Clay County (Miss.) T2—762 945
Clay County (Mo.) T2—778 16
Clay County (N.C.) T2—756 985
Clay County (Neb.) T2—782 357
Clay County (S.D.) T2—783 393
Clay County (Tenn.) T2—768 49
Clay County (Tex.) T2—764 542
Clay County (W. Va.) T2—754 67
Clay pigeons 799.313 2
Clayton County (Ga.) T2—758 432
Clayton County (Iowa) T2—777 36
Clean rooms
safety engineering 620.86
Cleaning
pneumatic engineering 621.54
technology 667.1
Cleaning crops 631.56
Cleaning house 648.5
Cleaning metals 671.7
Cleanliness 613.4
personal customs 391.64
personal grooming 646.71
personal health 613.4
Cleansing tissues 676.284 2
Clear-air turbulence
transportation hazard 363.124 12
Clear Creek County (Colo.) T2—788 61

Clearance (Banking) 332.178
central banking 332.113
commercial banking service 332.178
Clearfield County (Pa.) T2—748 61
Clearing banks 332.12
Clearing houses (Banking) 332.12
Clearing of land 631.61
Clearwater County (Idaho) T2—796 88
Clearwater County (Minn.) T2—776 83
Clearwater River (B.C.) T2—711 72
Clearwater River (Idaho) T2—796 85
Cleavage
geology 551.84
mineralogy 549.121
Cleburne County (Ala.) T2—761 64
Cleburne County (Ark.) T2—767 285
Cleethorpes (England : District) T2—428 33
Cleft lip
surgery 617.522
Cleft palate
surgery 617.522 5
Clematises 635.933 34
botany 583.34
floriculture 635.933 34
Clemency 364.65
law 345.077
penology 364.65
Cleopatra, Queen of Egypt
Egyptian history 932.021
Clerestories
Christian church architecture 726.594
Clergy 200.92
biography 200.92
Christian 270.092
biography 270.092
specific denominations 280
see Manual at 280
see Manual at 230–280
ecclesiology 262.1
occupational ethics 241.641
pastoral theology 253
personal religion 248.892
training 230.071 1
occupational ethics 174.1
religion 291.564 1
see Manual at 174.1
occupational group T7—2
role and function 291.61
see also Rabbis; Religious leaders
see Manual at 200.92 and 291–299
Clergymen's wives
biography 270.092
specific denominations 280
pastoral theology 253.22
Clerical services 651.37
Clerihews 808.817
history and criticism 809.17
specific literatures T3B—107
individual authors T3A—1
Clerks 651.370 92
occupational group T7—651
office services 651.37
social class 305.556
Clerks regular 255.5
church history 271.5
Clerks Regular of Somaschi 255.54
church history 271.54
Clerks Regular of the Mother of God 255.57
church history 271.57
Clermont (Qld.) T2—943 5
Clermont County (Ohio) T2—771 794
Cleroidea 595.763
Clethraceae 583.66
Cleveland (England) T2—428 5
Cleveland (Ohio) T2—771 32
Cleveland, Grover
United States history 973.85
1885–1889 973.85
1893–1897 973.87
Cleveland bay horse 636.14
Cleveland County (Ark.) T2—767 69
Cleveland County (N.C.) T2—756 775
Cleveland County (Okla.) T2—766 37
Cleveland Hills (England) T2—428 49
Clichés
dictionaries 413.1
specific languages T4—31
Click beetles 595.765
Client-server computing 004.36
Client-server processing 004.36
see also Processing modes—computer science
Clifford algebras 512.57
Clifton Forge (Va.) T2—755 811
Climacteric
human physiology 612.665
Climacteric disorders
gynecology 618.175
male
medicine 616.693
Climate 551.6
biophysics 571.49
ecology 577.22

Climate (continued)
  health 613.11
  influence on crime 364.22
  psychological influence 155.915
  social effects 304.25
  see Manual at 551.5 vs. 551.6
Climate control 551.68
Climate-induced illnesses
  medicine 616.988
  see also Environmental diseases (Human)
Climate types 551.62
Climatic changes
  crop damage 632.1
Climatological diseases
  medicine 616.988
  see also Environmental diseases (Human)
Climatologists 551.609 2
  occupational group T7—551
Climatology 551.6
Climatotherapy
  medicine 615.834
Climbing plants 582.18
  floriculture 635.974
Clinch County (Ga.) T2—758 812
Clinch River (Va. and Tenn.) T2—768 73
Clingfishes 597.62
Clinical chemistry 616.075 6
Clinical enzymology 616.075 6
Clinical medicine 616
  diagnosis 616.075
  see Manual at 616 vs. 616.075
Clinical psychology 616.89
  see also Mental illness
Clinics 362.12
  see also Health care facilities; Health services
Clinton (B.C.) T2—711 72
Clinton, Bill
  United States history 973.929
Clinton County (Ill.) T2—773 875
Clinton County (Ind.) T2—772 553
Clinton County (Iowa) T2—777 67
Clinton County (Ky.) T2—769 653
Clinton County (Mich.) T2—774 24
Clinton County (Mo.) T2—778 155
Clinton County (N.Y.) T2—747 54
Clinton County (Ohio) T2—771 765
Clinton County (Pa.) T2—748 54
Clip spot embroidery 677.77
Clipper ships 387.224
  design 623.812 24
Clipper ships (continued)
  engineering 623.822 4
  handling 623.882 24
  transportation services 387.224
  see also Ships
Clippings
  cataloging 025.342
  library treatment 025.172
Clive, Robert Clive, Baron
  Indian history 954.029 6
Cloaks 391
  commercial technology 687.147
  customs 391
  home sewing 646.457
  see also Clothing
Clock towers
  architecture 725.97
Clockcases
  art 739.3
  decorative arts 749.3
Clockmakers 681.113 092
  occupational group T7—681 1
Clocks 681.113
  art metalwork 739.3
  technology 681.113
Clockworks 681.112
Clocolan (South Africa : District) T2—685 5
Clog dancing 793.32
Clogs 391.413
  commercial technology 685.32
  customs 391.413
  see also Clothing
Cloisonné
  ceramic arts 738.42
Cloisters
  cathedral
    architecture 726.69
  monastic
    architecture 726.79
Clonal selection 571.964 6
  human immunology 616.079 5
Cloning 571.89
  biotechnology 660.65
  human immunology 616.079 5
  immunology 571.964 6
  plants 575.49
Clonmel (Ireland) T2—419 25
Clontarf, Battle of, 1014 941.501
Close air support (Tactics) 358.414 2
Close corporations 338.74
  law 346.066 8
  see also Corporations
Close-up photography 778.324

Closed-circuit television 384.556
see also Television
Closed-loop systems
automation engineering 629.83
Closed shop 331.889 2
Closed stacks 025.81
Closet drama 808.82
history and criticism 809.2
specific literatures T3B—2
individual authors T3A—2
Closets 643.5
Closing (Real estate) 346.043 73
Clostridium 579.364
Cloth
ship design 623.818 97
shipbuilding 623.820 7
Cloth covers
bookbinding 686.343
Clothes dryers
home economics 648.1
manufacturing technology 683.88
Clothing 391
armed forces 355.81
costume 355.14
arts 746.92
commercial manufacturing 687
fur 685.24
instruments 681.767 7
leather 685.22
customs 391
health 613.482
home economics 646.3
home sewing 646.4
product safety 363.19
law 344.042 35
see also Product safety
psychological influence 155.95
social welfare 361.05
see Manual at 391 vs. 646.3, 746.92
Clothing care
home economics 646.6
Clothing construction 646.4
commercial technology 687
home sewing 646.4
Clothing workers 687.092
occupational group T7—687
Cloud colors 551.567
Cloud County (Kan.) T2—781 25
Cloud seeding 551.687 6
Clouded leopard 599.75
Clouds 551.576
aeronautics 629.132 4
weather modification 551.687 6
Clove (Spice) 641.338 3
botany 583.765
see also Spices
Clovers 633.32
botany 583.74
forage crop 633.32
Clowns 791.33
occupational group T7—791 3
Cloze procedure
elementary education
reading 372.472
Club cars 385.33
engineering 625.23
see also Rolling stock
Club fungi 579.597
Club games 796.35
Club mosses 587.9
paleobotany 561.79
Clubhouse buildings
architecture 728.4
Clubmen 367.92
social group T7—367
Clubs 367
household management 647.94
Clubwomen 367.92
social group T7—367
Cluj (Romania : Judeţ) T2—498 4
Cluniacs 255.14
church history 271.14
Clupea 597.452
Clupeidae 597.45
Clupeomorpha 597.45
paleozoology 567.45
Clusiaceae 583.624
Cluster analysis 519.53
Cluster headaches
symptomatology
neurological diseases 616.849 1
see also Nervous system
Clusters of stars 523.85
Clutches (Machine parts) 621.825
Clutha District (N.Z.) T2—939 3
Clwyd (Wales) T2—429 3
Clyde, Firth of (Scotland) 551.461 37
T2—163 37
Clyde River (Scotland) T2—414 1
Clydebank (Scotland : District) T2—414 32
Clydesdale (Scotland : District) T2—414 69
Clydesdale horse 636.15
Cnidaria 593.5
paleozoology 563.5
Cnidospora 579.48

Co-dependency 362.291 3
  see also Codependency
Coach horses 636.14
Coaches (Railroad cars) 385.33
  engineering 625.23
  see also Rolling stock
Coaches (Sports) 796.092
  occupational group T7—796
Coaching (Driving)
  recreation 798.6
Coaching (Sports) 796.077
  see also Sports
Coaching horses
  recreation 798.6
Coagulants
  pharmacodynamics 615.718
  see also Cardiovascular system
Coagulation
  blood 573.159
    human physiology 612.115
    see also Cardiovascular system
  water supply treatment 628.162 2
Coahoma County (Miss.) T2—762 44
Coahuila (Mexico : State) T2—721 4
Coal 553.24
  chemical engineering 662.62
  economic geology 553.24
  heating buildings 697.042
  mining 622.334
    law 343.077 52
  pipeline transportation 388.57
  production economics 338.272 4
  prospecting 622.182 4
  public administration 354.44
  public utilities 363.6
    law 343.092 7
    see also Public utilities
  resource economics 333.822
    law 346.046 822
Coal County (Okla.) T2—766 67
Coal gasification 665.772
Coal mining 622.334
  law 343.077 52
  production economics 338.272 4
Coal oil 665.538 3
Coal slurry 662.623
  pipeline transportation 388.57
    technology 662.624
  technology 662.623
Coal tar 547.82
Coal tar chemicals 661.803
Coalition military forces 355.356
Coalition War, 1690–1697 949.204
Coarse fishing (Sports) 799.11
Coast artillery 358.168 2
  engineering 623.417
  military equipment 358.168 2
Coast artillery forces 358.16
Coast guard 363.286
  military service 359.97
  police services 363.286
Coast guard vessels 363.286
  design 623.812 63
  engineering 623.826 3
  police services 363.286
Coast Mountains (B.C.) T2—711 1
Coast Province (Kenya) T2—676 23
Coast Ranges T2—795
  California T2—794 1
  Oregon T2—795
  Washington T2—797 9
Coast Region (Tanzania) T2—678 23
Coasta Region (Ecuador) T2—866 3
Coastal defense 355.45
Coastal ecology 577.51
Coastal engineering 627.58
Coastal lands 551.457
  T2—146
  see also Coasts
Coastal pools 551.460 9
  T2—168
Coastal regions 551.457
  T2—146
  see also Coasts
Coastal wetlands
  biology 578.769
  ecology 577.69
  see also Wetlands
Coastal zones 551.457
  T2—146
  see also Coasts
Coasting
  snow sports 796.95
Coasts 551.457
  T2—146
  biology 578.751
  ecology 577.51
  geography 910.914 6
  geomorphology 551.457
  law 346.046 917
  physical geography 910.021 46
  recreational resources 333.784
  resource economics 333.917
Coastwise routes 387.524
Coated paper 676.283

Coaticook (Quebec :
Regional County
Municipality) T2—714 67
Coating 667.9
Coating latex 678.527
Coating metals 671.73
Coating paper 676.235
Coatings 667.9
Coatis 599.763
Coats 391
commercial technology 687.14
indoor garments 687.113
outdoor garments 687.14
customs 391
home sewing 646.45
indoor garments 646.433
outdoor garments 646.45
see also Clothing
Coats Island (N.W.T.) T2—719 4
Coats of arms 929.6
Cob (Building material) 693.22
Cobalt 669.733
chemical engineering 661.062 3
chemistry 546.623
economic geology 553.483
materials science 620.189 33
metallography 669.957 33
metallurgy 669.733
metalworking 673.733
mining 622.348 3
organic chemistry 547.056 23
applied 661.895
physical metallurgy 669.967 33
see also Chemicals; Metals
Cobalt soaps 668.125
Cobar (N.S.W.) T2—944 9
Cobb County (Ga.) T2—758 245
Cobbling 685.31
Cobourg Peninsula
National Park (N.T.) T2—942 95
Coburg (Germany) T2—433 11
Cocaine abuse 362.298
medicine 616.864 7
personal health 613.84
social welfare 362.298
see also Substance abuse
Cocas (Plants) 583.79
Coccidiosis
incidence 614.53
medicine 616.936
see also Communicable
diseases (Human)
Coccinellidae 595.769
Cochabamba (Bolivia :
Dept.) T2—842 3
Cochineal dyes 667.26
Cochise County (Ariz.) T2—791 53
Cochleas
human anatomy 611.85
human physiology 612.858
otology 617.882
see also Ears
Cochran County (Tex.) T2—764 845
Cochrane (Ont. : District) T2—713 142
Cockatiels 636.686 56
animal husbandry 636.686 56
zoology 598.71
Cockatoos 598.71
animal husbandry 636.686 5
Cocke County (Tenn.) T2—768 895
Cockfighting 791.8
Cockney dialect 427.1
T6—21
Cockroaches 595.728
control technology 628.965 7
Cocks (Mechanisms) 621.84
Cocksfoot (Grass) 633.22
botany 584.9
Coclé (Panama : Province) T2—728 721
Cocoa 641.337 4
beverage 641.337 4
commercial processing 663.92
home preparation 641.877
cooking with 641.637 4
food 641.337 4
Cocoa butter 665.354
chemical technology 665.354
cooking with 641.637 4
food 641.337 4
food technology 664.3
Coconino County (Ariz.) T2—791 33
Coconut milk
commercial processing 663.64
Coconut oil 665.355
Coconuts 641.346 1
botany 584.5
commercial processing 664.804 61
cooking 641.646 1
food 641.346 1
food crop 634.61
textiles 677.18
see also Textiles
Cocoons 595.714 6
Cocoparra National Park
(N.S.W.) T2—944 8
Cocos (Keeling) Islands 969.9
T2—699

Cod-liver oil
  pharmacology 615.34
COD mail 383.184
  see also Postal service
CODASYL databases
  computer science 005.754
Code generators
  computer science 005.45
Code of Manu 294.592 6
Code telegraphy 384.14
  wireless 384.524
  see also Telegraphy
Codependency 362.291 3
  alcoholism 362.292 3
    medicine 616.861 9
    social welfare 362.292 3
  devotional literature 291.432
    Christianity 242.4
  medicine 616.869
  pastoral theology 291.61
    Christianity 259.429
  religious guidance 291.442
    Christianity 248.862 9
  social theology 291.178 322 9
    Christianity 261.832 29
  social welfare 362.291 3
Codes
  computer science 005.72
Codes (Law) 348.023
  United States 348.732 3
Codes of conduct
  moral theology 291.5
    Christianity 241.5
    Judaism 296.36
Codex iuris canonici (1917) 262.93
Codex iuris canonici (1983) 262.94
Codiaeum 583.69
Codiales 579.835
Codification 348.004
  international law 341.026 7
  United States 348.730 4
Coding data 005.72
Coding programs 005.13
Coding theory 003.54
  T1—011 54
Codington County (S.D.) T2—783 23
Codling moth
  agricultural pests 634.049 78
Codons 572.86
Cods 641.392
  conservation technology 639.977 633
  cooking 641.692
  food 641.392
  resource economics 333.956 633
Cods (continued)
  zoology 597.633
Coefficient of expansion 536.41
Coefficient of restitution 531.382
Coelacanths 597.39
Coelenterata 593.5
  paleozoology 563.5
Coelesyria (Lebanon) T2—394 4
Coelomycetes 579.55
Coelophysis 567.912
Coenopteridales 561.73
Coenzymes 572.7
  chemistry 547.758
  see also Enzymes
Coercion
  social control 303.36
Coeur d'Alene Mountains
    (Idaho and Mont.) T2—796 91
Coevolution 576.87
Cofactors
  biochemistry 572.7
Coffee 641.337 3
  agricultural economics 338.173 73
  agriculture 633.73
  botany 583.93
  commercial processing
    economics 338.476 639 3
    technology 663.93
  cooking with 641.637 3
  food 641.337 3
  home preparation 641.877
Coffee cakes 641.865 9
  commercial processing 664.752 5
  home preparation 641.865 9
Coffee County (Ala.) T2—761 34
Coffee County (Ga.) T2—758 823
Coffee County (Tenn.) T2—768 64
Coffee grounds
  divination 133.324 4
Coffee substitutes 641.3
  commercial processing 663.97
  home preparation 641.877
Cofferdams 624.157
Coffey County (Kan.) T2—781 645
Coffin flies 595.774
Coffs Harbour (N.S.W.) T2—944 3
Cofimvaba (South Africa :
    District) T2—687 91
Cog railroads 385.6
  engineering 625.33
  transportation services 385.6
Cogeneration 333.793
  law 343.092 9
  resource economics 333.793

Cogeneration (continued)
  steam 621.199
Cognac 641.253
  commercial processing 663.53
Cognition
  epistemology 121
Cognitive psychology 153
  children 155.413
  education 370.152
  late adulthood 155.671 3
  see Manual at 153 vs. 153.4
Cognitive reading methods
  elementary education 372.474
Cognitive science 153
  see Manual at 153 vs. 006.3: Cognitive science
Cognitive therapy
  psychiatry 616.891 42
  see also Mental illness
Cohabiting 306.735
  customs 392.6
Coherent optics 535.2
Cohesion 541.33
  chemical engineering 660.293
  chemistry 541.33
Cohomology theory 514.23
Cohorts (Military units) 355.31
Coimbra (Portugal : District) T2—469 35
Coimbra da Luz, Carlos
  Brazilian history 981.062
Coinage
  law 343.032
  public revenue 336.16
Coins 332.404 2
  investment economics 332.63
  monetary economics 332.404 2
  numismatics 737.4
Coir
  textiles 677.18
    see also Textiles
Cojedes (Venezuela : State) T2—874 6
Coke
  chemical engineering 662.72
  heating buildings 697.042
Coke County (Tex.) T2—764 723
Coke gases 665.772
Coke-oven gas 665.772
Cola
  alkaloid crop 633.76
  beverage 641.337 6
    commercial processing 663.62
Colac (Vic.) T2—945 7
Colbert County (Ala.) T2—761 915
Colchagua (Chile : Province) T2—833 3
Colchester (England : District) T2—426 723
Colchester (N.S. : County) T2—716 12
Colchis 939.5
  T2—395
Cold 536.56
  biophysics 571.464
    humans 612.014 465
Cold (Disease)
  medicine 616.205
  see also Respiratory system
Cold-blooded vertebrates 597
  culture 639.3
  paleozoology 567
Cold climate
  health 613.111
Cold dishes
  cooking 641.79
Cold frames
  gardening 635.048 3
  manufacturing technology 681.763 1
Cold-molding glass powder 666.126
Cold sores
  medicine 616.52
  see also Skin
Cold-storing foods 664.028 52
  commercial preservation 664.028 52
  home preservation 641.452
Cold weather
  health 613.111
Cold-weather cooking 641.591 1
Cold-weather diseases
  medicine 616.988 1
  see also Environmental diseases (Human)
Cold-weather photography 778.75
Cold-working operations
  metals 671.3
Coldwater River (B.C.) T2—711 72
Cole County (Mo.) T2—778 55
Coleman County (Tex.) T2—764 725
Colemanite
  mineralogy 549.735
Coleoidea 594.5
Coleoptera 595.76
  paleozoology 565.76
Coleraine (Northern Ireland : Borough) T2—416 27
Coles County (Ill.) T2—773 72
Colesberg (South Africa : District) T2—687 13

Colfax County (N.M.) T2—789 22
Colfax County (Neb.) T2—782 532
Colic
  abdominal disorders 617.55
  gastrointestinal disorders
    pediatrics 618.923 3
Coligny (South Africa : District) T2—682 4
Coliiformes 598.75
  paleozoology 568.7
Colima (Mexico : State) T2—723 6
Colinus 598.627 3
Colitis
  medicine 616.344 7
  see also Digestive system
Collage 702.812
Collage painting 751.493
Collagen 572.67
  biochemistry 572.67
  chemistry 547.753
  human histology 611.018 2
  see also Musculoskeletal system; Proteins
Collagen diseases
  medicine 616.77
  see also Musculoskeletal system
Collards 641.353 47
  cooking 641.653 47
  food 641.353 47
  garden crop 635.347
Collateral kinsmen 306.87
  T1—085
  T7—046
Collect-on-delivery mail 383.184
  see also Postal service
Collected biography 920
  T1—092 2
  geographic treatment T1—092 2
    see Manual at T1—0922 vs. T1—093–T1—099
  see Manual at T1—0922
Collectibles T1—075
  see Manual at 745.1
Collecting 069.4
  T1—075
  descriptive research 001.433
  museology 069.4
  recreation 790.132
Collecting of accounts
  law 346.077
  management 658.88
Collection analysis
  library science 025.21
Collection development
  library science 025.21
Collection maintenance
  library operations 025.8
  library science 025.21
Collection management
  library science 025.21
Collections 069.5
  arts 700.74
  description T1—074
  fine arts 708
    temporary 707.4
    see Manual at 704.9: Use of standard subdivisions
  museology 069.5
  of texts 080
    see Manual at 080; *also at* 080 vs. 800; *also at* 081–089
  preparation T1—075 3
Collective bargaining 331.89
  economics 331.89
    see Manual at 331.2 vs. 331.89
  law 344.018 9
  personnel management 658.315 4
    public administration 352.68
  public administration 354.97
  women workers 331.479
Collective security 327.116
Collective settlements 307.77
  economics 335.9
Collectivism 335
  economics 335
  political ideology 320.53
  see Manual at 335 vs. 306.345, 320.53
Collectors
  social group T7—090 9
College administration 378.101
College administrators
  biography 378.009 2
  occupational group T7—371
  role and function 378.111
College admissions 378.161
College applications 378.161 6
College buildings 378.196
  architecture 727.3
  institutional housekeeping 647.993
  see also Educational buildings
College costs 378.38
College dropouts 378.169 13
College education 378
  see also Higher education

College enrollment 378.161 9
College entrance examinations 378.166 2
College entrance requirements 378.161 7
College extension 378.175
College graduates
  choice of vocation 331.702 35
  labor force 331.114 23
  social group 305.55
  unemployment 331.137 804
College-level accounting 657.044
College-level examinations 378.166 2
College libraries 027.7
  see also Academic libraries
College presidents
  biography 378.009 2
  occupational group T7—371
  role and function 378.111
College presses
  bibliographies of publications 011.54
  publishing 070.594
College readers (Reading comprehension textbooks)
  applied linguistics 418
    specific languages T4—86
College readers (Rhetoric textbooks) 808
  specific languages 808.04
    see Manual at 808.0427
College sports 796.043
  see also Sports
  see Manual at 796.08 vs. 796.04
College students
  guides to Christian life 248.834
  pastoral care 259.24
College teachers 378.12
  occupational group T7—372
College teaching 378.125
College trustees 378.101 1
Colleges 378.154 2
  T1—071 1
  area planning 711.57
  liability 344.075
  see also Higher education
Colleges without walls 378.03
  see also Higher education
Collembola 595.725
Colleton County (S.C.) T2—757 95
Collie (W.A.) T2—941 2
Collier County (Fla.) T2—759 44
Collies 636.737 4
Colligative properties
  chemical engineering 660.294 15
  chemistry 541.341 5
Collin County (Tex.) T2—764 556
Collingsworth County (Tex.) T2—764 831
Collision prevention seamanship 623.888 4
Collisions (Physics)
  nuclear particles 539.757
  solid-state physics 530.416
Colloid chemistry 541.345
  applied 660.294 5
  specific elements and compounds 546
Colloidal fuels 662.82
Colloids 541.345
  specific elements and compounds 546
Colloquial language 418
  specific languages T4—8
Collor de Mello, Fernando Affonso
  Brazilian history 981.064
Collotype printing 686.232 5
Collusion 364.134
  law 345.023 4
Cologne (Germany) T2—435 514
Cologne (Germany : Regierungsbezirk) T2—435 51
Colombia 986.1
  T2—861
  Panamanian history 972.870 3
Colombian literature 860
Colombians T5—688 61
Colombo (Sri Lanka) T2—549 3
Colon 573.379
  biology 573.379
  human anatomy 611.347
  human physiology 612.36
  surgery 617.554 7
  see also Digestive system
Colón (Honduras : Dept.) T2—728 313
Colón (Panama : Province) T2—728 732
Colón, Archipiélago de T2—866 5
Colon cancer
  incidence 614.599 943 47
  medicine 616.994 347
  see also Cancer (Human)
Colon Classification 025.435
Colonia (Uruguay) T2—895 11
Colonial architecture 724.1
Colonial Heights (Va.) T2—755 595
Colonial military forces 355.352
Colonial Phoenician architecture 722.32
Colonialism 325.3

Colonies (Territories) 321.08
see also Non-self-governing territories
Colonization 325.3
Colonnades 721.2
architecture 721.2
construction 690.12
Colonnettes 721.3
architecture 721.3
construction 690.13
Color 535.6
animal physiology 573.5
animals 591.472
arts 701.85
drawing 741.018
interior decoration 747.94
mineralogy 549.125
painting 752
physics 535.6
religious significance 291.37
Christianity 246.6
see also Symbolism—religious significance
technology 667
therapeutics 615.831
Color (Sound) 781.234
Color blindness
incidence 614.599 7
ophthalmology 617.759
see also Eyes
Color cinematography 778.534 2
Color materials
pottery 666.42
arts 738.12
technology 666.42
Color perception
psychology 152.145
Color photography 778.6
motion pictures 778.534 2
Color plants (Floriculture) 635.968
Color printing 686.230 42
Color television 621.388 04
Color therapy 615.831
Colorado 978.8
T2—788
Colorado County (Tex.) T2—764 253
Colorado Desert (Calif. and Mexico) T2—794 99
Colorado Plateau T2—791 3
Arizona T2—791 3
Colorado T2—788 1
Utah T2—792 5
Colorado River (Colo.-Mexico) T2—791 3
Arizona T2—791 3
Colorado T2—788 17
Utah T2—792 5
Colorado River (Tex.) T2—764
Colorado Springs (Colo.) T2—788 56
Colorado tick fever
incidence 614.574 2
medicine 616.924 2
see also Communicable diseases (Human)
Colorimetry 543.085 2
Coloring oils and gases 665.028 3
Coloring paper 676.234
Colorless sulfur bacteria 579.32
Colors (Flags) 929.92
armed forces 355.15
Colossians (Biblical book) 227.7
Colostomy 617.554 7
Colquitt County (Ga.) T2—758 975
Colugos 599.33
Columbia (S.C.) T2—757 71
Columbia County (Ark.) T2—767 59
Columbia County (Fla.) T2—759 83
Columbia County (Ga.) T2—758 635
Columbia County (N.Y.) T2—747 39
Columbia County (Or.) T2—795 47
Columbia County (Pa.) T2—748 38
Columbia County (Wash.) T2—797 46
Columbia County (Wis.) T2—775 81
Columbia River T2—797
British Columbia T2—711 6
Oregon T2—795 4
Washington T2—797
Columbia-Shuswap (B.C.) T2—711 68
Columbiana County (Ohio) T2—771 63
Columbiformes 598.65
paleozoology 568.6
Columbines 635.933 34
botany 583.34
floriculture 635.933 34
Columbium 669.79
chemistry 546.524
see also Chemicals; Niobium
Columbus (Ohio) T2—771 57
Columbus, Christopher
North American history 970.015
South American history 980.013
Columbus County (N.C.) T2—756 31
Column chromatography 543.089 4
Columnar epithelia
human histology 611.018 7

Columns 721.3
  architecture 721.3
  construction 690.13
  structural engineering 624.177 2
    concrete 624.183 42
Colusa County (Calif.) T2—794 33
Colwyn (Wales) T2—429 31
Colydiidea 595.769
Colymbiformes 598.44
COM devices 004.77
  manufacturing technology 681.6
Coma
  symptomatology
    neurological diseases 616.849
  see also Nervous system
Comal County (Tex.) T2—764 887
Comanche County (Kan.) T2—781 79
Comanche County (Okla.) T2—766 48
Comanche County (Tex.) T2—764 554
Comanche Indians T5—974 5
Comayagua (Honduras : Dept.) T2—728 372
Comb jellies 593.8
Combat 355.4
Combat aircraft 358.418 3
  engineering 623.746
  military equipment 358.418 3
Combat fatigue
  medicine 616.852 12
  see also Mental illness
Combat groups (Air force) 358.413 1
Combat readiness 355.033 2
Combat sports 796.8
  see also Sports
Combat squadrons (Air force) 358.413 1
Combat units 355.31
Combat vehicles 355.83
  engineering 623.74
  military equipment 355.83
Combat zones
  living conditions 355.129 4
Combatants
  law 343.013
  law of war 341.67
Combination of grades 371.25
Combinations (Enterprises) 338.8
  accounting 657.96
  economics 338.8
  international law 341.753
  management 658.046
    initiation 658.114 6
  see also International enterprises
  see Manual at 658.04 vs. 658.114, 658.402
Combinations (Mathematics) 511.64
  algebra 512.925
  arithmetic 513.25
  number theory 512.72
Combinatorial analysis 511.6
Combinatorial geometry 516.13
Combinatorial probabilities 519.2
Combinatorial set theory 511.322
Combinatorial topology 514.22
Combinatory logic 511.3
Combined operations (Armed forces) 355.46
Combined sewers 363.728 4
  social services 363.728 4
  technology 628.214
  see also Sewage treatment
Combines (Machines) 633.104 5
  manufacturing technology 681.763 1
Combing textiles 677.028 21
  arts 746.11
  manufacturing technology 677.028 21
Combretaceae 583.76
Combs 646.724
  customs 391.44
  manufacturing technology 688.5
  personal appearance 646.724
Combustion 541.361
  air pollution technology 628.532
  chemical engineering 660.296 1
  chemistry 541.361
  diesel engines 621.436 1
  heat engineering 621.402 3
Combustion gases
  human toxicology 615.91
COMECON (Economic organization) 341.242 7
  international commerce 382.914 7
  international economics 337.147
  international law 341.242 7
Comedians 792.702 809 2

Comedies (Drama) 792.23
literature 808.825 23
history and criticism 809.252 3
specific literatures T3B—205 23
individual authors T3A—2
motion pictures 791.436 17
radio programs 791.446 17
stage presentation 792.23
see also Theater
television programs 791.456 17
Comedy
arts T3C—17
literature 808.801 7
history and criticism 809.917
specific literatures T3B—080 17
history and criticism T3B—091 7
see Manual at T3B—7 vs. T3C—17
Comets 523.6
T2—993
Comfort equipment
aircraft 629.134 42
automobile 629.277
vehicles 629.040 289
Comfort stations 363.729 4
technology 628.45
see also Waste control
Comfreys 583.94
floriculture 635.933 94
Comics 741.5
drawing 741.5
journalism 070.444
Cominform 324.175
Coming-of-age customs 392.15
etiquette 395.24
Commagene T2—393 6
Command and control systems (Military) 355.330 41
Command functions (Armed forces) 355.330 41
Commandeering military resources 355.28
Commander Islands (Russia) T2—577
Commandments
Jewish law 296.18
moral theology 291.5
Christianity 241.5
Judaism 296.36
Commando raids 355.422
Commandos (Armed forces) 356.167
Commelinales 584.86
Commelinidae 584.8
Commemorations 394.2
see also Celebrations
Commemorative medals
numismatics 737.222
Commemorative stamps 769.563
Commencements
customs 394.2
Commensalism 577.852
Commentaries
journalism 070.442
Commerce 380.1
accounting 657.839
agent of social change 303.482
ethics 174.4
international law 341.754
law 343.08
see Manual at 343.078 vs. 343.08
literature 808.803 55
history and criticism 809.933 55
specific literatures T3B—080 355
history and criticism T3B—093 55
public administration 354.73
sociology 306.34
see Manual at 380; *also at* 380.1 vs. 658.8
Commercial air conditioning 697.931 6
Commercial airplanes 387.733 404 23
engineering 629.133 340 423
piloting 629.132 521 6
transportation services 387.733 404 23
see also Aircraft
Commercial areas 307.333
area planning 711.552 2
community sociology 307.333
land economics 333.77
Commercial art 741.6
Commercial artists 741.609 2
occupational group T7—741
Commercial aviation 387.7
see also Air transportation
Commercial banks 332.12
international law 341.751 12
international operations 332.15
law 346.082 12
services 332.17
see also Banks (Finance)
Commercial bookbinding 686.3
Commercial buildings
architecture 725.2
construction 690.52
institutional housekeeping 647.962
sale and rental 333.338 7
see also Buildings

Commercial catalogs 380.102 94
T1—029 4
see Manual at T1—074 vs. T1—0294; *also at* 338 vs. 060, 381, 382, 670.294, 910, T1—025, T1—0294, T1—0296; *also at* 380.1 and 381, 382
Commercial circulars 380.102 94
Commercial credit 332.742
Commercial crimes 364.168
law 345.026 8
Commercial fishing
economics 338.372 7
technology 639.2
see also Fisheries
Commercial gardening
economics 338.175
technology 635
Commercial general liability insurance 368.56
see also Insurance
Commercial insurance 368.094
see also Insurance
Commercial land use 333.77
community sociology 307.333
economics 333.77
Commercial languages 401.3
Commercial law 346.07
international law 341.754
Commercial leases
accounting 657.75
buildings 333.338 75
industrial lands 333.336 5
law 346.043 462
real property and equipment financial management 658.152 42
Commercial liability insurance 368.56
see also Insurance
Commercial miscellany 380.102 9
T1—029
see Manual at 380.1 and 381, 382
Commercial multi-peril insurance 368.094
see also Insurance
Commercial paper 332.77
exchange medium 332.55
Commercial policy 380.13
domestic commerce 381.3
international commerce 382.3
Commercial property 333.77
taxation 336.225
Commercial property insurance 368.12
see also Insurance
Commercial publishers 070.592
Commercial revenues
public finance 336.1
Commercial vehicles (Automotive) 388.34
engineering 629.22
transportation services 388.34
see also Automotive vehicles
Commercials 659.14
broadcast advertising 659.14
radio performances 791.443
television performances 791.453
Commewijne (Surinam : District) T2—883 7
Commission government
cities 320.854
Commissioned officers 355.009 2
occupational group T7—355
role and function 355.332
Commissioning
military personnel 355.223 6
Commissions (Governing boards) 352.25
libraries 021.82
Committees 302.34
legislative bodies 328.365
social psychology 302.34
Commodities 338.02
investment economics 332.632 8
production 338.02
speculation 332.632 8
Commodity brokers 332.62
public administration 354.88
Commodity exchanges 332.644
architecture 725.25
international law 341.752 44
law 343.08
public administration 354.88
Commodity futures 332.632 8
Commodity futures markets 332.644
Commodity options 332.632 8
Commodity options markets 332.644
Commodity standards (Money) 332.42
Commodores 359.009 2
role and function 359.331
Common carriers 388.041
sanitation services 363.729 3
public administration 353.94
see also Waste control
truck 388.324 3
see also Freight services; Passenger services

Common cold
  medicine 616.205
    see also Respiratory system
Common Communication
    Format 025.316
Common dolphin 599.532
Common herring 597.452
Common land 333.2
  landscape architecture 712.5
Common law 340.57
  see Manual at 340.57 vs.
      342–347
Common-law marriage 306.84
  law 346.016
Common lectionary 264.34
  preaching 251.6
Common Market 341.242 2
  see also European Union
Common mice 599.353
  see also Mice (Mus)
Common of the mass 264.36
  music 782.323 2
    choral and mixed voices 782.532 32
    single voices 783.093 232
Common partridge 598.623 2
Common people
  customs 390.24
    dress 391.024
Common quail 598.627 2
Common rats 599.352
  see also Rats (Rattus)
Common Slavic language 491.8
  T6—918
Common stocks 332.632 23
  speculation 332.632 28
Commons
  land economics 333.2
  landscape architecture 712.5
Commonwealth of Independent
    States 947.086
  T2—47
Commonwealth of Nations T2—171 241
Commonwealth of the
    Northern Mariana
    Islands T2—967
Communal land 333.2
Communal living 307.774
  economics 335.9
Communalism 302.14
Communauté régionale de
    l'Outaouais (Quebec) T2—714 221
Communauté urbaine de
    Montréal (Quebec) T2—714 28
Communauté urbaine de
    Québec (Quebec) T2—714 471
Communes 307.774
  economics 335.9
  production economics 338.7
    see Manual at 338.7 vs.
        335.9
Communicable diseases
    (Biology) 571.98
  agriculture 632.3
  plant crops 632.3
  veterinary medicine 636.089 69
Communicable diseases
    (Human) 362.196 9
  geriatrics 618.976 9
  incidence 614.5
    see Manual at 614.5
  law 344.043 69
  medicine 616.9
    see Manual at 616.1–616.8
        vs. 616.9; *also at* 616.9
        vs. 616.01
  nursing 610.736 99
  pediatrics 618.929
  social services 362.196 9
    public administration 353.63
Communication 302.2
  T1—014
  animals 591.59
    physiology 573.92
  ethics 175
    religion 291.565
      Christianity 241.65
  management 658.45
    see also Communication in
        management
    see Manual at 658.45 vs.
        651.7, 808.06665
  office services 651.7
    see Manual at 658.45 vs.
        651.7, 808.06665
  psychology 153.6
  sociology 302.2
Communication in management 658.45
  military administration 355.688 4
  public administration 352.384
Communication in teaching 371.102 2
Communication skills
  elementary education 372.6
Communications 384
  computer science 004.6
    see also Computer
        communications

Communications (continued)
  engineering 621.382
    see also Communications engineering
  international law 341.757
  law 343.099
  military science 358.24
    air forces 358.46
    land forces 358.24
    naval forces 359.983
  police services 363.24
  public administration 354.75
  social effects 303.483 3
  see Manual at 380
Communications engineering 621.382
  manned space flight 629.457
  military 623.73
  ships 623.856
  space flight 629.457
  spacecraft 629.474 3
  unmanned space flight 629.437
  unmanned spacecraft 629.464 3
Communications engineers 621.382 092
  occupational group T7—621 3
Communications equipment
  computer science 004.64
    engineering 621.398 1
  military equipment 355.85
Communications facilities 384.042
  architecture 725.23
  area planning 711.8
  construction 690.523
  military resources 355.27
  misuse 364.147
  railroads 385.316
Communications media 302.23
  religion 291.175
    Christianity 261.52
      evangelism 269.26
      use by local Christian church 253.78
        administration 254.3
    Judaism 296.37
  see also Mass media
Communications network architecture
  communications engineering 621.382 15
  computer science 004.65
    engineering 621.398 1
Communications protocols
  communications engineering 621.382 12
  computer science 004.62
Communications satellites 384.51
  see also Satellite communication
Communications services 384.043
  air forces 358.46
  armed forces 358.24
  naval forces 359.983
  police services 363.24
Communications workers 384.092
  occupational group T7—384
Communicative disorders 362.196 855
  geriatrics 618.976 855
  incidence 614.598 55
  medicine 616.855
  pediatrics 618.928 55
  social services 362.196 855
  special education 371.914
Communion (Part of service) 264.36
  music 782.323 5
Communion of saints 262.73
Communion service 264.36
  music 782.323
Communism 335.4
  economics 335.4
  political ideology 320.532
Communism and Christianity 261.21
Communism and Islam 297.273
Communist bloc T2—171 7
Communist ethics 171.7
Communist front organizations
  political science 324.3
Communist government 321.92
Communist Information Bureau 324.175
Communist International 324.175
Communist manifesto 335.422
Communist parties 324.217 5
  international organizations 324.175
Communist Party of the United States of America 324.273 75
Communists 335.409 2
  Marxist-Leninist 335.430 92
  political group T7—335
Communities 307
  psychological influence 155.94
  see Manual at 307
Community action (Social welfare) 361.8
  public administration 353.527 93
  see Manual at 361.6 vs. 361.7, 361.8
Community antenna television systems 384.554 6
  see also Television
Community-based corrections 365.6

Community centers
  adult education 374.8
  architecture 727.9
  area planning 711.55
  recreation centers 790.068
Community chests 361.8
Community colleges 378.154 3
  four-year 378.052
  two-year 378.154 3
  see also Higher education
Community development 307.14
  law 346.045
  public administration 354.279 3
Community ecology 577.82
  animals 591.782
  plants 581.782
Community health services 362.12
  see also Health services
Community information services
  libraries 021.28
Community mental health services 362.22
  see also Mental health services
Community nursing
  medicine 610.734 3
Community planning 307.12
  community sociology 307.12
  public administration 352.793
  see Manual at 307.12 vs. 711
Community property 346.042
Community-school partnerships 371.19
  elementary education 372.119
    reading 372.425
Community-school relations 306.432
  education 371.19
  higher education 378.103
  sociology 306.432
Community schools 371.03
Community service
  education 371.19
    higher education 378.103
    secondary education 373.119
  penology 364.68
Community suppers 642.4
Commutation of sentence 364.65
  law 345.077
  penology 364.65
Commutative algebra 512.24
Commutative groups 512.2
Commutators (Generator parts) 621.316
Commuter services 388.042
  urban 388.4
    see also Urban transportation
  see also Passenger services
Como (Italy : Province) T2—452 3
Comorans T5—969 694
Comoro Islands 969.4
  T2—694
Comoros 969.41
  T2—694 1
Comox-Strathcona (B.C.) T2—711 2
Compact disc read-only memory 004.565
  bibliographies 011.3
  cataloging 025.344
  engineering 621.397 6
  library treatment 025.174
  publishing 070.579 7
Compact discs 384
  bibliographies 011.38
  music 780
  see also Sound recordings
Compact discs (Computer) 004.565
  see also Compact disc read-only memory
Compact groups 512.55
Compact spaces 514.32
Companies 338.7
  law 346.066
  see also Business enterprises
Companies (Military units) 355.31
Companions of Muḥammad 297.648
Company law 346.066
Company meetings
  law 346.066 45
Company of New France
  Canadian history 971.016 2
Company records
  law 346.066 4
  records management 651.5
Company towns 307.767
Company unions 331.883 4
  see also Labor unions
Comparable worth 331.215 3
  law 344.012 153
Comparative advantage
  economics 338.604 6
  international commerce 382.104 2
Comparative anatomy 571.3
Comparative education 370.9
Comparative government 320.3
Comparative grammar 415
Comparative law 340.2
Comparative librarianship 020.9

Comparative linguistics 410
see Manual at 410
Comparative literature 809
Comparative physiology 571.1
Comparative psychology 156
Comparative religion 291
see Manual at 291
Comparison shopping 381.33
T1—029 7
consumer products 640.73
Comparisons of products and services T1—029 6
Compass 912.028
manufacturing technology 681.753
Compatibility
computer science 004
hardware 004
engineering 621.39
software 005
Compensation 331.21
economics 331.21
income distribution 339.21
law 344.012 1
legislators 328.333
personnel management 658.32
T1—068 3
armed forces 355.64
executives 658.407 2
public administration 352.67
public administration 354.98
see Manual at 331.29 vs. 331.22
Compensation differentials 331.22
see Manual at 331.29 vs. 331.22
Compensation plans 331.216
personnel management 658.322
Compensation scales 331.216
personnel management 658.322 2
Compensatory education 370.111
Competition 338.604 8
communications industry 384.041
economics 338.604 8
law 343.072 1
price determination 338.522
transportation services 388.049
Competition (Biology) 577.83
Competition (Social) 302.14
Competition law 343.072 1
Competitions T1—079
recreation 790.134
research 001.44
use in advertising 659.17
Compilers (Computer programs) 005.453
Complaints
marketing management 658.812
Complaints (Civil procedure) 347.053
Complement (Immunology) 571.968 8
humans 616.079 97
Complement fixation
human immunology 616.079 97
Complete fertilizers 631.813
chemical engineering 668.62
Completeness theorem 511.3
Complex groups (Sociology) 302.35
Complex-instruction set computing 004.3
see also Processing modes—computer science
Complex multiplication 516.35
Complex salts 546.345
chemical engineering 661.4
Complex-valued functions 515.7
Complex-variable functions 515.9
Complexes (Psychology) 154.24
Complexes (Topology) 514.223
Compline 264.15
music 782.324
see also Liturgy of the hours
Composers 780.92
occupational group T7—78
see Manual at 780.92: Composers
Composing machines 686.225 4
manufacturing technology 681.61
use 686.225 4
Compositae 583.99
Composite commodity standards 332.425
Composite current transmission 621.319 15
Composite foods 641.8
commercial technology 664.65
cooking 641.8
Composite materials
furniture 645.4
manufacturing technology 684.106
see also Furniture
handicrafts 745.59
materials science 620.118
Composite media 709.040 7
painting 759.067
Composite photography 778.8
Composite woods 674.83
Composites (Art) 702.81
two-dimensional 760
Composition (Arts) 701.8
architectural design 729.11
drawing 741.018
Composition (Law) 346.077

Composition (Music) 781.3
  elementary school education 372.874
Composition (Printing) 686.225
Composition (Writing) 808
  applied linguistics 418
    specific languages T4—8
  elementary education 372.623
  rhetoric 808
  see Manual at 808.001–808.7 vs. 070.52
Composition of atmosphere 551.511
Composition of ocean floor 551.460 83
Compost 631.875
Compound bridges 388
  construction 624.7
  see also Bridges
Compound engines
  aircraft 629.134 352
Compound liquors 641.255
  commercial processing 663.55
Compound microscopes 502.823
  biology 570.282 3
Compound musical bows 787.93
  instrument 787.931 9
  music 787.93
  see also Stringed instruments
Compounds (Chemicals) 546
  chemical engineering 661
  chemistry 546
Comprehensive high schools 373.25
  see also Secondary education
Compressed air 621.51
Compressed-air transmission 621.53
Compressed work week 331.257 22
  economics 331.257 22
  personnel management 658.312 1
Compressibility
  fluid mechanics 532.053 5
  gas mechanics 533.28
  liquid mechanics 532.58
Compressible flow
  aeronautics 629.132 323
Compression (Stress)
  materials science 620.112 42
Compromise of 1850 973.64
  Civil War (United States)
    cause 973.711 3
Compton (Quebec : County) T2—714 68
Compulsive behavior
  medicine 616.858 4
  see also Mental illness
Compulsive defrauding
  medicine 616.858 45
  see also Mental illness
Compulsive eating
  medicine 616.852 6
  see also Mental illness
Compulsive gambling 362.25
  medicine 616.858 41
  social welfare 362.25
  see also Mental illness
Compulsive lying
  medicine 616.858 45
  see also Mental illness
Compulsive shopping
  medicine 616.858 4
  see also Mental illness
Compulsory education 379.23
  law 344.079
Compulsory labor 331.117 3
Compulsory military service 355.223 63
  law 343.012 2
Computational linguistics 410.285
  see Manual at 410.285 vs. 006.35
Computed tomography
  medicine 616.075 72
Computer access control 005.8
  management 658.478
Computer-aided design 620.004 202 85
Computer-aided design/computer-aided manufacture 670.285
Computer-aided manufacture 670.427
Computer animation 006.696
Computer applications T1—028 5
  see Manual at T1—0285; *also at* T1—0285 vs. T1—0113
Computer architecture 004.22
  engineering 621.392
  see Manual at 004.21 vs. 004.22, 621.392
Computer art 700
  see Manual at 700
Computer-assisted instruction 371.334
  T1—078 5
  adult level 374.26
Computer-assisted printing 686.225 44
Computer communications 004.6
  T1—028 546
  communications services 384.3
  engineering 621.398 1
  international law 341.757 7
  law 343.099 44

Computer communications (continued)
programming 005.711
programs 005.713
see Manual at 005.713
public administration 354.75
sociology 302.23
see Manual at 004.6; also at 004.6 vs. 005.71; also at 004.6 vs. 384.3
Computer composition (Music) 781.34
Computer composition (Printing) 686.225 44
Computer control 629.89
Computer crimes 364.168
law 345.026 8
Computer engineering 621.39
see Manual at 004–006 vs. 621.39
Computer engineers 621.390 92
occupational group T7—621 3
Computer games 794.8
Computer graphics 006.6
T1—028 566
engineering 621.399
instructional use 371.334 66
T1—078 566
statistical presentation 001.422 602 8566
T1—072 8
Computer graphics programs 006.68
Computer hardware 004
engineering 621.39
see Manual at 004 vs. 005
Computer-human interaction 004.019
engineering 621.398 4
Computer industry 338.470 04
Computer input devices 004.76
engineering 621.398 6
Computer input-output devices 004.75
engineering 621.398 5
Computer integrated manufacturing systems 670.285
Computer interfacing 004.6
programming 005.711
programs 005.713
see Manual at 004.6; also at 004.6 vs. 005.71
Computer interfacing equipment 004.64
engineering 621.398 1
Computer languages 005.13
microprogramming 005.6
Computer literacy 004
elementary education 372.34
Computer mice 004.76
Computer modeling 003.3
T1—011 3
instructional use 371.397
see Manual at T1—0285 vs. T1—0113
Computer network resources 025.04
Computer networks 004.6
communications services 384.3
processing modes 004.3
see also Processing modes—computer science
see also Computer communications
Computer-operated equipment
printing composition 686.225 44
Computer organization 004.22
engineering 621.392
Computer output devices 004.77
engineering 621.398 7
Computer output microform devices 004.77
manufacturing technology 681.6
Computer output printers 004.77
manufacturing technology 681.62
Computer peripherals 004.7
engineering 621.398 4
Computer power supply
engineering 621.395
Computer-processed accounts
auditing 657.453
Computer programmers 005.109 2
occupational group T7—090 4
Computer programming 005.1
T1—028 551
see Manual at 005: Examples from 005; also at 005.1 vs. 005.3; also at 005.101; also at 005.11
Computer programs 005.3
T1—028 553
bibliographies 011.77
see Manual at 011.3 vs. 005.30296, 011.77
cataloging 025.344
library treatment 025.174
see Manual at 005: Examples from 005; also at 005.1 vs. 005.3; also at 005.3; also at 005.369
Computer reliability 004
software 005
hardware 004
engineering 621.39

Computer science 004
T1—028 5
see Manual at 004–006; *also at* 004–006 vs. 621.39
Computer scientists 004.092
occupational group T7—090 4
Computer security
data 005.8
management 658.478
armed services 355.343 3
public administration 352.379
Computer simulation 003.3
T1—011 3
see Manual at T1—0285 vs. T1—0113
Computer software 005.3
bibliographies 011.77
see Manual at 011.3 vs. 005.30296, 011.77
cataloging 025.344
library treatment 025.174
see Manual at 004 vs. 005
Computer sorting 005.741
library catalogs 025.317 7
Computer sound processing 006.45
Computer sound synthesis 006.5
T1—028 565
Computer systems 004
engineering 621.39
networks
processing modes 004.3
see also Processing modes—computer science
programs 005.3
Computer terminals 004.75
engineering 621.398 5
Computer testing 004.24
engineering 621.392
Computer viruses 005.84
Computer vision 006.37
engineering 621.399
see Manual at 006.37 vs. 006.42, 621.367, 621.391, 621.399
Computerized axial tomography
medicine 616.075 72
Computerized matching
personnel selection 658.311 2
Computerized office records 651.59
Computerized process control 629.895
chemical engineering 660.281 5
engineering 629.895
manufacturing technology 670.427 5
Computerized typesetting 686.225 44
Computers 004
access control 005.8
management 658.478
elementary education 372.34
engineering 621.39
instructional use 371.334
adult level 374.26
elementary level 372.133 4
law 343.099 9
music 780.285
composition 781.34
musical instrument 786.76
see also Electrophones
social effects 303.483 4
see Manual at 004.1; *also at* 004.1 vs. 004.3
Comtism 146.4
Conakry (Guinea) T2—665 2
Concealed weapons 364.143
law 345.024 3
Concealment
military engineering 623.77
Concentration
psychology of learning 153.153 2
Concentration camps 365.45
penology 365.45
World War II 940.531 7
see also Correctional institutions; Internment camps
Concentricycloidea 593.93
Concepción (Chile : Province) T2—833 9
Concepción (Paraguay) T2—892 138
Concepts
epistemology 121.4
psychology 153.23
Conceptual art 700
fine arts 709.040 75
painting 759.067 5
sculpture 735.230 475
see also Arts
Conceptualism
philosophy 149.1
Concert halls
architecture 725.81
music 781.539
Concert zithers 787.75
see also Stringed instruments
Concertantes 784.186
Concerti grossi 784.24

Concertinas 788.84
  instrument 788.841 9
  music 788.84
  see also Woodwind instruments
Concertinos 784.186 2
Concertos 784.23
  musical form 784.186
Concerts 780.78
Concho County (Tex.) T2—764 71
Conchostraca 595.32
Conciliation
  international politics 327.17
  labor economics 331.891 4
  law 347.09
Concord (N.H.) T2—742 72
Concord, Battle of, 1775 973.331 1
Concordances T1—03
Concordia Parish (La.) T2—763 73
Concrete 666.893
  architectural construction 721.044 5
  building construction 693.5
  building materials 691.3
  foundation materials 624.153 36
  materials science 620.136
  ship design 623.818 34
  ship hulls 623.845 4
  shipbuilding 623.820 7
  structural engineering 624.183 4
Concrete blocks 666.894
  building construction 693.4
  building materials 691.3
  manufacturing technology 666.894
  materials science 620.139
  structural engineering 624.183 2
Concrete music 786.75
Concrete pavements 625.84
Concrete poetry 808.814
  history and criticism 809.14
  specific literatures T3B—104
    individual authors T3A—1
Concubinage
  customs 392.6
Concussion idiophones 786.87
  see also Percussion instruments
Condemnation (Law) 343.025 2
Condemnation of Jesus Christ 232.962
Condensation 536.44
Condensation (Chemical reaction) 541.393
  chemical engineering 660.284 48
  organic chemistry 547.28
Condensation of moisture
  buildings 693.893
  meteorology 551.574
Condensed matter 530.41
Condensed milk 641.371 424
  cooking 641.671 424
  food 641.371 424
  processing 637.142 4
Condensers (Electrical) 621.315
  radio engineering 621.384 133
Condensers (Steam) 621.197
Condiments 641.338 2
  commercial processing 664.5
  cooking with 641.638 2
  food 641.338 2
Conditional equations 515.254
Conditional immortality 236.23
Conditional sales
  consumer credit 332.743
  law 346.074
    taxes 343.055 2
Conditioned reflexes
  comparative psychology 156.232 24
  psychology 152.322 4
Conditions of employment 331.2
  economics 331.2
    see Manual at 331.2 vs. 331.89
  law 344.012
    public employees 342.068 6
  personnel management 658.312
    armed forces 355.1
    public administration 352.67
  public administration 354.98
Conditions of employment (Physical) 331.25
  see also Work environment
Condominiums 643.2
  home economics 643.2
  law 346.043 3
Condoms
  health 613.943 5
    birth control 613.943 5
    disease prevention 613.95
  manufacturing technology 681.761
  see also Birth control
Condors 598.92
  conservation technology 639.978 92
  resource economics 333.958 92
Conduct of life
  armed forces 355.133

Conduct of life (continued)
ethics 170.44
religion 291.5
Christianity 241
Islam 297.5
Judaism 296.36
etiquette 395
parapsychology 131
personal religion 291.44
Buddhism 294.344 4
Christianity 248.4
Hinduism 294.544
Islam 297.57
Sufi 297.44
Judaism 296.7
psychology 158.1
Conducting 781.45
Conducting scores 780
treatises 780.264
Conduction of heat 536.23
Conduction of heat in fluids 536.25
Conductivity (Electrodynamics)
crystals 548.85
Conductometric analysis 543.087 11
Conductors (Music) 784.209 2
chorus 782.509 2
opera 782.109 2
orchestra 784.209 2
Conduits
road engineering 625.734
Condylarthra 569.62
Conecuh County (Ala.) T2—761 263
Conejos County (Colo.) T2—788 33
Cones 516.15
Confections 641.86
Confederate States of America 973.713
T2—75
Confederate sympathizers
United States history 973.718
Confederated Benedictines 255.11
church history 271.11
Confederation of Arab Republics T2—62
Confederation of the Rhine 943.06
Confederations 321.02
law 342.042
public administration 351
Conference calls 384.64
see also Telephone
Conference committees
legislative bodies 328.365 7
Conference on Data Systems Languages databases
computer science 005.754
Conferences 060
Confession (Christian rite) 234.166
public worship 265.62
theology 234.166
Confession (Law) 345.06
Confessionals 247.1
architecture 726.529 1
Confessions of faith 291.2
Christianity 238
Confidential communications 323.448
civil right 323.448
law 342.085 8
Confidentiality
office services 651
Confinement (Childbirth) 392.12
music 781.582
Confirmation (Religious rite) 291.38
Christianity 234.162
theology 234.162
public worship 265.2
etiquette 395.24
Judaism 296.442 4
liturgy 296.454 24
women's 296.443 4
liturgy 296.454 34
music 781.583
Conflict 303.6
international politics 327.16
law 341.5
social groups 305
sociology 303.6
subconscious psychology 154.24
Conflict management 303.69
business relationships 650.13
executive management 658.405 3
labor relations
personnel management 658.315
Conflict of interest
law 342.068 4
occupational ethics 174
political ethics 172
public administration 353.46
Conflict of laws 340.9
domestic 342.042
see Manual at 340.9
Conflict resolution 303.69
international relations 327.17
sociology 303.69
Conflicts of duties
ethical systems 171.6
Conformal mapping 516.36
calculus 515.9
differential geometry 516.36
Conformal projections 526.82

Conformal transformations 516.35
Conformation (Biochemical structure) 572.33
Conformity 303.32
  psychology 153.854
Confraternities 267
Confraternity Bible 220.520 5
Confucianism 181.112
  art representation 704.948 995 12
  arts 700.482 995 12
    T3C—382 995 12
  philosophy 181.112
  religion 299.512
Confucianist holidays
  customs 394.265 951 2
  see also Holidays
Confucianists
  biography 181.112
    religion 299.512 092
  religious group T7—299 512
Congenital diseases (Human)
  medicine 616.043
  see also Diseases (Human)
Congenital heart defects 616.120 43
  see also Cardiovascular system
Congers 597.43
Congestion (Mathematics) 519.82
Congestive heart failure
  medicine 616.129
  see also Cardiovascular system
Congleton (England) T2—427 13
Conglomerates (Enterprises) 338.804 2
  see also Combinations (Enterprises)
Congo (Brazzaville) 967.24
  T2—672 4
Congo (Democratic Republic) T2—675 1
Congo, French (Brazzaville) T2—672 4
Congo eels 597.85
Congo Free State 967.510 22
  T2—675 1
Congo-Kordofanian languages 496.3
  T6—963
Congo language 496.393 1
  T6—963 931
Congo literature 896.393 1
Congo River T2—675 1
Congolese (Brazzaville) T5—967 24
Congolese (Kinshasa) T5—967 51
Congregational Christian Churches of the United States 285.833
  see also Congregationalism
Congregational Churches of the United States 285.832
  see also Congregationalism
Congregational Methodist Church 287.2
  see also Methodist Church
Congregational systems
  Christian ecclesiology 262.4
Congregationalism 285.8
  church government 262.058
    parishes 254.058
  church law 262.985 8
  doctrines 230.58
    catechisms and creeds 238.58
  general councils 262.558
  guides to Christian life 248.485 8
  missions 266.58
  moral theology 241.045 8
  public worship 264.058
  religious associations 267.185 8
  religious education 268.858
  seminaries 230.073 58
  theology 230.58
Congregationalists
  biography 285.809 2
  religious group T7—258
Congregations
  Christianity
    denominations 280
    local church 250
    papal administration 262.136
  Judaism 296.65
  religion 291.65
Congress of Industrial Organizations (U.S.) 331.883 309 73
Congresses 060
Congresses (Legislative bodies) 328
Congruences
  Euclidean geometry 516.2
  number theory 512.72
Conic sections 516.15
Conies (Hyraxes) 599.68
Conies (Pikas) 599.329
Coniferales 585
  paleobotany 561.5
  see also Conifers
Conifers 585
  botany 585
  forestry 634.975
  ornamental arboriculture 635.977 5

Conifers (continued)
  ornamental gardening 635.935
  paleobotany 561.5
Conjugal rights of prisoners 365.6
Conjugales 579.837
Conjugated carbohydrates 572.567
  biochemistry 572.567
  chemistry 547.783
  see also Carbohydrates
Conjugated proteins 572.68
  biochemistry 572.68
  chemistry 547.754
  see also Proteins
Conjugation (Grammar) 415
  specific languages T4—5
Conjugation tables
  applied linguistics 418
    specific languages T4—82
Conjunctions (Grammar) 415
  specific languages T4—5
Conjunctiva
  human anatomy 611.84
  human physiology 612.841
  ophthalmology 617.77
  see also Eyes
Conjunctivitis
  incidence 614.599 7
  ophthalmology 617.773
  see also Eyes
Conjuring
  magic 133.43
  recreation 793.8
Connacht (Ireland) T2—417 1
Connarales 583.82
Connecticut 974.6
  T2—746
Connecticut River T2—74
  Connecticut T2—746
  Massachusetts T2—744 2
  New Hampshire T2—742
  Vermont T2—743
Connecting rods 621.827
  internal-combustion engines 621.437
  machine engineering 621.827
Connectionism
  artificial intelligence 006.32
Connections (Mathematics) 516.35
Connective tissues 571.56
  biology 571.56
  human anatomy 611.74
  human histology 611.018 2
  human physiology 612.75
  medicine 616.77
Connective tissues (continued)
  musculoskeletal system 573.735 6
  see also Musculoskeletal system
Connochaetes 599.645 9
Conodonts 562.2
Conrad I, Holy Roman Emperor
  German history 943.022
Conscience 170
  civil rights issues 323.442
  ethical systems 171.6
  religion 291.5
    Buddhism 294.35
    Christianity 241.1
    Hinduism 294.548
    Islam 297.5
    Judaism 296.36
Conscientious objection 355.224
  ethics 172.42
    religion 291.562 42
    see also War—ethics
  law 343.012 6
  social theology 291.178 73
    Buddhism 294.337 873
    Christianity 261.873
    Hinduism 294.517 873
    Judaism 296.382 7
Conscientious objectors 355.224
  see also Conscientious objection
Conscious mental processes 153
  children 155.413
  comparative psychology 156.3
Consciousness 153
  children 155.413
  philosophy 126
Consciousness-raising groups 305
Conscription (Draft) 355.223 63
  law 343.012 2
Consecrations (Christian rites) 265.92
Consequential loss
  insurance 368.08
Consequentialism
  ethics 171.5
CONSER Project 025.343 2
Conservation 620.004 6
  T1—028 8
  arts 702.88
  bibliographic materials 025.84
  museology 069.53
Conservation of biodiversity 333.951 6
Conservation of energy (Physics) 531.62
Conservation of mass-energy 530.11

Conservation of natural resources 333.72
  economics 333.72
  international law 341.762
  law 346.044
  public administration 354.334
  technology 639.9
  see Manual at 333.7–333.9 vs. 363.1, 363.73, 577; *also at* 333.72 vs. 304.28, 363.7
Conservation tillage 631.451
Conservationists 333.720 92
  occupational group T7—333
  of biological resources 333.951 609 2
    occupational group T7—333
    technologists 639.909 2
      occupational group T7—639 9
Conservatism
  political ideology 320.52
Conservative Judaism 296.834 2
  liturgy 296.450 47
Conservative parties 324.214
  international organizations 324.14
Conservative Party (Great Britain) 324.241 04
Conservative Party (New York State) 324.274 703
Conservative Party of Canada 324.271 04
Conservatories (Greenhouses) 631.583
  construction 690.892 4
  domestic architecture 728.924
  floriculture 635.982 3
  gardening 635.048 3
Consolatory devotions 291.432
  Christianity 242.4
  Judaism 296.72
Consolidated financial statements 657.3
Consolidation
  land economics 333.33
  management 658.16
  schools 379.153 5
Consonance
  musical element 781.238
Conspiracy 364.1
  law 345.02
Constance, Lake of T2—434 62
  Germany T2—434 62
  Switzerland T2—494 59
Constanţa (Romania : Judeţ) T2—498 3
Constantine (Algeria : Province) T2—655
Constantinople T2—496 18
  ancient T2—398
Constantinopolitan Creed 238.14
Constipation
  medicine 616.342 8
  see also Digestive system
Constituencies (Electoral politics) 324.63
Constituency services 328.331
Constitutional Act, 1791
  Canadian history 971.028
Constitutional amendments 342.03
Constitutional Church 284.8
Constitutional conventions 342.029 2
Constitutional history 342.029
Constitutional law 342
Constitutional monarchs 321.87
  public administration 352.233
Constitutional monarchy 321.87
Constitutional period (United States) 973.4
Constitutional reform 342.03
Constitutions 342.02
  organizations 060
Construction 624
  government control 354.642 8
  military engineering 623.047
  underwater engineering 627.702
  see Manual at 624 vs. 690
Construction engineers 624.092
  occupational group T7—624
  see also Construction workers
Construction equipment
  manufacturing technology 681.76
Construction industry 338.476 24
  accounting 657.869
  enterprises 338.762 4
  law 343.078 624
  public administration 354.64
  restrictive practices 338.826 24
Construction noise 363.741
  see also Noise
Construction services (Military) 358.22
  land 358.22
  naval 359.982
Construction specifications 692.3
Construction toys 790.133
  manufacturing technology 688.725
  see also Toys
Construction workers 624.092
  building trades 690.092
    occupational group T7—693
  civil engineering 624.092
    occupational group T7—624

Construction workers (continued)
  labor economics 331.762 4
  occupational group T7—624
  public administration 354.942 4
Constructions (Grammar) 415
  specific languages T4—5
Constructive accounting 657.1
Constructivism 709.040 57
  painting 759.065 7
  sculpture 735.230 457
Constructivism (Philosophy) 149
Consular law 342.041 2
  international law 341.35
Consular service 327.2
  public administration 353.132 63
Consulate (France) 944.046
Consulate buildings
  architecture 725.17
Consultants 001
  management 658.46
    public administration 352.373
  marketing management 658.83
  physicians 362.172
Consultative bodies
  public administration 352.743
Consumer attitudes
  marketing management 658.834 3
Consumer behavior
  marketing management 658.834 2
Consumer cooperatives 334.5
  management 658.870 7
Consumer credit 332.743
  law 346.073
  marketing management 658.883
Consumer education 381.33
  home economics 640.73
Consumer finance institutions 332.35
Consumer food prices 338.19
Consumer income
  macroeconomics 339.22
Consumer information 381.33
  home economics 640.73
  public administration 352.746
Consumer movements 381.32
Consumer preferences
  marketing management 658.834 3
Consumer price indexes 338.528
Consumer protection 381.34
  commerce 381.34
  law 343.071
  public administration 352.746
Consumer psychology
  marketing management 658.834 2
Consumer reports 381.33
  T1—029 6
  see Manual at 338 vs. 060, 381, 382, 670.294, 910, T1—025, T1—0294, T1—0296
Consumer research
  marketing management 658.834
Consumerism 381.3
Consumption 339.47
  ethics 178
    religion 291.568
      Christianity 241.68
    see also Ethical problems
  macroeconomics 339.47
  natural resources 333.713
    see Manual at 333.7–333.9
  sociology 306.3
Consumption-savings relationship 339.43
Contact allergies
  incidence 614.599 33
  medicine 616.973
  see also Diseases (Human)
Contact lenses
  manufacturing technology 681.41
  optometry 617.752 3
  see also Eyes
Contact printing (Photography) 771.44
Contactors (Generator parts) 621.316
Contagious diseases (Biology) 571.98
  agriculture 632.3
  plant crops 632.3
  veterinary medicine 636.089 69
Contagious diseases (Human) 362.196 9
  medicine 616.9
  social services 362.196 9
  see also Communicable diseases (Human)
Container gardening 635.986
  houseplants 635.965
Container-ship operations 387.544 2
Containers 688.8
  earthenware 666.68
    arts 738.38
    technology 666.68
  food board 676.34
  glass 666.19
    arts 748.8
    technology 666.19
  gold
    arts 739.228 4
  handicrafts 745.59

Containers (continued)
  ironwork
    arts 739.48
  paper 676.3
  paperboard 676.3
  plastic technology 668.497
  porcelain 666.58
    arts 738.28
    technology 666.58
  pottery 666.3
    arts 738
    technology 666.3
  sculpture 731.72
  silver
    arts 739.238 4
  technology 688.8
  warehouse management 658.785
  wooden 674.82
Contamination control 363.19
  see also Product safety
Contemplation 291.43
  Christianity 248.34
Contemplative religious orders 255.01
  church history 271.01
  women 255.901
    church history 271.901
Contempt of court 364.134
  law 345.023 4
Content-addressable memory 004.5
Content analysis T1—014
  linguistics 401.41
    specific languages T4—014 1
Content area reading
  elementary education 372.476
Contested elections
  procedures 324.65
Contests
  recreation 790.134
Contextual theology 291.2
  Christianity 230
  see Manual at 230
Continental drift 551.136
Continental shelves T2—141
  international law 341.448
  law 346.046 918
  resource economics 333.918
Continental wrestling 796.812 2
  see also Sports
Continents 551.41
  T2—141
  geography 910.914 1
  geomorphology 551.41
  physical geography 910.021 41
Contingency 123
Continuation schools 374.8
Continued fractions 515.243
  number theory 512.72
Continuing education 374
  T1—071 5
  see also Adult education
Continuo 781.47
Continuous bridges 388
  construction 624.33
  see also Bridges
Continuous casting
  metals 671.256
Continuous functions 511.33
  spaces 515.73
Continuous processes
  production management 658.533
Continuous radar systems 621.384 85
Continuous-time systems 003.8
Continuum hypothesis 511.322
Continuum mechanics 531
  see Manual at 530.12 vs. 531
Continuum physics 530
  theory 530.14
Contortions
  sports 796.47
Contour farming 631.455
Contour surveying 526.981
Contra Costa County
    (Calif.) T2—794 63
Contrabassoons 788.59
  instrument 788.591 9
  music 788.59
  see also Woodwind
    instruments
Contraception 363.96
  see also Birth control
Contract bridge 795.415
Contract carriers 388.041
  truck 388.324 3
  see also Freight services
Contract labor 331.542
  economics 331.542
  penology 365.65
  sociology 306.363
Contracting 346.02
  materials management 658.723
  see also Contracts
Contracting out
  armed forces 355.621 2
  management 658.723
  public administration 352.538
Contraction (Effect of heat) 536.41

Contractions
  heart 573.17
    human physiology 612.171
    see also Cardiovascular system
  muscles 573.75
    human physiology 612.741
    see also Musculoskeletal system
  skin 573.5
    human physiology 612.791
    see also Skin
Contractions (Linguistics) 411
  specific languages T4—11
  specific subject T1—014 8
Contractors (Builders) 690.092
Contracts 346.02
  armed forces 355.621 2
  civil rights issues 323.46
  construction 692.8
  international law 341.753
  materials management 658.723
    T1—068 7
  public administration 352.53
  see Manual at 346.02: Contracts
Contracts (Labor agreements) 331.891
  personnel management 658.315 4
    public administration 352.68
Contractual liability insurance 368.56
  see also Insurance
Contradiction (Principle of) 111
Contradictions
  logic 165
Contralto voices 782.68
  children's 782.78
    choral and mixed voices 782.78
    single voices 783.78
  general works 782.68
    choral and mixed voices 782.68
    single voices 783.68
  women's 782.68
    choral and mixed voices 782.68
    single voices 783.68
Contrapuntal forms 784.187
Contrastive linguistics 410
  applied linguistics 418
  see Manual at 410
Contributory negligence 346.032
Contrition (Christian rite) 234.166
  public worship 265.61
  theology 234.166

Control
  executive management 658.401 3
    military services 355.685
    public administration 352.35
  export trade 382.64
    see also Export trade
  public administration 352.8
    external control 352.8
    internal control 352.35
  social process 303.33
Control circuits 621.381 537
Control devices
  electrical engineering 621.317
  heating buildings 697.07
  transportation 388.041
    engineering 629.040 289
    transportation services 388.041
    see also Signals
Control line models 796.15
Control mechanisms (Biology) 571.7
  human physiology 612.022
  see also Endocrine system
Control of usage
  natural resources 333.717
    see Manual at 333.7–333.9
Control rods
  nuclear reactors 621.483 5
Control theory 003.5
  automation engineering 629.831 2
  mathematics 515.64
  systems 003.5
  see Manual at 003.5 vs. 629.8
Controlled-environment
    agriculture 631.583
  floriculture 635.982
  gardening 635.048 3
Controlled market price
    determination 338.523
Controlled money 332.427
Controlled subject vocabularies 025.49
Controlled transmission
    television 384.556
  see also Television
Controllers
  computer science 004.64
    engineering 621.398 1
  control engineering 629.895
Controllership
  executive management 658.401 3
  financial management 658.151
Controversial knowledge 001.9
  see Manual at 001.9 and 130

Contusions
  medicine 617.13
Contwoyto Lake (N.W.T.) T2—719 7
Conurbations 307.764
  see also Metropolitan areas
Conures 598.71
  animal husbandry 636.686 5
Convalescent homes 362.16
  see also Health care facilities; Health services
Convalescent serums
  pharmacology 615.375
Convalescents 305.908 14
  T1—087 7
  see also Sick persons
Convection of heat 536.25
Convection-oven cooking 641.58
Convective heating
  buildings 697.2
Convenience foods
  home serving 642.1
Convenience stores 381.147
  management 658.87
  see also Commerce
Convention centers
  architecture 725.91
  institutional housekeeping 647.969 1
Conventional housing
  architecture 728
  construction 690.8
Conventional war 355.02
Conventional weapons limitation 327.174 3
Conventions 060
  labor unions 331.874
  political nominations 324.56
Conventions (Treaties) 341.37
  texts 341.026
Convents 291.657
  architecture 726.7
  Christianity 255.9
    church history 271.9
    religious significance of buildings 246.97
Conventuals 255.37
  church history 271.37
Convergence 515.24
Conversation
  ethics 177.2
    religion 291.567 2
      Christianity 241.672
      Judaism 296.367 2
    see also Ethical problems
  etiquette 395.59
Conversation (continued)
  literature 808.856
    history and criticism 809.56
    specific literatures T3B—506
      individual authors T3A—5
  rhetoric 808.56
  social psychology 302.346
Conversational language study 418
  specific languages T4—83
Converse County (Wyo.) T2—787 16
Conversion (Law) 346.036
Conversion (Religious experience) 291.42
  Christianity 248.24
  Islam 297.574
  Judaism 296.714
Conversion tables (Measurement) 530.81
Conversion to metric system 389.16
  executive management 658.406 2
Converter substations
  electrical engineering 621.312 6
Converters
  electrical engineering 621.313
  electronic circuits 621.381 532 2
Convertible tops 629.26
Convertiplanes
  engineering 629.133 35
Converts 291.42
  Judaism 296.714
    outreach activity for 296.69
  missions for 291.72
Convex programming 519.76
Convex sets
  geometry 516.08
Convex surfaces 516.362
Conveyancing 346.043 8
Conveying equipment 621.867
  mining 622.66
  pneumatic engineering 621.54
Conveyor belts 621.867 5
  manufacturing technology 678.36
  materials handling 621.867 5
Convict labor 365.65
  economics 331.51
  law 344.035 65
  penology 365.65
Convicts 365.6
  T1—086 927
Convolutions
  cerebrum
    human physiology 612.825
    see also Nervous system
Convolvulaceae 583.94

Convulsions	
symptomatology	
neurological diseases	616.845
see also Nervous system	
Conway County (Ark.)	T2—767 31
Conway Range National Park (Qld.)	T2—943 6
Cook County (Ga.)	T2—758 876
Cook County (Ill.)	T2—773 1
Cook County (Minn.)	T2—776 75
Cook Inlet (Alaska)	551.466 34
	T2—164 34
Cook Islands	T2—962 3
Cook Strait (N.Z.)	551.465 78
	T2—164 78
Cooke County (Tex.)	T2—764 533
Cookies	641.865 4
commercial processing	664.752 5
home preparation	641.865 4
Cooking	641.5
customs	392.37
Cooking greens	641.354
commercial processing	664.805 4
cooking	641.654
food	641.354
garden crop	635.4
see Manual at 635.3 and 635.4, 635.5	
Cooking oils	
food technology	664.36
Cooking utensils	641.502 8
manufacturing technology	683.82
Cookout cooking	641.578
Cooks	641.509 2
occupational group	T7—641
Cookstown (Northern Ireland : District)	T2—416 43
Cool jazz	781.655
Coolants	621.564
nuclear engineering	621.483 36
refrigeration engineering	621.564
Coolgardie (W.A.)	T2—941 6
Coolidge, Calvin	
United States history	973.915
Cooling coils	621.56
buildings	697.932 2
Cooling-off periods	
economics	331.898 2
personnel management	658.315 4
Cooling systems	
automotive	629.256
buildings	697.93
ships	623.853 5
Cooling towers	621.197
Cooloola National Park (Qld.)	T2—943 2
Coon cat	636.83
Coonabarabran (N.S.W.)	T2—944 4
Cooper County (Mo.)	T2—778 51
Cooperage	674.82
Cooperation	158
social process	303.34
social psychology	302.14
Cooperation in higher education	378.104
Cooperation in research	
international law	341.767 5
Cooperative cataloging	025.35
Cooperative collection development	025.21
Cooperative education	371.227
higher education	378.37
secondary level	373.28
Cooperative information services	025.523
Cooperative learning	371.36
Cooperative marketing	334.681 380 1
management	658.84
Cooperatives	334
accounting	657.97
economics	334
law	346.066 8
property law	346.043 3
management	658.047
initiation	658.114 7
see Manual at 658.04 vs. 658.114, 658.402	
sociology	306.344
Coopers Creek (Qld. and S. Aust.)	T2—942 37
Coordinate constructions (Grammar)	415
specific languages	T4—5
Coordinate indexing	025.484
Coordinate systems	
geometry	516.16
Coordination (Social process)	303.3
Coordination biochemistry	572.51
Coordination chemistry	541.224 2
Coordination of movement	
psychology	152.385
Coos County (N.H.)	T2—742 1
Coos County (Or.)	T2—795 23
Coos Indians	T5—974 1
Coosa County (Ala.)	T2—761 59
Coosa River (Ga. and Ala.)	T2—761 6
Cootamundra (N.S.W.)	T2—944 8
Coots	598.32
Copán (Honduras : Dept.)	T2—728 384

Copeland (England) T2—427 84
Copenhagen (Denmark) T2—489 13
Copenhagen (Denmark : Amt) T2—489 14
Copepoda 595.34
Copiah County (Miss.) T2—762 52
Copiapó (Chile : Province) T2—831 45
Copiers
  manufacturing technology 681.6
    see also Photocopying
Copies
  arts 702.872
  paintings 751.5
  technical drawing 604.25
Copolymerization
  chemical engineering 668.92
  chemistry 547.28
Copper 669.3
  applied nutrition 613.285
  architectural construction 721.044 73
  biochemistry 572.518
    humans 612.015 24
  building construction 693.73
  building material 691.83
  chemical engineering 661.065 2
  chemistry 546.652
  decorative arts 739.511
  economic geology 553.43
  human toxicology 615.925 652
  materials science 620.182
  metabolism
    human physiology 612.392 4
  metallography 669.953
  metallurgy 669.3
  metalworking 673.3
  mining 622.343
  organic chemistry 547.056 52
    applied 661.895
  physical metallurgy 669.963
  structural engineering 624.182 2
  see also Chemicals; Metals
Copper Age 930.15
Copper-aluminum alloys 669.3
  see also Copper
Copper-beryllium alloys 669.3
  see also Copper
Copper soaps 668.125
Copper sulfate water treatment 628.166 2
Copperbelt Province (Zambia) T2—689 4
Copperleaves (Plants) 583.69
Coppermine (N.W.T.) T2—719 7
Copra 665.355
Coptic Church 281.72
  see also Eastern churches
Coptic language 493.2
  T6—932
  Biblical texts 220.49
Coptic literature 893.2
Coptic people T5—932
Coptic period 932.023
Copts T5—932
Copulation
  sociology 306.77
Copying machines
  manufacturing technology 681.6
    see also Photocopying
Copyright 346.048 2
  international law 341.758 2
  law 346.048 2
  library operations 025.12
  public administration 352.749
Copyright deposits
  library acquisitions 025.26
Coquet River (England) T2—428 87
Coquihalla River (B.C.) T2—711 37
Coquimbo (Chile : Region) T2—832 3
Coquitlam (B.C.) T2—711 33
Cor pulmonale
  medicine 616.12
  see also Cardiovascular system
Coraciiformes 598.78
  paleozoology 568.7
Coracles 386.229
  design 623.812 9
  engineering 623.829
  transportation services 386.229
Coral fungi 579.597
Coral Harbour (N.W.T.) T2—719 4
Coral reefs 578.778 9
  T2—142
  biology 578.778 9
  conservation technology 639.972
  ecology 577.789
  geography 910.914 2
  physical geography 910.021 42
  resource economics 333.955 3
Coral Sea 551.465 76
  T2—164 76
Coralberry 583.675
Corals 593.6
  paleozoology 563.6
Corby (England : District) T2—425 51
Cordage
  ship gear 623.862
  textiles 677.71

Cordaitales 561.59
Cordials 641.255
  commercial processing 663.55
Cordierite
  mineralogy 549.64
Cordillera (Paraguay) T2—892 135
Cordite 662.26
  military engineering 623.452 6
Córdoba (Argentina : Province) T2—825 4
Córdoba (Colombia : Dept.) T2—861 12
Córdoba (Spain : Province) T2—468 4
Cordoba caliphate 946.02
Cords (Textiles) 677.76
  textile arts 746.27
Corduroy 677.617
Core curriculum 375.002
Core memory 004.53
  engineering 621.397 3
Core of earth 551.112
Corfu (Greece : Nome) T2—495 5
Coriariaceae 583.77
Corinth (Greece : Nome) T2—495 22
  ancient T2—387
Corinth, Isthmus of (Greece) T2—495 22
Corinthia (Greece) T2—495 22
  ancient T2—387
Corinthians (Biblical books) 227.2
Cork 674.9
  forestry 634.985
Cork (Ireland) T2—419 56
Cork (Ireland : County) T2—419 5
Cork oak 583.46
Cork trees (Rutaceae) 635.977 377
  botany 583.77
  ornamental arboriculture 635.977 377
Corkboard
  materials science 620.195
Cormorants 598.43
Corms 584.146
  descriptive botany 584.146
  physiology 575.496
Corn 641.331 5
  botany 584.92
  cereal crop 633.15
  commercial processing 664.724
  cooking 641.631 5
  food 641.331 5
  forage crop 633.255
  garden crop 635.67
Corn earworm 632.78
Corn sugars 641.336
  commercial processing 664.133
  see also Sugar
Corn syrup 641.336
  commercial processing 664.133
Cornales 583.84
Corneas
  human anatomy 611.84
  human physiology 612.841
  ophthalmology 617.719
  see also Eyes
Cornetists 788.960 92
  occupational group T7—788
Cornets 788.96
  instrument 788.961 9
  music 788.96
  see also Brass instruments
Cornetts 788.99
  see also Brass instruments
Cornflower 583.99
Cornices 721.5
  architecture 721.5
  construction 690.15
Cornish fowl 636.587 2
  food 641.365 872
    cooking 641.665 872
Cornish language 491.67
  T6—916 7
Cornish literature 891.67
Cornish people T5—916 7
Cornishmen T5—916 7
Cornmeal
  commercial processing 664.724
Corns (Disorder)
  medicine 616.544
  see also Skin
Cornstalk pulp 676.14
Cornstarch
  food technology 664.22
Cornwall (England : County) T2—423 7
Cornwallis, Charles Cornwallis, Marquess
  Indian history 954.031 1
    1786–1793 954.031 1
    1805 954.031 2
Coromandel Peninsula (N.Z.) T2—933 23
Corona of sun 523.75
Coronary arteriosclerosis
  medicine 616.123 2
  see also Cardiovascular system

Coronary artery bypass surgery 617.412
see also Cardiovascular system
Coronary atherosclerosis
medicine 616.123 2
see also Cardiovascular system
Coronary heart disease
medicine 616.123
see also Cardiovascular system
Coronas (Electronics) 537.52
Coronatae 593.53
Coronations
customs 394.4
Coroners 614.109 2
law 347.016
occupational group T7—349
Coronie (Surinam : District) T2—883 2
Corowa (N.S.W.) T2—944 8
Corozal District (Belize) T2—728 21
Corpora quadrigemina
human physiology 612.826 4
see also Nervous system
Corporal punishment 364.67
education 371.542
law 345.077 3
penology 364.67
Corporate bonds 332.632 34
Corporate crime 364.168
law 345.026 8
Corporate divestiture
management 658.16
Corporate finance 338.604 1
management 658.15
Corporate governance 658.4
Corporate income tax 336.243
law 343.052 67
public administration 352.44
public finance 336.243
Corporate law 346.066
Corporate mergers 338.83
see also Mergers
Corporate organization 338.74
economics 338.74
law 346.066 2
management
initiation 658.114 5
internal organization 658.402
Corporate ownership
land economics 333.324
Corporate planning 658.401 2
Corporate profits
income distribution 339.21
Corporate reorganization 338.74
credit economics 332.75
law 346.066 26
management 658.16
production economics 338.74
Corporate retail chains 381.12
management 658.870 2
see also Commerce
Corporate securities 332.632 044
Corporate state (Government) 321.94
Corporation meetings
law 346.066 45
management use 658.456
Corporation records
law 346.066 4
records management 651.5
Corporation tax 336.207
law 343.067
Corporations 338.74
accounting 657.95
law 346.066 48
economics 338.74
law 346.066
income tax law 343.052 67
tax law 343.067
tort law 346.031
management 658.045
initiation 658.114 5
law 346.066 4
see Manual at 658.04 vs. 658.114, 658.402
Corps (Military units) 355.31
Corps of engineers 358.22
Corpus Christi (Tex.) T2—764 113
Corpus iuris canonici 262.923
Corpus striatum
human physiology 612.825
see also Nervous system
Corpuscular theory of light 535.12
Correctional institutions 365
accounting 657.832
area planning 711.556
buildings 365.5
architecture 725.6
institutional housekeeping 647.966
law 344.035
psychological influence 155.962
reform 365.7
Corrections 364.6
public administration 353.39
Corrections (Astronomy) 522.9
Correlation analysis 519.537

Correspondence (Letters) 383.122
see also Letters (Correspondence)
Correspondence analysis 519.537
Correspondence courses 371.356
adult education 374.4
T1—071 5
higher education 378.175 4
Correspondence schools 374.4
T1—071 5
Corrèze (France : Dept.) T2—446 7
Corrientes (Argentina : Province) T2—822 2
Corrodentia 595.732
Corrosion 620.112 23
Corrosion control
chemical process equipment 660.283 04
Corrosion-resistant construction
ship hulls 623.848
Corrosive materials 363.179
public safety 363.179
technology 604.7
see also Hazardous materials
Corrugated paperboard boxes 676.32
Corruption in government 364.132 3
law 345.023 23
public administration 353.46
Corryong (Vic.) T2—945 5
Cors anglais 788.53
instrument 788.531 9
music 788.53
see also Woodwind instruments
Corsages 745.923
Corse (Region) T2—449 45
Corse-de-Sud (France) T2—449 452
Corsica (Region) T2—449 45
ancient T2—379
Corsicans T5—58
Corson County (S.D.) T2—783 52
Cortés (Honduras : Dept.) T2—728 311
Cortes Island (B.C.) T2—711 1
Cortex
human anatomy 611.81
human physiology 612.825
see also Nervous system
Cortin
chemistry 547.734 5
Cortisone
pharmacology 615.364
see also Endocrine system
Cortland County (N.Y.) T2—747 72
Çorum İli (Turkey) T2—563
Coruña (Spain : Province) T2—461 1
Corundum 553.65
gems 553.84
materials science 620.198
mineralogy 549.523
Corvidae 598.864
Coryell County (Tex.) T2—764 515
Corynebacterium 579.373
Corythosaurus 567.914
Coryza
medicine 616.205
see also Respiratory system
Cosenza (Italy : Province) T2—457 85
Cosets 512.2
Coshocton County (Ohio) T2—771 65
Cosmetic surgery 617.95
Cosmetics 646.72
customs 391.63
health 613.488
manufacturing technology 668.55
personal care 646.72
product safety 363.196
law 344.042 3
see also Product safety
Cosmetologists 646.720 92
occupational group T7—646 7
Cosmetology 646.72
Cosmic dust 523.112 5
Cosmic noise
meteorology 551.527 6
Cosmic rays 539.722 3
biophysics 571.459
humans 612.014 486
meteorology 551.527 6
Cosmochemistry 523.02
Cosmogony 523.12
astronomy 523.12
philosophy 113
Cosmology 523.1
astronomy 523.1
philosophy 113
religion 291.24
Christianity 231.765
comparative religion 291.24
Hinduism 294.524
Judaism 296.3
philosophy of religion 215.2
Cosmonauts 629.450 092
occupational group T7—629 4
Cosmos (Flowers) 583.99
Cossacks T5—917 14
Cost accounting 657.42
Cost analysis 658.155 2
Cost-benefit analysis 658.155 4
public administration 352.43

Cost control 658.155 2
  public administration 352.85
Cost effectiveness
  financial management 658.155 4
Cost of living
  macroeconomics 339.42
Cost-output ratio 338.06
  agricultural industries 338.16
  economics 338.06
  mineral industries 338.26
  secondary industries 338.45
Cost reduction 658.155 2
Cost-volume-profit analysis 658.155 4
Costa e Silva, Arthur da
  Brazilian history 981.063
Costa Rica 972.86
  T2—728 6
Costa Rican literature 860
Costa Ricans T5—687 286
Costaceae 584.39
Costilla County (Colo.) T2—788 35
Costs 338.51
  accounting 657.42
  agricultural industries 338.13
  economics 338.51
  financial management 658.155 2
  macroeconomics 339.42
  mineral industries 338.23
  secondary industries 338.43
  transportation services 388.049
Costume 391
  literature 808.803 55
    history and criticism 809.933 55
    specific literatures T3B—080 355
      history and criticism T3B—093 55
  see also Clothing
  see Manual at 391 vs. 646.3, 746.92
Costume jewelry 391.7
  customs 391.7
  handicrafts 745.594 2
  making 688.2
Costume jewelry makers 688.209 2
  occupational group T7—688
Costumes 792.026
  commercial technology 687.16
  dramatic performances 792.026
    motion pictures 791.430 26
    stage 792.026
    television 791.450 26
  home sewing 646.478
  see also Clothing
  see Manual at 391 vs. 646.3, 746.92
Cot death
  pediatrics 618.92
Côte d'Azur (France) T2—449
Côte-de-Beaupré (Quebec) T2—714 48
Côte-de-Gaspé (Quebec) T2—714 79
Côte d'Ivoire 966.68
  T2—666 8
Côte-d'Or (France) T2—444 2
Côte-Nord (Quebec) T2—714 17
Côte-Nord (Quebec : Administrative region) T2—714 17
Côtes-d'Armor (France) T2—441 2
Côtes-du-Nord (France) T2—441 2
Cotillions 793.35
Cotingas 598.822
Cotingidae 598.822
Cotonou (Benin) T2—668 3
Cotopaxi (Ecuador) T2—866 14
Cotswold (England : District) T2—424 17
Cotswold Hills (England) T2—424 17
Cotswolds (England) T2—424 17
Cottage cheese 641.373 56
  cooking 641.673 56
  food 641.373 56
  processing 637.356
Cottage industries 338.634
Cottages
  architecture 728.37
  construction 690.837
Cottbus (Germany : Bezirk) T2—431 51
Cotters 621.883
Cottle County (Tex.) T2—764 751
Cotton
  agricultural economics 338.173 51
  botany 583.685
  fiber crop 633.51
  textiles 677.21
    arts 746.042 1
    see also Textiles
Cotton County (Okla.) T2—766 49
Cotton grasses 584.84
Cotton rats 599.357 2
Cottonseed meal 664.726
Cottonseed oil
  food technology 664.363
Cottontails 599.324
Cottonwood County (Minn.) T2—776 28
Cottonwoods 583.65
Coturnix 598.627 2
Cotylosauria 567.92

Couches 645.4
  manufacturing technology 684.12
  see also Furniture
Couching
  arts 746.44
Cougar 599.752 4
  conservation technology 639.979 752 4
  resource economics 333.959 752 4
Cough remedies
  pharmacodynamics 615.72
  see also Respiratory system
Coulometers 621.374 4
Coulometry 543.087 4
Council for Mutual Economic
    Assistance 341.242 7
  international commerce 382.914 7
  international economics 337.147
  international law 341.242 7
Council housing 363.585
  law 344.063 635
  see also Housing
Council of Europe T2—4
  law 341.242
Councillors of state
  occupational group T7—352 1
Councils
  Christian ecclesiology 262.5
Councils of ministers
  public administration 352.24
Coundres Island (Quebec) T2—714 49
Counseling 361.06
  armed forces 355.347
  crime prevention 364.48
  education 371.4
    law 344.079 4
  pastoral theology 291.61
    Christianity 253.5
    Judaism 296.61
  personnel management 658.385
    public administration 352.67
  prisoner services 365.66
  psychology 158.3
  social work 361.06
    older persons 362.66
  see Manual at T1—019:
      Counseling
Counted thread embroidery 746.443
Counter displays
  advertising 659.157
Counter-Reformation 270.6
  German history 943.03
Counterattacks (Military tactics) 355.422
Counterculture 306.1
Counterfactuals
  logic 160
Counterfeit cancellations
  philately 769.562
Counterfeit coins
  numismatics 737.4
Counterfeit covers
  philately 769.562
Counterfeit paper money
  arts 769.55
Counterfeit postage stamps
  philately 769.562
Counterfeiting 364.133
  economics 332.9
  law 345.023 3
Counterglow (Astronomy) 523.59
Counterintelligence 327.12
  armed forces 355.343 3
    see also Unconventional
      warfare
  see also Espionage
Countermining 623.31
Countermonopoly theory of
    unions 331.880 1
Counterpoint 781.286
Counters
  numismatics 737.3
Countersubjects
  musical element 781.248
Countertenor voices 782.86
  choral and mixed voices 782.86
  single voices 783.86
Counties 320.83
  government 320.83
  public administration 352.15
    support and control 353.335
    see Manual at 351.3–351.9
        vs. 352.13–352.19
Counting 513.211
Counting circuits 621.381 534
Counting machines
  manufacturing technology 681.14
Counting-out rhymes 398.84
Counting rhymes 398.84
Country and western music 781.642
  songs 782.421 642
Country clubs
  landscape architecture 712.7
Country music 781.642
  songs 782.421 642
Country Party 324.294 04
County charters 342.02
County Court (Great Britain) 347.420 21
County courts 347.02

County executives 352.232 15
County government buildings
  architecture 725.13
County planning
  civic art 711.3
  economics 338.9
Coupling (Nuclear particles) 539.75
Couplings 621.825
  railroad engineering 625.25
Coups d'état 321.09
  see Manual at 909, 930–990
    vs. 320.4, 321, 321.09
Courage
  ethics 179.6
  see also Virtues
Courland (Duchy) T2—479 6
Cournot, A. A. (Antoine
    Augustin)
  economic school 330.154 3
Course in Miracles 299.93
Court calendars 347.013
Court clerks 347.016
Court costs 347.077
Court decisions
  international law 341.026 8
  texts 348.044
    United States 348.734 4
Court management 347.013
Court of Appeal (Great Britain) 347.420 32
Court of Appeal (Scotland) 345.411 016 3
Court of Customs and Patent
    Appeals (United States) 347.732 8
Court of First Instance
    (Scotland) 345.411 016 2
Court of Session (Scotland) 347.411 023
Court of the Lord Lyon
    (Scotland) 347.411 04
Court records 347.013
  genealogy 929.3
Court reporters 347.016
Court reporting
  shorthand 653.18
Court rules 347.051
Court settings
  music 781.536
Court tennis 796.34
  see also Sports
Courtesy
  ethics 177.1
    see also Ethical problems
  etiquette 395
Courthouses
  architecture 725.15
Courtroom procedure 347.075
  criminal law 345.075
Courts (Law) 347.01
  England 347.420 1
  international law 341.55
  Scotland 347.411 01
  United States 347.731
Courts-martial 343.014 3
Courts of appeal 347.03
  England 347.420 3
  Scotland 347.411 03
  United States 347.732 4
Courts of last resort 347.035
Courtship 306.734
  customs 392.4
  ethics 177.65
    religion 291.567 65
      Christianity 241.676 5
      Judaism 296.367 65
    see also Ethical problems
  music 781.586
  personal living 646.77
  sociology 306.734
Courtship (Animal behavior) 591.562
Cousins 306.87
  T1—085
  T7—046
Couvade 392.12
Covasna (Romania : Judeţ) T2—498 4
Covenant relationship with God
  Christianity 231.76
  Judaism 296.311 72
Coventry (England) T2—424 98
Cover crops
  soil conservation 631.452
Coverdale Bible 220.520 1
Covered bridges 388
  construction 624.38
  see also Bridges
Covered-girder bridges 388
  construction 624.37
  see also Bridges
Coverlets
  manufacturing technology 677.626
Covers
  bookbinding 686.34
Covers (Philately) 769.565
Covington (Va.) T2—755 812
Covington County (Ala.) T2—761 27
Covington County (Miss.) T2—762 545
Cowardice
  ethics 179.6
  see also Vices

Cowbirds 598.874
Cowboys 636.213 092
  occupational group T7—636
Coweta County (Ga.) T2—758 423
Cowfishes 597.64
Cowichan Valley (B.C.) T2—711 2
Cowley County (Kan.) T2—781 89
Cowlitz County (Wash.) T2—797 88
Cowlitz River (Wash.) T2—797 82
Cowpeas 641.356 592
  see also Black-eyed peas
Cowpox
  incidence 614.521
  medicine 616.913
  see also Communicable diseases (Human)
Cowra (N.S.W.) T2—944 5
Cowries 594.32
Coyote 599.772 5
  conservation technology 639.979 772 5
  predator control technology 636.083 9
  resource economics 333.959 772 5
  small game hunting 799.259 772 5
Coypu 599.359
CPM (Management) 658.403 2
CPR (Resuscitation)
  medicine 616.102 5
  see also Cardiovascular system
CPU (Central processor) 004
  engineering 621.39
Crab culture 639.66
Crab fishing 639.56
Crabbing 639.56
  economics 338.372 538 6
Crabeater seal 599.796
Crabgrasses 584.92
Crabs 595.386
  conservation technology 639.975 386
  cooking 641.695
  fishing 639.56
  fishing industry 338.372 538 6
  food 641.395
    commercial processing 664.94
  resource economics 333.955 56
  zoology 595.386
Cracidae 598.64
Crack abuse 362.298
  medicine 616.864 7
  personal health 613.84
  social welfare 362.298
  see also Substance abuse
Crack resistance (Engineering)
  materials science 620.112 6
Crackers 641.815
  commercial processing 664.752
  cooking 641.815
Cracking processes
  petroleum 665.533
Cradle Mountain (Tas.) T2—946 3
Cradle Mountain-Lake Saint Clair National Park (Tas.) T2—946 3
Cradock (South Africa : District) T2—687 14
Craft (Ships) 387.2
  see also Ships
Craft unions 331.883 2
  see also Labor unions
Crafts 680
  arts 745
  public administrative support 353.77
  sociology 306.489
  see Manual at 680 vs. 745.5
Craftsmen's marks T1—027 8
Craig County (Okla.) T2—766 98
Craig County (Va.) T2—755 795
Craigavon (Northern Ireland : District) T2—416 64
Craighead County (Ark.) T2—767 98
Cranberries 641.347 6
  botany 583.66
  commercial processing 664.804 76
  cooking 641.647 6
  food 641.347 6
  horticulture 634.76
Cranbrook (B.C.) T2—711 65
Crane County (Tex.) T2—764 915
Crane flies 595.772
Cranes (Birds) 598.32
  conservation technology 639.978 32
  resource economics 333.958 32
Cranes (Hoisting machinery) 621.873
Cranial nerves 573.85
  human physiology 612.819
  medicine 616.87
  see also Nervous system
Craniata 596
  see also Vertebrates
Craniology 599.948
Craniotomy
  obstetrical surgery 618.83
Cranks (Mechanisms) 621.827
Crape myrtle 635.977 376
  botany 583.76
  ornamental arboriculture 635.977 376
Crappies 597.738
  sports fishing 799.177 38

Craps 795.12
Crash injuries
  medicine 617.102 8
Crassulaceae 583.72
Crater Lake National Park
  (Or.) T2—795 915
Craters (Depressions) 551.21
  T2—144
  geography 910.914 4
  geology 551.21
  physical geography 910.021 44
Craters of the Moon
  National Monument
  (Idaho) T2—796 59
Crates
  wooden 674.82
Craven (England : District) T2—428 41
Craven County (N.C.) T2—756 192
Crawfishes 595.384
  see also Crayfishes
Crawford County (Ark.) T2—767 35
Crawford County (Ga.) T2—758 562
Crawford County (Ill.) T2—773 75
Crawford County (Ind.) T2—772 28
Crawford County (Iowa) T2—777 45
Crawford County (Kan.) T2—781 98
Crawford County (Mich.) T2—774 77
Crawford County (Mo.) T2—778 62
Crawford County (Ohio) T2—771 27
Crawford County (Pa.) T2—748 97
Crawford County (Wis.) T2—775 74
Crawley (England) T2—422 61
Crawling
  physiology 573.79
Crayfish culture 639.64
Crayfishes 595.384
  cooking 641.695
  culture 639.64
  fishing 639.54
  food 641.395
  sports fishing 799.255 384
  zoology 595.384
Crayfishing 639.54
  sports 799.255 384
Crayon drawing 741.23
Cream 641.371 48
  cooking 641.671 48
  food 641.371 48
  processing 637.148
Cream cheese 641.373 52
  cooking 641.673 52
  food 641.373 52
  processing 637.352
Cream of tartar
  commercial processing 664.68
Cream puffs 641.865 9
  commercial processing 664.752 5
  home preparation 641.865 9
Creaming latex 678.522
Crease-resistant fabrics 677.681
  see also Textiles
Creation
  cosmogony 523.12
  nuclear particles 539.75
  philosophy 113
  religion 291.24
    Christianity 231.765
    comparative religion 291.24
    Islam 297.242
    Judaism 296.34
    philosophy of religion 213
Creation science 231.765 2
  see also Creationism
Creationism 231.765 2
  biological evolution 576.8
  public education 379.28
  see Manual at 231.7652 vs. 213, 500, 576.8
Creative ability 153.35
  see also Creativity
Creative activities
  child care 649.51
  education 371.3
Creative arts 700
  elementary education 372.5
Creative thinking 153.42
  see also Creativity
Creative writing
  elementary education 372.623
Creativity 153.35
  arts 701.15
  educational objective 370.118
  educational psychology 370.157
  promotion of
    personnel management 658.314
      executives 658.407 14
      public administration 352.66
Creativity (Literary) 801.92
Credibility
  Christian church 262.72
Credit 332.7
  economics 332.7
  international law 341.751 15
  law 346.073
  public administration 354.86
  see Manual at 332.7 vs. 332.1

Credit cards 332.765
  banking services 332.178
  credit economics 332.765
  law 346.073
  see Manual at 332.7 vs. 332.1
Credit cooperatives 334.2
Credit institutions 332.3
  accounting 657.833 3
  public administration 354.86
Credit insurance 368.87
  see also Insurance
Credit investigations
  marketing management 658.88
Credit management
  marketing 658.88
Credit money 332.420 42
Credit unions 334.22
  law 346.066 8
Creditors
  law 346.077
Credits (Education) 371.218
  higher education 378.161 8
Credo 264.36
  music 782.323 2
Cree Indians T5—973
Cree language 497.3
  T6—973
Cree literature 897.3
Creeds 291.2
  Christianity 238
Creek County (Okla.) T2—766 84
Creek Indians T5—973
Creek language 497.3
  T6—973
Creep (Geology) 551.307
Creep (Materials science) 620.112 33
Creepers (Birds) 598.82
Cremation 363.75
  customs 393.2
  social services 363.75
  see also Undertaking (Mortuary)
Crematoriums 363.75
  architecture 725.597
Cremona (Italy : Province) T2—452 7
Crenshaw County (Ala.) T2—761 36
Creodonta 569.7
Creole cooking 641.597 63
Creoles
  linguistics 417.22
  specific languages T4—7
    see Manual at T4—7
Creosote bush 583.79
Crepe myrtle 635.977 376
  botany 583.76
  ornamental arboriculture 635.977 376
Crepes 641.815
Creping paper 676.234
Creping textiles 677.028 25
Cresses 641.355 6
  botany 583.64
  cooking 641.655 6
  food 641.355 6
  garden crop 635.56
Creston (B.C.) T2—711 62
Crests 929.6
Creswick (Vic.) T2—945 3
Cretaceous period 551.77
  geology 551.77
  paleontology 560.177
Crete (Greece) 949.59
  T2—495 9
  ancient 939.18
  T2—391 8
Crete, Sea of (Greece) 551.462 8
  T2—163 88
Cretinism
  medicine 616.858 848 043
  see also Mental retardation
Creuse (France) T2—446 8
Creutzfeldt-Jakob disease
  medicine 616.83
  see also Nervous system
Crewe and Nantwich (England) T2—427 12
Crewelwork 746.446
Crib death
  pediatrics 618.92
Cribbage 795.411
Criblé engraving 765.6
Cricetidae 599.35
Cricetus 599.356
Cricket (Game) 796.358
  see also Sports
Cricket players 796.358 092
  sports group T7—796 35
Crickets 595.726
  culture 638.572 6
Cries (Rhymes) 398.87
Crime 364
  arts 700.455
  T3C—355
  correction 364.6
  international law 341.77
  law 345

Crime (continued)
  literature 808.803 55
    history and criticism 809.933 55
    specific literatures T3B—080 355
      history and criticism T3B—093 55
  social theology 291.178 33
    Christianity 261.833
Crime insurance 368.82
  government-sponsored
    violent crimes 368.48
  see also Insurance
Crime prevention 364.4
  criminology 364.4
    public administration 353.39
  individual action 362.88
  management 658.473
  penology 364.601
  police services 363.23
    public administration 353.36
  school programs 371.782
Crime victims 362.88
  T1—086 949
  see also Victims of crime
Crimea (Ukraine : Oblast) T2—477 1
Crimean Tatar language 494.388
  T6—943 88
Crimean Tatar literature 894.388
Crimean Tatars T5—943 88
Crimean War, 1853–1856 947.073 8
Crimes 364.1
  see also Criminal offenses
Crimes against humanity 364.135
  law 345.023 5
Crimes against peace 364.135
  law 345.023 5
Crimes against the state 364.131
  law 345.023 1
Crimes without victims 364.1
  law 345.02
Criminal abortion 364.185
  law 345.028 5
Criminal anthropology 364.2
Criminal courts 345.01
  England 345.420 1
  Scotland 345.411 01
Criminal Division of Courts of
    Appeal (Great Britain) 345.420 18
Criminal intent 345.04
Criminal investigation 363.25
  armed forces 355.133 23
  law 345.052
  police services 363.25
Criminal jurisdiction 345.01
  international law 341.488
Criminal justice 364
  criminology 364
  law 345
  police services 363.2
  public administration 353.4
Criminal justice information
    systems 025.063 64
Criminal law 345
  international law 341.77
  see Manual at 345
Criminal liability 345.04
Criminal offenses 364.1
  insurance against 368.82
    see also Insurance
  international law 341.77
  law 345.02
    see Manual at 345.02 vs.
      346.03
  see also Crime
  see Manual at 362–363 vs.
      364.1; *also at* 900:
      Historic events vs.
      nonhistoric events
Criminal procedure 345.05
  public administration 353.43
Criminal psychology 364.3
Criminal responsibility 345.04
Criminal trial practice 345.075
Criminal trials 345.07
Criminal usury 364.168
  law 345.026 8
Criminalistics 363.25
  see also Criminal investigation
Criminally insane persons 364.38
  correctional institutions 365.46
    see also Correctional
      institutions
Criminals 364.3
  T1—086 927
  T7—069 27
  see also Offenders
Criminologists 364.092
  occupational group T7—364
Criminology 364
Crinoidea 593.92
  paleozoology 563.92
Crinozoa 593.92
  paleozoology 563.92
Crioulo language 469.799 665 8
  T6—69
Crisis management 658.405 6
Crisp County (Ga.) T2—758 893
Criteria
  epistemology 121.65

Critical care 362.174
  medicine 616.028
  nursing 610.736 1
  social welfare 362.174
  see also Health services
Critical path method
  (Management) 658.403 2
Critical pedagogy 370.115
Critical phenomena 530.474
  see also Phase transformations
Critical philosophy 142
Critical points 530.474
  fluid state 530.424
  see also Phase transformations
Critical realism
  philosophy 149.2
Critical size
  nuclear engineering 621.483 1
Critical thinking 160
  educational psychology 370.152
  elementary education
    reading 372.474
  psychology 153.42
Criticism
  arts 701.18
  fine arts
    specific subjects 704.94
  literature 809
    specific literatures T3B—09
      see Manual at T3B—08
        and T3B—09:
        Preference order
    theory 801.95
    see Manual at 800: Literary
      criticism
Criticism of individuals T1—092
Crittenden County (Ark.) T2—767 94
Crittenden County (Ky.) T2—769 893
Cro-Magnon man 569.9
Croakers (Fishes) 597.725
Croatia T2—497 2
Croatian language 491.82
  T6—918 2
Croatian literature 891.82
Croatians T5—918 23
Croats T5—918 23
Crocheted fabrics 677.662
  arts 746.434
  manufacturing technology 677.662
  see also Textiles
Crocheted laces 677.662
  arts 746.22
  manufacturing technology 677.662
Crocheted rugs
  arts 746.73
  see also Rugs
Crocheting 677.028 2
  arts 746.434
  manufacturing technology 677.028 2
Crock-pot cooking 641.588 4
Crockett County (Tenn.) T2—768 225
Crockett County (Tex.) T2—764 875
Crocodiles 597.98
  big game hunting 799.279 8
  conservation technology 639.977 98
  paleozoology 567.98
  resource economics 333.957 98
  zoology 597.98
Crocuses 635.934 38
  botany 584.38
  floriculture 635.934 38
Crohn's disease
  medicine 616.344 5
  see also Digestive system
Cromwell, Oliver
  British history 941.064
  English history 942.064
  Scottish history 941.106 4
Cromwell, Richard
  British history 941.065
  English history 942.065
  Scottish history 941.106 5
Crook County (Or.) T2—795 83
Crook County (Wyo.) T2—787 13
Crop-dusting 632.94
Crop-hail insurance 368.121
  see also Insurance
Crop insurance 368.121
  see also Insurance
Crop rotation
  cultivation technique 631.582
  economics 338.162
  soil conservation 631.452
Crop yields 338.1
  agricultural technology 631.558
  economics 338.1
  see Manual at 338.1 vs.
    631.558
Crops 630
  economics 338.1
  pathology 632
  public administration 354.54
Croquet 796.354
  see also Sports
Croquet players 796.354 092
  sports group T7—796 35
Crosby County (Tex.) T2—764 848

Crosier Fathers 255.19
  church history 271.19
Cross-country races
  humans 796.428
  see also Sports
Cross-country skiing 796.932
  see also Sports
Cross County (Ark.) T2—767 93
Cross-cultural communication 303.482
Cross-cultural psychology 155.8
Cross-examination 347.075
  criminal law 345.075
Cross River languages 496.364
  T6—963 64
Cross River State (Nigeria) T2—669 44
Cross-stitch 746.443
Crossbills 598.885
Crossbreeding
  agriculture 631.523
    animal husbandry 636.082
    plant cultivation 631.523
Crosses
  religious significance 246.558
Crossing over (Genetics) 572.877
Crossings (Railroad) 385.312
  engineering 625.163
  transportation services 385.312
Crossopterygii 597.39
  paleozoology 567.39
Crossroads (South Africa) T2—687 35
Crossword-puzzle dictionaries 413.1
  specific languages T4—31
Crossword puzzles 793.732
Crotons 635.933 69
  botany 583.69
  floriculture 635.933 69
Croup
  medicine 616.201
  pediatrics 618.922 01
  see also Respiratory system
Crow Indians T5—975 2
Crow language 497.52
  T6—975 2
Crow Wing County
    (Minn.) T2—776 71
Crowbars 621.93
Crowberries 583.66
Crowd control 363.32
  public administration 353.36
Crowds 302.33
Crowley County (Colo.) T2—788 94
Crown Counsel (Scotland) 345.411 01
Crown Court (Great Britain) 345.420 14
Crown of thorns (Plant) 635.933 69
  botany 583.69
  floriculture 635.933 69
Crowns (Dentistry) 617.692
  see also Dentistry
Crows 598.864
  sports hunting 799.248 864
Crowsnest Pass (Alta.) T2—712 34
Croydon (London,
    England) T2—421 91
Crozet Islands 969.9
  T2—699
Cruciales 583.64
Crucible steel 669.142 9
Crucibles (Chemical apparatus) 542.2
Cruciferae 583.64
Crucifixes
  religious significance 246.558
Crucifixion of Jesus Christ 232.963
Crucifixion thorns 583.64
Crude drugs
  pharmacognosy 615.321
Crude gelatin 668.34
Cruelty
  ethics 179
    see also Ethical problems
Cruelty to animals
  criminology 364.187
    criminal law 345.028 7
  ethics 179.3
    religion 291.569 3
      see also Animals—
        treatment of—
        ethics—religion
Cruisers 359.835 3
  design 623.812 53
  engineering 623.825 3
  naval equipment 359.835 3
  naval units 359.325 3
Crumhorns 788.5
  see also Woodwind
    instruments
Crusades 909.07
  church history 270.4
  European history 940.18
  history 909.07
Crushed stone pavements 625.82
Crushers (Agricultural tools)
  manufacturing technology 681.763 1
Crushing
  chemical engineering 660.284 22
  ores 622.73
Crushing tools 621.914

Crust of earth 551.13
  compression 551.82
Crustacea 595.3
  see also Crustaceans
Crustaceans 595.3
  conservation technology 639.975 3
  cooking 641.695
  culture 639.6
  fishing 639.5
  fishing industry 338.372 53
  food 641.395
    commercial processing 664.94
  paleozoology 565.3
  resource economics 333.955 5
  zoology 595.3
Crutches
  manufacturing technology 681.761
Cryobiology 571.464 5
  humans 612.014 467
Cryogenic engineering 621.59
Cryogenic engineers 621.590 92
  occupational group T7—621
Cryogenics 536.56
  biophysics 571.464 5
    humans 612.014 467
  engineering 621.59
  materials science 620.112 16
Cryolite
  mineralogy 549.4
  synthetic 666.86
Cryometry 536.54
Cryosurgery 617.05
Cryotherapy
  medicine 615.832 9
Cryptanalysis 652.8
  armed forces 355.343 2
Cryptococcales 579.55
Cryptogamia 586
  paleobotany 561.6
Cryptography 652.8
  armed forces 358.24
  computer science 005.82
  recreation 793.73
Cryptophyta 579.82
Cryptozoic eon 551.71
  geology 551.71
  paleontology 560.171
Crystal conduction counters
  nuclear physics 539.776
Crystal devices
  electronics 621.381 52
Crystal gazing 133.322
Crystal growth 548.5
Crystal lattices 548.81
Crystalline lens
  human anatomy 611.84
  human physiology 612.844
  ophthalmology 617.742
  see also Eyes
Crystalline solids 530.413
Crystallization 548.5
  chemical engineering 660.284 298
  sugar production 664.115
Crystallograms 548.83
Crystallographers 548.092
  occupational group T7—548
Crystallographic mineralogy 549.18
Crystallographic properties
  materials science 620.112 99
Crystallography 548
  see Manual at 548 vs. 530.41;
    also at 549 vs. 548
Crystals 548
  occultism 133.254 8
    divination 133.322
Csongrád Megye
    (Hungary) T2—439 8
CT (Tomography)
  medicine 616.075 72
Ctenophora 593.8
  paleozoology 563.8
Ctenostomata 594.676
Ctenothrissiformes 567.5
Cuando Cubango (Angola) T2—673 5
Cuanza Norte (Angola) T2—673 2
Cuanza Sul (Angola :
    Province) T2—673 2
Cub Scouts 369.43
Cuba 972.91
  T2—729 1
Cuban communism 335.434 7
  economics 335.434 7
  political ideology 320.532 309 7291
Cuban itch
  medicine 616.913
  see also Communicable
    diseases (Human)
Cuban literature 860
Cubans T5—687 291
Cubature 515.43
Cube-doubling 516.204
Cube root 513.23
Cubes 516.15
Cubic equations 512.942
  algebra 512.942
  calculus 515.252

Cubism 709.040 32
  painting 759.063 2
  sculpture 735.230 432
Cubomedusae 593.53
Cuckoo shrikes 598.8
Cuckoos 598.74
Cucujoidea 595.769
Cuculiformes 598.74
  paleozoology 568.7
Cucumber tree 583.22
Cucumbers 641.356 3
  botany 583.63
  commercial processing 664.805 63
  cooking 641.656 3
  food 641.356 3
  garden crop 635.63
Cucurbitales 583.63
Cuenca (Spain : Province) T2—464 7
Cuicatec language 497.6
  T6—976
Cuitlatec language 497.9
  T6—979
Culberson County (Tex.) T2—764 94
Culicidae 595.772
Cullinan (South Africa : District) T2—682 3
Cullman County (Ala.) T2—761 73
Culpeper County (Va.) T2—755 392
Cultivated silk textiles 677.391
  see also Textiles
Cultivation 631.5
Cultivation (Tillage) 631.51
Cultivators 631.51
  manufacturing technology 681.763 1
Cults 291.9
  see Manual at 291: Denominations and sects; *also at* 299.93: New Age religions
Cultural anthropologists 306.092
  occupational group T7—309
Cultural anthropology 306
Cultural centers
  architecture 725.804 2
  area planning 711.57
Cultural contact 303.482
Cultural ethnology 305.8
Cultural exchanges 303.482
  law 344.08
  public administration 353.7
  sociology 303.482
Cultural influence
  psychology 155.92
Cultural institutions 306
Cultural levels (Social classes) 305.906 3
  T1—086 3
Cultural programs
  libraries 021.26
Cultural property
  historic preservation 363.69
    international law 341.767 7
    law 344.094
Cultural relations 303.482
  international law 341.767
Cultural Revolution 951.056
Culturally disadvantaged children 155.456 7
  home care 649.156 7
Culturally disadvantaged persons T1—086 33
Culture 306
  law 344.09
  public administrative support 353.7
  sociology 306
  see Manual at 305 vs. 306, 909, 930–990
Cultured skim milk 641.371 476
  cooking 641.671 476
  food 641.371 476
  processing 637.147 6
Cultured whole milk 641.371 46
  cooking 641.671 46
  food 641.371 46
  processing 637.146
Culverts (Drainage) 625.734 2
Cumacea 595.376
Cumberland (England) T2—427 8
Cumberland (N.S. : County) T2—716 11
Cumberland, Lake (Ky.) T2—769 63
Cumberland County (Ill.) T2—773 73
Cumberland County (Ky.) T2—769 683
Cumberland County (Me.) T2—741 91
Cumberland County (N.C.) T2—756 373
Cumberland County (N.J.) T2—749 94
Cumberland County (Pa.) T2—748 43
Cumberland County (Tenn.) T2—768 75
Cumberland County (Va.) T2—755 615
Cumberland Mountains T2—769 1
  Kentucky T2—769 1
  Tennessee T2—768 944
Cumberland Plateau T2—768 7
  Kentucky T2—769 1
  Tennessee T2—768 7
Cumberland Presbyterian Church 285.135
  see also Presbyterian Church

Cumberland River (Ky. and Tenn.) T2—768 5
Cumbernauld and Kilsyth (Scotland) T2—414 38
Cumbria (England) T2—427 8
Cumbrian Mountains (England) T2—427 8
Cuming County (Neb.) T2—782 232
Cumnock and Doon Valley (Scotland) T2—414 67
Cuna Indians T5—982
Cuna language 498.2
T6—982
Cundinamarca (Colombia) T2—861 46
Cuneo (Italy : Province) T2—451 3
Cunninghame (Scotland) T2—414 61
Cunoniaceae 583.72
Cup fungi 579.57
Cup games
soccer 796.334 64
Cupedidae 595.762
Cupesidae 595.762
Cupolas 721.5
architecture 721.5
construction 690.15
Cuprammonium rayon 677.462
see also Textiles
Cupressaceae 585.4
paleobotany 561.54
Cuprite
mineralogy 549.522
Cups
paper 676.34
Curaçao T2—729 86
Curassows 598.64
Curbs 625.888
Curculionidae 595.768
Curculionoidea 595.768
agricultural pests 632.768
Curfew
crime prevention 364.4
see also Crime prevention
Curia Romana 262.136
Curicó (Chile : Province) T2—833 4
Curium 546.442
see also Chemicals
Curling (Sport) 796.964
see also Sports
Currants 641.347 21
botany 583.72
cooking 641.647 21
food 641.347 21
horticulture 634.721
Currency 332.4
see also Money
Currency convertibility 332.45
Currency movements 332.042
Currency paper 676.282 6
Current assets
accounting 657.72
Current awareness services
information science 025.525
Current liabilities
accounting 657.74
Current transactions
balance of payments
international commerce 382.17
Curricula 375
T1—071
adult education 374.01
elementary education 372.19
higher education 378.199
law 344.077
public control 379.155
secondary education 373.19
Curriculum change 375.006
Curriculum development 375.001
Curriculum evaluation 375.006
Curriculum libraries 027.7
Curriculum planning 375.001
Curriculums 375
see also Curricula
Currituck County (N.C.) T2—756 132
Curry County (N.M.) T2—789 27
Curry County (Or.) T2—795 21
Curry powder 641.338 4
see also Hot spices
Curses
folklore 398.41
Curtains 645.3
arts 746.94
commercial technology 684.3
home sewing 646.21
household management 645.3
Curvature (Mathematics) 516.362
Curve fitting 511.42
Curves 516.15
algebraic geometry 516.352
differential geometry 516.36
integral geometry 516.36
Curvilinear coordinate system 516.16
Curzon, George Nathaniel Curzon, Marquis of
Indian history 954.035 5
Cuscatlán (El Salvador) T2—728 424
Cuscuses 599.232
Cuscutaceae 583.94

Cush T2—397 8
Cush sovereignty 932.015
Cushing's syndrome
  medicine 616.45
  see also Endocrine system
Cushites T5—935
Cushitic languages 493.5
  T6—935
Cushitic literatures 893.5
Cushitic peoples T5—935
Cusk eels 597.63
Custard apples 583.22
Custer County (Colo.) T2—788 52
Custer County (Idaho) T2—796 72
Custer County (Mont.) T2—786 33
Custer County (Neb.) T2—782 47
Custer County (Okla.) T2—766 17
Custer County (S.D.) T2—783 95
Custody of children 346.017 3
Custom production 338.642
Customary law 340.5
Customer relations
  marketing management 658.812
Customized vans 388.343 4
  driving 629.284 34
  engineering 629.223 4
  repair 629.287 34
  transportation services 388.343 4
  see also Trucks
Customizing automobiles 629.287
Customs (Social) 390
  music 781.58
  social control 303.372
  see Manual at 390
Customs (Tariff) 382.7
  commerce 382.7
  international law 341.754 3
  law 343.056
  public administration 352.448
  public finance 336.26
Customs administration 352.448
Customs buildings
  architecture 725.14
Customs courts 343.056 026 9
Customs unions 382.91
Cut flowers
  floriculture 635.966
  see also Flowers
Cut stock lumber 674.28
Cutaneous leishmaniasis
  medicine 616.936 4
  see also Communicable
    diseases (Human)
Cutaneous perception
  psychology 152.182
Cutaneous sensory disorders
  medicine 616.856
  see also Nervous system
Cutlass fishes 597.78
Cutlery 642.7
  cooking 641.502 8
  manufacturing technology 683.82
  table setting 642.7
Cuts
  road engineering 625.733
Cutting gems 736.202 8
Cutting glass 666.12
  arts 748.6
  technology 666.12
Cutting metals 671.53
  decorative arts 739.14
  machining process 671.35
  sculpture 731.41
Cutting tools 621.93
Cuttings (Plant propagation) 631.535
Cuttlefish 594.58
Cutwork
  arts 746.44
Cutworms 595.78
  agricultural pests 632.78
Cuyahoga County (Ohio) T2—771 31
Cuyahoga River (Ohio) T2—771 31
Cuzco (Peru : Dept.) T2—853 7
Cyanamide fertilizers 631.841
  chemical engineering 668.624 1
Cyanastraceae 584.35
Cyanite
  mineralogy 549.62
Cyanobacteria 579.39
Cyanophyta 579.39
Cybernetics 003.5
  T1—011 5
Cycadales 585.9
  paleobotany 561.591
Cycadeoidales 561.592
Cycads 585.9
  paleobotany 561.591
Cyclades (Greece) T2—495 85
  ancient T2—391 5
Cyclamens 635.933 675
  botany 583.675
  floriculture 635.933 675
Cyclanthales 584.62
Cyclarhidae 598.878
Cycles
  philosophy 116

Cycles (Vehicles)	388.347
engineering	629.227
repair	629.287 7
riding	629.284 7
sports	796.6
transportation services	388.347
Cyclic compounds	547.5
chemical engineering	661.8
Cyclic groups	512.2
Cyclical unemployment	331.137 047
Cycling	
sports	796.6
see also Sports	
Cycling paths	388.12
see also Bicycle paths	
Cyclists	796.609 2
sports group	T7—796 6
Cyclo rubber	678.68
Cycloacetylenes	547.513
chemical engineering	661.815
Cyclones	551.551 3
Cyclones (Tornadoes)	551.553
see also Tornadoes	
Cycloolefins	547.512
chemical engineering	661.815
Cycloparaffins	547.511
chemical engineering	661.815
Cyclopedias	030
Cyclopoida	595.34
Cyclops (Animals)	595.34
Cyclopteris	561.597
Cycloramas	745.8
decorative arts	745.8
painting	751.74
Cyclorrhapha	595.774
Cyclosilicates	
mineralogy	549.64
Cyclostomata (Jawless fish)	597.2
paleozoology	567.2
Cyclotomy (Number theory)	512.72
Cyclotrons	539.733
Cygninae	598.418
Cygnus	598.418
Cylinder recordings	
sound reproduction	621.389 32
Cylinders (Engine parts)	621.437
Cylinders (Shape)	516.15
Cylinders (Structural elements)	624.177 2
concrete	624.183 42
Cylindrical bark beetles	595.769
Cymbals	786.873
see also Percussion instruments	
Cymraeg literature	891.66
Cymric language	491.66
	T6—916 6
Cymric literature	891.66
Cymry	T5—916 6
Cynewulf	829.4
Cynic philosophy	183.4
Cynocephalidae	599.33
Cynocrambales	583.5
Cynomys	599.367
Cynon Valley (Wales : Borough)	T2—429 73
Cyperales	584.84
Cypress Hills (Alta. and Sask.)	T2—712 43
Cypress pine	585.4
Cypresses	585.4
forestry	634.975 5
lumber	674.144
Cyprinidae	597.482
Cypriniformes	597.48
paleozoology	567.48
Cyprinodontidae	597.665
Cyprinodontoidei	597.66
Cypriot architecture	
Phoenician	722.32
Cypriots	T5—895
Cyprus	956.93
	T2—569 3
ancient	939.37
	T2—393 7
Cyrenaic philosophy	183.5
Cyrenaica	T2—397 5
ancient	939.75
Cyrillic alphabet	491.8
printing	686.219 18
Cyrillic calligraphy	745.619 918
Cystic fibrosis	
medicine	616.37
see also Digestive system	
Cystitis	
medicine	616.623
see also Urinary system	
Cystoidea	563.95
Cythera Island (Greece)	T2—495 2
Cytinaceae	583.2
Cytochemistry	572
Cytodiagnosis	
medicine	616.075 82
Cytogenetics	572.8
humans	611.018 16
Cytological examination	
medicine	616.075 82
Cytology	571.6
humans	611.018 1

Cytometry
  diagnosis
    medicine 616.075 82
Cytopathology 571.936
  humans 611.018 15
Cytoplasm 571.65
Cytoplasmic inheritance 572.869
Cytoplasmic membranes 571.64
Cytoskeleton 571.654
Cytotaxonomy 578.012
Cytotoxic T cells 571.966
  human immunology 616.079 7
Czech language 491.86
  T6—918 6
Czech literature 891.86
Czech Republic 943.71
  T2—437 1
Czechoslovak Republic 943.703 2
  T2—437
Czechoslovakia 943.703
  T2—437
Czechoslovaks T5—918 6
Czechs T5—918 6
Częstochowa (Poland : Voivodeship) T2—438 5

D

D region (Ionosphere) 538.767 2
Da capo form 781.822 5
  instrumental 784.182 2
Daba language 493.7
  T6—937
Dacca (Bangladesh : Division) T2—549 22
Daces 597.482
  sports fishing 799.174 82
Dachshund 636.753 8
Dachshund (Miniature dog) 636.76
Dacia T2—398
Dacorum (England : District) T2—425 84
Dactylopteriformes 597.64
Dadaism
  fine arts 709.040 62
  literature 808.801 162
    history and criticism 809.911 62
    specific literatures T3B—080 116 2
      history and criticism T3B—091 162
  painting 759.066 2
  sculpture 735.230 462
Daddy longlegs 595.43
Dade County (Fla.) T2—759 38
Dade County (Ga.) T2—758 342
Dade County (Mo.) T2—778 745
Dādra and Nagar Haveli (India) T2—547 96
Daffodils 635.934 34
  botany 584.34
  floriculture 635.934 34
Dagari (African people) T5—963 5
Dagari language 496.35
  T6—963 5
Dagbani (African people) T5—963 5
Dagbani language 496.35
  T6—963 5
Dagestan (Russia) T2—475 2
Dagestan languages 499.964
  T6—999 64
Daggers 623.441
  art metalwork 739.72
  military engineering 623.441
Daggett County (Utah) T2—792 15
Daghestan languages 499.964
  T6—999 64
Dagomba (African people) T5—963 5
Dagomba language 496.35
  T6—963 5
Daguerreotype process 772.12
Dahlias 635.933 99
  botany 583.99
  floriculture 635.933 99
Dahomeans T5—966 83
Dahomey 966.83
  T2—668 3
Dahomey (African people) T5—963 37
Dahomey (Kingdom) 966.830 18
  T2—668 3
Dahūk (Iraq : Province) T2—567 2
Dai language (Chad) 493.7
  T6—937
Daily devotions 291.446
  Christianity 242.2
  Judaism 296.45
Dairy cattle
  animal husbandry 636.214 2
Dairy cooperatives 334.683 7
Dairy farmers 636.214 209 2
  occupational group T7—637
Dairy farming 636.214 2
Dairy industry 338.176 214 2
  law 343.076 621 42
  public administration 354.56
Dairy processing industry 338.476 37
Dairy processors
  occupational group T7—637

Dairy products 641.37
  cooking 641.67
  food 641.37
  processing 637
  product safety 363.192 9
    see also Food—product safety
Dairymen 636.214 209 2
  occupational group T7—637
Daisies 583.99
  floriculture 635.933 99
Dajabón (Dominican Republic : Province) T2—729 345
Dakar (Senegal) T2—663
Dakhla (Western Sahara) T2—648
Dakota County (Minn.) T2—776 56
Dakota County (Neb.) T2—782 224
Dakota Indians T5—975 2
Dakota language 497.52
  T6—975 2
Dakota literature 897.52
Dalby (Qld.) T2—943 3
Dale County (Ala.) T2—761 33
Dale Hollow Lake (Tenn. and Ky.) T2—768 49
Dalhousie, James Andrew Broun Ramsay, Marquis
  Indian history 954.031 6
Dallam County (Tex.) T2—764 812
Dallas (Tex.) T2—764 281 2
Dallas County (Ala.) T2—761 45
Dallas County (Ark.) T2—767 67
Dallas County (Iowa) T2—777 57
Dallas County (Mo.) T2—778 813
Dallas County (Tex.) T2—764 281 1
Dalmatia (Croatia) T2—497 2
Dalmatian (Dog) 636.72
Dalmatian language (Romance) 457.994 972
  T6—57
Dalmatian language (Slavic) 491.82
  T6—918 2
Dalmatian literature (Romance) 850
Dalmatian literature (Slavic) 891.82
Dalmatians (Romance people) T5—57
Dalmatians (Slavic people) T5—918 2
Daly River (N.T.) T2—942 95
Dama (Fallow deer) 599.655
Damages (Law) 347.077
Damascening 739.15
Damascus (Syria) T2—569 144
  ancient T2—394 3
Damascus (Syria : Province) T2—569 14
Damask 677.616
Damietta (Egypt : Province) T2—621
Dammar pines 585.3
  forestry 634.975 93
Damping
  aeronautics 629.132 364
Damping of sound
  physics 534.208
Dampness control
  construction
    buildings 693.893
Dams 627.8
  agricultural use 631.28
  ecology 577.272
  public administration 354.362 77
Damselfishes 597.72
Damselflies 595.733
Dan (African people) T5—963 4
Dan language 496.34
  T6—963 4
Dance 792.8
  elementary education 372.868
  see also Dancing
  see Manual at 792.78 vs. 792.8, 793.3
Dance bands 784.48
Dance flies 595.773
Dance forms 784.188
Dance halls
  architecture 725.86
Dance music 781.554
Dance of death
  arts 700.454 8
    T3C—354 8
  literature 808.803 548
    history and literature 809.933 548
    specific literatures T3B—080 354 8
      history and criticism T3B—093 548
Dance orchestras 784.48
Dance therapy
  medicine 615.851 55
Dancers 792.802 809 2
  occupational group T7—792 8
  see Manual at 791.092
Dances of the suite 793.3
  music 784.188 3
Dancing 792.8
  arts 700.455
    T3C—355
  customs 394.3
  ethics 175
  etiquette 395.3

Dancing (continued)
  literature 808.803 55
    history and criticism 809.933 55
    specific literatures T3B—080 355
      history and criticism T3B—093 55
  musical plays 792.62
  religious significance 291.37
    Christianity 246.7
    see also Arts—religious significance
  sociology 306.484
  see Manual at 792.78 vs. 792.8, 793.3
Dancing games 796.13
Dandelions 583.99
  cooking 641.655 1
  food 641.355 1
  garden crop 635.51
Dandruff
  medicine 616.546
  see also Skin
Dane County (Wis.) T2—775 83
Danes T5—398 1
Dangaleat language 493.7
  T6—937
Dangerous animals 591.65
Dani (New Guinea people) T5—991 2
Daniel (Biblical book) 224.5
Daniels County (Mont.) T2—786 213
Danios 597.482
Danish language 439.81
  T6—398 1
Danish literature 839.81
Danish pastry 641.865 9
  commercial processing 664.752 5
  home preparation 641.865 9
Danish people T5—398 1
Dannhauser (South Africa : District) T2—684 1
Dano-Norwegian language 439.82
  T6—398 2
Dano-Norwegian literature 839.82
Danube River T2—496
  Germany T2—433
Danville (Va.) T2—755 666
Danzig (Germany) T2—438 2
Daphnes 583.67
Daqahlīyah (Egypt) T2—621
DAR (Patriotic society) 369.135
  biography 369.135 092
Dar es Salaam (Tanzania : Region) T2–678 232
Dar'ā (Syria : Province) T2—569 14
Dard (Indic people) T5—914 99
Dard languages 491.499
  T6—914 99
Dard literatures 891.499
Dardanelles Strait (Turkey) 551.462 9
  T2—163 89
Dardic languages 491.499
  T6—914 99
Dardic literatures 891.499
Dardic peoples T5—914 99
Dare County (N.C.) T2—756 175
Darfur (Sudan) T2—627
Dārfūr al-Janūbīyah (Sudan : Province) T2—627
Dārfūr al-Shamālīyah (Sudan : Province) T2—627
Dargi language 499.964
  T6—999 64
Dargwa language 499.964
  T6—999 64
Dari language 491.56
  T6—915 6
Dari literature 891.56
Darien (Panama : Province) T2—728 74
Darien, Gulf of (Colombia) 551.463 5
  T2—163 65
Dark Ages 940.12
Dark matter (Astronomy) 523.112 6
Darke County (Ohio) T2—771 47
Darkling beetles 595.769
Darkroom techniques 771.4
Darkrooms (Photography) 771.1
Darling Downs (Qld.) T2—943 3
Darling Range (W.A.) T2—941 2
Darlington (England : District) T2—428 63
Darlington County (S.C.) T2—757 66
Darmstadt (Germany) T2—434 167
Darmstadt (Germany : Regierungsbezirk) T2—434 16
Darned laces
  arts 746.22
Darning 646.204
Darom (Israel : District) T2—569 49
Dart River (England) T2—423 592
Darters (Fish) 597.75
Dartford (England : District) T2—422 312
Dartmoor (England) T2—423 53
Dartmouth (N.S.) T2—716 225
Dartmouth Metropolitan Area (N.S.) T2—716 225
Darts 794.3
Darwin (N.T.) T2—942 95

Darwinism 576.82
Darwin's finches 598.883
Dascilloidea 595.763
Dassies 599.68
Dasycladales 579.836
Dasypodidae 599.312
Dasyuridae 599.27
DAT (Digital audio)
sound reproduction 621.389 3
Data backup 005.86
Data banks 025.04
see also Databases
Data bases 025.04
see also Databases
Data cells (Computer storage) 004.56
engineering 621.397 6
Data collection (Descriptive research) 001.433
T1—072 3
see Manual at T1—07201–T1—07209 vs. T1—0722–T1—0724
Data communications 004.6
see also Computer communications
Data compaction 005.746
Data compression 005.746
Data conversion 005.72
Data dictionaries 005.742
Data directories 005.742
Data encryption
computer science 005.82
Data entry 005.72
Data files 005.74
see Manual at 005.74
Data in computer systems 005.7
T1—028 557
Data preparation
computer science 005.72
Data processing 004
T1—028 5
office services 651.8
see Manual at T1—0285; *also at* T1—0285 vs. T1—0113; *also at* T1—0285 vs. T1—068; *also at* 510, T1—0151 vs. 004–006, T1—0285
Data record formats 005.72
Data recovery 005.86
Data representation 005.72
Data security 005.8
T1—028 558
management 658.478
Data structures 005.73
Data tapes 004.56
computer engineering 621.397 6
Data transmission 004.6
see also Computer communications
Databanks 025.04
see also Databases
Database architecture 005.74
Database design 005.74
Database management systems 005.74
Databases 025.04
civil rights issues 323.448 3
computer science 005.74
information science 025.04
law 343.099 9
management use 658.403 801 1
see Manual at 005.74
Dataflow computation 004.35
Dates (Chronology) 902.02
Dates (Fruit) 641.346 2
agriculture 634.62
botany 584.5
commercial processing 664.804 62
cooking 641.646 2
food 641.346 2
Dating (Archaeological technique) 930.102 85
Dating (Social practice) 306.73
customs 392.6
personal living 646.77
sociology 306.73
Daturas 583.952
Daughters 306.874
T1—085 4
T7—044 1
Daughters of the American Revolution 369.135
biography 369.135 092
Dauphin County (Pa.) T2—748 18
Dauphiné (France) T2—449 6
Dauplin (Man.) T2—712 72
D'Autray (Quebec) T2—714 43
DAV (Veterans) 369.186 3
Davao del Norte (Philippines) T2—599 7
Davao del Sur (Philippines) T2—599 7
Davao Oriental (Philippines) T2—599 7
Davenport (Iowa) T2—777 69
Davenport Range (N.T.) T2—942 91
Davenports 645.4
see also Furniture

Daventry (England :
  District) T2—425 56
David, King of Israel
  Biblical leader 222.409 2
  Palestinian history 933.02
David and Goliath story 222.430 950 5
Davidson County (N.C.) T2—756 68
Davidson County (Tenn.) T2—768 55
Davie County (N.C.) T2—756 69
Daviess County (Ind.) T2—772 385
Daviess County (Ky.) T2—769 864
Daviess County (Mo.) T2—778 183
Davis County (Iowa) T2—777 97
Davis County (Utah) T2—792 27
Davis Strait 551.461 42
  T2—163 42
Davison County (S.D.) T2—783 374
Da'wah 297.74
Dawes County (Neb.) T2—782 93
Dawn 525.7
  literature 808.803 3
    history and criticism 809.933 3
    specific literatures T3B—080 33
      history and criticism T3B—093 3
Dawson (Yukon) T2—719 1
Dawson County (Ga.) T2—758 263
Dawson County (Mont.) T2—786 24
Dawson County (Neb.) T2—782 46
Dawson County (Tex.) T2—764 854
Dawson Creek (B.C.) T2—711 87
Day camps 796.542 3
Day care 362.712
  law 344.032 712
  preschool education 372.21
  social welfare 362.712
Day County (S.D.) T2—783 142
Day language (Chad) 493.7
  T6—937
Day lilies 635.934 32
  botany 584.32
  floriculture 635.934 32
Day of the Lord
  Christianity 236.9
Daydreams 154.3
Daylesford (Vic.) T2—945 3
Daylight saving time 389.17
  law 343.07
Daymarks 387.155
  construction 627.924
  navigation aids 623.894 4
  transportation services 387.155
Dayr al-Zawr (Syria :
  Province) T2—569 12
Days 529.1
  chronology 529.1
  folklore 398.236
    history and criticism 398.33
  literature 808.803 3
    history and criticism 809.933 3
    specific literatures T3B—080 33
      history and criticism T3B—093 3
  music 781.522
Dayton (Ohio) T2—771 73
Daza (African people) T5—965
Daza language 496.5
  T6—965
DBS systems 384.552
DDT (Insecticide) 632.951 7
De Aar (South Africa :
  District) T2—687 13
De Baca County (N.M.) T2—789 44
De facto government
  international law 341.26
De Kalb County (Ala.) T2—761 66
De Kalb County (Ga.) T2—758 225
De Kalb County (Ill.) T2—773 28
De Kalb County (Ind.) T2—772 77
De Kalb County (Mo.) T2—778 153
De Kalb County (Tenn.) T2—768 532
De Klerk, F. W. (Frederik
  Willem)
  South African history 968.064
De Soto County (Fla.) T2—759 59
De Soto County (Miss.) T2—762 87
De Soto Parish (La.) T2—763 63
De Witt County (Ill.) T2—773 585
De Witt County (Tex.) T2—764 259
Deacidification
  bibliographic materials 025.84
Deacons 270.092
  biography 270.092
    specific denominations 280
    see Manual at 230–280
  ecclesiology 262.14
  pastoral theology 253
  see also Clergy—Christian
Dead
  disposal 363.75
    customs 393
    music 781.588
    see also Undertaking
      (Mortuary)
  objects of worship 291.213
Dead animal disposal 363.78
Dead letter services 383.186
  see also Postal service
Dead nettles 583.96

Dead reckoning 629.045
  seamanship 623.892 3
Dead Sea (Israel and
    Jordan) T2—569 4
Dead Sea Scrolls 296.155
  Old Testament works in 221.44
  pseudepigrapha 229.91
  Qumran community writings 296.155
Deaeration
  water supply treatment 628.165
Deaf-blind persons 305.908 161
  see also Blind persons
Deaf children 305.908 162
    T1—087 2
  home care 649.151 2
  see also Hearing-impaired
      persons
Deaf persons 305.908 162
    T1—087 2
    T7—081 62
  see also Hearing-impaired
      persons
Deaf Smith County (Tex.) T2—764 835
Deaf workers 331.592
Deafness
  incidence 614.599 8
  otology 617.8
  social welfare 362.42
  see also Ears
Deans of students 371.4
Dearborn (Mich.) T2—774 33
Dearborn County (Ind.) T2—772 11
Death 306.9
  arts 700.454 8
    T3C—354 8
  biology 571.939
  customs 393
  cytology 571.936
  demography 304.64
  ethics 179.7
    religion 291.569 7
      Buddhism 294.356 97
      Christianity 241.697
      Hinduism 294.548 697
      Judaism 296.369 7
  family sociology 306.88
  folklore 398.27
    history and criticism 398.354
  literature 808.803 548
    history and literature 809.933 548
    specific literatures T3B—080 354 8
      history and criticism T3B—093 548
Death (continued)
  medical ethics 174.24
    religion 291.564 24
      Christianity 241.642 4
      Judaism 296.364 24
  medicine 616.078
  music 781.588
  philosophy 113.8
    humans 128.5
  psychology 155.937
  religion 291.23
    Christianity 236.1
    Islam 297.23
    Judaism 296.33
    philosophy of religion 218
  religious rites 291.38
    Christianity 265.85
    Islam 297.385
    Judaism 296.445
      liturgy 296.454 5
    see also Rites—religion
  social services 363.75
    see also Undertaking
        (Mortuary)
  sociology 306.9
Death certificates
  public administration 353.59
Death of Jesus Christ 232.963
Death penalty 364.66
  law 345.077 3
Death Valley National Park
    (Calif. and Nev.) T2—794 87
Death watch beetles 595.763
Debarkation 355.422
Debaters 809.53
  collected biography 809.53
  occupational group T7—85
Debates
  literature 808.853
    history and criticism 809.53
    specific literatures T3B—503
      individual authors T3A—5
  rhetoric 808.53
Debating 808.53
Debit cards 332.76
  banking services 332.178
  credit economics 332.76
Debt collection
  law 346.077
  management 658.88
Debt limits
  public finance 336.346
Debt management (Business) 658.152 6
Debt management (Personal) 332.024 02

Debt management (Public) 336.36
  macroeconomic policy 339.523
  public administration 352.45
  public finance 336.36
Debtors
  law 346.077
Debtors' prisons 365.4
  see also Correctional institutions
Debugging (Computer science) 004.24
  engineering 621.392
  programs 005.14
Deburring metals 671.7
Debuts
  customs 392.15
  etiquette 395.24
  music 781.584
Decalcomania 745.74
Decalogue 222.16
  moral theology
    Christianity 241.52
    Judaism 296.36
Decapoda (Crustaceans) 595.38
  conservation technology 639.975 38
  resource economics 333.955 5
Decapoda (Mollusks) 594.58
  paleozoology 564.58
Decatur County (Ga.) T2—758 993
Decatur County (Ind.) T2—772 16
Decatur County (Iowa) T2—777 875
Decatur County (Kan.) T2—781 143
Decatur County (Tenn.) T2—768 32
Decay
  materials science 620.112 2
Decay (Sound)
  musical element 781.235
Decay schemes (Radioactivity) 539.752
Deccan (India) T2—548
Deceleration
  human biophysics 612.014 414
Decentralization
  executive management 658.402
  public administration 352.283
Deception 001.95
  military operations 355.41
Decidability 511.3
Decimal numbers 513.55
Decimal system 513.55
Decimalization of currency 332.404 8
Decision analysis
  management use 658.403 54
Decision making
  executive management 658.403
    T1—068 4
  military administration 355.683
  political science 320.019
  production management 658.503 6
  psychology 153.83
  public administration 352.33
  social psychology 302.3
Decision tables
  program design 005.120 28
Decision theory 003.56
    T1—011 56
Decision theory (Mathematics) 519.542
Decks (Buildings) 721.84
  architecture 721.84
  construction 690.184
  domestic
    architecture 728.93
    construction 690.893
Declaration of Independence, 1776 973.313
Declarative languages 005.13
Declaratory judgments 347.077
Declension (Grammar) 415
  specific languages T4—5
Decoding skills (Reading)
  elementary education 372.46
Decolorizing carbons 662.93
Decomposition
  materials science 620.112 2
Decomposition analysis 544.1
Decomposition method 519.4
Decompression sickness
  medicine 616.989 4
  see also Environmental diseases (Human)
Deconstruction
  philosophy 149
Decoration 745.4
  architecture 729
  arts 745.4
  automobile 629.262
Decorations (Awards) 929.81
  armed forces 355.134 2
    see also Military commemorations
  numismatics 737.223
Decorative arts 745
  see also Arts
Decorative coloring 745.7
Decorative lettering 745.61
Decorative sculpture 731.72

Decorative treatment
  glass 748.6
  metals 739.15
  pottery 666.45
    arts 738.15
    technology 666.45
  sculpture 731.4
Decorative values 701.8
  drawing 741.018
Decoupage 745.546
Decoys
  handicrafts 745.593 6
Decubitus ulcers
  medicine 616.545
  see also Skin
Dedications (Christian rites) 265.92
Deductive databases 006.33
Deductive mathematics 511.24
Deductive reasoning 162
  computer science 006.333
  logic 162
  psychology 153.433
Dee River (Grampian, Scotland) T2—412 4
Deeds 346.043 8
Deep-freezing foods 664.028 53
  commercial preservation 664.028 53
  home preservation 641.453
Deep sea cods 597.63
Deep-sea diving 627.72
Deep-sea fishing 639.22
  commercial 639.22
  sports 799.16
Deep-sea surveys 551.460 7
Deer 599.65
  agricultural pests 632.696 5
  animal husbandry 636.294
  big game hunting 799.276 5
  commercial hunting 639.116 5
  conservation technology 639.979 65
  resource economics 333.959 65
  zoology 599.65
Deer flies 595.773
Deer Lodge County (Mont.) T2—786 87
Deer mice 599.355
Defamation 364.156
  ethics 177.3
    see also Ethical problems
  law 345.025 6
    criminal law 345.025 6
    torts 346.034
Default
  credit economics 332.75
  public finance 336.368
Defecation
  human physiology 612.36
  see also Digestive system
Defendants 347.052
  criminal law 345.05
Defense (Legal) 347.05
  criminal law 345.050 44
Defense (Military operation) 355.4
  engineering 623.3
Defense (National security) 355.03
  international law 341.72
  law 343.01
Defense administration 355.6
Defense budgets 355.622 8
  specific jurisdictions 355.622 9
Defense contracts 355.621 2
  law 346.023
Defense departments 355.6
Defense industries 338.473 55
Defense mechanisms (Psychology) 155.2
Defense of home territory 355.45
Defense operations 355.4
Defenseless Mennonites 289.73
  biography 289.709 2
  see also Mennonite Church
Defiance County (Ohio) T2—771 14
Deficiency budgets (Public) 352.48
  see also Budgets (Public)
Deficiency diseases
  medicine 616.39
  see also Digestive system
Definite integrals 515.43
Defla (Algeria : Province) T2—653
Deflagrating explosives 662.26
Deflation (Economic) 332.41
Deflections
  structural analysis 624.171 4
Defluoridation
  water supply engineering 628.166 3
Defoid languages 496.33
  T6—963 3
Deformation 531.38
  crystals 548.842
  geology 551.8
  materials science 620.112 3
  naval architecture 623.817 6
  physics 531.38
  structural analysis 624.176
Deformities
  biology 571.976
  human teratology 616.043
  psychological influence 155.916

Degeneration (Pathology) 571.935
  cytology 571.936
  humans 616.07
Dehumidification
  chemical engineering 660.284 29
Dehumidifiers
  air conditioning
    buildings 697.932 3
Dehydrated foods
  cooking 641.614
Dehydrating foods 664.028 4
  commercial preservation 664.028 4
  home preservation 641.44
Dehydrogenases 572.791
  see also Enzymes
Dehydrogenation 547.23
  chemical engineering 660.284 43
Deinonychus 567.912
Deism 211.5
Deists 211.509 2
  religious group T7—291
Deities 291.211
  see also Gods and goddesses
DeKalb County (Ga.) T2—758 225
Dekkan (India) T2—548
Del Norte County (Calif.) T2—794 11
Delagoa Bay 551.467 24
  T2—165 24
Delareyville (South Africa : District) T2—682 4
Delaware 975.1
  T2—751
Delaware Bay (Del. and N.J.) 551.461 46
  T2—163 46
Delaware County (Ind.) T2—772 65
Delaware County (Iowa) T2—777 385
Delaware County (N.Y.) T2—747 36
Delaware County (Ohio) T2—771 535
Delaware County (Okla.) T2—766 91
Delaware County (Pa.) T2—748 14
Delaware Indians T5—973
Delaware language 497.3
  T6—973
Delaware River (N.Y.-Del. and N.J.) T2—749
Delaware Water Gap (N.J. and Pa.) T2—748 25
Delegate counts 324.5
Delegation of authority 658.402
  public administration 352.283
Deleterious animals 591.65
Deleterious microorganisms 579.165
Deleterious organisms 578.65
Deleterious plants 581.65
Delft (Netherlands) T2—492 38
Delftware 738.37
Delhi (India : Union Territory) T2—545 6
Delicts 346.03
  see Manual at 345.02 vs. 346.03
Delinquency in schools 371.782
Delinquent children 364.36
  T1—086 923
  see also Juvenile delinquents
Delinquent persons 305.906 92
  T1—086 92
Delinquent students 371.93
Delmarva Peninsula T2—752 1
  Maryland T2—752 1
  Virginia T2—755 1
Delmas (South Africa : District) T2—682 2
Delos Island (Greece) T2—495 85
Delphi (Greece) T2—383
Delphinapterus 599.542
Delphinidae 599.53
Delphiniums 635.933 34
  botany 583.34
  floriculture 635.933 34
Delphinus 599.532
Delta (B.C.) T2—711 33
Delta (Miss. : Region) T2—762 4
Delta Amacuro (Venezuela) T2—876 2
Delta County (Colo.) T2—788 18
Delta County (Mich.) T2—774 94
Delta County (Tex.) T2—764 273
Delta State (Nigeria) T2—669 36
Deltaplan (Netherlands)
  engineering 627.549 094 92
Deltas 551.456
  T2—146
  geography 910.914 6
  geomorphology 551.456
  physical geography 910.021 46
Delusions 001.96
Delyn (Wales) T2—429 33
Demai 296.123 1
  Mishnah 296.123 1
  Palestinian Talmud 296.124 1
Demand
  communications industry 384.041
  forecasts 338.02
    agricultural industries 338.17
    production economics 338.02
    secondary industries 338.47

Demand (continued)
  foreign exchange rate
    determination 332.456 2
  labor economics 331.123
  microeconomics 338.521 2
  natural resources 333.712
  transportation services 388.049
Demand deposits 332.175 2
Dematerialization (Spiritualism) 133.92
Dementia
  medicine 616.83
  see also Nervous system
Demineralization
  sewage treatment 628.358
  water supply treatment 628.166 6
Demobilization (Military
    science) 355.29
Democracy 321.8
  educational objective 370.115
Democratic centralism 335.43
  economics 335.43
  political ideology 320.532 2
Democratic government 321.8
Democratic Labor Party
    (Australia) 324.294 06
Democratic Party (U.S.) 324.273 6
Democratic Republic of the
    Congo T2—675 1
Democratic-Republican Party
    (U.S.) 324.273 6
Democratic socialism 335.5
  economics 335.5
  political ideology 320.531 5
Democritean philosophy 182.7
Demodulation
  electronics 621.381 536
Demodulators
  electronic circuits 621.381 536
Demographic anthropology 304.6
Demography 304.6
Demolition (Military) 623.27
Demolition charges
  military engineering 623.454 5
Demolition operations (Military) 358.23
  underwater 359.984
Demoniac possession 133.426
  occultism 133.426
  religion 291.42
Demonology 133.42
  religion 291.216
Demons 133.42
  religion 291.216
Demonstrations (Advertising) 659.15
Demonstrative evidence 347.064
Demospongiae 593.46
  paleozoology 563.4
Demotic language (Egyptian) 493.1
  T6—931
Demotic language (Modern
    Greek) 489.3
  T6—89
Demotic literature (Modern
    Greek) 889
Demotion
  armed forces 355.112
  personnel management 658.312 7
    employee discipline 658.314 4
    public administration 352.66
Demulcents (Digestive)
  pharmacodynamics 615.735
  see also Digestive system
Demythologizing (Bible) 220.68
Denali National Park and
    Preserve (Alaska) T2—798 3
Denbighshire (Wales) T2—429 3
Dendrobatidae 597.87
Dendrobiums 584.4
  floriculture 635.934 4
Dendrochirotacea 593.96
Dendrocolaptidae 598.822
Dendrologists 582.160 92
  occupational group T7—58
Dendrology 582.16
Denendeh T2—719 2
Dengue fever
  incidence 614.571
  medicine 616.921
  see also Communicable
    diseases (Human)
Denial
  epistemology 121.5
Denial of justice 364.134
  law 345.023 4
Denial of rights 364.132 2
  law 345.023 22
    government liability 342.088
  public administration 353.46
Denis-Riverin (Quebec) T2—714 79
Denizli İli (Turkey) T2—562
Denjoy integrals 515.43
Denman Island (B.C. :
    Island) T2—711 2
Denmark 948.9
  T2—489
  ancient 936.3
  T2—363
Denmark Strait 551.468 4
  T2—163 24

Denominations 291.9
  Christianity 280
    see also Christian denominations
  Judaism 296.8
  see Manual at 291: Denominations and sects
Dens
  home economics 643.58
Density 531.14
  gas mechanics 533.15
  liquid mechanics 532.4
  solid mechanics 531.54
Density pumps 621.699
Dent County (Mo.) T2—778 86
Dental assistants
  law 344.041 3
  role and function 617.602 33
  see also Dentistry
Dental care
  dentistry 617.6
  social services 362.197 6
  see also Dentistry
Dental diseases
  dentistry 617.6
  incidence 614.599 6
  see also Dentistry
Dental enamel
  dentistry 617.634
  see also Dentistry
Dental hygiene 617.601
  see also Dentistry
Dental insurance 368.382 3
  see also Insurance
Dental pulp
  dentistry 617.634 2
  see also Dentistry
Dental surgery 617.605
  see also Dentistry
  see Manual at 617.605 vs. 617.522
Dental technicians
  law 344.041 3
  role and function 617.602 33
  see also Dentistry
Dentin
  dentistry 617.634
  see also Dentistry
Dentinal material products 679.4
Dentistry 617.6
  anesthesiology 617.967 6
  law 344.041 3
  pediatrics 617.645
Dentists 617.600 92
  law 344.041 3
  occupational group T7—617 6
  role and function 617.602 32
  see also Dentistry
Dentition disorders
  dentistry 617.643
  incidence 614.599 6
  see also Dentistry
Denton County (Tex.) T2—764 555
D'Entrecasteaux Islands (Papua New Guinea) T2—954 1
Dentures
  dentistry 617.692
  see also Dentistry
Denver (Colo.) T2—788 83
Denver County (Colo.) T2—788 83
Deodorants
  pharmacodynamics 615.778
  see also Skin
Deodorization
  sewers 628.23
Deoxyribonucleic acid 572.86
  humans 611.018 16
  see Manual at 572.8
Department heads
  executive management 658.43
  public administration 352.293
Department stores 381.141
  management 658.871
  see also Commerce
Departments
  management 658.402
  public administration 351
    see also Executive departments
Departments (Territorial units) 320.83
  see also Counties
Departments of agriculture 354.5
Departments of commerce 354.73
Departments of defense 355.6
Departments of education 353.8
Departments of energy 354.4
Departments of foreign affairs 353.13
Departments of health 353.6
Departments of housing 353.55
Departments of interior 353.3
Departments of justice 353.4
Departments of labor 354.9
Departments of natural resources 354.3
Departments of state 351
  see also Executive departments
Departments of transportation 354.76

Departments of treasury 352.4
Dependence
  personality trait 155.232
Dependency grammar 415
  specific languages T4—5
Dependent children
  social welfare 362.713
Dependent states 321.08
  see also Semisovereign states
Depletion allowance 336.243 16
  tax law 343.052 34
Deportation 364.68
  law 342.082
  penology 364.68
Deposit insurance 368.854
  see also Insurance
Deposition (Geology) 551.303
Depository libraries
  acquisitions 025.26
  government relations 021.8
Deposits (Bank) 332.175 2
  government guaranty 332.1
  public revenues 336.15
Depreciation
  accounting 657.73
  tax law 343.052 34
Depressant abuse 362.299
  medicine 616.86
  personal health 613.8
  social welfare 362.299
  see also Substance abuse
Depression (Mental state) 362.25
  medicine 616.852 7
  social welfare 362.25
  see also Mental illness
Depressions (Economic)
  economic cycles 338.542
  personal finance 332.024 02
Depressions (Physiography) 551.44
  T2—144
  geography 910.914 4
  geomorphology 551.44
  physical geography 910.021 44
Depressive psychoses
  medicine 616.895
  see also Mental illness
Depressive reactions
  medicine 616.895
  see also Mental illness
Deputy chief executives
  executive management 658.42
  law 342.062
  occupational group T7—351
  political science 321
Deputy chief executives (continued)
  public administration 352.239
Deputy heads of departments
  executive management 658.43
  public administration 352.293
Dera Ismāīl Khān (Pakistan : District) T2—549 124
Derby (England) T2—425 17
Derbyshire (England) T2—425 1
Derbyshire Dales (England : District) T2—425 13
Derivation (Etymology) 412
  specific languages T4—2
Derivation (Morphology) 415
  specific languages T4—5
Derivatives (Speculation) 332.645
  multiple forms of investment 332.645
  securities 332.632
Derived spaces 514.320 3
Dermaptera 595.739
Dermatitis
  medicine 616.51
  see also Skin
Dermatitis (Atopic)
  medicine 616.521
  see also Skin
Dermatoglyphics 599.945
Dermatological allergies
  medicine 616.973
  see also Diseases (Human)
Dermatology 616.5
  see also Skin
Dermestoidea 595.763
Dermoptera 599.33
  paleozoology 569.33
Derricks 621.872
Derry (Northern Ireland) T2—416 21
Derry (Northern Ireland : County) T2—416 2
Derwent River (Derbyshire, England) T2—425 1
Derwent River (Yorkshire, England) T2—428 4
Derwentside (England) T2—428 68
Des Moines (Iowa) T2—777 58
Des Moines County (Iowa) T2—777 96
Des Moines River (Minn. and Iowa) T2—777
Des Plaines River (Wis. and Ill.) T2—773 2
Desai, Morarji Ranchodji
  Indian history 954.052
Desalinization 628.167

Descant recorders 788.364
see also Woodwind instruments
Descant viols 787.62
see also Stringed instruments
Descendants T1—085 4
T7—044
family relationships 306.874
Descent into hell of Jesus Christ 232.967
Deschutes County (Or.) T2—795 87
Deschutes River (Or.) T2—795 62
Description
literature 808.802 2
history and criticism 809.922
specific literatures T3B—080 22
history and criticism T3B—092 2
Descriptive bibliography 010.42
Descriptive biology 578
animals 590
microorganisms 579
plants 580
see Manual at 578 vs. 304.2, 508, 910
Descriptive cataloging 025.32
Descriptive geometry 516.6
applied 604.201 516 6
Descriptive government 320.4
Descriptive linguistics 410
see Manual at 410
Descriptive research 001.433
T1—072 3
public administrative support 352.75
see Manual at T1—07201–T1—07209 vs. T1—0722–T1—0724
Descriptive statistics 519.53
Descriptors (Terms) 025.49
Desegregation in education 379.263
Desert biology 578.754
Desert ecology 577.54
Desert plants 581.754
floriculture 635.952 5
Desert Storm, Operation, 1991 956.704 424
Desert tactics 355.423
Deserters 355.133 4
Algerian Revolution 965.046 8
Chaco War 989.207 168
Civil War (England) 942.062 8
Civil War (Spain) 946.081 8
Civil War (United States) 973.78
Crimean War 947.073 88
Falkland Islands War 997.110 248
Franco-German War 943.082 8
Hundred Years' War 944.025 8
Deserters (continued)
Indo-Pakistan War, 1971 954.920 518
Indochinese War 959.704 18
Iraqi-Iranian Conflict 955.054 28
Korean War 951.904 28
Mexican War 973.628
Napoleonic Wars 940.278
Persian Gulf War, 1991 956.704 428
South African War 968.048 8
Spanish-American War 973.898
Thirty Years' War 940.248
United States Revolutionary War 973.38
Vietnamese War 959.704 38
War of 1812 973.528
War of the Pacific 983.061 68
World War I 940.48
World War II 940.548
Desertification 333.736
geomorphology 551.415
land economics 333.736
Desertion (Domestic relations) 306.88
Desertion (Military) 355.133 4
law 343.014
see also Deserters
Deserts 551.415
T2—154
see also Arid lands
Desha County (Ark.) T2—767 85
Design
arts 745.4
automotive 629.231
elementary education 372.52
engineering 620.004 2
philosophy 124
road engineering 625.725
structural engineering 624.177 1
Design anthropometry 620.82
Design protection 346.048 4
international law 341.758 4
Designer drugs 362.299
medicine 616.86
personal health 613.8
social welfare 362.299
see also Substance abuse
Designs
diagrammatic T1—022 3
pictorial T1—022 2
textiles 677.022
see Manual at T1—0222 vs. T1—0223
Désirade (Guadeloupe) T2—729 76
Desjardins (Quebec) T2—714 59

Desks
  decorative arts 749.3
  household management 645.4
  manufacturing technology 684.14
Desktop publishing
  composition 686.225 444 16
Desktop typesetting 686.225 444 16
Desmidiaceae 579.837
Desmids 579.837
Desmophyceae 579.87
Desmostylia 569.5
Desolation Sound Provincial Marine Park (B.C.) T2—711 31
Despatch (South Africa) T2—687 5
Desserts 641.86
Destiny
  philosophy 123
  religion 291.22
    Christianity 234.9
Destitute persons 305.569
  T1—086 942
  see also Poor people
Destroyer escorts 359.835 4
  design 623.812 54
  engineering 623.825 4
  naval equipment 359.835 4
  naval units 359.325 4
Destroyers 359.835 4
  design 623.812 54
  engineering 623.825 4
  naval equipment 359.835 4
  naval units 359.325 4
Destruction of universe 523.19
Destructors
  military engineering 623.454 5
Desulfurization
  coal technology 662.623
Detail drawings
  construction 692.2
Detail finishing
  buildings 698
Detailing automobiles 629.287
Detection
  electronics 621.381 536
Detection of crime 363.25
  see also Criminal investigation
Detection of particles 539.77
Detection of radioactivity 539.77
Detective films 791.436 55
Detective plays
  literature 808.825 27
    history and criticism 809.252 7
    specific literatures T3B—205 27
Detective plays
  literature
    specific literatures (continued)
      individual authors T3A—2
Detective programs 791.446 55
  radio 791.446 55
  television 791.456 55
Detective stories 808.838 72
  history and criticism 809.387 2
  specific literatures T3B—308 72
    individual authors T3A—3
Detectives 363.250 92
  occupational group T7—363 2
Detectors
  electronic circuits 621.381 536
Detectors (Sensors)
  manufacturing technology 681.2
Detention 365
Detention homes 365.34
  see also Correctional institutions
Detergents 668.14
Deterioration
  materials science 620.112 2
Determinants 512.943 2
Determinative mineralogy 549.1
  see Manual at 549.1
Determinism 123
  literature 808.801 2
    history and criticism 809.912
    specific literatures T3B—080 12
      history and criticism T3B—091 2
Deterministic systems 003.7
Deterrence (Nuclear strategy) 355.021 7
Detmold (Germany : Regierungsbezirk) T2—435 65
Detonators 662.4
  military engineering 623.454 2
Detroit (Mich.) T2—774 34
Detroit River (Mich. and Ont.) T2—774 33
Deuel County (Neb.) T2—782 913
Deuel County (S.D.) T2—783 25
Deuterium 546.212
  see also Chemicals
Deuterium oxide
  chemical engineering 661.08
  chemistry 546.22
Deuteromycetes 579.55
Deuteromycotina 579.55
Deuteronomy (Bible) 222.15
Deuterons 539.723 2
Deutscher Bund 943.07

Deutzias 635.933 72
 botany 583.72
 floriculture 635.933 72
Deux-Montagnes (Quebec : County) T2—714 25
Deux-Montagnes (Quebec : Regional County Municipality) T2—714 25
Deux-Sèvres (France) T2—446 2
Devaluation of currency 332.414
 foreign exchange 332.452
Devanagari alphabet 491.1
Developable surfaces 516.362
Developed regions T2—172 2
Developing (Photography) 771.4
Developing apparatus
 photography 771.49
Developing regions T2—172 4
Developing solutions
 photography 771.54
Development
 biology 571.8
  see also Developmental biology
 economics 338.9
  see also Economic development
 sociology 303.44
Development banks 332.153
 domestic 332.28
 international 332.153
Developmental abnormalities 571.938
Developmental biology 571.8
 humans 612.6
 microorganisms 571.842 9
Developmental disabilities 571.938
Developmental genetics 571.85
Developmental immunology 571.963 8
Developmental linguistics 401.93
Developmental psychology 155
 comparative psychology 156.5
 see Manual at 155
Developmental reading 418.4
 specific languages T4—843
Developmentally disabled persons 305.908 16
 T1—087 5
 T7—081 6
 education 371.92
 social group 305.908 16
 social services 362.196 8
  mental retardation 362.3
  physical illness 362.196 8
  see also Health services
Developmentally disabled workers 331.595
Deveron River (Scotland) T2—412 25
Deviation (Social) 302.542
Device drivers
 programming 005.711
 programs 005.713
Devil 291.216
 art representation 704.948 7
 arts 700.482 912 16
 T3C—382 912 16
 Christianity 235.4
 Islam 297.216
 Judaism 296.316
 literature 808.803 829 1216
  history and criticism 809.933 829 1216
  specific literatures T3B—080 382 91216
   history and criticism T3B—093 829 1216
 occultism 133.422
Devil worship 291.216
 occultism 133.422
Devolution, War of, 1667–1668 944.033
Devon (England) T2—423 5
Devon cattle 636.226
Devonian period 551.74
 geology 551.74
 paleontology 560.174
Devonport (Tas.) T2—946 5
Devotional calendars 242.2
Devotional literature 291.432
 Buddhism 294.344 32
 Christianity 242
 Hinduism 294.543 2
 Islam 297.382
  Sufi 297.438 2
 Judaism 296.72
Devotional theology 291.4
 Buddhism 294.344
 Christianity 240
 Hinduism 294.54
 Islam 297.57
  Sufi 297.4
 Judaism 296.7
Dew 551.574 4
Dew points 536.44
Dewberries 641.347 17
 botany 583.73
 cooking 641.647 17
 food 641.347 17
 horticulture 634.717
Dewdney-Alouette (B.C) T2—711 37
Dewetsdorp (South Africa : District) T2—685 6

Dewey County (Okla.) T2—766 18
Dewey County (S.D.) T2—783 54
Dewey Decimal Classification 025.431
Dewey shorthand system 653.425
  1922 653.425
  1936 653.428
Dexter cattle 636.225
Dextrans 572.566
  biochemistry 572.566
  chemistry 547.782
  see also Carbohydrates
Dextrose 572.565
  biochemistry 572.565
  chemistry 547.781 3
  see also Carbohydrates
Dhaka (Bangladesh : Division) T2—549 22
Dhammapada 294.382 322
Dharma
  Hinduism 294.548
Dharmasastras 294.592 6
Dhī Qār (Iraq : Province) T2—567 5
Dhole 599.77
Diabetes 362.196 462
  medicine 616.462
  social services 362.196 462
  see also Endocrine system
Diabetes insipidus
  medicine 616.47
  see also Endocrine system
Diabetes mellitus 362.196 462
  cooking for 641.563 14
  medicine 616.462
  pediatrics 618.924 62
  social services 362.196 462
  see also Endocrine system
Diabrotica 595.764 8
  agricultural pests 632.764 8
Diachronic linguistics 417.7
  specific languages T4—7
  see Manual at 410
Diagenesis 552.03
Diagnosis
  medicine 616.075
Diagnostic cytology
  medicine 616.075 82
Diagnostic equipment
  manufacturing technology 681.761
Diagnostic graphology 155.282
  criminal investigation 363.256 5
  personnel selection 658.311 2
Diagnostic imaging
  medicine 616.075 4
    see Manual at 616.0757 vs. 616.0754, 616.07572
Diagnostic services 362.177
  see also Health services
Diagnostic tests
  elementary education
    reading 372.486
Diagnostic ultrasound
  medicine 616.075 43
Diagrams T1—022 3
  see Manual at T1—0222 vs. T1—0223
Dial-a-message telephone calls 384.646
  see also Telephone
Dialectical materialism
  Marxian theory 335.411 2
  philosophy 146.32
  see Manual at 335.4112 vs. 146.32
Dialecticianism (Chinese philosophy) 181.115
Dialectology 417.2
  specific languages T4—7
Dialects 417.2
  specific languages T4—7
    see Manual at T4—1–T4—5 and T4—8 vs. T4—7; *also at* 420–490: Dialects
Dialing systems
  telephone communications services 384.65
  wireless 384.535
Dialogue
  literature 808.802 6
    history and criticism 809.926
    specific literatures T3B—080 26
      history and criticism T3B—092 6
Dialysis
  chemistry 542.6
  qualitative chemistry 544.5
Diamagnetism 538.42
Diamonds 553.82
  economic geology 553.82
  glyptics 736.23
  jewelry 739.27
  mineralogy 549.27
  mining 622.382
  synthetic 666.88
Dianetics 299.936
Diapause 571.785
Diapensiales 583.67

Diaphragm (Body part)	573.26
biology	573.26
human anatomy	611.26
human physiology	612.2
surgery	617.547
see also Respiratory system	
Diaphragms (Birth control)	
health	613.943 5
see also Birth control	
Diaporthales	579.567
Diapsida	567.9
Diaries	920
	T1—092
biography	920
literature	808.883
specific literatures	T3B—803
individual authors	T3A—8
see Manual at T3A—8 + 03 and T3B—803, T3B—8 + 03	
Diarrhea	
medicine	616.342 7
see also Digestive system	
Diaspora (Jewish history)	909.049 24
Diaspore	
mineralogy	549.525
Diaspore clay	553.61
see also Clay	
Diastrophism	551.8
Diatessaron	226.1
Diathermy	
therapeutics	615.832 3
Diatomaceous earth	553.6
economic geology	553.6
mining	622.36
petrology	552.5
Diatoms	579.85
Diatonicism	781.262
Diatrymiformes	568.3
Díaz, Porfirio	
Mexican history	972.081 4
Díaz Ordaz, Gustavo	
Mexican history	972.083 1
Diazepam	
pharmacodynamics	615.788 2
see also Mental illness	
Diazines	547.593
chemical engineering	661.894
Diazotization	547.25
chemical engineering	660.284 45
Diazotype processes	773.7
Dice games	795.1
Dichapetalaceae	583.69
Dichondras	583.94
Dickens County (Tex.)	T2—764 741
Dickenson County (Va.)	T2—755 745
Dickey County (N.D.)	T2—784 54
Dickinson County (Iowa)	T2—777 123
Dickinson County (Kan.)	T2—781 56
Dickinson County (Mich.)	T2—774 955
Dickson County (Tenn.)	T2—768 44
Dicotyledons	583
forestry	634.972
paleobotany	561.3
see also Plants	
see Manual at 583–584	
Dictation (Office practice)	651.74
shorthand	653.14
Dictators	321.9
political group	T7—351
public administration	352.23
Dictatorship	321.9
Diction	418
applied linguistics	418
specific languages	T4—81
rhetoric	808
Dictionaries	413
specific languages	T4—3
see Manual at T4—3 vs. T4—81	
specific subject	T1—03
see Manual at T1—014 vs. T1—03	
Dictionary catalogs	025.315
bibliography	019
library science	025.315
Dictyoptera	595.728
Didactic poetry	808.815
history and criticism	809.15
specific literatures	T3B—105
individual authors	T3A—1
Didelphidae	599.276
Didjeridu	783.99
Dido language	499.964
	T6—999 64
Didymelales	583.43
Die casting	671.253
Diefenbaker, John G.	
Canadian history	971.064 2
Diefenbaker, Lake (Sask.)	T2—712 42
Dieffenbachias	635.934 64
botany	584.64
floriculture	635.934 64
Diegueño Indians	T5—975 7
Dielectric materials	
materials science	620.195
Dielectrics	537.24
crystals	548.85

Diencephalon
  human anatomy 611.81
  human physiology 612.826 2
  see also Nervous system
Dies (Tools) 621.984
Diesel-electric locomotives 385.366 2
  engineering 625.266 2
  transportation services 385.366 2
  see also Rolling stock
Diesel engines 621.436
  automotive 629.250 6
  ships 623.872 36
Diesel fuel 665.538 4
Diesel-hydraulic locomotives 385.366 4
  engineering 625.266 4
  transportation services 385.366 4
  see also Rolling stock
Diesel locomotives 385.366
  engineering 625.266
  transportation services 385.366
  see also Rolling stock
Diesel submarines 359.938 32
  design 623.812 572
  engineering 623.825 72
  naval equipment 359.938 32
Diet
  elementary education 372.37
  health 613.2
Diet cooking 641.563
Diet therapy
  medicine 615.854
    see Manual at 615.854
Dietary laws
  Islam 297.576
  Judaism 296.73
Dietary limitations
  cooking for 641.563
  religion 291.446
    Hinduism 294.544 6
    Judaism 296.73
Dietary regimens
  health 613.26
Dietetic salts
  food technology 664.4
Dietetics 613.2
  see Manual at 363.8 vs. 613.2, 641.3
Dieting (Weight loss)
  health 613.25
Difaqane 968.041
Difference algebras 512.56
Difference equations 515.625
Differentiable manifolds 516.36
Differentiable mappings 515.352
Differential algebras 512.56
Differential calculus 515.33
Differential diagnosis
  medicine 616.075
Differential-difference equations 515.38
Differential equations 515.35
Differential forms 515.37
Differential gear 621.833
  automotive engineering 629.245
Differential geometry 516.36
Differential inequalities 515.36
Differential invariants 515.37
Differential operators 515.724 2
Differential psychology 155
  comparative psychology 156.5
  education 370.151
  see Manual at 155
Differential topology 514.72
Differentials (Mathematics) 515.33
Differentiated teacher staffing 371.141 23
Diffraction crystallography 548.83
Diffraction of light 535.42
Diffuse nebulas 523.113 5
Diffusion 530.475
  chemical engineering 660.294
  chemistry 541.34
  gaseous-state physics 530.435
  liquid-state physics 530.425
  physics 530.475
  semiconductors 537.622 5
  solid-state physics 530.415
Diffusion analysis 544.5
Diffusion coating
  metals 671.736
Diffusion processes (Mathematics) 519.233
Diffusion welding 671.529
Digambara (Jainism) 294.493
Digby (N.S. : County) T2—716 32
Digenea 592.48
Digestants
  pharmacodynamics 615.734
  see also Digestive system
Digestion 573.3
  human physiology 612.3
  see also Digestive system
Digestive organs 573.3
  human physiology 612.3
  see also Digestive system
Digestive secretions 573.337 9
Digestive system 573.3
  anesthesiology 617.967 43
    specific organs 617.967 55
  biology 573.3

Digestive system (continued)
  geriatrics 618.976 3
  human allergies
    medicine 616.975
  human anatomy 611.3
  human cancer 362.196 994 3
    medicine 616.994 3
    social services 362.196 994 3
    see also Cancer (Human)
  human diseases 362.196 3
    incidence 614.593
    medicine 616.3
    social services 362.196 3
  human histology 611.018 93
  human physiology 612.3
  pediatrics 618.923
  pharmacodynamics 615.73
  surgery 617.43
    specific organs 617.55
  veterinary medicine 636.089 63
Digests T1—020 2
Digests of cases 348.046
  United States 348.734 6
Digests of laws 348.026
  United States 348.732 6
Digital audio technology
  sound reproduction 621.389 3
Digital circuits 621.381 5
  computer engineering 621.395
Digital codes (Computer) 005.72
Digital communications 384
  communications services 384
  computer science 004.6
  engineering 621.382
  see Manual at 004.6 vs. 621.382, 621.3981
Digital computers 004
  see also Computers
Digital instruments
  technology 681.1
Digital mainframe computers 004.12
  see also Mainframe computers
Digital microcomputers 004.16
  see also Microcomputers
Digital minicomputers 004.14
  see also Minicomputers
Digital supercomputers 004.11
  see also Supercomputers
Digital-to-analog converters
  computer engineering 621.398 14
  computer science 004.64
  electronic engineering 621.381 59
Digital video effects 778.593
Digitalis
  pharmacodynamics 615.711
  see also Cardiovascular system
Digitizer tablets 006.62
  computer engineering 621.399
Dihydroxy aromatics 547.633
Dik-diks 599.646
Dika 583.79
Dikes 627.42
  reclamation from sea 627.549
  road engineering 625.734
Dikes (Geology) 551.88
Dilation
  heart
    human physiology 612.171
    see also Cardiovascular system
Dilation and curettage
  surgery 618.145 8
  see also Female genital system
Dill 641.338 2
  botany 583.849
  see also Flavorings
Dilleniales 583.62
Dilleniidae 583.6
Dillon County (S.C.) T2—757 85
Diluents 661.807
  paint technology 667.624
Dimashq (Syria : Province) T2—569 14
Dîmbovița (Romania : Județ) T2—498 2
Dimension stock lumber 674.28
Dimensional analysis 530.8
Dimensioning T1—022 1
  technical drawing 604.243
Dimensions 530.81
  physics 530.81
  standardization 389.62
Diminishing marginal returns 338.512
Diminishing marginal utility 338.521 2
Dimmit County (Tex.) T2—764 455
Dimorphism
  crystallography 548.3
Dimouts
  military engineering 623.77
Dinagat (Philippines) T2—599 7
Dinefwr (Wales : Borough) T2—429 68
Dingaan, King of the Zulus
  Natal history 968.404 1
Dingo 599.772
  predator control technology 636.083 9
Dining car cooking 641.576

Dining cars 385.33
  engineering 625.23
  see also Rolling stock
Dining halls
  architecture 727.38
Dining rooms 643.4
  home economics 643.4
  interior decoration 747.76
Dinka (African people) T5—965
Dinka language 496.5
  T6—965
Dinner 642
  cooking 641.54
  customs 394.15
Dinnerware
  table setting 642.7
Dinocerata 569.62
Dinoflagellates 579.87
Dinophyceae 579.87
Dinornithiformes 568.5
Dinosaur National Monument (Colo. and Utah) T2—788 12
Dinosaurs 567.9
Dinwiddie County (Va.) T2—755 582
Dioceses
  Christian ecclesiology 262.3
Diodes
  semiconductor 621.381 522
Diola (African people) T5—963 2
Diola language 496.32
  T6—963 2
Diomedeidae 598.42
Diophantine analysis 512.74
Diophantine approximations 512.73
Diophantine equations 512.72
Diopsidae 595.774
Dioramas 745.8
  decorative arts 745.8
  painting 751.74
Diorites 552.3
Dioscoreaceae 584.357
Diouf, Abdou
  Senegalese history 966.305
Dioula (African people) T5—963 45
Dioula language 496.345
  T6—963 45
Diourbel (Senegal : Region) T2—663
Dioxin
  human toxicology 615.951 2
Diphenyl hydrocarbons 547.613
  chemical engineering 661.816
Diphenylmethane dyes 667.254
Diphtheria
  incidence 614.512 3
  medicine 616.931 3
  see also Communicable diseases (Human)
Diphthongs (Phonology) 414.6
  specific languages T4—16
Diplodocus 567.913
Diplomacy 327.2
  customs 399
  international law 341.33
Diplomas 371.291 2
  prints 769.5
Diplomatic causes of war 355.027 2
Diplomatic customs 399
Diplomatic history 327.09
  Algerian Revolution 965.046 2
  Chaco War 989.207 162
  Civil War (England) 942.062 2
  Civil War (Spain) 946.081 2
  Civil War (United States) 973.72
  Crimean War 947.073 82
  Falkland Islands War 997.110 242
  Franco-German War 943.082 2
  Hundred Years' War 944.025 2
  Indo-Pakistan War, 1971 954.920 512
  Indochinese War 959.704 12
  Iraqi-Iranian Conflict 955.054 22
  Korean War 951.904 22
  Mexican War 973.622
  Napoleonic Wars 940.272
  Persian Gulf War, 1991 956.704 422
  South African War 968.048 2
  Spanish-American War 973.892
  Thirty Years' War 940.242
  United States Revolutionary War 973.32
  Vietnamese War 959.704 32
  War of 1812 973.522
  War of the Pacific 983.061 62
  World War I 940.32
  World War II 940.532
Diplomatic immunities 327.2
  international law 341.33
Diplomatic languages 401.3
Diplomatic law 342.041 2
  international law 341.33
Diplomatic privileges 327.2
Diplomatic service 327.2
  public administration 353.132 63
Diplomats 327.209 2
  occupational group T7—352 2

Diplopia
  ophthalmology 617.762
  see also Eyes
Diplopoda 595.66
Diplura 595.724
Dipnoi 597.39
  paleozoology 567.39
Dipodomys 599.359 87
Dipole moments 537.243
Dipped latex 678.533
Dipped rubber 678.36
Dippers (Birds) 598.832
Dipperu National Park (Qld.) T2—943 5
Dipping animals 636.083 3
Dipping latex 678.527
Diprotodonta 599.2
Dips (Geology) 551.85
Dipsacales 583.92
Diptera 595.77
Dipterocarpaceae 583.624
Dīr District (Pakistan) T2—549 122
Direct advertising 659.133
Direct broadcast satellite systems 384.552
Direct-current machinery 621.313 2
Direct-current transmission 621.319 12
Direct distance dialing 384.64
  communications services 384.64
  engineering 621.385 7
Direct-driven hoists
  mining 622.67
Direct energy conversion
  electrical engineering 621.312 4
  nuclear to electric 621.312 5
Direct-fluid-pressure displacement pumps 621.699
Direct lighting 621.321 2
  see also Lighting
Direct-mail advertising 659.133
Direct-mail marketing 381.1
  management 658.84
Direct marketing 381.1
  management 658.84
Direct-metal sculpture 731.41
Direct nuclear generation of electricity 621.312 5
Direct-positive processes
  photography 772.1
Direct processes
  color photography 778.63
Direct selling 381.1
  management 658.84
Direct taxation 336.294
Directed lighting 621.321 4
  see also Lighting
Direction (Drama) 792.023 3
  motion pictures 791.430 233
  radio 791.440 233
  stage 792.023 3
  television 791.450 233
Direction finders
  aircraft engineering 629.135 1
  radio engineering 621.384 191
Direction finding 629.045
  air navigation 629.132 51
  marine navigation 623.893
  radio engineering 621.384 191
Directional derivatives 515.33
  geometry 516.36
Directional gyros
  aircraft 629.135 2
Director of Public Prosecutions (Great Britain) 345.420 1
Directories T1—025
  bibliographies 011.7
  see Manual at T1—025 vs. T1—0601–T1—0609; *also at* 338 vs. 060, 381, 382, 670.294, 910, T1—025, T1—0294, T1—0296
Directors (Drama) 792.023 309 2
  motion picture 791.430 233 092
    occupational group T7—791 4
  occupational group T7—792
  radio 791.440 233 092
    occupational group T7—791 4
  stage 792.023 309 2
    occupational group T7—792
  television 791.450 233 092
    occupational group T7—791 4
  see Manual at 791.092
Directors of corporations
  executive management 658.422
  law 346.066 42
Directors of religious education 291.750 92
  biography 291.750 92
  see Manual at 230–280
  Christianity 268.092
    biography 268.092
    role and function 268.3
  Judaism 296.680 92
    biography 296.680 92
    role and function 296.68
Directory (France) 944.045
Directory advertising 659.132
Dirichlet problem 515.353

Dirichlet series 515.243
Dirigibles 387.732 4
  engineering 629.133 24
  military engineering 623.743
  piloting 629.132 522
  transportation services 387.732 4
  see also Aircraft
Dirks 623.441
  art metalwork 739.72
  military engineering 623.441
Dirouilles (England) T2—423 49
Dirt roads 388.12
  engineering 625.74
  see also Roads
Disability
  psychological influence 155.916
  social welfare 362.4
Disability (Law) 346.013
Disability income insurance 368.386
  law 346.086 386
    workers' compensation 344.021
  see also Insurance
Disability insurance 368.382
  see also Insurance
Disabled American Veterans 369.186 3
Disabled children 305.908 16
  T1—087
  home care 649.151
  see also Disabled persons
Disabled persons 305.908 16
  T1—087
  T7—081 6
  architecture for 720.87
  clothing
    home sewing 646.401
  education 371.9
    law 344.079 11
  footwear for
    manufacturing technology 685.38
  government programs 353.539
  home care 649.8
  institutional buildings
    architecture 725.54
  legal status 346.013
    constitutional law 342.087
    private law 346.013
  libraries for 027.663
    administration 025.197 663
    collection
      development 025.218 766 3
    use studies 025.587 663
  museum services 069.17
Disabled persons (continued)
  publications for
    bibliographies 011.63
    reviews 028.163
  recreation 790.196
    indoor 793.019 6
    outdoor 796.087
  self-help devices 617.03
  social group 305.908 16
  social welfare 362.4
    public administration 353.539
      health services 353.66
  sports 796.087
    see Manual at 796.08 vs. 796.04
  see Manual at 362.1–362.4 vs. 610: Biographies
Disabled veterans 362.408 697
  legal status 343.011 6
  social welfare 362.408 697
Disabled workers 331.59
  economics 331.59
  government programs 354.908 7
  law 344.015 9
  social group 305.908 16
Disarmament 327.174
  ethics 172.4
    religion 291.562 4
      Christianity 241.624
    see also Political ethics
  international politics 327.174
  law 341.733
  social theology 291.178 7
    Christianity 261.87
    Judaism 296.382 7
Disassembling tools 621.93
Disaster insurance 368.122
  see also Insurance
Disaster nursing
  medicine 610.734 9
Disaster preparedness
  library operations 025.82
Disaster relief 363.348
  law 344.053 48
  public administration 353.95
Disaster technology 628.92
Disasters 904
  international law 341.766
  law 344.053 4
  management of enterprises 658.477
  personal safety 613.69
  psychology 155.935
  social effects 303.485

Disasters (continued)
  social services 363.34
    public administration 353.95
  see Manual at 900: Historic events vs. nonhistoric events
Discarding
  library collections 025.216
  museology 069.51
Discharge (Military personnel) 355.114
Discharged offenders 364.8
  labor economics 331.51
Disciples of Christ 286.6
  biography 286.609 2
  church government 262.066
    parishes 254.066
  church law 262.986 6
  doctrines 230.66
    catechisms and creeds 238.66
  guides to Christian life 248.486 6
  missions 266.66
  moral theology 241.046 6
  public worship 264.066
  religious associations 267.186 6
  religious education 268.866
  religious group T7—266
  seminaries 230.073 66
  theology 230.66
Discipline
  armed forces 355.13
    law 343.014
  education 371.5
  home child care 649.64
  labor economics 331.259 8
  labor unions 331.873
  legislators 328.366
  personnel management 658.314
    public administration 352.66
  prisons 365.643
Disco dancing 793.33
Discoglossoidea 597.86
Discographies 011.38
  music 016.780 266
Discomycetes 579.57
Discount 332.84
Discount brokers 332.62
Discount rates 332.84
  economics 332.84
    central banking 332.113
  macroeconomic policy 339.53
Discount stores 381.149
  management 658.879
  see also Commerce
Discourse analysis
  linguistics 401.41
    specific languages T4—014 1
  rhetoric 808.001 4
Discoveries in geography 910.9
  see Manual at 913–919: Add table: 04: Discovery and exploration
Discoveries in natural history 508
Discoveries in science 509
Discovery
  archaeological technique 930.102 82
Discovery (Law) 347.072
  criminal law 345.072
Discrete-time systems 003.83
Discriminant analysis 519.535
Discriminants
  number theory 512.74
Discrimination 305
  ethics 177.5
    see also Ethical problems
  social theology 291.178 34
    Christianity 261.834
    Judaism 296.38
Discrimination (Psychology) 152.1
  quantitative studies 152.82
Discrimination in education 379.26
  law 344.079 8
Discrimination in employment 331.133
  see also Equal employment opportunity
Discrimination in housing 363.51
  law 344.063 635 1
Discrimination learning
  psychology 153.152 8
Discs (Recording devices) 621.382 34
  sound reproduction 621.389 32
  television 384.558
    see also Video recordings
Discus fishes 597.74
  culture 639.377 4
Discus throwing 796.435
  see also Sports
Discussion
  public
    literature 808.853
      specific literatures T3B—503
        individual authors T3A—5
    rhetoric 808.53
  teaching method 371.37
Discussion groups
  adult education 374.22

Disease carriers
  law 344.043
  medicine 614.43
Disease control 614.44
  law 344.043
  public administration 353.628
  public health 614.44
Disease prevention
  medicine 613
  public health 614.44
Disease resistance 571.96
  humans 616.079
Disease vectors 571.986
Diseases (Biology) 571.9
  agriculture 632.3
    see Manual at 632.2–632.8
  conservation technology 639.964
  plant crops 632.3
  veterinary medicine 636.089 6
  see Manual at 571–575 vs. 630
Diseases (Human) 362.1
  geriatrics 618.97
  gynecology 618.1
  incidence 614.42
  medicine 616
    see Manual at 610 vs. 616; *also at* 616 vs. 612; *also at* 616 vs. 616.07; *also at* 616 vs. 617.4; *also at* 616 vs. 618.92; *also at* 616.1–616.8; *also at* 617 vs. 616
  pastoral theology 291.61
    Christianity 259.41
  pediatrics 618.92
  psychological influence 155.916
  religious rites 291.38
    Christianity 265.82
  social services 362.1
    see also Health services
  social theology 291.178 321
    Christianity 261.832 1
  sociology 306.461
  surgery 617
    see Manual at 617: Add table: 06; *also at* 617 vs. 616
  see Manual at 614.4–614.5 vs. 362.1–362.4
Diseconomies of scale 338.514 4
Disfigurement
  psychological influence 155.916
Dishes
  table setting 642.7
  see also Tableware
Dishwashers
  installation 696.184
  manufacturing technology 683.88
Disinfection
  public health 614.48
  sewage treatment 628.32
  water supply treatment 628.166 2
Disinformation activities
  international politics 327.14
Disk drives 004.563
  engineering 621.397 6
Disks (Computer) 004.563
  engineering 621.397 6
Disks (Recording devices) 621.382 34
Dislocation (Aftermath of war) 355.028
Dislocation (Crystallography) 548.842
Dislocations (Geology) 551.872
Dislocations (Injuries)
  medicine 617.16
Dismal Swamp (N.C. and Va.) T2—755 523
  North Carolina T2—756 135
  Virginia T2—755 523
Dismissal of employees
  economics 331.259 6
    unemployment 331.137
    worker security 331.259 6
  law 344.012 596
  personnel management 658.313
    public administration 352.69
Disordered solids 530.413
Disorderly conduct 364.143
  law 345.024 3
Dispatching 388.041
  production management 658.53
  see also Scheduling—transportation
Dispensaries 362.12
  armed forces 355.72
  see also Health care facilities; Health services
Dispensationalist theology 230.046 3
Dispensatories 615.13
Dispersion of light 535.4
Displaced persons 325.21
  see also Refugees
Display advertising 659.15
Display lighting 621.322 9
  see also Lighting
Display screens (Computer) 004.77
  engineering 621.398 7

Disposable personal income (Macroeconomics) 339.32
Disposal of dead 363.75
  see also Undertaking (Mortuary)
Disposal of government property 352.54
Disposal of military supplies 355.621 37
Disposal of public lands 333.16
  economics 333.16
  public administration 352.574
Dispute resolution 303.69
  international relations 327.17
  law 347.09
  sociology 303.69
Disruptive discharges 537.52
Disruptive students 371.93
Dissent 303.484
  social action 361.23
Dissenters (Protestant churches) 280.4
  see also Protestantism
Dissertations (Academic) 378.242
  bibliographies 011.75
  rhetoric 808.02
Dissociative disorders
  medicine 616.852 3
  see also Mental illness
Dissonance (Music) 781.239
Distance education 371.35
  adult level 374.4
    T1—071 5
  computers 371.334
  higher education 378.175
  radio 371.333 1
  television 371.335 8
Distance races 796.424
  see also Sports
Distant prospection (Parapsychology) 133.323
Distillation
  alcoholic beverages 663.16
  desalinization 628.167 2
Distilled liquor 641.25
  commercial processing 663.5
  cooking with 641.625
  home preparation 641.874
Distomatosis
  incidence 614.553
  medicine 616.963
  see also Communicable diseases (Human)
Distributed databases
  computer science 005.758
Distributed-parameter systems 003.78
Distributed processing 004.36
  architecture 004.368 2
  communications 004.618 6
    programming 005.712 76
    programs 005.713 76
  graphics programming 006.677 6
  graphics programs 006.687 6
  interfacing
    programming 005.712 76
    programs 005.713 76
  knowledge-based systems
    programming 006.337
  multimedia-systems
    programming 006.777 6
  multimedia-systems programs 006.787 6
  operating systems 005.447 6
  performance evaluation
    for design and improvement 004.368 4
  peripherals 004.718
  programming 005.276
  programs 005.376
  systems analysis 004.368 1
  systems design 004.368 1
  see also Processing modes—computer science
Distribution channels
  marketing management 658.84
Distribution management 658.8
    T1—068 8
  see Manual at 380.1 vs. 658.8; *also at* 658.8 and T1—0688; *also at* 658.8, T1—0688 vs. 659
Distribution theory (Mathematics) 515.782
Distribution theory of prime numbers 512.73
Distributions (Mathematics) 512.925
  algebra 512.925
  arithmetic 513.25
Distributive justice 340.115
  ethics 172.2
    religion 291.562 2
      Christianity 241.622
      Buddhism 294.356 22
      Hinduism 294.548 622
      Islam 297.562 2
      Judaism 296.362 2
Distributor brands
  sales promotion 658.827
District Court (Scotland) 345.411 012
District courts 347.02
  United States 347.732 2

District heating 697.03
  hot water 697.4
  resource economics 333.793
  steam 697.54
District nursing
  medicine 610.734 3
District of Columbia 975.3
  T2—753
Districting (Legislatures) 328.334 5
  law 342.053
Districts (Local government units) 320.83
  see also Counties
Distrito Especial de Bogotá (Colombia) T2—861 48
Distrito Federal (Brazil) T2—817 4
Distrito Federal (Mexico) T2—725 3
Distrito Federal (Venezuela) T2—877
Distrito Nacional (Dominican Republic) T2—729 375
Ditches
  agriculture 631.62
  road engineering 625.734
Ditsobotla (South Africa) T2—682 94
Diuretics
  pharmacodynamics 615.761
  see also Urinary system
Diurnal variations
  geomagnetism 538.742
Divehi language 491.487
  T6—914 8
Divehi literature 891.48
Divers 627.720 92
  springboard sports 797.240 92
  springboard sports group T7—797 2
  underwater sports 797.230 92
  underwater sports group T7—797 2
  underwater technologists 627.720 92
    occupational group T7—627
Diversification
  production economics 338.6
  production management 658.503 8
Divertimentos 784.185 2
Divestment
  management 658.16
Divide County (N.D.) T2—784 71
Divided catalogs 025.315
Dividends 332.632 21
  accounting 657.76
  financial management 658.155
  investment economics 332.632 21
  law 346.092 2
    income tax law 343.052 46
Dividers
  road engineering 625.795
Divination 133.3
  religion 291.32
    African religions 299.64
Divinatory graphology 137
Divinatory signs 133.334
Divine law
  Christianity 241.2
Divine Light Mission 294
Divine office (Religion) 264.15
  Anglican 264.030 15
  music 782.324
    choral and mixed voices 782.532 4
    single voices 783.093 24
  Roman Catholic 264.020 15
    texts 264.024
Divine right of kings 321.6
Diving 627.72
  engineering 627.72
  sports 797.2
    see also Sports
Divining rods 133.323
Divinity of Jesus Christ 232.8
Divinity schools 230.071 1
Divisibility 512.72
Division 512.92
  algebra 512.92
  arithmetic 513.214
Division algebras 512.24
Division of labor
  sociology 306.368
Divisional Court of Queen's Bench of High Court of Justice (Great Britain) 345.420 16
Divisionism 709.034 5
  painting 759.055
Divisions (Army units) 355.31
Divisions (Naval units) 359.31
Divorce 306.89
  ethics 173
    religion 291.563
      Buddhism 294.356 3
      Christianity 241.63
      Hinduism 294.548 63
      Islam 297.563
      Judaism 296.363
  Judaism 296.444 4
  law 346.016 6
  social theology 291.178 358 9
    Christianity 261.835 89
  social welfare 362.829 4
    see also Families—social welfare

Divorce (continued)
  sociology 306.89
Divorced persons 305.906 53
  T1—086 53
  Christian devotional literature 242.646
  family relationships 306.89
  guides to Christian life 248.846
  legal status 346.016 6
  psychology 155.643
  social group 305.906 53
Dixie County (Fla.) T2—759 812
Dixiecrat Party (U.S.) 324.273 3
Dixieland jazz 781.653
Dixon County (Neb.) T2—782 223
Dixon Entrance (B.C. and Alaska) 551.466 33
  T2—164 33
Diyālá (Iraq) T2—567 4
Diyarbakir Ili (Turkey) T2—566 7
Dizziness
  symptomatology
    neurological diseases 616.841
  see also Nervous system
Djakarta (Indonesia) T2—598 22
Djamena (Chad) T2—674 3
Djelfa (Algeria : Province) T2—653
Djibouti 967.71
  T2—677 1
Djiboutians T5—967 71
Djirbal language 499.15
  T6—991 5
DNA (Genetics) 572.86
  humans 611.018 16
  see Manual at 572.8; *also at* 576.5 vs. 572.8
DNA viruses 579.24
Dnepropetrovsk (Ukraine : Oblast) T2—477 4
Dnestr River (Ukraine and Moldova) T2—477 9
Dnieper River T2—477
Dniester River (Ukraine and Moldova) T2—477 9
Dnipropetrovs´ka oblast´ (Ukraine) T2—477 4
Do-it-yourself work 643.7
Dobby-weave fabrics 677.615
  see also Textiles
Doberman pinscher 636.736
Dobruja (Romania and Bulgaria) T2—498 3
  Bulgaria T2—499 4
  Romania T2—498 3
Dobsonflies 595.747
Dock (Plant) 583.57
Docks (Port facilities) 387.15
  engineering 627.31
  see also Port facilities
Doctors 610.92
  see also Physicians
Doctor's degree 378.2
Doctrinal controversies
  Christian church history 273
Doctrinal theology 291.2
  Buddhism 294.342
  Christianity 230
    see Manual at 261.5 vs. 231–239
  Hinduism 294.52
  Islam 297.2
    Sufi 297.41
  Judaism 296.3
  philosophy of religion 210
Document delivery services 025.6
Documentary evidence 347.064
  criminal investigation 363.256 5
  law 347.064
Documentary films
  journalism 070.18
Documentary hypothesis (Pentateuchal criticism) 222.106 6
Documentation 025
Dodders 583.94
Doddridge County (W. Va.) T2—754 56
Dodecanese T2—495 87
  ancient T2—391 6
Dodecaphony 781.268
Dōdekanēsos (Greece) T2—495 87
  ancient T2—391 6
Dodge County (Ga.) T2—758 532
Dodge County (Minn.) T2—776 153
Dodge County (Neb.) T2—782 235
Dodge County (Wis.) T2—775 82
Dodoma Region (Tanzania) T2—678 26
Dodos 598.65
Doe, Samuel K. (Samuel Kanyon)
  Liberian history 966.620 3
Dog breeds 636.71
  see Manual at 636.72–636.75
Dog family 599.77
Dog pounds 363.78
  see also Pest control
Dog racing 798.8
  see also Sports

Dog sled racing	798.83
see also Sports	
Dogbanes	583.93
Dogfishes	597.36
Dogmatism	
philosophy	148
Dogon (African people)	T5—963
Dogon language	496.3
	T6—963
Dogs	636.7
animal husbandry	636.7
experimental animals	
medicine	619.7
predator control technology	636.083 9
zoology	599.772
Dogwoods	635.977 384
botany	583.84
ornamental arboriculture	635.977 384
Doilies	642.7
arts	746.96
home sewing	646.21
table setting	642.7
Dolerites	552.3
Dolgan language	494.332
	T6—943 32
Dolichopodidae	595.773
Dolj (Romania)	T2—498 4
Doll clothing	688.722 1
handicrafts	745.592 21
manufacturing technology	688.722 1
see also Toys	
Doll furniture	688.723
handicrafts	745.592 3
manufacturing technology	688.723
see also Toys	
Dollhouses	688.723
handicrafts	745.592 3
manufacturing technology	688.723
see also Toys	
Dolls	688.722 1
ceramic arts	738.83
handicrafts	745.592 21
manufacturing technology	688.722 1
see also Toys	
Dolly Varden trout	597.554
Dolomite	553.516
economic geology	553.516
mineralogy	549.782
petrology	552.58
Dolores County (Colo.)	T2—788 26
Dolphins	599.53
animal husbandry	636.953
conservation technology	639.979 53
resource economics	333.959 53
Domaine-du-Roy (Quebec)	T2—714 14
Dombes (France)	T2—444 4
Domes	721.46
architecture	721.46
construction	690.146
structural engineering	624.177 5
concrete	624.183 45
Domestic animals	636
Domestic architecture	728
Domestic arts	640
Domestic cats	636.8
Domestic commerce	381
law	343.088
see also Domestic trade	
Domestic councils	
public administration	352.246
Domestic Court of Magistrates Court (Great Britain)	347.420 23
Domestic customs	392.3
Domestic employees	640.46
Domestic industries	338.634
Domestic investment	332.672
Domestic law	
relation to international law	341.04
Domestic medicine	616.024
Domestic order	
public administration	353.3
Domestic relations (Family)	306.8
law	346.015
Domestic safety	363.13
public administration	353.97
see also Safety	
Domestic sciences	640
Domestic settings	
music	781.535
Domestic system	
economics	338.634
Domestic trade	381
public administration	354.73
Domestic traders	381.092
occupational group	T7—381
Domestic wastes	363.728 8
social services	363.728 8
technology	628.4
water pollution engineering	628.168 2
see also Waste control	
Domestication (Agriculture)	631.52
animals	636.082
plants	631.52
Dominance	
applied psychology	158.2
social control	303.33
Dominica	972.984 1
	T2—729 841

Dominican Republic	972.93
	T2—729 3
Dominican Republic literature	860
Dominican Sisters	255.972
church history	271.972
Dominicans	255.2
church history	271.2
women	255.972
church history	271.972
Dominicans (Dominican Republic people)	T5—687 293
Dominion of Canada	971.05
	T2—71
Dominion theology	230.046
Dominoes	795.32
Don River (Russia)	T2—474 9
Don River (Scotland)	T2—412 32
Doña Ana County (N.M.)	T2—789 66
Donations	
financial management	658.153
tax law	343.052 32
Donatism	273.4
Donbas (Ukraine and Russia)	T2—477 4
Doncaster (England)	T2—428 27
Donegal (Ireland : County)	T2—416 93
Donets Basin (Ukraine and Russia)	T2—477 4
Donets River (Russia and Ukraine)	T2—477 4
Donetsʹk (Ukraine : Oblast)	T2—477 4
Donet͡sʹka oblastʹ (Ukraine)	T2—477 4
Doniphan County (Kan.)	T2—781 35
Donkeys	636.182
conservation technology	639.979 665
resource economics	333.959 665
Donley County (Tex.)	T2—764 832
Dooly County (Ga.)	T2—758 895
Door County (Wis.)	T2—775 63
Door furnishings	645.3
home sewing	646.21
household management	645.3
manufacturing technology	684
Door knockers	
artistic ironwork	739.48
Doors	721.822
architecture	721.822
construction	690.182 2
interior decoration	747.3
sculpture	731.542
Doors (Automobile bodies)	629.26
Doorstops	
rubber	678.34
Doorways	721.822
architecture	721.822
construction	690.182 2
Dopamine	
in nervous system	
human physiology	612.804 2
Doppelgänger	
literature	808.802 7
history and criticism	809.927
specific literatures	T3B—080 27
history and criticism	T3B—092 7
Doppler effect	534.3
Dorchester (Quebec)	T2—714 72
Dorchester County (Md.)	T2—752 27
Dorchester County (S.C.)	T2—757 94
Dordogne (France)	T2—447 2
Doris (Greece)	T2—383
Dormancy (Biology)	571.78
Dormers	721.5
architecture	721.5
construction	690.15
Dormice	599.359 6
Dormitories	
architecture	727.38
Dorsal muscles	
human anatomy	611.731
see also Musculoskeletal system	
Dorset (England)	T2—423 3
Dortmund (Germany)	T2—435 633
Dorval Island (Quebec)	T2—714 28
Dosage determination	
pharmacology	615.14
Dosimetry	
biophysics	
humans	612.014 48
radiotherapy	615.842
Dothideales	579.564
Dotted swiss embroidery	677.77
Douala (Cameroon)	T2—671 1
Douay Bible	220.520 2
Double basses	787.5
instrument	787.519
music	787.5
see also Stringed instruments	
Double-bassists	787.509 2
Double bassoons	788.59
instrument	788.591 9
music	788.59
see also Woodwind instruments	
Double cropping	631.58

Double helix 572.863 3
see Manual at 572.8
Double jeopardy 345.04
Double-reed bagpipes 788.49
see also Woodwind instruments
Double-reed instruments 788.5
see also Woodwind instruments
Double salts 546.343
chemical engineering 661.4
Double stars 523.841
Double sulfides
mineralogy 549.35
Double taxation 336.294
international law 341.484 4
law 343.052 6
public finance 336.294
Doubles (Literature) 808.802 7
history and criticism 809.927
specific literatures T3B—080 27
history and criticism T3B—092 7
Doubles (Tennis) 796.342 28
Doubling the cube 516.204
Doubs (France : Dept.) T2—444 6
Doubt
epistemology 121.5
Dougherty County (Ga.) T2—758 953
Douglas County (Colo.) T2—788 86
Douglas County (Ga.) T2—758 243
Douglas County (Ill.) T2—773 68
Douglas County (Kan.) T2—781 65
Douglas County (Minn.) T2—776 45
Douglas County (Mo.) T2—778 832
Douglas County (Neb.) T2—782 254
Douglas County (Nev.) T2—793 59
Douglas County (Or.) T2—795 29
Douglas County (S.D.) T2—783 383
Douglas County (Wash.) T2—797 31
Douglas County (Wis.) T2—775 11
Douglas squirrel 599.363
Douro Litoral (Portugal) T2—469 15
Dove, River (Derbyshire and Stafford, England) T2—425 13
Dovecotes
architecture 728.927
construction 690.892 7
Dover (Del.) T2—751 4
Dover (England : District) T2—422 352
Dover, Strait of 551.461 36
T2—163 36
Doves 598.65
conservation technology 639.978 65
resource economics 333.958 65
Doves (continued)
sports hunting 799.246 5
Dowayo (African people) T5—963 61
Dowayo language 496.361
T6—963 61
Down (Northern Ireland) T2—416 5
Down (Northern Ireland : District) T2—416 56
Downhill ski racing 796.935
see also Sports
Downhill skiing 796.935
see also Sports
Downs (Qld. : District) T2—943 3
Down's syndrome
medicine 616.858 842
see also Mental retardation
Downsizing of organizations
executive management 658.406
personnel management 658.313 4
production economics 338.64
worker security 331.259 6
Downtown 307.333 16
area planning 711.552 2
community redevelopment 307.342
community sociology 307.333 16
Downy mildew 579.546
agricultural disease 632.446
Dowry 392.5
Dowsing 133.323
Doxologies
Christian private prayer 242.72
Doyayo language 496.361
T6—963 61
DPI (Macroeconomics) 339.32
Dracaenas 584.352
Draft (Conscription) 355.223 63
law 343.012 2
Draft animals 636.088 2
Draft horses 636.15
Draft registration 355.223 6
Draft resistance 355.224
law 343.012 2
Drafted labor 331.117 32
Drafting (Drawing) 604.2
T1—022 1
Drafts (Credit) 332.77
exchange medium 332.55
law 346.096
Draftsmen 604.209 2
occupational group T7—604
Drag
aeronautics 629.132 34
Dragonfishes (Pegasiformes) 597.64
Dragonfishes (Stomiatoidei) 597.5

Dragonflies 595.733
Dragons 398.245 4
  see also Legendary animals
Dragoons 357.1
Drainage
  agriculture 631.62
  airport engineering 629.136 35
  engineering 627.54
  engineering geology 624.151 36
  mining 622.5
  road engineering 625.734
Drake Passage 551.469 3
  T2—167 3
Drakensberg Mountains T2—684 7
Drama (Greece : Nome) T2—495 7
Drama (Literature) 808.82
  criticism 809.2
    theory 808.2
  history 809.2
  rhetoric 808.2
  specific literatures T3B—2
    individual authors T3A—2
  see Manual at T3A—2, T3B—2 vs. T3A—1, T3B—102; *also at* T3B—2
Drama (Theater) 792
  see also Theater
Drama in Christian education 268.67
Dramatic monologues (Poetry) 808.812
  history and criticism 809.12
  specific literatures T3B—102
    individual authors T3A—1
  see Manual at T3A—2, T3B—2 vs. T3A—1, T3B—102
Dramatic music 781.552
Dramatic poetry 808.812
  history and criticism 809.12
  specific literatures T3B—102
    individual authors T3A—1
  see Manual at T3A—2, T3B—2 vs. T3A—1, T3B—102
Dramatic vocal forms 782.1
  music 782.1
  stage presentation 792.5
  see Manual at 782.1 vs. 792.5
Dramatists 809.2
  collected biography 809.2
    specific literatures T3B—200 9
  individual biography T3A—2
  occupational group T7—82
Draped figures 704.942 2
  drawing 743.5
  painting 757.23
Draperies 645.3
  arts 746.94
  commercial technology 684.3
  home sewing 646.21
  household management 645.3
  interior decoration 747.5
Draughts 794.2
Dravida languages 494.81
  T6—948 1
Dravida literatures 894.81
Dravidian languages 494.8
  T6—948
Dravidian literatures 894.8
Dravidians T5—948
Drawbacks
  international commerce 382.7
Drawbridges 388
  construction 624.8
  see also Bridges
Drawers (Artists) 741.092
  occupational group T7—743
Drawing (Delineating) 741
  arts 741
  elementary education 372.52
  technology 604.2
  T1—022 1
Drawing glass 666.124
Drawing metals 671.34
  decorative arts 739.14
  sculpture 731.41
Drawing paper 676.282 5
Drawing rooms 643.54
  home economics 643.54
  interior decoration 747.75
Drawings T1—022 2
  arts 741
Drawn work
  arts 746.44
Dream books 135.3
Dreams 154.63
  human physiology 612.821
  literature 808.803 53
    history and criticism 809.933 53
    specific literatures T3B—080 353
      history and criticism T3B—093 53
  parapsychology 135.3
Dred Scott decision, 1857
  Civil War (United States)
      cause 973.711 5

Dredgers (Ships)
  design 623.812 8
  engineering 623.828
Dredging 627.73
Dredging services
  ports 387.168
Dredging spoil 363.728 4
  engineering 627.73
  social services 363.728 4
  see also Waste control
Drenthe (Netherlands) T2—492 15
Dresden (Germany) T2—432 142
Dresden (Germany : Bezirk) T2—432 14
Dress accessories 391.44
  see also Accessories (Clothing)
Dressage 798.23
Dressers 645.4
  manufacturing technology 684.16
  see also Furniture
Dresses 391.2
  commercial technology 687.112
  customs 391.2
  home economics 646.34
  home sewing 646.432
  see also Clothing
Dressing
  child training 649.63
Dressing leather 675.24
Dressmakers 646.400 92
  commercial 687.112 092
    occupational group T7—687
  occupational group T7—646 4
Dressmaking 646.404
  commercial technology 687.112
  home sewing 646.404
Drew County (Ark.) T2—767 825
Dried eggs 641.375 4
  cooking 641.675 4
  food 641.375 4
  processing 637.54
Dried foods
  cooking 641.614
  home preparation 641.44
Dried milk 641.371 43
  cooking 641.671 43
  food 641.371 43
  processing 637.143
Dried skim milk 641.371 473
  cooking 641.671 473
  food 641.371 473
  processing 637.147 3
Driers (Paints) 667.622
Drift mining 622.2
Driftwood arrangements 745.925
Drill (Military training) 355.54
Drilling
  gas wells 622.338 1
  mining 622.23
  oil wells 622.338 1
  underwater engineering 627.75
Drilling muds 622.338 1
Drilling platforms 627.98
  petroleum extraction 622.338 19
Drilling ships
  design 623.812 8
  engineering 623.828
  petroleum extraction 622.338 19
Drilling tools 621.952
Drink driving 364.147
  causes of accidents 363.125 14
  law 345.024 7
Drinking
  customs 394.12
Drinking age 363.41
  law 344.054 1
Drinking glasses
  decorative arts 748.83
Drinking places 647.95
  architecture 725.72
  household management 647.95
  sanitation services 363.729 6
    public administration 353.94
    see also Waste control
Drinking water 363.61
  economics 333.912 2
  supply services 363.61
  treatment engineering 628.162
    nautical engineering 623.854 2
  see also Water
Drinks 641.2
  commercial processing 663
  home preparation 641.87
Drip-dry fabrics 677.68
  see also Textiles
Drive shafts
  automotive engineering 629.245
Driver information
  highway services 388.312 4
    urban 388.413 124
Drivers' licenses
  international law 341.756 86
  law 343.094 6
  public administration 354.765 284
Drives (Computer devices) 004.56
  engineering 621.397 6

Drives (Psychology)	153.8
physiological	152.5
Driveways	625.889
Driving belts	621.852
rubber technology	678.36
Driving family cars	
recreation	796.78
Driving horses (Breeds)	636.14
Driving horses (Recreation)	798.6
Driving motor vehicles	
recreation	796.7
Driving sports cars	
recreation	796.77
Drogheda (Ireland)	T2—418 256
Drôme (France)	T2—449 8
Dromedaries	636.295
Drones (Aircraft)	
control systems	629.132 6
military engineering	623.746 9
Dronning Maud Land	T2—989
Dronten (Netherlands)	T2—492 2
Dropouts (Education)	371.291 3
Drops	530.427
technology	620.43
Droseraceae	583.75
Drosophilidae	595.774
Drought-resistant plants	581.754
floriculture	635.952 5
Droughts	
agricultural economics	338.14
crop damage	632.12
meteorology	551.577 3
social services	363.349 29
agricultural industries	338.18
see also Disasters	
Drowning	
medicine	617.18
Drug abuse	362.29
see also Substance abuse	
Drug adulteration	363.194
criminology	364.142
criminal law	345.024 2
see also Drugs (Pharmaceuticals)—product safety	
Drug allergies	
incidence	614.599 358
medicine	616.975 8
see also Diseases (Human)	
Drug culture	306.1
Drug dependence	362.29
medicine	616.86
perinatal medicine	618.326 8
personal health	613.8
Drug dependence (continued)	
social welfare	362.29
see also Substance abuse	
Drug incompatibilities	
pharmacology	615.14
Drug interactions	
pharmacodynamics	615.704 5
Drug metabolism	
pharmacodynamics	615.7
Drug possession	364.177
law	345.027 7
see also Drug traffic	
Drug resistance in microorganisms	616.01
Drug shock therapy	
psychiatry	616.891 2
see also Mental illness	
Drug side effects	
pharmacodynamics	615.704 2
Drug testing	
personnel management	658.382 2
personnel selection	658.311 2
Drug therapy	
medicine	615.58
see Manual at 615.854	
psychiatry	616.891 8
see also Mental illness	
see Manual at 616–618 vs. 615.7	
Drug traffic	363.45
criminology	364.177
criminal law	345.027 7
international law	341.775
public administration	353.37
school problem	371.784
social problem	363.45
law	344.054 5
Drug use	362.29
see also Drug traffic; Substance abuse	
Drugs (Narcotics)	
customs	394.14
ethics	178.8
see also Ethical problems	
pharmacodynamics	615.782 2
see also Drug traffic; Substance abuse	
Drugs (Pharmaceuticals)	615.1
insurance	368.382 4
see also Insurance	
manufacturing technology	615.19
pharmacology	615.1
preservation	615.18

Drugs (Pharmaceuticals) (continued)
product safety 363.194
criminology 364.142
criminal law 345.024 2
law 344.042 33
public administration 353.998
see also Product safety
production economics 338.476 151
see Manual at 615.1 vs. 615.2–615.3; *also at* 615.2–615.3 vs. 615.7
Druidism 299.16
Druids
religious group T7—299 1
Drumheller (Alta.) T2—712 33
Drumlins 551.315
Drummers (Musicians) 786.909 2
occupational group T7—786
Drumming (Signaling)
social psychology 302.222
Drummond (Quebec : County) T2—714 563
Drummond (Quebec : Regional County Municipality) T2—714 563
Drums (Computer devices) 004.56
engineering 621.397 6
Drums (Fishes) 597.725
Drums (Music) 786.9
instrument 786.919
music 786.9
see also Percussion instruments
Drunk driving 364.147
causes of accidents 363.125 14
law 345.024 7
Drunkenness 362.292
criminology 364.173
criminal law 345.027 3
see also Alcoholism
Drupaceous fruits 641.342
botany 583.73
cooking 641.642
food 641.342
orchard crops 634.2
Druzes (Islamic sect) 297.85
Dry cells (Batteries) 621.312 423
Dry cleaning 667.12
Dry-climate plants 581.754
floriculture 635.952 5
Dry docks 623.83
Dry farming 631.586
Dry-weather photography 778.75
Dryers
home laundry 648.1
manufacturing technology 683.88
Drying clothes
home economics 648.1
Drying coal 662.623
Drying foods 664.028 4
commercial preservation 664.028 4
home preservation 641.44
Drying lumber 674.38
Drying processes 660.284 26
Dryopoidea 595.764 5
Drypoint 767.3
DTP (Publishing)
composition 686.225 444 16
Du Page County (Ill.) T2—773 24
Dual geometries 516.35
Dual nationality 323.634
international law 341.482
law 342.083
Dual personalities
medicine 616.852 36
see also Mental illness
Duala (African people) T5—963 962
Duala language 496.396 2
T6—963 962
Duala literature 896.396 2
Dualism
philosophy 147.4
Hindu 181.484
Dualism (Concept of God) 211.33
classes of religions 291.14
philosophy of religion 211.33
Duality (Mathematics) 515.782
Duarte (Dominican Republic) T2—729 367
Dubai (United Arab Emirates : Emirate) T2—535 7
Dubayy (United Arab Emirates : Emirate) T2—535 7
Dubbo (N.S.W.) T2—944 5
Dublin (Ireland) T2—418 35
Dublin (Ireland : County) T2—418 3
Dubois County (Ind.) T2—772 37
Dubuque County (Iowa) T2—777 39
Duchesne County (Utah) T2—792 22
Duck (Meat) 641.365 97
commercial processing 664.93
cooking 641.665 97
food 641.365 97
Duck-billed dinosaurs 567.914
Duck hunting
sports 799.244
Duck River (Tenn.) T2—768 434

Ducks	598.41
animal husbandry	636.597
conservation technology	639.978 41
resource economics	333.958 41
sports hunting	799.244
Duckweeds	584.64
Duct flutes	788.35
see also Woodwind instruments	
Ductility	
materials science	620.112 5
Dude farming	796.56
Dude ranching	796.56
Dudley (England)	T2—424 93
Due process of law	347.05
Dueling	394.8
customs	394.8
ethics	179.7
Duets	
chamber music	785.12
vocal music	783.12
Dufferin (Ont. : County)	T2—713 41
Dufferin and Ava, Frederick Temple Blackwood, Marquis of	
Indian history	954.035 4
Dugong	599.559
Dugongidae	599.559
Duikers	599.64
Duisburg (Germany)	T2—435 536
Dukes County (Mass.)	T2—744 94
Dukhobors	289.9
see also Christian denominations	
Dulcimers	787.74
see also Stringed instruments	
Duluth (Minn.)	T2—776 771
Dumbarton (Scotland : District)	T2—414 25
Dumfries and Galloway (Scotland)	T2—414 7
Dumfriesshire (Scotland)	T2—414 8
Dumping (Trade)	
law	343.087
Dumps (Solid waste)	363.728 5
technology	628.445 62
see also Waste control	
Dumyāṭ (Egypt : Province)	T2—621
Dún Laoghaire (Ireland)	T2—418 38
Dunaliellaceae	579.832
Dunbartonshire (Scotland)	T2—414 25
Dundas (Ont. : County)	T2—713 75
Dundee (Scotland)	T2—412 7
Dundee (South Africa : District)	T2—684 1
Dundy County (Neb.)	T2—782 86
Dune buggies	
engineering	629.222
see also Automobiles	
Dune stabilization	631.64
shore protection	627.58
Dunedin (N.Z.)	T2—939 2
Dunedin City (N.Z.)	T2—939 2
Dunes	551.375
see also Sand dunes	
Dunfermline (Scotland : District)	T2—412 98
Dung beetles	595.764 9
Dung flies	595.774
Dungannon (Northern Ireland : District)	T2—416 45
Dunkerque, Battle of, 1940	940.542 142 8
Dunkers	286.5
see also Baptists	
Dunklin County (Mo.)	T2—778 993
Dunn County (N.D.)	T2—784 82
Dunn County (Wis.)	T2—775 43
Duodecimal system	513.56
Duodenal ulcers	
medicine	616.343 3
see also Digestive system	
Duodenitis	
medicine	616.344
see also Digestive system	
Duodenum	573.378
biology	573.378
human anatomy	611.341
human physiology	612.33
medicine	616.34
surgery	617.554 1
see also Digestive system	
Duplex houses	
architecture	728.312
Duplex-process steel	669.142 3
Duplicating machines	
library services	025.12
manufacturing technology	681.6
office use	652.4
Duplin County (N.C.)	T2—756 382
Dupuit, Jules-Juvénal	
economic school	330.154 3
Durability engineering	620.004 54
Durable press fabrics	677.68
Durango (Mexico : State)	T2—721 5
Durazno (Uruguay : Dept.)	T2—895 24
Durban (South Africa)	T2—684 55

Durban-Pinetown
industrial area T2—684 55
Duress 345.04
Durham (England : City) T2—428 65
Durham (England : County) T2—428 6
Durham (Ont. : Regional municipality) T2—713 56
Durham County (N.C.) T2—756 563
Durham mission (Canadian history) 971.039
Duroc-Jersey swine 636.483
Düsseldorf (Germany) T2—435 534
Düsseldorf (Germany : Regierungsbezirk) T2—435 53
Dust
meteorology 551.511 3
technology 620.43
Dust control
buildings 697.932 4
mining 622.83
Dust diseases
human lungs
medicine 616.244
Dust storms 551.559
social services 363.349 29
see also Disasters
Dusting
housecleaning 648.5
Dusting in agriculture 632.94
Dusting-on processes
photographic printing 773.2
Dutch T5—393 1
Dutch East India Company
Indonesian history 959.802 1
Dutch East Indies 959.802 2
T2—598
Dutch elm disease 635.977 345
Dutch Guiana T2—883
Dutch language 439.31
T6—393 1
Dutch literature 839.31
Dutch Reformed Church in North America 285.732
see also Reformed Church (American Reformed)
Dutch Republic 949.204
T2—492
Dutch West Indies T2—729 86
Dutchess County (N.Y.) T2—747 33
Dutchman's breeches (Plant) 583.35
Duties (Tariff) 382.7
see also Customs (Tariff)
Duties of citizens 323.65
Dutra, Eurico Gaspar
Brazilian history 981.061
Duty
religion 291.5
Islam 297.5
Duval County (Fla.) T2—759 12
Duval County (Tex.) T2—764 463
Duvalier, François
Haitian history 972.940 72
Duvalier, Jean-Claude
Haitian history 972.940 72
Dvaita (Philosophy) 181.484 1
Dvaitādvaita (Philosophy) 181.484 3
Dwarf pea 641.356 57
see also Chick-peas
Dwarf potted trees 635.977 2
Dwarf sperm whales 599.547
Dwarfism (Pituitary)
medicine 616.47
see also Endocrine system
Dwarfs
physical anthropology 599.949
Dwellings 643.1
architecture 728
customs 392.36
health 613.5
home economics 643.1
literature 808.803 55
history and criticism 809.933 55
specific literatures T3B—080 355
history and criticism T3B—093 55
Dwyfor (Wales) T2—429 23
Dye lasers 621.366 4
Dye-producing plants
agriculture 633.86
economic botany 581.636
Dyeing 667.3
home economics 648.1
textile arts 746.6
Dyeing leather 675.25
Dyeing yarns
arts 746.13
Dyer County (Tenn.) T2—768 15
Dyerma language 496.5
T6—965
Dyes 547.86
chemistry 547.86
technology 667.2
Dyfed (Wales) T2—429 6
Dying 306.9
music 781.588
psychology 155.937
social aspects 306.9

Dying patients 362.175
pastoral theology 291.61
Christianity 259.417 5
social theology 291.178 321 75
Christianity 261.832 175
see also Terminal care
see Manual at 362.1–362.4 vs. 610: Biographies
Dynamic oceanography 551.47
Dynamic programming 519.703
Dynamic psychology 150.193
Dynamic systems 003.85
Dynamical systems (Mathematics) 515.352
Dynamics 531.11
air 533.62
engineering 620.107 4
atmosphere 551.515
engineering 620.104
fluids 532.05
engineering 620.106 4
gases 533.2
engineering 620.107 4
liquids 532.5
engineering 620.106 4
particles 531.163
engineering 620.43
physics 531.11
solids 531.3
engineering 620.105 4
Dynamism 146
Dynamite 662.27
military engineering 623.452 7
Dynamos 621.313 2
Dysentery
incidence 614.516
medicine 616.935
see also Communicable diseases (Human)
Dysfunctional families
pastoral theology 291.61
Christianity 259.1
social relationships 306.87
social theology 291.178 358 5
Christianity 261.835 85
Dyslexia
medicine 616.855 3
pediatrics 618.928 553
special education 371.914 4
see also Communicative disorders
Dysmenorrhea
gynecology 618.172
see also Female genital system
Dyspepsia
medicine 616.332
see also Digestive system
Dysphasia
medicine 616.855 2
see also Communicative disorders
Dyspnea
medicine 616.2
see also Respiratory system
Dysprosium
chemistry 546.417
see also Rare earths
Dystocia
obstetrics 618.5
Dystopias
arts T3C—372
literature 808.803 72
history and criticism 809.933 72
specific literatures T3B—080 372
history and criticism T3B—093 72
Dytikē Hellada (Greece) T2—495 27
Dytikē Makedonia (Greece) T2—495 62
Dytiscidae 595.762
Dyula (African people) T5—963 45
Dyula language 496.345
T6—963 45
Dzanani (South Africa : District) T2—682 91
Dzongkha language 495.4
T6—954

E

$E = mc^2$ 530.11
E document (Biblical criticism) 222.106 6
E-flat horns 788.974
see also Brass instruments
E region (Ionosphere) 538.767 3
Eagle County (Colo.) T2—788 44
Eagles 598.942
conservation technology 639.978 942
resource economics 333.958 942
Ealing (London, England) T2—421 84
Ear training (Music) 781.424
Eared seals 599.797
Earless seals 599.79
Early childhood education 372.21
Early Christian architecture 723.1
Early Christian art 709.021 2
religious significance 246.2
Early Christian decoration 745.442

Early Christian painting 759.021 2
Early Christian philosophy 189
Early Christian sculpture 734.222
Early Church 270.1
  see Manual at 281.1–281.4
Early County (Ga.) T2—758 962
Early school leavers 371.291 3
  secondary level 373.129 13
Earrings 391.7
  customs 391.7
  making 739.278
  see also Jewelry
Ears 573.89
  anesthesiology 617.967 8
  animal physiology 573.89
  descriptive zoology 591.4
  geriatrics 618.977 8
  human anatomy 611.85
  human diseases
    incidence 614.599 8
    otology 617.8
  human physiology 612.85
  pediatrics 618.920 978
  surgery 617.805 9
Earth 550
  astronomy 525
  extraterrestrial influences 001.94
  geologic history 551.7
  gravity 531.14
  internal structure 551.1
Earth currents (Geomagnetism) 538.748
Earth-fill dams 627.83
Earth roads 388.12
  engineering 625.74
  see also Roads
Earth sciences 550
  information systems 025.065 5
  see Manual at 550 vs. 910
Earth-sheltered buildings 720.473
Earth-sheltered houses 728.370 473
  architecture 728.370 473
  construction 690.837 047 3
Earth temperature
  meteorological effect 551.523
Earthenware 666.6
  arts 738.3
  technology 666.6
Earthquake engineering 624.176 2
Earthquake insurance 368.122 6
  see also Insurance
Earthquake-resistant construction 624.176 2
  buildings 693.852
Earthquakes 551.22
  disaster services 363.349 5
  social effects 303.485
  see also Disasters
Earth's age 551.701
Earthwork 624.152
  dam engineering 627.81
  mining 622.2
  railroad engineering 625.12
  road engineering 625.73
Earthworks (Art style) 709.040 76
Earthworm culture 639.75
Earthworms 592.64
  culture 639.75
Earthy materials 553.6
  economic geology 553.6
  mining 622.36
Earthy minerals 553.6
  economic geology 553.6
  mining 622.36
  synthetic 666.86
Earwigs 595.739
Easements 346.043 5
  international law 341.4
Easington (England : District) T2—428 67
East 950
  T2—5
East Africa 967.6
  T2—676
East Anglia (England) T2—426
East Asia T2—5
East Asian literatures 895
East Asians T5—95
East Avon River T2—423 19
East Azerbaijan (Iran) T2—553
East Baton Rouge Parish (La.) T2—763 18
East Bengal (Pakistan) T2—549 2
East Berbice (Guyana : District) T2—881 7
East Berlin (Germany) T2—431 552
East Cambridgeshire (England) T2—426 56
East Carroll Parish (La.) T2—763 82
East-Central State (Nigeria) T2—669 46
East China Sea 551.465 57
  T2—164 57
East Demerara (Guyana : District) T2—881 5
East Devon (England : District) T2—423 57

East Dorset (England : District) T2—423 34
East Feliciana Parish (La.) T2—763 16
East Flanders (Belgium) T2—493 14
East Friesland (Germany) T2—435 917
East Frisian Islands (Germany) T2—435 917
East Germanic languages 439.9
T6—399
East Germanic literatures 839.9
East Germany (Democratic Republic) 943.108 7
T2—431
East Hampshire (England) T2—422 74
East Hertfordshire (England : District) T2—425 83
East India Company
Indian history 954.031
East Indians T5—914
East Iranian languages (Ancient) 491.52
T6—915 2
East Iranian literatures (Ancient) 891.52
East Kilbride (Scotland : District) T2—414 54
East Kootenay (B.C.) T2—711 65
East Lansing (Mich.) T2—774 27
East Lindsey (England : District) T2—425 32
East London (South Africa : District) T2—687 55
East Lothian (Scotland) T2—413 6
East New Britain Province (Papua New Guinea) T2—958 5
East Northamptonshire (England : District) T2—425 54
East Orange (N.J.) T2—749 33
East Pakistan (Pakistan) T2—549 2
East Prussia (Poland and Russia) T2—438 3
Poland T2—438 3
Russia T2—472 4
East Punjab (India) T2—545 5
East Rand (South Africa) T2—682 2
East Redonda Island (B.C.) T2—711 1
East Riding of Yorkshire (England) T2—428 3
East Scandinavian languages 439.5
T6—395
East Scandinavian literatures 839.5
East Semites T5—921
East Semitic languages 492.1
T6—921
East Semitic literatures 892.1
East Sepik Province (Papua New Guinea) T2—957 5
East Siberian Sea (Russia) 551.468 5
T2—163 25
East Slavic languages 491.7
T6—917
East Slavic literatures 891.7
East Slavs T5—917
East Staffordshire (England) T2—424 65
East Suffolk (England) T2—426 46
East Sussex (England) T2—422 5
East Texas T2—764 14
East Thurlow Island (B.C.) T2—711 1
East York (Ont.) T2—713 541
East Yorkshire (England : Borough) T2—428 39
Eastbourne (England) T2—422 58
Easter 263.93
customs 394.266 7
devotional literature 242.36
sermons 252.63
Easter eggs 394.266 7
customs 394.266 7
handicrafts 745.594 4
Easter Island T2—961 8
Easter lily 635.934 32
botany 584.32
floriculture 635.934 32
Easter music 781.727
Easter Rebellion, 1916 941.508 21
Easter story 232.97
Eastern Aramaic languages 492.3
T6—923
Eastern Aramaic literatures 892.3
Eastern Arctic Inuit language 497.124
T6—971 24
Eastern Austronesian languages 499.4
T6—994
Eastern Canada T2—713
Eastern Canadian Inuit T5—971 24
Eastern Canadian Inuit language 497.124
T6—971 24
Eastern Canadian Inuktitut T5—971 24
Eastern Canadian Inuktitut language 497.124
T6—971 24
Eastern Canadian Inuktitut literature 897.124
Eastern churches 281.5
church government 262.015
parishes 254.015
church law 262.981 5

Eastern churches (continued)
doctrines 230.15
catechisms and creeds 238.19
general councils 262.515
guides to Christian life 248.481 5
liturgy 264.015
missions 266.15
monasticism 255.81
church history 271.81
women 255.981
church history 271.981
moral theology 241.041 5
public worship 264.015
religious associations 267.181 5
religious education 268.815
seminaries 230.073 15
theology 230.15
see Manual at 281.1–281.4
Eastern Desert (Egypt) T2—623
Eastern Empire 949.501 3
Eastern Equatoria (Sudan : Province)) T2—629 5
Eastern Europe 947
T2—47
Eastern front
World War I 940.414 7
Eastern Hemisphere T2—181 1
Eastern Highlands Province (Papua New Guinea) T2—956 9
Eastern Himalayan languages 495.49
T6—954 9
Eastern Himalayan literatures 895.49
Eastern Hindi languages 491.49
T6—914 9
Eastern Hindi literatures 891.49
Eastern languages (Adamawa-Eastern phylum) 496.361
T6—963 61
Eastern Macedonia and Thrace (Greece) T2—495 7
Eastern Malaysia T2—595 3
Eastern Mediterranean Sea 551.462 4
T2—163 84
Eastern Orthodox cathedrals
architecture 726.63
Eastern Orthodox Christians
biography 281.909 2
religious group T7—219
Eastern Orthodox Church 281.9
church government 262.019
parishes 254.019
church law 262.981 9
Eastern Orthodox Church (continued)
doctrines 230.19
catechisms and creeds 238.19
general councils 262.519
guides to Christian life 248.481 9
liturgy 264.019
missions 266.19
monasticism 255.819
church history 271.819
women 255.981 9
church history 271.981 9
moral theology 241.041 9
public worship 264.019
religious associations 267.181 9
religious education 268.819
seminaries 230.073 19
theology 230.19
see Manual at 281.1–281.4
Eastern Orthodox sacred music 781.711 9
public worship 782.322 19
music 782.322 19
religion 264.019 02
Eastern Province (Kenya) T2—676 24
Eastern Province (Zambia) T2—689 4
Eastern Region (China) T2—512
Eastern Region (Ecuador) T2—866 4
Eastern Region (Nigeria) T2—669 4
Eastern rite Catholics 281.5
see also Eastern churches
Eastern rite churches 281.5
see also Eastern churches
Eastern Roman Empire 949.501 3
Eastern Samar (Philippines) T2—599 5
Eastern Shore (Md. and Va.) T2—752 1
Eastern Siberia (Russia) T2—575
Eastern Townships (Quebec) T2—714 6
Eastern Turkic languages 494.32
T6—943 2
Eastertide 263.93
devotional literature 242.36
music 781.727
sermons 252.63
Eastland County (Tex.) T2—764 547
Eastleigh (England) T2—422 772
Eastwood (Scotland : District) T2—414 51
Easy dishes (Cooking) 641.512
Eating
animal physiology 573.35
child training 649.63
customs 394.12

Eating (continued)
  descriptive zoology 591.53
  gastronomy 641.013
  human physiology 612.31
Eating disorders
  medicine 616.852 6
  see also Digestive system; Mental illness
Eating places 647.95
  household management 647.95
  meal service 642.5
  sanitation services 363.729 6
    public administration 353.94
    see also Waste control
Eaton County (Mich.) T2—774 23
Eau Claire County (Wis.) T2—775 45
Ebenales 583.674
Ebla (Extinct city) T2—394 3
Eblaite language 492.6
  T6—926
Eblaite literature 892.6
Ebonies
  botany 583.674
  forestry 634.973 674
Ebro River (Spain) T2—465
EC (European Community) 341.242 2
  see also European Union
Ecbatana (Extinct city) T2—35
Eccentrics (Mechanisms) 621.827
Ecclesiastes 223.8
Ecclesiastical law 262.9
Ecclesiasticus (Bible) 229.4
Ecclesiology
  Christianity 262
ECG (Medicine) 616.120 754 7
  see also Cardiovascular system
Echeverría, Luis
  Mexican history 972.083 2
Echidnas 599.29
Echinococcosis
  incidence 614.554
  medicine 616.964
  see also Communicable diseases (Human)
Echinodera 592.55
Echinodermata 593.9
  paleozoology 563.9
Echinoidea 593.95
  paleozoology 563.95
Echinozoa 593.95
  paleozoology 563.95
Echiurida 592.3
  paleozoology 562.3
Echo-ranging devices
  geophysical prospecting 622.159 2
  marine navigation 623.893 8
Echocardiography
  medicine 616.120 754 3
  see also Cardiovascular system
Echoes
  physics 534.204
Echography
  diagnosis 616.075 43
Echoi 781.264
Echols County (Ga.) T2—758 814
Echuca (Vic.) T2—945 4
Eckankar 299.93
Eclairs 641.865 9
  commercial processing 664.752 5
  home preparation 641.865 9
Eclampsia
  obstetrics 618.75
Eclectic medicine
  therapeutic system 615.53
Eclecticism
  architecture 724.5
  philosophy 148
    ancient 186.3
Eclipses 523.99
  moon 523.38
  sun 523.78
Eclipsing binaries 523.844 4
Ecological anthropology 304.2
Ecological bioenergetics 577.13
Ecological chemistry 577.14
Ecological communities 577.82
Ecological genetics 576.58
Ecological niches 577.82
Ecological pyramids 577.16
Ecological succession 577.18
Ecological toxicology 571.95
Ecologists
  occupational group T7—577
Ecology 577
  animals 591.7
  elementary education 372.357
  ethics 179.1
    religion 291.569 1
      Buddhism 294.356 91
      Christianity 241.691
      Hinduism 294.548 691
      Judaism 296.369 1
  microorganisms 579.17
  physical anthropology 599.95
  plants 581.7

Ecology (continued)
social theology 291.178 362
Christianity 261.836 2
Judaism 296.38
sociology 304.2
specific environments 577
see Manual at 577 vs. 578.7
see Manual at 333.7–333.9 vs. 363.1, 363.73, 577; *also at* 577.26 vs. 579–590: Autecology
Econometrics 330.015 195
management decision making 658.403 3
Economic aggregates
macroeconomics 339.3
Economic anthropology 306.3
Economic assistance
international law 341.759
international politics 327.111
law 343.074
public administration 352.73
foreign aid 353.132 73
Economic biology 578.6
Economic botany 581.6
Economic causes of war 355.027 3
Economic classes 305.5
T1—086 2
T7—062
civil rights 323.322
customs 390.1
dress 391.01
relations with government 323.322
Economic concentration 338.8
Economic conditions 330.9
Economic cooperation
international economics 337.1
see Manual at 337.3–337.9 vs. 337.1
Economic development 338.9
international banking 332.153
law 343.074
natural resources 333.715
see Manual at 333.7–333.9; *also at* 333.7–333.9 vs. 363.1, 363.73, 577
production economics 338.9
public administration 354.27
see Manual at 300, 320.6 vs. 352–354: Public policy; *also at* 352
Economic fluctuations 338.54
Economic forecasting 330.011 2
Economic geography 330.9
Economic geology 553
see Manual at 553; *also at* 553 vs. 333.8, 338.2
Economic growth 338.9
macroeconomic policy 339.5
production economics 338.9
Economic history 330.9
Economic integration
international economics 337.1
Economic microbiology 579.16
Economic planning 338.9
Economic policy 338.9
Economic power (Legislative bodies) 328.341 3
Economic rent 333.012
Economic rights 330
see Manual at 361.614 vs. 330
Economic services for workers 331.255
personnel management 658.383
see also Conditions of employment
Economic situation 330.9
Economic sociology 306.3
Economic stabilization
law 343.034
macroeconomic policy 339.5
Economic strikes 331.892 2
see also Strikes (Work stoppages)
Economic systems 330.12
Economic zoology 591.6
Economics 330
information systems 025.063 3
international politics 327.111
literature 808.803 55
history and criticism 809.933 55
specific literatures T3B—080 355
history and criticism T3B—093 55
public administration 354
social theology 291.178 5
Christianity 261.85
Islam 297.273
see Manual at 297.26–297.27
Judaism 296.383
see Manual at 330 vs. 650
Economics libraries 026.33
Economics of the firm 338.5
Economies of scale 338.514 4
Economists 330.092
occupational group T7—339
Ecosystems 577
see Manual at 333.7–333.9 vs. 363.1, 363.73, 577

Ecotones 577
Ecotoxicology 571.95
  ecology 577.27
  pathology 571.95
  see Manual at 363.73 vs. 571.95, 577.27
Ecrehous (England) T2—423 49
Ecstasy
  psychology 152.42
Ectoparasitic diseases
  incidence 614.558
  medicine 616.968
  see also Communicable diseases (Human)
Ectopic pregnancy
  obstetrics 618.31
Ectoplasm 133.92
Ectoprocta 594.67
Ector County (Tex.) T2—764 862
Ecuador 986.6
  T2—866
Ecuadorian literature 860
Ecuadorians T5—688 66
Ecumenical councils 262.5
  Christian church history 270.2
    modern period 270.82
Ecumenical movement 280.042
  see Manual at 280.042 vs. 262.0011
Ecumenism 262.001 1
  see Manual at 280.042 vs. 262.0011
Eczema
  medicine 616.521
  see also Skin
Eddy, Mary Baker
  Christian Science writings 289.52
Eddy County (N.D.) T2—784 512
Eddy County (N.M.) T2—789 42
Eddy currents 621.310 42
Edema
  symptomatology 616.047
Eden (England : District) T2—427 86
Eden (N.S.W.) T2—944 7
Eden River (England) T2—427 86
Edenburg (South Africa : District) T2—685 7
Edentata 599.31
  paleozoology 569.31
Edgar, King of England
  English history 942.017 3
Edgar County (Ill.) T2—773 69
Edgecombe County (N.C.) T2—756 46
Edged weapons 623.441
  art metalwork 739.72
Edgefield County (S.C.) T2—757 37
Edgings (Floriculture) 635.963
Edible animals 641.306
  agriculture 636.088 3
  economic zoology 591.63
  food source 641.306
Edible bulbs 641.352
  cooking 641.652
  food 641.352
  garden crops 635.2
Edible organisms 641.3
  economic biology 578.63
Edible plants 641.303
  economic botany 581.632
  food 641.303
  see Manual at 583–585
Edible roots 641.351
  cooking 641.651
  food 641.351
  garden crop 635.1
Edinburgh (Scotland) T2—413 4
Edirne İli (Turkey) T2—496 1
Edisto River (S.C.) T2—757 9
Editing 808.027
  cinematography 778.535
  journalism 070.41
  video production 778.593
Editing music 780.149
Edition bookbinding 686.303 4
Editorial cartoons
  journalism 070.442
Editorial crusades 070.41
Editorial policy 070.41
Editorial techniques 808.027
Editorials 070.442
Edmonson County (Ky.) T2—769 752
Edmonton (Alta.) T2—712 334
Edmund I, King of England
  English history 942.017 2
Edmund II, King of England
  English history 942.017 4
Edmunds County (S.D.) T2—783 15
Edo (African people) T5—963 3
Edo language 496.33
  T6—963 3
Edo period (Japan) 952.025
Edo State (Nigeria) T2—669 32
Edoid languages 496.33
  T6—963 3
Edom 939.46
  T2—394 6
EDP (Computing) 004

Edred, King of England
  English history 942.017 2
Education 370
  T1—071
  law 344.07
  library role 021.24
  literature 808.803 55
    history and criticism 809.933 55
    specific literatures T3B—080 355
      history and criticism T3B—093 55
  prisoner services 365.66
  psychological influence 370.158
  public administrative support 353.8
    see Manual at 371 vs. 353.8, 371.2, 379
  public policy 379
  public support 379.11
  sociology 306.43
  value 370.13
  see also Public education
  see Manual at 370; *also at* 371 vs. 372–374, 378
Education and state 379
Education of employees 370.113
  see also Vocational education
Educational acceleration 371.28
Educational aid 379.11
  financial management 371.206
  international 379.129
Educational anthropology 306.43
Educational areas
  area planning 711.57
Educational buildings 371.6
  architecture 727
  construction 690.7
  higher education 378.196
  household management 647.99
  interior decoration 747.87
  special education 371.904 5
Educational consortia
  higher education 378.104
Educational counseling 371.422
Educational equalization 379.26
Educational exchanges 370.116
  international law 341.767 3
  law 344.08
Educational facilities 371.6
  see also Educational buildings
Educational films
  instructional use 371.335 23
  journalism 070.18
Educational games 790.1
  instructional use 371.337
  recreation 790.1
Educational guidance 371.422
Educational institutions 371
  accounting 657.832 7
Educational law 344.07
Educational leave 331.257 63
  labor economics 331.257 63
  personnel management 658.312 2
Educational media 371.33
Educational planning 371.207
Educational policy 379
  see Manual at 371 vs. 353.8, 371.2, 379
Educational psychology 370.15
  see Manual at 153.15 vs. 370.15
Educational research 370.72
Educational sociologists
  occupational group T7—309
Educational sociology 306.43
Educational technology 371.33
Educational tests 371.26
  see Manual at 371.262 vs. 371.264
Educational therapy
  medicine 615.851 6
Educational toys 790.133
  instructional use 371.337
  manufacturing technology 688.725
  recreation 790.133
  see also Toys
Educational vouchers 379.111
  private schools 379.32
Educationally disadvantaged students 371.826 94
Educators
  biography 370.92
  law 344.078
  occupational group T7—37
Eduyyot 296.123 4
  Babylonian Talmud 296.125 4
  Mishnah 296.123 4
  Palestinian Talmud 296.124 4
Edward, King of England, d. 924
  English history 942.016 5
Edward, King of England, ca. 963–978
  English history 942.017 3
Edward, King of England, ca. 1003–1066
  English history 942.019
Edward, the Confessor, King of England
  English history 942.019

Edward, the Elder, King of England
  English history 942.016 5
Edward, the Martyr, King of England
  English history 942.017 3
Edward I, King of England
  English history 942.035
Edward II, King of England
  English history 942.036
Edward III, King of England
  English history 942.037
Edward IV, King of England
  English history 942.044
Edward V, King of England
  English history 942.045
Edward VI, King of England
  English history 942.053
Edward VII, King of Great Britain
  British history 941.082 3
  English history 942.082 3
  Scottish history 941.108 23
Edward VIII, King of Great Britain
  British history 941.084
  English history 942.084
  Scottish history 941.108 4
Edwards County (Ill.) T2—773 791
Edwards County (Kan.) T2—781 782
Edwards County (Tex.) T2—764 882
Edwards Plateau (Tex.) T2—764 87
Edwy, King of England
  English history 942.017 2
EEC (Economic organization) 341.242 2
  see also European Union
Eelgrass 584.74
Eelpouts 597.63
Eels 597.43
Eels (Freshwater) 597.432
  commercial fishing 639.274 32
  cooking 641.692
  culture 639.374 32
  food 641.392
  sports fishing 799.174 32
Eelworms 592.57
  agricultural pests 632.625 7
Eerstehoek (South Africa : District) T2—682 96
Effect
  philosophy 122
Efficiency
  agricultural industries 338.16
  communications industry 384.041
Efficiency (continued)
  economics 338.06
  military administration 355.687 5
  mineral industries 338.26
  promotion of
    personnel management 658.314
    production management 658.515
  public administration 352.375
  secondary industries 338.45
  transportation services 388.049
Effigial slabs 736.5
Effingham County (Ga.) T2—758 722
Effingham County (Ill.) T2—773 796
Efik (African people) T5—963 642
Efik language 496.364 2
  T6—963 642
Efik literature 896.364 2
EFTA (Economic organization) 341.242
  international commerce 382.914 3
  international economics 337.143
  international law 341.242
Egadi Islands T2—458 24
Egba (African people) T5—963 33
Egba language 496.333
  T6—963 33
Egbert, King of England
  English history 942.016 1
Egg cells 571.845
Egg decorating 745.594 4
Egg production 636.514 2
Eggplants 641.356 46
  botany 583.952
  commercial processing 664.805 646
  cooking 641.656 46
  food 641.356 46
  garden crop 635.646
Eggs 591.468
  animal husbandry 636.514 2
    see Manual at 636.1–636.8 vs. 636.088
  cooking 641.675
  descriptive zoology 591.468
  food 641.375
  physiology 573.68
  processing 637.5
Eglise de Jésus-Christ sur la terre par le prophète Simon Kimbangu 289.93
  see also Christian denominations
Egmont National Park (N.Z.) T2—934 82
Ego (Psychology) 154.22

Egoism
  ethical systems 171.9
Egrets 598.34
Egypt 962
  T2—62
  ancient 932
    T2—32
Egyptian language 493.1
  T6—931
Egyptian literature
  Arabic 892.7
  Egyptian 893.1
Egyptians (Ancient) T5—931
  religion 299.31
Egyptians (Modern) T5—927 62
Ehime-ken (Japan) T2—523 2
Ehlers-Danlos syndrome
  medicine 616.77
  see also Musculoskeletal system
Eiders 598.415
Eidetic imagery (Psychology) 153.32
Eigenvalues 512.943 4
Eigenvectors 512.943 4
Eindhoven (Netherlands) T2—492 45
Einstein geometry 516.374
Einsteinium 546.449
  see also Chemicals
Eire 941.7
  T2—417
Eire (1937–1949) 941.708 22
Eisenhower, Dwight D. (Dwight David)
  United States history 973.921
EKG (Medicine) 616.120 754 7
  see also Cardiovascular system
El Asnam (Algeria : Province) T2—653
El Beni (Bolivia) T2—844 2
El Dorado County (Calif.) T2—794 41
El Loa (Chile) T2—831 35
El Oro (Ecuador) T2—866 31
El Paraíso (Honduras : Dept.) T2—728 34
El Paso County (Colo.) T2—788 56
El Paso County (Tex.) T2—764 96
El Progreso (Guatemala : Dept.) T2—728 153
El Salvador 972.84
  T2—728 4
El Seibo (Dominican Republic : Province) T2—729 384
Elaeagnales 583.82
Elaeocarpaceae 583.68
Elam T2—35
Elamite language 499.93
  T6—999 3
Elamite period 935.01
Elamites T5—999 3
Elands 599.642
Elasmobranchii 597.3
  paleozoology 567.3
Elastic cartilage 573.763 56
  human histology 611.018 3
  see also Musculoskeletal system
Elastic constants 531.381
Elastic deformation 531.382
  see also Elasticity
Elastic fibers 677.55
  see also Textiles
Elastic limit 531.382
  materials science 620.112 32
Elastic tissues
  human histology 611.018 2
Elasticity 531.382
  crystals 548.842
  fluid mechanics 532.053 5
  gas mechanics 533.28
  liquid mechanics 532.58
  materials science 620.112 32
  muscles 573.75
    human physiology 612.741
    see also Musculoskeletal system
  solid mechanics 531.382
Elastomer industry workers 678.092
  occupational group T7—678
Elastomers 678
  chemistry 547.842
  manufacturing technology 678
    equipment manufacture 681.766 8
  materials science 620.194
  structural engineering 624.189 4
Elastoplastics 678.73
Elateridae 595.765
Elateroidea 595.765
Elatinaceae 583.624
Elazığ İli (Turkey) T2—566 7
Elba (Italy) T2—455 6
Elbert County (Colo.) T2—788 87
Elbert County (Ga.) T2—758 163
Elbląg (Poland : Voivodeship) T2—438 2
Elbows (Human) 612.97
  physiology 612.97
  regional medicine 617.574

Elbows (Human) (continued)
  surgery 617.574
  see also Upper extremities (Human)
Elder abuse 362.6
  criminology 364.155 5
    criminal law 345.025 55
  social welfare 362.6
  see also Mental illness
Elderberries 641.347 4
  botany 583.92
  cooking 641.647 4
  food 641.347 4
  horticulture 634.74
Elderly persons 305.26
  T1—084 6
  see also Older persons
Elders (Plants) 583.92
Eleatic philosophy 182.3
Election (Christian doctrine) 234
Election campaigns 324.9
  see also Campaigns (Politics)
Election districts 328.334 5
Election fraud 324.66
  criminology 364.132 4
    criminal law 345.023 24
Election law 342.07
  see Manual at 342.07 vs. 324.6
Election officials 324.65
Election procedures 324.6
  law 342.07
  see Manual at 342.07 vs. 324.6
Election returns 324.9
Election systems 324.6
Electioneering 324.7
  law 342.078
Elections 324
  labor unions 331.874
Elective courses 375.004
  higher education 378.24
Electoral colleges 324.63
Electoral power (Legislative bodies) 328.345 4
Electoral systems 324.63
Electrets 537.24
Electric arcs 537.52
Electric automobiles
  engineering 629.229 3
Electric charge 537.21
Electric circuits 621.319 2
Electric clocks
  technology 681.116
Electric conductivity 537.62
Electric conductors 537.62
Electric control 629.804 3
Electric cooking 641.586
Electric currents
  measurement 621.374 4
  physics 537.6
Electric eels 597.48
Electric energy 333.793 2
  see also Electric power
Electric eyes 621.381 542
Electric furnace practice 669.142 4
Electric generators 621.313
Electric heating 621.402 8
  buildings 697.045
Electric lighting 621.32
  mining 622.474
  ships 623.852
  see also Lighting
Electric locomotives 385.363
  engineering 625.263
  transportation services 385.363
  see also Rolling stock
Electric meters 621.373
  watt-hour usage 621.374 5
Electric motors 621.46
  ships 623.872 6
Electric organs (Animals) 573.97
Electric potential 537.21
  measurement 621.374 3
Electric power 333.793 2
  area planning 711.8
  economics 333.793 2
  engineering 621.31
  law 343.092 9
  measurement 621.374 5
  mining 622.48
  public administration 354.49
Electric power generation 621.312 1
  nuclear steam generation 621.483
Electric power measurement 621.374 6
Electric power systems
  spacecraft 629.474 45
Electric propulsion 621.46
  automotive 629.250 2
  spacecraft 629.475 5
Electric railroads 385
  electrification 621.33
  see also Railroad transportation
Electric resistance 537.62
Electric shavers
  manufacturing technology 688.5

Electric shock therapy
  psychiatry 616.891 22
    see also Mental illness
Electric signs
  advertising 659.136
  engineering 621.322 9
Electric slow cooking 641.588 4
Electric submarines 359.938 32
  design 623.812 572
  engineering 623.825 72
  naval equipment 359.938 32
Electric trains
  toys 790.133
Electric utilities 333.793 2
  law 343.092 9
  see Manual at 333.7–333.9 vs. 363.6
Electric welding 671.521
Electrical appliances 643.6
  household equipment 643.6
  manufacturing technology 683.83
Electrical diagnosis
  medicine 616.075 47
Electrical energy 333.793 2
  see also Electric power
Electrical engineering 621.3
  military 623.76
Electrical engineers 621.309 2
  occupational group T7—621 3
Electrical equipment
  public safety 363.189
  use in chemistry 542.84
Electrical injuries
  medicine 617.122
Electrical machinery 621.310 42
Electrical power 333.793 2
  see also Electric power
Electrical properties
  crystals 548.85
  materials science 620.112 97
Electrical prospecting 622.154
Electrical systems
  aircraft 629.135 4
  automotive 629.254
  ships 623.850 3
Electrical toys 790.133
  manufacturing technology 688.728
  recreation 790.133
  see also Toys
Electrical zone melting 669.028 4
Electricians (Interior wiring) 621.319 240 92
  occupational group T7—621 3
Electricity 333.793 2
  astrophysics 523.018 7
  biophysics 571.47
    humans 612.014 42
  direct energy generation 621.312 4
  economics 333.793 2
  generation 621.312 1
  meteorology 551.563
  nuclear direct conversion 621.312 5
  nuclear steam generation 621.483
  physics 537
  plant management 658.26
  public administration 354.49
  solar generation 621.312 44
Electrification 333.793 2
  technology 621.319
Electroacoustical communications
  engineering 621.382 8
Electrobiochemistry 572.437
Electrocapillarity 537.24
Electrocardiography
  medicine 616.120 754 7
  see also Cardiovascular system
Electrochemical analysis 543.087 1
Electrochemistry 541.37
  biochemistry 572.437
  chemical engineering 660.297
  electrical engineering 621.312 42
Electroconvulsive therapy
  psychiatry 616.891 22
    see also Mental illness
Electrodeposited latex 678.538
Electrodeposited rubber 678.36
Electrodeposition
  latex 678.527
Electrodeposition analysis 543.087 4
Electrodes 541.372 4
  chemical engineering 660.297 24
  chemistry 541.372 4
Electrodiagnosis
  medicine 616.075 47
Electrodialysis 541.372
  chemical engineering 660.297 2
Electrodynamics 537.6
  engineering 621.31
Electrodynamometers 621.374 6
Electroencephalography
  medicine 616.804 754 7
  see also Nervous system
Electroforming metals 671.4
Electroluminescence 535.357

Electrolysis
  desalinization 628.167 3
Electrolyte conductivity 541.372
  chemical engineering 660.297 2
Electrolyte-water imbalances 571.937 5
  medicine 616.399 2
    see Manual at 612.01522 vs. 612.3923, 616.3992
  see also Digestive system
Electrolytic analysis 543.087 1
Electrolytic balance
  biochemistry
    humans 612.015 22
      see Manual at 612.01522 vs. 612.3923, 616.3992
Electrolytic dissociation 541.372 2
  chemical engineering 660.297 22
Electrolytic solutions 541.372
  chemical engineering 660.297 2
Electromagnetic analysis
  chemistry 543.087
Electromagnetic engineering 621.3
Electromagnetic engineers 621.309 2
  occupational group T7—621 3
Electromagnetic fields 530.141
  effects in semiconductors 537.622 6
Electromagnetic induction 621.34
Electromagnetic interaction 539.754 6
Electromagnetic radiation 539.2
Electromagnetic spectrum 539.2
Electromagnetic theory 530.141
Electromagnetic theory of light 535.14
Electromagnetic wave theory of matter 530.141
Electromagnetic waves 539.2
Electromagnetism 537
  astrophysics 523.018
  biophysics 571.47
    humans 612.014 42
  engineering 621.3
Electromagnets 621.34
  generator parts 621.316
Electrometallurgy 669.028 4
Electrometers 621.374 3
Electromyography 616.740 754 7
  see also Musculoskeletal system
Electron arrangement
  crystallography 548.81
  solid-state physics 530.411
Electron beam welding 671.521 4
Electron metallography 669.950 282
Electron microscopes 502.825
  biology 570.282 5
  manufacturing technology 681.413
Electron microscopy 502.825
  biology 570.282 5
Electron-nuclear double resonance 538.362
Electron optics
  physics 537.56
Electron paramagnetic resonance 538.364
Electron-ray tubes 621.381 542
Electron spin resonance 538.364
Electronic aids
  marine navigation 623.893
Electronic bands 784.6
Electronic bugging devices 621.389 28
Electronic bulletin boards 004.693
  communications services 384.33
  see also Computer communications
Electronic circuits 621.381 5
Electronic communications engineering 621.382
Electronic components 621.381 5
Electronic computers 004
  see also Computers
Electronic control 629.89
Electronic data processing 004
  T1—028 5
Electronic digital computers 004
  see also Computers
Electronic distance education 371.358
  adult level 374.26
  higher education 378.175 8
Electronic eavesdropping devices 621.389 28
Electronic engineering 621.381
Electronic engineers 621.381 092
  occupational group T7—621 3
Electronic equipment
  use in chemistry 542.84
Electronic field production (Video production) 778.594
Electronic flash photography 778.72
Electronic fuel injection systems
  automobiles 629.253
Electronic funds transfers 332.102 85
  law 346.082 102 85
Electronic games 794.8
Electronic interference 621.382 24

Electronic mail 004.692
  communications services 384.34
  internal office communications 651.79
  see also Computer communications
Electronic media
  sociology 302.234
Electronic music 786.74
Electronic musical instruments 786.7
  see also Electrophones
Electronic news gathering 070.195
Electronic noise 621.382 24
Electronic organs 786.59
  instrument 786.591 9
  music 786.59
  see also Keyboard instruments
Electronic programmed instruction 371.334
  adult education 374.26
Electronic properties
  crystals 548.85
  materials science 620.112 97
Electronic spreadsheets 005.3
  see Manual at 005.369
Electronic surveillance
  civil rights issue 323.448 2
  criminal investigation 363.252
  engineering 621.389 28
  law 345.052
Electronic systems
  aircraft 629.135 5
  automotive 629.254 9
  internal-combustion engines 621.437
  ships 623.850 4
Electronic therapy
  medicine 615.845
Electronic toys 790.133
  manufacturing technology 688.728
  recreation 790.133
  see also Toys
Electronic tubes 621.381 51
Electronics
  military engineering 623.043
  physics 537.5
  technology 621.381
Electrons 539.721 12
Electrooptical devices
  military communications engineering 623.731 4
Electrophones 786.7
  bands and orchestras 784
  chamber ensembles 785
    mixed 785.2–.5
    single type 785.67
Electrophones (continued)
  construction 786.719 23
    by hand 786.719 23
    by machine 681.867
  solo music 786.7
  see Manual at 784–788
Electrophoresis 541.372
  chemical engineering 660.297 2
Electrophotographic photocopying
  technology 686.44
Electrophotographic printing 686.233
Electrophysiology 572.437
  humans 612.014 27
  nerves 573.854 437
    human physiology 612.813
    see also Nervous system
Electroplating 671.732
Electrorefining 669.028 4
Electroshock therapy
  psychiatry 616.891 22
    see also Mental illness
Electrostatic photocopying
  technology 686.44
Electrostatic separation
  ores 622.77
Electrostatics 537.2
Electrostriction 537.24
Electrotherapy
  medicine 615.845
Electrowinning 669.028 4
Elegies (Music) 784.189 64
Ēleia (Greece) T2—495 27
  ancient T2—388
Elementary education 372
  law 344.074
  public administrative support 353.8
  public support 379.112
    law 344.076 82
  see Manual at 372.24 and 373.23
Elementary education of adults 374.012
Elementary number theory 512.72
Elementary school buildings
  architecture 727.1
Elementary school libraries 027.822 2
Elementary school teachers 372.11
Elementary school teaching 372.110 2
Elementary schools 372
  see also Elementary education
Elements (Chemicals) 546
  chemistry 546
  mineralogy 549.2

Elephant Butte Reservoir
  (N.M.) T2—789 62
Elephant fishes 597.47
Elephant seals 599.794
Elephant shrews 599.337
Elephantiasis
  incidence 614.555 2
  medicine 616.965 2
  see also Communicable
    diseases (Human)
Elephants 599.67
  animal husbandry 636.967
  big game hunting 799.276 7
  conservation technology 639.979 67
  resource economics 333.959 67
Elephant's ears (Plants) 584.64
Elephas 599.676
Eleuthera Island
  (Bahamas) T2—729 6
Elevated monorail systems 388.44
  engineering 625.44
  transportation services 388.44
  see also Local rail transit
    systems
Elevated rail transit systems 388.44
  engineering 625.44
  transportation services 388.44
  see also Local rail transit
    systems
Elevations (Physiography) 551.43
  T2—143
  see also Mountains
Elevator liability insurance 368.56
  see also Insurance
Elevators (Aircraft) 629.134 33
Elevators (Lifts) 621.877
  buildings 721.833
    architecture 721.833
    construction 690.183 3
  mining 622.68
Elevenses 642
  cooking 641.53
  customs 394.15
Elgin (Ont. : County) T2—713 34
Elgin, James Bruce, Earl
  Indian history 954.035 1
Elgin, Victor Alexander Bruce,
    Earl of
  Indian history 954.035 5
Elian philosophy 183.7
Elis (Greece) T2—495 27
  ancient T2—388
Elites 305.52
  T1—086 21
Elitist systems of government 321.5
Elixirs
  practical pharmacy 615.42
Elizabeth, Empress of Russia
  Russian history 947.062
Elizabeth I, Queen of England
  English history 942.055
Elizabeth II, Queen of Great
    Britain
  British history 941.085
  English history 942.085
  Scottish history 941.108 5
Elizabeth Islands (Mass.) T2—744 94
Elk (Moose) 599.657
  big game hunting 799.276 57
  conservation technology 639.979 657
Elk (Wapiti) 599.654 2
  big game hunting 799.276 542
  conservation technology 639.979 654 2
Elk County (Kan.) T2—781 915
Elk County (Pa.) T2—748 65
Elk Island National Park
    (Alta.) T2—712 33
Elkhart County (Ind.) T2—772 81
Elko County (Nev.) T2—793 16
Elks (Fraternal order) 366.5
  biography 366.509 2
  social group T7—366 5
Ellenborough, Edward Law, Earl
    of
  Indian history 954.031 5
Ellesmere Port and Neston
    (England) T2—427 17
Ellice Islands T2—968 2
Elliot (South Africa :
    District) T2—687 6
Elliotdale (South Africa :
    District) T2—687 91
Elliott County (Ky.) T2—769 255
Ellipses 516.15
Elliptic equations 515.353
Elliptic functions 515.983
Elliptic operators 515.724 2
Ellis County (Kan.) T2—781 19
Ellis County (Okla.) T2—766 155
Ellis County (Tex.) T2—764 281 5
Ellisras (South Africa :
    District) T2—682 5
Ellsworth County (Kan.) T2—781 535
Ellsworth Land (Antarctic
    regions) T2—989
Elmbridge (England) T2—422 145
Elminidae 595.764 5
Elmore County (Ala.) T2—761 52

Elmore County (Idaho) T2—796 29
Elms 635.977 345
  botany 583.45
  forestry 634.972 8
  lumber 674.142
  ornamental arboriculture 635.977 345
Elocution 808.5
Elopiformes 597.43
Elopomorpha 597.43
  paleozoology 567.43
Elqui (Chile : Province) T2—832 32
Elves 398.21
  see also Legendary beings
Ely, Isle of (England) T2—426 53
Emaciation
  medicine 616.396
  see also Digestive system
Emancipation of slaves 326.8
  see also Abolition of slavery
Emancipation Proclamation, 1863 973.714
Emanuel County (Ga.) T2—758 684
Ēmathia (Greece) T2—495 65
Embalming
  customs 393.3
Embankments
  flood-control engineering 627.42
  road engineering 625.733
  structural engineering 624.162
Embargoes
  international commerce 382.53
    see also Import trade
  international law 341.582
Embarrassment 152.4
Embassies 327.2
  architecture 725.17
  public administration 353.13
Embellishments (Music) 781.247
Emberizidae 598.883
Emberizinae 598.883
Embezzlement 364.162
  law 345.026 2
Embioptera 595.737
Embolisms
  arteries
    medicine 616.135
  veins
    medicine 616.145
  see also Cardiovascular system
Embossing leather 675.25
Embouchure 784.193 4
Embrithopoda 569.62
Embroidered rugs
  arts 746.74
  see also Rugs
Embroidery
  arts 746.44
Embryo
  human physiology 612.646
Embryo transplant
  ethics 176
    religion 291.566
      Christianity 241.66
    see also Reproduction—ethics
  gynecology 618.178 059
  see also Female genital system
Embryology 571.86
  human physiology 612.64
Embryophyta 580
  see also Plants
Embryotomy
  obstetrical surgery 618.83
Embumbulu (South Africa : District) T2—684 91
Emden (Lower Saxony, Germany) T2—435 917
Emeralds 553.86
  economic geology 553.86
  jewelry 739.27
  mining 622.386
Emergency care nursing
  medicine 610.736 1
Emergency labor 331.117 32
Emergency legislation 343.01
Emergency management
  management of enterprises 658.477
Emergency medical services 362.18
  law 344.032 18
  mental illness 362.204 251
Emergency medicine 616.025
Emergency planning 363.345 25
  public administration 353.95
  see also Disasters
Emergency surgery 617.026
Emergency telephone services 384.64
  see also Telephone
Emery County (Utah) T2—792 57
Emery wheels 621.923
Emetics
  pharmacodynamics 615.731
  see also Digestive system
Emigration 304.82
  law 342.082
  political science 325.2
Emigration from Mecca 297.634

Emilia-Romagna (Italy) T2—454
Eminent domain 343.025 2
  international law 341.484 6
  land economics 333.13
Emission (Physics)
  solid-state physics 530.416
Emission control devices
  automotive 629.252 8
Emission of light 535.3
Emmenagogues
  pharmacodynamics 615.766
Emmet County (Iowa) T2—777 125
Emmet County (Mich.) T2—774 88
Emmons County (N.D.) T2—784 78
Emnambithi (South Africa : District) T2—684 91
Emotional illness 362.2
  psychiatry 616.89
  social welfare 362.2
    see also Mental health services
  see also Mental illness
Emotionally disturbed children 305.908 24
  home care 649.154
  see also Mentally ill persons
Emotionally disturbed persons 305.908 24
  T1—087 4
  T7—082 4
  see also Mentally ill persons
Emotions 152.4
  children 155.412 4
  educational psychology 370.153
  literature 808.803 53
    history and criticism 809.933 53
    specific literatures T3B—080 353
      history and criticism T3B—093 53
  philosophy 128.37
Empangeni (South Africa) T2—684 3
Empathy
  psychology 152.41
Empedoclean philosophy 182.5
Emphysema
  medicine 616.248
  see also Respiratory system
Empididae 595.773
Empires 321.03
  T2—171 2
Empirical remedies
  therapeutics 615.88
    see Manual at 615.8809
Empiricism 146.44
  ethics 171.2
Employee absenteeism 331.259 8
  labor economics 331.259 8
  personnel management 658.314
Employee assistance programs 331.255
  economics 331.255
  personnel management 658.382
  see also Employee benefits
Employee benefits 331.255
  economics 331.255
  personnel management 658.325
  T1—068 3
    executives 658.407 25
    public administration 352.67
Employee development 370.113
  see also Vocational education
Employee discounts 331.255
  economics 331.255
  personnel management 658.383
Employee dismissal
  economics 331.259 6
    employment security 331.259 6
    unemployment 331.137
  law 344.012 596
  personnel management 658.313
    public administration 352.69
Employee evaluation 331.259
  military personnel 355.330 41
  personnel management 658.312 5
    executives 658.407 125
    libraries 023.9
  public administration 352.66
Employee fringe benefits 331.255
  see also Employee benefits
Employee housing 331.255
  economics 331.255
  personnel management 658.383
Employee malfeasance
  personnel management 658.314
Employee management 658.3
  see also Personnel management
Employee morale
  personnel management 658.314
Employee motivation
  personnel management 658.314
    executives 658.407 14
Employee organizations 331.88
  economics 331.88
  personnel management 658.315 3
    military personnel 355.33
    public administration 352.68
  women workers 331.478
Employee orientation
  personnel management 658.312 42

Employee participation in management 331.011 2
personnel management 658.315 2
public administration 352.68
Employee qualifications 331.114 2
see also Qualifications of employees
Employee representation in management 331.011 2
personnel management 658.315 2
Employee rights 331.011
law 344.010 1
Employee selection
personnel management 658.311 2
T1—068 3
libraries 023.9
public administration 352.65
Employee separation
economics 331.259 6
employment security 331.259 6
unemployment 331.137
law 344.012 596
personnel management 658.313
public administration 352.69
Employee stock ownership plans 331.216 4
labor economics 331.216 4
personnel management 658.322 5
Employee turnover
personnel management 658.314
Employee utilization
personnel management 658.312 8
public administration 352.66
Employees 331.11
bonding
insurance 368.83
economics 331.11
household 640.46
journalism for 070.486
see also Workers
see *Manual* at 331.1 vs. 331.11, 331.12
Employer-employee relationships
personnel management 658.315
libraries 023.9
public administration 352.68
public administration 354.97
Employer-supported services for workers 331.255
armed forces 355.34
economics 331.255
personnel management 658.38
executives 658.407 8
Employer-supported services for workers (continued)
public administration 352.67
see also Employee benefits
Employers' liability 346.031
Employers' liability insurance 368.56
see also Insurance
Employment 331.125
see *Manual* at 331.1 vs. 331.11, 331.12
Employment agencies 331.128
see also Employment services
Employment conditions 331.2
see also Conditions of employment
Employment interviewing
job hunting 650.14
personnel selection 658.311 24
Employment law 344.01
Employment rights 331.011
Employment security 331.259 6
law 344.012 596
public administration 354.98
Employment services 331.128
economics 331.128
public administration 354.96
social services 362.042 5
disabled persons 362.404 84
law 344.032 042 5
mentally retarded persons 362.384
older persons 362.64
sick persons 362.178 6
Employment subsidies 331.120 42
Emporia (Va.) T2—755 573
Empumalanga (South Africa : District) T2—684 91
Emu 598.53
Emulsins 572.756
see also Enzymes
Emulsions 541.345 14
chemical engineering 660.294 514
Emulsions (Pharmaceuticals)
practical pharmacy 615.45
Emzumbe (South Africa : District) T2—684 91
Ena language 496.394
T6—963 94
Enactment of laws 328.37
budgets 352.48
Enamel (Dental)
dentistry 617.634
see also Dentistry
Enameling
ceramic arts 738.4

Enameling glass
  arts 748.6
Enamels 666.2
  architectural decoration 729.6
  ceramic arts 738.4
  materials science 620.146
  technology 666.2
Encampment
  military operations 355.412
  military training 355.544
Encaustic painting 751.46
Encephalitis
  medicine 616.832
  see also Nervous system
Enclosures
  land economics 333.2
Encoding
  computer science 005.72
Encounter groups
  social psychology 302.14
  social work 361.06
Encryption 652.8
  computer science 005.82
Encyclicals 262.91
Encyclopedia yearbooks 030
  T1—03
Encyclopedias 030
  T1—03
Encyclopedists
  biography 030.92
  occupational group T7—093
End-blown flutes 788.35
  see also Woodwind instruments
End games (Chess) 794.124
End of the world
  controversial knowledge 001.9
  religion 291.23
    Christianity 236.9
End of universe 523.19
Endangered species 578.68
  see also entries beginning with Rare
Enderby (B.C.) T2—711 5
Enderby Land (Antarctic regions) T2—989
Endive 641.355 5
  botany 583.99
  food 641.355 5
  garden crop 635.55
Endocarditis
  medicine 616.11
  see also Cardiovascular system
Endocardium
  human anatomy 611.12
  human physiology 612.17
  medicine 616.11
  see also Cardiovascular system
Endocrine drugs
  pharmacology 615.36
  see also Endocrine system
Endocrine gynecology 618.1
  see also Female genital system
Endocrine secretions 573.44
  human physiology 612.4
  see also Endocrine system
Endocrine system 573.4
  anesthesiology 617.967 44
  biology 573.4
  geriatrics 618.976 4
  human anatomy 611.4
  human cancer 362.196 994 4
    incidence 614.599 944
    medicine 616.994 4
    social services 362.196 994 4
    see also Cancer (Human)
  human diseases 362.196 4
    incidence 614.594
    medicine 616.4
    social services 362.196 4
  human histology 611.018 94
  human physiology 612.4
  pediatrics 618.924
  pharmacodynamics 615.74
  surgery 617.44
  veterinary medicine 636.089 64
  see Manual at 573.44 vs. 571.74: Hormones
Endocrinology 573.4
  medicine 616.4
  see also Endocrine system
Endocrinotherapy 615.36
  see also Endocrine system
Endodontics 617.634 2
  see also Dentistry
Endogamy 306.82
Endometriosis
  gynecology 618.1
  see also Female genital system
Endometritis
  gynecology 618.142
  see also Female genital system
Endomycetales 579.562
Endoparasitic diseases (Biology) 571.999
  agriculture 632.623
  plant crops 632.623

Endoparasitic diseases (Biology) (continued)
  veterinary diseases 636.089 696 2
Endoparasitic diseases (Human)
  incidence 614.552
  medicine 616.962
  see also Communicable diseases (Human)
Endoplasmic reticulum 571.65
Endopterygota 595.7
  see also Insects
ENDOR (Physics) 538.362
Endoscopic surgery 617.05
Endoscopy
  medicine 616.075 45
  surgery 617.05
Endospore-forming gram-positive rods and cocci 579.36
Endosteum
  human histology 611.018 4
  see also Musculoskeletal system
Endothelium 571.555
Endothermic reactions 541.362
  chemical engineering 660.296 2
Endotoxins
  human toxicology 615.952 93
Endowment insurance 368.322
  see also Insurance
Endowments
  capital procurement 658.152 24
Endpapers
  handicrafts 745.54
Enemy sympathizers
  World War I 940.316 3
  World War II 940.531 63
Energism 146
Energy 333.79
  architectural consideration 720.472
  classical physics 531.6
  international law 341.755
  law 346.046 79
  philosophy 118
  physics 530
  plant management 658.2
  public administration 354.4
  quantum mechanics 530.12
  resource economics 333.79
  see Manual at 333.7–333.9 vs. 363.6
Energy budget (Nature)
  ecology 577.13
  meteorology 551.525
Energy conservation 333.791 6
  economics 333.791 6
  home economics 644
  housing program 363.583
  law 346.046 791 6
  management of enterprises 658.2
  public administration 354.43
  see also Energy
Energy development 333.791 5
  law 346.046 791 5
  public administration 354.427
  see also Energy
Energy engineering 621.042
  buildings 696
Energy flow (Nature)
  ecology 577.13
  meteorology 551.525
Energy levels (Nuclear physics) 539.725
Energy management 333.79
  business 658.2
  T1—068 2
  see also Energy
Energy metabolism 572.43
  human physiology 612.39
  see also Digestive system
Energy phenomena
  solid-state physics 530.416
  see Manual at 530.416 vs. 539.75
Energy policy 333.79
  see also Energy
Energy production 333.79
Energy resources 333.79
  economic geology 553.2
  economics 333.79
  extraction 622.33
    economics 338.2
  international law 341.755
  law 346.046 79
  public administration 354.4
  see also Energy
Energy supply 333.791 1
  see also Energy
Enets language 494.4
  T6—944
Enewetak Atoll (Marshall Islands) T2—968 3
Enfield (London, England) T2—421 89
Enga language 499.12
  T6—991 2
Enga Province (Papua New Guinea) T2—956 3

Engaged persons 306.734
T1—086 523
social group 305.906 523
social relationships 306.734
Engagement (Betrothal) 392.4
customs 392.4
etiquette 395.22
music 781.586
social aspects 306.81
Engcobo (South Africa : District) T2—687 91
Engineering 620
accounting 657.834
effect on natural ecology 577.272
law 343.078 62
Engineering analysis
structures 624.171
Engineering design 620.004 2
Engineering drawing 604.2
T1—022 1
Engineering geology 624.151
dams 627.81
railroads 625.122
roads 625.732
Engineering graphics 604.2
T1—022 1
Engineering installations (Armed forces) 355.74
Engineering materials 620.11
Engineering mechanics 620.1
Engineering optics 621.36
see Manual at 621.36 vs. 621.381045, 621.3827
Engineering services (Armed forces) 358.22
air force 358.47
navy 359.982
Engineering systems
ships 623.85
Engineers 620.009 2
occupational group T7—62
Engines 621.4
air-cushion vehicles 629.314
aircraft 629.134 35
automotive 629.25
military aircraft 623.746 049
ships 623.87
spacecraft 629.475
England 942
T2—42
ancient 936.2
T2—362
see Manual at 941
England, Northern T2—427
English (People) T5—21
see Manual at T5—201-T5—209 vs. T5—2101-T5—2109
English as a second language
applied linguistics
formal approach 428.24
audio-lingual approach 428.34
elementary education 372.652 1
English Channel 551.461 36
T2—163 36
English creole languages 427.9
T6—217
English folk music 781.622
English folk songs 782.421 622
English horns 788.53
instrument 788.531 9
music 788.53
see also Woodwind instruments
English language 420
T6—21
elementary education 372.6
rhetoric 808.042
English-language shorthand systems 653.42
English literature 820
English Longhorn cattle 636.226
English peas 641.356 56
commercial processing 664.805 656
see also Peas (Pisum sativum)
English Revised version Bible 220.520 4
English sparrow 598.887
English-speaking West Africa T2—660 917 521
English system (Measurement) 530.813
social aspects 389.15
English toy spaniel 636.76
Engraved seals
numismatics 737.6
Engraved stamps
numismatics 737.6
Engravers 769.92
occupational group T7—76
Engraving
graphic arts 760
Engraving gems 736.202 8
Engraving glass
arts 748.62
Enhanced recovery
oil extraction 622.338 2
Enhydra 599.769 5
Enigmas 001.94

Eniwetok Atoll (Marshall Islands) T2—968 3
Enjoyment
  psychology 152.42
Enlargers
  photography 771.49
Enlightenment
  European history 940.25
  religion 291.42
    Buddhism 294.344 2
    Hinduism 294.542
    Islam 297.57
Enlisted personnel 355.009 2
  role and function 355.338
Enlistment
  armed services 355.223
    law 343.012
Enna (Sicily : Province) T2—458 12
Enneagram 155.26
Enoch (Pseudepigrapha) 229.913
Enrollment
  higher education 378.161 9
Enseleni (South Africa : District) T2—684 91
Ensemble technique
  music 781.438
Entablatures 721.2
  construction 690.12
  see also Walls (Building element)
Entail 346.043 2
  land economics 333.323 4
Enteric fever
  incidence 614.511 2
  medicine 616.927 2
  see also Communicable diseases (Human)
Enteritis
  medicine 616.344
  see also Digestive system
Enterobacteriaceae 579.34
Enterobiasis
  incidence 614.555 4
  medicine 616.965 4
  see also Communicable diseases (Human)
Enteropneusta 593.99
  paleozoology 563.99
Entertainers 791.092
  occupational group T7—791
  see Manual at 791.092
Entertaining 793.2
  etiquette 395.3
  indoor amusements 793.2
Entertaining (continued)
  meal service 642.4
Entertainment advertising 659.13
Entertainment equipment
  automobile 629.277
Entertainment law 344.099
Entertainment media
  accounting 657.84
Entertainments (Parties) 793.2
  etiquette 395.3
  indoor amusements 793.2
  meal service 642.4
Entertainments (Performances) 790.2
  music 781.55
  see also Recreation
Enthusiasm
  psychology of learning 153.153 3
Entire functions 515.98
Entitlement spending 336.39
Entombment 363.75
  customs 393.1
  see also Undertaking (Mortuary)
Entomologists 595.709 2
  occupational group T7—595
Entomology 595.7
  agriculture 632.7
  medicine 616.968
  see also Communicable diseases (Human)
Entoprocta 594.66
  paleozoology 564.6
Entotrophi 595.724
Entrance examinations (Schools) 371.262
Entrance requirements (Schools) 371.217
Entre Douro e Minho (Portugal) T2—469 1
Entre Ríos (Argentina) T2—822 1
Entrees 641.82
Entrepreneurial management 658.421
Entrepreneurs 338.040 92
  T1—086 22
  executive management 658.421
  occupational group T7—338
  social class 305.554
  see Manual at 300 vs. 600: Biography and company history; *also at* 338.092
Entrepreneurship 338.04
  income distribution 339.21
  management 658.421
  production economics 338.04
Entropy 536.73
Enugu State (Nigeria) T2—669 49

Enumeration (Combinatorial
analysis) 511.62
Enumerative geometry 516.35
Enuresis
medicine 616.849
pediatrics 618.928 49
see also Nervous system
Environment 333.7
architectural consideration 720.47
economics 333.7
ethics 179.1
religion 291.569 1
Buddhism 294.356 91
Christianity 241.691
Hinduism 294.548 691
Judaism 296.369 1
literature 808.803 55
history and criticism 809.933 55
specific literatures T3B—080 355
history and criticism T3B—093 55
public administration 354.3
see Manual at 333.7–333.9 vs.
363.1, 363.73, 577; *also*
at 333.72 vs. 304.28,
363.7
Environment versus heredity
psychology 155.7
evolutional psychology 155.7
individual psychology 155.234
Environmental abuse 363.7
social effects 304.28
social problem 363.7
social theology 291.178 362 8
Christianity 261.836 28
see Manual at 333.72 vs.
304.28, 363.7
Environmental biology 577
Environmental biophysics 571.49
Environmental chemistry 577.14
Environmental control
spacecraft 629.477
Environmental design
arts 711
crime prevention 364.49
ergonomics 620.82
Environmental diseases
(Biology) 571.95
agriculture 632.1
plant crops 632.1
veterinary medicine 636.089 698
see Manual at 363.73 vs.
571.95, 577.27
Environmental diseases
(Human) 362.196 98
geriatrics 618.976 98
incidence 614.59
medicine 616.98
pediatrics 618.929 8
social services 362.196 98
Environmental engineering 628
T1—028 6
buildings 696
sanitary engineering 628
work environment 620.8
Environmental engineers 628.092
occupational group T7—628
Environmental factors
physical ethnology 599.972
Environmental health
engineering 628
Environmental impact studies 333.714
environmental protection 363.7
law 344.046
natural resources 333.714
see Manual at 333.7–333.9 vs.
363.1, 363.73, 577; *also*
at 333.714
Environmental impairment
liability insurance 368.563
see also Insurance
Environmental law 344.046
Environmental medicine 616.98
see also Environmental
diseases (Human)
Environmental monitoring 363.706 3
pollution 363.736 3
social services 363.706 3
see Manual at 333.7–333.9 vs.
363.1, 363.73, 577
Environmental pollution 363.73
see also Pollution
Environmental protection 363.7
engineering 628
executive management 658.408
international law 341.762
law 344.046
public administration 354.328
social services 363.7
see also Environment
see Manual at 363
Environmental psychology 155.9
Environmental sanitation 363.72
see also Sanitation
Environmental studies
elementary education 372.357
see also Environment

Environmental toxicology 571.95
ecology 577.27
medicine 615.902
pathology 571.95
Environmentalist parties 324.218 7
international organizations 324.187
Environments (Art style) 709.040 74
Envoys 327.209 2
occupational group T7—352 2
Envy 152.48
ethics 179.8
see also Vices
psychology 152.48
Enzyme technology 660.634
Enzymes 572.7
biochemistry 572.7
humans 612.015 1
chemistry 547.758
pharmacology 615.35
Eocene epoch 551.784
geology 551.784
paleontology 560.178 4
Eolithic Age 930.11
Eosuchia 567.94
Eotheria 569.29
Epacridaceae 583.66
Epeirogeny 551.8
Ēpeiros (Greece) T2—495 3
Ephedrales 585.8
Ephedras 585.8
Ephedrine abuse 362.299
medicine 616.864
personal health 613.84
social welfare 362.299
see also Substance abuse
Ephemerides 528
astrology 133.55
Ephemeroptera 595.734
Ephesians (Biblical book) 227.5
Ephesus (Extinct city) T2—392 3
Ephydridae 595.774
Epic poetry 808.813 2
history and criticism 809.132
specific literatures T3B—103 2
individual authors T3A—1
Epicurean philosophy 187
Epidemic diarrhea
incidence 614.517
medicine 616.342 7
see also Digestive system
Epidemic parotitis
incidence 614.544
medicine 616.313
see also Digestive system
Epidemic typhus
incidence 614.526 2
medicine 616.922 2
see also Communicable diseases (Human)
Epidemics (Mathematics) 519.85
Epidemiology 614.4
see Manual at 614.4
Epidermis 573.5
plants 575.451
see also Skin
Epidote
mineralogy 549.63
Epidural anesthesia
surgery 617.964
Epiglottis 573.925
human anatomy 611.22
medicine 616.22
surgery 617.533
see also Respiratory system
Epigrams 808.882
specific literatures T3B—802
individual authors T3A—8
Epigraphy 411.7
specific languages T4—11
Epilepsy
medicine 616.853
see also Nervous system
Epiphany 263.915
devotional literature 242.335
music 781.724
sermons 252.615
Epirus (Greece) T2—495 3
Epirus (Greece and Albania) T2—495 3
Albania T2—496 5
Greece T2—495 3
Epirus (Kingdom) T2—382
Episcopacy 262.12
Episcopal Church 283.73
church government 262.037 3
parishes 254.037 3
church law 262.983 73
doctrines 230.3
catechisms and creeds 238.3
guides to Christian life 248.483
liturgy 264.03
missions 266.3
moral theology 241.043
religious associations 267.183 73
religious education 268.837 3

Episcopal Church (continued)
  religious orders 255.83
    church history 271.83
    women 255.983
  seminaries 230.073 373
  theology 230.3
Episcopal palaces
  architecture 726.9
Episcopal systems
  Christian ecclesiology 262.3
Episcopalians
  biography 283.092
Episiotomy
  obstetrical surgery 618.85
Epistemology 121
Epistle of Jeremiah (Bible) 229.5
Epistles (Bible) 227
  pseudepigrapha 229.93
Epitaphs
  genealogy 929.5
Epithelial tissues 571.55
  human histology 611.018 7
Epithelium 571.55
  human histology 611.018 7
Epitomes T1—020 2
Eponym dictionaries 413.1
  specific languages T4—31
Epoxies 668.422 6
Epoxy resin 668.374
Epping Forest (England) T2—426 74
EPR (Magnetic resonance) 538.364
Epsom and Ewell
    (England) T2—422 15
Epsom salts
  pharmacodynamics 615.732
  see also Digestive system
Equal-area projections
  maps 526.85
Equal economic opportunity
  government programs 354.08
Equal educational opportunity 379.26
Equal employment opportunity 331.133
  economics 331.133
    labor unions 331.873 2
  government programs 354.908
  law 344.011 33
  personnel management 658.300 8
    government employees 352.608
  teachers 371.11
    higher education 378.124
Equal opportunity
  government programs 353.53
Equal pay for equal work 331.215 3
  economics 331.215 3
  law 344.012 153
Equal protection of the law 323.42
  law 340.11
  political science 323.42
Equal time (Election law) 342.078
Equality 305
  civil right 323.42
  political theory 320.011
  social theology 291.178 34
    Christianity 261.834
    Judaism 296.38
  sociology 305
Equateur (Zaire) T2—675 13
Equation of exchange theory 332.401
Equation of time 529.1
Equations 511.33
  algebra 512.94
  calculus 515.25
Equatoria Region (Sudan) T2—629 5
Equatorial Guinea 967.18
  T2—671 8
Equatorial Guineans T5—967 18
Equatorial Islands 996.4
  T2—964
Equatorial telescopes 522.4
Equestrian performers 791.320 92
  occupational group T7—791 3
Equestrian sculpture 731.81
Equestrian sports 798
  equipment technology 688.78
  see also Sports
Equestrian sportsmen 798.092
  sports group T7—798
Equidae 599.665
  animal husbandry 636.1
Equilibrium
  astronomy 521
  chemical engineering 660.299 2
  macroeconomic policy 339.5
Equinia
  incidence 614.564
  medicine 616.954
  see also Communicable
      diseases (Human)
Equipment T1—028 4
  armed forces 355.8
  educational use T1—078
  local Christian parishes 254.7
  management 658.27
    T1—068 2
    public administration 352.55
  office services 651.2

Equipment (continued)
  procurement 658.72
  teaching aids 371.33
    T1—078
Equipment research
  production management 658.577
Equipment sheds
  agricultural use 631.25
Equisetales 587.2
  paleobotany 561.72
Equisetum 587.2
Equitable remedies 347.077
Equity 346.004
Equivalent projections
  maps 526.85
Equus 599.665
Er Rachidia (Morocco :
    Province) T2—645
Érable (Quebec) T2—714 575
Eragrosteae 584.9
Erath County (Tex.) T2—764 551
Erbium
  chemistry 546.418
  see also Rare earths
Eremitical religious orders 255.02
  church history 271.02
  women 255.902
    church history 271.902
Erethizontidae 599.359 74
Eretrian philosophy (Ancient) 183.7
Erewash (England) T2—425 18
Erfurt (Germany : Bezirk) T2—432 24
Ergative constructions 415
  specific languages T4—5
Ergodic theory 515.42
Ergonomics 620.82
  computers 004.019
    engineering 621.398 4
Ergosterol
  chemistry 547.731
Ericales 583.66
Erie, Lake T2—771 2
  Ohio T2—771 2
  Ontario T2—713 3
Erie County (N.Y.) T2—747 96
Erie County (Ohio) T2—771 22
Erie County (Pa.) T2—748 99
Erinaceidae 599.332
Erinaceus 599.332 2
Eriocaulales 584.87
Eritrea 963.5
  T2—635
Eritreans T5—928
Erlangen (Germany) T2—433 22
Ermelo (South Africa :
    District) T2—682 7
Ermine 599.766 2
Erodiums 635.933 79
  botany 583.79
  floriculture 635.933 79
Erogeneity 155.31
Erosion 551.302
  agriculture 631.45
  by glaciers 551.313
  by water 551.352
  by wind 551.372
  engineering 627.5
  geology 551.302
  see Manual at
    551.302–551.307 vs.
    551.35
Erosions (Medicine)
  uterus and cervix
    gynecology 618.143
    see also Female genital
      system
Erotic literature 808.803 538
  history and criticism 809.933 538
  specific literatures T3B—080 353 8
    history and criticism T3B—093 538
Erotic painting 757.8
Erotica
  arts 700.453 8
    T3C—353 8
  literature 808.803 538
    history and criticism 809.933 538
    specific literatures T3B—080 353 8
      history and criticism T3B—093 538
Error analysis (Mathematics) 511.43
Error-correcting codes 005.72
Error correctors
  automation engineering 629.831 5
Error detectors
  automation engineering 629.831 5
Errors 001.96
  logic 165
  psychology of perception 153.74
Errors and omissions insurance 368.564
  see also Insurance
Erudition 001.2
Eruptive diseases
  incidence 614.52
  medicine 616.91
  see also Communicable
    diseases (Human)

Eruptive fevers
  incidence 614.526 3
  medicine 616.922 3
  see also Communicable diseases (Human)
Eruptive variables 523.844 6
Eruvin 296.123 2
  Babylonian Talmud 296.125 2
  Mishnah 296.123 2
  Palestinian Talmud 296.124 2
Erwinia 579.34
Erysipelas
  incidence 614.577
  medicine 616.942
  see also Communicable diseases (Human)
Erysiphales 579.567
Erythroblastosis fetalis
  pediatrics 618.921 5
  perinatal medicine 618.326 1
  see also Cardiovascular system
Erythrocytes 573.153 6
  human cancer
    medicine 616.994 18
  human histology 611.018 5
  human physiology 612.111
  medicine 616.151
  see also Cardiovascular system
Erythroxylaceae 583.79
Erzincan İli (Turkey) T2—566 7
Erzurum İli (Turkey) T2—566 2
Es Semara (Morocco : Province) T2—648
Esaki diodes 621.381 522
Escalators 621.867 6
  architecture 721.832
  building construction 690.183 2
Escalloniaceae 583.72
Escallonias 583.72
Escambia County (Ala.) T2—761 265
Escambia County (Fla.) T2—759 99
Escape equipment
  aircraft 629.134 386
  military aircraft 623.746 049
Escapements
  clockwork 681.112
Escapes 365.641
Eschatology 291.23
  Buddhism 294.342 3
  Christianity 236
  Hinduism 294.523
  Islam 297.23
Eschatology (continued)
  Judaism 296.33
  philosophy of religion 218
Escherichia 579.342
Eschrichtidae 599.522
Escrows 346.043 73
Escuintla (Guatemala : Dept.) T2—728 163
Esdras (Deuterocanonical book) 229.1
Eṣfahān (Iran : Province) T2—559 5
Eshowe (South Africa : District) T2—684 4
Eskimo T5—971
Eskimo-Aleut languages 497.1
  T6—971
Eskimo dogs 636.73
Eskimo languages 497.1
  T6—971
Eskimo literature 897.1
Eskişehir İli (Turkey) T2—563
Esmeralda County (Nev.) T2—793 35
Esmeraldas (Ecuador : Province) T2—866 35
Esocidae 597.59
Esophagus 573.359
  biology 573.359
  human anatomy 611.32
  human physiology 612.315
  medicine 616.32
  surgery 617.548
  see also Digestive system
Esoteric societies 366
Esox 597.59
ESP (Extrasensory perception) 133.8
Espaillat (Dominican Republic : Province) T2—729 362
Espartos 584.9
Esperance (W.A.) T2—941 7
Esperance National Park (W.A.) T2—941 7
Esperanto language 499.992
  T6—999 92
Esperanto literature 899.992
Espionage 327.12
  armed forces 355.343 2
  criminology 364.131
    criminal law 345.023 1
  ethics 172.4
    see also Political ethics
  industrial management 658.472
  international politics 327.12
  labor economics 331.894
  law of war 341.63
  public administration of 353.17

Espionage (continued)
  social theology 291.178 7
    Christianity 261.87
Espírito Santo (Brazil : State) T2—815 2
Esquimalt (B.C.) T2—711 28
ESR (Magnetic resonance) 538.364
Essaouira (Morocco : Province) T2—646
Essayists (Literature) 809.4
  collected biography 809.4
    specific literatures T3B—400 9
  individual biography T3A—4
  occupational group T7—84
Essays 080
  see Manual at 080 vs. 800
Essays (Literature) 808.84
  criticism 809.4
    theory 808.4
  history 809.4
  rhetoric 808.4
  specific literatures T3B—4
    individual authors T3A—4
Essen (Germany) T2—435 538
Essence (Philosophy) 111.1
Essences (Flavorings) 641.338 2
  see also Flavorings
Essenes 296.814
Essential hypertension
  medicine 616.132
  see also Cardiovascular system
Essential oils
  chemical engineering 661.806
  chemistry 547.71
Essequibo (Guyana : District) T2—881 2
Essequibo Islands (Guyana : District) T2—881 3
Essex (England) T2—426 7
Essex (Ont. : County) T2—713 31
Essex County (Mass.) T2—744 5
Essex County (N.J.) T2—749 31
Essex County (N.Y.) T2—747 53
Essex County (Va.) T2—755 34
Essex County (Vt.) T2—743 25
Essonne (France) T2—443 65
Estate planning 332.024 01
  law 346.052
    tax law 343.053
Estate tax 336.276
  law 343.053
  public administration 352.44
  public finance 336.276
Estates (Financial)
  accounting 657.47
  administration 346.056
Estates (Grounds)
  landscape architecture 712.6
Estcourt (South Africa : District) T2—684 7
Estelí (Nicaragua : Dept.) T2—728 524
Esterases 572.757
  see also Enzymes
Esterification 547.24
  chemical engineering 660.284 44
Esters 547.038
  aromatic chemistry 547.638
  chemical engineering 661.83
Esther (Biblical book) 222.9
Esther (Deuterocanonical book) 229.27
Esthonian language 494.545
  T6—945 45
Esthonian literature 894.545
Esthonians T5—945 45
Estill County (Ky.) T2—769 59
Estimated budgets (Public) 352.48
  see also Budgets (Public)
Estimates T1—029 9
  building construction 692.5
Estimation theory 519.5
  probabilities 519.287
  statistical mathematics 519.544
Estonia 947.98
  T2—479 8
Estonian language 494.545
  T6—945 45
Estonian literature 894.545
Estonians T5—945 45
Estrelleta (Dominican Republic : Province) T2—729 343
Estremadura (Portugal)
  historic province T2—469 4
  modern province T2—469 42
Estremadura (Spain) T2—462 6
Estrie (Quebec) T2—714 6
Estrildidae 598.886
Estrith dynasty 948.901 5
Estuaries 551.460 9
  biology 578.778 6
  ecology 577.786
  engineering 627.124
  public administration 354.36
  resource economics 333.916 4
  see Manual at T2—162
Etchemins (Quebec) T2—714 72
Etching
  graphic arts 767.2

Etching glass
  arts 748.63
Eternity
  philosophy 115
  religion 291.23
    Christianity 236.21
    Islam 297.23
    Judaism 296.33
Ethelbald, King of England
  English history 942.016 3
Ethelbert, King of England
  English history 942.016 3
Ethelred I, King of England
  English history 942.016 3
Ethelred II, King of England
  English history 942.017 4
Ethelwulf, King of England
  English history 942.016 2
Ethers 547.035
  aromatic chemistry 547.635
  chemical engineering 661.84
  human toxicology 615.951 35
Ethical education 370.114
Ethical problems 172–179
  religion 291.56
    Buddhism 294.356
    Christianity 241.6
      see Manual at 241.3–241.4 vs. 241.6
    Hinduism 294.548 6
    Islam 297.56
    Judaism 296.36
Ethical school
  economics 330.155
Ethical systems 171
Ethical wills
  Judaism 296.36
Ethicists 170.92
  see Manual at 170.92 vs. 171
Ethics 170
  religion 291.5
    Buddhism 294.35
    Christianity 241
    Hinduism 294.548
    Islam 297.5
      Sufi 297.45
    Judaism 296.36
  see Manual at 170
Ethics in government 172.2
  law 342.068 4
Ethics of the Fathers 296.123 47
Ethiopia 963
  T2—63
  ancient 939.78
    T2—397 8
Ethiopian Church 281.75
  see also Eastern churches
Ethiopian languages 492.8
  T6—928
Ethiopian literatures 892.8
Ethiopian War, 1895–1896 963.043
Ethiopians T5—928
Ethiopic language 492.81
  T6—928 1
  Biblical texts 220.46
Ethiopic literature 892.81
Ethnic cleansing
  sociology 304.663
Ethnic cooking 641.592
Ethnic groups 305.8
  T1—089
  T7—03
  civil rights 323.11
  criminology 364.34
  education 371.829
  geographic treatment T1—089 009
    see Manual at T1—09 vs. T1—089
  government programs 353.533 9
    specific groups 353.534
    see Manual at 353.53 vs. 351.08; *also at* 353.5339 and 353.534
  history 909.04
    specific places 930–990
  journalism for 070.484
  labor 331.6
    economics 331.6
    personnel management 658.300 89
  legal status 346.013
    constitutional law 342.087 3
    private law 346.013
  literature 808.898
    history and criticism 809.8
    specific literatures T3B—080 8
      history and criticism T3B—098
    see Manual at T3C—93–T3C—99, T3C—9174 vs. T3C—8
  military troops
    World War I 940.403
    World War II 940.540 4
  physical ethnology 599.97

Ethnic groups (continued)
  psychology 155.82
    see Manual at 155.89 vs. 155.84
  relations with government 323.11
  social theology 291.178 348
    Christianity 261.834 8
  social welfare 362.84
    public administration 353.533 9
      specific groups 353.534
      see Manual at 353.5339 and 353.534
  see Manual at T5; *also at* 305.8 vs. 306.089
Ethnic minorities 305.8
  see also Ethnic groups
Ethnic relations 305.8
Ethnographers 305.800 92
  occupational group T7—309
Ethnography 305.8
Ethnolinguistics 306.440 89
Ethnological jurisprudence 340.52
Ethnologists 305.800 92
  occupational group T7—309
Ethnology 305.8
  physical anthropology 599.97
Ethnomusicology 780.89
Ethnopsychology 155.82
  children 155.457
Ethology (Animal behavior) 591.5
Etiology
  medicine 616.071
    see Manual at 616.1–616.9: Add table: 071 vs. 01
Etiquette 395
  armed forces 355.133 6
  see Manual at 395
Etna, Mount (Sicily) T2—458 13
Etobicoke (Ont.) T2—713 541
Etorofu Island T2—524
Etowah County (Ala.) T2—761 67
Etruria T2—375
Etruscan architecture 722.62
Etruscan language 499.94
  T6—999 4
Etruscan sculpture 733.4
Etruscans 937.501
  T5—999 4
Ettrick and Lauderdale (Scotland) T2—413 85
Études 784.189 49
Etymology 412
  T1—014 2
  specific languages T4—2
  see Manual at 401.43 vs. 306.44, 401.9, 412, 415: Meaning
EU (European Union) 341.242 2
  see also European Union
Eubacteriales 579.3
Eubalaena 599.527 3
Euboea (Greece : Nome) T2—495 15
Euboea Island (Greece) T2—495 15
  ancient T2—384
Eucalyptus 583.766
  forestry 634.973 766
  medicinal crop 633.883 766
  ornamental arboriculture 635.977 376 6
Eucarida 595.38
Eucestoda 592.46
Eucharist 234.163
  public worship 264.36
    Anglican 264.030 36
      texts 264.03
    Roman Catholic 264.020 36
      texts 264.023
  theology 234.163
Eucharistic Liturgy 264.36
  see also Eucharist—public worship
Euclidean geometry 516.2
  metric differential 516.372
Eucommiales 583.43
Euechinoidea 593.95
Eugenics 363.92
  crime prevention 364.4
    see also Crime prevention
  health 613.94
  medical ethics 174.25
    see also Medical ethics
  social services 363.92
  sterilization services 363.97
Euglenida 579.84
Euglenoids 579.84
Euglenophyta 579.84
Eukaryotic cells 571.6
Eulerian integrals 515.52
Eumycetes 579.5
Eumycophyta 579.5
Eungella National Park (Qld.) T2—943 6
Euphausiacea 595.389

Euphoniums 788.975
 instrument 788.975 19
 music 788.975
 see also Brass instruments
Euphorbiales 583.69
Eupteleales 583.43
Eurarctos 599.785
Eurasia T2—5
Eurasian red squirrel 599.362
Eurasians T5—042
Eurasiatic languages 410
 T6—1
Eure (France) T2—442 4
Eure-et-Loir (France) T2—445 1
Eureka County (Nev.) T2—793 32
Euroa (Vic.) T2—945 5
Eurobonds 332.632 3
 investment economics 332.632 3
 public finance 336.31
Eurocommunism
 political ideology 320.532 309 4
Eurocurrency market 332.45
Eurodollar market 332.45
Europe 940
 T2—4
 ancient 936
 T2—36
Europe, Eastern 947
 T2—47
Europe, Northern 948
 T2—48
 ancient 936.3
 T2—363
Europe, Southeastern 949.6
 T2—496
 ancient 939.8
 T2—398
Europe, Southern 940
 T2—4
 ancient 938
 T2—38
Europe, Western 940
 T2—4
 ancient 936
 T2—36
European Arctic seawaters 551.468 4
 T2—163 24
European bison 599.643
European Common Market 341.242 2
 see also European Union
European Community 341.242 2
 see also European Union
European Economic Community 341.242 2
 see also European Union
European federation 321.040 94
European Free Trade
 Association 341.242
 international commerce 382.914 3
 international economics 337.143
 international law 341.242
European hedgehog 599.332 2
European Investment Bank
 economics 332.153 4
European Parliament 341.242 4
 legislative process 328.4
European philosophy 190
European polecat 599.766 28
European Union 341.242 2
 commerce 382.914 2
 economics 337.142
 international law 341.242 2
 economic functions 341.750 614
 public administration 352.114
European wildcat 599.752 6
Europium
 chemistry 546.415
 see also Rare earths
Eurotiales 579.565
Euryapsida 567.93
Eurylaimidae 598.822
Eurypterida 565.493
Eurytania (Greece) T2—495 15
Eurytanias Nomos (Greece) T2—495 15
Eustachian tubes
 human anatomy 611.85
 human physiology 612.854
 otology 617.86
 see also Ears
Euthanasia
 ethics 179.7
 religion 291.569 7
 Buddhism 294.356 97
 Christianity 241.697
 Hinduism 294.548 697
 Judaism 296.369 7
 law 344.041 97
Eutheria 599
 see also Mammals
Eutrophication 577.631 58
Eutychian Church 281.6
 see also Christian
 denominations
Euvoia (Greece) T2—495 15
Evaluation of employees 331.259
 see also Employee evaluation
Evaluation research 001.4
Evaluations of products
 and services T1—029 6

Evangelical and Reformed Church 285.734
  see also Reformed Church (American Reformed)
Evangelical churches 289.95
  see also Christian denominations
Evangelical Congregational Church 289.9
  see also Christian denominations
Evangelical Free Church of America 289.95
  see also Christian denominations
Evangelical Lutheran Church 284.131 2
  see also Lutheran church
Evangelical Lutheran Church in America 284.135
  see also Lutheran church
Evangelical Lutheran Synodical Conference of North America 284.132
  see also Lutheran church
Evangelical theology 230.046 24
Evangelical United Brethren Church 289.9
  see also Christian denominations
Evangelicalism 270.82
  independent denominations 289.95
  Protestantism 280.4
Evangeline Parish (La.) T2—763 57
Evangelische Kirche in Deutschland 284.143
  see also Lutheran church
  see Manual at 284.143
Evangelism 269.2
Evangelistic sermons 252.3
Evangelistic writings 243
Evangelization 266
Evans County (Ga.) T2—758 763
Evaporated foods
  cooking 641.614
Evaporated milk 641.371 422
  cooking 641.671 422
  food 641.371 422
  processing 637.142 2
Evaporating foods 664.028 4
  commercial preservation 664.028 4
  home preservation 641.44
Evaporation 536.44
  chemical engineering 660.284 26
  meteorology 551.572
Evaporation control
  water supply engineering 628.132
Evapotranspiration
  meteorology 551.572
Eve (Biblical person)
  Bible stories 222.110 950 5
Even language 494.1
  T6—941
Even-toed ungulates 599.63
Evening dress 391
  commercial technology 687.16
  customs 391
  home sewing 646.47
  see also Clothing
Evening prayer 264.15
  Anglican 264.030 15
    texts 264.034
  music 782.326
    choral and mixed voices 782.532 6
    single voices 783.093 26
Evening primroses 635.933 76
  botany 583.76
  floriculture 635.933 76
Evening schools
  adult education 374.8
  higher education 378.158
Evenki (Asian people) T5—941
Evenki (Russia : Okrug) T2—575
Evenki language 494.1
  T6—941
Evenskiĭ avtonomnyĭ okrug (Russia) T2—575
Evensong 264.030 15
  music 782.326
  texts 264.034
Eventing (Horsemanship) 798.24
  see also Sports
Events 900
  see also History
  see Manual at 900: Historic events vs. nonhistoric events
Events (Art style) 709.040 74
Everglades (Fla.) T2—759 39
Everglades National Park (Fla.) T2—759 39
Evergreen trees 582.16
  ornamental arboriculture 635.977 15
Evergreen trees (Conifers) 585
  ornamental arboriculture 635.977 5
Everlastings (Plants) 635.973
  botany 583.99
  floriculture 635.973

Everyday life
  art representation 704.949
  arts 700.455
    T3C—355
  literature 808.803 55
    history and criticism 809.933 55
    specific literatures T3B—080 355
      history and criticism T3B—093 55
Eviction 346.043 4
Evidence
  epistemology 121.65
Evidence (Law) 347.06
  criminal investigation 363.25
  criminal law 345.06
  law 347.06
Evidence procurement 363.252
Evil (Concept) 111.84
  ethics 170
    religion 291.5
      Christianity 241.3
      Islam 297.5
      Judaism 296.36
  religion 291.211 8
    Christianity 231.8
      freedom of choice 233.7
    comparative religion 291.211 8
    Islam 297.211 8
    Judaism 296.311 8
    philosophy of religion 214
Evil eye 133.425
Evil spirits 133.423
  religion 291.216
  see also Legendary beings
Evolutes 516.362
Evolution 576.8
  animals 591.38
  biochemistry 572.38
  biology 576.8
  ethical systems 171.7
  humans 599.938
  microorganisms 579.138
  molecular biology 572.838
  philosophy 116
  plants 581.38
  see Manual at 576.8 vs. 560
Evolution (Mathematics) 512.923
Evolution (Social change) 303.4
Evolution of stars 523.88
Evolution versus creation 291.24
  Christianity 231.765 2
    see Manual at 231.7652 vs. 213, 500, 576.8
  Judaism 296.34
  philosophy of religion 213
Evolutional psychology 155.7
Evolutionary cycles 576.84
Evolutionary genetics 572.838
Evolutionism
  philosophy 146.7
Evora (Portugal : District) T2—469 52
Evreĭskaia͡ avtonomnaia͡ oblast′ (Russia) T2—577
Evritania (Greece) T2—495 15
Evros (Greece) T2—495 7
Ewe (African people) T5—963 374
Ewe language 496.337 4
  T6—963 374
Ewe literature 896.337 4
Ewenki (Asian people) T5—941
Ewondo language 496.396
  T6—963 96
Ex-convicts 364.8
  labor economics 331.51
Examination of witnesses 347.075
  criminal investigation 363.254
  criminal law 345.075
Examinations (Educational tests) 371.26
  T1—076
  teacher-prepared tests 371.271
  see Manual at 371.262 vs. 371.264
Exanthems
  incidence 614.52
  medicine 616.91
  see also Communicable diseases (Human)
Excavation 624.152
  archaeological technique 930.102 83
  mining 622.2
  road engineering 625.733
Excelsior 674.84
Excelsior (South Africa : District) T2—685 5
Exceptional children
  education 371.9
  home care 649.15
  psychology 155.45
Exceptional students 371.9
Excess liability insurance 368.5
  see also Insurance
Excess profits tax 336.243 2
  law 343.052 44
  public finance 336.243 2
Exchange buildings
  architecture 725.25
Exchange rates
  foreign exchange 332.456

Exchanges
library acquisitions 025.26
library-government relations 021.8
Excise tax 336.271
law 343.055 3
public administration 352.44
public finance 336.271
Excitation
solid-state physics 530.416
Excited states
solid-state physics 530.416
Excitons
solid-state physics 530.416
Excluded classes 305.568
T1—086 94
Exclusionary rule 347.062
Excretion 573.49
animals 573.49
biology 573.49
human physiology 612.46
plants 575.79
see also Urinary system
Excretory organs 573.49
human anatomy 611.61
human physiology 612.46
see also Urinary system
Exe River (England) T2—423 5
Execution of wills 346.056
Executions of judgment 347.077
Executive ability 658.409
Executive advisory bodies 352.743
Executive agencies 351
see also Administrative agencies
Executive branch of government 351
control by legislature 328.345 6
law 342.06
sociology 306.24
Executive budgets 352.48
see also Budgets (Public)
Executive buildings
architecture 725.12
Executive councils
public administration 352.24
Executive departments 351
description and duties 351
government publications
bibliographies 011.534
law 342.064
organization and structure 352.29
see Manual at 352.29
see Manual at 352–354
Executive development
personnel management 658.407 124
public administration 352.39
Executive investigations
official misconduct 353.463
Executive-judicial relations 320.404
law 342.044
Executive leadership 658.409 2
public administration 352.39
Executive-legislative relations 328.345 6
law 342.044
Executive management 658.4
T1—068 4
military administration 355.68
public administration 352.3
schools 371.207
higher education 378.107
see Manual at 658.4 and T1—0684; *also at* 658.4 vs. 658.42, 658.43
Executive mansions
architecture 725.17
Executive messages
public administration 352.238
Executive orders (Compilations) 348.025
United States 348.732 5
Executive orders (Treatises) 342.060 263 6
Executive power 352.235
law 342.06
Executive privilege 352.235
law 342.06
Executive recruiting 658.407 111
Executive secretaries
office management 651.3
Executives
personal aspects 658.409
personnel management 658.407
public administration 352.39
Exegesis
sacred books 291.82
Bible 220.6
Koran 297.122 6
Talmud 296.120 6
Exemptions
customs duties 382.78
see also Customs (Tariff)
Exercise 613.71
child care 649.57
human physiology 612.044
musculoskeletal system 612.76
physical fitness 613.71
therapeutics 615.82
see Manual at 613.71 vs. 646.75, 796

Exercise therapy
  medicine 615.82
Exercises (Education) T1—076
Exeter (England) T2—423 56
Exhibit cases
  museology 069.31
Exhibition animals
  care and training 636.081 1
Exhibition buildings
  architecture 725.91
Exhibitions 907.4
  T1—074
  advertising 659.152
  arts 700.74
  civilization 907.4
  commerce 381.1
  customs 394.6
  fine arts 708
    temporary 707.4
    see Manual at 704.9: Use of standard subdivisions
  public administrative support 352.76
  technology 607.34
Exhibits
  museology 069.5
  preparation T1—075 3
  see also Exhibitions
Exile
  literature 808.803 55
    history and criticism 809.933 55
    specific literatures T3B—080 355
      history and criticism T3B—093 55
Exiles 305.906 91
  T1—086 91
  see also Refugees
Existence 111.1
Existence of God 212.1
  Christianity 231
  comparative religion 291.211
  Judaism 296.311
  philosophy of religion 212.1
Existential psychology 150.192
Existentialism 142.78
  ethics 171.2
  literature 808.803 84
    history and criticism 809.933 84
    specific literatures T3B—080 384
      history and criticism T3B—093 84
Existentialist theology 230.046
Exmoor Hills (England) T2—423 85
Exobasidiales 579.59
Exocrine secretions
  human physiology 612.4
Exodontics 617.66
  see also Dentistry
Exodus (Bible) 222.12
Exogamy 306.82
Exogenous processes (Geology) 551.3
Exopterygota 595.73
Exorcism
  occultism 133.427
  religious rite 291.38
    Christianity 265.94
    see also Rites—religion
Exorcists 200.92
  biography 200.92
  religious role and function 291.61
  see Manual at 200.92 and 291–299
Exoskeleton 591.477
  descriptive zoology 591.477
  physiology 573.77
Exothermic reactions 541.362
  chemical engineering 660.296 2
Expanding universe theories 523.18
Expanding vaults 721.45
  architecture 721.45
  construction 690.145
Expansion (Effect of heat) 536.41
Expansion of enterprises
  executive management 658.406
Expansions (Mathematics) 511.4
Expatriation 323.64
Expectant mothers
  employment economics 331.44
Expectant parents' handbooks 649.102 42
  medicine 618.24
Expectation
  probabilities 519.287
  statistical mathematics 519.54
Expectorants
  pharmacodynamics 615.72
  see also Respiratory system
Expediting
  materials management
    receiving operations 658.728
    shipping operations 658.788 6
Expeditionary forces 355.352
Expense statements
  financial management 658.151 2
Expenses
  financial management 658.155
Experience
  philosophical anthropology 128.4
  religion 291.42
    see also Religious experience

Experiment in International Living 373.011 62
Experimental animals 619
care and maintenance 636.088 5
medicine 619
Experimental arts 700.411
T3C—11
Experimental biology 570.724
Experimental literary works 808.887
specific literatures T3B—807
individual authors T3A—8
Experimental medicine 619
ethics 174.28
see also Medical ethics
Experimental research 001.434
T1—072 4
public administrative support 352.745
see Manual at T1—07201–T1—07209 vs. T1—0722–T1—0724
Experimental schools 371.04
higher education 378.03
Experimentation on animals
ethics 179.4
see also Animals—treatment of—ethics
medicine 619
Expert system shells 006.338
Expert systems 006.33
Expert testimony 347.067
criminal law 345.067
Expert witnesses 347.067
criminal law 345.067
Expertizing
antiques 745.102 88
arts 702.88
Experts 001
management use 658.46
Exploding wire phenomena 537.5
Explorations 910.9
geography 910.9
oceanography 551.460 7
recreation 796.52
science 508
see Manual at 629.43, 629.45 vs. 919.904; *also at* 913–919: Add table: 04: Discovery and exploration
Explorers 910.92
occupational group T7—91
Explorers (Organization) 369.43
Explosion 541.361
chemical engineering 660.296 1
chemistry 541.361
Explosion insurance 368.12
see also Insurance
Explosions
mine safety engineering 622.82
social services 363.349 7
see also Disasters
Explosive technologists 662.209 2
occupational group T7—662
Explosives 662.2
control 363.33
public administration 353.36
law 344.053 3
military engineering 623.452
public safety 363.179 8
see also Hazardous materials
Exponents 512.922
algebra 512.922
arithmetic 513.22
Export controls 382.64
law 343.087 8
Export credit 332.742
law 346.073
Export-Import Bank of the United States 332.154 097 3
Export licensing 382.64
law 343.087 8
Export marketing 382.6
commerce 382.6
management 658.848
Export subsidies 382.63
Export tax 382.7
public finance 336.263
see also Customs (Tariff)
Export trade 382.6
commerce 382.6
law 343.087 8
management 658.848
public administration 354.74
Exposition (Rhetoric) 808.066
speaking 808.5
writing 808.066
Expositions 907.4
see also Exhibitions
Expository writing 808.066
Exposure meters 771.37
Exposure of the dead
customs 393.4

Express freight services	388.044
air	387.744
bus	388.322 2
ferry	386.6
inland waterway	386.244
marine	387.544
railroad	385.23
special purpose	385.5
truck	388.324
Express mail	383.18
Expression	
drama	792.028
motion pictures	791.430 28
radio	791.440 28
stage	792.028
television	791.450 28
Expressionism	
architecture	724.6
fine arts	709.040 42
literature	808.801 15
history and criticism	809.911 5
specific literatures	T3B—080 115
history and criticism	T3B—091 15
painting	759.064 2
sculpture	735.230 442
Expressive movements	302.222
psychology	152.384
see also Gestures	
see Manual at 153.69 vs. 152.384	
Expressways	388.122
see also Roads	
Expropriation	338.924
international law	341.484 6
law of war	341.67
land economics	333.13
law	343.025 2
production economics	338.924
Extemporaneous speaking	
rhetoric	808.51
Extemporization (Music)	781.36
Extended care facilities	362.16
mental illness	362.23
see also Mental health services	
physical illness	362.16
see also Health care facilities; Health services	
Extended coverage endorsement	368.129
see also Insurance	
Extended family	306.857
Extended school year	371.236
Extenders (Chemicals)	661.807
Extenders (Paints)	667.623
Extension cords	
electrical engineering	621.319 24
Extension education	371.35
higher education	378.175
Extension services	T1—071 5
Extension theory	512.4
Exterior algebra	512.57
Exterior ballistics	
military engineering	623.514
Exterior lighting	621.322 9
see also Lighting	
Exterior painting	
buildings	698.12
Extermination camps	
European history	940.531 8
External affairs	327
public administration	353.1
External ears	573.89
animal physiology	573.89
descriptive zoology	591.4
human anatomy	611.85
human diseases	
incidence	614.599 8
otology	617.81
human physiology	612.851
see also Ears	
External storage	
computer science	004.56
engineering	621.397 6
Exterritoriality	
international law	341.4
Extinct animals	560
recently extinct	591.68
Extinct birds	568
recently extinct	598.168
Extinct mammals	569
recently extinct	599.168
Extinct plants	561
recently extinct	581.68
Extinction (Biology)	576.84
Extortion	364.165
law	345.026 5
Extortion insurance	368.82
see also Insurance	
Extrachromosomal DNA	572.869
Extraction (Chemical engineering)	660.284 2
oils and gases	665.028 2
Extraction (Dentistry)	617.66
Extraction (Mining)	622
petroleum	622.338
Extraction (Obstetrics)	618.82
Extractive industries	338

Extractive industry workers 331.794
labor economics 331.794
public administration 354.942 2
Extractive metallurgy 669
Extracts
practical pharmacy 615.42
Extracurricular activities 371.8
Extradition 345.052
international law 341.488
Extralegislative powers (Legislative bodies) 328.345
Extramarital relations 306.736
ethics 176
see also Sexual relations—ethics
social problem 363.48
social theology 291.178 357 36
Christianity 261.835 736
see also Sexual relations
Extrameridional instruments 522.4
Extrasensory perception 133.8
Extrasensory perception of animals 133.89
Extraterrestrial biophysics 571.499
humans 612.014 5
Extraterrestrial civilization 999
Extraterrestrial engineering 620.419
Extraterrestrial intelligence 999
Extraterrestrial life 576.839
Extraterrestrial rovers
engineering 629.295
Extraterrestrial worlds 999
T2—99
earth sciences 559.9
see Manual at 559.9
see Manual at T2—99 vs. T2—19; *also at* 520 vs. 500.5, 523.1, 530.1, 919.9
Extraterritoriality
international law 341.4
Extrauterine pregnancy
obstetrics 618.31
Extravehicular activity (Manned space flight) 629.458 4
Extremadura (Spain) T2—462 6
Extreme unction 234.167
public worship 265.7
theology 234.167
Extremities
bones
human anatomy 611.718
human physiology 612.75
medicine 616.71
surgery 617.471
Extremities (continued)
fractures
medicine 617.158
human anatomy 611.98
human physiology 612.98
joints
medicine 616.72
surgery 617.580 59
muscles
human anatomy 611.738
regional medicine 617.58
surgery 617.580 59
see also Musculoskeletal system
Extrinsic variables (Stars) 523.844 4
Extroversion 155.232
educational psychology 370.153
personality trait 155.232
Extruded latex 678.538
Extruded rubber 678.35
Extruding metals 671.34
decorative arts 739.14
sculpture 731.41
Extruding plastics 668.413
Extruding rubber 678.27
Eyadéma, Gnassingbé
Togolese history 966.810 42
Eyak language 497.2
T6—972
Eye banks 362.178 3
see also Health services
Eyeballs
human anatomy 611.84
human physiology 612.84
ophthalmology 617.74
see also Eyes
Eyeglasses
customs 391.44
manufacturing technology 681.411
optometry 617.752 2
see also Eyes
Eyelids
human physiology 612.847
ophthalmology 617.771
see also Eyes
Eyes 573.88
anesthesiology 617.967 7
animal physiology 573.88
descriptive zoology 591.4
geriatrics 618.977 7
human anatomy 611.84

Eyes (continued)
  human diseases 362.197 7
    incidence 614.599 7
    ophthalmology 617.7
    social services 362.197 7
  human physiology 612.84
  nursing 610.736 77
  pediatrics 618.920 977
  personal care 646.726
  surgery 617.71
Eyre, Lake (S. Aust.) T2—942 38
Eyre Peninsula (S. Aust.) T2—942 38
Ezekiel (Biblical book) 224.4
Ezingolweni (South Africa : District) T2—684 91
Ezra (Biblical book) 222.7

F

F region (Ionosphere) 538.767 4
Fabales 583.74
  see also Legumes
Fabian socialism 335.14
  political ideology 320.531 2
Fabliaux 808.813
  history and criticism 809.13
  specific literatures T3B—103
    individual authors T3A—1
Fabric furnishings 645.046
  commercial technology 684.3
  see also Furnishings
Fabricating equipment 621.9
Fabrics 677.028 64
  home economics 646.11
  home furnishings 645.046
  home sewing 646.11
  textile technology 677.028 64
  see also Textiles
Facades
  architectural design 729.1
Face
  anthropometry 599.948
  human anatomy 611.92
  human physiology 612.92
  personal care 646.726
  regional medicine 617.52
  surgery 617.520 59
Facial bones
  fractures
    medicine 617.156
  human anatomy 611.716
  human physiology 612.75
  medicine 616.71
Facial bones (continued)
  surgery 617.471
  see also Musculoskeletal system
Facility management 658.2
  see also Plant management
Facsimile transmission 384.14
  engineering 621.382 35
  postal service 383.141
    see also Postal service
  wireless 384.524
  see also Telegraphy
Facsimiles
  bibliographies 011.47
Fact books 030
Fact finding 001.4
  T1—072
  legislative activity 328.345 2
  public administration 352.743
    maladministration 353.46
  public safety 363.106 5
Factor algebras 512.57
Factor analysis 519.535 4
Factor proportions
  economics 338.512
Factorial series 515.243
Factories
  architecture 725.4
  institutional housekeeping 647.964
  landscape architecture 712.7
  manufacturing industries 338.476 7
  manufacturing technology 670
  organization of production 338.65
Factoring 512.923
  algebra 512.923
  arithmetic 513.23
Factorization
  number theory 512.74
Factors of production 338.01
  agricultural economics 338.14
  income distribution 339.21
  microeconomics 338.512
  mineral industries 338.26
  secondary industries 338.45
Factory operations engineering 670.42
Factory outlets 381.15
  see also Outlet stores
Factory ships 387.248
  design 623.812 48
  engineering 623.824 8
  transportation services 387.248
  see also Ships
Factory system
  economics 338.65

Facts (Philosophy) 111
Faculae 523.74
Facultatively anaerobic gram-negative rods 579.34
Faculty 371.1
  higher education 378.12
  see also Teachers; entries beginning with Teacher
Faculty psychology 150.192
Faeroe Islands 949.15
  T2—491 5
Faeroes 949.15
  T2—491 5
Faeroese dialect 439.699
  T6—396 99
Faeroese literature 839.699
Faeroese people T5—396 9
Fagales 583.46
Fagoideae 583.46
Faience 738.37
Failure (Materials science) 620.112
Fair employment 331.133
  see also Equal employment opportunity
Fair linens
  arts 746.96
Fair organs 786.68
  see also Mechanical musical instruments
Fair trade 338.522
  law 343.07
Fairbanks North Star Borough (Alaska) T2—798 6
Fairfax (Va.) T2—755 292
Fairfax County (Va.) T2—755 291
Fairfield County (Conn.) T2—746 9
Fairfield County (Ohio) T2—771 58
Fairfield County (S.C.) T2—757 49
Fairgrounds
  area planning 711.552 2
  landscape architecture 712.5
Fairies 398.21
  see also Legendary beings
Fairness doctrine (Broadcasting)
  law 343.099 45
Fairs
  customs 394.6
  distribution channels 381.18
    management 658.84
    see also Commerce
  see also Exhibitions
Fairways (Navigation) 387.1
  engineering 627.23
  see also Ports
Fairy chess 794.18
Fairy shrimps 595.32
Fairy tales 398.2
Faith 121.7
  epistemology 121.7
  religion 291.22
    Christianity 234.23
      knowledge of God 231.042
    Islam 297.22
    Judaism 296.32
    philosophy of religion 218
Faith and reason 210
  Christianity 231.042
  Judaism 296.311
  philosophy of religion 210
Faith healing
  medicine 615.852
  religion 291.31
    Christianity 234.131
    see also Spiritual healing—religion
  see Manual at 615.852 vs. 291.31, 234.131
Fal River (England) T2—423 78
Falangism 335.6
  economics 335.6
  political ideology 320.533
Falasha T5—924
Falcón (Venezuela) T2—872 4
Falconidae 598.96
Falconiformes 598.9
  paleozoology 568.9
Falconry 799.232
Falcons 598.96
  animal husbandry 636.686 9
  conservation technology 639.978 96
  resource economics 333.958 96
Faliscan languages 479.4
  T6—794
Falkirk (Scotland : District) T2—413 18
Falkland Islands 997.11
  T2—971 1
Falkland Islands War 997.110 24
Fall 508.2
  music 781.524 6
  see also Seasons
Fall of humankind 233.14
Fall River County (S.D.) T2—783 97
Fallacies 001.96
  logic 165
Falling bodies 531.14
  solid mechanics 531.5
Fallon County (Mont.) T2—786 35

Fallopian tubes
  gynecology 618.12
  human anatomy 611.65
  human physiology 612.62
  surgery 618.120 59
  see also Female genital system
Fallow deer 599.655
Fallowing 631.581 2
Falls Church (Va.) T2—755 293
Falls County (Tex.) T2—764 286
False arrest 346.033 4
False Dmitri I
  Russian history 947.045
False Dmitri II
  Russian history 947.045
False imprisonment 346.033 4
False killer whales 599.53
False memory syndrome
  adult child abuse victims
    psychotherapy 616.858 223 90651
  adult child sexual abuse victims
    psychotherapy 616.858 369 0651
  psychotherapy 616.891 4
False scorpions 595.47
Falsetto voices 782.86
  choral and mixed voices 782.86
  single voices 783.86
Falster (Denmark) T2—489 3
Families 306.85
  applied psychology 158.24
  government programs 353.533 1
  histories 929.2
    see Manual at 929.2
  influence on crime 364.253
  law 346.015
  psychological influence 155.924
  recreation 790.191
    indoor 793.019 1
    outdoor 796
  religion
    guides to life 291.441
      Christianity 248.4
      see also Family life—religion
    pastoral theology 291.61
      Christianity 259.1
    social theology 291.178 358 5
      Christianity 261.835 85
    worship 291.43
      Christianity 249
      Judaism 296.45
  social welfare 362.82
    law 344.032 82
Families
  social welfare (continued)
    public administration 353.533 1
  sociology 306.85
Families of clergymen
  pastoral theology 253.22
Family 306.85
  system of government 321.1
  see also Families
Family abuse 362.829 2
  sociology 306.87
  see also Family violence
Family behavior (Animals) 591.563
Family budgets
  home economics 640.42
  macroeconomics 339.41
Family cars
  driving 629.283
    recreation 796.78
  engineering 629.222
  repair 629.287 2
  see also Automobiles
Family Compact 971.038
Family corporations 338.74
  law 346.066 8
  see also Corporations
Family counseling 362.828 6
  Christian pastoral counseling 259.12
Family dissolution 306.88
Family ethics 173
  religion 291.563
    Buddhism 294.356 3
    Christianity 241.63
    Hinduism 294.548 63
    Islam 297.563
    Judaism 296.363
Family histories 929.2
  see Manual at 929.2; *also at* 929.2 vs. 929.7
Family law 346.015
Family leave 331.257 63
  personnel management 658.312 2
Family life 306.85
  applied psychology 158.24
  customs 392.3
  elementary education 372.82
  home economics 646.78
  psychological influence 155.924
  religion 291.441
    Buddhism 294.344 41
    Christianity 248.4
    Hinduism 294.544 1
    Islam 297.577
    Judaism 296.74

Family living 646.7
  elementary education 372.82
Family meals 642.1
Family names 929.42
Family planning 363.96
  see also Birth control
Family psychotherapy
  psychiatry 616.891 56
  see also Mental illness
Family purity
  Judaism 296.742
Family relationships 306.87
  home economics 646.78
Family rooms 643.55
  home economics 643.55
  interior decoration 747.791
Family size
  demography 304.634
Family socialization 303.323
Family violence 362.829 2
  criminology 364.155 5
    criminal law 345.025 55
  psychiatry 616.858 22
  social theology 291.178 327
    Christianity 261.832 7
  social welfare 362.829 2
    law 344.032 829 2
  sociology 306.87
Famine 363.8
Fan-jet engines
  aircraft 629.134 353 7
Fan vaults 721.45
  architecture 721.45
  construction 690.145
Fanagalo 496.398 6
  T6—963 986
Fanakalo 496.398 6
  T6—963 986
Fancies (Music) 784.187 6
Fancy-weave fabrics 677.61
  see also Textiles
Fanfares 784.189 24
Fang (African people) T5—963 96
Fang language 496.396
  T6—963 96
Fannin County (Ga.) T2—758 293
Fannin County (Tex.) T2—764 265
Fans (Machinery) 621.61
Fans (Ornamental) 391.44
  customs 391.44
  handicrafts 745.594
Fantasias 784.189 4
Fantastic fiction 808.838 766
  history and criticism 809.387 66
Fantastic fiction (continued)
  specific literatures T3B—308 766
    individual authors T3A—3
Fantasy 154.3
  arts 700.415
    T3C—15
  literature 808.801 5
    history and criticism 809.915
    specific literatures T3B—080 15
      history and criticism T3B—091 5
    see also Fantasy fiction
  motion pictures 791.436 15
  psychology 154.3
  radio programs 791.446 15
  television programs 791.456 15
Fantasy fiction 808.838 766
  history and criticism 809.387 66
  specific literatures T3B—308 766
    individual authors T3A—3
Fantasy games 793.93
  see Manual at 793.932 vs. 794.822
Fante (African people) T5—963 385
Fante language 496.338 5
  T6—963 385
Fante literature 896.338 5
Fanti (African people) T5—963 385
Fanti language 496.338 5
  T6—963 385
Fanti literature 896.338 5
Far East 950
  T2—5
Far East international organizations 341.247 3
Far North District (N.Z.) T2—931 3
Far Western Rand (South Africa) T2—682 2
Farces
  literature 808.825 232
    history and criticism 809.252 32
    specific literatures T3B—205 232
      individual authors T3A—2
Fareham (England) T2—422 775
Fares
  transportation services 388.049
  see Manual at 383–388: Offers for sale vs. Economic aspects
Fargo (N.D.) T2—784 13
Faribault County (Minn.) T2—776 22
Farm accounting 657.863
Farm advertising 659.131 5
Farm buildings 631.2
  architecture 728.92

Farm buildings (continued)
  construction 690.892
  use 631.2
Farm costs 338.13
Farm cottages
  architecture 728.6
Farm forestry 634.99
Farm income 338.13
Farm investment 338.13
Farm law 343.076
Farm loans 332.71
  law 346.073
Farm manure 631.861
Farm-owner insurance 368.096
  see also Insurance
Farm pests 632.6
  see Manual at 632.2–632.8
Farm prices 338.13
Farm produce
  public administration 354.59
Farm production quotas
  law 343.076 1
Farm profits 338.13
Farm property 333.76
  resource economics 333.76
  taxation 336.225
Farm roads
  use 631.28
Farm tenancy 333.335 53
  economics 333.335 53
  law 346.043 48
Farm tractors 629.225 2
  see also Tractors
Farm valuation 333.335 2
  real estate economics 333.335 2
  tax economics 336.225
Farmers 630.92
  T1—088 63
  occupational group T7—63
  social class 305.555
Farmhouses
  agriculture 631.21
  architecture 728.6
  construction 690.86
Farming 630
Farmowner-ranchowner
  insurance 368.096
  see also Insurance
Farms 630
  animal husbandry 636.01
Faro (Game) 795.42
Faro (Portugal : District) T2—469 6
Faroe Islands 949.15
  T2—491 5
Farquhar Islands
  (Seychelles) T2—696
Fārs (Iran) T2—557 2
Farsi language 491.55
  T6—915 5
Farsi literature 891.55
Faruk I, King of Egypt
  Egyptian history 962.052
Fasciae
  human anatomy 611.74
  human physiology 612.75
  medicine 616.75
  see also Musculoskeletal
    system
Fascism 335.6
  economics 335.6
  political ideology 320.533
Fascist government 321.94
Fascist parties 324.213 8
Fascist period (Italy) 945.091
Fashion 391
  arts 746.92
  customs 391
  see Manual at 391 vs. 646.3,
    746.92
Fashion design 746.92
Fashion designers 746.920 92
  occupational group T7—746
Fashion drawing 741.672
Fashion modeling 746.92
  advertising 659.152
Fast days 291.36
  Christianity 263.9
    devotional literature 242.3
    sermons 252.6
  cooking 641.567
  customs 394.2
  Islam 297.53
  Judaism 296.43
  see also Holy days
Fast foods
  home serving 642.1
Fasteners 621.88
  buildings 721.8
    architecture 721.8
    construction 690.18
Fastening equipment 621.97
Fasting
  health 613.25
  religious practice 291.447
    Buddhism 294.344 47
    Christianity 248.47
    Hinduism 294.544 7

Fasting
religious practice (continued)
Islam 297.53
Sufi 297.45
Judaism 296.7
Fatalism
philosophy 149.8
Fate
philosophy 123
Father (God)
Christian doctrines 231.1
Jewish doctrine 296.311 2
Father and child 306.874 2
Fatherhood 306.874 2
Fathers 306.874 2
T1—085 1
T7—043 1
family relationships 306.874 2
guides to Christian life 248.842 1
psychology 155.646 2
Fatigue (Human)
muscle tissues
physiology 612.744
see also Musculoskeletal system
production management 658.544
psychology 152.188 6
Fatigue (Materials) 620.112 6
Fatigue strength 620.112 6
Fats 572.57
applied nutrition 613.284
biochemistry 572.57
humans 612.015 77
chemistry 547.77
food technology 664.3
industrial 665
metabolism
human physiology 612.397
see also Lipids
Fatty acids 572.57
applied nutrition 613.284
biochemistry 572.57
humans 612.015 77
chemistry 547.77
metabolism
human physiology 612.397
recovery from pulp 676.5
see also Lipids
Fatty-alcohol sulfates 668.14
Fatty degeneration
medicine 616.396
see also Digestive system
Fatty tissues 571.57
human histology 611.018 2
Faucets 621.84
Faulk County (S.D.) T2—783 213
Faulkner County (Ark.) T2—767 74
Fault-tolerant computing 004.2
engineering 621.392
firmware 005.6
programming 005.1
Faults (Geology) 551.872
Fauquier County (Va.) T2—755 275
Fauresmith (South Africa : District) T2—685 7
Fauvism 709.040 43
painting 759.064 3
sculpture 735.230 443
Fax (Transmission) 384.14
see also Facsimile transmission
Fayette County (Ala.) T2—761 87
Fayette County (Ga.) T2—758 426
Fayette County (Ill.) T2—773 797
Fayette County (Ind.) T2—772 623
Fayette County (Iowa) T2—777 35
Fayette County (Ky.) T2—769 47
Fayette County (Ohio) T2—771 813
Fayette County (Pa.) T2—748 84
Fayette County (Tenn.) T2—768 21
Fayette County (Tex.) T2—764 251
Fayette County (W. Va.) T2—754 71
Faysal I, King of Iraq
Iraqi history 956.704 1
Faysal II, King of Iraq
Iraqi history 956.704 2
Fayyūm (Egypt : Province) T2—622
Fear 152.46
literature 808.803 53
history and criticism 809.933 53
specific literatures T3B—080 353
history and criticism T3B—093 53
social psychology 302.17
Feast days
Christianity 263.9
devotional literature 242.3
sermons 252.6
cooking 641.567
customs 394.2
religion 291.36
see also Holy days
Feather products
manufacturing technology 679.47
Featherbedding 331.889 6
Feathers 598.147
animal husbandry 636.514 5
nonpoultry 636.61
descriptive zoology 598.147

Feathers (continued)
  physiology 573.597
Features
  journalism 070.44
Febrifuges
  pharmacodynamics 615.75
Feces
  human physiology 612.36
  see also Digestive system
Federal administration 351
Federal aid
  education 379.121
    law 344.076 3
  higher education 379.121 4
    law 344.076 84
  private schools 379.32
Federal and Islamic Republic of
    the Comoros 969.41
    T2—694 1
Federal Capital Territory
    (Nigeria) T2—669 68
Federal cases
  United States 348.734
Federal courts (United States) 347.732
  reports 348.734 1
Federal District (Brazil) T2—817 4
Federal District (Mexico) T2—725 3
Federal government 321.02
  law 342.042
  public administration 351
Federal law (Treatises) 340
  United States 349.73
Federal laws (Compilations) 348.02
  United States 348.732
Federal Party (U.S.) 324.273 22
Federal-provincial relations 321.023
Federal Register (United States) 351.730 5
Federal regulations
    (Compilations) 348.025
  United States 348.732 5
Federal regulations
    (Treatises) 342.060 263 6
  United States 342.730 602 636
Federal Republic of Germany 943.087
    T2—43
Federal Reserve System (U.S.) 332.110 973
Federal-state relations 321.023
Federal statutes (Compilations) 348.022
  United States 348.732 2
Federalism 321.02
Federalist Party (U.S.) 324.273 22
Federation of Arab
    Republics T2—62
Federation of Rhodesia and
    Nyasaland 968.903
    T2—689
Federation of South Arabia T2—533 5
Federations 321.02
  law 342.042
  public administration 351
Fee-based library services 025.11
Fee simple 346.043 2
  land economics 333.323 2
Fee splitting
  medical ethics 174.26
Feed additives 636.085 57
Feedback circuits
  electronics 621.381 535
Feedback control systems 629.83
Feeding animals 636.084
Feeding behavior (Animals) 591.53
Feeding-bottle nipples
  latex technology 678.533
Feeding children 649.3
Feedlot runoff
  water pollution engineering 628.168 46
Feedlot wastes
  animal husbandry 636.083 8
Feedlots 636.084 3
Feeds 636.085 5
  animal husbandry 636.085 5
  commercial processing 664.66
    grain and seeds 664.76
Feelings 152.4
  educational psychology 370.153
Fees
  public administration 352.44
  public revenues 336.16
Feet (Human) 612.98
  physiology 612.98
  regional medicine 617.585
  surgery 617.585 059
  see also Lower extremities
    (Human)
Fe'fe' (Cameroon people) T5—963 6
Fe'fe' language 496.36
    T6—963 6
Fejér Megye (Hungary) T2—439 7
Feldspar
  materials science 620.198
  mineralogy 549.68
  synthetic 666.86
Felidae 599.75
  animal husbandry 636.8
  paleozoology 569.75
Felis 599.752
Felling trees 634.98

Fellowships 371.223
T1—079
higher education 378.33
research 001.44
see also Scholarships
Feloidea 599.74
paleozoology 569.74
Felsites 552.22
Felt 677.63
see also Textiles
Felting textiles 677.028 24
Female circumcision
gynecology 618.16
Female genital organs 573.66
see also Female genital system
Female genital system 573.66
anesthesiology 617.968 1
biology 573.66
geriatrics 618.978 1
gynecology 618.1
human anatomy 611.65
human cancer 362.196 994 65
incidence 614.599 946 5
medicine 616.994 65
social services 362.196 994 65
see also Cancer (Human)
human diseases 362.198 1
incidence 614.599 21
medicine 618.1
social services 362.198 1
human physiology 612.62
nursing 610.736 78
pediatrics 618.920 98
surgery 618.105 9
Female reproductive system 573.66
animals 573.66
plants 575.66
see also Female genital system
Female sexual disorders
gynecology 618.17
see also Female genital system
Females (Human) 305.4
T1—082
T7—042
grooming 646.704 2
see also Women
Femininity 155.333
Femininity of God 291.211 4
Christianity 231.4
Judaism 296.311 2
Feminism 305.42
social aspects 305.42
social theology 291.178 344 2
Christianity 261.834 42
Feminism
social theology (continued)
Judaism 296.38
Feminist theology 291.208 2
Christianity 230.082
Judaism 296.308 2
Feminist views T1—082
Feminists 305.42
Femurs
human anatomy 611.718
see also Musculoskeletal system
Fencers 796.860 92
sports group T7—796 8
Fences 631.27
agricultural use 631.27
landscape architecture 717
Fencing (Offense) 364.162
law 345.026 2
Fencing (Swordplay) 796.86
see also Sports
Fenders
automobile 629.26
Feng shui 133.333 7
Fenians 941.708 1
Canadian history 971.048
Irish history 941.708 1
Fenland (England) T2—426 53
Fennec fox 599.776
Fens, The (England) T2—426
Fentress County (Tenn.) T2—768 69
Feral children
psychology 155.456 7
Feral livestock
agricultural pests 632.696
conservation technology 639.966
Ferdinand I, Holy Roman Emperor
German history 943.032
Ferdinand II, Holy Roman Emperor
German history 943.042
Ferdinand III, Holy Roman Emperor
German history 943.043
Ferdinand V, King of Spain
Spanish history 946.03
Ferdinand VI, King of Spain
Spanish history 946.056
Ferdinand VII, King of Spain
Spanish history 946.072
Fergus County (Mont.) T2—786 292
Fermanagh (Northern Ireland) T2—416 3

Fermat's last theorem	512.74
Fermentation	547.29
alcoholic beverages	663.13
biochemistry	572.49
chemical engineering	660.284 49
food technology	664.024
Fermented cider	
commercial processing	663.2
Fermions	539.721
Fermium	546.449
see also Chemicals	
Fernando de Noronha (Brazil	T2—813 4
Fernando Po (Equatorial Guinea)	T2—671 86
Ferns	587.3
floriculture	635.937 3
Ferrara (Italy : Province)	T2—454 5
Ferrets (Black-footed)	599.766 29
conservation technology	639.979 766 29
resource economics	333.959 766 29
Ferrets (Domestic polecat)	636.976 628
animal husbandry	636.976 628
zoology	599.766 28
Ferrimagnetism	538.45
Ferroalloying metals	669.73
economic geology	553.46
metallography	669.957 3
metallurgy	669.73
metalworking	673.73
physical metallurgy	669.967 3
Ferroconcrete	624.183 41
building construction	693.54
foundation materials	624.153 37
structural engineering	624.183 41
Ferroelectricity	537.244 8
Ferromagnetism	538.44
Ferrotype process	772.14
Ferrous metals	669.1
architectural construction	721.044 71
building construction	693.71
building materials	691.7
decorative arts	739.4
materials science	620.17
metallography	669.951
metallurgy	669.1
metalworking	672
physical metallurgy	669.961
ship design	623.818 21
shipbuilding	623.820 7
structural engineering	624.182 1
see also Chemicals; Metals	
Ferry County (Wash.)	T2—797 25
Ferry transportation	386.6
public administration	354.78
transportation services	386.6
Ferry transportation workers	386.609 2
occupational group	T7—386
Ferryboats	386.223 4
design	623.812 34
engineering	623.823 4
transportation services	386.223 4
see also Ships	
Fertility	
demography	304.632
Fertilization (Biology)	571.864
Fertilization in vitro	
ethics	176
religion	291.566
Christianity	241.66
see also Reproduction—ethics	
medicine	618.178 059
Fertilizer spreaders	631.816
manufacturing technology	681.763 1
Fertilizers	631.8
agricultural economics	338.162
chemical engineering	668.62
use	631.8
water pollution engineering	628.168 41
Fès (Morocco : Province)	T2—643
Fescues	633.28
botany	584.9
Festivals	394.26
	T1—079
arts	700.79
customs	394.26
performing arts	791.6
religion	291.36
Christianity	263
Judaism	296.43
Festuca	633.28
botany	584.9
Festuceae	584.9
Fetal complications	
obstetrics	618.53
Fetal disorders	
medicine	618.32
Fetal dystocia	
obstetrics	618.53
Fetal erythroblastosis	
pediatrics	618.921 5
perinatal medicine	618.326 1
see also Cardiovascular system	
Fetishism	
religion	291.21

Fetishism (Sexual) 306.77
Fetus
  human physiology 612.647
Feudal Age
  European history 940.14
  Japanese history 952.02
Feudal law 340.55
Feudal tenure 321.3
  land economics 333.322
  political science 321.3
Feudalism 321.3
  land economics 333.322
  political science 321.3
Feuds
  influence on crime 364.256
Fever
  result of injury
    medicine 617.22
  symptomatology 616.047
Fever blisters
  medicine 616.52
  see also Skin
Fever therapy
  medicine 615.832 5
Few-bodies problem 530.14
Fez (Morocco : Province) T2—643
Fianarantsoa (Madagascar : Province) T2—691
Fiat money 332.427
Fiber (Diet)
  health 613.263
Fiber bundles 514.224
  combinatorial topology 514.224
  integral geometry 516.362
Fiber crops 633.5
Fiber glass 666.157
  materials science 620.144
  sculpture material 731.2
  ship design 623.818 38
  ship hulls 623.845 8
  shipbuilding 623.820 7
  textiles 677.52
    arts 746.045 2
    see also Textiles
Fiber optic sensors
  manufacturing technology 681.25
Fiber optics 621.369 2
Fiber spaces 514.224
  combinatorial topology 514.224
  integral geometry 516.362
Fiberboards 676.183
Fibers
  materials science 620.197
  textile materials 677.028 32
Fibers (Histology)
  human 611.018 2
Fibonacci numbers 512.72
Fibrin
  human physiology 612.115
  see also Cardiovascular system
Fibrinolytic agents
  pharmacodynamics 615.718
  see also Cardiovascular system
Fibrinoplastin
  human physiology 612.115
  see also Cardiovascular system
Fibrocartilage
  human histology 611.018 3
  see also Musculoskeletal system
Fibrositis
  medicine 616.74
  see also Musculoskeletal system
Fibrous cartilage
  human histology 611.018 3
  see also Musculoskeletal system
Fibrous tunics
  human physiology 612.841
  see also Eyes
Fibulas
  human anatomy 611.718
  see also Musculoskeletal system
Ficksburg (South Africa : District) T2—685 1
Fiction 808.83
  criticism 809.3
    theory 808.3
  folklore 398.2
  history 809.3
  rhetoric 808.3
  specific literatures T3B—3
    individual authors T3A—3
  see Manual at T3B—3
Fiction writers 809.3
  collected biography 809.3
    specific literatures T3B—300 9
  individual biography T3A—3
  occupational group T7—83
Fictions
  logic 165
Ficus 583.45

Ficus elastica 635.933 45
  see also Rubber plant (Ficus)
Fiddle makers 787.219 092
Fiddlers 787.209 2
Fiddles 787.2
  instrument 787.219
  music 787.2
  see also Stringed instruments
Fidelity bonds
  insurance 368.83
    see also Insurance
Fiduciary accounting 657.47
Fiduciary trusts 346.059
  income tax law 343.052 64
  tax law 343.064
Field artillery 358.128 2
  engineering 623.412
  military equipment 358.128 2
Field artillery forces 358.12
Field athletics 796.43
  see also Sports
Field crops 633
  feeds 636.086
  public administration 354.54
  see Manual at 633–635
Field-effect transistors 621.381 528 4
Field effects
  solid-state physics 530.416
Field extensions
  number theory 512.74
Field glasses
  manufacturing technology 681.412 5
Field hockey 796.355
  see also Sports
Field hockey players 796.355 092
  sports group T7—796 35
Field houses 796.068
  architecture 725.827
Field mice (Apodemus) 599.358 5
Field offices
  public administration 352.288
Field peas 633.369
  botany 583.74
  field crop 633.369
Field theory (Mathematics) 512.3
Field theory (Physics) 530.14
Field theory (Psychological system) 150.198 4
Field training (Armed forces) 355.544
Field trips 371.384
  education 371.384
  museum services 069.15
Field work
  descriptive research 001.433
    T1—072 3
Fielding
  baseball 796.357 24
  cricket 796.358 23
Fields (Mathematics) 512.3
  number theory 512.74
Fife (Scotland) T2—412 9
Fifes 788.33
  instrument 788.331 9
  music 788.33
  see also Woodwind instruments
Fifth Republic (France) 944.083
Fighter-bombers 358.428 3
  engineering 623.746 3
  military equipment 358.428 3
Fighter forces (Air warfare) 358.43
Fighters (Aircraft) 358.438 3
  engineering 623.746 4
  military equipment 358.438 3
Fighting
  animal behavior 591.566
Fighting animals
  animal husbandry 636.088 8
Figs 641.343 7
  botany 583.45
  commercial processing 664.804 37
  cooking 641.643 7
  food 641.343 7
  orchard crop 634.37
Figueiredo, João Baptista de Oliveira
  Brazilian history 981.063
Figuig (Morocco : Province) T2—643
Figure skating 796.912
  see also Sports
Figured bass 781.47
Figured madras fabrics 677.615
  see also Textiles
Figures of speech
  rhetoric 808
Figurines 666.68
  ceramic arts 738.82
  ceramic technology 666.68
    earthenware 666.68
    porcelain 666.58
  glyptics 736.224
Figworts 583.95
Fiji 996.11
  T2—961 1

Fiji Sea 551.465 77
T2—164 77
Fijian language 499.5
T6—995
Fijian literature 899.5
Fijians T5—995
Filarial diseases
incidence 614.555 2
medicine 616.965 2
see also Communicable diseases (Human)
Filariasis
incidence 614.555 2
medicine 616.965 2
see also Communicable diseases (Human)
Filberts 641.345 4
agriculture 634.54
botany 583.48
cooking 641.645 4
food 641.345 4
File cabinets 651.54
manufacturing technology 684.16
use in records management 651.54
File clerks
occupational group T7—651
office services 651.374 3
File compression 005.746
File formats
computer science 005.741
File management systems
computer science
data file programs 005.74
systems programming 005.426
systems programs 005.436
see Manual at 005.74 vs. 005.436
File managers
computer science
data file programs 005.74
systems programming 005.426
systems programs 005.436
see Manual at 005.74 vs. 005.436
File organization
computer science
data files 005.741
systems programs 005.436
see Manual at 005.74 vs. 005.436
File processing
databases 005.74
File structure
computer science
data files 005.741
see Manual at 005.74 vs. 005.436
File system management
computer science
systems programming 005.426
systems programs 005.436
see Manual at 005.74 vs. 005.436
Filefishes 597.64
Filers (Clerks) 651.374 3
occupational group T7—651
Files (Data)
computer science 005.74
Files (Tools) 621.924
Filicales 587.3
paleobotany 561.73
Filicopsida 587.3
paleobotany 561.73
Filing
library operations 025.317 7
records management 651.53
Filing rules
library science 025.317 7
Filipino language 499.211
T6—992 11
Filipino literature 899.211
Filipinos T5—992 1
Fillers
plastic technology 668.411
Filling stations
architecture 725.38
automotive engineering 629.286
Fillings
dentistry 617.675
see also Dentistry
Fillmore, Millard
United States history 973.64
Fillmore County (Minn.) T2—776 16
Fillmore County (Neb.) T2—782 342
Fills
road engineering 625.733
Film genres 791.436
see Manual at T3B—102–T3B—108, T3B—205, T3B—308 vs. T3C—1, T3C—3
Film music 781.542
Film reviews 791.437 5
Films (Photographic material) 771.532 4
development 771.43

Films (Photographic records) 791.43
  bibliographies 011.37
  cataloging 025.347 3
  library treatment 025.177 3
  see also Motion pictures
Filmscripts 791.437
  see also Screenplays
Filmstrips 778.2
  bibliographies 011.37
  cataloging 025.347 3
  instructional use 371.335 22
  library treatment 025.177 3
Filters
  air conditioning
    buildings 697.932 4
  cameras 771.356
  chemistry 542.6
  electronic circuits 621.381 532 4
  radio engineering 621.384 12
Filtration
  chemical engineering 660.284 245
  sewage treatment 628.352
  water supply treatment 628.164
Fin whale 599.524 6
Finance 332
  agricultural industries 338.13
  churches 262.006 81
    local church 254.8
  communications industry 384.041
  ethics 174.4
    see also Ethical problems
  insurance 368.01
  library operations 025.11
  management 658.15
    see also Financial management
  mineral industries 338.23
  production economics 338.604 1
  public administration 354.8
  secondary industries 338.43
  transportation services 388.049
  see Manual at 332, 336 vs. 339; *also at* 332 vs. 338, 658.15
Finance departments (Public administration) 352.4
Financial accounting 657.48
Financial administration 658.15
  see also Financial management
Financial aid (Welfare) 361.05
  crime prevention 364.44
Financial assistance
  public administration 352.73
    foreign aid 353.132 73
Financial clerks
  office services 651.37
Financial control
  management 658.151
    public administration 352.43
Financial crime 364.168
  law 345.026 8
Financial decision making
  management 658.15
Financial economics 332
  see Manual at 332, 336 vs. 339; *also at* 332 vs. 338, 658.15
Financial futures 332.632
Financial independence (Personal finance) 332.024 01
Financial institutions 332.1
  accounting 657.833 3
  architecture 725.24
  public administration 354.8
Financial management 658.15
  T1—068 1
  armed services 355.622
  public administration 352.4
  schools 371.206
    higher education 378.106
  see Manual at 332 vs. 338, 658.15; *also at* 658.15 and T1—0681
Financial patronage T1—079
  research 001.44
Financial planning
  management 658.15
  personal finance 332.024
Financial power (Legislative bodies) 328.341 2
Financial reports 657.3
  management use 658.151 2
  see also Financial statements
Financial security
  personal finance 332.024 01
Financial statements 657.3
  accounting 657.3
  law 346.063
    corporate law 346.066 48
  management use 658.151 2
    public administration 352.43
  see Manual at 657 vs. 658.1511, 658.1512
Financial strength measurement
  accounting 657.48

Financial success 650.12
Financial support T1—079
  research 001.44
Financial support by governments
  libraries 021.83
Financiers 332.092
  occupational group T7—332
Finback whale 599.524 6
Finches 598.88
  animal husbandry 636.686 2
Fine art museums 708
  architecture 727.7
Fine arts 700
  investment economics 332.63
  public administrative support 353.77
  see also Arts
Fine bookbinding 686.302
Fine particle technology 620.43
Fines 364.68
  penology 364.68
  personnel management 658.314 4
  public revenues 336.16
Finger Lakes (N.Y.) T2—747 8
Finger painting 751.49
Finger rings 391.7
  customs 391.7
  making 739.278 2
  see also Jewelry
Finger spelling 419
Finger techniques
  music 784.193 68
Fingering (Music) 784.193 68
Fingerprint files 363.24
Fingerprints
  anthropometry 599.945
  criminal investigation 363.258
Finish carpentry
  construction 694.6
Finished lumber 674.4
Finishing leather 675.25
Finishing machines
  textile technology 677.028 55
Finishing metals 671.7
Finishing paper 676.234
Finishing textiles 677.028 25
Finishing woodwork
  buildings 698.3
Finistère (France) T2—441 1
Finite (Philosophy) 111.6
Finite differences 515.62
Finite element analysis
  engineering 620.001 515 35
Finite mathematics 510
Finland 948.97
  T2—489 7
Finland, Gulf of 551.461 34
  T2—163 34
Finlay River (B.C.) T2—711 87
Finney County (Kan.) T2—781 44
Finnic languages 494.54
  T6—945 4
Finnic literatures 894.54
Finnic peoples T5—945 4
Finnish Evangelical Lutheran Church 284.133 4
  see also Lutheran church
Finnish language 494.541
  T6—945 41
Finnish literature 894.541
Finnish spitz 636.72
Finnmark fylke (Norway) T2—484 6
Finno-Ugrians T5—945
Finno-Ugric languages 494.5
  T6—945
Finno-Ugric literatures 894.5
Finns T5—945 41
Finol Linares, José
  Brazilian history 981.061
Fins
  aircraft 629.134 33
Finsler geometry 516.375
Fiordland National Park (N.Z.) T2—939 6
Fipa-Mambwe languages 496.391
  T6—963 91
Fiqh 340.59
  religious law 297.14
  secular law 340.59
Fire
  folklore 398.26
    history and criticism 398.364
  literature 808.803 6
    history and criticism 809.933 6
    specific literatures T3B—080 36
      history and criticism T3B—093 6
  religious worship 291.212
Fire-bellied toads 597.86
Fire clays 553.67
  see also Fireclays
Fire control (Artillery)
  military gunnery 623.558
Fire detectors 628.922 5
Fire ecology 577.2
Fire engines 628.925 9
  construction 629.225
  use 628.925 9
Fire escapes 628.922

Fire fighters 363.370 92
  occupational group T7—363 3
Fire fighting 628.925
  forestry 634.961 8
  on ships 623.888 6
  social services 363.378
  see also Fire safety
Fire fighting equipment
  airport engineering 629.136 8
  military airport engineering 623.668
  ships 623.865
Fire hazards 363.37
  technology 628.92
  see also Fire safety
Fire insurance 368.11
  allied lines 368.12
    see Manual at 368.12
  see also Insurance
Fire prevention 363.377
  law 344.053 77
  management of enterprises 658.477
  technology 628.922
Fire prevention equipment
  aircraft 629.134 43
Fire-resistant clothing
  commercial technology 687.16
  see also Clothing
Fire-resistant construction
  ship hulls 623.848
Fire-resistant paints 667.69
Fire retardants 628.922 3
Fire safety 363.37
  law 344.053 7
  mining technology 622.82
  public administration 353.979
  social services 363.37
  technology 628.922
Fire stations 363.37
  architecture 725.19
  construction 690.519
Fire thorns 635.933 73
  botany 583.73
  floriculture 635.933 73
Firearms 683.4
  art metalwork 739.74
  military engineering 623.4
  see also Guns (Small arms)
Fireclays 553.67
  ceramic technology 666.72
  economic geology 553.67
  materials science 620.143
Fireflies 595.764 4
Fireless cooking 641.588
Firemen 363.370 92
  occupational group T7—363 3
Firenze (Italy : Province) T2—455 1
Fireplaces
  architecture 721.8
  construction 697.1
  furniture arts 749.62
  home economics 644.1
Fireproofing 628.922 3
  buildings 693.82
Fires 363.37
  crop damage 632.18
  see also Fire safety
Fireweeds (Asteraceae) 583.99
Fireweeds (Onagraceae) 583.76
Fireworks 662.1
Firing artillery 623.558
Firing clays
  arts 730.028
  pottery 666.443
    arts 738.143
    technology 666.443
  sculpture 731.47
Firing glass 666.126
Firing metallurgical furnaces 669.83
Firing of employees
  economics 331.259 6
    employment security 331.259 6
    unemployment 331.137
  law 344.012 596
  personnel management 658.313
    public administration 352.69
Firmware
  hardware 004
    engineering 621.395
  microprograms 005.6
    see Manual at 005.6
Firmware development 005.6
Firs 585.2
  forestry 634.975 4
  lumber 674.144
First aid 362.18
  emergency surgery 617.026 2
  health services 362.18
  medicine 616.025 2
First aid stations 362.18
  armed forces 355.72
First-class mail 383.122
  see also Postal service
First editions 094.4
First Empire (France) 944.05
First International 324.17
First names 929.44
First Republic (Austria) 943.605 1

First Republic (France) 944.042
First Republic (Spain) 946.073
Firth of Clyde (Scotland) 551.461 37
T2—163 37
Firth of Forth (Scotland) 551.461 36
T2—163 36
Fiscal policy 336.3
law 343.034
macroeconomics 339.52
public finance 336.3
Fiscal tariffs 382.72
see also Customs (Tariff)
Fischer-Tropsch processes 662.662 3
Fish 597
see also Fishes
Fish culture 639.3
economics 338.371 3
enterprises 338.763 93
Fish culturists
occupational group T7—639 3
Fish farmers 639.309 2
Fish farming 639.3
freshwater 639.31
Fish hatcheries 639.311
Fish lice 595.36
Fish-liver oils
pharmacology 615.34
Fish oil 665.2
Fish ponds 639.31
ecology 577.636
Fisher (Mammal) 599.766 5
Fisher County (Tex.) T2—764 732
Fisheries 338.372 7
economics 338.372 7
enterprises 338.763 92
international law 341.762 2
law 343.076 92
products 338.372 7
commerce 380.143 7
public administration 354.57
technology 639.2
see Manual at 338.37 vs. 333.954; *also at* 338.372
Fishermen 639.209 2
commercial 639.209 2
occupational group T7—639 2
occupational group T7—639 2
sports 799.109 2
sports group T7—799 1
Fishery law 343.076 92
Fishery technology 639.2
Fishes 597
art representation 704.943 27
conservation technology 639.977
Fishes (continued)
cooking 641.692
drawing 743.67
food 641.392
commercial processing 664.94
paleozoology 567
production economics 338.372 7
public administration 354.57
resource economics 333.956
international law 341.762 2
law 346.046 956
sports fishing 799.1
zoology 597
Fishing
commercial technology 639.2
economics 338.372 7
enterprises 338.763 92
game laws 346.046 956 9
industrial law 343.076 92
international law 341.762 2
public administration 354.57
sports 799.1
public administrative support 353.78
see also Sports
see Manual at 338.372
Fishing equipment
sports
technology 688.791
Fishing industries 338.372 7
see also Fisheries
Fishpond ecology 577.636
Fishponds 639.31
ecology 577.636
Fishways 639.977
Fishworms
culture 639.75
Fission (Nuclear) 539.762
Fission reactors 621.483
Fissionable materials
economic geology 553.493
nuclear engineering 621.483 35
Fissipedia 599.7
paleozoology 569.7
Fitting
clothing 646.408
commercial tailoring 687.044
home sewing 646.408
Fitzroy River (Qld.) T2—943 5
Five Confucian Classics 299.512 82
Five dynasties (China) 951.018
Five pillars of Islam 297.31
Five scrolls (Bible) 221.044

Fixation
  microscopy 502.82
Fixation (Histology) 570.282 7
Fixatives
  painting material
    arts 751.2
Fixed assets 332.041 4
  see also Fixed capital
Fixed capital 332.041 4
  accounting 657.73
  financial management 658.152 42
Fixed costs 338.514 2
  financial management 658.155 3
Fixed liabilities
  accounting 657.75
Fixed rate securities 332.632 044
Fixing solutions
  photography 771.54
Fjord-du-Saguenay
    (Quebec) T2—714 16
Flacourtiaceae 583.625
Flag officers 355.009 2
  role and function 355.331
Flag signals
  military engineering 623.731 2
  nautical engineering 623.856 12
Flagella 571.67
Flagellates 579.82
Flageolets 788.35
  see also Woodwind
      instruments
Flagler County (Fla.) T2—759 19
Flags 929.92
  armed forces 355.15
  law 344.09
Flagstaff (South Africa :
    District) T2—687 91
Flagstones 553.53
  economic geology 553.53
  quarrying 622.353
  road engineering 625.81
Flame 541.361
Flame-resistant fabrics 677.689
  see also Textiles
Flame throwers 623.445
Flamenco 781.626 104 68
  dance 793.319 468
  music 781.626 104 68
    dance 784.188 2
    songs 782.421 626 10468
  poetry 861.009 946 8
Flameproof fabrics 677.689
  see also Textiles
Flamingos 598.35
Flammability testing 628.922 2
Flammable materials 363.179 8
  fire safety technology 628.922 2
  public safety 363.179 8
  technology 604.7
  see also Hazardous materials
Flanders T2—493 1
Flanders (Belgium) T2—493 1
Flanders (France) T2—442 8
Flannel 677.624
  see also Textiles
Flaps (Aircraft) 629.134 33
Flare stars 523.844 6
Flares
  nautical equipment 623.86
Flash welding 671.521 3
Flashbulb photography 778.72
Flashcards
  cataloging 025.349 6
  library treatment 025.179 6
Flat-backed lutes 787.85
  see also Stringed instruments
Flat-file databases
  computer science 005.752
Flat racing
  horses 798.4
  see also Sports
Flatcars 385.34
  engineering 625.24
  see also Rolling stock
Flatfishes 597.69
  sports fishing 799.176 9
Flathead County (Mont.) T2—786 82
Flathead Lake (Mont.) T2—786 832
Flats 643.2
  apartment house management 647.92
  apartment management 643.2
  architecture 728.314
Flattery
  ethics 177.3
    see also Ethical problems
Flatware
  table setting 642.7
Flatworms 592.4
Flavorings 641.338 2
  agriculture 633.82
  commercial processing 664.5
  cooking with 641.638 2
  economic botany 581.632
  food 641.338 2

Flax
  botany 583.79
  fiber crop 633.52
  textiles 677.11
    arts 746.041 1
    see also Textiles
Flaxseed oil 665.352
Flea beetles 595.764 8
  agricultural pests 632.764 8
Flea-borne typhus
  incidence 614.526 2
  medicine 616.922 2
  see also Communicable diseases (Human)
Flea markets 381.192
  management 658.87
  see also Commerce
Fleabanes 583.99
Fleas 595.775
  disease carriers
    medicine 614.432 4
Fleets (Naval units) 359.31
Fleming County (Ky.) T2—769 56
Flemings T5—393 2
Flemish T5—393 2
Flemish dialect 439.31
  T6—393 1
Flemish literature 839.31
Flesh flies 595.774
Fleshing leather 675.22
Fleshy-finned fishes 597.39
Fleuve (Senegal) T2—663
Flevoland (Netherlands) T2—492 2
Flexibilia 563.92
Flexible algebras 512.24
Flexible manufacturing systems 670.427
  see Manual at 670.427 vs. 670.285
Flexible polymers
  chemistry 547.843
Flexible scheduling 371.242
Flexible working periods 331.257 2
  personnel management 658.312 1
Flexure
  effect on materials 620.112 44
Flickers (Woodpeckers) 598.72
Fliers 629.130 92
Flies 595.77
  agricultural pests 632.77
  disease carriers 571.986
    medicine 614.432 2
Flies (House flies) 595.774
  control technology 628.965 7
Flight (Aeronautics) 629.13
  literature 808.803 56
    history and criticism 809.933 56
    specific literatures T3B—080 356
      history and criticism T3B—093 56
Flight (Animals)
  behavior 591.5
  physiology 573.798
Flight attendants 387.742 092
  occupational group T7—387 7
Flight from Mecca 297.634
Flight guides
  aeronautics 629.132 54
Flight instrumentation
  aircraft 629.135 2
Flight into Egypt 232.92
Flight navigators 629.132 510 92
Flight operations systems
  spacecraft 629.474 2
  unmanned spacecraft 629.464 2
Flight simulators
  aeronautics 629.132 520 78
  manned space flight 629.450 078
Flight tests
  aircraft 629.134 53
Flightless birds 598.16
Flights (Air force units) 358.413 1
Flights (Naval air units) 359.943 4
Flin Flon (Man.) T2—712 72
Flinders Chase National Park (S. Aust.) T2—942 35
Flinders Island (Tas.) T2—946 7
Flinders Ranges (S. Aust.) T2—942 37
Flint 553.65
Flint (Mich.) T2—774 37
Flint River (Ga.) T2—758 9
Flintshire (Wales) T2—429 33
Floater insurance 368.2
  see also Insurance
Floating 532.25
Floating airports
  engineering 629.136 1
Floating bridges 388
  construction 624.87
  see also Bridges
Floating debts
  public finance 336.32
Floating dry docks 623.83
Floating exchange rates 332.456 2
Floating foundations 624.156
Floats (Parades)
  performing arts 791.6
Flocculation
  water supply treatment 628.162 2

Flood barriers 627.42
Flood control 363.349 36
  engineering 627.4
  public administration 354.362 7
  social services 363.349 36
Flood control facilities
  area planning 711.8
Flood control ponds 627.44
Flood insurance 368.122 2
  see also Insurance
Flood wreckage studies 627.4
Flooding
  military engineering 623.31
Floodlighting 621.321 4
  exterior 621.322 9
  see also Lighting
Floodplains 551.442
  biology 578.766
  ecology 577.66
  geography 910.914 4
  geomorphology 551.442
  physical geography 910.021 44
Floods
  crop damage 632.17
  engineering control 627.4
  hydrology 551.489
  social services 363.349 3
  see also Disasters
Floor coverings 645.1
  building construction 698.9
  household management 645.1
Floor exercise (Sports) 796.47
  see also Sports
Floor systems
  bridge engineering 624.283
Floors 721.6
  architecture 721.6
  construction 690.16
  interior decoration 747.4
Floppy disks 004.563
  engineering 621.397 6
Floral arts 745.92
Floral oils 668.542
  customs 391.63
Floral waters 668.542
  customs 391.63
Florence (Italy : Province) T2—455 1
Florence County (S.C.) T2—757 84
Florence County (Wis.) T2—775 32
Flores (Uruguay) T2—895 26
Flores Island (Indonesia) T2—598 6
Flores Sea (Indonesia) 551.465 74
  T2—164 74
Floriculture 635.9
Florida 975.9
  T2—759
Florida (Uruguay : Dept.) T2—895 25
Florida, Straits of 551.464 63
  T2—163 63
Florida Keys (Fla.) T2—759 41
Florida Panhandle T2—759 9
Florideophycideae 579.89
Flórina (Greece : Nome) T2—495 62
Flotation
  ores 622.752
Flotillas (Naval units) 359.31
Flounders 597.69
  cooking 641.692
  food 641.392
  sports fishing 799.176 9
Flour 641.331
  commercial processing 664.720 7
    wheat 664.722 72
  cooking 641.631
  food 641.331
Flour beetles 595.769
Flow
  air mechanics 533.62
  engineering 620.106 4
  fluid mechanics 532.051
  gas mechanics 533.21
  liquid mechanics 532.51
Flow-charting
  computer programming 005.120 28
Flow cytometry
  diagnosis
    medicine 616.075 82
Flow meters
  manufacturing technology 681.28
Flow-of-funds accounts
  macroeconomics 339.26
Flow-of-funds measurement
  accounting 657.48
Flowcharting
  computer programming 005.120 28
Flower arrangements 745.92
Flower beds 635.962
Flower flies 595.774
Flower gardening 635.9
Flower language 302.222
Flowering plants 580
  landscape architecture 716
  see also Plants
  see Manual at 580 vs. 582.13;
    also at 583–584
Flowering trees 635.977 13
  botany 582.16
  ornamental arboriculture 635.977 13

Flowers 582.13
  art representation 704.943 4
  arts 700.464
    T3C—364
  cooking 641.659
  descriptive botany 582.13
  drawing 743.7
  dress customs 391.44
  food 641.359
  gardening 635.9
  literature 808.803 64
    history and criticism 809.933 64
    specific literatures T3B—080 364
      history and criticism T3B—093 64
  painting 758.42
  physiology 575.6
  see Manual at 580 vs. 582.13;
    also at 635.9 vs. 582.1
Flowmeters
  manufacturing technology 681.28
Floyd County (Ga.) T2—758 35
Floyd County (Ind.) T2—772 19
Floyd County (Iowa) T2—777 26
Floyd County (Ky.) T2—769 22
Floyd County (Tex.) T2—764 841
Floyd County (Va.) T2—755 712
Fluctuations (Mathematics) 519.85
Flues
  heating
    buildings 697.8
Flugelhorns 788.97
  instrument 788.971 9
  music 788.97
  see also Brass instruments
Fluid balance
  biochemistry
    humans 612.015 22
      see Manual at 612.01522
        vs. 612.3923,
        616.3992
Fluid balance disorders
  medicine 616.399 2
  see also Digestive system
  see Manual at 612.01522 vs.
    612.3923, 616.3992
Fluid mechanics 532
  engineering 620.106
Fluid metabolism
  biochemistry
    humans 612.015 22
Fluid phases
  fluid-state physics 530.424
Fluid-power technology 620.106
Fluid-state lasers 621.366 2
Fluid-state physics 530.42
Fluidics 629.804 2
Fluidization
  chemical engineering 660.284 292
Fluidized-bed combustion 621.402 3
Fluidized nuclear reactors 621.483 4
Fluids
  biochemistry
    humans 612.015 22
  heat transfer 536.25
  state of matter 530.42
Fluke-caused diseases
  incidence 614.553
  medicine 616.963
  see also Communicable
    diseases (Human)
Flukes (Worms) 592.48
Fluorescence 535.352
  mineralogy 549.125
Fluorescence spectroscopy 543.085 84
Fluorescent lighting 621.327 3
  see also Lighting
Fluoridation 614.599 6
  dental disease prevention 614.599 6
    see also Dentistry
  water supply engineering 628.166 3
Fluorine 553.95
  chemical engineering 661.073 1
  chemistry 546.731
  economic geology 553.95
  organic chemistry 547.02
    applied 661.891
  see also Chemicals
Fluorite
  mineralogy 549.4
Fluoroscopy
  medicine 616.075 72
Fluorspar
  mineralogy 549.4
Flute concertos 784.283 2
Flute family 788.3
  see also Woodwind
    instruments
Flutes 788.32
  instrument 788.321 9
  music 788.32
  see also Woodwind
    instruments
Flutists 788.320 92
  occupational group T7—788
Flutter
  aeronautics 629.132 362
Fluvanna County (Va.) T2—755 47
Flux (Metallurgy) 669.84

Fly fishing 799.124
Fly River Province (Papua New Guinea) T2—954 9
Fly tying (Fishing)
technology 688.791 24
Flycatchers (New World) 598.823
Flycatchers (Old World) 598.848
Flying (Aeronautics) 629.132 5
sports 797.5
see also Sports
see also Flight (Aeronautics)
Flying (Animals)
behavior 591.5
physiology 573.798
Flying discs (Game) 796.2
see also Sports
Flying fishes 597.66
Flying foxes 599.49
Flying jeeps
engineering 629.133 35
military engineering 623.746 047
Flying lemurs 599.33
Flying reptiles 567.918
Flying saucers 001.942
Flying squirrels 599.369
FM radio stations 384.545 3
see also Radio stations
FM radio systems 621.384 152
Foam glass 666.157
Foam latex 678.532
Foamed plastics 668.493
Foams 541.345 14
chemical engineering 660.294 514
Foard County (Tex.) T2—764 748
Focusing apparatus 771.37
Foehns (Winds) 551.518 5
Foggia (Italy : Province) T2—457 57
Fogs 541.345 15
colloid chemistry 541.345 15
applied 660.294 515
meteorology 551.575
Foils
use in cooking 641.589
Foix (Ariège, France) T2—448 8
Fokís (Greece) T2—495 15
Folding boxes 676.32
Folds (Geology) 551.875
Foliage plants 635.975
Foliations 514.72
Folk arts 745
Folk beliefs
folklore 398.41
Folk dancers 793.319 2
social group T7—793 3
Folk dancing 793.31
see Manual at 792.78 vs. 792.8, 793.3
Folk high schools 374.83
Folk literature 398.2
see also Literature
see Manual at 398.2; *also at* 398.2 vs. 291.13; *also at* 398.2 vs. 398.3–398.4; *also at* 398.2093–398.2099; *also at* 800 vs. 398.2
Folk medicine
folklore 398.27
history and criticism 398.353
therapeutics 615.882
see Manual at 398.27, 398.353 vs. 615.882; *also at* 615.882
Folk music 781.62
modes 781.263
songs 782.421 62
see Manual at 781.62 vs. 780.89
Folk musicians 781.620 092
occupational group T7—781 6
Folk rock 781.66
Folk singers 782.421 620 092
Folk songs 782.421 62
Folklore 398
history and criticism 398.09
Folklorists 398.092
occupational group T7—39
Folkways 306
sociology 390
Follicles
hair
human anatomy 611.78
medicine 616.546
see also Hair
Fon (African people) T5—963 37
Fon language 496.337
T6—963 37
Fond du Lac County (Wis.) T2—775 68
Fondues 641.81
Foochow dialect 495.17
T6—951 7
Food 641.3
armed forces supplies 355.81
commercial processing
economics 338.476 64
technology 664
cooking 641.5
customs 394.1

Food (continued)
  elementary education 372.37
  health 613.2
  home economics 641.3
  home preservation 641.4
  literature 808.803 55
    history and criticism 809.933 55
    specific literatures T3B—080 355
      history and criticism T3B—093 55
  nutritional content 613.2
    public administration 353.997
  preservation techniques 664.028
    commercial 664.028
    home 641.4
  product safety 363.192
    criminology 364.142
      criminal law 345.024 2
    law 344.042 32
    public administration 353.997
    see also Product safety
  social welfare 361.05
    public administration 353.56
  see Manual at 363.8 vs. 613.2, 641.3; *also at* 630 vs. 579–590, 641.3: Interdisciplinary numbers
Food addiction 362.27
  medicine 616.852 6
  social welfare 362.27
  see also Mental illness
Food additives 641.3
  commercial technology 664.06
    preservation 664.028 7
  food 641.3
  home preservation 641.47
  human toxicology 615.954
  law 344.042 32
  see also Food—product safety
Food adulteration 363.192
  criminology 364.142
    criminal law 345.024 2
  see also Food—product safety
Food allergies
  incidence 614.599 35
  medicine 616.975
  see also Diseases (Human)
Food biotechnology 664.024
Food board 676.288
Food cartons 676.34
Food chains (Ecology) 577.16
Food colors
  commercial 664.062
Food demand
  economics 338.19
Food guides 641.31
Food habits (Animals) 591.53
Food industry (Production) 338.19
  law 343.076
Food inspection 363.192 64
  see also Food—product safety
Food microbiology 664.001 579
Food plants 641.303
  agriculture 630
  economic botany 581.632
  food 641.303
Food poisons
  human toxicology 615.954
Food processing industry 338.476 64
Food production 338.19
Food rationing 363.856
Food relief 363.883
  international law 341.766
  law 344.033
Food reserves
  economics 338.19
Food safety 363.192
  see also Food—product safety
Food services
  employee services 658.383
  schools 371.716
Food services industry 338.476 479 5
Food stamp programs 363.882
Food stocks
  economics 338.19
  see also Food supply
Food storage (Plant physiology) 575.78
Food supply 363.8
  economics 338.19
  social welfare 363.8
    law 344.033
  spacecraft 629.477 3
  see Manual at 363.5, 363.6, 363.8 vs. 338; *also at* 363.8 vs. 338.19; *also at* 363.8 vs. 613.2, 641.3
Food taboos
  customs 394.16
  religion 291.446
    Hinduism 294.544 6
    Islam 297.576
    Judaism 296.73
Food technologists 664.009 2
  occupational group T7—664
Food technology 664
  equipment manufacturing technology 681.766 4
Food webs (Ecology) 577.16

Foodstuffs 641.3
see also Food
Foot forces (Military) 356
Foot warfare 356
Foot washing
Christian rite 265.9
Football 796.33
electronic games 794.863 3
equipment technology 688.763 3
see also Sports
Football cards 796.332 075
Football players 796.330 92
American football 796.332 092
Australian football 796.336 092
Canadian football 796.335 092
rugby 796.333 092
soccer 796.334 092
sports group T7—796 33
Football rattles 786.886
see also Percussion instruments
Footings
walls 721.2
construction 690.12
see also Walls (Building element)
Footpaths 388.12
see also Pedestrian paths
Footwear 391.413
commercial technology 685.3
customs 391.413
see also Clothing
For-hire carriers 388.041
truck 388.324 3
see also Freight services; Passenger services
Forage crops 633.2
feeds 636.086
Forage grasses 633.2
agriculture 633.2
botany 584.9
Foraminifera 579.44
paleozoology 561.994
Forbes (N.S.W.) T2—944 5
Force (Energy)
philosophy 118
Force (International politics) 327.117
Force and energy 531.6
Forces (Mechanics) 531.113
Forcing (Plants) 631.583
floriculture 635.982
gardening 635.048 3
Forcipulata 593.93
paleozoology 563.93
Ford, Gerald R.
United States history 973.925
Ford County (Ill.) T2—773 62
Ford County (Kan.) T2—781 76
Forearm techniques
music 784.193 62
Forebrain
human physiology 612.825
see also Nervous system
Forecasting 003.2
T1—011 2
business 338.544
investments 332.678
management decision making 658.403 55
marketing management 658.818
occultism 133.3
social change 303.49
weather 551.63
see Manual at 003.2
Forecasting methods
economics 338.544 2
Forecasts 003.2
T1—011 2
business 338.544 3
social change 303.49
see Manual at 003.2
Foreclosure 346.043 64
Forehand
tennis 796.342 22
Foreign affairs 327
Foreign affairs departments 353.13
Foreign aid 338.91
economics 338.91
international law 341.759
law 343.074 8
international relations 327.111
law 342.041 2
military science 355.032
public administration 353.132 73
Foreign assistance 338.91
see also Foreign aid
Foreign bodies
removal from wounds
medicine 617.146
Foreign economic assistance 338.91
see also Foreign aid
Foreign economic policies 337
Foreign economic relations 337
Foreign enterprises 338.88
see also International enterprises
Foreign exchange 332.45
international law 341.751 45
law 343.032

Foreign income
  tax economics 336.24
  tax law 343.052 48
Foreign intelligence 327.12
  see also Espionage
Foreign investment 332.673
  international law 341.752
  law 346.092
Foreign labor 331.62
  law 344.016 2
Foreign language groups
  journalism for 070.484
Foreign languages
  elementary education 372.65
Foreign legions 355.359
Foreign licensing
  management 658.18
Foreign loans 336.343 5
  international law 341.751 15
  law 346.073
  public finance 336.343 5
  role of banks 332.15
Foreign merchants 382.092
Foreign missions
  Christianity 266.023
Foreign news
  journalism 070.433 2
    see Manual at 070.433
Foreign-owned enterprises 338.88
  see also International enterprises
Foreign policy 327.1
Foreign relations 327
  law 342.041 2
  public administration 353.13
  see also International relations
Foreign service (Diplomatic service)
  public administration 353.132 63
Foreign shorthair cats 636.82
Foreign students 371.826 91
Foreign study 370.116
Foreign trade 382
  commerce 382
  international law 341.754
  law 343.087
  public administration 354.74
Foreign traders 382.092
  occupational group T7—382
Foreign words 412
  specific languages T4—24
Foreigners T1—086 91
Forenames 929.44
Forensic medicine 614.1
Forensic orations 347.075
Forensic pathology 614.1
Forensic psychiatry 614.1
Forensic psychology 347.066 019
  criminal law 345.066 019
Forensic science 363.25
  see also Criminal investigation
Forensic toxicology 614.1
Foreordination (Christian doctrine) 234.9
Forest biology 578.73
Forest County (Pa.) T2—748 68
Forest County (Wis.) T2—775 31
Forest ecology 577.3
Forest fires 363.379
  forestry 634.961 8
  social services 363.379
  see also Fire safety
Forest Heath (England) T2—426 43
Forest lands 333.75
  T2—152
  biology 578.73
  ecology 577.3
  economics 333.75
    sale and rental 333.335 7
  geography 910.915 2
  landscape architecture 719.33
  law 346.046 75
  physical geography 910.021 52
  recreational resources 333.784
  see Manual at 338.1749 vs. 333.75
Forest management 634.92
Forest nurseries 634.956 4
Forest of Bowland T2—427 685
Forest of Dean (England : District) T2—424 13
Forest products 634.98
Forest reserves 333.75
  see also Forest lands
Forest saltwater wetlands
  biology 578.769 7
  ecology 577.697
  see also Wetlands
Forest thinning 634.953
Forest wetlands
  biology 578.768 3
  ecology 577.683
  see also Wetlands
Forest yaws
  incidence 614.534
  medicine 616.936 4
  see also Communicable diseases (Human)

Forestation 333.751 52
see also Afforestation
Foresters 634.909 2
occupational group T7—634
Forestry 634.9
public administration 354.55
Forestry law 346.046 75
industry 343.076 49
protection 346.046 75
Forests 333.75
T2—152
see also Forest lands
Forfeit games 793.5
Forge welding 671.529
Forgeries
arts 702.874
books 098.3
museology 069.54
paintings 751.58
Forgery 364.163
economics
financial instruments 332.9
law 345.026 3
Forget-me-nots 635.933 94
botany 583.94
floriculture 635.933 94
Forgetting 153.125
Forging 671.332
blacksmithing 682
decorative arts 739.14
sculpture 731.41
Forgiveness (Christian doctrine) 234.5
Fork lifts 621.863
Forlì (Italy : Province) T2—454 8
Form (Concept)
arts 701.8
drawing 741.018
philosophy 117
Form books
law 347.055
Form criticism
sacred books 291.82
Bible 220.663
Talmud 296.120 663
Form letters
office use 651.752
Formal analysis
music 781.8
Formal dress 391
commercial technology 687.16
customs 391
home sewing 646.47
see also Clothing
Formal grammars 511.3
programming languages 005.131
Formal groups 512.2
Formal languages 511.3
programming languages 005.131
Formal usage (Language) 418
specific languages T4—8
Formaldehyde
human toxicology 615.951 36
Format publishing 686
Formations
sports
American football 796.332 22
soccer 796.334 22
Formentera (Spain) T2—467 56
Former Yugoslav Republic of Macedonia T2—497 6
Formicariidae 598.822 6
Formicidae 595.796
Formosa 951.249
T2—512 49
Formosa (Argentina : Province) T2—823 5
Formosa Strait 551.465 57
T2—164 57
Formosan native peoples T5—992 5
Forms
public administration 352.387
Forms (Law) 347.055
Forms (Mathematics) 512.944
Forms of address
etiquette 395.4
Forms of music 781.8
instrumental 784.18
vocal 782
Formula feeds 636.085 57
commercial processing 664.768
Formula plans
investments 332.678
Formularies
pharmacology 615.13
Formulas T1—021 2
Forrest County (Miss.) T2—762 18
Forster (N.S.W.) T2—944 2
Forsyth County (Ga.) T2—758 265
Forsyth County (N.C.) T2—756 67
Forsythias 635.933 87
botany 583.87
floriculture 635.933 87
Fort Beaufort (South Africa : District) T2—687 5
Fort Bend County (Tex.) T2—764 135
Fort Franklin (N.W.T.) T2—719 6
Fort Gibson Lake (Okla.) T2—766 87

Fort Gibson Reservoir (Okla.) T2—766 87
Fort Lauderdale (Fla.) T2—759 35
Fort Loudon Lake (Tenn.) T2—768 85
Fort Macleod (Alta.) T2—712 34
Fort McMurray (Alta.) T2—712 32
Fort Nelson (B.C.) T2—711 87
Fort Nelson-Liard (B.C.) T2—711 87
Fort Nelson River (B.C.) T2—711 87
Fort Norman (N.W.T.) T2—719 6
Fort Peck Lake (Mont.) T2—786 17
Fort Qu'Appelle (Sask.) T2—712 44
Fort Simpson (N.W.T.) T2—719 3
Fort Smith (N.W.T.) T2—719 3
Fort Smith (N.W.T. : Region) T2—719 3
see Manual at T2—7193–T2—7197
Fort St. John (B.C.) T2—711 87
Fort Wayne (Ind.) T2—772 74
Fort Worth (Tex.) T2—764 531 5
Forth, Firth of (Scotland) 551.461 36
T2—163 36
Forth River (Scotland) T2—413 1
Fortification
basic training 355.544
military engineering 623.1
Fortresses
architecture 725.18
military engineering 623.1
Forts
architecture 725.18
military engineering 623.1
military installations 355.7
Fortune-tellers 133.309 2
occupational group T7—13
Fortune-telling 133.3
Forty Hours devotion
Roman Catholic liturgy 264.027 4
Forums (Discussion and debate)
rhetoric 808.53
Forward exchange 332.45
Forward play
sports
rugby 796.333 23
soccer 796.334 23
Fossa 599.742
Fossil fuels 553.2
chemistry 547.82
economic geology 553.2
electric generation 621.312 132
public administration 354.44
resource economics 333.82
Fossil gums 553.29
mining 622.339
Fossil resins 553.29
mining 622.339
Fossils 560
Foster children 306.874
T1—085 4
T7—044 1
family relationships 306.874
home care 649.145
psychology 155.445
social welfare 362.733
Foster County (N.D.) T2—784 516
Foster homes 362.733
crime prevention 364.44
social welfare 362.733
see also Children—social welfare
Foster parents 306.874
T1—085
T7—043 1
family relationships 306.874
social welfare 362.733
Fotonovelas 741.5
Foucault's pendulum 525.36
Found objects
handicrafts 745.584
sculpture material 731.2
Foundation engineering 624.15
Foundation soils 624.151
railroad engineering 625.122
road engineering 625.732
Foundations (Building elements) 721.1
architecture 721.1
bridge engineering 624.284
construction 690.11
structural engineering 624.15
Foundations (Organizations) 060
law 346.064
social welfare 361.763 2
Founders of religions 291.63
Founding (Metalworking) 671.2
Fountain County (Ind.) T2—772 47
Fountains
landscape architecture 714
sculpture 731.72
Fouquieriaceae 583.628
Four Corners Region T2—792 59
Four-horned antelopes 599.642
Four-o'clock (Plant) 635.933 53
botany 583.53
floriculture 635.933 53
Four-year colleges 378.154 2
Four-year junior colleges 378.154 3

Fourier analysis 515.243 3
Fourier transform 515.723
Fourierism (Socialist school)
  economics 335.23
Fouriesburg (South Africa : District) T2—685 1
Fourth-class mail 383.125
  see also Postal service
Fourth dimension 530.11
Fourth International 324.175
Fourth of July 394.263 4
Fourth Republic (France) 944.082
Fowling 799.24
Fox hunting
  sports 799.259 775
Fox River (Wis.) T2—775 6
Fox squirrel 599.362
Fox trot 793.33
Foxes 599.775
  conservation technology 639.979 775
  resource economics 333.959 775
  small game hunting 799.259 775
  trapping 639.117 75
Foxgloves 635.933 95
  botany 583.95
  floriculture 635.933 95
Fractals
  mathematics 514.742
Fractional calculus 515.83
Fractional distillation
  chemical engineering 660.284 25
  petroleum 665.532
Fractionation
  air
    gas technology 665.82
  oils and gases 665.028 3
Fractions 513.26
Fracture
  crystals 548.842
  mineralogy 549.121
Fracture mechanics 620.112 6
Fracture strength
  materials science 620.112 6
Fractures
  medicine 617.15
Fragile X syndrome
  medicine 616.858 8
  see also Mental retardation
Fragrance plants (Floriculture) 635.968
Frame harps 787.95
  see also Stringed instruments
Frame-shaped drums 786.95
  see also Percussion instruments
Frame zithers 787.73
  see also Stringed instruments
Framed soaps 668.124
Frames
  naval architecture 623.817 73
  optical instruments
    manufacturing technology 681.43
  structural engineering 624.177 3
  wood construction 694.2
France 944
  T2—44
  ancient 936.4
    T2—364
France. Assemblée nationale constituante (1789–1791)
  French history 944.041
France. Assemblée nationale législative (1791–1792)
  French history 944.041
France. Convention nationale
  French history 944.043
France. Estates-General
  French history 944.041
France. Etats généraux
  French history 944.041
France. Legislative Assembly (1791–1792)
  French history 944.041
France. National Assembly (1789–1791)
  French history 944.041
France. National Convention
  French history 944.043
France, Southern T2—448
Franche-Comté (France) T2—444 5
Francheville (Quebec) T2—714 451
Franchises
  governmental
    public revenue 336.11
  international law 341.758
  law 346.048
  retail 381.13
    management 658.870 8
    see also Commerce
Francis I, Holy Roman Emperor
  German history 943.055
Francis I, King of France
  French history 944.028
Francis II, King of France
  French history 944.029
Francis Case, Lake (S.D.) T2—783 38

Franciscans 255.3
  church history 271.3
  women 255.973
    church history 271.973
Francisco Morazán (Honduras) T2—728 371
Francium 669.725
  chemistry 546.386
  metallurgy 669.725
  see also Chemicals
Franco, Francisco
  Spanish history 946.082
Franco, Itamar
  Brazilian history 981.064
Franco-German War, 1870–1871 943.082
Franco-Provençal language 449
  T6—49
Franco-Provençal literature 849
Franco-Prussian War, 1870–1871 943.082
Francolins 598.623
Franconia (Germany) T2—433
Franconian dialect 437.3
  T6—32
Franconian emperors
  German history 943.023
Franconian Jura (Germany) T2—433
Frankfort (Ky.) T2—769 432
Frankfort (South Africa : District) T2—685 1
Frankfurt am Main (Germany) T2—434 164
Frankfurt an der Oder (Germany) T2—431 532
Frankfurt an der Oder (Germany : Bezirk) T2—431 53
Frankia 579.37
Franking privileges 383.120 2
  see also Postal service
Fränkische Alb (Germany) T2—433
Frankish rule
  Italian history 945.02
Franklin (N.W.T.) T2—719 5
Franklin (State) 976.803
  T2—768
Franklin (Va.) T2—755 553
Franklin County (Ala.) T2—761 913
Franklin County (Ark.) T2—767 34
Franklin County (Fla.) T2—759 91
Franklin County (Ga.) T2—758 135
Franklin County (Idaho) T2—796 42
Franklin County (Ill.) T2—773 94
Franklin County (Ind.) T2—772 15
Franklin County (Iowa) T2—777 28
Franklin County (Kan.) T2—781 66
Franklin County (Ky.) T2—769 432
Franklin County (Mass.) T2—744 22
Franklin County (Me.) T2—741 72
Franklin County (Miss.) T2—762 27
Franklin County (Mo.) T2—778 63
Franklin County (N.C.) T2—756 54
Franklin County (N.Y.) T2—747 55
Franklin County (Neb.) T2—782 377
Franklin County (Ohio) T2—771 56
Franklin County (Pa.) T2—748 44
Franklin County (Tenn.) T2—768 63
Franklin County (Tex.) T2—764 213
Franklin County (Va.) T2—755 68
Franklin County (Vt.) T2—743 13
Franklin County (Wash.) T2—797 33
Franklin D. Roosevelt Lake (Wash.) T2—797 23
Franklin District (N.Z.) T2—933 1
  Auckland Region T2—932 7
  Waikato Region T2—933 1
Franklin Parish (La.) T2—763 77
Franz Josef Land (Russia) T2—985
Fraser Canyon (B.C.) T2—711 37
Fraser-Cheam (B.C.) T2—711 37
Fraser-Fort George (B.C.) T2—711 82
Fraser Island (Qld.) T2—943 2
Fraser Plateau (B.C.) T2—711 75
Fraser River (B.C.) T2—711 3
Fraserburg (South Africa : District) T2—687 17
Fraternal insurance 368.363
  see also Insurance
Fraternal organizations 366
Fraternities
  education 371.855
Fraud 364.163
  criminology 364.163
  law 345.026 3
  occultism 133
  prevention
    management 658.473
Fraudulent claims 364.163
  criminology 364.163
  insurance 368.014
  law 345.026 3
Fraudulent elections 324.66
  criminology 364.132 4
    criminal law 345.023 24
Frazil ice 551.344
Freaks (Circuses) 791.35
Fréchet algebras 512.55
Frederick, the Great
  German history 943.053

Frederick I, Holy Roman Emperor
German history 943.024
Frederick II, King of Prussia
German history 943.053
Frederick III, Emperor of Germany
German history 943.028
Frederick III, German Emperor
German history 943.084
Frederick Barbarossa, Holy Roman Emperor
German history 943.024
Frederick County (Md.) T2—752 87
Frederick County (Va.) T2—755 992
Fredericksburg (Va.) T2—755 366
Fredericton (N.B.) T2—715 515
Frederiksberg (Denmark) T2—489 13
Frederiksborg (Denmark) T2—489 1
Fredholm equations 515.45
Free aerophones 788.29
see also Wind instruments
Free algebras 512.24
Free assistance (Social welfare) 361.02
see also Welfare services
Free balloons
engineering 629.133 22
military engineering 623.742
Free Church of Scotland 285.234
see also Presbyterian Church
Free churches 280.4
see also Protestantism
Free enterprise 330.122
economics 330.122
sociology 306.342
Free labor 331.117 2
sociology 306.366
Free land 333.16
Free love 306.735
Free mail 383.120 2
see also Postal service
Free market price determination 338.522
Free materials
bibliographies 011.03
Free Methodist Church of North America 287.2
see also Methodist Church
Free-piston engines 621.433 5
Free ports 387.13
see also Ports
Free press and fair trial 347.05
Free products
catalogs T1—029 4
Free radicals (Chemicals) 541.224
Free reeds 788.8
see also Woodwind instruments
Free schools (Alternative schools) 371.04
Free services
catalogs T1—029 4
Free Soil Party 324.273 2
Free television 384.554
Free thought 211.4
Free time
sociology 306.481 2
Free trade 382.71
see also Customs (Tariff)
Free universities (Alternative higher education) 378.03
see also Higher education
Free will
philosophy 123.5
religion 291.22
Christianity 233.7
soteriology 234.9
Islam 297.227
Judaism 296.32
Freeborn County (Minn.) T2—776 18
Freedmen's Bureau
United States history 973.714
Freedom
philosophy 123.5
Freedom of action 323.44
Freedom of association 323.47
Freedom of conscience 323.442
Freedom of contract 323.46
Freedom of publication 323.445
law 342.085 3
Freedom of religion 323.442
see also Religious freedom
Freedom of speech 323.443
law 342.085 3
Freedom of the press 323.445
law 342.085 3
Freemasonry 366.1
Freemasons 366.1
biography 366.109 2
social group T7—366 1
Freesias 635.934 38
botany 584.38
floriculture 635.934 38
Freestone County (Tex.) T2—764 232
Freestyle skiing 796.937
see also Sports
Freestyle wrestling 796.812 3
see also Sports
Freetown (Sierra Leone) T2—664

Freeways 388.122
see also Roads
Freewill Baptists 286.2
see also Baptists
Freeze-dried foods
cooking 641.614
Freeze-drying foods 664.028 45
commercial preservation 664.028 45
home preservation 641.44
Freezers 621.57
kitchen appliances 641.453 028
low-temperature engineering 621.57
Freezing 536.42
Freezing foods 664.028 53
commercial preservation 664.028 53
home preservation 641.453
Fregatidae 598.43
Frei Montalva, Eduardo
Chilean history 983.064 5
Freiburg (Germany : Regierungsbezirk) T2—434 62
Freiburg (Switzerland) T2—494 53
Freiburg im Breisgau (Germany) T2—434 626
Freight and freightage 388.044
see also Freight services
Freight cars 385.34
engineering 625.24
see also Rolling stock
Freight insurance 368.2
see also Insurance
Freight services 388.044
air 387.744
airport services 387.736 4
international law 341.756 78
law 343.097 8
automobile 388.321
bus 388.322 2
international law 341.756 882
law 343.094 82
terminal services 388.33
ferries 386.6
ground 388.044
international law 341.756
law 343.093 2
inland waterway 386.244
international law 341.756 68
law 343.096 8
port services 386.864
international law 341.756
law 343.093 2
marine 387.544
international law 341.756 68
law 343.096 8
Freight services
marine (continued)
port services 387.164
port services 387.164
engineering 623.888 1
public administration 354.764
railroad 385.24
international law 341.756 58
law 343.095 8
special purpose 385.5
terminal services 385.264
truck 388.324
international law 341.756 883
law 343.094 83
terminal services 388.33
urban 388.413 24
terminal services 388.473
Freight terminals 388.044
architecture 725.3
area planning 711.7
construction 690.53
inland waterway 386.853
ports 387.153
Freighters (Ships) 387.245
engineering 623.824 5
see also Ships
Fremantle (W.A.) T2—941 1
Fremont County (Colo.) T2—788 53
Fremont County (Idaho) T2—796 56
Fremont County (Iowa) T2—777 77
Fremont County (Wyo.) T2—787 63
French (People) T5—41
French and Indian War, 1756–1763 940.253 4
North American history 973.26
French Broad River (N.C. and Tenn.) T2—768 895
French bulldog 636.72
French Cameroons T2—671 1
French-Canadian literature 840
French-Canadians T5—114
French Community T2—171 244
French Congo (Brazzaville) T2—672 4
French creole languages 447.9
T6—417
French Equatorial Africa 967.203
T2—672
Central African history 967.410 3
Chadian history 967.430 2
Congolese history 967.240 3
Gabonese history 967.210 2
French Flanders T2—442 8
French folk music 781.624 1

French folk songs 782.421 624 1
French Guiana 988.2
T2—882
French Guinea 966.520 3
T2—665 2
French horns 788.94
instrument 788.941 9
music 788.94
see also Brass instruments
French Indochina 959.703
T2—597
Cambodian history 959.603
Laotian history 959.403
Vietnamese history 959.703
French Island (Vic.) T2—945 2
French language 440
T6—41
French literature 840
French pastry 641.865 9
commercial processing 664.752 5
home preparation 641.865 9
French Polynesia T2—962
French Revolution 944.04
French Riviera (France) T2—449
French Somaliland 967.710 32
T2—677 1
French-speaking West Africa T2—660 917 541
French Sudan 966.230 3
T2—662 3
French Territory of the Afars and Issas 967.710 34
T2—677 1
French West Indies T2—729 76
Frenchmans Cap National Park (Tas.) T2—946 6
Frequency allocation
radio 384.545 24
television 384.552 1
Frequency bridges
electric engineering 621.374 7
Frequency distributions 519.532
Frequency meters
electric engineering 621.374 7
Frequency-modulation radio systems 621.384 152
Frequency modulators
electronic circuits 621.381 536 3
Frequency synthesizers 621.381 548 6
Fresco painting 751.44
Frescoes 751.73
Fresh water 553.7
T2—169
economic geology 553.7
hydrology 551.48
Freshwater animals 591.76
Freshwater aquariums 639.34
Freshwater biological resources 333.952 8
Freshwater biology 578.76
see Manual at 578.76–578.77 vs. 551.46
Freshwater ecology 577.6
Freshwater eels 597.432
see also Eels (Freshwater)
Freshwater fishes 597.176
culture 639.31
see also Fishes
Freshwater fishing 639.21
commercial 639.21
sports 799.11
Freshwater hatchetfishes 597.48
Freshwater hydrology 551.48
Freshwater lagoons 551.482
T2—169 2
biology 578.763
ecology 577.63
Freshwater plants 581.76
Freshwater zebra fishes 597.482
Fresno (Calif.) T2—794 83
Fresno County (Calif.) T2—794 82
Freudian psychology 150.195 2
Freycinet National Park (Tas.) T2—946 4
Friaries
architecture 726.7
church history 271
religious significance of buildings 246.97
Fribourg (Switzerland) T2—494 53
Friction 531.113 4
fluid mechanics 532.053 3
gas mechanics 533.28
liquid mechanics 532.58
machine engineering 621.89
solid mechanics 531.4
Friction drums 786.98
see also Percussion instruments
Friction idiophones 786.86
set 786.86
single 786.888
see also Percussion instruments
Friction resistance
materials science 620.112 92

Frictional unemployment 331.137 045
Friday
  Islamic observance 297.36
Friedel-Crafts reaction 547.21
  chemical engineering 660.284 41
Friedreich's ataxia
  medicine 616.83
  see also Nervous system
Friendly fire casualties (Military science) 355.422
Friendly Islands 996.12
  T2—961 2
Friendly societies 334.7
  economics 334.7
  insurance 368
    see also Insurance
Friends (Religious society) 289.6
  biography 289.609 2
  see also Society of Friends
Friends of the library
    organizations 021.7
Friendship 177.62
  applied psychology 158.25
  ethics
    religion 291.567 62
  literature 808.803 53
    history and criticism 809.933 53
    specific literatures T3B—080 353
      history and criticism T3B—093 53
  philosophy 177.62
  psychological influence 155.925
  social psychology 302.34
  see also Ethical problems
Friesian language 439.2
  T6—392
Friesians T5—392
Friesland (Germany) T2—435 917
Friesland (Netherlands) T2—492 13
Frieze (Fabric) 677.617
  see also Textiles
Frigate birds 598.43
Frigid zones T2—11
  biology 578.091 1
  diseases
    medicine 616.988 1
    see also Environmental diseases (Human)
  ecology 577.091 1
  health 613.111
Frigidity
  medicine 616.858 32
  see also Mental illness
Fringe benefits 331.255
  economics 331.255
  personnel management 658.325
    T1—068 3
    executives 658.407 25
  public administration 354.98
Fringes
  arts 746.27
Fringes (Judaism) 296.461
Fringillidae 598.883
Frio County (Tex.) T2—764 442
Frisbees® 796.2
  see also Sports
Frisian language 439.2
  T6—392
Frisian literature 839.2
Friuli-Venezia Giulia (Italy) T2—453 9
Friulian dialect 459.9
  T6—599
Friulian literature 859.9
Frobisher Bay (N.W.T.) T2—719 5
Frogbits 584.73
Frogfishes 597.62
Frogmen (Navy) 359.984
Frogmouths 598.99
Frogs 597.89
  farming 639.378 9
  food 641.396
    commercial processing 664.95
    cooking 641.696
    home preservation 641.495
  zoology 597.89
Frogs (Track crossings) 625.163
Fromm, Erich
  psychological system 150.195 7
Fronds (Plants) 581.48
  descriptive botany 581.48
  physiology 575.57
Front axles
  automotive engineering 629.247
Front-end systems 025.04
  computer science 005.758
  information science 025.04
Front Range (Colo. and Wyo.) T2—788 6
Front yards
  landscape architecture 712.6
Frontenac (Ont.) T2—713 71
Frontenac (Quebec : County) T2—714 69
Frontier County (Neb.) T2—782 835
Frontier defense 355.45
Frontier troops 355.351
Fronts (Meteorology) 551.551 2

Frosinone (Italy : Province) T2—456 22
Frost 551.38
  cold spell 551.525 3
    weather forecasting 551.642 53
    weather modification 551.682 53
  geologic agent 551.38
  hydrometeorology 551.574 4
Frost injury to crops 632.11
Frostbite
  medicine 616.58
  see also Skin
Froths 541.345 14
  chemical engineering 660.294 514
Frottole 782.43
Frozen desserts 641.86
  commercial processing 637.4
  home preparation 641.86
Frozen dinners
  commercial processing 664.65
  home serving 642.1
Frozen foods
  cooking 641.615 3
Frozen human embryos 346.017
Frozen seawater
  geology 551.343
Frozen yogurt 641.862
  commercial processing 637.4
  home preparation 641.862
Fructose 572.565
  biochemistry 572.565
  chemistry 547.781 3
  see also Carbohydrates
Fruit 581.464
  see also Fruits
Fruit arrangements 745.924
Fruit culture 634
Fruit flies 595.774
  agricultural pests 634.049 774
Fruit growers 634.092
  occupational group T7—634
Fruit juices 641.34
  commercial processing 663.63
  cooking with 641.64
  food 641.34
  home preparation 641.875
Fruits 581.464
  art representation 704.943 4
  commercial preservation 664.8
  cooking 641.64
  descriptive botany 581.464
  drawing 743.7
  food 641.34
  forest products 634.987
  home preservation 641.4
Fruits (continued)
  orchard crop 634
  paleobotany 561.14
  physiology 575.67
  product safety 363.192 9
    see also Food—product safety
Frustration 152.47
Frying 641.77
Frying pans
  electric cooking 641.586
Fthiótis (Greece) T2—495 15
Fu'ād I, King of Egypt
  Egyptian history 962.051
Fu'ād II, King of Egypt
  Egyptian history 962.052
Fucales 579.888
Fuchsias 635.933 76
  botany 583.76
  floriculture 635.933 76
Fucus 579.888
Fuel alcohols 662.669 2
Fuel cells 621.312 429
Fuel engineers 662.609 2
  occupational group T7—662
Fuel oils 665.538 4
Fuel resources
  economics 333.82
  extraction
    economics 338.2
  law 346.046 82
  public administration 354.4
Fuel systems
  automotive 629.253
Fueling 388.041
  aircraft 387.736 4
  boats 387.168
  buses 388.33
    urban 388.473
  ships 387.168
  trains 385.26
  trucks 388.33
    urban 388.473
Fuels 662.6
  aircraft 629.134 351
  automotive 629.253 8
  chemical engineering 662.6
  heat engineering 621.402 3
  heating buildings 697.04
  marine engines 623.874
  metallurgical furnaces 669.81
  military supplies 355.83
  nuclear reactors 621.483 35
  public administration 354.4

Fuels (continued)
  resource economics 333.82
  spacecraft 629.475
  steam engineering 621.182
  unmanned spacecraft 629.465
Fuelwood 333.953 97
Fugitive slaves
  Civil War (United States)
    cause 973.711 5
Fugue (Mind)
  medicine 616.852 32
  see also Mental illness
Fugues 784.187 2
Fujairah (United Arab Emirates : Emirate) T2—535 7
Fujayrah (United Arab Emirates : Emirate) T2—535 7
Fuji, Mount (Japan) T2—521 66
Fuji-san (Japan) T2—521 66
Fujian Sheng (China) T2—512 45
Fujiyama (Japan) T2—521 66
Fukien Province (China) T2—512 45
Fukui-ken (Japan) T2—521 55
Fukuoka-ken (Japan) T2—522 2
Fukushima-ken (Japan) T2—521 17
Fulah (African people) T5—963 22
Fulah language 496.322
  T6—963 22
Fulah literature 896.322
Fulani (African people) T5—963 22
Fulani Empire 966.950 1
  T2—669 5
Fulani language 496.322
  T6—963 22
Fulani literature 896.322
Full employment policies 331.120 42
  macroeconomics 339.5
  see Manual at 331.12042 vs. 331.1377
Full orchestras 784.2
Full-scale plants
  chemical engineering 660.280 73
Full scores 780
  treatises 780.264
Full-text databases 025.04
  computer science 005.759
  information science 025.04
Full-year school 371.236
Fuller's earth 553.61
  economic geology 553.61
  mining 622.361
Fulmars 598.42
Fulton County (Ark.) T2—767 22
Fulton County (Ga.) T2—758 23
Fulton County (Ill.) T2—773 48
Fulton County (Ind.) T2—772 87
Fulton County (Ky.) T2—769 99
Fulton County (N.Y.) T2—747 47
Fulton County (Ohio) T2—771 115
Fulton County (Pa.) T2—748 72
Fumariaceae 583.35
Fumaroles 551.23
Fumes (Pollutants) 363.738 7
  see also Pollution
Fumigants 668.65
  agricultural use 632.950 4
  chemical engineering 668.65
Fumigation
  agricultural pest control 632.94
  public health 614.48
Fumitories (Plants) 583.35
Funchal (Madeira Islands : District) T2—469 8
Function
  architectural design 729.2
Function theory 515
Functional analysis 515.7
Functional income distribution
  macroeconomics 339.21
Functional organization
  executive management 658.402
Functional programming 005.114
Functionalism
  architecture 724.6
  fine arts 709.040 2
  linguistics 410.18
    specific languages T4—018
  painting 759.062
  psychology 150.193
  sculpture 735.230 42
Functionals 515.74
Functions (Mathematics) 511.33
  calculus 515.25
  number theory 512.73
Functions of complex variables 515.9
Functions of real variables 515.8
Functions of several complex variables 515.94
Functions of several real variables 515.84
Functor theory 515.7
Functors 512.55
Fund raising 658.152 24
  T1—068 1
  capital procurement 658.152 24
  local Christian church 254.8
  social welfare 361.706 81
  study and teaching T1—079

Fundamental education 370.111
  adult level 374.012
Fundamental interactions
    (Nuclear physics) 539.754
Fundamental particles 539.72
Fundamental theology
    (Christianity) 230.01
Fundamentalism
  Christianity 270.82
    independent denominations 289.95
    Protestantism 280.4
  Islam 297.09
    see Manual at 320.55 vs.
      297.09, 322.1
Fundamentalist theology 230.046 26
Fundy, Bay of 551.461 45
  T2—163 45
Funeral homes 363.75
  see also Undertaking
    (Mortuary)
Funeral music 781.588
Funeral sermons
  Christianity 252.1
Funerals 393.9
  Buddhist rites 294.343 8
  Christian rites 265.85
  customs 393.9
  etiquette 395.23
  flower arrangements 745.926
  Hindu rites 294.538
  Islamic rites 297.385
  Jewish rites 296.445
    liturgy 296.454 5
  religious rites 291.38
Fungal diseases (Biology) 571.995
  agriculture 632.4
  plant crops 632.4
  veterinary medicine 636.089 696 9
Fungal diseases (Human)
  incidence 614.559
  medicine 616.969
  see also Communicable
    diseases (Human)
Fungal viruses 579.27
Fungi 579.5
  medical microbiology 616.015
  paleobotany 561.92
  physiology 571.295
Fungi Imperfecti 579.55
Fungicides 668.652
  agricultural use 632.952
  chemical engineering 668.652
Fungus diseases (Biology) 571.995
  agriculture 632.4
  plant crops 632.4
  veterinary medicine 636.089 696 9
Fungus diseases (Human)
  incidence 614.559
  medicine 616.969
  see also Communicable
    diseases (Human)
Fungus weevils 595.768
Funicular railroads 385.6
  engineering 625.32
  transportation services 385.6
  see also Railroad
    transportation
Funj Sultanate 962.402 3
  T2—624
Funnies 741.5
  drawing 741.5
  journalism 070.444
Fur 599.714 7
  descriptive zoology 599.714 7
  physiology 573.58
Fur-bearing animals 599.7
  animal husbandry 636.97
  conservation technology 639.979 7
  resource economics 333.959 7
  small game hunting 799.259 7
  trapping 639.117
  zoology 599.7
Fur clothing 391
  commercial technology 685.24
  customs 391
  home sewing 646.4
  see also Clothing
Fur farming 636.97
Fur goods
  commercial technology 685
Fur processing 675.3
  economics 338.476 753
Fur seals 599.797 3
  conservation technology 639.979 797 3
  resource economics 333.959 797 3
Fur trapping 639.117
  economics 338.372 97
Furans 547.592
  chemical engineering 661.8
Furloughs
  armed forces 355.113
  penology 365.643
Furnaces
  heat engineering 621.402 5
  heating buildings 697.07
    steam 697.507

Furnaces (continued)
  steam engineering 621.183
Furnariidae 598.822 5
Furnas County (Neb.) T2—782 384
Furneaux Islands (Tas.) T2—946 7
Furnishings 645
  commercial technology 684
  customs 392.36
  home cleaning 648.5
  household management 645
  interior decoration 747
  libraries 022.9
  schools 371.63
    see also School equipment
Furniture 645.4
  cleaning 648.5
  customs 392.36
  decorative arts 749
  household management 645.4
  libraries 022.9
  manufacturing technology 684.1
  office services 651.23
  ships 623.866
Furniture arrangement 645.4
Furniture covers 645.4
  home sewing 646.21
  household management 645.4
  textile arts 746.95
Furniture designers 749.2
  occupational group T7—749
Furniture makers 684.100 92
  occupational group T7—684
Furriers 675.309 2
  occupational group T7—675
Furs
  handicrafts 745.537
  home sewing materials 646.1
  processing 675.3
  products
    commercial technology 685
Further education 374
  T1—071 5
  see also Adult education
Furuncles
  medicine 616.523
  see also Skin
Fusarium 579.567 7
Fused aromatic compounds 547.615
  chemical engineering 661.816
Fused heterocyclic compounds 547.596
Fuselages
  aircraft 629.134 34
Fuses (Detonators) 662.4
  military engineering 623.454 2
Fuses (Electrical) 621.317
Fusibility
  crystals 548.86
Fusion (Melting) 536.42
Fusion (Thermonuclear) 539.764
Fusion reactors 621.484
Future interests (Law) 346.042
Future life
  occultism 133.901 3
  philosophy 129
  religion 291.23
    Buddhism 294.342 3
    Christianity 236.2
    Hinduism 294.523
    Islam 297.23
    Judaism 296.33
  see Manual at 133.9013 vs. 129
Futures 332.645
Futurism
  fine arts 709.040 33
  literature 808.801 14
    history and criticism 809.911 4
    specific literatures T3B—080 114
      history and criticism T3B—091 14
  painting 759.063 3
  sculpture 735.230 433
Futurology 003.2
  occultism 133.3
  social change 303.49
Fuzzy sets 511.322
Fylde (England) T2—427 662
Fylde (England : Borough) T2—427 662
Fyn (Denmark) T2—489 4
Fyns amt (Denmark) T2—489 4
Fyodor I, Czar of Russia
  Russian history 947.044
Fyodor III, Czar of Russia
  Russian history 947.049

G

Gã (African people) T5—963 378
Gã language 496.337 8
  T6—963 378
Gã literature 896.337 8
Gabbros 552.3
Gables 721.5
  architecture 721.5
  construction 690.15
Gabon 967.21
  T2—672 1
Gabonese T5—967 21

Gaborone (Botswana) T2—688 3
Gabrovo (Bulgaria : Okrŭg) T2—499 2
Gabrovski okrŭg (Bulgaria) T2—499 2
Gadaba (Dravidian people) T5—948 2
Gadaba (Munda people) T5—959 5
Gadaba language (Dravidian) 494.82
T6—948 2
Gadaba language (Munda) 495.95
T6—959 5
Gadba (Dravidian people) T5—948 2
Gadba (Munda people) T5—959 5
Gadba language (Dravidian) 494.82
T6—948 2
Gadba language (Munda) 495.95
T6—959 5
Gadidae 597.632
Gadiformes 597.63
paleozoology 567.63
Gadolinium
chemistry 546.416
see also Rare earths
Gadsden County (Fla.) T2—759 925
Gadus 597.633
Gaelic football 796.33
see also Sports
Gaelic languages 491.6
T6—916
Irish 491.62
T6—916 2
Scottish 491.63
T6—916 3
Gaelic literatures 891.6
Irish 891.62
Scottish 891.63
Gaels T5—916
Gaetulia 939.77
T2—397 7
Gagauz language 494.36
T6—943 6
Gage County (Neb.) T2—782 286
Gagon (Quebec) T2—714 115
Gain sharing 331.216 4
labor economics 331.216 4
personnel management 658.322 5
Gaines County (Tex.) T2—764 855
Gaining weight diets
health 613.24
Gairdner, Lake (S. Aust.) T2—942 38
Gaitas 788.49
see also Woodwind instruments
Galagos 599.83
Galapagos Islands T2—866 5
Galaţi (Romania : Judeţ) T2—498 1
Galatia T2—393 2
Galatians (Biblical book) 227.4
Galax 583.67
Galax (Va.) T2—755 715
Galaxies 523.112
see Manual at 520 vs. 523.1, 523.112, 523.8
Galbulidae 598.72
Galcha language 491.57
T6—915 7
Galcha literature 891.57
Galchah language 491.57
T6—915 7
Galchah literature 891.57
Galena
mineralogy 549.32
Galicia (Poland and Ukraine) T2—438 6
Poland T2—438 6
Ukraine T2—477 9
Galicia (Spain : Region) T2—461
Galician dialect 469.794
T6—69
Galician literature 869
Galilee (Israel) T2—569 45
ancient T2—33
Gall bladder 573.38
see also Gallbladder
Gall gnats 595.772
Galla (African people) T5—935
Galla language 493.55
T6—935 5
Galla literature 893.55
Gallatin County (Ill.) T2—773 97
Gallatin County (Ky.) T2—769 365
Gallatin County (Mont.) T2—786 662
Gallbladder 573.38
biology 573.38
human anatomy 611.36
human physiology 612.35
medicine 616.365
surgery 617.556 5
see also Digestive system
Gallegan dialect 469.794
T6—69
Gallegan literature 869
Galleons 387.22
design 623.812 2
engineering 623.822
transportation services 387.22
see also Ships
Galleries (Museums) 069
T1—074

Galleys (Ships) 387.21
design 623.812 1
engineering 623.821
handling 623.882 1
transportation services 387.21
see also Ships
Galli 598.6
Gallia Cisalpina T2—372
Gallia County (Ohio) T2—771 89
Gallia Transalpina T2—364
Galliards 793.3
music 784.188 2
Gallican schismatic churches 284.8
see also Old Catholic churches
Galliformes 598.6
paleozoology 568.6
sports hunting 799.246
Gallinules 598.32
Gallipoli Campaign, 1915 940.426
Gallium 669.79
chemical engineering 661.067 5
chemistry 546.675
metallurgy 669.79
see also Chemicals
Gallo-Roman period 936.402
Galloway (Scotland : District) T2—414 9
Galloway cattle 636.223
Galls
agriculture 632.2
Gallus (Jungle fowl) 598.625
Gallus domesticus 636.5
see also Chickens
Galois theory 512.3
Galops 793.3
music 784.188 4
Galvanometers 621.374 4
Galveston County (Tex.) T2—764 139
Galway (Ireland) T2—417 45
Galway (Ireland : County) T2—417 4
Gama grass 584.9
Gambai dialect 496.5
T6—965
Gambel's quail 598.627
Gambia 966.51
T2—665 1
Gambia River T2—665 1
Gambians T5—966 51
Gambier Island (B.C.) T2—711 31
Gambier Islands (French Polynesia) T2—962 2
Gamblers 795.092
occupational group T7—795
Gambling 306.482
criminology 364.172
criminal law 345.027 2
customs 394.3
ethics 175
horse racing 798.401
law 344.099
mathematics 519.2
occupational ethics 174.6
public control 363.42
law 344.054 2
public administration 353.37
recreation 795
sociology 306.482
Game animals 591.63
animal husbandry 636.088 8
conservation technology 639.9
economic zoology 591.63
food 641.391
cooking 641.691
mammals 599.163
resource economics 333.954 9
see Manual at 338.37 vs. 333.954
Game birds 598.163
animal husbandry 636.63
conservation technology 639.978 163
economic zoology 598.163
food 641.391
cooking 641.691
resource economics 333.958 29
sports hunting 799.24
see also Birds
Game fishes 597.163
conservation technology 639.977 163
resource economics 333.956 9
sports fishing 799.12
Game fishes (Salmonids) 597.55
conservation technology 639.977 55
resource economics 333.956 55
sports fishing 799.175 5
Game fishing 799.12
Game laws 346.046 954 9
Game protection 333.954 916
technology 639.9
Game reserves 333.954 916
Game theory 519.3
Gamekeepers 639.909 2
Games 790.1
camp sports 796.545
cataloging 025.349 6
customs 394.3
ethics 175
folk literature 398.8

Games (continued)
  indoor 793
  library treatment 025.179 6
  management decision making 658.403 53
  outdoor 796
    see also Sports
  sociology 306.487
  see also Recreation
Games of chance 795
  equipment technology 688.75
  probabilities 519.2
  see Manual at 795.015192 vs. 519.2
Games of skill 790.1
  indoor 794
  outdoor 796
Gametes 571.845
Gametogenesis 571.845
Gaming
  instructional use 371.397
Gamka River (South Africa) T2—687 16
Gamma decay 539.752 4
Gamma functions 515.52
Gamma globulins
  pharmacology 615.39
Gamma particles 539.722 2
Gamma radiation
  biophysics 571.459
    humans 612.014 486
Gamma-ray astronomy 522.686 2
Gamma-ray electronics 537.535
Gamma-ray photography
  engineering 621.367 3
Gamma-ray spectroscopes
  manufacturing technology 681.414 8
Gamma-ray spectroscopy 543.085 86
  analytical chemistry 543.085 86
  engineering 621.361 6
  physics 537.535 2
Gamma rays 539.722 2
Gamo Gofa Kifle Hāger (Ethiopia) T2—633
Ganapataism 294.551 5
Ganda (African people) T5—963 957
Ganda language 496.395 7
  T6—963 957
Ganda literature 896.395 7
Gandhi, Indira
  Indian history 954.045
    1966–1971 954.045
    1971–1977 954.051
    1980–1984 954.052
Gandhi, Rajiv
  Indian history 954.052
Ganges River (India and Bangladesh) T2—541
Ganglia
  human anatomy 611.83
  human physiology 612.81
  see also Nervous system
Gangrene
  medicine 616.047
Gangs
  criminology 364.106 6
  social psychology 302.34
Gangsterism 364.106 6
Ganoidei 597.42
Gansu Sheng (China) T2—514 5
Ganyesa (South Africa : District) T2—682 94
Gaols 365.34
  see also Correctional institutions
Gaonim 296.120 092
GAR (Organization) 369.15
Garage sales 381.195
  management 658.87
  see also Commerce
Garages
  architecture 725.38
  automotive engineering 629.286
  construction 690.538
  domestic
    architecture 728.98
    construction 690.898
Garamond type 686.224 7
Garavance 641.356 57
  see also Chick-peas
Garbage collection
  technology 628.442
Garbage disposal 363.728 8
  technology 628.445
  use as fertilizer 631.875
  see also Waste control
Garbage-disposal units
  installation 696.184
  manufacturing technology 683.88
Garbanzo 641.356 57
  see also Chick-peas
Garcia, Carlos
  Philippine history 959.904 4
Garcinias 583.624
Gard (France) T2—448 3
Garda, Lake (Italy) T2—452 6
Garden County (Neb.) T2—782 915

Garden crops 635
  see Manual at 633–635
Garden eggs 641.356 46
  see also Eggplants
Garden furniture 645.8
  see also Outdoor furniture
Garden legumes 641.356 5
  cooking 641.656 5
  food 641.356 5
  horticulture 635.65
Garden lighting 621.322 9
  see also Lighting
Garden peas 641.356 56
  commercial processing 664.805 656
  see also Peas (Pisum sativum)
Garden Route (South Africa) T2—687 4
Garden sculpture 731.72
Gardeners 635.092
  occupational group T7—635
Gardenias 635.933 93
  botany 583.93
  floriculture 635.933 93
Gardening 635
  landscape architecture 712
Gardens 635
  biology 578.755 4
  ecology 577.554
  landscape architecture 712
  literature 808.803 64
    history and criticism 809.933 64
    specific literatures T3B—080 364
      history and criticism T3B—093 64
Garfield, James A. (James Abram)
  United States history 973.84
Garfield County (Colo.) T2—788 16
Garfield County (Mont.) T2—786 27
Garfield County (Neb.) T2—782 764
Garfield County (Okla.) T2—766 28
Garfield County (Utah) T2—792 52
Garfield County (Wash.) T2—797 44
Garfish 597.66
Gargoyles
  architectural decoration 729.5
Garibaldi (Fish) 597.72
Garibaldi Provincial Park (B.C.) T2—711 31
Garland County (Ark.) T2—767 41
Garlic 641.352 6
  botany 584.33
  cooking 641.652 6
  food 641.352 6
  garden crop 635.26
Garlic (continued)
  pharmacology 615.324 33
Garment workers 687.092
  occupational group T7—687
Garments 391
  see also Clothing
Garnets 553.87
  mineralogy 549.62
  see also Semiprecious stones
Garnishes 641.81
Garnishment 347.077
  civil procedure 347.077
  commercial law 346.077
Garo language 495.4
  T6—954
Garonne River (Spain and France) T2—447
Garrard County (Ky.) T2—769 525
Garrett County (Md.) T2—752 97
Garrison Reservoir (N.D.) T2—784 75
Garrya 583.84
Gars 597.41
Garvin County (Okla.) T2—766 56
Gary (Ind.) T2—772 99
Garza County (Tex.) T2—764 852
Gas analysis
  chemistry 543.08
  quantitative 545.7
Gas appliances
  chemistry 542.7
Gas chromatography 543.089 6
  chemical engineering 660.284 23
Gas-detection prospecting 622.159
Gas dynamics 533.2
Gas engineering 665.7
  equipment manufacturing technology 681.766 5
Gas engineers 665.709 2
  occupational group T7—665
Gas equipment
  household appliances 643.6
    manufacturing technology 683.88
Gas exchange
  human physiology 612.22
    see also Respiratory system
Gas fitting
  buildings 696.2
Gas heating
  buildings 697.043
Gas lighting 621.324
  see also Lighting
Gas mechanics 533
  engineering 620.107
Gas oil 665.538 4

Gas pipes
  buildings
    installation 696.2
Gas supply facilities
  area planning 711.8
Gas tubes
  electronics 621.381 513
Gas-turbine engines 621.433
  aircraft 629.134 353
  automotive 629.250 3
  ships 623.872 33
Gas-turbine locomotives 385.362
  engineering 625.262
  transportation services 385.362
  see also Rolling stock
Gas welding 671.522
Gascogne (France) T2—447 7
Gasconade County (Mo.) T2—778 61
Gascony (France) T2—447 7
Gascoyne River (W.A.) T2—941 3
Gaseous-state lasers 621.366 3
Gaseous-state physics 530.43
Gaseous wastes 363.728
  social services 363.728
  technology 628.53
  see also Waste control
Gases
  chemical engineering 660.043
  expansion and contraction 536.412
  heat transfer 536.25
  pneumatics 533
  sound transmission 534.24
  specific heat 536.65
  state of matter 530.43
Gases (Fuels) 665.7
  cooking 641.584
  dowsing 133.323 7
  mine safety engineering 622.82
  natural 553.285
    see also Natural gas
  plant management 658.26
  public administration 354.46
  public safety 363.179 8
  public utilities 363.63
    see also Public utilities
  see also Hazardous materials
Gases (Noxious)
  human toxicology 615.91
  mine safety engineering 622.82
  pollution 363.738 7
    see also Pollution
Gases in atmosphere 551.511 2
Gasohol 662.669 2
Gasoline 665.538 27
  public safety 363.179 8
  see also Hazardous materials
Gasoline engines 621.434
Gaspé (Quebec : County) T2—714 79
Gaspé Peninsula (Quebec) T2—714 77
Gaspée (Ship), Burning of, 1772 973.311 2
Gasteropelecidae 597.48
Gasterosteidae 597.672
Gasterosteiformes 597.67
  paleozoology 567.67
Gaston County (N.C.) T2—756 773
Gastric analysis
  diagnosis
    general disease 616.075 63
Gastric indigestion
  medicine 616.332
  see also Digestive system
Gastric secretions 573.363 79
  human physiology 612.32
  see also Digestive system
Gastric ulcers
  medicine 616.334
  see also Digestive system
Gastritis
  medicine 616.333
  see also Digestive system
Gastroenteritis
  medicine 616.33
  see also Digestive system
Gastroenterology 616.33
  see also Digestive system
Gastroesophageal reflux
  medicine 616.32
  see also Digestive system
Gastrointestinal diseases
  medicine 616.33
  see also Digestive system
Gastrointestinal organs 573.36
  human anatomy 611.33
  human physiology 612.32
  see also Digestive system
Gastrojejunal ulcers
  medicine 616.343 4
  see also Digestive system
Gastromycetes 579.599
Gastronomy 641.013
Gastropoda 594.3
  paleozoology 564.3
Gastrotricha 592.53
Gastrulation 571.865
Gataga River (B.C.) T2—711 85

Gatehouses
  architecture 728.9
  construction 690.89
Gates
  canal engineering 627.135 2
  dam engineering 627.882
Gates County (N.C.) T2—756 153
Gates of the Arctic National Park and Preserve (Alaska) T2—798 6
Gateshead (England : Metropolitan Borough) T2—428 73
Gateways
  architecture 725.96
  landscape architecture 717
Gathas 295.82
Gatineau (Quebec : County) T2—714 221
Gatineau-Hull Region (Quebec) T2—714 221
Gatineau Park (Quebec) T2—714 221
Gatineau River (Quebec) T2—714 221
GATT (Commerce) 382.92
  law 341.754 3
Gauge fields
  physics 530.143 5
Gaul 936.4
  T2—364
Gauley River (W. Va.) T2—754 69
Gaulish language 491.6
  T6—916
Gaulish literature 891.6
Gauls T5—916
Gauntlets
  manufacturing technology 685.43
Gaur 599.642 2
Gauss geometry 516.9
Gaussian processes 519.23
Gautama Buddha 294.363
  art representation 704.948 943 63
  arts 700.482 943 63
  T3C—382 943 63
Gavial 597.98
Gaviiformes 598.442
  paleozoology 568.4
Gävleborg (Sweden) T2—487
Gavottes 793.319 44
  music 784.188 3
Gawler (S. Aust.) T2—942 32
Gay liberation movement 305.906 64
Gay marriage 306.848
Gay men 305.389 664
  T1—086 642
Gay women 305.489 664
  T1—086 643
Gay workers 331.53
Gays 305.906 64
  T1—086 64
  Christian pastoral theology 259.086 64
  female 305.489 664
  labor economics 331.53
  male 305.389 664
Gaza (Mozambique : Province) T2—679 2
Gaza Strip T2—531
Gazankulu (South Africa) T2—682 92
Gazehounds 636.753 2
Gazella 599.646 9
Gazelles 599.646 9
Gazetteers 910.3
Gazettes (Official publications) 351.05
Gaziantep İli (Turkey) T2—564
Gbandi (Liberian people) T5—963 48
Gbandi language 496.348
  T6—963 48
Gbaya (African people) T5—963 61
Gbaya language 496.361
  T6—963 61
GCSE (Educational tests) 373.126 2
Gdańsk (Poland : Voivodeship) T2—438 2
GDP (Macroeconomics) 339.31
Gê Indians T5—984
Gê language 498.4
  T6—984
Gê-Pano-Carib languages 498.4
  T6—984
Gear-cutting tools 621.944
Gear-driven hoists
  mining 622.67
Gears 621.833
  clockwork 681.112
Geary County (Kan.) T2—781 29
Geauga County (Ohio) T2—771 336
GED tests 373.126 2
Gedling (England) T2—425 28
Geelong (Vic.) T2—945 2
Geese 598.417
  animal husbandry 636.598
  conservation technology 639.978 417
  resource economics 333.958 417
  sports hunting 799.244 7
Ge'ez language 492.81
  T6—928 1
Ge'ez literature 892.81
Gegenschein 523.59
Geiger-Müller counters
  nuclear physics 539.774

Geisel, Ernesto
  Brazilian history 981.063
Gelatin process
  printing 686.232 5
Gelatins 641.864
  commercial processing 664.26
  home preparation 641.864
Gelderland (Netherlands) T2—492 18
Gels 541.345 13
  chemical engineering 660.294 513
Gelsenkirchen (Germany) T2—435 618
Gem County (Idaho) T2—796 27
Gemini (Zodiac) 133.526 4
Gemini project 629.454
Gempylidae 597.78
Gems 553.8
  carving 736.2
  economic geology 553.8
  jewelry 739.27
  materials science 620.198
  mining 622.38
  occultism 133.255 38
    divination 133.322
  prospecting 622.188
  synthetic 666.88
Gender identity 305.3
  social aspects 305.3
Gene mapping 572.863 3
  humans 611.018 16
Gene pools 576.58
Gene splicing
  biotechnology 660.65
Gene therapy
  law 344.041 96
  medicine 616.042
Genealogical registers 929.3
Genealogists 929.109 2
  occupational group T7—99
Genealogy 929.1
  see Manual at 929.1
General accounting offices 352.43
  audit reports 352.439
General Agreement on Tariffs and Trade (1947) 382.92
  law 341.754 3
General anesthesia
  surgery 617.962
General Carrera (Chile : Province) T2—836 25
General certificate of education examination (United Kingdom) 371.262
  A level 378.166 2
  GCSE 373.126 2
General Conference Mennonite Church 289.73
  see also Mennonite Church
General educational development tests 373.126 2
General paresis
  medicine 616.892
  see also Nervous system
General services agencies 352.5
General Society of Colonial Wars (U.S.) 369.12
General Society of Mayflower Descendants 369.12
General staffs 355.330 42
General stores 381.14
  management 658.874
  see also Commerce
General strikes 322.2
  economics 331.892 5
    see also Strikes (Work stoppages)
General topology 514.322
Generalists T7—09
Generalized functions 515.782
Generalized system of preference 382.753
  see also Customs (Tariff)
Generals 355.009 2
  role and function 355.331
Generating electricity 621.312 1
Generating functions 515.55
Generating machinery
  electrical engineering 621.313
Generating steam 621.18
Generation gap 305.2
  family relationships 306.874
Generation of sound
  physics 534.1
  see also Sound
Generative grammar 415
  specific languages T4—5
Generative organs 573.6
  see also Genital system
Genes 572.86
  humans 611.018 16
  see Manual at 572.8
Genesee County (Mich.) T2—774 37
Genesee County (N.Y.) T2—747 92
Genesee River (Pa. and N.Y.) T2—747 88
Genesis (Bible) 222.11
Genetic algorithms
  computer science 005.1
    artificial intelligence 006.31

Genetic code 572.863 3
Genetic disorders (Biology) 571.948
Genetic disorders (Human)
  medicine 616.042
  see also Diseases (Human)
Genetic engineering 660.65
  agriculture 631.523 3
    pest resistance 632.9
  animal husbandry 636.082 1
  ethics 174.957
    medical 174.25
    see also Ethical problems
  medical
    law 344.041 96
Genetic evolution 572.838
Genetic factors
  influence on crime 364.24
  physical ethnology 599.972
Genetic psychology 155.7
Genetic recombination 572.877
Genetic regulation 572.865
Genetic replication 572.864 5
Genetic resources 333.953 4
  animals 333.954
  economics 333.953 4
  plants 333.953 4
Genetic screening
  crime prevention 364.41
Genetic transcription 572.884 5
Genetic transduction 571.964 8
Genetic transformation 571.964 8
Genetic translation 572.645
Geneticists 576.509 2
  occupational group T7—57
Genetics 576.5
  animal husbandry 636.082 1
  animals 591.35
  humans 599.935
    sociology 304.5
  microorganisms 579.135
  plants 581.35
  social theology 291.178 365
    Christianity 261.836 5
  sociology 304.5
  see Manual at 576.5 vs. 572.8
Genets 599.742
Geneva (Switzerland : Canton) T2—494 51
Geneva, Lake (Switzerland and France) T2—494 52
  France T2—444 9
  Switzerland T2—494 52
Geneva Conventions 341.65
Geneva County (Ala.) T2—761 292
Genghis Khan
  Asian history 950.2
Geniculate bodies
  human physiology 612.826 2
  see also Nervous system
Genital herpes
  incidence 614.547
  medicine 616.951 8
  see also Communicable diseases (Human)
Genital organs 573.6
  see also Genital system
Genital system 573.6
  animals 573.6
  geriatrics 618.976 65
  human anatomy 611.6
  human cancer 362.196 994 6
    incidence 614.599 946
    medicine 616.994 6
    social services 362.196 994 6
    see also Cancer (Human)
  human diseases 362.196 65
    incidence 614.596 5
    medicine 616.65
    social services 362.196 65
  human histology 611.018 96
  human physiology 612.6
  pediatrics 618.926 5
  pharmacodynamics 615.766
  veterinary medicine 636.089 665
  see also Female genital system; Male genital system
Genitalia 573.6
  see also Genital system
Genitourinary system 573.6
  human physiology 612.46
  see also Genital system; Urinary system
Geniuses 305.908 29
  T1—087 9
  T7—082 9
  psychology 153.98
Genoa (Italy : Province) T2—451 82
Genocide 364.151
  ethics 179.7
    see also Ethical problems
  international law 341.778
  law 345.025 1
  sociology 304.663
Genome mapping 572.863 3
  humans 611.018 16

Genomes 572.86
  humans 611.018 16
  see Manual at 572.8
Genotypes 576.53
Genova (Italy : Province) T2—451 82
Genre paintings 754
Gent (Belgium) T2—493 142
Gentianales 583.93
Gentians 583.93
Gentleness 179.9
  see also Virtues
Gentry
  genealogy 929.7
Gentry County (Mo.) T2—778 145
Geobotanical prospecting 622.12
Geochemical prospecting 622.13
Geochemistry 551.9
Geodesics
  geometry 516.362
Geodesists 526.109 2
  occupational group T7—526
Geodesy 526.1
Geodetic astronomy 526.6
Geodetic coordinates 526.6
  spherical astronomy 522.7
Geodetic surveying 526.3
Geographers 910.92
  occupational group T7—91
Geographic myths 398.234
  see also Legendary places
Geographic subjects
  painting 758.991
Geographic treatment T1—09
  fine arts 709
    see Manual at 704.9: Use of standard subdivisions; *also at* 709.012–709.05 vs. 709.3–709.9; *also at* 753–758: Use of standard subdivisions
  see Manual at T1—09; *also at* T1—093–T1—099 and T2—3–T2—9; *also at* 380: Add table: 09 vs. 065
Geographical positions
  geodetic astronomy 526.64
Geography 910
  Bible 220.91
  elementary education 372.891
  see Manual at 578 vs. 304.2, 508, 910; *also at* 909, 930–990 vs. 910
Geologic time 551.701
Geological age measurements 551.701
Geological ages 551.7
  see Manual at 551.7
Geological instruments
  manufacturing technology 681.755
Geological prospecting 622.12
Geological surveys
  specific areas 554–559
Geologists 551.092
  occupational group T7—553
Geology 551
  specific areas 554–559
Geomagnetic reversals 538.727
Geomagnetism 538.7
Geomancy 133.333
Geometric abstractionism 709.040 52
  painting 759.065 2
  sculpture 735.230 452
Geometric design 709.040 3
  painting 759.063
  sculpture 735.230 43
Geometric number theory 512.75
Geometric probability 519.2
Geometric progressions 512.93
  algebra 512.93
  arithmetic 513.4
Geometric shapes 516.15
Geometrical crystallography 548.81
Geometrical optics 535.32
Geometries over algebras 516.186
Geometries over groups 516.186
Geometries over rings 516.186
Geometroidea 595.78
Geometry 516
  famous problems 516.204
Geometry of numbers 512.75
Geomorphologists 551.410 92
  occupational group T7—553
Geomorphology 551.41
Geomyidae 599.359 9
Geonavigation
  nautical 623.892
Geonim 296.120 092
Geophysical prospecting 622.15
Geophysics 550
  see Manual at 550 vs. 910
Geopolitics 320.12
  international relations 327.101
George (South Africa : District) T2—687 4
George, Lake (N.Y.) T2—747 51
George I, King of Great Britain
  British history 941.071
  English history 942.071
  Scottish history 941.107 1

George II, King of Great Britain
  British history 941.072
  English history 942.072
  Scottish history 941.107 2
George III, King of Great Britain
  British history 941.073
  English history 942.073
  Scottish history 941.107 3
George IV, King of Great Britain
  British history 941.074
  English history 942.074
  Scottish history 941.107 4
George V, King of Great Britain
  British history 941.083
  English history 942.083
  Scottish history 941.108 3
George VI, King of Great Britain
  British history 941.084
  English history 942.084
  Scottish history 941.108 4
George County (Miss.) T2—762 165
Georgetown (Guyana) T2—881 5
Georgetown County (S.C.) T2—757 89
Georgia 975.8
  T2—758
Georgia (Republic) 947.58
  T2—475 8
Georgia, Strait of (B.C.) 551.466 33
  T2—164 33
Georgian architecture 724.19
Georgian Bay (Ont. : Bay) T2—713 15
Georgian language 499.969
  T6—999 69
Georgian literature 899.969
Georgians
  (Transcaucasians) T5—999 69
Geotectonics 551.8
Geothermal energy 333.88
  economics 333.88
  public administration 354.48
Geothermal engineering 621.44
Geothermal prospecting 622.159
Gera (Germany : Bezirk) T2—432 22
Geraldton (W.A.) T2—941 2
Geraniales 583.79
Geraniums (Pelargoniums) 635.933 79
  botany 583.79
  floriculture 635.933 79
Gerberas 583.99
  floriculture 635.933 99
Gerbils 636.935 83
  animal husbandry 636.935 83
  zoology 599.358 3
Geriatric cardiology 618.976 12
  see also Cardiovascular system
Geriatric disorders 362.198 97
  incidence 614.599 297
  medicine 618.97
  social services 362.198 97
Geriatric gynecology 618.978 1
  see also Female genital system
Geriatric nursing
  medicine 610.736 5
Geriatric preventive measures 613.043 8
Geriatric surgery 617.97
Geriatric therapeutics 615.547
Geriatricians 618.970 092
  occupational group T7—618
  role and function 618.970 232
Geriatrics 618.97
  see Manual at 618.977 vs. 617
Germ cells 571.845
Germ plasm 333.953 4
  agriculture 631.523
    animal breeding 636.082 1
    plant cultivation 631.523
  resource economics 333.953 4
    animals 333.954
    plants 333.953 4
Germ warfare 358.38
  see also Biological warfare
German Confederation 943.07
German Democratic Republic 943.108 7
  T2—431
German Empire 943.083
  T2—43
German folk music 781.623 1
German folk songs 782.421 623 1
German historical school
  (Economics) 330.154 2
German language 430
  T6—31
German literature 830
German measles
  incidence 614.524
  medicine 616.916
  pediatrics 618.929 16
  see also Communicable diseases (Human)
German New Guinea 995.302 1
  T2—953
German police dog 636.737 6
German Pomerania T2—431 7

German Reformed Church (U.S.) 285.733
see also Reformed Church (American Reformed)
German shepherd dog 636.737 6
Germania Inferior T2—364
Germania Superior T2—364
Germanic languages 430
T6—3
Germanic literatures 830
Germanic people T5—3
Germanic regions 943
T2—43
ancient 936.3
T2—363
Germanic religion 293
Germanium
chemical engineering 661.068 4
chemistry 546.684
metallurgy 669.79
see also Chemicals
Germans T5—31
Germans (Dances) 793.35
Germany 943
T2—43
ancient 936.3
T2—363
Germany (East) 943.108 7
T2—431
Germany (West) 943.087
T2—43
Germination 571.862
Germiston (South Africa : District) T2—682 2
Germplasm 333.953 4
see also Germ plasm
Gerona (Spain : Province) T2—467 1
Gerontology 305.26
human physiology 612.67
social aspects 305.26
social welfare 362.6
Gerrymandering 328.334 55
Gers (France) T2—447 71
Gerunds 415
specific languages T4—5
Gesneriaceae 583.95
Gestalt psychology 150.198 2
Gestalt therapy
psychiatry 616.891 43
see also Mental illness
Gestures 302.222
drama 792.028
motion pictures 791.430 28
stage 792.028
television 791.450 28
preaching 251.03
psychology 153.69
expressive movements 152.384
nonverbal communication 153.69
social psychology 302.222
Gettysburg, Battle of, 1863 973.734 9
Geysers 551.23
Gezira (Sudan : Province) T2—626 4
Ghana 966.7
T2—667
Ghana Empire 966.101 6
T2—661
Ghanaians T5—966 7
Gharbīyah (Egypt) T2—621
Ghardaia (Algeria : Province) T2—657
Ghazi I, King of Iraq
Iraqi history 956.704 2
Ghazni dynasty 954.022 3
Ghent (Belgium) T2—493 142
Ghettos 307.336 6
Ghor dynasty 954.022 5
Ghost pipefishes 597.67
Ghost sharks 597.38
Ghosts 133.1
arts 700.475
T3C—375
fiction 808.838 733
history and criticism 809.387 33
specific literatures T3B—308 733
individual authors T3A—3
folklore 398.25
history and criticism 398.47
literature 808.803 75
history and criticism 809.933 75
specific literatures T3B—080 375
history and criticism T3B—093 75
occultism 133.1
Giant ferns 587.33
Giant forest hog 599.633
Giant otter 599.769
Giant panda 599.789
conservation technology 639.979 789
resource economics 333.959 789
Giant perches 597.72
Giant Schnauzer 636.73
Giant slalom skiing 796.935
see also Sports
Giant stars 523.88

Giants
physical anthropology 599.949
Giant's Castle Game Reserve (South Africa) T2—684 7
Giardiasis
medicine 616.34
see also Digestive system
Gibberellins
chemistry 547.734 2
Gibbons 599.882
Gibb's phase rule
thermochemistry 541.363
Gibraltar 946.89
T2—468 9
Gibraltar, Strait of 551.462 1
T2—163 81
Gibraltar Range National Park (N.S.W.) T2—944 3
Gibson County (Ind.) T2—772 35
Gibson County (Tenn.) T2—768 23
Gibson Desert (W.A.) T2—941 5
Giessen (Germany : Regierungsbezirk) T2—434 14
Gift revenues
public finance 336.16
Gift tax 336.276
law 343.053 5
public administration 352.44
public finance 336.276
Gift wrappings 745.54
Gifted children
home care 649.155
psychology 155.455
see also Gifted persons
Gifted persons 305.908 29
T1—087 9
T7—082 9
special education 371.95
Gifts
financial management 658.153
library acquisitions 025.26
library-government relations 021.8
military rewards 355.134 9
sales promotion 658.82
Gifts of the Holy Spirit 234.13
Gifu-ken (Japan) T2—521 62
Gigantism (Pituitary)
medicine 616.47
see also Endocrine system
Giglio Island (Italy) T2—455 7
Gila County (Ariz.) T2—791 55
Gila monsters 597.95
Gila River (N.M. and Ariz.) T2—791 7
Gīlān (Iran) T2—551
Gilbert Islands T2—968 1
Gilchrist County (Fla.) T2—759 78
Gilding
bookbinding 686.36
decorative arts 745.75
Giles County (Tenn.) T2—768 61
Giles County (Va.) T2—755 782
Gilgandra (N.S.W.) T2—944 5
Gill fungi 579.6
Gilles de la Tourette syndrome
medicine 616.83
see also Nervous system
Gillespie County (Tex.) T2—764 65
Gilliam County (Or.) T2—795 65
Gillingham (England) T2—422 325
Gills 573.28
descriptive zoology 591.4
physiology 573.28
Gilmer County (Ga.) T2—758 295
Gilmer County (W. Va.) T2—754 27
Gilpin County (Colo.) T2—788 62
Gilt-edged securities 332.632 044
see Manual at 332.632044 vs. 332.6323
Gilyak language 494.6
T6—946
Gimps 677.76
Gin 641.255
commercial processing 663.55
Gin rummy 795.418
Ginger 641.338 3
botany 584.39
see also Spices
Ginger ales
commercial processing 663.62
Ginger lily
botany 584.39
Gingivitis
dentistry 617.632
see also Dentistry
Ginkgo tree 635.977 57
botany 585.7
ornamental arboriculture 635.977 57
Ginkgoales 585.7
paleobotany 561.57
Ginning cotton 677.212 1
Ginsengs
botany 583.84
medicinal crops 633.883 84
pharmacology 615.323 84
Gippsland (Vic.) T2—945 6
Giraffe 599.638
Giraffidae 599.638

Girder bridges	388
construction	624.37
see also Bridges	
Girders	624.177 23
naval architecture	623.817 723
structural engineering	624.177 23
Giresun İli (Turkey)	T2—565
Girl Guides Association	369.463
Girl Scout camps	796.542 2
Girl Scouts	369.463
Girls	305.23
	T1—083
criminal offenders	364.36
education	371.823
health	613.042 42
home care	649.133
journalism for	070.483 27
psychology	155.433
publications for	
bibliographies	011.624 2
recreation	790.194
indoor	793.019 4
outdoor	796.083
sex hygiene	613.955
social aspects	305.23
Girls' clubs	369.46
Girls' societies	369.46
Gironde (France)	T2—447 1
Gisborne District (N.Z.)	T2—934 4
Gisborne Region (N.Z.)	T2—934 4
Gisu (African people)	T5—963 95
Gisu language	496.395
	T6—963 95
Gittin	296.123 3
Babylonian Talmud	296.125 3
Mishnah	296.123 3
Palestinian Talmud	296.124 3
Giurgiu (Romania : Judeţ)	T2—498 2
Given names	929.44
Giyani (South Africa : District)	T2—682 92
Giza (Egypt)	T2—622
ancient	T2—32
Gjoa Haven (N.W.T.)	T2—719 7
Glacial action	551.313
Glacial drift (Geologic landforms)	551.315
Glacial drift (Geologic material)	551.314
Glacier Bay National Park and Preserve (Alaska)	T2—798 2
Glacier County (Mont.)	T2—786 52
Glacier National Park (B.C.)	T2—711 68
Glacier National Park (Mont.)	T2—786 52
Glaciers	551.312
ecology	577.586
Glaciology	551.31
Glades County (Fla.)	T2—759 51
Gladiolus	635.934 38
botany	584.38
floriculture	635.934 38
Gladstone (Qld.)	T2—943 5
Gladwin County (Mich.)	T2—774 72
Glamorgan (Wales)	T2—429 7
Glamorgan, Vale of (Wales)	T2—429 89
Glanders	
incidence	614.564
medicine	616.954
see also Communicable diseases (Human)	
Glands	571.79
biology	571.79
endocrine system	573.4
human anatomy	611.4
human physiology	612.4
medicine	616.4
see also Endocrine system	
Glanford (England : Borough)	T2—428 32
Glaris (Switzerland : Canton)	T2—494 74
Glarus (Switzerland : Canton)	T2—494 74
Glascock County (Ga.)	T2—758 666
Glasgow (Scotland)	T2—414 43
Glass	666.1
architectural construction	721.044 96
building construction	693.96
building materials	691.6
decorative arts	748
materials science	620.144
optical components	
manufacturing technology	681.42
sculpture material	731.2
ship design	623.818 38
ship hulls	623.845 8
shipbuilding	623.820 7
structural engineering	624.183 8
technology	666.1
Glass artists	748.092
occupational group	T7—748
Glass beads	748.85
Glass breakage insurance	368.6
see also Insurance	
Glass carp	597.482

Glass harmonicas 786.866
  see also Percussion instruments
Glass insurance 368.6
  see also Insurance
Glass painting 748.502 82
Glass sand 553.622
Glass sponges 593.44
Glass staining 748.502 82
Glass underpainting 751.76
Glassblowing
  decorative arts 748.202 82
Glasscock County (Tex.) T2—764 872
Glassware 642.7
  decorative arts 748.2
  manufacturing technology 666.19
  table setting 642.7
Glaucoma
  incidence 614.599 7
  ophthalmology 617.741
  see also Eyes
Glaucomys 599.369
Glauconite
  mineralogy 549.67
Glaze (Meteorology) 551.574 4
Glazes
  pottery 666.427
    arts 738.127
    technology 666.427
Glaziers 698.509 2
  occupational group T7—698
Glazing
  arts 730.028
  ceramic arts 738.144
  sculpture 731.4
Glazing leather 675.25
Glazing pottery 666.444
  arts 738.144
  technology 666.444
Glazing windows 698.5
Glen Canyon National Recreation Area (Utah and Ariz.) T2—792 59
Glen Innes (N.S.W.) T2—944 4
Glencoe (South Africa : District) T2—684 1
Glengarry (Ont.) T2—713 75
Glenn County (Calif.) T2—794 31
Gliders (Aircraft) 387.733 3
  engineering 629.133 33
  piloting 629.132 523
  transportation services 387.733 3
  see also Aircraft
Gliding
  aeronautics 629.132 31
  sports 797.55
  see also Sports
Gliridae 599.359 6
Global analysis 514.74
Global differential geometry 516.362
Global warming 363.738 74
  see also Greenhouse effect
Globes
  cataloging 025.346
  library treatment 025.176
Globular clusters 523.855
Globulins 572.66
  biochemistry 572.66
  chemistry 547.752
  see also Proteins
Glockenspiels 786.843
  see also Percussion instruments
Glomerulonephritis
  medicine 616.612
  see also Urinary system
Gloria 264.36
  music 782.323 2
Glossaries
  applied linguistics 418
    specific languages T4—81
Glossinidae 595.774
Glossolalia 234.132
Glossopteris 561.597
Glottis 573.925
  human anatomy 611.22
  medicine 616.22
  see also Respiratory system
Gloucester (England) T2—424 14
Gloucester (N.B.) T2—715 12
Gloucester (N.S.W.) T2—944 2
Gloucester County (N.J.) T2—749 81
Gloucester County (Va.) T2—755 32
Gloucestershire (England) T2—424 1
Glove compartments
  automobile 629.277
Glove makers 685.409 2
  occupational group T7—685 4
Gloves 391.412
  commercial technology 685.4
  customs 391.412
  home sewing 646.48
  see also Clothing
Glowworms 595.764 4
Gloxinias 635.933 95
  botany 583.95
  floriculture 635.933 95

Glucose 572.565
  biochemistry 572.565
  chemistry 547.781 3
  see also Carbohydrates
Glue 668.3
  see also Adhesives
Glue abuse 362.299
  medicine 616.86
  personal health 613.8
  social welfare 362.299
  see also Substance abuse
Gluing
  bookbinding 686.35
Gluttony 178
  moral theology 291.568
  see also Vices
Glycerin 668.2
Glycogen 572.566
  biochemistry 572.566
  chemistry 547.782
  see also Carbohydrates
Glycoproteins 572.68
  biochemistry 572.68
  chemistry 547.754
  see also Proteins
Glycosides 572.567
  biochemistry 572.567
  chemistry 547.783
  see also Carbohydrates
Glyndŵr (Wales) T2—429 37
Glynn County (Ga.) T2—758 742
Glyptics 736.2
Glyptographers 736.209 2
  occupational group T7—736
Gmelina 583.96
  forestry 634.973 96
Gnats 595.772
Gneisses 552.4
Gnetales 585.8
Gneticae 585.8
  paleobotany 561.58
Gnetum 585.8
Gnosticism 299.932
  Christian heresy 273.1
GNP (Macroeconomics) 339.31
Gnus 599.645 9
Go (Game) 794.4
Goa, Daman and Diu (India) T2—547 99
Goajira Indians T5—983 9
Goajiro language 498.39
  T6—983 9
Goalkeeping
  ice hockey 796.962 27
  soccer 796.334 26
Goat (Meat) 641.363 9
  commercial processing 664.92
  cooking 641.663 9
  food 641.363 9
Goat hair textiles 677.33
  see also Textiles
Goatfishes 597.7
Goats 636.39
  animal husbandry 636.39
  zoology 599.648
Goat's milk 641.371 7
  cooking 641.671 7
  food 641.371 7
  processing 637.17
Goatsuckers 598.99
Gobi Desert (Mongolia and China) T2—517 3
Gobies 597.7
Gobiesociformes 597.62
God 211
  art representation 704.948
  arts 700.482 11
  T3C—382 11
  Buddhism 294.342 11
  Christianity 231
  comparative religion 291.211
  Hinduism 294.521 1
  Islam 297.211
  Judaism 296.311
  literature 808.803 821 1
    history and criticism 809.933 821 1
    specific literatures T3B—080 382 11
      history and criticism T3B—093 821 1
  philosophy of religion 211
Goddess religions 291.14
Goddesses 291.211 4
  arts 700.482 912 114
  T3C—382 912 114
  literature 808.803 829 12114
    history and criticism 809.933 829 12114
    specific literatures T3B—080 382 912114
      history and criticism T3B—093 829 12114
  see also Gods and goddesses
Gödel's theorem 511.3
Gods 291.211
  see also Gods and goddesses
Gods and goddesses 291.211
  African 299.63
  art representation 704.948

Gods and goddesses (continued)
arts 700.482 912 11
T3C—382 912 11
Australian 299.921 5
Buddhist 294.342 11
Celtic 299.16
Chinese 299.51
classical 292.211
Egyptian 299.31
folklore 398.21
history and criticism 398.45
Germanic 293.211
Greek 292.211
Hawaiian 299.924 2
Hindu 294.521 1
literature 808.803 829 1211
history and criticism 809.933 829 1211
specific literatures T3B—080 382 91211
history and criticism T3B—093 829 1211
Native American 299.73
North American 299.73
South American 299.83
Norse 293.211
Polynesian 299.924
Roman 292.211
Scandinavian 293.211
Semitic 299.2
Shinto 299.561 211
Goedelic languages 491.6
T6—916
Goedelic literatures 891.6
Goethite
mineralogy 549.525
Gogebic County (Mich.) T2—774 983
Gogo languages 496.391
T6—963 91
Goiás (Brazil : State) T2—817 3
Goidelic languages 491.6
T6—916
Goidelic literatures 891.6
Going public
financial management 658.152 24
Goiter
medicine 616.442
surgery 617.539
see also Endocrine system
Gojam Kifle Hāger
(Ethiopia) T2—633
Gold 669.22
chemical engineering 661.065 6
chemistry 546.656
economic geology 553.41
materials science 620.189 22
Gold (continued)
metallography 669.952 2
metallurgy 669.22
metalworking 673.22
mining 622.342 2
monetary law 343.032
physical metallurgy 669.962 2
production economics 338.274 1
prospecting 622.184 1
see also Chemicals; Metals
Gold Coast 966.703
T2—667
Gold coins 332.404 2
investment economics 332.63
monetary economics 332.404 2
numismatics 737.43
Gold movements 332.042
Gold standard 332.422 2
foreign exchange 332.452
Golden (B.C.) T2—711 68
Golden algae 579.86
Golden eagle 598.942 3
Golden Ears Provincial
Park (B.C.) T2—711 37
Golden Gate Highlands
National Park (South
Africa) T2—685 1
Golden hamsters 599.356
Golden Rule
Christianity 241.54
Judaism 296.36
Golden Valley County
(Mont.) T2—786 311
Golden Valley County
(N.D.) T2—784 95
Goldeneyes 598.415
Goldenrods 583.99
Goldfinches 598.885
Goldfish 639.374 84
culture 639.374 84
zoology 597.484
Goldi T5—941
Goldi language 494.1
T6—941
Golds T5—941
Goldsmithing 739.22
Golf 796.352
equipment technology 688.763 52
see also Sports
Golf courses 796.352 068
Golfers 796.352 092
sports group T7—796 35
Golgi apparatus 571.656
Goliad County (Tex.) T2—764 123

Gomel′ (Belarus : Oblast) T2—478 1
Gómez, Juan Vicente
  Venezuelan history 987.063 13
Gond (Dravidian people) T5—948 2
Gonder Kifle Hāger
    (Ethiopia) T2—634
Gondi language 494.823
  T6—948 23
Gondi literature 894.823
Gondola cars 385.34
  engineering 625.24
  see also Rolling stock
Gonga (African people) T5—935
Gongola State (Nigeria) T2—669 88
Gongs 786.884 3
  see also Percussion
    instruments
Gonorhynchiformes 597.5
Gonorrhea
  incidence 614.547 8
  medicine 616.951 5
  see also Communicable
    diseases (Human)
Gonystylus 583.68
  forestry 634.973 68
Gonzales County (Tex.) T2—764 257
Goochland County (Va.) T2—755 455
Good and evil 111.84
  ethics 170
    religion 291.5
      Christianity 241
      Islam 297.5
      Judaism 296.36
  religion 291.211 8
    Christianity 231.8
      freedom of choice 233.7
    comparative religion 291.211 8
    Islam 297.2
      freedom of choice 297.227
      theodicy 297.211 8
    Judaism 296.311 8
      freedom of choice 296.32
    philosophy of religion 214
Good Friday 263.925
  devotional literature 242.35
  music 781.726
  sermons 252.625
Good Hope, Cape of
    (South Africa : Cape) T2—687 35
Good luck charms 133.443
Good luck spells 133.443
Good News Bible 220.520 82
Goodeniaceae 583.98
Goodhue County (Minn.) T2—776 14
Gooding County (Idaho) T2—796 36
Goodness of God 214
  Christianity 231.8
  comparative religion 291.211 2
  Islam 297.211 2
  Judaism 296.311 2
  philosophy of religion 214
Goodwood (South Africa :
    District) T2—687 35
Goose hunting
  sports 799.244 7
Gooseberries 641.347 25
  botany 583.72
  cooking 641.647 25
  food 641.347 25
  horticulture 634.725
Goosefishes 597.62
Goosefoots (Plants) 583.53
Gophers (Ground squirrels) 599.365
Gophers (Pocket gophers) 599.359 9
Gorbachev, Mikhail Sergeevich
  Russian history 947.085 4
Gordioida 592.59
Gordon (Scotland :
    District) T2—412 32
Gordon County (Ga.) T2—758 362
Gordonia (South Africa :
    District) T2—687 12
Gore District (N.Z.) T2—939 7
Gorges 551.442
  T2—144
  geography 910.914 4
  geomorphology 551.442
  physical geography 910.021 44
Gorgonzola cheese 641.373 53
  cooking 641.673 53
  food 641.373 53
  processing 637.353
Gorilla 599.884
  big game hunting 799.278 84
  conservation technology 639.979 884
  resource economics 333.959 884
Gorizia (Italy : Province) T2—453 92
Gorj (Romania) T2—498 4
Gor′ki (Russia : Oblast) T2—474 1
Gor′kovskaia oblast′
    (Russia) T2—474 1
Gorno-Altay (Russia) T2—573
Gorno-Badakhshan
    Autonomous Oblast
    (Tajikistan) T2—586
Goroka (Papua New
    Guinea) T2—956 9

Gorzów Wielkopolski
(Poland : Voivodeship) T2—438 1
Gosford (N.S.W.) T2—944 2
Goshen County (Wyo.) T2—787 18
Gospel music 782.254
choral and mixed voices 782.525 4
single voices 783.092 54
Gospel stories retold 226.095 05
Gospels (Bible) 226
pseudepigrapha 229.8
Gosper County (Neb.) T2—782 387
Gosport (England) T2—422 78
Gossip
ethics 177.2
religion 291.567 2
Christianity 241.672
Judaism 296.367 2
see also Ethical problems
social psychology 302.24
Götaland (Sweden) T2—486
Göteborgs och Bohus län
(Sweden) T2—486
Gothic architecture 723.5
Gothic art 709.022
religious significance 246.1
Gothic calligraphy 745.619 75
Gothic decoration 745.442
Gothic fiction 808.838 729
history and criticism 809.387 29
specific literatures T3B—308 729
individual authors T3A—3
see Manual at T3B—308729
vs. T3B—3085
Gothic language 439.9
T6—399
literature 839.9
Gothic music 780.902
Gothic novels 808.838 729
history and criticism 809.387 29
specific literatures T3B—308 729
individual authors T3A—3
see Manual at T3B—308729
vs. T3B—3085
Gothic painting 759.022
Gothic revival architecture 724.3
Gothic sculpture 734.25
Gothic tracery 729.5
Gothic type 686.224 7
Goths (Germanic people) T5—39
Italian history 945.01
Gotlands län (Sweden) T2—486
Gouache 751.422
Goulart, João Belchior Marques
Brazilian history 981.062
Goulburn (N.S.W.) T2—944 7
Goulburn River (Vic.) T2—945 4
Gourds 583.63
floriculture 635.933 63
Gourmet cooking 641.514
Gout
medicine 616.399 9
see also Digestive system
Gove County (Kan.) T2—781 152
Governing boards
executive management 658.422
T1—068 4
hospitals 362.110 684
libraries 021.82
public administration 352.25
Government 320
ethics 172.2
see also Political ethics
see Manual at 320; *also at*
320.9, 320.4 vs. 351
Government accounting 657.835
law 343.034
Government advisory boards 352.743
Government agencies 351
see also Administrative
agencies
Government audit procedures 657.835 045
Government bills 332.632 32
see also Government
securities
Government bonds 332.632 32
see also Government
securities
Government buildings
architecture 725.1
area planning 711.551
Government certificates 332.632 32
see also Government
securities
Government cities
area planning 711.45
Government contracts 352.53
armed forces 355.621 2
law 346.023
Government corporations
law 346.067
public administration 352.266
public revenue source 336.19
Government documents
cataloging 025.343 4
Government employees 352.63
see also Government workers
Government expenditures 336.39
see also Public expenditures

Government gazettes 351.05
Government grants
  production economics 338.922
Government information services
  international relations 327.11
    libraries 027.65
    public administration 353.132 74
Government institutions
  sociology 306.2
Government investment 332.671 52
  domestic 332.672 52
  international 332.673 12
Government liability
  law 342.088
  public administration 352.885
Government libraries 027.5
  see Manual at 027.5
Government loans
  credit economics 332.7
  economic development 338.922
  law 343.074 2
  public revenues 336.15
Government notes 332.632 32
  see also Government securities
Government of Ireland Act, 1920 941.608 21
Government ownership
  land economics 333.1
Government procurement 352.53
  armed forces 355.621 2
Government property
  land economics 333.1
  law 343.02
  management 352.5
Government publications
  bibliographies 011.53
  cataloging 025.343 4
  library treatment 025.173 4
Government publishers 070.595
Government savings banks 332.21
Government securities 332.632 32
  investment economics 332.632 32
  law 346.092 2
    income tax law 343.052 46
  public administration 352.45
  public finance 336.31
  purchase
    central banking 332.114
  see Manual at 332.632044 vs. 332.6323: Gilt-edged securities
Government service 352.63
Government spending 336.39
  see also Public expenditures
Government-sponsored insurance 368.4
  law 344.02
  public administration 353.54
  see also Insurance
Government subsidies
  production economics 338.922
Government work force 352.63
Government workers 352.63
  administrative law 342.068
  biography 351.092
  labor economics 331.795
    labor force 331.119 042
    labor market 331.129 042
  occupational group T7—352 7
  pensions
    public administration 353.549
  public administration 352.63
  social class 305.553
Governmental investigations
  official misconduct 353.463
Governmental organizations 351
  see also Administrative agencies
Governmental social action 361.6
  see Manual at 361.6 vs. 361.7, 361.8
Governments-in-exile
  World War II 940.533 6
Governors (Control devices)
  internal-combustion engines 621.437
Governors (Executives) 321
  occupational group T7—351
  public administration 352.232 13
Governors-general (Commonwealth of Nations)
  public administration 352.233
Graaff-Reinet (South Africa : District) T2—687 14
Grace (Religious doctrine) 291.22
  Christianity 234
Gracias a Dios (Honduras : Dept.) T2—728 32
Grackles 598.874
Grade repetition 371.285
Grade schools 372
  see also Elementary education
Grade separations (Roads) 388.13
Grades (Military ranks) 355.33
Grading (Leveling)
  road engineering 625.733
Grading (Students) 371.272

Grading clothing
  commercial technology 687.042
Grading crops 631.567
Grading lumber 674.5
Gradual 264.36
  music 782.323 5
Graduate Record Examination 378.166 2
Graduate schools 378.155
Graduation from school 371.291 2
Graduations (Commencements)
  customs 394.2
Grady County (Ga.) T2—758 986
Grady County (Okla.) T2—766 54
Graffiti 080
  literature 808.882
    specific literatures T3B—802
      individual authors T3A—8
  painting 751.73
Graft (Crime) 364.132 3
  law 345.023 23
  public administration 353.46
Grafting (Plant propagation) 631.541
  equipment manufacturing
    technology 681.763 1
  fruit crops 634.044 1
  ornamental plants 635.915 41
Grafting (Surgery) 617.95
Grafton (N.S.W.) T2—944 3
Grafton County (N.H.) T2—742 3
Graham County (Ariz.) T2—791 54
Graham County (Kan.) T2—781 163
Graham County (N.C.) T2—756 97
Graham shorthand system 653.424 4
Grahamstown (South
    Africa) T2—687 5
Grain (Cereal) 641.331
  animal feed
    commercial processing 664.762
  commercial processing 664.7
  see also Cereals
Grain amaranths 641.331
  see also Amaranths
Grain beetles 633.104 976
Grain elevators 633.104 68
Grain legumes
  field crop 633.3
  see also Legumes
Grain sorghums 633.174
  grain crop 633.174
Grainger County (Tenn.) T2—768 932
Graining (Woodwork)
  buildings 698.32
Gram-negative aerobic rods and
    cocci 579.33
Gram-positive cocci 579.35
Graminales 584.9
  paleobotany 561.49
Grammar 415
  applied linguistics 418
    specific languages T4—8
  elementary education 372.61
  linguistics 415
    specific languages T4—5
  see Manual at 401.43 vs.
      306.44, 401.9, 412, 415:
      Meaning
Grammar schools (United
    Kingdom) 373.241
  see also Secondary education
Grammar schools (United
    States) 372
  see also Elementary education
Grammarians 415.092
  occupational group T7—4
Grammatical relations 415
  specific languages T4—5
Grammatidae 597.73
Grampian (Scotland) T2—412 1
Grampian Mountains
    (Scotland) T2—412 1
Grampians (Scotland) T2—412 1
Gran Colombia 986.104
 T2—861
  Colombian history 986.104
  Ecuadorian history 986.604
  Panamanian history 972.870 3
  Venezuelan history 987.05
Granada (Nicaragua :
    Dept.) T2—728 515
Granada (Spain : Province) T2—468 2
Granadillas 583.626
Granadine Confederation 986.105 3
  Colombian history 986.105 3
  Panamanian history 972.870 3
Granaries 633.104 68
Granby River (B.C.) T2—711 62
Grand Alliance, War of the,
    1688–1697 940.252 5
Grand Army of the Republic 369.15
Grand Bahama (Bahamas) T2—729 6
Grand Bahama Island T2—729 6
Grand Canyon National
    Park (Ariz.) T2—791 32
Grand County (Colo.) T2—788 65
Grand County (Utah) T2—792 58
Grand Forks (B.C.) T2—711 62
Grand Forks County (N.D.) T2—784 16
Grand Isle County (Vt.) T2—743 12

Grand jury 345.072
Grand Lake (Ohio) T2—771 415
Grand Manan Island (N.B.) T2—715 33
Grand Prairie (Tex.) T2—764 51
Grand Rapids (Mich.) T2—774 56
Grand River (Mich.) T2—774 15
Grand Teton National Park (Wyo.) T2—787 55
Grand Traverse Bay (Mich.) T2—774 64
Grand Traverse County (Mich.) T2—774 64
Grand unified theory 530.142
Grand'Anse (Haiti : Dept.) T2—729 466
Grandchildren 306.874 5
  T1—085 4
  T7—044 2
Grande Prairie (Alta.) T2—712 31
Grandparents 306.874 5
  T1—085 3
  T7—043 2
Grandstands
  architecture 725.827
Granit (Quebec) T2—714 69
Granite 553.52
  building material 691.2
  economic geology 553.52
  petrology 552.3
  quarrying 622.352
Granite Belt National Park (Qld.) T2—943 3
Granite County (Mont.) T2—786 88
Granite mosses 588.2
Granma (Cuba) T2—729 163
Grant, Ulysses S. (Ulysses Simpson)
  United States history 973.82
Grant County (Ark.) T2—767 71
Grant County (Ind.) T2—772 69
Grant County (Kan.) T2—781 723
Grant County (Ky.) T2—769 395
Grant County (Minn.) T2—776 44
Grant County (N.D.) T2—784 87
Grant County (N.M.) T2—789 692
Grant County (Neb.) T2—782 783
Grant County (Okla.) T2—766 23
Grant County (Or.) T2—795 78
Grant County (S.D.) T2—783 24
Grant County (W. Va.) T2—754 92
Grant County (Wash.) T2—797 32
Grant County (Wis.) T2—775 77
Grant Parish (La.) T2—763 67
Grants
  capital procurement 658.152 24
  education 379.11
    T1—079
    financial management 371.206
    public policy 379.11
    student aid 371.223
      higher education 378.33
      see also Scholarships
  production economics 338.922
  public administration 352.73
  research 001.44
    T1—079
  students T1—079
Grants-in-aid (Government) 336.185
  law 343.034
  public administration 352.73
  public finance 336.185
Granulocytes 571.968
  human immunology 616.079 9
Granville County (N.C.) T2—756 535
Grape ferns 587.33
Grape wine 641.22
  commercial processing 663.2
  cooking with 641.622
  home preparation 641.872
Grapefruit 641.343 2
  commercial processing 664.804 32
  cooking 641.643 2
  food 641.343 2
  orchard crop 634.32
Grapes 641.348
  botany 583.86
  commercial processing 664.804 8
  cooking 641.648
  food 641.348
  viticulture 634.8
Graph theory 511.5
Graphic artists 760.092
  occupational group T7—76
Graphic arts 760
Graphic arts paper 676.282
Graphic design
  arts 741.6
Graphic designers 741.609 2
Graphic expressions
  psychology 152.384 5
Graphic novels 741.5
Graphic representation 604.2
  T1—022 1
Graphic statics
  mechanics 531.12
  solids 531.2
  structural analysis 624.171 2

Graphical user interfaces
  systems programs 005.437
  see Manual at 005.269 and 005.284, 005.3684, 005.384
Graphics
  computer science 006.6
    T1—028 566
  engineering 621.399
  statistical presentation 001.422 6
    T1—072 8
Graphics programming languages 006.663
Graphics terminals 006.62
Graphics utilities 006.68
Graphite 553.26
  chemical engineering 662.92
  economic geology 553.26
  materials science 620.198
  mineralogy 549.27
  mining 622.336
  synthetic 666.86
Graphitic anthracite coal
  properties 662.622 5
Graphology 155.282
  criminal investigation 363.256 5
  divination 137
  personnel selection 658.311 2
Graphs 511.5
    T1—022
Graptolitoidea 563.55
Grass skiing 796.2
  see also Sports
Grass wax 665.12
Grass wetlands
  biology 578.768 4
  ecology 577.684
  see also Wetlands
Grasses 584.9
  botany 584.9
  cereal crops 633.1
  floriculture 635.964
  forage crops 633.2
  ornamental gardening 635.934 9
  paleobotany 561.49
Grasshoppers 595.726
  agricultural pests 632.726
  culture 638.572 6
Grasslands 333.74
    T2—153
  biology 578.74
  ecology 577.4
  economics 333.74
  geography 910.915 3
Grasslands (continued)
  geomorphology 551.453
  physical geography 910.021 53
Gratiot County (Mich.) T2—774 49
Gratitude 179.9
  see also Virtues
Graubünden (Switzerland) T2—494 73
Graubünden National Park T2—494 73
Graupel 551.578 7
Gravel 553.626
  economic geology 553.626
  materials science 620.191
  quarrying 622.362 6
Gravel pavements 625.82
Graves County (Ky.) T2—769 93
Graves' disease
  medicine 616.443
  see also Endocrine system
Graves registration service (Armed forces) 355.699
Gravesham (England) T2—422 315
Gravestone inscriptions
  genealogy 929.5
Gravimetric analysis 543.083
Gravitation 531.14
  see also Gravity
Gravitational interaction 539.754
Gravitational prospecting 622.152
Gravity 531.14
  astromechanics 629.411 1
  biophysics 571.435
    humans 612.014 412
  celestial mechanics 521.1
  mechanics 531.14
  solid mechanics 531.5
Gravity concentration of ores 622.751
Gravity determinations
  geodesy 526.7
Gravity planes
  mining 622.66
Gray County (Kan.) T2—781 74
Gray County (Tex.) T2—764 827
Gray fox 599.776
Gray kangaroos 599.222
Gray partridge 598.623 2
Gray seal 599.793
Gray squirrel 599.362
Gray whale 599.522
  conservation technology 639.979 522
  resource economics 333.959 522
Gray wolf 599.773
Graylings 597.559
Grays Harbor County (Wash.) T2—797 95

Graysby 597.736
Grayson County (Ky.) T2—769 842
Grayson County (Tex.) T2—764 557
Grayson County (Va.) T2—755 717
Grazing 591.54
  animal husbandry 636.084 5
  descriptive zoology 591.54
Grazing lands 333.74
GRE (Graduate Record Examination) 378.166 2
Great apes 599.88
Great Australian Bight (W.A. and S. Aust.) 551.467 76
  T2—165 76
Great Barrier Island (N.Z.) T2—932 4
Great Barrier Reef (Qld.) T2—943
Great Basin 979
  T2—79
Great Basin National Park T2—793 15
Great Bear Lake (N.W.T.) T2—719 3
Great Belt (Denmark) 551.461 34
  T2—163 34
Great blue shark 597.34
Great Britain 941
  T2—41
  ancient 936.1
  T2—361
  see Manual at 941
Great Britain. Attorney-General 345.420 1
Great Britain. Children's Hearings (Scotland) 345.411 08
Great Britain. County Court 347.420 21
Great Britain. Court of Appeal 347.420 32
Great Britain. Court of Appeal. Civil Division 347.420 35
Great Britain. Court of Appeal. Criminal Division 345.420 18
Great Britain. Court of Appeal (Scotland) 345.411 016 3
Great Britain. Court of First Instance (Scotland) 345.411 016 2
Great Britain. Court of Session (Scotland) 347.411 023
Great Britain. Court of Session. Inner House (Scotland) 347.411 035
Great Britain. Court of Session. Outer House (Scotland) 347.411 024
Great Britain. Court of the Lord Lyon (Scotland) 347.411 04
Great Britain. Crown Counsel (Scotland) 345.411 01
Great Britain. Crown Court 345.420 14
Great Britain. Director of Public Prosecutions 345.420 1
Great Britain. District Court (Scotland) 345.411 012
Great Britain. High Court of Justice 347.420 25
Great Britain. High Court of Justice. Chancery Division 347.420 26
Great Britain. High Court of Justice. King's Bench Division 347.420 27
Great Britain. High Court of Justice. Queen's Bench Division 347.420 27
Great Britain. High Court of Justice. Queen's Bench Division. Divisional Court 345.420 16
Great Britain. High Court of Justiciary (Scotland) 345.411 016
Great Britain. House of Lords (Court of last resort) 347.420 39
Great Britain. House of Lords (Court of last resort) (Scotland) 347.411 039
Great Britain. Licensing Appeals Court (Scotland) 347.411 04
Great Britain. Licensing Courts (Scotland) 347.411 04
Great Britain. Lord Advocate (Scotland) 345.411 01
Great Britain. Magistrates Court 345.420 12
Great Britain. Magistrates Court. Domestic Court 347.420 23
Great Britain. Privy Council. Judicial Committee 347.420 4
Great Britain. Sheriff Court (Scotland) 347.411 021
  criminal law 345.411 014
Great Britain. Sheriff-Principal (Scotland) 347.411 032
Great Britain. Solicitor-General (Scotland) 345.411 01
Great Britain. Supreme Court of Judicature 347.420 29
Great Dane 636.73
Great Dividing Range T2—94
Great Earthquake, 1692 972.920 32
Great Glen (Scotland) T2—411 75
Great grandchildren 306.874 5
  T1—085 4
  T7—044 2
Great grandparents 306.874 5
  T1—085 3
  T7—043 2

Great Grimsby (England)	T2—428 34	
Great Indian Desert (India and Pakistan)	T2—544	
Great Karoo (South Africa)	T2—687 15	
Great Karroo (South Africa)	T2—687 15	
Great Lake (Tas.)	T2—946 3	
Great Lakes	T2—77	
Canada	T2—713	
United States	T2—77	
Great Moravian Empire		943.702 1
	T2—437	
Great Northern War, 1700–1721		947.05
Great Ouse River (England)	T2—426	
Great Plains	T2—78	
Colorado	T2—788 7	
Montana	T2—786 1	
New Mexico	T2—789 2	
Texas	T2—764 8	
Wyoming	T2—787 1	
Great Pyrenee (Dog)		636.73
Great Rift Valley	T2—676	
Great Salt Lake (Utah)	T2—792 42	
Great Salt Lake Desert (Utah)	T2—792 43	
Great Sand Dunes National Monument (Colo.)	T2—788 49	
Great Sandy Desert (W.A.)	T2—941 5	
Great schism, 1054		270.38
Great Slave Lake (N.W.T.)	T2—719 3	
Great Smoky Mountains (N.C. and Tenn.)	T2—768 89	
North Carolina	T2—756 96	
Tennessee	T2—768 89	
Great Smoky Mountains National Park (N.C. and Tenn.)	T2—768 89	
Great Trek, 1835–1838		968.042
Great Valley (Calif.)	T2—794 5	
Great Victoria Desert (W.A.)	T2—941 5	
Great War, 1914–1918		940.3
Great whales		599.5
Great White Brotherhood		299.93
Great white shark		597.33
Great Yarmouth (England)	T2—426 18	
Greater Anchorage Area Borough (Alaska)	T2—798 35	
Greater Antilles	T2—729	
Greater Manchester (England)	T2—427 3	
Greater Vancouver (B.C.)	T2—711 33	
Grebes		598.443
Grebo language		496.33
	T6—963 3	
Greco-Roman wrestling		796.812 2
see also Sports		
Greco-Turkish War, 1896–1897		949.507 2
Greece		949.5
	T2—495	
ancient		938
	T2—38	
Greed		178
moral theology		291.568
see also Vices		
Greek architecture		722.8
Greek calligraphy		745.619 8
Greek language		480
	T6—8	
Biblical texts		220.48
printing		686.218
Greek language (Modern)		489.3
	T6—89	
Greek law		
ancient		340.538
Greek-letter societies		371.85
	T1—06	
Greek literature		880
Greek literature (Modern)		889
Greek philosophy		180
modern		199.495
Greek religion		292.08
Greek revival architecture		724.23
Greek sculpture		733.3
Greeks (Ethnic group)	T5—8	
ancient	T5—81	
modern	T5—89	
Greeks (National group)	T5—893	
Greeley County (Kan.)	T2—781 413	
Greeley County (Neb.)	T2—782 49	
Green algae		579.83
Green bacteria		579.38
Green Bay (Wis. and Mich.)	T2—775 63	
Green County (Ky.)	T2—769 695	
Green County (Wis.)	T2—775 86	
Green fodder		
forage crop		633.2
Green integral		515.43
Green Lake County (Wis.)	T2—775 59	
Green manures		631.874
Green monkeys		599.862
Green Mountains (Vt.)	T2—743	
Green peppers		641.356 43
see also Sweet peppers		
Green River (Ky. : River)	T2—769 8	

Green River (Wyo.-Utah)	T2—792 5
Utah	T2—792 5
Wyoming	T2—787 85
Green seaweeds	579.83
Greenbrier County (W. Va.)	T2—754 88
Greenbrier River (W. Va.)	T2—754 88
Greenbriers	584.356
Greene County (Ala.)	T2—761 42
Greene County (Ark.)	T2—767 993
Greene County (Ga.)	T2—758 612
Greene County (Ill.)	T2—773 84
Greene County (Ind.)	T2—772 42
Greene County (Iowa)	T2—777 466
Greene County (Miss.)	T2—762 173
Greene County (Mo.)	T2—778 78
Greene County (N.C.)	T2—756 393
Greene County (N.Y.)	T2—747 37
Greene County (Ohio)	T2—771 74
Greene County (Pa.)	T2—748 83
Greene County (Tenn.)	T2—768 91
Greene County (Va.)	T2—755 375
Greenhouse effect	363.738 74
crop damage	632.1
ecology	577.276
meteorology	551.525 3
pollution aspects	363.738 74
social effects	304.28
weather forecasting	551.642 5
Greenhouse gardening	635.048 3
floriculture	635.982 3
Greenhouses	631.583
agriculture	631.583
architecture	728.924
construction	690.892 4
floriculture	635.982 3
gardening	635.048 3
Greenland	998.2
	T2—982
Greenland halibut	597.694
Greenland right whale	599.527 6
Greenland Sea	551.468 4
	T2—163 24
Greenlandic Inuit	T5—971 2
Greenlandic Inuit language	497.12
	T6—971 2
Greenlandic Inuktitut language	497.12
	T6—971 2
Greenlandic language	497.12
	T6—971 2
Greenlee County (Ariz.)	T2—791 51
Greenlets	598.878
Greenockite	
mineralogy	549.32
Greensands	
petrology	552.5
Greensville County (Va.)	T2—755 572
Greenup County (Ky.)	T2—769 293
Greenville County (S.C.)	T2—757 27
Greenwich (London, England)	T2—421 62
Greenwood (B.C.)	T2—711 62
Greenwood County (Kan.)	T2—781 913
Greenwood County (S.C.)	T2—757 33
Greer County (Okla.)	T2—766 443
Greeting card verse	808.818
history and criticism	809.18
specific literatures	T3B—108
individual authors	T3A—1
Greeting cards	
handicrafts	745.594 1
illustration	741.684
Greetings	
etiquette	395.4
Gregg County (Tex.)	T2—764 189
Gregg shorthand systems	653.427
Gregorian calendar	529.43
Gregorian chants	782.322 2
Gregory County (S.D.)	T2—783 59
Grenada	972.984 5
	T2—729 845
Grenada County (Miss.)	T2—762 635
Grenades	623.451 14
Grenadiers	356.162
Grenadiers (Fishes)	597.63
Grenadine (Textile)	677.652
Grenadines	T2—729 844
Grenville (Ont. : County)	T2—713 73
Grevena (Greece : Nome)	T2—495 62
Grevilleas	635.933 89
botany	583.89
floriculture	635.933 89
Grey (Ont. : County)	T2—713 18
Grey Cup	796.335 648
Grey District (N.Z.)	T2—937 2
Greyhound	636.753 4
Greyhound racing	798.85
Greylag goose	598.417 3
Greytown (South Africa)	T2—684 7
Gridiron street patterns	
area planning	711.41
Gridirons (American football)	796.332 068
Grief	152.4
at death	155.937
Christianity	
pastoral theology	259.6

Grief
  at death
    Christianity (continued)
      personal religion 248.866
      prayers and meditations 242.4
    psychology 155.937
Grievances (Labor) 331.889 6
  economics 331.889 6
  law 344.018 896
  personnel management 658.315 5
    public administration 352.68
Grievances against government
  public administration 352.885
Griffith (N.S.W.) T2—944 8
Griggs County (N.D.) T2—784 34
Grilling (Cooking) 641.76
Grills (Cooking equipment)
  electric cooking 641.586
  outdoor cooking 641.578 4
Grills (Screens)
  ironwork
    arts 739.48
Grimes County (Tex.) T2—764 243
Grimoire 133.43
Grimsby (England) T2—428 34
Grinding
  chemical engineering 660.284 22
  ores 622.73
Grinding coal 662.623
Grinding metals 671.35
Grinding tools 621.92
Grindstones 621.923
Griqualand East (South Africa) T2—684 6
Grise Fiord (N.W.T.) T2—719 5
Grisons 599.766
Grisons (Switzerland) T2—494 73
Grizzly bear 599.784
  conservation technology 639.979 784
  resource economics 333.959 784
Groblersdal (South Africa : District) T2—682 3
Grodno (Belarus : Oblast) T2—478 8
Groined arches 721.44
  architecture 721.44
  construction 690.144
Groined vaults 721.44
  architecture 721.44
  construction 690.144
Groningen (Netherlands : Province) T2—492 12
Grooming 646.7
  child training 649.63
Grooming behavior (Animals) 591.563
Grooming of animals 636.083 3
Groote Eylandt (N.T.) T2—942 95
Grosbeaks 598.883
Gross domestic product 339.31
Gross national product 339.31
Grosse Île (Montmagny, Quebec) T2—714 735
Grosseto (Italy : Province) T2—455 7
Grossulariaceae 583.72
Grotesque
  arts T3C—15
  literature 808.801 5
    history and criticism 809.915
    specific literatures T3B—080 15
      history and criticism T3B—091 5
Grottoes 551.447
  T2—144
  see also Caves
Ground bass 781.827
  instrumental 784.182 7
Ground beetles 595.762
Ground cover 635.964
  floriculture 635.964
  landscape architecture 716
Ground-effect machines
  engineering 629.3
Ground forces (Military science) 355
Ground inspections
  aircraft 629.134 52
Ground ivy 583.96
Ground operations (Armed forces) 355.4
  see also Land operations
Ground photogrammetry 526.982 5
Ground squirrels 599.365
Ground substances (Histology)
  human 611.018 2
Ground surveying 526.9
Ground testing facilities
  spacecraft 629.478
Ground tests
  aircraft 629.134 52
Ground transportation 388
  engineering 629.049
  law 343.094
  military engineering 623.61
  public administration 354.76
  safety 363.12
    see also Transportation safety
  transportation services 388
    urban 388.4
      see also Urban transportation

Ground transportation facilities
 area planning 711.7
Ground warfare 355.02
Ground wood process 676.122
Ground zithers 787.73
 see also Stringed instruments
Groundhog 599.366
Grounding devices 621.317
 radio engineering 621.384 133
Grounding prevention
 seamanship 623.888 4
Groundnuts (Peanuts) 641.356 596
 see also Peanuts
Grounds
 landscape architecture 712
 prisons 365.5
Grounds management 658.2
 libraries 022.1
 museums 069.21
 public administration 352.57
 see also Plant management
Groundsels 583.99
Groundwater 553.79
 T2—169 8
 artificial recharge 627.56
 economic geology 553.79
 economics 333.910 4
 hydrology 551.49
 public administration 354.36
 water supply engineering 628.114
Group banking 332.16
Group behavior 302.3
Group counseling 158.35
Group decision making
 management use 658.403 6
Group dynamics 302.3
Group homes 363.59
 chronically ill persons 362.16
 see also Health care facilities; Health services
 disabled persons 362.404 85
 homeless persons 362.5
 maladjusted young people 362.74
 mentally ill persons 362.223
 see also Mental health services
 mentally retarded persons 362.385
 older persons 362.61
 see also Halfway houses
Group insurance 368.3
 see also Insurance
Group practice
 medicine 610.65
Group psychotherapy
 prisoner services 365.66
 psychiatry 616.891 52
 see also Mental illness
Group relations training
 social psychology 302.14
Group sex 306.77
Group teaching 371.395
Group work
 education 371.36
 social welfare 361.4
Groupers 597.736
Grouping of students 371.25
Groupoids 512.2
Groups (Air force) 358.413 1
Groups (Mathematics) 512.2
Groups (Naval air force) 359.943 4
Groups of figures
 art representation 704.942 6
 painting 757.6
Groupware 005.376
Grouse 598.63
 conservation technology 639.978 63
 resource economics 333.958 63
 sports hunting 799.246 3
Growing points (Plants) 575.48
Growlers (Ice formations) 551.342
Growth 571.8
 animals 571.81
 cells 571.849
 developmental biology 571.8
 human physiology 612.6
 microorganisms 571.849 29
 plants 571.82
Growth (Social development) 303.44
Growth regulators
 agriculture 631.89
 chemical engineering 668.6
Grues, Île aux (Quebec) T2—714 735
Grues Island (Quebec) T2—714 735
Gruidae 598.32
Gruiformes 598.32
 paleozoology 568.3
Grundy County (Ill.) T2—773 265
Grundy County (Iowa) T2—777 537
Grundy County (Mo.) T2—778 215
Grundy County (Tenn.) T2—768 78
Grunts (Fishes) 597.7
Grylloblattodea 595.726
GSP (Tariff) 382.753
 see also Customs (Tariff)
Guadalajara (Spain : Province) T2—464 9

Guadalcanal (Solomon Islands)	T2—959 33
Guadalquivir River (Spain)	T2—468
Guadalupe County (N.M.)	T2—789 25
Guadalupe County (Tex.)	T2—764 34
Guadalupe Mountains National Park (Tex.)	T2—764 94
Guadalupe River (Tex.)	T2—764 12
Guadeloupe	972.976
	T2—729 76
Guaicuru languages	498
	T6—98
Guainía (Colombia)	T2—861 67
Guairá (Paraguay)	T2—892 128
Guajira (Colombia : Dept.)	T2—861 17
Guajiro language	498.39
	T6—983 9
Guam	T2—967
Guanabara (Brazil : State)	T2—815 3
Guanacaste (Costa Rica : Province)	T2—728 66
Guanaco	599.636 7
animal husbandry	636.296 6
Guanaco wool textiles	677.32
see also Textiles	
Guanajuato (Mexico : State)	T2—724 1
Guanche language	493.3
	T6—933
Guangdong Sheng (China)	T2—512 7
Guangxi Zhuangzu Zizhiqu (China)	T2—512 8
Guano	
agricultural use	631.866
Guans	598.64
Guantánamo (Cuba : Province)	T2—729 167
Guaraní Indians	T5—983 82
Guaraní language	498.382
	T6—983 82
Guaraní literature	898.382
Guaranteed minimum income	362.582
law	344.032 582
public administration	353.54
Guaranteed-wage plans	331.23
Guarantees	343.08
Guarantees (Insurance)	368.85
Guaranty (Suretyship)	346.074
Guard animals	636.088 6
Guard dogs	636.73
Guarda (Portugal : District)	T2—469 31
Guardian and ward	346.018
Guárico (Venezuela : State)	T2—874 7
Guatemala	972.81
	T2—728 1
Guatemala (Guatemala : Dept.)	T2—728 11
Guatemalan literature	860
Guatemalans	T5—687 281
Guavas	641.344 21
botany	583.765
commercial processing	664.804 421
cooking	641.644 21
food	641.344 21
orchard crop	634.421
Guaviare (Colombia)	T2—861 66
Guayama (P.R. : District)	T2—729 58
Guayaquil, Gulf of	551.466 1
	T2—164 1
Guayas (Ecuador : Province)	T2—866 32
Guaycuruan languages	498
	T6—98
Guaymi Indians	T5—978
Guaymi language	497.8
	T6—978
Guayule	583.99
Guelma (Algeria : Province)	T2—655
Guelmim (Morocco : Province)	T2—646
Guelph (Ont.)	T2—713 43
Guenons	599.862
Guernsey (England)	T2—423 42
Guernsey cattle	636.224
Guernsey County (Ohio)	T2—771 92
Guernsey lily	635.934 34
floriculture	635.934 34
Guerrero (Mexico : State)	T2—727 3
Guerrilla tactics	355.425
Guerrilla troops	356.15
Guerrilla warfare	355.021 8
Guests	
seating at table	642.6
Guevara, Ernesto	
Cuban communism	335.434 7
GUI (User interface)	
systems programs	005.437
Guiana	988
	T2—88
Guidance	
crime prevention	364.48
education	371.4
manned space flight	629.453
social welfare	361.06
older persons	362.66
space flight	629.41
unmanned space flight	629.433

Guidance systems
  spacecraft 629.474 2
  unmanned spacecraft 629.464 2
Guidebooks 910.202
  see Manual at 913–919: Add table: 04: Guidebooks; *also at* 913–919 vs. 796.51: Walkers' guides
Guidebooks of exhibits T1—074
Guided aircraft
  control systems 629.132 6
  military engineering 623.746 9
Guided-light communication 621.382 75
Guided missile forces 358.17
  in space 358.8
  navy 359.981 7
Guided missiles 358.171 82
  engineering 623.451 9
  military equipment 358.171 82
Guided missiles in space 358.882
  engineering 623.451 98
  military equipment 358.882
Guided-way systems 388.42
  see also Local rail transit systems
Guides to religious life 291.44
  Buddhism 294.344 4
  Christianity 248.4
  Hinduism 294.544
  Islam 297.57
    Sufi 297.44
  Judaism 296.7
Guiding equipment (Tools) 621.992
Guild socialism 335.15
Guild system 338.632
Guildford (England) T2—422 162
Guilford County (N.C.) T2—756 62
Guillain-Barré syndrome
  medicine 616.87
  see also Nervous system
Guilt
  psychology 152.4
  religion 291.22
    Christianity 233.4
    Judaism 296.32
Guilt (Law) 345.04
Guinea 966.52
  T2—665 2
Guinea, Gulf of 551.464 73
  T2—163 73
Guinea-Bissau 966.57
  T2—665 7
Guinea-Bissauans T5—966 57
Guinea fowl 636.593
  animal husbandry 636.593
  zoology 598.64
Guinea pigs 636.935 92
  animal husbandry 636.935 92
  experimental animals
    medicine 619.93
  zoology 599.359 2
Guineans T5—966 52
Guipúzcoa (Spain) T2—466 1
Guiros 786.886
  see also Percussion instruments
Guitar concertos 784.278 7
Guitarfishes 597.35
Guitarists 787.870 92
  occupational group T7—787
Guitars 787.87
  instrument 787.871 9
  music 787.87
  see also Stringed instruments
Guizhou Sheng (China) T2—513 4
Gujar (South Asian people) T5—914 7
Gujarat (India) T2—547 5
Gujarati T5—914 7
Gujarati language 491.47
  T6—914 71
Gujarati literature 891.47
Gulches 551.442
  T2—144
  geography 910.914 4
  geomorphology 551.442
  physical geography 910.021 44
Gulf Coast (U.S.) 976
  T2—76
Gulf County (Fla.) T2—759 947
Gulf Islands (B.C.) T2—711 28
Gulf of Aden 551.467 32
  T2—165 32
Gulf of Alaska (Alaska) 551.466 34
  T2—164 34
Gulf of Aqaba 551.467 33
  T2—165 33
Gulf of Bothnia 551.461 34
  T2—163 34
Gulf of California (Mexico) 551.466 1
  T2—164 1
Gulf of Darien (Colombia) 551.463 5
  T2—163 65
Gulf of Finland 551.461 34
  T2—163 34
Gulf of Guayaquil 551.466 1
  T2—164 1

Gulf of Guinea 551.464 73
T2—163 73
Gulf of Honduras 551.463 5
T2—163 65
Gulf of Lions (France) 551.462 2
T2—163 82
Gulf of Martaban (Burma) 551.467 65
T2—165 65
Gulf of Mexico 551.463 4
T2—163 64
Gulf of Oman 551.467 36
T2—165 36
Gulf of Panama (Panama) 551.466 1
T2—164 1
Gulf of Paria (Venezuela and Trinidad and Tobago) 551.464 66
T2—163 66
Gulf of Riga (Latvia and Estonia) 551.461 34
T2—163 34
Gulf of Saint Lawrence 551.461 44
T2—163 44
Gulf of Siam 551.465 72
T2—164 72
Gulf of Suez 551.467 33
T2—165 33
Gulf of Taranto (Italy) 551.462 6
T2—163 86
Gulf of Tehuantepec (Mexico) 551.466 1
T2—164 1
Gulf of Thailand 551.465 72
T2—164 72
Gulf of Urabá (Colombia) 551.463 5
T2—163 65
Gulf of Venice (Italy) 551.462 5
T2—163 85
Gulf Province (Papua New Guinea) T2—954 7
Gulf Stream 551.471 1
Gulf War, 1980–1988 955.054 2
Gulf War, 1991 956.704 42
Gulfs
  resource economics 333.916 4
Gullah dialect 427.975 799
T6—217
Gulls 598.338
Gum-bichromate processes 773.5
Gum trees (Eucalypti) 583.766
  see also Eucalyptus
Gumatj language 499.15
T6—991 5
Gumma-ken (Japan) T2—521 33
Gums (Mouth parts)
  animal physiology 573.35
  descriptive zoology 596.14
  human anatomy 611.31
  human diseases
    dentistry 617.632
    incidence 614.599 6
  human physiology 612.31
  see also Dentistry; Digestive system
Gums (Substances) 572.567 2
  biochemistry 572.567 2
  chemistry 547.783
  commercial processing 668.37
  fossil 553.29
  materials science 620.192 4
  see also Carbohydrates
Gümüşhane İli (Turkey) T2—565
Gun control 363.33
  civil rights issues 323.43
  law 344.053 3
  public administration 353.36
  public safety 363.33
Gun mounts 623.43
Gun salutes
  armed forces 355.134 9
Guncotton 662.26
  military engineering 623.452 6
Gundis 599.359
Gundogs 636.752
Gunma-ken (Japan) T2—521 33
Gunmetal 669.3
  materials science 620.182
  metallography 669.953
  metallurgy 669.3
  metalworking 673.3
  physical metallurgy 669.963
Gunneras 635.933 82
  botany 583.82
  floriculture 635.933 82
Gunnery 623.55
Gunnison County (Colo.) T2—788 41
Gunpowder 662.26
  military engineering 623.452 6
Guns (Artillery) 355.821
  see also Artillery
Guns (Small arms) 683.4
  art metalwork 739.744 2
  civil rights issues 323.43
  control 363.33
  law 344.053 3
  military engineering 623.442
  military equipment 355.824 2
  military training 355.547

Guns (Small arms) (continued)
  shooting game 799.213
  sports 799.202 83
  target shooting 799.31
Gunshot wounds
  medicine 617.145
Gunsmithing 683.4
Gunsmiths 683.400 92
  occupational group T7—683
Guntersville Lake (Ala. and Tenn.) T2—761 94
Guppies 597.667
  culture 639.376 67
Gupta dynasty 934.06
Gur languages 496.35
  T6—963 5
Gur literatures 896.35
Gurage (African people) T5—928
Gurage language 492.8
  T6—928
Gurage literature 892.8
Gurma (African people) T5—963 5
Gurma language 496.35
  T6—963 5
Gurnards 597.68
Guru Granth 294.682
Gurung language 495.4
  T6—954
Gurus 200.92
  biography 200.92
  Buddhist 294.309 2
    biography 294.309 2
      specific sects 294.39
    role and function 294.361
  Hindu 294.509 2
    biography 294.509 2
      specific sects 294.55
    role and function 294.561
  role and function 291.61
  Sikh 294.609 2
    biography 294.609 2
    role and function 294.663
  see Manual at 200.92 and 291–299
Gusii (African people) T5—963 95
Gusii language 496.395
  T6—963 95
Gustation 573.878
  human physiology 612.87
Gustatory organs
  human anatomy 611.87
  see also Nervous system
Gustatory perception
  psychology 152.167
Guthrie, Edwin R. (Edwin Ray)
  psychological system 150.194 34
Guthrie County (Iowa) T2—777 49
Gutters
  road engineering 625.734
Guttiferae 583.624
Guyana 988.1
  T2—881
Guyandotte River (W. Va.) T2—754 4
Guyane 988.2
  T2—882
Guyanese T5—914 1
Guyenne (France) T2—447
Guysborough (N.S. : County) T2—716 21
Guzmán Blanco, Antonio
  Venezuelan history 987.062
Gwent (Wales) T2—429 9
Gwinnett County (Ga.) T2—758 223
Gwydir River (N.S.W.) T2—944 4
Gwynedd (Wales) T2—429 2
Gymnascales 579.565
Gymnasiums (Secondary schools) 373.241
  see also Secondary education
Gymnasiums (Sports) 796.406 8
  architecture 725.85
  sports 796.406 8
Gymnastic exercises 613.714
Gymnastics 796.44
  see also Sports
Gymnasts 796.440 92
  sports group T7—796 4
Gymnolaemata 594.676
Gymnophiona 597.82
  paleozoology 567.8
Gymnosomata 594.34
Gymnosperms 585
  forestry 634.975
  paleobotany 561.5
Gympie (Qld.) T2—943 2
Gynecologic cancer
  incidence 614.599 946 5
  medicine 616.994 65
  see also Cancer (Human)
Gynecologic disorders 362.198 1
  see also Female genital system
Gynecologic nursing
  medicine 610.736 78
Gynecologic surgery 618.105 9
  see also Female genital system
Gynecologists 618.100 92
  law 344.041 2
  occupational group T7—618 1

Gynecologists (continued)
role and function 618.102 32
see also Female genital system
Gynecology 618.1
anesthesiology 617.968 1
geriatrics 618.978 1
pediatrics 618.920 98
surgery 618.105 9
see also Female genital system
Gynoplasty 618.105 92
see also Female genital system
Győr-Sopron Megye (Hungary) T2—439 7
Gypsies T5—914 97
Gypsum 553.635
economic geology 553.635
mineralogy 549.755
mining 622.363 5
petrology 552.5
Gypsum plasters 666.92
Gypsy language 491.497
T6—914 97
Gypsy literature 891.497
Gypsy moth
agricultural pests 634.049 78
Gyrinidae 595.762
Gyrocompasses
aircraft engineering 629.135 1
Gyrodynamics 531.34
Gyrohorizons 629.135 2
Gyropilots 629.135 2
Gyroscopes
manufacturing technology 681.753

H

Haakon County (S.D.) T2—783 56
Haar integral 515.43
Haarlem (Netherlands) T2—492 35
Habad Lubavitch Hasidism 296.833 22
Habakkuk (Biblical book) 224.95
Habeas corpus 347.05
criminal law 345.056
Habersham County (Ga.) T2—758 125
Habit breaking 152.33
Habitat improvement (Wildlife)
technology 639.92
Habitations
animals 591.564
Habits
child training 649.6
customs 390
psychology 152.33
Habituations 362.29
see also Substance abuse
Habré, Hissein
Chadian history 967.430 43
Habyarimana, Juvénal
Rwandan history 967.571 04
Hackberries 583.45
Hackensack River (N.Y. and N.J.) T2—749 21
Hackney (London, England) T2—421 44
Hackney horse 636.14
Haddocks 641.392
cooking 641.692
food 641.392
zoology 597.632
Hades 291.23
see also Hell
Hadith 297.124
Ḥadj 297.352
Hadrian's Wall (England) T2—428 81
Hadrons 539.721 6
Hadrosauridae 567.914
Haematopodidae 598.33
Haemodoraceae 584.354
Hafnium 669.79
chemical engineering 661.051 4
chemistry 546.514
metallurgy 669.79
see also Chemicals
Hagfishes 597.2
Haggadah (Passover) 296.453 71
Haggai (Biblical book) 224.97
Ḥagigah 296.123 2
Babylonian Talmud 296.125 2
Mishnah 296.123 2
Palestinian Talmud 296.124 2
Hagiographa (Bible) 223
Hague (Netherlands) T2—492 382
Hahnium
chemistry 546.52
see also Chemicals
Haida Indians T5—972
Haida language 497.2
T6—972
Haifa (Israel : District) T2—569 46
Haiku 808.814 1
history and criticism 809.141
specific literatures T3B—104 1
individual authors T3A—1
Hail 551.578 7
crop damage 632.14
weather forecasting 551.647 87

Hail insurance 368.122
  crops 368.121
  see also Insurance
Hail Mary 242.74
Haile Selassie I, Emperor of Ethiopia
  Ethiopian history 963.055
    as emperor 963.055
    as regent and king 963.054
Hailstones 551.578 7
Hailstorms 551.554
  social services 363.349 24
  see also Disasters
Hainan Province (China) T2—512 9
Hainaut (Belgium) T2—493 42
Haines Borough (Alaska) T2—798 2
Hair 599.147
  animal husbandry 636.088 45
  animal physiology 573.58
  descriptive zoology 599.147
  geriatrics 618.976 546
  human anatomy 611.78
  human diseases
    incidence 614.595 46
    medicine 616.546
  human physiology 612.799
  pediatrics 618.925 46
  personal care 646.724
  pharmacodynamics 615.779
  surgery 617.477 9
Hair analysis
  criminal investigation 363.256 2
Hair dyeing
  personal care 646.724
Hair follicles
  medicine 616.546
  see also Hair
Hair removal
  surgery 617.477 9
Hair seals 599.79
Hair styles 646.724
  customs 391.5
Hair transplantation 617.477 905 92
Haircutting 646.724
Hairdressers 646.724 092
  occupational group T7—646 7
Hairdressing 646.724
  customs 391.5
Hairstyling 646.724
Hairweaving 646.724
Hairworms 592.59
Haiti 972.94
  T2—729 4
Haitian Creole 447.972 94
  T6—417
Haitian literature 840
Haitians T5—969 729 4
Hajdú-Bihar Megye (Hungary) T2—439 9
Ḥajj 297.352
Hakeas 583.89
Hakes 641.392
  cooking 641.692
  food 641.392
  zoology 597.632
Hakka dialect 495.17
  T6—951 7
Hakkâri İli (Turkey) T2—566 2
Hala 584.66
Ḥalab (Syria : Province) T2—569 13
Halakhah 296.18
  Midrash 296.141
  Talmud 296.127 4
  see Manual at 296.18 vs. 340.58
Haldimand (Ont. : County) T2—713 36
Haldimand-Norfolk (Ont.) T2—713 36
Hale County (Ala.) T2—761 43
Hale County (Tex.) T2—764 842
Half-life (Nuclear physics) 539.752
Halfback play
  rugby 796.333 24
  soccer 796.334 24
Halfbeaks 597.66
Halfmoons 597.7
Halftone cuts
  printing 686.232 7
Halfway houses 365.34
  corrections 365.34
    juvenile offenders 365.42
  maladjusted young people 362.74
  see also Correctional institutions; Group homes
Haliaeetus leucocephalus 598.943
Haliburton (Ont. : County) T2—713 61
Halibuts 641.392
  conservation technology 639.977 695
  cooking 641.692
  fishing 639.276 95
  food 641.392
  resource economics 333.956 695
  zoology 597.695
Halicarnassus (Extinct city) T2—392 4
Halichoerus 599.793
Halides
  mineralogy 549.4
Halifax (N.S.) T2—716 225

Halifax (N.S. : County) T2—716 22
Halifax, Edward Frederick Lindley Wood, Earl of
Indian history 954.035 8
Halifax County (N.C.) T2—756 48
Halifax County (Va.) T2—755 661
Halifax Metropolitan Area (N.S.) T2—716 225
Halite
mineralogy 549.4
see also Salt (Sodium chloride)
Hall Beach (N.W.T.) T2—719 5
Hall County (Ga.) T2—758 272
Hall County (Neb.) T2—782 41
Hall County (Tex.) T2—764 753
Hall effects in semiconductors 537.622 6
Ḥallah 296.123 1
Mishnah 296.123 1
Palestinian Talmud 296.124 1
Hallands län (Sweden) T2—486
Halle (Germany : Bezirk) T2—431 84
Halley's comet 523.642
Hallmarks 929.9
T1—027 8
Halloween 394.264 6
Hallucinations
psychology 154.4
Hallucinogen abuse 362.294
medicine 616.863 4
personal health 613.83
social welfare 362.294
see also Substance abuse
Hallucinogenic drugs
pharmacodynamics 615.788 3
Halobacteriaceae 579.321
Halocarbons 547.02
aliphatic chemistry 547.42
chemical engineering 661.891
human toxicology 615.951 2
Halogen gases
technology 665.83
Halogen salts
chemical engineering 661.42
Halogenated compounds
aromatic chemistry 547.62
chemical engineering 661.891
human toxicology 615.951 2
organic chemistry 547.02
Halogenated rubber 678.68
Halogenation 547.223
chemical engineering 660.284 423
Halogens
biochemistry 572.556
chemical engineering 661.073
chemistry 546.73
organic chemistry 547.02
applied 661.891
see also Chemicals
Halophilic bacteria 579.321
Haloragales 583.82
Halton (England : Borough) T2—427 18
Halton (Ont.) T2—713 533
Ham 641.364
see also Pork
Ham radio
engineering 621.384 16
see Manual at 621.38416 vs. 621.38454
Hamadān (Iran : Province) T2—555 2
Ḥamāh (Syria : Province) T2—569 13
Hamamelidales 583.44
Hamamelididae 583.4
Hamber Provincial Park (B.C.) T2—711 68
Hamblen County (Tenn.) T2—768 923
Hambleton (England : District) T2—428 49
Hamburg (Germany) T2—435 15
Häme (Finland : Lääni) T2—489 73
Hämeen lääni (Finland) T2—489 73
Hamilton (N.Z.) T2—933 4
Hamilton (Ont.) T2—713 52
Hamilton (Scotland : District) T2—414 57
Hamilton (Vic.) T2—945 7
Hamilton City (N.Z.) T2—933 4
Hamilton County (Fla.) T2—759 84
Hamilton County (Ill.) T2—773 95
Hamilton County (Ind.) T2—772 56
Hamilton County (Iowa) T2—777 52
Hamilton County (Kan.) T2—781 415
Hamilton County (N.Y.) T2—747 52
Hamilton County (Neb.) T2—782 354
Hamilton County (Ohio) T2—771 77
Hamilton County (Tenn.) T2—768 82
Hamilton County (Tex.) T2—764 549
Hamilton-Wentworth (Ont.) T2—713 52
Hamiltonian systems 514.74
Hamitic languages 493
T6—93
Hamitic literatures 893
Hamitic peoples T5—93
Hamito-Semitic languages 492
T6—92

Hamito-Semitic literatures		892
Hamlin County (S.D.)	T2—783 26	
Hammering metals		
sculpture		731.41
Hammers		621.973
Hammersmith and Fulham (London, England)	T2—421 33	
Hammurabi, King of Babylonia		
Mesopotamian history		935.02
Hampden County (Mass.)	T2—744 26	
Hampshire (England)	T2—422 7	
Hampshire County (Mass.)	T2—744 23	
Hampshire County (W. Va.)	T2—754 95	
Hampshire swine		636.484
Hampton (Va.)	T2—755 412	
Hampton County (S.C.)	T2—757 97	
Hamsters		636.935 6
animal husbandry		636.935 6
experimental animals		
medicine		619.93
zoology		599.356
Han dynasty		931.04
Hanafites (Islamic sect)		297.811
Hanbalites (Islamic sect)		297.814
Hancock County (Ga.)	T2—758 623	
Hancock County (Ill.)	T2—773 43	
Hancock County (Ind.)	T2—772 58	
Hancock County (Iowa)	T2—777 24	
Hancock County (Ky.)	T2—769 862	
Hancock County (Me.)	T2—741 45	
Hancock County (Miss.)	T2—762 14	
Hancock County (Ohio)	T2—771 19	
Hancock County (Tenn.)	T2—768 946	
Hancock County (W. Va.)	T2—754 12	
Hand bells		786.884 85
instrument		786.884 851 9
music		786.884 85
see also Percussion instruments		
Hand bookbinding		686.302
Hand composition		
printing		686.225 3
Hand County (S.D.)	T2—783 282	
Hand-forged tools		
manufacturing technology		682.4
Hand grenades		623.451 14
Hand haulage		
mining		622.65
Hand production		
paper		676.22
Hand-propelled boats		387.29
design		623.812 9
engineering		623.829
transportation services		387.29
see also Ships		
Hand pumps		621.64
hydraulic		621.252
Hand sewing		646.204 2
bookbinding		686.35
home economics		646.204 2
Hand techniques		
music		784.193 65
Hand tools		621.908
use in home woodworking		684.082
Handbags		391.44
customs		391.44
manufacturing technology		685.51
see also Clothing		
Handball		796.312
see also Sports		
Handbill paper		676.286
Handcars		385.32
engineering		625.22
transportation services		385.32
see also Rolling stock		
Handedness		
educational psychology		370.155
psychology		152.335
Handguns		683.43
manufacturing technology		683.43
military engineering		623.443
Handicapped persons		305.908 16
	T1—087	
	T7—081 6	
see also Disabled persons		
Handicapped workers		331.59
see also Disabled workers		
Handicraft industries		
arts economics		338.477 455
economics		338.476 8
production organization		338.642 5
see Manual at 680 vs. 745.5		
Handicrafters		745.509 2
occupational group	T7—745	
Handicrafts		680
arts		745.5
elementary education		372.55
see Manual at 680 vs. 745.5		
Handkerchiefs		391.44
see also Accessories (Clothing)		
Handreading		133.6

Hands (Human) 612.97
physiology 612.97
regional medicine 617.575
surgery 617.575 059
see also Upper extremities (Human)
Handwork
textile arts 746.4
Handwriting 652.1
elementary education 372.634
Handwriting analysis 155.282
criminal investigation 363.256 5
divination 137
personnel selection 658.311 2
Handwriting recognition
computer science 006.425
Hang gliders
engineering 629.14
Hang gliding
engineering 629.14
sports 797.55
see also Sports
Hangars 387.736 2
architecture 725.39
see also Airports
Hangings 645.2
commercial technology 684.3
home sewing 646.21
household management 645.2
interior decoration 747.3
textile arts 746.3
Hankel functions 515.53
Hankey (South Africa : District) T2—687 4
Hannover (Germany) T2—435 954
Hannover (Germany : Regierungsbezirk) T2—435 95
Hanover (South Africa : District) T2—687 13
Hanover, House of 941.07
British history 941.07
English history 942.07
genealogy 929.72
Scottish history 941.107
Hanover County (Va.) T2—755 462
Hansen's disease
incidence 614.546
medicine 616.998
see also Communicable diseases (Human)
Hansford County (Tex.) T2—764 814
Hanson County (S.D.) T2—783 373
Hants (England) T2—422 7
Hants (N.S.) T2—716 35
Hanukkah 296.435
customs 394.267
liturgy 296.453 5
Haploid cells 571.845
Haplosclerida 593.46
Haplotaxida 592.64
Happenings (Art style) 709.040 74
Happiness 170
applied psychology 158
literature 808.803 53
history and criticism 809.933 53
specific literatures T3B—080 353
history and criticism T3B—093 53
parapsychology 131
psychology of emotions 152.42
Hapsburg, House of 943.6
Austrian history 943.6
Dutch history 949.202
genealogy 929.736
German history 943
Hungarian history 943.904 2
Spanish history 946.04
Haptophyceae 579.86
Haralson County (Ga.) T2—758 38
Harare (Zimbabwe) T2—689 1
Harari (African people) T5—928
Harari language 492.8
T6—928
Harari literature 892.8
Harbor patrols 363.286
Harbor piloting 623.892 9
Harbor police 363.286
Harbor seal 599.792 3
Harborough (England) T2—425 44
Harbors 387.1
engineering 627.2
see also Ports
Hard bop 781.655
Hard cheeses
processing 637.354
Hard disk management 004.563
systems programming 005.426
systems programs 005.436
Hard disks (Computer) 004.563
engineering 621.397 6
Hard fiber crops 633.57
Hard rock 781.66
Hard-Shell Baptists 286.4
Hardanger
arts 746.44
Hardanger fiddles 787.6
see also Stringed instruments
Hardecanute, King of England
English history 942.018 3

Hardee County (Fla.) T2—759 57
Hardeman County (Tenn.) T2—768 28
Hardeman County (Tex.) T2—764 747
Hardening metals 671.36
Hardin County (Ill.) T2—773 98
Hardin County (Iowa) T2—777 535
Hardin County (Ky.) T2—769 845
Hardin County (Ohio) T2—771 44
Hardin County (Tenn.) T2—768 31
Hardin County (Tex.) T2—764 157
Harding, Warren G. (Warren Gamaliel)
  United States history 973.914
Harding County (N.M.) T2—789 24
Harding County (S.D.) T2—783 42
Hardinge, Henry Hardinge, Viscount
  Indian history 954.031 5
Hardinge of Penshurst, Charles Hardinge, Baron
  Indian history 954.035 6
Hardness
  crystals 548.842
  materials science 620.112 6
  mineralogy 549.121
Hardware 683
Hardware (Computer) 004
  engineering 621.39
  see Manual at 004 vs. 005
Hardware description languages 621.392
Hardwicke Island (B.C. : Island) T2—711 1
Hardwoods
  forestry 634.972
  lumber 674.142
Hardy County (W. Va.) T2—754 93
Harelip
  surgery 617.522
Hārergē Kifle Hāger (Ethiopia) T2—632
Hares 599.328
  animal husbandry 636.932 8
Harford County (Md.) T2—752 74
Harghita (Romania) T2—498 4
Hariana (India) T2—545 58
Haringey (London, England) T2—421 88
Harlan County (Ky.) T2—769 154
Harlan County (Neb.) T2—782 382
Harlem jazz 781.653
Harlow (England) T2—426 73
Harmful animals 591.65
Harmful microorganisms 579.165
Harmful organisms 578.65
Harmful plants 581.65
Harmon County (Okla.) T2—766 445
Harmonic analysis 515.243 3
  abstract 515.785
Harmonic functions 515.53
Harmonic organization 781.25
Harmonic rhythm 781.256
Harmonicas (Mouth organs) 788.82
  instrument 788.821 9
  music 788.82
  see also Woodwind instruments
Harmonicas (Musical glasses) 786.866
  see also Percussion instruments
Harmonies of Bible 220.65
Harmonies of Gospels 226.1
Harmoniums 786.55
  instrument 786.551 9
  music 786.55
  see also Keyboard instruments
Harmonization 781.434
Harmony
  arts 701.8
  musical element 781.25
Harness horses 636.14
Harness makers 685.109 2
  occupational group T7—685 1
Harness racehorses 636.175
Harness racing 798.46
  equipment technology 688.78
  see also Sports
Harnesses 636.108 37
  animal husbandry 636.083 7
  horse rearing 636.108 37
  manufacturing technology 685.1
Harnett County (N.C.) T2—756 362
Harney County (Or.) T2—795 95
Harold I, King of England
  English history 942.018 2
Harold II, King of England
  English history 942.019
Harp-lutes 787.98
  see also Stringed instruments
Harp seal 599.792 9
Harp zithers 787.73
  see also Stringed instruments
Harpacticoida 595.34
Harper County (Kan.) T2—781 845
Harper County (Okla.) T2—766 153
Harpists 787.909 2
  occupational group T7—787
Harps 787.9
  see also Stringed instruments

Harpsichordists 786.409 2
  occupational group T7—786
Harpsichords 786.4
  instrument 786.419
  music 786.4
  see also Keyboard instruments
Harquebuses
  art metalwork 739.744 25
Harrier (Dog) 636.753 6
Harriers (Birds) 598.94
Harris County (Ga.) T2—758 466
Harris County (Tex.) T2—764 141
Harrisburg (Pa.) T2—748 18
Harrismith (South Africa : District) T2—685 1
Harrison, Benjamin
  United States history 973.86
Harrison, William Henry
  United States history 973.58
Harrison County (Ind.) T2—772 21
Harrison County (Iowa) T2—777 47
Harrison County (Ky.) T2—769 413
Harrison County (Miss.) T2—762 13
Harrison County (Mo.) T2—778 17
Harrison County (Ohio) T2—771 68
Harrison County (Tex.) T2—764 192
Harrison County (W. Va.) T2—754 57
Harrison Lake (Fraser-Cheam, B.C.) T2—711 37
Harrisonburg (Va.) T2—755 921
Harrogate (England : Borough) T2—428 42
Harrow (London, England) T2—421 86
Harrows
  manufacturing technology 681.763 1
Harsha
  Indian history 934.07
Hart (England) T2—422 723
Hart County (Ga.) T2—758 155
Hart County (Ky.) T2—769 715
Hartebeests 599.645
Hartford (Conn.) T2—746 3
Hartford County (Conn.) T2—746 2
Hartlepool (England) T2—428 57
Hartley County (Tex.) T2—764 823
Hartswater (South Africa : District) T2—687 11
Hartz Mountains National Park (Tas.) T2—946 2
Harvest mouse 599.35
Harvest music 781.524 6
Harvesting 631.55
  equipment manufacturing technology 681.763 1
Harvesting (continued)
  production efficiency 338.163
Harvestmen (Arachnids) 595.43
Harvey County (Kan.) T2—781 85
Haryana (India) T2—545 58
Harz Mountains (Germany) T2—431 82
Ḥasakah (Syria : Province) T2—569 12
Hashing (Computer science) 005.741
Hashish
  agriculture 633.79
Hashish abuse 362.295
  medicine 616.863 5
  personal health 613.835
  social welfare 362.295
  see also Substance abuse
Hasidism 296.833 2
  liturgy 296.450 44
Haskell County (Kan.) T2—781 732
Haskell County (Okla.) T2—766 77
Haskell County (Tex.) T2—764 736
Hasmonean period 933.04
Hassan II, King of Morocco
  Moroccan history 964.05
Hastings (England) T2—422 59
Hastings (Ont. : County) T2—713 585
Hastings, Battle of, 1066 942.021
Hastings, Francis Rawdon-Hastings, Marquess of
  Indian history 954.031 3
Hastings, Warren
  Indian history 954.029 8
Hastings District (N.Z.) T2—934 65
Hatay Ili (Turkey) T2—564
Hatcheries
  fish culture 639.311
Hatchetfishes (Gasteropelecidae) 597.48
Hatchetfishes (Sternoptychidae) 597.5
Hate 179.8
  psychology 152.4
  see also Vices
Hatha yoga
  health 613.704 6
Hato Mayor (Dominican Republic : Province) T2—729 381
Hatred 179.8
  psychology 152.4
  see also Vices
Hats 391.43
  see also Headgear
Hattah Lakes National Park (Vic.) T2—945 9
Hatteras, Cape (N.C.) T2—756 175

Hatters 646.502 092
  occupational group T7—646 5
Haulage
  mining 622.6
Haunted places 133.12
  see Manual at 133.109 vs. 133.129
Hauraki District (N.Z.) T2—933 27
Hausa (African people) T5—937
Hausa language 493.72
  T6—937 2
Hausa literature 893.72
Hausa states 966.970 1
Haut-Rhin (France) T2—443 833
Haut-Richelieu (Quebec) T2—714 61
Haut-Saint-François (Quebec) T2—714 68
Haut-Saint-Laurent (Quebec) T2—714 31
Haut-Saint-Maurice (Quebec) T2—714 45
Haute-Corse (France) T2—449 456
Haute-Côte-Nord (Quebec) T2—714 17
Haute-Garonne (France) T2—448 6
Haute-Loire (France) T2—448 13
Haute-Marne (France) T2—443 32
Haute-Normandie (France) T2—442 4
Haute-Saône (France) T2—444 53
Haute-Savoie (France) T2—444 9
Haute-Vienne (France) T2—446 6
Haute-Yamaska (Quebec) T2—714 63
Haute-Zaire (Zaire : Region) T2—675 15
Hautes-Alpes (France) T2—449 7
Hautes-Pyrénées (France) T2—447 8
Hauts-de-Seine (France) T2—443 64
Havana (Cuba) T2—729 123
Havana (Cuba : Province) T2—729 124
Havant (England : Borough) T2—422 795
Havering (London, England) T2—421 74
Hawaii 996.9
  T2—969
Hawaii County (Hawaii) T2—969 1
Hawaii Island (Hawaii) T2—969 1
Hawaiian language 499.42
  T6—994 2
Hawaiian literature 899.42
Hawaiian religion 299.924 2
Hawaiians (Native people) T5—994 2
Hawea, Lake (N.Z.) T2—939 5
Hawfinches 598.885
Hawkes Bay Province (N.Z.) T2—934 6
Hawke's Bay Region (N.Z.) T2—934 6
Hawkesbury River (N.S.W.) T2—944 2
Hawkins County (Tenn.) T2—768 95
Hawks 598.944
  animal husbandry 636.686 9
Hawthorns 583.73
Hay
  animal feed 636.086
  forage crop 633.2
Hay (South Africa : District) T2—687 11
Hay fever
  incidence 614.599 3
  medicine 616.202
  see also Respiratory system
Hay Mohamed-Ain Sebaa (Morocco : Prefecture) T2—643
Hay River (N.W.T.) T2—719 3
Haya-Jita languages 496.395
  T6—963 95
Hayes, Rutherford Birchard
  United States history 973.83
Hayes County (Neb.) T2—782 832
Hays County (Tex.) T2—764 888
Haywood County (N.C.) T2—756 94
Haywood County (Tenn.) T2—768 223
Hazardous machinery 363.18
  law 344.047 2
  public administration 353.99
  see also Safety
Hazardous materials 363.17
  ecological effect 577.27
  public administration 353.993
  public safety 363.17
    international law 341.765
    law 344.047 2
  technology 604.7
    see Manual at 604.7 vs. 660.2804
  transportation 388.044
    international law 341.756 92
    law 343.093 22
    technology 604.7
    transportation services 388.044
  see Manual at 363.17; *also at* 363.176 vs. 604.7

Hazardous wastes 363.728 7
law 344.046 22
public administration 353.994
social services 363.728 7
technology 628.42
see also Waste control
Hazelnuts 641.345 4
see also Filberts
Hazelton (B.C.) T2—711 85
Hazelton Mountains (B.C.) T2—711 85
Hazing
education 371.58
HBO (Television) 384.555 4
see also Television
Head 591.4
animal physiology 573.995
anthropometry 599.948
descriptive zoology 591.4
human anatomy 611.91
human physiology 612.91
regional medicine 617.51
surgery 617.510 59
Head muscles
human anatomy 611.732
see also Musculoskeletal system
Head start (Education) 372.21
Head teachers 371.1
biography 371.100 92
public control 379.157
Headaches
symptomatology
neurological diseases 616.849 1
see also Nervous system
Headgear 391.43
commercial technology 687.4
customs 391.43
home economics 646.3
home sewing 646.5
see also Clothing
Headings (Cataloging) 025.322
Headmasters
biography 371.200 92
public control 379.157
role and function 371.201 2
Heads of government 321
occupational group T7—351
Heads of state 321
occupational group T7—351
public administration 352.23
Headstanders 597.48
Healesville (Vic.) T2—945 2
Healing
religion 291.31
Christianity 234.131
see also Spiritual healing—religion
see Manual at 615.852 vs. 291.31, 234.131
therapeutics 615.5
Health 613
child care 649.4
elementary education 372.37
medicine 613
social theology 291.178 321
Christianity 261.832 1
Judaism 296.38
sociology 306.461
see Manual at 613 vs. 615.8
Health care 362.1
see also Health services
Health care facilities 362.1
architecture 725.51
law 344.032 1
public administration 353.68
safety 363.15
sanitation services 363.729 7
public administration 353.94
see also Waste control
social welfare 362.1
see also Health services
Health centers 362.12
see also Health care facilities; Health services
Health cooking 641.563
Health foods 641.302
cooking 641.563 7
food 641.302
Health insurance 368.382
government-sponsored 368.42
law 344.022
law 346.086 382
public administration 353.69
see also Insurance
see Manual at 362.1042 vs. 368.382
Health maintenance organizations 362.104 258
insurance 368.382
see also Insurance
law 344.032 104 258
see also Health services
Health promotion
medicine 613
public administration 353.627 4

Health protection service
  public administration 353.628
Health resorts
  personal health 613.122
Health services 362.1
  Algerian Revolution 965.046 7
  armed forces 355.345
  Chaco War 989.207 167
  Civil War (England) 942.062 7
  Civil War (Spain) 946.081 7
  Civil War (United States) 973.775
  Crimean War 947.073 87
  Falkland Islands War 997.110 247
  for employees
    personnel management 658.382
      public administration 352.67
  Franco-German War 943.082 7
  Hundred Years' War 944.025 7
  Indo-Pakistan War, 1971 954.920 517
  Indochinese War 959.704 17
  Iraqi-Iranian Conflict 955.054 27
  Korean War 951.904 27
  labor economics 331.255
  law 344.032 1
  Mexican War 973.627 5
  Napoleonic Wars 940.277
  pastoral theology 291.61
    Christianity 259.41
  Persian Gulf War, 1991 956.704 427
  prisoner services 365.66
  public administration 353.6
  social theology 291.178 321
    Christianity 261.832 1
  social welfare 362.1
  South African War 968.048 7
  Spanish-American War 973.897 5
  student welfare 371.71
  Thirty Years' War 940.247
  United States Revolutionary War 973.375
  Vietnamese War 959.704 37
  War of 1812 973.527 5
  War of the Pacific 983.061 67
  World War I 940.475
  World War II 940.547 5
  see also Health care facilities
  see Manual at 362.1–362.4 vs. 610; *also at* 362.1042 vs. 368.382; *also at* 610 vs. 362.17; *also at* 614.4–614.5 vs. 362.1–362.4
Health surveys 614.42
Healthy persons T7—081 2
Heard County (Ga.) T2—758 422
Hearing 573.89
  human physiology 612.85
  psychology 152.15
  see also Ears
Hearing devices
  audiology 617.89
  see also Ears
Hearing examiners (Law) 342.066 4
Hearing-impaired children 305.908 162
  T1—087 2
  home care 649.151 2
  see also Hearing-impaired persons
Hearing-impaired persons 305.908 162
  T1—087 2
  T7—081 62
  education 371.912
  library services 027.663
  social group 305.908 162
  social welfare 362.42
Hearing impairment
  otology 617.8
  see also Ears
Hearings
  legislative 328.345
Hearsay evidence 347.064
Heart 573.17
  biology 573.17
  human anatomy 611.12
  human physiology 612.17
  see also Cardiovascular system
Heart attacks
  medicine 616.123 025
    myocardial infarction 616.123 7
  see also Cardiovascular system
Heart depressants
  pharmacodynamics 615.716
  see also Cardiovascular system
Heart diseases
  cooking for 641.563 11
  medicine 616.12
  surgery 617.412
  see also Cardiovascular system
Heart failure
  medicine 616.129
  see also Cardiovascular system

Heart pacers (Electronic)
  medicine 617.412 064 5
  see also Cardiovascular
    system
Heart stimulants
  pharmacodynamics 615.711
  see also Cardiovascular
    system
Heart surgery 617.412
  see also Cardiovascular
    system
Heart transplants 617.412 059 2
  see also Cardiovascular
    system; Organ transplants
Heart valve disease
  medicine 616.125
  see also Cardiovascular
    system
Heat 536
  astrophysics 523.013
  biophysics 571.467
    humans 612.014 462
  crop damage 632.12
  effect on matter 536.4
    see Manual at 536.4 vs.
      530.474
  pathological effect 571.934 67
    medicine 616.989
    see also Environmental
      diseases (Human)
  physics 536
Heat capacity 536.6
Heat conductivity
  materials science 620.112 96
Heat distribution systems 621.402 8
Heat engineering 621.402
Heat engineers 621.402 092
  occupational group T7—621 4
Heat engines 621.402 5
Heat exchange
  engineering 621.402 2
  metallurgical furnaces 669.85
Heat exchangers 621.402 5
Heat exhaustion
  medicine 616.989
  see also Environmental
    diseases (Human)
Heat loss
  electric circuits 621.319 21
Heat of fusion 536.42
Heat of vaporization 536.44
Heat perception 152.182 2
HEAT projectiles
  engineering 623.451 7
Heat pumps 621.402 5
  refrigeration engineering 621.563
Heat rash
  medicine 616.56
  see also Skin
Heat-resistant glass 666.155
Heat storage 621.402 8
  solar engineering 621.471 2
Heat stress (Biology) 571.934 67
Heat stress (Human)
  medicine 616.989
  see also Environmental
    diseases (Human)
Heat transfer 536.2
  chemical engineering 660.284 27
  engineering 621.402 2
  physics 536.2
Heat treatment
  metals 671.36
Heat weapons 623.446
Heaters
  buildings 697.07
Heathcote (Vic.) T2—945 3
Heather 583.66
  floriculture 635.933 66
Heaths (Ericaceae) 583.66
Heaths (Shrublands)
  biology 578.738
  ecology 577.38
Heating
  aircraft 629.134 42
  automobile 629.277 2
  buildings 697
    customs 392.36
  household management 644.1
  library buildings 022.8
  museums 069.29
  plant management 658.25
  vehicles 629.040 289
Heating, ventilating, air
    conditioning 697
Heating coils
  air conditioning buildings 697.932 2
Heating engineers 697.009 2
  occupational group T7—697
Heating equipment 621.402 5
  air conditioning buildings 697.932 2
  furniture arts 749.62
  installation in buildings 697.07
  ships 623.853 7
Heating from central stations
  resource economics 333.793
Heating oil 665.538 4

Heaven 291.23
  Christianity 236.24
  Islam 297.23
  Judaism 296.33
Heavenly bodies 520
  folklore 398.26
    history and criticism 398.362
Heavier-than-air aircraft 387.733
  engineering 629.133 3
  military engineering 623.746
  transportation services 387.733
  see also Aircraft
Heavy equipment
  capital procurement 658.152 42
  household appliances 643.6
    manufacturing technology 683.88
Heavy ions 539.723 4
Heavy spar 553.662
Heavy water
  chemical engineering 661.08
  chemistry 546.22
Hebei Sheng (China) T2—511 52
Hebrew language 492.4
  T6—924
  Biblical texts 220.44
  Midrashic texts 296.140 4
  printing 686.219 24
  Talmudic texts 296.120 4
Hebrew literature 892.4
Hebrew schools 296.680 83
Hebrews T5—924
Hebrews (Biblical book) 227.87
Hebrides (Scotland) T2—411 4
Hebron (Jordan : District) T2—569 51
Hecate Strait (B.C.) 551.466 33
  T2—164 33
Hedge laurels 583.72
Hedgehogs 599.332
Hedgerows
  biology 578.755 5
  ecology 577.555
Hedges
  agricultural use 631.27
  floriculture 635.976
Hedging (Finance) 332.645
Hedmark fylke (Norway) T2—482 4
Hedonism
  ethical systems 171.4
Heel-and-toe races 796.429
  see also Sports
Hegirah 297.634
Hei-Lung Chiang (China and Russia) T2—577
Heidelberg (Cape of Good Hope, South Africa : District) T2—687 3
Heidelberg (Germany) T2—434 645
Heidelberg (Transvaal, South Africa : District) T2—682 1
Heidelberg man 569.9
Heilbron (South Africa : District) T2—685 2
Heilongjiang Sheng (China) T2—518 4
Heilungkiang Province (China) T2—518 4
Heisei period 952.049
Heisenberg representation 530.122
Hejaz (Saudi Arabia) T2—538
Helena (Mont.) T2—786 615
Heliconiaceae 584.39
Heliconias 584.39
  floriculture 635.934 39
Helicopter accidents 363.124 93
  see also Air safety
Helicopters 387.733 52
  engineering 629.133 352
  military engineering 623.746 047
  piloting 629.132 525 2
  transportation services 387.733 52
  see also Aircraft
Heliographs
  military engineering 623.731 2
  nautical engineering 623.856 12
Heliotherapy
  medicine 615.831 4
Heliothis 595.78
  agricultural pests 632.78
Heliotropes (Plants) 583.94
Heliports 387.736
  engineering 629.136 16
  military engineering 623.661 6
  see also Airports
Helium 553.971
  chemistry 546.751
  economic geology 553.971
  gas technology 665.822
  see also Chemicals
Helium extraction 665.73
Hell 291.23
  art representation 704.948 9
    Christianity 704.948 2
  arts T3C—382 912 3
  Christianity 236.25
  Islam 297.23

Hell (continued)
  literature 808.803 829 123
    history and criticism 809.933 829 123
    specific literatures T3B—080 382 9123
      history and criticism T3B—093 829 123
Hellbender (Salamander) 597.85
Hellebores 583.34
  floriculture 635.933 34
Hellenic languages 480
  T6—8
Hellenic literatures 880
Hellenic sculpture 733.3
Hellenistic Greek language 487.4
  T6—87
Hellenistic movement (Judaism) 296.81
Hellenistic period
  Egyptian history 932.021
  Greek history 938.08
  Mesopotamian history 935.06
  Palestinian history 933.03
Hellenistic World T2—38
Helmets (Armor) 623.441
  art metalwork 739.75
Helmets (Headgear) 391.43
  see also Headgear
Helminthologists 592.309 2
  occupational group T7—595
Helminthology 592.3
  agriculture 632.623
  medicine 616.962
  plant crops 632.623
  veterinary medicine 636.089 696 2
  see also Communicable diseases (Human)
Helotiales 579.57
Help facilities (Computer) 005.3
  development 005.15
Helping behavior 158.3
Helsinki (Finland) T2—489 71
Helvetic Republic 949.405
  T2—494
Hemangiomas
  medicine 616.993 13
  see also Diseases (Human)
Hemapheresis
  pharmacology 615.39
Hematheia (Greece) T2—495 65
Hematite
  mineralogy 549.523
Hematology 616.15
  diagnosis
    general disease 616.075 61
  see also Cardiovascular system
Hematopoiesis 573.155
  human physiology 612.41
  see also Blood-forming system
Hematopoietic system 573.155
  human anatomy 611.41
  human physiology 612.41
  medicine 616.41
  see also Blood-forming system
Hematuria
  medicine 616.63
  see also Urinary system
Hemiascomycetes 579.562
Hemic disorders
  medicine 616.15
  see also Cardiovascular system
Hemichordata 593.99
  paleozoology 563.99
Hemimetabola 595.73
Hemiprocnidae 598.762
Hemiptera 595.754
Hemispheres T2—181
Hemlocks 585.2
  forestry 634.975 3
  lumber 674.144
  ornamental arboriculture 635.977 52
Hemoconia
  human physiology 612.117
  see also Cardiovascular system
Hemodialysis
  medicine 617.461 059
  see also Urinary system
Hemoglobin
  chemistry 547.754
  human physiology 612.111 1
  medicine 616.151
  see also Cardiovascular system; Proteins
Hemolytic anemia
  medicine 616.152
  see also Cardiovascular system
Hemolytic disease of the newborn
  pediatrics 618.921 5
  perinatal medicine 618.326 1
  see also Cardiovascular system
Hemophilia
  medicine 616.157 2

Hemophilia (continued)
  pediatrics 618.921 572
  see also Cardiovascular system
Hemopoiesis 573.155
  human physiology 612.41
  see also Blood-forming system
Hemopoietic system 573.155
  human anatomy 611.41
  human physiology 612.41
  see also Blood-forming system
Hemorrhage
  medicine 616.157
  see also Cardiovascular system
Hemorrhagic diseases
  medicine 616.157
  see also Cardiovascular system
Hemorrheology
  humans 612.118 1
  see also Cardiovascular system
Hemorrhoids
  medicine 616.35
  see also Digestive system
Hemp 677.12
  botany 583.45
  fiber crop 633.53
  textiles 677.12
    arts 746.041 2
    see also Textiles
Hemp (Agavaceae) 584.352
Hemp (Apocynaceae) 583.93
Hemp (Cannabaceae) 583.45
Hemp (Musaceae) 584.39
Hemp pulp 676.14
Hemphill County (Tex.) T2—764 817
Hempstead County (Ark.) T2—767 54
Henan Sheng (China) T2—511 8
Henbanes 583.952
Henderson County (Ill.) T2—773 413
Henderson County (Ky.) T2—769 87
Henderson County (N.C.) T2—756 92
Henderson County (Tenn.) T2—768 263
Henderson County (Tex.) T2—764 227
Henderson Island (Pitcairn Island) T2—961 8
Hendricks County (Ind.) T2—772 53
Hendry County (Fla.) T2—759 46
Hennenman (South Africa : District) T2—685 3
Hennepin County (Minn.) T2—776 57
Henrico County (Va.) T2—755 453
Henry I, King of England
  English history 942.023
Henry I, King of France
  French history 944.021
Henry II, King of England
  English history 942.031
Henry II, King of France
  French history 944.028
Henry III, King of England
  English history 942.034
Henry III, King of France
  French history 944.029
Henry IV, King of England
  English history 942.041
Henry IV, King of France
  French history 944.031
Henry V, King of England
  English history 942.042
Henry VI, King of England
  English history 942.043
Henry VII, King of England
  English history 942.051
Henry VIII, King of England
  English history 942.052
Henry County (Ala.) T2—761 31
Henry County (Ga.) T2—758 435
Henry County (Ill.) T2—773 38
Henry County (Ind.) T2—772 64
Henry County (Iowa) T2—777 95
Henry County (Ky.) T2—769 385
Henry County (Mo.) T2—778 462
Henry County (Ohio) T2—771 15
Henry County (Tenn.) T2—768 34
Henry County (Va.) T2—755 692
Hepatic jaundice
  medicine 616.362 5
  see also Digestive system
Hepaticae 588.3
Hepatitis
  medicine 616.362 3
  see also Digestive system
Hepatopsida 588.3
Heptarchy 942.015
Heraclitean philosophy 182.4
Hērakleion (Greece : Nome) T2—495 9
Heraldic design 929.6
  decorative arts 745.66
  insignia 929.6
Heraldry 929.6
Hérault (France) T2—448 4
Herb gardens 635.7

Herb teas 641.357
  agriculture 635.7
  commercial processing 663.96
  cooking with 641.657
  food 641.357
  home preparation 641.877
Herbaceous plants 582.12
  landscape architecture 716
Herbaceous vines 582.189
Herbals
  pharmacognosy 615.321
    see Manual at 615.1 vs. 615.2–615.3
Herbariums 580.74
Herbert (South Africa : District) T2—687 11
Herbicides
  agricultural use 632.954
  chemical engineering 668.654
Herbivorous animals 591.54
Herbivorous Saurischia 567.913
Herbs 581.63
  botany 581.63
  commercial processing 664.805 7
  cooking with 641.657
  food 641.357
  garden crop 635.7
  pharmacognosy 615.321
    see Manual at 615.1 vs. 615.2–615.3
Herculaneum (Extinct city) T2—377
Herdbooks 636.082 2
Herders (People) 636.084 509 2
Herders (Work animals)
  care and training 636.088 6
Herding (Animal husbandry) 636.084 5
Herding dogs 636.737
Heredia (Costa Rica : Province) T2—728 64
Hereditary diseases (Biology) 571.948
Hereditary diseases (Human)
  medicine 616.042
  see also Diseases (Human)
Hereditary metabolic disorders
  medicine 616.390 42
  see also Digestive system
Hereditary societies 369.2
  biography 369.209 2
  social group T7—369 2
Heredity 576.5
  animals 591.35
  humans 599.935
  influence on crime 364.24
  plants 581.35
Heredity (continued)
  psychology 155.7
    evolutional psychology 155.7
    individual psychology 155.234
Heredity versus environment
  psychology 155.7
    evolutional psychology 155.7
    individual psychology 155.234
Hereford (England) T2—424 46
Hereford and Worcester (England) T2—424 4
Hereford cattle 636.222
Herero (African people) T5—963 99
Herero language 496.399
  T6—963 99
Heresy
  Christianity 262.8
    church history 273
    polemics 239
  criminology 364.188
  Judaism 296.67
    polemics 296.35
    religious authority 296.67
  law 345.028 8
Herkimer County (N.Y.) T2—747 61
Herm (England) T2—423 46
Hermanus (South Africa : District) T2—687 3
Hermaphroditism (Biology) 571.886
Hermaphroditism (Human)
  medicine 616.694
Hermeneutics 121.686
  philosophy 121.686
  sacred books 291.82
    Bible 220.601
    Koran 297.122 601
    Talmud 296.120 601
Hermetism 135.45
Hermit crabs 595.387
  culture 639.67
Hermite polynomials 515.55
Hermitian spaces 515.73
Hernandiaceae 583.23
Hernando County (Fla.) T2—759 71
Hernando Island (B.C.) T2—711 31
Hernia
  abdominal surgery 617.559 059
  regional medicine 617.559
Heroes
  literature 808.803 52
    history and criticism 809.933 52
    specific literatures T3B—080 352
      history and criticism T3B—093 52

Heroin abuse 362.293
  medicine 616.863 2
  personal health 613.83
  social welfare 362.293
  see also Substance abuse
Heroism
  literature 808.803 53
    history and criticism 809.933 53
    specific literatures T3B—080 353
      history and criticism T3B—093 53
Herons 598.34
Herpes simplex type 1
  medicine 616.52
  see also Skin
Herpes simplex type 2
  incidence 614.547
  medicine 616.951 8
  see also Communicable diseases (Human)
Herpes zoster
  medicine 616.522
  see also Skin
Herpesviridae 579.243 4
Herpesvirus diseases
  incidence 614.575
  medicine 616.925
  see also Communicable diseases (Human)
Herpetologists 597.909 2
  occupational group T7—597
Herpetology 597.9
Herrera (Panama : Province) T2—728 724
Herring (Clupea harengus) 641.392
  conservation technology 639.977 452
  cooking 641.692
  fishing 639.274 52
  food 641.392
  resource economics 333.956 452
  zoology 597.452
Herring family 597.45
Herschel (South Africa : District) T2—687 91
Hertford County (N.C.) T2—756 155
Hertfordshire (England) T2—425 8
Hertsmere (England : Borough) T2—425 895
Hertzog, James Barry Munnik
  South African history 968.054
Hesperioidea 595.788
Hesperonesian languages 499.2
  T6—992
Hesperornithiformes 568.23
Hesse (Germany) T2—434 1
Hessen (Germany) T2—434 1
Hetero nitrogen compounds 547.593
  chemical engineering 661.894
Hetero oxygen compounds 547.592
  chemical engineering 661.8
Hetero sulfur compounds 547.594
  chemical engineering 661.896
Heterobasidiomycetes 579.59
Heterocyclic compounds 547.59
  chemical engineering 661.8
Heterogeneous grouping of students 371.252
Heterogeneous reactions 541.393
  chemical engineering 660.299 3
  organic chemistry 547.139 3
Heterogenesis 571.884
Heteromyidae 599.359 8
Heterophony 781.283
Heteroptera 595.754
Heterosexuality 306.764
Heterosexuals 305.906 62
  T1—086 62
Heterosomata 597.69
Hettinger County (N.D.) T2—784 86
Heveas 583.69
  rubber crop 633.895 2
Heves Megye (Hungary) T2—439 8
Hewu (South Africa : District) T2—687 92
Hexacorallia 593.6
Hexactinellida 593.44
  paleozoology 563.4
Hexadecimal system 513.57
Hexagonal chess 794.18
Hexapoda 595.7
  see also Insects
Hexateuch (Bible) 222.1
Hi-fi
  sound reproduction systems 621.389 332
Hiatal hernia
  regional medicine 617.559
Hibernation 591.565
  behavior 591.565
  physiology 571.787
Hibiscuses 583.685
  floriculture 635.933 685
Hickman County (Ky.) T2—769 98
Hickman County (Tenn.) T2—768 434
Hickories 583.49
Hickory County (Mo.) T2—778 496
Hidalgo (Mexico : State) T2—724 6
Hidalgo County (N.M.) T2—789 693
Hidalgo County (Tex.) T2—764 492
Hidatsa Indians T5—975 2

Hide-and-seek (Game) 796.14
Hides
  animal husbandry 636.088 44
  descriptive zoology 599.614 7
  physiology 573.519 6
  processing 675.2
Hierarchical databases
  computer science 005.755
Hierarchical systems 003.7
Hierarchy
  armed forces 355.33
Hieroglyphic Hittite language 491.998
  T6—919 98
Hieroglyphics
  Egyptian language 493.1
Hierotherapy
  medicine 615.852
  see Manual at 615.852 vs. 291.31, 234.131
High altitude
  biophysics 571.49
High-altitude plants
  floriculture 635.952 8
High-alumina cement 666.95
High blood pressure
  medicine 616.132
  see also Cardiovascular system
High-calorie cooking 641.563 4
High-calorie diet
  health 613.24
High-compression-ignition engines 621.436
  automotive 629.250 6
High-contrast photography 778.8
High Court of Justice (Great Britain) 347.420 25
High Court of Justiciary (Scotland) 345.411 016
High-energy forming 671.3
High-energy physics 539.76
High-explosive ammunition
  engineering 623.451 7
High explosives 662.27
High-fat cooking 641.563 8
High-fat diet
  health 613.284
High-fiber diet
  health 613.263
High-fidelity systems
  sound reproduction 621.389 332
High Holy Days 296.431
  liturgy 296.453 1
High jump 796.432
  see also Sports
High-level languages 005.13
High-octane-rating gasoline 665.538 25
High Peak (England : Borough) T2—425 11
High polymers
  chemistry 547.84
High-protein diet
  health 613.282
High-rise buildings 720.483
  see also Tall buildings
High school administration 373.12
High school dropouts 373.129 13
High school enrollment 373.121 9
High school equivalency certificate 373.126 2
High school equivalency programs 373.238
  see also Secondary education
High school graduates
  choice of vocation 331.702 33
  labor force 331.114 23
  unemployment 331.137 804
High school postgraduate programs 373.238
High school students 373.18
High school teachers 373.11
High school teaching 373.110 2
High schools 373
  T1—071 2
  see also Secondary education
High seas 551.46
  law 341.45
  see also Oceans
High-speed cinematography 778.56
High-speed local networks 004.68
  see also Computer communications
High-speed photography 778.37
High-styrene resins 678.73
High-temperature biology 571.467
  humans 612.014 462
High-temperature injury (Biology) 571.934 67
High-temperature injury (Human) 617.11
High temperatures 536.57
  chemical engineering 660.296 87
  chemistry 541.368 7
  effect on materials 620.112 17
High-tension electric transmission 621.319 13
High Veld (South Africa) T2—682

High-velocity armor-piercing
ammunition 623.451 8
High voice 783.3
High-voltage accelerators 539.732
Higher criticism
Bible 220.66
Higher education 378
T1—071 1
finance
law 344.076 84
law 344.074
public administrative support 353.88
public support 379.118
Highland cattle 636.223
Highland County (Ohio) T2—771 845
Highland County (Va.) T2—755 89
Highland Region
(Scotland) T2—411 5
Highland Rim T2—768 4
Kentucky T2—769 6
Tennessee T2—768 4
Highlands (Papua New Guinea) 995.6
T2—956
Highlands (Scotland) T2—411 5
Highlands County (Fla.) T2—759 55
Highly volatile petroleum
products 665.538 2
Highveld (South Africa) T2—682
Highway accidents 363.125
see also Highway safety
Highway engineers 625.709 2
occupational group T7—625
Highway maps 912
Highway patrol 363.233 2
Highway post offices 383.42
see also Postal service
Highway safety 363.125
engineering 625.702 89
law 343.094
public administration 353.98
social services 363.125
Highway transportation 388.31
see also Road transportation
Highways 388.1
engineering 625.7
transportation services 388.1
see also Roads
Hijacking 364.155 2
international law 341.772
law 345.025 52
Hijrah 297.634
Hikers 796.510 92
sports group T7—796 5
Hiking 796.51
Hilbert spaces 515.733
Hilbert transform 515.723
Hildebrand, Bruno
economic school 330.154 2
Hildesheim (Germany) T2—435 958
Hill climbing 796.522
Hill County (Mont.) T2—786 14
Hill County (Tex.) T2—764 283
Hillingdon (London,
England) T2—421 83
Hills 551.436
T2—143
see also Mountains
Hillsboro County (N.H.) T2—742 8
Hillsborough County (Fla.) T2—759 65
Hillsborough County
(N.H.) T2—742 8
Hillsdale County (Mich.) T2—774 29
Himachal Pradesh (India) T2—545 2
Himalaya Mountains T2—549 6
Himalayan cat 636.83
Ḥimṣ (Syria : Province) T2—569 12
Hinayana Buddhism 294.391
Hinchinbrook Island
National Park (Qld.) T2—943 6
Hinckley and Bosworth
(England) T2—425 49
Hindi language 491.43
T6—914 31
Hindi literature 891.43
Hindis T5—914 3
Hinds County (Miss.) T2—762 51
Hindu architecture 720.954
Hindu calendar 529.324 5
religion 294.536
Hindu education 294.575
Hindu ethics 294.548
Hindu holidays 294.536
customs 394.265 45
see also Holidays
Hindu Kush Mountains
(Afghanistan and
Pakistan) T2—581
Hindu medicine
therapeutic system 615.53
Hindu philosophy 181.4
Hindu sacred music 781.745
public worship 782.345
music 782.345
religion 294.538
religion 294.537
Hindu sculpture 730.954
Hindu temples and shrines 294.535
architecture 726.145

Hinduism 294.5
art representation 704.948 945
arts 700.482 945
T3C—382 945
Islamic polemics 297.294
Hinduism and Islam 294.517 2
Hindu view 294.517 2
Islamic view 297.284 5
Hindus
biography 294.509 2
religious group T7—294 5
Hinsdale County (Colo.) T2—788 39
Hip bones
human anatomy 611.718
see also Musculoskeletal system
Hip muscles
human anatomy 611.738
see also Musculoskeletal system
Hippies 305.568
T1—086 9
Hippoboscidae 595.774
Hippocampus 597.679 8
Hippocastanaceae 583.78
Hippocrateaceae 583.85
Hippocratic oath 174.22
Hippocratic theory of temperaments 155.262
Hippoglossus 597.695
Hippopotamidae 599.635
Hippopotamuses 599.635
Hippotraginae 599.645
Hippuridales 583.82
Hips (Human) 612.98
medicine 616.72
physiology 612.98
regional medicine 617.581
surgery 617.581 059
see also Lower extremities (Human)
Hiring halls 331.889 4
Hiring of employees
personnel management 658.311 2
public administration 352.65
Hiroshima-ken (Japan) T2—521 95
Hiroshima-shi (Japan) T2—521 954
Hirudinea 592.66
Hirundinidae 598.826
Hishkaryana language 498
T6—98
Hispanic Americans T5—68
Hispanic Americans (U.S.) T5—680 73
education 371.829 680 73
Hispaniola T2—729 3
Hister beetles 595.763
Histeroidea 595.763
Histochemical examination
medicine 616.075 83
Histochemistry 572
Histogenesis 571.835
humans 611.018
Histological examination
medicine 616.075 83
Histology 571.5
humans 611.018
Histones 572.66
biochemistry 572.66
chemistry 547.752
see also Proteins
Histopathology 571.9
humans 611.018
see also Pathology
Histophysiology 571.5
humans 611.018
Historians 907.202
occupational group T7—97
Historians of religion 200.92
Historic buildings
law 344.094
preservation 363.69
technology 721.028 8
see Manual at 913–919: Historic sites and buildings
Historic political parties 324.212
Historic preservation 363.69
law 344.094
public administrative support 353.77
social services 363.69
see Manual at 930–990: Historic preservation
Historical bibliography 002
Historical books (Old Testament) 222
Historical books (Pseudepigrapha) 229.911
Historical criticism
sacred books 291.82
Bible 220.67
Koran 297.122 67
Talmud 296.120 67
Historical drama 792.14
literature 808.825 14
history and criticism 809.251 4
specific literatures T3B—205 14
individual authors T3A—2

Historical drama (continued)
  stage presentation 792.14
    see also Theater
Historical events 900
  art representation 704.949 9
  arts 700.458
    T3C—358
  literature 808.803 58
    history and criticism 809.933 58
    specific literatures T3B—080 358
      history and criticism T3B—093 58
  see also History
  see Manual at 900: Historic events vs. nonhistoric events
Historical fiction 808.838 1
  history and criticism 809.381
  specific literatures T3B—308 1
    individual authors T3A—3
Historical geography 911
Historical geology 551.7
  see Manual at 551.7; *also at* 551.7 vs. 560
Historical linguistics 417.7
  specific languages T4—7
  see Manual at 410
Historical materialism
  Marxian theory 335.411 9
Historical novels 808.838 1
  history and criticism 809.381
  specific literatures T3B—308 1
    individual authors T3A—3
Historical pageants
  performing arts 791.624
Historical periods 909
    T1—090 1–090 5
  specific places 930–990
  see Manual at T1—0901–T1—0905
Historical remedies
  therapeutics 615.88
    see Manual at 615.8809
Historical research 001.432
    T1—072 2
  public administrative support 352.744
  see Manual at T1—07201–T1—07209 vs. T1—0722–T1—0724
Historical school (Economics) 330.154 2
Historical themes
  arts 700.458
    T3C—358
  folklore 398.27
    history and criticism 398.358
Historical themes (continued)
  literature 808.803 58
    history and criticism 809.933 58
    specific literatures T3B—080 358
      history and criticism T3B—093 58
  painting 758.99
Historical treatment T1—09
  see Manual at T1—09
Historicism
  philosophy 149
  philosophy of history 901
Historicity of Jesus Christ 232.908
Historiographers 907.202
Historiography 907.2
    T1—072 2
History 900
    T1—09
  Biblical events 220.95
  elementary education 372.89
  specific places 930–990
    see Manual at 930–990 vs. 355.009
  world 909
  see Manual at 305 vs. 306, 909, 930–990; *also at* 900; *also at* 909, 930–990 vs. 320; *also at* 909, 930–990 vs. 400
History (Theology) 291.211 7
  Christianity 231.76
  Islam 297.211 4
  Judaism 296.311 7
Hit-and-run tactics 355.422
Hitchcock County (Neb.) T2—782 845
Hitler, Adolf
  German history 943.086
Hittite language 491.998
    T6—919 98
Hittite literature 891.998
Hittites T5—919 9
HIV (Viruses)
  medical microbiology 616.979 201
Hives (Disease)
  medicine 616.51
  see also Skin
Hixkaryana language 498
    T6—98
Hlabisa (South Africa : District) T2—684 3
Hlanganani (South Africa : District) T2—684 91
Hluhluwe Game Reserve (South Africa) T2—684 91

HMO (Social welfare) 362.104 258
insurance 368.382
see also Insurance
see also Health services
Hmong (Asian people) T5—959 42
Hmong language 495.972
T6—959 72
Hmong literature 895.972
Hmong-Mien languages 495.97
T6—959 7
Ho language (Munda) 495.95
T6—959 5
Hoarding food (Animals) 591.53
Hoarfrost 551.574 4
Hoatzin 598.64
Hoaxes 001.95
books 098.3
Hobart (Tas.) T2—946 1
Hobbies T1—023
recreation 790.13
sociology 306.487
see also Recreation
Hobgoblins 133.14
Hoboes 305.568
T1—086 942
Hoceïma (Morocco : Province) T2—642
Hockey (Field sports) 796.355
see also Sports
Hockey (Ice sports) 796.962
electronic games 794.869 62
see also Sports
Hockey cards 796.962 075
Hockey players (Ice sports) 796.962 092
sports group T7—796 9
Hocking County (Ohio) T2—771 835
Hocking River (Ohio) T2—771 97
Hockley County (Tex.) T2—764 846
Hodgeman County (Kan.) T2—781 47
Hodgkin's disease
incidence 614.599 944 6
medicine 616.994 46
see also Cancer (Human)
Hoedowns 793.34
music 784.188 7
Hoëveldrif (South Africa : District) T2—682 7
Hofmeyr (South Africa : District) T2—687 14
Hog plums (Anacardiaceae) 583.77
Hog plums (Rosaceae) 583.73
Hogs 636.4
see also Pigs
Hohenstaufen dynasty 943.024
Hohenzollern (Germany) T2—434 73
Hoisting
mining 622.6
Hoisting equipment 621.862
Hokan languages 497.57
T6—975 7
Hoke County (N.C.) T2—756 365
Hokkaido (Japan) T2—524
Hokuriku Region (Japan) T2—521 5
Holderness (England : Borough) T2—428 38
Holding companies 338.86
economics 338.86
law 346.066 8
see also Combinations (Enterprises)
Holding equipment 621.992
Holguín (Cuba : Province) T2—729 164
Holiday work 331.257 4
economics 331.257 4
personnel management 658.312 1
Holidays 394.26
cooking 641.568
customs 394.26
flower arrangements 745.926
folklore 398.236
history and criticism 398.33
handicrafts 745.594 1
interior decoration 747.93
labor economics 331.257 6
law 344.091
literature 808.803 34
history and criticism 809.933 34
specific literatures T3B—080 334
history and criticism T3B—093 34
personnel management 658.312 2
religion 291.36
Buddhism 294.343 6
Christianity 263.9
devotional literature 242.3
sermons 252.6
Hinduism 294.536
Islam 297.36
Judaism 296.43
liturgy 296.453
Holiness 291.22
Christian church attribute 262.72
Christian doctrine 234.8
Holistic medicine 610
health 613
therapeutics 615.5
Holistic psychology 150.193

Holland 949.2
T2—492
ancient 936.4
T2—364
Holland (England : County) T2—425 39
Holland (Kingdom) 949.205
T2—492
Hollies 635.977 385
botany 583.85
ornamental arboriculture 635.977 385
Hollow blocks 666.894
architectural construction 721.044 4
building construction 693.4
ceramic technology 666.894
Hollow ware
rubber 678.34
Hollyhocks 635.933 685
botany 583.685
floriculture 635.933 685
Holman (N.W.T.) T2—719 7
Holmes County (Fla.) T2—759 965
Holmes County (Miss.) T2—762 625
Holmes County (Ohio) T2—771 64
Holmium
chemistry 546.417
see also Rare earths
Holocaust, 1933–1945 940.531 8
arts 700.458
T3C—358
Christian theology 231.76
European history 940.531 8
interreligious relations 261.26
Jewish theology 296.311 74
literature 808.803 58
history and criticism 809.933 58
specific literatures T3B—080 358
history and criticism T3B—093 58
Holocephali 597.38
paleozoology 567.38
Holography 774
arts 774
engineering 621.367 5
Holometabola 595.7
see also Insects
Holostei 597.41
paleozoology 567.41
Holothurioidea 593.96
paleozoology 563.96
Holstein-Friesian cattle 636.234
Holt County (Mo.) T2—778 115
Holt County (Neb.) T2—782 745
Holy, The 211
Holy Communion 234.163
public worship 264.36
Anglican 264.030 36
texts 264.03
Roman Catholic 264.020 36
texts 264.023
theology 234.163
Holy day work
economics 331.257 4
personnel management 658.312 1
Holy days 291.36
Buddhism 294.343 6
Christianity 263.9
devotional literature 242.3
sermons 252.6
customs 394.265
see Manual at 263.9, 291.36 vs. 394.265–394.267
Hinduism 294.536
Islam 297.36
Judaism 296.43
liturgy 296.453
see also Holidays
Holy Family 232.92
art representation 704.948 56
arts T3C—382 329 2
Holy Ghost 231.3
Holy Hours 264.7
Holy Orders 234.164
public worship 265.4
theology 234.164
Holy places 291.35
see also Sacred places
Holy Roman Empire 943
T2—43
church history 270
German history 943
Holy Shroud 232.966
Holy Spirit 231.3
baptism in 234.13
Holy war (Islam) 297.72
Holy Week 263.925
devotional literature 242.35
music 781.726
Roman Catholic liturgy 264.027 2
sermons 252.625
Homalozoa 563.92
Home affairs departments 353.3
Home and school associations 371.192 06
Home aquariums 639.34
Home-based enterprises
management 658.041
Home Box Office 384.555 4
see also Television

Home brewing 641.873
Home buying 643.12
Home care services 362.14
  mental illness 362.24
    see also Mental health services
  see also Health services
Home computers 004.16
  see also Microcomputers
Home Counties T2—422
Home defense (Military science) 355.45
Home departments 353.3
Home economics 640
  customs 392.3
  elementary education 372.82
Home economists 640.92
  occupational group T7—64
Home finance 332.722
Home furnishings 645
  household management 645
  manufacturing technology 684
Home gardens 635
  landscape architecture 712.6
Home guards 355.37
  active units 355.351
  reserve units 355.37
Home improvement 690.802 86
  home economics 643.7
  see Manual at 690 vs. 643.7
Home inspection 643.12
Home instruction 371.39
Home libraries (Rooms) 643.58
  home economics 643.58
  interior decoration 747.73
Home loan associations 332.32
  law 346.082 32
  public administration 354.86
Home meals 642.1
Home medicine 616.024
Home missions 266.022
Home movies 791.433
Home ownership 363.583
  public administrative support 353.55
Home remedies
  therapeutics 615.88
Home rental 643.12
Home repairs 690.802 88
  home economics 643.7
  see Manual at 690 vs. 643.7
Home reserves (Armed forces) 355.37
Home rule
  law 342.042
  local government 320.8
Home safety 363.13
  see also Safety
Home schooling 371.042
Home schools 371.042
Home selection 643.12
Home sites
  selection 643.12
Home video systems 778.59
  engineering 621.388
  video production 778.59
Home workshops 684.08
Homel′ (Belarus : Voblasts) T2—478 1
Homelands (South Africa) T2—682 9
  Cape of Good Hope T2—687 9
  Natal T2—684 9
  Orange Free State T2—685 9
  Transvaal T2—682 9
Homeless persons 305.569
  T1—086 942
  social theology 291.178 325
    Christianity 261.832 5
  social welfare 362.5
  see also Poor people
Homel′skaîa voblasts′ (Belarus) T2—478 1
Homemakers 640.92
  T1—088 649
  legal status 346.016 3
  social group T7—649
Homemaking 640
Homeomorphisms 514
Homeopathy
  therapeutic system 615.532
Homeostasis
  biology 571.75
    see also Endocrine system
  human physiology 612.022
Homeowner's insurance 368.096
  liability 368.56
  see also Insurance
Homes 640
  customs 392.36
  home economics 640
  social services 363.59
    older persons 362.61
    see also Group homes
Homework 371.302 81
Homicidal behavior
  medicine 616.858 44
  see also Mental illness
Homicide 364.152
  ethics 179.7
  law 345.025 2

Homiletic illustrations
  Christianity 251.08
Homiletics
  Christianity 251
  see also Preaching
Homilies 291.43
  Christianity 252
Homing
  manned space flight 629.453
  space flight 629.41
  unmanned space flight 629.433
Homing systems
  spacecraft 629.474 2
  unmanned spacecraft 629.464 2
Hominidae 599.9
  paleozoology 569.9
Hominoidea 599.88
  paleozoology 569.88
Homo (Genus) 599.9
  paleozoology 569.9
Homobasidiomycetes 579.59
Homogeneous coordinate system 516.16
Homogeneous equations
  calculus 515.253
Homogeneous grouping of students 371.254
Homogeneous reactions 541.393
  chemical engineering 660.299 3
  organic chemistry 547.139 3
Homogeneous spaces 514
Homogenization
  milk processing 637.141
Homoiothermy 571.76
Homological algebra 512.55
Homology theory 514.23
Homonym dictionaries 413.1
  specific languages T4—31
Homophony 781.285
Homoptera 595.752
Homosexual marriage 306.848
Homosexuality 306.766
  arts 700.453
  T3C—353
  ethics 176
    religion 291.566
      Buddhism 294.356 6
      Christianity 241.66
      Hinduism 294.548 66
      Judaism 296.366
  literature 808.803 53
    history and criticism 809.933 53
    specific literatures T3B—080 353
      history and criticism T3B—093 53
Homosexuality (continued)
  medicine 616.858 3
    see Manual at 616.8583
  social problem 363.49
  social theology 291.178 357 66
    Christianity 261.835 766
Homosexuals 305.906 64
  T1—086 64
  Christian pastoral theology 259.086 64
  female 305.489 664
  T1—086 643
  male 305.389 664
  T1—086 642
Homotopy theory 514.24
Honan Province (China) T2—511 8
Honduran literature 860
Hondurans T5—687 283
Honduras 972.83
  T2—728 3
Honduras, Gulf of 551.463 5
  T2—163 65
Honesty 179.9
  see also Virtues
Honey 641.38
  cooking 641.68
  food 641.38
  processing 638.16
Honey bush 583.78
Honey eaters 598.8
  conservation technology 639.978 8
  resource economics 333.958 8
Honey guides 598.72
Honeybees 638.1
  apiculture 638.1
  zoology 595.799
Honeycomb structures
  naval architecture 623.817 79
  structural engineering 624.177 9
Honeydew melon 641.356 117
  cooking 641.656 117
  food 641.356 117
  garden crop 635.611 7
Honeymoons
  customs 392.5
Honeysuckles 635.933 92
  botany 583.92
  floriculture 635.933 92
Honeyworts 583.94
Hong Kong 951.25
  T2—512 5
Honolulu (Hawaii) T2—969 31
Honolulu County (Hawaii) T2—969 3

Honor rolls (Military) 355.134
  World War I 940.467
  World War II 940.546 7
  see also Military commemorations
Honor societies
  education 371.852
Honorary degrees 378.25
Honorary insignia
  armed forces 355.134 2
Honorary titles T1—079
Honors
  awards 929.81
  research 001.44
Honors work 371.394 2
Honshū (Japan) T2—521
Honsyū (Japan) T2—521
Hood, Mount (Or.) T2—795 61
Hood County (Tex.) T2—764 522
Hood River County (Or.) T2—795 61
Hooded seal 599.796
Hoofed mammals 599.6
  see also Ungulates
Hookahs 688.4
Hooked rugs
  arts 746.74
  see also Rugs
Hooker County (Neb.) T2—782 777
Hooke's law 531.382
Hookworm infestations
  incidence 614.555 4
  medicine 616.965 4
  see also Communicable diseases (Human)
Hoopstad (South Africa : District) T2—685 3
Hoover, Herbert
  United States history 973.916
Hop, skip, and jump 796.432
  see also Sports
Hop, step, and jump 796.432
  see also Sports
Hop tree 635.977 377
  botany 583.77
  ornamental arboriculture 635.977 377
Hopbushes 583.78
Hope
  Christianity 234.25
  psychology 152.4
Hope (B.C.) T2—711 37
Hope Island (B.C.) T2—711 2
Hopefield (South Africa : District) T2—687 3
Hopeh Province (China) T2—511 52
Hopetown (South Africa : District) T2—687 13
Hopewell (Va.) T2—755 586
Hopf algebras 512.55
Hopi Indians T5—974 5
Hopi language 497.45
  T6—974 5
Hopkins County (Ky.) T2—769 823
Hopkins County (Tex.) T2—764 274
Hoplocarida 595.379 6
Hoppers (Insects) 595.752
  agricultural pests 632.752
Hoppers (Railroad cars) 385.34
  engineering 625.24
  see also Rolling stock
Hops 641.23
  agriculture 633.82
  botany 583.45
  brewing additive 641.23
Horary astrology 133.56
Horayot 296.123 4
  Babylonian Talmud 296.125 4
  Mishnah 296.123 4
  Palestinian Talmud 296.124 4
Hordaland fylke (Norway) T2—483 6
Hordeeae 584.9
Horehounds 583.96
Horizontal bars 796.44
Horizontal combinations (Enterprises) 338.804 2
  see also Combinations (Enterprises)
Horizontal property
  law 346.043 3
Hormic psychology 150.193
Hormones 571.74
  animal physiology 573.44
  biochemistry 571.74
    humans 612.405
  chemistry 547.734
  human physiology 612.405
  pharmacology 615.36
  see also Endocrine system
  see Manual at 573.44 vs. 571.74: Hormones
Hormozgān (Iran) T2—557 5
Hormuz, Strait of 551.467 35
  T2—165 35
Horn carving 736.6
Horn concertos 784.289 4
Horn of Africa T2—63
Horn players 788.940 92
  occupational group T7—788
Hornbeams 583.48

Hornbills 598.78
Hornby Island (B.C.) T2—711 2
Horned dinosaurs 567.915
Horned liverworts 588.3
Horney, Karen
  psychological system 150.195 7
Horns 788.94
  English 788.53
    instrument 788.531 9
    music 788.53
    see also Woodwind instruments
  French 788.94
    instrument 788.941 9
    music 788.94
    see also Brass instruments
  instrument 788.941 9
  music 788.94
  see also Brass instruments
Horns (Animals) 591.47
  descriptive zoology 591.47
  physiology 573.59
Hornworts (Anthocerotidae) 588.3
Hornworts (Ceratophyllaceae) 583.29
Horology 529.7
Horoscopes 133.54
Horowhenua District (N.Z.) T2—935 9
Horror
  arts 700.416 4
    T3C—164
  literature 808.801 64
    history and criticism 809.916 4
    specific literatures T3B—080 164
      history and criticism T3B—091 64
  motion pictures 791.436 164
  psychology 152.4
  radio programs 791.446 164
  television programs 791.456 164
Horror fiction 808.838 738
  history and criticism 809.387 38
  specific literatures T3B—308 738
    individual authors T3A—3
Horry County (S.C.) T2—757 87
Hors d'oeuvres 641.812
Horse cavalry 357.1
Horse chestnuts 583.78
Horse-drawn streetcars 388.46
  engineering 625.66
  transportation services 388.46
Horse flies 595.773
Horse racers 798.400 92
  sports group T7—798
Horse racing 798.4
  electronic games 794.884
  equipment technology 688.78
  law 344.099
  see also Sports
  see Manual at 798.2
Horse shows 798.24
Horse sports 798
  see also Sports
Horsefly River (B.C.) T2—711 75
Horsehair worms 592.59
Horsemanship
  sports 798.2
    see also Sports
    see Manual at 798.2
Horseradish 641.338 4
  see also Hot spices
Horses 636.1
  animal husbandry 636.1
  remount services 357.2
  zoology 599.665 5
Horseshoe crabs 595.492
  paleozoology 565.492
Horseshoe shrimps 595.36
Horseshoe worms 592.3
Horseshoeing 682.1
Horseshoes (Game) 796.24
  see also Sports
Horsetails (Plants) 587.2
Horsham (England : District) T2—422 64
Horsham (Vic.) T2—945 8
Horta (Azores : District) T2—469 9
Horticulture 635
Horticulturists 635.092
  occupational group T7—635
Hose (Clothing) 391.413
  commercial technology 687.3
  customs 391.413
  home sewing 646.42
  see also Clothing
Hosea (Biblical book) 224.6
Hoses
  rubber 678.36
Hosiery 391.413
  commercial technology 687.3
  customs 391.413
  home sewing 646.42
  see also Clothing
Hospices (Inns) 647.94
Hospices (Terminal care facilities) 362.175 6
  pastoral theology 291.61
    Christianity 259.417 56

Hospices (Terminal care facilities) (continued)
social theology 291.178 321 756
Christianity 261.832 175 6
social welfare 362.175 6
see also Health care facilities; Health services
Hospital chaplaincy 259.411
Hospital cooking 641.579
Hospital insurance 368.382 7
public administration 353.69
see also Insurance
Hospital libraries 027.662
administration 025.197 662
collection development 025.218 766 2
use studies 025.587 662
Hospital meal service 642.5
Hospital ships 359.836 4
design 623.812 64
military
engineering 623.826 4
naval equipment 359.836 4
naval units 359.326 4
Hospital ward management 362.173 068
Hospitalers of St. John of Jerusalem 255.791 2
church history 271.791 2
Hospitality
ethics 177.1
see also Ethical problems
etiquette 395.3
Hospitals 362.11
accounting 657.832 2
animal husbandry 636.083 2
architecture 725.51
armed forces 355.72
Civil War (United States) 973.776
construction 690.551
institutional housekeeping 647.965 1
landscape architecture 712.7
law 344.032 11
liability law 346.031
pastoral theology 291.61
Christianity 259.411
social theology 291.178 321 1
Christianity 261.832 11
social welfare 362.11
United States Revolutionary War 973.376
World War I 940.476
World War II 940.547 6
see also Health services
Host-virus relationships
medical microbiology 616.019 4
Hostage taking
criminology 364.154
criminal law 345.025 4
Hostas 635.934 32
botany 584.32
floriculture 635.934 32
Hostels 647.94
Hostile environments
biology 578.758
ecology 577.58
Hot air balloons
engineering 629.133 22
sports 797.51
see also Sports
Hot-air heating
buildings 697.3
Hot cake mixes 664.753
Hot cakes 641.815
Hot lines (Counseling) 361.06
mental illness 362.204 251
suicide 362.288 1
Hot-metal dipping 671.733
Hot peppers 641.338 4
see also Hot spices
Hot rods 796.72
driving 629.284 86
engineering 629.228 6
repair 629.287 86
sports 796.72
see also Sports
Hot spices 641.338 4
agriculture 633.84
commercial processing 664.54
cooking with 641.638 4
economic botany 581.632
food 641.338 4
Hot Spring County (Ark.) T2—767 42
Hot springs 551.23
Hot Springs County (Wyo.) T2—787 43
Hot Springs National Park (Ark.) T2—767 41
Hot-water bottles
rubber 678.34
Hot-water heating
buildings 697.4
Hot-water pipes
buildings 696.6
Hot-water supply
buildings 696.6
household management 644.6
Hot weather
health 613.113
Hot-weather cooking 641.591 3
Hot-weather photography 778.75

Hot-working operations
  metals 671.3
Hotbeds 631.583
  floriculture 635.982
  gardening 635.048 3
  manufacturing technology 681.763 1
Hotel cooking 641.572
Hotel industry 338.476 479 4
  law 343.078 647 94
Hotel meal service 642.5
Hotelkeepers 647.940 92
  occupational group T7—647
Hotels 647.94
  accounting 657.837
  architecture 728.5
  area planning 711.557
  household management 647.94
  landscape architecture 712.7
  sanitation services 363.729 8
    law 344.046 4
    see also Waste control
Hotlines (Counseling) 361.06
  mental illness 362.204 251
  suicide 362.288 1
Hottentot language 496.1
  T6—961
Hottentots T5—961
Houghton County (Mich.) T2—774 993
Hounds 636.753
  see Manual at 636.72–636.75: Hounds
Hound's tongues 583.94
Hounslow (London, England) T2—421 82
Houphouët-Boigny, Félix
  Ivorian history 966.680 51
Hourglasses
  technology 681.111
Hours of work 331.257
  economics 331.257
  personnel management 658.312 1
    public administration 352.67
House bats 599.47
House churches 250
House flies 595.774
  control technology 628.965 7
House mouse 599.353
  see also Mice (Mus)
House of Lords (Court of last resort) (Great Britain) 347.420 39
House of Lords (Court of last resort) (Scotland) 347.411 039
House organs T1—05
  journalism 070.486
  management use 658.455
House painting 698.1
House plants 635.965
House selling 333.338 3
House sparrow 598.887
House-to-house fighting 355.426
Houseboating
  sports 797.129
Houseboats 643.2
  architecture 728.78
  construction 690.878
  home economics 643.2
Housebound persons 305.908 14
  T1—087 7
  T7—081 4
Housecleaning 648.5
Household appliance makers 683.809 2
  occupational group T7—683
Household appliances 643.6
  manufacturing technology 683.8
  product safety 363.19
    see also Product safety
Household biology 578.755 4
Household budgets
  home economics 640.42
  macroeconomics 339.41
Household ecology 577.554
Household employees 640.46
  home economics 640.46
  public households 647.2
Household equipment 643
  home economics 643
Household expenses 640.42
Household finances 640.42
  see Manual at 332.024 vs. 640.42
Household furnishings 645
  household management 645
  manufacturing technology 684
Household garbage
  use as fertilizer 631.875
Household income
  macroeconomics 339.22
Household management 640
  public households 647
Household pests
  control technology 628.96
Household sanitation 648
Household security 643.16
Household utilities 644
Household wastes 363.728 8
  see also Waste control

Househusbands 640.92
T1—088 649
legal status 346.016 3
social group 305.336 49
T7—649
Housekeepers 640.92
occupational group T7—64
Housekeeping 648
public households 647
Houseleeks 583.72
Houseparents 362.732
see also Children—social welfare
Houseplants 635.965
interior decoration 747.98
Houses 643.1
architecture 728.37
construction 690.837
customs 392.36
home economics 643.1
see Manual at 363.5 vs. 643.1
Houses (Astrology) 133.530 42
Housewives 640.92
T1—088 649
legal status 346.016 3
social group 305.436 49
T7—649
Housing 363.5
animal husbandry 636.083 1
armed forces 355.12
construction 690.8
home economics 643.1
psychological influence 155.945
public administration 353.55
social services 363.5
sociology 307.336
see Manual at 363.5, 363.6, 363.8 vs. 338; *also at* 363.5 vs. 307.336, 307.34; *also at* 363.5 vs. 643.1
Housing allowances 363.582
armed forces 355.12
see also Housing
Housing conditions 363.51
see also Housing
Housing cooperatives 334.1
Housing renewal
area planning 711.59
community sociology 307.34
Housing succession 307.336
Houston (Tex.) T2—764 141 1
Houston County (Ala.) T2—761 295
Houston County (Ga.) T2—758 515
Houston County (Minn.) T2—776 11
Houston County (Tenn.) T2—768 36
Houston County (Tex.) T2—764 235
Hove (England) T2—422 54
Hover flies 595.774
Hovercraft
engineering 629.3
Howard County (Ark.) T2—767 483
Howard County (Ind.) T2—772 85
Howard County (Iowa) T2—777 312
Howard County (Md.) T2—752 81
Howard County (Mo.) T2—778 285
Howard County (Neb.) T2—782 43
Howard County (Tex.) T2—764 858
Howe Sound (B.C.) T2—711 31
Howell County (Mo.) T2—778 85
Howick (South Africa) T2—684 7
Howitzers 355.822
engineering 623.42
military equipment 355.822
Howland Island T2—969 9
Howler monkeys 599.855
Hrodzen (Belarus : Voblasts) T2—478 8
Hrodzenskaîa voblasts′ (Belarus) T2—478 8
Huambisa language 498.372
T6—983 72
Huambo (Angola : Province) T2—673 4
Huancavelica (Peru : Dept.) T2—852 8
Huánuco (Peru : Dept.) T2—852 2
Huasco (Chile : Province) T2—831 48
Huastec language 497.415
T6—974 15
Hubbard County (Minn.) T2—776 85
Hubei Sheng (China) T2—512 12
Huckaback fabrics 677.615
Huckleberries 641.347 32
botany 583.66
cooking 641.647 32
food 641.347 32
horticulture 634.732
Hudson Bay 551.468 7
T2—163 27
Hudson Bay Region T2—714 111
Hudson County (N.J.) T2—749 26
Hudson River (N.Y. and N.J.) T2—747 3
Hudspeth County (Tex.) T2—764 95
Huehuetenango (Guatemala : Dept.) T2—728 171
Huelva (Spain : Province) T2—468 7

Huerfano County (Colo.) T2—788 51
Huerta, Adolfo de la
  Mexican history 972.082 1
Huesca (Spain : Province) T2—465 55
Hugh Capet, King of France
  French history 944.021
Hughes County (Okla.) T2—766 72
Hughes County (S.D.) T2—783 29
Hugoniaceae 583.79
Huguenots 284.5
  biography 284.509 2
  persecution of 272.4
  religious group T7—245
  see also Christian denominations
Huichol language 497.45
  T6—974 5
Huíla (Angola) T2—673 5
Huila (Colombia : Dept.) T2—861 54
Huku language 496.394
  T6—963 94
Hull (England) T2—428 37
Hull (Quebec : County) T2—714 221
Hull, Clark Leonard
  psychological system 150.194 34
Ḥullin 296.123 5
  Babylonian Talmud 296.125 5
  Mishnah 296.123 5
Hulls (Ships)
  engineering 623.84
Humacao (P.R. : District) T2—729 59
Human anatomy 611
  see Manual at 599.94 vs. 611; *also at* 612 vs. 611
Human behavior
  psychology 150
  social psychology 302
Human body
  folklore 398.27
    history and criticism 398.353
Human chromosome abnormalities
  medicine 616.042
Human-computer interaction 004.019
  engineering 621.398 4
Human ecology 304.2
  biology 599.95
  social theology 291.178 362
    Christianity 261.836 2
    Judaism 296.38
  see Manual at 578 vs. 304.2, 508, 910
Human engineering 620.82
Human evolution 599.938
Human experimentation in medicine 619.98
  ethics 174.28
    see also Medical ethics
  law 344.041 96
Human factors engineering 620.82
  computers 621.39
Human figures
  art representation 704.942
  arts 700.45
  T3C—35
  drawing 743.4
  painting 757
Human genetics 599.935
Human geography 304.2
Human immunodeficiency viruses
  medical microbiology 616.979 201
Human information processing 153
Human life
  folklore 398.27
    history and criticism 398.35
    persons 398.22
  origin
    religion 291.22
      Christianity 233.11
      Islam 297.221
      Judaism 296.32
      philosophy of religion 213
  philosophy 128
Human milk diet 613.269
Human physiology 612
  see Manual at 612 vs. 611; *also at* 612.1–612.8; *also at* 616 vs. 612
Human pigmentation
  physical anthropology 599.95
Human qualities
  folklore 398.27
    history and criticism 398.353
Human races 305.8
  physical ethnology 599.97
  see also Ethnic groups
Human relations
  applied psychology 158.2
  business 650.13
  personnel management 658.314 5
    executives 658.407 145
    public administration 352.66
Human relations training
  personnel management 658.312 44
    executives 658.407 124 4
    public administration 352.669

Human reproduction 612.6
see also Genital system
Human reproductive technology
health 613.94
infertility
gynecology 618.178 06
medicine 616.692 06
Human resource development 370.113
see also Vocational education
Human resource management 658.3
T1—068 3
see also Personnel management
Human resources 331.11
armed forces 355.22
economics 331.11
utilization
economics 331.125
see *Manual* at 331.1 vs. 331.11, 331.12
Human resources management 658.3
see also Personnel management
Human rights 323
see also Civil rights
Human sacrifice
religion 291.34
Human services 361
see also Welfare services
Human settlement 307.14
Human variation
physical anthropology 599.94
Humane law 344.049
Humanism
arts T3C—384
ethics 171.2
literature 808.803 84
history and criticism 809.933 84
specific literatures T3B—080 384
history and criticism T3B—093 84
philosophy 144
philosophy of religion 211.6
Humanistic education 370.112
Humanistic Judaism 296.834
Humanistic psychology 150.198
Humanitarians 361.740 92
social group T7—361
Humanities 001.3
law 344.097
public administrative support 353.77
Humanity
arts 700.45
T3C—35
literature 808.803 5
history and criticism 809.933 5
specific literatures T3B—080 35
history and criticism T3B—093 5
Humanity of Jesus Christ 232.8
Humankind 301
see also Humans
Humans 301
anthropology 301
effect on natural ecology 577.27
paleozoology 569.9
philosophy 128
physical anthropology 599.9
physiology 612
religion 291.22
Buddhism 294.342 2
Christianity 233
Hinduism 294.522
Islam 297.22
Judaism 296.32
philosophy of religion 218
sociology 301
zoology 599.9
Humansdorp (South Africa : District) T2—687 4
Humayun, Emperor of Hindustan
Indian history 954.025 3
Humber, River (England) T2—428 3
Humberside (England) T2—428 3
Humboldt County (Calif.) T2—794 12
Humboldt County (Iowa) T2—777 272
Humboldt County (Nev.) T2—793 54
Humboldt Current 551.476 1
Humboldt River (Nev.) T2—793 16
Humeri
human anatomy 611.717
see also Musculoskeletal system
Humidification
chemical engineering 660.284 293
Humidifiers
air conditioning
buildings 697.932 3
Humidistats
air conditioning
buildings 697.932 3
Humidity
health 613.14
meteorology 551.571

Humidity control
  air conditioning
    buildings 697.932 3
  spacecraft 629.477 5
Humility 179.9
  see also Virtues
Humiriaceae 583.79
Hummingbirds 598.764
  conservation technology 639.978 764
  resource economics 333.958 764
Humor 152.43
  journalism 070.444
  literary criticism 809.7
    theory 808.7
  literary history 809.7
  literature 808.87
    specific literatures T3B—7
  psychology 152.43
  rhetoric 808.7
  sociology 306.481
  specific subjects T1—020 7
  see Manual at T1—0207 vs.
    T3B—7, T3A—8 + 02,
    T3B—802, T3B—8 + 02,
    T3A—8 + 07, T3B—807,
    T3B—8 + 07; *also at*
    T3B—7 vs. T3C—17
Humorists 809.7
  collected biography 809.7
    specific literatures T3B—700 9
  occupational group T7—87
Humorous poetry 808.817
  history and criticism 809.17
  specific literatures T3B—107
    specific literatures T3A—1
Humors (Psychology) 155.262
Humpback whale 599.525
Humpbacked flies 595.774
Humphreys County (Miss.) T2—762 48
Humphreys County (Tenn.) T2—768 37
Humus
  soil science 631.417
Hunan Province (China) T2—512 15
Hundred Days, 1815 944.05
Hundred Years' War,
    1337–1453 944.025
Hunedoara (Romania :
    Judet) T2—498 4
Hungarian language 494.511
    T6—945 11
Hungarian literature 894.511
Hungarian partridge 598.623 2
Hungarians T5—945 11
Hungary 943.9
    T2—439
  ancient 939.8
    T2—398
Hunger
  human physiology 612.391
  psychology 152.188 6
  social theology 291.178 326
    Christianity 261.832 6
  social welfare 363.8
  see also Digestive system
Hunger strikes
  social conflict 303.61
Hunt County (Tex.) T2—764 272
Hunter River (N.S.W.) T2—944 2
Hunterdon County (N.J.) T2—749 71
Hunters
  commercial 639.109 2
    occupational group T7—639 1
  occupational group T7—639 1
  sports 799.292
  sports group T7—799 2
Hunting 799.2
  art representation 704.943 2
  commercial 639.1
    production economics 338.372 9
    public administration 354.349
  ethics 179.3
    see also Ethical problems
  game laws 346.046 954 9
  painting 758.3
  products 338.372 9
    commerce 380.143 2–.1439
  public administration 354.349
  sports 799.2
    public administrative
        support 353.78
    see also Sports
Hunting animals
  animal husbandry 636.088 8
Hunting dogs 636.75
  sports 799.234
Hunting lodges
  architecture 728.7
Huntingdon (Quebec :
    County) T2—714 31
Huntingdon County (Pa.) T2—748 73
Huntingdonshire
    (England : District) T2—426 54
Huntington County (Ind.) T2—772 71
Huntsville (Ala.) T2—761 97
Huon pine 585.3
  forestry 634.975 93
Hupeh Province (China) T2—512 12

Hurdlers 796.426 092
  sports group T7—796 4
Hurdles (Race)
  horses 798.45
  humans 796.426
  see also Sports
Hurdy-gurdies 787.69
  instrument 787.691 9
  music 787.69
  see also Stringed instruments
Hurling (Game) 796.35
  see also Sports
Huron (Ont. : County) T2—713 22
Huron, Lake (Mich. and Ont.) T2—774
  Michigan T2—774
  Ontario T2—713 2
Huron County (Mich.) T2—774 44
Huron County (Ohio) T2—771 25
Huron Indians T5—975 5
Huron language 497.55
  T6—975 5
Hurrian languages 499.9
  T6—999
Hurricanes 551.552
  meteorology 551.552
  social services 363.349 22
  weather forecasting 551.645 2
  weather modification 551.685 2
  see also Disasters
Hurunui District (N.Z.) T2—938 1
  Canterbury Region T2—938 1
  Nelson-Marlborough Region T2—937 9
Husband and wife 306.872
  law 346.016 3
Husbands 306.872
  T1—086 55
  family relationships 306.872
  guides to Christian life 248.842 5
Huskers
  manufacturing technology 681.763 1
Huskies 636.73
Husking 631.56
Hussein, Saddam
  Iraqi history 956.704 4
Hussein Onn, Datuk
  Malaysian history 959.505 3
Hussite Wars, 1419–1436 943.702 24
Hussites 284.3
  religious group T7—243
  see also Christian denominations
Hutchinson County (S.D.) T2—783 384
Hutchinson County (Tex.) T2—764 821
Hutias 599.359
Hutterite Brethren 289.73
  biography 289.709 2
  see also Mennonite Church
Hutu (African people) T5—963 946 1
HVAC (Building systems) 697
HVAP ammunition 623.451 8
Hwang Ho (China) T2—511
Hyacinths 635.934 32
  botany 584.32
  floriculture 635.934 32
Hyaenidae 599.743
Hyaline cartilage
  human histology 611.018 3
  see also Musculoskeletal system
Hyalospongiae 593.44
  paleozoology 563.4
Hybrid computers 004.19
  architecture 004.259
  communications 004.619
    programming 005.712 9
    programs 005.713 9
  engineering 621.391 9
  graphics programming 006.679
  graphics programs 006.689
  interfacing 004.619
    programming 005.712 9
    programs 005.713 9
  knowledge-based systems
    programming 006.337
  multimedia-systems
    programming 006.779
  multimedia-systems programs 006.789
  operating systems 005.449
  performance evaluation 004.190 297
    for improvement and design 004.259
  peripherals 004.719
  programming 005.29
  programs 005.39
  systems analysis 004.259
  systems design 004.259
Hybrids
  agriculture 631.523
    animal husbandry 636.082
    plant cultivation 631.523
Hydatid diseases
  incidence 614.554
  medicine 616.964
  see also Communicable diseases (Human)
Hyde County (N.C.) T2—756 184
Hyde County (S.D.) T2—783 283

Hyderabad (India : State) T2—548 4
Hyderabad (Pakistan : District) T2—549 182
Hydnaceae 579.6
Hydrangeaceae 583.72
Hydrangeas 635.933 72
  botany 583.72
  floriculture 635.933 72
Hydras 593.55
Hydraulic control 629.804 2
Hydraulic engineering 627
Hydraulic engineers 627.092
  occupational group T7—627
Hydraulic fluids 621.204 24
Hydraulic machinery 621.2
Hydraulic mining 622.292 7
Hydraulic-power engineering 621.2
Hydraulic-power engineers 621.209 2
  occupational group T7—621
Hydraulic pumps 621.252
Hydraulic rams 621.27
Hydraulic transmission 621.26
Hydraulic turbines 621.24
Hydraulics 532
  see also Liquid mechanics
Hydrides
  chemical engineering 661.08
Hydrobatidae 598.42
Hydrocarbons 547.01
  alicyclic chemical engineering 661.815
  alicyclic chemistry 547.51
  aliphatic chemical engineering 661.814
  aliphatic chemistry 547.41
  aromatic chemical engineering 661.816
  aromatic chemistry 547.61
  chemical engineering 661.81
  human toxicology 615.95
Hydrocephalus
  medicine 616.858 843
  see also Mental retardation
Hydrocharitales 584.73
Hydrochloric acid
  chemical engineering 661.23
Hydrodynamics 532.5
Hydroelectric power 333.914
  see also Water power
Hydroelectric power plants 621.312 134
Hydroelectricity 333.914
  see also Water power
Hydrofoils 387.204 4
  engineering 623.820 4
  transportation services 387.204 4
  see also Ships
Hydrogen 553.92
  chemical engineering 661.08
  chemistry 546.2
  economic geology 553.92
  gas technology 665.81
  organic chemistry 547
  see also Chemicals
Hydrogen embrittlement 620.162 3
Hydrogen-ion concentration 541.372 8
  chemical engineering 660.297 28
Hydrogen sulfide
  gas technology 665.89
  human toxicology 615.91
Hydrogenation 547.23
  carbonaceous gas technology 662.662 3
  chemical engineering 660.284 43
  coal technology 662.662 2
  petroleum distillates 665.533
  physical chemistry 541.393
Hydrographic currents
  navigation tables 623.894 9
Hydrographic surveying 526.99
Hydrography 551.46
Hydroida 593.55
Hydroids 593.55
Hydrolases 572.793
  see also Enzymes
Hydrological cycle 551.48
Hydrology (Fresh waters) 551.48
Hydrolysis 541.393
  chemical engineering 660.284 425
  organic chemistry 547.225
Hydromechanics 532
  engineering 620.106
  soil physics 631.432
  see also Liquid mechanics
Hydrometallurgy 669.028 3
Hydrometeorology 551.57
Hydrophiloidea 595.763
Hydrophobia
  incidence 614.563
  medicine 616.953
  see also Communicable diseases (Human)
Hydrophyllaceae 583.94
Hydroplanes 387.231 4
  engineering 623.823 14
  transportation services 387.231 4
  see also Ships
Hydroponics 631.585
Hydroquinones 547.633
Hydroscaphidae 595.762
Hydrosols 541.345 14
  chemical engineering 660.294 514

Hydrosphere 551.46
Hydrostatics 532.2
Hydrosulfites 547.063
  chemical engineering 661.896
Hydrotherapy
  medicine 615.853
Hydrous sulfates
  mineralogy 549.755
Hydroxides
  mineralogy 549.53
Hydroxy compounds 547.03
  aliphatic chemistry 547.43
  aromatic chemistry 547.63
  chemical engineering 661.8
Hydroxyketone dyes 667.256
Hydrozoa 593.55
Hyenas 599.743
Hyeniales 561.72
Hygiene 613
  customs 391.64
  elementary education 372.37
  personal 613
  veterinary medicine 636.089 3
Hygienists 613.092
Hylidae 597.87
Hylobates 599.882
Hylobatidae 599.882
Hymen
  gynecology 618.1
  human anatomy 611.67
  human physiology 612.62
  see also Female genital system
Hymenoptera 595.79
Hymenostomatida 579.495
Hymns 782.27
  choral and mixed voices 782.527
  religion 291.38
    Christianity 264.23
    Judaism 296.462
    private devotions 291.43
  single voices 783.092 7
Hyndburn (England : Borough) T2—427 625
Hyōgo-ken (Japan) T2—521 87
Hyperactive children
  home care 649.153
Hyperactive students 371.93
Hyperactivity
  medicine 616.858 9
  pediatrics 618.928 589
  see also Nervous system
Hyperadrenalism
  medicine 616.45
  see also Endocrine system
Hyperbola 516.15
Hyperbolic equations 515.353
Hyperbolic geometry 516.9
Hyperboloids 516.15
Hyperborean languages 494.6
  T6—946
Hyperborean literatures 894.6
Hyperfunctions 515.9
Hypergeometric polynomials 515.55
Hypericaceae 583.624
Hyperkinesia
  medicine 616.858 9
  see also Nervous system
Hyperons 539.721 64
Hyperopia
  optometry 617.755
Hyperparathyroidism
  medicine 616.445
  see also Endocrine system
Hyperpinealism
  medicine 616.48
  see also Endocrine system
Hypersensitivity
  incidence 614.599 3
  medicine 616.97
  see also Diseases (Human)
Hypersonic flow 533.276
  air mechanics 533.62
    aeronautics 629.132 306
Hypertension
  medicine 616.132
  see also Cardiovascular system
Hypertext databases
  computer science 005.759 2
Hyperthyroidism
  medicine 616.443
  see also Endocrine system
Hypertrichosis
  medicine 616.546
Hypertrophic arthritis
  medicine 616.722 3
  see also Musculoskeletal system
Hypertrophies
  skin
    medicine 616.544
    see also Skin
Hyperventilation
  medicine 616.208
  see also Respiratory system
Hyphochytridiomycetes 579.53
Hyphomycetes 579.55

Hypnotherapy
  medicine 615.851 2
Hypnotic regression
  occultism 133.901 35
Hypnotics
  pharmacodynamics 615.782
Hypnotism 154.7
  parapsychology 133.89
Hypoadrenalism
  medicine 616.45
  see also Endocrine system
Hypochondria
  medicine 616.852 5
  see also Mental illness
Hypocreales 579.567 7
Hypoglycemia
  medicine 616.466
  see also Endocrine system
Hypoparathyroidism
  medicine 616.445
  see also Endocrine system
Hypopituitarism
  medicine 616.47
  see also Endocrine system
Hypostatic union 232.8
Hypothalamus 573.459
  biology 573.459
  human anatomy 611.81
  human physiology 612.826 2
  see also Nervous system
Hypothermia
  medicine 616.989
  therapeutics 615.832 9
  see also Environmental diseases (Human)
Hypotheses
  logic 167
  mathematics 511.3
Hypothesis testing (Statistics) 519.56
Hypothyroidism
  medicine 616.444
  see also Endocrine system
Hypoxidaceae 584.354
Hypsilophodon 567.914
Hyracoidea 599.68
Hyraxes 599.68
Hyrcania T2—396
Hyssop 583.96
Hysterectomies
  surgery 618.145 3
  see also Female genital system
Hysteresis (Magnetism) 538.3
Hysteria
  medicine 616.852 4
  see also Mental illness
Hystricidae 599.359 7
Hystricomorpha 599.359

I

Ialomiţa (Romania) T2—498 2
I͡Ambolski okrŭg (Bulgaria) T2—499 5
I͡Aroslavskai͡a oblast′ (Russia) T2—473 2
Iaşi (Romania : Judeţ) T2—498 1
Iatrogenic diseases
  medicine 615.5
Ibadan (Nigeria) T2—669 25
Ibadites 297.833
Ibaraki-ken (Japan) T2—521 31
Iberia (Kingdom) 939.5
  T2—395
Iberia Parish (La.) T2—763 49
Iberian Peninsula 946
  T2—46
  ancient 936.6
  T2—366
Iberville (Quebec : County) T2—714 61
Iberville Parish (La.) T2—763 44
Ibexes 599.648
Ibibio (African people) T5—963 64
Ibibio language 496.364
  T6—963 64
Ibis 598.34
Ibiza Island (Spain) T2—467 56
Ibizan hound 636.753 2
Ibn Ḥanbal, Aḥmad ibn Muḥammad
  Hadith 297.124
Ibn Mājah, Muḥammad ibn Yazīd
  Hadith 297.124 6
Ibo (African people) T5—963 32
Ibo language 496.332
  T6—963 32
Ibo literature 896.332
Ibrāhīm (Patriarch)
  Islam 297.246 3
Ica (Peru : Province) T2—852 7
Icacinaceae 583.85
Icarianism (Socialist school) 335.2
ICBM (Missiles) 358.175 482
  engineering 623.451 954
  military equipment 358.175 482

Ice 551.31
  building construction 693.91
  economic geology 553.7
  geology 551.31
  manufacturing technology 621.58
  mineralogy 549.522
Ice age 551.792
  geology 551.792
  paleontology 560.179 2
Ice bugs 595.726
Ice carving 736.94
Ice control
  road engineering 625.763
Ice cream 641.862
  commercial processing 637.4
  home preparation 641.862
Ice crossings
  railroad engineering 625.147
  road engineering 625.792
Ice dancing 796.912
  see also Sports
Ice fishing 799.122
Ice formation
  aeronautics 629.132 4
Ice games 796.96
  see also Sports
Ice hockey 796.962
  electronic games 794.869 62
  see also Sports
Ice hockey players 796.962 092
  sports group T7—796 9
Ice milk 641.862
  commercial processing 637.4
  home preparation 641.862
Ice plants (Sea figs) 583.53
Ice roads 388.12
  engineering 625.792
  see also Roads
Ice skaters 796.910 92
  sports group T7—796 9
Ice skates
  manufacturing technology 685.361
Ice skating 796.91
  see also Sports
Ice sports 796.9
  equipment technology 688.769
  see also Sports
Ice storms 551.559
Icebergs 551.342
Iceboating 796.97
  see also Sports
Icebreakers 387.28
  design 623.812 8
Icebreakers (continued)
  engineering 623.828
  see also Ships
Icebreaking services 387.54
İçel İli (Turkey) T2—564
Iceland 949.12
  T2—491 2
Iceland pony 636.16
Icelanders T5—396 1
Icelandic language 439.69
  T6—396 91
Icelandic literature 839.69
Icelandic people T5—396 1
Ices 641.863
  commercial processing 637.4
  home preparation 641.863
Ichneumonoidea 595.79
Ichneumons 595.79
Ichthyologists 597.092
  occupational group T7—597
Ichthyology 597
Ichthyornithiformes 568.23
Ichthyosauria 567.937
Ichthyosis
  medicine 616.544
  see also Skin
Iconography
  drawing 743.9
  fine arts 704.9
    see Manual at 704.9
  painting 753–758
    see Manual at 753–758
Icons
  fine arts 704.948
    Christianity 704.948 2
  religious significance 291.37
    Christianity 246.53
    see also Symbolism—
      religious significance
Ictaluridae 597.492
Ictalurus 597.492
Icteridae 598.874
Id (Psychology) 154.22
'Īd al-Aḍḥā 297.36
'Īd al-Fiṭr 297.36
Ida County (Iowa) T2—777 422
Idaho 979.6
  T2—796
Idaho County (Idaho) T2—796 82
Ideal states 321.07
  see also Utopias
Idealism 141
  arts T3C—13
  education 370.12

Idealism (continued)
  literature 808.801 3
    history and criticism 809.913
    specific literatures T3B—080 13
      history and criticism T3B—091 3
Ideals (Mathematics) 512.4
  algebra 512.4
  number theory 512.74
Ideas
  epistemology 121.4
  psychology 153.2
Ideation
  epistemology 121
  psychology 153.2
Idée fixe
  musical element 781.248
Identification
  arts 702.87
Identification cards 929.9
Identification marks 929.9
  T1—027
Identification of criminals 363.258
Identity (Human) 155.2
  philosophy 126
Identity (Principle of) 111.82
Ideographs 411
  specific languages T4—11
Ideologies (Political science) 320.5
  see also Political ideologies
Ideology 140
  philosophical system 145
  see Manual at 140
Idioms
  dictionaries 413.1
    specific languages T4—31
Idiophones 786.82
  see also Percussion instruments
Idlib (Syria : Province) T2—569 13
Idolatry 291.218
Idols 291.218
Idoma (African people) T5—963 3
Idoma language 496.33
  T6—963 3
Idomoid languages 496.33
  T6—963 3
Idris I, King of Libya
  Libyan history 961.204 1
Idutywa (South Africa : District) T2—687 91
Ife (Kingdom) 966.928 01
  T2—669 28
Ifrane (Morocco : Province) T2—643
Ifugao (Philippines) T2—599 1
Ig (Immunoglobulin) 571.967
  humans 616.079 8
Igala (African people) T5—963 33
Igbo (African people) T5—963 32
Igbo language 496.332
  T6—963 32
Igbo literature 896.332
Igboid languages 496.33
  T6—963 3
Igloolik (N.W.T.) T2—719 5
Igloos
  construction 693.91
Igneous rocks 552.1
Ignition 541.361
  chemical engineering 660.296 1
  chemistry 541.361
Ignition systems
  automotive 629.254
  internal-combustion engines 621.437
Iguanodon 567.914
Ijo (African people) T5—963
Ijo language 496.3
  T6—963
Ijoid languages 496.3
  T6—963
IJssel Lake (Netherlands) T2—492 2
IJssel River (Netherlands) T2—492 18
Ikhnaton, King of Egypt
  Egyptian history 932.014
Īlām (Iran : Province) T2—555 2
Ilamba-Irangi languages 496.394
  T6—963 94
Île aux Grues (Quebec) T2—714 735
Ile-de-France (France) T2—443 4
Ile de la Tortue (Haiti) T2—729 42
Île-de-Montréal (Quebec) T2—714 27
Île d'Orléans (Quebec) T2—714 48
Île-Jésus (Quebec) T2—714 27
Ileitis
  medicine 616.344 5
  see also Digestive system
Ileostomy 617.554 1
Îles-de-la-Madeleine (Quebec) T2—714 797
Ileum 573.378
  biology 573.378
  human anatomy 611.341
  surgery 617.554 1
  see also Digestive system
Ilía (Greece) T2—495 27
  ancient T2—388
Ilium (Extinct City) T2—392 1

Ill persons 305.908 14
T1—087 7
see also Sick persons
Ille-et-Vilaine (France) T2—441 5
Illecillewaet River (B.C.) T2—711 68
Illegitimacy 306.874
law 346.017
Illegitimate children 305.906 945
T1—086 945
family relationships 306.874
social group 305.906 945
social welfare 362.708 694 5
Illiciales 583.3
Illicit distilling 364.133
law 345.023 3
Illinois 977.3
T2—773
Illinois River (Ill.) T2—773 5
Illiteracy 302.224 4
see also Literacy
Illiterate persons 305.906 33
T1—086 33
Illizi (Algeria : Province) T2—657
Illness 362.1
medicine 616
see also Diseases (Human)
Illuminating engineering 621.32
see also Lighting
Illumination 621.32
see also Lighting
Illumination (Decorative arts) 745.67
Illuminations (Performing arts) 791.6
Illusions 001.96
psychology of perception 153.74
sensory perception 152.1
Illustration
arts 741.6
see Manual at 741.6 vs. 800
Illustrations T1—022
notable books 096.1
see Manual at T1—0222 vs. T1—0223
Illustrators 741.609 2
occupational group T7—74
Illyria T2—398
Illyrian language (Slavic) 491.82
T6—918 2
Illyrian languages (Ancient Indo-European) 491.993
T6—919 93
Ilmenite
mineralogy 549.523
ILO (Labor office) 354.921 1
law 341.763
Ilocos Norte (Philippines) T2—599 1
Ilocos Sur (Philippines) T2—599 1
Iloilo (Philippines : Province) T2—599 5
Iloko language 499.21
T6—992 1
Ilorin (Nigeria) T2—669 57
Īlubabor Kife Hāger (Ethiopia) T2—633
Image processing 621.367
computer science 006.42
engineering 621.399
see Manual at 006.37 vs. 006.42, 621.367, 621.391, 621.399
Imagery (Psychology) 153.32
Images
fine arts 704.9
religious significance 291.37
Christianity 246.53
see also Symbolism—religious significance
religious worship 291.218
Imaginary wars
military analysis 355.48
Imagination 153.3
educational psychology 370.157
philosophy 128.3
Imamate 297.61
Imams 297.092
biography 297.092
specific sects 297.8
role and function 297.61
see Manual at 297.092
Imbabura (Ecuador) T2—866 12
Imbibition processes 773.3
Imbros Island T2—562
ancient T2—391 1
IMF (Fund) 332.152
law 341.751 152
Imidazoles 547.593
chemical engineering 661.894
Imitation furs 675.3
Imitation-leather covers
bookbinding 686.343
Imitation leathers 675.4
Imitative learning
psychology 153.152 3
Immaculate Conception of Mary 232.911
Immigrants 305.906 91
T1—086 91
labor economics 331.62
Immigration 304.82
influence on crime 364.256

Immigration (continued)
  international law 341.484 2
  law 342.082
  political science 325.1
  public administration 353.484
Immorality 170
  religion 291.5
    Christianity 241
    see also Moral theology
Immortality
  philosophy 129
  religion 291.23
    Christianity 236.22
    Islam 297.23
    Judaism 296.33
    philosophy of religion 218
Immune deficiency diseases (Biology) 571.974
  veterinary medicine 636.089 697 9
Immune deficiency diseases (Human)
  incidence 614.599 39
  medicine 616.979
  see also Diseases (Human)
Immune reactions 571.964 6
  humans 616.079 5
Immune recognition 571.964 6
  human immunology 616.079 5
Immune response 571.964 6
  humans 616.079 5
Immune system 571.96
  human diseases
    medicine 616.97
    see also Diseases (Human)
  humans 616.079
  see Manual at 616.079 vs. 571.96
Immunity 571.96
  humans 616.079
  see Manual at 616.079 vs. 571.96
Immunity of legislators 328.348
Immunization
  disease control 614.47
  law 344.043
Immunoassays
  medicine 616.075 6
Immunochemistry 571.964
  medicine 616.079
    diagnosis 616.075 6
Immunocytochemistry 571.964
  medicine 616.079
Immunodiagnosis
  medicine 616.075 6
Immunogenetics 571.964 8
  medicine 616.079 6
Immunoglobulins 571.967
  humans 616.079 8
Immunologic diseases
  medicine 616.97
  see also Diseases (Human)
Immunologic drugs
  pharmacology 615.37
Immunology 571.96
  humans 616.079
  see Manual at 616.079 vs. 571.96
Immunotherapy 615.37
Imo State (Nigeria) T2—669 46
Impact strength
  materials science 620.112 5
Impact studies (Environmental) 333.714
  see also Environmental impact studies
Impala 599.646
Impatiens 583.79
Impeachment 342.068
  chief executives 342.062
  judges 347.014
Impeachment power (Legislative bodies) 328.345 3
Impendle (South Africa : District) T2—684 7
Imperia (Italy : Province) T2—451 87
Imperial County (Calif.) T2—794 99
Imperial system (Measurement) 530.813
  social aspects 389.15
Imperial Valley (Calif. and Mexico) T2—794 99
Imperialism 325.32
  international relations 327.1
Impersonation 792.028
  motion pictures 791.430 28
  radio 791.440 28
  stage 792.028
  television 791.450 28
Impetigo
  medicine 616.524
  see also Skin
Import quotas 382.52
  see also Import trade
Import tax 382.7
  public finance 336.264
  see also Customs (Tariff)
Import trade 382.5
  law 343.087 7
  public administration 354.74

Imposition
  printing 686.225 6
Impotence
  medicine 616.692
  neurotic
    medicine 616.858 32
  see also Male genital system; Mental illness
Impoverished persons 305.569
  T1—086 942
  see also Poor people
Impressing equipment 621.984
Impression
  printing 686.23
Impressionism
  fine arts 709.034 4
  literature 808.801 1
    history and criticism 809.911
    specific literatures T3B—080 11
      history and criticism T3B—091 1
  music 780.904
  painting 759.054
Imprisonment 365
Impromptus 784.189 4
Improper integrals 515.43
Improvisation (Drama) 792.028
  motion pictures 791.430 28
  radio 791.440 28
  stage 792.028
  television 791.450 28
Improvisation (Music) 781.36
Improvisatory forms 784.189 4
Impulse control disorders
  medicine 616.858 4
  see also Mental illness
İmroz Island T2—562
In-house training 331.259 2
  personnel management 658.312 43
  see also Vocational education
In-laws 306.87
  T1—085
  T7—04
In-line skating 796.21
  see also Sports
In-service training 331.259 2
  T1—071 55
  libraries 023.8
  museums 069.63
  see also Vocational education
In-situ processing 622.22
  see Manual at 622.22, 622.7 vs. 662.6, 669
In vitro fertilization
  medicine 618.178 059
Inactive files (Records management)
  storage 651.56
Inadunata 563.92
Inanda (South Africa : District) T2—684 4
Inaudible sound 534.5
Inaugural addresses
  public administration 352.238 6
Inaugurations
  customs 394.4
  music 781.57
Inboard motorboats 387.231 4
  design 623.812 314
  engineering 623.823 14
  transportation services 387.231 4
  see also Ships
Inboard motors 623.872 3
Inboard-outboard motorboats 387.231 5
  design 623.812 315
  engineering 623.823 15
  transportation services 387.231 5
  see also Ships
Inborn errors of metabolism
  medicine 616.390 42
  see also Digestive system
Inbreeding 576.544
  agriculture 631.523
    animal husbandry 636.082
    plant cultivation 631.523
  genetics 576.544
  sociology 306.82
Inca T5—983 23
Inca period 985.019
Incandescent lighting 621.326
  see also Lighting
Incantations (Occultism) 133.44
Incarcerated persons 365.6
  T1—086 927
Incarnation
  philosophy 129
Incarnation of Jesus Christ 232.1
Incense cedars 585.4
Incense trees 583.77
Incentive payments
  labor economics 331.216 4
  personnel management 658.322 5
    executives 658.407 225
    public administration 352.67
Incentives
  labor economics 331.216 4
  personnel management 658.314 2
    executives 658.407 142
  research 001.44

Incentives (continued)
  social control 303.35
Incest 306.877
  criminology 364.153 6
    criminal law 345.025 36
  medicine 616.858 36
  sociology 306.877
  see also Mental illness
Incidence geometry 516.12
Incidental music 781.552
Incineration
  sewage sludge disposal 628.37
  waste disposal 363.728
  waste technology 628.445 7
  see also Waste control
Incisions (Wounds)
  medicine 617.143
Inclined railroads 385.6
  engineering 625.3
  transportation services 385.6
  see also Railroad transportation
Inclines
  canal engineering 627.135 3
Inclosures
  land economics 333.2
Income
  agricultural industries 338.13
  analytical accounting 657.48
  financial management 658.155 4
  increase
    personal finance 332.024 01
  labor economics 331.21
  macroeconomics 339.3
  mineral industries 338.23
  secondary industries 338.43
  transportation services 388.049
Income accounts
  macroeconomics 339.3
Income-consumption relations
  macroeconomics 339.41
Income distribution
  macroeconomics 339.2
Income maintenance 362.582
  public administration 353.54
  social welfare 362.582
Income policy
  macroeconomics 339.5
Income redistribution
  macroeconomic policy 339.52
Income statements
  financial management 658.151 2
Income tax 336.24
  law 343.052
  public administration 352.44
  public finance 336.24
Income theory
  monetary economics 332.401
Incompatibilities
  logic 160
Incompressible airflow
  aeronautics 629.132 322
Inconvertible money 332.427
Incorporated banks 332.122
Incorporation
  law 346.066 22
  management 658.114 5
  public administration 352.84
Incorporation (Municipalities) 320.85
Incrustation
  architectural decoration 729.6
Incubi 133.423
  see also Legendary beings
Incunabula 093
  bibliographies 011.42
Indecent exposure 364.153
  law 345.025 3
Indemnification
  law of war 341.66
Indentured labor
  sociology 306.363
Independence County (Ark.) T2—767 26
Independence Day (United States) 394.263 4
Independence days 394.26
  see also Holidays
Independencia (Dominican Republic) T2—729 325
Independent agencies
  public administration 352.264
Independent Fundamental Churches of America 289.95
  see also Christian denominations
Independent Fundamentalist and Evangelical churches 289.95
  see also Christian denominations
Independent Methodists 287.533
  see also Methodist Church
Independent Order of Odd Fellows 366.3
  biography 366.309 2
Independent reading
  elementary education 372.454

Independent regulatory agencies 352.8
Independent retail stores 381.1
  management 658.870 1
  see also Commerce
Independent schools 371.02
  secondary education 373.222
  see also Private schools
Independent study 371.394 3
Indeterminacy composition 781.32
Indeterminate equations 515.253
Indeterminate sentence 364.62
Indeterminism 123
Index librorum prohibitorum 098.11
Index theorems 514.74
Indexing 025.3
  computer science 005.741
  information science 025.3
  museology 069.52
  subject 025.48
India 954
  T2—54
  ancient 934
    T2—34
India-Pakistan Conflict, 1971 954.920 51
India rubber tree 635.933 45
  see also Rubber plant (Ficus)
Indian corn 641.331 5
  see also Corn—food
Indian elephant 599.676
  conservation technology 639.979 676
  resource economics 333.959 676
Indian hemp 583.93
Indian languages (American) 497
  T6—97
  South America 498
    T6—98
Indian literatures (American) 897
  South America 898
Indian literatures (South Asian)
  Dravidian 894.8
  English 820
  Indic 891.1
Indian Ocean 551.467
  T2—165
  see Manual at T2—163 and T2—164, T2—165; *also at* T2—163, T2—164, T2—165 vs. T2—182
Indian Ocean Region T2—182 4
Indian pipe (Plant) 583.66
Indian River County (Fla.) T2—759 28
Indian sarsaparilla 583.93
Indian Territory (Okla.) T2—766 5
Indian tobacco 583.98
Indiana 977.2
  T2—772
Indiana County (Pa.) T2—748 89
Indianapolis (Ind.) T2—772 52
Indians (National group) T5—914 11
Indians of Central America T5—97
Indians of North America T5—97
Indians of South America T5—98
Indians of the West Indies T5—97
Indic languages 491.1
  T6—911
Indic literatures 891.1
Indic people T5—914
Indic religions 294
  art representation 704.948 94
  arts 700.482 94
    T3C—382 94
  Islamic polemics 297.294
  see Manual at 200.9 vs. 294, 299.5
Indic religions and Islam 294
  Indic view 294
  Islamic view 297.284
Indic rugs
  arts 746.754
  see also Rugs
Indicator species
  ecology 577.27
Indicatoridae 598.72
Indictment 345.072
Indigenous groups 306.08
  legal status 346.013
    constitutional law 342.087 2
    private law 346.013
  see Manual at 305.8 vs. 306.089
Indigo dyes 667.26
Indigo plants 583.74
Indigoid dyes 667.257
Indirect lighting 621.321 3
  see also Lighting
Indirect taxation 336.294
Indium 669.79
  chemical engineering 661.067 7
  chemistry 546.677
  economic geology 553.499
  metallurgy 669.79
  physical metallurgy 669.967 9
  see also Chemicals
Individual freedom 323
  see also Civil rights
Individual fulfillment
  educational goal 370.119

Individual land tenure
  economics 333.323
Individual psychology 155.2
  children 155.418 2
  late adulthood 155.671 82
  see Manual at 158 vs. 155.2
Individual retirement accounts 332.024 01
  tax law 343.052 33
Individualism
  economics 330.153
  philosophy 141.4
  political ideology 320.512
  social psychology 302.54
Individuality 155.2
  children 155.418 2
Individualized instruction 371.394
Individualized reading instruction
  elementary education 372.417
Indo-Aryan languages 491.1
  T6—911
Indo-Aryan literatures 891.1
Indo-Aryan period 934.02
Indo-Aryans T5—914
Indo-European languages 410
  T6—1
Indo-European literatures 800
Indo-European peoples T5—034
Indo-Germanic languages 410
  T6—1
Indo-Hittite languages 410
  T6—1
Indo-Iranian languages 491.1
  T6—911
Indo-Iranian literatures 891.1
Indo-jazz 781.657
Indo-Pakistan War, 1965 954.904 5
Indo-Pakistan War, 1971 954.920 51
Indochina (French Indochina) T2—597
Indochina (Southeast peninsula of Asia) 959
  T2—59
Indochinese War, 1946–1954 959.704 1
Indochinese War, 1961–1975 959.704 3
Indonesia 959.8
  T2—598
Indonesian language (Bahasa Indonesia) 499.221
  T6—992 21
Indonesian languages 499.22
  T6—992 2
Indonesian literature (Bahasa Indonesia) 899.221
Indonesian literatures 899.22
Indonesians T5—992 2
Indoor amusements 793
Indoor games 793
Indoor gardening (Floriculture) 635.965
Indoor hockey 796.355
  see also Sports
Indoor music 781.534
Indoor photography 778.72
Indoor recreation centers 790.068
  architecture 725.84
Indoor temperatures
  health 613.5
Indre (France : Dept.) T2—445 51
Indre-et-Loire (France) T2—445 4
Indri 599.83
Inductance meters 621.374 2
Induction accelerators 539.734
Induction heating 621.402
Induction of employees
  armed forces 355.223
  personnel management 658.312 42
  public administration 352.66
Induction welding 671.521 5
Inductive charging
  ores 622.77
Inductive mathematics 511.22
Inductive reasoning
  logic 161
  psychology 153.432
Inductors
  radio engineering 621.384 133
Indulgences (Christian rite) 265.66
Indus River T2—549 1
Indus script 490
  T6—9
Industrial accidents 363.11
  insurance 368.56
    government-sponsored 368.41
    see also Insurance
  see also Industrial safety
Industrial advertising 659.131 5
Industrial air conditioning 697.931 6
Industrial arbitration 331.891 43
  law 344.018 914 3
  personnel management 658.315 4
Industrial archaeology
  economic aspects 338.09
  historical aspects 900
  technological aspects 609
Industrial areas
  area planning 711.552 4
Industrial art 745.2
Industrial arts 600

Industrial banks 332.37
Industrial biochemistry 660.63
Industrial biology 660.6
Industrial botany 581.636
Industrial buildings
  architecture 725.4
  construction 690.54
  institutional housekeeping 647.964
  landscape architecture 712.7
  sale and rental 333.338 7
Industrial casualty insurance 368.7
  see also Insurance
Industrial chemicals 661
  human toxicology 615.902
Industrial chemistry 660
Industrial chemists 660.092
  occupational group T7—661
Industrial cities 307.766
  area planning 711.45
Industrial concentration 338.8
Industrial conditions 338.09
Industrial conflict
  sociology 306.34
Industrial costs 338.51
  see also Costs
Industrial credit 332.742
Industrial democracy 331.011 2
  theory of union role 331.880 1
Industrial design 745.2
Industrial development 338.9
  international banking 332.153
  public administration 354.27
Industrial diamonds 553.65
Industrial diseases
  health 613.62
  medicine 616.980 3
  see also Environmental diseases (Human)
Industrial drawing 604.2
  T1—022 1
Industrial economics 338
Industrial engineering 670
Industrial engineering (Production management) 658.5
  see Manual at 658.5 and T1—0685
Industrial espionage 364.16
  ethics 174.4
  law 343.072
  management 658.472
Industrial fats 665
Industrial gases 665.7
  equipment manufacturing technology 681.766 5
Industrial hazards 363.11
  see also Industrial safety
Industrial health 613.62
  see Manual at 363.11 vs. 613.62
Industrial insurance 368.3
  accident 368.56
    government-sponsored 368.41
  life 368.362
  see also Insurance
Industrial land use
  community sociology 307.332
Industrial lands 333.77
  economics 333.77
    sale and rental 333.336
Industrial law 343.07
Industrial libraries 027.69
Industrial life insurance 368.362
  see also Insurance
Industrial management 658
Industrial marketing
  management 658.804
Industrial medicine 616.980 3
Industrial microbiology 660.62
Industrial-military complex 355.021 3
  economics 338.473 55
  military science 355.021 3
  sociology 306.27
Industrial minerals 553.6
Industrial mobilization 355.26
  law 343.01
Industrial noise 363.741
  see also Noise
Industrial nursing
  medicine 610.734 6
Industrial oils 665
Industrial organization 338.6
  economics 338.6
  executive management 658.402
Industrial parks
  area planning 711.552 4
Industrial pollution 363.731
  social welfare 363.731
  technology 628.5
  see also Pollution
Industrial procurement 658.72
Industrial productivity 338.06
  economics 338.06
  mineral industries 338.26
  promotion of
    production management 658.515
  secondary industries 338.45
Industrial project management 658.404

Industrial property 346.048
  international law 341.758
Industrial psychology 158.7
Industrial railroads 385.54
  see also Railroad transportation
Industrial relations 331
  sociology 306.34
  see also Labor relations
Industrial research
  production management 658.57
  technology 607.2
Industrial resources 338.09
  economics 338.09
  military science 355.26
Industrial revolution 909.81
  economic history 330.903 4
Industrial robots 629.892
  engineering 629.892
  factory operations engineering 670.427 2
Industrial sabotage 364.164
  law 345.026 4
Industrial safety 363.11
  engineering 620.86
  law 344.046 5
  personal health 613.62
  public administration 353.96
  social services 363.11
  see also Safety
Industrial sanitation 363.729 5
  engineering 628.51
  law 344.046 5
  see also Waste control
Industrial schools (Penology) 365.42
  see also Correctional institutions
Industrial sociology 306.36
Industrial stoichiometry 660.7
Industrial surveys 338.09
Industrial towns 307.766
  area planning 711.45
Industrial toxicology
  medicine 615.902
Industrial unions 331.883 3
  see also Labor unions
Industrial wastes 363.728
  pollution technology 628.5
  social services 363.728
  technology 628.4
  water pollution engineering 628.168 3
  see also Waste control
Industrial workers 331.794
  labor economics 331.794
  public administration 354.93
Industrial Workers of the World 331.886
Industrial yellow pages T1—029 4
  see Manual at 338 vs. 060, 381, 382, 670.294, 910, T1—025, T1—0294, T1—0296
Industries 338
  see also Industry
Industry 338
  art representation 704.949 6
  arts 700.455
    T3C—355
  economics 338
  law 343.07
  literature 808.803 55
    history and criticism 809.933 55
    specific literatures T3B—080 355
      history and criticism T3B—093 55
  location
    economic rationale 338.604 2
    production 338.09
  public administration 354
  relations with government 322.3
Industry-school relations 371.195
Indwe (South Africa : District) T2—687 6
Inequalities
  algebra 512.97
  calculus 515.26
  geometry 516.17
Inequality 305
  social theology 291.178 34
    Christianity 261.834
    Judaism 296.38
  sociology 305
Inerrancy (Bible) 220.132
Inert gases
  chemistry 546.75
  economic geology 553.97
  technology 665.822
Inertia 531.12
  aeronautics 629.132 364
  fluids 532.02
  gases 533.12
  liquids 532.2
Infallibility
  Christian church 262.72
  pope 262.131
Infancy 305.232
  music 781.582
  see also Infants
Infancy of Jesus Christ 232.92
Infant baptism 234.161 2
  music 781.582

Infant baptism (continued)
  public worship 265.12
  theology 234.161 2
Infant betrothal
  customs 392.4
Infant schools (United Kingdom) 372.241
  see also Elementary education
Infanticide
  customs 392.12
  demographic effect 304.668
Infantry 356.1
Infants 305.232
  T1—083 2
  T7—054 2
  cooking for 641.562 2
  health 613.043 2
  home care 649.122
  pediatrics 618.92
  psychology 155.422
  social aspects 305.232
Infections
  result of injury
    medicine 617.22
  symptomatology 616.047
Infectious diseases (Biology) 571.98
  veterinary medicine 636.089 69
Infectious diseases (Human) 362.196 9
  medicine 616.9
  social services 362.196 9
  see also Communicable diseases (Human)
Infectious mononucleosis
  incidence 614.575
  medicine 616.925
  see also Communicable diseases (Human)
Inference
  logic 160
  psychology 153.432
  statistical mathematics 519.54
Infertility
  gynecology 618.178
  medicine 616.692
  see also Genital system
Infield play
  baseball 796.357 24
Infiltration (Military tactics) 355.422
Infinite (Philosophy) 111.6
Infinite processes 515.24
Infinite series 515.243
Infinitesimal calculus 515.33
Infinitesimal geometry 516.36
Infinitives 415
  specific languages T4—5
Infirmaries 362.11
  armed forces 355.72
  see also Health care facilities; Health services
Inflammable materials 363.179 8
  fire safety technology 628.922 2
  public safety 363.179 8
  technology 604.7
  see also Hazardous materials
Inflammation
  result of injury
    medicine 617.22
  symptomatology 616.047 3
Inflammatory bowel disease
  medicine 616.344
  see also Digestive system
Inflation (Economic) 332.41
  accounting 657.48
  personal finance 332.024 02
Inflection (Grammar) 415
  specific languages T4—5
Inflection (Phonology) 414.6
  specific languages T4—16
Inflection tables (Grammar)
  applied linguistics 418
    specific languages T4—82
Influence
  psychology 155.9
  social psychology 302.13
Influence peddling 364.132 3
  law 345.023 23
  public administration 353.46
Influenza
  incidence 614.518
  medicine 616.203
  see also Respiratory system
Informatics
  computer science 004
  information science 020
Information
  civil rights issues 323.445
  sociology 306.42
Information and referral services 025.52
Information centers 027
  operations 025
  publishing 070.594
  relationships 021
  see also Libraries
Information control 363.31
  see also Censorship
Information display systems
  electronic engineering 621.381 542
Information exchange
  international law 341.767 2

Information management
  executive management 658.403 8
    see Manual at 658.4038 vs. 658.455
  military administration 355.688
  office services 651
  production management 658.503 6
  public administration 352.38
Information policy
  economics 338.926
    see Manual at 338.926 vs. 352.745, 500
Information retrieval
  information science 025.524
Information science 020
  see Manual at 020
Information scientists 020.92
  occupational group T7—092
Information security
  management 658.472
Information services 025.52
  public administration 352.74
Information sources
  use 028.7
Information storage and retrieval systems 025.04
  computer science 005.74
  law 343.099 9
  management use 658.403 801 1
Information technology
  computer science 004
  social effects 303.483 3
Information theory 003.54
  T1—011 54
  communications engineering 621.382 2
Informational programs
  management use 658.455
    see Manual at 658.4038 vs. 658.455
Informed consent 344.041 2
Informers
  criminal investigation 363.252
Infrared astronomy 522.683
Infrared photography 778.34
  arts 778.34
  engineering 621.367 2
Infrared radiation 535.012
  biophysics 571.454
    humans 612.014 482
  chemical effect 541.353 2
  chemical engineering 660.295 32
  engineering 621.362
  physics 535.012
  therapeutics 615.832 2
Infrared spectroscopes
  manufacturing technology 681.414 2
Infrared spectroscopy 543.085 83
  analytical chemistry 543.085 83
  engineering 621.361 2
  physics 535.842
Infrared technology 621.362
  military engineering 623.042
  see also Infrared radiation
Ingenika River (B.C.) T2—711 87
Ingestion 573.35
  animal physiology 573.35
  human physiology 612.31
  see also Digestive system
Ingestion disorders
  incidence 614.593
  medicine 616.3
  see also Digestive system
Ingham (Qld.) T2—943 6
Ingham County (Mich.) T2—774 26
Inglenooks
  furniture arts 749.62
Inglewood (Vic.) T2—945 4
Ingolstadt (Germany) T2—433 62
Ingot iron 669.142 3
Ingrian language 494.54
  T6—945 4
Ingroups 302.4
Ingush T5—999 641
Ingush language 499.964 1
  T6—999 641
Ingushetia (Russia) T2—475 2
Ingwavuma (South Africa : District) T2—684 91
Inhalant abuse 362.299
  medicine 616.86
  personal health 613.8
  social welfare 362.299
  see also Substance abuse
Inhalation
  human physiology 612.21
  see also Respiratory system
Inhalation anesthesia
  surgery 617.962
Inhalation therapy
  medicine 615.836
Inhalation toxicology
  medicine 615.91
Inhalatory medication
  administering 615.6
Inhambane (Mozambique : Province) T2—679 3
Inheritance law 346.052

Inheritance of acquired characteristics 576.827
Inheritance tax 336.276
  law 343.053 2
  public administration 352.44
  public finance 336.276
Inherited diseases (Human)
  medicine 616.042
  see also Diseases (Human)
Inini (French Guiana) T2—882
Initial-value problems 515.35
Initiation of business enterprises 338.71
  economics 338.71
  management 658.11
    T1—068 1
  see Manual at 338.09 vs. 332.67309, 338.6042, 346.07, 658.11, T1—0681, 658.21, T1—0682; *also at* 658.04 vs. 658.114, 658.402
Initiation rites
  Christianity 234.161
    public worship 265.1
    theology 234.161
  customs 392.14
  etiquette 395.24
  music 781.57
  religion 291.38
  see also Rites
Initiative
  personality trait 155.232
Initiative (Legislation) 328.22
Injecting medication 615.6
Injection molding of plastics 668.412
Injunctions 347.077
  labor economics 331.893
    law 344.018 93
    management measure 331.894
Injuries
  anesthesiology 617.967 1
  incidence 614.599
  medicine 617.1
Injurious animals 591.65
Injurious microorganisms 579.165
Injurious organisms 578.65
Injurious plants 581.65
Ink drawing 741.26
Ink painting 751.425
Inka T5—983 23
Inka period 985.019
Inkanyezi (South Africa : District) T2—684 91
Inks 667.4
Inland marine insurance 368.23
  see also Insurance
Inland Sea (Japan) 551.465 55
  T2—164 55
Inland seas 551.460 9
  T2—168
  biology 578.763 9
  ecology 577.639
  international law 341.444
Inland water transportation 386
  engineering 629.048
    waterways 627.1
  law 343.096 4
  public administration 354.78
  transportation services 386
Inland water transportation workers 386.092
  occupational group T7—386
Inland waterway mail 383.143
Inland waterways 386
  engineering 627.1
  hydrology 551.48
  land economics 333.915
  see also Inland water transportation
Inlay trim
  furniture arts 749.5
  wood handicrafts 745.512
Inlays
  dentistry 617.675
  see also Dentistry
Inmates (Prisoners) 365.6
  T1—086 927
Innate ideas 121.4
Innate reflexes
  psychology 152.322 3
Innate virtues (Christian doctrine) 234
Innatism 149.7
Inner-city residents
  government programs 353.533 3
Inner ears 573.89
  human physiology 612.858
  see also Ears
Inner Hebrides (Scotland) T2—411 8
Inner House of Court of Session (Scotland) 347.411 035
Inner Mongolia (China) T2—517 7
Inner Mongolia Autonomous Region (China) T2—517 7
Inner product spaces 515.733
Inner tubes 678.35

Innervation 573.85
  human heart 612.178
  human muscles 612.743
  human physiology 612.81
  human respiratory system 612.28
  human skin 612.798
  see also Nervous system
Innisfail (Qld.) T2—943 6
Innocent passage 341.4
Innomines 784.187 6
Innovation
  agent of social change 303.484
  executive management 658.406 3
Inns 647.94
  see also Hotels
Inoculation
  disease control 614.47
İnönü, İsmet
  Turkish history 956.102 5
Inorganic biochemistry 572.51
  humans 612.015 24
Inorganic chemistry 546
  applied 660
  see Manual at 541 vs. 546; *also at* 549 vs. 546
Inorganic drugs
  pharmacology 615.2
  see Manual at 615.1 vs. 615.2–615.3
Inorganic poisons
  human toxicology 615.92
Inorganic substances
  metabolism 572.514
    human physiology 612.392
    see also Digestive system
Inosilicates
  mineralogy 549.66
Input-output accounts
  macroeconomics 339.23
Input-output peripherals 004.75
  engineering 621.398 5
Input peripherals 004.76
  computer engineering 621.398 6
Inquiry
  epistemology 121.6
Inquisition (Church history) 272.2
Insanity 362.2
  legal defense 345.04
  literature 808.803 53
    history and criticism 809.933 53
    specific literatures T3B—080 353
      history and criticism T3B—093 53
  see also Mental illness
Inscriptions
  architectural design 729.19
  paleography 411.7
    specific languages T4—11
  prints 769.5
  stone 736.5
Insect control 363.78
  environmental engineering 628.965 7
  home economics 648.7
  social welfare 363.78
  technology
    agriculture 632.7
  see also Pest control
Insect culture 638
Insect culturists 638.092
  occupational group T7—638
Insect venom
  human toxicology 615.942
Insect waxes 665.13
Insecta 595.7
  see also Insects
Insecticide-producing plants
  agriculture 633.898
  economic botany 581.636
Insecticides 668.651
  agricultural economics 338.162
  agricultural use 632.951 7
  chemical engineering 668.651
Insectivora 599.33
  paleozoology 569.33
Insectivorous plants 583.75
  see also Carnivorous plants
Insects 595.7
  agricultural pests 632.7
  art representation 704.943 257
  coevolution with plants 576.875
  conservation technology 639.975 7
  control technology 628.965 7
  disease carriers
    medicine 614.432
  drawing 743.657
  food 641.396
    commercial processing 664.95
    cooking 641.696
    home preservation 641.495
  paleozoology 565.7
  resource economics 333.955 7
  zoology 595.7
Insider trading in securities 364.168
  law 345.026 8

Insignia 929.9
armed forces 355.134 2
rank and service 355.14
religious significance 291.37
Christianity 246.56
Insolvency
credit economics 332.75
law 346.078
commercial law 346.078
public finance 343.037
public finance 336.368
Insomnia
symptomatology
neurological diseases 616.849 8
see also Nervous system
Inspection
engineering 620.004 4
military administration 355.685
production management 658.568
public administration 352.83
external control 352.83
internal control 352.35
Inspection technology 670.425
Inspectors general
military administration 355.685
Inspiration
Bible 220.13
Instabilities in semiconductors 537.622 6
Installations (Armed forces) 355.7
Installment sales
consumer credit 332.743
law 346.074
taxes 343.055 2
Instant cameras 771.32
Instant photography 770
Instantaneous systems 003.8
Instinct
animals 591.512
Instinctive movements
psychology 152.324
Institutes (Adult education) T1—071 5
Institutes (Roman law) 340.54
Institutional care 361.05
children 362.732
older persons 362.61
Institutional cooking 641.57
Institutional exemptions
customs duties 382.782
see also Customs (Tariff)
Institutional grounds
landscape architecture 712.7
Institutional households
household management 647.96
Institutional housekeeping 647
see Manual at 647 vs. 647.068, 658.2, T1—0682
Institutional investment 332.671 54
domestic 332.672 54
international 332.673 14
Institutional investors 332.671 54
domestic 332.672 54
international 332.673 14
Institutional nursing
medicine 610.733
Institutional publishers 070.594
Institutional school
economics 330.155
Institutionalized children
psychology 155.446
Institutions (Sociology) 306
see Manual at 302–307 vs. 320
Instruction services
museology 069.15
Instructional materials 371.33
elementary education 372.133
reading 372.412
public control 379.156
Instructional materials centers 027.7
college libraries 027.7
school libraries 027.8
Instructional supervision 371.203
Instructional technology 371.33
Instructions to juries 347.075 8
criminal law 345.075
Instrument flying 629.132 521 4
Instrumental ensembles 784
see Manual at 784–788
Instrumental forms 784.18
Instrumentalism 144.5
Instrumentation T1—028 4
aircraft 629.135
analytical chemistry 543.07
qualitative 544.07
quantitative 545.07
physics 530.7
weather reporting 551.635
Instruments T1—028 4
Instruments (Musical) 784.19
see also Musical instruments
Insulating materials
building materials 691.95
materials science 620.195
Insulation
building construction 693.83
electrical circuits 621.319 37

Insulation (continued)
  heat engineering 621.402 4
  steam engineering 621.185
Insulators
  electrical circuits 621.319 37
Insulin 572.565
  biochemistry 572.565
  chemistry 547.734 5
  human physiology 612.34
  pharmacology 615.365
  see also Digestive system; Endocrine system
Insulin therapy
  psychiatry 616.891 2
    see also Mental illness
Insurance 368
  accounting 657.73
  financial management 658.153
  labor economics 331.255
  law 346.086
  malpractice 346.086 02
  personnel management 658.325 4
  public administration 354.85
Insurance agents 368.009 2
  occupational group T7—368
Insurance companies 368.006 5
  accounting 657.836
  credit functions 332.38
  see also Insurance
Insurance law 346.086
Insurance rates 368.011
Insured mail 383.182
  see also Postal service
Insurgency (Warfare) 355.021 8
Insurgent warfare 355.021 8
Intaglio printing 765
Intaglios 736.223
Intangible property 346.048
  international law 341.758
Intangible property risks 368.063
Integer programming 519.77
Integers 512.72
Integral calculus 515.43
Integral domains 512.4
Integral equations 515.45
Integral geometry 516.362
Integral inequalities 515.46
Integral operators 515.723
Integrals 515.43
Integrated circuits 621.381 5
  computer engineering 621.395
Integrated optics 621.369 3
Integrated pest management 632.9
Integrated programs 005.3
Integrated services digital networks 384
  engineering 621.382
Integration (Mathematics) 515.43
Integration in education 379.263
Integration theory 515.42
Integro-differential equations 515.38
Integument 573.5
  animal physiology 573.5
  descriptive zoology 591.47
  human anatomy 611.77
  human physiology 612.79
  medicine 616.5
  see also Skin
Intellect 153.9
  philosophy 128.3
  psychology 153.9
Intellectual freedom 323.44
  library policies 025.213
Intellectual history 001.09
Intellectual life 001.1
  sociology 306.42
Intellectual processes 153
  children 155.413
Intellectual property 346.048
  international law 341.758
  public administrative support 352.749
Intellectualism 149.7
Intellectuals 305.552
  T1—086 31
  civil rights 323.323 1
  relations with government 323.323 1
Intelligence 153.9
  comparative psychology 156.39
  educational psychology 370.152
  evolutional psychology 155.7
  philosophy 128.3
  psychology 153.9
Intelligence (Animals) 591.513
Intelligence (Information) 327.12
  armed forces 355.343 2
    see also Unconventional warfare
  executive management 658.47
    public administration 352.379
  international relations
    public administration 353.17
  military technology 623.71
  see also Espionage
Intelligence tests 153.93
Intelligent road transportation systems 388.312
  engineering 625.794

Intelligent vehicle-highway system 388.312
engineering 625.794
Intelligentsia 305.552
T1—086 31
Intensifying solutions
photography 771.54
Intensity of light 535.22
Intensive care 362.174
medicine 616.028
nursing 610.736 1
social welfare 362.174
see also Health services
Intentionality
philosophy 128
psychology 153.8
Inter-American Development Bank 332.153 8
Interactive multimedia 006.7
Interactive processing 004
Interactive video 006.7
cataloging 025.344
computer science 006.7
instructional use 371.334 67
T1—078 567
library treatment 025.174
performing arts 791.45
Interactive videotex 004.696
communications services 384.354
see also Computer communications
Interamerican Development Bank 332.153 8
Interception of communication
civil rights issue 323.448 2
Interceptor missiles 358.174 82
engineering 623.451 94
military equipment 358.174 82
Intercession of Jesus Christ 232.8
Interchangeability engineering 620.004 5
Interchangeability standards
commerce 389.62
Intercoastal routes 387.522
Intercom systems
office use 651.79
Intercontinental ballistic missiles 358.175 482
engineering 623.451 954
military equipment 358.175 482
Intercultural communication 303.482
Intercultural education 370.117
adult level 374.017
Intercultural marriage 306.845
Interdenominational cooperation 280.042
Interdependence
economics 338.9
Interdisciplinary approach to knowledge 001
Interest (Income) 332.82
financial economics 332.82
central banking 332.113
law 346.073
macroeconomics 339.21
public administration 354.86
tax 336.242 6
Interest (Psychology)
learning 153.153 3
Interest groups (Political science) 322.4
political process 324.4
relation to government 322.4
Interest rate futures 332.632 3
Interest rate options 332.632 3
Interfacial tension
chemical engineering 660.293
Interfacing (Computer) 004.6
T1—028 546
engineering 621.398 1
programming 005.711
programs 005.713
see Manual at 004.6
Interfacing protocols
computer science 004.62
Interfaith marriage 306.843
Judaism 296.444 3
social theology 291.178 358 43
Christianity 261.835 843
see also Marriage
Interfaith relations 291.172
see also Interreligious relations
Interference
communications engineering 621.382 24
electronic engineering 621.382 24
microwave electronics 621.381 31
radio engineering 621.384 11
television engineering 621.388 1
Interference eliminators
electronic circuits 621.381 532
radio engineering 621.384 12
Interference of light 535.47
Interferometry 535.470 287
chemical analysis 543.085 3
Interferons 571.964 4
human immunology 616.079 1
pharmacology 615.37
Intergalactic matter 523.112 5

Intergovernmental administration 353.33
Intergovernmental fiscal relations 336
economics 336
law 343.034
public administration 352.73
Intergovernmental grants 336.185
law 343.034
public administration 352.73
public finance 336.185
Intergovernmental publishers 070.595
Intergovernmental revenues
public finance 336.18
Intergovernmental tax relations 336.2
law 343.04
Interindustry accounts
macroeconomics 339.23
Interior arrangement
architectural design 729.24
Interior ballistics
military engineering 623.513
Interior decoration 747
arts 747
home economics 645
Interior decorators 747.2
occupational group T7—747
Interior departments 353.3
Interior design 729
see Manual at 729
Interior furnishings
arts 747
household management 645
textile arts 746.9
Interior lighting 621.322
see also Lighting
Interior of earth 551.11
Interior painting
buildings 698.14
Interior wiring 621.319 24
Interjections (Grammar) 415
specific languages T4—5
Interlake Region (Man.) T2—712 72
Interlibrary loans 025.62
Interlingua language 499.993
T6—999 93
Interlocking directorates 338.87
see also Combinations (Enterprises)
Interludes (Drama)
literature 808.824 1
history and criticism 809.241
specific literatures T3B—204 1
individual authors T3A—2
Interludes (Music) 784.189 3
Intermediate appellate courts 347.033
Intermediate elementary grades 372.242
see also Elementary education
Intermediate forms (Music) 784.189 3
Intermediate-range ballistic missiles 358.175 382
engineering 623.451 953
military equipment 358.175 382
Intermediate schools 372.242
Intermediate service (Penology) 364.68
Intermediate state (Christian doctrine) 236.4
Intermetallic compounds
metallurgy 669.94
Intermezzos 784.189 3
Intermolecular forces
chemistry 541.226
Internal auditing 657.458
Internal-combustion engines 621.43
automotive 629.25
electric generation 621.312 133
ships 623.872 3
see Manual at 629.046 vs. 621.43
Internal commerce 381
see also Domestic trade
Internal ears 573.89
human anatomy 611.85
human diseases
incidence 614.599 8
otology 617.882
human physiology 612.858
see also Ears
Internal friction
solid-state physics 530.416
Internal management auditing 658.401 3
public administration 352.43
Internal management audits 658.401 3
public administration 352.439
Internal medicine 616
Internal migration 304.809
community sociology 307.2
Internal organization 658.402
T1—068 4
public administration 352.28
see Manual at 658.04 vs. 658.114, 658.402
Internal respiration
human physiology 612.26
see also Respiratory system
Internal revenue 336.2
law 343.04

Internal storage (Computer) 004.53
  engineering 621.397 3
International administration 352.11
International arbitration 327.17
  international law 341.522
  international politics 327.17
International assistance
  economics 338.91
  social welfare 361.26
    governmental 361.6
International Association of Rebekah Assemblies 366.38
  biography 366.380 92
  social group T7—366 3
International Bank for Reconstruction and Development 332.153 2
  law 341.751 153 2
International banking 332.15
  law 346.082 15
International banks 332.15
International borrowing 336.343 5
  public administration 352.45
  public finance 336.343 5
International business enterprises 338.88
  see also International enterprises
International claims
  public administration 353.44
International commerce 382
  see also Foreign trade
International Committee of the Red Cross 361.77
International Communist Congress 324.175
International conflicts 327.16
  law 341.5
  see also Wars
International cooking 641.59
International cooperation 327.17
  law 341.7
International Court of Justice 341.552
International courts 341.55
International crimes 364.135
  law 341.77
International Criminal Police Organization 363.206 01
  law 341.77
International debt 336.343 5
  public administration 352.45
  public finance 336.343 5
International development economics 338.91
International Development Association 332.153
International disputes 327.16
  law 341.5
International economic assistance 338.91
International economic cooperation 337
International economic development 338.91
International economic law 341.75
International economic planning 337
International economic relations 337
International economics 337
International education 370.116
International enterprises 338.88
  accounting 657.96
  financial management 658.159 9
  management 658.049
    initiation 658.114 9
    organization 658.18
  see Manual at 338.888–338.889
International farm policies 338.181
International finance 332.042
  international law 341.751
International Finance Corporation 332.153
International fiscal law 341.751
International forces (Military) 355.357
International governmental organizations 341.2
  T1—060 1
  economic cooperation 337.1
    see Manual at 337.3–337.9 vs. 337.1
  international law 341.2
  public administration 352.11
  see also International organizations
  see Manual at 341.22–341.24
International grants
  public finance 336.188
International investment 332.673
International labor mobility 331.127 91
International Labour Office 354.921 1
  law 341.763
International languages 401.3
International law 341
  relation to domestic law 341.04
  see Manual at 341 vs. 327

International migration 304.82
  political science 325
International Monetary Fund 332.152
  law 341.751 152
International monetary systems 332.45
International news
  journalism 070.433 2
International offenses 364.135
  law 341.77
International Order of Job's Daughters 366.108 352
  biography 366.108 352
  social group T7—366 1
International Order of the Rainbow for Girls 366.108 352
  biography 366.108 352
  social group T7—366 1
International organizations 060
  T1—060 1
  bibliographies of publications 011.52
  see also International governmental organizations
International party organizations 324.1
  see Manual at 324.2 vs. 324.1
International planning
  civic art 711.2
  social services 361.26
    governmental 361.6
International politics 327.1
  history 900
International postal conventions 383.41
  law 341.757 3
International Red Cross Committee 361.77
International relations 303.482
  ethics 172.4
    religion 291.562 4
      Christianity 241.624
      Islam 297.562 4
    see also Political ethics
  international law 341.3
  legislative control 328.346
  political science 327
  public administration 353.13
  social theology 291.178 7
    Christianity 261.87
    Islam 297.272
    Judaism 296.382 7
  sociology 303.482
  see Manual at 341 vs. 327
International security forces
  law 341.72
International Serials Data Program 025.343 2
International settlements (Banking) 332.155
International social services 361.26
International Socialist Congress 324.174
International Society for Krishna Consciousness 294.551 2
International Standard Bibliographic Description 025.324
International Standard Book Number 025.3
International Standard Serial Number 025.343 2
International style of architecture 724.6
International territories 321
  public administration 353.159
International trade 382
  management 658.848
  see also Foreign trade
International trusteeships 321.08
  see also Semisovereign states
International understanding
  educational objective 370.116
International unions 331.880 91
  see also Labor unions
International welfare services
  governmental 361.6
Internationalism 327.17
Internationals (Political party organizations) 324.1
Internet 004.678
  see also Computer communications
  see Manual at 004.678 vs. 025.04, 384.33
Internet resources 025.04
Internment (Military)
  service status 355.113
Internment camps 365.45
  Civil War (United States) 973.71
  Mexican War 973.621
  penology 365.45
  South African War 968.048 1
  Spanish-American War 973.891
  Vietnamese War 959.704 31
  World War I 940.317
  World War II 940.531 7
  see also Correctional institutions
Interoccupational mobility 305.9
  economics 331.127 2
Interoceanic canals 386.42
  engineering 627.137

Interoceanic canals (continued)
  law 343.096 4
  transportation services 386.42
Interparliamentary unions 328.060 1
Interpersonal communication
  psychology 153.6
Interpersonal relations 302
  applied psychology 158.2
  business 650.13
  personnel management 658.314 5
    executives 658.407 145
    public administration 352.66
  sociology 302
  see Manual at 302–307 vs. 155.92, 158.2
Interplanetary matter 523.5
Interpol 363.206 01
  law 341.77
Interpolation 511.42
Interpretation 121.68
  archaeological technique 930.102 85
  musical technique 781.46
Interpretation of tongues 234.13
Interpreters 418.020 92
  occupational group T7—4
  specific languages T4—802 092
Interpreters (Computer science)
  programming languages 005.452
Interpreting
  linguistics 418.02
    specific languages T4—802
Interpretive dancing 792.8
Interproduct price competition 338.522
Interprovincial relations
  law 342.042
  public administration 352.133
Interracial marriage 306.846
Interregional commerce 381.5
  see also Commerce
Interregnum, 1254–1273 943.025
Interreligious marriage 306.843
  Judaism 296.444 3
  social theology 291.178 358 43
    Christianity 261.835 843
  see also Marriage
Interreligious relations 291.172
  Buddhism 294.337 2
  Christianity 261.2
  Hinduism 294.517 2
  Islam 297.28
  Judaism 296.39
Interrogation
  criminal investigation 363.254
    law 345.052
Intersections (Mathematics) 516.35
Intersections (Roads) 388.13
  engineering 625.7
  transportation services 388.13
  urban 388.411
Interstate agreements 342.042
  public administration 352.133
Interstate banking 332.16
Interstate commerce 381.5
  law 343.088
  see also Commerce
Interstate planning
  civic art 711.3
  economics 338.9
Interstate relations (Federal systems)
  law 342.042
  public administration 352.133
Interstellar matter 523.112 5
  Milky Way 523.113 5
Interstitial nerve tissues
  human histology 611.018 8
  see also Nervous system
Interurban railroads 385.5
  engineering 625.6
  transportation services 385.5
Interval analysis (Mathematics) 511.42
Intervals (Music) 781.237
Intervention (International law) 341.584
Interventionism
  economics 330.126
Interviewing 158.39
  applied psychology 158.39
  job hunting 650.14
  marketing research 658.83
  personnel selection 658.311 24
    public administration 352.65
  social work 361.322
Interviews 080
Intestinal obstructions
  medicine 616.342
  surgery 617.554
  see also Digestive system
Intestinal secretions 573.373 79
  human physiology 612.33
  see also Digestive system
Intestine 573.37
  biology 573.37
  human anatomy 611.34
  human physiology 612.33
  medicine 616.34
  surgery 617.554
  see also Digestive system
Intibucá (Honduras : Dept.) T2—728 381

Intimacy
  applied psychology 158.2
Intonation (Linguistics) 414.6
  specific languages T4—16
Intoxications 362.29
  medicine 616.86
  social welfare 362.29
  see also Substance abuse
Intractable pain
  symptomatology 616.047 2
Intrafamily relationships 306.87
Intragovernmental revenues
  public finance 336.18
Intramural sports 796.042
  see also Sports
Intraocular lenses
  optometry 617.752 4
Intrauterine contraceptives
  health 613.943 5
  see also Birth control
Intravenous anesthesia
  surgery 617.962
Intravenous medication
  administering 615.6
Intravenous therapy
  medicine 615.855
Intrinsic variables (Stars) 523.844 2
Introductory forms (Music) 784.189 2
Introit 264.36
  music 782.323 5
Introversion 155.232
  educational psychology 370.153
  personality trait 155.232
Intrusions (Geology) 551.88
Intuition 153.44
  epistemology 121.3
  ethical systems 171.2
  psychology 153.44
Intuitionism 143
Intuitive mathematics 511.22
Inuit T5—971 2
Inuit languages 497.12
  T6—971 2
Inuit literatures 897.12
Inuktitut T5—971 2
Inuktitut (Eastern Canada) T5—971 24
Inuktitut language (Eastern Canada) 497.124
  T6—971 24
Inuktitut languages 497.12
  T6—971 2
Inuktitut literature (Eastern Canada) 897.124
Inuktitut literatures 897.12
Inupiaq T5—971 2
Inupiaq language 497.12
  T6—971 2
Inupiat language 497.12
  T6—971 2
Inupik language 497.12
  T6—971 2
Inuvik (N.W.T. : Region) T2—719 6
  see Manual at T2—7193–T2—7197
Invariant theory 512.74
  algebra 512.944
Invariants 512.5
Invasion
  engineering defense 623.31
Invasion of privacy 323.448
  criminology 364.156
  law 345.025 6
    criminal law 345.025 6
    torts 346.033
  political science 323.448
Inventions 608
  see Manual at 608 vs. 609
Inventions (Musical form) 784.187 4
Inventories (Lists) T1—021 6
Inventory
  accounting 657.72
  financial economics 332.041 2
  financial management 658.152 44
  government property 352.54
  library operations 025.82
  materials management 658.787
  military supplies 355.621 32
Inventory (Mathematics) 519.83
Invercargill District (N.Z.) T2—939 8
Inverclyde (Scotland : District) T2—414 28
Inverell (N.S.W.) T2—944 4
Invermere (B.C.) T2—711 65
Inverness (N.S. : County) T2—716 91
Inverness (Scotland : District) T2—411 75
Inversion (Genetics) 572.877
Inversions (Mathematics) 511.33
Inversive geometry 516.9
Invertebrate viruses 579.23
Invertebrates 592
  agricultural pests 632.62
  conservation technology 639.972
  harvest and culture 639.4
  paleozoology 562
  resource economics 333.955
  zoology 592

Inverters
  electronic circuits 621.381 532 2
Investigation (Research) 001.4
  T1—072
Investigative power (Legislative bodies) 328.345 2
Investment 332.6
  see also Investments
Investment banking 332.66
  law 346.066 2
Investment banks 332.66
Investment casting
  metals 671.255
Investment company securities 332.632 7
Investment counselors 332.62
  economics 332.62
  law 346.092 6
Investment guarantees 368.853
  see also Insurance
Investment guides 332.678
Investment income
  financial management 658.155 4
  income tax law 343.052 46
Investment law 346.092
  international law 341.752
Investment manuals 332.678
Investment prospectuses 332.6
Investment tax credit
  income tax law 343.052 37
Investment trusts 332.632 7
Investments 332.6
  banking services 332.175 4
  capital formation 332.041 5
  economics 332.6
  financial management 658.152
  international law 341.752
  law 346.092
  macroeconomics 339.43
  public administration 354.88
  public revenues 336.15
Invitations
  etiquette 395.4
Involuntary movement
  psychology 152.32
Involuntary muscle tissues
  human histology 611.018 6
  see also Musculoskeletal system
Involutes 516.362
Involution 512.922
Involutional psychoses
  medicine 616.895
  see also Mental illness
Inyo County (Calif.) T2—794 87
Iōannina (Greece : Nome) T2—495 3
Iodine 553.6
  chemical engineering 661.073 4
  chemistry 546.734
  economic geology 553.6
  organic chemistry 547.02
    applied 661.891
  see also Chemicals
Iodometry 545.23
Ion exchange 541.372 3
  chemical engineering 660.297 23
Ion-exchange chromatography 543.089 3
Ion-exchange separations 543.089 3
Ion implantation
  solid-state physics 530.416
Ion optics
  physics 537.56
Ion propulsion 621.465
  spacecraft 629.475 5
Ion transport 571.64
Ionia T2—392 3
Ionia County (Mich.) T2—774 54
Ionian Islands (Greece) T2—495 5
  ancient T2—382
Ionian Sea 551.462 6
  T2—163 86
Ionic equilibriums 541.372 3
  chemical engineering 660.297 23
Ionic philosophy 182.1
Ionioi Nēsoi (Greece) T2—495 5
Ionization 530.444
  chemical engineering 660.297 22
  chemistry 541.372 2
  meteorology 551.561
  plasma physics 530.444
Ionization chambers
  nuclear physics 539.772
Ionization of gases 530.444
  electronic physics 537.532
Ionized gases 530.44
Ionizing radiations 539.722
Ionosphere 538.767
  T2—161 4
  meteorology 551.514 5
Ionospheric probes
  unmanned 629.435 2
Ions
  chemical engineering 660.297 2
  electrochemistry 541.372
Iosco County (Mich.) T2—774 74
Iowa 977.7
  T2—777
Iowa County (Iowa) T2—777 653
Iowa County (Wis.) T2—775 78

Iowa River (Iowa) T2—777 6
IPM (Pest management) 632.9
Ipswich (England) T2—426 49
Ipswich (Qld.) T2—943 2
IQ tests 153.93
Iqaluit (N.W.T.) T2—719 5
Iquique (Chile : Province) T2—831 27
IRA (Retirement account) 332.024 01
  tax law 343.052 33
Iran 955
  T2—55
  ancient 935
  T2—35
Iran-Iraq War, 1980–1988 955.054 2
Irangi (African people) T5—963 94
Irangi language 496.394
  T6—963 94
Iranian-Iraqi Conflict, 1980–1988 955.054 2
Iranian languages 491.5
  T6—915
Iranian literatures 891.5
Iranians (National group) T5—915 5
Iraq 956.7
  T2—567
  ancient 935
  T2—35
Iraq-Kuwait Crisis, 1990–1991 956.704 42
Iraqi-Iranian Conflict, 1980–1988 955.054 2
Iraqis T5—927 567
Irbid (Jordan : Province) T2—569 54
Irbīl (Iraq : Province) T2—567 2
IRBM (Missiles) 358.175 382
  engineering 623.451 953
  military equipment 358.175 382
Iredell County (N.C.) T2—756 793
Ireland 941.7
  T2—417
  see Manual at 941
Ireland (Island) 941.5
  T2—415
  ancient 936.15
  T2—361 5
Irian Barat T2—951
Irian Jaya 995.1
Irian Jaya (Indonesia) T2—951
Iridales 584.38
Iridium 669.7
  chemical engineering 661.064 3
  chemistry 546.643
  metallography 669.957
  metallurgy 669.7
Iridium (continued)
  physical metallurgy 669.967
  see also Chemicals
Iringa Region (Tanzania) T2—678 25
Irion County (Tex.) T2—764 874
Irises (Eyes)
  human physiology 612.842
  ophthalmology 617.72
  see also Eyes
Irises (Plants) 635.934 38
  botany 584.38
  floriculture 635.934 38
Irish T5—916 2
Irish Free State 941.708 22
  T2—417
Irish Gaelic language 491.62
  T6—916 2
Irish Gaelic literature 891.62
Irish Gaels T5—916 2
Irish harps 787.95
  see also Stringed instruments
Irish language 491.62
  T6—916 2
Irish literature
  English 820
  Gaelic 891.62
Irish Sea 551.461 37
  T2—163 37
Irish wolfhounds 636.753 5
Irkutsk (Russia : Oblast) T2—575
Irkutskaîa oblast′ (Russia) T2—575
Iron 669.141
  applied nutrition 613.285
  biochemistry 572.517
    humans 612.015 24
  building construction 693.71
  building material 691.7
  chemical engineering 661.062 1
  chemistry 546.621
  economic geology 553.3
  materials science 620.17
  metabolism
    human physiology 612.392 4
  metallography 669.951 41
  metallurgy 669.141
  metalworking 672
  mining 622.341
  organic chemistry 547.056 21
    applied 661.895
  physical metallurgy 669.961 41
  prospecting 622.183
  ship design 623.818 21
  shipbuilding 623.820 7

Iron (continued)
  structural engineering 624.182 1
  see also Chemicals; Metals
Iron Age 930.16
Iron County (Mich.) T2—774 975
Iron County (Mo.) T2—778 883
Iron County (Utah) T2—792 47
Iron County (Wis.) T2—775 22
Iron industry 338.273
  metallurgy 338.476 691
  mining 338.273
Iron law of wages 331.210 1
Iron soaps 668.125
Iron workers 669.109 2
  metallurgy 669.109 2
    occupational group T7—669
  metalworking 672.092
    occupational group T7—672
  occupational group T7—672
Ironbarks (Eucalypti) 583.766
  see also Eucalyptus
Ironing
  home economics 648.1
Irons (Golf equipment) 796.352 33
Ironwoods 583.48
Ironwoods (Betulaceae) 583.48
Ironwoods (Hamamelidaceae) 583.44
Ironwoods (Rhamnaceae) 583.86
Ironwork
  blacksmithing 682.4
  decorative arts 739.4
Irony
  literature 808.801 8
    history and criticism 809.918
    specific literatures T3B—080 18
      history and criticism T3B—091 8
Iroquoian languages 497.55
  T6—975 5
Iroquois County (Ill.) T2—773 64
Iroquois Indians T5—975 5
Iroquois language 497.55
  T6—975 5
Irradiating foods 664.028 8
Irregular street patterns
  area planning 711.41
Irregular troops 356.15
Irreligion
  religious attitude toward 291.172
    Christianity 261.21
Irreversible reactions
  chemical engineering 660.299 3
  chemistry 541.393
  organic chemistry 547.139 3
Irrigation 333.913
  agriculture 631.587
  engineering 627.52
  land economics 333.913
  law 346.046 913
  public administration 354.367
  sewage effluent technology 628.362 3
  water pollution engineering 628.168 41
Irrigation canals
  engineering 627.52
Irritability 573.85
  cytology 571.67
  muscles 573.752 8
    human physiology 612.741
    see also Musculoskeletal system
  nerves 573.85
    human physiology 612.816
    see also Nervous system
  sense of touch 573.875
  sensory functions
    human physiology 612.88
  skin 573.5
    human physiology 612.791
    see also Skin
Irritable bowel syndrome
  medicine 616.342
  see also Digestive system
Irritable colon
  medicine 616.342
  see also Digestive system
Irwin County (Ga.) T2—758 855
Isaac (Biblical patriarch) 222.110 92
Isabel (Solomon Islands) T2—959 36
Isabela (Philippines : Province) T2—599 1
Isabella I, Queen of Spain
  Spanish history 946.03
Isabella II, Queen of Spain
  Spanish history 946.072
Isabella County (Mich.) T2—774 51
Isagogics
  Bible 220.61
Isaiah (Biblical book) 224.1
Isanti County (Minn.) T2—776 64
ISBD (Bibliographic description) 025.324
ISBN (Standard book number) 025.3
Ischemic heart diseases
  medicine 616.123
  see also Cardiovascular system
Ischia Island (Italy) T2—457 3

ISDN (Digital networks) 384
  engineering 621.382
ISDP (Program) 025.343 2
Isère (France) T2—449 9
Isernia (Italy : Province) T2—457 194
Iṣfahān (Iran : Province) T2—559 5
Ishikawa-ken (Japan) T2—521 54
Isiswazi language 496.398 7
  T6—963 987
Isla de la Juventud T2—729 125
Isla de Pinos T2—729 125
Isla Gorge National Park (Qld.) T2—943 5
Islam 297
  art representation 704.948 97
  arts 700.482 97
  T3C—382 97
Islam and Buddhism 294.337 2
  Buddhist view 294.337 2
  Islamic view 297.284 3
Islam and Christianity 261.27
  Christian view 261.27
  Islamic view 297.283
Islam and Hinduism 294.517 2
  Hindu view 294.517 2
  Islamic view 297.284 5
Islam and Indic religions 294
  Indic view 294
  Islamic view 297.284
Islam and Judaism 296.397
  Islamic view 297.282
  Jewish view 296.397
Islam and Sikhism 294.617 2
  Islamic view 297.284 6
  Sikh view 294.617 2
Islāmābād (Pakistan) T2—549 142
Islamic calendar 529.327
Islamic education 297.77
  see Manual at 291.75 vs. 200.71
Islamic ethics 297.5
Islamic fundamentalism 297.09
  see Manual at 320.55 vs. 297.09, 322.1
Islamic holidays 297.36
  customs 394.265 7
  see also Holidays
Islamic law 340.59
  see Manual at 340.59 vs. 297.14
Islamic legends 297.18
Islamic philosophy 181.07
Islamic regions T2—176 71
Islamic schools (General education) 371.077
Islamic shrines 297.35
  architecture 726.2
Island Carib Indians T5—979
Island County (Wash.) T2—797 75
Islands 551.42
  T2—142
  biology 578.752
  ecology 577.52
  geography 910.914 2
  geomorphology 551.42
  physical geography 910.021 42
Islands authorities (Scotland) T2—411 2
Islands of Langerhans 573.377
  biology 573.377
  human anatomy 611.37
  human physiology 612.34
  medicine 616.46
  surgery 617.557
  see also Digestive system; Endocrine system
Islands of the Arctic T2—98
  Canada T2—719 5
Islands of the Atlantic 997
  T2—97
Islands of the Pacific 990
  T2—9
Islas de la Bahía (Honduras) T2—728 315
Islas Malvinas 997.11
  T2—971 1
Isle of Anglesey (Wales) T2—429 21
Isle of Capri (Italy) T2—457 3
Isle of Ely (England) T2—426 53
Isle of Man (England) T2—427 9
Isle of Orléans (Quebec) T2—714 48
Isle of Pines T2—729 125
Isle of Wight (England) T2—422 8
Isle of Wight County (Va.) T2—755 54
Isle of Youth T2—729 125
Isle Royale (Mich.) T2—774 997
Isle Royale National Park (Mich.) T2—774 997
Islington (London, England) T2—421 43
Islwyn (Wales : Borough) T2—429 93
Ismailia (Egypt : Province) T2—621 5
Ismailis (Islamic sect) 297.822
Isobutylene rubber 678.72
Isoetales 587.9
  paleobotany 561.79

Isolation
  disease control 614.45
  social psychology 302.545
Isomerases 572.79
  see also Enzymes
Isomers 547.122 52
  inorganic chemistry 541.225 2
  organic chemistry 547.122 52
Isometric exercises 613.714 9
Isometric projection
  technical drawing 604.245
Isomorphism
  crystallography 548.3
Isonitriles 547.044
  chemical engineering 661.894
Isopoda 595.372
Isoptera 595.736
Isotope structure 539.74
Isotopes
  chemical engineering 660.298 8
  radiochemistry 541.388
Isparta İli (Turkey) T2—564
Isrā' 297.633
Israel 956.94
  T2—569 4
  ancient 933
  T2—33
  Biblical geography and history 220.9
  Christian theology 231.76
  Jewish theology 296.311 73
Israel-Arab War, 1948–1949 956.042
Israel-Arab War, 1967 956.046
Israel-Arab War, 1973 956.048
Israel-Lebanon-Syria Conflict, 1982–1985 956.052
Israelis T5—924
Israelites T5—924
Issaquena County (Miss.) T2—762 412
ISSN (Standard serial number) 025.343 2
Issuing houses 332.66
Istanbul (Turkey) T2—496 18
  ancient T2—398
İstanbul İli (Turkey) T2—496 18
  Asia T2—563
  Europe T2—496 18
Isthmus of Corinth (Greece) T2—495 22
Isthmus of Suez (Egypt) T2—621 5
Istiophoridae 597.78
Istria (Croatia) T2—497 2
  ancient T2—373
Isuridae 597.33
Italian folk music 781.625 1
Italian folk songs 782.421 625 1
Italian greyhound 636.76
Italian language 450
  T6—51
Italian literature 850
Italian Peninsula 945
  T2—45
  ancient 937
  T2—37
Italian Riviera (Italy) T2—451 8
Italian Somaliland T2—677 3
Italianate revivals
  architecture 724.52
Italians T5—51
Italic calligraphy 745.619 77
Italic languages 470
  T6—7
Italic literatures 870
Italic peoples T5—4
Italic type 686.224 7
Italo-Ethiopian War, 1935–1936 963.056
Italy 945
  T2—45
  ancient 937
  T2—37
Italy, Central T2—456
Italy, Southern T2—457
  ancient T2—377
Itapúa (Paraguay) T2—892 126
Itasca County (Minn.) T2—776 78
Itawamba County (Miss.) T2—762 982
Iterative methods (Mathematics) 511.4
Ithaca (N.Y.) T2—747 71
Ithaca Island (Greece) T2—495 5
  ancient T2—383
Ithna Asharites (Islamic sect) 297.821
Itzá dialect 497.415 27
  T6—974 152
IUD (Contraceptive)
  health 613.943 5
  see also Birth control
Ivan, the Terrible
  Russian history 947.043
Ivan III, Grand Duke of Russia
  Russian history 947.041
Ivan IV, Czar of Russia
  Russian history 947.043
Ivan VI, Emperor of Russia
  Russian history 947.061
Ivano-Frankivs′k (Ukraine : Oblast) T2—477 9
Ivano-Frankivs′ka oblast′ (Ukraine) T2—477 9
Ivanovo (Russia : Oblast) T2—473 3

Ivanovskaia͡ oblastʹ (Russia) T2—473 3
Ivies 635.933 84
  botany 583.84
  floriculture 635.933 84
Ivorians T5—966 68
Ivory
  manufacturing technology 679.43
Ivory carving 736.62
Ivory Coast 966.68
  T2—666 8
Ivory Coast people T5—966 68
Iwate-ken (Japan) T2—521 14
IWW (Labor) 331.886
Ixonanthaceae 583.79
Ixopo (South Africa : District) T2—684 7
Izabal (Guatemala : Dept.) T2—728 131
Izard County (Ark.) T2—767 27
İzmir İli (Turkey) T2—562

J

J document (Biblical criticism) 222.106 6
Jacamars 598.72
Jacanas 598.33
Jacanidae 598.33
Jack County (Tex.) T2—764 544
Jack-in-the-pulpits 584.64
Jackals 599.772
Jackets (Clothing) 391
  commercial technology 687.147
    indoor garments 687.113
    outdoor garments 687.147
  customs 391
  home sewing 646.457
    indoor garments 646.433
    outdoor garments 646.457
  see also Clothing
Jackrabbits 599.328
Jacks (Fishes) 597.72
Jacks (Lifting mechanisms) 621.877
Jackson (Miss.) T2—762 51
Jackson, Andrew
  United States history 973.56
Jackson County (Ala.) T2—761 95
Jackson County (Ark.) T2—767 97
Jackson County (Colo.) T2—788 66
Jackson County (Fla.) T2—759 93
Jackson County (Ga.) T2—758 145
Jackson County (Ill.) T2—773 994
Jackson County (Ind.) T2—772 23
Jackson County (Iowa) T2—777 64
Jackson County (Kan.) T2—781 335
Jackson County (Ky.) T2—769 183
Jackson County (Mich.) T2—774 28
Jackson County (Minn.) T2—776 235
Jackson County (Miss.) T2—762 12
Jackson County (Mo.) T2—778 41
Jackson County (N.C.) T2—756 95
Jackson County (Ohio) T2—771 85
Jackson County (Okla.) T2—766 45
Jackson County (Or.) T2—795 27
Jackson County (S.D.) T2—783 572
Jackson County (Tenn.) T2—768 51
Jackson County (Tex.) T2—764 127
Jackson County (W. Va.) T2—754 31
Jackson County (Wis.) T2—775 51
Jackson Parish (La.) T2—763 92
Jacksonville (Fla.) T2—759 12
Jacob (Biblical patriarch) 222.110 92
Jacobi polynomials 515.55
Jacobite Church 281.63
  see also Eastern churches
Jacob's ladders (Plants)
  botany 583.94
Jacobsdal (South Africa : District) T2—685 8
Jacquard-weave fabrics 677.616
  see also Textiles
Jacquard-weave rugs
  arts 746.72
  see also Rugs
Jacques-Cartier (Quebec) T2—714 47
Jacques-Cartier River (Quebec) T2—714 47
Jade 553.876
  economic geology 553.876
  glyptics 736.24
  jewelry 739.27
  materials science 620.198
  mining 622.387 6
  occultism 133.255 387 6
    divination 133.322
  prospecting 622.188 76
Jadīda (Morocco : Province) T2—643
Jadite 553.876
  see also Jade
Jaegers 598.338
Jaén (Spain : Province) T2—468 3
Jagellon dynasty 943.802 3
Jagersfontein (South Africa : District) T2—685 7
Jaguar 599.755
  big game hunting 799.277 55
  conservation technology 639.979 755
  resource economics 333.959 755

Jahangir, Emperor of Hindustan
  Indian history 954.025 6
Jahn-Teller effect (Physics) 530.416
Jail breaks 365.641
Jails 365.34
  see also Correctional institutions
Jain architecture 720.954
Jain philosophy 181.044
Jain sculpture 730.954
Jain temples and shrines 294.435
  architecture 726.144
Jainism 294.4
  art representation 704.948 944
  arts 700.482 944
    T3C—382 944
Jains
  biography 294.409 2
  religious group T7—294 4
Jaipuri dialect 491.479 7
  T6—914 79
Jaipuri literature 891.479
Jakarta (Indonesia) T2—598 22
Jakun language 499.28
  T6—992 8
Jalapa (Guatemala : Dept.) T2—728 142
Jalisco (Mexico) T2—723 5
Jamaica 972.92
  T2—729 2
Jamaica bayberry 583.765
Jamaican literature 810
Jamaicans T5—969 729 2
James (Biblical book) 227.91
James, William
  personality theory 155.264
James I, King of England
  British history 941.061
  English history 942.061
  Scottish history 941.106 1
James I, King of Scotland
  Scottish history 941.104
James II, King of England
  British history 941.067
  English history 942.067
  Scottish history 941.106 7
James II, King of Scotland
  Scottish history 941.104
James III, King of Scotland
  Scottish history 941.104
James IV, King of Scotland
  Scottish history 941.104
James V, King of Scotland
  Scottish history 941.104
James VI, King of Scotland
  Scottish history 941.106 1
    1567–1603 941.105
    1603–1625 941.106 1
James Bay Region (Ont. and Quebec) T2—714 115
James City County (Va.) T2—755 425 1
James River (N.D. and S.D.) T2—783 3
  North Dakota T2—784 5
  South Dakota T2—783 3
James River (Va.) T2—755 4
Jameson raid, 1895–1896 968.204 75
Jammu and Kashmir (India) T2—546
Jams 641.852
  commercial processing 664.152
  home preparation 641.852
Jämtlands län (Sweden) T2—488
Jan Mayen Island T2—983
Jansenism 273.7
  denominations 284.84
Jansenists
  religious group T7—248
Jansenville (South Africa : District) T2—687 14
Janūb Sīnā' (Egypt) T2—531
Japan 952
  T2—52
Japan, Sea of 551.465 54
  T2—164 54
Japan Current 551.475 5
Japanese T5—956
Japanese beetles 595.764 9
  agricultural pests 632.764 9
Japanese calendar 529.329 56
Japanese cedar 585.5
Japanese chess 794.18
Japanese chin 636.76
Japanese flower arrangements 745.922 52
Japanese flowering cherry 635.977 373
Japanese ink painting 751.425 2
Japanese language 495.6
  T6—956
Japanese literature 895.6
Japanese macaque 599.864 4
Japanese medlars 641.341 6
  see also Loquats
Japanese quail 598.627 2
Japanese religions 299.56

Japanese river fever
  incidence 614.526 4
  medicine 616.922 4
  see also Communicable diseases (Human)
Japanese spaniel 636.76
Japanning
  decorative arts 745.726
  technology 667.8
Jar cutting
  decorative arts 748.202 86
Jarai T5—992 2
Jardins-de-Napierville (Quebec) T2—714 35
Jargon 417.2
  specific languages T4—7
Jars 688.8
  glass 666.192
  see also Bottles
Jasmines 583.87
  botany 583.87
  floriculture 635.933 87
  perfume crop 633.81
Jasper County (Ga.) T2—758 583
Jasper County (Ill.) T2—773 74
Jasper County (Ind.) T2—772 977
Jasper County (Iowa) T2—777 594
Jasper County (Miss.) T2—762 575
Jasper County (Mo.) T2—778 72
Jasper County (S.C.) T2—757 98
Jasper County (Tex.) T2—764 159
Jasper National Park (Alta.) T2—712 332
Jatakas 294.382 325
Jaundice
  medicine 616.362 5
  see also Digestive system
Java (Indonesia) T2—598 2
Java man 569.9
Java Sea 551.465 74
  T2—164 74
Java War, 1825–1830 959.802 2
Javan pig 599.633 2
Javanese T5—992 2
Javanese language 499.222
  T6—992 22
Javanese literature 899.222
Javelin hurling 796.435
  see also Sports
Jawara, Dawda Kairaba
  Gambian history 966.510 31
Jawless fishes 597.2
Jaws
  fractures
    medicine 617.156
Jaws (continued)
  human anatomy 611.92
  human physiology 612.92
  surgery 617.522
Jay County (Ind.) T2—772 67
Jays 598.864
  conservation technology 639.978 864
  resource economics 333.958 864
Jaza'ir (Algeria : Province) T2—653
Jazīrah (Sudan : Province) T2—626 4
Jazz 781.65
  songs 782.421 65
Jazz bands 784.416 5
Jazz dancing 793.3
Jazz ensembles 785.065
Jazz musicians 781.650 92
  occupational group T7—781 6
Jazz pianists 786.216 509 2
Jazz saxophonists 788.716 509 2
Jazz singers 782.421 650 92
Jazz trumpeters 788.921 650 92
Jazz vocals 782.421 65
Jé Island (Quebec) T2—714 271
Jealousy 152.48
  ethics 179.8
  psychology 152.48
  see also Vices
Jean I, King of France
  French history 944.024
Jean II, King of France
  French history 944.025
Jeep cavalry 357.54
Jeeps 388.342
  driving 629.283
  engineering 629.222
  military engineering 623.747 22
  repair 629.287 2
  transportation services 388.342
  see also Automobiles
Jeff Davis County (Ga.) T2—758 827
Jeff Davis County (Tex.) T2—764 934
Jefferson, Thomas
  United States history 973.46
    1801–1805 973.46
    1805–1809 973.48
Jefferson City (Mo.) T2—778 55
Jefferson County (Ala.) T2—761 78
Jefferson County (Ark.) T2—767 79
Jefferson County (Colo.) T2—788 84
Jefferson County (Fla.) T2—759 87
Jefferson County (Ga.) T2—758 663
Jefferson County (Idaho) T2—796 58
Jefferson County (Ill.) T2—773 793
Jefferson County (Ind.) T2—772 13

Jefferson County (Iowa) T2—777 94
Jefferson County (Kan.) T2—781 37
Jefferson County (Ky.) T2—769 44
Jefferson County (Miss.) T2—762 283
Jefferson County (Mo.) T2—778 67
Jefferson County (Mont.) T2—786 67
Jefferson County (N.Y.) T2—747 57
Jefferson County (Neb.) T2—782 332
Jefferson County (Ohio) T2—771 69
Jefferson County (Okla.) T2—766 52
Jefferson County (Or.) T2—795 85
Jefferson County (Pa.) T2—748 62
Jefferson County (Tenn.) T2—768 924
Jefferson County (Tex.) T2—764 145
Jefferson County (W. Va.) T2—754 99
Jefferson County (Wash.) T2—797 98
Jefferson County (Wis.) T2—775 85
Jefferson Davis County (Miss.) T2—762 543
Jefferson Davis Parish (La.) T2—763 55
Jefferson Parish (La.) T2—763 38
Jeffersonian Republicans (Political party) 324.273 26
Jehovah's Witnesses 289.92
  biography 289.920 92
  religious group T7—289
  see also Christian denominations
Jejunitis
  medicine 616.344
  see also Digestive system
Jejunum 573.378
  biology 573.378
  human anatomy 611.341
  surgery 617.554 1
  see also Digestive system
Jelenia Góra (Poland : Voivodeship) T2—438 5
Jellies 641.852
  commercial processing 664.152
  home preparation 641.852
Jelly fungi 579.59
Jellyfish 593.53
Jenkins County (Ga.) T2—758 693
Jenkins' Ear, War of, 1739–1741 946.055
Jennings County (Ind.) T2—772 17
Jerauld County (S.D.) T2—783 32
Jerboas 599.35
Jeremiah (Biblical book) 224.2
Jerome County (Idaho) T2—796 35
Jersey (England) T2—423 41
Jersey cattle 636.224
Jersey City (N.J.) T2—749 27
Jersey County (Ill.) T2—773 855
Jerusalem T2—569 442
  ancient T2—33
  sacred place
    Christianity 263.042 569 442
    Judaism 296.482
Jerusalem (Israel : District) T2—569 44
Jerusalem (Jordan : District) T2—569 52
Jerusalem artichoke sugar 641.336
  commercial processing 664.139
  see also Sugar
Jerusalem artichoke syrup
  commercial processing 664.139
Jerusalem artichokes 641.352 4
  agriculture 635.24
  cooking 641.652 4
  food 641.352 4
Jerusalem Bible 220.520 7
Jerusalem Talmud 296.124
Jessamine County (Ky.) T2—769 483
Jessamines 583.87
  see also Jasmines
Jesuits 255.53
  church history 271.53
Jesus Christ 232
  art representation 704.948 53
  arts 700.482 32
  T3C—382 32
  biography 232.901
    Gospel text and criticism 226
    see Manual at 230–280
  Islam 297.246 5
  Jewish interpretations 232.906
  rationalistic interpretations 232.9
  see Manual at 232
Jet (Precious stone) 553.87
  see also Semiprecious stones
Jet engines 621.435 2
  aircraft 629.134 353
  see Manual at 629.046 vs. 621.43
Jet fuel 665.538 25
Jet planes 387.733 49
  engineering 629.133 349
  military engineering 623.746 044
  military equipment 358.418 3
  transportation services 387.733 49
  see also Aircraft
Jet pumps 621.691
  hydraulic 621.252
Jet skiing 797.37
  see also Sports
Jet streams (Meteorology) 551.518 3

Jethou (England)	T2—423 47
Jetties	
engineering	627.24
Jevons, William Stanley	
economic school	330.157
Jewelers	739.270 92
occupational group	T7—739
Jewell County (Kan.)	T2—781 22
Jewelry	391.7
customs	391.7
making	739.27
costume jewelry	688.2
handicrafts	745.594 2
fine jewelry	739.27
Jewelweeds	583.79
Jewish apocalypses	
pseudepigrapha	229.913
Jewish architecture	
ancient	722.33
Jewish Autonomous Region (Russia)	T2—577
Jewish Bible	221
see Manual at 221	
Jewish calendar	529.326
religion	296.43
Jewish-Christian dialogue	261.26
Christian theology	261.26
Jewish theology	296.396
Jewish Christians (Sects)	289.9
see also Christian denominations	
Jewish cooking	641.567 6
Jewish day schools	371.076
Jewish education	296.68
see Manual at 291.75 vs. 200.71	
Jewish holidays	296.43
customs	394.267
liturgy	296.453
see also Holidays	
Jewish philosophy	181.06
Jewish Publication Society Bible	221.520 8
Jewish religious schools	296.680 83
Jewish sacred music	781.76
public worship	782.36
music	782.36
religion	296.462
Jewish sculpture	732.3
Jews	T5—924
civilization	909.049 24
social aspects	305.892 4
Jews (Religious group)	T7—296
biography	296.092
specific denominations	296.8
role of leaders	296.61
Jew's harps	786.887
see also Percussion instruments	
Jiangsu Sheng (China)	T2—511 36
Jiangxi Sheng (China)	T2—512 22
Jigawa State (Nigeria)	T2—669 77
Jigs (Tools)	621.992
Jigsaw puzzles	793.73
Jihad	297.72
Jihočeský kraj (Czech Republic)	T2—437 1
Jihomoravský kraj (Czech Republic)	T2—437 2
Jijel (Algeria : Province)	T2—655
Jījil (Algeria : Province)	T2—655
Jilin Sheng (China)	T2—518 8
Jim Hogg County (Tex.)	T2—764 482
Jim Wells County (Tex.)	T2—764 465
Jimi River (Papua New Guinea)	T2—956 5
Jimsonweed	583.952
Jindjibandji language	499.15
	T6—991 5
Jinn	297.217
Jinnah, Mahomed Ali	
Pakistani history	954.904 2
Jinotega (Nicaragua : Dept.)	T2—728 522
Jipijapa	584.62
Jita language	496.395
	T6—963 95
Jitterbug	793.33
Jivaran languages	498.37
	T6—983 7
Jivaro language	498.372
	T6—983 72
Jivaro literature	898.372
Jivaroa language	498.372
	T6—983 72
Jivaroa literature	898.372
Jivaroan languages	498.37
	T6—983 7
Jizah (Egypt)	
ancient	T2—32
Jīzah (Egypt : Province)	T2—622
Jnana yoga	294.543 6
Jo Daviess County (Ill.)	T2—773 343
Joachim, Saint	232.933
private prayers to	242.75
Job (Biblical book)	223.1

Job analysis	658.306
military personnel	355.614
personnel management	658.306
public administration	352.64
Job banks	331.128
Job burnout	158.723
Job classification	658.306
military personnel	355.614
personnel management	658.306
public administration	352.64
Job control languages	005.434
Job creation	331.12
government policy	331.120 42
see Manual at 331.12042 vs. 331.1377	
public administration	354.927
Job description	658.306
military personnel	355.614
personnel management	658.306
libraries	023.7
public administration	352.64
Job enrichment	
personnel management	658.314 23
Job evaluation	
personnel management	658.306
Job hunting	650.14
see also Résumé writing	
Job information	331.128
Job openings	331.124
Job opportunities	331.124
Job rights	331.011
law	344.010 1
Job satisfaction	
personnel management	658.314 22
public administration	352.66
psychology	158.7
Job security	331.259 6
law	344.012 596
public administration	354.98
Job sharing	331.257 2
Job stress	158.72
Job training	370.113
see also Vocational education	
Job vacancies	331.124
Jobbers (Wholesalers)	
commerce	381.2
management	658.86
Jobs	
openings	331.124
personal success	650.14
Jockeys	798.400 92
occupational group	T7—798
Joel (Biblical book)	224.7
Jogging	613.717 2

Johannesburg (South Africa : District)	T2—682 21
John (Biblical books)	226.5
epistles	227.94
gospel	226.5
Revelation	228
John, King of England	
English history	942.033
John, the Baptist, Saint	232.94
John I, King of France	
French history	944.024
John II, King of France	
French history	944.025
John IV, Negus of Ethiopia	
Ethiopian history	963.042
John Brown's Raid, 1859	
Civil War (United States)	
cause	973.711 6
John Dories	597.64
Johnson, Andrew	
United States history	973.81
Johnson, Lyndon B. (Lyndon Baines)	
United States history	973.923
Johnson County (Ark.)	T2—767 33
Johnson County (Ga.)	T2—758 676
Johnson County (Ill.)	T2—773 996
Johnson County (Ind.)	T2—772 515
Johnson County (Iowa)	T2—777 655
Johnson County (Kan.)	T2—781 675
Johnson County (Ky.)	T2—769 245
Johnson County (Mo.)	T2—778 455
Johnson County (Neb.)	T2—782 276
Johnson County (Tenn.)	T2—768 99
Johnson County (Tex.)	T2—764 524
Johnson County (Wyo.)	T2—787 35
Johnston County (N.C.)	T2—756 41
Johnston County (Okla.)	T2—766 68
Johnston Island	T2—969 9
Johore	T2—595 1
Joinery	684.08
construction	694.6
ship hulls	623.844
woodworking	684.08
Joining equipment	621.97
Joining metals	671.5
decorative arts	739.14
sculpture	731.41
Joint chiefs of staff	355.330 42
Joint committees	
legislative bodies	328.365 7
Joint custody	346.017 3

Joint stock companies 338.7
  see also Unincorporated business enterprises
Joint tenancy 346.042
Joint ventures 338.7
  law 346.068 2
  management of enterprises 658.044
    initiation 658.114 4
    see Manual at 658.04 vs. 658.114, 658.402
  see also Business enterprises
Joints (Body parts) 573.78
  diseases
    medicine 616.72
  extremities
    surgery 617.580 59
  human anatomy 611.72
  human physiology 612.75
  surgery 617.472
  see also Musculoskeletal system
Joints (Geology) 551.84
Jokes
  literature 808.882
    specific literatures T3B—802
      individual authors T3A—8
  see Manual at T1—0207 vs. T3B—7, T3A—8 + 02, T3B—802, T3B—8 + 02, T3A—8 + 07, T3B—807, T3B—8 + 07; also at T3A—8 + 02, T3B—802, T3B—8 + 02 vs. 398.6, 793.735
Joliette (Quebec : County) T2—714 42
Joliette (Quebec : Regional County Municipality) T2—714 42
Jonah (Biblical book) 224.92
Jonathan, Leabua
  Lesotho history 968.850 31
Jones County (Ga.) T2—758 567
Jones County (Iowa) T2—777 63
Jones County (Miss.) T2—762 55
Jones County (N.C.) T2—756 21
Jones County (S.D.) T2—783 577
Jones County (Tex.) T2—764 733
Jongley (Sudan : Province) T2—629 3
Jönköpings län (Sweden) T2—486
Jonquils 635.934 34
  botany 584.34
  floriculture 635.934 34
Jordan 956.95
  T2—569 5
Jordan algebras 512.24
Jordan River T2—569 4
Jordanians T5—927 569 5
Jos (Nigeria) T2—669 52
Joseph (Son of Jacob) 222.110 92
Joseph, Saint 232.932
  private prayers to 242.75
Joseph I, Emperor of Germany
  German history 943.051
Joseph II, Holy Roman Emperor
  German history 943.057
Joseph Bonaparte, King of Spain
  Spanish history 946.06
Josephine County (Or.) T2—795 25
Josephson effect (Physics) 530.416
Joshua (Biblical book) 222.2
Joshua Tree National Park (Calif.) T2—794 97
Joual 447.971
  T6—41
Joubertina (South Africa : District) T2—687 4
Joule's law 536.71
Journalism 070.4
  civil rights issues 323.445
  sociology 302.23
Journalists 070.92
  occupational ethics 174.909 7
  occupational group T7—097
Journals (Diaries) 920
  T1—092
  see also Diaries
Journals (Mechanisms) 621.821
Journals (Serials) 050
  T1—05
  see also Serials
Joy 152.42
Joysticks (Computer) 004.76
  engineering 621.398 6
Ju-chen (Manchurian people) T5—941
Ju-chen language 494.1
  T6—941
Juab County (Utah) T2—792 44
Juan Carlos I, King of Spain
  Spanish history 946.083
Juan de Fuca Strait (B.C. and Washington) 551.466 32
  T2—164 32
Jubilees
  customs 394.4
Judaea T2—33
Judah T2—33
Judaism 296
  art representation 704.948 96

Judaism (continued)
  arts 700.482 96
    T3C—382 96
  Christian polemics 239.2
  Islamic polemics 297.292
Judaism and Christianity 261.26
  Christian view 261.26
  Jewish view 296.396
Judaism and Islam 296.397
  Islamic view 297.282
  Jewish view 296.397
Judas's betrayal of Jesus Christ 232.961
Jude (Biblical book) 227.97
Judeo-Arabic language 492.77
    T6—927
Judeo-Arabic literature 892.7
Judeo-German language 439.1
    T6—391
Judeo-German literature 839.1
Judeo-Spanish language 467.949 6
    T6—67
Judeo-Spanish literature 860
Judges 347.014
  occupational ethics 174.3
  occupational group T7—343
Judges (Biblical book) 222.32
Judges (Rulers)
  Palestinian history 933.02
Judging competitions T1—079
Judging livestock 636.081 1
Judgment
  epistemology 121
  psychology 153.46
Judgment Day 291.23
  Christianity 236.9
  Islam 297.23
Judgments (Law) 347.077
Judicial administration 347.013
Judicial assistance 345.052
  international law 341.78
Judicial branch of government 347
Judicial Committee of the Privy Council (Great Britain) 347.420 4
Judicial discretion 347.012
Judicial error 347.012
Judicial-executive relations 320.404
  law 342.044
Judicial institutions
  sociology 306.25
Judicial-legislative relations 320.404
  law 342.044
Judicial power 347.012
  chief executives 352.235
  legislatures 328.345 3
Judicial process 347.05
Judicial review 347.012
Judicial statistics 347.013
Judith (Deuterocanonical book) 229.24
Judith Basin County (Mont.) T2—786 62
Judo 796.815 2
  see also Sports
Juggling 793.87
Juglandales 583.49
Jujitsu 796.815 2
  see also Sports
Jujubes 641.342
  botany 583.86
  cooking 641.642
  food 641.342
  orchard crop 634.2
Jujuy (Argentina : Province) T2—824 1
Jukeboxes 621.389 33
Jula language 496.345
    T6—963 45
Julian calendar 529.42
Juliana, Queen of the Netherlands
  Dutch history 949.207 2
July Monarchy 944.063
Jum'ah 297.36
Jump rope rhymes 398.8
Jumpers (Athletes) 796.432 092
  sports group T7—796 4
Jumping
  field sports 796.432
  horses 798.25
  skiing 796.933
  see also Sports
Jumping mice 599.35
Juncaginaceae 584.74
Juncales 584.82
Juncos 598.883
Junction diodes 621.381 522
Junction transistors 621.381 528 2
Juncture (Linguistics) 414.6
  specific languages T4—16
June beetles 595.764 9
June bugs 595.764 9
Juneau (Alaska) T2—798 2
Juneau County (Wis.) T2—775 55
Juneberries 641.347 4
  botany 583.73
  cooking 641.647 4
  food 641.347 4
  horticulture 634.74
Junee (N.S.W.) T2—944 8

Jungermanniales 588.3
Jungian psychology 150.195 4
  personality theory 155.264
Jungle diseases
  medicine 616.988 3
  see also Environmental diseases (Human)
Jungle fowl 598.625
Jungle tactics 355.423
Jungles 333.75
  T2—152
  biology 578.734
  ecology 577.34
  see also Forest lands
Juniata County (Pa.) T2—748 47
Juniata River (Pa.) T2—748 45
Junín (Peru : Dept.) T2—852 4
Junior colleges 378.154 3
  see also Higher education
Junior high schools 373.236
  see also Secondary education
Junior schools (United Kingdom) 372
  see also Elementary education
Junipers 585.4
Junk bonds 332.632 34
Junqali (Sudan : Province) T2—629 3
Jupiter (Planet) 523.45
  T2—992 5
  astrology 133.536
  unmanned flights to 629.435 45
Jura (France) T2—444 7
Jura (Switzerland) T2—494 36
Jura Mountains (France and Switzerland) T2—494 3
  France T2—444 5
  Switzerland T2—494 3
Jurassic period 551.766
  geology 551.766
  paleontology 560.176 6
Jurchen (Manchurian people) T5—941
Jurchen language 494.1
  T6—941
Juries 347.075 2
  criminal law 345.075
Jurisdiction
  courts 347.012
    criminal law 345.01
    see Manual at 347: Jurisdiction
Jurisdiction (continued)
  government 342.041
    international law 341.4
    persons 342.08
    territory 342.041 3
Jurisdictional strikes 331.892 2
  see also Strikes (Work stoppages)
Jurisprudence 340
Juristic persons 346.013
Jurists 340.092
Jurists (Judges) 347.014 092
Jury instructions 347.075 8
Jury selection 347.075 2
Jury trial 347.052
  criminal law 345.056
Just war theory
  ethics 172.42
    religion 291.562 42
      Christianity 241.624 2
Justice
  ethics 172.2
    religion 291.562 2
      Buddhism 294.356 22
      Christianity 241.622
      Hinduism 294.548 622
      Islam 297.562 2
      Judaism 296.362 2
  law 340.11
  literature 808.803 53
    history and criticism 809.933 53
    specific literatures T3B—080 353
      history and criticism T3B—093 53
  political science 320.011
  public administration 353.4
  social theology 291.178
    Christianity 261.8
    Islam 297.27
    Judaism 296.38
Justice of God 214
  Christianity 231.8
  comparative religion 291.211 8
  Judaism 296.311 8
  philosophy of religion 214
  see also Theodicy
Justices of the peace 347.016
  occupational ethics 174.3
  occupational group T7—349
Justification (Christian doctrine) 234.7
Jute 677.13
  agricultural economics 338.173 54
  botany 583.68
  fiber crop 633.54

Jute (continued)
  textiles 677.13
    arts 746.041 3
    economics 338.476 771 3
    see also Textiles
Jute pulp 676.14
Jutiapa (Guatemala : Dept.) T2—728 143
Jutland (Denmark) T2—489 5
Juvenile courts 345.081
Juvenile delinquency 364.36
  school problem 371.782
Juvenile delinquents 364.36
  T1—086 923
  T7—069 23
  home care 649.153
  law 345.03
  pastoral care of 259.5
  penal institutions 365.42
    see also Correctional institutions
Juvenile justice 364.36
  criminology 364.36
  law 345.08
Juvenile literature 808.899 282
  history and criticism 809.892 82
  reviews 028.162
  rhetoric 808.068
  specific literatures T3B—080 928 2
    history and criticism T3B—099 282
Juvenile procedure 345.08

K

K-mesons 539.721 62
K-theory
  algebra 512.55
  topology 514.23
Kabardian language 499.962 4
  T6—999 624
Kabardino-Balkaria (Russia) T2—475 2
Kabbalah 296.16
  see also Cabala
Kabuki theater 792.095 2
Kabwari language 496.394
  T6—963 94
Kabyle language 493.34
  T6—933 4
Kabyle literature 893.34
Kabyles T5—933
Kacem (Morocco : Province) T2—643
Kachin language 495.4
  T6—954
Kadarites (Islamic sect) 297.835
Kaduna State (Nigeria) T2—669 73
Kaffraria T2—687 5
Kafiri languages 491.49
  T6—914 9
Kafiri literatures 891.49
Kafirs (Afghanistan people) T5—914 9
Kafr al-Shaykh (Egypt) T2—621
Kafr el Sheikh (Egypt) T2—621
Kagawa-ken (Japan) T2—523 5
Kagera Region (Tanzania) T2—678 27
Kagoshima-ken (Japan) T2—522 6
Kahoolawe (Hawaii) T2—969 22
Kahraman Maraş İli (Turkey) T2—565
Kaikoura District (N.Z.) T2—937 8
Kaipara District (N.Z.) T2—931 8
Kaka languages 496.396
  T6—963 96
Kakapo 598.71
  conservation technology 639.978 71
  resource economics 333.958 71
Kako languages 496.396
  T6—963 96
Kala-azar
  incidence 614.534
  medicine 616.936 4
  see also Communicable diseases (Human)
Kalahari Desert T2—688 3
  Botswana T2—688 3
  South Africa T2—687 11
Kalahari Gemsbok National Park (South Africa) T2—687 12
Kalām (Islam) 297.2
Kalam District (Pakistan) T2—549 122
Kalamazoo County (Mich.) T2—774 17
Kalanga language 496.394
  T6—963 94
Kalāt District (Pakistan) T2—549 153
Kalâtdlisut language 497.12
  T6—971 2
Kalawao County (Hawaii) T2—969 24
Kalbarri National Park (W.A.) T2—941 2
Kale 641.353 47
  cooking 641.653 47
  food 641.353 47
  garden crop 635.347
Kalenjin language 496.5
  T6—965
Kalgoorlie (W.A.) T2—941 6

Kalimantan (Indonesia) T2—598 3
Kalimantan Barat (Indonesia) T2—598 3
Kalimantan Island T2—598 3
Kalimantan Selatan (Indonesia) T2—598 3
Kalimantan Tengah (Indonesia) T2—598 3
Kalimantan Timur (Indonesia) T2—598 3
Kalinga-Apayao (Philippines) T2—599 1
Kalinin (Russia : Oblast) T2—472 8
Kaliningrad (Russia : Oblast) T2—472 4
Kaliningradskaîa oblast′ (Russia) T2—472 4
Kalininskaîa oblast′ (Russia) T2—472 8
Kalisz (Poland : Voivodeship) T2—438 4
Kalkaska County (Mich.) T2—774 65
Kallitype processes 772.16
Kalmar län (Sweden) T2—486
Kalmar Union 948.03
  Danish history 948.902
  Norwegian history 948.102
  Swedish history 948.501 8
Kalmias 583.66
Kalmuck language 494.2
  T6—942
Kalmyk language 494.2
  T6—942
Kalmykia (Russia) T2—474 8
Kaluga (Russia : Oblast) T2—472 6
Kaluzhskaîa oblast′ (Russia) T2—472 6
Kamakura period 952.021
Kamba (African people) T5—963 953
Kamba language 496.395 3
  T6—963 953
Kamchatka (Russia : Oblast) T2—577
Kamchatskaîa oblast′ (Russia) T2—577
Kamerun 967.110 2
  T2—671 1
Kames 551.315
Kamhlushwa (South Africa : District) T2—682 96
Kamloops (B.C.) T2—711 72
Kamouraska (Quebec : County) T2—714 75
Kamouraska (Quebec : Regional County Municipality) T2—714 75
Kampala (Uganda) T2—676 1
Kampuchea 959.6
  T2—596
Kanabec County (Minn.) T2—776 63
Kanagawa-ken (Japan) T2—521 36
Kananaskis Country (Alta.) T2—712 332
Kanarese T5—948 14
Kanarese language 494.814
  T6—948 14
Kanarese literature 894.814
Kanawha County (W. Va.) T2—754 37
Kanawha River (W. Va.) T2—754 3
Kandh (Dravidian people) T5—948 2
Kandh language 494.824
  T6—948 24
Kandh literature 894.824
Kandiyohi County (Minn.) T2—776 48
Kane County (Ill.) T2—773 23
Kane County (Utah) T2—792 51
Kanem (Kingdom) 967.430 1
  T2—674 3
Kanem-Bornu (Kingdom) 966.980 1
Kanem-Bornu Empire T2—669 8
Kanembu (African people) T5—965
Kanembu language 496.5
  T6—965
Kangaroo Island (S. Aust.) T2—942 35
Kangaroo mice 599.359 8
Kangaroo rats 599.359 87
Kangaroos 599.222
  big game hunting 799.272 22
  conservation technology 639.979 222
  resource economics 333.959 222
KaNgwane (South Africa) T2—682 96
Kankakee County (Ill.) T2—773 63
Kankan (Guinea) T2—665 2
Kannada language 494.814
  T6—948 14
Kannada literature 894.814
Kano State (Nigeria) T2—669 78
Kansas 978.1
  T2—781
Kansas City (Kan.) T2—781 39
Kansas City (Mo.) T2—778 411
Kansas City jazz 781.653
Kansas River (Kan.) T2—781 3
Kansu Province (China) T2—514 5
Kantianism 142.3
Kantō Region (Japan) T2—521 3
Kanuri language 496.5
  T6—965

Kaolin 553.61
  economic geology 553.61
  mining 622.361
Kaolinite
  mineralogy 549.67
Kaonde language 496.393
  T6—963 93
Kaons 539.721 62
Kapiti Coast District (N.Z.) T2—936 1
Kapok
  botany 583.68
  fiber crop 633.56
  materials science 620.195
  textiles 677.23
    see also Textiles
Kaposi's sarcoma
  incidence 614.599 947 7
  medicine 616.994 77
  see also Cancer (Human)
Kara-Kalpak language 494.34
  T6—943 4
Kara Sea 551.468 5
  T2—163 25
Karachaevo-Cherkesiia (Russia) T2—475 2
Karachay-Balkar language 494.38
  T6—943 8
Karachay-Cherkessia (Russia) T2—475 2
Karachi (Pakistan : District) T2—549 183
Karagwe (Kingdom) 967.610 1
  T2—676 1
Karaim language 494.38
  T6—943 8
Karaites 296.81
Karak (Jordan : Province) T2—569 563
Karakalpak (Uzbekistan) T2—587
Karakalpak language 494.34
  T6—943 4
Karakoram Range T2—546
Karanga (African people) T5—963 975
Karanga kingdoms 968.910 1
Karanga language 496.397 5
  T6—963 975
Karate 796.815 3
  physical fitness 613.714 8
  see also Sports
Karbalā' (Iraq : Province) T2—567 5
Karditsa (Greece : Nome) T2—495 4
Karelia (Russia) T2—471 5
Karelian language 494.54
  T6—945 4
Karelian literature 894.54
Karelians T5—945 4
Karen (Asian people) T5—95
Karen languages 495
  T6—95
Kari languages (Bantu) 496.39
  T6—963 9
Karl-Marx-Stadt (Germany) T2—432 162
Karl-Marx-Stadt (Germany : Bezirk) T2—432 16
Karlsruhe (Germany) T2—434 643
Karlsruhe (Germany : Regierungsbezirk) T2—434 64
Karma 291.22
  Buddhism 294.342 2
  Hinduism 294.522
Karma yoga 294.543 6
Karnak (Egypt) T2—32
Karnataka (India) T2—548 7
Karnes County (Tex.) T2—764 444
Kärnten (Austria) T2—436 6
Karo, Joseph ben Ephraim
  Jewish legal codes 296.182
Karoo (South Africa) T2—687 15
Karoo, Great (South Africa) T2—687 15
Karoo, Little (South Africa) T2—687 16
Karoo, Northern (South Africa) T2—687 13
Karoo, Upper (South Africa) T2—687 13
Karoo National Park (South Africa) T2—687 15
Karpathos Island (Greece) T2—495 87
  ancient T2—391 7
Karroo (South Africa) T2—687 15
Karroo, Great (South Africa) T2—687 15
Karroo, Little (South Africa) T2—687 16
Karroo, Northern (South Africa) T2—687 13
Karroo, Upper (South Africa) T2—687 13
Karroo National Park (South Africa) T2—687 15
Kars İli (Turkey) T2—566 2
Karsts 551.447
  T2—144
  see also Caves
Karting 796.76
  see also Sports

Karts (Racing cars) 796.76
driving 629.284 8
engineering 629.228
repair 629.287 8
sports 796.76
see also Sports
Kartvelian languages 499.968
T6—999 68
Kasai-Occidental (Zaire) T2—675 123
Kasai-Oriental (Zaire) T2—675 126
Kasem language 496.35
T6—963 5
Kasena language 496.35
T6—963 5
Kashmir T2—546
India T2—546
Pakistan T2—549 13
Kashmiri language 491.499
T6—914 99
Kashmiri literature 891.499
Kashmiris T5—914 99
Kashrut 296.73
Kashubian language 491.85
T6—918 5
Kashubian literature 891.85
Kashubians T5—918 5
Kashubs T5—918 5
Kassalā (Sudan : Province) T2—625
Kassel (Germany) T2—434 124
Kassel (Germany : Regierungsbezirk) T2—434 12
Kastamonu İli (Turkey) T2—563
Kastoria (Greece : Nome) T2—495 62
Katanga (Zaire) T2—675 18
Katanning (W.A.) T2—941 2
Katharevusa language (Modern Greek) 489.3
T6—89
Katharevusa literature (Modern Greek) 889
Katherine (N.T.) T2—942 95
Katherine Gorge National Park (N.T.) T2—942 95
Kativik Regional Administration (Quebec) T2—714 111
Katmai National Park and Preserve (Alaska) T2—798 4
Katoomba (N.S.W.) T2—944 5
Katowice (Poland : Voivodeship) T2—438 5
Katsina State (Nigeria) T2—669 76
Katsura tree 583.43
Kattang language 499.15
T6—991 5
Kattegat (Denmark and Sweden) 551.461 34
T2—163 34
Katydids 595.726
Kauai (Hawaii) T2—969 41
Kauai County (Hawaii) T2—969 4
Kaufman County (Tex.) T2—764 277
Kaunda, Kenneth D. (Kenneth David)
Zambian history 968.940 41
Kauris 585.3
forestry 634.975 93
Kavala (Greece : Nome) T2—495 7
Kavieng (Papua New Guinea) T2—958 3
Kavirondo language (Nilotic) 496.5
T6—965
Kaw River (Kan.) T2—781 3
Kawau Island (N.Z. : Island) T2—932 1
Kawerau (N.Z.) T2—934 26
Kawerau District (N.Z.) T2—934 26
Kay County (Okla.) T2—766 24
Kayaking 797.122 4
see also Sports
Kayseri İli (Turkey) T2—564
Kazak language 494.345
T6—943 45
Kazak literature 894.345
Kazakh language 494.345
T6—943 45
Kazakh literature 894.345
Kazakhs T5—943 45
Kazakhstan T2—584 5
Kazaks T5—943 45
Kazoo 783.99
Kearney County (Neb.) T2—782 394
Kearny County (Kan.) T2—781 425
Kearsarge and Alabama, Battle of, 1864 973.754
Keats Island (B.C. : Island) T2—711 31
Kebbi State (Nigeria) T2—669 63
Kechika River (B.C.) T2—711 85
Kechua Indians T5—983 23
Kechua language 498.323
T6—983 23
Kechua literature 898.323
Kechuan languages 498.323
T6—983 23
Kedah T2—595 1
Keeling Islands 969.9
T2—699
Keene's cement 666.92

Keeshond 636.72
Keewatin (N.W.T.) T2—719 4
  see Manual at T2—7193–T2—7197
Kefa Kifle Hāger (Ethiopia) T2—633
Keffa (Ethiopia) T2—633
Kegs
  wooden 674.82
Keiskammahoek (South Africa : District) T2—687 92
Keith County (Neb.) T2—782 89
Kejimkujik National Park (N.S.) T2—716 33
Kekchí Indians T5—974 15
Kekchí language 497.415
  T6—974 15
Kelaa des Srarhna (Morocco : Province) T2—646
Kelantan T2—595 1
Kele languages 496.396
  T6—963 96
Kelim 296.123 6
Kelowna (B.C.) T2—711 5
Kelps 579.887
  resource economics 333.953 8
Kemerovo (Russia : Oblast) T2—573
Kemerovskaîa oblast′ (Russia) T2—573
Kemper County (Miss.) T2—762 683
Kempo 796.815 9
  see also Sports
Kempsey (N.S.W.) T2—944 3
Kempton Park (South Africa : District) T2—682 2
Kenaf
  botany 583.685
  fiber crop 633.56
Kenai Fjords National Park (Alaska) T2—798 3
Kenai Peninsula (Alaska) T2—798 3
Kenai Peninsula Borough (Alaska) T2—798 3
Kendall County (Ill.) T2—773 263
Kendall County (Tex.) T2—764 886
Kendo 796.86
  see also Sports
Kenedy County (Tex.) T2—764 473
Kenhardt District (South Africa) T2—687 12
Kenitra (Morocco : Province) T2—643
Kennebec County (Me.) T2—741 6
Kennebec River (Me.) T2—741 22
Kennedy, John F. (John Fitzgerald)
  United States history 973.922
Kennelly-Heaviside layers 538.767 3
Kennels (Dog housing) 636.708 31
Kennet (England : District) T2—423 17
Kenora (Ont. : District) T2—713 112
  Patricia Portion T2—713 1
Kenosha County (Wis.) T2—775 98
Kensington and Chelsea (London, England) T2—421 34
Kent (England) T2—422 3
Kent (N.B. : County) T2—715 22
Kent (Ont.) T2—713 33
Kent County (Del.) T2—751 4
Kent County (Md.) T2—752 36
Kent County (Mich.) T2—774 55
Kent County (R.I.) T2—745 4
Kent County (Tex.) T2—764 738
Kentani (South Africa : District) T2—687 91
Kenton County (Ky.) T2—769 35
Kentrikē Makedonia (Greece) T2—495 65
Kentucky 976.9
  T2—769
Kentucky Lake (Ky. and Tenn.) T2—769 895
Kentucky River T2—769 3
Kenya 967.62
  T2—676 2
Kenyans T5—967 62
Kenyatta, Jomo
  Kenyan history 967.620 41
Keogh plans 332.024 01
  tax law 343.052 33
Keokuk County (Iowa) T2—777 91
Kephallēnia (Greece) T2—495 5
Kepler's laws 521.3
Kerala (India) T2—548 3
Keratin 572.67
  chemistry 547.753
  see also Proteins
Keratinous material products 679.4
Keratosis
  medicine 616.544
  see also Skin
Kerbs 625.888
Kerensky, Aleksandr Fyodorovich
  Russian history 947.084 1
Keres language 497.9
  T6—979

Keresan languages 497.9
T6—979
Kerguelen Islands 969.9
T2—699
Keritot 296.123 5
  Babylonian Talmud 296.125 5
  Mishnah 296.123 5
Kerkyra (Greece : Nome) T2—495 5
Kermadec Islands T2—939 9
Kerman (Iran) T2—558 2
Kermānshāhān (Iran : Province)) T2—555 2
Kern County (Calif.) T2—794 88
Kerosene 665.538 3
Kerosene lamps 621.323
  see also Lighting
Kerr County (Tex.) T2—764 884
Kerrier (England : District) T2—423 76
Kerry (Ireland) T2—419 6
Kershaw County (S.C.) T2—757 61
Keski-Suomen lääni (Finland) T2—489 73
Keski-Suomi (Finland) T2—489 73
Kesteven (England) T2—425 35
Kestrels 598.96
Ket language 494.6
T6—946
Ketchikan Gateway Borough (Alaska) T2—798 2
Ketchup 641.814
  commercial processing 664.58
  home preparation 641.814
Kete language 496.393
T6—963 93
Kethubim 223
Ketones 547.036
  aromatic chemistry 547.636
  chemical engineering 661.85
Kettering (England) T2—425 52
Kettle River (B.C. and Wash.) T2—711 62
Kettle-shaped drums 786.93
  see also Percussion instruments
Kettledrums 786.93
  see also Percussion instruments
Kettles (Geologic landforms) 551.315
Ketubbot 296.123 3
  Babylonian Talmud 296.125 3
  Mishnah 296.123 3
  Palestinian Talmud 296.124 3
Ketuvim 223
Keuka Lake (N.Y.) T2—747 82
Kewa language 499.12
T6—991 2
Kewaunee County (Wis.) T2—775 62
Keweenaw County (Mich.) T2—774 995
Keweenaw Peninsula (Mich.) T2—774 99
Key West (Fla.) T2—759 41
Key word indexing 025.486
Keya Paha County (Neb.) T2—782 725
Keyboard bands 784.6
Keyboard electrophones 786.59
  see also Keyboard instruments
Keyboard idiophones 786.83
  see also Percussion instruments
Keyboard instruments 786
  bands and orchestras 784
  chamber ensembles 785
    mixed 785.2
    single type 785.62–.65
  construction 786.192 3
    by hand 786.192 3
    by machine 681.86
  solo music 786
  see Manual at 784–788
Keyboard stringed instruments 786
  see also Keyboard instruments
Keyboard wind instruments 786.5
  see also Keyboard instruments
Keyboarding 652.3
Keyboards (Computer) 004.76
  engineering 621.398 6
Keynesian economic school 330.156
Keys 683.32
Khabarovsk (Russia : Kray) T2—577
Khabarovskiĭ kraĭ (Russia) T2—577
Khairpūr District (Pakistan) T2—549 17
Khakass (Russia) T2—575
Khakasskai͡a respublika (Russia) T2—575
Khalaj language 494.36
T6—943 6
Khalji dynasty 954.023 4
Khalkha Mongolian language 494.23
T6—942 3
Khalkha Mongolian literature 894.23
Khama, Seretse
  Botswana history 968.830 31
Khamti T5—959 19
Khantia-Mansia (Russia) T2—573
Khanty T5—945 1

Khanty language 494.51
T6—945 1
Khanty literature 894.51
Kharia language 495.95
T6—959 5
Kharias T5—959 5
Kharijites 297.83
Kharkiv (Ukraine : Oblast) T2—477 5
Kharkivs´ka oblast´ (Ukraine) T2—477 5
Khartoum (Sudan : Province) T2—626 2
Khasi language 495.93
T6—959 3
Khasis T5—959 3
Khaskovo (Bulgaria : Oblast) T2—499 6
Khaskovo (Bulgaria : Okrŭg) T2—499 6
Khaskovska oblast (Bulgaria) T2—499 6
Khaskovski okrŭg (Bulgaria) T2—499 6
Khat
alkaloidal crop 633.7
botany 583.85
Khemisset (Morocco : Province) T2—643
Khenchela (Algeria : Province) T2—655
Khenifra (Morocco : Province) T2—643
Kherson (Ukraine : Oblast) T2—477 3
Khersons´ka oblast´ (Ukraine) T2—477 3
Khmel´nyts´ka oblast´ (Ukraine) T2—477 8
Khmel´nyts´kyy (Ukraine : Oblast) T2—477 8
Khmer T5—959 3
Khmer language 495.932
T6—959 32
Khmer literature 895.932
Khmer Republic 959.6
T2—596
Khoi-Khoi language 496.1
T6—961
Khoi language 496.1
T6—961
Khoikhoi (African people) T5—961
Khoikhoi language 496.1
T6—961
Khoisan languages 496.1
T6—961
Khoisan literatures 896.1
Khomeini, Ruhollah
Iranian history 955.054 2
Khond (Dravidian people) T5—948 2
Khond language 494.824
T6—948 24
Khond literature 894.824
Khorāsān (Iran) T2—559 2
Khotanese language 491.53
T6—915 3
Khotanese literature 891.53
Khouribga (Morocco : Province) T2—643
Khowar language 491.499
T6—914 99
Khowar literature 891.499
Khrushchev, Nikita Sergeevich
Russian history 947.085 2
Khuddakanikāya 294.382 32
Khulna (Bangladesh : Division) T2—549 25
Khurasan (Iran) T2—559 2
Khuṭbah 297.37
Khūzestān (Iran) T2—556
Kiangsi Province (China) T2—512 22
Kiangsu Province (China) T2—511 36
Kibbutzim 307.776
Kicking
American football 796.332 27
Kidder County (N.D.) T2—784 57
Kiddushin 296.123 3
Babylonian Talmud 296.125 3
Mishnah 296.123 3
Palestinian Talmud 296.124 3
Kidnap and ransom insurance 368.82
see also Insurance
Kidnap insurance 368.82
see also Insurance
Kidnapping 364.154
law 345.025 4
Kidney beans 641.356 52
botany 583.74
commercial processing 664.805 652
cooking 641.656 52
field crop 633.372
food 641.356 52
garden crop 635.652
Kidney failure
medicine 616.614
see also Urinary system
Kidney stones
medicine 616.622
see also Urinary system

Kidneys 573.496
  biology 573.496
  human anatomy 611.61
  human physiology 612.463
  medicine 616.61
  surgery 617.461
  see also Urinary system
Kielce (Poland : Voivodeship) T2—438 4
Kiev (Ukraine : Oblast) T2—477 7
Kievan Rus 947.7
  Belarussian history 947.8
  Russian history 947.02
  Ukrainian history 947.7
Kigali (Rwanda) T2—675 71
Kigoma Region (Tanzania) T2—678 28
Kikongo languages 496.393 1
  T6—963 931
Kikuyu (African people) T5—963 954
Kikuyu-Kamba languages 496.395 3
  T6—963 953
Kikuyu language 496.395 4
  T6—963 954
Kikuyu literature 896.395 4
Kilayim 296.123 1
  Mishnah 296.123 1
  Palestinian Talmud 296.124 1
Kildare (Ireland : County) T2—418 5
Kilimanjaro, Mount (Tanzania) T2—678 26
Kilimanjaro National Park (Tanzania) T2—678 26
Kilimanjaro Region (Tanzania) T2—678 26
Kiliwa language 497.57
  T6—975 7
Kilkenny (Ireland : County) T2—418 9
Kilkis (Greece : Nome) T2—495 65
Killarney (Ireland) T2—419 65
Killer cells 571.968
  human immunology 616.079 9
Killer whale 599.536
  conservation technology 639.979 536
  resource economics 333.959 536
Killifishes 597.665
Kilmarnock and Loudoun (Scotland) T2—414 63
Kiln drying lumber 674.384
Kilns 666.436
  decorative arts 738.136
  sculpture 731.3
  technology 666.436
Kim, Il-sŏng
  Korean history 951.930 43
Kimbala languages 496.393
  T6—963 93
Kimball County (Neb.) T2—782 973
Kimberley (B.C.) T2—711 65
Kimberley (South Africa : District) T2—687 11
Kimberley (W.A.) T2—941 4
Kimble County (Tex.) T2—764 878
Kimbundu language 496.393 2
  T6—963 932
Kimbundu literature 896.393 2
Kin recognition (Animals) 591.563
Kinbasket Lake (B.C.) T2—711 68
Kincardine and Deeside (Scotland) T2—412 4
Kindergarten 372.218
  see also Elementary education
Kindergarten teachers 372.11
Kindergarten teaching 372.110 2
Kindness
  ethics 177.7
  see also Virtues
Kinematics 531.112
  fluids 532.05
  gases 533.2
  liquid mechanics 532.5
  meteorology 551.515 1
  solids 531.3
Kinesiology
  health 613.7
Kinetic art 709.040 73
  sculpture 735.230 473
Kinetic energy 531.6
Kinetic theories (Statistical mechanics) 530.136
Kinetic theory of gases 533.7
Kinetics 531.113
  fluids 532.05
  gases 533.2
  liquid mechanics 532.5
  physical chemistry 541.394
    biochemistry 572.44
    enzymes 572.744
  solids 531.3
King, William Lyon Mackenzie
  Canadian history 971.062 2
    1921–1930 971.062 2
    1935–1948 971.063 2
King and Queen County (Va.) T2—755 352
King County (Tex.) T2—764 742
King County (Wash.) T2—797 77

King crabs 595.387
fishing 639.57
King George County (Va.) T2—755 25
King George's War, 1740–1748 940.253 2
North American history 973.26
King James version (Bible) 220.520 3
King Philip's War, 1675–1676 973.24
King vulture 598.92
King William County (Va.) T2—755 355
King William Island (N.W.T.) T2—719 7
King William's Town (South Africa : District) T2—687 5
King William's War, 1688–1697 940.252 5
North American history 973.25
Kinga language 496.391
T6—963 91
Kingaroy (Qld.) T2—943 2
Kingdom of God 231.72
eschatology 236
Kingfish 597.725
Kingfisher County (Okla.) T2—766 32
Kingfishers 598.78
Kinglake National Park (Vic.) T2—945 2
Kinglets 598.843
Kingman County (Kan.) T2—781 843
Kings (Biblical books) 222.5
Kings (Chessmen) 794.147
Kings (N.B.) T2—715 41
Kings (N.S. : County) T2—716 34
Kings (P.E.I.) T2—717 7
Kings (Rulers) 321
public administration 352.23
Kings Canyon National Park (Calif.) T2—794 82
Kings County (Calif.) T2—794 85
Kings County (N.Y.) T2—747 23
King's Lynn and West Norfolk (England : Borough) T2—426 13
Kingsburgh (South Africa) T2—684 55
Kingsbury County (S.D.) T2—783 273
Kingship of Jesus Christ 232.8
Kingston (Ont.) T2—713 72
Kingston (Tas.) T2—946 2
Kingston upon Hull (England) T2—428 37
Kingston upon Thames (London, England) T2—421 94
Kingswood (England : District) T2—423 94
Kinkajou 599.763
Kinki Region (Japan) T2—521 8
Kinney County (Tex.) T2—764 433
Kinnim 296.123 5
Kinorhyncha 592.55
Kinsei period 952.025
Kinshasa (Zaire) T2—675 112
Kinship 306.83
genealogy 929.2
system of descent 306.83
Kinsmen 306.87
T1—085
T7—04
Kinyarwanda language 496.394 61
T6—963 946 1
Kiowa County (Colo.) T2—788 93
Kiowa County (Kan.) T2—781 785
Kiowa County (Okla.) T2—766 47
Kiowa Indians T5—974 9
Kiowa language 497.49
T6—974 9
Kiowa-Tanoan languages 497.49
T6—974 9
Kiranti languages 495.49
T6—954 9
Kirantish languages 495.49
T6—954 9
Kirghiz T5—943 47
Kirghiz language 494.347
T6—943 47
Kirghiz literature 894.347
Kirghizia T2—584 3
Kiribati 996.81
T2—968 1
Kirin Province (China) T2—518 8
Kiritimati (Kiribati) T2—964
Kirkcaldy (Scotland : District) T2—412 95
Kirkcudbrightshire (Scotland : District) T2—414 92
Kirklareli İli (Turkey) T2—496 1
Kirkless (England) T2—428 13
Kirkwood (South Africa : District) T2—687 5
Kirlian photography 778.3
parapsychology 133.892
Kirmān (Iran) T2—558 2
Kirov (Russia : Oblast) T2—474 2
Kirovohrad (Ukraine : Oblast) T2—477 6
Kirovohrads'ka oblast' (Ukraine) T2—477 6
Kirovskaīa oblast' (Russia) T2—474 2
Kirşehir İli (Turkey) T2—564

Kirstenbosch Botanic Gardens (South Africa) T2—687 355
Kirundi language 496.394 65
T6—963 946 5
Kirundi literature 896.394 65
Kisangani (Zaire) T2—675 15
Kissi (African people) T5—963 2
Kissi language 496.32
T6—963 2
Kissimmee River (Fla.) T2—759 53
Kissing
customs 394
Kiswahili language 496.392
T6—963 92
Kiswahili literature 896.392
Kit Carson County (Colo.) T2—788 91
Kitchen linens
household equipment 643.3
Kitchen utensils 641.502 8
cooking 641.502 8
manufacturing technology 683.82
Kitchener (Ont.) T2—713 45
Kitchens 643.3
home economics 643.3
plumbing 696.184
residential interior decoration 747.797
Kites 629.133 32
recreation 796.158
Kites (Birds) 598.945
conservation technology 639.978 945
resource economics 333.958 945
Kitikmeot (N.W.T.) T2—719 7
see Manual at T2—7193–T2—7197
Kitimat (B.C.) T2—711 1
Kitimat-Stikine (B.C.) T2—711 1
Kitsap County (Wash.) T2—797 76
Kitsch 709.034 8
Kittens 636.807
Kittitas County (Wash.) T2—797 57
Kittson County (Minn.) T2—776 99
Kituba language 496.393 1
T6—963 931
Kiustendilski okrug (Bulgaria) T2—499 8
Kivu (Zaire) T2—675 17
Kivu, Lake (Rwanda and Zaire) T2—675 17
Rwanda T2—675 71
Zaire T2—675 17
Kiwi (Fruit) 641.344
botany 583.66
cooking 641.644
Kiwi (Fruit) (continued)
food 641.344
horticulture 634.4
Kiwis (Birds) 598.54
Kiyaka languages 496.393
T6—963 93
Klamath County (Or.) T2—795 91
Klamath Indians T5—974 1
Klamath Mountains (Calif. and Or.) T2—795 2
California T2—794 21
Oregon T2—795 2
Kleberg County (Tex.) T2—764 472
Kleptomania 362.27
medicine 616.858 42
social welfare 362.27
see also Mental illness
Klerk, F. W. de (Frederik Willem)
South African history 968.064
Klerksdorp (South Africa : District) T2—682 4
Klickitat County (Wash.) T2—797 53
Klinefelter's syndrome
medicine 616.680 42
see also Male genital system
Klip River (South Africa : District) T2—684 7
Klystrons 621.381 333
Knapp, Georg Friedrich
economic school 330.154 2
Kneelers
home sewing 646.21
household management 645.4
textile arts 746.95
Knees (Human) 612.98
physiology 612.98
regional medicine 617.582
surgery 617.582
see also Lower extremities (Human)
Knies, Karl
economic school 330.154 2
Knife combat
military training 355.548
Knighthood
genealogy 929.7
Knighthood orders 929.71
Christian religious orders 255.791
church history 271.791
Knights (Chessmen) 794.144
Knights Hospitalers of St. John of Jerusalem 255.791 2
church history 271.791 2

Knights of Labor 331.883 309 73
Knights of Malta 255.791 2
  church history 271.791 2
Knights of Pythias 366.2
  biography 366.209 2
  social group T7—366 2
Knights Templars 255.791 3
  church history 271.791 3
Knitted fabrics 677.661
  see also Textiles
Knitted laces
  arts 746.226
Knitted rugs
  arts 746.73
  see also Rugs
Knitting 677.028 245
  arts 746.432
  manufacturing technology 677.028 245
Knives 621.932
  art metalwork 739.72
  military engineering 623.441
Knob celery 641.351 28
  see also Celeriac
Knobs region (Ky.) T2—769 5
Knockers
  artistic ironwork 739.48
Knossos (Extinct city) T2—391 8
Knots 623.888 2
Knots (Mathematics) 514.224
Knott County (Ky.) T2—769 165
Knotted fabrics 677.66
  see also Textiles
Knotting (Seamanship) 623.888 2
Knotting textiles 677.028 2
  arts 746.422
  manufacturing technology 677.028 2
Know-Nothing Party 324.273 2
Knowledge 001
  psychology 153.4
  public administrative support 352.74
  sociology 306.42
  theory of 121
Knowledge acquisition
  computer science 006.331
Knowledge-based systems 006.33
Knowledge engineering
  computer science 006.332
Knowledge of God 212.6
  Christianity 231.042
  comparative religion 291.211
  philosophy of religion 212.6
Knowledge representation
  computer science 006.332
Knowsley (England) T2—427 54
Knox County (Ill.) T2—773 49
Knox County (Ind.) T2—772 39
Knox County (Ky.) T2—769 125
Knox County (Me.) T2—741 53
Knox County (Mo.) T2—778 315
Knox County (Neb.) T2—782 59
Knox County (Ohio) T2—771 52
Knox County (Tenn.) T2—768 85
Knox County (Tex.) T2—764 743
Knoxville (Tenn.) T2—768 85
Knysna (South Africa : District) T2—687 4
Koala 599.25
Kōbe-shi (Japan) T2—521 874
København (Denmark) T2—489 13
Københavns amt (Denmark) T2—489 14
Koblenz (Germany) T2—434 323
Koblenz (Germany : Regierungsbezirk) T2—434 32
Kobuk Valley National Park (Alaska) T2—798 6
Kocaeli İli (Turkey) T2—563
Kōchi-ken (Japan) T2—523 3
Kodashim 296.123 5
  Babylonian Talmud 296.125 5
  Mishnah 296.123 5
  Palestinian Talmud 296.124 5
Kodiak Island (Alaska) T2—798 4
Kodiak Island Borough (Alaska) T2—798 4
Koffiefontein (South Africa : District) T2—685 8
Kogi State (Nigeria) T2—669 56
Kohelet 223.8
Kohistani language 491.499
  T6—914 99
Kohistani literature 891.499
Kohistanis T5—914 99
Kohlrabi 641.353 47
  cooking 641.653 47
  food 641.353 47
Koi 639.374 83
Koine (Greek language) 487.4
  T6—87
Koksilah River (B.C.) T2—711 2
Kokstad (South Africa) T2—684 6
Kola Peninsula (Russia) T2—471 3
Kola trees 583.68
  alkaloidal crop 633.76
Köln (Germany) T2—435 514
Köln (Germany : Regierungsbezirk) T2—435 51

Komandorski Islands (Russia) T2—577
Komárom Megye (Hungary) T2—439 7
Komati River T2—679 1
 Mozambique T2—679 1
 South Africa T2—682 6
 Swaziland T2—688 7
Komga (South Africa : District) T2—687 5
Komi T5—945 3
Komi (Russia) T2—474 3
Komi language 494.53
 T6—945 3
Komi literature 894.53
Komi-Permiak (Russia) T2—474 3
Komi-Permiatskiĭ avtonomnyĭ okrug (Russia) T2—474 3
Kominform 324.175
Komondor 636.73
Konde language 496.391
 T6—963 91
Kongo (African people) T5—963 931
Kongo (Kingdom) 967.511 401
 T2—675 114
Kongo language 496.393 1
 T6—963 931
Kongo literature 896.393 1
Konin (Poland : Voivodeship) T2—438 4
Konjo languages 496.394
 T6—963 94
Konkani language 491.467
 T6—914 6
Konkani literature 891.46
Kono (African people) T5—963 4
Kono language 496.34
 T6—963 4
Konya İli (Turkey) T2—564
Koochiching County (Minn.) T2—776 79
Kootenai County (Idaho) T2—796 94
Kootenai River T2—711 65
Kootenay Boundary (B.C.) T2—711 62
Kootenay Lake (B.C.) T2—711 62
Kootenay National Park (B.C.) T2—711 65
Kootenay River T2—711 65
Kopparbergs län (Sweden) T2—487
Koppies (South Africa : District) T2—685 2
Koran 297.122
Koran stories 297.122 2
Koras 787.98
 see also Stringed instruments
Kordestān (Iran) T2—555 4
Kordofan (Sudan) T2—628
Kordofanian languages 496.3
 T6—963
Korea 951.9
 T2—519
Korea (North) 951.93
 T2—519 3
Korea (South) 951.95
 T2—519 5
Korea Strait 551.465 54
 T2—164 54
Korean language 495.7
 T6—957
Korean literature 895.7
Korean War, 1950–1953 951.904 2
Koreans T5—957
Koriak (Russia : Okrug) T2—577
Koriakskiĭ avtonomnyĭ okrug (Russia) T2—577
Korinthia (Greece) T2—495 22
 ancient T2—387
Kos Island (Greece) T2—495 87
Kosciusko County (Ind.) T2—772 82
Kosciusko National Park (N.S.W.) T2—944 7
Kosher cooking 641.567 6
Kosher observance 296.73
Kosovo i Metohija (Serbia) T2—497 1
Kosrae (Micronesia) T2—966
Kossuth County (Iowa) T2—777 21
Koster (South Africa : District) T2—682 4
Kostroma (Russia : Oblast) T2—473 3
Kostromskaia oblast′ (Russia) T2—473 3
Kosygin, Aleksey Nikolayevich
 Russian history 947.085 3
Koszalin (Poland : Voivodeship) T2—438 1
Kota language (Dravidian) 494.81
 T6—948 1
Kota literature (Dravidian) 894.81
Kountché, Seyni
 Nigerien (Niger) history 966.260 5
Kozanē (Greece : Nome) T2—495 62
Kpelle (African people) T5—963 4
Kpelle language 496.34
 T6—963 4
Kraft process 676.126
Kraft wrapping paper 676.287

Kraków (Poland : Voivodeship) T2—438 6
Kranskop (South Africa : District) T2—684 7
Krasnodar (Russia : Kray) T2—475 2
Krasnodarskiĭ kraĭ (Russia) T2—475 2
Krasnoi͡arskiĭ kraĭ (Russia) T2—575
Krasnoyarsk (Russia : Kray) T2—575
Krebs cycle 572.475
Krētē (Greece) T2—495 9
  ancient T2—391 8
Kretschmer, Ernst
  personality theory 155.264
Krill 595.389
Krio language 427.966 4
  T6—217
Kristianstads län (Sweden) T2—486
Kronobergs län (Sweden) T2—486
Kroonstad (South Africa : District) T2—685 2
Krosno (Poland : Voivodeship) T2—438 6
Kru (African people) T5—963 3
Kru languages 496.33
  T6—963 3
Kruger National Park (South Africa) T2—682 6
Krugersdorp (South Africa : District) T2—682 2
Krymskai͡a oblastʹ (Ukraine) T2—477 1
Krypton
  chemistry 546.754
  gas technology 665.822
  see also Chemicals
Ku Klux Klan 322.420 973
Ku-ring-gai Chase National Park (N.S.W.) T2—944 1
Kuala Lumpur (Malaysia) T2—595 1
Kuba (Kingdom) 967.512 601
  T2—675 126
Kuba languages 496.396
  T6—963 96
Kubitschek, Juscelino
  Brazilian history 981.062
Kublai Khan
  Asian history 950.2
Kuchean language 491.994
  T6—919 94
Kudus 599.642 3
Kudzu 583.74
Kui language 494.824
  T6—948 24
Kui literature 894.824
Kuĭbyshev (Russia : Oblast) T2—474 4
Kuĭbyshevskai͡a oblastʹ (Russia) T2—474 4
Kuils River (South Africa : District) T2—687 35
Kuki-Chin languages 495.4
  T6—954
Kumamoto-ken (Japan) T2—522 5
Kumasi (Ghana) T2—667
Kumquats 641.343 4
  cooking 641.643 4
  food 641.343 4
  orchard crop 634.34
Kuna Indians T5—982
Kuna language 498.2
  T6—982
Kunashiri Island (R.S.F.S.R.) T2—524
Kundalini yoga
  comparative religion 291.436
  Hinduism 294.543 6
Kunene (Angola : Province) T2—673 5
Kung fu 796.815 9
  see also Sports
Kuopio (Finland) T2—489 75
Kurdi language 491.597
  T6—915 97
Kurdi literature 891.597
Kurdish Autonomous Region (Iraq) T2—567 2
Kurdish language 491.597
  T6—915 97
Kurdish literature 891.597
Kurdistan T2—566 7
  Iran T2—555 4
  Iraq T2—567 2
  Turkey T2—566 7
Kurds T5—915 97
Kurdufān al Janūbīyah (Sudan) T2—628
Kurdufān al-Shamālīyah (Sudan) T2—628
Kŭrdzhali (Bulgaria : Okrŭg) T2—499 6
Kŭrdzhaliĭski okrŭg (Bulgaria) T2—499 6
Kurgan (Russia : Oblast) T2—573
Kurganskai͡a oblastʹ (Russia) T2—573
Kuria (African people) T5—963 95

Kuria language 496.395
T6—963 95
Kuril Islands (Russia) T2—577
Kurland (Duchy) T2—479 6
Kurmanji language 491.597
T6—915 97
Kurmanji literature 891.597
Kursk (Russia : Oblast) T2—473 5
Kurskaîa oblast′ (Russia) T2—473 5
Kurukh T5—948 3
Kurukh language 494.83
T6—948 3
Kurukh literature 894.83
Kuruman (South Africa : District) T2—687 11
Kushans T5—915
Kuskokwim River (Alaska) T2—798 4
Kūt (Iraq : Province) T2—567 5
Kütahya (Turkey : İli) T2—562
Kutchin Indians T5—972
Kutchin language 497.2
T6—972
Kuvasz (Dog) 636.73
Kuwait 953.67
T2—536 7
Kuwait-Iraq Crisis, 1990–1991 956.704 42
Kuwaitis T5—927 536 7
Kwa languages 496.337
T6—963 37
Kwa literatures 896.337
Kwa Zulu (South Africa) T2—684 91
Kwajalein Atoll (Marshall Islands) T2—968 3
KwaMapumulu (South Africa : District) T2—684 91
KwaNdebele (South Africa) T2—682 95
Kwangsi Chuang Autonomous Region (China) T2—512 8
Kwangtung Province (China) T2—512 7
Kwara State (Nigeria) T2—669 57
Kwashiorkor
medicine 616.396
see also Digestive system
KwaZulu (South Africa) T2—684 91
Kweichow Province (China) T2—513 4
Kwese language 496.393
T6—963 93
KWIC indexing 025.486
KWOC indexing 025.486
Kyabram (Vic.) T2—945 4
Kyanite
mineralogy 549.62
Kyïvs′ka oblast′ (Ukraine) T2—477 7
Kyklades (Greece) T2—495 85
Kyle and Carrick (Scotland) T2—414 64
Kymi (Finland : Lääni) T2—489 71
Kyogle (N.S.W.) T2—944 3
Kyoto (Japan) T2—521 864
Kyoto (Japan : Prefecture) T2—521 86
Kyrgyzstan T2—584 3
Kyrie 264.36
music 782.323 2
Kythēra Island (Greece) T2—495 2
Kyūshū Island (Japan) T2—522
Kyūshū Region (Japan) T2—522
Kyustendil (Bulgaria : Okrŭg) T2—499 8
Kyusyu Island (Japan) T2—522
Kyusyu Region (Japan) T2—522

L

La Altagracia (Dominican Republic : Province) T2—729 385
La Coruña (Spain : Province) T2—461 1
La Côte-de-Beaupré (Quebec) T2—714 48
La Côte-de-Gaspé (Quebec) T2—714 79
La Crosse County (Wis.) T2—775 71
La Estrelleta (Dominican Republic : Province) T2—729 343
La Guajira (Colombia : Dept.) T2—861 17
La Habana (Cuba) T2—729 123
La Habana (Cuba : Province) T2—729 124
La Haute-Côte-Nord (Quebec) T2—714 17
La Haute-Yamaska (Quebec) T2—714 63
La Jacques-Cartier (Quebec) T2—714 47
La Libertad (El Salvador : Dept.) T2—728 422
La Libertad (Peru : Dept.) T2—851 6
La Mancha (Spain) T2—464
La Matapédia (Quebec : Regional County Municipality) T2—714 775
La Mitis (Quebec) T2—714 771

La Moure County (N.D.) T2—784 53
La Nouvelle-Beauce (Quebec) T2—714 71
La Pampa (Argentina : Province) T2—821 3
La Paz (Bolivia : Dept.) T2—841 2
La Paz (El Salvador : Dept.) T2—728 425
La Paz (Honduras : Dept.) T2—728 36
La Paz County (Ariz.) T2—791 72
La Perouse Strait 551.465 53
  T2—164 53
La Plata County (Colo.) T2—788 29
La Porte County (Ind.) T2—772 91
La Rioja (Argentina : Province) T2—824 6
La Rioja (Spain) T2—463 54
La Rivière-du-Nord (Quebec) T2—714 24
La Romana (Dominican Republic : Province) T2—729 383
La Salle County (Ill.) T2—773 27
La Salle County (Tex.) T2—764 453
La Salle Parish (La.) T2—763 75
La Spezia (Italy : Province) T2—451 83
La Unión (El Salvador : Dept) T2—728 434
La Union (Philippines) T2—599 1
La Vallée-de-la-Gatineau (Quebec) T2—714 221
La Vallée-du-Richelieu (Quebec : Regional County Municipality) T2—714 36
La Vega (Dominican Republic) T2—729 369 7
La Vérendrye Provincial Park (Quebec) T2—714 21
Laadi language 496.393 1
  T6—963 931
Laâyoune (Morocco : Province) T2—648
Labanotation 792.82
Labeling
  library materials 025.7
  production management 658.564
  regulation 343.082
Labelle (Quebec : County) T2—714 225
Labels
  illustration 741.692
  stamps
    prints 769.57
Labette County (Kan.) T2—781 96
Labiatae 583.96
Labor 331
  economics 331
  ethics 174
    religion 291.564
      Christianity 241.64
      Judaism 296.364
    see also Ethical problems
  income distribution
    macroeconomics 339.21
  international law 341.763
  law 344.01
  literature 808.803 55
    history and criticism 809.933 55
    specific literatures T3B—080 355
      history and criticism T3B—093 55
  psychology 158.7
  public administration 354.9
  religion 291.178 5
    Christianity 261.85
      guides to life 248.88
    Judaism 296.383
  social aspects 306.36
  see also Laboring classes
Labor (Obstetrics) 618.4
  complications 618.5
Labor and capital 331.011
Labor banks 332.37
Labor conditions 331.2
Labor contracts 331.891
  see also Collective bargaining
Labor costs
  financial management 658.155 3
  production economics 338.512
Labor demand 331.123
Labor discipline
  labor economics 331.259 8
  personnel management 658.314
Labor economics 331
  see Manual at 331 vs. 658.3
Labor estimates T1—029 9
  building construction 692.5
Labor exchanges 331.128
Labor force 331.11
  see Manual at 331.1 vs. 331.11, 331.12
Labor grievances 331.889 6
  see also Grievances (Labor)
Labor groups
  relations with government 322.2
Labor injunctions
  economics 331.893
  law 344.018 93
Labor law 344.01
  international 341.763

Labor leaders 331.880 92
  occupational group T7—331 8
Labor-management bargaining 331.89
  see also Collective bargaining
Labor market 331.12
  government policy 331.120 42
    see Manual at 331.12042
      vs. 331.1377
  maladjustments 331.13
  see Manual at 331.1 vs.
    331.11, 331.12
Labor mobility
  economics 331.127
Labor movements 331.8
  economics 331.8
  relations with government 322.2
Labor need 331.123
Labor parties 324.217
  international organizations 324.17
Labor Party (Australia) 324.294 07
Labor productivity 331.118
  economics 331.118
  promotion of
    personnel management 658.314
Labor relations 331
  counseling
    personnel management 658.315 1
  economics 331
  law 344.01
  personnel management 658.315
    T1—068 3
    military personnel 355.33
    public administration 352.68
  public administration 354.9
  see Manual at 331 vs. 331.8;
    also at 331 vs. 658.3
Labor requirements 331.123
Labor rights 331.011
  law 344.010 1
Labor shortages 331.136
Labor supply 331.11
  see Manual at 331.1 vs.
    331.11, 331.12
Labor surpluses 331.136
Labor systems
  economics 331.117
  sociology 306.36
Labor theory of value
  Marxian theory 335.412
Labor turnover 331.126
  economics 331.126
  personnel management 658.314
Labor unions 331.88
  accounting 657.861
Labor unions (continued)
  benefits 331.873 5
  elections 331.874
  law 344.018 8
  personnel management 658.315 3
    public administration 352.68
  public administration 354.97
  relations with government 322.2
  social welfare 361.766
  women workers 331.478
Labor use
  agricultural industries 338.16
Labor violence
  economics 331.893
Laboratories 001.4
  architecture 727.5
  institutional housekeeping 647.995
  school facilities 371.623
Laboratory animals 619
  care and maintenance 636.088 5
  medicine 619
Laboratory diagnosis
  medicine 616.075 6
Laboratory manuals T1—078
  research T1—072
Laboratory method 371.382
Laboratory mice
  animal husbandry 636.935 3
Laboratory rats
  animal husbandry 636.935 2
Laborers 331.11
  social class 305.562
    T1—086 24
  see also Laboring classes;
    Workers
Laboring classes 305.562
  T1—086 23
  civil rights 323.322 3
  customs 390.1
    dress 391.01
  lower class T1—086 24
  middle class T1—086 23
  relation to government 323.322 3
  social welfare 362.85
    public administration 354.9
Laboulbeniales 579.567
Labour Party (Great Britain) 324.241 07
Labrador (Nfld.) 971.82
  T2—718 2
Labrador Current 551.471 4
Labrador Sea 551.461 43
  T2—163 43
Labuan T2—595 3
Labyrinth fishes 597.7

Labyrinthodontia	567.8
Labyrinths (Ears)	
human anatomy	611.85
human physiology	612.858
otology	617.882
see also Ears	
Lac la Biche (Alta.)	T2—712 33
Lac qui Parle County (Minn.)	T2—776 38
Lac-Saint-Charles (Quebec)	T2—714 471
Lac-Saint-Jean-Est (Quebec : Regional County Municipality)	T2—714 14
Lac-Saint-Jean Region (Quebec)	T2—714 14
Lacandón dialect	497.415 27
	T6—974 152
Lacandón Indians	T5—974 152
Laccadive, Minicoy, and Amindivi Islands (India)	T2—548 1
Laccadive Sea	551.467 37
	T2—165 37
Laccoliths	551.88
Lacerations (Wounds)	
medicine	617.143
Laces	677.653
arts	746.22
manufacturing technology	677.653
Lacewings	595.747
Lachlan River (N.S.W.)	T2—944 9
Lacings	677.76
Lackawanna County (Pa.)	T2—748 36
Laclede County (Mo.)	T2—778 815
Laconia (Greece)	T2—495 22
ancient	T2—389
Lacquering	667.75
decorative arts	745.726
furniture arts	749.5
woodwork	
buildings	698.34
Lacrimal apparatus	
ophthalmology	617.764
Lacrimal mechanisms	
human physiology	612.847
see also Eyes	
Lacrosse (Game)	796.347
see also Sports	
Lacrosse players	796.347 092
sports group	T7—796 34
Lactation	573.679
biology	573.679
human physiology	612.664
Lactation (continued)	
obstetrics	618.71
Lactobacillus	579.37
Lactococcus	579.355
Lactose	572.565
biochemistry	572.565
chemistry	547.781 5
see also Carbohydrates	
Lactose intolerance	
medicine	616.399 8
see also Digestive system	
Ladin language	459.9
	T6—599
Ladin literature	859.9
Ladino language	467.949 6
	T6—67
Ladino literature	860
Ladismith (South Africa : District)	T2—687 16
Ladoga Lake (Russia)	T2—471 5
Lady Frere (South Africa : District)	T2—687 91
Lady Grey (South Africa : District)	T2—687 6
Ladybrand (South Africa : District)	T2—685 5
Ladybugs	595.769
culture	638.576 9
Ladysmith (South Africa)	T2—684 7
Lae (Papua New Guinea)	T2—957 1
Lafayette County (Ark.)	T2—767 57
Lafayette County (Fla.)	T2—759 816
Lafayette County (Miss.)	T2—762 83
Lafayette County (Mo.)	T2—778 453
Lafayette County (Wis.)	T2—775 79
Lafayette Parish (La.)	T2—763 47
Lafourche Parish (La.)	T2—763 39
Lag b'Omer	296.439
liturgy	296.453 9
Laghouat (Algeria : Province)	T2—657
Lagomorpha	599.32
paleozoology	569.32
Lagoons	551.460 9
	T2—168
freshwater biology	578.763
freshwater ecology	577.63
freshwater hydrology	551.482
oceanography	551.460 9
Lagopus	598.633
Lagos (Chile : Region)	T2—835
Lagos State (Nigeria)	T2—669 1
LaGrange County (Ind.)	T2—772 79
Lagrange polynomials	515.55

Laguerre polynomials 515.55
Laguna (Philippines : Province) T2—599 1
Lahn River (Germany) T2—434 14
Lahnda language 491.419
T6—914 19
Lahnda literature 891.419
Lahore District (Pakistan) T2—549 143
Laingsburg (South Africa : District) T2—687 15
Laissez-faire economics 330.153
Laity (Church members) 262.15
T1—088 204
biography 270.092
specific denominations 280
see Manual at 280
church government 262.15
pastoral theology 253
religious group T7—204
social group 305.6
Lajemmerais (Quebec) T2—714 36
Lak-Dargwa languages 499.964
T6—999 64
Lak language 499.964
T6—999 64
Lake Abitibi (Ont. and Quebec) T2—713 142
Lake Athabasca (Sask. and Alta.) T2—712 41
Lake Barkley (Ky. and Tenn.) T2—769 79
Lake biology 578.763
Lake Champlain T2—747 54
New York T2—747 54
Vermont T2—743 1
Lake Champlain, Battle of, 1814 973.525 6
Lake Clark National Park and Preserve (Alaska) T2—798 6
Lake Constance T2—434 62
Germany T2—434 62
Switzerland T2—494 59
Lake County (Calif.) T2—794 17
Lake County (Colo.) T2—788 46
Lake County (Fla.) T2—759 22
Lake County (Ill.) T2—773 21
Lake County (Ind.) T2—772 99
Lake County (Mich.) T2—774 68
Lake County (Minn.) T2—776 76
Lake County (Mont.) T2—786 832
Lake County (Ohio) T2—771 334
Lake County (Or.) T2—795 93
Lake County (S.D.) T2—783 35
Lake County (Tenn.) T2—768 12
Lake Cumberland (Ky.) T2—769 63
Lake Diefenbaker (Sask.) T2—712 42
Lake District (England) T2—427 8
Lake ecology 577.63
Lake Erie T2—771 2
Ohio T2—771 2
Ontario T2—713 3
Lake Erie, Battle of, 1813 973.525 4
Lake Eyre (S. Aust.) T2—942 38
Lake Francis Case (S.D.) T2—783 38
Lake Gairdner (S. Aust.) T2—942 38
Lake Garda (Italy) T2—452 6
Lake Geneva (Switzerland and France) T2—494 52
France T2—444 9
Switzerland T2—494 52
Lake George (N.Y.) T2—747 51
Lake Hawea (N.Z.) T2—939 5
Lake Huron (Mich. and Ont.) T2—774
Michigan T2—774
Ontario T2—713 2
Lake ice 551.345
Lake Kivu (Rwanda and Zaire) T2—675 17
Rwanda T2—675 71
Zaire T2—675 17
Lake Ladoga (Russia) T2—471 5
Lake Le Roux (South Africa) T2—687 13
Lake liners 386.224 36
design 623.812 436
engineering 623.824 36
see also Ships
Lake Lucerne (Switzerland) T2—494 55
Lake Maggiore (Italy and Switzerland) T2—451 6
Italy T2—451 6
Switzerland T2—494 78
Lake Malawi T2—689 7
Lake Manapouri (N.Z.) T2—939 6
Lake Manitoba (Man.) T2—712 72
Lake Maracaibo (Venezuela) T2—872 3
Lake Martin (Ala.) T2—761 53
Lake Maurepas (La.) T2—763 32
Lake Mead (Ariz. and Nev.) T2—793 12
Lake Mead National Recreation Area (Ariz. and Nev.) T2—793 12
Lake Michigan T2—774
Lake Mweru (Zaire and Zambia) T2—675 18

Lake Nasser (Egypt and Sudan) T2—623
Lake Nipissing (Ont.) T2—713 147
Lake Nyasa T2—689 7
Lake Oahe (S.D. and N.D.) T2—783 5
Lake of Constance T2—434 62
  Germany T2—434 62
  Switzerland T2—494 59
Lake of the Ozarks (Mo.) T2—778 493
Lake of the Woods T2—776 81
  Canada T2—713 11
  Minnesota T2—776 81
Lake of the Woods County (Minn.) T2—776 81
Lake Ohau (N.Z.) T2—938 97
Lake Okeechobee (Fla.) T2—759 39
Lake Onega (Russia) T2—471 5
Lake Ontario (N.Y. and Ont.) T2—747 9
  New York T2—747 9
  Ontario T2—713 5
Lake Pedder National Park (Tas.) T2—946 2
Lake Pontchartrain (La.) T2—763 34
Lake Powell (Utah and Ariz.) T2—792 59
Lake Pukaki (N.Z.) T2—938 8
Lake Rudolf (Kenya and Ethiopia) T2—676 27
Lake Saint Clair (Mich. and Ont.) T2—774 39
  Michigan T2—774 39
  Ontario T2—713 31
Lake Saint Clair (Tas.) T2—946 3
Lake Saint Clair National Park (Tas.) T2—946 3
Lake Saint Marys (Ohio) T2—771 415
Lake Sakakawea (N.D.) T2—784 75
Lake States T2—77
Lake Superior T2—774 9
  Michigan T2—774 9
  Ontario T2—713 12
Lake Tahoe (Calif. and Nev.) T2—794 38
  California T2—794 38
  Nevada T2—793 57
Lake Tanganyika T2—678 28
Lake Taupo (N.Z.) T2—933 9
Lake Te Anau (N.Z.) T2—939 6
Lake Texoma (Okla. and Tex.) T2—766 61
Lake Titicaca (Peru and Bolivia) T2—841 2
  Bolivia T2—841 2
  Peru T2—853 6
Lake transportation 386.5
  see also Inland water transportation
Lake trout 597.554
Lake Turkana (Kenya and Ethiopia) T2—676 27
Lake Victoria T2—678 27
Lake Wakatipu (N.Z.) T2—939 5
Lake Wallenpaupack (Pa.) T2—748 23
Lake Wanaka (N.Z.) T2—939 5
Lake Winnebago (Wis.) T2—775 64
Lake Winnipeg (Man.) T2—712 72
Lake Winnipegosis (Man.) T2—712 72
Lake Winnipesaukee (N.H.) T2—742 4
Lakes 551.482
  T2—169 2
  biology 578.763
  ecology 577.63
  engineering 627.14
  hydrology 551.482
  influence on precipitation 551.577 5
  interactions with atmosphere 551.524 8
  international law 341.444
  landscape architecture 714
  law 346.046 916 3
  recreational resources 333.784 4
  recreational use 797
  resource economics 333.916 3
  water supply engineering 628.112
Lakes Entrance (Vic.) T2—945 6
Lakōnia (Greece) T2—495 22
  ancient T2—389
Lakota Indians T5—975 2
Lakshadweep (India) T2—548 1
Lama (Genus) 599.636 7
Lamaism 294.392 3
Lamar County (Ala.) T2—761 86
Lamar County (Ga.) T2—758 446
Lamar County (Miss.) T2—762 19
Lamar County (Tex.) T2—764 263
Lamarckism 576.827
Lamb (Meat) 641.363
  commercial processing 664.92
  cooking 641.663
  food 641.363
Lamb County (Tex.) T2—764 843
Lamba language 496.391
  T6—963 91
Lambayeque (Peru : Dept.) T2—851 4
Lambda calculus 511.3

Lambeth (London, England)	T2—421 65
Lambton (Ont.)	T2—713 27
Lamé	677.616
Lamellibranchia	594.4
Lamellicornia	595.764 9
Lamentations (Bible)	224.3
Lamiales	583.96
L'Amiante (Quebec)	T2—714 573
Laminar flow	532.052 5
air mechanics	533.62
gas mechanics	533.215
liquid mechanics	532.515
Laminariales	579.887
Laminated fabrics	677.69
see also Textiles	
Laminated glass	666.154
Laminated plastic	668.492
Laminated wood	674.835
materials science	620.12
Laminating plastics	668.414
Lamington National Park (Qld.)	T2—943 2
Lammermuir Hills (Scotland)	T2—413 6
Lamoille County (Vt.)	T2—743 35
Lamp shells	594.68
paleozoology	564.68
Lampasas County (Tex.)	T2—764 513
Lampblack	662.93
Lampedusa (Italy)	T2—458 22
Lampreys	597.2
Lampridiformes	597.64
Lamps	621.32
ceramic arts	738.8
furniture arts	749.63
manufacturing technology	683.83
mining	622.473
see also Lighting	
Lampshades	
handicrafts	745.593 2
Lampyridae	595.764 4
Lamut	T5—941
Lamut language	494.1
	T6—941
LAN (Computer network)	004.68
see also Computer communications	
Lanai (Hawaii)	T2—969 23
Lanao del Norte (Philippines)	T2—599 7
Lanao del Sur (Philippines)	T2—599 7
Lanark (Ont. : County)	T2—713 82
Lanark (Scotland : District)	T2—414 69
Lanaudière Region (Quebec)	T2—714 41
Lancashire (England)	T2—427 6
Lancaster (England : City)	T2—427 69
Lancaster, House of	942.04
English history	942.04
Irish history	941.504
Lancaster County (Neb.)	T2—782 293
Lancaster County (Pa.)	T2—748 15
Lancaster County (S.C.)	T2—757 45
Lancaster County (Va.)	T2—755 22
Lancelets	596.4
Lancers (Cavalry)	357.1
Lances	623.441
Lancewoods	
botany	583.22
forestry	634.973 22
Land	333
	T2—14
economics	333
see Manual at 333.7–333.9 vs. 333; *also at* 333.73–333.78 vs. 333, 333.1–333.5	
financial management	658.152 42
income distribution	
macroeconomics	339.21
investment economics	332.632 42
military reservations	355.79
property law	346.043
public administration	354.34
public land	352.57
resource economics	333.73
Land appraisal	333.332
Land art	709.040 76
Land-atmosphere interactions	551.523
microclimatology	551.66
Land banks	332.31
Land Between the Lakes (Ky. and Tenn.)	T2—769 79
Land birds	598
see also Birds	
Land breezes	551.518 5
Land carnivores	599.7
Land conservation	333.731 6
law	346.046 731 6
Land economics	333
Land forces (Military science)	355
Land gift	333.333
Land-grant colleges	378.054
see also Higher education	
Land grants	
economics	333.16
law	343.025 3

Land gunnery 623.551
Land management (Plant management) 658.2
  public land 352.57
Land nationalization 333.14
  economics 333.14
  law 343.025 2
Land operations 355.4
  Algerian Revolution 965.046 42
  Chaco War 989.207 164 2
  Civil War (England) 942.062 42
  Civil War (Spain) 946.081 42
  Crimean War 947.073 842
  Falkland Islands War 997.110 244 2
  Franco-German War 943.082 42
  Hundred Years' War 944.025 42
  Indo-Pakistan War, 1971 954.920 514 2
  Indochinese War 959.704 142
  Iraqi-Iranian Conflict 955.054 242
  Korean War 951.904 242
  Mexican War 973.623
  military analysis 355.48
  Napoleonic Wars 940.274 2
  Persian Gulf War, 1991 956.704 424 2
  South African War 968.048 4
  Spanish-American War 973.893
  Thirty Years' War 940.244 2
  United States Revolutionary War 973.33
  Vietnamese War 959.704 342
  War of 1812 973.523
  War of the Pacific 983.061 642
  World War I 940.41
  World War II 940.541
Land reclamation 333.731 53
  agriculture 631.6
  ecology 577.272
  hydraulic engineering 627.5
    from the sea 627.549
  law 346.046 731 53
  revegetation 631.64
Land redistribution
  economics 333.31
Land reform
  economics 333.31
  law 346.044
Land resettlement
  economics 333.31
Land resources 333.73
  economics 333.73
  public administration 354.34
  see Manual at 333.73–333.78 vs. 333, 333.1–333.5
Land sailing 796.68
  see also Sports
Land sale 333.333
Land settlement
  economics 333.31
Land slugs 594.38
Land snails 594.38
  see also Snails (Land)
Land subdivision 333.3
  law 346.043 77
  public administration 354.34
Land surveys 333.08
  economics 333.08
    public land 333.18
  technology 526.9
Land tenure 333.3
  agricultural sociology 306.349
  economics 333.3
  law 346.043 2
  sociology 306.32
  see Manual at 333.73–333.78 vs. 333, 333.1–333.5
Land titles 346.043 8
Land transfer 333.33
  economics 333.33
  law 346.043 6
Land transportation 388
  engineering 629.049
  military engineering 623.61
  see also Ground transportation
Land trusts
  law 346.068
Land use 333.73
  agricultural surveys 631.47
    see Manual at 631.474–631.479 vs. 631.494–631.499
  community sociology 307.33
  economics 333.73
  law 346.045
  see Manual at 333.73–333.78 vs. 333, 333.1–333.5
Land valuation 333.332
Land vehicles 388
  engineering 629.049
  transportation services 388
  see also Automotive vehicles
Land vertebrates 596
  see also Vertebrates
Landed gentry 305.523 2
  T1—086 21
Lander County (Nev.) T2—793 33
Landes (France : Dept.) T2—447 72

Landforms 551.41
T2—14
geography 910.914
geomorphology 551.41
physical geography 910.021 4
Landing
aeronautics 629.132 521 3
manned space flight 629.458 8
Landing (Military tactics) 355.422
Landing accidents 363.124 92
see also Air safety
Landing craft 359.835 6
design 623.812 56
engineering 623.825 6
naval equipment 359.835 6
naval units 359.325 6
Landing fields 387.736
see also Airports
Landing lights 629.135 1
Landing systems
aircraft 629.134 381
spacecraft 629.474 2
unmanned spacecraft 629.464 2
Landkreise 320.83
see also Counties
Landlord and tenant 333.54
land economics 333.54
law 346.043 4
Landlords' liability insurance 368.56
see also Insurance
Landowners 333.009 2
occupational group T7—333
Landowning classes 305.523 2
T1—086 21
Landsailing 796.68
see also Sports
Landscape architects 712.092
occupational group T7—71
Landscape architecture 712
engineering aspects 624
Landscape design 712
Landscapes
art representation 704.943 6
arts 700.42
T3C—32
drawing 743.836
literature 808.803 2
history and criticism 809.933 2
specific literatures T3B—080 32
history and criticism T3B—093 2
painting 758.1
Landshut (Germany) T2—433 58
Landslides 551.307
Landsmål language 439.83
T6—398 3
Landsmål literature 839.83
Lane County (Kan.) T2—781 45
Lane County (Or.) T2—795 31
Langbaurgh-on-Tees
(England) T2—428 54
Langeland (Denmark) T2—489 4
Langlade County (Wis.) T2—775 354
Langley (B.C.) T2—711 33
Language 400
T1—014
animal communication 591.59
elementary education 372.6
law 344.09
philosophy
philosophical works 121.68
see Manual at 401 vs.
121.68, 149.94, 410.1:
Philosophy of language
sociology 306.44
see Manual at 400 vs. 800;
also at 909, 930–990 vs.
400
Language acquisition 401.93
see Manual at 407.1, T1—071
vs. 401.93, 410.71,
418.0071, T4—80071
Language arts
elementary education 372.6
Language disorders
medicine 616.855
see also Communicative
disorders
Language for special purposes 418
applied linguistics 418
specific languages T4—8
Language groups
sociology 305.7
Language planning 306.449
Language policy 306.449
Language programs
public administration 353.7
Language regions T2—175
Language textbooks
audio-lingual approach T4—83
for nonnative speakers T4—834
formal approach T4—82
for nonnative speakers T4—824
see Manual at 420–490:
Language vs. subject
Language translators
engineering 621.389 4

Language usage 418
elementary education 372.61
specific languages T4—8
Languages 400
see also Language
Langue d'oc 449
T6—491
Langue d'oc literature 849
Languedoc (France) T2—448
Languedoc-Roussillon (France) T2—448
Lanier County (Ga.) T2—758 817
Laniidae 598.862
Lanolin 665.13
Lansdowne, Henry Charles Keith Petty-FitzMaurice, Marquess of
Indian history 954.035 4
Lansing (Mich.) T2—774 27
Lantern-eyed fishes 597.64
Lantern fishes 597.61
Lanthanide series
chemistry 546.41
economic geology 553.494
metallurgy 669.291
see also Rare earths
Lanthanum
chemistry 546.411
see also Rare earths
Lanuvian language 479.4
T6—794
Lao (Tai people) T5—959 191
Lao language 495.919 1
T6—959 191
Lao literature 895.919 1
Laoighis (Ireland) T2—418 7
Laois (Ireland) T2—418 7
Laos 959.4
T2—594
Lap robes
manufacturing technology 677.626
Laparoscopic surgery 617.550 59
gynecology 618.105 9
Laparoscopy
diagnosis 617.550 754 5
gynecology 618.107 545
surgery 617.550 59
Lapeer County (Mich.) T2—774 42
Lapidary work 736.202 8
Lapin lääni (Finland) T2—489 77
Laplace functions 515.53
Laplace transform 515.723
Lapland T2—489 77
Lapp language 494.55
T6—945 5
Lapp literature 894.55
Lappet embroidery 677.77
Lappi (Finland : Lääni) T2—489 77
Lapping tools 621.922
Lappish language 494.55
T6—945 5
Lappish literature 894.55
Lapps T5—945 5
Laprairie (Quebec : County) T2—714 34
Lapse
insurance 368.016
Laptev Sea (Russia) 551.468 5
T2—163 25
Laptop computers 004.16
see also Microcomputers
Lapwings 598.33
L'Aquila (Italy : Province) T2—457 11
Lara (Venezuela) T2—872 5
Laramie County (Wyo.) T2—787 19
Laramie Mountains (Wyo. and Colo.) T2—787 9
Larceny 364.162
see also Theft
Larceny insurance 368.82
see also Insurance
Larches 585.2
forestry 634.975 7
lumber 674.144
ornamental arboriculture 635.977 52
Lard
food technology 664.34
Large business 338.644
economics 338.644
management 658.023
personnel management 658.303
Large intestine 573.379
biology 573.379
human anatomy 611.347
human physiology 612.36
surgery 617.554 7
see also Digestive system
Large-print publications
bibliographies 011.63
cataloging 025.349
library treatment 025.179
Large-scale digital computers 004.12
see also Mainframe computers
Large-scale systems 003.71

Large-type publications
  bibliographies 011.63
  cataloging 025.349
  library treatment 025.179
Largemouth bass 597.738 8
  culture 639.377 388
  sports fishing 799.177 388
Lari 598.338
Laridae 598.338
Larimer County (Colo.) T2—788 68
Larisa (Greece : Nome) T2—495 4
Larks 598.825
Larkspurs 635.933 34
  botany 583.34
  floriculture 635.933 34
Larne (Northern Ireland : Borough) T2—416 16
Larue County (Ky.) T2—769 713
Larvacea 596.2
Laryngology 616.22
  see also Respiratory system
Larynx 573.925
  biology 573.925
  human anatomy 611.22
  human physiology 612.2
    speech 612.78
  medicine 616.22
  surgery 617.533
  see also Respiratory system
Las Animas County (Colo.) T2—788 96
Las Palmas (Canary Islands : Province) T2—649
Las Tunas (Cuba : Province) T2—729 162
Las Vegas (Nev.) T2—793 135
Las Villas (Cuba : Province) T2—729 14
Laser communications
  engineering 621.382 7
Laser optical discs 384.558
  see also Video recordings
Laser printing 686.233
Laser surgery 617.05
Laser warfare 358.39
Laser weapons
  engineering 623.446
Laser welding 671.52
Lasers 621.366
Lashley, Karl Spencer
  psychological system 150.194 32
Lasithi (Greece) T2—495 9
Lasqueti Island (B.C.) T2—711 31
Lassen County (Calif.) T2—794 26
Lassen Volcanic National Park (Calif.) T2—794 24
L'Assomption (Quebec : County) T2—714 416
L'Assomption (Quebec : Regional County Municipality) T2—714 416
Lassos
  sports 799.202 82
Last Judgment
  Christianity 236.9
Last Supper 232.957
Latah County (Idaho) T2—796 86
Latakia (Syria : Province) T2—569 13
Latches 683.31
Latent heat 536.4
  chemical engineering 660.296 2
  evaporation and condensation 536.44
  fusion and solidification 536.42
  thermochemistry 541.362
Latent structure analysis 519.535
Later Prophets (Biblical books) 224
Laterality
  psychology 152.335
Latex biscuits 678.522
Latex paints 667.63
Latexes
  chemistry 547.842 5
  manufacturing technology 678.5
Lathers 541.345 14
  chemical engineering 660.294 514
  colloid chemistry 541.345 14
Lathes 621.942
Lathing 693.6
  architectural construction 721.044 6
Latidae 597.72
Latimer County (Okla.) T2—766 76
Latin America 980
  T2—8
Latin American literature 860
Latin American Spanish dialects 467.98
  T6—61
Latin Americans T5—68
Latin calligraphy 745.619 7
Latin grammar schools 373.242
  see also Secondary education
Latin language 470
  T6—71
  Biblical texts 220.47
  see Manual at 471–475, 478 vs. 477
Latin literature 870
Latin peoples T5—4
Latin squares 511.64

Latina (Italy : Province) T2—456 23
Latinian languages 479.4
T6—794
Latitude 526.61
celestial navigation 527.1
Latium (Italy) T2—456 2
ancient T2—376
Latter-Day Saints
biography 289.309 2
religious group T7—283
Latter-Day Saints Church 289.3
see also Mormon Church
Lattice dynamics
solid-state physics 530.411
Lattice-girder bridges 388
construction 624.37
see also Bridges
Lattice plant 584.74
Lattice point geometry 516.35
Lattices (Crystals) 548.81
Lattices (Mathematics) 511.33
number theory 512.7
Latvia 947.96
T2—479 6
Latvian language 491.93
T6—919 3
Latvian literature 891.93
Latvians T5—919 3
Lauderdale County (Ala.) T2—761 99
Lauderdale County (Miss.) T2—762 676
Lauderdale County (Tenn.) T2—768 16
Lauds 264.15
music 782.324
see also Liturgy of the hours
Laughter
psychology 152.43
Launceston (Tas.) T2—946 5
Launch complexes
guided missiles 623.451 9
spacecraft 629.478
Launch vehicles
guided missiles 623.451 9
Launching
manned space flight 629.452
space flight 629.41
unmanned space flight 629.432
Launderers
occupational group T7—648
Laundering 667.13
home economics 648.1
Laundries 667.13
plumbing 696.183
sanitation services 363.729 9
see also Waste control
Laurales 583.23
Laurel County (Ky.) T2—769 143
Laurel wax 665.12
Laurels 583.23
Laurels (Ericaceae) 583.66
Laurels (Lauraceae) 583.23
Laurels (Saxifragales) 583.72
Laurens County (Ga.) T2—758 535
Laurens County (S.C.) T2—757 31
Laurentian Mountains
(Quebec) T2—714 24
Laurentian Plateau T2—714
Ontario T2—713 1
Quebec T2—714
Laurentides (Quebec) T2—714 24
Laurentides Provincial
Park (Quebec) T2—714 4
Laurier, Wilfred, Sir
Canadian history 971.056
Lava 552.22
Lava Beds National
Monument (Calif.) T2—794 21
Lavaca County (Tex.) T2—764 255
Laval (Quebec) T2—714 271
Lavalieres 391.7
customs 391.7
making 739.278
see also Jewelry
Lavalleja (Uruguay : Dept.) T2—895 21
Lavatories 643.52
home economics 643.52
plumbing 696.182
Lavenders (Plants) 583.96
Law 340
information systems 025.063 4
literature 808.803 55
history and criticism 809.933 55
specific literatures T3B—080 355
history and criticism T3B—093 55
religious 291.84
see also Religious law
specific jurisdictions 349.4–.9
see Manual at
340.02–340.09 vs. 349;
also at 342–349
specific socioeconomic
regions 349.1
see Manual at 340: Forms of
legal literature; *also at*
363 vs. 340, 353–354
Law (Theology)
Christianity 241.2
Judaism 296.18
Law and ethics 340.112

Law and gospel 241.2
Law and morality 340.112
Law and society 340.115
Law codification 348.004
  international law 341.026 7
  United States 348.730 4
Law enforcement 363.23
  armed forces 355.133 23
  law 345.052
  public administration 353.36
  see Manual at 363 vs. 340, 353–354: Law enforcement
Law libraries 026.34
Law of falling bodies 531.5
Law of God
  Christianity 241.2
Law of supply and demand
  microeconomics 338.521
Law reform 340.3
Law reports 348.04
  national 348.041
  provincial 348.043
  regional 348.042
  state 348.043
Law schools 340.071 1
Lawn bowling 796.315
  see also Sports
Lawn tennis 796.342
  see also Sports
Lawns
  floriculture 635.964 7
  landscape architecture 712.6
Lawrence, John Laird Mair, Baron
  Indian history 954.035 1
Lawrence County (Ala.) T2—761 92
Lawrence County (Ark.) T2—767 25
Lawrence County (Ill.) T2—773 76
Lawrence County (Ind.) T2—772 26
Lawrence County (Ky.) T2—769 26
Lawrence County (Miss.) T2—762 536
Lawrence County (Mo.) T2—778 75
Lawrence County (Ohio) T2—771 88
Lawrence County (Pa.) T2—748 93
Lawrence County (S.D.) T2—783 91
Lawrence County (Tenn.) T2—768 42
Lawrencium 546.449
  see also Chemicals
Laws (Compilations) 348.02
  United States 348.732
Laws (Enactment and repeal) 328.37
Laws of thermodynamics 536.71
Lawsuits 347.053
  procedure 347.050 4
Lawyers 340.092
  malpractice 347.050 41
  occupational ethics 174.3
  occupational group T7—344
  practice 347.050 4
Laxatives
  pharmacodynamics 615.732
  see also Digestive system
Lay brothers
  religious orders 255.093
    church history 271.093
Lay ministry 253
  ecclesiology 262.15
  pastoral theology 253
Lay sisters
  religious orders 255.909 3
    church history 271.909 3
Layering (Plant propagation) 631.534
Laying on of hands (Christian rite) 265.9
Laylat al-Barā'ah 297.36
Laylat al-Mi'rāj 297.36
Laylat al-Qadr 297.362
Laymen (Church members) 262.15
  see also Laity (Church members)
Layoffs of employees
  economics 331.259 6
    employment security 331.259 6
    unemployment 331.137
    union control 331.889 4
  law 344.012 596
  personnel management 658.313 4
    public administration 352.69
Layout
  plant management 658.23
  typesetting 686.225 2
Laz language 499.968
  T6—999 68
Lazarists 255.77
  church history 271.77
Lazio (Italy) T2—456 2
Le Bas-Richelieu (Quebec) T2—714 51
Le Centre-de-la-Mauricie (Quebec) T2—714 451
Le Chatelier's principle 541.392
Le Domaine-du-Roy (Quebec) T2—714 14
Le Fjord-du-Saguenay (Quebec) T2—714 16
Le Flore County (Okla.) T2—766 79
Le Granit (Quebec) T2—714 69

Le Haut-Richelieu (Quebec) T2—714 61
Le Haut-Saint-François (Quebec) T2—714 68
Le Haut-Saint-Laurent (Quebec) T2—714 31
Le Haut-Saint-Maurice (Quebec) T2—714 45
Le Roux, Lake (South Africa) T2—687 13
Le Sueur County (Minn.) T2—776 553
Le Val-Saint-François (Quebec) T2—714 65
Lea County (N.M.) T2—789 33
Leach mining wells 622.22
Lead 669.4
  architectural construction 721.044 74
  building construction 693.74
  building material 691.84
  chemical engineering 661.068 8
  chemistry 546.688
  decorative arts 739.54
  economic geology 553.44
  human toxicology 615.925 688
  materials science 620.183
  metallography 669.954
  metallurgy 669.4
  metalworking 673.4
  mining 622.344
  organic chemistry
    applied 661.895
  physical metallurgy 669.964
  pollution 363.738 4
    see also Pollution
  public safety 363.179 1
    see also Hazardous materials
  see also Chemicals; Metals
Lead soldiers
  handicrafts 745.592 82
Leaded glass
  arts 748.5
Leadership 303.34
  armed forces 355.330 41
  Christian church 262.1
    local church 253
  executive management 658.409 2
    public administration 352.39
  political parties 324.22
  psychology 158.4
  social control 303.34
Leadership role of chief executives 658.409 2
  public administration 352.236
Leading windows
  buildings 698.5
Leadworts 583.5
Leaf beetles 595.764 8
  agricultural pests 632.764 8
Leaf frogs 597.87
Leaf hoppers 595.752
Leaf insects 595.729
Leaf miner flies 595.774
Leaf miners
  agricultural pests 632.7
Leafhoppers
  agricultural pests 632.752
League of Arab States 341.247 7
  finance 336.091 68
League of Augsburg, War of the, 1688–1697 940.252 5
  North American history 973.25
League of Nations 341.22
  finance 336.091 62
  international law 341.22
  public administration 352.112
League of Nations treaties series 341.026 1
League soccer 796.334 63
Leake County (Miss.) T2—762 653
Leapfrog (Game) 796.14
Learned societies 060
  libraries 027.68
  publishing 070.594
Learned society buildings
  architecture 727.9
Learning 153.15
  animal behavior 591.514
  comparative psychology 156.315
  educational psychology 370.152 3
  psychology 153.15
    children 155.413 15
    see Manual at 153.15 vs. 370.15; *also at* 155.4–155.6 vs. 153.15
Learning (Scholarship) 001.2
Learning ability 153.9
Learning curves 153.158
Learning disabilities 371.9
  medicine 616.858 89
  see also Mental retardation
Learning-disabled persons T1—087
  education 371.9
Lease system
  penology 365.65
Leases
  accounting 657.75
  equipment
    financial management 658.152 42

Leases (continued)
  personal property
    law 346.047
  real property 333.5
    economics 333.5
    financial management 658.152 42
    law 346.043 46
Least squares 511.42
Leather 675
  handicrafts 745.531
  home sewing material 646.1
Leather clothing 391
  commercial technology 685.22
  customs 391
  home sewing 646.4
  see also Clothing
Leather covers
  bookbinding 686.342
Leather fungi 579.6
Leather goods
  commercial technology 685
Leather goods makers 685.092
  occupational group T7—685
Leather workers 675.209 2
  occupational group T7—675
Leatherjackets (Crane fly larvae) 595.772
  agricultural pests 633.104 977 2
Leavening agents 664.68
Leavenworth County (Kan.) T2—781 38
Leaves (Absences) 331.257 6
  armed forces 355.113
  labor economics 331.257 6
  personnel management 658.312 2
    public administration 352.67
Leaves (Plants) 581.48
  descriptive botany 581.48
  physiology 575.57
Lebanese T5—927 569 2
Lebanon 956.92
  T2—569 2
  ancient 939.44
    T2—394 4
Lebanon Conflict, 1982–1985 956.052
Lebanon County (Pa.) T2—748 19
Lebel-sur-Quévillon (Quebec) T2—714 115
Lebesgue integral 515.43
Lebowa (South Africa) T2—682 93
Lebowa-Kgomo (South Africa) T2—682 93
Lecce (Italy : Province) T2—457 53
Lecterns
  church architecture 726.529 2
Lectionaries (Public worship) 264.34
  Anglican 264.030 34
    texts 264.032
  preaching 251.6
  Roman Catholic 264.020 34
    texts 264.029
Lecture method 371.396
  Christian religious education 268.632
Lectures 080
  museum services 069.15
Lecturing
  rhetoric 808.51
Lecythidaceae 583.76
LED (Diodes) 621.381 522
Lee, Charles
  treason 973.383
Lee County (Ala.) T2—761 55
Lee County (Ark.) T2—767 89
Lee County (Fla.) T2—759 48
Lee County (Ga.) T2—758 943
Lee County (Ill.) T2—773 36
Lee County (Iowa) T2—777 99
Lee County (Ky.) T2—769 185
Lee County (Miss.) T2—762 935
Lee County (N.C.) T2—756 355
Lee County (S.C.) T2—757 67
Lee County (Tex.) T2—764 247
Lee County (Va.) T2—755 735
Leeaceae 583.86
Leeches 592.66
Leeching 615.899
Leeds (England : City) T2—428 19
Leeds (Ont. : County) T2—713 73
Leeds and Grenville (Ont.) T2—713 73
Leeks 641.352 6
  botany 584.33
  cooking 641.652 6
  food 641.352 6
  garden crop 635.26
Leelanau County (Mich.) T2—774 635
Leer (Germany : Landkreis) T2—435 917
Leeton (N.S.W.) T2—944 8
Leeward Islands (West Indies) 972.97
  T2—729 7
Leflore County (Miss.) T2—762 46
Left and right (Psychology) 152.335
Left-hand techniques
  music 784.193 66
Left-handedness
  educational psychology 370.155
  psychology 152.335
Leftist parties 324.217
  international organizations 324.17
Leftovers (Cooking) 641.552

Leg muscles
  human anatomy 611.738
  see also Musculoskeletal system
Leg techniques
  music 784.193 8
Lega-Kalanga languages 496.394
  T6—963 94
Legal accounting 657.834
Legal aid 362.58
  law 347.017
    criminal law 345.01
    welfare law 344.032 58
  social services 362.58
Legal codes 348.023
  United States 348.732 3
Legal counsel
  management use 658.12
Legal education 340.07
Legal ethics 174.3
Legal malpractice 347.050 41
Legal officers 347.016
  occupational group T7—349
Legal positivism 340.112
Legal procedure 347.05
Legal process 347.05
Legal profession 340.023
  see Manual at 340.023 vs. 347.0504
Legal reasoning 340.11
Legal responsibility 346.03
Legal schools 340.109
Legal services 347
Legal systems 340.5
Legal tender 332.420 42
Legal theories 340.109
Legal writing 808.066 34
  see Manual at 340 vs. 808.06634
Legalism (Chinese philosophy) 181.115
Legations 327.2
  architecture 725.17
  public administration 353.13
Legendary animals 398.245 4
  art representation 704.947
  arts 700.474
  T3C—374
  folklore 398.245 4
    history and criticism 398.469
  literature 808.803 74
    history and criticism 809.933 74
    specific literatures T3B—080 374
      history and criticism T3B—093 74
  mysteries 001.944
Legendary beings 398.21
  art representation 704.947
  arts 700.475
  T3C—375
  folklore 398.21
    history and criticism 398.45
  literature 808.803 75
    history and criticism 809.933 75
    specific literatures T3B—080 375
      history and criticism T3B—093 75
Legendary persons 398.22
  art representation 704.947
  see also Persons
Legendary places 398.234
  art representation 704.947
  arts 700.472
  T3C—372
  folklore 398.234
    history and criticism 398.42
  literature 808.803 72
    history and criticism 809.933 72
    specific literatures T3B—080 372
      history and criticism T3B—093 72
  mysteries 001.94
Legendre function 515.53
Legendre polynomials 515.55
Legendre transform 515.723
Legends
  art representation 704.947
  arts 700.47
  T3C—37
  folklore 398.2
    see Manual at 398.2 vs. 291.13
  literature 808.803 7
    history and criticism 809.933 7
    specific literatures T3B—080 37
      history and criticism T3B—093 7
  paintings 753.7
Leghorn (Poultry) 636.55
Legionella 579.33
Legionnaires' disease
  medicine 616.241
  see also Respiratory system
Legions (Military units) 355.31
Legislation (Compilations) 348.02
Legislation (Enactment and repeal) 328.37
Legislative bodies 328
  bibliographies of publications 011.532
  law 342.05
  see Manual at 909, 930–990 vs. 320: Political activities

Legislative branch	328
law	342.05
Legislative budgets	352.48
see also Budgets (Public)	
Legislative buildings	
architecture	725.11
Legislative calendars	328.4–.9
Legislative duties	328.34
law	342.052
Legislative-executive relations	328.345 6
law	342.044
Legislative functions	328.34
law	342.052
Legislative hearings	328.345
law	348.01
United States	348.731
see Manual at 350 vs. 342–347	
Legislative histories	348.01
United States	348.731
Legislative immunity	328.348
Legislative institutions	
sociology	306.23
Legislative investigation	328.345 2
Legislative journals	328.4–.9
Legislative-judicial relations	320.404
law	342.044
Legislative organization	328.36
law	342.057
Legislative oversight	328.345 6
Legislative powers	328.34
chief executives	352.235
law	342.052
Legislative privileges	328.347
Legislative procedures	328.1
law	342.057
Legislative process	328
Legislative reference bureaus	027.65
Legislative reform	328.304
Legislative representation	328.334
Legislators	
biography	328.092
law	342.055
occupational group	T7—328
personal privileges	328.347
role and function	328.33
Legitimacy of government	320.011
Legitimation	346.017
Legnica (Poland : Voivodeship)	T2—438 5
Legs	591.479
animal physiology	573.79
descriptive zoology	591.479
human physiology	612.98
regional medicine	617.584
surgery	617.584
see also Lower extremities (Human)	
Legumes	583.74
botany	583.74
commercial processing	664.805 65
cooking	641.656 5
edible fruits	641.344 6
cooking	641.644 6
food	641.344 6
orchard crop	634.46
food	641.356 5
forage crop	633.3
garden crop	635.65
see Manual at 633–635: Legumes (633.3 vs. 635.65)	
Leguminales	583.74
see also Legumes	
Lehigh County (Pa.)	T2—748 27
Lehurutshe (South Africa : District)	T2—682 94
Leicester (England)	T2—425 42
Leicestershire (England)	T2—425 4
Leiden (Netherlands)	T2—492 38
Leinster (Ireland)	T2—418
Leiopelmatidae	597.86
Leipzig (Germany)	T2—432 122
Leipzig (Germany : Bezirk)	T2—432 12
Leiria (Portugal : District)	T2—469 42
Leishmaniasis	
incidence	614.534
medicine	616.936 4
see also Communicable diseases (Human)	
Leisure	
educational objective	370.119
influence on crime	364.25
recreational arts	790.013 5
sociology	306.481 2
Leitmotif	781.248
Leitneriales	583.43
Leitrim (Ireland)	T2—417 6
Leix (Ireland)	T2—418 7
Lelystad (Netherlands)	T2—492 2
Lemhi County (Idaho)	T2—796 78
Lemmings	599.358 2
Lemmus	599.358 2

Lemnaceae 584.64
Lemnos Island (Greece) T2—495 82
  ancient T2—391 1
Lemon shark 597.34
Lemons 641.343 34
  commercial processing 664.804 334
  cooking 641.643 34
  food 641.343 34
  orchard crop 634.334
Lempira (Honduras) T2—728 382
Lemuridae 599.83
Lemurs 599.83
  conservation technology 639.979 83
  resource economics 333.959 83
Lenape Indians T5—973
Lenape language 497.3
  T6—973
Lenawee County (Mich.) T2—774 31
Lending institutions 332.1
  law 346.082
  public administration 354.86
Lenin, Vladimir Il´ich
  Russian history 947.084 1
Leningrad (Russia : Oblast) T2—472 1
Leningradskaia͡ oblast´
    (Russia) T2—472 1
Lenje-Tonga languages 496.391
  T6—963 91
Lennox and Addington
    (Ont.) T2—713 59
Lennox Hills (Scotland) T2—413 12
Leno-weave fabrics 677.652
  see also Textiles
Lenoir County (N.C.) T2—756 385
Lenses
  cameras 771.352
  manufacturing technology 681.423
Lent 263.92
  devotional literature 242.34
  sermons 252.62
Lenten cooking 641.566
Lenten music 781.725
Lentibulariaceae 583.95
Lentils 641.356 58
  botany 583.74
  cooking 641.656 58
  food 641.356 58
  garden crop 635.658
Leo (Cat genus) 599.755
Leo (Zodiac) 133.526 6
Leominster (England :
    District) T2—424 44
León (Nicaragua : Dept.) T2—728 512
León (Spain : Province) T2—462 1
León (Spain : Region) T2—462
Leon County (Fla.) T2—759 88
Leon County (Tex.) T2—764 233
Leopard seal 599.796
Leopards 599.755 4
  conservation technology 639.979 755 4
  resource economics 333.959 755 4
Leopold I, Holy Roman Emperor
  German history 943.044
Léopold III, King of the
    Belgians
  Belgian history 949.304 2
Leopoldville (Zaire) T2—675 112
Lepcha language 495.4
  T6—954
Lepidodendrales 561.79
Lepidoptera 595.78
  agricultural pests 632.78
Lepidosauria 597.94
  paleozoology 567.94
Leporidae 599.32
Lepospondyli 567.8
Leprosy
  incidence 614.546
  medicine 616.998
  see also Communicable
      diseases (Human)
Leptis Magna (Extinct city) T2—397 4
Leptodactylidae 597.87
Leptolepis 567
Leptons 539.721 1
Leptostraca 595.379 2
Leptureae 584.9
Lepus 599.328
L'Érable (Quebec) T2—714 575
Lérida (Spain : Province) T2—467 4
Lernaeopodoida 595.34
Les Basques (Quebec) T2—714 76
Les
    Chutes-de-la-Chaudière
    (Quebec) T2—714 59
Les Etchemins (Quebec) T2—714 72
Les Îles-de-la-Madeleine
    (Quebec) T2—714 797
Les Jardins-de-Napierville
    (Quebec) T2—714 35
Les Laurentides (Quebec) T2—714 24
Les Maskoutains (Quebec) T2—714 523
Les Moulins (Quebec) T2—714 24
Les Pays-d'en-Haut
    (Quebec) T2—714 24
Les Saintes Islands
    (Guadeloupe) T2—729 76

Lesbianism 306.766 3
social theology 291.178 357 663
Christianity 261.835 766 3
see also Homosexuality
Lesbians 305.489 664
T1—086 643
Christian pastoral theology 259.086 643
Lesbos (Greece) T2—495 82
Lesbos Island (Greece) T2—495 82
ancient T2—391 2
Leslie County (Ky.) T2—769 152
Lesotho 968.85
T2—688 5
Lesotho people T5—968 85
Lespedezas 633.364
botany 583.74
forage crop 633.364
Less developed countries T2—172 4
Lesser Antilles T2—729
Lesser celandine 583.34
Lesser panda 599.763
Lesser Slave Lake (Alta.) T2—712 31
Lesser Sunda Islands (Indonesia) T2—598 6
Lesson plans 371.302 8
Lesvos (Greece) T2—495 82
Leszno (Poland : Voivodeship) T2—438 4
Letaba (South Africa) T2—682 6
Letcher County (Ky.) T2—769 163
Lethal gases
human toxicology 615.91
Lethbridge (Alta.) T2—712 345
Lethrinidae 597.72
Lettering T1—022 1
architectural design 729.19
bookbinding 686.36
decorative arts 745.61
prints 769.5
stone 736.5
technical drawing 604.243
Letterpress
mechanical printing technique 686.231 2
Letters (Correspondence) 383.122
biography 920
T1—092
direct advertising 659.133
etiquette 395.4
office services 651.75
postal handling 383.122
see also Postal service
Letters (Literature) 808.86
criticism 809.6
theory 808.6
Letters (Literature) (continued)
history 809.6
rhetoric 808.6
specific literatures T3B—6
individual authors T3A—6
see Manual at T3A—6 and T3B—6
Letters of credit 332.77
law 346.096
Letters rogatory 341.78
Lettish language 491.93
T6—919 3
Lettish literature 891.93
Letts T5—919 3
Lettuce 641.355 2
botany 583.99
commercial processing 664.805 52
cooking 641.655 2
food 641.355 2
garden crop 635.52
Lëtzeburgesch dialect 437.949 35
T6—32
Leucite
mineralogy 549.68
Leucocytes 571.96
see also Leukocytes
Leukas (Greece) T2—495 5
Leukemia 362.196 994 19
incidence 614.599 941 9
medicine 616.994 19
social services 362.196 994 19
see also Cancer (Human); Cardiovascular system
Leukocytes 571.96
human cancer
medicine 616.994 19
see also Cancer (Human)
human histology 611.018 5
human immunology 616.079
human physiology 612.112
medicine 616.154
see also Cardiovascular system
Leukocytosis
medicine 616.15
see also Cardiovascular system
Leukopenia
medicine 616.15
see also Cardiovascular system
Leukorrhea
gynecology 618.173
see also Female genital system

Levant T2—56
Levees (Flood barriers) 627.42
Leveling (Surveying) 526.36
Levels of education 372–374
  see Manual at 371 vs. 372–374, 378
Lévis (Quebec : County) T2—714 59
Levitation (Spiritualism) 133.92
Leviticus 222.13
Levy County (Fla.) T2—759 77
Lewes (England : District) T2—422 57
Lewis and Clark County (Mont.) T2—786 615
Lewis County (Idaho) T2—796 84
Lewis County (Ky.) T2—769 295
Lewis County (Mo.) T2—778 345
Lewis County (N.Y.) T2—747 59
Lewis County (Tenn.) T2—768 432
Lewis County (W. Va.) T2—754 61
Lewis County (Wash.) T2—797 82
Lewisham (London, England) T2—421 63
Lexicographers 413.092
  occupational group T7—4
Lexicography 413.028
  T1—03
  specific languages T4—302 8
Lexicology 401.4
  specific languages T4—014
Lexington (Ky.) T2—769 47
Lexington (Mass.) T2—744 4
Lexington (Va.) T2—755 853
Lexington, Battle of, 1775 973.331 1
Lexington County (S.C.) T2—757 73
Leyte (Philippines) T2—599 5
Leyte Island (Philippines) T2—599 5
Lezghi language 499.964
  T6—999 64
Lezghian language 499.964
  T6—999 64
Lhasa apso 636.72
Lhomi language 495.4
  T6—954
Liability 346.02
  government 342.088
  schools 344.075
Liability insurance 368.5
  law 346.086 5
  see also Insurance
Liability risks 368.08
Liaoning Province (China) T2—518 2
Liard River T2—711 87
Libel 364.156
  law 345.025 6
    criminal law 345.025 6
    torts 346.034
Liberal Catholic Church 284.8
  see also Old Catholic churches
Liberal education 370.112
Liberal parties 324.216
  international organizations 324.16
Liberal Party (Great Britain) 324.241 06
Liberal Party of Australia 324.294 05
Liberal Party of Canada 324.271 06
Liberal Party of New York State 324.274 707
Liberal theology 230.046
Liberalism
  philosophy 148
  political ideology 320.51
Liberality
  ethics 177.7
Liberation theology 230.046 4
  political aspects 261.7
  Roman Catholic 230.2
  socioeconomic aspects 261.8
Liberia 966.62
  T2—666 2
Liberians T5—966 62
Libertad (El Salvador : Dept.) T2—728 422
Libertad (Peru : Dept.) T2—851 6
Libertador General Bernardo O'Higgins (Chile) T2—833 2
Libertarian parties 324.218
  international organizations 324.18
Libertarianism 320.512
Liberty (Personal freedom) 323.44
  philosophy 123.5
  public administrative support 353.48
Liberty (Political theory) 320.011
Liberty County (Fla.) T2—759 923
Liberty County (Ga.) T2—758 733
Liberty County (Mont.) T2—786 13
Liberty County (Tex.) T2—764 155
Libido 155.31
Libode (South Africa : District) T2—687 91
Libra (Zodiac) 133.527 2
Librarians 020.92
  library operations
    role and function 023.2
  occupational group T7—092

Libraries	027
accounting	657.832
armed forces	355.346
law	344.092
operations	025
see Manual at 020; *also at* 026–027	
public administrative support	352.744
publications for	
bibliographies	011.67
reviews	028.167
publishing	070.594
relationships	021
residential interior decoration	747.73
Libraries and museums	021.3
Library acquisitions	025.2
Library administration	025.1
Library aides	023.3
Library and state	021.8
Library assistants	023.3
Library boards	021.82
Library bookbinding	686.303 2
Library buildings	
architecture	727.8
area planning	711.57
institutional housekeeping	647.998
planning	022.3
Library catalogs	025.31
bibliography	017
library science	025.31
maintenance	025.317
Library clerks	023.3
Library collections	
maintenance	025.8
Library commissions	021.82
Library-community relations	021.2
Library consortia	021.65
Library consultants	023.2
Library cooperation	021.64
Library equipment	022.9
Library-government relations	021.8
Library information networks	021.65
Library materials	
preservation	025.84
selection policy	025.21
Library networks	021.65
Library of Congress	027.573
Library of Congress Classification	025.433
Library orientation	025.56
Library paraprofessionals	023.3
Library regulations	025.56
Library science	020
see Manual at 020	
Library signs	025.56
Library systems	
cooperation	021.65
operations	025
Library systems analysts	023.2
Library technicians	023.3
Library trustees	021.82
Library use studies	025.58
Librettos	780
treatises	780.268
Libreville (Gabon)	T2—672 1
Libya	961.2
	T2—612
ancient	939.74
	T2—397 4
Libyan Desert	T2—612
Libyans	T5—927 612
Lice	595.756
disease carriers	571.986
medicine	614.432 4
License agreements	343.07
international law	341.758
License fees	
public revenues	336.16
License plates	929.9
Licensing	352.84
economic law	343.07
enforcement	363.233
export trade	382.64
see also Export trade	
import trade	382.54
see also Import trade	
intangible property law	346.048
public administration	352.84
Licensing Appeals Court (Scotland)	347.411 04
Licensing Courts (Scotland)	347.411 04
Lichees	641.346
see also Litchis	
Lichens	579.7
Lichfield (England : District)	T2—424 68
Lichtenburg (South Africa : District)	T2—682 4
Licking County (Ohio)	T2—771 54
Lie algebras	512.55
Lie detectors	363.254
civil rights	323.448
criminal investigation	363.254
law of privacy	342.085 8
law of self-incrimination	345.056
personnel management	658.314
selection procedures	658.311 2
Lie groups	512.55

Liechtenstein 943.648
T2—436 48
ancient 936.3
T2—363
Lieder 782.421 68
Liège (Belgium : Province) T2—493 46
Liens
law 346.074
Liesegang rings 541.348 5
Lieutenant governors
public administration 352.239
Life
biological nature 570.1
civil rights issues 323.43
medical ethics 174.24
religion 291.564 24
Christianity 241.642 4
Judaism 296.364 24
origin 576.83
see also Origin of life
philosophy 113.8
respect for
ethics 179.1
religion 291.569 1
Buddhism 294.356 91
Christianity 241.691
Hinduism 294.548 691
Judaism 296.369 1
Life after death
occultism 133.901 3
philosophy 129
religion 291.23
Christianity 236.2
Islam 297.23
Judaism 296.33
philosophy of religion 218
see Manual at 133.9013 vs. 129
Life care communities 362.16
see also Health care facilities; Health services
Life cycle 571.8
animal behavior 591.56
animals 571.81
customs 392
developmental biology 571.8
etiquette 395.2
folklore 398.27
history and criticism 398.354
microorganisms 571.842 9
music 781.58
plants 571.82
Life estates 346.043 2
land economics 333.323 4
Life expectancy 304.645
human physiology 612.68
Life insurance 368.32
law 346.086 32
tax law 343.052 4
see also Insurance
Life on other planets 576.839
Life rafts
aircraft 629.134 43
Life sciences 570
see Manual at 560–590; *also at* 570–590
Life sciences and religion 291.175
Christianity 261.55
philosophy of religion 215.7
Life-support systems
spacecraft 629.477
Lifeboats 387.29
design 623.812 9
engineering 623.829
transportation services 387.29
see also Ships
Lifelong education 374
T1—071 5
see also Adult education
Lifesaving equipment
aircraft 629.134 43
ships 623.865
Liffey River (Ireland) T2—418 3
Lift (Aeronautics) 629.132 33
Lift bridges 388
construction 624.84
see also Bridges
Lift systems
air-cushion vehicles 629.313
Lifts (Canal engineering) 627.135 3
Lifts (Elevators) 621.877
see also Elevators (Lifts)
Ligaments 573.783 56
biology 573.783 56
human anatomy 611.72
human physiology 612.75
medicine 616.77
see also Musculoskeletal system
Ligands 541.224 2
Ligases 572.79
see also Enzymes
Light 535
arts 701.8
drawing 741.018
astrophysics 523.015
biophysics 571.455
humans 612.014 44

Light (continued)	
chemical effect	541.353 3
chemical engineering	660.295 33
engineering	621.36
health	613.19
meteorology	551.565
military engineering	623.042
physics	535
therapeutics	615.831
Light beacons	
construction	627.924
navigation aids	623.894 4
Light-emitting diodes	621.381 522
Light harness horses	636.17
Light lists	
navigation aids	623.894 5
Light metals	669.72
building construction	693.772
building materials	691.872
economic geology	553.492
metallography	669.957 2
metallurgy	669.72
metalworking	673.72
physical metallurgy	669.967 2
Light orchestras	784.4
Light pens	
bar-code scanners	006.42
engineering	621.399
computer graphics	006.62
engineering	621.399
computer input devices	004.76
engineering	621.398 6
Light spectroscopy	543.085 84
analytical chemistry	543.085 84
engineering	621.361 3
physics	535.843
Light trucks	388.343
driving	629.284 3
engineering	629.223
repair	629.287 3
transportation services	388.343
see also Trucks	
Light verse	808.818
history and criticism	809.18
specific literatures	T3B—108
individual authors	T3A—1
Lighter-than-air aircraft	387.732
engineering	629.133 2
military engineering	623.741
sports flying	797.51
transportation services	387.732
see also Aircraft	
Lighters (Ships)	387.245
towed	387.29
see also Ships	
Lighthouses	387.155
engineering	627.922
navigation aid	623.894 2
transportation services	387.155
Lighting	621.32
airport engineering	629.136 5
architectural design	729.28
automobile	629.271
cinematography	778.534 3
customs	392.36
dramatic performances	792.025
motion pictures	791.430 25
stage	792.025
television	791.450 25
engineering	621.32
household management	644.3
interior decoration	747.92
library buildings	022.7
mining	622.47
museums	069.29
photography	778.7
plant management	658.24
public areas	628.95
religious significance	291.37
Christianity	246.6
see also Symbolism—religious significance	
road transportation	388.312
video production	778.592
Lighting fixtures	621.32
ceramic arts	738.8
church architecture	726.529 8
furniture arts	749.63
household management	645.5
manufacturing technology	683.83
see also Lighting	
Lightning	551.563 2
crop damage	632.15
Lightning arresters	621.317
Lightning protection	
buildings	693.898
Lightships	387.28
engineering	623.828
navigation aids	623.894 3
see also Ships	
Lignin	
recovery from pulp	676.5
Lignin-derived plastics	668.45
Lignite	553.22
economic geology	553.22
mining	622.332

Lignite (continued)	
properties	662.622 2
Lignum vitaes	583.79
Liguria (Italy)	T2—451 8
ancient	T2—371
Ligurian language	491.993
	T6—919 93
Ligurian Sea	551.462 2
	T2—163 82
Lihou (England)	T2—423 49
Lihoumel (England)	T2—423 49
Lij Yasu, Negus of Ethiopia	
Ethiopian history	963.053
Lilacs	635.933 87
botany	583.87
floriculture	635.933 87
Lilaeaceae	584.74
L'Île d'Orléans (Quebec)	T2—714 48
Liliaceae	584.32
floriculture	635.934 32
Liliales	584.3
Lilies	584.3
floriculture	635.934 3
Liliidae	584.3
Liliopsida	584
see also Monocotyledons	
see Manual at 583–584	
Lille Bælt (Denmark)	551.461 34
	T2—163 34
Lillooet (B.C.)	T2—711 31
Lillooet Lake (B.C.)	T2—711 31
Lillooet River (B.C.)	T2—711 3
Lilongwe (Malawi)	T2—689 7
Lily of the valley	635.934 32
botany	584.32
floriculture	635.934 32
Lima (Peru : Dept.)	T2—852 5
Lima beans	641.356 53
botany	583.74
commercial processing	664.805 653
cooking	641.656 53
food	641.356 53
garden crop	635.653
Limarí (Chile : Province)	T2—832 35
Limavady (Northern Ireland : District)	T2—416 25
Limbo	236.4
Limbu language	495.49
	T6—954 9
Limburg (Belgium : Province)	T2—493 24
Limburg (Netherlands)	T2—492 48
Limburger cheese	641.373 53
cooking	641.673 53
Limburger cheese (continued)	
food	641.373 53
processing	637.353
Lime	553.68
economic geology	553.68
use as soil conditioner	631.821
Lime mortars	666.93
Limerick (Ireland)	T2—419 45
Limerick (Ireland : County)	T2—419 4
Limericks	808.817 5
history and criticism	809.175
specific literatures	T3B—107 5
individual authors	T3A—1
Limes (Fruit)	641.343 37
commercial processing	664.804 337
cooking	641.643 37
food	641.343 37
orchard crop	634.337
Limes (Lindens)	
botany	583.68
forestry	634.972 77
Limestone	553.516
building material	691.2
economic geology	553.516
petrology	552.58
quarrying	622.351 6
Limestone County (Ala.)	T2—761 98
Limestone County (Tex.)	T2—764 285
Liming leather	675.22
Limitation of actions	347.052
Limitation of rights	323.49
Limited companies	338.74
law	346.066 8
see also Corporations	
Limited editions	094.4
publishing	070.573
Limited government	320.512
Limited monarchies	321.87
Limited war	355.021 5
Limnocharitaceae	584.72
Limnology	551.48
biology	577.6
Limón (Costa Rica : Province)	T2—728 61
Limousin (France)	T2—446 6
Limousine services	388.321
urban	388.413 214
Limousines	388.342 32
driving	629.283 32
engineering	629.222 32
repair	629.287 232
transportation services	388.342 32
see also Automobiles	

Limpets 594.32
Limpopo River T2—679 2
  Mozambique T2—679 2
  South Africa T2—682 5
Linaceae 583.79
Linares (Chile : Province) T2—833 7
Linares, José Finol
  Brazilian history 981.061
Lincoln (England) T2—425 34
Lincoln (Neb.) T2—782 293
Lincoln (Ont. : County) T2—713 38
Lincoln, Abraham
  United States history 973.7
Lincoln County (Ark.) T2—767 823
Lincoln County (Colo.) T2—788 89
Lincoln County (Ga.) T2—758 165
Lincoln County (Idaho) T2—796 34
Lincoln County (Kan.) T2—781 532
Lincoln County (Ky.) T2—769 625
Lincoln County (Me.) T2—741 57
Lincoln County (Minn.) T2—776 365
Lincoln County (Miss.) T2—762 534
Lincoln County (Mo.) T2—778 37
Lincoln County (Mont.) T2—786 81
Lincoln County (N.C.) T2—756 782
Lincoln County (N.M.) T2—789 64
Lincoln County (Neb.) T2—782 82
Lincoln County (Nev.) T2—793 14
Lincoln County (Okla.) T2—766 35
Lincoln County (Or.) T2—795 33
Lincoln County (S.D.) T2—783 391
Lincoln County (Tenn.) T2—768 624
Lincoln County (W. Va.) T2—754 43
Lincoln County (Wash.) T2—797 35
Lincoln County (Wis.) T2—775 27
Lincoln County (Wyo.) T2—787 82
Lincoln Heath (England) T2—425 3
Lincoln National Park (S. Aust.) T2—942 38
Lincoln Parish (La.) T2—763 91
Lincoln Sea 551.468 7
  T2—163 27
Lincoln Wolds (England) T2—425 32
Lincolnshire (England) T2—425 3
Lindens
  botany 583.68
  forestry 634.972 7
Lindi (Tanzania : Region) T2—678 24
Lindley (South Africa : District) T2—685 1
Lindsey (England : County) T2—425 31
Lindsey, Parts of (England) T2—425 31
Lindsley shorthand system 653.425

Line and staff organization 658.402
  armed forces 355.330 4
  public administration 352.283
Line cuts
  printing 686.232 7
Line engraving 765.2
Line geometry 516.183
Line integrals 515.43
Line Islands 996.4
  T2—964
Line-outs 796.333 23
Line play
  American football 796.332 23
Linear A (Minoan) 492.6
  T6—926
  see Manual at T6—926
Linear accelerators 539.733
Linear algebras 512.5
Linear B (Minoan) 487.1
  T6—87
Linear closed-loop systems
  automation engineering 629.832
Linear differential equations 515.354
Linear equations 515.252
Linear operators 515.724 6
Linear programming 519.72
Linear systems 003.74
Linear topological spaces 515.73
Linen textiles 677.11
  see also Textiles
Lines 516.15
Lines (Electrical) 621.319 2
Lineups (Criminal investigation) 363.258
Lingala language 496.396 86
  T6—963 968 6
Lingala literature 896.396 86
Lingerie 391.42
  commercial technology 687.22
  customs 391.42
  home economics 646.34
  home sewing 646.420 4
  see also Clothing
Lingua francas 401.3
Linguatula 592.76
Linguistic change 417.7
  specific languages T4—7
Linguistic disorders
  special education 371.914
Linguistic groups
  sociology 305.7
Linguistic philosophies 149.94
  see Manual at 401 vs. 121.68, 149.94, 410.1: Philosophy of language

Linguistics 410
  see Manual at 410; *also at* 411–418 and T4—1–T4—8
Linguists
  language specialists
    specific languages T4—092
  linguistics specialists 410.92
    specific languages T4—092
  occupational group T7—4
  philologists 409.2
Linin network 571.66
Linkage editors 005.43
Linkers 005.43
Links (Mathematics) 514.224
Linlithgow, Victor Alexander John Hope, Marquess of
  Indian history 954.035 9
Linn County (Iowa) T2—777 62
Linn County (Kan.) T2—781 69
Linn County (Mo.) T2—778 24
Linn County (Or.) T2—795 35
Linoleum 645.1
  building construction 698.9
  household management 645.1
Linoleum-block printing 761.3
Linopteris 561.597
Linotype
  manufacturing technology 681.61
Linotype composition
  automatic 686.225 44
  manual 686.225 42
Linsangs 599.742
Linseed oil 665.352
Linters
  plastic technology 668.411
Lion 599.757
  big game hunting 799.277 57
  conservation technology 639.979 757
  resource economics 333.959 757
Lions, Gulf of (France) 551.462 2
  T2—163 82
Lions Bay (B.C.) T2—711 33
Lions International 369.5
  biography 369.5
  social group T7—369 5
Lion's River (South Africa : District) T2—684 7
Lip-reed instruments 788.9
  see also Brass instruments
Lipari Islands (Italy) T2—458 11
Lipases 572.757
  see also Enzymes
Lipetsk (Russia : Oblast) T2—473 5
Lipet͡skai͡a oblast′ (Russia) T2—473 5
Lipids 572.57
  biochemistry 572.57
    humans 612.015 77
  chemistry 547.77
  metabolic disorders 571.945 7
    medicine 616.399 7
  metabolism 572.574
    human physiology 612.397
    see also Digestive system
Lipizzaner horse 636.138
Lipolytic enzymes 572.757
  see also Enzymes
Lipoproteins 572.68
  biochemistry 572.68
  chemistry 547.754
  see also Proteins
Lipostraca 565.32
Liposuction 617.95
Lipotyphla 599.33
Lippe River T2—435 6
Lippizaner horse 636.138
Lippmann process 778.63
Lipreading
  education 371.912 7
Lips 591.4
  descriptive zoology 591.4
  human anatomy 611.317
  human physiology 612.31
    speech 612.78
  personal care 646.726
  physiology 573.355
  surgery 617.522
  see also Digestive system
Lipscomb County (Tex.) T2—764 816
Liquefaction of air
  technology 665.82
Liquefaction of coal
  technology 662.662 2
Liquefaction of gases
  physics of heat 536.44
Liqueurs 641.255
  commercial processing 663.55
Liquid chromatography 543.089 4
Liquid crystal displays 621.381 542 2
Liquid crystals 530.429
Liquid-drop model (Nuclear physics) 539.742
Liquid dynamics 532.5
Liquid-gas interface 530.427
Liquid-in-glass thermometry 536.51
Liquid mechanics 532
  engineering 620.106
  hydraulic engineering 627

Liquid mechanics (continued)
  physics 532
Liquid particle technology 620.43
Liquid phases
  liquid-state physics 530.424
Liquid polymers
  liquid-state physics 530.429
Liquid propellants 662.26
  aircraft 629.134 351
  military engineering 623.452 6
  spacecraft 629.475 22
Liquid soaps 668.124
Liquid-state lasers 621.366 2
Liquid-state physics 530.42
Liquid statics 532.2
Liquid wastes 363.728 4
  social services 363.728 4
  technology 628.43
  see also Waste control
Liquidation of corporations
  law 346.066 2
  management 658.1
Liquidity measurement
  accounting 657.48
Liquids
  chemical engineering 660.042
  expansion and contraction 536.413
  heat transfer 536.25
  sound transmission 534.23
  specific heat 536.63
  state of matter 530.42
Liquor laws 344.054 1
Liquor traffic 363.41
  law 344.054 1
  public administration 353.37
  social problem 363.41
Lisboa (Portugal : District) T2—469 425
Lisbon (Portugal : District) T2—469 425
Lisburn (Northern Ireland : District) T2—416 19
L'Islet (Quebec : County) T2—714 74
L'Islet (Quebec : Regional County Municipality) T2—714 74
Lismore (N.S.W.) T2—944 3
Listening
  applied linguistics 418
    specific languages T4—83
  child care 649.58
  elementary education 372.69
  music training method 781.424
  psychology
    communication 153.68
    perception 153.733
  recreation 790.138
Listeria 579.37
Lists T1—021 6
Litanies 264.13
  music 782.292
  Roman Catholic 264.027 4
Litchfield County (Conn.) T2—746 1
Litchis 641.346
  botany 583.78
  cooking 641.646
  food 641.346
  orchard crop 634.6
Literacy 302.224 4
  adult education 374.012 4
  educational policy 379.24
  elementary education 372.6
  linguistics 418.4
  sociology 302.224 4
Literacy programs 379.24
  adult education 374.012 4
Literary agents
  publishing 070.52
    see Manual at 808.001–808.7 vs. 070.52
Literary criticism 809
  sacred books 291.82
    Bible 220.66
    Talmud 296.120 66
  specific literatures T3B—09
    see Manual at T3B—08 and T3B—09: Preference order
  theory 801.95
  see Manual at 800: Literary criticism
Literary forgeries 098.3
Literary genres
  sacred books 291.82
    Bible 220.66
    Talmud 296.120 66
Literary hoaxes 098.3
Literary movements 808.801
  history and criticism 809.91
  specific literatures T3B—080 1
    history and criticism T3B—091
Literary style 800
  criticism 809
    specific literatures T3B—09
  rhetoric 808
Literary themes
  arts 700.457
    T3C—357
  folklore 398.27
    history and criticism 398.357

Literary themes (continued)
  literature 808.803 57
    history and criticism 809.933 57
    specific literatures T3B—080 357
      history and criticism T3B—093 57
Literature 800
  elementary education 372.64
  geographic treatment T3C—93–99
    see Manual at T3C—93–T3C—99; *also at* T3C—93–T3C—99, T3C—9174 vs. T3C—8
  history and criticism 809
  influence on crime 364.254
  see also Arts
  see Manual at 400 vs. 800; *also at* 741.6 vs. 800; *also at* 800; *also at* 909, 930–990 vs. 400
Literature (Black authors) 808.898 96
  specific literatures T3B—080 896
    history and criticism T3B—098 96
Literature and religion 291.175
  Christianity 261.58
Lithgow (N.S.W.) T2—944 5
Lithium 669.725
  chemical engineering 661.038 1
  chemistry 546.381
  economic geology 553.499
  metallurgy 669.725
  physical metallurgy 669.967 25
  see also Chemicals
Lithography 686.231 5
  graphic arts 763
Lithology 552
Lithops 583.53
Lithosphere 551
Lithuania 947.93
  T2—479 3
Lithuanian language 491.92
  T6—919 2
Lithuanian literature 891.92
Lithuanians T5—919 2
Litopterna 569.62
Little Barrier Island (N.Z.) T2—932 4
Little Belt (Denmark) 551.461 34
  T2—163 34
Little Big Horn, Battle of the, 1876 973.82
Little brown bats 599.472
Little Church of France 284.8
  see also Christian denominations
Little Colorado River (N.M. and Ariz.) T2—791 33
Little Kanawha River (W. Va.) T2—754 2
Little Karoo (South Africa) T2—687 16
Little Karroo (South Africa) T2—687 16
Little league (Baseball) 796.357 62
Little River County (Ark.) T2—767 55
Little Rock (Ark.) T2—767 73
Little Sisters of the Poor 255.95
  church history 271.95
Little theater 792.022 3
Liturgical dance 246.7
Liturgical drama
  music 782.298
    choral and mixed voices 782.529 8
    single voices 783.092 98
Liturgical music 782.29
  instrumental forms 784.189 93
  vocal forms 782.29
    choral and mixed voices 782.529
    single voices 783.092 9
Liturgical objects 291.37
  Christianity 247
  Judaism 296.461
Liturgical renewal 264.001
Liturgical year 263.9
  devotional literature 242.3
  sermons 252.6
Liturgy 291.38
  Christianity 264
  music 782.3
  see also Public worship
Liturgy of the hours 264.15
  Anglican 264.030 15
  Roman Catholic 264.020 15
    texts 264.024
Live-bearers 597.667
  culture 639.376 67
Live-forevers (Plants) 583.72
Live Oak County (Tex.) T2—764 447
Liver 573.38
  biology 573.38
  human anatomy 611.36
  human physiology 612.35
  medicine 616.362
  surgery 617.556 2
  see also Digestive system

Liver extracts
  pharmacology 615.367
  see also Digestive system
Liverpool (England) T2—427 53
Liverpool (N.S.) T2—716 24
Liverworts 588.3
Livestock 636
Livestock exhibition 636.081 1
Livestock feeding 636.084
Livestock feeds 636.085 5
  see also Feeds
Livestock judging 636.081 1
Livestock liability insurance 368.56
  see also Insurance
Livestock workers 636.009 2
Living Bible 220.520 83
Living chess 794.17
Living conditions
  armed forces 355.12
Living rooms 643.54
  home economics 643.54
  interior decoration 747.75
Living standard
  macroeconomics 339.47
Living stones 583.53
Livingston County (Ill.) T2—773 61
Livingston County (Ky.) T2—769 895
Livingston County (Mich.) T2—774 36
Livingston County (Mo.) T2—778 223
Livingston County (N.Y.) T2—747 85
Livingston Parish (La.) T2—763 14
Livonia T2—479 8
Livonian language 494.54
  T6—945 4
Livonian literature 894.54
Livonian War, 1557–1582 947.043
Livonians T5—945 4
Livorno (Italy : Province) T2—455 6
Lizard fishes 597.61
Lizards 597.95
Lizard's-tail (Plant) 583.25
Llama wool textiles 677.32
  see also Textiles
Llamas 636.296 6
Llanelli (Wales : Borough) T2—429 67
Llano County (Tex.) T2—764 62
Llano Estacado T2—764 8
  New Mexico T2—789 3
  Texas T2—764 8
Llanquihue (Chile :
    Province) T2—835 4
Lliw Valley (Wales :
    Borough) T2—429 83
Lloydminster (Sask. and
    Alta.) T2—712 42
Lloyds of London 368.012 060 4212
Loa (Chile) T2—831 35
Loaches 597.48
Loaders (Computer programs) 005.43
Loading equipment
  port engineering 627.34
  ships 623.867
Loading operations
  materials management 658.788 5
  ships 623.888 1
Loads (Structural analysis) 624.172
Loan brokers 332.34
Loan collections
  museology 069.56
Loan guarantees
  public administration 352.736
Loan services
  library science 025.6
  museology 069.13
Loan words 412
  specific languages T4—24
Loans 332.7
  capital management 658.152 24
  economics 332.7
    banking services 332.175 3
    central banking 332.113
  flotation
    public finance 336.344
  international law 341.751 15
  law 346.073
    economic assistance 343.074 2
  public administrative support 352.736
  public revenues 336.15
    administration 352.45
Loasaceae 583.94
Lobachevski geometry 516.9
Lobbying 324.4
  law 342.05
  legislative bodies 328.38
Lobeliaceae 583.98
Lobi (African people) T5—963 5
Lobi language 496.35
  T6—963 5
Lobster culture 639.64
Lobster fishing 639.54
Lobsters 641.395
  conservation technology 639.975 384
  cooking 641.695
  culture 639.64
  fishing 639.54
  fishing industry
    economics 338.372 538 4

Lobsters (continued)
  food 641.395
    commercial processing 664.94
  resource economics 333.955 54
  zoology 595.384
Local anesthesia
  surgery 617.966
Local-area networks 004.68
  see also Computer communications
Local bibliographies 015
Local Christian church 250
  ecclesiology 262.2
  specific denominations 280
  see Manual at 260 vs. 251–254, 259
Local courts 347.02
  Great Britain 347.420 2
  Scotland 347.411 02
  United States 347.734
Local finance 336.014
  law 343.03
  public administration 352.421 4
  public finance 336.014
Local government 320.8
  grants-in-aid 336.185
    public administration 352.734 4
  law 342.09
  public administration 352.14
    support and control 353.334
    see Manual at 351.3–351.9 vs. 352.13–352.19
Local heating
  buildings 697.02
Local laws (Compilations) 348.02
Local news
  journalism 070.433
    see Manual at 070.433
Local planning 307.12
  civic art 711.4
  community sociology 307.12
  law 346.045
  see Manual at 307.12 vs. 711
Local rail transit stations
  architecture 725.31
Local rail transit systems 388.42
  engineering 625.6
  law 343.098 3
  public administration 354.769
  transportation services 388.42
Local railroads 388.42
  engineering 625.6
  see also Local rail transit systems
Local religious organizations 291.65
Local support of education 379.123
Local taxation 336.201 4
  law 343.043
  public administration 352.442 14
  public finance 336.201 4
Local telephone service 384.64
  see also Telephone
Local transportation 388.4
  see also Urban transportation
Local wind systems 551.518 5
Localization (Auditory perception)
  psychology 152.158
Locally compact groups 512.55
Locals (Unions) 331.872
  see also Labor unions
Location of business enterprises 338.09
  see also Business enterprises—location
Location of plants
  management 658.21
  see also Business enterprises—location; Plant location—management
Loch Lomond (Scotland) T2—414 25
Loch Ness monster 001.944
Lochaber (Scotland) T2—411 85
Lockouts 331.894
  economics 331.894
  law 344.018 94
Locks (Canals)
  engineering 627.135 2
Locks (Fasteners) 683.32
Locksmithing 683.3
Locksmiths 683.309 2
  occupational group T7—683
Lockup (Printing) 686.225 6
Locomotion 573.79
  animal physiology 573.79
  human physiology 612.76
    see also Musculoskeletal system
  physical adaptation 591.479
  psychology 152.382
Locomotives 385.36
  engineering 625.26
  mining 622.66
  transportation services 385.36
    monorail 385.5
    special purpose 385.5
  see also Rolling stock

Locomotor ataxia
  medicine 616.838
  see also Nervous system
Locoweeds 583.74
Locris (Greece) T2—495 15
  ancient T2—383
Loculoascomycetes 579.564
Locusts 595.726
  agricultural pests 632.726
Locusts (Plants) 583.74
  forestry 634.973 74
Lodes 553.19
Lodi dynasty 954.024 5
Łódź (Poland : Voivodeship) T2—438 4
Lofoten (Norway) T2—484 4
Lofoten Islands (Norway) T2—484 4
Lofting
  ship hulls 623.842
Logan County (Ark.) T2—767 37
Logan County (Colo.) T2—788 75
Logan County (Ill.) T2—773 57
Logan County (Kan.) T2—781 135
Logan County (Ky.) T2—769 76
Logan County (N.D.) T2—784 56
Logan County (Neb.) T2—782 795
Logan County (Ohio) T2—771 463
Logan County (Okla.) T2—766 33
Logan County (W. Va.) T2—754 44
Loganberries 641.347 14
  cooking 641.647 14
  food 641.347 14
  horticulture 634.714
Loganiaceae 583.93
Logarithms 512.922
  algebra 512.922
  arithmetic 513.22
Logbooks
  aeronautics 629.132 54
Loggers 634.980 92
  occupational group T7—634
Logging 634.98
Logic (Reasoning) 160
  see Manual at 153.43 vs. 160
Logic circuits 621.395
Logic design
  computer circuits 621.395
Logic operators 511.3
Logic programming 005.115
  artificial intelligence 006.3
Logical atomism 146.5
Logical positivism 146.42
Logistics
  management 658.5
  military operations 355.411
Logooli language 496.395
  T6—963 95
Logos 232.2
Logroño (Spain : Province) T2—463 54
Loir-et-Cher (France) T2—445 3
Loire (France : Dept.) T2—445 81
Loire-Atlantique (France) T2—441 4
Loire-Inférieure (France) T2—441 4
Loire River (France) T2—445
Loiret (France) T2—445 2
Loja (Ecuador : Province) T2—866 25
Lokāyata 181.46
Lolland (Denmark) T2—489 3
Lollards 284.3
Lolo languages 495.4
  T6—954
Loloish languages 495.4
  T6—954
Lombardia (Italy) T2—452
Lombards
  Italian history 945.01
Lombardy (Italy) T2—452
Lombok (Indonesia) T2—598 6
Lomé (Togo) T2—668 1
Lomond, Loch (Scotland) T2—414 25
Łomża (Poland : Voivodeship) T2—438 3
London (England) T2—421
London (Ont.) T2—713 26
Londonderry (Northern Ireland) T2—416 21
Londonderry (Northern Ireland : County) T2—416 2
Loneliness 155.92
  applied psychology 158.2
Long County (Ga.) T2—758 762
Long-distance service 384.64
  see also Telephone
Long-haired cats 636.83
Long-horned flies 595.772
Long Island (N.Y.) T2—747 21
Long Island Sound (N.Y. and Conn.) 551.461 46
  T2—163 46
Long jump 796.432
  see also Sports
Long-legged flies 595.773
Long-necked lutes 787.8
  see also Stringed instruments
Long-period variable stars 523.844 26

Long-range ballistic missiles 358.175 482
  engineering 623.451 954
  military equipment 358.175 482
Long-range weather forecasting 551.636 5
Long-span bridges 388
  construction 624.3
  see also Bridges
Long-tailed shrews 599.336 2
Long-term capital 332.041 4
  financial management 658.152 42
Long-term care health insurance 368.382
  government-sponsored 368.42
  see also Insurance
Long-term care nursing
  medicine 610.736 1
Long-term loans receivable
  financial management 658.152 42
Long-wave electronics
  physics 537.534 2
Long-wave radio systems 621.384 153
Long waves (Economics) 338.54
Longevity 571.879
  human physiology 612.68
Longevity pay 331.216
  personnel management 658.322 2
Longford (Ireland : County) T2—418 12
Longhair cats 636.83
Longitude 526.62
  celestial navigation 527.2
Longreach (Qld.) T2—943 5
Lonoke County (Ark.) T2—767 78
Looking
  psychology 153.733
Lookout Mountain (Appalachian Mountains) T2—768 82
  Georgia T2—758 342
  Tennessee T2—768 82
Lookout towers
  forestry 634.93
Looms
  textile technology 677.028 54
Loons 598.442
Loosestrifes (Lythraceae) 583.76
Loosestrifes (Primulaceae) 583.675
López Mateos, Adolfo
  Mexican history 972.082 9
López Portillo, José
  Mexican history 972.083 3
Lophiiformes 597.62
Lopseed 583.96
Loquats 641.341 6
  botany 583.73
Loquats (continued)
  cooking 641.641 6
  food 641.341 6
  orchard crop 634.16
L'Or-Blanc (Quebec) T2—714 573
Lorain County (Ohio) T2—771 23
Loran
  marine navigation 623.893 2
  radio engineering 621.384 191
Loranthaceae 583.88
Lord Advocate (Scotland) 345.411 01
Lord Howe Island (N.S.W.) T2—948 1
Lord's Prayer 226.96
  music 782.295
  private devotions 242.722
Lord's Supper 234.163
  public worship 264.36
  theology 234.163
Lorestān (Iran) T2—556
Loreto (Peru : Dept.) T2—854 4
Loretteville (Quebec) T2—714 471
Loricata 597.98
Lories (Parrots) 598.71
  animal husbandry 636.686 5
Lorises 599.83
Lorisidae 599.83
Lorraine (France) T2—443 8
Lorries 388.344
  engineering 629.224
  see also Trucks
Los Alamos County (N.M.) T2—789 58
Los Andes (Chile : Province) T2—832 42
Los Angeles (Calif.) T2—794 94
Los Angeles County (Calif.) T2—794 93
Los Lagos (Chile : Region) T2—835
Los Ríos (Ecuador) T2—866 33
Los Santos (Panama : Province) T2—728 723
Losengo language 496.396 86
  T6—963 968 6
Losengo literature 896.396 86
Loss (Financial management) 658.155
Loss (Psychology) 155.93
Loss of citizenship 323.6
  penology 364.68
Loss of territory 320.12
Loss of vote 324.62
  penology 364.68
Lost-wax casting
  metals 671.255
  sculpture 731.456

Lot (France) T2—447 3
Lot-et-Garonne (France) T2—447 6
Lotbinière (Quebec : County) T2—714 58
Lotbinière (Quebec : Regional County Municipality) T2—714 58
Lothair II, Holy Roman Emperor
  German history 943.023
Lothian (Scotland) T2—413 2
Lotteries 795.38
  occupational ethics 174.6
  use in advertising 659.17
Lottery income
  public administration 352.44
  public finance 336.17
Lotto 795.38
Lotuses 635.933 3
  botany 583.3
  floriculture 635.933 3
Loudness
  acoustical engineering 620.21
Loudon County (Tenn.) T2—768 863
Loudoun County (Va.) T2—755 28
Louga (Senegal : Region) T2—663
Lough Neagh (Northern Ireland) T2—416
Louis VI, King of France
  French history 944.022
Louis VII, King of France
  French history 944.022
Louis VIII, King of France
  French history 944.023
Louis IX, King of France
  French history 944.023
Louis X, King of France
  French history 944.024
Louis XI, King of France
  French history 944.027
Louis XII, King of France
  French history 944.027
Louis XIII, King of France
  French history 944.032
Louis XIV, King of France
  French history 944.033
Louis XV, King of France
  French history 944.034
Louis XVI, King of France
  French history 944.035
    1774–1789 944.035
    1789–1792 944.041
Louis XVIII, King of France
  French history 944.061
    1814–1815 944.05
    1815–1824 944.061
Louis Philippe, King of the French
  French history 944.063
Louis Trichardt (South Africa) T2—682 5
Louisa County (Iowa) T2—777 926
Louisa County (Va.) T2—755 465
Louisbourg (N.S.) T2—716 955
Louisiana 976.3
  T2—763
Louisiana French Creole 447.976 3
  T6—417
Louisville (Ky.) T2—769 44
Lounge cars 385.33
  engineering 625.23
  see also Rolling stock
Loup County (Neb.) T2—782 767
Louse-borne typhus
  incidence 614.526 2
  medicine 616.922 2
  see also Communicable diseases (Human)
Louse flies 595.774
Louth (Ireland : County) T2—418 25
Love
  arts 700.454 3
    T3C—354 3
  ethics 177.7
    religion 291.567 7
      Buddhism 294.35
      Christianity 241.4
      Hinduism 294.548
      Islam 297.567 7
      Judaism 296.367 7
  folklore 398.27
    history and criticism 398.354
  God's love 212.7
    Christianity 231.6
    comparative religion 291.211 2
    philosophy of religion 212.7
  literature 808.803 543
    history and criticism 809.933 543
    specific literatures T3B—080 354 3
      history and criticism T3B—093 543
  philosophy 128.46
  psychology 152.41
  social interaction 302.3
Love charms 133.442
Love County (Okla.) T2—766 59

Love feasts
  Christian rite 265.9
Love spells 133.442
Love stories 808.838 5
  history and criticism 809.385
  specific literatures T3B—308 5
    individual authors T3A—3
Lovebirds 636.686 4
Lovech (Bulgaria : Oblast) T2—499 2
Lovech (Bulgaria : Okrŭg) T2—499 2
Loveshka oblast (Bulgaria) T2—499 2
Loveshki okrŭg (Bulgaria) T2—499 2
Loving County (Tex.) T2—764 912
Loving cups 739.228 4
Low Archipelago T2—963 2
Low birth weight
  pediatrics 618.920 11
Low budget cooking 641.552
Low budget interior decorating 747.1
Low-calorie cooking 641.563 5
Low-calorie diets
  health 613.25
Low-calorie food
  technology 664.63
Low-carbohydrate cooking 641.563 8
Low-carbohydrate diet
  health 613.283
Low-cholesterol cooking 641.563 8
Low-cholesterol diet
  health 613.284
Low-cost housing
  architecture 728.1
  construction 690.81
Low Countries 949.2
  T2—492
Low-dimensional topology 514.22
Low-fat cooking 641.563 8
Low-fat diet
  health 613.284
Low-fiber diet
  health 613.263
Low German language 439.4
  T6—394
Low German literature 839.4
Low Germanic languages 439
  T6—39
Low Germanic literatures 839
Low-income persons 305.569
  T1—086 24
  see also Poor people
Low power television stations 384.55
  see also Television
Low-protein diet
  health 613.282
Low-salt cooking 641.563 2
Low-temperature biology 571.464
  humans 612.014 465
Low-temperature technology 621.56
Low temperatures 536.56
  chemical engineering 660.296 86
  chemistry 541.368 6
  effect on materials 620.112 16
Low voice 783.5
Lowell (Mass.) T2—744 4
Lower Arrow Lake (B.C.) T2—711 62
Lower Austria (Austria) T2—436 12
Lower Avon River
    (England) T2—423 9
Lower Bavaria (Germany) T2—433 5
Lower California (Mexico) T2—722
Lower Canada 971.03
  Quebec 971.402
Lower classes 305.56
  T1—086 24
Lower criticism
  Bible 220.404 6
Lower Egypt T2—621
Lower extremities (Human) 612.98
  anatomy 611.98
  bones 612.75
    anatomy 611.718
    medicine 616.71
    physiology 612.75
    surgery 617.471
  fractures
    medicine 617.158
  joints
    medicine 616.72
    surgery 617.580 59
  muscles
    anatomy 611.738
  physiology 612.98
  regional medicine 617.58
  surgery 617.580 59
Lower Franconia
    (Germany) T2—433 3
Lower Guinea 967.1
  T2—671
Lower houses (Legislative
    bodies) 328.32
Lower Hutt City (N.Z.) T2—936 4
Lower middle classes 305.55
  T1—086 23
Lower Peninsula (Mich.) T2—774
Lower Saxony (Germany) T2—435 9
Lower Tugela (South
    Africa : District) T2—684 4

Lower Umfolozi (South Africa : District) T2—684 3
Lowland game birds 598.41
conservation technology 639.978 41
resource economics 333.958 41
sports hunting 799.244
Lowlands (Scotland) T2—413
Lowndes County (Ala.) T2—761 465
Lowndes County (Ga.) T2—758 864
Lowndes County (Miss.) T2—762 973
Lowveld (South Africa) T2—682 6
Loxodonta 599.674
Loxton (S. Aust.) T2—942 33
Loyalty Islands (New Caledonia) T2—959 7
Loyalty oaths 323.65
law 342.068 4
obligation of citizens 323.65
public personnel management 352.65
Loyalty of citizens 323.65
Lozère (France : Dept.) T2—448 15
Lozi (African people) T5—963 99
Lozi language 496.399
T6—963 99
L^p spaces 515.73
LPTV stations 384.55
see also Television
LSD abuse 362.294
medicine 616.863 4
personal health 613.83
social welfare 362.294
see also Substance abuse
LSP (Special-purpose language) 418
applied linguistics 418
specific languages T4—8
Luanda (Angola : Province) T2—673 2
Luapala Province (Zambia) T2—689 4
Luba (African people) T5—963 93
Luba (Kingdom) 967.518 01
T2—675 18
Luba languages 496.393
T6—963 93
Lubavitch Hasidism 296.833 22
Lubbock County (Tex.) T2—764 847
Lublin (Poland : Voivodeship) T2—438 4
Lubricants
automobiles 629.255
plastic technology 668.411
Lubricating grease 665.538 5
Lubricating oil 665.538 5
Lubrication 621.89
Lubumbashi (Zaire) T2—675 18
Lucania (Italy) T2—457 7
ancient T2—377
Lucanidae 595.764 9
Lucas County (Iowa) T2—777 863
Lucas County (Ohio) T2—771 12
Lucazi language 496.399
T6—963 99
Lucca (Italy : Province) T2—455 3
Luce County (Mich.) T2—774 925
Lucerne (Plant) 633.31
botany 583.74
forage crop 633.31
Lucerne (Switzerland) T2—494 55
Lucerne Lake (Switzerland) T2—494 55
Luchu Islands T2—522 9
Lucifer
Christianity 235.47
Lucioperca 597.758
Ludwigshafen am Rhein (Germany) T2—434 353
Luganda language 496.395 7
T6—963 957
Luganda literature 896.395 7
Lugbara (African people) T5—965
Lugbara language 496.5
T6—965
Lugdunensis T2—364
Lugeing 796.95
see also Sports
Luggage
manufacturing technology 685.51
Lugo (Spain : Province) T2—461 3
Luhans´k (Ukraine : Oblast) T2—477 4
Luhans´ka oblast´ (Ukraine) T2—477 4
Luhya language 496.395
T6—963 95
Luke (Gospel) 226.4
Lullabies 781.582
folk literature 398.8
music 781.582
songs 782.421 582
Lumber 674
Lumber industry 338.476 74
law 343.078 674
Lumber industry workers 674.092
occupational group T7—674
Lumbering 634.98
Lumbermen 634.980 92
Lumberyards 674.32
Lumbriculida 592.64

Luminescence 535.35
  materials science 620.112 95
  mineralogy 549.125
Luminescence spectroscopy 543.085 84
Luminism 709.034 4
  painting 759.054
Luminous paints 667.69
Luminous-tube lighting 621.327
  see also Lighting
Lumped-parameter systems 003.7
Lumpkin County (Ga.) T2—758 273
Luna County (N.M.) T2—789 68
Lunar flights 629.454
  manned 629.454
  unmanned 629.435 3
Lunch 642
  cooking 641.53
  customs 394.15
Lunch periods
  labor economics 331.257 6
  personnel management 658.312 1
Lunda (Kingdom) 967.340 1
  T2—673 4
Lunda languages 496.393
  T6—963 93
Lunda Norte (Angola) T2—673 4
Lunda Sul (Angola) T2—673 4
Lundu-Balong languages 496.396
  T6—963 96
Lüneburg (Germany : Regierungsbezirk) T2—435 93
Lunenburg (N.S. : County) T2—716 23
Lunenburg County (Va.) T2—755 643
Lung cancer
  incidence 614.599 942 4
  medicine 616.994 24
  see also Cancer (Human)
Lungfishes 597.39
Lungs 573.25
  biology 573.25
  human anatomy 611.24
  human physiology 612.2
  medicine 616.24
  surgery 617.542
  see also Respiratory system
Luo (African people) T5—965
Luo language (Africa) 496.5
  T6—965
Luorawetlin languages 494.6
  T6—946
Lupines 583.74
  field crop 633.367
  floriculture 635.933 74
Lupus erythematosus
  medicine 616.77
  see also Musculoskeletal system
Luristān (Iran) T2—556
Lusaka (Zambia) T2—689 4
Lusaka Province (Zambia) T2—689 4
Lusatian language 491.88
  T6—918 8
Lusatian literature 891.88
Lusatians T5—918 8
Lusengo language 496.396 86
  T6—963 968 6
Lusengo literature 896.396 86
Lusikisiki (South Africa : District) T2—687 91
Lusitania T2—366
Lust
  ethics 176
    religion 291.566
      Christianity 241.3
Lute family 787
  see also Stringed instruments
Lutes 787.83
  instrument 787.831 9
  music 787.83
  see also Stringed instruments
Lutetium
  chemistry 546.419
  see also Rare earths
Lutheran church 284.1
  church government 262.041
    parishes 254.041
  church law 262.984 1
  doctrines 230.41
    catechisms and creeds 238.41
  general councils 262.541
  guides to Christian life 248.484 1
  missions 266.41
  moral theology 241.044 1
  public worship 264.041
  religious associations 267.184 1
  religious education 268.841
  seminaries 230.073 41
  theology 230.41
Lutheran Church in America 284.133
  see also Lutheran church
Lutheran Church—Missouri Synod 284.132 2
  see also Lutheran church
Lutheran Free Church 284.131 4
  see also Lutheran church

Lutheran sacred music 781.714 1
public worship 782.322 41
music 782.322 41
religion 264.041 02
Lutherans
biography 284.109 2
religious group T7—241
Lutjanidae 597.72
Luton (England) T2—425 67
Lutra 599.769 2
Lutrinae 599.769
Luwian language 491.998
T6—919 98
Luxembourg 949.35
T2—493 5
ancient 936.4
T2—364
Luxembourg (Belgium) T2—493 48
Luxembourgeois dialect 437.949 35
T6—32
Luxembourgers T5—3
Luxembourgian dialect 437.949 35
T6—32
Luxemburg, House of 943.702 24
Czechoslovakian history 943.702 24
German history 943.027
Luxor (Egypt) T2—32
Luxury tax 336.271
law 343.055
public administration 352.44
public finance 336.271
Luyana languages 496.399
T6—963 99
Luyia language 496.395
T6—963 95
Luzern (Switzerland) T2—494 55
Luzerne County (Pa.) T2—748 32
Luzon (Philippines) T2—599 1
Luzon Strait (Philippines) 551.465 58
T2—164 58
L´viv (Ukraine : Oblast) T2—477 9
L´vivs´ka oblast´ (Ukraine) T2—477 9
Lwo languages (Africa) 496.5
T6—965
Lyases 572.79
see also Enzymes
Lycées (Secondary schools) 373.241
see also Secondary education
Lycia T2—392 8
Lycian language 491.998
T6—919 98
Lycidae 595.764 4
Lycoming County (Pa.) T2—748 51
Lycoperdales 579.599
Lycopodiales 587.9
Lycopsida 587.9
Lydenburg (South Africa : District) T2—682 6
Lydia (Kingdom) T2—392 2
Lydian language 491.998
T6—919 98
Lygeeae 584.9
Lyginopteridaceae 561.595
Lying
ethics 177.3
see also Ethical problems
Lyman County (S.D.) T2—783 58
Lyme disease
medicine 616.92
see also Communicable diseases (Human)
Lymexyloidea 595.763
Lymph 573.16
biology 573.16
human histology 611.018 5
human physiology 612.42
Lymph plasma
human histology 611.018 5
Lymphatic glands
human anatomy 611.46
human physiology 612.42
Lymphatic system 573.16
biology 573.16
geriatrics 618.976 42
human anatomy 611.42
glands 611.46
human cancer 362.196 994 42
glands
incidence 614.599 944 6
medicine 616.994 46
incidence 614.599 944 2
medicine 616.994 42
social services 362.196 994 42
see also Cancer (Human)
human diseases 362.196 42
incidence 614.594 2
medicine 616.42
social services 362.196 42
human histology 611.018 5
human physiology 612.42
pediatrics 618.924 2
pharmacodynamics 615.74
surgery 617.44
Lymphatitis
medicine 616.42
see also Lymphatic system
Lymphocytes 571.96
human histology 611.018 5

Lymphocytes (continued)
  human immunology 616.079
Lymphogranuloma venereum
  incidence 614.547
  medicine 616.951 8
  see also Communicable diseases (Human)
Lymphokines
  human immunology 616.079
Lymphomas
  incidence 614.599 944 6
  medicine 616.994 46
  see also Cancer (Human)
Lymphomatosis
  medicine 616.42
  see also Lymphatic system
Lynchburg (Va.) T2—755 671
Lynching 364.134
  law 345.023 4
Lynn County (Tex.) T2—764 851
Lynx 599.753
  conservation technology 639.979 753
  resource economics 333.959 753
Lyon (France) T2—445 823
Lyon County (Iowa) T2—777 114
Lyon County (Kan.) T2—781 62
Lyon County (Ky.) T2—769 813
Lyon County (Minn.) T2—776 363
Lyon County (Nev.) T2—793 58
Lyonnais (France) T2—445 8
Lyrebirds 598.822
Lyres 787.78
  instrument 787.781 9
  music 787.78
  see also Stringed instruments
Lyric poetry 808.814
  history and criticism 809.14
  specific literatures T3B—104
    individual authors T3A—1
Lyrics 780
  treatises 780.268
Lysergic acid diethylamide abuse 362.294
  medicine 616.863 4
  personal health 613.83
  social welfare 362.294
  see also Substance abuse
Lysosomes 571.655
Lyssavirus 579.256 6
Lythraceae 583.76
Lytton (B.C.) T2—711 72
Lytton, Edward Robert Bulwer Lytton, Earl of
  Indian history 954.035 3
Lzhedmitriĭ I, Czar of Russia
  Russian history 947.045
Lzhedmitriĭ II
  Russian history 947.045

M

Ma'ān (Jordan : Province) T2—569 57
Maas River T2—492 4
  Belgium T2—493 46
  Netherlands T2—492 4
Maasai language 496.5
  T6—965
Ma'aser Sheni (Tractate) 296.123 1
  Mishnah 296.123 1
  Palestinian Talmud 296.124 1
Ma'aserot (Tractate) 296.123 1
  Mishnah 296.123 1
  Palestinian Talmud 296.124 1
Maastricht (Netherlands) T2—492 48
Macaca 599.864
Macadam pavements 625.86
Macadamia nuts 641.345
  agriculture 634.5
  botany 583.89
  cooking 641.645
  food 641.345
Macao 951.26
  T2—512 6
Macapagal, Diosdado
  Philippine history 959.904 5
Macaques 599.864
Macaroni 641.822
  commercial processing 664.755
  cooking 641.822
Macau 951.26
  T2—512 6
Macaws 598.71
  animal husbandry 636.686 5
Maccabean period 933.04
Maccabees (Biblical books) 229.7
Macclesfield (England) T2—427 16
MacDonald, John Alexander, Sir
  Canadian history 971.051
    1867–1873 971.051
    1878–1891 971.054
Mace (Spice) 641.338 3
  see also Spices
Macedonia (Region) T2—495 6
  ancient T2—381
  Bulgaria T2—499 8
  Greece T2—495 6
  Macedonia (Republic) T2—497 6

Macedonia (Republic) T2—497 6
Macedonian language 491.819
  T6—918 19
Macedonian literature 891.819
Macedonian supremacy 938.07
Macedonians T5—918 19
Macerata (Italy : Province) T2—456 73
Maces (Weapons) 623.441
Mach number
  aeronautics 629.132 32
Machel, Samora
  Mozambican history 967.905 1
Machine composition
  printing 686.225 4
Machine design 621.815
Machine embroidery 677.77
  arts 746.440 28
  manufacturing technology 677.77
Machine engineering 621.8
Machine gunners 356.162
Machine guns 355.824 24
  military engineering 623.442 4
  military equipment 355.824 24
    infantry 356.162
Machine laces 677.653
Machine languages 005.136
Machine learning 006.31
Machine production
  paper 676.2
Machine-readable catalog
    records
  format 025.316
  maintenance 025.317
  retrospective conversion 025.317 3
Machine-Readable Cataloging
  format 025.316
Machine-readable data
    representation 005.72
Machine-readable materials 302.23
  bibliographies 011.3
    see Manual at 011.3 vs.
        005.30296, 011.77
  cataloging 025.344
  library treatment 025.174
  publishing 070.579 7
  see Manual at T1—0285:
      Machine-readable
      materials and programs
Machine sewing
  home economics 646.204 4
Machine sheds
  agricultural use 631.25
Machine-shop practice 670.423
  agriculture 631.304
Machine shorthand 653.3
Machine theory
  computer engineering 621.39
  computer science 004
  mathematics 511.3
Machine tools 621.902
Machine translating
  linguistics 418.020 285
Machinery 621.8
Machinery insurance 368.7
  see also Insurance
Machines in production 338.06
Machining metals 671.35
  decorative arts 739.14
  sculpture 731.41
Machmeters 629.135 2
Macías Nguema, Francisco
  Equatorial Guinean history 967.180 31
Mackay (Qld.) T2—943 6
Mackenzie (B.C.) T2—711 82
Mackenzie (N.W.T.) T2—719 3
Mackenzie, Alexander
  Canadian history 971.052
MacKenzie District (N.Z.) T2—938 8
Mackenzie Mountains
    (N.W.T. and Yukon) T2—719 3
Mackenzie River (N.W.T.) T2—719 6
Mackerel 641.392
  cooking 641.692
  fishing 639.277 82
  food 641.392
  zoology 597.782
Mackerel sharks 597.33
Mackinac, Straits of
    (Mich.) T2—774 923
Mackinac County (Mich.) T2—774 923
Maclear (South Africa :
    District) T2—687 6
Macleay River (N.S.W.) T2—944 3
Macomb County (Mich.) T2—774 39
Macon (Ga.) T2—758 552
Macon County (Ala.) T2—761 49
Macon County (Ga.) T2—758 513
Macon County (Ill.) T2—773 582
Macon County (Mo.) T2—778 27
Macon County (N.C.) T2—756 982
Macon County (Tenn.) T2—768 484
Macoupin County (Ill.) T2—773 83
Macpherson, John, Sir
  Indian history 954.031 1
Macquarie perch 597.73
Macramé 746.422 2
Macro-Algonkian languages 497.3
  T6—973

Macro-Gê languages	498.4
	T6—984
Macro processors	005.45
Macrobiotic diet	
health	613.264
Macrocystis	579.887
Macroeconomic policy	339.5
Macroeconomic theory	339.3
Macroeconomics	339
see Manual at 332, 336 vs. 339	
Macroinstructions	
programming	005.13
programs	005.3
Macromolecules	572
biochemistry	572
chemistry	547.7
Macrophages	571.968 5
human immunology	616.079 95
Macropodidae	599.22
Macropus	599.222
Macroscelidea	599.337
paleozoology	569.337
Macrosudanic languages	496.5
	T6—965
Macrotonality	781.265
Macrouridae	597.63
Macrura	595.384
Madadeni (South Africa : District)	T2—684 91
Madagascar	969.1
	T2—691
Madang Province (Papua New Guinea)	T2—957 3
Madawaska (N.B. : County)	T2—715 54
Madders	583.93
Madeira Islands	T2—469 8
Madeira vine	583.53
Madeleine, Îles de la (Quebec)	T2—714 797
Madera County (Calif.)	T2—794 81
Madhvāchārya (Philosophy)	181.484 1
Madhya Pradesh (India)	T2—543
Madhyamika Buddhism	294.392
Madikwe (South Africa : District)	T2—682 94
Madison (Wis.)	T2—775 83
Madison, James	
United States history	973.51
Madison County (Ala.)	T2—761 97
Madison County (Ark.)	T2—767 15
Madison County (Fla.)	T2—759 85
Madison County (Ga.)	T2—758 152
Madison County (Idaho)	T2—796 55
Madison County (Ill.)	T2—773 86
Madison County (Ind.)	T2—772 57
Madison County (Iowa)	T2—777 81
Madison County (Ky.)	T2—769 53
Madison County (Miss.)	T2—762 623
Madison County (Mo.)	T2—778 91
Madison County (Mont.)	T2—786 663
Madison County (N.C.)	T2—756 875
Madison County (N.Y.)	T2—747 64
Madison County (Neb.)	T2—782 54
Madison County (Ohio)	T2—771 55
Madison County (Tenn.)	T2—768 27
Madison County (Tex.)	T2—764 237
Madison County (Va.)	T2—755 38
Madison Parish (La.)	T2—763 81
Madness	362.2
see also Mental illness	
Madonna and Child	
art representation	704.948 55
arts	T3C—382 329 2
Madras (India : State)	T2—548 2
Madre de Dios (Peru : Dept.)	T2—854 2
Madrid (Spain : Province)	T2—464 1
Madrid Hurtado, Miguel de la	
Mexican history	972.083 4
Madrigals	782.43
choral and mixed voices	782.543
single voices	783.094 3
Madriz (Nicaragua)	T2—728 523
Madtoms	597.492
Madura Island (Indonesia)	T2—598 2
Madurese language	499.22
	T6—992 2
Mafia	364.106
Mafikeng (South Africa)	T2—682 94
Mafraq (Jordan : Province)	T2—569 597
Magadan (Russia : Oblast)	T2—577
Magadanskaia͡ oblast´ (Russia)	T2—577
Magahi language	491.454 7
	T6—914 54
Magahi literature	891.454
Magallanes (Chile : Province)	T2—836 44
Magallanes y Antártica Chilena (Chile)	T2—836 4
Magar	T5—95
Magari language	495.49
	T6—954 9
Magazine illustration	741.652

Magazines 050
T1—05
see also Serials
Magdalen Islands (Quebec) T2—714 797
Magdalena (Colombia : Dept.) T2—861 16
Magdeburg (Germany) T2—431 822
Magdeburg (Germany : Bezirk) T2—431 82
Magellan, Strait of (Chile and Argentina) 551.469 4
T2—167 4
Maggiore, Lake (Italy and Switzerland) T2—451 6
Italy T2—451 6
Switzerland T2—494 78
Maggots 595.771 39
agricultural pests 632.77
Magherafelt (Northern Ireland : District) T2—416 29
Maghreb T2—61
Magi (Christian doctrines) 232.923
Magic 133.43
folklore 398.2
history and criticism 398.4
literature 808.803 7
history and criticism 809.933 7
specific literatures T3B—080 37
history and criticism T3B—093 7
recreation 793.8
religious practice 291.3
sociology 306.4
Magic squares 511.64
Magicians (Occultists) 133.430 92
see also Legendary beings
Magicians (Performers) 793.809 2
occupational group T7—793 8
Magicians (Religious leaders) 200.92
biography 200.92
role and function 291.61
see Manual at 200.92 and 291–299
Magicians' manuals 133.43
Magisterium 262.8
Magistrates Court (Great Britain) 345.420 12
Magma 551.13
Magnēsia (Greece) T2—495 4
Magnesia ad Maeandrum (Extinct city) T2—392 3
Magnesia cement 666.95
Magnesite
mineralogy 549.782
Magnesium 669.723
applied nutrition 613.285
biochemistry 572.523 92
humans 612.015 24
chemical engineering 661.039 2
chemistry 546.392
economic geology 553.492 9
materials science 620.187
metabolism 572.523 92
human physiology 612.392 4
metallography 669.957 23
metallurgy 669.723
metalworking 673.723
mining 622.349 29
organic chemistry 547.053 92
applied 661.895
physical metallurgy 669.967 23
see also Chemicals; Metals
Magnesium soaps 668.125
Magnet schools 373.241
see also Secondary education
Magnetic bubble memory 004.56
engineering 621.397 63
Magnetic-core memory 004.53
engineering 621.397 3
Magnetic currents (Earth) 538.748
Magnetic diagnosis
medicine 616.075 48
Magnetic disks (Computer) 004.563
engineering 621.397 6
Magnetic drums 004.56
engineering 621.397 6
Magnetic engineering 621.34
Magnetic engineers 621.340 92
occupational group T7—621 3
Magnetic fields (Earth) 538.7
Magnetic induction 538.4
Magnetic ink character recognition 006.4
engineering 621.399
Magnetic levitation trains 388.42
see also Local rail transit systems
Magnetic observations (Earth) 538.79
Magnetic phenomena 538.3
Magnetic properties 538.3
crystals 548.85
materials science 620.112 97
Magnetic prospecting 622.153
Magnetic relaxation 538.3
Magnetic resonance 538.36
Magnetic resonance imaging
medicine 616.075 48

Magnetic resonance spectroscopes	
manufacturing technology	681.414 8
Magnetic resonance spectroscopy	
engineering	621.361 7
Magnetic separation	
ores	622.77
Magnetic spectroscopy	543.087 7
Magnetic storms (Earth)	538.744
Magnetic substances	538.4
Magnetic surveys (Earth)	538.78
Magnetic tapes	
engineering	621.382 34
music	786.75
see also Electrophones	
Magnetic tapes (Computer)	004.56
engineering	621.397 6
Magnetic testing	
materials science	620.112 78
Magnetic therapy	
medicine	615.845
Magnetic variations (Geomagnetism)	538.74
Magnetism	538
astrophysics	523.018 8
biophysics	571.47
humans	612.014 42
physics	538
Magnetite	
mineralogy	549.526
Magnetochemistry	541.378
chemical engineering	660.297 8
Magnetohydrodynamic generation	621.312 45
Magnetohydrodynamic power systems	
spacecraft	629.474 45
Magnetohydrodynamic propulsion	
spacecraft	629.475 5
Magnetohydrodynamics	538.6
Magnetosphere	538.766
meteorology	551.514
Magnetostriction	538.3
Magnetotherapy	
medicine	615.845
Magnetrons	621.381 334
Magnets	538.4
artificial	621.34
natural	538.4
Magnolia vine	583.3
Magnoliales	583.22
Magnolias	635.977 322
botany	583.22
ornamental arboriculture	635.977 322
Magnoliidae	583.2
Magnoliopsida	583
see also Dicotyledons	
see Manual at 583–584	
Magoffin County (Ky.)	T2—769 215
Magpie larks	598.8
Magpies	598.864
Magsaysay, Ramon	
Philippine history	959.904 3
Magyar language	494.511
	T6—945 11
Magyar literature	894.511
Magyars	T5—945 11
Mah jong	795.34
Mahabharata	294.592 3
Mahajanga (Madagascar : Province)	T2—691
Maharashtra (India)	T2—547 92
Mahasanghika Buddhism	294.391
Mahaska County (Iowa)	T2—777 84
Mahathir bin Mohamad	
Malaysian history	959.505 4
Mahayana Buddhism	294.392
Mahé Island (Seychelles)	T2—696
Mahili͡oŭ (Belarus : Voblasts)	T2—478 2
Mahili͡oŭskai͡a voblastsʹ (Belarus)	T2—478 2
Mahl language	491.487
	T6—914 8
Mahl literature	891.48
Mahlabatini (South Africa : District)	T2—684 91
Mahnomen County (Minn.)	T2—776 94
Mahoganies	
botany	583.77
forestry	634.973 77
Mahomet, Prophet	297.63
Mahoning County (Ohio)	T2—771 39
Mahoning River (Ohio and Pa.)	T2—771 39
Mahratta	T5—948
Mahri	T5—929
Mahri language	492.9
	T6—929
Mahri literature	892.9
Mahzorim	296.453
Maiasaura	567.914
Maidenhair ferns	587.3
Maidenhair tree	635.977 57
botany	585.7

Maidenhair tree (continued)
  ornamental arboriculture 635.977 57
Maidstone (England : Borough) T2—422 375
Maiduguri (Nigeria) T2—669 85
Mail 383
  see also Postal service
Mail art 709.04
Mail cars 385.33
  engineering 625.23
  see also Rolling stock
Mail fraud 364.136
  law 345.023 6
Mail handling 383.1
  office services 651.759
Mail openers
  office use 651.759
Mail-order catalogs T1—029 4
  direct advertising 659.133
  see also Commercial catalogs
Mail-order houses 381.142
  management 658.872
  see also Commerce
Mail sealers
  office use 651.759
Mail service 383.1
  see also Postal service
Maimonides, Moses
  Jewish legal writings 296.181
Main dishes (Cooking) 641.82
Main memory (Computer) 004.53
  engineering 621.397 3
Main River (Germany) T2—434
Main-sequence stars 523.88
Maine 974.1
  T2—741
Maine (France) T2—441 6
Maine, Gulf of 551.461 45
  T2—163 45
Maine coon cat 636.83
Maine-et-Loire (France) T2—441 8
Mainframe computers 004.12
  architecture 004.252
  communications 004.612
    programming 005.712 2
    programs 005.713 2
  engineering 621.391 2
  graphics programming 006.672
  graphics programs 006.682
  interfacing 004.612
    programming 005.712 2
    programs 005.713 2
  knowledge-based systems
    programming 006.337
Mainframe computers (continued)
  multimedia-systems programming 006.772
  multimedia-systems programs 006.782
  operating systems 005.442
  performance evaluation 004.120 297
    for design and improvement 004.252
  peripherals 004.712
  programming 005.22
  programs 005.32
  systems analysis 004.252
  systems design 004.252
  see Manual at 004.11–004.16
Mainstream jazz 781.654
Mainstreaming
  education 371.904 6
    gifted students 371.952
    grouping of students 371.252
  library services 027.663
Maintainability engineering 620.004 5
Maintenance 620.004 6
  T1—028 8
  plant management 658.202
  T1—068 2
    public administration 352.564
  public administration 352.54
Maintenance (Domestic relations) 346.016 6
Maintenance facilities
  spacecraft 629.478
Mainz (Rhineland-Palatinate, Germany) T2—434 351
Maithili language 491.454 7
  T6—914 54
Maithili literature 891.454
Maitland (N.S.W.) T2—944 2
Maize 641.331 5
  botany 584.92
  see also Corn—food
Majingai dialect 496.5
  T6—965
Majolica 738.372
Major County (Okla.) T2—766 29
Major medical insurance 368.382 8
  see also Insurance
Major Prophets (Biblical books) 224
Major surgery 617.025
Majorca (Spain) T2—467 54
Majority (Age)
  customs 392.15
  etiquette 395.24
  law 346.013 5
  music 781.584

Maka-Njem languages 496.396
T6—963 96
Makasar Strait 551.465 73
T2—164 73
Make-ahead meals
cooking 641.555
Make-work arrangements
economics 331.120 42
unions 331.889 6
Makedonia (Greece : Periphereia) T2—495 6
Makeup 646.72
dramatic performances 792.027
motion pictures 791.430 27
stage 792.027
television 791.450 27
see also Cosmetics
Makhshirin 296.123 6
Makira and Ulawa (Solomon Islands) T2—959 38
Makkot 296.123 4
Babylonian Talmud 296.125 4
Mishnah 296.123 4
Palestinian Talmud 296.124 4
Mako sharks 597.33
Makonde (African people) T5—963 97
Makonde language 496.397
T6—963 97
Makua languages 496.397
T6—963 97
Makula and Temotu Province (Solomon Islands) T2—959 39
Makurdi (Nigeria) T2—669 54
Malabo (Equatorial Guinea) T2—671 86
Malabsorption
medicine 616.342 3
see also Digestive system
Malacca (State) T2—595 1
Malacca, Strait of 551.467 65
T2—165 65
Malachi (Biblical book) 224.99
Malachite
mineralogy 549.785
Malacology 594
Malacostraca 595.37
paleozoology 565.37
Maladjusted students 371.93
Maladjusted young people
delinquent T1—086 923
mentally ill 305.908 24
T1—087 4
T7—082 4
social group 305.908 24
social welfare 362.74
Málaga (Spain : Province) T2—468 5
Malagasy T5—993
Malagasy language 499.3
T6—993
Malagasy literature 899.3
Malagasy Republic T2—691
Malaita (Solomon Islands) T2—959 37
Malamulele (South Africa : District) T2—682 92
Malan, D. F. (Daniel François)
South African history 968.056
Malanje (Angola) T2—673 4
Malaria
incidence 614.532
medicine 616.936 2
see also Communicable diseases (Human)
Malaspina Peninsula (B.C.) T2—711 31
Malatya İli (Turkey) T2—565
Malawi 968.97
T2—689 7
Malawi (Kingdom) 968.970 1
T2—689 7
Malawi, Lake T2—689 7
Malawi people T5—968 97
Malawians T5—968 97
Malay Archipelago T2—598
Malay Archipelago inner seas 551.465 73
T2—164 73
Malay language 499.28
T6—992 8
Malay languages 499.2
T6—992
Malay literature 899.28
Malay Peninsula T2—595 1
Malay-Polynesian languages 499.2
T6—992
Malaya T2—595 1
Malayalam language 494.812
T6—948 12
Malayalam literature 894.812
Malayalis T5—948 12
Malayan languages 499.2
T6—992
Malayan literatures 899.2
Malayo-Polynesian languages 499.2
T6—992

Malayo-Polynesians T5—992
Malays (Asian people) T5—992 8
Malaysia 959.5
T2—595
Malaysia, East T2—595 3
Malaysians T5—992 8
Malcolm Island (B.C.) T2—711 2
Maldive Islands T2—549 5
Maldives 954.95
T2—549 5
Maldivian language 491.487
T6—914 8
Maldivian literature 891.48
Maldivians T5—914 1
Maldon (England : District) T2—426 756
Maldon (Vic.) T2—945 3
Maldonado (Uruguay : Dept.) T2—895 15
Male breast (Human)
medicine 616.49
surgery 617.549
Male genital system 573.65
anesthesiology 617.967 463
biology 573.65
human anatomy 611.63
human cancer 362.196 994 63
incidence 614.599 946 3
medicine 616.994 63
social services 362.196 994 63
see also Cancer (Human)
human diseases 362.196 65
incidence 614.596 5
medicine 616.65
social services 362.196 65
human physiology 612.61
surgery 617.463
Male reproductive system 573.65
animals 573.65
plants 575.65
see also Male genital system
Male sexual disorders
medicine 616.69
see also Male genital system
Malenkov, Georgi
Russian history 947.085 2
Males (Human) 305.31
T1—081
T7—041
see also Men
Malfeasance by employees
labor economics 331.259 8
personnel management 658.314
Malfeasance in office 364.132
law 345.023 2
public administration 353.46
Malheur County (Or.) T2—795 97
Mali 966.23
T2—662 3
Mali Empire 966.201 7
T2—662
Malians T5—966 23
Malicious mischief insurance 368.12
see also Insurance
Malicious prosecution 346.033 4
Malignant cholera
incidence 614.514
medicine 616.932
see also Communicable diseases (Human)
Malignant tumors (Human)
medicine 616.994
see Manual at 616.994 vs. 616.992
see also Cancer (Human)
Malikites (Islamic sect) 297.813
Malinke (African people) T5—963 45
Malinke language 496.345
T6—963 45
Malis (Greece) T2—383
Mallard 598.413 4
Malleability
materials science 620.112 5
Malleco (Chile) T2—834 5
Mallee (Vic. : District) T2—945 9
Mallet games 796.35
Mallophaga 595.757
Mallorca (Spain) T2—467 54
Mallows 583,685
Malls (Shopping) 381.1
see also Shopping malls
Malmesbury (South Africa : District) T2—687 3
Malmöhus län (Sweden) T2—486
Malnutrition
medicine 616.39
see also Digestive system
Malone shorthand system 653.426
Malpighiaceae 583.79
Malpractice 346.033
Malpractice insurance 368.564
see also Insurance
Malta 945.85
T2—458 5
ancient T2—378

Maltases 572.756
  see also Enzymes
Malted alcoholic beverages 641.23
  commercial processing 663.3
  home preparation 641.873
Malted nonalcoholic beverages 641.26
  commercial processing 663.6
  home preparation 641.875
Maltese T5—927 9
Maltese (Dog) 636.76
Maltese language 492.79
  T6—927 9
Maltese literature 892.79
Malthusian economic school 330.153
Malto language 494.83
  T6—948 3
Malto literature 894.83
Maltose 572.565
  biochemistry 572.565
  chemistry 547.781 5
  see also Carbohydrates
Maluku (Indonesia) T2—598 5
Malvaceae 583.685
Malvales 583.68
Malvern Hills (England) T2—424 47
Malvinas Islands 997.11
  T2—971 1
Mam language 497.415
  T6—974 15
Mambwe language 496.391
  T6—963 91
Mammal nest beetles 595.764 2
Mammalia 599
  see also Mammals
Mammalogists 599.092
  occupational group T7—599
Mammals 599
  agricultural pests 632.69
  animal husbandry 636
  art representation 704.943 29
  big game hunting 799.26
  commercial hunting 639.11
  conservation technology 639.9
  control technology 628.969
    agriculture 632.69
  drawing 743.69
  paleozoology 569
  resource economics 333.954
  small game hunting 799.259
  zoology 599
  see Manual at 599: Sources of taxonomic information
Mammaplasty 618.190 592
Mammary glands 573.679
  biology 573.679
  gynecology 618.19
  human anatomy 611.49
  human cancer
    incidence 614.599 944 9
    medicine 616.994 49
    see also Cancer (Human)
  human physiology 612.664
  surgery 618.190 59
Mammee apple 583.624
Mammography
  medicine 618.190 757 2
Mammoth Cave National Park (Ky.) T2—769 754
Man 301
  see also Humans
Man, Isle of (England) T2—427 9
Man-machine ratios
  production management 658.514
Man-machine systems
  ergonomics 620.82
    computer science 004.019
      engineering 621.398 4
Man-made environments
  biology 578.755
  ecology 577.55
Man-made fibers
  paper 676.7
  textiles 677.4
    arts 746.044
    see also Textiles
Manabí (Ecuador) T2—866 34
Managed care plans 362.104 258
  insurance 368.382
    see also Insurance
Managed currency 332.46
Management 658
  T1—068
  armed forces 355.6
  personal aspects 658.409
  public administration 351
  see Manual at T1—0285 vs. T1—068; *also at* T1—068 vs. 353–354; *also at* 330 vs. 650; *also at* 658 and T1—068
Management accounting 658.151 1
  public administration 352.43
  see Manual at 657 vs. 658.1511, 658.1512
Management auditing 658.401 3
  public administration 352.43

Management audits 658.401 3
  public administration 352.439
Management by objectives 658.401 2
  public administration 352.36
Management consultants 658.46
  public administration 352.373
Management environment 658.409 5
  public administration 352.39
Managerial accounting 658.151 1
  public administration 352.43
  see Manual at 657 vs. 658.1511, 658.1512
Managerial finance 658.15
  see also Financial management
Managerial occupations 331.714
Managerial success 658.409
Managers 338.092
  T1—086 22
  labor economics 331.761 658
  occupational group T7—658
  social class 305.554
Managing change 658.406
  military administration 355.686 7
  public administration 352.367
Managing your boss 650.13
Managua (Nicaragua : Dept.) T2—728 513
Manakins 598.822
Manapouri, Lake (N.Z.) T2—939 6
Manassas (Va.) T2—755 273 4
Manassas Park (Va.) T2—755 273 6
Manatee County (Fla.) T2—759 62
Manatees 599.55
  conservation technology 639.979 55
  resource economics 333.959 55
Manawatu District (N.Z.) T2—935 6
Manawatu-Wanganui Region (N.Z.) T2—935
Mancha T2—464
Manche 551.461 36
  T2—163 36
Manche (France) T2—442 1
Manchester (England) T2—427 33
Manchester (N.H.) T2—742 8
Manchester terrier (Standard dog) 636.755
Manchester terrier (Toy dog) 636.76
Manchineels 583.69
Manchu T5—941
Manchu dynasty 951.03
Manchu languages 494.1
  T6—941
Manchu literatures 894.1
Manchuria T2—518
Manda languages 496.391
  T6—963 91
Mandab, Strait of 551.467 32
  T2—165 32
Mandalas 291.37
  Buddhism 294.343 7
  Hinduism 294.537
Mandarin Chinese language 495.1
  T6—951 1
Mandarin duck 598.412
Mandates 321.08
  establishment
    World War I 940.314 26
    World War II 940.531 426
  see also Semisovereign states
Mande (African people) T5—963 45
Mande languages 496.34
  T6—963 4
Mande literatures 896.34
Mandeb, Bab el 551.467 32
  T2—165 32
Mandekan languages 496.345
  T6—963 45
Mandela, Nelson
  South African history 968.065
Mandingo (African people) T5—963 45
Mandingo languages 496.345
  T6—963 45
Mandinka (African people) T5—963 45
Mandinka languages 496.345
  T6—963 45
Mandolins 787.84
  instrument 787.841 9
  music 787.84
  see also Stringed instruments
Mandrakes
  botany 583.952
  medicinal crop 633.883 952
Mandrakes (Mayapples) 583.34
Maneuvers (Military) 355.4
  training 355.52
Manganese 669.732
  chemical engineering 661.054 1
  chemistry 546.541
  economic geology 553.462 9
  human toxicology 615.925 541
  materials science 620.189 32
  metallography 669.957 32
  metallurgy 669.732
  metalworking 673.732
  mining 622.346 29
  organic chemistry 547.055 41
    applied 661.895

Manganese (continued)
  physical metallurgy 669.967 32
  see also Chemicals; Metals
Manganese group
  chemical engineering 661.054
  chemistry 546.54
Mangbetu language 496.5
  T6—965
Mange
  medicine 616.57
  see also Skin
Mangoes 641.344 4
  botany 583.77
  cooking 641.644 4
  food 641.344 4
  orchard crop 634.44
Mangosteens 641.346 55
  agriculture 634.655
  botany 583.624
  cooking 641.646 55
  food 641.346 55
Mangrove swamps 577.698
  biology 578.769 8
  ecology 577.698
  see also Wetlands
Mangroves 583.763
  Arecaceae 584.5
  Myrtales 583.763
  Verbenaceae 583.96
Mangue Indians T5—976
Mangue language 497.6
  T6—976
Manguindanao (Philippines) T2—599 7
Manhattan (New York, N.Y.) T2—747 1
Manholes
  sewers 628.25
Manic-depressive psychoses
  medicine 616.895
  see also Mental illness
Manic psychoses
  medicine 616.895
  see also Mental illness
Manica (Mozambique : (Province) T2—679 4
Manicaland Province (Zimbabwe) T2—689 1
Manicheism 299.932
  Christian heresy 273.2
Manicouagan (Quebec : Regional County Municipality) T2—714 17
Manicure tools
  manufacturing technology 688.5
Manicuring 646.727
Maniema (Zaire) T2—675 17
Manifold topology 514.3
Manifolds (Mathematics) 516.07
  geometry 516.07
  topology 514.3
Manihiki Atoll (Cook Islands) T2—962 4
Manila (Philippines) T2—599 16
Manila hemp
  botany 584.39
  fiber crop 633.571
Manila paper 676.287
Manioc 641.336 82
  see also Cassava
Manipur (India) T2—541 7
Manisa İli (Turkey) T2—562
Manistee County (Mich.) T2—774 62
Manitoba 971.27
  T2—712 7
Manitoba, Lake (Man.) T2—712 72
Manitoulin (Ont.) T2—713 135
Manitowoc County (Wis.) T2—775 67
Manjimup (W.A.) T2—941 2
Mankind 301
  see also Humans
Mankwe (South Africa : District) T2—682 94
Manned space flight
  engineering 629.45
  see Manual at 629.43, 629.45 vs. 919.904
Manned spacecraft
  engineering 629.47
Manners 390
  child training 649.6
  etiquette 395
Mannheim (Germany) T2—434 646
Manning Provincial Park (B.C. : Provincial Park) T2—711 5
Manor houses
  architecture 728.8
Manpower 331.11
  armed forces 355.22
    civilians 355.23
  military law 343.012
Manpower planning
  management 658.301
Mansel Island (N.W.T.) T2—719 5
Mansfield (England : District) T2—425 23

Mansi T5—945 1
Mansi language 494.51
T6—945 1
Mansi literature 894.51
Mansions
architecture 728.8
Manslaughter 364.152 5
law 345.025 25
Mantels
furniture arts 749.62
Mantis shrimps 595.379 6
Mantises 595.727
culture 638.572 7
Mantle of earth 551.116
Mantodea 595.727
Mantova (Italy : Province) T2—452 8
Mantras 291.37
Buddhism 294.343 7
Hinduism 294.537
Mantua (Italy : Province) T2—452 8
Manual alphabet 419
Manual arts
elementary education 372.5
Manual of arms 355.547
Manufactured gases 665.7
Manufacturers 338.476 709 2
Manufacturers' outlets 381.15
see also Outlet stores
Manufacturing
ethics 174.4
production management 658.5
see Manual at 658.5 and T1—0685
technology 670
see Manual at 671–679 vs. 680
Manufacturing industries 338.476 7
accounting 657.867
public administration 354.66
Manufacturing wastes
water pollution engineering 628.168 37
Manufacturing workers 670.92
labor economics 331.767
occupational group T7—67
public administration 354.947
Manukau City (N.Z.) T2—932 5
Manures 631.86
animal husbandry 636.083 8
Manus (Papua New Guinea people) T5—991 2
Manus Province (Papua New Guinea) T2—958 1
Manuscript editing 808.027
publishing 070.51
Manuscript illumination 745.67
Manuscript selection
publishing 070.51
Manuscripts 091
bibliographies 011.31
cataloging 025.341 2
library treatment 025.171 2
music 780
treatises 780.262
Manx T5—916 4
Manx cat 636.822
Manx language 491.64
T6—916 4
Manx literature 891.64
Manxmen T5—916 4
Many-bodies problem 530.144
astronomy 521
Mao, Tse-tung
Chinese history 951.05
Maoism 335.434 5
economics 335.434 5
political ideology 320.532 309 51
Maori T5—994 42
Maori language 499.442
T6—994 42
Maori literature 899.442
Maori Wars, 1843–1847 993.021
Maori Wars, 1860–1870 993.022
Map-coloring problem 514.223
Map drawing 526.022 1
Map makers 526.092
occupational group T7—526
Map making 526
military engineering 623.71
military intelligence service 355.343 2
Map projections 526.8
Map reading 912.014
Maple Ridge (B.C.) T2—711 37
Maple sugar 641.336 4
agriculture 633.64
commercial processing 664.132
cooking 641.636 4
food 641.336 4
see also Sugar
Maple syrup 641.336 4
agriculture 633.64
commercial processing 664.132
cooking 641.636 4
food 641.336 4
see also Sugar
Maples 583.78
forestry 634.972 2
lumber 674.142
ornamental arboriculture 635.977 378

Maplewood (N.J.) T2—749 33
Mappings (Mathematics) 511.33
topology 514
Maps 912
T1—022 3
aeronautics 629.132 54
cartography 526
military engineering 623.71
cataloging 025.346
geography 912
library treatment 025.176
printing 686.283
publishing 070.579 3
see Manual at 912 vs. T1—0223
Maps (Mathematics) 511.33
Mapuche Indians T5—98
Mapuche language 498
T6—98
Mapudungu Indians T5—98
Mapudungu language 498
T6—98
Mapulaneng (South Africa : District) T2—682 93
Mapumulo (South Africa : District) T2—684 91
Maputaland (South Africa) T2—684 91
Maputo (Mozambique : Province) T2—679 1
Maputo River T2—684 2
Mozambique T2—679 1
South Africa T2—684 2
Maqurrah (Kingdom) 962.502 2
T2—625
Mar Thoma Church 281.5
see also Eastern churches
Mara Region (Tanzania) T2—678 27
Maracaibo, Gulf of (Colombia and Venezuela) 551.463 5
T2—163 65
Maracaibo Lake (Venezuela) T2—872 3
Maracas 786.885
see also Percussion instruments
Marakwet (African people) T5—965
Marakwet language 496.5
T6—965
Maramureş (Romania : Judeţ) T2—498 4
Maranhão (Brazil) T2—812 1
Marantaceae 584.39
Maraş İli (Turkey) T2—565
Maratha T5—948
Marathi language 491.46
T6—914 6
Marathi literature 891.46
Marathon (Ancient site) T2—385
Marathon County (Wis.) T2—775 29
Marathon races 796.425 2
see also Sports
Marattiales 587.33
paleobotany 561.73
Marble 553.512
building material 691.2
economic geology 553.512
petrology 552.4
quarrying 622.351 2
Marbled polecat 599.766
Marbles (Game) 796.2
see also Sports
Marbling
bookbinding 686.36
Marbling (Woodwork)
buildings 698.32
MARC format 025.316
Marcgraviaceae 583.624
March flies 595.772
March flies (Bibionidae) 595.772
March flies (Tabanidae) 595.773
Marchantiales 588.3
Marche (France : Province) T2—446 8
Marche (Italy) T2—456 7
Marches 784.189 7
Marches (Italy) T2—456 7
Marching bands 784.83
Marcos, Ferdinand E. (Ferdinand Edralin)
Philippine history 959.904 6
Mardi Gras 394.25
customs 394.25
recreation 791.6
Mardin İli (Turkey) T2—566 7
Mareeba (Qld.) T2—943 6
Maremma (Italy) T2—455 7
Marengo County (Ala.) T2—761 392
Mare's tails (Plants) 583.82
Marfan syndrome
medicine 616.77
see also Musculoskeletal system
Margarine
food technology 664.32
Margay 599.752
Margiana T2—396
Margin 332.645
multiple forms of investment 332.645
stocks 332.632 28

Marginal costs 338.514 2
  management 658.155 3
Marginal productivity theory
  land economics 333.012
  wages 331.210 1
Marginal utility school
    (Economics) 330.157
Marginalist school (Economics) 330.157
Mari T5—945 6
Mari El (Russia) T2—474 6
Mari language 494.56
  T6—945 6
Mari literature 894.56
Maria-Chapdelaine
    (Quebec) T2—714 14
Maria Island National Park
    (Tas.) T2—946 4
María Trinidad Sánchez
    (Dominican Republic :
    Province) T2—729 364
Mariana Islands 996.7
  T2—967
Maribo amt (Denmark) T2—489 3
Marico (South Africa :
    District) T2—682 3
Marico River (South Africa
    and Botswana) T2—682 3
Maricopa County (Ariz.) T2—791 73
Maricopa Indians T5—975 7
Maricopa language 497.57
  T6—975 7
Mariculture 639.8
Marie Galante T2—729 76
Maries County (Mo.) T2—778 592
Marigolds 635.933 99
  botany 583.99
  floriculture 635.933 99
Marijuana
  agriculture 633.79
  botany 583.45
  customs 394.14
  human toxicology 615.952 345
  pharmacodynamics 615.782 7
  pharmacology 615.323 45
Marijuana abuse 362.295
  medicine 616.863 5
  personal health 613.835
  social welfare 362.295
  see also Substance abuse
Marimbas 786.843
  see also Percussion
    instruments
Marin County (Calif.) T2—794 62
Marinas 387.15
  engineering 627.38
  see also Port facilities
Marinduque (Philippines) T2—599 1
Marine animals 591.77
Marine aquariums 597.177 073
  fish culture 639.342
Marine archaeology 930.102 804
Marine architecture 623.81
Marine biological resources
  public administration 354.57
  resource economics 333.956
Marine biology 578.77
  see Manual at 578.76–578.77
    vs. 551.46
Marine botany 579.177
Marine carnivores 599.79
Marine ecology 577.7
Marine engineering 623.87
Marine fishes 597.177
  culture 639.32
  see also Fishes
Marine forces (Military service) 359.96
Marine geology 551.460 8
Marine hatchetfishes 597.5
Marine insurance 368.2
  see also Insurance
Marine invertebrates
  resource economics 333.955
Marine lizards 567.95
Marine mammals 599.5
  paleozoology 569.5
  resource economics 333.959 5
Marine navigation 623.89
Marine pollution 363.739 4
  see also Water pollution
Marine reptiles (Fossils) 567.937
Marine resources 333.916 4
  public administration 354.369
Marine safety technology 623.888
Marine scenes
  art representation 704.943 7
  painting 758.2
Marine science 551.46
  see also Oceans
Marine transportation 387.5
  see also Ocean transportation
Marine transportation facilities 387.15
  see also Port facilities
Marine transportation safety 363.123
  see also Water
    transportation—safety
Marine transportation workers 387.509 2
  occupational group T7—387 5

Marine waters 551.46
  see also Oceans
Marine zoology 591.77
Mariner project 629.435 4
Marines (Armed forces) 359.96
Marinette County (Wis.) T2—775 33
Maring (Papua New Guinea people) T5—991 2
Mariology (Christian doctrines) 232.91
Marion County (Ala.) T2—761 89
Marion County (Ark.) T2—767 193
Marion County (Fla.) T2—759 75
Marion County (Ga.) T2—758 482
Marion County (Ill.) T2—773 794
Marion County (Ind.) T2—772 52
Marion County (Iowa) T2—777 83
Marion County (Kan.) T2—781 57
Marion County (Ky.) T2—769 51
Marion County (Miss.) T2—762 21
Marion County (Mo.) T2—778 353
Marion County (Ohio) T2—771 514
Marion County (Or.) T2—795 37
Marion County (S.C.) T2—757 86
Marion County (Tenn.) T2—768 79
Marion County (Tex.) T2—764 193
Marion County (W. Va.) T2—754 54
Marionettes 791.53
  making
    handicrafts 745.592 24
  see also Puppets
Mariopteris 561.597
Mariotype process 773.1
Mariposa County (Calif.) T2—794 46
Marital property law 346.016 6
Marital psychotherapy
  psychiatry 616.891 56
Marital rights 346.016 3
Maritime (Russia: Kray) T2—577
Maritime law 343.096
  international law 341.756 6
Maritime Provinces 971.5
  T2—715
Marjoram 641.357
  botany 583.96
  see also Herbs
Mark (Gospel) 226.3
Markazī (Iran) T2—552 7
Marker drawing 741.26
Markerwaard (Netherlands) T2—492 2
Market analysis procedure
  management 658.83
  T1—068 8
Market analysis reports 380.1
Market economies 330.122
Market research procedure
  management 658.83
  T1—068 8
Market research reports 380.1
Market segmentation
  management 658.802
Market study procedure
  management 658.835
  T1—068 8
Market study reports 380.1
Marketing 380.1
  law 343.084
  management 658.8
  T1—068 8
    see Manual at 658.8 and T1—0688; *also at* 658.8, T1—0688 vs. 659
  see also Commerce
  see Manual at 380.1 vs. 658.8
Marketing channels
  management 658.84
Marketing firms 380.1
Marketing management 658.8
  T1—068 8
  see Manual at 658.8 and T1—0688; *also at* 658.8, T1—0688 vs. 659
Marketing survey procedure
  management 658.83
  T1—068 8
Marketing survey reports 380.1
Markets 380.1
  area planning 711.552 2
  marketing management 658.84
  retail 381.1
    management 658.87
  see also Commerce
Markham River (Papua New Guinea) T2—957 1
Marking (Students) 371.272
Markov chains 519.233
Markov processes 519.233
Markov risk 519.287
Marks of identification 929.9
  T1—027
Marl 553.68
Marlboro County (S.C.) T2—757 64
Marlborough District (N.Z.) T2—937 5
Marlborough Province (N.Z.) T2—937 5

Marlins 597.78
  sports fishing 799.177 8
Marmalades 641.852
  commercial processing 664.152
  home preparation 641.852
Marmara, Sea of (Turkey) 551.462 9
  T2—163 89
Marmarica T2—397 6
  ancient 939.76
Marmosets 599.84
Marmota 599.366
Marmots 599.366
Marne (France) T2—443 2
Marne River (France) T2—443
Maronites 281.5
Maronites (Religious order) 255.18
  church history 271.18
Marowijne (Surinam : District) T2—883 8
Marquard (South Africa : District) T2—685 5
Marquesan language 499.42
  T6—994 2
Marquesas Islands T2—963 1
Marquesic languages 499.42
  T6—994 2
Marquetry
  furniture arts 749.5
  wood handicrafts 745.512
Marquette County (Mich.) T2—774 96
Marquette County (Wis.) T2—775 58
Marquisettes 677.652
Marrakech (Morocco : Province) T2—646
Marriage 306.81
  arts 700.454 3
  T3C—354 3
  citizenship issues 323.636
  customs 392.5
  ethics 173
    religion 291.563
      Buddhism 294.356 3
      Christianity 241.63
      Hinduism 294.548 63
      Islam 297.563
      Judaism 296.363
  folklore 398.27
    history and criticism 398.354
  law 346.016
  literature 808.803 543
    history and criticism 809.933 543
    specific literatures T3B—080 354 3
      history and criticism T3B—093 543
  music 781.587
Marriage (continued)
  personal religion 291.441
    Buddhism 294.344 41
    Christianity 248.4
    Hinduism 294.544 1
    Islam 297.577
    Judaism 296.74
  religion 291.441
    Christianity 248.4
    Islam 297.577
    Judaism 296.74
  religious doctrine 291.22
    Christianity 234.165
  religious law 291.84
    Christianity 262.9
    Judaism 296.444
  rites 291.38
    Christianity 265.5
    Judaism 296.444
      liturgy 296.454 4
    see also Public worship
  social theology 291.178 358 1
    Christianity 261.835 81
Marriage counseling
  pastoral theology 291.61
    Christianity 259.14
    Judaism 296.61
  psychotherapy 616.891 56
  social welfare 362.828 6
Married persons 306.872
  T1—086 55
  Christian devotional literature 242.644
  family relationships 306.872
  guides to religious life 291.441
    Christianity 248.844
    Islam 297.577
    Judaism 296.74
    see also Marriage—personal religion
  psychology 155.645
  social group 305.906 55
Married women 306.872
  family relationships 306.872
  labor economics 331.43
Marrucinian language 479.7
  T6—797
Mars (Planet) 523.43
  T2—992 3
  astrology 133.535
  manned flights to 629.455 3
  unmanned flights to 629.435 43
Marsá Maṭrūḥ (Egypt) T2—621
Marseille (France) T2—449 12
Marseilles T2—449 12

Marsh flies 595.774
Marsh rabbit 599.324
Marshall County (Ala.) T2—761 94
Marshall County (Ill.) T2—773 515
Marshall County (Ind.) T2—772 88
Marshall County (Iowa) T2—777 55
Marshall County (Kan.) T2—781 31
Marshall County (Ky.) T2—769 91
Marshall County (Minn.) T2—776 97
Marshall County (Miss.) T2—762 88
Marshall County (Okla.) T2—766 61
Marshall County (S.D.) T2—783 13
Marshall County (Tenn.) T2—768 585
Marshall County (W. Va.) T2—754 16
Marshall Islands 996.83
T2—968 3
Marshals (Law) 347.016
occupational group T7—349
Marshals (Police) 363.282
Marshes 551.41
see also Wetlands
Marsian language 479.7
T6—797
Marsiliales 587.3
Marsupial cats 599.27
Marsupial mice 599.27
Marsupial moles 599.27
Marsupial rats 599.27
Marsupialia 599.2
Marsupials 599.2
conservation technology 639.979 2
paleozoology 569.2
resource economics 333.959 2
Marsupicarnivora 599.27
Martaban, Gulf of (Burma) 551.467 65
T2—165 65
Martens 599.766 5
Martes 599.766 5
Martha's Vineyard (Mass.) T2—744 94
Martial artists 796.809 2
sports group T7—796 8
Martial arts 796.8
physical fitness 613.714 8
see also Sports
Martial law 342.062 8
Martin, Lake (Ala.) T2—761 53
Martin County (Fla.) T2—759 31
Martin County (Ind.) T2—772 382
Martin County (Ky.) T2—769 243
Martin County (Minn.) T2—776 232
Martin County (N.C.) T2—756 45
Martin County (Tex.) T2—764 857
Martingales 519.287
Martinicans T5—969 729 82
Martiniquais T5—969 729 82
Martinique 972.982
T2—729 82
Martins 598.826
Martinsville (Va.) T2—755 693
Martyrs 200.92
biography 200.92
Christian 272.092
see Manual at 230–280
role and function 291.61
see Manual at 200.92 and 291–299
Marwari language 491.479 7
T6—914 79
Marwari literature 891.479
Marxian parties 324.217
international organizations 324.17
Marxian socialism 335.4
economics 335.4
political ideology 320.531 5
see Manual at 335.4 vs. 335.401, 335.411
Marxism 335.4
economics 335.4
political ideology 320.531 5
see Manual at 335.4 vs. 335.401, 335.411
Marxism-Leninism 335.43
economics 335.43
political ideology 320.532 2
Marxist-Christian dialogue
Christian theology 261.21
Marxist-Leninists 335.430 92
Marxists 335.409 2
Mary, Blessed Virgin, Saint 232.91
art representation 704.948 55
arts T3C—351
private prayers to 242.74
see Manual at 230–280
Mary, Queen of Scots
Scottish history 941.105
Mary I, Queen of England
English history 942.054
Mary II, Queen of England
British history 941.068
English history 942.068
Scottish history 941.106 8
Mary Tudor, Queen of England
English history 942.054
Maryborough (Qld.) T2—943 2
Maryborough (Vic.) T2—945 3
Maryland 975.2
T2—752

Masaba language	496.395
	T6—963 95
Masaba-Luhya languages	496.395
	T6—963 95
Masai (African people)	T5—965
Masai language	496.5
	T6—965
Masai literature	896.5
Masaya (Nicaragua : Dept.)	T2—728 514
Masbate (Philippines : Province)	T2—599 5
Mascara (Algeria : Province)	T2—651
Mascarene Islands	T2—698
Mascots (Occultism)	133.44
Masculinity	155.332
Masers	621.381 336
Maseru (Lesotho)	T2—688 5
Mashona (African people)	T5—963 975
Mashonaland Central Province (Zimbabwe)	T2—689 1
Mashonaland East Province (Zimbabwe)	T2—689 1
Mashonaland West Province (Zimbabwe)	T2—689 1
Maskinongé (Quebec : County)	T2—714 44
Maskinongé (Quebec : Regional County Municipality)	T2—714 44
Maskoutains (Quebec)	T2—714 523
Masks	391.434
commercial technology	687.4
customs	391.434
home construction	646.478
see also Clothing	
Masks (Sculpture)	731.75
Masochism	
medicine	616.858 35
sociology	306.776
see also Mental illness	
Mason County (Ill.)	T2—773 553
Mason County (Ky.)	T2—769 323
Mason County (Mich.)	T2—774 61
Mason County (Tex.)	T2—764 66
Mason County (W. Va.)	T2—754 33
Mason County (Wash.)	T2—797 97
Masonry	693.1
Masonry (Secret order)	366.1
Masonry adhesives	666.9
building materials	691.5
materials science	620.135
Masonry dams	627.82
Masonry materials	
architectural construction	721.044 1
materials science	620.13
structural engineering	624.183
Masons	693.109 2
occupational group	T7—693
Masons (Secret order)	366.1
Masques	782.15
literature	808.825
history and criticism	809.25
specific literatures	T3B—205
individual authors	T3A—2
music	782.15
stage presentation	792.6
see also Theater	
Mass (Christian rite)	264.36
Anglican	264.030 36
texts	264.03
music	782.323
choral and mixed voices	782.532 3
single voices	783.093 23
Roman Catholic	264.020 36
texts	264.023
Mass (Substance)	531.14
air mechanics	533.6
gas mechanics	533.15
liquid mechanics	532.4
solid mechanics	531.5
Mass communication	302.2
communications services	384
law	343.099
social aspects	302.2
Mass culture	306
Mass deacidification	
bibliographic materials	025.84
Mass-energy equivalence	530.11
Mass hysteria	302.17
Mass media	302.23
accounting	657.84
election campaigns	324.73
influence on crime	364.254
instructional use	371.358
adult level	374.26
higher education	378.175 8
law	343.099
religion	291.175
Christianity	261.52
evangelism	269.26
use by local Christian church	253.78
administration	254.3
Judaism	296.37
sociology	302.23
see Manual at 302.2308	

Mass media music	781.54
Mass movement (Geology)	551.307
Mass spectrometry	543.087 3
analytical chemistry	543.087 3
physics	539.602 87
Mass spectroscopy	543.087 3
analytical chemistry	543.087 3
physics	539.602 87
Mass transfer	530.475
chemical engineering	660.284 23
gaseous-state physics	530.435
liquid-state physics	530.425
physics	530.475
semiconductors	537.622 5
solid-state physics	530.415
Mass transit	388.4
see also Urban transportation	
Mass transport (Physics)	530.475
see also Mass transfer	
Mass transportation	388.042
law	343.093 3
transportation services	388.042
urban	388.4
see also Urban transportation	
see also Passenger services	
Mass wasting (Geology)	551.307
Massa-Carrara (Italy : Province)	T2—455 4
Massa e Carrara (Italy : Province)	T2—455 4
Massac County (Ill.)	T2—773 997
Massachusetts	974.4
	T2—744
Massachusetts Bay (Mass.)	551.461 45
	T2—163 45
Massacre of innocents	232.92
Massage	615.822
for appearance	646.75
therapeutics	615.822
Massif Central (France)	T2—445 9
Mastectomy	616.994 490 59
see also Cancer (Human)	
Master and servant	
law	346.024
Master's degree	378.2
Masters Golf Tournament	796.352 66
Masterton District (N.Z.)	T2—936 8
Mastication	
human physiology	612.311
rubber	678.22
see also Digestive system	
Mastiffs	636.73
Mastigomycotina	579.53
Mastoid processes	
human anatomy	611.85
human physiology	612.854
otology	617.87
see also Ears	
Masts	623.862
Masturbation	
sociology	306.772
Masvingo Province (Zimbabwe)	T2—689 1
Mặt trận dân tộc giải phóng miền nam Việt Nam	959.704 332 2
Matabeleland North Province (Zimbabwe)	T2—689 1
Matabeleland South Province (Zimbabwe)	T2—689 1
Mataco-Guaicuru languages	498
	T6—98
Mataco languages	498
	T6—98
Matagalpa (Nicaragua : Dept.)	T2—728 525
Matagalpa language	497.8
	T6—978
Matagalpan Indians	T5—978
Matagami (Quebec)	T2—714 115
Matagorda County (Tex.)	T2—764 132
Matamata Piako District (N.Z.)	T2—933 53
Matane (Quebec : County)	T2—714 775
Matane (Quebec : Regional County Municipality)	T2—714 775
Matanuska-Susitna Borough (Alaska)	T2—798 3
Matanzas (Cuba : Province)	T2—729 13
Matapédia (Quebec)	T2—714 775
Matapédia (Quebec : Regional County Municipality)	T2—714 775
Matawini (Quebec)	T2—714 41
Match-cover advertising	659.13
Match covers	741.694
Matches	662.5
Matching numbers contests	790.134
Maté	641.337 7
agriculture	633.77
beverage	641.337 7
botany	583.85
commercial processing	663.96
cooking with	641.637 7
home preparation	641.877
Mate selection	
customs	392.4

Mate selection (continued)
  sociology 306.82
Matera (Italy : Province) T2—457 72
Materia medica 615.1
  see also Drugs (Pharmaceuticals)
Material remains 930.1
Materialism 146.3
  Christian polemics 239.7
  Indian philosophy 181.46
  Islamic polemics 297.298
Materialization (Spiritualism) 133.92
Materials T1—028 4
  engineering 620.11
  foundation engineering 624.153
  manufacturing technology 670
  standards and specifications
    production management 658.562
Materials costs
  financial management 658.155 3
Materials engineers 620.110 92
  occupational group T7—620 1
Materials estimates T1—029 9
  building construction 692.5
Materials handling
  materials management 658.781
Materials-handling equipment 621.86
  ships 623.867
Materials management 658.7
  T1—068 7
  public administration 352.55
  schools 371.67
  see Manual at 658.7 and T1—0687
Materials science 620.11
Matériel (Armed forces) 355.8
Maternal behavior (Animals) 591.563
Maternal complications
  obstetrics 618.51
Maternal deaths
  incidence 614.599 279
  obstetrics 618.79
Maternal dystocia
  obstetrics 618.51
Maternally acquired antibodies 571.963 8
Maternity garments 392
  commercial technology 687.16
  customs 392
  home economics 646.34
  home sewing 646.47
  see also Clothing
Maternity insurance 368.424
  law 344.022 4
  see also Insurance
Maternity leave 331.44
  economics 331.44
  personnel management 658.312 2
Maternity services 362.198 2
  see also Health services
Mathematical analysis 515
Mathematical crystallography 548.7
Mathematical economics
  school 330.154 3
Mathematical games 793.74
Mathematical geography 526
Mathematical logic 511.3
  computer programming
    languages 005.131
Mathematical models 511.8
  T1—015 118
  systems 003
    T1—011
Mathematical optimization 519.3
Mathematical physics 530.15
Mathematical programming 519.7
  management decision making 658.403 3
Mathematical recreations 793.74
Mathematical systems 511.2
Mathematicians 510.92
  occupational group T7—51
Mathematics 510
  T1—015 1
  elementary education 372.7
  see Manual at 510; *also at* 510, T1—0151 vs. 003, T1—011; *also at* 510, T1—0151 vs. 004–006, T1—0285
Mathews County (Va.) T2—755 31
Mathieu functions 515.54
Mating 591.562
Matins 264.15
  Anglican 264.030 15
    texts 264.033
  music 782.324
    Anglican church 782.325
  see also Liturgy of the hours
Mato Grosso (Brazil : State) T2—817 2
Mato Grosso do Sul (Brazil) T2—817 1
Matriarchal family 306.859
Matriarchy (System of government) 321.1
Matrices 512.943 4
Matriculation 371.21
Matrilineal kinship 306.83

Matrimony 306.81
  sacrament 234.165
    public worship 265.5
    theology 234.165
  see also Marriage
Matrix algebra 512.943 4
Matrix mechanics 530.122
Maṭrūḥ (Egypt) T2—621
Mats 642.7
  arts 746.96
  home sewing 646.21
  table setting 642.7
MATS (Air transportation) 358.44
Matter 530
  philosophy 117
  physics 530
  structure 539.1
Matter at high temperatures 536.57
Matter at low temperatures 536.56
Matthew (Gospel) 226.2
Matthias, Holy Roman Emperor
  German history 943.035
Matthiola 583.64
Matting
  arts 746.41
Mattresses 645.4
  manufacturing technology 684.15
  see also Furniture
Matumbi languages 496.397
  T6—963 97
Maturation 571.87
  developmental psychology 155
  human physiology 612.6
Maturity
  developmental psychology
    adulthood 155.6
  human physiology 612.663
  individual psychology
    character development 155.25
Maui (Hawaii) T2—969 21
Maui County (Hawaii) T2—969 2
Maule (Chile : Region) T2—833 5
Maumee River (Ind. and Ohio) T2—771 1
Maundy Thursday 263.925
  devotional literature 242.35
  music 781.726
  sermons 252.625
Maurelle Island (B.C.) T2—711 1
Maurepas, Lake (La.) T2—763 32
Mauretania 939.71
  T2—397 1
Mauretania Caesariensis T2—397 1
Mauretania Tingitana T2—397 1
Mauricie Region (Quebec) T2—714 45
Mauritania 966.1
  T2—661
Mauritanians T5—966 1
Mauritians T5—914 1
Mauritius 969.82
  T2—698 2
Maury County (Tenn.) T2—768 59
Maurya dynasty 934.04
Maverick County (Tex.) T2—764 435
Mawlid al-Nabī 297.36
Maxamed Siyaad Barre
  Somali history 967.730 52
Maxima 511.66
Maximilian, Emperor of Mexico
  Mexican history 972.07
Maximilian I, Holy Roman Emperor
  German history 943.029
Maximilian II, Emperor of Germany
  German history 943.033
Maxims 398.9
Maximum-security prisons 365.33
  see also Correctional institutions
Maxwell's equations (Physics) 530.141
Maxwell's thermodynamic formulas 536.71
May Day 394.262 7
Maya (Middle American people) T5—974 152
Maya language 497.415 2
  T6—974 152
Maya literature 897.415 2
Mayaguana Island (Bahamas) T2—729 6
Mayagüez (P.R. : District) T2—729 56
Mayan calendar 529.329 784 152
Mayan languages 497.415
  T6—974 15
Mayan period 972.810 16
Mayans T5—974 152
Mayapple 583.34
Mayas T5—974 152
Maydeae 584.92
Mayenne (France : Dept.) T2—441 6
Mayes County (Okla.) T2—766 93
Mayflies 595.734
Mayflower 583.34
Mayo (Ireland : County) T2—417 3
Mayo, Richard Southwell Bourke, Earl of
  Indian history 954.035 2

Mayonnaise 641.814
  food technology 664.37
  home preparation 641.814
Mayor-council government 320.854
Mayors 320.854
  occupational group T7—351
  public administration 352.232 16
Mayotte 969.45
  T2—694 5
Maypop 583.626
Maysān (Iraq) T2—567 5
Māzandarān (Iran) T2—552 3
Mazaruni-Potaro (Guyana : District) T2—881 9
Mazdaism 295
Maze puzzles 793.738
Mazurkas 793.319 438
  music 784.188 4
Mbabane (Swaziland) T2—688 7
Mbai language (Moissala) 496.5
  T6—965
Mbala (Zairian people, Bandundu region) T5—963 93
Mbala language (Bandundu region, Zaire) 496.393
  T6—963 93
Mbasogo, Teodoro Obiang Nguema
  Equatorial Guinean history 967.180 32
Mbete languages 496.396
  T6—963 96
Mbeya Region (Tanzania) T2—678 28
MBO (Management by objectives) 658.401 2
  public administration 352.36
Mbole-Ena languages 496.394
  T6—963 94
Mboshi languages 496.396
  T6—963 96
Mbosi language 496.396
  T6—963 96
Mbukushu language 496.399
  T6—963 99
Mbum language 496.361
  T6—963 61
Mbundu (Angolan people, Benguela Province) T5—963 99
Mbundu (Angolan people, Luanda Province) T5—963 932
Mbundu language (Benguela Province, Angola) 496.399
  T6—963 99
Mbundu language (Luanda Province, Angola) 496.393 2
  T6—963 932
McBride (B.C.) T2—711 82
McClain County (Okla.) T2—766 55
McCone County (Mont.) T2—786 26
McCook County (S.D.) T2—783 372
McCormick County (S.C.) T2—757 36
McCracken County (Ky.) T2—769 95
McCreary County (Ky.) T2—769 135
McCulloch County (Tex.) T2—764 67
McCurtain County (Okla.) T2—766 64
McDonald County (Mo.) T2—778 736
McDonough County (Ill.) T2—773 42
McDowell County (N.C.) T2—756 89
McDowell County (W. Va.) T2—754 49
McDuffie County (Ga.) T2—758 632
McGregor River (B.C.) T2—711 82
McHenry County (Ill.) T2—773 22
McHenry County (N.D.) T2—784 62
McIntosh County (Ga.) T2—758 737
McIntosh County (N.D.) T2—784 55
McIntosh County (Okla.) T2—766 74
McKean County (Pa.) T2—748 63
McKenzie County (N.D.) T2—784 81
McKinley, William
  United States history 973.88
McKinley County (N.M.) T2—789 83
McLean County (Ill.) T2—773 59
McLean County (Ky.) T2—769 826
McLean County (N.D.) T2—784 75
McLennan County (Tex.) T2—764 284
McLeod County (Minn.) T2—776 52
McMinn County (Tenn.) T2—768 865
McMullen County (Tex.) T2—764 452
McNairy County (Tenn.) T2—768 29
McNaughton Lake (B.C.) T2—711 68
McPherson County (Kan.) T2—781 55
McPherson County (Neb.) T2—782 793
McPherson County (S.D.) T2—783 16
Mdantsane (South Africa : District) T2—687 92
Mdutjana (South Africa : District) T2—682 95
Mead, Lake (Ariz. and Nev.) T2—793 12
Meade County (Kan.) T2—781 75
Meade County (Ky.) T2—769 852
Meade County (S.D.) T2—783 44
Meadow beauties 583.76
Meadow mice (Voles) 599.354
Meadowlarks 598.874

Meadows 333.74
  biology 578.746
  ecology 577.46
  see also Grasslands
Meagher County (Mont.) T2—786 612
Meal (Milling products)
  commercial processing 664.720 7
    wheat 664.722 73
Meals 642
  customs 394.1
  transportation services 388.042
    see also Passenger services
Mealworms 595.769
Mean 519.533
Mean value theorems 515.33
Meaning
  epistemology 121.68
  linguistics 401.43
    specific languages T4—014 3
    see Manual at 401.43 vs. 306.44, 401.9, 412, 415
Measles
  incidence 614.523
  medicine 616.915
  pediatrics 618.929 15
  see also Communicable diseases (Human)
Measure theory 515.42
  calculus 515.783
Measurement 530.8
  T1—028 7
Measurement systems 530.81
  physics 530.81
  social aspects 389.15
Measurement theory 530.801
Measures 530.81
  see also Weights and measures
Measuring instruments
  electric measurement 621.37
  electronics 621.381 548
  manufacturing technology 681.2
  physics 530.7
Meat 641.36
  commercial preservation technology 664.902 8
  commercial processing
    economics 338.476 649
    technology 664.9
  cooking 641.66
  food 641.36
  home preservation 641.49
Meat (continued)
  product safety 363.192 9
    see also Food—product safety
Meat loaf 641.824
  commercial processing 664.92
  cooking 641.824
Meat pies 641.824
  commercial processing 664.92
  cooking 641.824
Meat processing industry 338.476 649
  see also Meat
Meath (Ireland) T2—418 22
Meatless high-protein foods
  technology 664.64
Meats 641.36
  see also Meat
Mecca (Saudi Arabia) T2—538
  Islamic religion 297.352
Mechanical bands 784.6
Mechanical barriers
  military engineering 623.31
Mechanical chess players 794.17
Mechanical conveyer systems
  office services 651.79
Mechanical deformation
  materials science 620.112 3
Mechanical drawing 604.2
  T1—022 1
Mechanical engineering 621
  military applications 623.045
Mechanical engineers 621.092
  occupational group T7—621
Mechanical forces 530
  biophysics 571.43
    humans 612.014 41
  materials science 620.112 3
Mechanical musical instruments 786.6
  bands and orchestras 784
  chamber ensembles 785
    single type 785.66
  construction 786.619 23
    by hand 786.619 23
    by machine 681.866
  solo music 786.6
  see Manual at 784–788
Mechanical pencils
  manufacturing technology 681.6
Mechanical processes
  printing 686.231
  wood pulp 676.122
Mechanical properties
  materials science 620.112 92

Mechanical separation
  ores 622.75
Mechanical stokers
  steam engineering 621.183
Mechanical systems
  ships 623.850 1
Mechanical toys 790.133
  manufacturing technology 688.728
  recreation 790.133
  see also Toys
Mechanical working
  metals 671.3
Mechanics 530
  atmosphere 551.515
  classical physics 531
  engineering 620.1
  foundation soils 624.151 36
  physics 530
  quantum physics 530.12
  structures 624.171
  see Manual at 530.12 vs. 531
Mechanics' liens 346.024
Mechanics of materials 620.112 3
Mechanics of particles
  classical physics 531.16
Mechanics of points 531.1
Mechanism (Philosophy) 146.6
Mechanisms
  engineering 621.8
Mechanization
  agricultural economics 338.161
  control engineering 629.8
  economics 338.064
  factory operations engineering 670.427
  mineral industries 338.26
  production management 658.514
  secondary industries 338.45
  social effects 303.483
Mechanized bells 786.64
  see also Mechanical musical instruments
Mechanized cavalry 357.5
Mechanotherapy
  medicine 615.822
Mechitarists 255.17
  church history 271.17
Mecklenburg (Germany : State) T2—431 7
Mecklenburg County (N.C.) T2—756 76
Mecklenburg County (Va.) T2—755 645
Mecklenburg-Vorpommern (Germany) T2—431 7
Mecoptera 595.744
Mecosta County (Mich.) T2—774 52
Medal of Honor Legion (U.S.) 369.11
Medallions
  numismatics 737.22
Medals
  armed forces 355.134 2
  numismatics 737.22
  religious significance 291.37
    see also Symbolism—religious significance
  research incentive 001.44
Médéa (Algeria : Province) T2—653
Media 302.23
  see also Mass media
Media (Ancient empire) 935.04
  T2—35
Media centers 027
  see also Libraries
Media kits
  cataloging 025.349 6
  library treatment 025.179 6
Media production
  elementary education 372.672
Median 519.533
Mediastinum
  human anatomy 611.27
  human physiology 612.2
  medicine 616.27
  surgery 617.545
  see also Respiratory system
Mediation
  international law 341.52
  labor economics 331.891 42
    public administration 354.97
  law 347.09
  personnel management 658.315 4
    public administration 352.68
  social conflict 303.69
Medicaid 368.420 097 3
  law 344.730 22
  public administration 353.690 973
Medicaid fraud 364.163
  law 345.730 263
Medical accounting 657.834
Medical anthropology 306.461
Medical assistants 610.737 092
  role and function 610.695 3
  services 610.737
Medical astrology 133.586 1
Medical bacteriology 616.014
Medical care 362.1
  see also Health services
Medical care facilities
  area planning 711.555

Medical chemistry 615.19
Medical climatology 616.988
  see also Environmental diseases (Human)
Medical economics 338.473 621
Medical emergencies 362.18
  medicine 616.025
  social services 362.18
Medical entomology 616.968
  see also Communicable diseases (Human)
Medical ethics 174.2
  religion 291.564 2
    Buddhism 294.356 42
    Christianity 241.642
    Hinduism 294.548 642
    Islam 297.564 2
    Judaism 296.364 2
Medical examinations 616.075
Medical examiners 614.109 2
  law 347.016
Medical genetics 616.042
  law 344.041 96
Medical geography 614.42
Medical gymnastics
  therapeutics 615.824
Medical helminthology 616.962
  see also Communicable diseases (Human)
Medical history taking 616.075 1
Medical installations (Armed forces) 355.72
Medical instruments 610.284
  manufacturing technology 681.761
  product safety 363.19
    public administration 353.99
    see also Product safety
Medical insurance 368.382 2
  public administration 353.69
  see also Insurance
Medical jurisprudence 614.1
Medical law 344.041
Medical libraries 026.61
Medical machinery
  manufacturing technology 681.761
Medical malpractice
  torts 344.041 1
Medical malpractice insurance 368.564 2
  see also Insurance
Medical meteorology 616.988
  see also Environmental diseases (Human)
Medical microbiology 616.01
  see Manual at 579.165 vs. 616.01; *also at* 616.1–616.9: Add table: 071 vs. 01; *also at* 616.9 vs. 616.01
Medical missionaries
  Christian 266.009 2
  role and function 610.695
Medical missions 362.1
  Christian 266
  social welfare 362.1
  see also Health services
Medical mycology 616.969
  see also Communicable diseases (Human)
Medical office buildings
  architecture 725.23
Medical parasitology 616.96
  see also Communicable diseases (Human)
Medical personnel 610.92
  law 344.041
  malpractice 344.041 1
  occupational group T7—61
  role and function 610.69
  see Manual at 362.1–362.4 vs. 610: Biographies; *also at* 610.69
Medical physics 610.153
Medical protozoology 616.016
Medical radiology 616.075 7
  see Manual at 616.0757 vs. 616.0754, 616.07572
Medical records management 651.504 261
Medical rehabilitation 617.03
Medical sciences 610
  folklore 398.27
    history and criticism 398.353
  information systems 025.066 1
Medical screening 362.177
  public administration 353.628
  see also Health services
Medical services 362.1
  armed forces 355.345
  see also Health services
Medical shorthand 653.18
Medical social work 362.104 25
Medical supplies 610.284
  armed forces 355.88
  product safety 363.19
    public administration 353.99
    see also Product safety

Medical technicians 610.737 092
  role and function 610.695 3
  services 610.737
Medical virology 616.019 4
Medical wastes 363.728 8
  law 344.046 22
  see also Waste control
Medicare 368.426 009 73
  law 344.730 226
  public administration 353.690 973
Medicare fraud 364.163
  law 345.730 263
Medicare supplement insurance 368.382
  see also Insurance
Medication methods 615.6
Medications 615.1
  see also Drugs (Pharmaceuticals)
Médici, Emílio Garrastazu
  Brazilian history 981.063
Medicinal plants 615.321
  agriculture 633.88
  economic botany 581.634
  pharmacognosy 615.321
Medicinal teas
  pharmacognosy 615.321
  see also Herb teas
Medicine 610
  applied science 610
  economics 338.473 621
  law 344.041
  literature 808.803 56
    history and criticism 809.933 56
    specific literatures T3B—080 356
      history and criticism T3B—093 56
  sociology 306.461
  see Manual at 610 vs. 362.17; *also at* 610 vs. 616
Medicine and religion 291.175
  Christianity 261.561
  Judaism 296.376
Medicine Bow Mountains (Colo. and Wyo.) T2—787 86
Medicine Hat (Alta.) T2—712 34
Medicine shows 791.1
Medicines 615.1
  see also Drugs (Pharmaceuticals)
Medieval architecture 723
Medieval art 709.02
Medieval church modes 781.263
Medieval law 340.55
Medieval music 780.902
Medieval painting 759.02
Medieval period 909.07
  T1—090 2
  Austrian history 943.602
  church history 270.3
  Danish history 948.901
  English history 942.03
  European history 940.1
  French history 944.02
  German history 943.02
  Italian history 945.03
  Japanese history 952.02
  Norwegian history 948.101
  Scandinavian history 948.02
  specific centuries 909.1–.4
  Swedish history 948.501
  see Manual at T1—0940902 vs. T1—0902
Medieval philosophy
  Oriental 181
  western 189
Medieval remedies
  therapeutics 615.899
Medieval sculpture 734
Medigap 368.382
  see also Insurance
Medina (England : Borough) T2—422 82
Medina (Saudi Arabia) T2—538
  Islamic religion 297.355 38
Medina County (Ohio) T2—771 35
Medina County (Tex.) T2—764 42
Meditation 158.12
  religion 291.435
    Buddhism 294.344 35
    Christianity 248.34
    Hinduism 294.543 5
    Islam 297.382
      Sufi 297.438 2
    Judaism 296.72
Meditations 158.128
  religion 291.432
    Buddhism 294.344 32
    Christianity 242
    Hinduism 294.543 2
    Islam 297.382 4
      Sufi 297.438 24
    Judaism 296.72
Meditations (Music) 784.189 6
Mediterranean Region T2—182 2
Mediterranean Sea 551.462
  T2—163 8
Medium-security prisons 365.33
  see also Correctional institutions

Term		Number
Mediums of exchange		332.4
Mediumship (Spiritualism)		133.91
Medlars		641.341 5
botany		583.73
cooking		641.641 5
food		641.341 5
orchard crop		634.15
Medulla		
human histology		611.018 4
Medulla oblongata		
human anatomy		611.81
human physiology		612.828
see also Nervous system		
Medullosaceae		561.595
Medusas		593.53
Meeker County (Minn.)	T2—776 49	
Meetings		060
management use		658.456
Megachiroptera		599.49
paleozoology		569.4
Megaloptera		595.747
Megalopteris		561.597
Mégantic (Quebec)	T2—714 575	
Megapodiidae		598.64
Megaptera		599.525
Megaric philosophy		183.6
Megaris (Greece)	T2—384	
Megasporangia		575.665
Megaspores		571.845
Meghalaya (India)	T2—541 64	
Megillah (Tractate)		296.123 2
Babylonian Talmud		296.125 2
Mishnah		296.123 2
Palestinian Talmud		296.124 2
Megillot (Bible)		221.044
Mehedinţi (Romania)	T2—498 4	
Meighen, Arthur		
Canadian history		971.061 3
1920–1921		971.061 3
1926		971.062 2
Meigs County (Ohio)	T2—771 99	
Meigs County (Tenn.)	T2—768 836	
Meiji period		952.031
Me'ilah		296.123 5
Babylonian Talmud		296.125 5
Mishnah		296.123 5
Meiosis		571.845
Meirionnydd (Wales)	T2—429 29	
Mékinac (Quebec)	T2—714 45	
Meknès (Morocco : Province)	T2—643	
Mekong River	T2—597	
Melaka (State)	T2—595 1	
Melamines		668.422 4
Melancholy		
literature		808.803 53
history and criticism		809.933 53
specific literatures	T3B—080 353	
history and criticism	T3B—093 53	
Melanconiales		579.55
Melanesia		995
	T2—95	
Melanesian languages		499.5
	T6—995	
Melanesian literatures		899.5
Melanesians	T5—995	
Melanoma		
incidence		614.599 947 7
medicine		616.994 77
see also Cancer (Human)		
Melanommatales		579.564
Melastomataceae		583.76
Melayu Asli languages		499.28
	T6—992 8	
Melbourne (Vic.)	T2—945 1	
Meleagrididae		598.645
Meles		599.767 2
Meliaceae		583.77
Melilla (Spain)	T2—642	
Melilotus		633.366
botany		583.74
forage crop		633.366
Melinae		599.767
Meliorism		
philosophy		149.5
Mellette County (S.D.)	T2—783 63	
Mellivorinae		599.767
Melmoth (South Africa)	T2—684 3	
Melodeons		788.863
instrument		788.863 19
music		788.863
see also Woodwind instruments		
Melodrama		792.27
literature		808.825 27
history and criticism		809.252 7
specific literatures	T3B—205 27	
individual authors	T3A—2	
stage presentation		792.27
see also Theater		
Melody		781.24
Meloidea		595.769
Melons		641.356 1
botany		583.63
commercial processing		664.805 61
cooking		641.656 1
food		641.356 1
garden crop		635.61

Melos Island (Greece) T2—495 85
Melting 536.42
  chemical engineering 660.284 296
Melting metals 671.24
Melton (England : Borough) T2—425 46
Melville (Sask.) T2—712 44
Melville Peninsula (N.W.T.) T2—719 5
Membership lists T1—06
Membrane processes
  chemical engineering 660.284 24
  desalinization 628.167 4
  water supply treatment 628.164
Membranes (Cytology) 571.64
Membranophones 786.9
  see also Percussion instruments
Memoirs 920
  T1—092
Memorabilia T1—075
Memorandums
  office use 651.755
Memorial buildings 725.94
  see also Monuments
Memorials 394.4
  see also Military commemorations
Memorizing
  music training method 781.426
Memory 153.12
  educational psychology 370.152 2
  human physiology 612.82
  philosophy 128.3
Memory (Computer) 004.5
  engineering 621.397
Memory disorders
  symptomatology 616.84
  see also Nervous system
Memory management 005.435
  programming 005.425
  programs 005.435
Memphis (Extinct city) T2—32
Memphis (Tenn.) T2—768 19
Memphrémagog (Quebec) T2—714 64
Memphrémagog Lake (Quebec) T2—714 64
Men 305.31
  T1—081
  T7—041
  art representation 704.942 3
  arts T3C—352 041
  biography 920.71
  criminal offenders 364.373
Men (continued)
  drawing 743.43
  etiquette 395.142
  grooming 646.704 4
  guides to Christian life 248.842
  guides to religious life 291.440 81
  health 613.042 34
  journalism for 070.483 46
  literature 808.803 520 41
    history and criticism 809.933 520 41
    specific literatures T3B—080 352 041
      history and criticism T3B—093 520 41
  painting 757.3
  physical fitness 613.704 49
  psychology 155.632
  recreation 790.194
    indoor 793.019 4
    outdoor 796.081
  sex hygiene 613.952
  social aspects 305.31
  social theology 291.178 343 1
    Christianity 261.834 31
  see Manual at T1—081 and T1—082, T1—08351, T1—08352, T1—08421, T1—08422
Menabe (Kingdom) 969.101
  T2—691
Ménage à trois 306.735
Menaḥot 296.123 5
  Babylonian Talmud 296.125 5
  Mishnah 296.123 5
Menarche
  human physiology 612.662
  see also Female genital system
Menard County (Ill.) T2—773 555
Menard County (Tex.) T2—764 877
Mende (African people) T5—963 48
Mende-Bandi languages 496.348
  T6—963 48
Mende language 496.348
  T6—963 48
Mende literature 896.348
Mendelevium 546.449
  see also Chemicals
Mendel's laws 576.52
Mendicant religious orders 255.06
  church history 271.06
Mending books 025.7
Mending textiles
  home economics 646.2
    clothes 646.6
Mendip (England : District) T2—423 83

Mendip Hills (England) T2—423 83
Mendocino County (Calif.) T2—794 15
Mendoza (Argentina : Province) T2—826 4
Menelik II, Negus of Ethiopia
  Ethiopian history 963.043
Menger, Carl
  economic school 330.157
Mengistu Haile-Mariam
  Ethiopian history 963.071
Menhadens 597.45
  fishing 639.274 5
Ménière's disease 617.882
  see also Ears
Menifee County (Ky.) T2—769 583
Menindee Lake (N.S.W.) T2—944 9
Meninges 573.862 5
  human anatomy 611.81
  human histology 611.018 8
  human physiology 612.82
  medicine 616.82
  see also Nervous system
Meningitis
  medicine 616.82
  see also Nervous system
Menispermaceae 583.34
Mennonite Church 289.7
  church government 262.097
    parishes 254.097
  church law 262.989 7
  doctrines 230.97
    catechisms and creeds 238.97
  general councils 262.597
  guides to Christian life 248.489 7
  missions 266.97
  moral theology 241.049 7
  public worship 264.097
  religious associations 267.189 7
  religious education 268.897
  seminaries 230.073 97
  theology 230.97
Mennonite cooking 641.566
Mennonites
  biography 289.709 2
  religious group T7—287
Menominee County (Mich.) T2—774 953
Menominee County (Wis.) T2—775 356
Menominee Indians T5—973
Menopause
  disorders
    gynecology 618.175
  human physiology 612.665
  see also Female genital system
Menorca (Spain) T2—467 52
Menorrhagia
  gynecology 618.172
  see also Female genital system
Men's clothing 391.1
  commercial technology 687.081
  customs 391.1
  home economics 646.32
  home sewing 646.402
  see also Clothing
Men's liberation movement 305.32
Men's prisons 365.44
  see also Correctional institutions
Men's voices 782.8
  choral and mixed voices 782.8
  single voices 783.8
Mensk (Belarus : Voblasts) T2—478 6
Menskaia voblasts′ (Belarus) T2—478 6
Menstruation
  gynecology 618.172
  human physiology 612.662
  see also Female genital system
Mensuration 530.8
  T1—028 7
  forestry 634.928 5
Mensuration (Geometry) 516.15
Mental arithmetic 513.9
Mental deficiency 362.3
  medicine 616.858 8
  social welfare 362.3
  see also Mental retardation
Mental disorders 362.2
  see also Mental illness
Mental health
  social welfare 362.2
  see also Mental health services
Mental health facilities 362.21
  see also Mental health services
Mental health insurance 368.382 5
  see also Insurance
Mental health law 344.044
Mental health personnel 616.890 092
  law 344.044
  role and function 616.890 23
Mental health services 362.2
  for employees
    personnel management 658.382
      public administration 352.67
  law 344.044

Mental health services (continued)
  pastoral theology 291.61
    Christianity 259.42
  public administration 353.64
  social theology 291.178 322
    Christianity 261.832 2
  students 371.713
  see also Health services
Mental illness 362.2
  arts T3C—353
  Christian religious guidance 248.862
  geriatrics 618.976 89
  influence on crime 364.24
  literature 808.803 53
    history and criticism 809.933 53
    specific literatures T3B—080 353
      history and criticism T3B—093 53
  nursing 610.736 8
  pastoral theology 291.61
    Christianity 259.42
  pediatrics 618.928 9
  psychiatry 616.89
  social theology 291.178 322
    Christianity 261.832 2
  social welfare 362.2
    see also Mental health services
Mental retardation 362.3
  geriatrics 618.976 858 8
  medicine 616.858 8
  nursing 610.736 8
  pediatrics 618.928 588
  social welfare 362.3
    public administration 353.65
Mental tests 153.93
Mental therapies
  medicine 615.851
  psychiatry 616.891 6
    see also Mental illness
Mentally disabled persons 305.908 24
  T1—087 4
  T7—082 4
  education 371.92
    law 344.079 12
  institutional buildings
    architecture 725.53
  legal status 346.013 8
    constitutional law 342.087
    private law 346.013 8
  social group 305.908 24
Mentally healthy persons 305.908 22
  T7—082 2
Mentally ill persons 305.908 24
  T1—087 4
  T7—082 4
  criminal offenders 364.38
    correctional institutions 365.46
      see also Correctional institutions
  education 371.94
    law 344.079 14
  guides to Christian life 248.862
  legal status 346.013 8
    constitutional law 342.087
    private law 346.013 8
  social group 305.908 24
  social welfare 362.2
    law 344.044
    see also Mental health services
  see Manual at 362.1–362.4 vs. 610: Biographies
Mentally retarded children 305.908 26
  T1—087 4
  home care 649.152 8
  see also Mentally retarded persons
Mentally retarded persons 305.908 26
  T1—087 4
  T7—082 6
  education 371.928
    law 344.079 128
  legal status 346.013 8
    constitutional law 342.087
    private law 346.013 8
  social group 305.908 26
  social welfare 362.3
Menticide
  psychology 153.853
Mentoring
  education 371.102
Menuridae 598.822
Menus 642
Menzies, Robert Gordon, Sir
  Australian history 994.05
    1939–1941 994.042
    1949–1966 994.05
Mephitinae 599.768
Meprobamate
  pharmacodynamics 615.788 2
  see also Mental illness
Merbein (Vic.) T2—945 9
Mercantile credit 332.742
  marketing management 658.882
Mercantilism (Economic school) 330.151 3
Mercator projection 526.82

Merced County (Calif.)	T2—794 58
Mercedarians	255.45
church history	271.45
Mercenary troops	355.354
Mercer County (Ill.)	T2—773 395
Mercer County (Ky.)	T2—769 485
Mercer County (Mo.)	T2—778 213
Mercer County (N.D.)	T2—784 83
Mercer County (N.J.)	T2—749 65
Mercer County (Ohio)	T2—771 415
Mercer County (Pa.)	T2—748 95
Mercer County (W. Va.)	T2—754 74
Mercerizing textiles	677.028 25
Merchandisers	380.109 2
occupational group	T7—381
Merchandising	380.1
management	658.8
Merchant marine	387.5
see also Ocean transportation	
Merchant seamen	387.509 2
occupational group	T7—387 5
technologists	623.880 92
Merchant ships	387.2
design	623.812
engineering	623.82
freight services	387.544
power-driven	387.24
design	623.812 4
engineering	623.824
transportation services	387.24
transportation services	387.2
wind-driven	387.224
design	623.812 24
engineering	623.822 4
handling	623.882 24
transportation services	387.224
see also Ships	
Merchants	380.109 2
Mercia supremacy	942.015 7
Mercuries (Plants)	583.69
Mercury (Element)	669.71
chemical engineering	661.066 3
chemistry	546.663
economic geology	553.454
human toxicology	615.925 663
metallurgy	669.71
mining	622.345 4
organic chemistry	547.056 63
applied	661.895
physical metallurgy	669.967 1
toxicology	571.954 663
see also Chemicals; Metals	
Mercury (Planet)	523.41
	T2—992 1
astrology	133.533
unmanned flights to	629.435 41
Mercury fulminate	662.27
Mercury project	629.454
Mercury-vapor lighting	621.327 4
see also Lighting	
Mergansers	598.415
Merge sort (Computer science)	005.741
Mergers	338.83
accounting	657.96
banks	332.16
economics	338.83
law	346.066 26
management	658.16
Merging data	005.741
Mergini	598.415
Mérida (Spain)	T2—462 7
Mérida (Venezuela : State)	T2—871 3
Meridian (Miss.)	T2—762 677
Meridional instruments	522.3
Merina (Kingdom)	969.101
	T2—691
Merino sheep	636.36
Merioneth (Wales)	T2—429 29
Meristem	575.48
Merit (Christian doctrine)	234
Merit awards	
personnel management	658.322 6
Merit system (Civil service)	352.63
Meriwether County (Ga.)	T2—758 455
Merkaz (Israel : District)	T2—569 47
Mermaids	398.21
see also Legendary beings	
Mermen	398.21
see also Legendary beings	
Meromorphic functions	515.982
Meropidae	598.78
Merostomata	565.49
Merovingian dynasty	944.013
French history	944.013
German history	943.013
Merreden (W.A.)	T2—941 2
Merrick County (Neb.)	T2—782 423
Merrimac, Battle of Monitor and, 1862	973.752
Merrimack County (N.H.)	T2—742 72
Merrimack River (N.H. and Mass.)	T2—742 72
Merritt (B.C.)	T2—711 72
Mersey River (England)	T2—427 5
Merseyside (England)	T2—427 5
Merthyr Tydfil (Wales)	T2—429 75

Merton (London, England) T2—421 93
Mesa County (Colo.) T2—788 17
Mesa Verde National Park (Colo.) T2—788 27
Mesabi Range (Minn.) T2—776 77
Mescal 641.25
  commercial processing 663.5
Mescaline abuse 362.294
  medicine 616.863 4
  personal health 613.83
  social welfare 362.294
  see also Substance abuse
Mesencephalon
  human anatomy 611.81
  human physiology 612.826 4
  see also Nervous system
Mesentery
  human anatomy 611.38
  human physiology 612.33
  surgery 617.558
  see also Digestive system
Mesilinka River (B.C.) T2—711 87
Mesmerism 154.7
Meso-American native languages 497
  T6—97
Meso-American native literatures 897
Meso-American native peoples T5—97
Mesocricetus 599.356
Mesogastropoda 594.32
Mesolithic Age 930.13
Mesons 539.721 62
Mesopotamia 956.7
  T2—567
  ancient 935
  T2—35
Mesopotamian architecture 722.51
Mesopotamian sculpture 732.5
Mesosauria 567.937
Mesosphere 551.514
Mesozoic era 551.76
  geology 551.76
  paleontology 560.176
Mesquite 583.748
Mess services (Armed forces) 355.341
Messapian language 491.993
  T6—919 93
Messenger services
  internal office communication 651.79
  office services 651.374 3
Messēnia (Greece) T2—495 22
  ancient T2—389
Messiahs
  Christianity 232.1
  Judaism 296.336
  role and function 291.61
  see Manual at 200.92 and 291–299
Messianic Judaism 289.9
  see also Christian denominations
Messianic prophecies
  Christianity 232.12
  Judaism 296.336
Messianism 291.23
  Judaism 296.336
Messina (Sicily : Province) T2—458 11
Messina (South Africa : District) T2—682 5
Messina, Strait of (Italy) 551.462 6
  T2—163 86
Meta (Colombia) T2—861 56
Metabolic diseases (Biology) 571.944
Metabolic diseases (Human)
  medicine 616.39
  see also Digestive system
Metabolism 572.4
  bone diseases
    medicine 616.716
    see also Musculoskeletal system
  human physiology 612.39
  inborn errors
    medicine 616.390 42
  medicine 616.39
  pharmacodynamics 615.739
  see also Digestive system
Metacarpals
  human anatomy 611.717
  see also Musculoskeletal system
Metaethics 170.42
Metagenesis 571.884
Metal engraving 765
Metal forming 671.3
Metal furniture 645.4
  manufacturing technology 684.105
  see also Furniture
Metal intaglio engraving 765
Metal manufacturing equipment
  manufacturing technology 681.767 1
Metal-oxide-semiconductor memory 004.53
  engineering 621.397 32
Metal products 671.8
Metal relief engraving 761.8

Metal spraying 671.734
Metal-work 671
  see also Metalworking
Metalanguage 410.1
Metalinguistics 410.1
Metallic compounds 546.3
Metallic fillings
  dentistry 617.675
  see also Dentistry
Metallic glass 669.94
Metallic inlays
  dentistry 617.675
  see also Dentistry
Metallic salt processes
  photography 772
Metallic soaps 668.125
Metallic solids 530.413
Metallic wood-boring beetles 595.763
Metallizing 671.734
Metallography 669.95
Metallurgical furnaces 669.8
Metallurgists 669.092
  occupational group T7—669
Metallurgy 669
  equipment manufacturing
    technology 681.766 9
Metals 669
  applied nutrition 613.285
  architectural construction 721.044 7
  architectural decoration 729.6
  biochemistry 572.51
    humans 612.015 24
  building construction 693.7
  building materials 691.8
  chemistry 546.3
  decorative arts 739
  dowsing 133.323 3
  economic geology 553.4
  foundation materials 624.153 6
  handicrafts 745.56
  human toxicology 615.925 3
  materials science 620.16
  metabolism 572.514
    human physiology 612.392 4
  metallography 669.95
  military resources 355.242
  mineralogy 549.23
  mining 622.34
  organic chemistry 547.05
    aliphatic 547.45
    applied 661.895
  prospecting 622.184
  sculpture material 731.2
  ship design 623.818 2
Metals (continued)
  shipbuilding 623.820 7
  structural engineering 624.182
  textiles 677.53
    see also Textiles
  toxicology 571.954 3
  see also Chemicals
Metalworkers 669.092
  metallurgy 669.092
  metalworking 671.092
    occupational group T7—671
  occupational group T7—671
Metalworking 671
  home workshops 684.09
  production economics 338.476 71
  ship hulls 623.843
  technology 671
Metamathematics 510.1
Metamorphic rocks 552.4
Metamorphosis (Biology) 571.876
Metaphysics 110
Metatarsals
  human anatomy 611.718
  see also Musculoskeletal
    system
Metatheria 599.2
  paleozoology 569.2
Metcalfe, Charles Theophilus
    Metcalfe, Baron
  Indian history 954.031 4
Metcalfe County (Ky.) T2—769 693
Metchosin (B.C.) T2—711 28
Meteor showers 523.53
Meteorite craters 551.397
Meteorites 523.51
  mineralogy 549.112
  petrology 549.112
Meteoroids 523.51
    T2—993
  effect on space flight 629.416
Meteorologists 551.509 2
  occupational group T7—551
Meteorology 551.5
    T1—015 515
  aeronautics 629.132 4
  agriculture 630.251 5
  see Manual at 551.5 vs. 551.6
Meteors 523.51
Meter (Music) 781.226
Meter (Prosody) 808.1
Methane
  biogas technology 665.776
Methane producing bacteria 579.321
Methanogenic bacteria 579.321

Methodist Church 287
  church government 262.07
    parishes 254.07
  church law 262.987
  doctrines 230.7
    catechisms and creeds 238.7
  guides to Christian life 248.487
  missions 266.7
  moral theology 241.047
  public worship 264.07
  religious associations 267.187
  religious education 268.87
  seminaries 230.073 7
  theology 230.7
Methodist Church (U.S.) 287.631
  see also Methodist Church
Methodist Episcopal Church 287.632
  see also Methodist Church
Methodist Episcopal Church, South 287.633
  see also Methodist Church
Methodist New Connexion 287.53
  see also Methodist Church
Methodist Protestant Church 287.7
  see also Methodist Church
Methodist sacred music 781.717
  public worship 782.322 7
    music 782.322 7
    religion 264.070 2
Methodists
  biography 287.092
  religious group T7—27
Methodology (Principles) T1—01
Metric differential geometries 516.37
Metric geometry 516.1
  Euclidean 516.2
Metric system 530.812
  elementary education 372.35
  law 343.075
  social aspects 389.15
Metric topology 514.3
Metrication 389.16
Metritis
  puerperal diseases
    obstetrics 618.73
Metrology
  commerce 389.1
Metronomes
  technology 681.118
Metropolitan areas 307.764
  area planning 711.43
  government 320.85
  public administration 352.167
Metropolitan Toronto (Ont.) T2—713 541
Metropolitana (Chile) T2—833 1
Meurthe-et-Moselle (France) T2—443 823
Meuse (France) T2—443 81
Meuse River T2—492 4
  Belgium T2—493 46
  Netherlands T2—492 4
Mevleviyeh 297.482
Mexican-American Border Region T2—721
Mexican Americans T5—687 207 3
Mexican hairless 636.76
Mexican literature 860
Mexican Revolution, 1910–1917 972.081 6
Mexican War, 1845–1848 973.62
Mexicans T5—687 2
Mexico 972
  T2—72
Mexico (Mexico) T2—725 2
Mexico, Gulf of 551.463 4
  T2—163 64
Mexico, Valley of (Mexico) T2—725
Mexico City (Mexico) T2—725 3
Mezereum 583.67
Mezuzot 296.461
Mezzo-soprano voices 782.67
  children's 782.77
    choral and mixed voices 782.77
    single voices 783.77
  general works 782.67
    choral and mixed voices 782.67
    single voices 783.67
  women's 782.67
    choral and mixed voices 782.67
    single voices 783.67
Mezzotinting 766.2
Mfecane 968.041
Mgeni River (South Africa) T2—684 7
Mhala (South Africa : District) T2—682 92
Miami (Fla.) T2—759 381
Miami Beach (Fla.) T2—759 381
Miami County (Ind.) T2—772 84
Miami County (Kan.) T2—781 68
Miami County (Ohio) T2—771 48
Miami River (Ohio) T2—771 7
Miao (Asian people) T5—959 42
Miao language 495.972
  T6—959 72
Miao literature 895.972

Miao-Yao languages 495.97
T6—959 7
MIAs 355.113
see also Missing in action
Mica 553.674
economic geology 553.674
mineralogy 549.67
mining 622.367 4
synthetic 666.86
technology 666.72
Micah (Biblical book) 224.93
Mice (Computer) 004.76
Mice (Muridae) 599.35
see also Rodents
Mice (Mus) 599.353
agricultural pests 632.693 53
animal husbandry 636.935 3
experimental animals
medicine 619.93
household sanitation 648.7
Michael, Czar of Russia
Russian history 947.047
Michael the Brave (Wallachia)
Romanian history 949.801 5
Michelias 635.977 322
botany 583.22
ornamental arboriculture 635.977 322
Michigan 977.4
T2—774
Michigan, Lake T2—774
Michoacán (Mexico : State) T2—723 7
Michoacán de Ocampo (Mexico) T2—723 7
Micmac Indians T5—973
Micmac language 497.3
T6—973
MICR (Computer science) 006.4
engineering 621.399
Microanalysis 543.081
quantitative 545.84
Microascales 579.565
Microassembly languages 005.6
Microbes 579
see also Microorganisms
Microbial diseases (Biology) 571.98
Microbial diseases (Human)
medicine 616.9
social services 362.196 9
see also Communicable diseases (Human)
Microbiologists 579.092
occupational group T7—579
Microbiology 579
applied 660.62
medicine 616.01
see Manual at 579.165 vs. 616.01; *also at* 616.1–616.9: Add table: 071 vs. 01; *also at* 616.9 vs. 616.01
Microcephaly
medicine 616.858 844
see also Mental retardation
Microchemical analysis 543.081 3
qualitative 544.83
Microchiroptera 599.4
paleozoology 569.4
Microcircuits 621.381 5
Microclimatology 551.66
ecology 577.22
Microcode 005.6
Microcomputer workstations 004.16
see also Microcomputers
Microcomputers 004.16
architecture 004.256
communications 004.616
programming 005.712 6
programs 005.713 6
engineering 621.391 6
graphics programming 006.676
graphics programs 006.686
interfacing 004.616
programming 005.712 6
programs 005.713 6
knowledge-based systems
programming 006.337
multimedia-systems
programming 006.776
multimedia-systems programs 006.786
operating systems 005.446
performance evaluation 004.160 297
for design and improvement 004.256
peripherals 004.716
programming 005.26
programs 005.36
systems analysis 004.256
systems design 004.256
see Manual at 004.11–004.16
Microcoryphia 595.723
Microeconomics 338.5
Microelectronic circuits 621.381 5
Microelectronics 621.381
social effects 303.483 4
Microfiche 302.23
bibliographies 011.36
see also Microforms

Microfilaments 571.654
Microfilms 302.23
  bibliographies 011.36
  see also Microforms
Microform catalogs 025.313
Microforms 302.23
  bibliographies 011.36
  cataloging 025.349 4
  library treatment 025.179 4
  production
    office records 651.58
    technology 686.43
  publishing 070.579 5
Microhylidae 597.89
Microlithography
  electronics 621.381 531
Micrometeorology 551.66
  ecology 577.22
Micronesia T2—965
Micronesia (Federated States) T2—966
Micronesian languages 499.52
  T6—995 2
Micronesians T5—995 2
Micronutrients 572.515
  see also Trace elements
Microorganisms 579
  air pollution control 628.536
  cell biology 571.629
    see Manual at 571.629 vs. 571.29
  cell culture 571.638 29
  food technology 664.024
  paleontology 561.9
  physiology 571.29
    see Manual at 571–575; *also at* 571.629 vs. 571.29
  see Manual at 579–590
Micropedology 631.433
Microphones 621.382 84
  radio engineering 621.384 133
Microphotography
  technology 686.43
Microprocessors 004.16
  see also Microcomputers
Microprogramming 005.6
  T1—028 556
  see Manual at 005.6
Microprograms 005.6
  T1—028 556
Micropterus 597.738 8
Microreproductions 302.23
  bibliographies 011.36
  see also Microforms
Microscopes 502.82
  biology 570.282
  manufacturing technology 681.413
Microscopic analysis
  chemistry 543.081 2
Microscopic metallography 669.950 282
Microscopic objects
  photography 778.31
Microscopic petrology 552.8
Microscopy 502.82
  biology 570.282
  medical diagnosis 616.075 8
  natural sciences 502.82
Microsporangia 575.65
Microstructure
  materials science 620.112 99
Microsurgery 617.05
Microtomy 502.82
  biology 570.282 7
Microtonality 781.269
Microtubules 571.654
Microtus 599.354
Microwave aids
  marine navigation 623.893 3
Microwave cooking 641.588 2
Microwave dinners
  home serving 642.1
Microwave electronics
  engineering 621.381 3
  physics 537.534 4
Microwave spectroscopes
  manufacturing technology 681.414 8
Microwave spectroscopy 543.085 82
  analytical chemistry 543.085 82
  engineering 621.361 5
  physics 537.534 4
Microwaves 537.534 4
  biophysics 571.453
    humans 612.014 481
Mid Bedfordshire (England) T2—425 63
Mid Devon (England : District) T2—423 54
Mid Glamorgan (Wales) T2—429 7
Mid Suffolk (England) T2—426 45
Mid Sussex (England : District) T2—422 65
Mid Wales T2—429 5
Mid-Western State (Nigeria) T2—669 3

Midair collisions 363.124 92
see also Air safety
Midbrain
human anatomy 611.81
human physiology 612.826 4
see also Nervous system
Middelburg (Cape of Good Hope, South Africa : District) T2—687 14
Middelburg (Transvaal, South Africa : District) T2—682 7
Middle age 305.244
Middle-aged persons 305.244
T1—084 4
T7—056 4
guides to Christian life 248.84
health 613.043 4
psychology 155.66
social aspects 305.244
Middle-aged workers 331.394
Middle Ages 909.07
T1—090 2
see also Medieval period
Middle America 972
T2—72
Middle American native languages 497
T6—97
Middle American native literatures 897
Middle American native peoples T5—97
Middle Atlantic States 974
T2—74
Middle classes 305.55
T1—086 22
customs 390.1
dress 391.01
Middle Congo 967.240 3
T2—672 4
Middle-distance races 796.423
see also Sports
Middle ears
human anatomy 611.85
human diseases
incidence 614.599 8
otology 617.84
human physiology 612.854
see also Ears
Middle East 956
T2—56
ancient 939.4
T2—394
Middle Egypt T2—622
Middle English language 427.02
T6—219
Middle Franconia (Germany) T2—433 2
Middle French language 447.02
T6—41
Middle games (Chess) 794.123
Middle High German language 437.02
T6—31
Middle-income classes 305.55
T1—086 22
Middle Indic languages 491.3
T6—913
Middle Indic literatures 891.3
Middle Iranian languages 491.53
T6—915 3
Middle Iranian literatures 891.53
Middle Italian language 457.02
T6—51
Middle kingdom (Egypt) 932.013
Middle latitude zones T2—12
Middle management 658.43
public administration 352.284
see Manual at 658.4 vs. 658.42, 658.43
Middle Persian language 491.53
T6—915 3
Middle Persian literature 891.53
Middle Portuguese language 469.702
T6—69
Middle Russian language 491.770 2
T6—917 1
Middle schools 373.236
see also Secondary education
Middle Spanish language 467.02
T6—61
Middle Stone Age 930.13
Middle voice 783.4
Middle Volga languages 494.56
T6—945 6
Middle Volga literatures 894.56
Middle West T2—77
Middledrift (South Africa : District) T2—687 92
Middlesbrough (England : Borough) T2—428 53
Middlesex (England) T2—421 8
Middlesex (Ont.) T2—713 25
Middlesex County (Conn.) T2—746 6
Middlesex County (Mass.) T2—744 4
Middlesex County (N.J.) T2—749 41
Middlesex County (Va.) T2—755 33
Middot 296.123 5

Midges 595.772
  agricultural pests 632.772
Midget car racing 796.76
  see also Sports
MIDI (Musical instrument digital interface) 784.190 285 46
Midi-Pyrénées (France) T2—448 6
Midland County (Mich.) T2—774 48
Midland County (Tex.) T2—764 861
Midlands (England) T2—424
Midlands Province (Zimbabwe) T2—689 1
Midlothian (Scotland) T2—413 5
Midrash 296.14
Midway, Battle of, 1942 940.542 6
Midway Islands T2—969 9
Midwest T2—77
Midwife toads 597.86
Midwifery
  law 344.041 5
  medicine 618.2
Midwives
  law 344.041 5
  role and function 618.202 33
Mie-ken (Japan) T2—521 81
Mifepristone
  pharmacodynamics 615.766
Mifflin County (Pa.) T2—748 46
Mignonettes 635.933 64
  botany 583.64
  floriculture 635.933 64
Migraine
  medicine 616.857
  see also Nervous system
Migrant agricultural workers
  economics 331.544
Migrant workers 331.544
  T1—086 24
  economics 331.544
  social class 305.562
  social welfare 362.85
Migration 304.8
  political science 325
Migration (Animals) 591.568
Migratory animals 591.568
Migratory birds 598.156 8
Mihai II, Viteazul, Voivode of Wallachia
  Romanian history 949.801 5
Mikhaĭlovgradska oblast (Bulgaria) T2—499 1
Mikhaĭlovgradski okrŭg (Bulgaria) T2—499 1
Mikhaylovgrad (Bulgaria : Oblast) T2—499 1
Mikhaylovgrad (Bulgaria : Okrŭg) T2—499 1
Mikkeli (Finland) T2—489 75
Mikva'ot (Tractate) 296.123 6
Mikveh 296.75
Mila (Algeria : Province) T2—655
Milam County (Tex.) T2—764 288
Milan (Italy : Province) T2—452 1
Milano (Italy : Province) T2—452 1
Mildew 579.53
  agricultural disease 632.43
  materials science 620.112 23
Mildura (Vic.) T2—945 9
Miletus T2—392 3
Milieu therapy
  psychiatry 616.891 44
  see also Mental illness
Militarism 355.021 3
  ethics 172.42
    see also War—ethics
  social theology 291.178 73
    Buddhism 294.337 873
    Christianity 261.873
    Hinduism 294.517 873
    Judaism 296.382 7
  sociology 303.66
Military accounting 657.835
Military administration 355.6
Military air transportation service 358.44
Military aircraft 358.418 3
  armed forces equipment 358.418 3
  engineering 623.746
Military alliances 355.031
  armed forces 355.356
Military arts 355
Military assistance 355.032
  international law 341.728
  law 342.041 2
Military attachés 355.032
Military bands 784.84
Military bases 355.7
  international law 341.725
  law 343.01
Military buildings
  architecture 725.18
Military camps 355.7
Military capability 355.033 2
Military commemorations 355.16
  Algerian Revolution 965.046 6
  Chaco War 989.207 166
  Civil War (England) 942.062 6

Military commemorations (continued)
  Civil War (Spain) 946.081 6
  Civil War (United States) 973.76
  Crimean War 947.073 86
  Falkland Islands War 997.110 246
  Franco-German War 943.082 6
  Hundred Years' War 944.025 6
  Indo-Pakistan War, 1971 954.920 516
  Indochinese War 959.704 16
  Iraqi-Iranian Conflict 955.054 26
  Korean War 951.904 26
  Mexican War 973.626
  Napoleonic Wars 940.276
  Persian Gulf War, 1991 956.704 426
  South African War 968.048 6
  Spanish-American War 973.896
  Thirty Years' War 940.246
  United States Revolutionary War 973.36
  Vietnamese War 959.704 36
  War of 1812 973.526
  War of the Pacific 983.061 66
  World War I 940.46
  World War II 940.546
Military consultants 355.687 3
Military contracts 355.621 2
Military cooking 641.57
Military courts 343.014 3
Military customs 355.1
Military dependents
  living conditions 355.12
  social services 355.34
Military deserters 355.133 4
  see also Deserters
Military discipline 355.13
  law 343.014
Military districts 355.31
Military engineering 623
Military engineers 623.092
  occupational group T7—623 1
Military geography 355.47
Military government 355.49
Military health 613.67
Military history 355.009
  Algerian Revolution 965.046 4
  Chaco War 989.207 164
  Civil War (England) 942.062 4
  Civil War (Spain) 946.081 4
  Civil War (United States) 973.73
  Crimean War 947.073 84
  Falkland Islands War 997.110 244
  Franco-German War 943.082 4
  Hundred Years' War 944.025 4
Military history (continued)
  Indo-Pakistan War, 1971 954.920 514
  Indochinese War 959.704 14
  Iraqi-Iranian Conflict 955.054 24
  Korean War 951.904 24
  Mexican War 973.623
  Napoleonic Wars 940.274
  Persian Gulf War, 1991 956.704 424
  South African War 968.048 4
  Spanish-American War 973.893
  Thirty Years' War 940.244
  United States Revolutionary War 973.33
  Vietnamese War 959.704 34
  War of 1812 973.523
  War of the Pacific 983.061 64
  World War I 940.4
  World War II 940.54
  see Manual at 930–990 vs. 355.009
Military housing 355.12
Military hygiene 355.345
  engineering 623.75
Military-industrial complex 355.021 3
  economics 338.473 55
  military science 355.021 3
  sociology 306.27
Military intelligence 355.343 2
  technology 623.71
  see also Unconventional warfare
Military law 343.01
Military life 355.1
  Algerian Revolution 965.046 8
  Chaco War 989.207 168
  Civil War (England) 942.062 8
  Civil War (Spain) 946.081 8
  Civil War (United States) 973.783
  Crimean War 947.073 88
  Falkland Islands War 997.110 248
  Franco-German War 943.082 8
  Hundred Years' War 944.025 8
  Indo-Pakistan War, 1971 954.920 518
  Indochinese War 959.704 18
  Iraqi-Iranian Conflict 955.054 28
  Korean War 951.904 28
  Mexican War 973.628
  Napoleonic Wars 940.278
  Persian Gulf War, 1991 956.704 428
  South African War 968.048 8
  Spanish-American War 973.898
  Thirty Years' War 940.248
  United States Revolutionary War 973.38

Military life (continued)
  Vietnamese War 959.704 38
  War of 1812 973.528
  War of the Pacific 983.061 68
  World War I 940.483–.484
  World War II 940.548 3–.5484
Military mail 355.693
Military maneuvers 355.4
  training 355.52
Military medals 355.134 2
  numismatics 737.223
Military medicine 616.980 23
Military missions 355.032
  international law 341.728
  law 342.041 2
Military models 355.48
  handicrafts 745.592 82
  war gaming 355.48
Military music 781.599
  songs 782.421 599
Military occupation 355.028
  law of war 341.66
  operations 355.49
Military offenses (Law) 343.014 3
Military operations 355.4
  World War I 940.41
  World War II 940.541
  see also Military history
Military Order of Foreign Wars of the United States 369.11
Military pacts 355.031
Military penology 365.48
  law 343.014 6
Military pensions 331.252 913 55
  law 343.011 2
Military personnel 355.009 2
  occupational group T7—355
  role and function 355.33
Military police 355.133 23
Military policy 355.033 5
Military prisons 365.48
  law 344.035 48
  penology 365.48
  see also Correctional institutions
Military procurement 355.621 2
Military records management 355.688 7
Military relations 355.031
Military religious orders 255.791
  church history 271.791
Military resources 355.2
Military schools (Secondary education) 373.243
  see also Secondary education
Military schools (Service academies) 355.007 11
  see Manual at 378 vs. 355.00711
Military science 355
Military sealift commands 359.985
Military service (Conditions of work) 355.1
Military service (Manpower procurement) 355.223
  ethics 172.42
    see also War—ethics
  law 343.012
Military services 355
  see also Armed services
Military situation 355.03
Military societies 369.2
  biography 369.209 2
  social group T7—369 2
Military sociology 306.27
Military songs 782.421 599
Military supplies 355.8
Military supply ships 359.985 83
  design 623.812 65
  engineering 623.826 5
  naval equipment 359.985 83
  naval units 359.985 3
Military surgery 617.99
Military training 355.5
Military transportation 358.25
  air forces 358.44
  engineering 623.6
  land forces 358.25
  naval forces 359.985
Military transports (Ships) 359.985 83
  see also Transports (Ships)
Military units 355.31
  Civil War (United States) 973.74
  Mexican War 973.624
  Spanish-American War 973.894
  United States Revolutionary War 973.34
  War of 1812 973.524
  World War I 940.412–.413
  World War II 940.541 2–.5413
  see also Military history
  see Manual at 930–990: Wars: Military units
Militia 355.37
Milk 641.371
  animal husbandry 636.088 42
    cow's milk 636.214 2
    see Manual at 636.1–636.8 vs. 636.088

Milk (continued)
  cooking 641.671
  food 641.371
  processing 637.1
Milk River (Mont. and Alta.) T2—786 1
Milk substitutes
  commercial processing 663.64
Milkfish 641.392
  cooking 641.692
  culture 639.375
  food 641.392
  zoology 597.5
Milking 637.124
Milkweeds 583.93
Milkworts 583.82
Milky Way 523.113
Mill, John Stuart
  economic school 330.153
Millard County (Utah) T2—792 45
Mille Lacs County (Minn.) T2—776 68
Milled soaps 668.124
Millennium
  Christianity 236.9
Milleporina 593.55
Miller County (Ark.) T2—767 56
Miller County (Ga.) T2—758 964
Miller County (Mo.) T2—778 56
Millets 641.331 71
  botany 584.92
  commercial processing 664.72
  cooking 641.631 71
  food 641.331 71
  food crop 633.171
  forage crop 633.257 1
Milliammeters 621.374 4
Milliners 646.504 092
  occupational group T7—646 5
Millinery 646.504
  commercial technology 687.42
  home construction 646.504
Milling grains 664.72
Milling metals 671.35
Milling plants
  ore dressing 622.79
Milling tools 621.91
Millipedes 595.66
Millmerran (Qld.) T2—943 3
Mills
  architecture 725.4
  construction 690.54
Mills County (Iowa) T2—777 74
Mills County (Tex.) T2—764 512
Milne Bay Province (Papua New Guinea) T2—954 1
Milos
  botany 584.92
Milton Keynes (England) T2—425 91
Milwaukee (Wis.) T2—775 95
Milwaukee County (Wis.) T2—775 94
Mimamsa (Philosophy) 181.42
Mime 792.3
  see also Theater
Mimicry (Biology)
  animals 591.473
Mimidae 598.844
Mimosaceae 583.748
Mimosas 583.748
  ornamental arboriculture 635.977 374 8
Mĭn dialect 495.17
  T6—951 7
Mina (African people) T5—963 374
Mina dialect 496.337 4
  T6—963 374
Minarets 297.351
  architecture 726.2
Minas Gerais (Brazil) T2—815 1
Mind 128.2
  philosophy 128.2
  psychology 150
Mind reading 133.82
Mindanao Island (Philippines) T2—599 7
Mindoro (Philippines) T2—599 3
Mindoro Occidental (Philippines) T2—599 3
Mindoro Oriental (Philippines) T2—599 3
Mine clearance (Military) 623.26
Mine drainage 622.5
  water pollution engineering 628.168 32
Mine health 363.119 622
  social services 363.119 622
  technology 622.8
Mine laying (Military) 623.26
Mine railroads 622.66
Mine roof control 622.28
Mine safety 363.119 622
  social services 363.119 622
  technology 622.8
  see also Safety
Mine shafts 622.25
Mine surveys 622.14
Mine timbering 622.28
Mined lands 333.765
  economics 333.765
  reclamation technology 631.64

Minelayers 359.836 2
  design 623.812 62
  engineering 623.826 2
  naval equipment 359.836 2
  naval units 359.326 2
Miner County (S.D.) T2—783 34
Mineral commodities 338.27
  investment economics 332.644 2
Mineral County (Colo.) T2—788 38
Mineral County (Mont.) T2—786 84
Mineral County (Nev.) T2—793 51
Mineral County (W. Va.) T2—754 94
Mineral drugs
  pharmacology 615.2
Mineral fertilizers 631.8
  economic geology 553.64
  see also Fertilizers
Mineral industries 338.2
  enterprises 338.762 2
  law 343.077
  products 338.27
    commerce 380.142
  public administration 354.39
Mineral oils
  processing 665.4
Mineral pigments 553.662
Mineral resources
  land economics 333.85
  law 346.046 85
  military science 355.242
  public administration 354.39
Mineral rights
  law 346.043
    private ownership 346.043
    public control 346.046 85
  public revenue 336.12
  sale and rental 333.339
Mineral springs
  health 613.122
  therapeutics 615.853
Mineral surveys
  prospecting 622.13
Mineral waters 553.73
  commercial processing 663.61
  economic geology 553.73
  health 613.287
  therapeutics 615.853
Mineral waxes
  processing 665.4
Mineralized beverages 641.26
  commercial processing 663.62
Mineralogists 549.092
  occupational group T7—549
Mineralogy 549
  see Manual at 549 vs. 546; *also at* 549 vs. 548; *also at* 552 vs. 549
Minerals 553
  applied nutrition 613.285
    animal husbandry 636.085 27
  biochemistry 572.51
    humans 612.015 24
  economic geology 553
  economics 338.2
    resources 333.85
    see Manual at 553 vs. 333.8, 338.2
  folklore 398.26
    history and criticism 398.365
      legendary 398.465
      real 398.365
  metabolism 572.514
    human physiology 612.392
  mineralogy 549
  synthetic 666.86
Miners 622.092
  labor economics 331.762 2
  occupational group T7—622
  public administration 354.942 2
Mines (Excavations) 622.2
  environment technology 622.4
  psychological influence 155.964
  public administration 354.39
Mines (Weapons) 355.825 115
  engineering 623.451 15
  laying and clearing 623.26
  military equipment 355.825 115
Minesweepers 359.836 2
  design 623.812 62
  engineering 623.826 2
  naval equipment 359.836 2
  naval units 359.326 2
Ming dynasty 951.026
Minganie (Quebec) T2—714 17
Mingo County (W. Va.) T2—754 48
Minho (Portugal) T2—469 12
Miniature aircraft 629.133 1
Miniature automobiles 629.221 2
Miniature books 099
Miniature cameras 771.32
Miniature dachshund 636.76
Miniature golf 796.352 2
  see also Sports
Miniature paintings 751.77
Miniature pinscher 636.76
Miniature portraits
  painting 757.7

Miniature railroads 625.19
Miniature Schnauzer 636.755
Miniature scores 780
  treatises 780.265
Miniature trains 625.19
Miniature trees 635.977 2
Miniatures 688.1
  T1—022 8
  handicrafts 745.592 8
    see Manual at 745.5928
  manufacturing technology 688.1
Miniaturization
  electronics 621.381 52
Minibikes 388.347 5
  engineering 629.227 5
  see also Motorcycles
Minicomputers 004.14
  architecture 004.254
  communications 004.614
    programming 005.712 4
    programs 005.713 4
  engineering 621.391 4
  graphics programming 006.674
  graphics programs 006.684
  interfacing 004.614
    programming 005.712 4
    programs 005.713 4
  knowledge-based systems
    programming 006.337
  multimedia-systems
      programming 006.774
  multimedia-systems programs 006.784
  operating systems 005.444
  performance evaluation 004.140 297
    for design and improvement 004.254
  peripherals 004.714
  programming 005.24
  programs 005.34
  systems analysis 004.254
  systems design 004.254
  see Manual at 004.11–004.16
Minidoka County (Idaho) T2—796 33
Minima 511.66
Minimal brain dysfunction
  medicine 616.858 9
  pediatrics 618.928 589
  see also Nervous system
Minimal curves 516.362
Minimal surfaces 516.362
Minims (Religious order) 255.49
  church history 271.49
Minimum-security prisons 365.33
  see also Correctional
      institutions
Minimum tillage 631.581
Minimum wage 331.23
Mining 622
  engineering 622
  enterprises 338.762 2
    accounting 657.862
  labor economics 331.762 2
  law 343.077
  production economics 338.2
  public administration 354.39
Mining bureaus 354.39
Mining engineers 622.092
  occupational group T7—622
Mining equipment
  manufacturing technology 681.76
Mining law 343.077
Mining towns 307.766
Ministates 321.06
Minister of justice's advisory
    opinions 348.05
Ministerial authority 262.8
Ministers (Christian clergy) 270.092
  biography 270.092
    specific denominations 280
    see Manual at 230–280
  ecclesiology 262.14
  pastoral theology 253
  see also Clergy—Christian;
      Religious leaders
Ministers of state 352.293
Ministries of state 351
  see also Executive
      departments; entries
      beginning with
      Departments
Minivans
  engineering 629.222
  see also Automobiles
Minke whale 599.524
Minkowski geometry 516.374
Minks 599.766 27
  animal husbandry 636.976 627
  conservation technology 639.979 766 27
  resource economics 333.959 766 27
  trapping 639.117 662 7
  zoology 599.766 27
Minna (Nigeria) T2—669 65
Minneapolis (Minn.) T2—776 579
Minneapolis Metropolitan
    Area (Minn.) T2—776 579
Minnedosa (Man.) T2—712 73
Minnehaha County (S.D.) T2—783 371

Minnesang (Poetry) 808.814
  history and criticism 809.14
  specific literatures T3B—104
    individual authors T3A—1
Minnesota 977.6
  T2—776
Minnesota River (S.D. and Minn.) T2—776 3
Minnows 597.482
Minoan architecture 722.61
Minoan Linear A 492.6
  T6—926
  see Manual at T6—926
Minoan Linear B 487.1
  T6—87
Minor arts 745
  see also Arts
Minor Clerks Regular 255.56
  church history 271.56
Minor Prophets (Bible) 224.9
Minor surgery 617.024
  obstetrics 618.85
Minor tractates (Talmud) 296.123 7
Minorca (Spain) T2—467 52
Minorities 305.56
  T1—08
  civil rights 323.1
  education 371.82
  government programs 353.53
    see Manual at 353.53 vs. 351.08
  legal status 346.013
  libraries for 027.63
  relation to government 323.1
  social welfare
    public administration 353.53
Minorities (Racial, ethnic, national) 305.8
  T1—089
  civil rights 323.11
  education 371.829
  government programs 353.533 9
    specific groups 353.534
  journalism for 070.484
  labor 331.6
    economics 331.6
    personnel management 658.300 89
  legal status 346.013
    constitutional law 342.087 3
    private law 346.013
Minorities (Racial, ethnic, national) (continued)
  literature 808.898
    history and criticism 809.8
    specific literatures T3B—080 8
      history and criticism T3B—098
    see Manual at T3C—93–T3C—99, T3C—9174 vs. T3C—8
  psychology 155.8
  relations with government 323.11
  social welfare 362.84
    public administration 353.533 9
      specific groups 353.534
  see also Ethnic groups; Minorities
  see Manual at 305.8 vs. 306.089
Minority enterprises 338.642 2
  economics 338.642 2
  financial management 658.159 208
  management 658.022 08
Minority groups (Racial, ethnic, national) 305.8
Minors 305.23
  see also Young people
Minquiers (England) T2—423 48
Minsk (Belarus : Oblast) T2—478 6
Minstrel shows 791.12
Mint (Herb) 641.338 2
  botany 583.96
  see also Flavorings
Minting policies 332.46
Minto, Gilbert Elliot, Earl of
  Indian history 954.031 3
Minto, Gilbert John Murray Kynynmond Elliot, Earl of
  Indian history 954.035 6
Minuets 793.3
  music 784.188 35
Minūfīyah (Egypt) T2—621
Minutes
  office records 651.77
Minyā (Egypt : Province T2—622
Miocene epoch 551.787
  geology 551.787
  paleontology 560.178 7
Mirabel (Quebec : Regional County Municipality) T2—714 25

Miracle plays
  literature 808.825 16
    history and criticism 809.251 6
    specific literatures T3B—205 16
      individual authors T3A—2
  stage presentation 792.16
    see also Theater
Miracles 291.211 7
  Christianity 231.73
    of Jesus Christ 232.955
      Gospels 226.7
    of Mary 232.917
    spiritual gift 234.13
  Judaism 296.311 6
  philosophy of religion 212
Mirages 551.565
Miʻrāj 297.633
Miramichi River (N.B.) T2—715 21
Miranda (Venezuela : State) T2—873 5
Mirliton 783.99
Mirounga 599.794
Mirrors
  automobile 629.276
  decorative arts 748.8
  furniture 645.4
    decorative arts 749.3
    see also Furniture
  manufacturing technology 681.428
Misamis Occidental (Philippines) T2—599 7
Misamis Oriental (Philippines) T2—599 7
Misappropriation of funds 364.132 3
  law 345.023 23
  public administration 353.46
Miscarriage
  obstetrics 618.392
Miscegenation 306.846
Miscellaneous facts
  books 030
Misconduct by employees
  labor economics 331.259 8
  personnel management 658.314
Misconduct in office 364.132
  law 345.023 2
  public administration 353.46
Mishnah 296.123
Mishnaic period 956.940 2
Mishneh Torah 296.181 2
Misinformation campaigns
  international politics 327.14
Misiones (Argentina) T2—822 3
Misiones (Paraguay) T2—892 125
Miskito Indians T5—978
Miskito language 497.8
  T6—978
Missals 264.36
  Anglican 264.030 36
    texts 264.03
  Roman Catholic 264.020 36
    texts 264.023
Missaukee County (Mich.) T2—774 66
Missile forces 358.17
Missile-hurling weapons
  art metalwork 739.73
Missiles
  military engineering 623.451
  military equipment 358.171 82
  see Manual at 629.046 vs. 621.43
Missing children 362.829 7
Missing in action 355.113
  Algerian Revolution 965.046 8
  Chaco War 989.207 168
  Civil War (England) 942.062 8
  Civil War (Spain) 946.081 8
  Civil War (United States) 973.78
  Crimean War 947.073 88
  Falkland Islands War 997.110 248
  Franco-German War 943.082 8
  Hundred Years' War 944.025 8
  Indo-Pakistan War, 1971 954.920 518
  Indochinese War 959.704 18
  Iraqi-Iranian Conflict 955.054 28
  Korean War 951.904 28
  Mexican War 973.628
  Napoleonic Wars 940.278
  Persian Gulf War, 1991 956.704 428
  South African War 968.048 8
  Spanish-American War 973.898
  Thirty Years' War 940.248
  United States Revolutionary War 973.38
  Vietnamese War 959.704 38
  War of 1812 973.528
  War of the Pacific 983.061 68
  World War I 940.48
  World War II 940.548
Missing persons
  police searches 363.233 6
Mission (B.C.) T2—711 37
Mission buildings
  architecture 726.9
Mission schools 371.07

Missionaries 291.720 92
  Christian 266.009 2
    occupational ethics 241.641
    see Manual at 230–280
  occupational ethics 174.1
    religion 291.564 1
    see Manual at 174.1
  occupational group T7—2
Missionaries of Charity 255.97
  church history 271.97
Missionary stories
  Christianity 266
Missions (Religion) 291.72
  Christianity 266
  Islam 297.74
Missisquoi (Quebec) T2—714 62
Mississippi 976.2
  T2—762
Mississippi County (Ark.) T2—767 95
Mississippi County (Mo.) T2—778 983
Mississippi River T2—77
  Arkansas T2—767 8
  Tennessee T2—768 1
Mississippi River Delta (La.) T2—763 3
Mississippi River Valley T2—77
Mississippian period 551.751
  geology 551.751
  paleontology 560.175 1
Missoula County (Mont.) T2—786 85
Missouri 977.8
  T2—778
Missouri Compromise, 1820 973.54
  Civil War (United States)
    cause 973.711 3
Missouri River T2—78
  Missouri T2—778
  Montana T2—786
  Nebraska T2—782 2
  North Dakota T2—784 7
  South Dakota T2—783 3
Mist (Weather) 551.575
Mistassini Territory T2—714 115
Mistletoes 583.88
Mists 541.345 15
  colloid chemistry 541.345 15
    applied 660.294 515
Misty Fjords National Monument (Alaska) T2—798 2
Misumalpan languages 497.8
  T6—978
Mitanni (Ancient kingdom) T2—35
Mitanni Kingdom 935.02
Mitchell (Qld.) T2—943 4
Mitchell County (Ga.) T2—758 973
Mitchell County (Iowa) T2—777 234
Mitchell County (Kan.) T2—781 23
Mitchell County (N.C.) T2—756 865
Mitchell County (Tex.) T2—764 729
Mites 595.42
  agricultural pests 632.654 2
  disease carriers
    medicine 614.433
Mithraism 299.15
Mitis (Quebec) T2—714 771
Mitochondria 571.657
Mitochondrial DNA 572.869
Mitosis 571.844
Mitral valves
  human anatomy 611.12
  human physiology 612.17
  medicine 616.125
  see also Cardiovascular system
Mittelfranken (Germany) T2—433 2
Mittelland (Switzerland) T2—494 5
Mitten makers 685.409 2
  occupational group T7—685 4
Mittens 391.412
  commercial technology 685.4
  customs 391.412
  home sewing 646.48
  see also Clothing
Mitzvot
  Jewish ethics 296.36
  Jewish law 296.18
Mixe Indians T5—974 1
Mixed-bloods (People) T5—04
Mixed descent T5—04
Mixed drinks 641.874
Mixed economies 330.126
Mixed equations 515.38
Mixed-level classrooms 371.25
Mixed marriage 306.84
Mixed-media arts 702.81
  two-dimensional 760
Mixed voices 782.5
Mixes (Pastry) 664.753
Mixing
  chemical engineering 660.284 292
Mixing paints
  buildings 698.102 83
Mixtec Indians T5—976
Mixtec language 497.6
  T6—976
Miyagi-ken (Japan) T2—521 15
Miyazaki-ken (Japan) T2—522 7
Mizoram (India) T2—541 66

Mkobola (South Africa : District) T2—682 95
Mkuze Game Reserve (South Africa) T2—684 91
Mmabatho (South Africa) T2—682 94
Mnemonics 153.14
Mnong (Indochinese people) T5—959 3
Moab (Kingdom) 939.46
T2—394 6
Moabite language 492.6
T6—926
Moats
architecture 725.98
military engineering 623.31
Moba language 496.35
T6—963 5
Mobile County (Ala.) T2—761 22
Mobile homes 643.2
architecture 728.79
automotive engineering 629.226
construction 690.879
home economics 643.2
law 346.043
recreation 796.79
see Manual at 643.2, 690.879, 728.79 vs. 629.226
Mobile libraries
public library use 027.4
Mobile radio stations 621.384 5
Mobile River (Ala.) T2—761 22
Mobile tactics 355.422
Mobiles 731.55
Mobility-impaired children
home care 649.151 6
see also Mobility-impaired persons
Mobility-impaired persons 305.908 166
T1—087 3
T7—081 66
education 371.916
social group 305.908 166
social welfare 362.43
Mobilization 355.28
World War I 940.402
World War II 940.540 2
see also Military history
Mobs 302.33
Mobs (Organized crime) 364.106
Mobutu Sese Seko
Zairian history 967.510 33
Mock oranges 583.72
Mockingbirds 598.844
Modality
linguistics 415
specific languages T4—5
logic 160
Mode 519.533
Model aircraft 629.133 1
recreation 796.154
see Manual at 796.15 vs. 629.0460228
Model airplanes 629.133 134
recreation 796.154
see Manual at 796.15 vs. 629.0460228
Model automobiles 629.221 2
recreation 796.156
see Manual at 796.15 vs. 629.0460228
Model boats 623.820 1
recreation 796.152
see Manual at 796.15 vs. 629.0460228
Model cars 629.221 2
recreation 796.156
see Manual at 796.15 vs. 629.0460228
Model land vehicles 629.221
recreation 796.156
see Manual at 796.15 vs. 629.0460228
Model makers 688.109 2
occupational group T7—688
Model ships 623.820 1
recreation 796.152
see Manual at 796.15 vs. 629.0460228
Model trains 625.19
recreation 790.133
see Manual at 796.15 vs. 629.0460228
Modeling
ceramic arts 738.142
elementary education 372.53
plastic arts 730.028
sculpture 731.42
use in child care 649.51
Modeling (Fashion design) 746.92
Modeling (Simulation) 003
T1—011
Modeling pottery 666.442
arts 738.142
technology 666.442
Models (Fashion) 746.920 92
occupational group T7—746

Models (For molding)
  sculpture 731.43
Models (Representations) 688.1
  T1—022 8
  arts 702.8
  cataloging 025.349 6
  educational use T1—078
  handicrafts 745.592 8
    see Manual at 745.5928
  library treatment 025.179 6
  manufacturing technology 688.1
  see also entries beginning with
    Model
Models (Simulations) 003
  T1—011
  management decision making 658.403 52
Modems 004.64
  engineering 621.398 14
Modena (Italy : Province) T2—454 2
Moderators
  nuclear engineering 621.483 37
Modern algebra 512
Modern architecture 724
Modern art 709.04
  religious significance 291.37
    Christianity 246.4
Modern dance 792.8
  see also Theater
Modern dance performers 792.802 809 2
  occupational group T7—792 8
Modern decoration 745.444
Modern geometry 516.04
Modern Greek language 489.3
  T6—89
Modern Greek literature 889
Modern history 909.08
  T1—090 3
  specific centuries 909.4–.8
Modern Indic languages 491.4
  T6—914
Modern Indic literatures 891.4
Modern jazz 781.655
Modern languages 410
Modern Latin peoples T5—4
Modern literature 808.800 3
  history and criticism 809.03
Modern music 780.903
Modern painting 759.06
Modern philosophy 190
  Oriental 181
  western 190
  see Manual at 140 vs.
    180–190; *also at* 190 vs.
    100, 109
Modern physics 539
Modern Prakrit languages 491.4
  T6—914
Modern Prakrit literatures 891.4
Modern sculpture 735
Modern world T2—4–9
Modernism
  arts 700.411 2
    T3C—112
  church history 273.9
  literature 808.801 12
    history and criticism 809.911 2
    specific literatures T3B—080 112
      history and criticism T3B—091 12
Modernization
  executive management 658.406
    military administration 355.686 7
    public administration 352.367
  production management 658.514
Modes (Music) 781.263
Modesty 179.9
  see also Virtues
Modoc County (Calif.) T2—794 23
Modoc Indians T5—974 1
Modular arithmetic 513.6
Modular coordination
  architectural design 729.23
Modular design 729.2
Modular forms (Mathematics) 512.73
Modular functions 515.982
Modular geometry 516.185
Modular houses 643.2
Modular programming 005.112
Modulation
  electronics 621.381 536
Modulation circuits
  radio engineering 621.384 12
Modulators
  electronic circuits 621.381 536
Modules
  algebra 512.4
  electronics 621.381 52
Modulus of rigidity 531.381
Moe (Vic.) T2—945 6
Mo‘ed (Order) 296.123 2
  Babylonian Talmud 296.125 2
  Mishnah 296.123 2
  Palestinian Talmud 296.124 2
Mo‘ed Katan 296.123 2
  Babylonian Talmud 296.125 2
  Mishnah 296.123 2
  Palestinian Talmud 296.124 2
Moesia T2—398
Moffat County (Colo.) T2—788 12

Mogadishu (Kingdom) 967.730 1
T2—677 3
Mogadishu (Somalia) T2—677 3
Mogalakwena River T2—682 93
Mogilev (Belarus : Oblast) T2—478 2
Mogilevskaîa oblast′ (Belarus) T2—478 2
Mogul Empire 954.025
T2—54
Mogul skiing 796.937
see also Sports
Mohamedia-Znata (Morocco : Prefecture) T2—643
Moḥammed, Prophet 297.63
Mohammed Reza Pahlavi, Shah of Iran
Iranian history 955.053
Mohave County (Ariz.) T2—791 59
Mohave Desert (Calif.) T2—794 95
Mohave Indians T5—975 7
Mohawk Indians T5—975 5
Mohawk language 497.55
T6—975 5
Mohawk River (N.Y.) T2—747 6
Mohegan Indians T5—973
Mohican Indians T5—973
Moḥism (Chinese philosophy) 181.115
Moi, Daniel Arap
Kenyan history 967.620 42
Moism (Chinese philosophy) 181.115
Moisture
meteorology 551.57
soil physics 631.432
Moistureproof construction
buildings 693.893
Mojave Desert (Calif.) T2—794 95
Mokerong (South Africa : District) T2—682 93
Molasses 641.336
commercial processing 664.118
cooking with 641.636
Moldavia T2—498 1
Moldova T2—476
Romania T2—498 1
Moldavia (Principality) 949.801 4
T2—498 1
Moldavian language 459
T6—591
Moldavians T5—59
Molded pulp 676.182
Molded rubber 678.34
Molding
arts 730.028
ceramic arts 738.142
Molding (continued)
sculpture 731.43
Molding glass 666.125
Molding latex 678.527
Molding plastics 668.412
Molding rubber 678.27
Moldmaking
metal casting 671.23
Moldova 947.6
T2—476
Molds (Fungi) 579.53
agricultural diseases 632.43
Molds (Tools) 621.984
Mole rats 599.35
Mole Valley (England) T2—422 165
Molecular biology 572.8
humans 611.018 16
see Manual at 572.8
Molecular botany 572.82
Molecular evolution 572.838
Molecular genetics 572.8
humans 611.018 16
Molecular physics 539.6
astronomy 523.019 6
Molecular properties
materials science 620.112 99
Molecular sieve chromatography 543.089 2
Molecular spectra 539.6
Molecular structure 541.22
biochemistry 572.33
chemistry 541.22
physics 539.12
Molecular weights 541.222
Molecules
chemistry 541.22
physics 539.6
Moles (Animals) 599.335
agricultural pests 632.693 35
Moles (Disorder)
medicine 616.55
see also Skin
Molinism 273.7
persecution of 272.5
Molise (Italy : Region) T2—457 19
Mollicutes 579.328
Mollies 597.667
Mollusca 594
see also Mollusks
Molluscoidea 594.6
paleozoology 564.6
Mollusks 594
conservation technology 639.974
control technology 628.964
cooking 641.694

Mollusks (continued)
  culture 639.4
  fishing 639.4
  fishing industry 338.372 4
  food 641.394
    commercial processing 664.94
  paleozoology 564
  resource economics 333.955 4
  zoology 594
Molokai (Hawaii) T2—969 24
Molopo (South Africa : District) T2—682 94
Molteno (South Africa : District) T2—687 6
Molucca Sea 551.465 73
  T2—164 73
Moluccas T2—598 5
Molybdates
  mineralogy 549.74
Molybdenite
  mineralogy 549.32
Molybdenum 669.734
  chemical engineering 661.053 4
  chemistry 546.534
  economic geology 553.464 6
  materials science 620.189 34
  metallography 669.957 34
  metallurgy 669.734
  metalworking 673.734
  mining 622.346 46
  organic chemistry 547.055 34
    applied 661.895
  physical metallurgy 669.967 34
  see also Chemicals; Metals
Momase region (Papua New Guinea) 995.7
  T2—957
Mombasa (Kenya) T2—676 23
Moment distribution method
  structural analysis 624.171 5
Moments of inertia
  aeronautics 629.132 364
Momentum 531.6
Momentum transfer
  chemical engineering 660.284 292
Momoyama period 952.024
Mon-Khmer languages 495.93
  T6—959 3
Mon-Khmer literatures 895.93
Mon-Khmer peoples T5—959 3
Mon language 495.93
  T6—959 3
Monachus 599.795
Monaco 944.949
  T2—449 49
Monads
  ontology 111
Monagas (Venezuela : State) T2—875 6
Monaghan (Ireland : County) T2—416 97
Monarchist parties 324.213
  international organizations 324.13
Monarchs 321
  occupational group T7—351
  public administration 352.23
Monashee Mountains (B.C.) T2—711 62
Monasteries 291.657
  architecture 726.7
  Buddhism 294.365 7
  Christianity 255
    church history 271
    religious significance of buildings 246.97
Monastic schools 371.07
Monasticism 291.657
  Buddhism 294.365 7
  Christianity 255
    church history 271
    personal religion 248.894
Monazite
  mineralogy 549.72
Moncton (N.B.) T2—715 235
Monera 579.3
Monetary law 343.032
Monetary policy 332.46
  economics 332.46
    central banking 332.112
    international 332.456 6
  international law 341.751 46
  law 343.032
  macroeconomics 339.53
Monetary reform
  international 332.456 6
Monetary stabilization 332.415
  international banking 332.152
Monetary standards 332.42
Monetary theory 332.401
Money 332.4
  arts 737.4
  economics 332.4
  international law 341.751 4
  law 343.032
  public administration 354.84
Money market funds 332.632 7

Money orders 332.76
  law 346.096
Money-saving cooking 641.552
Money-saving interior decorating 747.1
Mong language 495.972
  T6—959 72
Mong literature 895.972
Mongkut, King of Siam
  Thai history 959.303 4
Mongo (African people) T5—963 96
Mongo-Nkundu languages 496.396
  T6—963 96
Mongol dynasty 951.025
Mongol Empire 950.2
  T2—5
Mongolia 951.73
  T2—517 3
Mongolia (Region) 951.7
  T2—517
Mongolian language 494.23
  T6—942 3
Mongolian languages 494.2
  T6—942
Mongolian literature 894.23
Mongolian literatures 894.2
Mongolian People's Republic 951.73
  T2—517 3
Mongolians T5—942
Mongolism
  medicine 616.858 842
  see also Mental retardation
Mongoloid race T5—035
Mongols T5—942
Mongooses 599.742
Moniliales 579.55
Moniligastrida 592.64
Monimiaceae 583.23
Monism
  philosophy 147.3
Moniteau County (Mo.) T2—778 52
Monitor and Merrimac, Battle of, 1862 973.752
Monitorial system of education 371.39
Monitoring (Social control) 361.25
  see also Environmental monitoring
Monitors
  student discipline 371.59
Monitors (Computer)
  control programs 005.43
    firmware 005.6
  video display screens 004.77
    engineering 621.398 7
Monk seals 599.795
Monkeys 599.8
  see also Primates
Monklands (Scotland) T2—414 46
Monks 291.657
  Buddhist 294.365 7
  Christian 255
    biography 271.009 2
      see Manual at 230–280
    ecclesiology 262.24
    guides to Christian life 248.894 2
Monkshoods 583.34
Monmouth (Wales : District) T2—429 98
Monmouth County (N.J.) T2—749 46
Monmouthshire (Wales) T2—429 9
Mono County (Calif.) T2—794 48
Monochromatic photography 778.62
  motion pictures 778.534 2
Monocotyledons 584
  forestry 634.974
  paleobotany 561.4
  see also Plants
  see Manual at 583–584
Monocycles
  engineering 629.227 1
  repair 629.287 71
  riding 629.284 71
Monodon 599.543
Monodontidae 599.542
Monody 781.282
Monogamy 306.842 2
Monogenea 592.44
Monographs 002
  see also Books
Monohydric hydroxy aromatics 547.632
Monolithic circuits (Electronics) 621.381 5
Monologues (Drama)
  literature 808.824 5
    history and criticism 809.245
    specific literatures T3B—204 5
      individual authors T3A—2
  see Manual at T3A—2, T3B—2 vs. T3A—1, T3B—102
Monometallic standards 332.422
Monomotapas (Kingdom) 968.910 1
  T2—689 1
Monona County (Iowa) T2—777 44
Monongahela River (W. Va. and Pa.) T2—748 8
  Pennsylvania T2—748 8
  West Virginia T2—754 5

Monongalia County (W. Va.) T2—754 52
Mononucleosis
  incidence 614.575
  medicine 616.925
  see also Communicable diseases (Human)
Monophonic electrophones 786.73
  see also Electrophones
Monophysite churches 281.6
  see also Eastern churches
Monoplacophora 594.2
Monopoly 338.82
  economics 338.82
  international economics 338.884
  international law 341.753
  law 343.072
Monopulse radar systems
  engineering 621.384 85
Monorail railroads 385.5
  engineering 625.103
  transportation services 385.5
    urban 388.44
      see also Local rail transit systems
  see also Railroad transportation
Monorail rolling stock 385.5
  engineering 625.28
  transportation services 385.5
Monorail tracks 625.146
Monosaccharides 572.565
  biochemistry 572.565
  chemistry 547.781 3
  see also Carbohydrates
Monosodium glutamate
  food technology 664.4
Monotheism 211.34
  Christianity 231
  comparative religion 291.211
  Islam 297.211
  Judaism 296.311
  philosophy of religion 211.34
Monotheistic religions 291.14
Monotony studies
  production management 658.544
Monotremata 599.29
  paleozoology 569.29
Monotropaceae 583.66
Monotype
  manufacturing technology 681.61
Monotype composition
  automatic 686.225 44
  manual 686.225 42
Monroe, James
  United States history 973.54
Monroe County (Ala.) T2—761 25
Monroe County (Ark.) T2—767 87
Monroe County (Fla.) T2—759 41
Monroe County (Ga.) T2—758 563
Monroe County (Ill.) T2—773 91
Monroe County (Ind.) T2—772 255
Monroe County (Iowa) T2—777 865
Monroe County (Ky.) T2—769 685
Monroe County (Mich.) T2—774 32
Monroe County (Miss.) T2—762 975
Monroe County (Mo.) T2—778 325
Monroe County (N.Y.) T2—747 88
Monroe County (Ohio) T2—771 96
Monroe County (Pa.) T2—748 25
Monroe County (Tenn.) T2—768 883
Monroe County (W. Va.) T2—754 78
Monroe County (Wis.) T2—775 54
Monrovia (Liberia) T2—666 2
Monseñor Nouel (Dominican Republic : Province) T2—729 369 3
Monserrat 972.975
Monsoons 551.518 4
Monster flower 583.2
Monsteras 584.64
Monsters
  arts 700.47
    T3C—37
  literature 808.803 7
    history and criticism 809.933 7
    specific literatures T3B—080 37
      history and criticism T3B—093 7
  unexplained phenomena 001.944
Monstrilloida 595.34
Mont-Tremblant Provincial Park (Quebec) T2—714 4
Montage 702.813
Montagnais Indians T5—973
Montagnais language 497.3
  T6—973
Montagnards (Vietnamese people) T5—959 3
Montagu (South Africa : District) T2—687 3
Montague County (Tex.) T2—764 541
Montana 978.6
  T2—786
Montana (Bulgaria : Oblast) T2—499 1
Montcalm (Quebec : County) T2—714 415

Montcalm (Quebec : Regional County Municipality) T2—714 415
Montcalm County (Mich.) T2—774 53
Monte-Carlo (Monaco) T2—449 49
Monte Carlo method 519.282
Monte Cristi (Dominican Republic : Province) T2—729 352
Monte Plata (Dominican Republic : Province) T2—729 377
Montenegrins T5—918 22
Montenegro T2—497 45
Monterey Bay (Calif.) 551.466 32
T2—164 32
Monterey County (Calif.) T2—794 76
Montessori method 371.392
Montevideo (Uruguay : Dept.) T2—895 13
Montezuma County (Colo.) T2—788 27
Montgomery (Wales : District) T2—429 51
Montgomery County (Ala.) T2—761 47
Montgomery County (Ark.) T2—767 43
Montgomery County (Ga.) T2—758 832
Montgomery County (Ill.) T2—773 82
Montgomery County (Ind.) T2—772 48
Montgomery County (Iowa) T2—777 75
Montgomery County (Kan.) T2—781 93
Montgomery County (Ky.) T2—769 553
Montgomery County (Md.) T2—752 84
Montgomery County (Miss.) T2—762 642
Montgomery County (Mo.) T2—778 382
Montgomery County (N.C.) T2—756 74
Montgomery County (N.Y.) T2—747 46
Montgomery County (Ohio) T2—771 72
Montgomery County (Pa.) T2—748 12
Montgomery County (Tenn.) T2—768 45
Montgomery County (Tex.) T2—764 153
Montgomery County (Va.) T2—755 785
Months 529.2
Montmagny (Quebec : County) T2—714 735
Montmagny (Quebec : Regional County Municipality) T2—714 735
Montmorency County (Mich.) T2—774 83
Montmorency No 1 (Quebec) T2—714 48
Montmorency No 2 (Quebec) T2—714 48
Monto (Qld. : Shire) T2—943 5
Montour County (Pa.) T2—748 39
Montpelier (Vt.) T2—743 4
Montréal (Quebec : Administrative region) T2—714 27
Montréal Island (Quebec) T2—714 28
Montreal Urban Community (Quebec) T2—714 28
Montrose County (Colo.) T2—788 19
Montserrat T2—729 75
Monumental brasses
  arts 739.522
Monumental reliefs 731.549
Monuments 725.94
  architecture 725.94
  law 344.094
  sculpture 731.76
  World War I 940.465
  World War II 940.546 5
  see also Military commemorations
Mood (Grammar) 415
  specific languages T4—5
Moods 152.4
Moody County (S.D.) T2—783 36
Mooi River (South Africa : District) T2—684 7
Moon 523.3
T2—991
  astrology 133.532
  international law 341.47
  manned flights to 629.454
  unmanned flights to 629.435 3
Moon cars
  engineering 629.295
Moonfishes (Citharinidae) 597.48
Moonfishes (Perciformes) 597.7
Moons 523.98
Moonseeds 583.34
Moonworts 587.33
Mooré (African people) T5—963 5
Moore County (N.C.) T2—756 352
Moore County (Tenn.) T2—768 627
Moore County (Tex.) T2—764 822
Mooré language 496.35
T6—963 5

Mooring areas 387.15
  engineering 627.22
  see also Port facilities
Mooring structures 387.15
  engineering 627.32
  see also Port facilities
Moorish architecture 723.3
Moorish period
  Spanish history 946.02
Moorreesburg (South Africa : District) T2—687 3
Moors
  biology 578.768 7
  ecology 577.687
Moors (Bogs)
  biology 578.768 7
  ecology 577.687
  see also Wetlands
Moors (Heaths)
  biology 578.738
  ecology 577.38
Moose 599.657
  big game hunting 799.276 57
  conservation technology 639.979 657
  resource economics 333.959 657
Moose Jaw (Sask.) T2—712 44
Moosehead Lake (Me.) T2—741 2
Mopán dialect 497.415 27
  T6—974 152
Mopeds 388.347 5
  engineering 629.227 5
  see also Motorcycles
Mops 679.6
Moquegua (Peru : Dept.) T2—853 4
Mora County (N.M.) T2—789 54
Moraceae 583.45
  edible fruits 641.343 6
    cooking 641.643 6
    orchard crop 634.36
Moraines (Geologic landforms) 551.315
Moraines (Geologic material) 551.314
Moral determinants
  individual psychology 155.234
Moral development
  psychology 155.25
Moral education 370.114
Moral judgment 170
  psychology 155.232
Moral offenses
  criminology 364.17
    criminal law 345.027
  social control 363.4
Moral philosophers 170.92
  see Manual at 170.92 vs. 171
Moral philosophy 170
  see Manual at 170
Moral Rearmament 267.16
Moral renewal (Christianity) 248.25
Moral sense
  ethical systems 171.2
Moral theology 291.5
  Buddhism 294.35
  Christianity 241
    see Manual at 241 vs. 261.8
  Hinduism 294.548
  Islam 297.5
    Sufi 297.45
  Judaism 296.36
Moral training
  home child care 649.7
Morale
  armed forces 355.123
  personnel management 658.314
    public administration 352.66
Morality 170
  public control 363.4
    criminology 364.17
      criminal law 345.027
    public administration 353.37
  religion 291.5
    see also Moral theology
  see also Ethics
Morality plays
  literature 808.825 16
    history and criticism 809.251 6
    specific literatures T3B—205 16
      individual authors T3A—2
  stage presentation 792.16
    see also Theater
Moravia (Czech Republic) 943.72
  T2—437 2
Moravian Church 284.6
  see also Christian denominations
Moravian dialects 491.867
  T6—918 6
Moravian literature 891.86
Moravians (Ethnic group) T5—918 6
Moravians (Religious group) T7—246
  biography 284.609 2
Moray (Scotland) T2—412 23
Morays 597.43
Morazán (El Salvador) T2—728 433
Morbihan (France) T2—441 3
Mordell conjecture 516.352
Mordellidae 595.769
Mordovii͡a (Russia) T2—474 6

Mordvin	T5—945 6
Mordvin language	494.56
	T6—945 6
Mordvin literature	894.56
Mordvinia (Russia)	T2—474 6
Moré (African people)	T5—963 5
Moré language	496.35
	T6—963 5
Møre og Romsdal fylke (Norway)	T2—483 9
Morehouse Parish (La.)	T2—763 84
Morelos (Mexico)	T2—724 9
Morels	579.578
Mores	306
customs	390
sociology	306
Moretele (South Africa : District)	T2—682 94
Morgan County (Ala.)	T2—761 93
Morgan County (Colo.)	T2—788 74
Morgan County (Ga.)	T2—758 595
Morgan County (Ill.)	T2—773 463
Morgan County (Ind.)	T2—772 513
Morgan County (Ky.)	T2—769 253
Morgan County (Mo.)	T2—778 53
Morgan County (Ohio)	T2—771 94
Morgan County (Tenn.)	T2—768 74
Morgan County (Utah)	T2—792 26
Morgan County (W. Va.)	T2—754 96
Morgan horse	636.177
Morgues	363.75
architecture	725.597
Morice Lake (B.C.)	T2—711 82
Morice River (B.C.)	T2—711 82
Moridae	597.63
Mormon Church	289.3
church government	262.093
parishes	254.093
church law	262.989 3
doctrines	230.93
catechisms and creeds	238.93
general councils	262.593
guides to Christian life	248.489 3
missions	266.93
moral theology	241.049 3
public worship	264.093
religious associations	267.189 3
religious education	268.893
seminaries	230.073 93
temples	246.958 93
theology	230.93
Mormon tea	585.8
Mormons	
biography	289.309 2
Mormons (continued)	
religious group	T7—283
Mormyriformes	597.47
Morning-blooming plants	
floriculture	635.953
Morning glories	635.933 94
botany	583.94
floriculture	635.933 94
Morning prayer	264.15
Anglican	264.030 15
texts	264.033
music	782.325
choral and mixed voices	782.532 5
single voices	783.093 25
Mornington (Vic.)	T2—945 2
Morobe Province (Papua New Guinea)	T2—957 1
Moroccans	T5—927 64
Morocco	964
	T2—64
Morocco (Spanish zone)	T2—642
Morogoro Region (Tanzania)	T2—678 25
Morona-Santiago (Ecuador)	T2—866 43
Morone	597.732
Moroni (Comoros)	T2—694 1
Moronidae	597.732
Morphine abuse	362.293
medicine	616.863 2
personal health	613.83
social welfare	362.293
see also Substance abuse	
Morphing	
computer graphics	006.696
Morphisms (Mathematics)	512.55
Morphology	571.3
microorganisms	571.633 29
Morphology (Grammar)	415
specific languages	T4—5
Morrill County (Neb.)	T2—782 95
Morris County (Kan.)	T2—781 58
Morris County (N.J.)	T2—749 74
Morris County (Tex.)	T2—764 217
Morrison County (Minn.)	T2—776 69
Morrison plan	371.39
Morrow County (Ohio)	T2—771 516
Morrow County (Or.)	T2—795 67
Morse code telegraphy	384.14
wireless	384.524
see also Telegraphy	
Mortal sin	241.31
Mortality	
demography	304.64

Mortar (Material) 620.135
  see also Masonry
    adhesives—materials
    science
Mortars (Weapons) 355.822
  engineering 623.42
  military equipment 355.822
Mortgage banks 332.32
  law 346.082 32
  public administration 354.86
Mortgage bonds 332.632 3
Mortgage certificates 332.632 3
Mortgage defaults 332.72
Mortgage delinquencies 332.72
Mortgage insurance 368.852
  law 346.086 852
    economic assistance 343.074 2
  see also Insurance
Mortgages 332.72
  accounting 657.75
  credit economics 332.72
  investment economics 332.632 44
  law 346.043 64
  public administration 354.86
Morton County (Kan.) T2—781 715
Morton County (N.D.) T2—784 85
Morton National Park
    (N.S.W.) T2—944 6
Mortuary chapels
  architecture 726.8
Mortuary practice 363.75
  see also Undertaking
    (Mortuary)
Moruya (N.S.W.) T2—944 7
Morwell (Vic.) T2—945 6
MOS memory 004.53
  engineering 621.397 32
Mosaic diseases
  agriculture 632.8
Mosaic glass
  arts 748.5
Mosaic law (Bible) 222.1
Mosaics 738.5
  architectural decoration 729.7
Mosasauridae 567.95
Moscow (Russia : Oblast) T2—473 1
Moselle (France) T2—443 825
Moselle River T2—434 3
Moses
  Biblical leader 222.109 2
  Islam 297.246
Moshoeshoe II, King of Lesotho
  Lesotho history 968.850 31
Mosques 297.351
  architecture 726.2
  organization 297.65
Mosquito control 363.78
  social welfare 363.78
  technology 628.965 7
  see also Pest control
Mosquito Indians T5—978
Mosquito language 497.8
  T6—978
Mosquitoes 595.772
  disease carriers 571.986
    medicine 614.432 3
Moss animals 594.67
Mössbauer spectroscopy 543.085 86
  analytical chemistry 543.085 86
  physics 537.535 2
Mossel Bay (South Africa :
    District) T2—687 4
Mosses 588.2
  paleobotany 561.8
Mossi (African people) T5—963 5
Mossi (Kingdom) 966.250 1
  T2—662 5
Mossi languages 496.35
  T6—963 5
Mostaganem (Algeria :
    Province) T2—651
Mosul (Iraq) T2—567 4
Motacillidae 598.854
Motazilites 297.834
Motelkeepers 647.940 92
  occupational group T7—647
Motels 647.94
  see also Hotels
Motets 782.26
  choral and mixed voices 782.526
  single voices 783.092 6
Moth flies 595.772
Mother and child 306.874 3
Motherhood 306.874 3
Mothers 306.874 3
  T1—085 2
  T7—043 1
  Christian devotional literature 242.643 1
  family relationships 306.874 3
  guides to Christian life 248.843 1
  psychology 155.646 3
Mother's Day 394.262
Motherwell (Scotland :
    District) T2—414 49
Moths 595.78
  agricultural pests 632.78
  culture 638.578

Motility
  cytology 571.67
  microorganisms 571.672 9
Motion
  celestial bodies 521
  philosophy 116
  physics 531.11
  stars 523.83
Motion picture directors 791.430 233 092
  occupational group T7—791 4
Motion picture photography 778.53
Motion picture plays 791.437
  see also Screenplays
Motion picture projection 778.55
Motion picture scripts
  rhetoric 808.066 791
Motion picture theaters
  architecture 725.823
Motion pictures 791.43
  accounting 657.84
  bibliographies 011.37
  cataloging 025.347 3
  communications services 384.8
  ethics 175
    religion 291.565
      Christianity 241.65
  influence on crime 364.254
  instructional use 371.335 23
    adult level 374.26
  journalism 070.18
  library treatment 025.177 3
  performing arts 791.43
    sociology 306.485
    see Manual at 791.43, 791.45 vs. 778.5
  public administration 354.75
  sociology 302.234 3
  use in advertising 659.152
  see also entries beginning with Motion picture
  see Manual at 384.54, 384.55, 384.8 vs. 791.4
Motion sickness
  medicine 616.989 2
  see also Environmental diseases (Human)
Motion studies
  production management 658.542 3
  psychology 152.3
Motions (Law) 347.052
Motivation 153.8
  armed forces 355.123
  education
    gifted students 371.956
Motivation (continued)
  educational psychology 370.154
  elementary education
    reading 372.42
  learning psychology 153.153 4
  personnel management 658.314
    executives 658.407 14
    public administration 352.66
Motivation research
  marketing management 658.834 2
Motley County (Tex.) T2—764 752
Motocross 796.756
  see also Sports
Motor bicycles 388.347 5
  engineering 629.227 5
  see also Motorcycles
Motor functions
  human physiology 612.7
    localization in brain 612.825 2
  psychology 152.3
  see also Musculoskeletal system
Motor homes 388.346
  architecture 728.79
  camper cooking 641.575
  driving 629.284 6
  engineering 629.226
  recreation 796.79
  repair 629.287 6
  transportation services 388.346
  see also Automotive vehicles
  see Manual at 643.2, 690.879, 728.79 vs. 629.226
Motor horns
  music 786.99
    see also Percussion instruments
Motor land vehicles 388.34
  engineering 629.2
  transportation services 388.34
  see also Automotive vehicles
Motor learning
  psychology 152.334
Motor nerves
  human physiology 612.811
Motor organs 573.7
  human anatomy 611.7
  human physiology 612.7
  see also Musculoskeletal system
Motor scooter racing 796.75
  see also Sports
Motor skills
  educational psychology 370.155

Motor system 573.7
  human anatomy 611.7
  human physiology 612.7
  see also Musculoskeletal system
Motor vehicle engineers 629.209 2
  occupational group T7—629 2
Motor vehicle insurance 368.092
  inland marine 368.232
  liability 368.572
  see also Insurance
Motor vehicle racing 796.7
  see also Sports
Motor vehicle registration plates 929.9
Motor vehicle transportation facilities
  architecture 725.38
  area planning 711.73
Motor vehicles 388.34
  engineering 629.2
  transportation services 388.34
  see also Automotive vehicles
Motor yachting 797.125 6
Motor yachts 387.231 4
  engineering 623.823 14
  transportation services 387.231 4
  see also Ships
Motorboat racing 797.14
  see also Sports
Motorboating
  sports 797.125
    see also Sports
Motorboats 387.231
  design 623.812 31
  engineering 623.823 1
  handling 623.882 31
  transportation services 387.231
  see also Ships
Motorcycle accidents 363.125 9
  see also Highway safety
Motorcycle racers 796.750 92
  sports group T7—796 7
Motorcycle racing 796.75
  see also Sports
Motorcycle transportation facilities
  area planning 711.73
Motorcycle troops (Armed forces) 357.53
Motorcycles 388.347 5
  engineering 629.227 5
  repair 629.287 75
  riding 629.284 75
  sports 796.75
Motorcycles (continued)
  transportation services 388.347 5
  see also Automotive vehicles
  see Manual at 629.046 vs. 388
Motorized homes 388.346
  see also Motor homes
Motorized infantry 356.16
Motors 621.4
Motorscooters 388.347 5
  engineering 629.227 5
  repair 629.287 75
  see also Motorcycles
Motorways 388.122
  see also Roads
Moulins (Quebec) T2—714 24
Moultrie County (Ill.) T2—773 675
Mound builders (Birds) 598.64
Mount Aspiring National Park (N.Z.) T2—937 1
Mount Athos (Greece) T2—495 65
Mount Ayliff (South Africa : District) T2—687 91
Mount Buffalo National Park (Vic.) T2—945 5
Mount Cook National Park (N.Z.) T2—938 8
Mount Currie (South Africa : District) T2—684 6
Mount Desert Island (Me.) T2—741 45
Mount Elliott National Park (Qld.) T2—943 6
Mount Etna (Sicily) T2—458 13
Mount Field National Park (Tas.) T2—946 2
Mount Fletcher (South Africa : District) T2—687 91
Mount Frere (South Africa : District) T2—687 91
Mount Fuji (Japan) T2—521 66
Mount Gambier (S. Aust.) T2—942 34
Mount Hood (Or.) T2—795 61
Mount Isa (Qld.) T2—943 7
Mount Kaputar National Park (N.S.W.) T2—944 4
Mount Kilimanjaro (Tanzania) T2—678 26
Mount Lofty Ranges (S. Aust.) T2—942 32
Mount McKinley National Park (Alaska) T2—798 3
Mount Rainier National Park (Wash.) T2—797 782
Mount Revelstoke National Park (B.C.) T2—711 68

Mount Robson Provincial Park (B.C.) T2—711 82
Mount Spec National Park (Qld.) T2—943 6
Mount Waddington (B.C.) T2—711 2
Mount Whitney (Calif.) T2—794 86
Mountain ashes 583.73
Mountain biking 796.63
  see also Sports
Mountain building 551.82
Mountain climbing 796.522
  equipment technology 688.765 22
  see also Sports
Mountain goat 599.647 5
  conservation technology 639.979 647 5
  resource economics 333.959 647 5
Mountain laurel 583.66
Mountain lion 599.752 4
  conservation technology 639.979 752 4
  resource economics 333.959 752 4
Mountain Province (Philippines) T2—599 1
Mountain railroads 385.6
  engineering 625.3
  transportation services 385.6
  see also Railroad transportation
Mountain sickness
  medicine 616.989 3
  see also Environmental diseases (Human)
Mountain tactics 355.423
Mountain troops 356.164
Mountain tunnels 388
  construction 624.192
  see also Tunnels
Mountain winds 551.518 5
Mountain Zebra National Park (South Africa) T2—687 14
Mountaineering 796.522
  see also Sports
Mountaineers 796.522 092
  sports group T7—796 5
Mountains 551.432
  T2—143
  biology 578.753
  ecology 577.53
  geography 910.914 3
  geomorphology 551.432
  health 613.12
  land economics 333.73
  physical geography 910.021 43
  recreational resources 333.784
  recreational use 796.522
Mountbatten of Burma, Louis Mountbatten, Earl
  Indian history 954.035 9
Mounted forces 357
Mountrail County (N.D.) T2—784 74
Mourne Mountains (Northern Ireland) T2—416 58
Mourning 393.9
  music 781.588
  religion
    Christianity
      devotional literature 242.4
      religious guidance 248.866
      rites 265.85
    devotional literature 291.432
    Islam
      rites 297.385
    Judaism
      rites 296.445
        liturgy 296.454 5
    religious guidance 291.442
    rites 291.38
Mouse deer 599.63
Mousebirds 598.75
Mouth 591.4
  animal physiology 573.35
  descriptive zoology 591.4
  human anatomy 611.31
  human physiology 612.31
    speech 612.78
  medicine 616.31
  surgery 617.522
  see also Digestive system
Mouth-breeding frogs 597.87
Mouth organs 788.82
  instrument 788.821 9
  music 788.82
  see also Woodwind instruments
Moutse (South Africa : District) T2—682 95
Movable bridges 388
  construction 624.8
  see also Bridges
Movable dams 627.84
Movable property
  international law 341.48
  law 346.047
    private ownership 346.047
    public ownership 343.023
Movement 573.7
  animal behavior 591.5
  animal physiology 573.7

Movement (continued)
 arts 701.8
  drawing 741.018
 cytology 571.67
 human physiology 612.04
  musculoskeletal system 612.7
 plants 575.97
 psychology 152.3
 see also Musculoskeletal system
Movement disorders
 medicine 616.7
 see also Musculoskeletal system
Movement education
 elementary education 372.868
Movement perception
 psychology 153.754
  visual perception 152.142 5
Movie Channel, The 384.555 4
 see also Television
Movies 791.43
 see also Motion pictures
Moving and storage industry 388.044
 law 343.093 2
Moving household goods 648.9
 freight services 388.044
 personnel management 658.383
Moving sidewalks 388.41
Moving targets
 gun sports 799.313
 physics 531.112
Mower County (Minn.) T2—776 17
Mowing 631.55
Moxico (Angola : Province) T2—673 4
Moyle (Northern Ireland) T2—416 15
Mozambicans T5—967 9
Mozambique 967.9
 T2—679
Mozambique Channel 551.467 25
 T2—165 25
MP (Military Police) 355.133 23
Mpendle (South Africa : District) T2—684 7
Mpongwe language 496.396
 T6—963 96
Mqanduli (South Africa : District) T2—687 91
MRI (Imaging)
 medicine 616.075 48
MSG (Food additive)
 food technology 664.4
M'Sila (Algeria : Province) T2—655
Msinga (South Africa : District) T2—684 91
Mswari III, King of Swaziland
 Swazi history 968.870 3
Mthethwa (Kingdom) 968.403 8
 T2—684
Mtonjaneni (South Africa : District) T2—684 3
Mtunzini (South Africa : District) T2—684 4
Mtwara Region (Tanzania) T2—678 24
Mu-mesons 539.721 14
Mubārak, Muḥammad Ḥusnī
 Egyptian history 962.055
Mucilage 668.33
Mucocutaneous leishmaniasis
 medicine 616.936 4
 see also Communicable diseases (Human)
Mucous membranes
 human histology 611.018 7
Mud flows 551.307
Mud fuels 662.82
Mud puppies 597.85
Mudéjar architecture 720.946 090 2
Mudgee (N.S.W.) T2—944 5
Mudīrīyah al-Istiwā'īyah al-Gharbīyah (Sudan) T2—629 5
Mudīrīyah al-Istiwā'īyah al-Sharqīyah (Sudan) T2—629 5
Mudīrīyat al-Sharqīyah (Egypt) T2—621
Mudminnows 597.5
Muffin mixes 664.753
Mufflers (Automobile part) 629.252
Muffs 391.41
 commercial technology
  fur 685.24
 customs 391.41
 home sewing 646.48
 see also Clothing
Mugabe, Robert Gabriel
 Zimbabwean history 968.910 51
Muğla İli (Turkey) T2—562
Muḥammad, Prophet 297.63
Muhammad, Zahir Shah
 Afghan history 958.104 3
Muḥammad V, King of Morocco
 Moroccan history 964.04
  1927–1956 964.04
  1956–1961 964.05
Muhlenberg County (Ky.) T2—769 832
Mukhara (Kingdom) 962.502 2
 T2—625

Mukurra (Kingdom) 962.502 2
  T2—625
Mulattoes T5—044
Mulberries 583.45
  botany 583.45
  cooking 641.643 8
  food 641.343 8
  orchard crop 634.38
  ornamental arboriculture 635.977 345
Mulch tillage 631.451
Mule deer 599.653
  big game hunting 799.276 53
  conservation technology 639.979 653
  resource economics 333.959 653
Mules 636.183
Mulleins 583.95
Mullets 641.392
  cooking 641.692
  culture 639.377
  food 641.392
  zoology 597.7
Mullica River (N.J.) T2—749 61
Mulroney, Brian
  Canadian history 971.064 7
Multān District (Pakistan) T2—549 14
Multi-peril real property insurance 368.096
  see also Insurance
Multicultural education 370.117
  adult level 374.017
Multiculturalism
  sociolinguistics 306.446
Multidimensional algebra 512.5
Multiform functions 515.223
Multigraded classes 371.25
Multilateral agreements
  international economics 337.1
Multilateral economic cooperation 337.1
  see Manual at 337.3–337.9 vs. 337.1
Multilateral trade agreements 382.91
Multilateral treaties 341.37
  texts 341.026 5
Multilevel marketing
  management 658.84
Multilinear algebra 512.5
Multilinear forms
  algebraic geometry 516.35
Multilingual phrase books 418
Multilingual shorthand systems 653.41
Multilingualism 306.446
  linguistics 404.2
    specific languages T4—042
Multilingualism (continued)
  sociology 306.446
Multimedia authoring software 006.78
Multimedia systems
  cataloging 025.344
  computer science 006.7
  instructional use 371.334 67
    T1—078 567
  library treatment 025.174
Multinational enterprises 338.88
  see also International enterprises
Multinational forces (Military) 355.356
  internationally controlled 355.357
Multiphase flow
  liquid mechanics 532.56
Multiple access systems
  computer communications 004.6
    see also Computer communications
  processing modes 004.3
    see also Processing modes—computer science
Multiple art 709.040 78
  sculpture 735.230 478
Multiple banking 332.16
Multiple birth
  obstetrics 618.25
Multiple column tariffs 382.753
  see also Customs (Tariff)
Multiple cropping 631.58
Multiple deficiency states
  medicine 616.399
  see also Digestive system
Multiple dwellings
  architecture 728.31
Multiple flutes 788.37
  see also Woodwind instruments
Multiple-line insurance coverage 368.09
Multiple-loop systems
  automation engineering 629.833
Multiple myeloma
  incidence 614.599 947 1
  medicine 616.994
  see also Cancer (Human)
Multiple personalities
  medicine 616.852 36
  see also Mental illness
Multiple pregnancy
  obstetrics 618.25
Multiple-purpose buildings 720.49

Multiple sclerosis 362.196 834
  medicine 616.834
  social services 362.196 834
  see also Nervous system
Multiple stars 523.841
Multiplexers
  communications engineering 621.382 16
  computer communications 004.66
    engineering 621.398 1
Multiplexing
  communications engineering 621.382 16
  computer communications 004.66
    engineering 621.398 1
Multiplication 512.92
  algebra 512.92
  arithmetic 513.213
Multiplicative properties 512.73
Multiplier effect
  macroeconomics 339.43
Multiprocessing 004.35
  architecture 004.358 2
  communications 004.618 5
    programming 005.712 75
    programs 005.713 75
  graphics programming 006.677 5
  graphics programs 006.687 5
  interfacing
    programming 005.712 75
    programs 005.713 75
  knowledge-based systems
    programming 006.337
  multimedia-systems
      programming 006.777 5
  multimedia-systems programs 006.787 5
  operating systems 005.447 5
  performance evaluation
    for design and improvement 004.358 4
  peripherals 004.718
  programming 005.275
  programs 005.375
  systems analysis 004.358 1
  systems design 004.358 1
  see also Processing modes—
      computer science
Multiprocessors 004.35
  engineering 621.391
  see also Processing modes—
      computer science
Multiprogramming 005.434
  computer hardware 004.3
  systems programs 005.434
  see also Processing modes—
      computer science
Multistage programming 519.703
Multistory buildings 720.483
  see also Tall buildings
Multistory houses
  architecture 728.372
Multitasking (Computer science)
  computer hardware 004.3
  see also Processing modes—
      computer science
Multiuser processing (Computer
    science) 004.3
Multivariate analysis 519.535
Multnomah County (Or.) T2—795 49
Mumps
  incidence 614.544
  medicine 616.313
  pediatrics 618.923 13
  see also Digestive system
München (Germany) T2—433 64
Muncie (Ind.) T2—772 65
Munda languages 495.95
  T6—959 5
Munda literatures 895.95
Mundane astrology 133.5
Mundari language 495.95
  T6—959 5
Mundari literature 895.95
Mundas T5—959 5
Mundurucu language 498.38
  T6—983 8
Munduruku language 498.38
  T6—983 8
Munich (Germany) T2—433 64
Municipal annexation 320.859
Municipal bankruptcy 336.368
Municipal bonds 332.632 33
  law 346.092 2
Municipal charters 342.02
Municipal colleges 378.052
  see also Higher education
Municipal contracts 352.531 4
Municipal corporations 320.85
  law 342.09
Municipal courts 347.02
Municipal engineering 628
Municipal engineers 628.092
  occupational group T7—628
Municipal finance 336.014
  law 343.03
  public administration 352.421 4
  public finance 336.014
Municipal franchises
  public revenue 336.11
Municipal incorporation 320.85
Municipal theater 792.022

Municipal universities	378.052
see also Higher education	
Municipal wastes	363.728
see also Waste control	
Municipal water supply	363.61
engineering	628.1
see also Water supply	
Municipalities	320.85
Munson shorthand system	653.424 5
Münster (Germany : Regierungsbezirk)	T2—435 61
Munster (Ireland)	T2—419
Münster (Westphalia, Germany)	T2—435 614
Münster in Westfalen (Germany)	T2—435 614
Muntjacs	599.65
Muntz metal	669.3
materials science	620.182
metallography	669.953
metallurgy	669.3
metalworking	673.3
physical metallurgy	669.963
Muong (Vietnamese people)	T5—959 2
Muong language	495.92
	T6—959 2
Muons	539.721 14
Mural paintings	751.73
Murcia (Spain : Region)	T2—467 7
Murder	364.152 3
law	345.025 23
Mureş (Romania)	T2—498 4
Muriatic acid	
chemical engineering	661.23
Muridae	599.35
Murine typhus	
incidence	614.526 2
medicine	616.922 2
see also Communicable diseases (Human)	
Murjiites (Islamic sect)	297.837
Murmansk (Russia : Oblast	T2—471 3
Murmanskaîa oblast′ (Russia)	T2—471 3
Muromachi period	952.023
Murray Bridge (S. Aust.)	T2—942 32
Murray County (Ga.)	T2—758 31
Murray County (Minn.)	T2—776 27
Murray County (Okla.)	T2—766 57
Murray River (B.C.)	T2—711 87
Murray River (N.S.W.-S. Aust.)	T2—944
Murraysburg (South Africa : District)	T2—687 15
Murres	598.33
conservation technology	639.978 33
resource economics	333.958 33
sports hunting	799.248 33
Murrumbidgee River (N.S.W.)	T2—944 8
Murua Island (Papua New Guinea)	T2—954 1
Murui language	498
	T6—98
Murwillumbah (N.S.W.)	T2—944 3
Mus	599.353
see also Mice (Mus)	
Muş İli (Turkey)	T2—566 7
Mūsá	
Islam	297.246
Musaceae	584.39
Muscat and Oman	T2—535 3
Muscatine County (Iowa)	T2—777 68
Musci	588.2
Muscicapidae	598.848
Muscidae	595.774
Muscles	573.75
biology	573.75
drawing	
animals	743.6
humans	743.47
human anatomy	611.73
human physiology	612.74
medicine	616.74
pharmacodynamics	615.773
surgery	617.473
see also Musculoskeletal system	
Muscogee County (Ga.)	T2—758 473
Muscular dystrophy	362.196 748
medicine	616.748
pediatrics	618.927 48
social services	362.196 748
see also Musculoskeletal system	
Muscular rheumatism	
medicine	616.742
see also Musculoskeletal system	
Muscular tissue	
human histology	611.018 6
see also Musculoskeletal system	
Musculoskeletal system	573.7
anesthesiology	617.967 47
biology	573.7

Musculoskeletal system (continued)
  dislocations
    medicine 617.16
  fractures
    medicine 617.15
  geriatrics 618.976 7
  human anatomy 611.7
  human cancer 362.196 994 7
    incidence 614.599 947
    medicine 616.994 7
    social services 362.196 994 7
    see also Cancer (Human)
  human diseases 362.196 7
    incidence 614.597
    medicine 616.7
    social services 362.196 7
  human histology 611.018 97
  human physiology 612.7
  pediatrics 618.927
  pharmacodynamics 615.77
  sprains
    medicine 617.17
  surgery 617.47
  veterinary medicine 636.089 67
Museologists 069.092
  occupational group T7—096
Museology 069
  T1—075
Museum activities 069
  T1—075
Museum catalogs 069.52
  T1—074
Museum collections 069.5
  T1—074
Museum documentation 069.52
Museum equipment 069.3
Museum furnishings
  plant management 069.3
Museum furniture
  museology 069.33
Museum guidebooks T1—074
Museum labels 069.53
Museum libraries 027.68
Museum objects
  circulation 069.132
  selection 069.51
Museum registration methods 069.52
Museum science 069
Museum services 069.1
  T1—075 5
Museums 069
  T1—074
  architecture 727.6
Museums (continued)
  area planning 711.57
  arts 700.74
  fine arts 708
    see Manual at 704.9: Use of standard subdivisions
  institutional housekeeping 647.996
  law 344.093
  public administrative support 352.76
Museveni, Yoweri
  Ugandan history 967.610 44
Mushrooms 579.6
  agriculture 635.8
  commercial processing 664.805 8
  cooking 641.658
  food 641.358
  human toxicology 615.952 96
Music 780
  elementary education 372.87
  ethics 175
    religion 291.565
      Christianity 241.65
  literature 808.803 57
    history and criticism 809.933 57
    specific literatures T3B—080 357
      history and criticism T3B—093 57
  printing 686.284
  public administrative support 353.77
  publishing 070.579 4
  religion 291.37
    Buddhism 294.343 7
    Christianity 246.75
      attitude toward secular music 261.578
    Hinduism 294.537
    Jainism 294.437
    Judaism 296.462
    public worship 291.38
      Christianity 264.2
      Judaism 296.462
      see also Public worship
  sociology 306.484
  use in child care 649.51
  see Manual at 780
Music appreciation 781.17
  elementary education 372.872
Music boxes 786.65
  see also Mechanical musical instruments
Music dictionaries 780.3
Music editing 780.149
Music education 780.7
Music hall presentations 792.7
  see also Theater

Music halls
  architecture 725.81
Music instruction 780.7
Music libraries 026.78
Music theory 781
Music therapy
  medicine 615.851 54
Musical aptitude tests 153.947 8
Musical bows 787.92
  instrument 787.921 9
  music 787.92
  see also Stringed instruments
Musical chairs (Recreation) 793.4
Musical elements 781.2
Musical forms 781.8
  instrumental 784.18
  vocal 782
Musical glasses 786.866
  see also Percussion instruments
Musical instrument digital interface 784.190 285 46
Musical instrument makers 784.190 92
  craft producers 784.190 92
    occupational group T7—78
  mass producers 681.809 2
    occupational group T7—681 8
  occupational group T7—78
  see Manual at 784–788: Add table: 092
Musical instruments 784.19
  construction 784.192 3
    by hand 784.192 3
    by machine 681.8
  see Manual at 784–788
Musical notation 780.148
Musical pitch 781.232
Musical plays 782.14
  music 782.14
  stage presentation 792.6
    see also Theater
  see Manual at 782.1 vs. 792.5
Musical saws 786.888
  see also Percussion instruments
Musical sound 781.23
Musical temperament 784.192 8
Musical traditions 781.6
Musicals 782.14
  music 782.14
  stage presentation 792.6
    see also Theater
  see Manual at 782.1 vs. 792.5
Musicians 780.92
  occupational group T7—78
  see Manual at 780.92: Musicians; *also at* 781.6; *also at* 784–788: Add table: 092; *also at* 791.092
Musicology 780.72
Musique concrète 786.75
Muskegon County (Mich.) T2—774 57
Muskellunge 597.59
  sports fishing 799.175 9
Muskets
  art metalwork 739.744 25
  military engineering 623.442 5
  see also Guns (Small arms)
Muskhogean Indians T5—973
Muskhogean languages 497.3
  T6—973
Muskie 597.59
  sports fishing 799.175 9
Muskingum County (Ohio) T2—771 91
Muskingum River (Ohio) T2—771 91
Muskmelons 641.356 11
  cooking 641.656 11
  food 641.356 11
  garden crop 635.611
Muskogean Indians T5—973
Muskogean languages 497.3
  T6—973
Muskogee County (Okla.) T2—766 82
Muskoka (Ont. : District municipality) T2—713 16
Muskox 599.647 8
Muskrats 599.357 9
  conservation technology 639.979 357 9
  resource economics 333.959 357 9
  trapping 639.113 579
Muslim ibn al-Ḥajjāj al-Qushayrī
  Hadith 297.124 3
Muslims 297.092
  biography 297.092
    specific sects 297.8
  religious group T7—297 1
  see Manual at 297.092
Musophagidae 598.74
Mussel shrimps 595.33
Mussels 641.394
  cooking 641.694
  fishing 639.42
  food 641.394
    commercial processing 664.94
  zoology 594.4

Musselshell County (Mont.) T2—786 312
Mussolini, Benito
  Italian history 945.091
Mustache shrimps 595.36
Mustaches 646.724
  care 646.724
  customs 391.5
Mustang 636.13
  zoology 599.665 5
Mustard 641.338 4
  botany 583.64
  see also Hot spices
Mustela 599.766 2
Mustelidae 599.766
  conservation technology 639.979 766
  resource economics 333.959 766
Mustelinae 599.766
Muswellbrook (N.S.W.) T2—944 2
Mutagens
  biology 576.542
  medicine 616.042
Mutale (South Africa : District) T2—682 91
Mutarotation 541.7
Mutation (Genetics) 576.549
Mutazilites 297.834
Mute swan 598.418 7
Muthanná (Iraq : Province) T2—567 5
Mutiny 355.133 4
Mutton 641.363
  commercial processing 664.92
  cooking 641.663
  food 641.363
Mutual aid societies 334.7
  economics 334.7
  insurance 368
    see also Insurance
Mutual funds 332.632 7
  law 346.092 2
Mutual savings banks 332.21
Mutual security pacts 355.031
  law 341.72
Mutualism (Biology) 577.852
Mwanza Region (Tanzania) T2—678 27
Mweru, Lake (Zaire and Zambia) T2—675 18
Myalgia
  medicine 616.74
  see also Musculoskeletal system
Myanmar 959.1
  T2—591
Myasthenia gravis
  medicine 616.744 2
  see also Musculoskeletal system
Mycelia Sterilia 579.55
Mycenae (Extinct city) T2—388
Mycenaean architecture 722.61
Mycenaean Linear B 487.1
  T6—87
Mycetozoa 579.52
Mycobacteria 579.374
Mycologists 579.509 2
  occupational group T7—579
Mycology 579.5
  medical microbiology 616.015
  medicine 616.969
  see also Communicable diseases (Human)
Mycoplasmas 579.328
Mycoses (Biology) 571.995
Mycoses (Human)
  incidence 614.559
  medicine 616.969
  see also Communicable diseases (Human)
Mycota 579.5
Mycotoxins
  human toxicology 615.952 95
Mycrothyriales 579.564
Myctophiformes 597.61
Mydas flies 595.773
Myene language 496.396
  T6—963 96
Mykolaïvs´ka oblast´ (Ukraine) T2—477 3
Mykolayiv (Ukraine : Oblast) T2—477 3
Mykonos Island (Greece) T2—495 85
Mynas 598.863
  animal husbandry 636.68
Myocardial infarction
  medicine 616.123 7
  see also Cardiovascular system
Myocarditis
  medicine 616.124
  see also Cardiovascular system
Myocardium
  human anatomy 611.12
  human physiology 612.17
  medicine 616.124
  see also Cardiovascular system

Myodocopa 595.33
  paleozoology 565.33
Myomorpha 599.35
Myopia
  optometry 617.755
Myoporaceae 583.95
Myositis
  medicine 616.743
  see also Musculoskeletal system
Myotis 599.472
Myoxidae 599.359 6
Myriangiales 579.564
Myriapoda 595.6
  paleozoology 565.6
Myricales 583.43
Myristicaceae 583.22
Myrmecophagidae 599.314
Myrsinaceae 583.675
Myrtaceae 583.765
  edible fruits 641.344 2
    cooking 641.644 2
    food 641.344 2
    orchard crop 634.42
Myrtales 583.76
Myrtle wax 665.12
Myrtles 635.933 765
  botany 583.765
  floriculture 635.933 765
Myrtles (Oregon myrtle) 583.23
Myrtles (Wax myrtles) 583.43
Mysia (Turkey) T2—392 1
Mysidacea 595.375
Mysore (India : State) T2—548 7
Mystacocarida 595.36
Mysteries
  occultism 135
  unexplained phenomena 001.94
Mystery films 791.436 55
Mystery games 793.93
  see Manual at 793.932 vs. 794.822
Mystery plays (Religious)
  literature 808.825 16
    history and criticism 809.251 6
    specific literatures T3B—205 16
      individual authors T3A—2
  stage presentation 792.16
    see also Theater
Mystery plays (Suspense) 792.27
  literature 808.825 27
    history and criticism 809.252 7
    specific literatures T3B—205 27
      individual authors T3A—2
  see also Suspense drama
Mystery programs 791.446 55
  radio 791.446 55
  television 791.456 55
Mystery stories 808.838 72
  history and criticism 809.387 2
  specific literatures T3B—308 72
    individual authors T3A—3
Mystical body of Christ 262.77
Mystical Judaism 296.833
Mysticeti 599.5
  paleozoology 569.5
Mysticism 291.422
  Buddhism 294.344 22
  Christianity 248.22
  comparative religion 291.422
  Hinduism 294.542 2
  Islam 297.4
    see Manual at 297.4
  Judaism 296.712
  philosophy 149.3
    medieval western 189.5
Myth
  arts 700.415
    T3C—15
    see Manual at T3C—37 vs. T3C—15
  literature 808.801 5
    history and criticism 809.915
    specific literatures T3B—080 15
      history and criticism T3B—091 5
  see also Mythology
Mythical animals 398.245 4
  see also Legendary animals
Mythological interpretation
  Bible 220.68
Mythologists 291.130 92
Mythology 398.2
  African religions 299.62
  art representation 704.947
  arts 700.47
    T3C—37
    see Manual at T3C—37 vs. T3C—15
  Australian religion 299.921 5
  Buddhism 294.333
  Celtic religion 299.16
  Chinese religions 299.51
  Christianity 230

Mythology (continued)
  classical religion 292.13
  Egyptian religion 299.31
  folklore 398.2
  Germanic religion 293.13
  Greek religion 292.13
  Hawaiian religion 299.924 2
  Hinduism 294.513
  literature 808.803 7
    history and criticism 809.933 7
    specific literatures T3B—080 37
      history and criticism T3B—093 7
  Native American religions 299.72
    North American 299.72
    South American 299.82
  Norse religion 293.13
  paintings 753.7
  Polynesian religion 299.924
  religion 291.13
    sources 291.8
  Roman religion 292.13
  Scandinavian religion 293.13
  Semitic religions 299.2
  Shintoism 299.561 13
  see Manual at 398.2 vs. 291.13
Mythomania
  medicine 616.858 45
  see also Mental illness
Myxedemism
  medicine 616.858 848
  see also Mental retardation
Myxobacteria 579.32
Myxogastromycetidae 579.52
Myxomycetes 579.52
Myxomycophyta 579.52
Myxomycota 579.52
Myxomycotina 579.52
Myxophaga 595.762
Myzostomida 592.62

N

Na-Dene languages 497.2
  T6—972
Naâma (Algeria : Province) T2—657
Nablus (Jordan : District) T2—569 53
Naboomspruit (South Africa) T2—682 5
Nacogdoches County (Tex.) T2—764 182
Nador (Morocco : Province) T2—642
Naga languages 495.4
  T6—954
Nāgāland (India) T2—541 65
Nagano-ken (Japan) T2—521 63
Nagar Haveli (India) T2—547 96
Nagasaki-ken (Japan) T2—522 4
Nagasaki-shi (Japan) T2—522 44
Nagorno-Karabakh (Azerbaijan) T2—475 4
Nagoya-shi (Japan) T2—521 674
Naguib, Mohammed
  Egyptian history 962.053
Nahanni National Park (N.W.T.) T2—719 3
Nahatlatch River (B.C.) T2—711 37
Nahuas T5—974 52
Nahuatl language 497.452
  T6—974 52
Nahuatl literature 897.452
Nahum (Biblical book) 224.94
Naiads (Plants) 584.74
Nail-care tools
  manufacturing technology 688.5
Nails (Body parts) 599.814 7
  descriptive zoology 599.814 7
  geriatrics 618.976 547
  human anatomy 611.78
  human diseases
    incidence 614.595 47
    medicine 616.547
  human physiology 612.799
  pediatrics 618.925 47
  personal care 646.727
  pharmacodynamics 615.779
  physiology 573.59
  see also Skin
Nails (Fasteners) 621.884
  arts 739.48
Nairn (Scotland : District) T2—411 95
Nairobi (Kenya) T2—676 25
Nais 788.37
  see also Woodwind instruments
Najadales 584.74
Najaf (Iraq : Province) T2—567 5
Najd (Saudi Arabia) T2—538
Nakers 786.93
  see also Percussion instruments
Nakh languages 499.964 1
  T6—999 641
Nakhichevan (Azerbaijan) T2—475 4
Nakho-Daghestan languages 499.964
  T6—999 64

Nama language 496.1
T6—961
Namakgale (South Africa : District) T2—682 93
Namaqualand (South Africa) T2—687 2
Nambicuara Indians T5—984
Nambicuara language 498.4
T6—984
Nambikuara Indians T5—984
Nambikuara language 498.4
T6—984
Nambiquaran languages 498.4
T6—984
Namboku period 952.022
Name cards
prints 769.5
Names 929.97
cataloging 025.322
customs 392.12
divination 133.33
etymology 412
specific languages T4—2
geographic 910.014
gazetters 910.3
personal 929.4
Names of God
Islam 297.211 2
Judaism 296.311 2
Namibe (Angola : Province) T2—673 5
Namibia 968.81
T2—688 1
Namibians T5—968 81
Naming ceremonies
Judaism 296.443
Nampula (Mozambique) T2—679 7
Namur (Belgium : Province) T2—493 44
Nan-ching shih (China) T2—511 36
Nanai (Asian people) T5—941
Nanai language 494.1
T6—941
Nanaimo (B.C. : Regional District) T2—711 2
Nance County (Neb.) T2—782 425
Nande (Zairian people) T5—963 94
Nande languages 496.394
T6—963 94
Nandi (East African people) T5—965
Nandi (Zairian people) T5—963 94
Nandi language (Bantu) 496.394
T6—963 94
Nandi languages (Nilotic) 496.5
T6—965
Nang Klao, King of Siam
Thai history 959.303 3
Nangklao, King of Siam
Thai history 959.303 3
Nanjing Shi (China) T2—511 36
Nanking (China) T2—511 36
Nanostructure materials 620.5
Nanotechnology 620.5
Nantucket County (Mass.) T2—744 97
Nantucket Island (Mass.) T2—744 97
Nantucket Sound (Mass.) 551.461 46
T2—163 46
Napa County (Calif.) T2—794 19
Naphthalenes 547.615
chemical engineering 661.816
Naphthas 665.538 24
Naphuno (South Africa : District) T2—682 93
Napier City (N.Z.) T2—934 67
Napierville (Quebec : County) T2—714 35
Napkin folding 642.7
Napkins 642.7
arts 746.96
home sewing 646.21
table setting 642.7
Naples (Italy) T2—457 3
ancient T2—377
Naples (Italy : Province) T2—457 3
Napo (Ecuador : Province) T2—866 416
Napoleon I, Emperor of the French
French history 944.05
Napoleon III, Emperor of the French
French history 944.07
Napoleonic Wars 940.27
Napoli (Italy : Province) T2—457 3
Nappes (Geology) 551.872
Naqara 786.93
see also Percussion instruments
Naqshabandiyah 297.48
Nara-ken (Japan) T2—521 84
Narasimha Rao, P. V.
Indian history 954.052
Narbonensis T2—364
Narcissism
medicine 616.858 5
see also Mental illness
Narcissus 635.934 34
botany 584.34

Narcissus (continued)
  floriculture 635.934 34
Narcolepsy
  medicine 616.849 8
  see also Nervous system
Narcotic antagonists
  pharmacodynamics 615.782 2
Narcotics 362.29
  customs 394.14
  ethics 178.8
    see also Ethical problems
  pharmacodynamics 615.782 2
  see also Drug traffic;
      Substance abuse
Narcotics abuse 362.293
  medicine 616.863 2
  personal health 613.83
  social welfare 362.293
  see also Substance abuse
Narcotics traffic 363.45
  see also Drug traffic
Nardeae 584.9
Nariño (Colombia : Dept.) T2—861 62
Narooma (N.S.W.) T2—944 7
Narragansett Bay (R.I.) 551.461 46
  T2—163 46
Narration
  literature 808.802 3
    history and criticism 809.923
    specific literatures T3B—080 23
      history and criticism T3B—092 3
  rhetoric 808
Narrative
  literature 808.802 3
    history and criticism 809.923
    specific literatures T3B—080 23
      history and criticism T3B—092 3
Narrative poetry 808.813
  history and criticism 809.13
  specific literatures T3B—103
    individual authors T3A—1
Narrogin (W.A. : Shire) T2—941 2
Narrow-gage railroads 385.52
  see also Railroad
      transportation
Narwhal 599.543
Nasā'ī, Aḥmad ibn Shu'ayb
  Hadith 297.124 5
Nasal sinuses 573.26
  biology 573.26
  human anatomy 611.21
  human physiology 612.2
  medicine 616.212
  see also Respiratory system
Nash County (N.C.) T2—756 47
Nashim 296.123 3
  Babylonian Talmud 296.125 3
  Mishnah 296.123 3
  Palestinian Talmud 296.124 3
Nashville (Tenn.) T2—768 55
Nasopharynx
  medicine 616.212
  see also Respiratory system
Nass River (B.C.) T2—711 85
Nassau (Bahamas) T2—729 6
Nassau County (Fla.) T2—759 11
Nassau County (N.Y.) T2—747 245
Nasser, Gamal Abdel
  Egyptian history 962.053
Nasser, Lake (Egypt and
    Sudan) T2—623
Nasturtiums (Brassicaceae) 583.64
Nasturtiums (Tropaeolaceae) 635.933 79
  botany 583.79
  floriculture 635.933 79
Natal (South Africa) 968.4
  T2—684
Natalia 968.404 2
  T2—684
Natantia 595.388
Natchez (Miss.) T2—762 26
Natchitoches Parish (La.) T2—763 65
Nathalia (Vic.) T2—945 4
Nation of Islam 297.87
Nation River (B.C.) T2—711 82
Nation-states 321.05
National advertising 659.131 2
National bankruptcy 336.368
National banks 332.122 3
National Baptist Convention of
    America 286.134
  see also Baptists
National Baptist Convention of
    the United States of
    America 286.133
  see also Baptists
National bibliographies 015
National borrowing 336.343 3
  public administration 352.45
  see also National debt
National Botanic Gardens
    of South Africa T2—687 355
National Capital (Papua
    New Guinea) T2—954 5
National Capital Region
    (Canada) T2—713 83
  Ontario T2—713 83
  Quebec T2—714 221

National cemeteries 363.75
  landscape architecture 718.8
  see also Cremation—social services
National characteristics 305.8
  psychology 155.89
National conferences of bishops 262.12
National Council of the Churches of Christ in the United States of America 277.308 206
National Country Party 324.294 04
National dances 793.31
  see Manual at 792.78 vs. 792.8, 793.3
National debt 336.343 3
  law 343.037
  macroeconomic policy 339.523
  public administration 352.45
  public finance 336.343 3
National flags 929.92
National forests 333.75
  see also Forest lands
National Front (Colombia) 986.106 33
National groups 305.8
  T1—089
  T7—03
  literature 808.898
    history and criticism 809.8
    specific literatures T3B—080 8
      history and criticism T3B—098
    see Manual at T3C—93–T3C—99, T3C—9174 vs. T3C—8
  see also Ethnic groups
National guards 355.37
National health insurance 368.42
  law 344.022
National income 339.32
  macroeconomics
    distribution 339.2
National income theory of wages 331.210 1
National Liberation Front of South Viet Nam 959.704 332 2
National libraries 027.5
National-local relations 320.404 9
  law 342.042
  public administration 353.334
National Merit Scholarship Qualifying Test 378.166 2
National minorities 305.8
  see also Ethnic groups
National parks 363.68
  conservation of natural resources 333.72
  see also Parks
  see Manual at 333.7–333.9 vs. 508, 913–919, 930–990
National planning
  civic art 711.2
  economics 338.9
National product
  macroeconomics 339.3
National-provincial relations 320.404 9
  law 342.042
  public administration 353.333
National psychology 155.89
  see Manual at 155.89 vs. 155.84
National Republican Party (U.S.) 324.273 23
National resources
  conservation 339.49
National security 355.03
  law 343.01
    police powers 342.041 8
  public administration 353.1
National security councils 353.122 4
National self-determination 320.15
National service (Selective service) 355.223 63
  law 343.012 2
National Service Life Insurance 368.364
  see also Insurance
National socialism 335.6
  economics 335.6
  political ideology 320.533
National Socialist White People's Party 324.273 38
National Society of the Colonial Dames of America 369.12
National songs 782.421 599
National-state relations 320.404 9
  law 342.042
  public administration 353.333
National states 321.05
National states (South Africa) T2—682 9
  Cape of Good Hope T2—687 9
  Natal T2—684 9
  Orange Free State T2—685 9
  Transvaal T2—682 9
National taxation 336.201 2
  law 343.043
  public finance 336.201 2
National territory 320.12
  international law 341.42

National Union Party (U.S. : 1854–) 324.273 4
National unions 331.872
  see also Labor unions
National universities 378.055
  see also Higher education
Nationalism 320.54
  arts 700.458
    T3C—358
  literature 808.803 58
    history and criticism 809.933 58
    specific literatures T3B—080 358
      history and criticism T3B—093 58
  music 780.903 4
Nationalist China T2—512 49
Nationalist parties 324.218 3
  international organizations 324.183
Nationality (Citizenship) 323.6
  see also Citizenship
Nationality clubs 369.2
Nationalization of industry 338.924
  law 343.07
Nationalization of property 333.14
  international law 341.484 6
  land economics 333.14
  law 343.025 2
Native American languages 497
    T6—97
  South America 498
    T6—98
Native American literatures 897
  South America 898
Native American peoples T5—97
  South America T5—98
Native elements 549.2
  see also Chemicals
Native metals 549.23
  see also Metals
Native peoples 306.08
  legal status 346.013
    constitutional law 342.087 2
    private law 346.013
Native plants
  floriculture 635.951
  resource economics 333.953 3
Nativism 149.7
Nativity of Jesus Christ 232.92
NATO (Alliance) 355.031 091 821
  law 341.72
Natrona County (Wyo.) T2—787 93
Natural areas
  biological resource conservation 333.951 6
  land conservation 333.731 6
Natural areas (continued)
  wildlife conservation 333.954 16
Natural childbirth
  obstetrics 618.45
Natural communities 577.82
Natural dyes
  technology 667.26
Natural environments
  health 613.1
Natural foods 641.302
Natural gas 553.285
  economic geology 553.285
  extraction 622.338 5
  extractive economics 338.272 85
    law 343.077 2
  pipeline transportation 388.56
    engineering 665.744
  prospecting 622.182 85
  public administration 354.46
  public utilities 363.63
    law 343.092 6
    see also Public utilities
  resource economics 333.823 3
    law 346.046 823 3
  technology 665.7
    economics 338.476 657
  see also Petroleum
Natural gas vehicles 388.34
  engineering 629.220 43
  repair 629.287 043
  transportation services 388.34
  see also Automotive vehicles
Natural history 508
  animals 590
  biology 578
  microorganisms 579
  plants 580
  see also Nature
  see Manual at 578 vs. 304.2, 508, 910
Natural landscapes
  landscape architecture 719
Natural language processing
  computer science 006.35
  see Manual at 410.285 vs. 006.35
Natural law
  ethical systems 171.2
  law 340.112
  moral theology
    Christianity 241.2
Natural leather 675.2
Natural magnets 538.4

Natural monuments
  landscape architecture 719.32
Natural numbers 513.2
  number theory 512.72
Natural phenomena 508
  see also Nature
Natural radioactivity 539.752
Natural religion 210
Natural resource management 333.7
  see Manual at 333.7–333.9 vs. 363.1, 363.73, 577
Natural resources 333.7
  conservation 333.72
    see Manual at 333.72 vs. 304.28, 363.7
  economics 333.7
    see Manual at 333.7–333.9; *also at* 333.7–333.9 vs. 333
  ethics 178
    religion 291.568
      Christianity 241.68
    see also Ethical problems
  law 346.044
  public administration 354.3
  see Manual at 333.7–333.9 vs. 363.1, 363.73, 577; *also at* 333.7–333.9 vs. 363.6
Natural rights 323.01
  international law 341.481 01
  law 340.112
Natural sciences 500
  see also Science
Natural selection 576.82
Natural stone 553.5
  see also Stone
Natural theology 210
Naturalism 146
  ethics 171.2
  fine arts 709.034 3
  literature 808.801 2
    history and criticism 809.912
    specific literatures T3B—080 12
      history and criticism T3B—091 2
  painting 759.053
Naturalization 323.623
  law 342.083
  public administration 353.484
Nature 508
  art representation 704.943
  arts 700.46
    T3C—36
  Christian doctrine 231.7
  elementary education 372.357
Nature (continued)
  folklore 398.24
    history and criticism 398.36
    living 398.24
    nonliving 398.26
  literature 808.803 6
    history and criticism 809.933 6
    specific literatures T3B—080 36
      history and criticism T3B—093 6
  painting 758
  philosophy 113
  religious worship 291.212
  respect for
    ethics 179.1
      religion 291.569 1
        Christianity 241.691
      see also Ethical problems
Nature reserves
  biological resource conservation 333.951 6
Nature study
  elementary education 372.357
Nature versus nurture
  psychology
    evolutional psychology 155.7
    individual psychology 155.234
Natures of Jesus Christ 232.8
Naturopathy
  therapeutic system 615.535
Nauru 996.85
  T2—968 5
Nautical almanacs 528
Nautical engineering 623.8
Nautical engineers 623.809 2
  occupational group T7—623 8
Nautical facilities 387.15
  see also Port facilities
Nautical health 613.68
Nautical instruments 623.863
Nautiloidea 594.52
  paleozoology 564.52
Navajo County (Ariz.) T2—791 35
Navajo Indians T5—972
Navajo language 497.2
  T6—972
Navajo literature 897.2
Navajo rugs
  arts 746.72
  see also Rugs
Naval administration 359.6
Naval air forces 359.94
Naval aircraft 359.948 34
  military engineering 623.746
  naval equipment 359.948 34

Naval architecture 623.81
Naval artillery 359.981 282
  engineering 623.418
  naval equipment 359.981 282
Naval artillery services 359.981 2
Naval aviation 359.94
Naval bases 359.7
  military engineering 623.64
  World War I 940.453
  World War II 940.545 3
  see also Naval operations
Naval defense 359.03
Naval design 623.81
Naval disarmament 327.174 3
Naval engineering 623.8
Naval engineers 623.809 2
  occupational group T7—623 8
Naval forces 359
Naval gunnery 623.553
Naval health 613.68
Naval maneuvers 359.4
  training 359.52
  see also Naval operations
Naval medicine 616.980 24
Naval officers 359.009 2
  role and function 359.332
Naval operations 359.4
  Algerian Revolution 965.046 45
  Civil War (England) 942.062 45
  Civil War (Spain) 946.081 45
  Civil War (United States) 973.75
  Crimean War 947.073 845
  Falkland Islands War 997.110 244 5
  Hundred Years' War 944.025 45
  Indo-Pakistan War, 1971 954.920 514 5
  Indochinese War 959.704 145
  Iraqi-Iranian Conflict 955.054 245
  Korean War 951.904 245
  Mexican War 973.625
  Napoleonic Wars 940.274 5
  Persian Gulf War, 1991 956.704 424 5
  Spanish-American War 973.895
  Thirty Years' War 940.244 5
  United States Revolutionary War 973.35
  Vietnamese War 959.704 345
  War of 1812 973.525
  World War I 940.45
  World War II 940.545
Naval ordnance 359.8
  engineering 623.825 1
  naval equipment 359.8
Naval personnel 359.009 2
  occupational group T7—359
Naval reserves 359.37
Naval schools (Secondary education) 373.243
  see also Secondary education
Naval warfare 359
Naval weapons 359.8
  engineering 623.8
  naval equipment 359.8
Navarra (Spain) T2—465 2
Navarro County (Tex.) T2—764 282
Naves 726.592
Navigable waters
  land economics 333.915
Navigation 629.045
  air transportation 629.132 51
    international law 341.756 76
    law 343.097 6
  animal physiology 573.87
  aquatic sports 797.1
  engineering 629.045
  maritime transportation 623.89
    international law 341.756 66
    law 343.096 6
  space flight 629.453
Navigation Acts
  United States history 973.311 2
Navigation aids 387.155
  hydraulic engineering 627.92
  transportation services 387.155
Navigation instrumentation
  aircraft engineering 629.135 1
Navigation systems
  spacecraft 629.474 2
  unmanned spacecraft 629.464 2
Navigators 629.045 092
  occupational group T7—629
Navy beans 641.356 52
  see also Kidney beans
Navy life 359.1
Naxos Island (Greece) T2—495 85
  ancient T2—391 5
Nayarit (Mexico) T2—723 4
Nāys 788.35
  see also Woodwind instruments
Nazi government 321.94
Nazi parties 324.213 8
Nazir 296.123 3
  Babylonian Talmud 296.125 3
  Mishnah 296.123 3
  Palestinian Talmud 296.124 3
Nazism 335.6
  economics 335.6
  political ideology 320.533

Nazko River (B.C.) T2—711 75
Ndebele (South Africa) T2—682 95
Ndebele (South African people) T5—963 977
Ndebele (Zimbabwean people) T5—963 98
Ndebele language (South Africa) 496.397 7
T6—963 977
Ndebele language (Zimbabwe) 496.398
T6—963 98
Ndonga languages 496.399
T6—963 99
Ndumu Game Reserve (South Africa) T2—684 91
Ndwanwe (Kingdom) 968.403 8
T2—684
Ndwedwe (South Africa : District) T2—684 91
Neagh, Lough (Northern Ireland) T2—416
Neamţ (Romania) T2—498 1
Neanderthal man 569.9
Near-death experience
occultism 133.901 3
Near East 956
T2—56
ancient 939.4
T2—394
Near-space exploration
unmanned 629.435 2
Nearshore biology 578.778
Nearshore ecology 577.78
Neath (Wales : District) T2—429 84
Neat's-foot oil 665.2
Nebaliacea 595.379 2
Nebiim 224
Nebo (South Africa : District) T2—682 93
Nebraska 978.2
T2—782
Nebraska Panhandle T2—782 9
Nebuchadnezzar II, King of Babylonia
Mesopotamian history 935.04
Necessity
philosophy 123.7
Nechako Plateau (B.C.) T2—711 82
Nechako Reservoir (B.C.) T2—711 82
Nechako River (B.C.) T2—711 82
Neches River (Tex.) T2—764 15
Neck
fractures
medicine 617.151
human anatomy 611.93
Neck (continued)
human physiology 612.93
regional medicine 617.53
surgery 617.530 59
Neck muscles
human anatomy 611.733
see also Musculoskeletal system
Necklaces 391.7
customs 391.7
making 739.278
see also Jewelry
Necks (Geology) 551.88
Neckwear 391.41
see also Accessories (Clothing)
Necrologies 920
Necromancy 133.9
Necropneumonia
medicine 616.245
see also Respiratory system
Nectarines 641.342 57
cooking 641.642 57
food 641.342 57
orchard crop 634.257
Nectria 579.567 7
Nedarim 296.123 3
Babylonian Talmud 296.125 3
Mishnah 296.123 3
Palestinian Talmud 296.124 3
Nederlandsche Oost-Indische Compagnie
Indonesian history 959.802 1
Needle biopsy
medicine 616.075 8
Needlefishes 597.66
Needlepoint 746.442
Needlepoint laces 677.653
arts 746.224
manufacturing technology 677.653
Needlework
elementary education 372.54
textile arts 746.4
Ñeembucú (Paraguay : Dept.) T2—892 124
Ñeengatú language 498.382 9
T6—983 829
Ñeengatú literature 898.382 9
Nefertiti, Queen of Egypt
Egyptian history 932.014
Nega'im 296.123 6
Negation
logic 160

Negative income tax 362.582
  law 344.032 582
Negatives (Photography) 771.43
Negeri Sembilan T2—595 1
Negev (Israel) T2—569 49
Neglected children
  social welfare 362.76
    see also Child abuse
Negligence (Law) 346.032
Negotiable instruments 332.76
  law 346.096
Negotiable order of withdrawal
    accounts 332.175 2
Negotiation 302.3
  executive management 658.405 2
  psychology 158.5
  social psychology 302.3
Negro Methodist churches 287.8
  see also Methodist Church
Negro race T5—036
Negroes T5—96
Negroid race T5—036
Negros Island (Philippines) T2—599 5
Negros Occidental
    (Philippines) T2—599 5
Negros Oriental
    (Philippines) T2—599 5
Nehemiah (Biblical book) 222.8
Nehru, Jawaharlal
  Indian history 954.042
Nei Monggol Zizhiqu
    (China) T2—517 7
Neighborhood centers
  recreation centers 790.068
Neighborhoods 307.336 2
Neighbors
  applied psychology 158.25
  psychological influence 155.925
Neisseria 579.33
Nejd (Saudi Arabia) T2—538
Nelson (B.C.) T2—711 62
Nelson and Hay National
    Park (W.A.) T2—941 2
Nelson City (N.Z.) T2—937 6
Nelson County (Ky.) T2—769 495
Nelson County (N.D.) T2—784 35
Nelson County (Va.) T2—755 493
Nelson Lakes National
    Park (N.Z.) T2—937 4
Nelson-Marlborough
    Region (N.Z.) T2—937 5
Nelson Province (N.Z.) T2—937 5
Nelson River (Man.) T2—712 71
Nelspruit (South Africa :
    District) T2—682 6
Nelumbonales 583.3
Nemaha County (Kan.) T2—781 332
Nemaha County (Neb.) T2—782 278
Nemata 592.57
Nemathelminthes 592.5
Nematocera 595.772
Nematoda 592.57
  agricultural pests 632.625 7
  paleozoology 562.57
Nematode-caused diseases
    (Biology) 571.999
  agriculture 632.625 7
  plant crops 632.625 7
  veterinary medicine 636.089 696 5
Nematode-caused diseases
    (Human)
  incidence 614.555
  medicine 616.965
  see also Communicable
      diseases (Human)
Nematomorpha 592.59
Nemertea 592.32
  paleozoology 562.32
Nemertina 592.32
Nene River (England) T2—425 5
Nenets language 494.4
  T6—944
Nenets National District
    (Russia) T2—471 1
Nenet͡skiĭ natsionalʹnyĭ
    okrug (Russia) T2—471 1
Neo-Aristotelianism 149.91
Neo-Babylonian Empire 935.04
  T2—35
Neo-Confucianism 181.112
Neo-impressionism 709.034 5
  painting 759.055
Neo-Kantianism 142.3
Neo-Persian Empire 935.07
  T2—35
Neo-scholasticism 149.91
Neo-Thomism 149.91
Neobehaviorism 150.194 34
Neocene period 551.786
  geology 551.786
  paleontology 560.178 6
Neoclassical architecture 724.2
Neoclassical economics 330.157
Neoclassical school (Economics) 330.157
Neoclassicism
  music 780.904
  painting 759.051

Neodymium
  chemistry 546.413
  see also Rare earths
Neofiber 599.357 9
Neogastropoda 594.32
Neogene period 551.786
  geology 551.786
  paleontology 560.178 6
Neolithic Age 930.14
Neon
  chemistry 546.752
  gas technology 665.822
  see also Chemicals
Neon lighting 621.327 5
  see also Lighting
Neonatal development
  humans 612.652
Neonatal medicine 618.920 1
Neonates
  pediatrics 618.920 1
Neonatology 618.920 1
Neoplasms (Biology) 571.978
Neoplasms (Human)
  incidence 614.599 9
  medicine 616.992
    see Manual at 616.994 vs. 616.992
  see also Diseases (Human)
Neoplasticism 709.040 52
  painting 759.065 2
  sculpture 735.230 452
Neoplatonism 186.4
  ancient 186.4
  Christian polemics 239.4
  modern 141.2
Neopsychoanalytic systems 150.195 7
Neorealism
  philosophy 149.2
Neornithes 598
  paleozoology 568
Neosho County (Kan.) T2—781 95
Neotoma 599.357 3
Neotropical fruit bats 599.45
Nepal 954.96
  T2—549 6
Nepalese T5—914 95
Nepali T5—914 95
Nepali language 491.495
  T6—914 95
Nepali literature 891.495
Nepean River (N.S.W.) T2—944 6
Nepenthales 583.75
Nephews 306.87
  T1—085
  T7—046
Nephrite 553.876
  see also Jade
Nephritis
  medicine 616.612
  see also Urinary system
Nephrology 616.61
  see also Urinary system
Neptune (Planet) 523.481
  T2—992 8
  astrology 133.539 1
Neptunium 546.432
  see also Chemicals
Nerve tissues 573.85
  human histology 611.018 8
  see also Nervous system
Nerves 573.85
  biology 573.85
  human anatomy 611.83
  human physiology 612.81
  surgery 617.483
  see also Nervous system
Nervous system 573.8
  anesthesiology 617.967 48
  biology 573.8
  geriatrics 618.976 8
  human anatomy 611.8
  human cancer 362.196 994 8
    incidence 614.599 948
    medicine 616.994 8
    social services 362.196 994 8
    see also Cancer (Human)
  human diseases 362.196 8
    incidence 614.598
    medicine 616.8
    social services 362.196 8
  human histology 611.018 98
  human physiology 612.8
  pediatrics 618.928
  perinatal medicine 618.326 8
  pharmacodynamics 615.78
  surgery 617.48
  veterinary medicine 636.089 68
  see also Innervation
Neshoba County (Miss.) T2—762 685
Nesosilicates
  mineralogy 549.62
Ness County (Kan.) T2—781 46
Nesting 591.564
Nestorian churches 281.8
  see also Eastern churches
Nests 591.564

Net national product 339.32
Net-winged beetles 595.764 4
Net worth
  personal finance 332.024 01
Netball 796.324
  see also Sports
Netball players 796.324 092
Netherlanders T5—393 1
Netherlandish languages 439.3
  T6—393
Netherlandish literatures 839.3
Netherlandish peoples T5—393
Netherlands 949.2
  T2—492
  ancient 936.4
  T2—364
Netherlands Antilles T2—729 86
Netherlands New Guinea T2—951
Neto, António Agostinho
  Angolan history 967.304 1
Nets (Devices)
  fishing 639.202 84
    sports 799.13
  hunting
    sports 799.202 82
Nets (Mathematics)
  topology 514.223
Nets (Surveying) 526.33
Netsukes 736.68
Netted fabrics 677.664
  see also Textiles
Netting
  arts 746.422 4
Nettles 583.45
Network affiliates
  television 384.550 65
Network analysis
  management 658.403 2
  telephony 621.385 1
Network architecture
  communications engineering 621.382 15
  computer science 004.65
Network databases
  computer science 005.754
Network operating systems 005.447 6
Network programs 791.443
  radio performances 791.443
  television performances 791.453
Network protocols
  communications engineering 621.382 12
  computer science 004.62
Network topology
  communications engineering 621.382 15
  computer science 004.65
Networks (Communications) 384.540 65
  facilities 384.545 5
  organizations 384.540 65
  performing arts 791.44
  see also Television networks
  see Manual at 384.54065 vs. 384.5453, 384.5455
Networks (Electrical) 621.319 2
Neubrandenburg (Germany : Bezirk) T2—431 72
Neuchâtel (Switzerland : Canton) T2—494 38
Neuenburg (Switzerland : Canton) T2—494 38
Neufchâtel cheese 641.373 53
  cooking 641.673 53
  food 641.373 53
  processing 637.353
Neumann function 515.53
Neumes 780.148
Neuquén (Argentina : Province) T2—827 2
Neural computers 006.32
Neural nets (Computer science) 006.32
Neural networks (Computer science) 006.32
Neuralgias
  medicine 616.87
  see also Nervous system
Neurasthenia
  medicine 616.852 8
  see also Mental illness
Neurilemma
  human histology 611.018 8
  see also Nervous system
Neuritis
  medicine 616.87
  see also Nervous system
Neuroanatomy 573.833
  human 611.8
  see also Nervous system
Neurobiology 573.8
  humans 612.8
  see also Nervous system
Neuroblastoma
  pediatrics 618.929 948
Neurochemistry 573.84
  human physiology 612.804 2
  see also Nervous system
Neurofibromatosis
  medicine 616.993 83
  see also Diseases (Human)

Neuroglia
human histology 611.018 8
see also Nervous system
Neurolinguistics
disorders
medicine 616.855
see also Communicative disorders
human physiology 612.78
Neurological diseases 573.839
symptomatology 616.84
see also Nervous system
Neurological language disorders
medicine 616.855 2
see also Communicative disorders
Neurological nursing
medicine 610.736 8
Neurology
medicine 616.8
see also Nervous system
Neuromuscular diseases
medicine 616.744
see also Musculoskeletal system
Neurons 573.853 6
human histology 611.018 8
see also Nervous system
Neuropharmacology 615.78
see also Nervous system
Neurophysiology 573.8
humans 612.8
see also Nervous system
Neuropsychiatry 616.8
see also Mental illness
Neuropsychopharmacology 615.78
see also Mental illness
Neuroptera 595.747
Neuropteris 561.597
Neuroses 362.25
medicine 616.852
social welfare 362.25
see also Mental illness
Neurosurgery 617.48
see also Nervous system
Neurosyphilis
medicine 616.892
see also Nervous system
Neuse River (N.C.) T2—756 19
Neuston 592.176
Neutral countries T2—171 83
law of war 341.64
World War I 940.335
World War II 940.533 5
Neutralist blocs T2—171 6
Neutrality
law of war 341.64
Neutralization (Chemistry)
analytical chemistry 545.22
Neutrinos 539.721 5
Neutron radiation
biophysics 571.459
humans 612.014 486
Neutron stars 523.887 4
Neutrons 539.721 3
Neuvo León (Mexico : State) T2—721 3
Nevada 979.3
T2—793
Nevada County (Ark.) T2—767 52
Nevada County (Calif.) T2—794 37
Nevi
medicine 616.55
see also Skin
Nevi'im 224
Nevi'im aḥaronim 224
Nevi'im rishonim 222
Nevis T2—729 73
Nevşehir İli (Turkey) T2—564
New Academy (Philosophy) 186.2
New Age movement 299.93
Christian polemics 239.93
occultism 133
Christian viewpoint 261.513
parapsychology 133
religion 299.93
see Manual at 299.93
New Age religions 299.93
see Manual at 299.93
New American Bible 220.520 5
New Britain Island (Papua New Guinea) T2—958 5
New Brunswick 971.51
T2—715 1
New Brunswick (N.J.) T2—749 42
New Caledonia 995.97
T2—959 7
New Caledonia (Canada) 971.102
T2—711
New Castile (Spain) T2—464
New Castle County (Del.) T2—751 1
New Century Bible 220.520 8
New Delhi (India) T2—545 6
New Democratic Party 324.271 07
New England 974
T2—74
New England National Park (N.S.W.) T2—944 4

New English Bible 220.520 6
New Forest (England : District) T2—422 75
New France, Company of
  Canadian history 971.016 2
New Glasgow (N.S.) T2—716 13
New Granada 986.102
  T2—861
  Colombian history 986.102
  Ecuadorian history 986.602
  Panamanian history 972.870 2
  Venezuelan history 987.03
New Granada (Republic) 986.105 2
  T2—861
  Colombian history 986.105 2
  Panamanian history 972.870 3
New Guinea 995
  T2—95
New Guinea (Territory) 995.302 2
  T2—953
New Hampshire 974.2
  T2—742
New Hanover (South Africa : District) T2—684 7
New Hanover County (N.C.) T2—756 27
New Haven (Conn.) T2—746 8
New Haven County (Conn.) T2—746 7
New Hebrides T2—959 5
New International version (Bible) 220.520 81
New Ireland Province (Papua New Guinea) T2—958 3
New Jersey 974.9
  T2—749
New Jerusalem Bible 220.520 7
New Jerusalemites
  biography 289.409 2
  religious group T7—284
New Kent County (Va.) T2—755 43
New King James Bible 220.520 8
New Kingdom (Egypt) 932.014
New left 320.53
New London County (Conn.) T2—746 5
New Madrid County (Mo.) T2—778 985
New Mexico 978.9
  T2—789
New nations
  establishment
    World War I 940.314 25
    World War II 940.531 425
New Norfolk (Tas.) T2—946 2
New Norse language 439.83
  T6—398 3
New Norse literature 839.83
New Orleans (La.) T2—763 35
New Orleans, Battle of, 1815 973.523 9
New Orleans jazz 781.653
New Plymouth District (N.Z.) T2—934 82
New product development management 658.575
New Providence Island (Bahamas) T2—729 6
New Quebec (Quebec) T2—714 11
New religions 291.046
  see Manual at 291: Denominations and sects
New religious movements 291.046
  see Manual at 291: Denominations and sects
New Revised Standard version Bible 220.520 43
New River (N.C.-W. Va.) T2—754 7
  North Carolina T2—756 83
  Virginia T2—755 7
  West Virginia T2—754 7
New Siberian Islands (Russia) T2—988
New South Wales T2—944
New Southwest 979
  T2—79
New Stone Age 930.14
New Testament 225
New Testament Greek language 487.4
  T6—87
New Testament pseudepigrapha 229.92
New Testament theology 230.041 5
New Thought 299.93
  Christian 289.98
    see also Christian denominations
New towns 307.768
  area planning 711.45
New Valley (Egypt : Province) T2—622
New Westminster (B.C.) T2—711 33
New World flycatchers 598.823
New World monkeys 599.85
New World pitcher plants 583.36
New World polecats 599.768
New World porcupines 599.359 74
New World seedeaters 598.883
New World vultures 598.92

New Year 394.261 4
  customs 394.261 4
    Jewish 394.267
  Jewish 296.431 5
    liturgy 296.453 15
New York (N.Y.) T2—747 1
New York (State) 974.7
  T2—747
New York Bay (N.Y.) 551.461 46
  T2—163 46
New York County (N.Y.) T2—747 1
New York jazz 781.653
New York Metropolitan Area T2—747 1
New Zealand 993
  T2—93
  see Manual at T2—93
New Zealand literature 820
New Zealand red pine 585.3
New Zealand Wars, 1843–1847 993.021
New Zealand Wars, 1860–1870 993.022
New Zealanders T5—23
Newar T5—95
Newari language 495.49
  T6—954 9
Newari literature 895.49
Newark (N.J.) T2—749 32
Newark and Sherwood (England : District) T2—425 24
Newaygo County (Mich.) T2—774 58
Newberry County (S.C.) T2—757 39
Newborn infants
  pediatrics 618.920 1
Newbury (England : District) T2—422 91
Newcastle (N.S.W.) T2—944 2
Newcastle (South Africa : District) T2—684 1
Newcastle-under-Lyme (England : District) T2—424 62
Newcastle upon Tyne (England) T2—428 76
Newfoundland 971.8
  T2—718
Newfoundland (Dog) 636.73
Newham (London, England) T2—421 76
Newport (R.I.) T2—745 7
Newport (Wales : District) T2—429 91
Newport County (R.I.) T2—745 6
Newport News (Va.) T2—755 416
Newry and Mourne (Northern Ireland) T2—416 58
News agencies
  journalism 070.435
News gathering 070.43
News media 070.1
News sources
  journalism 070.431
Newsletters 050
  journalism 070.175
  see also Serials
Newspaper columns
  journalism 070.44
Newspaper illustration 741.65
Newspapers 070
  T1—05
  bibliographies 011.35
  journalism 070.172
  postal handling 383.123
    see also Postal service
  publishing 070.572 2
  sociology 302.232 2
Newsprint 676.286
Newsreel journalism 070.18
Newsreel photography 778.538 07
Newton County (Ark.) T2—767 16
Newton County (Ga.) T2—758 593
Newton County (Ind.) T2—772 974
Newton County (Miss.) T2—762 672
Newton County (Mo.) T2—778 732
Newton County (Tex.) T2—764 162
Newtownabbey (Northern Ireland) T2—416 18
Newts 597.85
Nez Perce County (Idaho) T2—796 85
Nez Percé Indians T5—974 1
Nezikin 296.123 4
  Babylonian Talmud 296.125 4
  Mishnah 296.123 4
  Palestinian Talmud 296.124 4
Ngaanyatjara language 499.15
  T6—991 5
Ngala language 496.396 86
  T6—963 968 6
Ngambai dialect 496.5
  T6—965
Nganasan language 494.4
  T6—944
Ngo language 496.36
  T6—963 6
Ngombe languages 496.396
  T6—963 96
Ngonde (African people) T5—963 91
Ngonde language 496.391
  T6—963 91

Ngondi languages 496.396
T6—963 96
Ngoni (Tanzania-Malawi people) T5—963 91
NGOs (International agencies) 060
social welfare 361.77
Ngotshe (South Africa : District) T2—684 2
Ngqeleni (South Africa : District) T2—687 91
Nguema, Francisco Macías
Equatorial Guinean history 967.180 31
Ngundi languages 496.396
T6—963 96
Nguni (African people) T5—963 98
Nguni kingdoms 968.403 8
Nguni languages 496.398
T6—963 98
Ngurus 788.38
see also Woodwind instruments
Nheengatu language 498.382 9
T6—983 829
Nheengatu literature 898.382 9
Nhengatu language 498.382 9
T6—983 829
Nhengatu literature 898.382 9
NI (Macroeconomics) 339.32
Niagara (Ont. : Regional municipality) T2—713 38
Niagara County (N.Y.) T2—747 98
Niagara Escarpment T2—713
Niagara Falls (N.Y. and Ont.) T2—713 39
New York T2—747 99
Ontario T2—713 39
Niagara Falls (N.Y.) T2—747 98
Niagara Falls (Ont.) T2—713 38
Niagara Peninsula (Ont.) T2—713 38
Niagara River (N.Y. and Ont.) T2—713 38
New York T2—747 98
Ontario T2—713 38
Niamey (Niger) T2—662 6
Niassa (Mozambique : Province) T2—679 9
Nicaragua 972.85
T2—728 5
Nicaragua Canal 386.445
Nicaraguan literature 860
Nicaraguans T5—687 285
Nice (County) T2—449 41
Nice (France) T2—449 414
Nicene Creed 238.142
Niches 721.48
architecture 721.48
construction 690.148
Niches (Ecology) 577.82
Nichiren Shoshu 294.392 8
Nicholas I, Emperor of Russia
Russian history 947.073
Nicholas II, Emperor of Russia
Russian history 947.083
Nicholas County (Ky.) T2—769 417
Nicholas County (W. Va.) T2—754 69
Nickel 669.733 2
biochemistry 572.526 25
building construction 693.773 32
building material 691.873 32
chemical engineering 661.062 5
chemistry 546.625
decorative arts 739.56
economic geology 553.485
human toxicology 615.925 625
materials science 620.188
metallography 669.957 332
metallurgy 669.733 2
metalworking 673.733 2
mining 622.348 5
physical metallurgy 669.967 332
see also Chemicals; Metals
Nickerie (Surinam : District) T2—883 1
Nicola River (B.C.) T2—711 72
Nicolet (Quebec : County) T2—714 55
Nicolet-Yamaska (Quebec) T2—714 54
Nicollet County (Minn.) T2—776 32
Nicotine
human toxicology 615.952 395 2
Niddah (Tractate) 296.123 6
Babylonian Talmud 296.125 6
Mishnah 296.123 6
Palestinian Talmud 296.124 6
Niddah practice 296.742
Nidulariales 579.599
Nidwald (Switzerland) T2—494 762
Nidwalden (Switzerland) T2—494 762
Nieces 306.87
T1—085
T7—046
Niederbayern (Germany) T2—433 5
Niederösterreich (Austria) T2—436 12
Niedersachsen (Germany) T2—435 9
Nielim language 496.361
T6—963 61
Nielloing
decorative arts 739.15
Nièvre (France) T2—445 6

Niğde İli (Turkey) T2—564
Nigei Island (B.C.) T2—711 2
Nigel (South Africa : District) T2—682 2
Niger 966.26
T2—662 6
Niger-Congo languages 496.3
T6—963
Niger-Kordofanian languages 496.3
T6—963
Niger people T5—966 26
Niger River T2—662
Niger State (Nigeria) T2—669 65
Nigeria 966.9
T2—669
Nigerian Civil War, 1967–1970 966.905 2
Nigerians T5—966 9
Nigeriens (People of Niger) T5—966 26
Night-blooming plants
  floriculture 635.953
Night crawlers 592.64
  culture 639.75
Night flying 629.132 521 4
Night journey of Muḥammad 297.633
Night photography 778.719
Night schools
  adult education 374.8
  higher education 378.158
Night skies
  meteorology 551.566
Night work 331.257 4
  personnel management 658.312 1
Nightclothes 391.42
  commercial technology 687.165
  customs 391.42
  home sewing 646.475
  see also Clothing
Nightclub presentations 792.7
  see also Theater
Nighthawks 598.99
Nightingales 598.842
Nightjars 598.99
Nightshades 583.952
Nihilism
  literature 808.803 84
    history and criticism 809.933 84
    specific literatures T3B—080 384
      history and criticism T3B—093 84
  philosophy 149.8
Niigata-ken (Japan) T2—521 52
Niihau (Hawaii) T2—969 42
Nijmegen (Netherlands) T2—492 18
Nika language 496.395
T6—963 95
Nikolaevskaia oblast′ (Ukraine) T2—477 3
Nikolayev (Ukraine : Oblast) T2—477 3
Nīl (Sudan) T2—625
Nīl al-Abyaḍ (Sudan) T2—626 4
Nīl al Azraq (Sudan) T2—626 4
Nile River T2—62
Nile River Delta T2—621
Nilo-Hamitic peoples T5—965
Nilo-Saharan languages 496.5
T6—965
Nilotic-Kavirondo language 496.5
T6—965
Nilotic languages 496.5
T6—965
Nilotic peoples T5—965
Nimbarka (Philosophy) 181.484 3
Nīnawá (Iraq : Province) T2—567 4
Nineveh (Extinct city) T2—35
Nineveh (Iraq : Province) T2—567 4
Ningsia Hui Autonomous Region (China) T2—517 5
Ningxia Huizu Zizhiqu (China) T2—517 5
Niobium 669.79
  chemical engineering 661.052 4
  chemistry 546.524
  economic geology 553.499
  metallurgy 669.79
  physical metallurgy 669.967 9
  see also Chemicals
Niobrara County (Wyo.) T2—787 15
Niobrara River (Wyo. and Neb.) T2—782 7
Nipa palm 584.5
Nipissing (Ont. : District) T2—713 147
Nipissing, Lake (Ont.) T2—713 147
Nirvana
  Buddhism 294.342 3
  Hinduism 294.523
Niter 553.64
  mineralogy 549.732
Nith River (Scotland) T2—414 86
Nithsdale (Scotland : District) T2—414 86
Nitidulidae 595.769
Nitrate fertilizers 631.842
  chemical engineering 668.624 2
Nitrates 553.64
  chemical engineering 661.65
  economic geology 553.64

Nitrates (continued)
  mineralogy 549.732
  mining 622.364
Nitration 547.26
  chemical engineering 660.284 46
Nitric acid
  chemical engineering 661.24
Nitrification 572.545
Nitrifying bacteria
  agricultural use 631.847
Nitrifying crops 631.847
Nitriles 547.044
  chemical engineering 661.894
Nitro compounds 547.041
  chemical engineering 661.894
Nitro dyes 667.252
Nitrocellulose 662.26
  textiles 677.461
    see also Textiles
Nitrocellulose glue 668.33
Nitrogen 553.93
  animal nutrition 572.544 1
    animal husbandry 636.085 21
  biochemistry 572.54
  chemical engineering 661.071 1
  chemistry 546.711
  economic geology 553.93
  gas technology 665.824
  organic chemistry 547.04
    aliphatic 547.44
    applied 661.894
    aromatic 547.64
  see also Chemicals
Nitrogen cycle
    (Biogeochemistry) 577.145
Nitrogen fertilizers 631.84
  chemical engineering 668.624
Nitrogen fixation 572.545
Nitrogen removal
  sewage treatment 628.357
Nitrogen salts
  chemical engineering 661.65
Nitroglycerin
  military engineering 623.452 7
Nitrosation 547.26
  chemical engineering 660.284 46
Nitroso compounds 547.041
  chemical engineering 661.894
Nitroso dyes 667.252
Nitrous oxide abuse 362.299
  medicine 616.86
  personal health 613.8
  social welfare 362.299
  see also Substance abuse
Niue T2—962 6
Niuean language 499.48
  T6—994 8
Niueans T5—994 8
Nivation 551.38
Nivernais (France) T2—445 6
Nivkh language 494.6
  T6—946
Nixon, Richard M. (Richard
    Milhous)
  United States history 973.924
Nizhegorod (Russia :
    Oblast) T2—474 1
Nizhegorodskai͡a oblastʹ
    (Russia) T2—474 1
Nizhniy Novgorod
    (Russia : Oblast) T2—474 1
Njabi languages 496.396
  T6—963 96
Njem language 496.396
  T6—963 96
Nkandla (South Africa :
    District) T2—684 91
Nkoya languages 496.393
  T6—963 93
Nkrumah, Kwame
  Ghanaian history 966.705
Nkundo language 496.396
  T6—963 96
Nkundu language 496.396
  T6—963 96
NMR (Physics) 538.362
NMR imaging
  medicine 616.075 48
NMSQT (Merit scholarship test) 378.166 2
NNP (Macroeconomics) 339.32
Nō
  literature 895.620 51
  theater 792.095 2
No-fault insurance 368.5
  law 346.086 5
  see also Insurance
No-fault motor vehicle insurance 368.572 8
  law 346.086 572 8
  see also Insurance
No-tillage 631.581 4
Noah (Biblical person)
  Bible stories 222.110 950 5
Nobatia (Kingdom) 962.502 2
  T2—625
Nobelium 546.449
  see also Chemicals

Nobility (Social class) 305.522 3
T1—086 21
customs 390.23
dress 391.023
Noble County (Ind.) T2—772 76
Noble County (Ohio) T2—771 95
Noble County (Okla.) T2—766 27
Noble gases
chemistry 546.75
economic geology 553.97
technology 665.822
Nobles County (Minn.) T2—776 24
Nobles of the Mystic Shrine 366.16
biography 366.160 92
social group T7—366 1
Nocardia 579.37
Noctuoidea 595.78
Nocturnal animals 591.518
Nocturnes 784.189 66
Nodaway County (Mo.) T2—778 124
Nodes (Plant stems) 575.454
Nofretete, Queen of Egypt
Egyptian history 932.014
Nogai language 494.34
T6—943 4
Nógrád Megye (Hungary) T2—439 8
Noh
literature 895.620 51
theater 792.095 2
Noise 363.74
communications engineering 621.382 24
electronic engineering 621.382 24
engineering 620.23
law 344.046 38
psychology 152.15
environmental psychology 155.911 5
public administration 354.338
social welfare 363.74
Noise control equipment
plant management 658.28
Nolan County (Tex.) T2—764 728
Nolanaceae 583.95
Noltingham Island
(N.W.T. : Island) T2—719 5
Nomads 305.906 91
T1—086 91
Nomenclature T1—014
Nominal groups (Grammar) 415
specific languages T4—5
Nominalism 149.1
Nominals (Nouns) 415
specific languages T4—5
Nominating conventions
(Political parties) 324.56
Nomination (Political parties) 324.5
Nomination hearings 352–354
legislative function 328.345 5
see Manual at 300, 320.6 vs.
352–354: Nomination
hearings
Nomography 511.5
Non-Austronesian languages of
Oceania 499.1
T6—991
Non-Euclidean geometry 516.9
Non-self-governing territories 321.08
T2—171 9
international law 341.28
public administration 353.15
specific territories 351.3–.9
Non-Trinitarian concepts
Christianity
God 231.044
Jesus 232.9
Nonaffiliated commercial
television 384.550 65
Nonalcoholic beverages 641.26
commercial processing 663.6
cooking with 641.62
home preparation 641.875
Nonaqueous solvents 541.348 2
Nonassociative algebras 512.24
Nonbeing 111.5
Nonbook materials
cataloging 025.34
library treatment 025.17
Noncombat services (Armed
forces) 355.34
Noncombatants
law of war 341.67
World War I 940.316 1
World War II 940.531 61
Noncommercial radio 384.54
Noncommercial television 384.554
Noncommissioned officers 355.009 2
role and function 355.338
Noncommissioned officers'
clubs 355.346
Noncommunicable diseases
(Biology) 571.9
Noncommunicable diseases
(Human)
incidence 614.59
medicine 616.98
see also Environmental
diseases (Human)

Nonconformists (British churches) 280.4
see also Protestantism
Noncrystalline solids 530.413
Nondairy coffee whiteners
commercial processing 663.64
Nondestructive testing
materials science 620.112 7
Nondifferentiable functions 515.8
Nondominant groups 305.56
T1—086 93
see also Minorities
Nondramatic vocal forms 782.2
choral and mixed voices 782.52
None (Divine office) 264.15
music 782.324
see also Liturgy of the hours
Nonelectronic data processing 004.9
Nonets
chamber music 785.19
vocal music 783.19
Nonexplosive ammunition
military engineering 623.459
Nonferrous metals 669
architectural construction 721.044 7
building construction 693.72–.77
building materials 691.8
economic geology 553.4
materials science 620.18
metallography 669.95
metallurgy 669
metalworking 673
mining 622.34
physical metallurgy 669.96
ship design 623.818 2
shipbuilding 623.820 7
structural engineering 624.182 2–.1829
see also Chemicals; Metals
Nongoma (South Africa : District) T2—684 91
Nongovernmental organizations (International agencies) 060
social welfare 361.77
Nongraded schools 371.255
Nonimpact printing 686.233
Nonlinear closed-loop systems
automation engineering 629.836
Nonlinear differential equations 515.355
Nonlinear equations 515.252
Nonlinear functional analysis 515.724 8
Nonlinear operators 515.724 8
Nonlinear optics 535.2
engineering 621.369 4
Nonlinear programming 519.76
Nonlinear systems 003.75
Nonlinguistic communication 302.222
T1—014
Nonliterate peoples
psychology 155.81
Nonliterate persons 305.906 33
T1—086 33
Nonliterate societies 301.7
government 321.1
Nonloom weaving
arts 746.42
Nonmechanized data processing 004.9
Nonmetals
biochemistry 572
chemistry 546.7
materials science 620.193
mineralogy 549.27
solid-state physics 530.413
see also Chemicals
Nonmotor land vehicles 388.341
manufacturing technology 688.6
transportation services 388.341
Nonobjectivity (Art style) 709.040 56
painting 759.065 6
sculpture 735.230 456
Nonoscine Passeriformes 598.822
Nonparametric statistical methods 519.5
Nonphonetic shorthand systems
English language 653.422
Nonprescription drugs 615.1
see also Drugs (Pharmaceuticals)
Nonprocedural languages 005.13
Nonprofit organizations 060
accounting 657.98
law 346.064
libraries 027.68
management 658.048
initiation 658.114 8
social welfare 361.763
Nonrigid airships 387.732 7
engineering 629.133 27
military engineering 623.743 7
transportation services 387.732 7
see also Aircraft
Nonrigid materials
architectural construction 721.044 98
building construction 693.98
Nonsporting dog 636.72
Nonstriated muscle tissues
human histology 611.018 6
see also Musculoskeletal system

Nontax revenues 336.1
  public administration 352.44
  public finance 336.1
Nontheistic religions 291.14
Nonverbal communication 302.222
  T1—014
  psychology 153.69
  social psychology 302.222
  see Manual at 153.69 vs. 152.384
Nonverbal intelligence tests 153.933 4
  individual 153.932 4
Nonviolence 303.61
  ethics 179.7
    religion 291.569 7
      Buddhism 294.356 97
      Christianity 241.697
      Hinduism 294.548 697
      Islam 297.569 7
      Judaism 296.369 7
  social conflict 303.61
Nonwestern art music 781.69
Nonwoven fabrics 677.6
  see also Textiles
Noodles 641.822
  commercial processing 664.755
  cooking 641.822
Noord-Brabant (Netherlands) T2—492 45
Noord-Holland (Netherlands) T2—492 35
Nootka Indians T5—979
Nootka language 497.9
  T6—979
Nord (France : Dept.) T2—442 8
Nord (Haiti : Dept.) T2—729 432
Nord-Est (Haiti : Dept.) T2—729 436
Nord-Kivu (Zaire) T2—675 17
Nord-Norge T2—484 3
Nord-Ouest (Haiti) T2—729 42
Nord-Pas-de-Calais (France) T2—442 7
Nord-Trøndelag fylke (Norway) T2—484 2
Norddeutscher Bund 943.081
  T2—43
Nordic combination (Skiing) 796.932
  see also Sports
Nordic people T5—3
Nordic skiing 796.932
  see also Sports
Nordjyllands amt (Denmark) T2—489 5
Nordland fylke (Norway) T2—484 4
Nordrhein-Westfalen (Germany) T2—435 5
Nore River (Ireland) T2—418 9
Norfolk (England) T2—426 1
Norfolk (Ont. : County) T2—713 36
Norfolk (Va.) T2—755 521
Norfolk Broads (England) T2—426 17
Norfolk County (Mass.) T2—744 7
Norfolk Island T2—948 2
Noricum T2—363
Norites 552.3
Norman architecture 723.4
Norman County (Minn.) T2—776 93
Normandie (France) T2—442
Normandy (France) T2—442
Normandy Invasion, 1944 940.542 142
Normans T5—395
Normative ethics 170.44
Normed linear spaces 515.732
Nornalup National Park (W.A.) T2—941 2
Norrbottens län (Sweden) T2—488
Norris Lake (Tenn.) T2—768 935
Norrland (Sweden) T2—488
Norse religion 293
Norseman (W.A.) T2—941 7
Norte de Santander (Colombia) T2—861 24
North Africa 961
  T2—61
  ancient 939.7
    T2—397
North Africans T5—93
North America 970
  T2—7
  see Manual at T2—7 vs. T2—1812; *also at* T2—73 vs. T2—71
North American catfishes 597.492
  see also Catfishes (Channel catfish)
North American native languages 497
  T6—97
North American native literatures 897
North American native peoples T5—97
North American red squirrels 599.363
North Americans T5—1
  see Manual at T5—1

North Atlantic Ocean 551.461 1
T2—163 1
see Manual at T2—1631 and T2—1635
North Atlantic Treaty Organization 355.031 091 821
law 341.72
North Battleford (Sask.) T2—712 42
North Bedfordshire (England) T2—425 61
North Borneo T2—595 3
North Brabant (Netherlands) T2—492 45
North Canadian River (Okla.) T2—766 1
North Carolina 975.6
T2—756
North Cascades National Park (Wash.) T2—797 73
North Caucasian languages 499.96
T6—999 6
North central Caucasian languages 499.964 1
T6—999 641
North Central State (Nigeria) T2—669 73
North Central States 977
T2—77
North Channel (Huron, Lake, Mich. and Ont.) T2—713 132
North Channel (Ireland and Scotland) 551.461 37
T2—163 37
North Coast (South Africa) T2—684 4
North Cornwall (England) T2—423 71
North Cotabato (Philippines) T2—599 7
North Dakota 978.4
T2—784
North Devon (England : District) T2—423 52
North Dorset (England) T2—423 32
North Down (Northern Ireland) T2—416 53
North Downs T2—422 3
North Dravidian languages 494.83
T6—948 3
North Dravidian literatures 894.83
North Dravidians T5—948 3
North East Derbyshire (England) T2—425 14
North East Fife (Scotland) T2—412 92
North East Frontier Agency, India T2—541 63
North East Polder T2—492 16
North-Eastern Province (Kenya) T2—676 22
North-Eastern Region (China) T2—518
North-Eastern State (Nigeria) T2—669 8
North Friesland (Germany) T2—435 12
North frigid zone T2—113
North Frisian Islands (Denmark and Germany) T2—435 12
North German Confederation 943.081
T2—43
North Germanic languages 439.5
T6—395
North Germanic literatures 839.5
North Hertfordshire (England) T2—425 81
North Holland (Netherlands) T2—492 35
North Island (N.Z.) T2—931
North Kesteven (England : District) T2—425 35
North Korea 951.93
T2—519 3
North Land (Russia) T2—987
North Norfolk (England : District) T2—426 12
North Okanagan (B.C.) T2—711 5
North Ossetia (Russia) T2—475 2
North Pacific Ocean 551.465 4
T2—164 4
see Manual at T2—1644 and T2—1648, T2—1649
North Platte River T2—787 16
North Polar Sea 551.468
T2—163 2
North Pole T2—163 2
North Queensland tick typhus
incidence 614.526 6
medicine 616.922 6
see also Communicable diseases (Human)
North Rhine-Westphalia (Germany) T2—435 5
North Riding of Yorkshire (England) T2—428 4
North Saanich (B.C.) T2—711 28
North Saskatchewan River (Alta. and Sask.) T2—712 33
North Sea 551.461 36
T2—163 36
North Shore City (N.Z.) T2—932 2

North Shropshire (England) T2—424 53
North Slope Borough (Alaska) T2—798 7
North Solomons Province (Papua New Guinea) 995.92
T2—959 2
North temperate zone T2—123
North Thompson River (B.C.) T2—711 72
North Tyneside (England) T2—428 79
North Vancouver (B.C.) T2—711 33
North Vietnam T2—597
North Wales T2—429 1
North Warwickshire (England : Borough) T2—424 81
North West district (Guyana : District) T2—881 1
North-West Frontier Province (Pakistan) T2—549 12
North West Leicestershire (England : District) T2—425 48
North-Western Province (Zambia) T2—689 4
North-Western Region (China) T2—514
North-Western State (Nigeria) T2—669 6
North Wiltshire (England : District) T2—423 12
North York (Ont.) T2—713 541
North Yorkshire (England) T2—428 4
North Yorkshire Moors (England) T2—428 46
Northam (W.A.) T2—941 2
Northampton (England) T2—425 57
Northampton County (N.C.) T2—756 49
Northampton County (Pa.) T2—748 22
Northampton County (Va.) T2—755 15
Northampton Uplands (England) T2—425 56
Northamptonshire (England) T2—425 5
Northavon (England : District) T2—423 91
Northbrook, Thomas George Baring, Earl of
Indian history 954.035 2
Northeast Caucasian languages 499.964
T6—999 64
Northeast Turkic languages 494.33
T6—943 3
Northeastern India T2—541
Northeastern States 974
T2—74
Northern Aegean (Greece) T2—495 82
Northern Australia T2—942 9
Northern Bantu languages 496.394
T6—963 94
Northern Baptists 286.131
see also Baptists
Northern Britain 941.1
T2—411
ancient 936.11
T2—361 1
Northern coastal region (Papua New Guinea) 995.7
T2—957
Northern Darfur (Sudan : Province) T2—627
Northern dynasties
Chinese history 951.015
Northern England T2—427
Northern Europe 948
T2—48
ancient 936.3
T2—363
Northern fur seal 599.797 3
Northern Hemisphere T2—181 3
Northern Ireland 941.6
T2—416
Northern Karoo (South Africa) T2—687 13
Northern Kordofan (Sudan) T2—628
Northern lights 538.768
Northern Mariana Islands T2—967
Northern Neck (Va.) T2—755 2
Northern Norway T2—484 3
Northern Ontario T2—713 1
Northern Province (Papua New Guinea) T2—954 2
Northern Province (Sudan) T2—625
Northern Province (Zambia) T2—689 4
Northern Region (China) T2—511
Northern Region of Nigeria (Nigeria) T2—669 5
Northern Rhodesia 968.940 2
T2—689 4
Northern Samar (Philippines) T2—599 5
Northern Sotho language 496.397 71
T6—963 977 1
Northern Sotho literature 896.397 71

Northern Sporades (Greece) T2—495 4
 ancient T2—391 1
Northern territories 971.9
 T2—719
Northern Territory T2—942 9
Northern Turkic languages 494.33
 T6—943 3
Northern Yemen T2—533 2
Northern Yemenis T5—927 533 2
Northland Region (N.Z.) T2—931 3
Northmen T5—395
Northumberland (England) T2—428 8
Northumberland (N.B.) T2—715 21
Northumberland (Ont.) T2—713 57
Northumberland County (Pa.) T2—748 31
Northumberland County (Va.) T2—755 21
Northumbria supremacy 942.015 3
Northumbrian pipes 788.49
 see also Woodwind instruments
Northwest, Old 977
 T2—77
Northwest, Pacific T2—795
Northwest Caucasian languages 499.962
 T6—999 62
Northwest Rebellion, 1885 971.054
Northwest Semitic languages 492
 T6—92
Northwest Semitic literatures 892
Northwest Territories T2—719 2
 see Manual at T2—7193–T2—7197
Northwest Turkic languages 494.38
 T6—943 8
Northwestern Bantu languages 496.396
 T6—963 96
Norton (Va.) T2—755 744
Norton County (Kan.) T2—781 155
Norton Sound (Alaska) 551.466 34
 T2—164 34
Norway 948.1
 T2—481
 ancient 936.3
 T2—363
Norway rat 599.352
 see also Rats (Rattus)
Norwegian elkhound 636.753
Norwegian language 439.82
 T6—398 2
Norwegian literature 839.82
Norwegian Sea 551.468 4
 T2—163 24
Norwegians T5—398 2
Norwich (England) T2—426 15
Nose 599.14
 animal physiology 573.26
 descriptive zoology 599.14
 fractures
  medicine 617.156
 human anatomy 611.21
 human physiology 612.2
  smelling 612.86
  speech 612.78
 medicine 616.212
 surgery 617.523
 see also Respiratory system
Nose flutes 788.3
 see also Woodwind instruments
Nostocales 579.39
Nostratic hypothesis 417.7
 T6—1
Notacanthiformes 597.43
Notaries 347.016
 occupational group T7—349
Notaspidea 594.34
Notched flutes 788.35
 see also Woodwind instruments
Note rows 781.268
Note-taking (Study technique) 371.302 81
Notebook computers 004.16
 see also Microcomputers
Notebooks
 literature 808.883
  specific literatures T3B—803
   individual authors T3A—8
Notes payable 657.74
 accounting 657.74
 financial management 658.152 6
Nothingness 111.5
Nothosauria 567.937
Notio Aigaio (Greece) T2—495 85
Notions 646.19
 commercial technology 687.8
 home sewing 646.19
Notodelphyoida 595.34
Notostraca 595.32
Notoungulata 569.62
Notre-Dame Mountains (Quebec) T2—714 7
Nottingham (England) T2—425 27
Nottinghamshire (England) T2—425 2
Nottoway County (Va.) T2—755 637

Noturus 597.492
Nouakchott (Mauritania) T2—661
Noun phrases 415
  specific languages T4—5
Nouns 415
  specific languages T4—5
Noupoort (South Africa : District) T2—687 13
Nouveau-Québec (Quebec) T2—714 11
Nouveau-Québec (Quebec : Administrative region) T2—714 115
Nouvelle-Beauce (Quebec) T2—714 71
Nova Scotia 971.6
  T2—716
Novaîa Zemlîa (Russia) T2—986
Novara (Italy : Province) T2—451 6
Novas 523.844 6
Novaya Zemlya (Russia) T2—986
Novelettes 808.83
  history and criticism 809.3
  specific literatures T3B—3
    individual authors T3A—3
Novelists 809.3
  collected biography 809.3
    specific literatures T3B—300 9
  individual biography T3A—3
  occupational group T7—83
Novellas 808.83
  history and criticism 809.3
  specific literatures T3B—3
    individual authors T3A—3
Novels 808.83
  history and criticism 809.3
  specific literatures T3B—3
    individual authors T3A—3
Novelties
  manufacturing technology 688.726
Novenas 264.7
Novgorod (Russia : Oblast) T2—472 2
Novices
  social group 305.909 09
  T7—090 9
Novitiate (Monastic life) 248.894 25
  women 248.894 35
Novo Estado (Portugal) 946.904 2
Novogrodskaîa oblast´ (Russia) T2—472 2
Novosibirsk (Russia : Oblast) T2—573
Novosibirskaîa oblast´ (Russia) T2—573
NOW accounts 332.175 2
Nowata County (Okla.) T2—766 97
Nowra (N.S.W.) T2—944 7
Nowy Sącz (Poland : Voivodeship) T2—438 6
Noxubee County (Miss.) T2—762 955
Nqamakwe (South Africa : District) T2—687 91
NQR (Physics) 538.362
Nqutu District of KwaZulu (South Africa) T2—684 91
Nsikazi (South Africa : District) T2—682 96
Ntcham language 496.35
  T6—963 5
Ntomba language 496.396 8
  T6—963 968
Ntuzuma (South Africa : District) T2—684 91
Nubia T2—397 8
Nubian languages 496.5
  T6—965
Nubians T5—965
Ñuble (Chile) T2—833 8
Nuckolls County (Neb.) T2—782 372
Nuclear accidents 363.179 9
  public safety 363.179 9
  technology 621.483 5
  see also Hazardous materials
Nuclear activation analysis 543.088 2
  qualitative 544.982
  quantitative 545.822
Nuclear activities 539.75
  see Manual at 530.416 vs. 539.75
Nuclear chemistry 541.38
  applied 660.298
Nuclear disarmament 327.174 7
  international law 341.734
Nuclear energy 333.792 4
  economics 333.792 4
  international law 341.755
  law 343.092 5
  physics 539.7
  public administration 354.47
Nuclear energy industry 333.792 4
Nuclear energy insurance 368.7
  see also Insurance
Nuclear engineering 621.48
  military applications 623.044
Nuclear engineers 621.480 92
  occupational group T7—621 48
Nuclear envelope 571.66
Nuclear family 306.855
Nuclear fission 539.762
Nuclear forces 355.021 7

Nuclear fuels
  engineering 621.483 35
  public administration 354.47
Nuclear fusion 539.764
Nuclear hazards insurance 368.7
  see also Insurance
Nuclear heating
  buildings 697.79
Nuclear interactions 539.75
  see Manual at 530.416 vs. 539.75
Nuclear liability insurance 368.7
  see also Insurance
Nuclear magnetic resonance 538.362
  imaging
    medicine 616.075 48
  spectroscopy 543.087 7
Nuclear medicine 616.075 75
Nuclear membrane 571.66
Nuclear missile forces 358.17
Nuclear missiles 358.171 82
  engineering 623.451 9
  military equipment 358.171 82
Nuclear models 539.74
Nuclear nonproliferation 327.174 7
  international law 341.734
Nuclear physicists 539.709 2
  occupational group T7—539
Nuclear physics 539.7
  astronomy 523.019 7
Nuclear power plants 621.483
  law 343.092 5
Nuclear power systems
  auxiliary systems
    spacecraft 629.474 43
  propulsion 621.485
    see also Nuclear propulsion
Nuclear-powered automobiles
  engineering 629.229 6
Nuclear-powered submarines 359.938 34
  design 623.812 574
  engineering 623.825 74
  naval equipment 359.938 34
Nuclear propulsion 621.485
  aircraft 629.134 355
  automotive 629.250 9
  ships 623.872 8
  spacecraft 629.475 3
Nuclear quadrupole resonance 538.362
Nuclear reactions 539.76
Nuclear reactors 621.483
Nuclear safety 363.179 9
  public administration 353.999
  public safety 363.179 9
Nuclear safety (continued)
  technology 621.483 5
  see also Hazardous materials
Nuclear spectroscopy 543.087 7
Nuclear structure 539.74
Nuclear warfare 355.021 7
  civil defense 363.35
    see also Civil defense
  ethics 172.422
    religion 291.562 422
      Christianity 241.624 22
    see also War—ethics
  operations 355.43
  social theology 291.178 732
    Christianity 261.873 2
    Judaism 296.382 7
  see also Disasters
Nuclear weapons 355.825 119
  control 327.174 7
    international law 341.734
  engineering 623.451 19
  military equipment 355.825 119
  see also Nuclear warfare
Nuclear winter 577.274
Nuclei as particles 539.723 2
Nucleic acids 572.8
  biochemical genetics 572.8
  chemistry 547.79
  humans 611.018 16
Nucleolus 571.66
Nucleons 539.721 2
Nucleoplasm 571.66
Nucleoproteins 572.84
  chemistry 547.754
  see also Proteins
Nucleosides 572.85
Nucleosomes 572.87
Nucleotide sequences 572.863 3
Nucleotides 572.85
  humans 611.018 16
Nucleus (Cells) 571.66
Nuclide structure 539.74
Nuda 593.8
Nudes
  art representation 704.942 1
  drawing 743.4
  painting 757.22
Nudibranchia 594.36
Nudism
  health 613.194
Nudity
  arts 700.453
    T3C—353
Nueces County (Tex.) T2—764 113

Nueces River (Tex.) T2—764 11
Nuer (African people) T5—965
Nuer language 496.5
T6—965
Nueva Asunción
(Paraguay : Dept.) T2—892 25
Nueva Ecija (Philippines :
Province) T2—599 1
Nueva Esparta (Venezuela) T2—875 4
Nueva Segovia
(Nicaragua) T2—728 521
Nueva Vizcaya
(Philippines) T2—599 1
Nuisance (Law) 346.036
Nukuoro language 499.46
T6—994 6
Nullification movement
United States history 973.561
Numayrī, Ja'far Muḥammad
Sudanese history 962.404
Numbat 599.27
Number
philosophy 119
Number systems 513.5
Number theoretic functions 512.73
Number theory 512.7
Numbers 513.2
fortune-telling 133.335 4
Numbers (Biblical book) 222.14
Numeracy 513
elementary education 372.72
Numeration systems 513.5
Numerical algebra 512
Numerical analysis 515
applied mathematics 519.4
Numerical calculations
applied mathematics 519.4
Numerical control
machine tools 621.902 3
Numerical differentiation 515.623
Numerical integration 515.624
Numerical interpretation
Bible 220.68
Numerical taxonomy 578.012
Numerology 133.335
Numidia 939.72
T2—397 2
Numididae 598.64
Numismatics 737
Numismatists 737.092
occupational group T7—737
Nunavut T2—719 2
Nuneaton and Bedworth
(England : Borough) T2—424 83
Nunggubuyu language 499.15
T6—991 5
Nuns 291.657
Buddhist 294.365 7
Christian 255.9
biography 271.900 2
see Manual at 230–280
ecclesiology 262.24
guides to Christian life 248.894 3
Nuoro (Sardinia :
Province) T2—459 2
Nuove musiche 780.903 2
Nupe (African people) T5—963 3
Nupe language 496.33
T6—963 3
Nupoid languages 496.33
T6—963 3
Nuremberg (Germany) T2—433 24
Nuremberg war crimes trials 341.690 268
Nuri (Afghanistan people) T5—914 9
Nuristani languages 491.49
T6—914 9
Nuristani literatures 891.49
Nürnberg (Germany) T2—433 24
Nurse and patient 610.730 699
Nurse and physician 610.730 699
Nurse practitioners 610.730 92
role and function 610.730 692
see also Nurses
Nurseries (For children) 643.53
home economics 643.53
interior decoration 747.77
Nurseries (For plants) 631.52
floriculture 635.915 2
forestry 634.956 4
Nursery catalogs 631.520 294
Nursery practice 631.52
floriculture 635.915 2
forestry 634.956 4
Nursery rhymes 398.8
Nursery schools 372.216
see also Elementary education
Nurses 610.730 92
health services 362.173
see also Health services
law 344.041 4
malpractice 344.041 4
occupational group T7—613
role and function 610.730 69
Nurses' aides 610.730 92
role and function 610.730 698
see also Nurses

Nursing
  medicine 610.73
    see also Nurses
    see Manual at 610.73
Nursing (Breast feeding) 649.33
  child rearing 649.33
  health 613.269
  human physiology 612.664
Nursing homes 362.16
  mental illness 362.23
  physical illness 362.16
  see also Health care facilities; Health services; Mental health services
Nursing orders (Christianity) 255.07
  church history 271.07
  women 255.907
    church history 271.907
Nusa Tenggara (Indonesia) T2—598 6
Nutation
  celestial mechanics 521.9
Nuthatches 598.82
Nutmeg 641.338 3
  botany 583.22
  see also Spices
Nutria 599.359
Nutrition 363.8
  animal husbandry 636.085 2
  biology 572.4
    requirements 572.39
  elementary education 372.37
  health 613.2
  human physiology 612.3
  plants
    nutrient absorption 575.76
  social welfare 363.8
    law 344.033
    see Manual at 363.82 vs. 614.5939
  see also Digestive system
  see Manual at 363.8 vs. 613.2, 641.3
Nutritional diseases
  medicine 616.39
  see also Digestive system
  see Manual at 363.82 vs. 614.5939
Nutritional requirements 572.39
Nutritional services
  health services 362.176
    see also Health services
  public administration 353.56
  schools 371.716
Nutritionists 613.209 2
  occupational group T7—641
Nutritive organs 573.3
  human anatomy 611.3
  human physiology 612.3
  see also Digestive system
Nuts 581.464
  commercial processing 664.804 5
  cooking 641.645
  descriptive botany 581.464
  food 641.345
  forest products 634.987
  orchard crop 634.5
  physiology 575.67
Nuts (Fasteners) 621.882
Nyakyusa-Konde language 496.391
  T6—963 91
Nyalas 599.642 3
Nyamwezi (African people) T5—963 94
Nyamwezi language 496.394
  T6—963 94
Nyanja (African people) T5—963 918
Nyanja language 496.391 8
  T6—963 918
Nyanja literature 896.391 8
Nyankore language 496.395 6
  T6—963 956
Nyanza Province (Kenya) T2—676 29
Nyasa, Lake T2—689 7
Nyasaland 968.970 2
  T2—689 7
Nyaya (Philosophy) 181.43
Nyctaginaceae 583.53
Nyctibiidae 598.99
Nye County (Nev.) T2—793 34
Nyerere, Julius K. (Julius Kambarage)
  Tanzanian history 967.804 1
Nyika (Nika) language 496.395
  T6—963 95
Nyika-Safwa languages 496.391
  T6—963 91
Nyika-Taita languages 496.395
  T6—963 95
Nylons (Plastics) 668.423 5
  textiles 677.473
    see also Textiles
Nymphaeales 583.29
Nymphomania
  medicine 616.858 33
  see also Mental illness
Nyngan (N.S.W.) T2—944 9

Nynorsk language 439.83
T6—398 3
Nynorsk literature 839.83
Nyoro-Ganda languages 496.395 6
T6—963 956
Nytrils
textiles 677.474 4
see also Textiles
Nyunga (Australian people) T5—991 5
Nyungar dialects 499.15
T6—991 5
Nzima (African people) T5—963 385
Nzima language 496.338 5
T6—963 385

O

Oadby and Wigston (England) T2—425 43
Oahe, Lake (S.D. and N.D.) T2—783 5
Oahu (Hawaii) T2—969 3
Oak Bay (B.C.) T2—711 28
Oakey (Qld.) T2—943 3
Oakland (Calif.) T2—794 66
Oakland County (Mich.) T2—774 38
Oaks 583.46
forestry 634.972 1
lumber 674.142
Oarfishes 597.64
OAS (Alliance) 341.245
Oatlands (Tas.) T2—946 3
Oats 641.331 3
botany 584.9
commercial processing technology 664.72
cooking 641.631 3
food 641.331 3
food crop 633.13
forage crop 633.253
Oaxaca (Mexico) T2—727 4
Ob-Ugric languages 494.51
T6—945 1
Obadiah (Biblical book) 224.91
OBE (Parapsychology) 133.95
Obedience
home child care 649.64
Obedience (Christian doctrine) 234.6
Obedience training (Pets) 636.088 7
Oberbayern (Germany) T2—433 6
Oberfranken (Germany) T2—433 1
Oberholzer (South Africa : District) T2—682 2
Oberösterreich (Austria) T2—436 2
Oberpfalz (Germany) T2—433 4
Obesity
low-calorie cooking 641.563 5
medicine 616.398
reducing diet 613.25
see also Digestive system
Obiang Nguema Mbasogo, Teodoro
Equatorial Guinean history 967.180 32
Obion County (Tenn.) T2—768 13
Obituaries 920
Obituary sermons
Christianity 252.9
Object-oriented databases
computer science 005.757
Object-oriented programming 005.117
Objective knowledge 121.4
Objectivism 149
Objectivity
epistemology 121.4
Oblates 255.76
church history 271.76
women 255.97
church history 271.97
Obligations of citizens 323.65
Oblong books 099
Oboe concertos 784.285 2
Oboes 788.52
instrument 788.521 9
music 788.52
see also Woodwind instruments
Obote, A. Milton (Apollo Milton)
Ugandan history 967.610 41
1962–1971 967.610 41
1980–1985 967.610 43
Obregón, Alvaro
Mexican history 972.082 2
O'Brien County (Iowa) T2—777 14
Obscenity
criminology 364.174
criminal law 345.027 4
ethics 176.7
religion 291.566 7
Christianity 241.667
law 344.054 7
postal handling 383.120 5
social problem 363.47

Observatories
  architecture 727.5
  astronomy 522.1
Obsessive-compulsive neurosis
  medicine 616.852 27
  see also Mental illness
Obsidian 552.22
  glyptics 736.28
Obstacle courses (Military training) 355.544
Obstetrical disorders 618.2
  incidence 614.599 22
Obstetrical nursing
  medicine 610.736 78
Obstetrical surgery 618.8
Obstetricians 618.200 92
  law 344.041 2
  malpractice 344.041 21
  occupational group T7—618 1
  role and function 618.202 32
Obstetrics 618.2
  anesthesiology 617.968 2
  veterinary medicine 636.089 82
Obstructions
  intestine
    medicine 616.342
    surgery 617.554
    see also Digestive system
Obstructive pulmonary disease
  medicine 616.24
  see also Respiratory system
Obwalden (Switzerland) T2—494 764
Ocarinas 788.38
  see also Woodwind instruments
Occasionalism 147
Occident 909.098 21
  T2—182 1
Occidental flower arrangements 745.922 4
Occidental Mindoro (Philippines) T2—599 3
Occidental region (Paraguay) T2—892 2
Occitan language 449
  T6—491
Occlusion disorders
  dentistry 617.643
  incidence 614.599 6
  see also Dentistry
Occult sciences 133
  see Manual at 133 vs. 130; *also at* 133 vs. 200
Occultations 523.99
Occultism 133
  literature 808.803 7
    history and criticism 809.933 7
    specific literatures T3B—080 37
      history and criticism T3B—093 7
  religious practice 291.3
  see Manual at 133 vs. 130; *also at* 133 vs. 200
Occultism and religion 291.175
  Christianity 261.513
Occultists 133.092
  social group T7—13
Occupational aptitude tests 153.94
Occupational diseases
  health 613.62
  law 344.043 698 03
  medicine 616.980 3
  workers' compensation law 344.021 8
  see also Environmental diseases (Human)
Occupational ethics 174
  see also Ethical problems
Occupational groups 305.9
  T1—088
  customs 390.4
    dress 391.04
  journalism for 070.486
  see Manual at T1—088 vs. T1—024; *also at* 305.9 vs. 305.5
Occupational guidance 331.702
  see also Vocational guidance
Occupational health 613.62
  see Manual at 363.11 vs. 613.62
Occupational health nursing
  medicine 610.734 6
Occupational licensing 354.928 4
  law 344.017
  public administration 354.928 4
Occupational medicine 616.980 3
Occupational mobility 305.9
  economics 331.127 2
Occupational requirements
  personnel selection 658.311 2
Occupational safety 363.11
  see also Industrial safety
Occupational specialties 331.702
  T1—023
  see also Vocational guidance
Occupational stress 158.72
Occupational therapy
  medicine 615.851 5

Occupational training 370.113
T1—071 5
see also Vocational education
Occupations 331.7
T1—023
active employment 331.125
collective bargaining 331.890 4
compensation 331.28
demand 331.123
economics 331.7
employment conditions 331.204
industrial relations 331.04
labor force 331.119
labor market 331.129
labor unions 331.881
opportunities 331.124
pensions 331.252 9
public administration 354.9
social groups 305.9
sociology of production 306.36
strikes 331.892 8
unemployment 331.137 8
Occupied countries 355.49
aftermath of war 355.028
World War I 940.33
World War II 940.533 6
see Manual at 930–990: Wars: Occupied countries
Occupied territory 355.49
Ocean-atmosphere interactions 551.524 6
Ocean basins T2—182
see Manual at T2—163, T2—164, T2—165 vs. T2—182
Ocean bottom 551.460 84
composition 551.460 83
international law 341.762 1
topography 551.460 84
Ocean bottom vehicles
engineering 629.292
Ocean County (N.J.) T2—749 48
Ocean currents 551.470 1
Ocean dumping 363.728
law 344.046 26
see also Waste control
Ocean engineering 620.416 2
Ocean Falls (B.C.) T2—711 1
Ocean floor 551.460 84
see also Ocean bottom
Ocean floor mining 622.295
Ocean floor vehicles
engineering 629.292
Ocean liners 387.243 2
design 623.812 432
engineering 623.824 32
see also Ships
Ocean marine insurance 368.22
see also Insurance
Ocean sunfishes 597.64
Ocean temperatures 551.460 1
meteorological effect 551.524 6
Ocean thermal power conversion 333.914
Ocean transportation 387.5
international law 341.756 62
law 343.096 2
public administration 354.78
transportation services 387.5
Ocean travel 910.45
Oceana County (Mich.) T2—774 59
Oceania 995
T2—95
Oceanic languages 499.4
T6—994
Oceanographers 551.460 092
occupational group T7—55
Oceanography 551.46
see also Oceans
Oceans 551.46
T2—162
biology 578.77
ecology 577.7
geologic agent 551.36
influence on precipitation 551.577 5
interactions with atmosphere 551.524 6
international law 341.45
physical geology 551.46
public administration 354.369
resource economics 333.916 4
see Manual at T2—162
Ocelot 599.752
animal husbandry 636.89
Ochil Hills (Scotland) T2—412 8
Ochiltree County (Tex.) T2—764 815
Ochnaceae 583.624
Ochotona 599.329
Ochotonidae 599.329
Oconee County (Ga.) T2—758 193
Oconee County (S.C.) T2—757 21
Oconee River (Ga.) T2—758 6
Oconto County (Wis.) T2—775 37
Ocotepeque (Honduras : Dept.) T2—728 383
Ocotillo 583.628
OCR (Computer science) 006.424
Octal system (Numeration) 513.54

Octets
  chamber music 785.18
  vocal music 783.18
Octopoda 594.56
  paleozoology 564.56
Octopuses 594.56
  cooking 641.694
  food 641.394
    commercial processing 664.94
Ocular neuromuscular
    mechanism
  human physiology 612.846
  ophthalmology 617.762
  see also Eyes
Odd Fellows 366.3
  biography 366.309 2
  social group T7—366 3
Odd-toed ungulates 599.66
Odendaalsrus (South
    Africa : District) T2—685 3
Odes 808.814 3
  history and criticism 809.143
  specific literatures T3B—104 3
    individual authors T3A—1
Odes of Solomon 229.912
Odes′ka oblast′ (Ukraine) T2—477 2
Odessa (Ukraine : Oblast) T2—477 2
Odi (South Africa : District) T2—682 94
Odobenidae 599.799
Odocoileus 599.652
Odocoileus hemionus 599.653
Odonata 595.733
Odontoceti 599.5
  paleozoology 569.5
Odontopteris 561.597
Oea (Libya) T2—397 4
Oestridae 595.774
Off-road biking 796.63
  see also Sports
Off-road vehicles 388.34
  driving 629.283 042
  engineering 629.220 42
  military engineering 623.747
  repair 629.287 042
  transportation services 388.34
  see also Automotive vehicles
Off-shore mining 622.295
Offaly (Ireland) T2—418 6
Offenbach am Main
    (Germany) T2—434 163
Offenders 364.3
  T1—086 927
  criminology 364.3
  law 345.03
Offenders (continued)
  pastoral care of 259.5
  punishment 364.6
  welfare services 364.6
Offenses against military
    discipline 355.133 4
Offenses against property 364.16
  law 345.026
Offenses against public morals 364.17
  law 345.027
Offenses against public safety 364.142
  law 345.024 2
Offenses against religion 364.188
  law 345.028 8
Offenses against the person 364.15
  law 345.025
Offensive arms
  art metalwork 739.7
  customs 399
Offerings (Religion) 291.34
  Christianity 248.6
  Judaism 296.492
Offertory 264.36
  music 782.323 5
Office buildings
  architecture 725.23
  construction 690.523
  institutional housekeeping 647.962 3
Office employees 651.309 2
  see also Office workers
Office equipment
  armed forces 355.81
  manufacturing technology 681.6
  office services 651.2
  procurement 658.72
Office etiquette 395.52
Office furniture
  manufacturing technology 684
  office services 651.23
  procurement 658.72
Office hours (Religion) 264.15
  Anglican 264.030 15
  music 782.324
  Roman Catholic 264.020 15
    texts 264.024
Office layout
  plant management 658.23
Office management 651.3
Office of chief executive
  management 658.42
  public administration 352.237
Office security
  office services 651
  public administration 352.379

Office services 651
Office supplies
  armed forces 355.81
  office services 651.29
  procurement 658.72
Office workers 651.309 2
  labor economics 331.761 651 3
  occupational group T7—651
  personnel management 651.306 83
    public administration 352.63
  social class 305.556
Officers (Armed forces) 355.009 2
  role and function 355.332
Officers' clubs 355.346
Officers of corporations
  executive management 658.4
  law 346.066 42
Officers' training (Armed forces) 355.55
Official ceremonies and observances 394.4
  armed forces 355.17
  customs 394.4
Official gazettes 351.05
  see also Serials
Official residences
  architecture 725.17
Official secrets 342.068 4
Official strikes 331.892 2
  see also Strikes (Work stoppages)
Offline processing 004.3
  see also Processing modes—computer science
Offset printing 686.231 5
Offshore petroleum drilling 622.338 19
Offshore structures 627.98
Offspring 306.874
  T1—085 4
  T7—044 1
Ogasawara-guntō (Japan) T2—528
Ogeechee River (Ga.) T2—758 6
Ogemaw County (Mich.) T2—774 75
Oglala Indians T5—975 2
Ogle County (Ill.) T2—773 32
Oglethorpe County (Ga.) T2—758 175
Ogres 398.21
  see also Legendary beings
Ogun State (Nigeria) T2—669 23
Ogwr (Wales : Borough) T2—429 71
Ohau, Lake (N.Z.) T2—938 97
O'Higgins (Chile) T2—833 2
Ohio 977.1
  T2—771
Ohio County (Ind.) T2—772 123
Ohio County (Ky.) T2—769 835
Ohio County (W. Va.) T2—754 14
Ohio River T2—77
  Kentucky T2—769
  West Virginia T2—754 1
Ohio River Valley T2—77
Ohmmeters 621.374 2
Oholot 296.123 6
Oil (Petroleum) 553.282
  economic geology 553.282
  extraction 622.338 2
  extractive economics 338.272 82
    law 343.077 2
  pipeline technology 665.544
  processing 665.5
    economics 338.476 655
    enterprises 338.766 55
  prospecting 622.182 82
  public administration 354.45
  public utilities 363.6
    law 343.092 6
    see also Public utilities
  resource economics 333.823 2
    law 346.046 823 2
  see also Petroleum
Oil beetles 595.769
Oil depletion allowance 336.243 16
  tax law 343.052 34
Oil gas 665.773
Oil heating
  buildings 697.044
Oil lamps 621.323
  see also Lighting
Oil painting 751.45
Oil palms 633.851
  agriculture 633.851
  botany 584.5
Oil pollution 363.738 2
  law 344.046 332
  water supply engineering 628.168 33
  see also Pollution
Oil processes
  photographic printing 773.8
Oil-producing plants
  agriculture 633.85
Oil sands 553.283
  processing 665.4
  see also Tar sands
Oil shale 553.283
  economic geology 553.283
  mining 622.338 3
    law 343.077 2
  processing 665.4
Oil-soluble paint 667.62

Oil spills 363.738 2
law 344.046 332
water pollution engineering 628.168 33
Oil well flooding 622.338 2
Oil wells 622.338 2
Oilbird 598.99
Oiling
woodwork
buildings 698.33
Oils
hydraulic-power technology 621.204 24
industrial 665
materials science 620.198
Oils (Food)
applied nutrition 613.284
food technology 664.3
metabolism
human physiology 612.397
Oils (Paints) 667.622
Oilseed plants
agriculture 633.85
Ointments
practical pharmacy 615.45
Oirat-Kalmyk language 494.2
T6—942
Oise (France) T2—443 5
Ōita-ken (Japan) T2—522 8
Ojibwa Indians T5—973
Ojibwa language 497.3
T6—973
Ojibwa literature 897.3
Okaloosa County (Fla.) T2—759 982
Okanagan Lake (B.C.) T2—711 5
Okanagan-Similkameen (B.C.) T2—711 5
Okanogan County (Wash.) T2—797 28
Okapi 599.638
Okayama-ken (Japan) T2—521 94
Okeechobee, Lake (Fla.) T2—759 39
Okeechobee County (Fla.) T2—759 53
Okefenokee Swamp (Ga. and Fla.) T2—758 752
Okfuskee County (Okla.) T2—766 73
Okhahlamba (South Africa : District) T2—684 91
Okhotsk, Sea of 551.465 53
T2—164 53
Okinawa Island (Japan) T2—522 94
Okinawa-ken (Japan) T2—522 9
Oklahoma 976.6
T2—766
Oklahoma City (Okla.) T2—766 38
Oklahoma County (Okla.) T2—766 38
Oklahoma Panhandle (Okla.) T2—766 13
Oklahoma Territory T2—766 1
Okmulgee County (Okla.) T2—766 83
Oko languages 496.33
T6—963 3
Okpe language 496.33
T6—963 3
Okra 641.356 48
botany 583.685
commercial processing 664.805 648
cooking 641.656 48
food 641.356 48
garden crop 635.648
Oktibbeha County (Miss.) T2—762 953
Oktoberfest 394.264 4
Olacaceae 583.88
Olancho (Honduras) T2—728 33
Öland (Sweden) T2—486
Old-age and survivors' insurance 368.3
government-sponsored 368.43
law 344.023
see also Insurance
Old age pensions 331.252
see also Pensions
Old Bulgarian language 491.817 01
T6—918 17
Old Bulgarian literature 891.81
Old Castile (Spain) T2—463 5
Old Catholic churches 284.8
church government 262.048
parishes 254.048
church law 262.984 8
doctrines 230.48
catechisms and creeds 238.48
guides to Christian life 248.484 8
missions 266.48
moral theology 241.044 8
public worship 264.048
religious education 268.848
theology 230.48
Old Catholics
biography 284.8
religious group T7—248
Old Church Slavic language 491.817 01
T6—918 17
Old English language 429
T6—29
Old English literature 829
Old French language 447.01
T6—41
Old Frisian language 439.2
T6—392
Old Frisian literature 839.2

Old-growth forests 333.75
see also Forest lands
Old High German language 437.01
T6—31
Old Icelandic language 439.6
T6—396 1
Old Icelandic literature 839.6
Old Indic language 491.29
T6—912 9
Old Indic literature 891.29
Old Italian language 457.01
T6—51
Old Kingdom (Egypt) 932.012
Old Latin language 477
T6—71
Old Low Franconian language 439.31
T6—393 1
Old Low Franconian literature 839.31
Old Low German language 439.4
T6—394
Old Low German literature 839.4
Old Low Germanic languages 439
T6—39
Old Low Germanic literatures 839
Old Norse language 439.6
T6—396 1
Old Norse literature 839.6
Old Northwest 977
T2—77
Old Persian language 491.51
T6—915 1
Old Persian literature 891.51
Old persons 305.26
T1—084 6
see also Older persons
Old Portuguese language 469.701
T6—69
Old Prussian language 491.91
T6—919 1
Old Prussian literature 891.91
Old Russian language 491.770 1
T6—917 1
Old Saxon language 439.4
T6—394
Old Saxon literature 839.4
Old School Baptists 286.4
see also Baptists
Old Southwest 976
T2—76
Old Spanish language 467.01
T6—61
Old Stone Age 930.12
Old Testament 221
see Manual at 221
Old Testament Apocrypha 229
Old Testament pseudepigrapha 229.91
Old Testament theology
  Christianity 230.041 1
Old Turkic language 494.31
T6—943 1
Old World badger 599.767 2
Old World flycatchers 598.848
Old World fruit bats 599.49
Old World monkeys 599.86
Old World pitcher plants 583.75
Old World polecats 599.766 2
Old World porcupines 599.359 7
Old World rabbit 599.322
Old World vultures 598.94
Old World warblers 598.843
Oldenburg (Germany) T2—435 914
Older persons 305.26
T1—084 6
T7—056 5
  accident insurance
    government-sponsored 368.426
    see also Insurance
  architecture for 720.846
  civil rights 323.354
  cooking for 641.562 7
  customs 390.084 6
  etiquette 395.126
  geriatrics 618.97
  government programs 353.537
  health 613.043 8
  health insurance
    government-sponsored 368.426
    see also Insurance
  home care 649.8
  institutional buildings
    architecture 725.56
  institutional care 362.61
  legal status 346.013
    constitutional law 342.087
    private law 346.013
  libraries for 027.622
  personal living 646.79
  physical fitness 613.704 46
  physiology 612.67
  psychology 155.67
  recreation 790.192 6
    indoor 793.019 26
    outdoor 796.084 6
  relations with government 323.354
  religion 200.846
    Christianity 270.084 6
      devotional literature 242.65
      guides to life 248.85

Older persons
  religion
    Christianity (continued)
      pastoral care of 259.3
      social theology 261.834 26
    guides to life 291.440 846
    social theology 291.178 342 6
  social aspects 305.26
  social welfare 362.6
    law 344.032 6
    public administration 353.537
Older workers 331.398
  see also Older persons
Oldham (England) T2—427 393
Oldham County (Ky.) T2—769 383
Oldham County (Tex.) T2—764 824
Oleales 583.87
Oleanders 635.933 93
  botany 583.93
  floriculture 635.933 93
Oleasters 635.933 82
  botany 583.82
  floriculture 635.933 82
Olefins 547.412
  chemical engineering 661.814
  textiles 677.474 5
    see also Textiles
Oleomargarine
  food technology 664.32
Olfaction 573.877
  human physiology 612.86
Olfactory nerves 573.877
Olfactory organs 573.877
  human anatomy 611.86
  human physiology 612.86
  see also Nervous system
Olfactory perception
  psychology 152.166
Oligarchy 321.5
Oligocene epoch 551.785
  geology 551.785
  paleontology 560.178 5
Oligochaeta 592.64
Oligomenorrhea
  gynecology 618.172
  see also Female genital system
Oligopoly 338.82
  economics 338.82
  international economics 338.884
Oligosaccharides 572.565
  biochemistry 572.565
  chemistry 547.781 5
  see also Carbohydrates
Olive oil 641.346 3
  cooking with 641.646 3
  food 641.346 3
  food technology 664.362
Oliver County (N.D.) T2—784 843
Olives 641.346 3
  agriculture 634.63
  botany 583.87
  commercial processing 664.804 63
  cooking 641.646 3
  food 641.346 3
Olivetans 255.13
  church history 271.13
  women 255.97
    church history 271.97
Olmsted County (Minn.) T2—776 155
Olsztyn (Poland :
    Voivodeship) T2—438 3
Olt (Romania) T2—498 2
Oltenia (Romania) T2—498 4
Olympia (Greece : Ancient
    sanctuary) T2—388
Olympia (Wash.) T2—797 79
Olympic Games 796.48
  summer 796.48
  winter 796.98
  see also Sports
Olympic Mountains
    (Wash.) T2—797 94
Olympic National Park
    (Wash.) T2—797 98
Olympic Peninsula (Wash.) T2—797 94
Olyreae 584.9
Omagh (Northern Ireland :
    District) T2—416 47
Omaha (Neb.) T2—782 254
Oman 953.53
  T2—535 3
Oman, Gulf of 551.467 36
  T2—165 36
Omanis T5—927 535 3
Ombudsmen 352.88
  law 342.066 7
  legislative branch 328.345 2
  military administration 355.685
  public administration 352.88
    agency ombudsmen 352.35
Omens 133.334
  religion 291.32
Omentum
  human anatomy 611.38
  human physiology 612.33
  surgery 617.558
  see also Digestive system

Omineca Mountains (B.C.) T2—711 85
Omineca River (B.C.) T2—711 82
Omissions insurance 368.564
  see also Insurance
Omnipotence of God 212.7
  see also Attributes of God
Omniscience of God 212.7
  see also Attributes of God
Omotic languages 493.59
  T6—935 9
Omotic peoples T5—935
Omsk (Russia : Oblast) T2—573
Omskaîa oblast´ (Russia) T2—573
On-the-job training 331.259 2
  T1—071 55
  see also Vocational education
Onagraceae 583.76
Onchocerciasis
  incidence 614.555 2
  medicine 616.965 2
  see also Communicable diseases (Human)
Oncogenic viruses 579.256 9
Oncology 616.992
  cancer 616.994
    see also Cancer (Human)
Oncopods 592.7
  paleozoology 562.7
Oncorhynchus 597.56
Oncoviruses 579.256 9
Ondatra 599.357 9
Ondes martenot 786.73
  see also Electrophones
Ondo State (Nigeria) T2—669 28
One-act plays
  literature 808.824 1
    history and criticism 809.241
    specific literatures T3B—204 1
      individual authors T3A—2
One-dish cooking 641.82
One old cat 796.357 8
One-person cooking 641.561
One-room schools 372.125
Onega Lake (Russia) T2—471 5
Oneida County (Idaho) T2—796 41
Oneida County (N.Y.) T2—747 62
Oneida County (Wis.) T2—775 25
Oneida Lake (N.Y.) T2—747 62
Ongoye (South Africa : District) T2—684 91
Onions 641.352 5
  botany 584.33
  commercial processing 664.805 25
  cooking 641.652 5
Onions (continued)
  food 641.352 5
  garden crop 635.25
Onionskin paper 676.282 3
Online catalogs 025.313 2
Online help facilities 005.3
  development 005.15
Online information systems 025.04
  see also Information storage and retrieval systems
Online processing 004
Only children 306.874
  T1—085 4
  T7—044 1
  family relationships 306.874
  home care 649.142
  psychology 155.442
Onomastics 929.97
  etymology 412
    specific languages T4—2
  geographic names 910.014
    gazetters 910.3
  personal names 929.4
Onondaga County (N.Y.) T2—747 65
Onslow County (N.C.) T2—756 23
Ontario 971.3
  T2—713
Ontario (Ont. : County) T2—713 56
Ontario, Lake (N.Y. and Ont.) T2—747 9
  New York T2—747 9
  Ontario T2—713 5
Ontario, Northern T2—713 1
Ontario County (N.Y.) T2—747 86
Ontology 111
Ontonagon County (Mich.) T2—774 985
Onychophora 592.74
Onygenales 579.565
Onyx 553.87
  see also Semiprecious stones
Onyx marble 553.55
  economic geology 553.55
  quarrying 622.355
Oolites 552.58
Oomycetes 579.54
Op art 709.040 72
  painting 759.067 2
  sculpture 735.230 472
Op-ed pages 070.442
Opah 597.64
Opals 553.873
  mineralogy 549.68
  see also Semiprecious stones
Open classroom grouping 371.256

Open classroom instruction 371.394 1
Open clusters (Stars) 523.852
Open economies 330.122
Open-field system
  land economics 333.2
Open fires
  heating buildings 697.1
Open-hearth furnace practice 669.142 2
Open learning
  adult education 374.4
Open-loop systems
  automation engineering 629.82
Open-market operations 332.114
  central banking 332.114
  macroeconomic policy 339.53
Open-pit mining 622.292
Open plan schools 371.256
  instruction 371.394 1
Open shop 331.889 2
Open stacks 025.81
Open Systems Interconnection 004.62
Open universities (Alternative higher education) 378.03
  see also Higher education
Openings (Buildings) 721.82
  architecture 721.82
  construction 690.182
Openings (Chess) 794.122
Openings (Physiography) T2—144
Openwork fabrics 677.65
Opera glasses
  manufacturing technology 681.412 5
Opera houses
  architecture 725.822
  history 792.509
Opera reviews 792.545
Opera singers 782.109 2
  occupational group T7—782
Operant conditioning 153.152 6
Operas 782.1
  music 782.1
  stage presentation 792.5
    see also Theater
  see Manual at 782.1 vs. 792.5
Operating budgets (Public) 352.48
  see also Budgets (Public)
Operating rooms (Surgery) 617.917
Operating systems 005.43
  graphics programming 006.678 2
  graphics programs 006.688 2
  knowledge-based systems programming 006.337
  multimedia-systems programming 006.778 2
Operating systems (continued)
  multimedia-systems programs 006.788 2
  programming 005.42
Operation Desert Storm, 1991 956.704 424
Operational amplifiers 621.395
Operational audits 658.401 3
  public administration 352.439
Operational calculus 515.72
Operations (Mathematics) 511.33
  number theory 512.72
Operations income
  financial management 658.155 4
Operations research 003
  T1—011
  management decision making 658.403 4
  see Manual at 003
Operative gynecology 618.105 9
  see also Female genital system
Operative surgery 617.91
Operator algebras 512.55
Operator errors 363.120 1
  see also Transportation safety
Operator theory 515.724
Operators (Mathematics) 515.724
Operettas 782.12
  music 782.12
  stage presentation 792.5
    see also Theater
Ophicleides 788.99
  see also Brass instruments
Ophidiidae 597.63
Ophioglossales 587.33
  paleobotany 561.73
Ophiurida 593.94
Ophiuroidea 593.94
  paleozoology 563.94
Ophthalmic nursing
  medicine 610.736 77
Ophthalmologists 617.709 2
  occupational group T7—617 7
  role and function 617.702 32
Ophthalmology 617.7
  anesthesiology 617.967 7
  geriatrics 618.977 7
  nursing 610.736 77
  pediatrics 618.920 977
  see also Eyes
Opiliaceae 583.88
Opilioacariformes 595.42
Opiliones 595.43
Opisthobranchia 594.34
Opisthocomidae 598.64
Opium
  pharmacodynamics 615.782 2

Opium (continued)
  pharmacology 615.323 35
Opium abuse 362.293
  medicine 616.863 2
  personal health 613.83
  social welfare 362.293
  see also Substance abuse
Opium War, 1840–1842 951.033
Opole (Poland :
    Voivodeship) T2—438 5
Opossum shrimps 595.375
Opossums 599.276
Opossums (America) 599.276
Opossums (Australasia) 599.23
Opotiki District (N.Z.) T2—934 28
Oppland fylke (Norway) T2—482 5
Opposition parties (Legislatures) 328.369
Optic nerves 573.882 8
  animal physiology 573.882 8
  human anatomy 611.84
  human diseases
    incidence 614.599 7
    ophthalmology 617.732
  human physiology 612.843
  see also Eyes
Optical analysis
  chemistry 543.085
Optical art 709.040 72
  painting 759.067 2
  sculpture 735.230 472
Optical binaries 523.841
Optical character recognition 006.424
  computer engineering 621.399
Optical communications
  engineering 621.382 7
  see Manual at 621.36 vs.
    621.381045, 621.3827
Optical components
  cameras 771.35
Optical computers
  engineering 621.391
Optical crystallography 548.9
Optical data processing 621.367
  computer science 006.42
    engineering 621.399
  see Manual at 006.37 vs.
    006.42, 621.367, 621.391,
    621.399
Optical detectors
  manufacturing technology 681.25
Optical diagnosis
  medicine 616.075 45
Optical digital discs 004.565
  engineering 621.397 67
Optical disc technology 621.382 7
Optical-fiber cable
  computer science 004.64
    engineering 621.398 1
Optical-fiber communication 621.382 75
Optical glass 666.156
Optical illusions 152.148
Optical instruments
  manufacturing technology 681.4
Optical metallography 669.950 282
Optical pattern recognition
  computer science 006.42
    engineering 621.399
    see Manual at 006.37 vs.
      006.42, 621.367,
      621.391, 621.399
Optical properties
  materials science 620.112 95
Optical rotation
  chemistry 541.7
Optical scanning
  computer science 006.42
    engineering 621.399
Optical spectroscopes
  manufacturing technology 681.414
Optical spectroscopy
  physics 535.84
Optical storage devices 004.565
  engineering 621.397 67
Optical surgery 617.71
  see also Eyes
Opticians 681.409 2
  occupational group T7—681 4
Optics 535
  engineering 621.36
    see Manual at 621.36 vs.
      621.381045, 621.3827
  see also Light
Optimal control
  automation engineering 629.831 2
Optimism
  philosophy 149.5
Optimization (Mathematics) 519.3
Optimization (Systems) 003
  T1—011
Optoacoustic communications
  engineering 621.382 8
Optoelectronic devices 621.381 52
Optoelectronics 621.381 045
  see Manual at 621.36 vs.
    621.381045, 621.3827
Optometry 617.75
  see also Eyes
Or-Blanc (Quebec) T2—714 573

Oracles 133.324 8
  religion 291.32
Oral communication 302.224 2
  management use 658.452
  office services 651.73
  rhetoric 808.5
Oral contraceptives
  health 613.943 2
  pharmacodynamics 615.766
  see also Birth control
Oral hygiene
  dentistry 617.601
  see also Dentistry
Oral interpretation 808.54
Oral medication
  administering 615.6
Oral presentations
  elementary education 372.66
Oral reading
  elementary education 372.452
Oral region
  medicine 617.522
  surgery 617.522 059
Oral sex
  sociology 306.774
Oral surgery 617.522 059
  dentistry 617.605
    see also Dentistry
  see Manual at 617.605 vs. 617.522
Oral traditions
  folklore 398.2
Oral traditions (Religion) 291.83
  Bible 220.663
  Buddhism 294.383
  Hinduism 294.593
  Judaism 296.1
Oran (Algeria : Province) T2—651
Orange (N.J.) T2—749 33
Orange (N.S.W.) T2—944 5
Orange County (Calif.) T2—794 96
Orange County (Fla.) T2—759 24
Orange County (Ind.) T2—772 27
Orange County (N.C.) T2—756 565
Orange County (N.Y.) T2—747 31
Orange County (Tex.) T2—764 147
Orange County (Va.) T2—755 372
Orange County (Vt.) T2—743 63
Orange Free State 968.504 5
  T2—685
Orange Free State (South Africa) 968.5
  T2—685
Orange jessamine 635.977 377
  botany 583.77
Orange jessamine (continued)
  ornamental arboriculture 635.977 377
Orange River T2—687
Orange River Colony 968.504 9
  T2—685
Orange River Sovereignty 968.504 2
  T2—685
Orange roughy 597.64
Orange Walk District (Belize) T2—728 26
Orangeburg County (S.C.) T2—757 79
Oranges 641.343 1
  botany 583.77
  commercial processing 664.804 31
  cooking 641.643 1
  food 641.343 1
  orchard crop 634.31
Orangutan 599.883
Oraon T5—948 3
Oraon language 494.83
  T6—948 3
Oraon literature 894.83
Oratories (Chapels)
  architecture 726.595
Oratorios 782.23
  choral and mixed voices 782.523
Orators 809.5
  collected biography 809.5
    specific literatures T3B—500 9
  individual biography T3A—5
  occupational group T7—85
Oratory 808.51
Orbital flights
  manned 629.454
Orbitals (Quantum chemistry) 541.28
Orbits (Astromechanics) 521.3
  astronautics 629.411 3
  astronomy 521.3
    comets 523.63
    earth 525.3
    moon 523.33
Orbits (Eye sockets)
  human anatomy 611.84
  ophthalmology 617.78
  see also Eyes
Orbits (Nuclear particles) 539.725
Orchard grass 633.22
  botany 584.9
Orchards 634
Orchestra conductors 784.209 2
  occupational group T7—784
Orchestral harps 787.95
  see also Stringed instruments
Orchestral music 784.2

Orchestras 784.2
  see Manual at 784–788
Orchestras with solo instruments 784.23
Orchestras with toy instruments 784.46
Orchestras with vocal parts 784.22
Orchestration 781.374
Orchidales 584.4
Orchids 584.4
  floriculture 635.934 4
Orcinus 599.536
Ord River (W.A. : River) T2—941 4
Order
  philosophy 117
Order of DeMolay for Boys 366.108 351
  biography 366.108 351
  social group T7—366 1
Order of the Eastern Star 366.18
  biography 366.180 92
  social group T7—366 1
Order statistics 519.5
Ordered algebraic structures 511.33
Ordered solids 530.413
Ordered topological spaces 514.32
Ordering
  library acquisitions 025.23
  materials management 658.72
Orderlies (Hospital) 610.730 92
  role and function 610.730 698
  see also Nurses
Orders (Awards) 929.81
  armed forces 355.134 2
  numismatics 737.223
Orders (Societies) 366
Orders of knighthood 929.71
Ordinances (Compilations) 348.02
Ordinary differential equations 515.352
Ordinary differentiation 515.33
Ordinary language philosophy 149.94
Ordinary of the mass 264.36
  music 782.323 2
Ordination of clergy 291.61
  Christianity 262.14
    ecclesiology 262.14
    sacrament 234.164
      public worship 265.4
      theology 234.164
  Judaism 296.61
Ordination of women 291.610 82
  Christianity 262.14
  Judaism 296.610 82
Ordnance 355.8
  engineering 623.4
    air ordnance 623.746 1
    naval ordnance 623.825 1
Ordnance (continued)
  military equipment 355.8
    air ordnance 358.418
    naval ordnance 359.8
  see Manual at 355 vs. 623
Ordos
  Roman Catholic liturgy 264.021
Ordovician period 551.731
  geology 551.731
  paleontology 560.173 1
Ordu İli (Turkey) T2—565
Orduña (Spain) T2—466 9
Ore dressing 622.7
  see Manual at 622.22, 622.7 vs. 662.6, 669
Ore processing 622.7
Oreamnos 599.647 5
Örebro län (Sweden) T2—487
Oregano 641.357
  see also Herbs
Oregon 979.5
  T2—795
Oregon County (Mo.) T2—778 875
Oregon myrtle 583.23
Orel (Russia : Oblast) T2—473 5
Orenburg (Russia : Oblast) T2—474 3
Orenburgskaia oblast′ (Russia) T2—474 3
Orense (Spain : Province) T2—461 5
Ores 553
  see Manual at 553
Oresund (Denmark and Sweden) 551.461 34
  T2—163 34
Organ banks 362.178 3
  see also Health services
Organ builders 786.519 092
Organ cases
  church architecture 726.529 7
Organ concertos 784.265
Organ culture 571.538
  humans 612.028
Organ donation 362.178 3
  law 344.041 94
Organ transplants 362.197 95
  law 344.041 94
  medical ethics 174.25
    see also Medical ethics
  social services 362.197 95
  surgery 617.95
Organelles 571.65
Organic chemicals
  chemical engineering 661.8
Organic chemistry 547
  applied 661.8

Organic compounds 547
  biochemistry 572
    humans 612.015 7
  human toxicology 615.95
  pollution
    ecology 577.278
  toxicology 571.957
Organic drugs
  pharmacology 615.3
  see Manual at 615.1 vs. 615.2–615.3
Organic evolution 576.8
Organic farming 631.584
Organic fertilizers 631.86
  chemical engineering 668.63
Organic gardening 635.048 4
  floriculture 635.987
Organic geochemistry 553.2
Organic materials
  materials science 620.117
Organic poisons 363.179 1
  human toxicology 615.95
  public safety 363.179 1
  see also Hazardous materials
Organic solids 530.413
Organically grown foods 641.302
  agriculture 631.584
  home economics 641.302
Organismic psychology 150.193
Organists 786.509 2
  occupational group T7—786
Organization (Management) 658.1
  T1—068 1
  executive 658.402
  production 658.51
  public administration 352.2
  see Manual at 658.04 vs. 658.114, 658.402
Organization of African Unity 341.249
  public administration 352.116
Organization of American States 341.245
  public administration 352.117
Organization of production 338.6
  economics 338.6
  management 658.51
  T1—068 5
Organizational behavior 302.35
  management 658
  see Manual at 302.35 vs. 658, T1—068
Organizational change
  executive management 658.406
    public administration 352.367
Organizations 060
  T1—06
  business enterprises 338.7
  law 346.06
  organizational behavior 302.35
  religious 291.65
    see also Religious organizations
  social 366
  see Manual at T1—025 vs. T1—0601-T1—0609; *also at* T1—0601-T1—0609; *also at* T1—072 vs. T1—0601-T1—0609
Organized crime 364.106
  law 345.02
Organized strikes 331.892 2
  see also Strikes (Work stoppages)
Organohalogen compounds 547.02
Organometallic compounds 547.05
  aliphatic chemistry 547.45
  chemical engineering 661.895
  human toxicology 615.951 5
Organonitrogen compounds 547.04
  aliphatic chemistry 547.44
  aromatic chemistry 547.64
Organophosphorus compounds 547.07
  aliphatic chemistry 547.47
Organosilicon compounds 547.08
  aliphatic chemistry 547.48
Organosulfur compounds 547.06
  aliphatic chemistry 547.46
  aromatic chemistry 547.66
Organotherapy
  pharmacology 615.36
Organs (Musical instruments) 786.5
  instrument 786.519
  music 786.5
  see also Keyboard instruments
Oribi Gorge Nature Reserve (South Africa) T2—684 5
Orient 950
  T2—5
Oriental architecture 720.95
  ancient 722.1
Oriental arts 709.5
Oriental churches 281.5
  see also Eastern churches
Oriental flower arrangements 745.922 5
Oriental horses 636.11
Oriental languages 490
  T6—9

Oriental law 340.58
Oriental Mindoro
  (Philippines) T2—599 3
Oriental philosophy 181
Oriental region (Paraguay) T2—892 1
Oriental rugs
  arts 746.750 95
  see also Rugs
Oriental sculpture 730.95
  ancient 732.7
Oriental shorthair cats 636.82
Oriental sores
  incidence 614.534
  medicine 616.936 4
  see also Communicable
    diseases (Human)
Orientation (Geography) 912.014
Orientation of employees
  personnel management 658.312 42
  public administration 352.66
Orientational perception
  psychology 152.188 2
Oriente (Cuba : Province) T2—729 16
Oriente (Ecuador) T2—866 4
Orienteering 796.58
  see also Sports
Origami 736.982
Origin of life 576.83
  philosophy 113.8
  religion 291.24
    Christianity 231.765
    philosophy of religion 213
Origin of races
  physical ethnology 599.972
Origin of the state 320.11
Origin of universe 523.12
  philosophy 113
  religion 291.24
    Christianity 231.765
    philosophy of religion 213
Original sin 233.14
Orinoco River (Venezuela) T2—87
Orioles 598.874
Orissa (India) T2—541 3
Oristano (Sardinia :
  Province) T2—459 4
Oriya T5—914 5
Oriya language 491.456
  T6—914 56
Oriya literature 891.456
Orkney (Scotland) T2—411 32
Orkney Islands (Scotland) T2—411 32
Orlah 296.123 1
  Mishnah 296.123 1
Orlah (continued)
  Palestinian Talmud 296.124 1
Orléanais (France) T2—445
Orléans, Île de (Quebec) T2—714 48
Orléans, Isle of (Quebec) T2—714 48
Orleans County (N.Y.) T2—747 91
Orleans County (Vt.) T2—743 23
Orleans Parish (La.) T2—763 35
Orléansville (Algeria :
  Province) T2—653
Orlicz spaces 515.73
Orlovskaîa oblast´ (Russia) T2—473 5
Ormiston Gorge National
  Park (N.T.) T2—942 91
Ornamental birds 636.68
  economic zoology 598.163
  see also Birds
Ornamental bookbinding 686.36
Ornamental fans
  decorative arts 736.7
  dress customs 391.44
Ornamental glass
  architectural decoration 729.8
Ornamental nails
  ironwork 739.48
Ornamental plants 635.9
  economic botany 581.636
  see also Plants
  see Manual at 583–585; *also*
    at 633–635: Other crops;
    also at 635.9 vs. 582.1
Ornamental woodwork
  furniture arts 749.5
  handicrafts 745.51
Ornaments
  arts 745
    glass 748.8
    stone 736.5
    wood 736.4
  handicrafts 745.594
  manufacturing technology 688.726
Ornaments (Music) 781.247
Orne (France) T2—442 3
Ornithischia 567.914
Ornithologists 598.092
  occupational group T7—598
Ornithology 598
Ornithopoda 567.914
Ornithopters
  engineering 629.133 36
Ornithorhynchidae 599.29
Oro (Ecuador) T2—866 31
Oro Province (Papua New
  Guinea) T2—954 2

Orobanchaceae 583.95
Orogeny 551.82
Oromo (African people) T5—935
Oromo language 493.55
T6—935 5
Oromo literature 893.55
Orphanages 362.732
see also Children—social welfare
Orphans 305.906 945
T1—086 945
social group 305.906 945
social services 362.73
Orpines 583.72
Orthochromatic photography 778.62
Orthodontics 617.643
see also Dentistry
Orthodox Eastern Church 281.9
see also Eastern Orthodox Church
Orthodox Judaism 296.832
Orthogonal polynomials 515.55
Orthogonal series 515.243
Orthographic projection
technical drawing 604.245
Orthography 411
applied linguistics 418
specific languages T4—81
elementary education 372.632
linguistics 411
specific languages T4—152
Orthomorphic projections 526.82
Orthopedic appliances 617.9
manufacturing technology 681.761
Orthopedic nursing
medicine 610.736 77
Orthopedic shoes
manufacturing technology 685.38
Orthopedic surgery 617.47
Orthopedics 616.7
see also Musculoskeletal system
Orthoptera 595.726
Orthopters
engineering 629.133 36
Orthoptics 617.762
see also Eyes
Orthorrhapha 595.773
Ortiz Rubio, Pascual
Mexican history 972.082 43
Oruro (Bolivia : Dept.) T2—841 3
Oryctolagus 599.322
Oryx 599.645
conservation technology 639.979 645
Oryx (continued)
resource economics 333.959 645
Oryzeae 584.9
Osage County (Kan.) T2—781 643
Osage County (Mo.) T2—778 58
Osage County (Okla.) T2—766 25
Osage Indians T5—975 2
Osage orange 583.45
Osaka (Japan) T2—521 834
Osaka (Japan : Prefecture) T2—521 83
Osborne County (Kan.) T2—781 215
Oscan language 479.9
T6—799
Oscans T5—79
Osceola County (Fla.) T2—759 25
Osceola County (Iowa) T2—777 116
Osceola County (Mich.) T2—774 69
Oscillations
solid-state physics 530.416
solids 531.32
Oscillatoriales 579.39
Oscillators
electronic circuits 621.381 533
radio engineering 621.384 12
Oscillographs 621.374 7
electronic engineering 621.381 548 3
Oscilloscopes 621.381 548 3
Oscines 598.8
see Manual at 598.824–598.88
Osco-Umbrian languages 479.9
T6—799
Osco-Umbrian literatures 879.9
Osco-Umbrians T5—79
Oscoda County (Mich.) T2—774 78
Osee (Biblical book) 224.6
Osetin language 491.59
T6—915 9
Osetin literature 891.59
Oshkosh (Wis.) T2—775 64
OSI (Computer communication) 004.62
Osilinka River (B.C.) T2—711 85
Oslo fylke (Norway) T2—482 1
Osmanli language 494.35
T6—943 5
Osmanli literature 894.35
Osmium 669.7
chemical engineering 661.064 1
chemistry 546.641
metallography 669.957
metallurgy 669.7
physical metallurgy 669.967
see also Chemicals
Osmosis 530.425
physics 530.425

Osmosis (continued)	
solution chemistry	541.341 5
water supply treatment	628.164
Osnabrück (Germany)	T2—435 911
Osorno (Chile : Province)	T2—835 3
Osoyoos (B.C.)	T2—711 5
Osprey	598.93
Osseous tissues	
human histology	611.018 4
see also Musculoskeletal system	
Ossete language	491.59
	T6—915 9
Ossete literature	891.59
Ossetic language	491.59
	T6—915 9
Ossetic literature	891.59
Ossets	T5—915 9
Ossicles	
human anatomy	611.85
human physiology	612.854
otology	617.842
see also Ears	
Ostariophysi	597.48
Osteichthyes	597
see also Fishes	
Osteitis	
medicine	616.712
see also Musculoskeletal system	
Osteitis deformans	
medicine	616.712
see also Musculoskeletal system	
Osteoarthritis	
medicine	616.722 3
see also Musculoskeletal system	
Osteochondritis	
medicine	616.712
see also Musculoskeletal system	
Osteoglossomorpha	597.47
paleozoology	567.47
Osteomyelitis	
medicine	616.715
see also Musculoskeletal system	
Osteopathy	610
therapeutic system	615.533
Osteoporosis	
medicine	616.716
see also Musculoskeletal system	
Östergötlands län (Sweden)	T2—486
Østfold fylke (Norway)	T2—482 3
Ostfriesland (Germany)	T2—435 917
Ostia (Italy)	T2—456 3
ancient	T2—376
Ostinato	781.827
instrumental	784.182 7
Østlandet (Norway)	T2—482
Ostracoda	595.33
paleozoology	565.33
Ostriches	598.524
animal husbandry	636.694
Ostrołęka (Poland : Voivodeship)	T2—438 4
Ostropales	579.57
Ostyak language	494.51
	T6—945 1
Ostyak literature	894.51
Ostyak Samoyed language	494.4
	T6—944
Ostyaks	T5—945 1
Osun State (Nigeria)	T2—669 26
Oswego County (N.Y.)	T2—747 67
Oswestry (England)	T2—424 51
Otago Province (N.Z.)	T2—939
Otago Region (N.Z.)	T2—939 1
Otariidae	599.797
Otariinae	599.797 5
OTC market	332.643
Otero County (Colo.)	T2—788 95
Otero County (N.M.)	T2—789 65
Other minds	
epistemology	121.2
Otididae	598.32
Oto language (Siouan)	497.52
	T6—975 2
Oto-Manguean languages	497.6
	T6—976
Otoe County (Neb.)	T2—782 273
Otologists	617.809 2
occupational group	T7—617 8
role and function	617.802 32
see also Ears	
Otology	617.8
anesthesiology	617.967 8
geriatrics	618.977 8
pediatrics	618.920 978
surgery	617.805 9
see also Ears	
Otomanguean languages	497.6
	T6—976
Otomí Indians	T5—976

Otomí language 497.6
T6—976
Otorhinolaryngology 617.51
Otorohanga District (N.Z.) T2—933 7
Otsego County (Mich.) T2—774 84
Otsego County (N.Y.) T2—747 74
Ottawa (Ont.) T2—713 84
Ottawa-Carleton (Ont.) T2—713 83
Ottawa County (Kan.) T2—781 26
Ottawa County (Mich.) T2—774 15
Ottawa County (Ohio) T2—771 212
Ottawa County (Okla.) T2—766 99
Ottawa River (Quebec and Ont.) T2—713 8
  Ontario T2—713 8
  Quebec T2—714 2
Otter shrews 599.33
Otter Tail County (Minn.) T2—776 89
Otterhound 636.753 6
Otters 599.769
  animal husbandry 636.976 9
  conservation technology 639.979 769
  resource economics 333.959 769
  small game hunting 799.259 769
Otters (River otters) 599.769 2
  animal husbandry 636.976 92
  conservation technology 639.979 769 2
  resource economics 333.959 769 2
  small game hunting 799.259 769 2
Ottoman Empire 956.015
T2—56
  Algerian history 965.02
  Arabian history 953.03
  Egyptian history 962.03
  Iraqi history 956.703
  Jordanian history 956.950 3
  Lebanese history 956.920 34
  Libyan history 961.202
  North African history 961.023
  Palestinian history 956.940 3
  Syrian history 956.910 3
  Tunisian history 961.103
  Turkish history 956.101 5
Ottoman Turkish language 494.35
T6—943 5
Ottoman Turkish literature 894.35
Ouachita County (Ark.) T2—767 66
Ouachita Mountains (Okla. and Ark.) T2—766 6
  Arkansas T2—767 4
  Oklahoma T2—766 6
Ouachita Parish (La.) T2—763 87
Ouachita River (Ark. and La.) T2—763 7
Ouagadougou (Burkina Faso) T2—662 5
Ouargla (Algeria : Province) T2—657
Ouarzazate (Morocco : Province) T2—646
Ouds 787.82
  see also Stringed instruments
Oudtshoorn (South Africa : District) T2—687 16
Oued (Algeria : Province) T2—657
Ouest (Haiti : Dept.) T2—729 452
Ouija board 133.932 5
Oujda (Morocco : Province) T2—643
Oulu (Finland) T2—489 76
Oum el Bouaghi (Algeria : Province) T2—655
Ounce (Snow leopard) 599.755 5
Ouray County (Colo.) T2—788 22
Ouse River (England) T2—428 4
Out-of-body experience 133.95
Outagamie County (Wis.) T2—775 39
Outaouais (Quebec : Administrative region) T2—714 22
Outaouais Region (Quebec) T2—714 22
Outaouais Regional Community (Quebec) T2—714 221
Outboard motorboats 387.231 3
  design 623.812 313
  engineering 623.823 13
  transportation services 387.231 3
  see also Ships
Outboard motors 623.872 34
Outcrops (Geology) 551.85
Outdoor advertising 659.134 2
Outdoor cooking 641.578
Outdoor education 371.384
Outdoor furniture 645.8
  cleaning 648.5
  customs 392.36
  decorative arts 749.8
  household management 645.8
  manufacturing technology 684.18
Outdoor games 796
  see also Sports
Outdoor life 796.5
  equipment technology 688.765
Outdoor markets 381.18
  management 658.87
  see also Commerce
Outdoor music 781.532
Outdoor photography 778.71

Outdoor recreation centers 790.068
Outdoor safety
  public administration 353.97
Outdoor sports 796
  equipment technology 688.76
  see also Sports
Outer Banks (N.C.) T2—756 1
Outer ears 573.89
  animal physiology 573.89
  descriptive zoology 591.4
  human physiology 612.851
  see also Ears
Outer garments
  commercial technology 687
    fur 685.24
    leather 685.22
Outer Hebrides (Scotland) T2—411 4
Outer House of Court of Session
    (Scotland) 347.411 024
Outer Mongolia 951.73
  T2—517 3
Outer space 520
  T2—19
  astronomy 520
  international law 341.47
  resource economics 333.94
    see Manual at 333.94 vs.
      338.0919
  see Manual at 520 vs. 500.5,
    523.1, 530.1, 919.9
Outfield play
  baseball 796.357 25
Outgroups 302.4
Outlaw strikes 331.892 4
  see also Strikes (Work
    stoppages)
Outlet stores 381.15
  retail 381.15
    management 658.870 5
  wholesale 381.2
    management 658.86
  see also Commerce
Outlets
  electrical engineering 621.319 24
Outlines T1—020 2
Outpatient departments 362.12
  see also Health services
Outpatient surgery 617.024
Output peripherals 004.77
  computer engineering 621.398 7
Ovaries 573.665
  biology 573.665
  gynecology 618.11
  human anatomy 611.65
Ovaries (continued)
  human physiology 612.62
  plants 575.665
  surgery 618.110 59
  see also Female genital system
Ovenbirds 598.822 5
Ovens River (Vic.) T2—945 5
Over-the-counter drugs 615.1
  see also Drugs
      (Pharmaceuticals)
Over-the-counter market 332.643
Overberg (South Africa) T2—687 3
Overcoats 391
  commercial technology 687.144
  customs 391
  home sewing 646.452
  see also Clothing
Overeaters Anonymous, inc.
    (U.S.) 362.27
Overflows
  sewer systems 628.21
Overglaze painting 666.45
  arts 738.15
  technology 666.45
Overhead costs
  financial management 658.155 3
Overhead electrical lines 621.319 22
Overijssel (Netherlands) T2—492 16
Overindulgence
  ethics 178
Overland air-cushion vehicles
  engineering 629.322
  military engineering 623.748 2
Overland mail 383.143
  see also Postal service
Overpopulation 363.91
Overseas service 384.64
  see also Telephone
Oversewing
  bookbinding 686.35
Overshoes 678.33
Oversight 658.401 3
  legislative function 328.345 6
  management 658.401 3
  military administration 355.685
  public administration 352.35
    independent agencies 352.88
Overtime pay 331.216 2
  labor economics 331.216 2
  personnel management 658.322 2
Overtime work 331.257 2
  personnel management 658.312 1
Overton County (Tenn.) T2—768 684

Overtures 784.189 26
  musical form 784.189 26
  orchestral music 784.218 926
Overwater air-cushion vehicles 387.2
  engineering 629.324
  military engineering 623.748 4
  transportation services 387.2
    inland water 386.22
    ocean 387.2
Overweight persons
  cooking for 641.563 5
  reducing diet 613.25
Ovibos 599.647 8
Oviducts
  gynecology 618.12
  surgery 618.120 59
Oviedo (Spain : Province) T2—461 9
Ovimbundu (African people) T5—963 99
Oviraptor 567.912
Ovis 599.649
Ovis canadensis 599.649 7
Owen County (Ind.) T2—772 43
Owen County (Ky.) T2—769 393
Owenism 335.12
Owensboro (Ky.) T2—769 864
Owl Creek Mountains (Wyo.) T2—787 43
Owls 598.97
  conservation technology 639.978 97
  resource economics 333.958 97
Owners' liability insurance 368.56
  see also Insurance
Ownership
  communications industry 384.041
  real property law 346.043 2
  transportation services 388.049
Ownership equity
  accounting 657.76
Ownership flags 929.92
Ownership marks 929.9
  T1—027 7
  animal husbandry 636.081 2
Owsley County (Ky.) T2—769 176
Owyhee County (Idaho) T2—796 21
Oxalidaceae 583.79
Oxazines 547.595
Oxazoles 547.592
  chemical engineering 661.8
Oxdiazines 547.595
Oxdiazoles 547.595
Oxen 599.642 2
  animal husbandry 636.216
Oxford (England) T2—425 74
Oxford (Ont. : County) T2—713 46
Oxford County (Me.) T2—741 75
Oxfordshire (England) T2—425 7
Oxidases 572.791
  see also Enzymes
Oxidation 541.393
  chemical engineering 660.284 43
  organic chemistry 547.23
Oxidation ditches 628.351
Oxidation ponds 628.351
Oxidation-reduction methods
  analytical chemistry 545.23
Oxides
  mineralogy 549.5
Oxidizing enzymes 572.791
  see also Enzymes
Oxidoreductases 572.791
  see also Enzymes
Oxpeckers 598.863
Oxy compounds 547.03
  aliphatic chemistry 547.43
  aromatic chemistry 547.63
  chemical engineering 661.8
Oxygen
  biochemistry 572.53
    human 612.22
  chemical engineering 661.072 1
  chemistry 546.721
  economic geology 553.94
  gas technology 665.823
  organic chemistry 547.03
    applied 661.8
  therapeutics 615.836
  see also Chemicals
Oxygen supply
  human physiology 612.22
    see also Respiratory system
Oxynotidae 597.36
Oxytocin
  chemistry 547.734 5
Oyampi language 498.38
  T6—983 8
Oyo (Kingdom) 966.925 01
  T2—669 25
Oyo State (Nigeria) T2—669 25
Oystercatchers 598.33
Oysters 641.394
  conservation technology 639.974 4
  cooking 641.694
  fishing 639.41
  fishing industry 338.372 44
  food 641.394
    commercial processing 664.94
  resource economics 333.955 41

Oysters (continued)
zoology 594.4
Ozark County (Mo.) T2—778 835
Ozark Mountains T2—767 1
Arkansas T2—767 1
Missouri T2—778 8
Oklahoma T2—766 8
Ozark Plateau T2—767 1
see also Ozark Mountains
Ozarks T2—767 1
see also Ozark Mountains
Ozarks, Lake of the (Mo.) T2—778 493
Ozaukee County (Wis.) T2—775 92
Ozobrome process 773.1
Ozokerite 553.27
processing 665.4
see also Asphalt
Ozone
gas technology 665.89
Ozone layer 551.514 2
Ozone layer depletion 363.738 75
ecology 577.276
meteorology 551.514 2
pollution aspects 363.738 75
Ozone treatment
water supply engineering 628.166 2
Ozotype process 773.1

P

P-adic numbers 512.74
P document (Biblical criticism) 222.106 6
P.K. le Roux Dam (South Africa) T2—687 13
Paarl (South Africa : District) T2—687 3
Pabok (Quebec) T2—714 79
Pacas 599.359
Pacemakers (Electronic cardiac)
medicine 617.412 064 5
see also Cardiovascular system
Pacers (Horses) 636.175
Pachycephalosaurus 567.914
Pacific, War of the, 1879–1883 983.061 6
Pacific Area T2—182 3
Pacific Coast (B.C.) T2—711 1
Pacific Coast (North America) 979
T2—79
Pacific County (Wash.) T2—797 92
Pacific fur seal 599.797 3
Pacific international organizations 341.246
Pacific Islands (Trust Territory) 996.5
T2—965
Pacific Northwest T2—795
Pacific Ocean 551.465
T2—164
see Manual at T2—163 and T2—164, T2—165; *also at* T2—163, T2—164, T2—165 vs. T2—182
Pacific Ocean islands 990
T2—9
Pacific Region T2—182 3
Pacific Rim National Park (B.C.) T2—711 2
Pacific settlement of disputes 303.69
international law 341.52
international relations 327.17
sociology 303.69
Pacifism 303.66
ethics 172.42
religion 291.562 42
Christianity 241.624 2
international politics 327.172
social theology 291.178 73
Buddhism 294.337 873
Christianity 261.873
Hinduism 294.517 873
Judaism 296.382 7
sociology 303.66
Pacifists 303.66
biography
international politics 327.172 092
World War I 940.316 2
World War II 940.531 62
Packaging 658.564
electronics 621.381 046
engineering 688.8
law 343.075
production management 658.564
sales promotion 658.823
Packers (Agricultural tools)
manufacturing technology 681.763 1
Packet switching (Data transmission)
communications engineering 621.382 16
computer communications 004.66
computer engineering 621.398 1
Packing clothes
home economics 646.6
Packing crops 631.56
Packing for shipment
materials management 658.788 4
PACs (Action committees) 324.4
law 342.078

Padded toys
  making 688.724
    handicrafts 745.592 4
    technology 688.724
  see also Toys
Paddle tennis 796.34
  see also Sports
Paddlefishes 597.42
Paddy rice 641.331 8
  see also Rice
Padova (Italy : Province) T2—453 2
Padre Island (Tex.) T2—764 47
Padua (Italy : Province) T2—453 2
Paelignian language 479.7
  T6—797
Paeoniales 583.62
Paez Indians T5—982
Paez language 498.2
  T6—982
Paezan languages 498.2
  T6—982
Pagalu (Equatorial Guinea) T2—671 86
Paganism 292
  Christian polemics 239.3
Page County (Iowa) T2—777 78
Page County (Va.) T2—755 94
Page design
  typesetting 686.225 2
Pageantry
  performing arts 791.6
Pageants 394.5
  customs 394.5
  performing arts 791.62
  see Manual at 394.5 vs. 791.6
Paget's disease of bone
  medicine 616.712
  see also Musculoskeletal system
Paging systems
  engineering 621.389 2
Pahang T2—595 1
Pahari T5—914 96
Pahari languages 491.49
  T6—914 9
Pahari literatures 891.49
Pahlavi language 491.53
  T6—915 3
Pahlavi literature 891.53
Paid assistance (Social welfare) 361.04
  see also Welfare services
Paid vacations 331.257 6
  labor economics 331.257 6
  personnel management 658.312 2
Pails
  manufacturing technology 683.82
Pain
  human physiology 612.88
  symptomatology 616.047 2
    neurological diseases 616.849
  see also Nervous system
Pain perception
  psychology 152.182 4
Paint 667.6
  architectural decoration 729.4
  household management 645.2
Paint removers 667.6
Paint thinners 667.624
Painted Desert (Ariz.) T2—791 33
Painted glass
  arts 748.5
Painters (Arts) 759
  occupational group T7—75
Painters (Building trades) 698.109 2
  occupational group T7—698
Painting 667.6
  arts 750
  buildings 698.1
    woodwork 698.35
  decorative arts 745.723
  elementary education 372.52
  interior decoration 747.3
  literature 808.803 57
    history and criticism 809.933 57
    specific literatures T3B—080 357
      history and criticism T3B—093 57
  technology 667.6
  textile arts 746.6
  use in child care 649.51
Painting metals
  decorative arts 739.15
Painting pottery 666.45
  arts 738.15
  technology 666.45
Paintings 750
Pair skating 796.912
  see also Sports
País Vasco (Spain) T2—466
Paiute Indians T5—974 5
Paiwan (Taiwan people) T5—992 5
Pakistan 954.91
  T2—549 1
Pakistan (1947–1971) 954.9
  T2—549
Pakistanis T5—914 122
Palaces
  architecture 728.82
    official residences 725.17

Palaces
  architecture (continued)
    private residences 728.82
Palaeanodonta 569.31
Palaeognathae 598.5
  paleozoology 568.5
Palaic language 491.998
  T6—919 98
Palate
  human anatomy 611.315
  human physiology 612.31
    speech 612.78
  regional medicine 617.522 5
  surgery 617.522 5
  see also Digestive system
Palatinate (Germany) T2—434 35
Palau 996.6
  T2—966
Palawan (Philippines) T2—599 4
Palawan Island
    (Philippines) T2—599 4
Palencia (Spain : Province) T2—462 2
Paleo-Asiatics T5—946
Paleobotanists 561.092
Paleobotany 561
Paleocene epoch 551.783
  geology 551.783
  paleontology 560.178 3
Paleoclimatology 551.609 01
  specific areas 551.69
Paleoecology 560.45
  botanical 561.1
  zoological 560.45
Paleogene period 551.782
  geology 551.782
  paleontology 560.178 2
Paleogeography 551.7
Paleography 417.7
  handwriting 411.7
    specific languages T4—11
Paleolithic Age 930.12
  fine arts 709.011 2
  painting 759.011 2
  sculpture 732.22
Paleomagnetism 538.727
Paleontologists 560.92
  occupational group T7—56
Paleontology 560
  see Manual at 551.7 vs. 560;
    also at 560; *also at* 576.8
    vs. 560
Paleopalynology 561.13
Paleosiberian languages 494.6
  T6—946
Paleosiberian literatures 894.6
Paleosiberian peoples T5—946
Paleovolcanism 551.210 901
Paleozoic era 551.72
  geology 551.72
  paleontology 560.172
Paleozoology 560
Palermo (Sicily : Province) T2—458 23
Palestine 956.94
  T2—569 4
  ancient 933
  T2—33
  Biblical geography and history 220.9
Palestine Liberation
    Organization
  history 956.940 5
  political party 324.256 940 83
  revolutionary
      organization 322.420 956 94
Palestinian Arabs T5—927 4
Palestinian architecture
  ancient 722.33
Palestinian sculpture 732.3
Palestinian Talmud 296.124
Palestinians T5—927 4
Pali language 491.37
  T6—913 7
Pali literature 891.37
Palindromes 793.734
Palladium 669.7
  chemical engineering 661.063 6
  chemistry 546.636
  metallography 669.957
  metallurgy 669.7
  physical metallurgy 669.967
  see also Chemicals
Pallets
  wooden 674.82
Palm Beach County (Fla.) T2—759 32
Palm reading 133.6
Palm Sunday 263.925
  devotional literature 242.35
  music 781.726
  sermons 252.625
Palm Valley National Park
    (N.T.) T2—942 91
Palma (Majorca) T2—467 542
Palma de Mallorca
    (Majorca) T2—467 542
Palmae 584.5
  see also Palms
Palmales 584.5
  see also Palms
Palmerston North (N.Z.) T2—935 8

Palmerston North City (N.Z.) T2—935 8
Palmettos 584.5
  see also Palms
Palmistry 133.6
Palmists 133.609 2
  occupational group T7—13
Palms 584.5
  botany 584.5
  forestry 634.974
  ornamental arboriculture 635.977 45
  ornamental gardening 635.934 5
  paleobotany 561.45
Palmtop computers 004.16
  see also Microcomputers
Palmyra (Extinct city) T2—394 3
Palmyra Atoll (Line Islands) T2—969 9
Palo Alto County (Iowa) T2—777 155
Palo Pinto County (Tex.) T2—764 552
Palomino horse 636.13
Palouse River (Idaho and Wash.) T2—797 39
Palpigradi 595.452
Pama-Maric languages 499.15
  T6—991 5
Pama-Nyungan languages 499.15
  T6—991 5
Pamir T2—586
Pamir languages 491.59
  T6—915 9
Pamir literatures 891.59
Pamiri T5—915 9
Pamlico County (N.C.) T2—756 194
Pamlico Sound (N.C.) 551.461 48
  T2—163 48
Pampa (Argentina : Province) T2—821 3
Pampanga (Philippines) T2—599 1
Pampas 333.74
  T2—145
  see also Prairies
Pampas grass 584.9
Pamphlets
  bibliographies 011.33
  cataloging 025.342
  library treatment 025.172
Pamphylia T2—392 9
Pamplona (Spain) T2—465 2
Pan (Chimpanzees) 599.885
Pan-Africanism 320.549 096
Pan-Arabism 320.540 917 4927
Pan fishing 799.12
Pan-Germanism 320.540 943
Pan movements 320.54
Pan pipes 788.37
  see also Woodwind instruments
Pan-Slavism 320.549 094 7
Panama 972.87
  T2—728 7
Panama (Panama : Province) T2—728 731
Panama, Gulf of (Panama) 551.466 1
  T2—164 1
Panama Canal (Panama) 386.44
  T2—728 75
Panama Canal Zone T2—728 75
Panama hat palm 584.62
Panamanian literature 860
Panamanians T5—687 287
Panay Island (Philippines) T2—599 5
Pancake mixes 664.753
Pancakes 641.815
Panchromatic photography 778.62
Pancreas 573.377
  biology 573.377
  human anatomy 611.37
  human physiology 612.34
  medicine 616.37
  surgery 617.557
  see also Digestive system
Pancreatic secretions
  human physiology 612.34
  see also Digestive system
Panda (Giant) 599.789
  conservation technology 639.979 789
  resource economics 333.959 789
Panda (Lesser) 599.763
Pandanales 584.66
Pandemics
  social effects 303.485
Pandionidae 598.93
Pando (Bolivia : Dept.) T2—844 3
Panel heating
  buildings 697.72
Paneling
  household management 645.2
  interior decoration 747.3
Panentheism 211.2
  philosophy 147
Pangasinan (Philippines) T2—599 1
Pangnirtung (N.W.T.) T2—719 5
Pangolins 599.31
Panic
  social psychology 302.17

Panic disorders
psychiatry 616.852 23
see also Mental illness
Panic grasses 584.92
forage crop 633.257 1
Panicoideae 584.92
forage crops 633.27
Panics (Economics) 338.542
Panicum 584.92
food crop 633.171
see also Millets
Panjabi language 491.42
T6—914 2
Panjabi literature 891.42
Pannonia T2—398
Panoan languages 498.4
T6—984
Panoan peoples T5—984
Panola County (Miss.) T2—762 84
Panola County (Tex.) T2—764 187
Panoramas 745.8
decorative arts 745.8
paintings 751.74
Panoramic photography 778.36
Panpipes 788.37
instrument 788.371 9
music 788.37
see also Woodwind instruments
Panpsychism 141
Pans
cooking 641.502 8
manufacturing technology 683.82
Pansies 635.933 625
botany 583.625
floriculture 635.933 625
Pantelleria Island (Italy) T2—458 24
Pantheism 211.2
philosophy 147
Pantheistic religions 291.14
Panther (Puma) 599.752 4
conservation technology 639.979 752 4
resource economics 333.959 752 4
Panthera 599.755
Pantodonta 569.62
Pantomime 792.3
see also Theater
Pants 391
commercial technology 687.113
customs 391
home sewing 646.433
see also Clothing
Papa Doc
Haitian history 972.940 72
Papacy 262.13
Papago Indians T5—974 5
Papago language 497.45
T6—974 5
Papakura District (N.Z.) T2—932 6
Papal administration 262.136
Papal bulls and decrees 262.91
Papal infallibility 262.131
Papal schism, 1378–1417 282.090 23
Papal States T2—456
Papal systems (Ecclesiology) 262.3
Paparoa National Park (N.Z.) T2—937 3
Papaverales 583.35
Papaws (Annonaceae) 641.344 1
botany 583.22
cooking 641.644 1
food 641.344 1
orchard crop 634.41
Papaws (Caricaceae, Papayas) 641.346 51
see also Papayas
Papayas 641.346 51
agriculture 634.651
botany 583.626
commercial processing 664.804 651
cooking 641.646 51
food 641.346 51
Paper 676
handicrafts 745.54
manufacturing technology 676
materials science 620.197
photographic materials 771.532 3
sculpture material 731.2
Paper airplanes 745.592
Paper bags 676.33
Paper boxes 676.32
handicrafts 745.54
Paper chromatography 543.089 52
Paper covers
bookbinding 686.344
Paper cups 676.34
Paper cutting 736.98
Paper dolls 769.53
Paper folding 736.98
Paper industry workers 676.092
occupational group T7—676
Paper money 332.404 4
arts 769.55
economics 332.404 4
printing 686.288
Paper plates 676.34
Paper production 676.2
Paper recycling 676.142

Paper standard
  foreign exchange 332.454
Paper-tape devices 004.56
  engineering 621.397 6
Paper work
  child care 649.51
  elementary education 372.55
Paperbacks 002
  bibliographies 011.32
  publishing 070.573
  reviews 028.132
Paperboard 676.288
  materials science 620.197
  structural engineering 624.189 7
Paperboard boxes 676.32
  handicrafts 745.54
Paperhangers 698.609 2
  occupational group T7—698
Paperhanging 698.6
  interior decoration 747.3
Papermaking 676
  equipment manufacturing
      technology 681.767 6
Paperweights
  glass
    decorative arts 748.84
Paphiopedeliums 635.934 4
  botany 584.4
  floriculture 635.934 4
Paphlagonia T2—393 1
Papiamento dialect 467.972 986
  T6—68
Papiamento literature 860
Papier-mâché
  handicrafts 745.542
  sculpture material 731.2
Papilionoidea 595.789
Papillomavirus 579.244 5
Papillon 636.76
Papineau (Quebec :
    County) T2—714 227
Papineau (Quebec :
    Regional County
    Municipality) T2—714 227
Papio 599.865
Papovaviridae 579.244 5
Pappophoreae 584.9
Paprika 641.338 4
  botany 583.952
  see also Hot spices
Papua 995.4
  T2—954
Papua (Territory) 995.402 2
  T2—954
Papua and New Guinea
    (Territory) 995.304
  T2—953
Papua New Guinea 995.3
  T2—953
Papuan languages 499.12
  T6—991 2
Papuan literatures 899.12
Papuans T5—991 2
Papular eruptions
  medicine 616.51
  see also Skin
Papyrus 584.84
Pará (Brazil : State) T2—811 5
Para (Surinam) T2—883 4
Parables in the Gospels 226.8
Parabola 516.15
Parabolic equations 515.353
Parabolic functions 515.9
Paracanthopterygii 597.62
  paleozoology 567.62
Parachute troops 356.166
Parachutes 629.134 386
Parachuting
  sports 797.56
    see also Sports
Parades 394.5
  circuses 791.38
  customs 394.5
  performing arts 791.6
  see Manual at 394.5 vs. 791.6
Paradisaeidae 598.865
Paradise 291.23
  Christianity 236.24
  Islam 297.23
Paradoxes
  logic 165
Paraffin (Kerosene) 665.538 3
Paraffin (Wax) 547.77
  natural 665.4
  petroleum product 665.538 5
Paraffins (Alkanes) 547.411
  chemical engineering 661.814
Paragraphs
  rhetoric 808
Paraguarí (Paraguay) T2—892 123
Paraguay 989.2
  T2—892
Paraguay River T2—892
Paraguay tea 641.337 7
  see also Maté
Paraguayan literature 860
Paraguayan War, 1865–1870 989.205
Paraguayans T5—688 92

Parah 296.123 6
Paraíba (Brazil : State) T2—813 3
Paraíso (Honduras : Dept.) T2—728 34
Parakeets 598.71
  animal husbandry 636.686 5
Parakeets (Lovebirds) 636.686 4
  animal husbandry 636.686 4
  zoology 598.71
Paralegals 340.092
  malpractice 347.050 41
  practice 347.050 4
Paralipomena (Biblical books) 222.6
Parallax
  stars 523.81
Parallax corrections 522.9
Parallel bars 796.44
  see also Sports
Parallel processing 004.35
  see also Processing modes—
    computer science
Parallel processors 004.35
  engineering 621.391
  see also Processing modes—
    computer science
Parallelism 147
Paralympics 796.045 6
  see also Sports
Paralysis
  symptomatology
    neurological diseases 616.842
  see also Nervous system
Paralysis agitans
  medicine 616.833
  see also Nervous system
Paramagnetism 538.43
Paramaribo (Surinam :
    District) T2—883 5
Paramecium 579.495
Parametric statistical methods 519.5
Paramyxoviridae 579.256
Paraná (Brazil : State) T2—816 2
Paraná River
    (Brazil-Argentina) T2—822
  Argentina T2—822
  Brazil T2—816
Paranoia
  medicine 616.897
  see also Mental illness
Paranormal phenomena 130
  see Manual at 001.9 and 130;
    also at 133 vs. 130
Paraphotic phenomena 535.01
  engineering 621.36
Paraphotic spectroscopes
  manufacturing technology 681.414
Paraphotic spectroscopy 543.085 8
  analytical chemistry 543.085 8
  physics 535.84
Paraphrase
  musical element 781.377
  musical forms 781.826
    instrumental 784.182 6
Paraplegia
  medicine 617.58
  neurology 616.837
  see also Nervous system
Parapsychologists 133.092
  occupational group T7—13
Parapsychology 133
  see Manual at 133 vs. 130;
    also at 133 vs. 200
Parapsychology and religion 291.175
  Christianity 261.513
Pararthropoda 592.7
  paleozoology 562.7
Parasaurolophus 567.914
Parasites 578.65
Parasitic animals 591.65
Parasitic diseases (Biology) 571.999
  agriculture 632.62
  plant crops 632.62
  veterinary medicine 636.089 696
Parasitic diseases (Human)
  incidence 614.55
  medicine 616.96
  see also Communicable
    diseases (Human)
Parasitic plants 581.65
  agricultural pests 632.52
Parasitic skin diseases
  medicine 616.57
  see also Skin
Parasitiformes 595.429
Parasitism (Biology)
  animals 591.785 7
  ecology 577.857
  pathology 571.999
  plants 581.785 7
  veterinary medicine 636.089 696
Parasitism (Human diseases)
  medicine 616.96
  see also Communicable
    diseases (Human)
Parasitology
  medicine 616.96
    see also Communicable
      diseases (Human)

Parasols
  customs 391.44
Parasympathetic nervous system
  human physiology 612.89
  medicine 616.88
  see also Nervous system
Parathyroid extracts
  pharmacology 615.362
  see also Endocrine system
Parathyroid glands 573.478
  biology 573.478
  human anatomy 611.44
  human physiology 612.44
  medicine 616.445
  surgery 617.539
  see also Endocrine system
Paratroops 356.166
Paratyphoid fever
  incidence 614.511 4
  medicine 616.927 4
  see also Communicable diseases (Human)
Parazoa 593.4
  paleozoology 563.4
Parc provincial des Laurentides (Quebec) T2—714 4
Parcels
  postal handling 383.125
    see also Postal service
Parchment papers 676.284 5
Parchments (Skins)
  manufacturing technology 685
Pardon 364.65
  law 345.077
  penology 364.65
Parenchyma 571.585
Parent abuse 362.829 2
  see also Family violence
Parent-child relations 306.874
  law 346.017
  psychological influence 155.924
  sociology 306.874
Parent participation in schools 371.192
  elementary education 372.119 2
    reading 372.425
Parent-school relations 371.192
Parent-teacher associations 371.192 06
Parent-teacher conferences 371.103
Parent-teacher relations 371.192
Parental behavior (Animals) 591.563
Parental kidnapping 362.829 7
  law 344.032 829 7
Parental kidnapping (continued)
  social welfare 362.829 7
  see also Families—social welfare
Parental leave 331.257 63
  personnel management 658.312 2
Parental rights 346.017
Parenteral medication
  administering 615.6
Parenteral therapy
  medicine 615.855
Parenthood
  child rearing 649.1
  customs 392.3
Parenting 649.1
  home economics 649.1
  personal religion 291.441
    Christianity 248.845
    Judaism 296.74
  sociology 306.874
Parents 306.874
  T1—085
  T7—043 1
  Christian devotional literature 242.645
  family relationships 306.874
  guides to religious life 291.441
    Christianity 248.845
    Judaism 296.74
  psychology 155.646
  social welfare 362.82
    see also Families—social welfare
Pareto, Vilfredo
  economic school 330.154 3
Pari-mutuel betting 798.401
Paria, Gulf of (Venezuela and Trinidad and Tobago) 551.464 66
  T2—163 66
Parianeae 584.9
Paridae 598.824
Paris (France) T2—443 61
Paris Commune, 1871 944.081 2
Paris metropolitan area (France) T2—443 6
Parish houses
  architecture 726.4
Parish libraries 027.67
Parish missions 266.022
Parish welfare work 361.75
Parishes 250
  administration 254
  ecclesiology 262.22
  see Manual at 260 vs. 251–254, 259

Park buildings
  architecture 725.7
Park County (Colo.) T2—788 59
Park County (Mont.) T2—786 661
Park County (Wyo.) T2—787 42
Park police 363.28
Park Range (Colo. and Wyo.) T2—788 66
Parke County (Ind.) T2—772 465
Parker County (Tex.) T2—764 553
Parking 388.474
  see also Parking facilities
Parking aprons 625.889
Parking facilities 388.474
  architecture 725.38
  area planning 711.73
  construction 690.538
  law 343.098 2
  public administration 354.765
  urban transportation services 388.474
Parking turnouts 625.77
Parkinson's disease
  medicine 616.833
  see also Nervous system
Parks 363.68
  area planning 711.558
  community redevelopment 307.346
  land economics 333.783
  landscape architecture 712.5
    reserved lands 719.32
  law 346.046 783
  public administration 353.78
  recreation centers 790.068
  social services 363.68
  see Manual at T2—4–T2—9: Physiographic features and regions
Parkways 388.122
  see also Roads
Parliamentary papers 328.4–.9
Parliamentary rules 060.42
  legislatures 328.1
Parliaments 328
Parlors 643.54
  home economics 643.54
  interior decoration 747.75
Parma (Italy : Province) T2—454 4
Parmer County (Tex.) T2—764 836
Parmesan cheese 641.373 54
  cooking 641.673 54
  food 641.373 54
  processing 637.354
Parnassiaceae 583.72
Parochial schools 371.071
Parody 808.87
  literary criticism 809.7
    theory 808.7
  literary history 809.7
  literature 808.87
    specific literatures T3B—7
  musical element 781.377
  musical form 781.826
    instrumental 784.182 6
  rhetoric 808.7
Parole 364.62
  law 345.077
  penology 364.62
  public administration 353.39
Parole administration 364.620 68
Paronym dictionaries 413.1
  specific languages T4—31
Paros Island (Greece) T2—495 85
Parotid gland
  surgery 617.522
Parramatta (N.S.W.) T2—944 1
Parrot fever (Biology)
  veterinary medicine 636.686 539
Parrot fever (Human)
  incidence 614.566
  medicine 616.958
  see also Communicable diseases (Human)
Parrotfishes 597.7
Parrots 598.71
  animal husbandry 636.686 5
  conservation technology 639.978 71
  resource economics 333.958 71
Parry Sound (Ont. : District) T2—713 15
Parseeism 295
Parsers (Computer science)
  natural languages 006.35
  programming languages 005.45
Parsi language (Dari) 491.56
  T6—915 6
Parsi language (Modern Persian) 491.55
  T6—915 5
Parsi language (Pahlavi) 491.53
  T6—915 3
Parsi literature (Dari) 891.56
Parsi literature (Modern Persian) 891.55
Parsi literature (Pahlavi) 891.53
Parsley 641.357
  botany 583.849
  see also Herbs
Parsnip River (B.C.) T2—711 82

Parsnips 641.351 4
botany 583.849
commercial processing 664.805 14
cooking 641.651 4
food 641.351 4
garden crop 635.14
Parsonages
architecture 726.9
Part songs 783.1
Part-time employment 331.257 2
personnel management 658.312 1
Part-time enterprises
management 658.041
Part-whole relationships 111.82
Part-word method (Reading)
elementary education 372.465
Parthenogenesis 571.887
Parthia T2—396
Parthian Empire 935.06
Parti québécois 324.271 409 84
Partial differential equations 515.353
Partial differential operators 515.724 2
Partial differentiation 515.33
Partially ordered sets 511.32
Participatory democracy 323.042
Participatory management 331.011 2
personnel management 658.315 2
see also Employee participation in management
Participles 415
specific languages T4—5
Particle acceleration 539.73
Particle beams 539.73
Particle board 674.836
Particle colliders 539.73
Particle mechanics
classical physics 531.16
see Manual at 530.475 vs. 530.12, 531.16
Particle physics 539.72
Particle radiation 539.72
biophysics 571.459
humans 612.014 486
nuclear physics 539.72
Particles (Grammar) 415
specific languages T4—5
Particles (Matter)
classical mechanics 531.16
meteorology 551.511 3
nuclear physics 539.72
technology 620.43
Parties
cooking 641.568
indoor amusements 793.2
interior decoration 747.93
Parties (Politics) 324.2
see also Political parties
Partisan troops 356.15
Partitas 784.185 4
Partition chromatography 543.089 2
Partitions (Building element) 721.2
architecture 721.2
construction 690.12
see also Walls (Building element)
Partitions (Mathematics)
number theory 512.73
Partitions, 1772–1795 (Poland) 943.802 5
Partnership associations 338.7
see also Unincorporated business enterprises
Partnerships 338.73
accounting 657.92
economics 338.73
law 346.068 2
income tax law 343.052 662
tax law 343.066 2
management 658.042
initiation 658.114 2
see Manual at 658.04 vs. 658.114, 658.402
Partridgeberry 583.93
Partridges 598.623
sports hunting 799.246 23
Parts of Holland (England) T2—425 39
Parts of Kesteven (England) T2—425 35
Parts of Lindsey (England) T2—425 31
Parts of speech (Grammar) 415
specific languages T4—5
Parturition
human physiology 612.63
obstetrics 618.4
disorders 618.5
Party costumes
home sewing 646.478
see also Clothing
Party finance (Politics) 324.21
Party leadership (Politics) 324.22
Party organization (Politics) 324.21
legislative bodies 328.369
political process 324.21
sociology 306.26
Parulidae 598.872
Parvoviridae 579.247

Parys (South Africa :
  District) T2—685 2
Pas (Man.) T2—712 72
Pas-de-Calais (France) T2—442 7
Pasadena (Calif.) T2—794 93
Pasargadae (Extinct city) T2—35
Pasco (Peru : Dept.) T2—852 3
Pasco County (Fla.) T2—759 69
Pashto language 491.593
  T6—915 93
Pashto literature 891.593
Pashtoon T5—915 93
Pashtun T5—915 93
Pasquotank County (N.C.) T2—756 142
Passacaglias 781.827
  instrumental 784.182 7
Passaic County (N.J.) T2—749 23
Passaic River (N.J.) T2—749 3
Passamaquoddy Indians T5—973
Passamaquoddy language 497.3
  T6—973
Passau (Germany) T2—433 55
Passementerie 677.76
  arts 746.27
Passenger automobiles 388.342
  driving 629.283
  engineering 629.222
  military engineering 623.747 2
  repair 629.287 2
  transportation services 388.342
  see also Automobiles
Passenger services 388.042
  air 387.742
    airport services 387.736 4
    international law 341.756 78
    law 343.097 8
  automobile 388.321
    urban 388.413 21
  bus 388.322
    international law 341.756 882
    law 343.094 82
    terminal services 388.33
    urban 388.413 22
      terminal services 388.473
  ferries 386.6
  ground 388.042
    international law 341.756
    law 343.093 3
  inland waterway 386.242
    international law 341.756 68
    law 343.096 8
    port services 386.862
  international law 341.756
  law 343.093 3
Passenger services (continued)
  marine 387.542
    international law 341.756 68
    law 343.096 8
    port services 387.162
  ports 387.162
  public administration 354.763
  railroad 385.22
    international law 341.756 58
    law 343.095 8
    special purpose 385.5
    terminal services 385.262
    urban 388.42
      terminal services 388.472
Passenger ships
  power-driven 387.243
    design 623.812 43
    engineering 623.824 3
  see also Merchant ships; Ships
Passenger terminals
  architecture 725.3
  area planning 711.7
  construction 690.53
  inland waterway 386.852
  ports 387.152
  railroad 385.262
Passenger-train cars 385.33
  engineering 625.23
  see also Rolling stock
Passenger transportation 388.042
  see also Passenger services
Passer sparrows 598.887
Passeres 598.8
  see Manual at 598.824–598.88
Passeriformes 598.8
  paleozoology 568.8
Passerines 598.8
Passifloraceae 583.626
  edible fruits 641.344 2
    cooking 641.644 2
    food 641.344 2
    orchard crop 634.42
Passiflorales 583.626
Passing
  American football 796.332 25
Passion fruit 641.344 25
  cooking 641.644 25
  food 641.344 25
  orchard crop 634.425
Passion of Jesus Christ 232.96
  music 782.23

Passion plays
  literature 808.825 16
    history and criticism 809.251 6
    specific literatures T3B—205 16
      individual authors T3A—2
  religious significance 246.723
  stage presentation 792.16
    see also Theater
Passionflowers 583.626
  floriculture 635.933 626
Passionists 255.62
  church history 271.62
Passiontide 263.92
  devotional literature 242.34
  music 781.725 5
  sermons 252.62
Passive resistance
  political action 322.4
  social conflict 303.61
Passive smoking
  human toxicology 615.952 395 2
  respiratory diseases 616.200 471
    see also Respiratory system
Passover 296.437
  customs 394.267
  liturgy 296.453 7
Passover Haggadah 296.453 71
Passports 323.67
  international law 341.484 2
  law 342.082
  political science 323.67
  public administration 353.13
Past lives (Occultism) 133.901 35
Pasta 641.822
  commercial processing 664.755
  cooking 641.822
Pastaza (Ecuador : Province) T2—866 42
Pasteboard 676.288
Pastel drawing 741.235
Pasteurella 579.34
Pasteurella diseases
  incidence 614.573
  medicine 616.923
  see also Communicable diseases (Human)
Pasteurization
  alcoholic beverages 663.15
  milk processing 637.141
Pastoral counseling 291.61
  Christianity 253.5
  Judaism 296.61
Pastoral Epistles 227.83
Pastoral psychology 291.61
  Christianity 253.52
Pastoral systems 636.084 5
Pastoral themes
  arts 700.421 734
    T3C—321 734
  literature 808.803 217 34
    history and criticism 809.933 217 34
    specific literatures T3B—080 321 734
      history and criticism T3B—093 217 34
Pastoral theology 291.61
  Christianity 253
  Islam 297.61
  Judaism 296.61
Pastors 270.092
  biography 270.092
    specific denominations 280
    see Manual at 230–280
  ecclesiology 262.14
  pastoral theology 253
  see also Clergy—Christian; Religious leaders
Pastries 641.865
  commercial processing 664.752 5
  home preparation 641.865
Pastry mixes 664.753
Pasture lands 333.74
  sale and rental 333.335
Pastures 633.202
Pasturing animals 636.084 5
Patagonia (Argentina and Chile) T2—827
  Argentina T2—827
  Chile T2—836 44
Patagonian weasel 599.766 3
Patañjali's philosophy 181.452
Patchwork
  arts 746.46
Patellas
  human anatomy 611.718
  see also Musculoskeletal system
Patent law 346.048 6
Patent leather 675.25
Patent medicines
  therapeutics 615.886
Patents 346.048 6
  international law 341.758 6
  law 346.048 6
  public administration 352.749
Patents (Collections) 608
  T1—027 2
Paternity 346.017 5

Paternity leave 331.257 63
  personnel management 658.312 2
Paternosters (England) T2—423 49
Pâtés 641.812
Path spaces (Mathematics) 514.224
Pathogenic microorganisms 579.165
  medical microbiology 616.01
  see Manual at 579.165 vs. 616.01
Pathogenicity 571.9
  see also Pathology
Pathological aging 571.939
Pathological anatomy 571.933
  humans 616.07
Pathological biochemistry 571.94
  human metabolic diseases 616.39
Pathological gambling
  medicine 616.858 41
  see also Mental illness
Pathological physiology 571.9
  see also Pathology
Pathological psychology 616.89
  see also Mental illness
Pathology 571.9
  cytology 571.936
    humans 611.018 15
  humans 616.07
    see Manual at 616 vs. 616.07
  surgery 617.07
  see Manual at 571–575 vs. 630
Pathophysiology 571.9
  see also Pathology
Patience 179.9
  see also Virtues
Patience (Game) 795.43
Patient compliance
  medicine 615.5
Patients' libraries 027.662
Patinating
  decorative arts 739.15
Patio furniture 645.8
  see also Outdoor furniture
Patio gardening 635.967 1
Patio lighting 621.322 9
  see also Lighting
Patios 721.84
  architecture 721.84
  construction 690.184
  domestic 643.55
    architecture 728.93
    construction 690.893
    home economics 643.55
Patmos Island (Greece) T2—495 87
Patois 417.2
  specific languages T4—7
Patriarchal family 306.858
Patriarchate 262.13
Patriarchs 200.92
  Biblical 222.110 922
  biography 200.92
  Christian 270.092
    biography 270.092
      specific denominations 280
      see Manual at 230–280
    ecclesiology 262.13
    see also Clergy—Christian
Patriarchy (System of government) 321.1
Patricia Portion (Ont.) T2—713 1
Patrick County (Va.) T2—755 695
Patrilineal kinship 306.83
Patriotic holidays 394.26
  law 344.091
  see also Holidays
Patriotic music 781.599
  songs 782.421 599
Patriotic pageants 394.5
  customs 394.5
  performing arts 791.624
Patriotic societies 369.2
  biography 369.209 2
  social group T7—369 2
Patristic philosophy 189.2
Patristics (Christianity) 270
Patrol
  military operation 355.413
  police services 363.232
Patrol boats (Military) 359.835 8
  design 623.812 58
  engineering 623.825 8
  naval equipment 359.835 8
  naval units 359.325 8
Patrol boats (Police) 363.286
  design 623.812 63
  engineering 623.826 3
  police services 363.286
Patron and client 306.2
Patronage 306.2
Patronage of individuals T1—079
Pattern lumber 674.43
Pattern perception
  visual
    psychology 152.142 3
Pattern poetry 808.814
  history and criticism 809.14
  specific literatures T3B—104

Pattern recognition
computer science 006.4
T1—028 564
engineering 621.399
Patternmaking
clothing 646.407 2
commercial technology 687.042
home sewing 646.407 2
metal casting 671.23
metal rolling 671.821
Patterns (Geometry) 516.15
Patterns (Sewing) 646.407
design 646.407 2
home sewing 646.407
Patuxent River (Md.) T2—752 4
Paucituberculata 599.27
Paul I, Emperor of Russia
Russian history 947.071
Paulatuk (N.W.T.) T2—719 6
Paulding County (Ga.) T2—758 373
Paulding County (Ohio) T2—771 17
Pauline epistles 227
Paulpietersburg (South Africa : District) T2—684 2
Pauropoda 595.64
Pauses (Linguistics) 414.6
specific languages T4—16
Pavans 793.3
music 784.188 23
Pavements
airport runways 629.136 34
road surfaces 625.8
Pavia (Italy : Province) T2—452 9
Paving roads 625.8
Pavlovian conditioning 153.152 6
Pavlovian psychological system 150.194 4
Pavo 598.625 8
Pawnbrokers 332.34
Pawnbroking 332.34
law 346.025
Pawnee County (Kan.) T2—781 49
Pawnee County (Neb.) T2—782 284
Pawnee County (Okla.) T2—766 26
Pawnee Indians T5—979
Pawns (Chess) 794.142
Pay-cable television 384.555 4
see also Television
see Manual at 384.555 vs. 384.5554
Pay differentials 331.22
see Manual at 331.29 vs. 331.22
Pay equity 331.215 3
law 344.012 153
Pay telephones
engineering 621.386 9
Pay television 384.555
see also Television
see Manual at 384.555 vs. 384.5554
Pay television (Canada) 384.555 4
see also Television
Payette County (Idaho) T2—796 24
Payments in lieu of taxes
public finance 336.185
Payne County (Okla.) T2—766 34
Payroll accounting 657.74
Payroll administration 658.321
armed forces 355.64
public administration 352.47
Payroll tax 336.242 2
law 343.052 42
public finance 336.242 2
Pays de la Loire (France) T2—441 6
Pays-d'en-Haut (Quebec) T2—714 24
Paysandú (Uruguay : Dept.) T2—895 31
Paz (Bolivia : Dept.) T2—841 2
Paz (El Salvador : Dept.) T2—728 425
Paz (Honduras : Dept.) T2—728 36
Pazardzhik (Bulgaria : Okrŭg) T2—499 7
Pazardzhishki okrŭg (Bulgaria) T2—499 7
PCB (Chemical)
human toxicology 615.951 2
PCP abuse 362.294
medicine 616.863 4
personal health 613.83
social welfare 362.294
see also Substance abuse
PDA (Computer) 004.16
see also Microcomputers
Pea beans 641.356 52
see also Kidney beans
Peace 303.66
arts 700.458
T3C—358
ethics 172.42
religion 291.562 42
Christianity 241.624 2
Islam 297.562 42
international law 341.73
international politics 327.172
literature 808.803 58
history and criticism 809.933 58
specific literatures T3B—080 358
history and criticism T3B—093 58

Peace (continued)
  social theology 291.178 73
    Buddhism 294.337 873
    Christianity 261.873
    Hinduism 294.517 873
    Islam 297.27
    Judaism 296.382 7
Peace conferences 341.73
Peace Corps (U.S.) 361.6
Peace movements 327.172
  sociology 303.66
Peace pipe 399
Peace River (Alta.) T2—712 31
Peace River (B.C. and Alta.) T2—712 31
  Alberta T2—712 31
  British Columbia T2—711 87
Peace River (B.C. : Region) T2—711 87
Peace River (Fla.) T2—759 57
Peace River-Liard (B.C.) T2—711 87
Peace treaties 341.66
Peaceful occupation
  international law 341.722
Peaceful settlement of disputes 303.69
  international law 341.52
  international relations 327.17
  sociology 303.69
Peacekeeping forces 355.357
  international law 341.584
Peach County (Ga.) T2—758 556
Peaches 641.342 5
  botany 583.73
  commercial processing 664.804 25
  cooking 641.642 5
  food 641.342 5
  orchard crop 634.25
Peafowl 598.625 8
  animal husbandry 636.595
Pe'ah 296.123 1
  Mishnah 296.123 1
  Palestinian Talmud 296.124 1
Peak District (England) T2—425 11
Peanut flour 664.726
Peanut meal 664.726
Peanut worms 592.35
Peanuts 641.356 596
  agricultural economics 338.175 659 6
  botany 583.74
  commercial processing
    economics 338.476 648 056596
    technology 664.805 659 6
  cooking 641.656 596
  field crop 633.368
Peanuts (continued)
  food 641.356 596
  garden crop 635.659 6
Pearl Harbor, Attack on, 1941 940.542 6
Pearl oysters
  culture 639.412
Pearl River (Miss. and La.) T2—762 5
Pearl River County (Miss.) T2—762 15
Pearlfishes 597.63
Pears 641.341 3
  botany 583.73
  commercial processing 664.804 13
  cooking 641.641 3
  food 641.341 3
  orchard crop 634.13
Pearson, Lester B.
  Canadian history 971.064 3
Pearston (South Africa : District) T2—687 14
Peas 641.356 5
  botany 583.74
  commercial processing 664.805 65
  cooking 641.656 5
  field crop 633.3
  food 641.356 5
  garden crop 635.65
Peas (Pisum sativum) 641.356 56
  botany 583.74
  commercial processing 664.805 656
  cooking 641.656 56
  food 641.356 56
  garden crop 635.656
Peasants 305.563 3
  T1—088 63
Peasants' War, 1524–1525 943.031
Peat 553.21
  economic geology 553.21
  mining 622.331
  properties 662.622 1
  use as soil conditioner 631.826
Peat bogs
  biology 578.768 7
  ecology 577.687
  see also Wetlands
Peat coal 553.21
  see also Peat
Peat mosses 588.29
Peatlands
  biology 578.768 7
  ecology 577.687
  see also Wetlands
Pecans 641.345 2
  agriculture 634.52
  botany 583.49

Pecans (continued)
  cooking 641.645 2
  food 641.345 2
Peccaries 599.634
Pecopteris 561.597
Pecos County (Tex.) T2—764 923
Pecos River (N.M. and Tex.) T2—764 9
  New Mexico T2—789 4
  Texas T2—764 9
Pectins 572.566
  biochemistry 572.566
  chemistry 547.782
  food technology 664.25
  see also Carbohydrates
Pedaliaceae 583.95
Pedaling
  music 784.193 8
Peddie (South Africa : District) T2—687 92
Pedernales (Dominican Republic : Province) T2—729 323
Pedestals 721.3
  architecture 721.3
  construction 690.13
Pedestrian facilities 388.41
  area planning 711.74
  landscape architecture 717
  use 388.41
Pedestrian malls 388.411
  area planning 711.74
  landscape architecture 717
Pedestrian paths 388.12
  area planning 711.74
  use 388.12
    local 388.411
Pedestrian traffic 388.41
  law 343.098 1
Pedi (African people) T5—963 977 1
Pedi language 496.397 71
  T6—963 977 1
Pediatric cardiology 618.921 2
  see also Cardiovascular system
Pediatric disorders
  incidence 614.599 292
  medicine 618.92
Pediatric gynecology 618.920 98
  see also Female genital system
Pediatric nursing
  medicine 610.736 2
Pediatric preventive measures 613.043 2
Pediatric services 362.198 92
  see also Health services
Pediatric surgery 617.98
Pediatric therapeutics 615.542
Pediatricians 618.920 009 2
  occupational group T7—618 9
  role and function 618.920 023 2
Pediatrics 618.92
  see Manual at 616 vs. 618.92; *also at* 618.92097 vs. 617
Pedicuring 646.727
Pedigrees
  animal husbandry 636.082 2
Pediments 721.5
  architecture 721.5
  construction 690.15
Pedodontics 617.645
  see also Dentistry
Pee Dee River (N.C. and S.C.) T2—757 8
Peeblesshire (Scotland) T2—413 82
Peel (Ont. : Regional municipality) T2—713 535
Peer counseling of students 371.404 7
Peer group
  influence on crime 364.253
  socialization 303.327
Peer review
  health services 362.106 8
Peerage
  genealogy 929.7
Pegasiformes 597.64
Pegmatite dikes 553.16
  determinative mineralogy 549.116
Peiping (China) T2—511 56
Peking (China) T2—511 56
Peking man 569.9
Pekingese (Dog) 636.76
Pelagian Islands T2—458 22
Pelagianism 273.5
Pelargoniums 635.933 79
  botany 583.79
  floriculture 635.933 79
Pelecaniformes 598.43
  paleozoology 568.4
Pelecanoididae 598.42
Pelicans 598.43
Pella (Greece : Nome) T2—495 65
Pellagra
  medicine 616.393
  see also Digestive system
Pelly Bat (N.W.T.) T2—719 7
Pelobatoidea 597.86
Peloncillo Mountains (Ariz. and N.M.) T2—789 693

Peloponnesian War, 431–404 B.C. 938.05
Peloponnēsos (Greece) T2—495 2
Peloponnēsos (Greece : Periphereia) T2—495 22
Peloponnesus (Greece) T2—495 2
ancient T2—386
Peloponnesus (Greece : Periphereia) T2—495 22
Pelvic bone
medicine 616.71
see also Musculoskeletal system
Pelvic muscles
human anatomy 611.736
see also Musculoskeletal system
Pelvic region
human anatomy 611.96
human physiology 612.96
regional medicine 617.55
surgery 617.55
Pelycosauria 567.93
Pemba (Tanzania) 967.81
T2—678 1
Pemba North (Tanzania) T2—678 1
Pemba South (Tanzania) T2—678 1
Pemberton (B.C.) T2—711 31
Pembina County (N.D.) T2—784 19
Pembrokeshire (Wales) T2—429 62
Pemiscot County (Mo.) T2—778 996
Pemón language 498.4
T6—984
Pen-and-ink drawing 741.26
P'en ching 635.977 2
Pen computers 004.16
see also Microcomputers
Penal colonies 365.34
see also Correctional institutions
Penal institutions 365
see also Correctional institutions
Penal reform 364.6
Penalties
personnel management 658.314 4
Penance 291.34
Christianity 234.166
public worship 265.6
theology 234.166
Penang T2—595 1
Penas 787.6
see also Stringed instruments
Pencil drawing 741.24
Pencil fishes 597.48
Pencils
wood-cased 674.88
Pend Oreille County (Wash.) T2—797 21
Pende (African people) T5—963 93
Pende languages 496.393
T6—963 93
Pender County (N.C.) T2—756 25
Pendle (England) T2—427 645
Pendleton County (Ky.) T2—769 33
Pendleton County (W. Va.) T2—754 91
Pendulum motion 531.324
Pendulums 531.324
clockworks 681.112
dowsing 133.323
fortune-telling 133.3
Penetration
materials science 620.112 6
Penguins 598.47
Penicillin
pharmacology 615.329 565 4
Penicillium 579.565 4
Peninsular Malaysia T2—595 1
Peninsular War, 1807–1814 940.27
Penis 573.656
biology 573.656
human anatomy 611.64
human physiology 612.61
medicine 616.66
see also Male genital system
Penitentiaries 365.34
see also Correctional institutions
Penjing 635.977 2
Penmanship 652.1
elementary education 372.634
Pennines (England) T2—428
Pennington County (Minn.) T2—776 965
Pennington County (S.D.) T2—783 93
Pennsylvania 974.8
T2—748
Pennsylvania Dutch T5—310 748
Pennsylvania Dutch dialect 437.974 8
T6—38
Pennsylvania German dialect 437.974 8
T6—38
Pennsylvania Germans T5—310 748
Pennsylvanian period 551.752
geology 551.752
paleontology 560.175 2
Penny stocks 332.632 23
speculation 332.632 28

Penny whistles 788.35
 see also Woodwind instruments
Pennyroyal (Ky.) T2—769 6
Penobscot County (Me.) T2—741 3
Penobscot River (Me.) T2—741 3
Penology 364.6
 public administration 353.39
Penrith (N.S.W.) T2—944 1
Pens (Writing)
 manufacturing technology 681.6
Pensacola (Fla.) T2—759 99
Pension funds
 investments by 332.671 54
  domestic 332.672 54
Pension reform 331.252 2
 see also Pensions
Pension trusts
 tax law 343.064
Pensions 331.252
 accounting 657.75
 annuities
  insurance 368.37
 economics 331.252
 law 344.012 52
 personnel management 658.325 3
  executives 658.407 253
 public administration 353.54
 social security 368.43
Penstemon 635.933 95
 botany 583.95
 floriculture 635.933 95
Penstocks
 dam engineering 627.882
Pentaerythritol tetranitrate 662.27
Pentane 665.773
Pentastomida 592.76
Pentateuch 222.1
Pentatonicism 781.265
Pentecost 263.94
 devotional literature 242.38
 Jewish 296.438
  liturgy 296.453 8
 music 781.729 3
 sermons 252.64
Pentecostal churches 289.94
 see also Christian denominations
Pentecostalism 270.82
 independent denominations 289.94
 Protestantism 280.4
Pentecostals
 biography 289.940 92
 religious group T7—289
Penthouse gardens
 landscape architecture 712.6
Penticton (B.C.) T2—711 5
Pentland Hills (Scotland) T2—413 5
Penutian languages 497.41
 T6—974 1
Penutian peoples T5—974 1
Penwith (England) T2—423 75
Penza (Russia : Oblast) T2—474 6
Penzenskaîa oblast′ (Russia) T2—474 6
Peonies 635.933 62
 botany 583.62
 floriculture 635.933 62
Peons 305.56
 T1—086 25
People movers
 engineering 621.868
People of God (Church) 262.7
People's Democratic Republic of Korea 951.93
 T2—519 3
People's Party of America 324.273 27
People's Republic of China T2—51
Peoria County (Ill.) T2—773 52
Peperomias 583.25
Pepin County (Wis.) T2—775 47
Pepos 641.356 1
 see also Melons
Pepper-shrikes 598.878
Pepperbushes 583.66
Peppers 641.338 4
 botany 583.952
 see also Hot spices; Sweet peppers
Peppers (Piperaceae) 641.338 4
 botany 583.25
 see also Hot spices
Peppers (Solanaceae) 641.338 4
 botany 583.952
 food 641.338 4
  hot peppers 641.338 4
  sweet peppers 641.356 43
 see also Hot spices; Sweet peppers
Peppertype processes 773.2
Peptic ulcers
 medicine 616.343
 see also Digestive system
Peptides 572.65
 biochemistry 572.65
 chemistry 547.756
 see also Proteins

Peptones 572.65
  biochemistry 572.65
  chemistry 547.756
  see also Proteins
Pequot War, 1636–1638 973.22
Peracarida 595.37
  paleozoology 565.37
Perak T2—595 1
Peramelidae 599.26
Peramelina 599.26
Peravia (Dominican Republic : Province) T2—729 373
Percentage 513.24
Percentage renting
  agricultural land economics 333.335 563
  land economics 333.563
Perception 153.7
  educational psychology 370.155
  epistemology 121.34
  psychology 153.7
    sensory 152.1
  see Manual at 153.7 vs. 152.1
Perception theory 003.52
  T1—011 52
  computer pattern recognition 006.4
Perceptrons 006.32
Perch trout 597.73
Percheron horse 636.15
Perches 597.75
  sports fishing 799.177 5
Perching birds 598.8
Percichthyidae 597.73
Percidae 597.75
Perciformes 597.7
  paleozoology 567.7
Percoidea 597.72
Percoidei 597.7
Percolation (Statistical physics) 530.13
Percolation theory 530.13
Percopsiformes 597.62
Percussed idiophones 786.84
  set 786.84
  single 786.884
  see also Percussion instruments
Percussion bands 784.68
Percussion caps 662.4
  military engineering 623.454 2
Percussion ensembles 785.68
Percussion instruments 786.8
  bands and orchestras 784
  chamber ensembles 785
    mixed 785.2–.5
    single type 785.68
Percussion instruments (continued)
  construction 786.819 23
    by hand 786.819 23
    by machine 681.868
  solo music 786.8
  see Manual at 784–788
Perdix perdix 598.623 2
Pereira, Aristides
  Cape Verdean history 966.580 31
Perennials (Plants) 582.16
  floriculture 635.932
Perfect binding
  bookbinding 686.35
Perfectionism
  ethical systems 171.3
  personality trait 155.232
Perforating tools 621.95
Performance (Law) 346.022
Performance art 700
  fine arts 702.81
Performance auditing 658.401 3
  public administration 352.43
Performance audits 658.401 3
  public administration 352.439
Performance contracting
  students 371.393
  teachers 371.15
Performance evaluation
  computer science 004.029 7
    engineering 621.390 297
    for design and improvement 004.24
      engineering 621.392
    see Manual at 004.24
  executive management 658.401 3
    military services 355.685
    public administration 352.35
Performance evaluation of employees 658.312 5
  public administration 352.66
Performance rating
  personnel management 658.312 5
    executives 658.407 125
Performance scores 780
  treatises 780.264
Performance standards
  commerce 389.63
  production management 658.562
Performance techniques
  music 781.43
Performance tests
  automotive vehicles 629.282 4

Performances 790.2
  music 780.78
  see also Public performances
Performers (Entertainers) 791.092
  occupational group T7—791
  see Manual at 791.092
Performing arts 790.2
  public administrative support 353.77
  see Manual at 780.079 vs. 790.2
Performing arts centers
  architecture 725.83
  area planning 711.558
Perfume-producing plants
  agriculture 633.81
  economic botany 581.636
Perfumes 668.54
  customs 391.63
Pergamum (Turkey) T2—392 1
Pericardium 573.172 5
  biology 573.172 5
  human anatomy 611.11
  human physiology 612.17
  medicine 616.11
  see also Cardiovascular system
Peridotites 552.3
Peridural anesthesia
  surgery 617.964
Perimetrium 573.667 25
  gynecology 618.13
  human physiology 612.62
  see also Female genital system
Perinatal medicine 618.32
Perinatology 618.32
Perineum
  human anatomy 611.96
  human physiology 612.96
  surgery 617.555
Period costumes
  home sewing 646.478
  see also Clothing
Period furniture 749.2
Period novels 808.838 1
  history and criticism 809.381
  specific literatures T3B—308 1
    individual authors T3A—3
Periodic law 541.24
Periodic table 546.8
Periodicals 050
  T1—05
  see also Serials
Periodicity (Biology) 571.77
Periodicity (Chemistry) 541.24
Periodontics 617.632
  see also Dentistry
Periodontitis
  dentistry 617.632
  see also Dentistry
Periosteum 573.762 5
  human histology 611.018 4
  see also Musculoskeletal system
Periostitis
  medicine 616.712
  see also Musculoskeletal system
Peripheral control units 004.64
  engineering 621.398 1
Peripheral nerves 573.85
  human physiology 612.81
  medicine 616.87
  see also Nervous system
Peripheral vascular diseases
  medicine 616.131
  see also Cardiovascular system
Peripherals (Computer) 004.7
  T1—028 547
  engineering 621.398 4
Perischoechinoidea 593.95
Periscopes 623.46
Perissodactyla 599.66
  paleozoology 569.66
Peritoneal dialysis
  medicine 617.461 059
  see also Urinary system
Peritoneum 573.325
  human anatomy 611.38
  human physiology 612.33
  medicine 616.38
  surgery 617.558
  see also Digestive system
Peritonitis
  puerperal diseases
    obstetrics 618.73
Periuterine diseases
  gynecology 618.13
  see also Female genital system
Periwinkles (Plants)
  botany 583.93
Perjury 364.134
  law 345.023 4
Perkins County (Neb.) T2—782 88
Perkins County (S.D.) T2—783 45
Perlis T2—595 1
Perm´ (Russia : Oblast) T2—474 3

Permafrost 551.384
  engineering geology 624.151 36
Permanent deformation 531.385
  materials science 620.112 33
  see also Plasticity
Permanent education 374
  T1—071 5
  see also Adult education
Permanent magnetic fields (Earth) 538.72
Permanent-mold casting
  metals 671.253
Permanent waving 646.724
Permanent way (Railroad) 385.312
  engineering 625.1
  transportation services 385.312
Permeability
  foundation soils 624.151 36
Permiaks T5—945 3
Permian languages 494.53
  T6—945 3
Permian literatures 894.53
Permian period 551.756
  geology 551.756
  paleontology 560.175 6
Permians T5—945 3
Permic languages 494.53
  T6—945 3
Permic literatures 894.53
Permiculture 631.58
Permskaîa oblast′ (Russia) T2—474 3
Permutation groups 512.2
Permutations (Mathematics) 511.64
  algebra 512.925
  arithmetic 513.25
Pernambuco (Brazil) T2—813 4
Pernik (Bulgaria : Okrŭg) T2—499 8
Pernin shorthand system 653.425
Pernishki okrŭg (Bulgaria) T2—499 8
Peromyscus 599.355
Perón, Isabel
  Argentine history 982.064
Perón, Juan Domingo
  Argentine history 982.062
    1946–1955 982.062
    1973–1974 982.064
Perón, María Estela
  Argentine history 982.064
Peronosporales 579.546
Perouse Strait 551.465 53
  T2—164 53
Peroxidation
  chemical engineering 660.284 43
  organic chemistry 547.23
Peroxisomes 571.655
Perquimans County (N.C.) T2—756 144
Perry County (Ala.) T2—761 44
Perry County (Ark.) T2—767 39
Perry County (Ill.) T2—773 93
Perry County (Ind.) T2—772 29
Perry County (Ky.) T2—769 173
Perry County (Miss.) T2—762 175
Perry County (Mo.) T2—778 694
Perry County (Ohio) T2—771 59
Perry County (Pa.) T2—748 45
Perry County (Tenn.) T2—768 38
Persecutions (Christian church history) 272
Persepolis (Iran) T2—35
Pershing County (Nev.) T2—793 53
Persia T2—55
  ancient T2—35
Persian cat 636.832
Persian Empire 935.05
  Egyptian history 932.016
  Mesopotamian history 935.05
  Palestinian history 933.03
Persian Gulf 551.467 35
  T2—165 35
Persian Gulf (Iran : Province) T2—557 5
Persian Gulf States 953.6
  T2—536
Persian Gulf War, 1980–1988 955.054 2
Persian Gulf War, 1991 956.704 42
Persian language 491.55
  T6—915 5
Persian literature 891.55
Persian rugs
  arts 746.755
  see also Rugs
Persian Wars, 500–479 B.C. 938.03
Persians T5—915 5
Persimmons 641.344 5
  botany 583.674
  cooking 641.644 5
  food 641.344 5
  orchard crop 634.45
Persistence
  insurance 368.016
Person County (N.C.) T2—756 573
Person of Jesus Christ 232.8
Personal actions (Law) 347.053
Personal analysis
  applied psychology 158.1
Personal appearance 646.7
  customs 391.6

Personal appearance (continued)
  ethics 177.4
    see also Ethical problems
Personal beauty
  arts 700.453
    T3C—353
Personal budgets
  home economics 640.42
Personal cleanliness 613.4
  customs 391.64
  grooming 646.71
  health 613.4
Personal computers 004.16
  see also Microcomputers
Personal conduct
  public administrative control 353.37
Personal counseling
  education 371.46
  see also Counseling
Personal digital assistants 004.16
  see also Microcomputers
Personal efficiency
  business 650.1
    executives 658.409 3
Personal exemptions
  customs duties 382.782
    see also Customs (Tariff)
Personal finance 332.024
  see Manual at 332.024 vs. 640.42
Personal fulfillment
  ethical systems 171.3
Personal grooming 646.7
Personal grooming accessories
  manufacturing technology 688.5
Personal health 613
Personal hygiene 613
Personal improvement
  applied psychology 158.1
Personal income
  macroeconomics 339.32
    distribution 339.22
    see Manual at 339.32 vs. 339.22
Personal income tax 336.242
  law 343.052 62
  public administration 352.44
  public finance 336.242
Personal injury (Law) 346.032 3
Personal liability insurance 368.56
  see also Insurance
Personal liberty 323.44
  see also Liberty (Personal freedom)
Personal living 646.7
Personal loans 332.743
Personal names 929.4
Personal narratives
  Chaco War 989.207 160 92
  Civil War (England) 942.062 092
  Civil War (United States) 973.781–.782
  Crimean War 947.073 809 2
  Franco-German War 943.082 092
  Hundred Years' War 944.025 092
  Indo-Pakistan War, 1971 954.920 510 92
  Indochinese War 959.704 109 2
  Iraqi-Iranian Conflict 955.054 209 2
  Korean War 951.904 209 2
  Mexican War 973.620 92
  South African War 968.048 092
  Spanish-American War 973.890 92
  Thirty Years' War 940.240 92
  United States Revolutionary War 973.309 2
  Vietnamese War 959.704 309 2
  War of 1812 973.520 92
  War of the Pacific 983.061 609 2
  World War I 940.481–.482
  World War II 940.548 1–.548 2
  see Manual at 930–990: Wars: Personal narratives
Personal property
  international law 341.48
  law 346.047
    private ownership 346.047
    public ownership 343.023
Personal property tax 336.23
  law 343.054
  public administration 352.44
  public finance 336.23
Personal religion 291.4
  Buddhism 294.344
  Christianity 240
  Hinduism 294.54
  Islam 297.57
    Sufi 297.4
  Judaism 296.7
Personal risks 368.07
Personal safety 613.6
    T1—028 9
Personal security
  civil rights issues 323.43
Personal selling
  management 658.85
    T1—068 8
  retail commerce 381.1
Personal shorthand 653.18

Personal space
  sociology 304.23
Personal survival
  occultism 133.901 3
  see Manual at 133.9013 vs. 129
Personales 583.95
Personalism
  philosophy 141.5
Personality 155.2
  applied psychology 158.1
  children 155.418 2
  educational psychology 370.153
  folklore 398.27
    history and criticism 398.353
  late adulthood 155.671 82
  philosophy 126
  sex psychology 155.32
Personality (Law) 346.012
Personality assessment 155.28
Personality disorders
  medicine 616.858
  see also Mental illness
Personality inventories 155.283
Personality tests 155.28
Personality types 155.26
Personalized reading instruction
  elementary education 372.417
Personifications (Religion) 291.214
Personnel
  libraries 023
  museums 069.63
  office services 651.3
Personnel administration 658.3
  see also Personnel management
Personnel information
  management 658.301
Personnel management 658.3
  T1—068 3
  armed forces 355.61
  executives 658.407
  libraries 023
  museums 069.63
  public administration 352.6
  schools 371.201
    higher education 378.11
  see Manual at 331 vs. 658.3; *also at* 658.3 and T1—0683
Personnel planning 658.301
Personnel policy 658.301
Personnel selection
  management 658.311 2
Personnel transports
  military engineering 623.746 5
Personnel utilization
  management 658.312 8
  public administration 352.66
Persons T1—092
  T2—2
  arts 700.451
    T3C—351
    see Manual at T3C—353–T3C—358 vs. T3C—352
  biography 920
  folklore 398.22
    history and criticism 398.352
  individuals T1—092
    collected T1—092 2
    see Manual at T1—092
  international law 341.48
  kinds T1—08
    government programs 353.53
      see Manual at 353.53 vs. 352.1
    see Manual at T1—08
  law 346.012
  literature 808.803 51
    history and criticism 809.933 51
    specific literatures T3B—080 351
      history and criticism T3B—093 51
  objects of worship 291.213
Persoonia 583.89
Perspective
  arts 701.82
  technical drawing 604.245
Perspiration
  human physiology 612.792 1
  see also Skin
Persuasion 303.342
  logic 168
  political science 320.014
  psychology 153.852
  rhetoric 808
  social process 303.342
PERT (Network analysis) 658.403 2
Perth (Ont. : County) T2—713 23
Perth (W.A.) T2—941 1
Perth and Kinross (Scotland) T2—412 8
Perturbation theory 515.35
Perturbations
  celestial mechanics 521.4
Pertussis
  incidence 614.543
  medicine 616.204

Pertussis (continued)
  pediatrics 618.922 04
  see also Respiratory system
Peru 985
  T2—85
Peru-Bolivian Confederation 984.044
  Bolivian history 984.044
  Peruvian history 985.05
Peru Current 551.476 1
Perugia (Italy : Province) T2—456 51
Peruvian lily 635.934 34
  botany 584.34
  floriculture 635.934 34
Peruvian literature 860
Peruvians T5—688 5
Pesach 296.437
  customs 394.267
  liturgy 296.453 7
Pesaḥim 296.123 2
  Babylonian Talmud 296.125 2
  Mishnah 296.123 2
  Palestinian Talmud 296.124 2
Pesaro e Urbino (Italy : Province) T2—456 77
Pescara (Italy : Province) T2—457 17
Peshawar District (Pakistan) T2—549 123
Pessimism
  philosophy 149.6
Pest control 363.78
  agriculture 632.9
    see Manual at 632.95 vs. 632.2–632.8
  conservation technology 639.966
  control technology 628.96
  disease carriers
    medicine 614.43
  household sanitation 648.7
  law 344.046
  public administration 354.339
  social welfare 363.78
Pest Megye (Hungary) T2—439 1
Pest resistance
  materials science 620.112 2
Pest-resistant construction 693.84
Pesticide pollution 363.738 4
  see also Pesticides—pollution
Pesticide resistance
  agriculture 632.950 42
Pesticides 668.65
  adverse effects
    agriculture 632.950 42
    bee keeping 638.159
    wildlife conservation 639.969
Pesticides (continued)
  agricultural use 632.95
    see Manual at 632.95 vs. 632.2–632.8
  chemical engineering 668.65
  human toxicology 615.902
  pest control technology 628.96
  pollution 363.738 4
    ecology 577.279
    environmental engineering 628.529
    law 344.046 334
    see also Pollution
  public safety 363.179 2
    see also Hazardous materials
  toxicology 571.959
  water pollution engineering 628.168 42
Pests 591.65
  agriculture 632.6
    see Manual at 632.2–632.8
  see also Pest control
PET (Tomography) 616.075 75
Pet food 636.088 7
  animal husbandry 636.088 7
  manufacturing technology 664.66
Pet names 929.97
Petals 575.69
Petauridae 599.23
Petén (Guatemala : Dept.) T2—728 12
Peter (Biblical books) 227.92
Peter I, Emperor of Russia
  Russian history 947.05
Peter II, Emperor of Russia
  Russian history 947.061
Peter III, Emperor of Russia
  Russian history 947.062
Peter Lougheed Provincial Park (Alta.) T2—712 332
Peterborough (England : District) T2—426 51
Peterborough (Ont.) T2—713 67
Peterborough (Ont. : County) T2—713 67
Petersburg (Va.) T2—755 581
Petit basset griffon vendén 636.753 6
Petition
  civil right 323.48
PETN (Explosives) 662.27
Petorca (Chile : Province) T2—832 48
Petra (Extinct city) 939.48
  T2—394 8
Petrels 598.42
Petri nets 511.3

Petrified Forest National
Park (Ariz.) T2—791 37
Petrified wood 561.16
Petrochemicals
chemical engineering 661.804
human toxicology 615.951
Petrogenesis 552.03
Petroglyphs 709.011 3
Petrography 552
Petrolatum 665.538 5
Petroleum 553.28
chemistry 547.83
dowsing 133.323 7
economic geology 553.28
extraction 622.338
equipment manufacturing
technology 681.766 5
extractive economics 338.272 8
law 343.077 2
pipeline transportation 388.55
processing 665.5
economics 338.476 655
enterprises 338.766 55
prospecting 622.182 8
public administration 354.45
resource economics 333.823
law 346.046 823
Petroleum chemicals
chemical engineering 661.804
Petroleum coke 665.538 8
Petroleum County (Mont.) T2—786 28
Petroleum engineers 665.509 2
occupational group T7—665
Petroleum gas 665.773
Petroleum geology 553.28
Petroleum industry 338.272 8
law 343.077 2
Petrologists 552.009 2
occupational group T7—552
Petrology 552
see Manual at 552 vs. 549
Petrusburg (South Africa :
District) T2—685 7
Pets 636.088 7
see Manual at 800 vs.
398.245, 590, 636
Pettis County (Mo.) T2—778 48
Petty officers 359.009 2
role and function 359.338
Petunias 635.933 952
botany 583.952
floriculture 635.933 952
Pews 247.1
architecture 726.529 3
Pewter
decorative arts 739.533
Pezizales 579.578
pH 541.372 8
chemical engineering 660.297 28
Phacidiales 579.57
Phaeophyceae 579.88
Phaeophyta 579.88
Phaethontidae 598.43
Phages 579.26
Phagocytes 571.968
human immunology 616.079 9
Phalaborwa (South Africa :
District) T2—682 6
Phalacrocoracidae 598.43
Phalaenopsis 584.4
floriculture 635.934 4
Phalanger 599.232
Phalangeridae 599.232
Phalangeroidea 599.23
Phalanges
human anatomy 611.718
see also Musculoskeletal
system
Phalangida 595.43
Phalansterianism (Socialist
school)
economics 335.23
Phalanxes (Military units) 355.31
Phalarideae 584.9
Phalaropes 598.33
Phalaropodidae 598.33
Phallales 579.599
Phanarists
Romanian history 949.801 5
Phanerites 552.3
Phanerozoic eon 551.7
Phanerozonia 593.93
paleozoology 563.93
Phantasms 133.14
Pharaoh hound 636.753 6
Phareae 584.9
Pharisees 296.812
Pharmaceutical chemistry 615.19
Pharmaceutical drugs 615.1
see also Drugs
(Pharmaceuticals)
Pharmaceutical industry 338.476 151
Pharmaceutical services
insurance 368.382 4
see also Insurance
social welfare 362.178 2
see also Health services

Pharmacists 615.109 2
  law 344.041 6
  occupational group T7—615
Pharmacodynamics 615.7
  see Manual at 615.1 vs. 615.7; *also at* 615.2–615.3 vs. 615.7; *also at* 615.7 vs. 615.9; *also at* 616–618 vs. 615.7
Pharmacognosy 615.321
Pharmacokinetics 615.7
Pharmacologists 615.109 2
  occupational group T7—615
Pharmacology 615.1
  veterinary medicine 636.089 51
  see Manual at 615; *also at* 615.1 vs. 615.7
Pharmacopoeias 615.11
Pharmacy 615.1
  law 344.041 6
  see Manual at 615.1 vs. 615.4
Pharyngeal diseases
  medicine 616.32
  surgery 617.532
  see also Digestive system
Pharynx
  human anatomy 611.32
  human physiology 612.31
  medicine 616.32
  surgery 617.532
  see also Digestive system
Phascolarctidae 599.25
Phase changes 530.474
  see also Phase transformations
Phase diagrams 530.474
  metallurgy 669.94
  see also Phase transformations
Phase equilibria 530.474
  see also Phase transformations
Phase-locked loops
  electronic circuits 621.381 536 4
Phase modulators
  electronic circuits 621.381 536 4
Phase stability 530.474
  see also Phase transformations
Phase transformations 530.474
  chemical engineering 660.296 3
  fluid-state physics 530.424
  physics 530.474
  solid-state physics 530.414
  thermochemistry 541.363
  see Manual at 536.4 vs. 530.474
Phase transitions 530.474
  see also Phase transformations
Phasemeters 621.374 9
Phases
  moon 523.32
Phasianidae 598.62
Phasianus colchicus 598.625 2
Phasmatodea 595.729
Phasmida 595.729
Pheasants 598.625
  animal husbandry 636.594
  conservation technology 639.978 625
  resource economics 333.958 625
  sports hunting 799.246 25
Phelps County (Mo.) T2—778 594
Phelps County (Neb.) T2—782 392
Phencyclidine abuse 362.294
  medicine 616.863 4
  personal health 613.83
  social welfare 362.294
  see also Substance abuse
Phenolics 668.422 2
Phenology 578.42
Phenols 547.632
  chemical engineering 661.82
Phenomenalism 142.7
Phenomenological psychology 150.192
Phenomenology 142.7
Phenotypes 576.53
Phenylketonuria
  medicine 616.399
  see also Digestive system
Phigalia (Extinct city) T2—388
Philadelphia (Pa.) T2—748 11
Philadelphia County (Pa.) T2—748 11
Philanthropists 361.740 92
  social group T7—361
Philanthropy
  ethics 177.7
    see also Ethical problems
  social welfare 361.74
Philately 769.56
Philemon (Biblical book) 227.86
Philesiaceae 584.35
Philinoglossacea 594.34
Philip I, King of France
  French history 944.022
Philip II, King of France
  French history 944.023
Philip II, King of Spain
  Spanish history 946.043
Philip III, King of France
  French history 944.024

Philip III, King of Spain
  Spanish history 946.051
Philip IV, King of France
  French history 944.024
Philip IV, King of Spain
  Spanish history 946.052
Philip V, King of France
  French history 944.024
Philip V, King of Spain
  Spanish history 946.055
Philip VI, King of France
  French history 944.025
Philippians (Biblical book) 227.6
Philippine-American War, 1898–1901 959.903 1
Philippine Independent Church 284.8
  see also Old Catholic churches
Philippine languages 499.21
  T6—992 1
Philippine literatures 899.21
Philippine people T5—992 1
Philippine Sea 551.465 58
  T2—164 58
Philippines 959.9
  T2—599
Philippolis (South Africa : District) T2—685 7
Philipstown (South Africa : District) T2—687 13
Phillip Island (Vic.) T2—945 2
Phillips County (Ark.) T2—767 88
Phillips County (Colo.) T2—788 77
Phillips County (Kan.) T2—781 17
Phillips County (Mont.) T2—786 16
Philodendrons 635.934 64
  botany 584.64
  floriculture 635.934 64
Philologists 409.2
  linguistics specialists 410.92
  occupational group T7—4
Philology 400
  linguistics 410
  see Manual at 400 vs. 800
Philosophers 180–190
  ancient 180
  medieval western 189
  modern 190
  occupational group T7—11
  Oriental 181
  see Manual at 180–190
Philosopher's stone 540.112
  folklore 398.26
    history and criticism 398.465
Philosophical anthropology 128
Philosophy 100
  T1—01
  literature 808.803 84
    history and criticism 809.933 84
    specific literatures T3B—080 384
      history and criticism T3B—093 84
  see Manual at T1—01; *also at* 190 vs. 100, 109; *also at* 200 vs. 100
Philosophy and religion 291.175
  Christianity 261.51
  Islam 297.261
  Judaism 296.371
Philosophy of nature 113
Philosophy of religion 210
Philosophy of science 501
Philydraceae 584.35
Phiomorpha 599.359
Phlebitis
  medicine 616.142
  see also Cardiovascular system
Phlebotomy
  diagnosis
    general disease 616.075 61
  therapeutics 615.899
Phloem 575.452
Phlogiston theory 540.118
Phlorina (Greece : Nome) T2—495 62
Phloxes 635.933 94
  botany 583.94
  floriculture 635.933 94
Phobias
  medicine 616.852 25
  see also Mental illness
Phoca 599.792
Phocidae 599.79
Phocis (Greece) T2—495 15
  ancient T2—383
Phocoenidae 599.539
Phoenicia 939.44
  T2—394 4
Phoenician architecture 722.31
Phoenician language 492.6
  T6—926
Phoenician literature 892.6
Phoenician sculpture 732.944
Phoenicians T5—926
Phoenicopteriformes 598.35
  paleozoology 568.3
Phoenix 398.245 4
  see also Legendary animals
Phoenix (Ariz.) T2—791 73
Phoka (African people) T5—963 91

Phōkis (Greece) T2—495 15
Pholidota 599.31
  paleozoology 569.31
Phonemics 414
  specific languages T4—15
Phonetic method (Reading)
  elementary education 372.465
Phonetic shorthand systems
  English language 653.423–.428
Phonetics 414.8
  elementary education 372.465
  specific languages T4—158
Phonics
  elementary education 372.465
Phonocardiography
  medicine 616.120 754 4
  see also Cardiovascular system
Phonodiscs 384
  see also Sound recordings
Phonograph records 384
  see also Sound recordings
Phonographs 621.389 33
Phonology 414
  specific languages T4—15
Phonons
  solid-state physics 530.416
Phonorecords 384
  see also Sound recordings
Phoridae 595.774
Phoronida 592.3
  paleozoology 562.3
Phosphatases 572.757
  see also Enzymes
Phosphates 553.64
  chemical engineering 661.43
  economic geology 553.64
  mineralogy 549.72
  mining 622.364
Phosphenes 547.071
  chemical engineering 661.87
Phosphinic acids 547.076
  chemical engineering 661.87
Phosphoacids 547.074
  chemical engineering 661.87
Phosphoalcohols 547.073
  chemical engineering 661.87
Phosphoaldehydes 547.075
  chemical engineering 661.87
Phosphoketones 547.075
  chemical engineering 661.87
Phospholipids 572.57
  see also Lipids
Phosphonic acids 547.077
  chemical engineering 661.87
Phosphonium compounds 547.071
  chemical engineering 661.87
Phosphoproteins 572.68
  biochemistry 572.68
  chemistry 547.754
  see also Proteins
Phosphorescence 535.353
Phosphoric acid
  chemical engineering 661.25
Phosphorus
  applied nutrition 613.285
  biochemistry 572.553
    humans 612.015 24
  chemical engineering 661.071 2
  chemistry 546.712
  metabolism
    human physiology 612.392 4
  organic chemistry 547.07
    aliphatic 547.47
    applied 661.87
  see also Chemicals
Phosphorus fertilizers 631.85
  chemical engineering 668.625
Phosphorus salts
  chemical engineering 661.43
Photo-offset printing 686.232 5
Photo-optics 621.367
Photobacterium 579.34
Photobiochemistry 572.435
Photoceramic processes 773.6
Photochemistry 541.35
  atmosphere 551.511
  chemical engineering 660.295
Photocomposition 686.225 44
Photoconductive cells 621.381 542
Photoconductivity 537.54
Photocopying 686.4
  equipment manufacturing technology 681.65
  library services 025.12
  office use 652.4
  technology 686.4
Photoduplication 686.4
  see also Photocopying
Photoelasticity
  materials science 620.112 95
Photoelectric devices 621.381 542
Photoelectric photometry
  astronomy 522.623
Photoelectricity 537.54
Photoelectronic devices 621.381 542
Photoemission 537.54

Photoemissive cells 621.381 542
Photoenamel processes 773.6
Photoengraving 686.232 7
Photogrammetry 526.982
  military engineering 623.72
Photograph files
  police records 363.24
Photographers 770.92
  occupational group T7—77
  see Manual at 779
Photographic chemicals 771.5
  chemical engineering 661.808
Photographic equipment 771
  manufacturing technology 681.418
Photographic photometry
  astronomy 522.622
Photographic projection 778.2
  motion picture 778.55
Photographic surveying 526.982
Photographs 779
  T1—022 2
  arts 779
  criminal investigation 363.258
  see Manual at 779
Photography 770
  arts 770
  astronomy 522.63
  engineering 621.367
  military engineering 623.72
  nuclear physics 539.778
  technique 771
  see Manual at 778.3 vs. 621.367
Photogravure 686.232 7
Photointaglio 686.232 7
Photoionization of gases 530.444
Photojournalism 070.49
  education 371.897
Photolithography 686.232 5
Photoluminescence 535.355
Photomacrography 778.324
  cinematography 778.56
  video production 778.596
Photomechanical printing 686.232
Photometers
  manufacturing technology 681.415
Photometry 535.220 287
  analytical chemistry 543.085 2
    quantitative 545.812
  astronomy 522.62
Photomicrography 778.31
  biology 570.282
  cinematography 778.56
  video production 778.596
Photomontage 778.8
Photomultipliers 621.381 542
Photon propulsion 629.475 4
Photons 539.721 7
Photonuclear reactions 539.756
Photopsychography 778.3
Photosensitive surfaces
  chemical engineering 661.808
  photography 771.53
Photosensitivity
  animals 573.88
    see also Eyes
Photosensitivity diseases
  medicine 616.5
  see also Skin
Photosphere
  sun 523.74
Photostating
  technology 686.45
Photostats
  technical drawing 604.25
Photosynthesis 572.46
Photosynthetic bacteria 579.38
Phototherapy
  medicine 615.831
Phototransistors 621.381 528
Phototubes 621.381 542
Photovoltaic cells 621.381 542
Photovoltaic effect 537.54
Photovoltaic generation 621.312 44
Phrase books 418
  specific languages T4—83
Phrases (Grammar) 415
  specific languages T4—5
Phrenology 139
Phrygia T2—392 6
Phrygian language 491.993
  T6—919 93
Phrynophiurida 593.94
Phthiōtis (Greece) T2—495 15
Phthiraptera 595.756
Phuthaditjhaba (South Africa) T2—685 91
Phutthalœtla Naphālai, King of Siam
  Thai history 959.303 2
Phutthayǫtfā Čhulālōk, King of Siam
  Thai history 959.303 1
Phycologists 579.809 2
  occupational group T7—579
Phycology 579.8
Phycomycetes 579.53
Phylacteries 296.461 2

Phyllocarida 595.379 2
Phyllodocida 592.62
Phyllosilicates
  mineralogy 549.67
Phyllostomatidae 599.45
Phyllostomidae 599.45
Phylogeny 576.88
  animals 591.38
  microorganisms 579.138
  plants 581.38
Physarales 579.52
Physeter 599.547
Physeteridae 599.547
Physical allergies
  medicine 616.977
  see also Diseases (Human)
Physical anthropologists 599.909 2
  occupational group T7—599
Physical anthropology 599.9
Physical biochemistry 572.43
  humans 612.015 83
Physical chemistry 541.3
  applied 660.29
  see Manual at 541 vs. 546
Physical conditions of work 331.25
  see also Work environment
Physical constants 530.81
Physical crystallography 548.8
Physical diagnosis
  medicine 616.075 4
Physical distribution of goods
  management 658.788
Physical education 613.7
  elementary school 372.86
  health 613.7
  sports 796.07
Physical environment
  influence on crime 364.22
  psychological influence 155.91
Physical ethnologists 599.970 92
  occupational group T7—599
Physical ethnology 599.97
Physical evidence
  criminal investigation 363.256 2
  criminal law 345.064
  law 347.064
Physical fitness 613.7
  health 613.7
  public administration 353.627 4
Physical geography 910.02
  see Manual at 550 vs. 910;
    also at 909, 930–990 vs.
    910
Physical geology 551
Physical gerontology 612.67
Physical illness 362.1
  medicine 616
  see also Diseases (Human)
Physical instruments
  manufacturing technology 681.753
Physical metallurgy 669.9
Physical mineralogy 549.12
Physical oceanography 551.46
Physical operations
  chemical engineering 660.284 2
Physical optics 535.2
Physical sciences 500.2
  see Manual at 530 vs. 500.2
Physical therapy
  medicine 615.82
  psychiatry 616.891 3
    see also Mental illness
Physical training
  health 613.7
Physical typology
  influence on crime 364.24
Physical units 530.81
Physical yoga
  health 613.704 6
Physically disabled persons 305.908 16
  T1—087
  T7—081 6
  education 371.91
  social group 305.908 16
  social welfare 362.4
Physically handicapped persons 305.908 16
  T1—087
  T7—081 6
  see also Physically disabled
    persons
Physically healthy persons T7—081 2
Physician and patient 610.696
Physicians 610.92
  health services 362.172
    see also Health services
  law 344.041 2
  malpractice 344.041 21
  occupational group T7—61
  role and function 610.695 2
Physicians' liability insurance 368.564 2
  see also Insurance
Physicists 530.092
  occupational group T7—53

Physics 530
  ecology 577.13
  engineering 621
  see Manual at 530 vs. 500.2; *also at* 530 vs. 540; *also at* 530 vs. 621
Physics and religion 291.175
  Christianity 261.55
  philosophy of religion 215.3
Physiocracy (Economic school) 330.152
Physiognomy
  divination 138
Physiographic features T2—1
  see Manual at T2—1; *also at* T2—4–T2—9: Physiographic features and regions
Physiographic regions T2—1
  folklore 398.23
    history and criticism 398.322
  see Manual at T2—1; *also at* T2—4–T2—9: Physiographic features and regions
Physiological balance 571.75
  see also Endocrine system
Physiological drives 152.5
Physiological genetics 572.8
  humans 611.018 16
Physiological optics
  humans 612.84
  see also Eyes
Physiological pathology 571.9
  see also Pathology
Physiology 571
  animals 571.1
  domestic animals 636.089 2
  humans 612
    see Manual at 612 vs. 611; *also at* 612.1–612.8; *also at* 616 vs. 612
  plants 571.2
  see Manual at 571–575; *also at* 571–575 vs. 630
Physiotherapy
  medicine 615.82
Phytoflagellates 579.82
Phytogeography 581.9
Phytolaccaceae 583.53
Phytomastigophorea 579.82
Phytophthora 579.546
Phytoplankton 579.817 76
  freshwater 579.817 6
PI (Macroeconomics) 339.32
  distribution 339.22
  see Manual at 339.32 vs. 339.22
Pi-mesons 539.721 62
P'i p'as 787.82
  see also Stringed instruments
Piacenza (Italy : Province) T2—454 6
Pianists 786.209 2
  occupational group T7—786
Piano accordions 788.865
  instrument 788.865 19
  music 788.865
  see also Woodwind instruments
Piano concertos 784.262
Piano-vocal scores 780
  treatises 780.264
Pianolas 786.66
  see also Mechanical musical instruments
Pianos 786.2
  instrument 786.219
  music 786.2
  see also Keyboard instruments
Piarists 255.58
  church history 271.58
Piast dynasty 943.802 2
Piatt County (Ill.) T2—773 673
Piauí (Brazil) T2—812 2
Picardie (France) T2—442 6
Picardy (France) T2—442 6
Piccolos 788.33
  instrument 788.331 9
  music 788.33
  see also Woodwind instruments
Picenum T2—374
Pichincha (Ecuador : Province) T2—866 13
Pici 598.72
Piciformes 598.72
  paleozoology 568.7
Pickaback plants 583.72
Pickaway County (Ohio) T2—771 815
Pickens County (Ala.) T2—761 85
Pickens County (Ga.) T2—758 255
Pickens County (S.C.) T2—757 23
Pickerels 597.59
Picketing 331.892 7
Pickett County (Tenn.) T2—768 687
Pickled foods
  cooking 641.616

Pickling foods 664.028 6
  commercial preservation 664.028 6
  home preservation 641.46
Pickup trucks 388.343 2
  driving 629.284 32
  engineering 629.223 2
  repair 629.287 32
  transportation services 388.343 2
  see also Trucks
Picnic areas
  road engineering 625.77
Picnic cooking 641.578
Picnics 642.3
Picornaviridae 579.257 2
Pictorial arts 760
Pictorial journalism 070.49
Pictorial materials T1—022 2
Pictou (N.S. : County) T2—716 13
Picture dictionaries 413.1
  specific languages T4—31
  specific subject T1—03
Picture frames 684
  furniture arts 749.7
  wooden 674.88
Picture framing 749.7
Pictures T1—022 2
  cataloging 025.347 1
  fine arts 760
  instructional use 371.335 2
  library treatment 025.177 1
  textile arts 746.3
Pidgin English 427.9
  T6—217
Pidgins 417.22
  specific languages T4—7
    see Manual at T4—7
Pidyon haben 296.442 3
  liturgy 296.454 23
Pie mixes 664.753
Piecework 331.216 4
  labor economics 331.216 4
  personnel management 658.322 5
Piedmont (Italy : Region) T2—451
Piedmont (U.S. : Region) T2—75
  Alabama T2—761 5
  Georgia T2—758 4
  Maryland T2—752 7
  North Carolina T2—756 5
  South Carolina T2—757 3
  Virginia T2—755 6
Piemonte (Italy) T2—451
Pier foundations 624.158
Pierce, Franklin
  United States history 973.66
Pierce County (Ga.) T2—758 792
Pierce County (N.D.) T2—784 591
Pierce County (Neb.) T2—782 56
Pierce County (Wash.) T2—797 78
Pierce County (Wis.) T2—775 42
Pieria (Greece) T2—495 65
Pierre (S.D.) T2—783 29
Piers (Columns) 721.3
  architecture 721.3
  construction 690.13
  structural engineering 624.16
Piers (Port facilities) 387.15
  engineering 627.31
  see also Port facilities
Pies 641.865 2
  commercial processing 664.752 5
  home preparation 641.865 2
Piet Retief (South Africa :
    District) T2—682 7
Pietermaritzburg (South
    Africa : District) T2—684 75
Pietersburg (South Africa :
    District) T2—682 5
Pietism 273.7
Piezoelectricity 537.244 6
Piezomagnetism 538.3
Pig iron 669.141 3
Pigeon English 427.9
  T6—217
Pigeons 598.65
  agricultural pests 632.686 5
  animal husbandry 636.596
  sports hunting 799.246 5
Piggyback transportation 385.72
  public administration 354.764
Pigment processes
  photographic printing 773
Pigmentation
  human physiology 612.792 7
    see also Skin
  physical anthropology 599.95
Pigmented cells
  human histology 611.018 2
Pigments 547.869
  biochemistry 572.59
    humans 612.015 28
  chemistry 547.869
  economic geology 553.662
  paint technology 667.623
  painting material
    arts 751.2
  technology 667.29
Pigmy hippopotamus 599.635
Pigmy shrew 599.336 2

Pigs 636.4
  agricultural pests 632.696 33
  animal husbandry 636.4
  big game hunting 799.276 332
  pest control
    conservation technology 639.966
  zoology 599.633
Pikas (Conies) 599.329
Pike County (Ala.) T2—761 35
Pike County (Ark.) T2—767 485
Pike County (Ga.) T2—758 453
Pike County (Ill.) T2—773 453
Pike County (Ind.) T2—772 36
Pike County (Ky.) T2—769 23
Pike County (Miss.) T2—762 23
Pike County (Mo.) T2—778 36
Pike County (Ohio) T2—771 847
Pike County (Pa.) T2—748 24
Pike perches 597.758
Pikes (Fishes) 597.59
  conservation technology 639.977 59
  resource economics 333.956 59
  sports fishing 799.175 9
Piketberg (South Africa : District) T2—687 3
Piła (Poland : Voivodeship) T2—438 4
Pilanesberg Game Reserve (South Africa) T2—682 94
Pilasters 721.3
  architecture 721.3
  construction 690.13
Pilchards 641.392
  cooking 641.692
  food 641.392
  zoology 597.45
Pile foundations 624.154
Pile rugs
  arts 746.75
  see also Rugs
Pile-weave fabrics 677.617
  see also Textiles
Pileas 583.45
Pilgrimage to Mecca 297.352
Pilgrimages 291.351
  Christianity 263.041
  Islam 297.35
  Judaism 296.481
Pilgrim's Rest (South Africa : District) T2—682 6
Piling (Foundation engineering) 624.154
Pilipino language 499.211
  T6—992 11
Pilipino literature 899.211
Pill beetles 595.763
Pill bugs 595.372
Pillars of Islam 297.31
Pillow lava 552.26
Pillowcases 643.53
  arts 746.97
  home sewing 646.21
  household equipment 643.53
Pills
  practical pharmacy 615.43
Pills (Contraceptives)
  health 613.943 2
  pharmacodynamics 615.766
  see also Birth control
Pilot ejection seats 629.134 386
Pilot errors
  air transportation 363.124 14
  see also Transportation safety
Pilot guides
  aeronautics 629.132 54
  seamanship 623.892 2
Pilot plants
  chemical engineering 660.280 72
Pilot whales 599.53
Piloting
  aeronautics 629.132 52
  commercial aircraft 629.132 521 6
  manned space flight 629.458 2
  military aeronautics 623.746 048
  private aircraft 629.132 521 7
  seamanship 623.892 2
Piloting services 387.166
  inland ports 386.866
  law 343.096 7
Piloting systems
  spacecraft 629.474 2
  unmanned spacecraft 629.464 2
Pilotless aircraft
  military engineering 623.746 9
Pilots
  aircraft 629.130 92
    occupational group T7—629 1
Pilot's license 343.097 5
Piltdown man 569.9
Pima Bajo language 497.45
  T6—974 5
Pima County (Ariz.) T2—791 77
Pima Indians T5—974 5
Pima language 497.45
  T6—974 5
Pimento (Allspice) 641.338 3
  botany 583.765
  see also Spices

Pimientos (Peppers) 641.356 43
  botany 583.952
  see also Sweet peppers
Pinaceae 585.2
  paleobotany 561.52
Pinal County (Ariz.) T2—791 75
Pinang T2—595 1
Pinar del Río (Cuba : Province) T2—729 11
Pinball games 794.75
Pinching beetles 595.764 9
Pindus Mountains (Greece) T2—495 3
Pine beetles 595.763
  forestry pests 634.975 167 63
Pine County (Minn.) T2—776 62
Pine Point (N.W.T.) T2—719 3
Pine River (B.C.) T2—711 87
Pineal gland
  human anatomy 611.47
  human physiology 612.492
  light sensing 573.88
  medicine 616.48
  see also Endocrine system
Pineapples 641.347 74
  botany 584.85
  commercial processing 664.804 774
  cooking 641.647 74
  fiber crop 633.576
  food 641.347 74
  horticulture 634.774
Pinecone fishes 597.64
Pinellas County (Fla.) T2—759 63
Pines 585.2
  forestry 634.975 1
  lumber 674.144
  ornamental arboriculture 635.977 52
Pinetown (South Africa : District) T2—684 5
Piney Woods (Miss. : Region) T2—762 5
Pinhole photography 771
Pinicae 585
Pinks (Flowers) 635.933 53
  botany 583.53
  floriculture 635.933 53
Pinnacles 721.5
  architecture 721.5
  construction 690.15
Pinnipedia 599.79
  paleozoology 569.79
Pinochle 795.416
Piñons 585.2
Pinophyta 585
  paleobotany 561.5
Pins
  numismatics 737.24
Pintupi dialect 499.15
  T6—991 5
Pioneer (Space probes) 629.435 4
Pions 539.721 62
Piophilidae 595.774
Piotrków Trybunalski (Poland : Voivodeship) T2—438 4
Pious societies
  Christianity 267
Pipe fitters 696.209 2
  occupational group T7—696
Pipe fitting
  buildings 696.2
Pipe-threading tools 621.944
Pipefishes 597.679
Pipeline processing 004.3
  see also Processing modes—computer science
Pipeline processors 004.3
  engineering 621.391
Pipeline transportation 388.5
  gas technology 665.744
  law 343.093
  petroleum technology 665.544
  public administration 354.764
  transportation services 388.5
Pipelines
  engineering 621.867 2
Piperales 583.25
Pipes (Conduits) 621.867 2
  chemical engineering 660.283
  machine engineering 621.867 2
  metalworking 671.832
  road engineering 625.734
  ship power plants 623.873
  water supply engineering 628.15
Pipes (Tobacco) 688.42
Pipestone County (Minn.) T2—776 26
Pipeworts 584.87
Pipil language 497.452
  T6—974 52
Pipits 598.854
Pipoidea 597.86
Pipridae 598.822
Piracy 364.164
  international law 341.772
  law 345.026 4
Piranhas 597.48
Pirates' expeditions 910.45
Pirin Macedonia T2—499 8
Pirke Avot 296.123 47
Pisa (Italy : Province) T2—455 5

Pisaca literatures 891.499
Pisacha languages 491.499
T6—914 99
Pisacha literatures 891.499
Piscataquis County (Me.) T2—741 25
Pisces 597
see also Fishes
Pisces (Zodiac) 133.527 7
Pisé
building construction 693.22
Pisidia T2—392 7
Pistachios 641.345 74
agriculture 634.574
botany 583.77
commercial processing 664.804 574
cooking 641.645 74
food 641.345 74
Pistils 575.66
Pistoia (Italy : Province) T2—455 2
Pistols 683.432
art metalwork 739.744 32
manufacturing technology 683.432
military engineering 623.443 2
shooting game 799.213
sports 799.202 833
target shooting 799.31
see also Guns (Small arms)
Piston-driven airplanes 387.733 43
engineering 629.133 343
transportation services 387.733 43
see also Aircraft
Piston engines
aircraft 629.134 352
Piston-turbine engines
aircraft 629.134 352
Pistons 621.84
internal-combustion engines 621.437
Pisum sativum 641.356 56
see also Peas (Pisum sativum)
Pit bull terriers 636.755 9
Pitakas 294.382
Pitcairn Island T2—961 8
Pitch (Aeronautics) 629.132 364
Pitch (Linguistics) 414.6
specific languages T4—16
Pitch (Natural asphalt) 553.27
see also Asphalt
Pitch (Petroleum product) 665.538 8
Pitch (Sound)
musical element 781.232
perception
psychology 152.152
Pitcher plants 583.75
Pitcher plants (New World) 583.36
Pitcher plants (Old World) 583.75
Pitching (Aeronautics) 629.132 364
Pitching (Baseball) 796.357 22
Pitching (Golf) 796.352 34
Pitching games 796.24
Pith 571.585
Pithecanthropus erectus 569.9
Pitkin County (Colo.) T2—788 43
Pitman shorthand systems 653.424
Pitt County (N.C.) T2—756 44
Pitt Meadows (B.C.) T2—711 37
Pitt River (B.C.) T2—711 37
Pittas 598.822
Pittidae 598.822
Pittosporaceae 583.72
Pittsburg County (Okla.) T2—766 75
Pittsburgh (Pa.) T2—748 86
Pittsylvania County (Va.) T2—755 665
Pituitary gland 573.45
biology 573.45
human anatomy 611.47
human physiology 612.492
medicine 616.47
see also Endocrine system
Pituitary hormones 573.454
pharmacology 615.363
see also Endocrine system
Piura (Peru : Dept.) T2—851 3
Piute County (Utah) T2—792 53
Piyyutim 296.452
Pizza 641.824
Place names 910.014
Place settings
table service 642.6
Placebo effect
medicine 615.5
Placement (Education) 371.264
colleges and universities 378.166 4
see Manual at 371.262 vs. 371.264
Placement of workers 331.128
economics 331.128
personnel management 658.312 8
public administration 352.66
Placement tests (Education) 371.262
Placenta
human physiology 612.63
obstetrical surgery 618.87
obstetrics 618.34
Placental complications
obstetrics 618.56
Placental dystocia
obstetrics 618.56

Placental extracts
  pharmacology 615.39
Placental mammals 599
  see also Mammals
Placer County (Calif.) T2—794 38
Placer deposits 553.13
Placer mining 622.292 7
Places 900
  T1—09
  arts 700.42
    T3C—32
  folklore 398.23
    history and criticism 398.32
  legendary 398.234
    see also Legendary places
  literature 808.803 2
    history and criticism 809.933 2
    specific literatures T3B—080 32
      history and criticism T3B—093 2
Placodermi 567.2
Placodontia 567.93
Plagiarism
  composition 808
Plague (Bubonic)
  incidence 614.573 2
  medicine 616.923 2
  see also Communicable diseases (Human)
Plaice 597.694
Plain-woven rugs
  arts 746.72
  see also Rugs
Plains 551.453
  T2—145
  geography 910.914 5
  geomorphology 551.453
  physical geography 910.021 45
Plains Indians T5—970 78
Plainsong 782.292
Plaintiffs 347.052
Planarians 592.42
Planctosphaeroidea 593.99
  paleozoology 563.99
Plane geometry 516.05
  analytic 516.32
  Euclidean 516.22
Plane surveying 526.9
Plane trees 583.44
  forestry 634.973 44
  ornamental arboriculture 635.977 344
Plane trigonometry 516.242
Planers 621.912
Planes (Geometry) 516.05
Planes (Tools) 621.912
Planetariums 520.74
Planetary atmospheres
  astronautic engineering 629.415
Planetary flights 919.920 4
  unmanned 629.435 4
Planetary nebulas 523.113 5
Planetary rings 523.98
Planetary transits 523.99
Planetary wind systems 551.518 3
Planetoids 523.44
  T2—992 4
Planets 523.4
  T2—992
  astrology 133.53
  astronomy 523.4
  international law 341.47
Planing mills 674.42
Plank roads
  engineering 625.83
Plankton 578.776
  ecology 577.76
    freshwater 577.6
  freshwater 578.76
Planned economies 330.124
Planning 320.6
  executive management 658.401 2
    T1—068 4
  higher education 378.107
  military administration 355.684
  production management 658.503
  public administration 352.34
    community development 354.279 3
  public policy 320.6
  sales management 658.810 1
  social action 361.25
Planographic printing 686.231 5
  graphic arts 763
Plans 912
  T1—022 3
  architectural design 729.2
  geography 912
  see Manual at T1—0222 vs. T1—0223
Plant arrangements 745.92
Plant biotechnology 630
Plant breeding 631.52
  forestry 634.956
Plant closing 338.604 2
  labor economics 331.259 6
    employment security 331.259 6
    unemployment 331.137
  labor law 344.012 596
  production economics 338.604 2
Plant communities 581.782

- Plant containers
  - manufacturing technology 681.763 1
- Plant crops 630
  - public administration 354.54
  - *see Manual at* 633–635
- Plant culture 630
  - equipment manufacturing technology 681.763 1
- Plant diseases 571.92
  - agricultural economics 338.14
  - agriculture 632.3
    - *see Manual at* 632.2–632.8
- Plant ecology 581.7
- Plant genetics 581.35
  - agriculture 631.523 3
- Plant injuries
  - agriculture 632
- Plant introduction 631.523
- Plant layout
  - management 658.23
- Plant lice 595.752
  - agricultural pests 632.752
- Plant location
  - management 658.21
    - libraries 022.1
    - museums 069.21
  - schools 371.61
  - *see also* Business enterprises—location
  - *see Manual at* 338.09 vs. 332.67309, 338.6042, 346.07, 658.11, T1—0681, 658.21, T1—0682
- Plant maintenance
  - management 658.202
- Plant management 658.2 T1—068 2
  - libraries 022
  - museums 069.2
  - public administration 352.56
  - schools 371.6
    - special education 371.904 5
  - *see Manual at* 647 vs. 647.068, 658.2, T1—0682; *also at* 658.2 and T1—0682
- Plant nutrients
  - agricultural economics 338.162
- Plant pathology 571.92
  - agriculture 632
- Plant pest control
  - environmental engineering 628.97
- Plant physiology 571.2
  - *see Manual at* 571–575
- Plant propagation 631.53
  - agriculture 631.53
  - forestry 634.956 5
- Plant protection 632.9
- Plant quarantine 632.93
- Plant regulators
  - agriculture 631.89
- Plant resources 333.953
  - public administration 354.349
- Plant respiration 572.472
- Plant sanitation 363.729 5
  - engineering 628.51
- Plant selection 631.52
- Plant shutdowns 338.604 2
  - *see also* Plant closing
- Plant spacing (Agriculture) 631.53
- Plant supports
  - manufacturing technology 681.763 1
- Plant training 631.546
- Plant varieties
  - agriculture 631.57
  - resource economics 333.953 4
- Plant viruses 579.28
  - agriculture 632.8
- Plantagenet, House of 942.03
  - English history 942.03
  - genealogy 929.72
  - Irish history 941.503
- Plantaginaceae 583.95
- Plantagos 583.95
- Plantain lilies 635.934 32
  - botany 584.32
  - floriculture 635.934 32
- Plantains (Fruits) 641.347 73
  - botany 584.39
  - commercial processing 664.804 773
  - cooking 641.647 73
  - food 641.347 73
  - horticulture 634.773
- Plantains (Plantagos) 583.95
- Plantation crops 633
  - *see Manual at* 633–635
- Plantation houses
  - architecture 728.8
- Plantations
  - community sociology 307.72
  - system of production
    - sociology 306.349
- Planting 631.53
  - equipment manufacturing technology 681.763 1

Plants 580
  agricultural pests 632.5
  agriculture 630
  art representation 704.943 4
  botany 580
  coevolution with insects 576.875
  comparative psychology 156.9
  conservation technology 639.99
  drawing 743.7
  folklore 398.242
    history and criticism 398.368
      legendary 398.468
      real 398.368
  food source 641.303
    see Manual at 583–585
  influence on precipitation 551.577 5
  landscape architecture 715
  literature 808.803 64
    history and criticism 809.933 64
    specific literatures T3B—080 364
      history and criticism T3B—093 64
  painting 758.5
  paleobotany 561
  physiology 571.2
    see Manual at 571–575
  resource economics 333.953
  see Manual at 579–590
Plants (Buildings and equipment)
  architecture 725.4
  construction 690.54
  location
    management 658.21
    see also Business enterprises—location
  management 658.2
   T1—068 2
    see also Plant management
  prisons 365.5
Plants in Bible 220.858
Plaquemines Parish (La.) T2—763 37
Plasma (Blood) 573.156
  biology 573.156
  human cancer
    medicine 616.994 18
    see also Cancer (Human)
  human histology 611.018 5
  human physiology 612.116
  pharmacology 615.39
  substitutes
    pharmacology 615.39
  see also Cardiovascular system
Plasma (Ionized gas) 530.44
  applied physics 621.044
  chemical engineering 660.044
  physics 530.44
Plasma chemistry 541.042 4
  engineering 660.044
Plasma engineering 621.044
Plasma membranes 571.64
Plasma motors 621.466
Plasma physics 530.44
  applied physics 621.044
Plasma propulsion 629.475 5
Plasmapheresis
  pharmacology 615.39
Plasmid DNA 572.869
Plasmids 572.869
Plasmodiophoromycetes 579.53
Plassey, Battle of, 1757 954.029 4
Plaster casting
  sculpture 731.452
Plaster of paris 666.92
Plasterers 693.609 2
  occupational group T7—693
Plastering 693.6
  architectural construction 721.044 6
Plastic arts 730
  see Manual at 731–735 vs. 736–739
Plastic deformation 531.385
  see also Plasticity
Plastic films 668.495
Plastic flow
  materials science 620.112 33
Plastic foams 668.493
Plastic furniture 645.4
  manufacturing technology 684.106
  see also Furniture
Plastic surgery 617.95
Plasticity 531.385
  crystals 548.842
  materials science 620.112 33
  physics 531.385
Plasticizers (Paints) 667.622
Plasticizers (Plastics) 668.411
Plastics 668.4
  architectural construction 721.044 992 3
  building materials 691.92
  construction materials 693.992 3
  handicrafts 745.572
  materials science 620.192 3
  sculpture material 731.2
  ship design 623.818 923
  shipbuilding 623.820 7
  structural engineering 624.189 23

Plastics casting
  sculpture 731.453
Plastics industry 338.476 684
  equipment manufacturing
    technology 681.766 8
Plastids 571.659
Plata, Rio de la (Argentina and
    Uruguay) 551.464 68
  T2—163 68
Plata, Río de la (Viceroyalty) 982.024
  T2—82
Platanaceae 583.44
Platanistidae 599.538
Plate-girder bridges 388
  construction 624.37
  see also Bridges
Plate glass 666.153
Plate glass insurance 368.6
  see also Insurance
Plate tectonics 551.136
Plateau State (Nigeria) T2—669 52
Plateaus 551.434
  T2—143
  see also Mountains
Platelets 573.159
  human cancer
    medicine 616.994 18
    see also Cancer (Human)
  human histology 611.018 5
  human physiology 612.117
  see also Cardiovascular
      system
Plates
  mechanical printing technique
    flat surfaces 686.231 5
    raised surfaces 686.231 4
  paper 676.34
Plates (Musical instruments) 786.82
  see also Bars (Musical
      instruments)
Plates (Photosensitive surfaces) 661.808
  chemical engineering 661.808
  photography 771.532 2
Plates (Structural elements) 624.177 65
  naval architecture 623.817 765
Platform diving 797.24
  see also Sports
Platform foundations 624.156
Platform speeches
  literature 808.851
    history and criticism 809.51
    specific literatures T3B—501
      individual authors T3A—5
  rhetoric 808.51
Platforms (Party programs) 324.23
Platinotype processes 772.3
Platinum 669.24
  chemical engineering 661.064 5
  chemistry 546.645
  economic geology 553.422
  materials science 620.189 24
  metallography 669.952 4
  metallurgy 669.24
  metalworking 673.24
  mining 622.342 4
  physical metallurgy 669.962 4
  see also Chemicals; Metals
Platinum metals 669.7
  chemical engineering 661.063
  chemistry 546.63
  economic geology 553.495
  metallography 669.957
  metallurgy 669.7
  physical metallurgy 669.967
  see also Metals
Platinum printing-out process 772.3
Platinumwork
  decorative arts 739.24
Platonism 184
  ancient 184
  modern 141.2
Platoons (Military units) 355.31
Platt National Park (Okla.) T2—766 57
Plattdeutsch 439.4
  T6—394
Plattdeutsch literature 839.4
Platte County (Mo.) T2—778 135
Platte County (Neb.) T2—782 52
Platte County (Wyo.) T2—787 17
Platte River (Neb.) T2—782
Platy 597.667
Platycopa 595.33
  paleozoology 565.33
Platyhelminthes 592.4
  paleozoology 562.4
Platypus 599.29
Platyrrhini 599.85
  paleozoology 569.85
Play 790
  child care 649.5
  psychology 155
    children 155.418
  recreation 790
  sociology 306.481
  see also Recreation
Play (Animals) 591.563
Play groups
  agent of socialization 303.327

Play groups (continued)
  social psychology 302.34
Player pianos 786.66
  see also Mechanical musical instruments
Playground equipment
  manufacturing technology 688.76
Playgrounds 796.068
Playing cards 795.4
  manufacturing technology 688.754
Playing time
  musical technique 781.432
Plays
  literature 808.82
    see also Drama (Literature)
  musical 782.14
    music 782.14
    stage presentation 792.6
  theater 792
    see also Theater
Playwrights 809.2
  collected biography 809.2
    specific literatures T3B—200 9
  individual biography T3A—2
Playwriting 808.2
Plazas
  area planning 711.55
Plea bargaining 345.072
Pleading (Law) 347.072
  criminal law 345.072
Pleasant Island 996.85
  T2—968 5
Pleasants County (W. Va.) T2—754 21
Pleasure
  ethical systems 171.4
  psychology 152.42
  sociology 306.481
Pleasure craft 387.204 23
  design 623.812 042 3
  engineering 623.820 23
  handling 623.881 23
  power-driven 387.231
    design 623.812 31
    engineering 623.823 1
    handling 623.882 31
    transportation services 387.231
  transportation services 387.204 23
  wind-driven 387.223
    design 623.812 23
    engineering 623.822 3
    handling 623.882 23
    transportation services 387.223
Pleasures of eating 641.013
Plecoptera 595.735
Plectomycetes 579.565
Plectral instruments 787.7
  see also Stringed instruments
Plectral lutes 787.8
  see also Stringed instruments
Pledges (Law) 346.025
Pleinairism 709.034 4
  painting 759.054
Pleistocene epoch 551.792
  geology 551.792
  paleontology 560.179 2
Pleosporales 579.564
Plesiosauria 567.937
Plettenberg Bay (South Africa) T2—687 4
Pleura 573.252 5
  biology 573.252 5
  human anatomy 611.25
  human physiology 612.2
  medicine 616.25
  surgery 617.543
  see also Respiratory system
Pleuracanthodii 567.3
Pleural pneumonia
  medicine 616.241
  see also Respiratory system
Pleuromeiales 561.79
Pleuronectidae 597.694
Pleuronectiformes 597.69
  paleozoology 567.69
Pleven (Bulgaria : Okrŭg) T2—499 2
Plevenski okrŭg (Bulgaria) T2—499 2
Pliocene epoch 551.788
  geology 551.788
  paleontology 560.178 8
Ploceidae 598.887
Płock (Poland : Voivodeship) T2—438 4
Ploieşti (Romania) T2—498 2
Plots
  literature 808.802 4
    history and criticism 809.924
    specific literatures T3B—080 24
      history and criticism T3B—092 4
  music 780
    treatises 782.002 69
Plotters (Computer devices) 006.62
  engineering 621.399
Plovdiv (Bulgaria : Oblast) T2—499 7
Plovdiv (Bulgaria : Okrŭg) T2—499 7
Plovdivska oblast (Bulgaria) T2—499 7
Plovdivski okrŭg (Bulgaria) T2—499 7

Plovers 598.33
Plowing 631.51
Plows 631.51
  manufacturing technology 681.763 1
Plucked board zithers 787.75
  see also Stringed instruments
Plucked drums 786.97
  see also Percussion instruments
Plucked idiophones 786.85
  set 786.85
  single 786.887
  see also Percussion instruments
Plumas County (Calif.) T2—794 29
Plumb-yews 585.3
Plumbaginales 583.5
Plumbago (Graphite) 553.26
  see also Graphite
Plumbers 696.109 2
  occupational group T7—696
Plumbing 696.1
  see also Water supply
Plumeria 583.93
  floriculture 635.933 93
Plums 641.342 2
  botany 583.73
  cooking 641.642 2
  food 641.342 2
  orchard crop 634.22
Pluralism
  philosophy 147.4
Pluriarcs 787.93
  instrument 787.931 9
  music 787.93
  see also Stringed instruments
Plush 677.617
Plush-capped finch 598.88
Pluto (Planet) 523.482
  T2—992 9
  astrology 133.539 2
Plutocracy 321.5
Plutonic rocks 552.3
Plutonium 669.293 4
  chemical engineering 661.043 4
  chemistry 546.434
  human toxicology 615.925 434
  metallography 669.952 934
  metallurgy 669.293 4
  physical metallurgy 669.962 934
  see also Chemicals
Plymouth (England) T2—423 58
Plymouth Brethren 289.9
  see also Christian denominations
Plymouth County (Iowa) T2—777 16
Plymouth County (Mass.) T2—744 82
Plymouth Rock chicken 636.582
Plywood 674.834
PMS (Syndrome)
  gynecology 618.172
  see also Female genital system
Pneumatic clocks
  technology 681.115
Pneumatic construction 693.98
  architecture 721.044 98
Pneumatic control 629.804 5
Pneumatic conveyor systems
  library equipment 022.9
  office use 651.79
Pneumatic engineering 621.51
Pneumatic engineers 621.510 92
  occupational group T7—621
Pneumatic pumps 621.69
Pneumatic tools 621.904
Pneumatics 533
  engineering 621.51
  physics 533
Pneumatotherapy
  medicine 615.836
Pneumoconiosis
  medicine 616.244
  see also Respiratory system
Pneumocystis carinii pneumonia
  medicine 616.241
  see also Respiratory system
Pneumonia
  medicine 616.241
  see also Respiratory system
Po River (Italy) T2—452
Poales 584.9
  paleobotany 561.49
Pocahontas County (Iowa) T2—777 19
Pocahontas County (W. Va.) T2—754 87
Pocket billiards 794.73
Pocket calculators 681.145
  mathematics 510.284
Pocket computers 004.16
  see also Microcomputers
Pocket gophers 599.359 9
Pocket mice 599.359 8
Pocket scores 780
  treatises 780.265
Pocono Mountains (Pa.) T2—748 2
Podargidae 598.99

Podiatry 617.585
Podicipediformes 598.443
  paleozoology 568.4
Podocarpaceae 585.3
  paleobotany 561.53
Podocarpuses 585.3
Podocopa 595.33
  paleozoology 565.33
Podophyllaceae 583.34
Podostemales 583.82
Poeciliidae 597.667
Poems 808.81
  music 780
    treatises 780.268
  see also Poetry
Poetic books (Old Testament) 223
  pseudepigrapha 229.912
Poetic drama
  literature 808.82
    history and criticism 809.2
    specific literatures T3B—2
      individual authors T3A—2
Poetics 808.1
Poetry 808.81
  criticism 809.1
    theory 808.1
  history 809.1
  rhetoric 808.1
  specific literatures T3B—1
    individual authors T3A—1
  see Manual at T3B—1
Poets 809.1
  collected biography 809.1
    specific literatures T3B—100 9
  individual biography T3A—1
  occupational group T7—81
Pogolo (African people) T5—963 91
Pogolo languages 496.391
  T6—963 91
Pogonophora 592.3
  paleozoology 562.3
Pohjois-Karjala (Finland) T2—489 75
Poikilothermy 571.76
Poinsett County (Ark.) T2—767 96
Poinsettias 635.933 69
  botany 583.69
  floriculture 635.933 69
Point-of-sale advertising 659.157
Point processes 519.23
Point set topology 514.322
Point sets 511.33
Pointe Coupee Parish (La.) T2—763 454
Pointers (Dogs) 636.752 5
Pointillism 709.034 5
  painting 759.055
Poison arrow frogs 597.87
Poison gas
  ethics 172.42
  military engineering 623.459 2
Poison gas projectiles 623.451 6
Poison hemlocks 583.849
Poison ivies 583.77
Poison oaks 583.77
Poisoning
  human toxicology 615.9
Poisonous animals 591.65
  human toxicology 615.94
Poisonous fishes 597.165
  human toxicology 615.945
Poisonous microorganisms 579.165
Poisonous organisms 578.65
Poisonous plants 581.659
  human toxicology 615.952
Poisons 363.179 1
  human toxicology 615.9
  public safety 363.179 1
  toxicology 571.95
  see also Hazardous materials
Poisson integral 515.43
Poisson-Stieltjes integral 515.43
Poisson's ratio 531.381
Poitou (France) T2—446
Poitou-Charentes (France) T2—446
Poker (Game) 795.412
Pokeweed 583.53
Polabian language 491.89
  T6—918 9
Polabian literature 891.89
Poland 943.8
  T2—438
Poland China swine 636.482
Polar bear 599.786
  conservation technology 639.979 786
  resource economics 333.959 786
Polar regions T2—11
  see also Frigid zones
Polarimeters
  manufacturing technology 681.25
Polarimetry
  analytical chemistry 543.085 6
    qualitative 544.956
    quantitative 545.816
  astronomy 522.65
Polaris missiles 359.981 782
  engineering 623.451 97
  military equipment 359.981 782

Polariscopic analysis 543.085 6
  qualitative 544.956
  quantitative 545.816
Polarization of light 535.52
Polarography 543.087 2
Polders
  engineering 627.549
Pole vaulting 796.434
  see also Sports
Polecats (New World) 599.768
Polecats (Old World) 599.766 2
Polela (South Africa : District) T2—684 7
Polemics
  Christianity 239
  comparative religion 291.2
  Islam 297.29
  Judaism 296.35
Polemoniales 583.94
Poles (People) T5—918 5
Polesine (Italy) T2—453 3
Police 363.2
  law 344.052
  public administration 353.36
  sociology 306.28
Police boats 363.286
  design 623.812 63
  engineering 623.826 3
  police services 363.286
Police buildings
  architecture 725.18
Police corruption 364.132 3
  law 345.023 23
  public administration 353.46
Police dogs 636.737 6
Police functions 363.23
Police officers 363.209 2
  occupational group T7—363 2
  role and function 363.22
Police patrols 363.232
Police powers (Constitutional law) 342.041 8
Police questioning 363.254
Police records 363.24
Police services 363.2
  see also Police
Police surveillance 363.232
Policy making 320.6
  executive management 658.401 2
  military administration 355.684
  political science 320.6
  public administration 352.34

Policy making (continued)
  social processes 303.3
  see Manual at 300, 320.6 vs. 352–354: Public policy
Policy studies 320.6
Poliomyelitis
  incidence 614.549
  medicine 616.835
  pediatrics 618.928 35
  see also Nervous system
Poliovirus 579.257 2
Polish language 491.85
  T6—918 51
Polish literature 891.85
Polish people T5—918 5
Polishing 667.72
  housecleaning 648.5
  woodwork
    buildings 698.33
Polishing gems 736.202 8
Polishing metals 671.72
Polishing wheels 621.922
Politeness
  ethics 177.1
Political action committees 324.4
  law 342.078
Political action groups 322.4
  law 342.078
  political process 324.4
  relation to government 322.4
Political alliances T2—171 2
Political buttons
  numismatics 737.242
Political campaign strategy 324.72
Political campaigns 324.9
  see also Campaigns (Politics)
Political causes of war 355.027 2
Political change 320.011
Political clubs 324.3
Political conditions 320.9
  see Manual at 909, 930–990 vs. 320: Political activities
Political corruption 364.132 3
  law 345.023 23
  public administration 353.46
Political crimes 364.131
  law 345.023 1
Political divisions
  historical geography 911
Political elites 305.524
  T1—086 21

Political ethics 172
  religion 291.562
    Buddhism 294.356 2
    Christianity 241.62
    Hinduism 294.548 62
    Islam 297.562
    Judaism 296.362
Political history 900
  see Manual at 900; *also at* 909, 930–990 vs. 320: Political history
Political ideologies 320.5
  party programs 324.23
  see also Politics and religion
  see Manual at 320.011 vs. 320.5
Political institutions
  description and appraisal 320.9
  social welfare 361.613
  sociology 306.2
  see Manual at 302–307 vs. 320; *also at* 320 vs. 306.2
Political justice 320.011
Political machines 324.21
  sociology 306.26
Political movements 320.5
  see Manual at 324 vs. 320.5, 320.9
Political music 781.599
  songs 782.421 599
Political parties 324.2
  sociology 306.26
  see Manual at 324.2094–324.2099 and 324.24–324.29; *also at* 324.24–324.29; *also at* 909, 930–990 vs. 320: Political activities
Political patronage 324.204
Political persecution 323.044
Political persuasion 320.014
Political philosophers 320.092
Political pins
  numismatics 737.242
Political prisoners 365.450 92
  labor economics 331.51
Political prisons 365.45
  see also Correctional institutions
Political process 324
  see Manual at 302–307 vs. 320
Political programs (Party platforms) 324.23
Political propaganda 320.014
Political refugees 325.21
  see also Refugees
Political rights 323.5
Political science 320
Political scientists 320.092
  occupational group T7—321
Political situation 320.9
  see Manual at 909, 930–990 vs. 320: Political activities
Political sociology 306.2
  see Manual at 320 vs. 306.2
Political songs 782.421 599
Political theories 320.011
  see Manual at 320.011 vs. 320.5
Politicians
  biography 324.209 2
  characteristics 324.22
  ethics 172.2
  occupational group T7—329
Politics 320
  arts 700.458
    T3C—358
  folklore 398.27
    history and criticism 398.358
  journalism 070.449 32
  literature 808.803 58
    history and criticism 809.933 58
    specific literatures T3B—080 358
      history and criticism T3B—093 58
  sociology 306.2
  see Manual at 320: Politics of specific subjects; *also at* 324 vs. 320
Politics and religion 322.1
  political science 322.1
  social theology 291.177
    Buddhism 294.337 7
    Christianity 261.7
    Hinduism 294.517 7
    Islam 297.272
      see Manual at 297.26–297.27
    Judaism 296.382
      see Manual at 322.1 vs. 296.382, 320.54095694
  see Manual at 322.1 vs. 261.7, 291.177
Politics as a profession 324.22
Polk, James K. (James Knox)
  United States history 973.61
Polk County (Ark.) T2—767 45

Polk County (Fla.) T2—759 67
Polk County (Ga.) T2—758 375
Polk County (Iowa) T2—777 58
Polk County (Minn.) T2—776 95
Polk County (Mo.) T2—778 77
Polk County (N.C.) T2—756 915
Polk County (Neb.) T2—782 352
Polk County (Or.) T2—795 38
Polk County (Tenn.) T2—768 875
Polk County (Tex.) T2—764 165
Polk County (Wis.) T2—775 17
Polkas 793.33
  music 784.188 44
Poll tax 336.25
  law 343.062
  public administration 352.44
  public finance 336.25
  qualification for voting 324.62
Polled Shorthorn cattle 636.226
Pollen 571.845
  paleobotany 561.13
Pollen control
  air conditioning
    buildings 697.932 4
Pollination 571.864 2
  coevolution 576.875
Polling 324.65
Pollocks 641.392
  cooking 641.692
  food 641.392
  zoology 597.632
Pollutants 363.738
  law 344.046 33
  see also Pollution
Pollution 363.73
  crop damage 632.19
  ecology 577.27
  human toxicology 615.902
  international law 341.762 3
  law 344.046 32
  public administration 354.335
    cleanup 353.93
  social effects 304.28
  social theology 291.178 362 8
    Christianity 261.836 28
  social welfare 363.73
  toxicology 571.95
  see Manual at 333.7–333.9 vs. 363.1, 363.73, 577; *also at* 363.73 vs. 571.95, 577.27
Pollution control equipment
  manufacturing technology 681.76
Pollution control technology 628.5
  T1—028 6
  aircraft 629.134 35
  automotive 629.25
  glassmaking 666.14
  paper manufacturing 676.042
  petroleum 665.538 9
  plastic technology 668.419 2
  rubber manufacturing 678.29
  water 628.168
  wood products 674.84
Pollution liability insurance 368.563
  see also Insurance
Polo 796.353
  see also Sports
Polo players 796.353 092
  sports group T7—796 35
Polonaises 793.3
  music 784.188 4
Polonium
  chemical engineering 661.072 8
  chemistry 546.728
  metallurgy 669.79
  see also Chemicals
Poltava (Ukraine : Oblast) T2—477 6
Poltavs′ka oblast′
    (Ukraine) T2—477 6
Poltergeists 133.142
Polyacrylics 668.423 2
  textiles 677.474 2
    see also Textiles
Polyamides 668.423 5
  textiles 677.473
    see also Textiles
Polyandry 306.842 3
Polybutadiene rubber 678.72
Polycarbonates 668.423
Polychaeta 592.62
Polychlorinated biphenyl
  human toxicology 615.951 2
Polycyclic current transmission 621.319 16
Polycythemia
  medicine 616.153
  see also Cardiovascular system
Polyesters 668.422 5
  textiles 677.474 3
    see also Textiles
Polyethers 668.423
Polyethylene 668.423 4
  textiles 677.474 5
    see also Textiles

Polyfluoro hydrocarbons 668.423 8
  textiles 677.474 8
    see also Textiles
Polygalales 583.82
Polygamists 306.842 3
  T1—086 59
Polygamy 306.842 3
  customs 392.5
Polyglandular disorders
  medicine 616.48
  see also Endocrine system
Polyglot Bibles 220.51
Polyglot dictionaries 413
  T1—03
Polygonales 583.57
Polygons 516.15
Polygraph tests 363.254
  see also Lie detectors
Polyhedra 516.15
Polyhydroxy aromatics 547.633
Polyisobutylenes 668.423 4
Polymer painting 751.49
Polymer sequence 572.33
Polymerization 547.28
  organic chemistry 547.28
  chemical engineering 668.92
  inorganic chemistry 541.393
Polymerization plastics 668.42
Polymers 547.7
  biochemistry 572.33
  chemical engineering 668.9
  inorganic chemistry 541.225 4
  liquid-state physics 530.429
  materials science 620.192
  organic chemistry 547.7
  shipbuilding 623.820 7
  state of matter 530.413
  structural engineering 624.189 2
Polymixiiformes 597.62
Polymorphism
  crystallography 548.3
Polynesia 996
  T2—96
Polynesian languages 499.4
  T6—994
Polynesian literatures 899.4
Polynesian religion 299.924
Polynesians T5—994
Polynomial equations 512.942
  algebra 512.942
  calculus 515.252
Polyolefins 668.423 4
Polyomavirus 579.244 5
Polypeptides 572.65
  biochemistry 572.65
  chemistry 547.756
  see also Proteins
Polyphaga 595.76
Polyphenyl hydrocarbons 547.613
  chemical engineering 661.816
Polyphony 781.284
Polyplacophora 594.27
Polyploidy 572.87
Polypodiales 587.3
Polypodiopsida 587.3
  paleobotany 561.73
Polyporales 579.597
Polypropylene 668.423 4
  textiles 677.474 5
    see also Textiles
Polypteriformes 597.42
  paleozoology 567.42
Polyradiculoneuritis
  medicine 616.87
  see also Nervous system
Polysaccharides 572.566
  biochemistry 572.566
  chemistry 547.782
  see also Carbohydrates
Polystyrenes 668.423 3
Polytheism 211.32
  comparative religion 291.211
  philosophy of religion 211.32
Polytheistic religions 291.14
Polytopes 516.35
Polyurethane rubber 678.72
Polyurethanes 668.423 9
  polyesters 668.422 5
  thermoplastic 668.423 9
Polyvinyls 668.423 6
  textiles 677.474 4
    see also Textiles
Polyzoa 594.67
Pomacanthidae 597.72
Pomacentridae 597.72
Pomaceous fruits 641.341
  botany 583.73
  cooking 641.641
  food 641.341
  orchard crops 634.1
Pombaline reforms 946.903 3
Pomegranates 641.346 4
  agriculture 634.64
  botany 583.76
  cooking 641.646 4
  food 641.346 4

Pomerania (Poland and Germany) T2—438 1
Germany T2—431 7
Poland T2—438 1
Pomeranian (Dog) 636.76
Pomerelia (Poland) T2—438 2
Pomo Indians T5—975 7
Pomo languages 497.57
T6—975 7
Pompeii (Extinct city) T2—377
Ponape (Micronesia) T2—966
Ponce (P.R. : District) T2—729 57
Pond Inlet (N.W.T.) T2—719 5
Pondera County (Mont.) T2—786 53
Pondicherry (India : Union Territory) T2—548 6
Pondoland (South Africa) T2—687 91
Ponds 551.482
T2—169 2
biology 578.763 6
ecology 577.636
fish culture 639.31
hydrology 551.482
landscape architecture 714
resource economics 333.916 3
Pondweeds 584.742
Pongidae 599.88
paleozoology 569.88
Pongo 599.883
Pongola River T2—684 2
Mozambique T2—679 1
South Africa T2—684 2
Ponies 636.16
Pons Variolii
human anatomy 611.81
human physiology 612.826 7
see also Nervous system
Ponta Delgada (Azores : District) T2—469 9
Pontchartrain, Lake (La.) T2—763 34
Pontederiaceae 584.35
Pontevedra (Spain : Province) T2—461 7
Pontiac (Quebec : County) T2—714 21
Pontiac (Quebec : Regional County Municipality) T2—714 21
Pontiac's Conspiracy, 1763–1764 973.27
Pontificale Romanum 264.025
Pontine Islands (Italy) T2—456 23
Pontine Marshes (Italy) T2—456 23
Pontoon bridges 388
construction 624.87
see also Bridges
Pontotoc County (Miss.) T2—762 932
Pontotoc County (Okla.) T2—766 69
Pontus T2—393 3
Pony express 383.18
Ponza Islands (Italy) T2—456 23
Poodle 636.728
Poodle (Toy dog) 636.76
Pooideae 584.9
forage crops 633.2
Pool (Game) 794.73
equipment technology 688.747 3
Pool halls
architecture 725.84
Pool players 794.730 92
sports group T7—794 7
Poole (Dorset, England) T2—423 37
Pools (Organizations) 338.87
see also Combinations (Enterprises)
Pools (Water)
landscape architecture 714
see also Ponds
Poor Clares 255.973
church history 271.973
Poor laws 362.5
social aspects 362.5
welfare law 344.032 5
Poor people 305.569
T1—086 942
government programs 353.533 2
institutional buildings 362.585
social theology 291.178 325
Buddhism 294.337 832 5
Christianity 261.832 5
Hinduism 294.517 832 5
Judaism 296.38
social welfare 362.5
public administration 353.533 2
welfare law 344.032 5
see also Poverty
Pop art 709.040 71
painting 759.067 1
sculpture 735.230 471
Popcorn 641.356 77
commercial processing 664.805 677
cooking 641.656 77
food 641.356 77
garden crop 635.677
Pope County (Ark.) T2—767 32
Pope County (Ill.) T2—773 991
Pope County (Minn.) T2—776 46
Popes 282.092
biography 282.092
ecclesiology 262.13

Popguns
  music 786.99
    see also Percussion instruments
Poplars 583.65
  forestry 634.972 3
  lumber 674.142
  ornamental arboriculture 635.977 365
Popoloca Indians T5—976
Popoloca language 497.6
  T6—976
Poppies 635.933 35
  botany 583.35
  floriculture 635.933 35
  narcotic crop 633.75
Popular culture 306
Popular education 370
  social education 370.115
Popular music 781.63
Popular practices (Islam) 297.39
Popular songs 782.421 63
  western 782.421 64
Population 304.6
  social problems 363.9
    see Manual at 363.9 vs. 304.66
  sociology 304.6
Population biology 577.88
  animals 591.788
  microorganisms 579.178 8
  plants 581.788
Population control 363.96
  conservation technology 639.93
  demography 304.66
  law 344.048
  public administration 353.59
  social theology 291.178 366 6
    Christianity 261.836 66
  see also Birth control
  see Manual at 363.9 vs. 304.66
Population density 304.61
Population dynamics (Ecology) 577.88
Population ecology 577.88
  animals 591.788
  microorganisms 579.178 8
  plants 581.788
Population exchange 325
Population genetics 576.58
Population geography 304.6
Population movement 304.8
  public administration 353.59
Population transfer 325
Populist Party (U.S.) 324.273 27
Populus 583.65
Poquoson (Va.) T2—755 422
Porcelain 666.5
  arts 738.2
  materials science 620.146
  technology 666.5
Porch furniture 645.8
  see also Outdoor furniture
Porches 721.84
  architecture 721.84
  construction 690.184
  home economics 643.55
Porcupine fishes 597.64
Porcupines (New World) 599.359 74
Porcupines (Old World) 599.359 7
Pordenone (Italy : Province) T2—453 94
Pore fungi 579.597
Porgies 597.72
  sports fishing 799.177 2
Porifera 593.4
  paleozoology 563.4
Porirua City (N.Z.) T2—936 2
Pork 641.364
  commercial processing 664.92
  cooking 641.664
  food 641.364
Pornography 363.47
  arts 700.453 8
  T3C—353 8
  criminology 364.174
    criminal law 345.027 4
    international law 341.77
  ethics 176.7
    religion 291.566 7
      Christianity 241.667
  fine arts 704.942 8
  law 344.054 7
  literature 808.803 538
    history and criticism 809.933 538
    specific literatures T3B—080 353 8
      history and criticism T3B—093 538
  painting 757.8
  social problem 363.47
    public administrative control 353.37
Porous materials
  materials science 620.116
Porous solids 530.413
Porphyria
  medicine 616.399
  see also Digestive system
Porphyries 552.3
Porphyrins 547.593
  chemical engineering 661.894

Porpoises 599.539
Port Alfred (South Africa) T2—687 5
Port Arthur (Tas.) T2—946 4
Port-au-Prince (Haiti) T2—729 452
Port Augusta (S. Aust.) T2—942 38
Port buildings 387.15
  see also Port facilities
Port Coquitlam (B.C.) T2—711 33
Port Cygnet (Tas.) T2—946 2
Port Elizabeth (South Africa : District) T2—687 52
Port Elizabeth-Uitenhage-Despatch industrial area T2—687 52
Port facilities 387.15
  architecture 725.34
  area planning 711.76
  engineering 627.3
  military engineering 623.64
  transportation services 387.15
    inland waterway 386.85
  see also Ports
Port Fairy (Vic.) T2—945 7
Port Harcourt (Nigeria) T2—669 42
Port Hedland (W.A.) T2—941 3
Port installations 387.15
  see also Port facilities
Port Kembla (N.S.W.) T2—944 6
Port Lincoln (S. Aust.) T2—942 38
Port Louis (Mauritius) T2—698 2
Port Macquarie (N.S.W.) T2—944 2
Port maintenance 387.16
Port Moody (B.C.) T2—711 33
Port Moresby (Papua New Guinea) T2—954 5
Port Nelson (Man.) T2—712 71
Port Nolloth (South Africa) T2—687 2
Port Pirie (S. Aust.) T2—942 32
Port Renfrew (B.C.) T2—711 28
Port Said (Egypt : Province) T2—621 5
Port Shepstone (South Africa : District) T2—684 5
Port St. Johns (South Africa : District) T2—687 91
Port Sudan (Sudan) T2—625
Portability
  computer software 005
Portable firearms
  military engineering 623.442
  see also Guns (Small arms)
Portable flight vehicles
  engineering 629.14
Portable heaters
  buildings 697.24
Portable lights
  mining 622.473
  nautical equipment 623.86
Portable radios 621.384 5
Portable steam engines 621.15
Portable telephones 384.53
  communications services 384.53
  engineering 621.384 56
  see also Radiotelephony
Portage County (Ohio) T2—771 37
Portage County (Wis.) T2—775 53
Portage la Prairie (Man.) T2—712 73
Portalegre (Portugal : District) T2—469 52
Portals
  sculpture 731.542
Porter County (Ind.) T2—772 98
Portes Gil, Emilio
  Mexican history 972.082 42
Portfolio analysis 332.6
Portfolio management 332.6
Portland (Me.) T2—741 91
Portland (Or.) T2—795 49
Portland (Vic.) T2—945 7
Portland cement 666.94
Portneuf (Quebec : County) T2—714 46
Portneuf Wildlife Reserve (Quebec) T2—714 46
Porto (Portugal : District) T2—469 15
Porto-Novo (Benin) T2—668 3
Portraits
  art representation 704.942
  drawing 743.42
  painting 757
Ports 387.1
  engineering 627.2
  inland waterway 386.8
  law 343.096 7
  public administration 354.78
  transportation services 387.1
  see also Port facilities
  see Manual at 386.8 vs. 387.1
Portsmouth (England) T2—422 792
Portsmouth (N.H.) T2—742 6
Portsmouth (Va.) T2—755 522
Portugal 946.9
  T2—469
  ancient 936.6
    T2—366
Portuguesa (Venezuela) T2—874 5
Portuguese (Ethnic group) T5—69

Portuguese (National group) T5—691
Portuguese folk music 781.626 9
Portuguese folk songs 782.421 626 9
Portuguese Guinea 966.570 2
T2—665 7
Portuguese language 469
T6—69
Portuguese literature 869
Portuguese man-of-war 593.55
Portuguese Timor T2—598 6
Portuguese water dog 636.73
Portulacaceae 583.53
Portulacas 583.53
Posey County (Ind.) T2—772 34
Posidoniaceae 584.74
Position classification 658.306
Position-finding devices
marine navigation 623.893
radio engineering 621.384 191
Positional astronomy 522
mathematical geography 526.6
Positives (Photography) 771.44
Positivism 146.4
ethics 171.2
Positron emission tomography
medicine 616.075 75
Positrons 539.721 4
Posology
pharmacology 615.14
Possums 599.23
Possums (America) 599.276
Possums (Australasia) 599.23
Post exchanges 355.341
Post-mortem examination
medicine 616.075 9
Post offices 383.42
architecture 725.16
see also Postal service
Post-production
video production 778.593
Post-traumatic stress disorder
medicine 616.852 1
see also Mental illness
Postage-due stamps
prints 769.57
Postage meters
office use 651.759
Postage stamps 383.23
investment economics 332.63
philately 769.56
postal service 383.23
see also Postal service
printing 686.288
Postal cards 383.122
see also Postal service
Postal clerks 383.492
occupational group T7—383
Postal codes 383.145 5
see also Postal service
Postal communication 383
see also Postal service
Postal insurance 368.2
see also Insurance
Postal law 343.099 2
Postal offenses 364.136
law 345.023 6
Postal organization 383.4
law 343.099 25
see also Postal service
Postal rates 383.23
law 343.099 23
Postal routes 383.143
law 343.099 25
Postal savings banks 332.22
Postal savings stamps
prints 769.57
Postal service 383
armed services 355.693
international law 341.757 3
law 343.099 2
public administration 354.759
Postal service workers 383.492
occupational group T7—383
Postal stationery
philately 769.566
Postal zones 383.145
see also Postal service
Postcard illustration 741.683
Postcards 383.122
philately 769.566
see also Postal service
Postclassical Greek language 487.3
T6—87
Postclassical Latin language 477
T6—71
Postcoordinate indexing 025.484
Postdoctoral programs 378.155
Posters 741.674
Postglacial epoch 551.793
geology 551.793
paleontology 560.179 3
Posthypnotic phenomena 154.774
Postimpressionism 709.034 6
painting 759.056
Postludes 784.189 3
Postmarks
philately 769.567

Postmasburg (South Africa : District) T2—687 11
Postmodernism 149.97
  arts 700.411 3
    T3C—113
  literature 808.801 13
    history and criticism 809.911 3
    specific literatures T3B—080 113
      history and criticism T3B—091 13
  philosophy 149.97
Postnatal development
  humans 612.6
Postoperative care
  surgery 617.919
Postpartum care
  obstetrics 618.6
Postpartum depression
  medicine 618.76
  see also Mental illness
Posts (Columns) 721.3
  architecture 721.3
  construction 690.13
Posts (Military installations) 355.7
  international law 341.725
  law 343.01
Posttraumatic stress disorder
  medicine 616.852 1
  see also Mental illness
Postulates
  mathematical logic 511.3
Posture 613.78
Postwar period (World War II) 909.825
  T1—090 45
Pot abuse 362.295
  medicine 616.863 5
  personal health 613.835
  social welfare 362.295
  see also Substance abuse
Pot gardening 635.986
Potable water 363.61
  see also Drinking water; Municipal water supply
Potaliaceae 583.93
Potamogetonaceae 584.742
Potamogetonales 584.74
Potash 546.383 22
  chemical engineering 661.334
Potash salts 553.636
  economic geology 553.636
  mining 622.363 6
Potassium 669.725
  chemical engineering 661.038 3
  chemistry 546.383
  metallurgy 669.725
Potassium (continued)
  mining 622.363 6
  organic chemistry 547.053 83
    applied 661.895
  physical metallurgy 669.967 25
  see also Chemicals
Potassium alkalis 546.383 22
  chemical engineering 661.33
Potassium bicarbonate 546.383 22
  chemical engineering 661.333
Potassium carbonate 546.383 22
  chemical engineering 661.334
Potassium fertilizers 631.83
  chemical engineering 668.623
Potassium hydroxide 546.383 22
  chemical engineering 661.332
Potassium minerals
  economic geology 553.636
Potato printing 761
Potato starch
  food technology 664.22
Potato whiskey 641.25
  commercial processing 663.5
Potatoes 641.352 1
  agriculture 635.21
  botany 583.952
  commercial processing 664.805 21
  cooking 641.652 1
  food 641.352 1
Potawatomi Indians T5—973
Potchefstroom (South Africa : District) T2—682 4
Potential energy 531.6
Potential offenders
  identification 364.41
Potential theory 515.9
Potentiometers 621.374 3
Potentiometry 543.087 12
Potenza (Italy : Province) T2—457 71
Potgietersrus (South Africa : District) T2—682 5
Potichomania
  handicrafts 745.546
Potomac River T2—752
  Maryland T2—752
  West Virginia T2—754 9
Potoos 598.99
Potosí (Bolivia : Dept.) T2—841 4
Pots 641.502 8
  cooking 641.502 8
  manufacturing technology 683.82
Potsdam (Germany) T2—431 572
Potsdam (Germany : Bezirk) T2—431 57

Pottawatomie County
(Kan.) T2—781 32
Pottawatomie County
(Okla.) T2—766 36
Pottawattamie County
(Iowa) T2—777 71
Potted plants 635.986
houseplants 635.965
Potted trees 635.977
houseplants 635.965
Potter County (Pa.) T2—748 55
Potter County (S.D.) T2—783 19
Potter County (Tex.) T2—764 825
Potters 738.092
occupational group T7—738
Potter's wheels 666.43
decorative arts 738.13
sculpture 731.3
technology 666.43
Pottery 666.3
arts 738
technology 666.3
Poultry 636.5
agricultural economics 338.176 5
zoology 598.6
Poultry (Meat) 641.365
commercial processing 664.93
economics 338.476 649 3
cooking 641.665
food 641.365
home preservation 641.493
Poured concrete 624.183 4
building construction 693.5
with reinforcement 693.541
without reinforcement 693.521
structural engineering 624.183 4
Poverty 362.5
influence on crime 364.2
law 344.032 5
macroeconomics 339.46
religious practice 291.447
Buddhism 294.344 47
Christianity 248.47
Hinduism 294.544 7
social services
institutional architecture 725.55
social theology 291.178 325
Buddhism 294.337 832 5
Christianity 261.832 5
Hinduism 294.517 832 5
Judaism 296.38
social welfare 362.5
public administration 353.533 2
Poverty (continued)
social welfare facilities 362.583
architecture 725.55
Poverty-stricken persons 305.569
T1—086 942
see also Poor people
Powder metal products 671.87
Powder metallurgy 671.37
Powder post beetles 595.763
Powder processes
photographic printing 773.2
Powder River County
(Mont.) T2—786 37
Powder rooms 643.52
home economics 643.52
interior decoration 747.78
Powder technology 620.43
Powdered eggs 641.375 4
cooking 641.675 4
food 641.375 4
processing 637.54
Powdered soaps 668.124
Powders
practical pharmacy 615.43
Powell, Lake (Utah and
Ariz.) T2—792 59
Powell County (Ky.) T2—769 585
Powell County (Mont.) T2—786 86
Powell River (B.C.) T2—711 31
Powell River (B.C. :
Regional District) T2—711 31
Power (Energy) 333.79
see also Electricity; Energy
Power (Social sciences) 303.3
international relations 327.101
political science 320.011
sociology 303.3
Power control devices 621.812
Power County (Idaho) T2—796 49
Power-driven ships 387.204 4
design 623.812 044
engineering 623.820 4
handling 623.881 4
see also Ships
Power electronics 621.317
Power equipment
agricultural use 631.37
textile technology 677.028 5
Power-factor meters 621.374 9
Power failure
electrical engineering 621.319
Power hammers 621.974

Power interruption insurance 368.7
see also Insurance
Power of attorney 346.029
Power plant insurance 368.7
see also Insurance
Power plants (Electric generation) 621.312 1
nuclear engineering 621.483
Power plants (Engines) 621.4
aircraft 629.134 35
ships 623.87
unmanned spacecraft 629.465
Power politics 327.1
Power residues 512.72
Power resources 333.79
see also Energy resources
Power series 515.243 2
Power shovels 621.865
Power supply
communications engineering 621.382 32
electronics 621.381 044
Power tools 621.9
use in home woodworking 684.083
Power transmission
machine engineering 621.85
Powers (Mathematics) 512.922
Poweshiek County (Iowa) T2—777 596
Powhatan County (Va.) T2—755 612
Powhatan Indians T5—973
POWs 355.113
see also Prisoners of war
Powys (Wales) T2—429 5
Poxviridae 579.243 2
Poznań (Poland : Voivodeship) T2—438 4
Practical astronomy 522
Practical ethics 170.44
Practical nurses 610.730 92
role and function 610.730 693
see also Nurses
Practical pharmacy 615.4
see Manual at 615.1 vs. 615.4
Practical politics 324.7
Practical printing 686.225
Practice of law 347.050 4
see Manual at 340.023 vs. 347.0504
Practice teaching 370.71
T1—071
Praenestian language 479.4
T6—794
Pragmatic reductionism (Psychology) 150.194 34
Pragmatics 306.44
psycholinguistics 401.9
sociolinguistics 306.44
see Manual at 401.43 vs. 306.44, 401.9, 412, 415: Meaning
Pragmatism 144.3
education 370.12
Prague (Czech Republic) T2—437 12
Praha (Czech Republic) T2—437 12
Prahova (Romania) T2—498 2
Praia (Cape Verde) T2—665 8
Prairie chickens 598.637
Prairie County (Ark.) T2—767 77
Prairie County (Mont.) T2—786 25
Prairie dogs 599.367
Prairie Provinces 971.2
T2—712
Prairies 333.74
T2—145
biology 578.744
ecology 577.44
geography 910.914 5
geomorphology 551.453
land economics 333.74
physical geography 910.021 45
Prajadhipok, King of Siam
Thai history 959.304 2
Prakrit languages 491.3
T6—913
Prakrit literatures 891.3
Praseodymium
chemistry 546.413
see also Rare earths
Prasinophyceae 579.83
Pratt County (Kan.) T2—781 815
Prawns 595.388
see also Shrimps
Prayer 291.43
Buddhism 294.344 3
Christianity 248.32
Hinduism 294.543
Islam 297.382
Sufi 297.438 2
Judaism 296.45
public worship 291.38
Buddhism 294.343 8
Christianity 264.1
Hinduism 294.538
Judaism 296.45
Prayer books 291.433
Buddhism 294.344 33
Christianity 242.8
public worship 264.13

Prayer books (continued)
  Hinduism 294.543 3
  Islam 297.382 4
    Sufi 297.438 24
  Judaism 296.45
Prayer desks
  church architecture 726.529 2
  church furniture 247.1
Prayer in public schools 379.28
  law 344.079 6
Prayer meetings
  Christianity
    public worship 264.7
Prayer of Manasseh (Bible) 229.6
Prayer plant 635.934 39
  botany 584.39
  floriculture 635.934 39
Prayer shawls 296.461
Prayers (Private devotions) 291.433
  Buddhism 294.344 33
  Christianity 242
  Hinduism 294.543 3
  Islam 297.382 4
    Sufi 297.438 24
  Judaism 296.45
Prayers (Public worship) 291.38
  Buddhism 294.343 8
  Christianity 264.13
  Hinduism 294.538
  Islam 297.382 4
    Sufi 297.438 24
  Judaism 296.45
Pre-Aryan period
  Indian history 934.01
Pre-Islamic prophets 297.246
Pre-Socratic philosophy 182
Preaching 291.61
  Christianity 251
  Islam 297.37
  Judaism 296.47
Preaching orders (Christianity) 255.04
  church history 271.04
Preble County (Ohio) T2—771 71
Precalculus 510
  see Manual at 510
Precambrian era 551.71
  geology 551.71
  paleontology 560.171
Precast concrete 624.183 414
  building construction 693.5
    with reinforcement 693.544
    without reinforcement 693.522
  manufacturing technology 666.893
  materials science 620.137
Precast concrete (continued)
  structural engineering 624.183 414
Precedence (Heraldry) 929.7
Precession
  celestial mechanics 521.9
    corrections 522.9
Precious metals 669.2
  decorative arts 739.2
  economic geology 553.42
  handicrafts 745.56
  materials science 620.189 2
  metallography 669.952
  metallurgy 669.2
  metalworking 673.2
  mining 622.342
  physical metallurgy 669.962
Precious stones 553.8
  see also Gems
Precipitates 541.348 5
  chemical engineering 660.294 85
Precipitation (Chemistry) 541.34
  engineering 660.284 24
Precipitation (Meteorology) 551.577
  geologic agent 551.35
  weather forecasting 551.647 7
  weather modification 551.687 7
PRECIS indexing 025.482
Precision (Information science) 025.04
Precision casting
  metals 671.255
Precision diving 797.24
  see also Sports
Precision engineering 620.004 5
Precision instruments
  technology 681
Preclassical Greek language 487.1
  T6—87
Preclassical Latin language 477
  T6—71
Preclassicism
  music 780.903 3
Precognition 133.86
Precoordinate indexing 025.482
Predation (Biology) 591.53
  plants 575.99
Predator control
  animal husbandry 636.083 9
  conservation technology 639.966
Predator-prey relations 591.53
Predatory animals 591.53
  small game hunting 799.259 7

Predelinquents 305.906 923
T1—086 923
social group 305.906 923
social welfare 362.74
Predestination 291.22
Christianity 234.9
Islam 297.227
Predicate and subject (Grammar) 415
specific languages T4—5
Predicate calculus 511.3
Prediction 003.2
probabilities 519.287
statistical mathematics 519.54
Predictions 003.2
occultism 133.3
religion 291.32
eschatological 291.23
Prefabricated houses 643.2
Prefabricated materials
architectural construction 721.044 97
building materials 691.97
construction 693.97
Preferential hiring
personnel management 658.311 2
public administration 352.650 8
union security arrangements 331.889 2
Preferred provider health insurance 368.382
see also Insurance
Preferred stocks 332.632 25
speculation 332.632 28
Prefixes 415
specific languages T4—5
Pregnancy 573.67
biology 573.67
cooking for 641.563
human physiology 612.63
obstetrics 618.2
psychology 155.646 3
veterinary medicine 636.089 82
Pregnancy programs in schools 371.714
Prehistoric archaeology 930.1
Prehistoric humans 569.9
Prehistoric religions 291.042
Prejudice 303.385
ethics 177.5
social theology 291.178 34
Christianity 261.834
Judaism 296.38
sociology 303.385
Preliminary hearings 345.072
Preliminary Scholastic Assessment Test 378.166 2
Preludes 784.189 28
Premarital counseling
Christian pastoral counseling 259.13
social welfare 362.828 6
see also Families—social welfare
Premarital sexual relations 306.73
customs 392.6
social problem 363.48
see also Sexual relations
Premature delivery
obstetrics 618.397
Premature infants
pediatrics 618.920 11
Premenstrual syndrome
gynecology 618.172
see also Female genital system
Premiers 321
cabinet governments 321.804 3
occupational group T7—351
public administration 352.23
Premium television 384.555 4
see also Television
see Manual at 384.555 vs. 384.5554
Premonstratensians 255.19
church history 271.19
Přemyslid dynasty 943.702 23
Prenatal care
obstetrics 618.24
Prentiss County (Miss.) T2—762 985
Prenuptial contracts 346.016
Preoperative care
surgery 617.919
Prep schools 373.222
see also Secondary education
Prepaid dental insurance 368.382 3
see also Insurance
Prepaid health insurance 368.382
see also Insurance
Preparation of food (Cooking) 641.5
Preparatory schools 373.222
see also Secondary education
Prepared doughs 664.753
Prepared ores 669.042
Prepared pianos 786.28
instrument 786.281 9
music 786.28
see also Keyboard instruments
Prepositional phrases 415
specific languages T4—5
Prepositions 415
specific languages T4—5

Prerelease guidance centers 365.34
see also Correctional institutions
Prerelease programs (Penology) 365.66
Presbyopia
optometry 617.755
Presbyterian Church 285
church government 262.05
parishes 254.05
church law 262.985
doctrines 230.5
catechism and creeds 238.5
general councils 262.55
guides to Christian life 248.485
missions 266.5
moral theology 241.045
public worship 264.05
religious associations 267.185
religious education 268.85
seminaries 230.073 5
theology 230.5
Presbyterian Church (U.S.A.) 285.137
see also Presbyterian Church
Presbyterian Church in the United States 285.133
see also Presbyterian Church
Presbyterian Church in the United States of America 285.132
see also Presbyterian Church
Presbyterian Church of Wales 285.235
see also Presbyterian Church
Presbyterian sacred music 781.715 1
public worship 782.322 51
music 782.322 51
religion 264.050 2
Presbyterians
biography 285.092
religious group T7—251
Presbyteries
Christian ecclesiology 262.4
Preschool children 305.233
T1—083 3
T7—054 3
home care 649.123
psychology 155.423
social aspects 305.233
Preschool education 372.21
child rearing 649.68
see also Elementary education
Preschool teachers 372.11
Prescott (Ont. : County) T2—713 85
Prescott and Russell (Ont.) T2—713 85
Prescribed burning
forestry 634.955
Prescription drug abuse 362.299
medicine 616.86
personal health 613.8
social welfare 362.299
see also Substance abuse
Prescription drugs 615.1
insurance 368.382 4
see also Insurance
pharmacology 615.1
see also Drugs (Pharmaceuticals)
Prescription filling 615.4
Prescription writing 615.14
Prescriptive linguistics 418
specific languages T4—8
see Manual at 410
Preseli (Wales : District) T2—429 62
Presentation (Parturition)
obstetrics 618.42
Presentation of Jesus Christ 232.928
Presentation religious orders 255.977
church history 271.977
Preservation 620.004 6
T1—028 8
arts 702.88
bibliographic materials 025.84
biological specimens 570.752
botanical specimens 580.752
lumber 674.386
museology 069.53
negatives and transparencies 771.45
positives (photographs) 771.46
zoological specimens 590.752
see also Historic preservation
Preserved Context Indexing System 025.482
Preserved foods
cooking 641.61
home economics 641.4
Preserves (Jams) 641.852
commercial processing 664.152
home preparation 641.852
Preserves (Whole fruits) 641.34
cooking with 641.64
food 641.34
home preparation 641.4
Presidente Hayes (Paraguay : Dept.) T2—892 23
Presidential government 321.804 2
Presidents 321
democratic systems 321.804 2
occupational group T7—351
public administration 352.23
Presidio County (Tex.) T2—764 933

Presque Isle County
  (Mich.) T2—774 82
Press 070
  civil rights issues 323.445
  influence on crime 364.254
Press control 363.31
  see also Censorship
Press law 343.099 8
Pressing clothes
  home economics 648.1
Pressing equipment 621.98
Pressing glass 666.123
Pressing metals 671.33
Pressing textiles 677.028 25
Pressure
  biophysics 571.437
    humans 612.014 415
  mechanics 531.1
Pressure cooking 641.587
Pressure distribution
  aeronautics 629.132 35
Pressure groups 322.43
  political process 324.4
  relation to government 322.43
Pressure perception
  psychology 152.182 3
Pressure regulators
  steam engineering 621.185
Pressure surge
  engineering 620.106 4
Pressure vessels 681.760 41
Pressure welding 671.529
Pressurization
  aircraft 629.134 42
  manned spacecraft 629.477 5
  spacecraft 629.477 5
Pressurizing oils and gases 665.028 2
Presswork
  printing 686.23
Preston (England :
  Borough) T2—427 665
Preston County (W. Va.) T2—754 82
Prestressed concrete 624.183 412
  building construction 693.542
  manufacturing technology 666.893
  materials science 620.137
  structural engineering 624.183 412
Presumptions (Law) 347.064
Pretoria (South Africa :
  District) T2—682 35
Pretoria-Witwatersrand-Vereeniging
  area (South Africa) T2—682 2
Pretrial procedure 347.072
  criminal law 345.072
Pretrial release 345.072
Preventive dentistry 617.601
  see also Dentistry
Preventive detention 345.052 7
Preventive medicine 613
  personal 613
  public 614.44
    animal husbandry 636.089 444
    public administration 353.628
    see Manual at 614.4–614.5
      vs. 362.1–362.4
Preveza (Greece) T2—495 3
Priapulida 592.3
  paleozoology 562.3
Price control (Government) 338.526
  economics 338.526
  law 343.083
  public administration 352.85
Price County (Wis.) T2—775 24
Price-demand relationship 338.521 2
Price determination 338.52
  economics 338.52
  marketing management 658.816
Price discrimination
  criminology 364.168
  trade law 343.072 5
Price-earnings ratio
  investment economics 332.632 21
Price fixing
  criminology 364.168
    criminal law 345.026 8
  trade law 343.072 5
Price indexes 338.528
Price leadership 338.523
Price levels 338.528
Price lists T1—029 4
Price statistics 338.528
Price-supply relationship 338.521 3
Price supports
  agricultural economics 338.18
    law 343.076 1
    public administration 354.528 5
  economics 338.52
  law 343.074 2
  public administration 352.85
Price trends T1—029 7
  collectibles T1—075
Prices 338.52
  agricultural industries 338.13
  economics 338.52
  land economics 333.332 3
  macroeconomics 339.42
  mineral industries 338.23

Prices (continued)
  regulation 338.526
    economics 338.526
    law 343.083
    public administration 352.85
  secondary industries 338.43
  stocks 332.632 22
  theories 338.521
Prickly heat
  medicine 616.56
  see also Skin
Pride 179.8
  literature 808.803 53
    history and criticism 809.933 53
    specific literatures T3B—080 353
      history and criticism T3B—093 53
  see also Vices
Prieska (South Africa :
    District) T2—687 12
Priesthood 291.61
  Christianity 262.1
    pastoral theology 253
  Jewish 296.495
Priesthood of believers 234
Priesthood of Jesus Christ 232.8
Priests 200.92
  biography 200.92
  Christian 270.092
    biography 270.092
      specific denominations 280
      see Manual at 230–280
    ecclesiology 262.14
    pastoral theology 253
    see also Clergy—Christian
  Jewish 296.495
  role and function 291.61
  see Manual at 200.92 and
      291–299
Prima facie evidence 347.064
Primaries (Elections) 324.54
  specific countries 324.24–.29
Primary batteries 621.312 423
Primary elections 324.54
  specific countries 324.24–.29
Primary epidermis (Plants) 575.451
Primary grades (United States) 372.241
  see also Elementary education
Primary groups (Sociology) 302.34
Primary industries 338
  economics 338
  law 343.076
Primary industries (continued)
  products 338.02
    commerce 380.14
      domestic 381.4
      foreign 382.4
      public administration 354.73
  public administration 354.3
Primary metal products 671.8
Primary productivity (Ecology) 577.15
Primary roads 388.12
  see also Roads
Primary school teaching 372.110 2
Primary schools (United
    Kingdom) 372
  see also Elementary education
Primary schools (United States) 372.241
  see also Elementary education
Primates 599.8
  animal husbandry 636.98
  conservation technology 639.979 8
  experimental animals
    medicine 619.98
  paleozoology 569.8
  resource economics 333.959 8
  zoology 599.8
Prime (Divine office) 264.15
  music 782.324
  see also Liturgy of the hours
Prime ministers 321
  cabinet governments 321.804 3
  occupational group T7—351
  public administration 352.23
Prime movers
  technology 621.4
Prime numbers 512.72
Primers (Detonators) 662.4
  military engineering 623.454 2
Primers (Readers) 418
  specific languages T4—86
    for nonnative speakers T4—864
Primitive art 700
  nonliterate peoples 709.011
Primitive Baptists 286.4
  see also Baptists
Primitive law 340.52
Primitive Methodist Church 287.4
  see also Methodist Church
Primitive religions 291.042
Primitive remedies
  therapeutics 615.899
Primitive societies 301.7
  psychology 155.81
Primitive weapons
  art metalwork 739.744 1

Primitivism
  arts 700.414 5
  T3C—145
  literature 808.801 45
    history and criticism 809.914 5
    specific literatures T3B—080 145
      history and criticism T3B—091 45
Primorskiĭ kraĭ (Russia) T2—577
Primor´ye (Russia : Kray) T2—577
Primroses 583.675
  floriculture 635.933 675
Primulales 583.675
Primulas 583.675
  floriculture 635.933 675
Prince (P.E.I.) T2—717 1
Prince Albert (Sask.) T2—712 42
Prince Albert (South Africa : District) T2—687 15
Prince Albert's yew 585.3
Prince Edward (Ont.) T2—713 587
Prince Edward County (Va.) T2—755 632
Prince Edward Island 971.7
  T2—717
Prince Edward Islands 969.9
  T2—699
Prince George (B.C.) T2—711 82
Prince George County (Va.) T2—755 585
Prince George's County (Md.) T2—752 51
Prince of Wales Island (N.W.T.) T2—719 7
Prince Rupert (B.C.) T2—711 1
Prince William County (Va.) T2—755 273 2
Princeton (B.C.) T2—711 5
Principal components analysis 519.535 4
Principals (Criminal law) 345.03
Principals (School)
  biography 371.200 92
  public control 379.157
  role and function 371.201 2
Print making
  graphic arts 760
Print media
  journalism 070.17
  sociology 302.232
Print specimens 686.224
Printed advertising 659.132
Printed books 094
Printed circuits 621.381 531
Printed music 780
  treatises 780.263
Printers 686.209 2
  occupational group T7—686 2
Printers (Equipment)
  computer science 004.77
  manufacturing technology 681.62
Printing 686.2
  photography 771.4
  textile arts 746.62
  textiles 667.38
Printing apparatus
  photography 771.49
Printing ink 667.5
Printing presses
  manufacturing technology 681.62
Printing solutions
  photography 771.54
Printing telegraphy 384.14
  wireless 384.524
  see also Telegraphy
Printmakers 769.92
  occupational group T7—76
  see Manual at 769.92
Prints
  arts 769
  cataloging 025.347 1
  library treatment 025.177 1
Prions (Subviral organisms) 579.29
Priories
  architecture 726.7
  church history 271
  religious significance of buildings 246.97
Pripet Marshes (Belarus and Ukraine) T2—478
Prisms 535.420 284
  geometry 516.15
  manufacturing technology 681.42
Prison administration 365.068
  public administration 353.39
Prison administrators 365.92
  occupational group T7—365
Prison camps 365.34
  military 365.48
  see also Correctional institutions
Prison chaplaincy 291.61
  Christianity 259.5
Prison discipline 365.643
  law 344.035 643
Prison farms 365.34
  see also Correctional institutions

Prison libraries 027.665
  administration 025.197 665
  collection development 025.218 766 5
  use studies 025.587 665
Prison life 365.6
Prison psychology 155.962
Prison reform 365.7
Prison security 365.641
Prisoner discharge 365.647
Prisoner-of-war camps 355.71
  living conditions 355.129 6
Prisoner release 365.647
Prisoners (Convicts) 365.6
  T1—086 927
  labor economics 331.51
  legal status 344.035 6
Prisoner's base 796.14
Prisoners exchange
  World War I 940.473
  World War II 940.547 3
Prisoners of war 355.113
  Algerian Revolution 965.046 7
  Chaco War 989.207 167
  Civil War (England) 942.062 7
  Civil War (Spain) 946.081 7
  Civil War (United States) 973.771
  Crimean War 947.073 87
  Falkland Islands War 997.110 247
  Franco-German War 943.082 7
  Hundred Years' War 944.025 7
  Indo-Pakistan War, 1971 954.920 517
  Indochinese War 959.704 17
  Iraqi-Iranian Conflict 955.054 27
  Korean War 951.904 27
  labor economics 331.51
  law 341.65
  Mexican War 973.627
  military operations 355.41
  Napoleonic Wars 940.277
  Persian Gulf War, 1991 956.704 427
  prisons and camps 355.71
    living conditions 355.129 6
  service status 355.113
  South African War 968.048 7
  Spanish-American War 973.897
  Thirty Years' War 940.247
  United States Revolutionary War 973.371
  Vietnamese War 959.704 37
  war customs 399
  War of 1812 973.527
  War of the Pacific 983.061 67
  World War I 940.472
  World War II 940.547 2
Prisoners-of-war camps 355.71
  living conditions 355.129 6
Prisons 365
  see also Correctional institutions
Privacy 323.448
  civil right 323.448
  law 342.085 8
Private accounting 657.63
Private airplanes
  engineering 629.133 340 422
  piloting 629.132 521 7
Private banks 332.123
Private bills
  enactment 328.378
Private carriers 388.041
  truck 388.324 3
  see also Freight services; Passenger services
Private colleges 378.04
  see also Higher education
Private companies 338.7
  law 346.066 8
  see also Business enterprises
Private detective services 363.289
Private duty nursing
  medicine 610.732
Private education 371.02
  see also Private schools
Private enterprise 338.61
Private international law 340.9
  see Manual at 340.9
Private investment 332.671 53
  domestic 332.672 53
  economics 332.671 53
  international 332.673 14
Private investors 332.671 53
  domestic 332.672 53
  economics 332.671 53
  international 332.673 14
Private land
  landscape architecture 712.6
  ownership
    economics 333.3
  subdivision
    economics 333.3
Private law 346
Private libraries 027.1
Private parks
  landscape architecture 712.6
Private police services 363.289
Private presses
  bibliographies of publications 011.55

Private publishers 070.593
Private schools 371.02
  elementary education 372.104 22
  finance 371.206
    law 344.076
  law 344.072
  public policy 379.3
  secondary education 373.222
  see Manual at 371 vs. 353.8, 371.2, 379
Private television 384.550 65
Private universities 378.04
  see also Higher education
Private welfare services 361.7
  see also Welfare services
  see Manual at 361.6 vs. 361.7, 361.8
Privateering
  naval operations 359.4
    see also Naval operations
Privatization 338.925
Privets 635.933 87
  botany 583.87
  floriculture 635.933 87
Privileges (Military awards) 355.134
Privileges of chief executives
  public administration 352.235
Privileges of diplomats 327.2
Privileges of legislators 328.347
Prize contests
  sales promotion 658.82
  use in advertising 659.17
Prize law 343.096
  international law 341.63
Prizes T1—079
  research 001.44
Pro-choice movement 363.46
  law 342.087 8
  social theology 291.178 366 67
    Christianity 261.836 667
    Judaism 296.38
  see also Abortion
Pro-life movement 363.46
  law 342.085
  social theology 291.178 366 67
    Christianity 261.836 667
    Judaism 296.38
  see also Abortion
Probabilistic number theory 512.76
Probabilities 519.2
  epistemology 121.63
  gambling 795.015 192
  insurance 368.01
Probabilities (continued)
  management decision making 658.403 4
  see Manual at 795.015192 vs. 519.2
Probability calculus 519.2
Probability distribution 519.24
Probate law 346.052
Probation 364.63
  law 345.077
  penology 364.63
  public administration 353.39
Probation after death 236.4
Probation of teachers 371.144
Problem of few bodies 530.14
Problem of *n* bodies 530.144
  astronomy 521
Problem of three bodies 530.14
  astronomy 521
Problem solving 153.43
  artificial intelligence 006.333
  educational psychology 370.152 4
  executive management 658.403
  psychology 153.43
  see Manual at 153.43 vs. 160
Problem students 371.93
Problems
  study and teaching T1—076
Proboscidea 599.67
  paleozoology 569.67
Proboscis worms 592.32
Procaryotes 579.3
Procedural rights 347.05
  public administration 352.88
Procedure (Law) 347.05
Procellariiformes 598.42
  paleozoology 568.4
Process
  philosophy of nature 116
Process analysis
  production management 658.5
Process control 003.5
  T1—011 5
  chemical engineering 660.281 5
  production management 658.5
Process design
  chemical engineering 660.281 2
Process management
  systems programming 005.424
  systems programs 005.434
Process metallurgy 669
Process philosophy 146.7
Process research
  production management 658.577
Process serving 347.072

Process theology 230.046
Processed cheese 641.373 58
  cooking 641.673 58
  food 641.373 58
  manufacturing 637.358
Processing (Libraries) 025.02
Processing centers
  library operations 025.02
Processing modes
  computer science 004.3
    T1—028 543
    see Manual at 004.1 vs. 004.3
Processions 394.5
  customs 394.5
  performing arts 791.6
  religious rites 291.38
    Christianity 265.9
  see Manual at 394.5 vs. 791.6
Processors
  computer hardware 004
    engineering 621.39
    see Manual at 004.1; *also at* 004.1 vs. 004.3
  programming-language translators 005.45
Prochlorales 579.39
Proctology 616.35
  see also Digestive system
Procurators fiscal 345.411 01
Procurement 658.72
  T1—068 7
  armed forces 355.621 2
  public administration 352.53
    specific forms of property 352.55–.57
Procurement of capital 658.152 2
  T1—068 1
Procyon 599.763 2
Procyonidae 599.763
Producer brands
  sales promotion 658.827
Producer gas 665.772
Producers' cooperatives 334.6
Product comparison T1—029 7
Product comparisons T1—029 6
Product control 363.19
  production management 658.56
  see also Product safety
Product design
  production management 658.575 2
Product development management 658.575
Product directories T1—029 4
  see Manual at 338 vs. 060, 381, 382, 670.294, 910, T1—025, T1—0294, T1—0296; *also at* 380.1 and 381, 382
Product evaluation 381.33
  T1—029 7
Product evaluations T1—029 6
Product improvement research
  production management 658.576
Product liability 346.038
  production management 658.56
Product liability insurance 368.562
  see also Insurance
Product life cycle management 658.5
Product listings T1—029
Product management 658.5
  marketing 658.8
  production 658.5
Product planning 658.503 8
Product recall 363.19
  law 344.042
  product safety 363.19
  production management 658.56
Product returns
  marketing management 658.812
Product safety 363.19
  criminology 364.142
    criminal law 345.024 2
  international law 341.765
  law 344.042
  production management 658.56
  social services 363.19
    public administration 353.99
Product servicing
  marketing management 658.812
Product specifications
  production management 658.562
Product standards
  production management 658.562
Production
  sociology 306.34
Production (Performing arts) 792.023 2
  ballet 792.84
  motion pictures 791.430 232
  musical plays 792.64
  opera 792.54
  radio 791.440 232
  stage 792.023 2
  television 791.450 232
Production capacity
  secondary industries 338.45

Production control
  management 658.5
Production controls (Economic
    programs) 338.9
  law 343.075
  public administration 354.28
Production cooperatives 334.6
Production economics 338
Production efficiency 338.06
  agricultural industries 338.16
  economics 338.06
  mineral industries 338.26
  promotion of
    management 658.515
  secondary industries 338.45
Production engineering 670
Production forecasting 338.544
Production forecasts 338.544 3
Production illustration 604.242
Production management 658.5
  T1—068 5
  see Manual at 658.5 and
    T1—0685
Production planning
  management 658.503
Production resources 338.09
Productivity
  agricultural industries 338.16
  labor economics 331.118
  mineral industries 338.26
  production economics 338.06
  promotion of
    personnel management 658.314
      executives 658.407 14
      public administration 352.66
    production management 658.515
  secondary industries 338.45
Products 338.02
  agricultural industries 338.17
    commerce 380.141
    production economics 338.17
  commerce 380.1
    public administration 354.73
  economics 338.02
  liability 346.038
  mineral industries 338.27
    commerce 380.142
    production economics 338.27
  secondary industries 338.47
    commerce 380.145
    production economics 338.47
    see Manual at 338.4 vs.
      338.47
Products research
  technology 607.2
Profanity 179.5
  customs 394
  ethics 179.5
    see also Ethical problems
Profession of faith
  Islam 297.34
Professional corporations 338.761
  accounting 657.834
  law 346.066 8
  mergers 338.836 1
  restrictive practices 338.826 1
Professional education 378.013
  T1—071 1
  see also Higher education
Professional employees 331.712
  social class 305.553
  see also Professional workers
Professional ethics 174
  see also Ethical problems
Professional fees
  labor economics 331.216 6
Professional liability 346.033
Professional liability insurance 368.564
  see also Insurance
Professional licensing 354.93
  law 344.017
Professional nurses 610.730 92
  role and function 610.730 692
  see also Nurses
Professional relationships T1—023
  economics 331.7
  ethics 174
    see also Ethical problems
Professional schools 378.155
  architecture 727.4
  area planning 711.57
Professional services 338.46
Professional sports 796.044
  law 344.099
  see also Sports
  see Manual at 796.08 vs.
    796.04
Professional workers 331.712
  labor economics 331.712
  personnel management 658.304 4
  public administration 354.93
  social class 305.553
  training
    personnel management 658.312 45
Professional writing 808.066
Professionals 305.553
  T1—086 22

Professionals (continued)
  labor economics 331.712
  social class 305.553
Professions 331.712
  T1—023
  economics 331.712
Professors 378.12
  occupational group T7—372
Profit and loss statements
  financial management 658.151 2
Profit sharing
  labor economics 331.216 4
  personnel management 658.322 5
Profitability measurement
  accounting 657.48
Profits 338.516
  agricultural industries 338.13
  financial management 658.155
  income distribution 339.21
  mineral industries 338.23
  production economics 338.516
  secondary industries 338.43
  taxes 336.243 2
    law 343.052 44
    public administration 352.44
    public finance 336.243 2
Progeny 306.874
  T1—085 4
  T7—044
Prognosis
  medicine 616.075
Progoneata 595.6
  paleozoology 565.6
Program auditing 658.401 3
  public administration 352.43
Program auditing (Computer-processed accounts) 657.453
Program audits 658.401 3
  public administration 352.439
Program compatibility 005
Program design 005.12
Program documentation
  preparation 005.15
  text 005.3
  see Manual at 005.15 vs. 808.066005
Program evaluation techniques (Network analysis) 658.403 2
Program languages 005.13
Program maintenance 005.16
Program music 781.56
Program notes (Music) 780.15
Program portability 005
Program reliability 005
Program verification 005.14
Programmable calculators 510.285 41
  see Manual at 004.1
Programmable controllers
  control engineering 629.895
Programmed instruction 371.394 4
  T1—077
  electronic 371.334
    adult education 374.26
Programming
  dramatic performances 792.023 6
    motion pictures 791.430 236
    radio 791.440 236
    stage 792.023 6
    television 791.450 236
Programming (Mathematics) 519.7
  see Manual at 005.1 vs. 510
Programming computers 005.1
  T1—028 551
  graphics 006.66
  knowledge-based systems 006.336
  multimedia systems 006.76
  see Manual at 005.1 vs. 510; *also at* 005.268 vs. 005.265, 005.269
Programming language translators 005.45
Programming languages 005.13
  computer graphics 006.663
  knowledge-based systems 006.336 3
  see Manual at 005.362
Programs (Broadcasting) 384.544 3
  communications 384.544 3
  radiobroadcasting 384.544 3
    communications 384.544 3
    performing arts 791.44
  television broadcasting 384.553 2
    communications 384.553 2
    performing arts 791.45
Programs (Computer) 005.3
  T1—028 553
  coding 005.13
  graphics 006.68
  multimedia systems 006.78
  see Manual at T1—0285: Machine-readable materials and programs
Programs (Party platforms) 324.23
Programs (Social action) 361.25
  public administration 351
Progreso (Guatemala : Dept.) T2—728 153
Progress 303.44

Progressions 512.93
algebra 512.93
arithmetic 513.4
Progressive Conservative Party of Canada 324.271 04
Progressive jazz 781.655
Progressive National Baptist Convention 286.135
see also Baptists
Progressive Party (U.S. : 1912) 324.273 27
Progressive Party (U.S. : 1924) 324.273 27
Progressive Party (U.S. : 1948) 324.273 7
Progressive taxation 336.293
Prohibited books 098.1
Prohibition Party (U.S.) 324.273 8
Prohibitive tariffs 382.73
see also Customs (Tariff)
Project Apollo 629.454
Project Gemini 629.454
Project management 658.404
public administration 352.365
Project Mariner 629.435 4
Project Mercury 629.454
Project method of teaching 371.36
Project Ranger 629.435 3
Projectiles 531.55
military engineering 623.451
physics 531.55
Projection welding 671.521 3
Projections T1—022 1
technical drawing 604.245
Projective geometry 516.5
Projective techniques
psychological testing 155.284
Projectors
manufacturing technology 681.418
Prokaryotes 579.3
paleozoology 561.91
Prolapse of uterus
gynecology 618.144
see also Female genital system
Proletarian dictatorship 321.92
Proletariat 305.562
T1—086 23
social class 305.562
Promethium
chemistry 546.414
see also Rare earths
Promiscuity
ethics 176
see also Sexual relations—ethics
Promissory notes 332.77
law 346.096
Promotion
armed forces 355.112
personal success 650.14
personnel management 658.312 6
employee motivation 658.314 2
public administration 352.66
Promotion (Students) 371.283
Pronghorn 599.639
conservation technology 639.979 639
resource economics 333.959 639
Pronouns 415
specific languages T4—5
Pronunciation 414
applied linguistics 418
specific languages T4—81
elementary education 372.622
linguistics 414
specific languages T4—152
singing 783.043
Proof theory
mathematical logic 511.3
Proofreading
printing 686.225 5
Proofs of God's existence 212.1
Propaganda 303.375
armed services 355.34
see also Unconventional warfare
Civil War (United States) 973.788
international politics 327.14
political parties 324.23
political science 320.014
social control 303.375
United States Revolutionary War 973.388
War of 1812 973.528
World War I 940.488
World War II 940.548 8
Propagation of sound 534.2
see also Sound
Propane 665.773
Propellants 662.26
aircraft 629.134 351
military explosives 623.452 6
Propeller-driven airplanes 387.733 43
engineering 629.133 343
military engineering 623.746 042
transportation services 387.733 43
see also Aircraft
Propellers
aircraft 629.134 36
ships 623.873
Proper integrals 515.43

Proper of the mass 264.36
  music 782.323 5
    choral and mixed voices 782.532 35
    single voices 783.093 235
Property
  economic theory 330.17
  law 346.04
  sociology 306.32
Property damage insurance 368.1
  see also Insurance
Property insurance 368.1
  commercial 368.12
  see also Insurance
Property law 346.04
Property loss insurance 368.1
  see also Insurance
Property management
  public administration 352.5
Property offenses 364.16
  law 345.026
Property rights 323.46
  law 346.042
Property risks 368.06
Property tax 336.22
  law 343.054
  public administration 352.44
  public finance 336.22
Prophecies 133.3
  occultism 133.3
  religion 291.32
    Biblical 220.15
    eschatological 291.23
      Christianity 236
      Judaism 296.33
    messianic
      Christianity 232.12
      Judaism 296.336
Prophecy (Concept) 291.211 7
  Christianity 231.745
    spiritual gift 234.13
  in Bible 220.15
  Islam 297.211 5
  Judaism 296.311 55
Prophetic books (Old Testament) 224
Prophetic books
    (Pseudepigrapha) 229.913
Prophetic message
  Bible 220.15
Prophetic office of Jesus Christ 232.8
Prophets 200.92
  biography 200.92
  Islam 297.246
Prophets (continued)
  role and function 291.61
  see Manual at 200.92 and
      291–299
Prophets (Biblical books) 224
Prophylaxis
  public health 614.44
Propjet engines
  aircraft 629.134 353 2
Proportion
  architectural design
    horizontal plane 729.23
    vertical plane 729.13
Proportion (Mathematics) 512.924
  algebra 512.924
  arithmetic 513.24
Proportional counters
  nuclear physics 539.773
Proportional representation 328.334 7
  law 342.053
Proportional taxation 336.293
Propositional calculus 511.3
Propositions
  logic 160
Proprietary libraries 027.2
Proprietor's income
  macroeconomics 339.21
Proprietorships 338.72
  accounting 657.91
  economics 338.72
  management 658.041
    initiation 658.114 1
    see Manual at 658.04 vs.
        658.114, 658.402
Proprioceptive organs
  human anatomy 611.8
  human physiology 612.88
  see also Nervous system
Proprioceptive perception
  psychology 152.188
Propulsion systems 621.4
  air-cushion vehicles 629.314
  spacecraft 629.475
  unmanned spacecraft 629.465
Prose literature 808.888
  specific literatures T3B—808
    individual authors T3A—8
Prosecution 345.050 42
Proselytizing
  Judaism 296.69
Prosencephalon
  human physiology 612.825
  see also Nervous system

Prosimii 599.83
  paleozoology 569.83
Prosobranchia 594.32
  paleozoology 564.32
Prosodic analysis (Linguistics) 414.6
  specific languages T4—16
Prosody 808.1
  linguistics 414.6
    specific languages T4—16
  see Manual at 808.1 vs. 414.6
Prospecting 622.1
Prospectors 622.109 2
  occupational group T7—622
Prosperity
  economics 338.542
Prostate 573.658
  biology 573.658
  human anatomy 611.63
  human physiology 612.61
  medicine 616.65
  see also Male genital system
Prosthetic dentistry 617.69
  see also Dentistry
Prosthetic devices 617.9
  manufacturing technology 681.761
Prosthetic ophthalmology 617.79
  see also Eyes
Prosthodontics 617.69
  see also Dentistry
Prostitution 306.74
  criminology 364.153 4
    criminal law 345.025 34
  ethics 176.5
    see also Sexual relations—ethics
  public control 363.44
    law 344.054 4
    public administration 353.37
  sociology 306.74
Protacanthopterygii 597.5
Protactinium
  chemistry 546.424
  metallurgy 669.292 4
  see also Chemicals; Metals
Proteales 583.89
Proteas 635.933 89
  botany 583.89
  floriculture 635.933 89
Proteases 572.76
  see also Enzymes
Protection of natural resources 333.72
  see also Conservation of natural resources
Protective adaptation 578.47
  animals 591.47
  plants 581.47
Protective barriers
  road engineering 625.795
Protective behaviors (Animals) 591.566
Protective clothing 391
  commercial technology 687.16
  customs 391
  see also Clothing
Protective coatings 667.9
Protective coloration (Biology) 578.47
  animals 591.472
  plants 581.47
Protective construction
  military engineering 623.38
Protective gloves
  manufacturing technology 685.43
Protective tariffs 382.73
  see also Customs (Tariff)
Protectorates 321.08
  see also Semisovereign states
Protein cooking 641.563 8
Protein deficiency 571.946
Protein plastics 668.43
Proteins 572.6
  applied nutrition 613.282
    animal husbandry 636.085 22
  biochemistry 572.6
    humans 612.015 75
  chemistry 547.75
  metabolic disorders 571.946
    medicine 616.399 5
  metabolism
    human physiology 612.398
    see also Digestive system
Proteinuria
  medicine 616.63
  see also Urinary system
Proteolytic enzymes 572.76
  see also Enzymes
Proterozoic era 551.715
  geology 551.715
  paleontology 560.171 5
Protest 303.6
  social action 361.23
Protest groups 322.4
Protest music 781.592
Protest stoppages 331.892 6
  see also Strikes (Work stoppages)
Protestant art
  religious significance 246.4

Protestant churches 280.4
  see also Protestantism
Protestant Methodists 287.53
  see also Methodist Church
Protestant regions T2—176 14
Protestantism 280.4
  church law 262.980 4
  conversion to 248.244
  doctrines 230.044
  guides to Christian life 248.480 4
  missions 266
  moral theology 241.040 4
  public worship 264
  religious associations 267.180 4
  religious education 268.804
  seminaries 230.071 1
  theology 230.044
Protestants
  biography 280.409 2
  religious group T7—204 4
Protista 579
  see also Microorganisms
Proto-Malay languages 499.28
  T6—992 8
Protobranchia 594.4
Protoceratops 567.915
Protocol (Diplomacy) 327.2
Protocols
  communications engineering 621.382 12
  computer communications 004.62
  interfacing 004.62
Protocols (Treaties)
  international law 341.37
    texts 341.026
Protolepidodendrales 561.79
Protomycetales 579.562
Protons 539.721 23
Protophytes 579
Protoplasm 571.6
Prototheria 599.29
  paleozoology 569.29
Protozoa 579.4
  medical microbiology 616.016
  paleontology 561.99
Protozoan diseases (Biology) 571.994
  agriculture 632.3
  plant crops 632.3
  veterinary medicine 636.089 693 6
Protozoan diseases (Human)
  incidence 614.53
  medicine 616.936
  see also Communicable diseases (Human)
Protozoologists 579.409 2
  occupational group T7—579
Protura 595.722
Provençal language 449
  T6—491
Provençal literature 849
Provence (France) T2—449
Provence-Alpes-Côte d'Azur (France) T2—449
Provence-Côte d'Azur (France) T2—449
Proverbs 398.9
Proverbs (Biblical book) 223.7
Providence (R.I.) T2—745 2
Providence County (R.I.) T2—745 1
Providence of God 214.8
  Christianity 231.5
  comparative religion 291.211 7
  Judaism 296.311 4
  philosophy of religion 214.8
Provident societies 334.7
  economics 334.7
  insurance 368
    see also Insurance
Province of Canada 971.04
  T2—71
Provinces 320.83
  public administration 352.14
    support and control 353.33
    see Manual at 351.3–351.9 vs. 352.13–352.19; *also at* 352.13 vs. 352.15
Provinces (Local government units) 320.83
  see also Counties
Provinces (State-level units) 321.023
  see also States (Members of federations)
Provincial administration 352.14
  see also Provinces—public administration
Provincial banks 332.122 4
Provincial-local relations 320.404 9
  law 342.042
  public administration 353.334
Provincial planning
  civic art 711.3
  economics 338.9
Provincial taxation 336.201 3
  law 343.043
  public administration 352.442 13
  public finance 336.201 3

Provincialisms
  linguistics 417.2
    specific languages T4—7
Provisional courts 342.066 4
Prowers County (Colo.) T2—788 98
Proximity topology 514.323
Proxy
  law 346.066 6
Prudence 179.9
  see also Virtues
Pruning 631.542
  equipment manufacturing
      technology 681.763 1
  fruit crops 634.044 2
  horticulture 635.044 2
  ornamental arboriculture 635.977
  ornamental plants 635.915 42
Prussia (Kingdom) T2—43
Prussia, East (Poland and
    Russia) T2—438 3
  Poland T2—438 3
  Russia T2—472 4
Prussia, West (Poland) T2—438 2
Prussian language, Old 491.91
  T6—919 1
Prussian literature, Old 891.91
Prussian Saxony T2—431 8
Przemyśl (Poland :
    Voivodeship) T2—438 6
Przewalski's horse 599.665 5
Psalms 223.2
  music 782.294
    choral and mixed voices 782.529 4
    single voices 783.092 94
Psalteries 787.75
  see also Stringed instruments
Psalters 264.15
  Anglican 264.030 15
    texts 264.038
  Roman Catholic 264.020 15
    texts 264.028
PSAT (Assessment test) 378.166 2
Pselaphidae 595.764 2
Pseudepigrapha 229.9
Pseudo-Demetrius I
  Russian history 947.045
Pseudo-Demetrius II
  Russian history 947.045
Pseudo gospels 229.8
Pseudoanalytic functions 515.98
Pseudoborniales 561.72
Pseudomonas 579.332
Pseudomorphism
  crystallography 548.3
Pseudonymous works
  bibliographies 014
Pseudopoda 571.67
Pseudoscorpiones 595.47
Psi phenomena 133.8
Psilophytales 561.74
Psilopsida 587.4
  paleobotany 561.74
Psilotales 587.4
  paleobotany 561.74
Psittaciformes 598.71
  paleozoology 568.7
Psittacosis (Biology)
  veterinary medicine 636.686 539
Psittacosis (Human)
  incidence 614.566
  medicine 616.958
  see also Communicable
      diseases (Human)
Pskov (Russia : Oblast) T2—472 3
Pskovskaîa oblast´ (Russia) T2—472 3
Psocoptera 595.732
Psophiidae 598.32
Psoriasis
  medicine 616.526
  see also Skin
Psychedelic drugs 615.788 3
Psychedelics abuse 362.294
  medicine 616.863 4
  personal health 613.83
  social welfare 362.294
  see also Substance abuse
Psychiatric clinics 362.22
  see also Mental health
      services
Psychiatric disorders
  medicine 616.89
  see also Mental illness
Psychiatric hospitals 362.21
  architecture 725.52
  see also Mental health
      services
Psychiatric insurance 368.382 5
  see also Insurance
Psychiatric nursing
  medicine 610.736 8
Psychiatric social work 362.204 25
Psychiatrists
  law 344.041 2
  malpractice 344.041 21

Psychiatry 616.89
  geriatrics 618.976 89
  pediatrics 618.928 9
  see also Mental illness
  see Manual at 616.89 vs. 150.195
Psychic messages 133.93
Psychic phenomena 133.8
Psychic therapy
  medicine 615.852
Psychoanalysis 150.195
  psychiatry 616.891 7
  psychology 150.195
  see also Mental illness
  see Manual at 616.89 vs. 150.195
Psychobiology 573.8
  humans 612.8
  see also Nervous system
Psychodidae 595.772
Psychodrama
  psychiatry 616.891 523
  see also Mental illness
Psychokinesis 133.88
Psycholinguistics 401.9
  specific languages T4—019
Psychological causes of war 355.027 5
Psychological characteristics
  influence on crime 364.24
Psychological fiction 808.838 3
  history and criticism 809.383
  specific literatures T3B—308 3
    individual authors T3A—3
Psychological principles T1—019
Psychological systems 150.19
  see Manual at 152–158 vs. 150.19
Psychological warfare 355.343 4
  see also Unconventional warfare
Psychologists 150.92
  occupational group T7—15
Psychology 150
  T1—019
  information systems 025.061 5
  see Manual at 302–307 vs. 150, T1—019
Psychology (Animals) 591.5
Psychology and religion 291.175
  Christianity 261.515
  Judaism 296.371
Psychology of religion 200.19
Psychometrics 150.151 95
  tests 150.287
Psychopathic personality
  medicine 616.858 2
  see also Mental illness
Psychopathology 616.89
  see also Mental illness
Psychopharmacology 615.78
  see also Mental illness
Psychophysiology
  humans 612.8
  see also Nervous system
Psychoses 362.26
  medicine 616.89
  puerperal diseases
    medicine 618.76
  social welfare 362.26
  see also Mental illness
Psychosexual disorders
  medicine 616.858 3
  see also Mental illness
Psychosomatic medicine 616.08
Psychosurgery 617.481
  see also Nervous system
Psychotherapy
  psychiatry 616.891 4
  see also Mental illness
Psychotropic drugs
  pharmacodynamics 615.788
Psychrometrics
  air conditioning
    buildings 697.931 5
PT boats 359.835 8
  design 623.812 58
  engineering 623.825 8
  naval equipment 359.835 8
  naval units 359.325 8
Ptarmigans 598.633
Pteranodon 567.918
Pteridophyta 587
  paleobotany 561.7
Pteridospermae 561.595
Pterobranchia 593.99
  paleozoology 563.99
Pteroclididae 598.65
Pterodactylus 567.918
Pteromedusae 593.55
Pterophyllum 597.74
Pteropoda 594.37
Pteropodidae 599.49
Pterosauria 567.918
Pterygota 595.7
  paleozoology 565.7
Ptilogonatidae 598.853
Ptolemaic dynasty 932.021

Puberty 612.661
  customs 392.14
  etiquette 395.24
  human physiology 612.661
  music 781.583
Public accounting 657.61
  law 346.063
Public address systems
  engineering 621.389 2
  office use 651.79
Public administration 351
  armed forces 355.6
  ethics 172.2
    see also Political ethics
  subordinate jurisdictions 352.14
    support and control 353.33
    see Manual at 351.3–351.9 vs. 352.13–352.19; *also at* 352.13 vs. 352.15
  see Manual at T1—068 vs. 353–354; *also at* 320.9, 320.4 vs. 351; *also at* 351; *also at* 363 vs. 340, 353–354
Public administrators 352.3
  biography 351.092
  executive management 352.3
  investigation
    public administration 353.46
  law 342.068
  occupational group T7—35
  role and function 352.3
Public behavior
  customs 390
  etiquette 395.53
Public borrowing 336.34
  see also Public debt
Public broadcasting 384.54
  radio 384.54
  television 384.554
Public buildings
  architecture 725
  interior decoration 747.85
  law 344.067 2
    public property 343.025 6
  plant management 352.56
  public works 363
    public administration 352.77
Public carriers 388.041
  see also Common carriers
Public colleges 378.05
  see also Higher education
Public contracts 352.53
  law 346.023
Public credit
  public finance 336.3
Public debt 336.34
  administration 352.45
  law 343.037
  macroeconomic policy 339.523
  public finance 336.34
  see Manual at 336.3409 vs. 336.343
Public defenders 345.01
Public discussion
  literature 808.853
    specific literatures T3B—503
      individual authors T3A—5
  rhetoric 808.53
Public education 370
  financial management 371.206
  government control 379.15
  law 344.071
  policy issues 379
  public support 379.11
    law 344.076
  revenue sources 379.13
  see also Education
Public elementary education 372
  see also Elementary education
Public employees 352.63
  see also Government workers
Public enterprise (Organization of production) 338.62
Public enterprises 338.74
  production economics 338.74
  public administration 352.266
  public revenue source 336.19
Public entertainment 791
  ethics 175
  music 781.55
Public expenditures 336.39
  administration 352.46
  law 343.034
  macroeconomic policy 339.522
  public finance 336.39
Public expenditures limitation
  law 343.034
Public facilities
  safety 363.1
    public administration 353.97
    see also Safety
  sanitation services 363.729
    public administration 353.94
    see also Waste control

Public finance 336
administration 352.4
economics 336
law 343.03
see Manual at 332, 336 vs. 339; *also at* 336 vs. 352.4; *also at* 336.093, 336.4–336.9 vs. 336.01
Public forests
economics
acquisition and disposal 333.11
Public health 362.1
international law 341.765
law 344.04
medicine 614
public administration 353.6
social welfare 362.1
Public health law 344.04
Public health nursing
medicine 610.734
Public health offenses 364.142
law 345.024 2
Public hearings
legislative 328.345
law 348.01
see Manual at 350 vs. 342–347
nomination of officials 351
see Manual at 300, 320.6 vs. 352–354: Nomination hearings
public administration 351
see Manual at T1—068 vs. 353–354
Public housekeeping 647
Public housing 363.585
household management 647.92
law 344.063 635
see also Housing
Public insolvency 336.368
Public investigations
official misconduct 353.463
Public investment 332.671 52
domestic 332.672 52
international 332.673 12
Public land sales 333.16
economics 333.16
law 343.025 3
Public lands 333.1
administration 352.57
economics 333.1
landscape architecture 712.5
law 343.025
revenue source 336.12
Public law 342
Public lending rights (Intellectual property) 346.048
Public liability insurance 368.56
see also Insurance
Public libraries 027.4
administration 025.197 4
collection development 025.218 74
public administrative support 353.73
publications for
bibliographies 011.67
use studies 025.587 4
Public life of Jesus Christ 232.95
Public lighting 628.95
Public limited companies 338.74
law 346.066 8
see also Corporations
Public opinion 303.38
Public order
public administration 353.3
Public order offenses 364.143
law 345.024 3
Public ownership
land economics 333.1
Public parks 363.68
see also Parks
Public performances 791
ethics 175
Public policy 320.6
law 342.041
see Manual at 300, 320.6 vs. 352–354: Public policy
Public preventive medicine 613
see also Preventive medicine
Public property
land economics 333.1
law 343.02
management 352.5
Public prosecutors 345.01
Public radio 384.54
Public records 352.387
archival treatment 025.171 4
civil rights issues 323.448 3
law 342.066 2
public administration 352.387
Public relations 659.2
armed forces 355.342
libraries 021.7
local churches 254.4
public administration 352.748
Public safety 363.1
see also Safety
Public safety offenses 364.142
law 345.024 2

Public sanitation 363.72
technology 628
see also Sanitation; Waste control
Public schools 371.01
elementary 372.104 21
finance
law 344.076
law 344.071
secondary education 373.224
see also Education
see Manual at 371 vs. 353.8, 371.2, 379
Public schools (United Kingdom) 371.02
secondary education 373.222
see also Private schools
Public securities
public finance 336.31
see also Government securities
Public service (Civil service) 352.63
Public service (Voluntarism) 361.37
public administrative support 352.78
Public service workers 352.63
see also Government workers
Public services
libraries 025.5
museums 069.1
T1—075 5
Public speaking 808.51
elementary education 372.622
Public speeches
literature 808.851
history and criticism 809.51
specific literatures T3B—501
individual authors T3A—5
Public spending 336.39
see also Public expenditures
Public structures
architecture 725
Public television 384.554
see also Television
Public toilets 363.729 4
technology 628.45
see also Waste control
Public transportation 388
see also Transportation
Public transportation vehicles 388.34
driving 629.283 3
engineering 629.222 3
transportation services 388.34
Public universities 378.05
see also Higher education
Public utilities 363.6
accounting 657.838
area planning 711.7
law 343.09
public administration 354.728
energy 354.428
social services 363.6
see Manual at 333.7–333.9 vs. 363.6; *also at* 363.5, 363.6, 363.8 vs. 338
Public utility workers 363.609 2
occupational group T7—363 6
Public welfare 361.6
law 344.031 6
see also Welfare services
Public works 363
law 344.06
public property 343.025 6
public administration 352.77
see Manual at 363
Public worship 291.38
Buddhism 294.343 8
Christianity 264
flower arrangements 745.926
Hinduism 294.538
Islam 297.38
Judaism 296.45
music 782.3
choral and mixed voices 782.53
single voices 783.093
see also Worship
Publicists
occupational group T7—659
Publicity 659
public administration 352.748
see Manual at 658.8, T1—0688 vs. 659
Publishers 070.509 2
occupational ethics 174.909 7
occupational group T7—097
relations with authors 070.52
Publishers' catalogs 015
Publishing 070.5
accounting 657.84
journalism 070.5
law 343.099 8
see Manual at 808.001–808.7 vs. 070.52
Pubs 647.95
architecture 725.72
Puddings 641.864
Puddling (Furnace practice) 669.141 4
Puebla (Mexico : State) T2—724 8
Pueblo County (Colo.) T2—788 55

Pueblo Indians T5—974
Puerperal diseases
  obstetrics 618.7
Puerperal perticemia
  obstetrics 618.74
Puerperal pyemia
  incidence 614.545
  obstetrics 618.74
Puerperal septicemia
  incidence 614.545
  obstetrics 618.74
Puerperium
  obstetrics 618.6
Puerto Plata (Dominican
    Republic) T2—729 358
Puerto Rican literature 860
Puerto Ricans T5—687 295
Puerto Rico 972.95
  T2—729 5
Puffballs 579.599
Puffbirds 598.72
Puffer fishes 597.64
Puffins 598.33
Pug (Dog) 636.76
Puget Sound (Wash.) 551.466 32
  T2—164 32
Puglia (Italy) T2—457 5
  ancient T2—377
Pukaki, Lake (N.Z.) T2—938 8
Pulaski County (Ark.) T2—767 73
Pulaski County (Ga.) T2—758 523
Pulaski County (Ill.) T2—773 998
Pulaski County (Ind.) T2—772 925
Pulaski County (Ky.) T2—769 63
Pulaski County (Mo.) T2—778 57
Pulaski County (Va.) T2—755 775
Puli 636.737
Pullovers 391
  commercial technology 687.146
  customs 391
  home sewing 646.454
  see also Clothing
Pulmonary abscesses
  medicine 616.244
  see also Respiratory system
Pulmonary embolisms
  medicine 616.249
  see also Respiratory system
Pulmonary heart disease
  medicine 616.12
  see also Cardiovascular
    system
Pulmonary thromboses
  medicine 616.249
  see also Respiratory system
Pulmonary tuberculosis
  incidence 614.542
  medicine 616.995
  see also Communicable
    diseases (Human)
Pulmonary valve
  human anatomy 611.12
  human physiology 612.17
  medicine 616.125
  see also Cardiovascular
    system
Pulmonata 594.38
Pulp 676.1
Pulp industry workers 676.109 2
  occupational group T7—676
Pulpboards 676.183
Pulpit platforms
  church architecture 726.593
Pulpits
  church architecture 726.529 2
Pulpwood
  forest products 634.983
Pulque 641.23
  commercial processing 663.49
Pulsars 523.887 4
Pulsating stars 523.844 25
Pulsating variables 523.844 25
Pulse
  human physiology 612.14
  musical element 781.222
  see also Cardiovascular
    system
Pulse circuits
  electronic circuits 621.381 534
Pulse detectors
  electronic circuits 621.381 536 5
Pulse generators
  electronic circuits 621.381 534
Pulse-jet engines
  aircraft 629.134 353 6
Pulse-modulated radar systems
  engineering 621.384 85
Pulse modulators
  electronic circuits 621.381 536 5
Pulse processes
  electronics 621.381 534
Puma 599.752 4
  conservation technology 639.979 752 4
  resource economics 333.959 752 4
Pumice 553.65
  petrology 552.23

Pumping stations
  sewer engineering 628.29
  water supply engineering 628.144
Pumpkins 641.356 2
  botany 583.63
  commercial processing 664.805 62
  cooking 641.656 2
  food 641.356 2
  garden crop 635.62
Pumps 621.69
  hydraulic 621.252
  ships 623.873
Punch (Beverage) 641.875
Punched card readers 004.76
  computer engineering 621.398 6
Punched cards 004.56
  electronic data processing 004.56
  nonelectronic data processing 004.9
Punching tools 621.96
Punctuated equilibrium 576.82
Punctuation 411
  specific languages T4—11
Puncture wounds
  medicine 617.143
Punic language 492.6
  T6—926
Punic Wars, 264–146 B.C. 937.04
Punishment
  armed forces 355.133 25
  law 345.077
  penology 364.6
  prisons 365.644
  social control 303.36
  social theology 291.178 336
    Christianity 261.833 6
Punjab (India) T2—545 52
Punjab (India : Province) T2—545
Punjab (India : State) T2—545 5
Punjab (Pakistan) T2—549 14
Punjabi language 491.42
  T6—914 2
Punjabi literature 891.42
Punjabis (South Asian people) T5—914 2
Punk rock 781.66
Puno (Peru : Dept.) T2—853 6
Puns
  dictionaries 413.1
    specific languages T4—31
Puntarenas (Costa Rica : Province) T2—728 67
Punting (Boating) 797.123
Punting (Kicking)
  American football 796.332 27
Punu language 496.396
  T6—963 96
Puppet films 791.433
Puppet masters 791.530 92
  occupational group T7—791 5
Puppeteers 791.530 92
  occupational group T7—791 5
Puppetry 791.53
  Christian religious use 246.725
    religious education 268.67
  elementary education 372.674
  production scripts 791.538
Puppets 791.53
  making 688.722 4
    handicrafts 745.592 24
    technology 688.722 4
  performing arts 791.53
  see also Toys
Puranas 294.592 5
Purari River (Gulf Province, Papua New Guinea) T2—954 7
Purbeck (England : District) T2—423 36
Purcell Mountains (B.C. and Mont.) T2—711 65
Purchase contracts
  accounting 657.75
  materials management 658.723
Purchase of real property 333.33
  economics 333.33
    private ownership 333.33
    public ownership 333.13
  law 346.043 62
    private ownership 346.043 62
    public ownership 343.025 2
Purchasing 658.72
  T1—068 7
  see also Procurement
Purchasing manuals 381.33
  T1—029 7
Purchasing power
  cost of living 339.42
  income-consumption relations 339.41
  value of money 332.41
  see Manual at 339.41, 339.42 vs. 332.41
Purchasing power parity 332.456
Pure food control 363.192
  see also Food—product safety
Pure Land Buddhism 294.392 6
Pure sciences 500
  see also Science

Purgatives
  pharmacodynamics 615.732
  see also Digestive system
Purgatory 291.23
  Christianity 236.5
Purification
  oils and gases 665.028 3
  petroleum distillates 665.534
Purified pulp 676.4
Purim 296.436
  liturgy 296.453 6
Purines 547.596
  chemical engineering 661.894
Puritanism 285.9
  doctrines 230.59
  moral theology 241.045 9
  persecution of others 272.8
Puritans
  biography 285.909 2
  religious group T7—25
Purple bacteria 579.38
Purple nonsulfur bacteria 579.385
Purpose
  philosophy 124
Purposive psychology 150.193
Purses 391.44
  customs 391.44
  manufacturing technology 685.51
Purslanes 583.53
Pursuit (Law enforcement) 363.232
Pursuit forces (Air warfare) 358.43
Pursuit planes 358.438 3
  engineering 623.746 4
  military equipment 358.438 3
Pus 571.937 9
Pushball 796.33
  see also Sports
Pushmataha County
    (Okla.) T2—766 65
Pushto language 491.593
  T6—915 93
Pushto literature 891.593
Puss in corner 796.14
Pustular eruptions
  medicine 616.52
  result of injury
    medicine 617.22
  see also Skin
Put 332.645
  multiple forms of investment 332.645
  stocks 332.632 28
Put and call transactions 332.645
  multiple forms of investment 332.645
  stocks 332.632 28

Putnam County (Fla.) T2—759 17
Putnam County (Ga.) T2—758 576
Putnam County (Ill.) T2—773 375
Putnam County (Ind.) T2—772 49
Putnam County (Mo.) T2—778 232
Putnam County (N.Y.) T2—747 32
Putnam County (Ohio) T2—771 18
Putnam County (Tenn.) T2—768 67
Putnam County (W. Va.) T2—754 35
Putonghua (Standard Chinese
    language) 495.1
  T6—951 1
Putters (Golf equipment) 796.352 35
Putting 796.352 35
Putumayo (Colombia :
    Intendancy) T2—861 63
Puy-de-Dôme (France) T2—445 91
Puzzles 793.73
PWV area (South Africa) T2—682 2
Pycnogonida 595.496
  paleozoology 565.49
Pyelitis
  medicine 616.613
  see also Urinary system
Pyelocystitis
  medicine 616.613
  see also Urinary system
Pyelonephritis
  medicine 616.613
  see also Urinary system
Pyemia
  incidence 614.577
  medicine 616.944
  puerperal diseases
    incidence 614.545
    obstetrics 618.74
  see also Communicable
      diseases (Human)
Pygmies (African people) T5—96
Pygmy right whale 599.52
Pygmy sperm whales 599.547
Pylorus 573.36
  biology 573.36
  human anatomy 611.33
  surgery 617.553
  see also Digestive system
Pyometra
  gynecology 618.142
  see also Female genital system
Pyorrhea
  dentistry 617.632
  see also Dentistry

Pyracanthas 635.933 73
  botany 583.73
  floriculture 635.933 73
Pyralidoidea 595.78
Pyramid power 001.94
Pyramidellacea 594.34
Pyramids (Buildings) 909
  Aztec 972.018
  Egyptian 932
  Incan 985.019
  Mayan 972.810 16
    Guatemala 972.810 16
    Mexico 972.650 16
  Mexican 972.01
  Toltec 972.017
Pyramids (Geometry) 516.15
Pyramids (Marketing) 381.1
  management 658.84
Pyrans 547.592
  chemical engineering 661.8
Pyrazoles 547.593
  chemical engineering 661.894
Pyrenees (France and Spain) T2—465
  France T2—448 9
  Spain T2—465
Pyrénées-Atlantiques (France) T2—447 9
Pyrénées-Orientales (France) T2—448 9
Pyrenomycetes 579.567
Pyridines 547.593
  chemical engineering 661.894
Pyrite
  mineralogy 549.32
Pyroclastic rocks 552.23
Pyrolaceae 583.66
Pyromagnetism 538.3
Pyromania
  medicine 616.858 43
  see also Mental illness
Pyrometallurgy 669.028 2
Pyrometers
  manufacturing technology 681.2
Pyrometry 536.52
Pyrophyllite
  mineralogy 549.67
Pyrotechnical devices
  military communications engineering 623.731 3
Pyrotechnics 662.1
Pyrotheria 569.62
Pyroxenes
  mineralogy 549.66
Pyrrhonic philosophy 186.1
Pyrroles 547.593
  chemical engineering 661.894
Pyrrophyta 579.87
Pythagorean philosophy 182.2
Pythagorean theorem 516.22
Pyuria
  medicine 616.633
  see also Urinary system

Q

Q fever
  incidence 614.526 5
  medicine 616.922 5
  see also Communicable diseases (Human)
Q hypothesis (Gospels) 226.066
Qacentina (Algeria : Province) T2—655
Qādarīyah (Islamic sect) 297.835
Qaddafi, Muammar
  Libyan history 961.204 2
Qādirīyah (Sufi order) 297.48
Qādisīyah (Iraq) T2—567 5
Qāhirah (Egypt : Province) T2—621 6
Qalyūbīyah (Egypt) T2—621
Qatar 953.63
  T2—536 3
Qataris T5—927 536 3
Qattara Depression (Egypt) T2—622
Qiblah 297.382
Qin dynasty 931.04
Qinā (Egypt : Province) T2—623
Qinghai Sheng (China) T2—514 7
Qirā'āt 297.122 404 5
Qohelet 223.8
Qoran 297.122
Quackery
  medicine 615.856
Quadra Island (B.C.) T2—711 2
Quadrants
  astronomy 522.4
Quadraphonic sound systems
  engineering 621.389 334
Quadratic equations 512.942
  algebra 512.942
  calculus 515.252
Quadratic forms 512.74
Quadratic programming 519.76
Quadratic residues 512.72
Quadrature 515.43
Quadrilaterals 516.15
Quadrilles 793.34

Quadros, Jânio
  Brazilian history 981.062
Quadruplets 306.875
  see also Siblings
Quagga 599.665 716 8
Quails 598.627
  conservation technology 639.978 627
  resource economics 333.958 627
  sports hunting 799.246 27
Quakers 289.6
  biography 289.609 2
  religious group T7—286
  see also Society of Friends
Qualifications of employees 331.114 2
  economics 331.114 2
  personnel management 658.306
    public administration 352.64
    selection 658.311 2
      public administration 352.65
    job analysis 658.306
      public administration 352.64
Qualitative analysis 544
  organic 547.34
  see Manual at 543 vs. 544–545
Quality control
  management 658.401 3
  military administration 355.685 7
  production management 658.562
  public administration 352.357
  statistical mathematics 519.86
Quality engineering 620.004 5
Quality of life 306
Quality of work life 306.361
  labor economics 331.25
Quality standards
  commerce 389.63
Quangos 352.8
  law 346.067
Quantitative analysis 545
  organic 547.35
  see Manual at 543 vs. 544–545
Quantity
  philosophy 119
Quantity standards
  commerce 389.62
Quantity surveying 692.5
  T1—029 9
Quantity theory
  monetary economics 332.401
Quantock Hills (England) T2—423 85
Quantum chemistry 541.28
Quantum chromodynamics 539.754 8
Quantum electrodynamics 537.67
Quantum electronics 537.5
Quantum field theory 530.143
Quantum flavor 539.721 67
Quantum mechanics 530.12
  see Manual at 530.12 vs. 531
Quantum physics 539
Quantum statistical mechanics 530.133
Quantum statistics 530.133
Quantum theory 530.12
Quantum theory of light 535.15
Quarantine
  disease control 614.46
  law 344.043
Quarks 539.721 67
Quarter (Law of war) 341.65
Quarter horse 636.133
Quarters (Time interval) 529.2
Quarters for military personnel 355.71
Quartets
  chamber music 785.14
  vocal music 783.14
Quartic equations 512.942
  algebra 512.942
  calculus 515.252
Quartz
  materials science 620.198
  mineralogy 549.68
Quartzites 552.4
Quasars 523.115
Quasi contract 346.029
Quasi-judicial agencies 352.8
Quaternary period 551.79
  geology 551.79
  paleontology 560.179
Quaternions 512.5
Quay County (N.M.) T2—789 26
Quays 387.15
  engineering 627.31
  see also Port facilities
Queanbeyan (N.S.W.) T2—944 7
Quebec (Province) 971.4
  T2—714
Québec (Quebec) T2—714 471
Québec (Quebec : Administrative region) T2—714 47
Québec (Quebec : County) T2—714 47
Quebec Act, 1774 971.022
Quebec Conference, 1864 971.049
Quebec Urban Community (Quebec) T2—714 471
Quechua Indians T5—983 23
Quechua language 498.323
  T6—983 23

Quechua literature 898.323
Quechuan languages 498.323
T6—983 23
Queen Anne's County (Md.) T2—752 34
Queen Anne's lace 583.849
Queen Anne's War, 1701–1714 940.252 6
North American history 973.25
Queen bees
apiculture 638.145
Queen Charlotte Islands (B.C.) T2—711 12
Queen Charlotte Sound (B.C.) 551.466 33
T2—164 33
Queen Charlotte Strait (B.C.) 551.466 33
T2—164 33
Queen Maud Land T2—989
Queens (Chessmen) 794.146
Queens (N.B.) T2—715 42
Queens (New York, N.Y.) T2—747 243
Queens (P.E.I.) T2—717 4
Queen's Bench Division of High Court of Justice (Great Britain) 347.420 27
Queens County (N.S. : County) T2—716 24
Queenscliff (Vic.) T2—945 2
Queensland T2—943
Queenstown (South Africa : District) T2—687 5
Queenstown (Tas.) T2—946 6
Queenstown-Lakes District (N.Z.) T2—939 5
Queleas 598.887
agricultural pests 632.688 87
Quenas 788.35
see also Woodwind instruments
Quenching metals 671.36
Quercoideae 583.46
Querétaro (Mexico : State) T2—724 5
Quesnay, François
economic school 330.152
Quesnel (B.C.) T2—711 75
Quesnel Lake (B.C.) T2—711 75
Quesnel River (B.C.) T2—711 75
Question
logic 160
Question-answering systems 006.3
Questionnaires
descriptive research 001.433
Questions and answers
study and teaching T1—076
Quetta District (Pakistan : District) T2—549 152
Queuing theory 519.82
management decision making 658.403 4
Quezaltenango (Guatemala : Dept.) T2—728 182
Quezon (Philippines : Province) T2—599 1
Quicas 786.98
see also Percussion instruments
Quiché (Guatemala) T2—728 172
Quiché Indians T5—974 15
Quiché language 497.415
T6—974 15
Quiches 641.82
Quiddity 111.1
Quietism 273.7
persecution of 272.5
Quileute Indians T5—979
Quileute language 497.9
T6—979
Quilling
handicrafts 745.54
Quillota (Chile : Province) T2—832 52
Quillworts 587.9
Quilting
arts 746.46
home sewing 646.21
Quilts 643.53
arts 746.46
household equipment 643.53
Quinary system (Numeration) 513.5
Quinces 641.341 4
botany 583.73
cooking 641.641 4
food 641.341 4
orchard crop 634.14
Quindío (Colombia) T2—861 34
Quinine
medicinal crop 633.883 93
Quinoidals 667.256
Quinolines 547.596
chemical engineering 661.894
Quinonization 547.23
chemical engineering 660.284 43
Quintana Roo (Mexico : State) T2—726 7
Quintets
chamber music 785.15
vocal music 783.15
Quintuplets 306.875
see also Siblings

Quirino, Elpidio
  Philippine history 959.904 2
Quitman County (Ga.) T2—758 924
Quitman County (Miss.) T2—762 453
Quito (Ecuador) T2—866 13
Quito Presidency 986.604
  T2—866
Quizzes
  recreation 793.73
Qumbu (South Africa : District) T2—687 91
Qumran community 296.815
  Dead Sea Scrolls 296.155
Qunayṭirah (Syria : Province) T2—569 14
Quoits 796.24
  see also Sports
Quorn (S. Aust.) T2—942 36
Quotas
  import trade 382.52
    see also Import trade
Quotations 080
  literature 808.882
    specific literatures T3B—802
      individual authors T3A—8
  see Manual at 080; *also at* 080 vs. 800; *also at* 081–089
Quran 297.122
Qwabe (Kingdom) 968.403 8
  T2—684
Qwaqwa (South Africa) T2—685 91

R

R and D (Research)
  production management 658.57
Rabat (Morocco) T2—643
Rabat-Salé (Morocco : Prefecture) T2—643
Rabaul (Papua New Guinea) T2—958 5
Rabbinical literature 296.1
Rabbinical seminaries 296.071 1
Rabbis 296.092
  biography 296.092
    specific denominations 296.8
  professional ethics 296.364 1
  role and function 296.61
  training 296.071 1
Rabbit hair textiles 677.35
  see also Textiles
Rabbits 599.32
  agricultural pests 632.693 2
  animal husbandry 636.932 2
  conservation technology 639.979 32
  experimental animals
    medicine 619.93
  resource economics 333.959 32
  small game hunting 799.259 32
  zoology 599.32
Rabies
  incidence 614.563
  medicine 616.953
  veterinary medicine 636.089 695 3
    incidence 636.089 456 3
  see also Communicable diseases (Human)
Rabies virus 579.256 6
Rabun County (Ga.) T2—758 123
Race discrimination 305.8
  law 342.087 3
Race discrimination in employment 331.6
  law 344.016
Race relations 305.8
  social theology 291.178 348
    Christianity 261.834 8
Race walking 796.429
  see also Sports
Racehorses 636.12
  sports 798.4
Racemization 541.7
Races (Ethnology) 305.8
  physical ethnology 599.97
  see also Minority groups (Racial, ethnic, national)
Races (Sports) 796
  see also Racing
Racetracks
  architecture 725.89
  automobiles 796.720 68
  horses 798.400 68
  humans 796.420 68
Rachidia (Morocco : Province) T2—645
Racial characteristics
  physical ethnology 599.972
  psychology 155.82
Racial conflict 305.8
  influence on crime 364.256
Racial discrimination 305.8
Racial groups 305.8
  T1—089
  T7—03

Racial groups (continued)
  literature 808.898
    history and criticism 809.8
    specific literatures T3B—080 8
      history and criticism T3B—098
    see Manual at T3C—93–T3C—99, T3C—9174 vs. T3C—8
  psychology 155.82
  see also Ethnic groups
Racial minorities 305.8
  see also Ethnic groups
Racially mixed people T5—04
Racine County (Wis.) T2—775 96
Racing 796
  aircraft 797.52
  animals 798
    dogs 798.8
    horses 798.4
  automobiles 796.72
  bicycles 796.62
  boats 797.14
  humans 796.42
  midget cars 796.76
  motor scooters 796.75
  motor vehicles 796.7
  motorcycles 796.75
  mountain bicycles 796.63
  soapboxes 796.6
  see also Sports
Racing animals
  animal husbandry 636.088 8
Racing cars 796.72
  driving 629.284 8
  engineering 629.228
  repair 629.287 8
  sports 796.72
    see also Sports
Racism 305.8
  ethics 177.5
    see also Ethical problems
  political ideology 320.56
  social theology 291.178 348
    Christianity 261.834 8
Racism in textbooks
  public control 379.156
Rack railroads 385.6
  engineering 625.33
  transportation services 385.6
  see also Railroad transportation
Racket games 796.34
  equipment technology 688.763 4
Racketeering 364.106 7
  law 345.02
Rackets (Game) 796.343
  see also Sports
Rackets players 796.343 092
  sports group T7—796 34
Racketts 788.5
  see also Woodwind instruments
Racon 621.384 892
  marine navigation 623.893 3
Racoons 599.763 2
  trapping 639.117 632
Racquetball 796.343
  see also Sports
Radar 621.384 8
  airport engineering 629.136 6
  electronic engineering 621.384 8
  marine navigation 623.893 3
  military engineering 623.734 8
  military gunnery 623.557
  nautical engineering 623.856 48
  weather reporting 551.635 3
Rade language 499.22
  T6—992 2
Radford (Va.) T2—755 786
Radha Soami Satsang 294
Radial street patterns
  area planning 711.41
Radiant energy 539.2
Radiant panel heating
  buildings 697.72
Radiant points
  astronomy 523.53
Radiation 539.2
  biophysics 571.45
    humans 612.014 48
  effect on materials 620.112 28
  effect on space flight 629.416
  meteorology 551.527
  physics 539.2
  solid-state physics 530.416
Radiation (Biological evolution) 576.84
Radiation biology 571.45
  humans 612.014 48
Radiation chemistry 541.382
  applied 660.298 2
Radiation injury (Biology) 571.934 5
  agriculture 632.3
  plant crops 632.3
  veterinary medicine 636.089 698 97

Radiation injury (Human)
  surgery 617.124
Radiation measurement 539.77
Radiation of heat 536.3
Radiation safety 363.179 9
  public administration 353.999
  see also Hazardous materials
Radiation sickness (Biology) 571.934 5
Radiation sickness (Human)
  medicine 616.989 7
  see also Environmental diseases (Human)
Radiation therapy
  medicine 615.842
Radiation warfare 358.39
Radiation weapons 358.398 2
  engineering 623.446
  military equipment 358.398 2
Radiative heating
  buildings 697.1
Radiators
  heating buildings 697.07
    steam 697.507
Radical theory 512.4
Radicalism
  agent of social change 303.484
  political ideology 320.53
Radicals (Chemicals) 541.224
Radiesthesia 133.323
Radio 384.5
  accounting 657.84
  communications services 384.5
  engineering 621.384
  influence on crime 364.254
  instructional use 371.333 1
    adult level 374.26
 T1—071 5
  international law 341.757 7
  journalism 070.194
  law 343.099 45
  marine navigation 623.893 2
  military engineering 623.734
  nautical engineering 623.856 4
  performing arts 791.44
    sociology 306.485
    see Manual at 384.54, 384.55, 384.8 vs. 791.4
  public administration 354.75
Radio (continued)
  religion 291.175
    Christianity 261.52
      evangelism 269.26
      preaching 251.07
      use by local Christian church 253.78
        administration 254.3
  sociology 302.234 4
Radio advertising 659.142
Radio astronomy 522.682
Radio beacons
  engineering 621.384 191
  marine navigation 623.893 2
Radio comment
  journalism 070.442
Radio communication 384.5
  see also Radio
Radio compasses
  aircraft engineering 629.135 1
  engineering 621.384 191
  marine navigation 623.893 2
Radio control
  airport engineering 629.136 6
  engineering 621.384 196
Radio direction finders
  aircraft engineering 629.135 1
Radio drama
  literature 808.822 2
    history and criticism 809.222
    specific literatures T3B—202 2
      individual authors T3A—2
  rhetoric 808.222
Radio engineers 621.384 092
  occupational group T7—621 3
Radio evangelism 269.26
Radio frequency allocation 384.545 24
Radio-frequency spectroscopes
  manufacturing technology 681.414 8
Radio genres 791.446
Radio music 781.544
Radio networks 384.540 65
  facilities 384.545 5
  organizations 384.540 65
  performing arts 791.44
  see Manual at 384.54065 vs. 384.5453, 384.5455
Radio news 070.194
Radio plays 791.447
  literature 808.822 2
    history and criticism 809.222
    specific literatures T3B—202 2
      individual authors T3A—2
  radio programs 791.447

Radio plays (continued)
  rhetoric 808.222
  see Manual at 791.437 and 791.447, 791.457, 792.9
Radio programs 384.544 3
  broadcasting 384.544 3
  performing arts 791.44
Radio relay
  telephone engineering 621.387 82
    see Manual at 621.3845 vs. 621.38782
Radio scripts 791.447
  rhetoric 808.066 791
  see also Radio plays
Radio speeches
  literature 808.851
    history and criticism 809.51
    specific literatures T3B—501
      individual authors T3A—5
Radio stations 384.545 3
  architecture 725.23
  engineering 621.384
  facilities 384.545 3
  organizations 384.540 65
  performing arts 791.44
  see Manual at 384.54065 vs. 384.5453, 384.5455
Radio telescopes 522.682
Radio towers
  architecture 725.23
Radio waves 537.534
  biophysics 571.453
    humans 612.014 481
  physics 537.534
  propagation and transmission 621.384 11
Radioactivation analysis 543.088 2
  quantitative 545.822
Radioactive fallout 363.738
  physics 539.753
  social problem 363.738
  see also Pollution
Radioactive materials
  public administration 353.999
  public safety 363.179 9
  see also Hazardous materials
Radioactive pollution 363.738
  ecology 577.277
  see also Pollution
Radioactive substances 539.752
Radioactive tracers in chemistry 543.088 4
Radioactive wastes 363.728 9
  environmental engineering 628.5
    air pollution 628.535
    water pollution 628.168 5
Radioactive wastes (continued)
  law 344.046 22
  public administration 353.999
  social services 363.728 9
  technology 621.483 8
  see also Waste control
Radioactivity 539.752
Radioactivity prospecting 622.159
Radiobiology 571.45
  humans 612.014 48
Radiobroadcasting 384.54
  see also Radio
  see Manual at 384.54, 384.55, 384.8 vs. 791.4
Radiochemical analysis 543.088
  quantitative 545.82
Radiochemistry 541.38
  chemical engineering 660.298
Radiocommunication 384.5
  see also Radio
Radioecology 577.277
Radioelements 539.752
Radiofrequency spectroscopy
  engineering 621.361 5
  physics 537.534
Radiogenetics 576.542
Radiographic testing
  materials science 620.112 72
Radiography
  engineering 621.367 3
  medicine 616.075 72
    see Manual at 616.0757 vs. 616.0754, 616.07572
Radioimmunoassay
  medicine 616.075 7
Radioisotope scanning
  medicine 616.075 75
Radioisotopes 539.752
  chemical engineering 660.298 84
  chemistry 541.388 4
  physics 539.752
  technology 621.483 7
  therapeutics 615.842 4
Radiolaria 579.45
  paleozoology 561.995
Radiology
  medicine 616.075 7
    see Manual at 616.0757 vs. 616.0754, 616.07572
Radiology services 362.177
  see also Health services
Radiolysis
  chemical engineering 660.298 2
  radiochemistry 541.382

Radionuclide imaging 616.075 75
Radionuclides 539.752
Radios 621.384 18
  automobile 629.277
Radioscopic diagnosis
  medicine 616.075 7
Radioscopic urinalysis
  medicine 616.075 7
Radiosondes
  weather reporting 551.635 2
Radiotelegraphy 384.52
  communications services 384.52
  engineering 621.384 2
  military engineering 623.734 2
  see also Radio
Radiotelephony 384.53
  communications services 384.53
  engineering 621.384 5
    see Manual at 621.3845 vs. 621.38782
  military engineering 623.734 5
  see also Radio
Radiotherapy
  medicine 615.842
Radishes 641.351 5
  botany 583.64
  commercial processing 664.805 15
  cooking 641.651 5
  food 641.351 5
  garden crop 635.15
Radium 669.725
  chemical engineering 661.039 6
  chemistry 546.396
  economic geology 553.493
  human toxicology 615.925 396
  metallurgy 669.725
  see also Chemicals
Radium therapy
  medicine 615.842 3
Radius (Bone)
  human anatomy 611.717
  see also Musculoskeletal system
Radnor (Wales : District) T2—429 54
Radom (Poland : Voivodeship) T2—438 4
Radon
  air pollution 363.738
    see also Pollution
  air pollution technology 628.535
  chemistry 546.756
  economic geology 553.97
  gas technology 665.822
  see also Chemicals
Rae (N.W.T.) T2—719 3
Rae Lakes (N.W.T.) T2—719 3
Raetia T2—363
Raeto-Romance languages 459.9
  T6—599
Raeto-Romance literatures 859.9
Raffia
  textile arts 746.41
  textiles 677.54
    see also Textiles
Raffia palm 584.5
Rafflesiales 583.2
Raft zithers 787.73
  see also Stringed instruments
Rafting (Sports) 797.121
  see also Sports
Rafts 386.229
  design 623.812 9
  engineering 623.829
  transportation services 386.229
Rag pulp 676.13
Rāgas 781.264
Ragoli-Kuria languages 496.395
  T6—963 95
Ragtime 781.645
Ragusa (Sicily : Province) T2—458 15
Ragweeds 583.99
Ragworts 583.99
Rail fastenings
  railroad engineering 625.15
Rail transit services 388.42
  see also Local rail transit systems
Railings
  church architecture 726.529 6
Railroad accidents 363.122
  see also Railroad safety
Railroad atlases 385.022 3
  specific areas 385.09
Railroad buildings 385.314
  architecture 725.33
  see also Railroad terminals
Railroad cars 385.32–.34
  engineering 625.2
  see also Rolling stock
Railroad construction workers 625.100 92
  occupational group T7—625
Railroad crossings 385.312
  engineering 625.163
  transportation services 385.312
Railroad engineers 625.100 92
  occupational group T7—625

Railroad freight stations 385.314
architecture 725.32
see also Railroad terminals
Railroad insurance
inland marine 368.233
see also Insurance
Railroad mail 383.143
see also Postal service
Railroad passenger stations 385.314
architecture 725.31
see also Railroad terminals
Railroad police 363.287 4
Railroad post offices 383.42
see also Postal service
Railroad safety 363.122
law 343.095
public administration 353.98
Railroad stations 385.314
see also Railroad terminals
Railroad terminals 385.314
architecture 725.31
area planning 711.75
engineering 625.18
special purpose 625.3–.6
institutional housekeeping 647.963 1
law 343.095 2
transportation services 385.314
special purpose 385.5
urban 388.472
Railroad ties 625.143
Railroad tracks 385.312
engineering 625.14
interurban railroads 625.65
local railroads 625.65
military engineering 623.631
transportation services 385.312
Railroad transportation 385
engineering 625.1
international law 341.756 5
law 343.095
local transit 388.42
see also Local rail transit systems
public administration 354.767
transportation services 385
Railroad transportation workers 385.092
occupational group T7—385
Railroad workers 385.092
construction 625.100 92
occupational group T7—625
occupational group T7—385
Railroad yards 385.314
engineering 625.18
law 343.095 2
transportation services 385.314
Railroads 385
electrification
technology 621.33
engineering 625.1
landscape architecture 713
military engineering 623.63
mining 622.66
transportation services 385
see also Railroad transportation
Rails (Birds) 598.32
Rails (Railroads) 625.15
Rain 551.577
crop damage 632.16
meteorology 551.577
weather forecasting 551.647 7
weather modification 551.687 7
Rain forests 333.75
T2—152
biology 578.734
ecology 577.34
see also Forest lands
Rainbows 551.567
Raincoats 391
commercial technology 687.145
customs 391
home sewing 646.453
see also Clothing
Rainfall 551.577
Rains County (Tex.) T2—764 275
Rainy Lake (Minn. and Ont.) T2—776 79
Rainy River (Minn. and Ont.) T2—776 79
Rainy River (Ont. : District) T2—713 117
Raised-character publications
publishing 070.579 2
Raja yoga 181.45
Hinduism 294.543 6
philosophy 181.45
Rajasthan (India) T2—544
Rajasthani language 491.479
T6—914 79
Rajasthani literature 891.479
Rajasthani-speaking people T5—914 7
Rajiformes 597.35
paleozoology 567.35
Rajput (Indic people) T5—914 7
Rājshāhi (Bangladesh : Division) T2—549 24

Raleigh (N.C.) T2—756 55
Raleigh County (W. Va.) T2—754 73
Rallidae 598.32
Rallies (Automobile sport) 796.73
  see also Sports
Ralls County (Mo.) T2—778 355
RAM (Computer memory) 004.53
  engineering 621.397 3
Rama I, King of Siam
  Thai history 959.303 1
Rama II, King of Siam
  Thai history 959.303 2
Rama III, King of Siam
  Thai history 959.303 3
Rama IV, King of Siam
  Thai history 959.303 4
Rama V, King of Siam
  Thai history 959.303 5
Rama VI, King of Siam
  Thai history 959.304 1
Rama VII, King of Siam
  Thai history 959.304 2
Rama VIII, King of Thailand
  Thai history 959.304 3
Rama IX, King of Thailand
  Thai history 959.304 4
Ramadan 297.362
Ramakrishna movement 294.555
Raman effect 535.846
Raman spectroscopes
  manufacturing technology 681.414 6
Raman spectroscopy 543.085 84
  analytical chemistry 543.085 84
  engineering 621.361 3
  physics 535.846
Rāmānujāchārya (Philosophy) 181.483
Ramayana 294.592 2
Rameses II, King of Egypt
  Egyptian history 932.014
Ramie
  botany 583.45
  fiber crop 633.55
  textiles 677.15
    see also Textiles
Ramjet engines
  aircraft 629.134 353 5
Ramos, Nereu
  Brazilian history 981.062
Ramphastidae 598.72
Ramps 721.83
  architecture 721.83
  canal engineering 627.135 3
  construction 690.183
Ramses II, King of Egypt
  Egyptian history 932.014
Ramsey County (Minn.) T2—776 58
Ramsey County (N.D.) T2—784 36
Ramu languages 499.12
  T6—991 2
Ranales 583.34
Ranch-style houses
  architecture 728.373
Ranchers 636.010 92
  occupational group T7—636
Ranches 636.01
Ranchowner insurance 368.096
  see also Insurance
Randall County (Tex.) T2—764 834
Randburg (South Africa : District) T2—682 2
Randfontein (South Africa : District) T2—682 2
Randolph County (Ala.) T2—761 57
Randolph County (Ark.) T2—767 24
Randolph County (Ga.) T2—758 932
Randolph County (Ill.) T2—773 92
Randolph County (Ind.) T2—772 66
Randolph County (Mo.) T2—778 283
Randolph County (N.C.) T2—756 61
Randolph County (W. Va.) T2—754 85
Random-access memory 004.53
  engineering 621.397 3
Random fields 519.23
Random processes 519.23
Random walks 519.282
Ranganathan's Colon Classification 025.435
Range finders
  military engineering 623.46
  photography 771.37
Range management 636.084 5
  animal husbandry 636.084 5
  forage agriculture 633.202
Rangelands
  animal husbandry 636.084 5
  biology 578.74
  ecology 577.4
Rangeley Lakes (Me. and N.H.) T2—741 7
Ranger project 629.435 3
Rangers (Armed forces) 356.167
Ranges (Stoves)
  manufacturing technology 683.88
Rangifer 599.658

Rangitikei District (N.Z.) T2—935 5
  Hawke's Bay Region T2—934 64
  Manawatu-Wanganui Region T2—935 5
Ranidae 597.89
Rank (Heraldry) 929.7
Rankin County (Miss.) T2—762 59
Rankin Inlet (N.W.T.) T2—719 4
Ranks (Military grades) 355.33
Ranoidea 597.89
Ransom County (N.D.) T2—784 315
Ransom insurance 368.82
  see also Insurance
Ranunculales 583.34
Ranunculidae 583.3
Rao, P. V. Narasimha
  Indian history 954.052
Rap (Music) 782.421 649
Rapanui language 499.4
  T6—994
Rapateaceae 584.86
Rape (Crime) 364.153 2
  law 345.025 32
Rape prevention 362.883
Rape victims 362.883
  see also Victims of crime
Rapes (Plants) 583.64
  oil crop 633.853
Rapeseed
  oil crop 633.853
Raphidiodea 595.747
Rapid calculations 513.9
Rapid reading 418.4
  specific languages T4—843 2
Rapid transit 388.4
  see also Urban transportation
Rapid transit facilities
  architecture 725.33
  area planning 711.75
Rapid transit railroads 388.42
  engineering 625.4
  see also Local rail transit systems
Rapides Parish (La.) T2—763 69
Rappahannock County (Va.) T2—755 395
Rappahannock River (Va.) T2—755 2
Rapping (Spiritualism) 133.92
Raptors (Birds) 598.9
  conservation technology 639.978 9
  resource economics 333.958 9
Rapture (Christian doctrine) 236.9
Raqqah (Syria : Province) T2—569 12
Rare animals 591.68
  resource economics 333.954 2
Rare birds 598.168
  resource economics 333.958 22
Rare book libraries 026.09
Rare books 090
  bibliographies 011.44
  cataloging 025.341 6
  library treatment 025.171 6
Rare earths 669.291
  chemical engineering 661.041
  chemistry 546.41
  economic geology 553.494
  materials science 620.189 291
  metallography 669.952 91
  metallurgy 669.291
  physical metallurgy 669.962 91
  see also Chemicals
Rare fishes 597.168
  resource economics 333.956 8
Rare gases
  chemistry 546.75
  economic geology 553.97
  technology 665.822
Rare mammals 599.168
  resource economics 333.954 2
Rare plants 581.68
  resource economics 333.953 2
Rare reptiles 597.916 8
  resource economics 333.957 2
Rare species 578.68
  law 346.046 95
  resource economics 333.952 2
Rarefied-gas electronics 537.53
Raritan River (N.J.) T2—749 44
Rarotongan language 499.44
  T6—994 4
Ras al Khaimah (United Arab Emirates : Emirate) T2—535 7
Ra's al Khaymah (United Arab Emirates : Emirate) T2—535 7
Ras Tafari
  Ethiopian history 963.055
    as emperor 963.055
    as regent and king 963.054
Ras Tafari movement 299.676
Raspberries 641.347 11
  botany 583.73
  commercial processing 664.804 711
  cooking 641.647 11
  food 641.347 11
  horticulture 634.711

Rasps 621.924
Rastafari, Jah
  Ethiopian history 963.055
    as emperor 963.055
    as regent and king 963.054
Rastafarians
  biography 299.676 092
  religious group T7—299 6
Rat control 363.78
  social welfare 363.78
  technology 628.969 3
    agriculture 632.693 52
  see also Pest control
Rat kangaroos 599.22
Ratchet wheels 621.837
Ratchets 621.837
  music 786.886
    see also Percussion instruments
Rates
  communications industry 384.041
  insurance 368.011
  transportation services 388.049
  see Manual at 383–388: Offers for sale vs. Economic aspects
Rates (United Kingdom) 336.22
  law 343.054 2
  public finance 336.22
Ratio 512.924
  algebra 512.924
  arithmetic 513.24
Ration coupons
  prints 769.57
Rational functions 512.96
Rational psychology 150.192
Rationalism 149.7
  Christian polemics 239.7
  philosophy 149.7
  philosophy of religion 211.4
  political ideology 320.512
Rationality 128.33
Rationing 333.717
  law 343.07
  public administration 352.86
  social welfare 361.6
  see Manual at 333.7–333.9 vs. 363.6
Ratites 598.5
  animal husbandry 636.69
  paleozoology 568.5
Rats (Muridae) 599.35
  see also Rodents
Rats (Rattus) 599.352
  agricultural pests 632.693 52
  animal husbandry 636.935 2
  experimental animals
    medicine 619.93
  household sanitation 648.7
  pest control 363.78
    social welfare 363.78
    technology 628.969 3
      agriculture 632.693 52
    see also Pest control
  small game hunting 799.259 352
  zoology 599.352
Ratsiraka, Didier
  Malagasy history 969.105 2
Rattan
  basketwork crop 633.58
Rattan furniture 645.4
  manufacturing technology 684.106
  see also Furniture
Rattan palm 584.5
Rattan textiles 677.54
  see also Textiles
Ratting
  sports hunting 799.259 352
Rattle drums 786.96
  see also Percussion instruments
Rattled idiophones 786.885
  see also Percussion instruments
Rattles
  musical instruments 786.885
    see also Percussion instruments
Rattlesnake ferns 587.33
Rattus 599.352
  see also Rats (Rattus)
Rauwolfias 583.93
Ravalli County (Mont.) T2—786 89
Ravenna (Italy : Province) T2—454 7
Ravens 598.864
Ravines 551.442
  T2—144
  geography 910.914 4
  geomorphology 551.442
  physical geography 910.021 44
Raw food diet
  health 613.26
Raw materials 333.7
  economics 333.7
  military resources 355.24
Rāwalpindi (Pakistan : District) T2—549 142

Rawlings, Jerry J.
  Ghanaian history 966.705
Rawlins County (Kan.) T2—781 125
Ray County (Mo.) T2—778 19
Ray-finned fishes 597
  see also Fishes
Ray tracing
  computer graphics 006.693
Rayon
  textiles 677.46
    arts 746.044 6
    see also Textiles
Rays (Fishes) 597.35
  cooking 641.692
  food 641.392
Rays (Nuclear physics) 539.722
Razgrad (Bulgaria : Oblast) T2—499 3
Razgrad (Bulgaria : Okrŭg) T2—499 3
Razgradska oblast
    (Bulgaria) T2—499 3
Razgradski okrŭg
    (Bulgaria) T2—499 3
Razing buildings 690.26
Razors
  manufacturing technology 688.5
Reaction kinetics 541.394
  biochemistry 572.44
  chemical engineering 660.299 4
  enzymes 572.744
Reaction-time studies 152.83
Reactions
  biochemistry 572.43
  chemical engineering 660.299
  chemistry 541.39
Reactions (Classical mechanics) 531.113
Reactor physics
  nuclear engineering 621.483 1
Reactors
  nuclear engineering 621.483
Read Island (B.C. : Island) T2—711 1
Read-only memory 004.53
  engineering 621.397 3
Readability
  rhetoric 808
Reader advisory services
  library operations 025.54
Readers (Textbooks) 418
  applied linguistics 418
    specific languages T4—86
      for new literates T4—862
        see Manual at T4—862
      for nonnative
          speakers T4—864
        see Manual at T1—014
          vs. T4—864
  rhetoric 808
    specific languages 808.04
      see Manual at 808.0427
  see Manual at 420–490:
      Language vs. subject
Readers' theater
  elementary education 372.676
Reading 418.4
  child care 649.58
  elementary education 372.4
  library science 028
  recreation 790.138
  sociology 306.488
  specific languages T4—84
Reading (England) T2—422 93
Reading, Rufus Daniel Isaacs,
    Marquess of
  Indian history 954.035 7
Reading aids
  library science 028
Reading aloud
  child care 649.58
  rhetoric 808.545
Reading comprehension
  elementary education 372.47
Reading disorders
  special education 371.914 4
Reading failure
  elementary education 372.43
Reading for content 371.302 81
Reading groups
  adult education 374.22
Reading interests 028.9
Reading is Fundamental
    (Reading program)
  elementary education 372.423
Reading programs
  elementary education 372.42
Reading readiness 372.414
Reading-skill strategies
  elementary education 372.45
Ready-mix concrete 666.893
Ready reckoners (Arithmetic) 513.9
Ready-to-eat cereals
  commercial processing 664.756

Reagan, Ronald
  United States history 973.927
Reagan County (Tex.) T2—764 873
Reagents
  analytical chemistry 543.01
    quantitative 545.01
Real County (Tex.) T2—764 883
Real estate 333.3
  accounting 657.833 5
  investment economics 332.632 4
  land economics 333.3
  see Manual at 333.73–333.78 vs. 333, 333.1–333.5
Real estate business 333.33
  law 346.043 7
  malpractice 346.043 71
Real estate finance 332.72
Real estate investment trusts 332.632 47
Real estate market 333.332 2
Real estate sales tax
  law 343.054 6
Real estate syndication 332.632 47
Real numbers 512.7
Real property 333.3
  credit economics 332.72
  investment economics 332.632 4
  land economics 333.3
  law 346.043
    private ownership 346.043
    public ownership 343.025
  public administration 354.34
  see Manual at 333.73–333.78 vs. 333, 333.1–333.5; *also at* 346.043 vs. 333.1–333.5
Real property insurance 368.096
  see also Insurance
Real property market 333.332 2
Real property tax 336.22
  law 343.054
  public administration 352.44
  public finance 336.22
Real-time processing 004.33
  architecture 004.338 2
  communications 004.618 3
    programming 005.712 73
    programs 005.713 73
  graphics programming 006.677 3
  graphics programs 006.687 3
  interfacing
    programming 005.712 73
    programs 005.713 73
  knowledge-based systems
    programming 006.337
Real-time processing (continued)
  multimedia-systems programming 006.777 3
  multimedia-systems programs 006.787 3
  operating systems 005.447 3
  performance evaluation
    for design and improvement 004.338 4
  peripherals 004.718
  programming 005.273
  programs 005.373
  systems analysis 004.338 1
  systems design 004.338 1
  see also Processing modes—computer science
  see Manual at 004 vs. 004.33
Real-time programming 005.273
Real-valued functions 515.7
Real variable functions 515.8
Realia
  cataloging 025.349
  library treatment 025.179
Realism
  education 370.12
  fine arts 709.034 3
  literature 808.801 2
    history and criticism 809.912
    specific literatures T3B—080 12
      history and criticism T3B—091 2
  painting 759.053
  philosophy 149.2
  sculpture 735.22
Realistic fiction 808.838 3
  history and criticism 809.383
  specific literatures T3B—308 3
    individual authors T3A—3
Reality
  philosophy 111
Reamers 621.954
Reaping 631.55
Reapportionment (Legislatures) 328.334 5
Rear axles
  automotive engineering 629.245
Reason 128.33
  epistemology 121.3
  ethical systems 171.2
  philosophical anthropology 128.33
Reason (Theology)
  Christianity 231.042
Reasoning 153.43
  artificial intelligence 006.333
  educational psychology 370.152 4
  logic 160

Reasoning (continued)
  psychology 153.43
    subconscious 154.24
  see Manual at 153.43 vs. 160
Rebates
  law 343.072
Rebekah (Biblical matriarch) 222.110 92
Rebellion (Political offense) 364.131
  law 345.023 1
Rebuses 793.73
Recall (Elections) 324.68
Recall (Information science) 025.04
Recall (Memory) 153.123
Recataloging
  library operations 025.393
Receivership
  accounting 657.47
  credit economics 332.75
  law 346.078
Receiving operations
  materials management 658.728
Receiving sets
  radio 621.384 18
Recent epoch 551.793
  geology 551.793
  paleontology 560.179 3
Recently extinct species 578.68
  see also entries beginning with Rare
Receptionists
  office services 651.374 3
Receptions
  meal service 642.4
Receptive processes (Psychology) 152.1
Recession (Economics) 338.542
Recidivists 364.3
  T1—086 927
  see also Offenders
Recipes T1—021 2
  cooking 641.5
Reciprocal equations 515.253
Reciprocal trade 382.9
  law 343.087
Reciprocating engines
  aircraft 629.134 352
Reciprocating pumps 621.65
  hydraulic 621.252
Reciprocating steam engines 621.164
Reciprocity (Mathematics)
  number theory 512.74
Recitals
  music 780.78
Recitation
  Koran 297.122 404 5
  rhetoric 808.54
Recitation (Education) 371.37
Recitations
  literature 808.854
    history and criticism 809.54
    specific literatures T3B—504
      individual authors T3A—5
Recklinghausen's disease
  medicine 616.993 83
  see also Diseases (Human)
Reclaimed rubber 678.29
Reclamation of land 333.731 53
  see also Land reclamation
Reclassification
  library operations 025.396
Recognition (International law) 341.26
Recognition (Psychology) 153.124
Recognition of unions 331.891 2
Recoil
  military gunnery 623.57
Recollection (Psychology) 153.123
Recombinant DNA 660.65
Recombination (Genetics) 572.877
Reconciliation (Christian doctrine) 234.5
Reconnaissance (Military operations) 355.413
Reconnaissance aircraft 358.458 3
  military engineering 623.746 7
  military equipment 358.458 3
Reconnaissance forces (Air warfare) 358.45
Reconnaissance surveys (Geodesy) 526.31
Reconnaissance topography
  military engineering 623.71
Reconstruction (Aftermath of war) 355.028
  United States history 973.8
  World War I 940.314 4
  World War II 940.531 44
Reconstruction (Linguistics) 417.7
  specific languages T4—7
Reconstructionist Judaism 296.834 4
  liturgy 296.450 48
Record buildings
  architecture 725.15
Record keeping
  accounting 657.2

Recorders (Musical instruments) 788.36
  instrument 788.361 9
  music 788.36
  see also Woodwind instruments
Recording
  music 781.49
Recording devices
  communications engineering 621.382 34
  physical quantities 530.7
    manufacturing technology 681.2
Recordings (Sound) 384
  bibliographies 011.38
  see also Sound recordings
Records management 651.5
  office services 651.5
  public administration 352.387
Recovering substance abusers T1—087 4
Recovery
  economics 338.542
Recovery (Law) 346.043 2
Recovery from addiction
  devotional literature 291.432
    Christianity 242.4
  pastoral theology 291.61
    Christianity 259.429
  rehabilitation 616.860 3
  religious guidance 291.442
    Christianity 248.862 9
  social services 362.291 86
  social theology 291.178 322 9
    Christianity 261.832 29
  therapy 616.860 6
  see Manual at 616.86 vs. 158.1, 248.8629, 291.442, 362.29
Recreation 790
  agent of socialization 303.327
  armed forces 355.346
  child care 649.5
  church work 253.7
  crime prevention 364.44
  ethics 175
    religion 291.565
      Christianity 241.65
  human physiology 612.044
  influence on crime 364.25
  law 344.099
  prisoner services 365.66
  public administrative support 353.78
  social welfare 361.05
  sociology 306.48
  see Manual at 790
Recreation centers 790.068
  architecture 725.804 2
  see also Recreation facilities
Recreation facilities 790.068
  architecture 725.8
  community redevelopment 307.346
  recreation 790.068
  sanitation services 363.729 2
    see also Waste control
  social services 363.68
Recreation leaders 790.092
  occupational group T7—79
Recreation safety 363.14
  law 344.047 6
  see also Safety
Recreational activities 790.1
Recreational areas (Public areas)
  area planning 711.558
Recreational areas (Residential areas) 643.55
  home economics 643.55
  interior decoration 747.791
Recreational arts 790
  see also Arts; Recreation
Recreational equipment
  manufacturing technology 688.7
Recreational equipment makers 688.709 2
  occupational group T7—688
Recreational lands 333.78
  community sociology 307.334
  economics 333.78
    government acquisition and disposal 333.11
Recreational music 781.594
Recreational reading 790.138
  library science 028.8
Recreational therapy
  medicine 615.851 53
Recreational vehicles 388.346
  engineering 629.226
  pleasure driving 796.79
  transportation services 388.346
  see also Motor homes
Recreational water resources 333.784
Recreational waters
  hydraulic engineering 627.046
Recruiting
  armed forces 355.223
    law 343.012
  personnel management 658.311 1
    executives 658.407 111
    libraries 023.9
    public administration 352.65

Rectal anesthesia
surgery 617.962
Rectifiers
electrical engineering 621.313 7
electronic circuits 621.381 532 2
radio engineering 621.384 12
Rectum 573.379
biology 573.379
human anatomy 611.35
human physiology 612.36
medicine 616.35
surgery 617.555
see also Digestive system
Recurrent education 374
T1—071 5
see also Adult education
Recursion theory 511.35
Recursive functions 511.35
Recycling paper 676.142
Recycling technology 628.445 8
Recycling waste 363.728 2
see also Waste control
Red algae 579.89
Red cedars 585.4
Red corpuscles 573.153 6
human histology 611.018 5
human physiology 612.111
see also Cardiovascular system
Red Crescent 361.763 4
see also Welfare services
Red Cross 361.77
international 361.77
national 361.763 4
World War I 940.477 1
World War II 940.547 71
see also Welfare services
Red Cross nursing
medicine 610.734
Red deer 599.654 2
big game hunting 799.276 542
conservation technology 639.979 654 2
Red Deer (Alta.) T2—712 33
Red Deer River (Alta. and Sask.) T2—712 33
Red drum 597.725
Red dwarfs 523.88
Red fox 599.775
Red kangaroo 599.222 3
Red Lake County (Minn.) T2—776 963
Red meat 641.36
commercial processing 664.92
home preservation 641.492
see also Meat
Red panda 599.763
Red peppers 641.356 43
botany 583.952
see also Sweet peppers
Red River (Minn.-Man.) T2—784 1
see also Red River of the North
Red River (Tex.-La.) T2—766 6
Louisiana T2—763 6
Oklahoma T2—766 6
Red River County (Tex.) T2—764 212
Red River of the North T2—784 1
Manitoba T2—712 74
Minnesota T2—776 9
North Dakota T2—784 1
Red River Parish (La.) T2—763 64
Red River Rebellion, 1869–1870 971.051
Red River Valley (Minn.-Man.) T2—784 1
see also Red River of the North
Red Sea 551.467 33
T2—165 33
Red Sea (Sudan : Province) T2—625
Red Sea Province (Egypt) T2—623
Red seaweeds 579.89
Red squirrels (Eurasia) 599.362
Red squirrels (North America) 599.363
Red tide 579.87
Red Willow County (Neb.) T2—782 843
Red wine 641.222 3
commercial processing 663.223
sparkling 641.222 4
commercial processing 663.224
Red wolf 599.773
Redaction criticism
sacred books 291.82
Bible 220.66
Talmud 296.120 66
Redbridge (London, England) T2—421 73
Redbuds 635.977 374 9
botany 583.749
ornamental arboriculture 635.977 374 9
Reddersburg (South Africa : District) T2—685 6
Redditch (England) T2—424 43
Redemption 291.22
Christian doctrine 234.3
Christology 232.3
Judaism 296.32
Redemption (Public debt)
public finance 336.363

Redemptorists 255.64
  church history 271.64
Redevelopment
  community sociology 307.34
Rediscount 332.84
Redistricting (Legislatures) 328.334 5
Redpolls (Birds) 598.885
Reduced-instruction set computing 004.3
  see also Processing modes—computer science
Reducing
  dietetics 613.25
  for appearance 646.75
Reducing enzymes 572.791
  see also Enzymes
Reducing solutions
  photography 771.54
Reduction (Chemical reaction) 541.393
  engineering 660.284 43
  organic chemistry 547.23
Reduction in force
  economics 331.259 6
    employment security 331.259 6
    unemployment 331.137
  law 344.012 596
  personnel management 658.313 4
    public administration 352.69
Reductionism (Psychology) 150.194
Reductive algebras 512.55
Redwood (Sequoia) 585.5
  forestry 634.975 8
  lumber 674.144
Redwood County (Minn.) T2—776 35
Redwood National Park (Calif.) T2—794 12
Reed instruments 788.4
  see also Woodwind instruments
Reed organs 786.55
  instrument 786.551 9
  music 786.55
  see also Keyboard instruments
Reedbucks 599.645
Reedfishes 597.42
Reeds 584.9
Reefs 551.424
  T2—142
  biology 578.778 9
  ecology 577.789
  geography 910.914 2
  geomorphology 551.424
  physical geography 910.021 42
Reel-to-reel tapes (Computer) 004.56
  engineering 621.397 6
Reelfoot Lake (Tenn.) T2—768 12
Reeling textiles 677.028 22
  arts 746.12
  manufacturing technology 677.028 22
Reels (Dances) 793.34
Reengineering
  executive management 658.406 3
Reentry problems
  space flight 629.415
Reeves County (Tex.) T2—764 924
Refectories
  architecture 726.79
Refereeing (Recreation) 790.1
  American football 796.332 3
  basketball 796.323 3
  Canadian football 796.335 3
  golf 796.352 4
  ice hockey 796.962 3
  rugby 796.333 3
  soccer 796.334 3
  tennis 796.342 3
  see also Sports
Reference
  philosophy 121.68
Reference books 028.7
  bibliographies 011.02
  reviews 028.12
  use 028.7
Reference groups
  social psychology 302.52
Reference services 025.52
Reference works 028.7
  bibliographies 011.02
  reviews 028.12
  use 028.7
Referendum (Legislation) 328.23
Referral services
  physicians 362.172
Refined grain
  commercial processing 664.720 7
Reflecting circles 522.4
Reflection of light
  physics 535.323
Reflection of sound
  engineering 620.21
  physics 534.204
Reflex disturbances
  symptomatology
    neurological diseases 616.849
  see also Nervous system

Reflexes
  psychology 152.322
Reflexology
  psychology 150.194 4
Reforestation 333.751 53
  law 346.046 751 53
  resource economics 333.751 53
  silviculture 634.956
  see Manual at 338.1749 vs. 333.75: 15
Reform Judaism 296.834 1
  liturgy 296.450 46
Reform movements 303.484
  agent of social change 303.484
  relation to government 322.44
  social action 361.24
Reform schools 365.42
  see also Correctional institutions
Reformation 270.6
  European history 940.23
  German history 943.03
Reformation of offenders 364.601
Reformatories 365.34
  juvenile offenders 365.42
  see also Correctional institutions
Reformed Christians 284.2
  American 285.7
    biography 285.709 2
    religious group T7—257
  biography 284.209 2
  European 284.2
    biography 284.209 2
    religious group T7—242
  religious group T7—242
Reformed Church 284.2
  church government 262.042
    parishes 254.042
  church law 262.984 2
  doctrines 230.42
    catechisms and creeds 238.42
  guides to Christian life 248.484 2
  missions 266.42
  moral theology 241.044 2
  public worship 264.042
  religious associations 267.184 2
  religious education 268.842
  seminaries 230.073 42
  theology 230.42
Reformed Church (American Reformed) 285.7
  church government 262.057
    parishes 254.057
  church law 262.985 7
  doctrines 230.57
    catechisms and creeds 238.57
  guides to Christian life 248.485 7
  missions 266.57
  moral theology 241.045 7
  public worship 264.057
  religious associations 267.185 7
  religious education 268.857
  seminaries 230.073 57
  theology 230.57
Reformed Church in America 285.732
  see also Reformed Church (American Reformed)
Reformed Church in the United States 285.733
  see also Reformed Church (American Reformed)
Reformed Episcopal Church 283.3
  see also Anglican Communion
Reformed Hinduism 294.556
Reformed natural gas 665.773
Reformed Presbyterian churches 285.136
  see also Presbyterian Church
Reformed refinery gas 665.773
Refraction errors
  optometry 617.755
    incidence 614.599 7
  see also Eyes
Refraction of light 535.324
  astronomical corrections 522.9
Refraction of sound
  acoustical engineering 620.21
Refractivity
  materials science 620.112 95
Refractometry 543.085 3
Refractory materials 553.67
  economic geology 553.67
  materials science 620.143
  metallurgical furnaces 669.82
  technology 666.72
Refrigerants
  refrigeration engineering 621.564
Refrigerating foods 664.028 52
  commercial preservation 664.028 52
  home preservation 641.452
Refrigeration 621.56
  alcoholic beverages 663.15
  nautical engineering 623.853 5

Refrigeration engineers 621.560 92
  occupational group T7—621
Refrigerator cars 385.34
  engineering 625.24
  see also Rolling stock
Refrigerators 621.57
  kitchen appliances 641.452 028
  low-temperature engineering 621.57
Refugees 325.21
  T1—086 91
  Algerian Revolution 965.046 086 91
  asylum 323.631
  Chaco War 989.207 160 8691
  citizenship law 342.083
  Civil War (England) 942.062 086 91
  Civil War (United States) 973.708 691
  Crimean War 947.073 808 691
  Franco-German War 943.082 086 91
  Hundred Years' War 944.025 086 91
  immigration law 342.082
  Indo-Pakistan War, 1971 954.920 510 8691
  Indochinese War 959.704 108 691
  international law 341.486
  Iraqi-Iranian Conflict 955.054 208 691
  Korean War 951.904 208 691
  Mexican War 973.620 869 1
  Persian Gulf War, 1991 956.704 420 8691
  political science 325.21
  political status 323.631
  social group 305.906 91
  social theology 291.178 328
    Christianity 261.832 8
  social welfare 362.87
    public administration 353.533 8
  South African War 968.048 086 91
  Spanish-American War 973.890 869 1
  Thirty Years' War 940.240 869 1
  Vietnamese War 959.704 308 691
  War of 1812 973.520 869 1
  War of the Pacific 983.061 608 691
  World War I 940.308 691
  World War II 940.530 869 1
Refugio County (Tex.) T2—764 119
Refuse 363.728
  military sanitation 623.754
  waste technology 628.44
    rural 628.744
  see also Waste control
Regals (Music) 786.55
  instrument 786.551 9
  music 786.55
  see also Keyboard instruments
Regattas 797.14
Regeneration (Christian
    doctrine) 234.4
Regeneration (Developmental
    biology) 571.889
Regensburg (Germany) T2—433 47
Reggae 781.646
  songs 782.421 646
Regge poles 539.721
Reggio di Calabria (Italy :
    Province) T2—457 83
Reggio Emilia (Italy :
    Province) T2—454 3
Reggio nell'Emilia (Italy :
    Province) T2—454 3
Regiments (Military units) 355.31
Regina (Sask.) T2—712 445
Région parisienne (France) T2—443 6
Regional anatomy
  animals 573.993 3
  humans 611.9
Regional anesthesia
  surgery 617.964
Regional bibliographies 015
Regional development 338.9
  economics 338.9
  law 343.074 6
Regional field offices
  public administration 352.288
Regional histology 571.59
  animals 573.99
  plants 575.435 9
Regional medicine 617.5
  geriatrics 618.977 5
  pediatrics 618.920 975
  see Manual at 617.5
Regional physiology 571.59
  animals 573.99
  humans 612.9
  plants 575.4
Regional planning 307.12
  civic art 711.3
  community sociology 307.12
  economics 338.9
  law 346.045
  see Manual at 307.12 vs. 711
Regional surgery 617.5
  anesthesiology 617.967 5
  see Manual at 617.5
Regional treatment T1—09
Regions T2—1
  see Manual at T2—1
Regions (Local government
    units) 320.83
  see also Counties

Regions (State-level units) 321.023
  see also States (Members of federations)
Registered mail 383.182
  see also Postal service
Registered nursing assistants 610.730 92
  role and function 610.730 693
  see also Nurses
Registration 352.84
  see also Licensing
Registration for military service 355.223 6
Registration of voters 324.64
Registration plates 929.9
Regression analysis 519.536
Regressive taxation 336.293
Regular Baptists 286.1
  see also Baptists
Regulation (Public administration) 352.8
Regulation of conduct
  armed forces 355.133
Regulations (Compilations) 348.025
  United States 348.732 5
Regulatory agencies 352.8
  decisions 348.045
    United States 348.734 5
  law 342.066 4
  rulings 348.045
    United States 348.734 5
  see Manual at 352
Rehabilitation
  health services 362.178 6
    medicine 617.03
    see also Health services
  housing services 363.583
  natural resources 333.715 3
  prisoner services 365.66
  social services 362.042 5
Rehabilitation (Restoration of rights) 345.077
Rehabilitation training 362.042 5
  labor economics 331.259 2
  personnel management 658.312 44
    public administration 352.669
Rehabilitative therapy 617.06
Rehearsal
  musical technique 781.44
Reigate and Banstead (England) T2—422 17
Reign of Terror, 1793–1794 944.044
Reimbursement health insurance 368.382
  see also Insurance
Reincarnation
  occultism 133.901 35
  philosophy 129
  religion 291.237
    Buddhism 294.342 37
    Hinduism 294.523 7
  see Manual at 133.9013 vs. 129
Reindeer 599.658
  animal husbandry 636.294
  conservation technology 639.979 658
  resource economics 333.959 658
Reinforced concrete
  architectural construction 721.044 54
  building construction 693.54
  foundation materials 624.153 37
  materials science 620.137
  ship design 623.818 341
  ship hulls 623.845 41
  shipbuilding 623.820 7
  structural engineering 624.183 41
Reinforced plastics 668.494
Reinforcement (Psychology) 153.85
Reinforcing plastics 668.416
Reinstatement (Military personnel) 355.114
Reinsurance 368.012 2
  law 346.086 012 2
Reinventing government 352.2
Reitz (South Africa : District) T2—685 1
Relapsing fevers
  incidence 614.574 4
  medicine 616.924 4
  see also Communicable diseases (Human)
Relation (Philosophy) 111
Relational databases
  computer science 005.756
Relational grammar 415
  specific languages T4—5
Relations (Mathematics) 511.33
Relative indexing 025.482
Relatives (Persons) 306.87
  T1—085
  T7—04
Relativism 149
  epistemology 121
  ethics 171.7
Relativistic particles 539.72
Relativity theory 530.11
  philosophy 115
Relaxation
  physical fitness 613.79

Relaxation (Physics)
  solid-state physics 530.416
Relaxing (Hairdressing) 646.724
Relay communication
  engineering 621.382 5
Relay races 796.427
  see also Sports
Relay systems
  radio engineering 621.384 156
Relays (Electrical) 621.317
  electronic circuits 621.381 537
Relevance (Information science) 025.04
Reliability
  computer software 005
Reliability engineering 620.004 52
Reliability theory 519.287
Relics
  Christianity 235.2
Relics of Passion of Jesus Christ 232.966
Relief (Sculpture) 731.54
  architectural decoration 729.5
Relief (Welfare) 361.05
  see also Welfare services
Relief printing 761
Relief supply exemptions
  customs duties 382.788
    see also Customs (Tariff)
Relief valves
  steam engineering 621.185
Relief work 361.3
  see also Welfare services
Religion 200
  art representation 704.948
  arts 700.482
    T3C—382
  elementary education 372.84
  law 344.096
  literature 808.803 82
    history and criticism 809.933 82
    specific literatures T3B—080 382
      history and criticism T3B—093 82
  painting 755
  public administrative support 353.7
  sociology 306.6
  see Manual at 133 vs. 200;
    also at 200 vs. 100
Religion and culture 291.17
  Christianity 261
  Islam 297.27
  Judaism 296.38
  sociology 306.6
Religion and politics 322.1
  social theology 291.177
  see also Politics and religion
Religion and secular disciplines 291.175
  Buddhism 294.337 5
  Christianity 261.5
    see Manual at 261.5; *also at*
      261.5 vs. 231–239
  Hinduism 294.517 5
  Islam 297.26
    see Manual at
      297.26–297.27
  Judaism 296.37
  philosophy of religion 215
Religion and state 322.1
  social theology 291.177
  see also Politics and religion
Religion historians 200.92
Religion in public schools 379.28
  law 344.079 6
Religions 291
  see also Religion
  see Manual at 291
Religious (Members of Christian
    orders) 255
  biography 271.009 2
    see Manual at 230–280
  church history 271
  ecclesiology 262.24
  guides to Christian life 248.894
  occupational group T7—204
Religious arts 700.482
    T3C—382
  fine arts 704.948
  religious significance 291.37
    see also Arts—religious
      significance
Religious authority 291.65
  Christianity 262.8
  Judaism 296.67
Religious broadcasting
  Christianity 269.26
Religious buildings
  architecture 726
  area planning 711.56
  household management 647.98
  interior decoration 747.86
  religious significance 291.35
    Christianity 246.9
    Judaism 296.46
Religious conflict 306.6
  influence on crime 364.256
Religious dance
  religious significance 291.37
    Christianity 246.7
    see also Arts—religious
      significance

Religious dietary limitations 291.446
  cooking for 641.567
  Hinduism 294.544 6
  Islam 297.576
  Judaism 296.73
Religious education 291.75
  Buddhism 294.375
  Christianity 268
    see Manual at 268 vs. 230.071
  Hinduism 294.575
  Islam 297.77
  Judaism 296.68
  see Manual at 291.75 vs. 200.71
Religious experience 291.42
  Buddhism 294.344 2
  Christianity 248.2
  Hinduism 294.542
  Islam 297.57
    Sufi 297.4
  Judaism 296.71
Religious freedom 323.442
  civil right 323.442
  law 342.085 2
  social theology 291.177 2
    Christianity 261.72
    Judaism 296.382
    see also Politics and religion—social theology
Religious groups T1—088 2
  journalism for 070.482
  legal status 346.013
    constitutional law 342.087
    private law 346.013
  libraries for 027.67
  relations with state 322.1
  sociology 305.6
  see Manual at T1—088 vs. T1—024; *also at* T1—0882 and 200; *also at* T1—0882 vs. T1—09; *also at* 322.1 vs. 261.7, 291.177
Religious holidays 291.36
  customs 394.265
    see Manual at 263.9, 291.36 vs. 394.265–394.267
  see also Holidays; Holy days
Religious ideologies 320.55
Religious institutions
  accounting 657.832
Religious language 210.14
  Christianity 230.014
Religious law 291.84
  Buddhism 294.384
  Christianity 262.9
  Hinduism 294.594
  Islam 297.14
  Judaism 296.18
    see Manual at 296.18 vs. 340.58
Religious leaders 200.92
  biography 200.92
  Buddhist 294.309 2
    biography 294.309 2
      specific sects 294.39
    role and function 294.361
  Christian 270.092
    biography 270.092
      specific denominations 280
        see Manual at 280
      see Manual at 230–280
    ecclesiology 262.1
    occupational ethics 241.641
    pastoral theology 253
    personal religion 248.892
    training 230.071 1
  Hindu 294.509 2
    biography 294.509 2
      specific sects 294.55
    role and function 294.561
  Islamic 297.092
    biography 297.092
      specific sects 297.8
    role and function 297.61
    see Manual at 297.092
  Jewish 296.092
    biography 296.092
      specific denominations 296.8
    professional ethics 296.364 1
    role and function 296.61
    training 296.071 1
  occupational ethics 174.1
    religion 291.564 1
    see Manual at 174.1
  occupational group T7—2
  role and function 291.61
  social group 305.92
  see Manual at 200.92 and 291–299
Religious life 291.44
  Buddhism 294.344 4
  Christianity 248.4
  Hinduism 294.544

Religious life (continued)
  Islam 297.57
    Sufi 297.44
  Judaism 296.7
  see also Monasticism
Religious medals
  numismatics 737.224
  religious significance 291.37
    see also Symbolism—
      religious significance
Religious mythology 291.13
  art representation 704.948
  arts 700.482 911 3
    T3C—382 911 3
  literature 808.803 829 113
    history and criticism 809.933 829 113
    specific literatures T3B—080 382 9113
      history and criticism T3B—093 829 113
  see also Mythology
Religious observances 291.3
  Christianity 263
  Judaism 296.4
  private 291.446
    Christianity 248.46
    Judaism 296.7
Religious orders 291.657
  Buddhism 294.365 7
  Christianity 255
    church history 271
    ecclesiology 262.24
    organization 255
Religious organizations 291.65
  Christianity 260
    associations for religious
      work 267
    denominations 280
    local church 250
      specific local churches 280
    religious orders 255
    see Manual at 260 vs.
      251–254, 259
  congregations 291.65
  Islam 297.65
  Judaism 296.67
  publishing 070.594
  relations with state 322.1
  sociology 306.6
  welfare services 361.75
  see Manual at 322.1 vs. 261.7,
    291.177
Religious pageants
  performing arts 791.622
  religious significance 291.37
    Christianity 246.72
Religious plays
  literature 808.825 16
    history and criticism 809.251 6
    specific literatures T3B—205 16
      individual authors T3A—2
  religious significance 291.37
    Christianity 246.72
      religious education 268.67
  stage presentation 792.16
    see also Theater
Religious pluralism 291.172
  Buddhism 294.337 2
  Christianity 261.2
  Hinduism 294.517 2
  Islam 297.28
  Judaism 296.39
Religious political parties 324.218 2
  international organizations 324.182
Religious publishers 070.594
Religious rites 291.38
  see also Rites—religion
Religious schools (General
    education) 371.07
  libraries 027.83
Religious services 291.38
  armed forces 355.347
  penal institutions 365.66
  see also Rites—religion
Religious socialization 303.325
Religious studies 200.71
  see Manual at 291.75 vs.
    200.71
Religious symbolism 291.37
  art representation 704.948
  painting 755
  see also Symbolism—
      religious significance
Religious therapy
  medicine 615.852
  see Manual at 615.852 vs.
    291.31, 234.131
Reliquaries
  Christianity 247
Relishes 641.812
Relizane (Algeria :
    Province) T2—651
Remarriage 306.84
  ethics 173
  Judaism 296.444
  social theology 291.178 358 4
    Christianity 261.835 84
Remedial education
  adult level 374.012

Remedial readers (Textbooks)
applied linguistics 418
specific languages T4—862
see Manual at T4—862
Remedial reading 418.4
elementary education 372.43
specific languages T4—842
Remedies (Legal actions) 347.077
Reminiscences 920
T1—092
biography 920
literature 808.883
specific literatures T3B—803
individual authors T3A—8
Remodeling of buildings 690.24
architecture 720.286
home economics 643.7
see Manual at 690 vs. 643.7
Remodeling of clothes 646.4
Remonstrant churches 284.9
see also Christian denominations
Remonstrants
biography 284.9
religious group T7—249
Remote control 620.46
radio engineering 621.384 196
Remote-control models 796.15
recreation 796.15
technology 629.046 022 8
see Manual at 796.15 vs. 629.0460228
Remote sensing technology 621.367 8
Remotely controlled vehicles 629.046
Remount services 357.2
Removal from office
recall elections 324.68
Renaissance architecture 724.12
Renaissance art 709.024
religious significance 246.4
Renaissance decoration 745.443
Renaissance music 780.903 1
Renaissance painting 759.03
Renaissance period
European history 940.21
Italian history 945.05
Renaissance revival architecture 724.52
Renaissance sculpture 735.21
Renal disease
medicine 616.61
see also Urinary system
Renal failure
medicine 616.614
see also Urinary system
Renal hypertension
medicine 616.132
see also Cardiovascular system
Rendering oils and gases 665.028 2
Rendezvous
manned space flight 629.458 3
Renegotiation of government contracts 352.53
Renewable energy resources 333.794
economics 333.794
engineering 621.042
Renewal theory 519.287
Renfrew (Ont. : County) T2—713 81
Renfrew (Scotland : District) T2—414 41
Renmark (S. Aust.) T2—942 33
Rennellese language 499.46
T6—994 6
Reno (Nev.) T2—793 55
Reno County (Kan.) T2—781 83
Renovation 690.24
home economics 643.7
see Manual at 690 vs. 643.7
Rensselaer County (N.Y.) T2—747 41
Rent
income distribution
macroeconomics 339.21
land economics 333.5
law 346.043 44
public revenue 336.11
Rent (Economic theory) 333.012
Rent control 363.583
law 346.043 44
Rent subsidies 363.582
Rental collections
museology 069.56
Rental libraries 027.3
Rental services
museology 069.13
Renting
land economics 333.5
Renting homes 643.12
Renville County (Minn.) T2—776 34
Renville County (N.D) T2—784 64
Reorganization
internal 658.402
management 658.16
public administration 352.2
Reorganized Church of Jesus Christ of Latter Day Saints 289.333
see also Mormon Church
Reoviridae 579.254

Repairs 620.004 6
T1—028 8
buildings 690.24
see Manual at 690 vs. 643.7
home economics 643.7
library materials 025.7
Reparations
law of war 341.66
revenue source 336.182
World War I 940.314 22
World War II 940.531 422
Reparative surgery 617.95
Repatriation 323.64
Repayment (Public debt)
public finance 336.363
Repeal of laws 328.37
Repentance 291.22
Christianity 234.5
Islam 297.22
Judaism 296.32
Repetition learning
psychology 153.152 2
Report writing (Study technique) 371.302 81
Reporters 070.430 92
occupational group T7—097
Reporting
executive management 658.45
military administration 355.688
public administration 352.38
financial management 658.151 2
journalism 070.43
Reports
audits 657.452
financial management 658.151 2
office records 651.78
Repossession 347.077
installment sales 346.074
Repoussé
decorative arts 739.14
sculpture 731.41
Representation 324.63
electoral politics 324.63
legislative districts 328.334 5
political right 323.5
Representation theory 515.722 3
Representations
fine arts 704.9
number theory 512.72
Representations of groups 512.2
Repression 323.044
Reprieve (Penology) 364.63
Reprimands
personnel management 658.314 4
Reprints
bibliographies 011.47
Reprisals
international relations 327.117
law 341.582
Reproducers
sound engineering 621.389 33
Reproduction 571.8
animals 573.6
biology 571.8
ethics 176
religion 291.566
Buddhism 294.356 6
Christianity 241.66
Hinduism 294.548 66
Judaism 296.366
human physiology
elementary education 372.372
microorganisms 571.842 9
plants 575.6
see also Genital system
see Manual at 571.8 vs. 573.6, 575.6
Reproduction (Memory) 153.123
Reproductions
arts 702.872
paintings 751.5
Reproductive adaptation 578.46
animals 591.46
plants 581.46
Reproductive behavior (Animals) 591.56
Reproductive hormones 571.837 4
see also Sex hormones
Reproductive organs 573.6
see also Genital system
Reproductive system 573.6
animals 573.6
see also Genital system
biology 573.6
descriptive botany 581.46
plant physiology 575.6
Reprography 686
equipment manufacturing technology 681.6
library services 025.12
office use 652.4
Reptantia 595.38
Reptiles 597.9
art representation 704.943 279
big game hunting 799.279
commercial hunting 639.14
conservation technology 639.977 9
drawing 743.679

Reptiles (continued)
farming 639.39
food 641.396
cooking 641.696
paleozoology 567.9
resource economics 333.957
zoology 597.9
Republic County (Kan.) T2—781 24
Republic of Korea 951.95
T2—519 5
Republic of South Africa 968
T2—68
Republic of the Congo (Brazzaville) 967.24
T2—672 4
Republican Party (U.S. : 1792–1828) 324.273 26
Republican Party (U.S. : 1854–) 324.273 4
Republican River (Neb. and Kan.) T2—781 2
Kansas T2—781 2
Nebraska T2—782 37
Republics 321.86
Repudiation of debt
public finance 336.368
Repulse Bay (N.W.T.) T2—719 4
Requiem mass 264.36
music 782.323 8
choral and mixed voices 782.532 38
single voices 783.093 238
Required courses 375.002
higher education 378.24
Requisition
military resources 355.28
Reredoses 247.1
architecture 726.529 6
Res judicata 347.077
Rescission (Law) 346.022
Rescue aircraft
military engineering 623.746 6
Rescue operations 363.348 1
disaster relief 363.348 1
engineering 628.92
fire safety 363.378 1
technology 628.922
mining technology 622.89
seamanship 623.888 7
Research 001.4
T1—072
public administrative support 352.74
see Manual at T1—072 vs. T1—0601–T1—0609
Research and development
air force supplies 358.407
military science 355.07
naval forces 359.07
production management 658.57
public administration 354.27
noneconomic fields 352.7
public contract law 346.023
Research buildings
architecture 727.5
interior decoration 747.875
Research ethics 174
Research methods 001.42
Research reports
rhetoric 808.02
Researchers 001.409 2
occupational group T7—090 1
Resedaceae 583.64
Reservation systems
transportation 388.042
air service 387.742 2
see also Passenger services
Reservations (Military installations) 355.7
Reserve Officer Training Corps 355.223 207 1173
Reserve requirements
central banking 332.113
Reserve status (Armed forces) 355.113
Reserve training (Armed forces) 355.223 2
Reserves (Armed forces) 355.37
Reserves (Capital management) 658.152 26
Reserves (Natural resources) 333.711
Reservoir engineering
oil extraction 622.338 2
Reservoirs 627.86
biology 578.763
ecology 577.63
flood control 627.44
landscape architecture 719.33
recreational resources 333.784 6
recreational use 797
water supply engineering 628.132
Resettlement
community sociology 307.2
housing services 363.583
see also Housing
public administration 353.59
Residency (Training) T1—071 55
Residential buildings 643.1
architecture 728
construction 690.8
economics 333.338
home economics 643.1

Residential buildings (continued)
  interior decoration 747
  sanitation services 363.729 8
    see also Waste control
Residential cities
  area planning 711.45
Residential finance 332.722
Residential land 333.77
  area planning 711.58
  community sociology 307.336
  resource economics 333.77
  taxation 336.225
Residents (Students)
  training T1—071 55
Residues
  petroleum 665.538 8
  wood 674.84
Residues (Mathematics) 512.72
Resignation of employees
  armed forces 355.114
  personnel management 658.313
    public administration 352.69
Resin-derived plastics 668.45
Resin-producing plants
  agriculture 633.895
  economic botany 581.636
Resins
  chemistry 547.843 4
  commercial processing 668.37
  fossil 553.29
  materials science 620.192 4
  recovery from pulp 676.5
Resist-dyeing
  textile arts 746.66
Resistance
  materials science 620.112
Resistance meters 621.374 2
Resistance movements
  World War II 940.533 6
Resistance thermometry 536.502 87
Resistance to government 323.044
Resistance warfare 355.021 8
Resistance welding 671.521 3
Resistant construction
  buildings 693.8
  ship hulls 623.848
Resistivity
  skin
    human physiology 612.791
    see also Skin
Resistivity in semiconductors 537.622 6
Resistors
  radio engineering 621.384 133
Resolute (N.W.T.) T2—719 5
Resolutions (Legislation)
  enactment 328.377
Resonance
  musical technique 781.48
    instrumental 784.193 2
Resonance accelerators 539.733
Resorcinols 547.633
Resource development
  international banking 332.153
  natural resources 333.715
    see Manual at 333.7–333.9
Resource recovery 363.728 2
  see also Waste control
Resources
  education and research T1—07
    see Manual at 016 vs. 026, T1—07
  military science 355.2
  natural 333.7
    see also Natural resources
Respiration 572.47
  animals 573.2
  biochemistry 572.47
  human physiology 612.2
  microorganisms 572.472 9
  plants 572.472
  see also Respiratory system
Respiratory allergies
  medicine 616.202
  see also Respiratory system
Respiratory diseases
  medicine 616.2
  see also Respiratory system
Respiratory organs 573.2
  human physiology 612.2
  see also Respiratory system
Respiratory system 573.2
  biology 573.2
  geriatrics 618.976 2
  human anatomy 611.2
  human cancer 362.196 994 2
    incidence 614.599 942
    medicine 616.994 2
    social services 362.196 994 2
    see also Cancer (Human)
  human diseases 362.196 2
    incidence 614.592
    medicine 616.2
    social services 362.196 2
  human histology 611.018 92
  human physiology 612.2
  nursing 610.736 92
  pediatrics 618.922
  pharmacodynamics 615.72

Respiratory system (continued)
surgery 617.54
veterinary medicine 636.089 62
Respiratory therapy
medicine 615.836
Responsa (Jewish law) 296.185
Responses
music 782.292
Responsibility
executive management 658.402
law 346.03
military administration 355.685
public administration 352.35
Responsive readings
public worship 291.38
Christianity 264.4
Judaism 296.45
Rest
animal physiology 573.79
human physiology 612.76
physical fitness 613.79
Rest areas
road engineering 625.77
Rest homes 362.16
see also Health care facilities; Health services
Rest periods
labor economics 331.257 6
personnel management 658.312 1
Restaurant cooking 641.572
Restaurant meal service 642.5
Restaurants 647.95
accounting 657.837
architecture 725.71
area planning 711.557
household management 647.95
Restaurateurs 647.950 92
occupational group T7—642
Restigouche (N.B.) T2—715 11
Restigouche River (N.B. and Quebec) T2—715 11
Restionales 584.8
Restitution (Law of war) 341.66
Restitution coefficient 531.382
Restoration 620.004 6
T1—028 8
arts 702.88
museology 069.53
wooden furniture 684.104 42
Restoration (France), 1815–1848 944.06
Restoration (Great Britain), 1660–1688 941.066
English history 942.066
Scottish history 941.106 6
Restoration (Spain), 1814–1833 946.072
Restoration (Spain), 1871–1873 946.073
Restoration of natural resources 333.715 3
Restorative surgery 617.95
Restoring torques
aeronautics 629.132 364
Restormel (England : Borough) T2—423 72
Restraint
social control 303.36
Restraint of trade (Competition) 338.604 8
criminology 364.168
criminal law 345.026 8
economics 338.604 8
international law 341.753
law 343.072 3
Restrictive environments
psychology 155.96
Restrictive practices 338.82
economics 338.82
international economics 338.884
Rests (Music) 781.236
Résumé writing 808.066 65
see also Job hunting
Résumés (Employment) 650.14
Resurfacing
road maintenance 625.761
Resurrection 291.23
Christianity 236.8
Islam 297.23
Judaism 296.33
Resurrection of Jesus Christ 232.5
life 232.97
Resurrection plants 587.9
Resuscitation
therapeutics 615.804 3
Retail advertising 659.131 4
Retail chains 381.12
management 658.870 2
see also Commerce
Retail credit
marketing management 658.883
Retail marketing 381.1
management 658.87
see also Commerce
see Manual at 381.1 vs. 381.4, 658.87
Retail salesmanship
domestic commerce 381.1
etiquette 395.53
management 658.85

Retail stores 381.1
  management 658.87
  see Manual at 381.1 vs. 381.4, 658.87
Retail trade 381.1
  accounting 657.839
  law 343.088 7
  marketing management 658.87
  see also Commerce
  see Manual at 381.1 vs. 381.4, 658.87
Retail trade buildings
  architecture 725.21
Retained profits
  capital formation 332.041 52
Retaining walls 721.2
  architecture 721.2
  construction 690.12
  railroad engineering 625.13
  structural engineering 624.164
  see also Walls (Building element)
Retalhuleu (Guatemala : Dept.) T2—728 183
Retarded persons 305.908 26
  T1—087 4
  see also Mentally retarded persons
Retarding (Plants) 631.583
  floriculture 635.982
  gardening 635.048 3
Retention (Memory) 153.122
Retention of records 651.51
Rethymnē (Greece) T2—495 9
Reticular tissues
  human histology 611.018 2
Reticulated beetles 595.762
Reticuloendothelial system
  human immunology 616.079 9
Reticulosis
  medicine 616.156
  see also Cardiovascular system
Retinas
  human anatomy 611.84
  human diseases
    incidence 614.599 7
    ophthalmology 617.735
  human physiology 612.843
  see also Eyes
Retinitis pigmentosa
  ophthalmology 617.735
Retired persons 305.906 96
  T1—086 96
  psychology 155.672
Retirement 306.38
  armed forces 355.114
  financial planning 332.024 01
  personnel management 658.313 2
    public administration 352.69
  psychology 155.672
  sociology 306.38
Retirement age
  economics 331.252
  personnel management 658.313 2
Retirement benefits 331.252
Retirement counseling
  personnel management 658.385
Retirement enterprises
  management 658.041
Retirement guides
  personal living 646.79
Retirement income
  pensions 331.252
    see also Pensions
  tax economics 336.242 8
  tax law 343.052 4
Retracts 514.24
Retraining
  labor economics 331.259 24
  law 344.012 592 4
  personnel management 658.312 43
  social welfare 362.042 5
  vocational education 370.113
  see also Vocational education
Retreats (Military tactics) 355.422
Retreats (Religion)
  Christianity 269.6
Retribution
  penology 364.601
Retrieval of information
  information science 025.524
Retrievers 636.752 7
Retrospective conversion
  library operations 025.317 3
Retroviridae 579.256 9
Retroviruses 579.256 9
  medical microbiology 616.019 4
Return to Orthodox Judaism 296.715
Returned merchandise
  marketing management 658.812
Réunion 969.81
  T2—698 1
Reusability
  computer software 005
Revegetation 631.64

Revelation (Biblical book) 228
Revelation of God 212.6
  Bible 220.13
  Christianity 231.74
  comparative religion 291.211 7
  Islam 297.211 5
  Judaism 296.311 5
  philosophy of religion 212.6
Revelstoke (B.C.) T2—711 68
Revenue 336.02
  financial management 658.155 4
  law 343.036
  public administration 352.44
  public finance 336.02
Revenue budgets (Public) 352.48
  see also Budgets (Public)
Revenue cutters 363.286
  design 623.812 63
  engineering 623.826 3
  police services 363.286
Revenue offenses 364.133
  law 345.023 3
Revenue sharing 336.185
  law 343.034
  public administration 352.73
  public finance 336.185
Revenue stamps 336.272
  prints 769.572
  public finance 336.272
Revenue tariffs 382.72
  see also Customs (Tariff)
Reveries 154.3
Reverse dictionaries 413.1
  specific languages T4—31
Reverse osmosis
  desalinization 628.167 44
Reversible reactions
  chemical engineering 660.299 3
  chemistry 541.393
  organic chemistry 547.139 3
Review
  study and teaching T1—076
Reviews
  ballet 792.845
  books 028.1
  films 791.437 5
  musical plays 792.645
  opera 792.545
  radio programs 791.447 5
  television programs 791.457 5
Revised English Bible 220.520 6
Revised Standard version Bible 220.520 42
Revised versions of Bible 220.520 4
Revival meetings 269.24
Revolution 303.64
  ethics 172.1
  political science 321.094
  social change 303.4
  social conflict 303.64
  social theology 291.177
    Buddhism 294.337 7
    Christianity 261.7
    Hinduism 294.517 7
    Judaism 296.382
  see Manual at 909, 930–990
    vs. 320.4, 321, 321.09
Revolution of 1911–1912 951.036
Revolutionary activities 322.42
Revolutionary groups 322.42
Revolutionary unions
  labor economics 331.886
Revolutionary warfare 355.021 8
Revolvers 683.436
  art metalwork 739.744 36
  manufacturing technology 683.436
  military engineering 623.443 6
  see also Guns (Small arms)
Revues 782.14
  music 782.14
  stage presentation 792.6
    see also Theater
Rewards
  armed forces 355.134
  social control 303.35
Reweaving 646.25
  clothing care 646.6
  home sewing 646.25
Rex cat 636.822
Reye's syndrome
  medicine 616.83
  pediatrics 618.928 3
  see also Nervous system
Reynolds County (Mo.) T2—778 885
Reza Shah Pahlavi, Shah of Iran
  Iranian history 955.052
RFD (Mail delivery) 383.145
  see also Postal service
Rh factor
  human physiology 612.118 25
  incompatibility
    pediatrics 618.921 5
    perinatal medicine 618.326 1
  see also Cardiovascular
    system
Rhabdocoela 592.42
Rhabdoviridae 579.256 6
Rhacopteris 561.597

Rhade (Vietnamese people) T5—992 2
Rhaetian languages 459.9
T6—599
Rhaetians T5—5
Rhaeto-Romanic languages 459.9
T6—599
Rhaeto-Romanic literatures 859.9
Rhagionidae 595.773
Rhamnales 583.86
Rhapsodies (Music) 784.189 45
Rhea County (Tenn.) T2—768 834
Rheas 598.522
Rheiformes 598.522
paleozoology 568.5
Rheims-Douay Bible 220.520 2
Rheinhessen-Pfalz (Germany : Regierungsbezirk) T2—434 35
Rheinland-Pfalz (Germany) T2—434 3
Rhenish Prussia (Germany) T2—434 3
Rhenium 669.7
chemical engineering 661.054 5
chemistry 546.545
metallurgy 669.7
physical metallurgy 669.967
see also Chemicals
Rheology 531.113 4
Rheostats 621.317
Rhesus monkey 599.864 3
Rheto-Romance languages 459.9
T6—599
Rheto-Romance literatures 859.9
Rhetoric 808
see Manual at 808.001–808.7 vs. 070.52
Rheumatic fever
incidence 614.597 23
medicine 616.991
pediatrics 618.929 91
see also Communicable diseases (Human)
Rheumatic heart disease
medicine 616.127
see also Cardiovascular system
Rheumatism
medicine 616.723
see also Musculoskeletal system
Rheumatoid arthritis
medicine 616.722 7
see also Musculoskeletal system
Rheumatology 616.723
see also Musculoskeletal system
Rhinbund 943.06
Rhine, Confederation of the 943.06
Rhine Province (Germany) T2—434 3
Rhine River (Germany) T2—434
Rhineland-Palatinate (Germany) T2—434 3
Rhinencephalon
human physiology 612.825
see also Nervous system
Rhinoceroses 599.668
conservation technology 639.979 668
resource economics 333.959 668
Rhinocerotidae 599.668
Rhinology 616.212
see also Respiratory system
Rhipiceroidea 595.763
Rhizobium 579.334
Rhizocephala 595.35
Rhizomes 581.46
descriptive botany 581.46
physiology 575.497
Rhizomyidae 599.35
Rhizophoraceae 583.763
Rhizopodea 579.43
Rhizopus 579.53
Rhizostomeae 593.53
Rhode Island 974.5
T2—745
Rhode Island Red chicken 636.584
Rhode Island Sound (Mass. and R.I.) 551.461 46
T2—163 46
Rhodes (Greece : Island) T2—495 87
ancient T2—391 6
Rhodesia (1964–1980) 968.910 4
T2—689 1
Rhodesia and Nyasaland 968.903
T2—689
Rhodesian man 569.9
Rhodesian ridgeback 636.753 6
Rhodesians T5—968 91
Rhodium 669.7
chemical engineering 661.063 4
chemistry 546.634
metallography 669.957
metallurgy 669.7

Rhodium (continued)
  physical metallurgy 669.967
  see also Chemicals
Rhodobacter 579.385
Rhododendrons 583.66
  floriculture 635.933 66
Rhodope (Greece) T2—495 7
Rhodope Mountains T2—499 7
Rhodophyceae 579.89
Rhodophyta 579.89
Rhodopseudomonas 579.385
Rhoeadales 583.35
Rhondda (Wales) T2—429 72
Rhône (France) T2—445 82
Rhône-Alpes (France) T2—445 8
Rhône River (Switzerland and France) T2—445 8
Rhubarb 641.354 8
  botany 583.57
  commercial processing 664.805 48
  cooking 641.654 8
  food 641.354 8
  garden crop 635.48
Rhuddlan (Wales : Borough) T2—429 32
Rhyme 808.1
Rhymes
  folk literature 398.8
Rhyming 808.1
Rhyming dictionaries 413.1
  specific languages T4—31
Rhyming games 398.8
Rhymney Valley (Wales : District) T2—429 76
Rhynchobdellida 592.66
Rhynchocephalia 597.945
  paleozoology 567.945
Rhynchocoela 592.32
Rhyolite 552.22
Rhythm (Linguistics) 414.6
  specific languages T4—16
Rhythm (Musical element) 781.224
Rhythm and blues 781.643
Rhythm bands 784.68
Rhythm method (Birth control)
  health 613.943 4
  see also Birth control
Rhythm perception 153.753
Rhythmic arts
  religious significance 291.37
    Christianity 246.7
    see also Arts—religious significance
Rhythmic gymnastics 796.44
  see also Sports
Rîâzanskaîâ oblast´ (Russia) T2—473 3
Rib vaults 721.45
  architecture 721.45
  construction 690.145
Ribatejo (Portugal) T2—469 45
Ribble, River T2—427 685
Ribble Valley (England : Borough) T2—427 685
Ribbon seal 599.792
Ribbon worms 592.32
Ribbons 677.76
Ribe amt (Denmark) T2—489 5
Ribes 583.72
  edible fruits 641.347 2
    cooking 641.647 2
    food 641.347 2
  horticulture 634.72
Ribonucleic acid 572.88
Ribose 572.565
  biochemistry 572.565
  chemistry 547.781 3
  see also Carbohydrates
Ribosomes 571.658
Ribs
  human anatomy 611.712
  medicine 616.71
  surgery 617.471
  see also Musculoskeletal system
Ricardo, David
  economic rent theory 333.012
  economic school 330.153
Ricciaceae 588.3
Rice 641.331 8
  agricultural economics 338.173 18
  botany 584.9
  commercial processing
    economics 338.476 647 25
    technology 664.725
  cooking 641.631 8
  food 641.331 8
  food crop 633.18
Rice County (Kan.) T2—781 543
Rice County (Minn.) T2—776 555
Rice Lake (Ont.) T2—713 57
Ricercares 784.187 6
Rich (Social class) 305.523 4
  T1—086 21
Rich County (Utah) T2—792 13
Richard I, King of England
  English history 942.032

Richard II, King of England
  English history 942.038
Richard III, King of England
  English history 942.046
Richards Bay (South Africa) T2—684 3
Richardson County (Neb.) T2—782 282
Richelieu (Quebec : County) T2—714 51
Richelieu River (Quebec) T2—714 3
Richland County (Ill.) T2—773 77
Richland County (Mont.) T2—786 23
Richland County (N.D.) T2—784 12
Richland County (Ohio) T2—771 28
Richland County (S.C.) T2—757 71
Richland County (Wis.) T2—775 75
Richland Parish (La.) T2—763 86
Richmond (B.C.) T2—711 33
Richmond (Cape of Good Hope, South Africa : District) T2—687 13
Richmond (N.S. : County) T2—716 98
Richmond (Natal, South Africa : District) T2—684 7
Richmond (Quebec : County) T2—714 65
Richmond (Va.) T2—755 451
Richmond County (Ga.) T2—758 64
Richmond County (N.C.) T2—756 34
Richmond County (N.Y.) T2—747 26
Richmond County (Va.) T2—755 23
Richmond River (N.S.W.) T2—944 3
Richmond upon Thames (London, England) T2—421 95
Richmondshire (England : District) T2—428 48
Ricinulei 595.455
Rickets
  medicine 616.395
  see also Digestive system
Rickettsiae
  medical microbiology 616.019 2
Rickettsial diseases (Biology) 571.993 27
  agriculture 632.8
  plant crops 632.8
  veterinary medicine 636.089 692 2
Rickettsial diseases (Human)
  incidence 614.526
  medicine 616.922
  see also Communicable diseases (Human)
Rickettsialpox
  incidence 614.526 3
  medicine 616.922 3
  see also Communicable diseases (Human)
Rickettsias 579.327
Rickshaws 388.341
  manufacturing technology 688.6
Riddles 398.6
  folk literature 398.6
  jokes
    literature 808.882
      specific literatures T3B—802
        individual authors T3A—8
  recreation 793.735
  see Manual at T3A—8 + 02, T3B—802, T3B—8 + 02 vs. 398.6, 793.735
Ridesharing 388.413 212
Riding-club buildings
  architecture 725.88
Riding horses (Breeds) 636.13
Riding horses (Recreation) 798.23
Riel's Rebellion, 1869–1870 971.051
Riel's Rebellion, 1885 971.054
Riemann integral 515.43
Riemann surfaces 515.93
Riemannian geometry 516.373
Riemannian hypothesis 512.73
Riesz spaces 515.73
Rieti (Italy : Province) T2—456 24
RIF (Layoff)
  economics 331.259 6
    employment security 331.259 6
    unemployment 331.137
  law 344.012 596
  personnel management 658.313 4
    public administration 352.69
Rif language 493.3
  T6—933
Rif Mountains (Morocco) T2—642
Riffle beetles 595.764 5
Rifle grenades 623.451 14
Rifles 683.422
  art metalwork 739.744 25
  manufacturing technology 683.422
  military engineering 623.442 5
  military equipment 355.824 25
  shooting game 799.213
  sports 799.202 832
  target shooting 799.31
  see also Guns (Small arms)
Rift Valley Province (Kenya) T2—676 27

Rift valleys 551.872
Riga, Gulf of (Latvia and Estonia) 551.461 34
T2—163 34
Rigging equipment
aircraft 629.134 37
Right and wrong 170
religion 291.5
Right-eyed flounders 597.694
Right-hand techniques
music 784.193 67
Right of assembly 323.47
law 342.085 4
Right of asylum 323.631
international law 341.488
law 342.083
Right of petition 323.48
law 342.085 4
Right of privacy 323.448
Right of property 323.46
Right of way 346.043 5
railroads
economics
sale and rental 333.336
Right to bear arms 323.43
Right to counsel 345.056
Right to die
ethics 179.7
religion 291.569 7
Christianity 241.697
Judaism 296.369 7
law 344.041 97
medical ethics 174.24
religion 291.564 24
Christianity 241.642 4
Judaism 296.364 24
Right to education 379.26
law 344.079
Right to hold office 323.5
Right to information 323.445
law 342.066 2
Right to labor 331.889 2
government policy 331.898
Right to learn 379.26
law 344.079
Right to life 323.43
ethics 179.7
religion 291.569 7
Christianity 241.697
Judaism 296.369 7
law 342.085
Right to life (Prenatal)
ethics 179.76
religion 291.569 76
Christianity 241.697 6
Judaism 296.369 76
law 342.085
social theology 291.178 366 67
Christianity 261.836 667
Judaism 296.38
Right to life movement
social theology 291.178 366 67
Christianity 261.836 667
Judaism 296.38
Right to read 379.24
Right to representation 323.5
Right to strike 331.892 01
Right to vote 324.62
law 342.072
Right to work 331.889 2
government policy 331.898
Right whale 599.527 3
Righteousness (Christian doctrine) 234
Rightist parties 324.213
international organizations 324.13
Rights of man 323
see also Civil rights
Rigid airships 387.732 5
engineering 629.133 25
military engineering 623.743 5
transportation services 387.732 5
see also Aircraft
Rigid bodies
mechanics 531
Rigidity
materials science 620.112 5
Rigveda 294.592 12
Riksmål language 439.82
T6—398 2
Riksmål literature 839.82
Riley County (Kan.) T2—781 28
Rimouski (Quebec : County) T2—714 771
Rimouski-Neigette (Quebec) T2—714 771
Ring-necked pheasant 598.625 2
sports hunting 799.246 252
Ringed seal 599.792
Ringgold County (Iowa) T2—777 873
Ringkøbing amt (Denmark) T2—489 5
Rings (Jewelry) 391.7
customs 391.7
making 739.278 2
see also Jewelry

Rings (Mathematics) 512.4
  number theory 512.74
Rings (Planets) 523.98
Ringworm
  medicine 616.57
  see also Skin
Rinks
  architecture 725.86
Rinzai 294.392 7
Rio Arriba County (N.M.) T2—789 52
Rio Blanco County (Colo.) T2—788 15
Rio Branco (Brazil : Territory) T2—811 4
Rio de Janeiro (Brazil : State) T2—815 3
Rio de la Plata (Argentina and Uruguay) 551.464 68
  T2—163 68
Río de la Plata (Viceroyalty) 982.024
  T2—82
Rio de Oro T2—648
Rio Grande T2—764 4
  Colorado T2—788 3
  Mexico T2—721
  New Mexico T2—789 6
  Texas T2—764 4
Rio Grande County (Colo.) T2—788 37
Rio Grande do Norte (Brazil) T2—813 2
Rio Grande do Sul (Brazil) T2—816 5
Rio Grande Valley T2—764 4
Rio Maputo T2—684 2
  Mozambique T2—679 1
  South Africa T2—684 2
Río Muni T2—671 83
Río Negro (Argentina) T2—827 3
Río Negro (Uruguay) T2—895 28
Río San Juan (Nicaragua) T2—728 531
Rioja (Argentina : Province) T2—824 6
Rioja (Spain) T2—463 54
Ríos (Ecuador) T2—866 33
Riot and civil commotion insurance 368.125
  see also Insurance
Riot control 363.32
Riot insurance 368.125
  see also Insurance
Rioting 364.143
  law 345.024 3
Riots 303.623
  political action 322.4
  prisons 365.641
  social conflict 303.623
Riots (continued)
  social services 363.349 7
  see also Disasters
Riparian biology 578.768
Riparian ecology 577.68
Riparian rights
  law 346.043 2
Ripened cheeses 641.373 53
  cooking 641.673 53
  food 641.373 53
  processing 637.353
Ripley County (Ind.) T2—772 14
Ripley County (Mo.) T2—778 894
Ripon, George Frederick Samuel Robinson, Marquess of
  Indian history 954.035 3
Risaralda (Colombia : Dept.) T2—861 32
RISC (Computer science) 004.3
  see also Processing modes—computer science
Rishonim 296.180 92
Risk
  economics 338.5
  insurance 368
Risk assessment
  natural resources 333.714
    see Manual at 333.7–333.9 vs. 363.1, 363.73, 577
  public safety 363.102
  social services 361.1
Risk management
  financial management 658.155
  insurance 368
  see Manual at 368 vs. 658.155
Risk of consequential loss 368.08
Risk perception
  social psychology 302.12
Risorgimento 945.083
Ritavi (South Africa : District) T2—682 92
Ritchie County (W. Va.) T2—754 24
Rites 390
  customs 390
  magic 133.43
  religion 291.38
    African religions 299.64
    Buddhism 294.343 8
    Christianity 264
    comparative religion 291.38
    Hinduism 294.538
    Islam 297.38
    Judaism 296.45
  music 782.3

Rites
religion (continued)
Native American religions 299.74
witchcraft 133.43
Ritual bath
Judaism 296.75
Ritual purity
Islam 297.38
Judaism
family purity 296.742
Ritual slaughter (Dietary laws) 291.446
Islam 297.576
Judaism 296.73
Rituale Romanum 264.025
Rituals 291.38
Roman Catholic liturgy 264.025
see also Rites—religion
Rivas (Nicaragua : Dept.) T2—728 517
River basins
land economics 333.73
River beds 551.442
T2—144
geography 910.914 4
geomorphology 551.442
physical geography 910.021 44
River boats 386.224 36
design 623.812 436
engineering 623.824 36
freight services 386.244
passenger services 386.242
transportation services 386.224 36
see also Ships
River dogfishes 597.41
River dolphins 599.538
River Humber (England) T2—428 3
River ice 551.345
River mouths
engineering 627.124
River otters 599.769 2
see also Otters (River otters)
River police 363.287 2
River steamers 386.224 36
see also River boats
River transportation 386.3
see also Inland water transportation
River Trent (England) T2—425
River Wye (Wales and England) T2—429 5
Rivera (Uruguay : Dept.) T2—895 34
Rivers 551.483
T2—169 3
biology 578.764
ecology 577.64
Rivers (continued)
geography 910.916 93
hydraulic engineering 627.12
hydrology 551.483
interactions with atmosphere 551.524 8
international law 341.442
landscape architecture 714
law 346.046 916 2
recreational resources 333.784 5
recreational use 797
resource economics 333.916 2
travel 910.916 93
water supply engineering 628.112
Rivers State (Nigeria) T2—669 42
Riversdale (South Africa : District) T2—687 3
Riverside County (Calif.) T2—794 97
Riverweeds 583.82
Riveting 671.59
decorative arts 739.14
sculpture 731.41
ship hulls 623.843 2
Riveting equipment 621.978
Rivets 621.884
Riviera T2—449
France T2—449
Italy T2—451 8
Rivière-du-Loup (Quebec : County) T2—714 76
Rivière-du-Loup (Quebec : Regional County Municipality) T2—714 76
Rivière-du-Nord (Quebec) T2—714 24
Rivne (Ukraine : Oblast) T2—477 9
Rivnensʹka oblastʹ (Ukraine) T2—477 9
Rizal (Philippines : Province) T2—599 1
Rize İli (Turkey) T2—566 2
RNA (Genetics) 572.88
RNA viruses 579.25
Roach (Fish) 597.482
sports fishing 799.174 82
Roaches 595.728
Road accidents 363.125
see also Highway safety
Road camps (Penology) 365.34
see also Correctional institutions
Road engineers 625.709 2
occupational group T7—625
Road maintenance 625.761
Road maps 912
Road oils 665.538 8

Road repair 625.761
Road running 796.425
  see also Sports
Road safety 363.125
  see also Highway safety
Road tests
  automotive vehicles 629.282 4
Road transportation 388.31
  international law 341.756 8
  law 343.094
  public administration 354.77
  urban 388.413 1
Roadability tests
  automotive vehicles 629.282 5
Roadbeds
  railroad engineering 625.123
    interurban railroads 625.65
    local railroads 625.65
  road engineering 625.733
Roadrunners 598.74
Roads 388.1
  agricultural use 631.28
  area planning 711.7
  ecological effect 577.272
  engineering 625.7
  forestry 634.93
  land economics 333.77
    acquisition and disposal 333.11
    urban land use 333.77
  landscape architecture 713
  law 343.094 2
  military engineering 623.62
  public administration 354.77
  transportation services 388.1
  urban 388.411
  use 388.314
    urban 388.413 14
Roadside areas 625.77
  road transportation 388.312
Roadside barriers 625.795
Roadside biology 578.755
Roadside ecology 577.55
Roadside shrines
  architecture 726.9
Roadside signs
  outdoor advertising 659.134 2
Roadsteads 387.1
  hydraulic engineering 627.22
  see also Ports
Roan antelope 599.645
Roane County (Tenn.) T2—768 84
Roane County (W. Va.) T2—754 36
Roanoke (Va.) T2—755 791
Roanoke County (Va.) T2—755 792
Roanoke Island (N.C.) T2—756 175
Roanoke River (Va. and N.C.) T2—756 16
  North Carolina T2—756 16
  Virginia T2—755 6
Roarers (Musical instruments) 783.99
Roasters
  electric cooking 641.586
Roasting
  home cooking 641.71
Robalos 597.72
Robben Island (South Africa) T2—687 35
Robber flies 595.773
Robbery 364.155 2
  law 345.025 52
Robbery insurance 368.82
  see also Insurance
Robert II, King of France
  French history 944.021
Robert-Cliche (Quebec) T2—714 71
Roberts County (S.D.) T2—783 12
Roberts County (Tex.) T2—764 818
Robertson (South Africa : District) T2—687 3
Robertson County (Ky.) T2—769 415
Robertson County (Tenn.) T2—768 464
Robertson County (Tex.) T2—764 239
Robeson County (N.C.) T2—756 332
Robins (American) 598.842
Robinson Gorge National Park (Qld.) T2—943 5
Robotics 629.892
Robots 629.892
  elementary education 372.358
  engineering 629.892
  factory operations engineering 670.427 2
  social effects 303.483 4
Rocha (Uruguay : Dept.) T2—895 16
Rochdale (England) T2—427 392
Roches Douvres (England) T2—423 49
Roches moutonnées 551.315
Rochester (N.Y.) T2—747 89
Rochester upon Medway (England) T2—422 323
Rochford (England : District) T2—426 775
Rock (Music) 781.66
  attitude of Christianity toward 261.578
  songs 782.421 66
Rock art 709.011 3
  painting 759.011 3
  sculpture 732.23
Rock bass 597.738

Rock climbing 796.522 3
  see also Sports
Rock County (Minn.) T2—776 25
Rock County (Neb.) T2—782 743
Rock County (Wis.) T2—775 87
Rock cutting
  road engineering 625.733
Rock failure
  mining 622.28
Rock-fill dams 627.83
Rock fragmentation
  frost action 551.382
Rock gardens 635.967 2
Rock Island County (Ill.) T2—773 393
Rock mechanics
  engineering geology 624.151 32
  railroad engineering 625.122
  road engineering 625.732
Rock musicians 781.660 92
  occupational group T7—781 6
Rock 'n' roll 781.66
Rock pools
  biology 578.769 9
  ecology 577.699
Rock rats 599.359
Rock River (Wis. and Ill.) T2—773 3
Rock salt 553.632
  mineralogy 549.4
  see also Salt (Sodium chloride)
Rock singers 782.421 660 92
Rock songs 782.421 66
Rock whiting 597.72
Rock wool
  materials science 620.195
Rockbridge County (Va.) T2—755 852
Rockcastle County (Ky.) T2—769 623
Rockdale County (Ga.) T2—758 215
Rocket engines 621.435 6
  aircraft 629.134 354
  spacecraft 629.475 2
  see Manual at 629.046 vs. 621.43
Rocket fuels 662.666
Rocket launchers (Crew-served weapons) 355.822
  engineering 623.42
  military equipment 355.822
    field artillery 358.128 2
Rocket launchers (Portable weapons) 356.162
  engineering 623.442 6
  military equipment 356.162
Rocket planes
  engineering 629.133 38
  military engineering 623.746 045
Rocket propellants 662.666
Rocket-propelled guided missiles 358.171 82
  engineering 623.451 9
  military equipment 358.171 82
Rocket weapons 358.171 82
  engineering 623.451 9
  military equipment 358.171 82
Rocketry 621.435 6
Rockets 621.435 6
  see Manual at 629.046 vs. 621.43
Rockets (Ordnance) 355.825 43
  engineering 623.454 3
  military equipment 355.825 43
Rockfalls 551.307
Rockfishes 597.68
  cooking 641.692
  food 641.392
Rockhampton (Qld.) T2—943 5
Rockingham County (N.C.) T2—756 63
Rockingham County (N.H.) T2—742 6
Rockingham County (Va.) T2—755 922
Rockland County (N.Y.) T2—747 28
Rockroses 583.625
Rocks 552
  determinative mineralogy 549.114
  petrology 552
  structural engineering 624.183 2
Rockwall County (Tex.) T2—764 278
Rockweeds 579.888
Rocky Mountain National Park (Colo.) T2—788 69
Rocky Mountain Trench (B.C. and Mont.) T2—711
Rocky Mountains T2—78
  Alberta T2—712 33
  British Columbia T2—711
  Canada T2—711
  Colorado T2—788
  Montana T2—786 5
  New Mexico T2—789 5
  United States T2—78
  Utah T2—792 2
  Wyoming T2—787 2
Rococo architecture 724.19
Rococo art 709.033 2
Rococo decoration 745.443
Rococo music 780.903 3

Rococo painting 759.047
Rodent control 363.78
  see also Rodents—pest control
Rodent-resistant construction 693.844
Rodentia 599.35
  see also Rodents
Rodenticides 668.651
  agricultural use 632.951
  chemical engineering 668.651
Rodents 599.35
  animal husbandry 636.935
  disease carriers 571.986
    medicine 614.438
  experimental animals
    medicine 619.93
  paleozoology 569.35
  pest control 363.78
    social welfare 363.78
    technology 628.969 3
      agriculture 632.693 5
      home economics 648.7
  zoology 599.35
Rodeos 791.84
Rodney District (N.Z.) T2—932 1
Rodopē (Greece) T2—495 7
Rodopi Mountains T2—499 7
Rodrigues Island (Mauritius) T2—698 2
Rodríguez, Abelardo L. (Abelardo Luján)
  Mexican history 972.082 44
Rods (Musical instruments) 786.82
  concussed 786.872
  friction 786.862
    set 786.862
    single 786.888
  percussed 786.842
    set 786.842
    single 786.884 2
  plucked 786.85
    set 786.85
    single 786.887
  see also Percussion instruments
Rods (Structural elements) 624.177 4
Roe deer 599.659
Roentgenology
  medicine 616.075 72
    see Manual at 616.0757 vs. 616.0754, 616.07572
Rogaland fylke (Norway) T2—483 4
Roger Mills County (Okla.) T2—766 16
Rogers County (Okla.) T2—766 94
Rogue River (Or.) T2—795 21
Role conflict 302.15
Role playing
  psychiatry 616.891 523
    see also Mental illness
Role-playing games 793.93
  see Manual at 793.932 vs. 794.822
Role theory 302.15
Rolette County (N.D.) T2—784 592
Roll (Aeronautics) 629.132 364
Roll on/roll off shipping 387.544 2
Roller bearings 621.822
Roller painting 751.49
Roller skates
  manufacturing technology 685.362
Roller skating 796.21
  see also Sports
Rollerblading 796.21
Rollers (Agricultural tools)
  manufacturing technology 681.763 1
Rollers (Birds) 598.78
Rolling metals 671.32
  decorative arts 739.14
  sculpture 731.41
Rolling stock 385.37
  engineering 625.2
  law 343.095 5
  military 358.25
    engineering 623.633
  mining 622.66
  monorail 385.5
    engineering 625.28
  operation 385.204 4
  production economics 338.476 252
  public administration 354.767
  rapid transit 388.42
    engineering 625.4
  special purpose 385.5
    engineering 625.3–.6
  transportation services 385.37
  see Manual at 629.046 vs. 388
Rolls 641.815
  commercial processing 664.752
  cooking 641.815
Rolls of honor
  armed forces 355.134
    World War I 940.467
    World War II 940.546 7
    see also Military commemorations
Rolong (African people) T5—963 977 5
Rolong dialect 496.397 757
  T6—963 977 5

ROM (Computer memory) 004.53
  engineering 621.397 3
Roma (Italy) T2—456 32
  ancient T2—376
Roma (Italy : Province) T2—456 3
Roma (People) T5—914 97
Roman architecture 722.7
Roman calligraphy 745.619 78
Roman Catholic cathedrals
  architecture 726.64
Roman Catholic Church 282
  canon law 262.9
  church government 262.02
    parishes 254.02
  conversion to 248.242
  doctrines 230.2
    catechisms and creeds 238.2
  general councils 262.52
  guides to Christian life 248.482
  Inquisition 272.2
  liturgy 264.02
  missions 266.2
  moral theology 241.042
  papacy 262.13
  persecution under Queen
      Elizabeth 272.7
  public worship 264.02
  religious associations 267.182
  religious education 268.82
  religious orders 255
    church history 271
    women 255.9
      church history 271.9
  seminaries 230.073 2
  social teaching 261.808 822
  theology 230.2
  see Manual at 281.1–281.4
Roman Catholic sacred music 781.712
  public worship 782.322 2
    music 782.322 2
    religion 264.020 2
Roman Catholic schisms 284.8
  see also Old Catholic churches
Roman Catholic schools 371.071 2
Roman Catholics 282.092
  religious group T7—22
Roman-Dutch law 340.56
Roman Empire 937.06
  T2—37
  Egyptian history 932.022
  English history 936.204
  French history 936.402
  Greek history 938.09
  Palestinian history 933.05
Roman Empire (continued)
  Spanish history 936.603
Roman Kingdom 937.01
  T2—37
Roman law 340.54
Roman philosophy 180.937
Roman religion 292.07
Roman Republic 937.02
  T2—37
Roman revival architecture 724.22
Roman sculpture 733.5
Roman type 686.224 7
Romana (Dominican
    Republic : Province) T2—729 383
Romance language literatures 840
Romance languages 440
  T6—4
Romances (Music) 784.189 68
Romances (Prose) 808.83
  history and criticism 809.3
  medieval 808.83
    history and criticism 809.3
    specific literatures T3B—3
      individual authors T3A—3
  modern 808.838 5
    history and criticism 809.385
    specific literatures T3B—308 5
      individual authors T3A—3
    see Manual at
        T3B—308729 vs.
        T3B—3085
Romances (Verse) 808.813 3
  specific literatures T3B—103 3
    individual authors T3A—1
Romanesque architecture 723.4
Romanesque art 709.021 6
  religious significance 246.2
Romanesque decoration 745.442
Romanesque painting 759.021 6
Romanesque revival architecture 724.52
Romanesque sculpture 734.24
Romania 949.8
  T2—498
  ancient 939.8
    T2—398
Romanian language 459
  T6—591
Romanian literature 859
Romanians T5—59
Romanies T5—914 97
Romanov, House of 947.046
  genealogy 929.77
Romans (Ancient people) T5—71
Romans (Biblical book) 227.1

Romansh language 459.9
T6—599
Romansh literature 859.9
Romantic fiction 808.838 5
history and criticism 809.385
specific literatures T3B—308 5
individual authors T3A—3
Romantic school
economics 330.155
Romanticism
arts 700.414 5
T3C—145
decoration 745.444 1
fine arts 709.034 2
literature 808.801 45
history and criticism 809.914 5
specific literatures T3B—080 145
history and criticism T3B—091 45
music 780.903 4
painting 759.052
philosophy 141.6
sculpture 735.22
Romany language 491.497
T6—914 97
Romany literature 891.497
Romblon (Philippines : Province) T2—599 5
Rome (Italy) T2—456 32
ancient T2—376
Rome (Italy : Province) T2—456 3
Rommelpots 786.98
see also Percussion instruments
Ronde bosse
ceramic arts 738.4
Rondônia (Brazil : State) T2—811 1
Rondos 781.824
instrumental 784.182 4
Ronga language 496.397 8
T6—963 978
Rood screens 247.1
architecture 726.529 6
Roodepoort (South Africa : District) T2—682 2
Roof failure (Mining) 622.28
Roof furniture 645.8
see also Outdoor furniture
Roof gardening 635.967 1
Roofers 695.092
occupational group T7—695
Roofing 695
Roofing paper 676.289
Roofing tiles 666.732
Roofs 721.5
architecture 721.5
construction 690.15
Rooks (Birds) 598.864
Rooks (Chessmen) 794.143
Rooks County (Kan.) T2—781 18
Rooming houses 647.94
Roosevelt, Franklin D. (Franklin Delano)
United States history 973.917
Roosevelt, Theodore
United States history 973.911
Roosevelt County (Mont.) T2—786 22
Roosevelt County (N.M.) T2—789 32
Root canal surgery 617.634 205 9
see also Dentistry
Root celery 641.351 28
see also Celeriac
Root crops 635.1
agriculture 635.1
cooking 641.651
food 641.351
Root extraction (Mathematics) 512.923
arithmetic 513.23
Roots (Mathematics)
number theory 512.72
Roots (Plants) 581.498
descriptive botany 581.498
physiology 575.54
Rope climbing 796.46
see also Sports
Roper River (N.T.) T2—942 95
Ropes 677.71
knotting and splicing 623.888 2
materials science 620.197
power transmission 621.853
sculpture material 731.2
ship gear 623.862
structural engineering 624.189 7
Roraima (Brazil) T2—811 4
Rorquals 599.524
Rorschach personality theory 155.264
Rorschach tests 155.284 2
Rosa (Roses) 583.734
Rosales 583.73
Rosary 242.74
Roscher, Wilhelm
economic school 330.154 2
Roscommon (Ireland : County) T2—417 5
Roscommon County (Mich.) T2—774 76
Rosé 641.222 3
commercial processing 663.223

Rose apples 583.765
Rose of Sharon 635.933 685
  botany 583.685
  floriculture 635.933 685
Roseau County (Minn.) T2—776 98
Rosebud County (Mont.) T2—786 32
Rosefinches 598.885
Rosellas (Birds) 598.71
Rosemaling 745.723
Rosemary 641.357
  botany 583.96
  see also Herbs
Roses 635.933 734
  botany 583.734
  floriculture 635.933 734
Roses, Wars of the, 1455–1485 942.04
Rosetta stone 493.1
Rosh Hashanah 296.431 5
  customs 394.267
  liturgy 296.453 15
Rosh Hashanah (Tractate) 296.123 2
  Babylonian Talmud 296.125 2
  Mishnah 296.123 2
  Palestinian Talmud 296.124 2
Rosicrucianism 135.43
Rosicrucians 135.430 92
  social group T7—13
Rosidae 583.7
Roskilde amt (Denmark) T2—489 1
Ross and Cromarty (Scotland) T2—411 72
Ross County (Ohio) T2—771 82
Ross Sea (Antarctic regions) 551.469 4
  T2—167 4
Ross seal 599.796
Rossendale (England) T2—427 63
Rossland (B.C.) T2—711 62
Rostock (Germany : Bezirk) T2—431 74
Rostov (Russia : Oblast) T2—474 9
Rostovskaia͡ oblast′ (Russia) T2—474 9
Rostral furniture
  church architecture 726.529 2
Rot
  agriculture 632.4
  materials science 620.112 23
Rotary blowers 621.62
Rotary fans 621.62
Rotary files (Records management) 651.54
Rotary International 369.52
  biography 369.520 92
  social group T7—369 5
Rotary pumps 621.66
  hydraulic 621.252
Rotary steam engines 621.16
Rotation
  celestial bodies 521
  earth 525.35
  sun 523.73
Rotation groups 512.2
Rotation of crops
  cultivation technique 631.582
  economics 338.162
  soil conservation 631.452
Rotational motion 531.113
  classical mechanics 531.113
  fluid mechanics 532.059 5
  gas mechanics 533.295
  liquid mechanics 532.595
  solid bodies 531.34
ROTC (Reserve training) 355.223 207 1173
Rote learning
  education 371.39
  psychology 153.152 2
Rother (England) T2—422 52
Rotherham (England : Metropolitan Borough) T2—428 23
Rotifera 592.52
Rotifers 592.52
Rotisseries
  electric cooking 641.586
Rotor ships 387.22
  engineering 623.822
  transportation services 387.22
  see also Ships
Rotors
  aircraft 629.134 36
Rotorua District (N.Z.) T2—934 23
  Bay of Plenty Region T2—934 23
  Waikato Region T2—933 67
Rotterdam (Netherlands) T2—492 385
Rottweiler 636.73
Rouen (France) T2—442 5
Rouergue (France) T2—447 4
Rough carpentry 694.2
Rough lumber 674.28
Roughness
  materials science 620.112 92
Roughy (Trachichthyidae) 597.64
Roulette 795.23
Roumania 949.8
  T2—498
  ancient 939.8
  T2—398
Round-backed lutes 787.82
  see also Stringed instruments

Round dances 793.33
Roundabouts
  urban 388.411
Roundhouses 385.314
  architecture 725.33
Roundworm-caused diseases (Human)
  incidence 614.555
  medicine 616.965
  see also Communicable diseases (Human)
Roundworms 592.57
Roussillon (France : Province) T2—448 9
Roussillon (Quebec) T2—714 34
Routes
  air 387.72
  bus 388.322 1
    urban 388.413 22
  maritime 387.52
  truck 388.324 2
    urban 388.413 24
Routing
  production management 658.53
  transportation 388.041
    see also Scheduling—transportation
Routt County (Colo.) T2—788 14
Rouville (Quebec) T2—714 53
Rouville (Quebec : Regional County Municipality) T2—714 53
Rouxville (South Africa : District) T2—685 6
Rouyn-Noranda (Quebec : Regional County Municipality) T2—714 13
Rove beetles 595.764 2
Rovigo (Italy : Province) T2—453 3
Row houses
  architecture 728.312
Rowan County (Ky.) T2—769 57
Rowan County (N.C.) T2—756 71
Rowan trees 583.73
Rowboat racing 797.14
  see also Sports
Rowboating 797.123
  see also Sports
Rowboats 386.229
  design 623.812 9
  engineering 623.829
  transportation services 386.229
Roxas, Manuel
  Philippine history 959.904 1
Roxburgh (Scotland : District) T2—413 92
Royal commissions 352.743
Royal fern 587.3
Royal houses
  genealogy 929.7
Royal Natal National Park (South Africa) T2—684 7
Royal National Park (N.S.W.) T2—944 6
Royal office of Jesus Christ 232.8
Royal tennis 796.34
Royalty 305.522 2
  T1—086 21
  customs 390.22
    dress 391.022
RSFSR (Russia) 947
  T2—47
RU486 (Drug)
  pharmacodynamics 615.766
Ruanda language 496.394 61
  T6—963 946 1
Ruanda literature 896.394 61
Ruanda-Rundi languages 496.394 6
  T6—963 946
Ruanda-Urundi 967.57
  T2—675 7
Ruapehu District (N.Z.) T2—935 2
Rub'al-Khali T2—538
Rubato 781.46
Rubber 678.2
  chemistry 547.842 6
  handicrafts 745.57
  materials science 620.194
  shipbuilding 623.820 7
  structural engineering 624.189 4
Rubber bands 678.35
Rubber hydrochloride 678.68
Rubber industry workers 678.209 2
  occupational group T7—678
Rubber plant (Ficus) 635.933 45
  botany 583.45
  floriculture 635.933 45
  rubber crop 633.895
Rubber products 678.3
Rubber-stamp printing 761
Rubber stamps
  manufacturing technology 681.6
Rubber tree (Hevea) 633.895 2
  botany 583.69
  rubber crop 633.895 2
Rubbings
  graphic arts 760
  research technique 739.522

Rubella
  incidence 614.524
  medicine 616.916
  see also Communicable diseases (Human)
Rubeola
  incidence 614.523
  medicine 616.915
  pediatrics 618.929 15
  see also Communicable diseases (Human)
Rubiaceae 583.93
Rubidium 669.725
  chemical engineering 661.038 4
  chemistry 546.384
  metallurgy 669.725
  see also Chemicals
Rubies 553.84
  economic geology 553.84
  jewelry 739.27
  mining 622.384
  synthetic 666.88
Rubus berries 641.347 1
  botany 583.73
  see also Cane fruits
Rudders 623.862
  aircraft 629.134 33
Rudolf, Lake (Kenya and Ethiopia) T2—676 27
Rudolf II, Holy Roman Emperor
  German history 943.034
Rues (Plants) 583.77
Ruffed grouse 598.635
  sports hunting 799.246 35
Rugby 796.333
  see also Sports
Rugby (England) T2—424 85
Rugby League 796.333 8
Rugby players 796.333 092
  sports group T7—796 33
Rugby Union 796.333
Rugs 645.1
  arts 746.7
  building construction 698.9
  household management 645.1
  interior decoration 747.5
  manufacturing technology 677.643
Ruhr River (Germany) T2—435 5
Ruiz Cortines, Adolfo
  Mexican history 972.082 8
Rukwa Region (Tanzania) T2—678 28
Rule of law 340.11
Rule of the road at sea
  international law 341.756 66
  law 343.096 6
  seamanship 623.888 4
Ruled surfaces 516.362
Rules committees (Legislatures) 328.365 8
Rules of order 060.42
  legislatures 328.1
Rum 641.259
  commercial processing 663.59
Rumania 949.8
  T2—498
  ancient 939.8
  T2—398
Rumanians T5—59
Rumbas 793.33
  music 784.188 8
Ruminants 599.63
  animal husbandry 636.2
  paleozoology 569.63
Rummy 795.418
Rumor
  social psychology 302.24
Runaway children 305.906 923
  T1—086 923
  social group 305.906 923
  social welfare 362.74
Rundi (African people) T5—963 946 5
Rundi language 496.394 65
  T6—963 946 5
Rundi literature 896.394 65
Runes 430
  divination 133.33
Runnels County (Tex.) T2—764 724
Runners (Athletes) 796.420 92
  sports group T7—796 4
Runners (Stolons) 581.46
  agricultural propagation 631.533
  descriptive botany 581.46
  physiology 575.499
Running
  animal behavior 591.5
  animal physiology 573.79
  humans
    physical fitness 613.717 2
    sports 796.42
      see also Sports
Running boards 629.26
Running gear
  railroad engineering 625.21
Runnymede (England) T2—422 11
Runoff (Hydrology) 551.488

Runways (Airports)
  engineering 629.136 3
  military airports 623.663
  transportation services 387.736 2
Rupert's Land 971.201
  T2—712
Ruppiaceae 584.74
Rupture strength
  materials science 620.112 6
Rupununi (Guyana : District) T2—881 8
Rural areas T2—173 4
  social services to residents 361.917 34
    public administration 353.533 4
  see also Rural government
Rural churches 250.917 34
  administration 254.24
  pastoral theology 253.091 734
Rural collection 383.145
  see also Postal service
Rural communities 307.72
  psychological influence 155.944
Rural delivery 383.145
  see also Postal service
Rural development 307.141 2
  law 343.074 5
  public administration 354.279 4
Rural education 370.917 34
Rural electrification 333.793 2
Rural exodus 307.24
Rural families 306.852
Rural free delivery 383.145
  see also Postal service
Rural government 320.84
  public administration 352.17
    control by higher jurisdictions 353.337
  public administrative support 352.794
  see also Rural areas
Rural health services 362.104 257
Rural lands 333.76
  economics 333.76
    sale and rental 333.335
  see *Manual* at 333.76 vs. 333.73
Rural municipalities 320.84
Rural sanitation 363.720 917 34
  technology 628.7
    see *Manual* at 628.7
Rural schools 371.009 173 4
Rural sociology 307.72
Rural-urban migration 307.24
Ruscaceae 584.355
Ruse (Bulgaria : Oblast) T2—499 3
Ruse (Bulgaria : Okrŭg) T2—499 3
Rusenska oblast (Bulgaria) T2—499 3
Rusenski okrŭg (Bulgaria) T2—499 3
Rush County (Ind.) T2—772 61
Rush County (Kan.) T2—781 48
Rushcliffe (England : Borough) T2—425 29
Rushes 584.82
  textile arts 746.41
  textiles 677.54
  see also Textiles
Rushes (Cyperaceae) 584.84
Rushes (Juncaceae) 584.82
Rushmoor (England : District) T2—422 725
Rushwork 746.41
Rushworth (Vic.) T2—945 4
Rusk County (Tex.) T2—764 185
Rusk County (Wis.) T2—775 19
Russell (Ont. : County) T2—713 85
Russell County (Ala.) T2—761 485
Russell County (Kan.) T2—781 51
Russell County (Ky.) T2—769 655
Russell County (Va.) T2—755 755
Russia 947
  T2—47
  Asia 957
    T2—57
Russian blue cat 636.82
Russian calligraphy 745.619 917 1
Russian folk music 781.629 171
Russian folk songs 782.421 629 171
Russian language 491.7
  T6—917 1
Russian literature 891.7
Russian Orthodox Church 281.947
  see also Eastern Orthodox Church
Russian Revolution, 1905 947.083
Russian Revolution, 1917 947.084 1
Russian Soviet Federated Socialist Republic 947
  T2—47
Russian turnip 641.351 26
  see also Rutabagas
Russians T5—917 1
Russo-Finnish War, 1939–1940 948.970 32
Russo-Japanese War, 1904–1905 952.031
Russo-Turkish War, 1877–1878 947.081
Rust
  materials science 620.112 23
Rust diseases
  agriculture 632.492

Rust flies 595.774
Rust fungi 579.592
Rust-resistant paints 667.69
Rustenburg (South Africa : District) T2—682 3
Rusts (Fungi) 579.592
  agricultural diseases 632.492
Rutabagas 641.351 26
  botany 583.64
  commercial processing 664.805 126
  cooking 641.651 26
  food 641.351 26
  garden crop 635.126
Rutales 583.77
Ruth (Biblical book) 222.35
Ruthenians (Ethnic group) T5—917 91
Ruthenium 669.7
  chemical engineering 661.063 2
  chemistry 546.632
  metallography 669.957
  metallurgy 669.7
  physical metallurgy 669.967
  see also Chemicals
Rutherford County (N.C.) T2—756 913
Rutherford County (Tenn.) T2—768 57
Rutherfordium
  chemistry 546.51
  see also Chemicals
Rutherglen (Vic.) T2—945 5
Rutile
  mineralogy 549.524
Rutland (England) T2—425 45
Rutland County (Vt.) T2—743 7
Ruvuma Region (Tanzania) T2—678 25
RV (Vehicle) 388.346
  engineering 629.226
  see also Motor homes
Rwanda 967.571
  T2—675 71
Rwanda language 496.394 61
  T6—963 946 1
Rwanda literature 896.394 61
Rwanda-Rundi languages 496.394 6
  T6—963 946
Rwandans T5—967 571
Ryazan (Russia : Oblast) T2—473 3
Rye 641.331 4
  botany 584.9
  commercial processing 664.72
  cooking 641.631 4
  food 641.331 4
  food crop 633.14
  forage crop 633.254
Ryedale (England : District) T2—428 46
Rynchopidae 598.338
Ryukyu Islands T2—522 9
Ryukyuans T5—956
Rzeszów (Poland : Voivodeship) T2—438 6

S

's-Gravenhage (Netherlands) T2—492 382
Saam language 494.55
  T6—945 5
Saam literature 894.55
Saami (European people) T5—945 5
Saami language 494.55
  T6—945 5
Saami literature 894.55
Saanich (B.C.) T2—711 28
Saanich Peninsula (B.C.) T2—711 28
Saar River (France and Germany) T2—434 2
Saarbrücken (Germany) T2—434 21
Saarland (Germany) T2—434 2
Saba (Netherlands Antilles) T2—729 77
Sabah T2—595 3
Sabbath 296.41
  Christianity 263.1
  Judaism 296.41
Sabbatianism 296.82
Sabbatical leave 331.257 63
  economics 331.257 63
  education 371.104
    higher education 378.121
  personnel management 658.312 2
Sabbatical Year (Judaism) 296.439 1
Sabellian languages 479.7
  T6—797
Sabellian literatures 879.7
Sabellianism 273.3
Sabers 623.441
  art metalwork 739.722
Sabiaceae 583.78
Sabie (South Africa) T2—682 6
Sabine County (Tex.) T2—764 177
Sabine Lake (La. and Tex.) T2—763 52
Sabine language 479.7
  T6—797
Sabine Parish (La.) T2—763 62
Sabine River (Tex. and La.) T2—764 14
Sable (Carnivorous mammal) 599.766 5

Sable antelope 599.645
Sable Island (N.S.) T2—716 99
Sabotage 364.164
  armed forces 355.343 7
  labor economics 331.893
  law 345.026 4
Sabrata (Extinct city) T2—397 4
Sac County (Iowa) T2—777 424
Sacatepéquez (Guatemala) T2—728 162
Saccharides 572.56
  biochemistry 572.56
  chemistry 547.78
  see also Carbohydrates
Saccharolytic enzymes 572.756
  see also Enzymes
Saccharomyces 579.563
Saccharomycetaceae 579.562
Saccorhiza 579.887
Sachs Harbour (N.W.T.) T2—719 6
Sachsen (Germany) T2—432 1
Sachsen-Anhalt (Germany) T2—431 8
Sackville (N.B.) T2—715 23
Sacoglossa 594.35
Sacramental furniture 247.1
  architecture 726.529 1
Sacramentals 264.9
Sacramentaries
  Roman Catholic 264.020 36
    texts 264.023
Sacramento (Calif.) T2—794 54
Sacramento County (Calif.) T2—794 53
Sacramento Mountains (N.M.) T2—789 65
Sacramento River (Calif.) T2—794 5
Sacraments 234.16
  public worship 265
    Anglican 264.030 8
      texts 264.035
    Roman Catholic 264.020 8
      texts 264.025
  theology 234.16
Sacred books 291.82
  Buddhism 294.382
  Christianity 220
    Latter-Day Saints 289.32
  Hinduism 294.592
  Islam 297.122
  Judaism 296.1
    Bible 221
      see Manual at 221
  see Manual at 133 vs. 200
Sacred Heart religious orders 255.93
  church history 271.93
Sacred music 781.7
  public worship 291.38
    see also Public worship
  religious significance 291.37
    see also Music—religion
  vocal forms 782.22
    choral and mixed voices 782.522
    instrumental forms 784.189 92
    single voices 783.092 2
Sacred places 291.35
  Buddhist 294.343 5
  Christianity 263.042
  Hindu 294.535
  Islam 297.35
  Jain 294.435
  Judaism 296.48
  public worship 291.38
  Sikh 294.635
Sacred songs 782.25
  choral and mixed voices 782.525
  single voices 783.092 5
Sacred vocal music 782.22
Sacrifice of Jesus Christ 232.4
Sacrifices (Religion) 291.34
  Judaism 296.492
Sacrilege
  criminology 364.188
  law 345.028 8
Sacristies
  architecture 726.596
Ṣadaqah 297.54
Sadat, Anwar
  Egyptian history 962.054
Saddle block anesthesia
  surgery 617.964
Saddle fungi 579.578
Saddle horses 636.13
Saddlers 685.109 2
  occupational group T7—685 1
Saddlery 636.108 37
  animal husbandry 636.083 7
  horse rearing 636.108 37
  manufacturing technology 685.1
Sadducees 296.813
Sadism
  medicine 616.858 35
  sociology 306.775
  see also Mental illness
Sadomasochism
  medicine 616.858 35
  sociology 306.775
  see also Mental illness
Safe-deposit services 332.178
Safes 683.34

Safety 363.1
international law 341.765
law 344.047
management 658.408
T1—068 4
personal safety T1—028 9
personnel management 658.382
public administration 352.67
public administration 353.9
social services 363.1
see Manual at 363; *also at* 363.1
Safety engineering 620.86
T1—028 9
automotive 629.204 2
design 629.231
construction 690.22
military 623.75
roads 625.702 89
transportation 629.040 289
Safety equipment 621.992
aircraft 629.134 43
automobile 629.276
plant management 658.28
ships 623.865
Safety management 658.408
T1—068 4
Safety regulations 363.1
public administration 353.9
see Manual at 363.1: Safety regulations
Safety training
personnel management 658.312 44
public administration 352.669
Safety valves
steam engineering 621.185
Safflower 583.99
Saffron (Crocus) 584.38
Safi (Morocco : Province) T2—646
Safwa language 496.391
T6—963 91
Saga-ken (Japan) T2—522 3
Sagadahoc County (Me.) T2—741 85
Sagas
Old Norse literature 839.63
Sage 641.357
botany 583.96
see also Herbs
Sage grouse 598.636
Sagebrushes 583.99
Saginaw Bay (Mich.) T2—774 47
Saginaw County (Mich.) T2—774 46
Saginaw River (Mich.) T2—774 47
Sagitta 592.38
Sagittariidae 598.9
Sagittarius (Zodiac) 133.527 4
Sago 641.336 8
cooking 641.636 8
food 641.336 8
starch crop 633.68
Saguache County (Colo.) T2—788 49
Saguenay (Quebec) T2—714 17
Saguenay-Lac-Saint-Jean (Quebec : Administrative region) T2—714 14
Saguenay River (Quebec) T2—714 16
Saguia el Hamra T2—648
Sahara T2—66
Saharan languages 496.5
T6—965
Sahel T2—66
Saïda (Algeria : Province) T2—651
Saiga 599.647
Sail yachting 797.124 6
Sailboarding 797.33
see also Sports
Sailboat racing 797.14
see also Sports
Sailboating 797.124
see also Sports
Sailfishes 597.78
sports fishing 799.177 8
Sailing ships 387.204 3
design 623.812 043
engineering 623.820 3
handling 623.881 3
naval equipment 359.832
naval units 359.322
transportation services 387.204 3
see also Ships
Sailors 387.509 2
merchant seamen 387.509 2
occupational group T7—387 5
navy personnel 359.009 2
occupational group T7—359
occupational group T7—387 5
sports 797.109 2
sports group T7—797 1
technologists 623.880 92
occupational group T7—623 8
Sails 623.862
Saimiri 599.852
Saint Albans (England : District) T2—425 85
Saint-Augustin-de-Desmaures (Quebec) T2—714 471
Saint Barthélemy T2—729 76
Saint Bernard (Dog) 636.73

Saint Bernard Parish (La.) T2—763 36
Saint Charles County (Mo.) T2—778 39
Saint Charles Parish (La.) T2—763 33
Saint Christopher T2—729 73
Saint Christopher-Nevis 972.973
T2—729 73
Saint Christopher-Nevis-Anguilla T2—729 73
Saint Clair, Lake (Mich. and Ont.) T2—774 39
Michigan T2—774 39
Ontario T2—713 31
Saint Clair, Lake (Tas.) T2—946 3
Saint Clair County (Ala.) T2—761 69
Saint Clair County (Ill.) T2—773 89
Saint Clair County (Mich.) T2—774 41
Saint Clair County (Mo.) T2—778 466
Saint Clair River (Mich. and Ont.) T2—774 41
Michigan T2—774 41
Ontario T2—713 27
Saint Croix (V.I.) T2—729 722
Saint Croix County (Wis.) T2—775 41
Saint Croix River (Me. and N.B.) T2—741 42
Maine T2—741 42
New Brunswick T2—715 33
Saint Croix River (Wis. and Minn.) T2—775 1
Saint-Denis (Réunion) T2—698 1
Saint Edmundsbury (England) T2—426 44
Saint-Emile (Quebec) T2—714 471
Saint Eustatius (Netherlands Antilles) T2—729 77
Saint-Foy (Quebec) T2—714 471
Saint Francis County (Ark.) T2—767 91
Saint Francois County (Mo.) T2—778 68
Saint-François River (Wolfe-Yamaska, Quebec) T2—714 5
Saint Gall (Switzerland : Canton) T2—494 72
Saint George's Channel (Ireland and Wales) 551.461 37
T2—163 37
Saint Helena 997.3
T2—973
Saint Helena Parish (La.) T2—763 15
Saint Helens (Merseyside, England : District) T2—427 57
Saint Hyacinthe (Quebec : County) T2—714 523
Saint James Parish (La.) T2—763 31
Saint-Jean (Quebec : County) T2—714 38
Saint John (N.B. : County) T2—715 32
Saint John (V.I.) T2—729 722
Saint John River (Me. and N.B.) T2—715 5
Saint John the Baptist Parish (La.) T2—763 32
Saint Johns County (Fla.) T2—759 18
Saint Johns River (Fla.) T2—759 1
Saint Joseph County (Ind.) T2—772 89
Saint Joseph County (Mich.) T2—774 19
Saint Joseph religious orders 255.976
church history 271.976
Saint Kitts T2—729 73
Saint Kitts-Nevis 972.973
T2—729 73
Saint Kitts-Nevis-Anguilla T2—729 73
Saint Landry Parish (La.) T2—763 46
Saint-Laurent, Louis Stephen
Canadian history 971.063 3
Saint-Laurent du Maroni (French Guiana) T2—882
Saint Lawrence, Gulf of 551.461 44
T2—163 44
Saint Lawrence County (N.Y.) T2—747 56
Saint Lawrence River T2—714
New York T2—747 56
Ontario T2—713 7
Quebec T2—714
Saint Lawrence Seaway 386.509 714
T2—714
Ontario T2—713 7
Quebec T2—714
Saint Louis (Mo.) T2—778 66
Saint-Louis (Senegal) T2—663
Saint Louis County (Minn.) T2—776 77
Saint Louis County (Mo.) T2—778 65
Saint Lucia 972.984 3
T2—729 843
Saint Lucia Game Reserve (South Africa) T2—684 3
Saint Lucie County (Fla.) T2—759 29
Saint Martin T2—729 76
Guadeloupe T2—729 76
Netherlands Antilles T2—729 77
Saint Martin Parish (La.) T2—763 48
Saint Mary Parish (La.) T2—763 42
Saint Marys, Lake (Ohio) T2—771 415

Saint Marys County (Md.) T2—752 41
Saint Marys River (Ga. and Fla.) T2—759 11
Saint Marys River (Mich. and Ont.) T2—774 91
Saint-Maurice (Quebec : County) T2—714 451
Saint Paul (Minn.) T2—776 581
Saint Paul Island 969.9
T2—699
Saint Petersburg (Russia) T2—472 1
Saint Pierre and Miquelon 971.88
T2—718 8
Saint-Simonism (Socialist school) 335.22
Saint Tammany Parish (La.) T2—763 12
Saint Thomas (V.I.) T2—729 722
Saint Vincent T2—729 844
Saint Vincent and the Grenadines 972.984 4
T2—729 844
Sainte Genevieve County (Mo.) T2—778 692
Saintes Islands (Guadeloupe) T2—729 76
Saintonge (France) T2—446 4
Saints 200.92
  art representation 704.948 63
  biography 200.92
  Christian 270.092
    biography 270.092
      specific denominations 280
      see Manual at 230–280
    doctrines 235.2
  Islam
    Sufis 297.409 2
  objects of worship 291.213
  religious group T7—2
  role and function 291.61
  see Manual at 200.92 and 291–299
Saints' days 263.98
  devotional literature 242.37
  sermons 252.67
Saipan T2—967
Saitama-ken (Japan) T2—521 34
Saite period 932.015
Saivism 294.551 3
Saka language 491.53
T6—915 3
Saka literature 891.53
Sakakawea, Lake (N.D.) T2—784 75
Sakarya İli (Turkey) T2—563
Sake 641.23
  commercial processing 663.49
Sakhalin (Russia : Oblast) T2—577
Sakhalin Ula (China and Russia) T2—577
Sakhalinskai͡a oblast′ (Russia) T2—577
Salad dressings 641.814
  food technology 664.37
  home preparation 641.814
Salad greens 641.355
  commercial processing 664.805 5
  cooking 641.655
  food 641.355
  garden crop 635.5
    see Manual at 635.3 and 635.4, 635.5
Salad oils
  food technology 664.36
Salads 641.83
Ṣalāḥ ad-Dīn (Iraq : Province) T2—567 4
Sălaj (Romania) T2—498 4
Salamanca (Spain : Province) T2—462 5
Salamanders 597.85
Salamandroidea 597.85
Salar language 494.36
T6—943 6
Salaries 331.21
  personnel management 658.32
    executives 658.407 2
    public administration 352.67
  public administration 354.98
  see also Wages
Salary scales 331.216
  personnel management 658.322 2
Ṣalāt 297.382 2
Salazar, Antonio de Oliveira
  Portuguese history 946.904 2
Salcedo (Dominican Republic : Province) T2—729 363
Sale of businesses
  law 346.065
  management 658.16
Sale of real property 333.333
  economics 333.333
    private ownership 333.333
    public ownership 333.16
  law 346.043 63
    private ownership 346.043 63
    public ownership 343.025 3
Salem (Or.) T2—795 37
Salem (Va.) T2—755 793

Salem County (N.J.) T2—749 91
Salerno (Italy : Province) T2—457 4
Sales
  commerce 380.1
  law 346.072
  management 658.81
Sales clerks 381.092
  occupational group T7—381
Sales finance institutions 332.35
Sales forecasting
  marketing management 658.818
Sales management 658.81
  T1—068 8
Sales meetings 658.810 6
Sales personnel
  domestic commerce 381.092
  occupational group T7—381
  organization 658.810 2
Sales planning 658.810 1
Sales promotion 658.82
Sales tax 336.271 3
  law 343.055 2
  public administration 352.44
  public finance 336.271 3
Salesmanship
  domestic commerce 381
  etiquette 395.53
  management 658.85
Salesmen
  domestic commerce 381.092
  occupational group T7—381
Salford (England : City) T2—427 32
Salian emperors
  German history 943.023
Salicales 583.65
Salientia 597.8
Salinas de Gortari, Carlos
  Mexican history 972.083 5
Salinas River (Calif.) T2—794 76
Saline County (Ark.) T2—767 72
Saline County (Ill.) T2—773 992
Saline County (Kan.) T2—781 545
Saline County (Mo.) T2—778 47
Saline County (Neb.) T2—782 327
Saline water 553.72
Saline water conversion
  water supply engineering 628.167
Salinity
  sea water 551.460 1
  soil science 631.416
Salisbury (England : District) T2—423 19
Salisbury (S. Aust.) T2—942 32
Salisbury Island (N.W.T.) T2—719 5
Salisbury Plain T2—423 19
Salish Indians T5—979
Salishan Indians T5—979
Salishan languages 497.9
  T6—979
Saliva 573.353 79
  human physiology 612.313
  see also Digestive system
Salivary glands 573.353 79
  biology 573.353 79
  human anatomy 611.316
  human physiology 612.313
  medicine 616.316
  see also Digestive system
Salix 583.65
Salmo 597.57
Salmo salar 597.56
Salmon 641.392
  commercial fishing 639.275 6
  conservation technology 639.977 56
  cooking 641.692
  culture 639.375 6
    economics 338.371 375 6
  food 641.392
  resource economics 333.956 56
  sports fishing 799.175 6
  zoology 597.56
Salmon Arm (B.C.) T2—711 68
Salmon River (Idaho) T2—796 82
Salmon River Mountains (Idaho) T2—796 7
Salmonella 579.344
Salmonella diseases (Biology) 571.993 44
  veterinary medicine 636.089 692 7
Salmonella diseases (Human)
  incidence 614.511
  medicine 616.927
  see also Communicable diseases (Human)
Salmonidae 597.55
  conservation technology 639.977 55
  culture 639.375 5
  resource economics 333.956 55
  sports fishing 799.175 5
Salmoniformes 597.5
  paleozoology 567.5
Salon orchestras 784.4
Salpingitis
  gynecology 618.12
  see also Female genital system
Salsify 641.351 6
  botany 583.99
  cooking 641.651 6
  food 641.351 6

Salsify (continued)
  garden crop 635.16
Salt (Sodium chloride) 553.632
  applied nutrition 613.285
  biochemistry 572.523 822 4
    humans 612.015 24
  chemistry 546.382 24
  cooking with 641.6
  economic geology 553.632
  food technology 664.4
  metabolism 572.523 822 4
    human physiology 612.392 6
  mineralogy 549.4
  mining 622.363 2
Salt-free cooking 641.563 2
Salt-free diet
  health 613.285
Salt Lake City (Utah) T2—792 258
Salt Lake County (Utah) T2—792 25
Salt lakes 551.460 9
  biology 578.763 9
  ecology 577.639
  resource economics 333.916 4
Salt marshes
  biology 578.769
  ecology 577.69
  see also Wetlands
Salta (Argentina : Province) T2—824 2
Saltarellos 793.319 45
  music 784.188 2
Salto (Uruguay : Dept.) T2—895 35
Salton Sea (Calif.) T2—794 99
Saltpeter 553.64
  economic geology 553.64
  mineralogy 549.732
Salts 546.34
  biochemistry 572.51
  chemical engineering 661.4
  chemistry 546.34
  economic geology 553.63
  metabolism 572.51
    human physiology 612.392 6
  see also Chemicals; Salt (Sodium chloride)
Saltwater biology 578.77
Saltwater desalinization 628.167
Saltwater ecology 577.7
Saltwater fishes 597.177
  culture 639.32
  see also Fishes
Saltwater fishing 639.22
  commercial 639.22
  sports 799.16
Saltwater intrusion 363.738
  engineering 628.114
  social problem 363.738
  see also Pollution
Saltwater lagoons 551.460 9
  T2—168
Saltwater wetlands
  biology 578.769
  ecology 577.69
  see also Wetlands
Saltwater zebra fishes 597.68
Saluda County (S.C.) T2—757 38
Saluki 636.753 2
Salvador, El 972.84
  T2—728 4
Salvadoran literature 860
Salvadorans T5—687 284
Salvage operations
  disaster relief 363.348 1
  international law 341.756 68
  maritime law 343.096 8
  maritime transportation 387.55
  underwater engineering 627.703
Salvation 291.22
  Christianity 234
  Islam 297.22
  Judaism 296.32
  see also Humans—religion
Salvation Army 287.96
  religious group T7—27
  see also Christian denominations
Salvator Rosa National Park (Qld.) T2—943 5
Salvelinus 597.554
Salviniales 587.3
Salzburg (Austria : Land) T2—436 3
Samaná (Dominican Republic : Province) T2—729 365
Samar (Philippines) T2—599 5
Samara (Russia : Oblast) T2—474 4
Samaria T2—33
Samaritan Aramaic language 492.29
  T6—922 9
Samaritan language 492.29
  T6—922 9
  Biblical texts 220.45
Samaritan literature 892.29
Samaritans T5—922
Samaritans (Judaism) 296.817
Samarium
  chemistry 546.415
  see also Rare earths

Samarskaia͡ oblast′
  (Russia) T2—474 4
Samaveda 294.592 13
Samba (Game) 795.418
Sambar 599.654
Sambas 793.33
  music 784.188 8
Same language 494.55
  T6—945 5
Same literature 894.55
Samhitas 294.592 1
Sami (European people) T5—945 5
Sami language 494.55
  T6—945 5
Sami literature 894.55
Samnan (Iran) T2—552 3
Samnium T2—377
Samoa T2—961 3
Samoan Islands T2—961 3
Samoan language 499.462
  T6—994 62
Samoan literature 899.462
Samoans T5—994 62
Samoic Outlier languages 499.46
  T6—994 6
Samos (Greece : Nome) T2—495 82
Samos Island (Greece) T2—495 82
  ancient T2—391 4
Samothrace Island
  (Greece) T2—495 7
  ancient T2—391 1
Samoyed T5—944
Samoyed (Dog) 636.73
Samoyedic languages 494.4
  T6—944
Samoyedic literatures 894.4
Sample preparation
  analytical chemistry 543.02
    qualitative 544.02
Samples
  sales promotion 658.82
Sampling techniques 001.433
  T1—072 3
Sampling theory 519.52
Sampson County (N.C.) T2—756 375
Samsun Ili (Turkey) T2—563
Samuel (Biblical books) 222.4
San (African people) T5—961
San Andres Mountains
  (N.M.) T2—789 67
San Andrés y Providencia
  (Colombia) T2—861 8
San Antonio (Chile :
  Province) T2—832 58
San Antonio (Tex.) T2—764 351
San Antonio River (Tex.) T2—764 12
San Augustine County
  (Tex.) T2—764 175
San Benito County (Calif.) T2—794 75
San Bernardino County
  (Calif.) T2—794 95
San Bernardino Mountains
  (Calif.) T2—794 95
San Cristóbal (Dominican
  Republic : Province) T2—729 374
San Diego (Calif.) T2—794 985
San Diego County (Calif.) T2—794 98
San Felipe (Chile :
  Province) T2—832 45
San Francisco (Calif.) T2—794 61
San Francisco Bay (Calif.) 551.466 32
  T2—164 32
San Francisco Bay Area
  (Calif.) T2—794 6
San Francisco County
  (Calif.) T2—794 61
San Gabriel Mountains
  (Calif.) T2—794 93
San hsiens 787.85
  see also Stringed instruments
San Jacinto County (Tex.) T2—764 167
San Joaquin County
  (Calif.) T2—794 55
San Joaquin River (Calif.) T2—794 8
San Jose (Calif.) T2—794 74
San José (Costa Rica :
  Province) T2—728 63
San José (Uruguay : Dept.) T2—895 12
San Juan (Argentina :
  Province) T2—826 3
San Juan (Dominican
  Republic : Province) T2—729 342
San Juan (P.R. : District) T2—729 51
San Juan County (Colo.) T2—788 25
San Juan County (N.M.) T2—789 82
San Juan County (Utah) T2—792 59
San Juan County (Wash.) T2—797 74
San Juan Mountains (Colo.
  and N.M.) T2—788 3
San Juan River (B.C.) T2—711 28
San Juan River
  (Colo.-Utah) T2—792 59
San languages 496.1
  T6—961
San Luis (Argentina :
  Province) T2—826 2
San Luis Obispo County
  (Calif.) T2—794 78

San Luis Potosí (Mexico : State) T2—724 4
San Luis Valley (Colo. and N.M.) T2—788 3
San Marcos (Guatemala : Dept.) T2—728 184
San Marino 945.49
T2—454 9
San Martín (Peru : Dept.) T2—854 5
San Mateo County (Calif.) T2—794 69
San Miguel (El Salvador : Dept.) T2—728 432
San Miguel County (Colo.) T2—788 23
San Miguel County (N.M.) T2—789 55
San Patricio County (Tex.) T2—764 115
San Pedro (Paraguay : Dept.) T2—892 136
San Pedro de Macorís (Dominican Republic : Province) T2—729 382
San Saba County (Tex.) T2—764 68
San Salvador (El Salvador : Dept.) T2—728 423
San Salvador Island (Bahamas) T2—729 6
San Sebastián (Spain) T2—466 1
San Vicente (El Salvador : Dept.) T2—728 427
Sanaga languages 496.396
T6—963 96
Sanatoriums 362.16
architecture 725.51
mental illness 362.23
physical illness 362.16
see also Health care facilities; Health services; Mental health services
Sanborn County (S.D.) T2—783 33
Sánchez Ramírez (Dominican Republic : Province) T2—729 368
Sancti Spíritus (Cuba : Province) T2—729 145
Sanctification (Christian doctrine) 234.8
Sanctifying grace 234.1
Sanctions (International politics) 327.117
international law 341.582
Sanctuaries
architecture 726.593
Sanctus 264.36
music 782.323 2
Sand 553.622
economic geology 553.622
materials science 620.191
mining 622.362 2
petrology 552.5
Sand casting
metals 671.252
sculpture 731.45
Sand dollars 593.95
Sand dunes 551.375
biology 578.758 3
ecology 577.583
geomorphology 551.375
land economics 333.73
Sand fleas 595.378
Sand grouse 598.65
Sand painting 751.49
Sand yachting 796.68
see also Sports
Sandalwood
botany 583.88
forestry 634.973 88
Sandaun Province (Papua New Guinea) T2—957 7
Sandblasting 621.54
glass arts 748.6
pneumatic engineering 621.54
Sanders County (Mont.) T2—786 833
Sandlot baseball 796.357 62
Sandoval County (N.M.) T2—789 57
Sandpaper blocks
music 786.863
see also Percussion instruments
Sandpipers 598.33
Sandstone 553.53
building material 691.2
economic geology 553.53
petrology 552.5
quarrying 622.353
Sandusky Bay (Ohio) T2—771 214
Sandusky County (Ohio) T2—771 214
Sandwell (England : Metropolitan Borough) T2—424 94
Sandwich construction 624.177 9
naval architecture 623.817 79
Sandwich panels 674.835
architectural construction 721.044 92
construction materials 693.92
Sandwiches 641.84
Sangamon County (Ill.) T2—773 56
Sangamon River (Ill.) T2—773 55
Sango language 496.361 6
T6—963 616

Sango literature 896.361 6
Sangre de Cristo Mountains (Colo. and N.M.) T2—788 49
Sanhedrin 296.67
Sanhedrin (Tractate) 296.123 4
  Babylonian Talmud 296.125 4
  Mishnah 296.123 4
  Palestinian Talmud 296.124 4
Sanikiluaq (N.W.T.) T2—719 5
Sanilac County (Mich.) T2—774 43
Sanitariums 362.16
  see also Sanatoriums
Sanitary engineering 628
  military engineering 623.75
  see Manual at 628.7
Sanitary engineers 628.092
  occupational group T7—628
Sanitary landfills 363.728
  technology 628.445 64
    sewage sludge 628.364
    water pollution engineering 628.168 25
  see also Waste control
Sanitary napkins 677.8
Sanitation 363.72
  armed forces 355.345
  customs 392.36
  home economics 648
  law 344.046 4
    enforcement 363.233
  mining 622.49
  public administration 353.93
    public facilities 353.94
  ships 623.854 6
  social services 363.72
  spacecraft 629.477 4
  World War I 940.475 2
  World War II 940.547 52
  see also Waste control
Sanitation equipment
  plant management 658.28
Sanitation facilities
  area planning 711.8
Sanitation services 363.72
  see also Sanitation
Sanitoriums 362.16
  see also Sanatoriums
Sankara, Thomas
  Burkinan history 966.250 5
Śaṅkarācārya (Philosophy) 181.482
Sankhya (Philosophy) 181.41
Şanliurfa İli (Turkey) T2—565
Sanpete County (Utah) T2—792 563
Sansevierias 584.352
Sanskrit language 491.2
  T6—912
  Vedas 294.592 104 1
Sanskrit literature 891.2
Santa Ana (El Salvador : Dept.) T2—728 412
Santa Ana Mountains (Calif.) T2—794 96
Santa Bárbara (Honduras) T2—728 385
Santa Barbara County (Calif.) T2—794 91
Santa Barbara Islands (Calif.) T2—794 91
Santa Catarina (Brazil : State) T2—816 4
Santa Clara County (Calif.) T2—794 73
Santa Cruz (Argentina : Province) T2—827 5
Santa Cruz (Bolivia : Dept.) T2—843
Santa Cruz, Andrés
  Bolivian history 984.044
Santa Cruz County (Ariz.) T2—791 79
Santa Cruz County (Calif.) T2—794 71
Santa Cruz de Tenerife (Canary Islands : Province) T2—649
Santa Fe (Argentina : Province) T2—822 4
Santa Fe County (N.M.) T2—789 56
Santa Lucia Range (Calif.) T2—794 78
Santa Rosa (Guatemala) T2—728 144
Santa Rosa County (Fla.) T2—759 985
Santal (South Asian people) T5—959 5
Santalales 583.88
Santali language 495.95
  T6—959 5
Santander (Colombia : Dept.) T2—861 25
Santander (Spain : Province) T2—463 51
Santarém (Portugal : District) T2—469 45
Santee River (S.C.) T2—757 8
Santeria 299.674
Santiago (Chile) T2—833 15
Santiago (Chile : Province) T2—833 1
Santiago (Dominican Republic) T2—729 356
Santiago de Compostela (Spain) T2—461 1
Santiago de Cuba (Cuba : Province) T2—729 165

Santiago del Estero
  (Argentina : Province) T2—825 2
Santiago Rodríguez
  (Dominican Republic :
  Province) T2—729 353
Santirs 787.74
  see also Stringed instruments
Santo Domingo
  (Dominican Republic) T2—729 375
Santoríni Island (Greece) T2—495 85
Santos
  fine arts 704.948 2
  religious significance 246.53
Santos, José Eduardo dos
  Angolan history 967.304 2
Sanzas 786.85
  see also Percussion
    instruments
São Francisco River
  (Brazil) T2—814 2
São Paulo (Brazil : State) T2—816 1
São Tomé (Sao Tome and
  Principe) T2—671 5
Sao Tome and Principe 967.15
  T2—671 5
Sao Tomeans T5—967 15
Saône-et-Loire (France) T2—444 3
Saône River (France) T2—444
Sap 575.75
  forest product 634.986
Sap beetles 595.769
Sapindales 583.78
Sapodilla 583.674
  see also Sapotaceae
Saponification 547.770 459 3
  chemical engineering 660.284 425
  lipid chemistry 547.770 459 3
  organic chemistry 547.225
Saponins 572.567
  see also Carbohydrates
Sapotaceae 583.674
  edible fruits 641.344 3
    cooking 641.644 3
    food 641.344 3
    orchard crop 634.43
Sapphires 553.84
  economic geology 553.84
  glyptics 736.25
  jewelry 739.27
  mining 622.384
  synthetic 666.88
Saprolegniales 579.542
Sara Gambai dialect 496.5
  T6—965
Saracenic architecture
  medieval 723.3
Saragossa (Spain :
  Province) T2—465 53
Sarah (Biblical matriarch) 222.110 92
Sarajevo (Bosnia and
  Hercegovina) T2—497 42
Saramacca (Surinam :
  District) T2—883 3
Sarangis 787.6
  see also Stringed instruments
Sarans
  textiles 677.474 4
    see also Textiles
Sarasota County (Fla.) T2—759 61
Saratoga County (N.Y.) T2—747 48
Saratov (Russia : Oblast) T2—474 6
Saratovskaîa oblast′
  (Russia) T2—474 6
Saravastivada Buddhism 294.391
Sarawak T2—595 4
Sarcodina 579.43
Sarcoidosis
  medicine 616
  see also Diseases (Human)
Sarcoma
  medicine 616.994
  see also Cancer (Human)
Sarcomastigophora 579.4
Sarcophagidae 595.774
Sarcopterygii 597.39
  paleozoology 567.39
Sardegna T2—459
Sardines 641.392
  conservation technology 639.977 45
  cooking 641.692
  food 641.392
  resource economics 333.956 45
  zoology 597.45
Sardines (Young herring) 641.392
  zoology 597.452
  see also Herring (Clupea
    harengus); Sardines
Sardinia T2—459
  ancient T2—379
Sardinian language 457.9
  T6—56
Sardinian literature 850
Sardinians T5—56
Sardis (Extinct city) T2—392 2
Sargasso Sea 551.464 62
  T2—163 62
  biology 578.776 362
  ecology 577.763 62

Sargassum 579.888
Sargent County (N.D.) T2—784 314
Sargodha District (Pakistan) T2—549 14
Sark (England) T2—423 45
Sarmatia 939.5
T2—395
Sarney, José
Brazilian history 981.064
Sarpy County (Neb.) T2—782 256
Sarraceniales 583.36
Sarsaparillas 584.356
Sarthe (France) T2—441 7
Sasakian geometry 516.373
Sashes (Clothing) 391.44
see also Accessories (Clothing)
Saskatchewan 971.24
T2—712 4
Saskatchewan River (Sask. and Man.) T2—712 42
Saskatoon (Sask.) T2—712 425
Sasolburg (South Africa : District) T2—685 25
Sasquatch 001.944
Sassafras
botany 583.23
food 641.338 2
see also Flavorings
Sassafras tea 641.338 2
commercial processing 663.96
cooking with 641.638 2
home preparation 641.877
Sassanian Empire 935.07
T2—35
Sassari (Sardinia : Province) T2—459 3
Sassou Nguesso, Denis
Congolese history 967.240 52
SAT (Assessment test) 378.166 2
Satan
Christianity 235.47
Islam 297.216
Judaism 296.316
occultism 133.422
Satanism 133.422
religion 299
Satellite cells
human histology 611.018 8
see also Nervous system
Satellite communication 384.51
communications services 384.51
engineering 621.382 5
international law 341.757 7
Satellite communication (continued)
law 343.099 4
radio 384.545 6
engineering 621.384 156
television 384.552
engineering 621.388 53
Satellite dishes (Television) 384.552
engineering 621.388 35
Satellite insurance 368.2
see also Insurance
Satellites (Moons) 523.98
T2—992
Satire 808.87
literary criticism 809.7
theory 808.7
literary history 809.7
literature 808.87
specific literatures T3B—7
rhetoric 808.7
see Manual at T1—0207 vs. T3B—7, T3A—8 + 02, T3B—802, T3B—8 + 02, T3A—8 + 07, T3B—807, T3B—8 + 07; *also at* T3B—7 vs. T3C—17
Satirical poetry 808.817
history and criticism 809.17
specific literatures T3B—107
individual authors T3A—1
Satirists 809.7
collected biography 809.7
specific literatures T3B—700 9
occupational group T7—87
Satisfaction (Christian rite) 265.63
Satu Mare (Romania : Judeţ) T2—498 4
Saturating paper 676.284 4
Saturday
music 781.522 8
Saturn (Planet) 523.46
T2—992 6
astrology 133.537
Satyromania
medicine 616.858 33
see also Mental illness
Sauces 641.814
commercial processing 664.58
cooking 641.814
Saudi Arabia 953.8
T2—538
Saudi Arabians T5—927 538
Saudis T5—927 538
Sauger 597.758

Sauk County (Wis.)	T2—775 76
Saul, King of Israel	
Biblical leader	222.430 92
Palestinian history	933.02
Saunas	
architecture	725.73
domestic	728.96
public	725.73
construction	
domestic	690.896
public	690.573
personal care	646.75
Saunders County (Neb.)	T2—782 296
Sauraism	294.551 7
Saurauiaceae	583.66
Sauria	597.95
paleozoology	567.95
Saurischia	567.912
Sauropodomorpha	567.913
Sauropterygia	567.937
Saururaceae	583.25
Sausage	641.36
cooking	641.66
food	641.36
Sautéing	641.77
Sautrantika Buddhism	294.391
Savannah (Ga.)	T2—758 724
Savannah River (Ga. and S.C.)	T2—758 1
Georgia	T2—758 1
South Carolina	T2—757 9
Savannas	333.74
	T2—153
biology	578.748
ecology	577.48
see also Grasslands	
Savings	332.041 5
capital management	658.152 26
financial economics	332.041 5
macroeconomics	339.43
Savings accounts	332.175 2
Savings and loan associations	332.32
law	346.082 32
public administration	354.86
Savings banks	332.21
Savings-consumption relationship	339.43
Savings departments	332.175 2
Savings stamps	
prints	769.57
Savoie (France)	T2—444 8
Savona (Italy : Province)	T2—451 84
Savories	641.812
Savoy (Duchy)	T2—444 8
Savu Sea	551.465 74
	T2—164 74
Sawdust	674.84
fuel	662.65
Sawfishes	597.35
Sawflies	595.79
agricultural pests	632.79
Ṣawm	297.53
Ṣawm Ramaḍān	297.362
Sawmill operations	674.2
Saws	621.93
music	786.888
see also Percussion instruments	
Sawtooth Mountains (Idaho)	T2—796 72
Sawtooth Range (Idaho)	T2—796 29
Sawyer County (Wis.)	T2—775 16
Saxhorns	788.97
instrument	788.971 9
music	788.97
see also Brass instruments	
Saxifragales	583.72
Saxifrages	583.72
floriculture	635.933 72
Saxons	
English history	942.017
Saxony (Germany)	T2—432 1
Saxony (Prussia)	T2—431 8
Saxony, House of	943.022
Saxony-Anhalt (Germany)	T2—431 8
Saxophones	788.7
instrument	788.719
music	788.7
see also Woodwind instruments	
Saxophonists	788.709 2
occupational group	T7—788
Say, Jean Baptiste	
economic school	330.153
Sayan Mountains (Russia)	T2—575
Sayyid dynasty	954.024 2
Scabies	
medicine	616.57
see also Skin	
Scalar field theory	515.63
Scalds	
medicine	617.11
Scale insects	595.752
agricultural pests	632.752
Scale mosses	588.3
Scales (Integument)	591.477
descriptive zoology	591.477
physiology	573.595

Scales (Maps) 912.014 8
Scales (Music) 781.246
Scalic formations (Music) 781.246
Scallops 641.394
  conservation technology 639.974 4
  cooking 641.694
  fishing and culture 639.46
  food 641.394
    commercial processing 664.94
  resource economics 333.955 46
  zoology 594.4
Scalp diseases
  medicine 616.546
  see also Skin
Scaly anteaters 599.31
Scaly reptiles 597.94
Scaly-tailed possums 599.232
Scandentia 599.338
  paleozoology 569.338
Scandinavia 948
  T2—48
  ancient 936.3
    T2—363
Scandinavian languages 439.5
  T6—395
Scandinavian literatures 839.5
Scandinavian religion 293
Scandinavians T5—395
Scandium 669.290 1
  chemical engineering 661.040 1
  chemistry 546.401
  economic geology 553.494 2
  metallurgy 669.290 1
  see also Chemicals; Metals
Scaphopoda 594.29
  paleozoology 564.29
Scapolite
  mineralogy 549.68
Scapulas
  human anatomy 611.717
  see also Musculoskeletal system
Scarabaeidae 595.764 9
Scarabaeoidea 595.764 9
Scarabs
  glyptics 736.209 32
Scarborough (England : Borough) T2—428 47
Scarborough (Ont.) T2—713 541
Scarlatina
  incidence 614.522
  medicine 616.917
  see also Communicable diseases (Human)
Scarlet fever
  incidence 614.522
  medicine 616.917
  see also Communicable diseases (Human)
Scarves 391.41
  see also Accessories (Clothing)
Scarves (Table linen) 642.7
  arts 746.96
  home sewing 646.21
  table setting 642.7
Scatophagidae 595.774
Scattering (Physics) 539.758
  solid-state physics 530.416
Scattering of heat 536.3
Scattering of light 535.43
  meteorology 551.566
Scavenger cells 571.968
  human immunology 616.079 9
Scenarios
  music 780
    treatises 782.002 69
Scene paintings 751.75
Scene understanding
  artificial intelligence 006.37
Scenery
  dramatic performances 792.025
    motion pictures 791.430 25
    stage 792.025
    television 791.450 25
Scenic rivers 333.784 5
  law 346.046 784 5
  natural resources 333.784 5
Scent hounds 636.753 6
Schaffhausen (Switzerland : Canton) T2—494 58
Schaffhouse (Switzerland : Canton) T2—494 58
Scheduling
  broadcasting services 384.544 2
    radio 384.544 2
    television 384.553 1
  education 371.242
  production management 658.53
  transportation 388.041
    air 387.740 42
    automobile 388.321
    bus 388.322 042
      urban 388.413 22
    ferries 386.6
    inland waterway 386.240 42
    marine 387.540 42

Scheduling
  transportation (continued)
    railroad 385.204 2
      urban 388.42
    truck 388.324 042
      urban 388.413 24
Scheelite
  mineralogy 549.74
Schefferville (Quebec) T2—714 115
Schenectady County (N.Y.) T2—747 44
Scheuchzeriaceae 584.74
Schiffli embroidery 677.77
Schipperke 636.72
Schism between Eastern and Western Church 270.38
Schisms
  Christianity 262.8
    church history 273
Schistosomiasis
  incidence 614.553
  medicine 616.963
  see also Communicable diseases (Human)
Schists 552.4
Schizanthuses 635.933 952
  botany 583.952
  floriculture 635.933 952
Schizomida 595.45
Schizomycetes 579.3
Schizophrenia 362.26
  medicine 616.898 2
  social welfare 362.26
  see also Mental illness
Schizophyta 579.3
Schleicher County (Tex.) T2—764 876
Schleswig-Holstein (Germany) T2—435 12
Schleswig-Holstein War, 1864 943.076
Schley County (Ga.) T2—758 495
Schmalkaldic War, 1546–1547 943.031
Schmoller, Gustav von
  economic school 330.154 2
Schnauzers 636.73
Schoharie County (N.Y.) T2—747 45
Scholars
  social group T7—090 1
Scholarship 001.2
Scholarships 371.223
  T1—079
  higher education 378.34
  research 001.44
Scholastic Assessment Test 378.166 2
Scholastic philosophy 189.4
  modern 149.91
School adjustment 370.158
School administration 371.2
  see Manual at 371 vs. 353.8, 371.2, 379
School administrators
  biography 371.200 92
  occupational group T7—371
  public control 379.157
  role and function 371.201 1
School and society 306.432
School attendance 371.294
  compulsory education 379.23
  law 344.079 2
School attendance districts 379.153 5
School boards 353.822 5
  local public education 379.153 1
  public education 353.822 5
School bonds 379.13
School boys T1—083 41
School buildings 371.6
  see also Educational buildings
School cafeterias 371.716
School calendar 371.23
School camps 796.542 2
School children 305.234
  T1—083 4
  T7—054 4
  home care 649.124
  psychology 155.424
  social aspects 305.234
  transportation 371.872
  see also entries beginning with Student
School choice 379.111
School closings 379.153 5
School cooking 641.571
School credits 371.218
School custodians 371.68
School day 371.244
  law 344.079 2
School desegregation 379.263
  law 344.079 8
School discipline 371.5
School districts 379.153 5
  liability 344.075
School dropouts 371.291 3
School enrollment 371.219
  secondary education 373.121 9
School environment
  psychological influence 370.158

School equipment 371.67
  higher education 378.196 7
  special education 371.904 5
School etiquette 395.5
School excursions 371.384
School facilities 371.6
  see also Educational buildings
School furniture 371.63
  see also School equipment
School girls T1—083 42
School grounds 371.61
  landscape architecture 712.7
School hygiene 371.71
School integration 379.263
School journalism 371.897
School leavers 371.291 3
  secondary level 373.129 13
School-leaving age 379.23
School libraries 027.8
  administration 025.197 8
  collection development 025.218 78
  use studies 025.587 8
School library reading programs
  elementary education 372.427
School location 371.61
School lunch programs 371.716
  law 344.079 42
School management 371.2
School meal service 642.5
School media centers 027.8
School milk programs 371.716
School newspapers
  journalism 371.897 4
School nursing 371.712
School orchestras 784.44
School plays
  elementary education 372.66
School policy 371
  see Manual at 371 vs. 353.8, 371.2, 379
School principals
  biography 371.200 92
  public control 379.157
  role and function 371.201 2
School psychologists 371.713
School resource centers 027.8
School safety programs 363.119 371
School schedules 371.242
School sites 371.61
School social services 371.7
School social workers 371.46
School socialization 303.324
School staff 371.201
School superintendents
  biography 371.200 92
  public control 379.157
  role and function 371.201 1
School supervision 371.203
School supplies 371.67
  see also School equipment
School systems 371
  see Manual at 371 vs. 353.8, 371.2, 379
School tablet paper 676.286
School taxes 379.13
School vandalism 371.782
School violence 371.782
School week 371.242
School year 371.23
  law 344.079 2
School yearbooks
  journalism 371.897 6
Schoolcraft County (Mich.) T2—774 935
Schooling 370
  see also Education
Schools 371
  T1—071
  accounting 657.832 7
  area planning 711.57
  centralization 379.153 5
  fire hazards 363.379
    see also Fire safety
  law 344.07
  liability 344.075
  public finance 379.11
    law 344.076
  standards
    public policy 379.158
  see also Education; entries beginning with Student
  see Manual at 371 vs. 353.8, 371.2, 379; *also at* 371 vs. 372–374, 378
Schools (Styles)
  fine arts 709
    see Manual at 709.012–709.05 vs. 709.3–709.9
  see Manual at 704.9; *also at* 753–758
Schools of thought T1—01
  philosophy 140
    see Manual at 140 vs. 180–190
  see Manual at T1—01
Schrödinger wave mechanics 530.124
Schuyler County (Ill.) T2—773 475

Schuyler County (Mo.) T2—778 262
Schuyler County (N.Y.) T2—747 81
Schuylkill County (Pa.) T2—748 17
Schuylkill River (Pa.) T2—748 1
Schwaben (Germany : Regierungsbezirk) T2—433 7
Schweinfurt (Germany) T2—433 36
Schweizer-Reneke (South Africa : District) T2—682 4
Schwerin (Germany : Bezirk) T2—431 76
Schwyz (Switzerland : Canton) T2—494 752
Sciaenidae 597.725
Sciaenops 597.725
Sciaridae 595.772
Sciatica
  medicine 616.87
  see also Nervous system
Science 500
  T1—015
  art representation 704.949 5
  arts 700.456
  T3C—356
  elementary education 372.35
  folklore 398.26
    history and criticism 398.36
  information systems 025.065
  law 344.095
  libraries 026.5
  literature 808.803 56
    history and criticism 809.933 56
    specific literatures T3B—080 356
      history and criticism T3B—093 56
  public administrative support 352.745
  social effects 303.483
    see Manual at 303.48 vs. 306.4; *also at* 303.483 vs. 306.45, 306.46
  sociology 306.45
    see Manual at 303.48 vs. 306.4; *also at* 303.483 vs. 306.45, 306.46
  use in agricultural industries 338.16
  see also Knowledge
  see Manual at 500 vs. 001; *also at* 500 vs. 600
Science and religion 291.175
  Buddhism 294.337 5
  Christianity 261.55
  Hinduism 294.517 5
  Islam 297.265
  Judaism 296.375
  philosophy of religion 215
Science fair projects 507.8
Science fiction 808.838 762
  arts 700.415
  T3C—15
  history and criticism 809.387 62
  motion pictures 791.436 15
  radio programs 791.446 15
  specific literatures T3B—308 762
    individual authors T3A—3
  television programs 791.456 15
Science laboratories 507.2
  architecture 727.55
Science museums 507.4
  architecture 727.65
Science policy
  economics 338.926
    see Manual at 338.926 vs. 352.745, 500
Science projects in schools 507.8
Sciences (Knowledge) 001
  see also Knowledge
Sciences (Natural sciences) 500
  see also Science
Scientific instruments
  manufacturing technology 681.75
Scientific method 001.42
  T1—072
Scientific principles 500
  T1—015
  see Manual at T1—015 vs. T1—0245–T1—0246
Scientific recreations 793.8
Scientific socialism 335.423
Scientific surveys 508
Scientific toys 790.133
  manufacturing technology 688.725
  recreation 790.133
  see also Toys
Scientific travels 508
Scientific writing 808.066 5
Scientists 509.2
  Islamic polemics 297.298
  occupational group T7—5
  works for T1—024 5
    see Manual at T1—015 vs. T1—0245–T1—0246
Scientology 299.936
Scilly, Isles of (England) T2—423 79
Scintillation
  atmospheric optics 551.565
Scintillation counters
  nuclear physics 539.775
Sciomyzidae 595.774
Scioto County (Ohio) T2—771 87

Scioto River (Ohio) T2—771 5
Sciuridae 599.36
  paleozoology 569.36
Sciurus 599.362
Scleras
  human anatomy 611.84
  human physiology 612.841
  ophthalmology 617.719
  see also Eyes
Sclerenchyma 571.585
Scleroderma
  medicine 616.544
  see also Skin
Scleroproteins 572.67
  biochemistry 572.67
  chemistry 547.753
  see also Proteins
Scolioidea 595.79
Scoliosis
  medicine 616.73
Scolopacidae 598.33
Scolytidae 595.768
Scombridae 597.782
Scombroidei 597.78
Sconces
  furniture arts 749.63
Scooters 388.347 5
  engineering 629.227 5
  see also Motorcycles
Scopelomorpha 597.61
  paleozoology 567.61
Score reading 781.423
  elementary education 372.873
Scores (Music) 780
  cataloging 025.348 8
  library treatment 025.178 8
  treatises 780.26
  see Manual at 780.26; *also at* 782
Scoring systems
  contract bridge 795.415 4
Scorpaeniformes 597.68
  paleozoology 567.68
Scorpio (Zodiac) 133.527 3
Scorpion fishes 597.68
Scorpion flies 595.744
Scorpion venom
  human toxicology 615.942
Scorpions 595.46
Scotch broom 583.74
Scotia Sea 551.469 3
  T2—167 3
Scotland 941.1
  T2—411
  ancient 936.11
    T2—361 1
  see Manual at 941
Scotland. Children's Hearings 345.411 08
Scotland. Court of Appeal 345.411 016 3
Scotland. Court of First Instance 345.411 016 2
Scotland. Court of Session 347.411 023
Scotland. Court of Session. Inner House 347.411 035
Scotland. Court of Session. Outer House 347.411 024
Scotland. Court of the Lord Lyon 347.411 04
Scotland. Crown Counsel 345.411 01
Scotland. District Court 345.411 012
Scotland. High Court of Justiciary 345.411 016
Scotland. House of Lords (Court of last resort) 347.411 039
Scotland. Licensing Appeals Court 347.411 04
Scotland. Licensing Courts 347.411 04
Scotland. Lord Advocate 345.411 01
Scotland. Sheriff Court 347.411 021
  criminal law 345.411 014
Scotland. Sheriff-Principal 347.411 032
Scotland. Solicitor-General 345.411 01
Scotland County (Mo.) T2—778 312
Scotland County (N.C.) T2—756 335
Scots T5—916 3
Scots language (English dialect) 427.941 1
  T6—21
Scott County (Ark.) T2—767 44
Scott County (Ill.) T2—773 455
Scott County (Ind.) T2—772 183
Scott County (Iowa) T2—777 69
Scott County (Kan.) T2—781 43
Scott County (Ky.) T2—769 425
Scott County (Minn.) T2—776 54
Scott County (Miss.) T2—762 655
Scott County (Mo.) T2—778 97
Scott County (Tenn.) T2—768 71
Scott County (Va.) T2—755 732
Scottburgh (South Africa) T2—684 5
Scottish deerhound 636.753 2
Scottish English dialect 427.941 1
  T6—21
Scottish Gaelic language 491.63
  T6—916 3
Scottish Gaelic literature 891.63

Scottish Gaels T5—916 3
Scottish Highlands
(Scotland) T2—411 5
Scottish literature
English 820
Gaelic 891.63
Scotts Bluff County (Neb.) T2—782 98
Scottsdale (Tas.) T2—946 4
Scouring compounds 668.127
Scouts (Boy and girl) 369.409 2
social group T7—369 4
Scows 387.29
design 623.812 9
engineering 623.829
transportation services 387.29
see also Ships
Scranton (Pa.) T2—748 37
Scrap metal 363.728 8
metallurgy 669.042
social services 363.728 8
see also Waste control
Scraped idiophones 786.886
see also Percussion
instruments
Scratch pad paper 676.286
Scratchboard drawing 741.29
Screamers (Birds) 598.41
Screen process printing 686.231 6
Screening
chemical engineering 660.284 22
ores 622.74
sewage treatment 628.34
water supply treatment 628.162 2
Screenplays 791.437
literature 808.823
history and criticism 809.23
specific literatures T3B—203
individual authors T3A—2
motion pictures 791.437
music 780
treatises 780.268
rhetoric 808.23
see Manual at 791.437 and
791.447, 791.457, 792.9
Screens 645.4
church architecture 726.529 6
church furniture 247.1
decorative arts 749.3
see also Furniture
Screenwriting 808.23
Screven County (Ga.) T2—758 695
Screw-cutting tools 621.944
Screw pines 584.66
Screwdrivers 621.972
Screws 621.882
Scribes
Judaism 296.461 509 2
Script-geometric shorthand
systems 653.426
Script shorthand systems 653.428
Scripts
motion pictures 791.437
see also Screenplays
puppetry 791.538
radio 791.447
stage productions 792.9
television 791.457
Scripture readings
public worship
Christianity 264.34
Scriptures (Religion) 291.82
see also Sacred books
Scrollwork
furniture arts 749.5
wood handicrafts 745.513
Scrophulariales 583.95
Scrotum 573.655 25
biology 573.655 25
human anatomy 611.63
human physiology 612.61
medicine 616.67
see also Male genital system
Scrub typhus
incidence 614.526 4
medicine 616.922 4
see also Communicable
diseases (Human)
Scrublands
biology 578.738
ecology 577.38
Scrummaging 796.333 23
Scuba diving
sports 797.23
see also Sports
Scuds (Amphipoda) 595.378
Sculptors 730.92
occupational group T7—731
Sculptural stone 553.5
see also Stone
Sculpture 730
architectural decoration 729.5
elementary education 372.53
see Manual at 731–735 vs.
736–739
Scunthorpe (England) T2—428 31
Scups 597.72
Scurry County (Tex.) T2—764 731

Scurvy
medicine 616.394
see also Digestive system
Scyphozoa 593.53
paleozoology 563.5
Scyros Island (Greece) T2—495 15
ancient T2—391 1
Scythia 939.51
T2—395 1
Scythian languages 491.53
T6—915 3
Scythian literatures 891.53
Scythians T5—915
Scytho-Dravidians T5—948
see Manual at T5—948 vs. T5—914
SDI (Information service) 025.525
SDI (Strategic Defense Initiative) 358.174
Sea, air, land teams (Military units) 359.984
Sea anemones 593.6
Sea basins T2—182
see Manual at T2—163, T2—164, T2—165 vs. T2—182
Sea basses 597.736
Sea birds 598.177
conservation technology 639.978 177
resource economics 333.958 287
Sea breams 597.72
Sea breezes 551.518 5
Sea caves
biology 578.769 9
ecology 577.699
Sea cows 599.55
Sea cucumbers 593.96
Sea fans 593.6
Sea figs 583.53
Sea-floor spreading 551.136
Sea forces 359
Sea grass wetlands
biology 578.769 4
ecology 577.694
see also Wetlands
Sea hares 594.37
Sea horses 597.679 8
Sea ice 551.343
Sea Islands T2—757 99
Georgia T2—758 7
South Carolina T2—757 99
Sea Islands Creole 427.975 799
T6—217
Sea lavenders 583.5
Sea-level changes 551.458
Sea lilies 593.92
Sea lions 599.797 5
Sea mail 383.142
see also Postal service
Sea mats (Bryozoa) 594.67
Sea of Azov (Ukraine and Russia) 551.462 9
T2—163 89
Sea of Crete (Greece) 551.462 8
T2—163 88
Sea of Japan 551.465 54
T2—164 54
Sea of Marmara (Turkey) 551.462 9
T2—163 89
Sea of Okhotsk 551.465 53
T2—164 53
Sea otter 599.769 5
conservation technology 639.979 769 5
resource economics 333.959 769 5
Sea pens 593.6
Sea slugs 594.34
Sea snails 594.32
Sea songs 782.421 595
Sea spiders 595.496
Sea squirts 596.2
Sea urchins 593.95
harvest and culture 639.7
Sea walnuts 593.8
Sea warfare 359
Seabed 551.460 84
international law 341.762 1
see also Ocean bottom
Seabed mining 622.295
Seabees (Naval forces) 359.982
Seadromes
engineering 629.136 1
Seafaring life 910.45
music about 781.595
Seafood 641.392
commercial processing 664.94
cooking 641.692
home preservation 641.494
Seahorses 597.679 8
Sealants 668.38
building materials 691.99
materials science 620.199
structural engineering 624.189 9
Sealers (Hunters) 639.290 92
occupational group T7—639 2
Sealing (Hunting) 639.29
economics 338.372 979
international law 341.762 2
Sealing devices 621.885

Seals (Animals) 599.79
conservation technology 639.979 79
hunting 639.29
resource economics 333.959 79
Seals (Devices) 929.9
insignia 929.9
numismatics 737.6
SEALs (Military units) 359.984
Seam welding 671.521 3
Seamanship 623.88
Seamen 387.509 2
navy enlisted personnel 359.009 2
role and function 359.338
see also Sailors
Seamstresses 646.209 2
occupational group T7—646 4
Seaplanes 387.733 47
engineering 629.133 347
transportation services 387.733 47
see also Aircraft
Seaports 387.1
see also Ports
Search algorithms 005.741
Search and seizure
criminal investigation 363.252
law 345.052 2
Search for moving target 531.112
Search strategy
information science 025.524
Search trees (Computer science) 005.741
Searching data 005.741
Searcy County (Ark.) T2—767 195
Seas 551.46
T2—162
see also Oceans
Seascapes
art representation 704.943 7
drawing 743.837
painting 758.2
Seashells 594.147 7
Seashores 551.457
T2—146
biology 578.769 9
ecology 577.699
health 613.12
see also Coasts
Seasickness
medicine 616.989 2
see also Environmental diseases (Human)
Seasonal adaptation 578.43
animals 591.43
plants 581.43
Seasonal changes
health 613.13
Seasonal cooking 641.564
Seasonal holidays 394.26
see also Holidays
Seasonal houses
architecture 728.7
Seasonal music 781.524
Seasonal parties 793.22
Seasonal unemployment 331.137 044
Seasoning lumber 674.38
Seasonings 641.338 2
cooking with 641.638 2
Seasons 508.2
astronomy 525.5
biological adaptation 578.43
ecological effect 577.23
folklore 398.236
history and criticism 398.33
influence on crime 364.22
literature 808.803 3
history and criticism 809.933 3
specific literatures T3B—080 33
history and criticism T3B—093 3
music 781.524
natural history 508.2
Seat belts
aircraft 629.134 43
automobiles 363.125 7
engineering 629.276
highway safety 363.125 7
law 343.094 4
Seat ejectors
aircraft 629.134 386
Seats
automobile 629.26
Seattle (Wash.) T2—797 772
Seatwork 371.3
Seawalls 627.58
flood control 627.42
port engineering 627.24
shore protection 627.58
Seawater 551.460 1
desalinization 628.167
oceanography 551.460 1
water supply evaluation 628.116
Seawater intrusion 363.738
engineering 628.114
social problem 363.738
see also Pollution
Seawater supply
ship sanitation 623.854 3
Seaweeds 579.88
culture 639.89

Seaweeds (continued)
  resource economics 333.953 8
Sebaceous glands 573.537 9
  biology 573.537 9
  human anatomy 611.77
  human physiology 612.792 1
  medicine 616.53
  see also Skin
Sebastian County (Ark.) T2—767 36
Seborrhea
  medicine 616.53
  see also Skin
Secernentea 592.57
Secession
  United States history 973.713
Second-class mail 383.123
  see also Postal service
Second Coming of Christ 236.9
Second Empire (France) 944.07
Second International 324.174
Second language acquisition 401.93
  applied linguistics 418
    audio-lingual approach T4—834
    formal approach T4—824
Second Republic (Austria) 943.605 3
Second Republic (France) 944.07
Second Republic (Spain) 946.081
Secondary batteries 621.312 424
Secondary consciousness
  psychology 154.3
Secondary education 373
  T1—071 2
  law 344.074
  public administrative support 353.8
  public support 379.113
    law 344.076 83
  see Manual at 372.24 and 373.23
Secondary industries 338.4
  enterprises 338.7
  international enterprises 338.88
  law 343.078
    see Manual at 343.078 vs. 343.08
  mergers 338.83
  products 338.47
    commerce 380.145
      domestic 381.45
      foreign 382.45
      public administration 354.73
  public administration 354.6
  restrictive practices 338.82
  see Manual at 338.4 vs. 338.47
Secondary recovery
  oil extraction 622.338 2
Secondary roads 388.12
  see also Roads
Secondary school buildings
  architecture 727.2
Secondary school graduates
  choice of vocation 331.702 33
  labor force 331.114 23
  unemployment 331.137 804
Secondary school libraries 027.822 3
Secondary school teaching 373.110 2
Secondary schools 373
  T1—071 2
  see also Secondary education
Secondary sexual characteristics 591.46
Secondary storage (Computer) 004.56
  engineering 621.397 6
Secondhand stores 381.19
  management 658.87
  see also Commerce
Secret agents
  criminal investigation 363.252
Secret codes
  computer science 005.82
Secret police 363.283
Secret societies 366
Secretarial accounting 657.2
Secretarial bookkeeping 657.2
Secretariat (United Nations) 352.113
Secretaries 651.374 109 2
  occupational group T7—651
  office services 651.374 1
Secretaries of state 352.293
  see Manual at 352.293
Secretary bird 598.9
Secretion 571.79
  biology 571.79
  human physiology 612.4
  medicine 616.332
  see also Endocrine system
Secretory organs 571.79
  biology 571.79
  human anatomy 611.4
  human physiology 612.4
  see also Endocrine system
Sectionalist parties 324.218 4
Sects (Religion) 291.9
  Buddhism 294.39
    sources 294.385
  Christianity 280
    see also Christian denominations

Sects (Religion) (continued)
  Hinduism 294.55
    sources 294.595
  Islam 297.8
  Jainism 294.49
  Judaism 296.8
    sources 296.15
  sources 291.85
  see Manual at 291: Denominations and sects
Secular holidays 394.26
  see also Holidays
Secular humanism 211.6
  Christian polemics 239.7
Secular institutes
  Christianity 255.095
    church history 271.095
    women 255.909 5
      church history 271.909 5
Secular trends (Economics) 338.54
Secular vocal music 782.4
  choral and mixed voices 782.54
  single voices 783.094
Secularism 211.6
Secured transactions
  law 346.074
Securities 332.632
  investment economics 332.632
  law 346.092
    corporate law 346.066 6
    income tax law 343.052 46
  printing 686.288
  public administration 354.88
Securities exchange 332.642
  international 332.65
  international law 341.752 42
Securities fraud 364.163
  law 345.026 8
Securities violations 364.168
  law 345.026 8
Security classification (Government documents) 352.379
  armed forces 355.343 3
  law 342.068 4
  public administration 352.379
Security electronics 621.389 28
Security measures
  household security 643.16
  library operations 025.82
  management 658.47
    armed forces 355.343 3
    public administration 352.379
  museology 069.54
  office services 651
Security measures (continued)
  penology 365.641
Sedang language 495.93
  T6—959 3
Sedative abuse 362.299
  medicine 616.86
  personal health 613.8
  social welfare 362.299
  see also Substance abuse
Sedatives
  pharmacodynamics 615.782
Seder service 296.453 71
Sedgefield (England) T2—428 62
Sedgemoor (England : District) T2—423 81
Sedges 584.84
  forage crop 633.26
Sedgwick County (Colo.) T2—788 76
Sedgwick County (Kan.) T2—781 86
Sediment transport 551.303
  by water 551.353
  by wind 551.373
Sedimentary rocks 552.5
Sedimentation 551.303
  in water 551.353
  sewage treatment 628.353
    primary 628.34
    secondary 628.353
  water supply treatment 628.162 2
Sedimentology 552.5
  surface processes 551.3
Sediments 551.304
  glacier borne 551.314
  ocean floor
    composition 551.460 83
  river engineering 627.122
  water borne 551.354
  wind borne 551.374
Seditious libel 364.131
  law 345.023 1
Seduction
  criminology 364.153
    criminal law 345.025 3
Sedums 583.72
  floriculture 635.933 72
Seed arrangements
  decorative arts 745.928
Seed-bearing plants 580
  see also Plants
Seed catalogs 631.521 029 4
  see also Nursery catalogs
Seed ferns 561.595

Seed-hair fibers
  textiles 677.2
    see also Textiles
Seed industry 338.17
Seed oil 665.35
  food technology 664.3
  industrial oils 665.35
Seed plants 580
  see also Plants
Seed shrimps 595.33
Seeding clouds 551.687 6
Seedless plants 586
Seedlings
  nursery production 631.52
    forestry 634.956 2
  planting 631.536
    forestry 634.956 5
Seeds 581.467
  animal feeds
    commercial processing 664.76
  descriptive botany 581.467
  food
    commercial processing 664.7
  forest products 634.987
  nursery production 631.521
    forestry 634.956 2
    ornamental plants 635.915 21
  paleobotany 561.14
  physiology 575.68
  sowing 631.531
    forestry 634.956 5
    ornamental plants 635.915 31
Sees
  Christian ecclesiology 262.3
Sefton (England) T2—427 59
Segmented worms 592.6
Segovia (Spain : Province) T2—463 57
Segregation in education 379.263
  law 344.079 8
Sei whale 599.524
Seibo (Dominican Republic : Province) T2—729 384
Seiches 551.470 23
Seine (France) T2—443 6
Seine-et-Marne (France) T2—443 7
Seine-et-Oise (France) T2—443 6
Seine-Inférieure (France) T2—442 5
Seine-Maritime (France) T2—442 5
Seine River (France) T2—443 4
Seine-Saint-Denis (France) T2—443 62
Seining
  sports 799.13
Seismic prospecting 622.159 2
Seismic sea waves 551.470 24
Seismic waves 551.22
Seismography 551.220 287
Seismology 551.22
Seismosaurus 567.913
Sekgosese (South Africa : District) T2—682 93
Sekhukhuneberg Range T2—682 93
Sekhukhuneland (South Africa : District) T2—682 93
Selachii 597.3
  paleozoology 567.3
Selaginellales 587.9
Selangor T2—595 1
Selby (England : District) T2—428 45
Select committees
  legislative bodies 328.365 7
Selected laws 348.024
  United States federal laws 348.732 4
Selection of animals 636.081
Selection procedures
  personnel management 658.311 2
    public administration 352.65
Selective dissemination of information 025.525
Selective service 355.223 63
  law 343.012 2
Selenides
  mineralogy 549.32
Selenium
  biochemistry 572.555
  chemical engineering 661.072 4
  chemistry 546.724
  metallurgy 669.79
  organic chemistry 547.057 24
    applied 661.895
  see also Chemicals
Selenography 919.91
Seleucid Empire 935.06
  T2—35
Self
  literature 808.803 84
    history and criticism 809.933 84
    specific literatures T3B—080 384
      history and criticism T3B—093 84
  philosophy 126
  psychology 155.2
Self-acceptance 155.2
Self-actualization 155.2
  applied psychology 158.1
Self-confidence 155.2
  applied psychology 158.1
Self-contained communities 307.77

Self-control 179.9
  psychology 153.8
    development 155.25
  see also Virtues
Self-defense 613.66
  military training 355.548
  personal safety 613.66
Self-defense (Law) 345.04
Self-destructive behavior
  medicine 616.858 2
  see also Mental illness
Self-determination of states 320.15
  international law 341.26
Self-development reading
  library science 028.8
Self-employed persons
  income tax 336.242 3
    law 343.052 6
    public finance 336.242 3
Self-esteem 155.2
  applied psychology 158.1
Self-financing capital 332.041 52
Self-help groups
  adult education 374.22
Self-incrimination 345.056
Self instruction 371.394 3
Self-organizing systems 003.7
Self-publishing 070.593
Self-realization 155.2
  applied psychology 158.1
  ethical systems 171.3
Self-reliance 179.9
  see also Virtues
Self-respect 155.2
  applied psychology 158.1
Seljuk dynasty 956.014
  Middle Eastern history 956.014
  Turkish history 956.101 4
Selkirk (Man.) T2—712 74
Selkirk Mountains T2—711 68
Selkirkshire (Scotland : District) T2—413 85
Selkup language 494.4
  T6—944
Selling
  commerce 380.1
  management 658.81
  T1—068 8
  see also Commerce
Selosesha (South Africa : District) T2—682 94
Selwyn District (N.Z.) T2—938 5
Semaeostomeae 593.53
Semang (Asian people) T5—991 1
Semang languages 495.93
  T6—959 3
Semantics
  linguistics 401.43
    specific languages T4—014 3
    see Manual at 401.43 vs. 306.44, 401.9, 412, 415: Meaning
  philosophical system 149.94
  philosophy 121.68
  see Manual at 401 vs. 121.68, 149.94, 410.1: Philosophy of language
Semaphores
  military engineering 623.731 2
  nautical engineering 623.856 12
Semara (Morocco : Province) T2—648
Semi-indirect lighting 621.321 3
  see also Lighting
Semi-industrial unions 331.883 3
  see also Labor unions
Semiarid lands 551.415
  T2—154
  see also Arid lands
Semibituminous coal 553.24
  properties 662.622 4
  prospecting 622.182 4
  see also Coal
Semicircular canals
  human physiology 612.858
  otology 617.882
  see also Ears
Semiconductivity 537.622
  materials science 620.112 972
Semiconductor circuits 621.381 5
Semiconductor memory 004.53
  engineering 621.397 32
Semiconductors 621.381 52
  chemical engineering 660.297 7
  electrochemistry 541.377
  physics 537.622
  radio engineering 621.384 134
  television engineering 621.388 32
Semidiesel engines 621.436
  ships 623.872 36
Semidiesel locomotives 385.366
  engineering 625.266
  transportation services 385.366
  see also Rolling stock
Semigeometric shorthand systems 653.426
Semigroups 512.2

Semimetals
  chemistry 546.71
  economic geology 553.499
  mineralogy 549.25
Semimicroanalysis 543.081 5
  qualitative 544.85
  quantitative 545.845
Seminaries 200.711
  Christianity 230.071 1
  Judaism 296.071 1
Seminars 371.37
  higher education 378.177
Seminole County (Fla.) T2—759 23
Seminole County (Ga.) T2—758 996
Seminole County (Okla.) T2—766 71
Seminole Indians T5—973
Seminole War, 1818 973.54
Seminole War, 1835–1842 973.57
Semionotiformes 597.41
Semiotics 302.2
  linguistics 401.41
    specific languages T4—014 1
    specific subjects T1—014
  philosophy 121.68
  social aspects 302.2
  see Manual at 401 vs. 121.68, 149.94, 410.1: Philosophy of language
Semiprecious stones 553.87
  carving 736.2
  economic geology 553.87
  jewelry 739.27
  materials science 620.198
  mining 622.387
  occultism 133.255 387
    divination 133.322
  prospecting 622.188 7
  synthetic 666.88
Semiregular variable stars 523.844 26
Semirigid airships 387.732 6
  engineering 629.133 26
  military engineering 623.743 6
  transportation services 387.732 6
  see also Aircraft
Semiscript shorthand systems 653.426
Semiskilled workers 331.794
  labor economics 331.794
  labor force 331.114 22
  personnel management 658.304 4
  unemployment 331.137 804
Semisovereign states 321.08
  international law 341.27
  public administration 353.15
    specific states 351.3–.9
Semites T5—92
  religion 299.2
Semitic languages 492
  T6—92
  Biblical texts 220.4
Semitic literatures 892
Semitic peoples T5—92
  religion 299.2
Semnān (Iran) T2—552 3
Sena language 496.391
  T6—963 91
Senari language 496.35
  T6—963 5
Seneca County (N.Y.) T2—747 69
Seneca County (Ohio) T2—771 24
Seneca Indians T5—975 5
Senegal 966.3
  T2—663
Senegal languages 496.321
  T6—963 21
Sénégal Oriental (Senegal) T2—663
Senegalese T5—966 3
Senegambia 966.305
  T2—663
Senekal (South Africa : District) T2—685 1
Senescence 571.878
  see also Aging
Senga-Sena languages 496.391
  T6—963 91
Senile dementia
  geriatrics 618.976 898 3
  medicine 616.898 3
  see also Mental illness
Senior citizens 305.26
  T1—084 6
  see also Older persons
Senior high schools 373.238
  see also Secondary education
Seniority
  labor economics 331.259 6
  personnel management 658.312
Sennas 583.749
Senoic languages 495.93
  T6—959 3
Sensation 152.1
  biology 573.87
  epistemology 121.35
  see also Sense organs
Sensationalism (Philosophical school) 145
Sensations (Art styles) 709.040 7
Sense knowledge 121.35

Sense organs 573.87
  animal physiology 573.87
  descriptive zoology 591.4
  human anatomy 611.8
  human histology 611.018 98
  human physiology 612.8
  see also Nervous system
Senses 573.87
  psychology 152.1
  see also Sense organs
Sensitive plants 583.748
Sensitivity in plants 575.98
Sensitivity training
  applied psychology 158.2
  social psychology 302.14
Sensitometry 661.808
Sensorineural deafness
  otology 617.886
  see also Ears
Sensors
  manufacturing technology 681.2
Sensory evaluation
  food 664.072
Sensory functions 573.87
  human physiology 612.8
  localization in brain
    human physiology 612.825 5
  see also Nervous system; Sense organs
  see Manual at 612.8 vs. 152
Sensory influences
  psychology 155.911
Sensory nerves 573.872 8
  human physiology 612.811
  see also Nervous system
Sensory perception 152.1
  comparative psychology 156.21
  educational psychology 370.155
  epistemology 121.35
  psychological influence 155.911
  see Manual at 153.7 vs. 152.1; *also at* 612.8 vs. 152
Sentences (Grammar) 415
  specific languages T4—5
Sentences (Legal decisions) 345.077
  penology 364.6
Sentencing 345.077 2
Sentiments 152.4
Senufo (African people) T5—963 5
Senufo language 496.35
  T6—963 5
Sepals 575.69
Separated persons 305.906 53
  T1—086 53
  family relationships 306.89
  social group 305.906 53
Separation (Domestic relations) 306.89
  ethics 173
  Judaism 296.444 4
  law 346.016 68
  social theology 291.178 358 9
    Christianity 261.835 89
Separation from parents
  child psychology 155.44
Separation from service
  personnel management 658.313
    public administration 352.69
Separation of powers 320.404
  law 342.044
Separation processes
  chemical engineering 660.284 2
Separatist parties 324.218 4
Sephardic liturgy 296.450 42
Sepik-Ramu languages 499.12
  T6—991 2
Sepik River (New Guinea) T2—957 5
Sepioidea 594.58
Sepoy Mutiny, 1857–1858 954.031 7
Sept-Rivières (Quebec) T2—714 17
Septets
  chamber music 785.17
  vocal music 783.17
Septic tanks
  technology 628.742
Septicemia
  incidence 614.577
  medicine 616.944
  puerperal diseases
    incidence 614.545
    obstetrics 618.74
  see also Communicable diseases (Human)
Septuagint 221.48
Sepulchral slabs 736.5
Sequatchie County (Tenn.) T2—768 77
Sequatchie River (Tenn.) T2—768 77
Sequence 264.36
  music 782.323 5
Sequences (Mathematics) 515.24
Sequences of integers 512.72
Sequencing
  production management 658.53
Sequential analysis 519.54
Sequential machines 511.3
Sequoia National Park (Calif.) T2—794 86

Sequoias 585.5
  forestry 634.975 8
Sequoyah County (Okla.) T2—766 81
Serbia 949.71
  T2—497 1
  ancient 939.8
    T2—398
Serbian language 491.82
  T6—918 2
Serbian literature 891.82
Serbians T5—918 22
Serbo-Croatian language 491.82
  T6—918 2
Serbo-Croatian literature 891.82
Serbs T5—918 22
Serenades 784.185 6
Serengeti National Park
    (Tanzania) T2—678 27
Serer (African people) T5—963 21
Serer language 496.321
  T6—963 21
Serfdom 306.365
Serfs 305.563
  T1—086 25
  customs 390.25
    dress 391.025
Serging 646.204 4
Sergipe (Brazil) T2—814 1
Serial publications 050
  T1—05
  see also Serials
Serialism
  music 781.33
Serials 050
  T1—05
  bibliographies 011.34
  cataloging 025.343 2
  indexes 050
  journalism 070.175
  library treatment 025.173 2
  postal handling 383.123
    see also Postal service
  publishing 070.572
  sociology 302.232 4
Sericulture 638.2
Series (Mathematics) 515.243
Series (Publications)
  bibliographies 011.48
Serigraphy 764.8
Sermon on the Mount 226.9
  Christian moral theology 241.53
Sermon outlines 251.02
Sermon preparation 251.01
  see also Preaching
Sermons 291.43
  Christianity 252
  Islam 297.37
  Jewish 296.47
Serobacterins
  pharmacology 615.372
Serology
  medicine 616.079 5
    diagnosis 616.075 6
Serous membranes
  human histology 611.018 7
Serows 599.647
Serpentine 553.55
  building material 691.2
  economic geology 553.55
  mineralogy 549.67
  petrology 552.4
  quarrying 622.355
Serpents 597.96
  paleozoology 567.96
Serpents (Musical instruments) 788.99
  see also Brass instruments
Serrai (Greece : Nome) T2—495 65
Serranidae 597.736
Serums
  pharmacology 615.37
Serval 599.752
Servants
  home economics 640.46
    public households 647.2
  legal status 346.024
Servian language 491.82
  T6—918 2
Servian literature 891.82
Servians T5—918 22
Service (Tennis) 796.342 21
Service academies (Armed
    forces) 355.007 11
  see Manual at 355.00711
Service clubs 369.5
  biography 369.509 2
  social group T7—369 5
Service comparison T1—029 7
Service comparisons T1—029 6
Service contracts 346.024
  armed forces 355.621 2
  public administration 352.538
Service directories 338.470 002 94
  T1—029 4
  see Manual at 338 vs. 060,
    381, 382, 670.294, 910,
    T1—025, T1—0294,
    T1—0296

Service districts
  local public administration 352.19
Service evaluation T1—029 7
Service evaluations T1—029 6
Service industries 338.4
  accounting 657.83
  commerce 380.145
    domestic 381.45
    foreign 382.45
  enterprises 338.761
  international enterprises 338.887 1
  labor economics 331.793
  law 343.078
  mergers 338.836 1
  production efficiency 338.456 1
  public administration 354.68
  restrictive practices 338.826 1
  see Manual at 338.4 vs. 338.47
Service listings T1—029
Service marks 929.95
  T1—027 5
Service periods (Armed forces) 355.11
Service stations
  automotive engineering 629.286
Service workers 331.793
  labor economics 331.793
    labor force 331.119 042
    labor market 331.129 042
Serviceberries 583.73
Servicemen missing in action 355.113
  see also Missing in action
Serviettes 642.7
  arts 746.96
  home sewing 646.21
  table setting 642.7
Serving at table 642.6
Servites 255.47
  church history 271.47
Servitudes 346.043 5
  international law 341.4
Servomechanisms
  automation engineering 629.832 3
Sesames 583.95
  botany 583.95
  food 641.338 5
    cooking 641.638 5
  oil crop 633.85
Sesamoids
  human anatomy 611.718
  see also Musculoskeletal system
Seshego (South Africa : District) T2—682 93
Sesotho language 496.397 72
  T6—963 977 2
Sesquilinear forms
  algebraic geometry 516.35
Session laws 348.022
Sessions (Legislative bodies) 328.35
Set algebra 511.324
Set idiophones 786.84
  see also Percussion instruments
Set theory 511.322
SETI (Search for extraterrestrial intelligence) 999
Sétif (Algeria : Province) T2—655
Seto-naikai (Japan) 551.465 55
  T2—164 55
Sets 511.32
Settat (Morocco : Province) T2—643
Setters (Dogs) 636.752 6
Setting (Literature) 808.802 2
  history and criticism 809.922
  specific literatures T3B—080 22
    history and criticism T3B—092 2
Setting (Performances) 792.025
  motion pictures 791.430 25
  stage 792.025
  television 791.450 25
Settlement (Insurance) 368.014
Settlement (Population) 307.14
  land reform 333.31
  public administration 353.59
Settlement (Real estate) 346.043 73
Settling
  water supply treatment 628.162 2
Setúbal (Portugal : District) T2—469 42
Seven last words on cross 232.963 5
Seven Weeks' War, 1866 943.076
Seven Years' War, 1756–1763 940.253 4
  North American history 973.26
Seveners (Islamic sect) 297.822
Sevenoaks (England) T2—422 36
Seventh-Day Adventist Church 286.732
  religious group T7—267
  see also Adventists
Seventh-Day Baptists 286.3
  see also Baptists
Severance pay 331.216
  personnel management 658.322 2
Severance tax 336.271 6
  law 343.055
  public finance 336.271 6

Severn River (Wales and England) T2—424
  England T2—424
  Wales T2—429 51
Severnaîa Zemlîa (Russia) T2—987
Severnaya Zemlya (Russia) T2—987
Severočeský kraj (Czech Republic) T2—437 1
Severomoravský kraj (Czech Republic) T2—437 2
Sevier County (Ark.) T2—767 47
Sevier County (Tenn.) T2—768 893
Sevier County (Utah) T2—792 55
Seville (Spain : Province) T2—468 6
Sewage disposal 363.728 4
  social services 363.728 4
  technology 628.36
  see also Sewage treatment
Sewage effluent 363.728 4
  disposal technology 628.362
  social services 363.728 4
  water pollution engineering 628.168 2
  see also Sewage treatment
Sewage irrigation 628.362 3
Sewage lagoons
  sanitary engineering 628.351
Sewage sludge 363.728 4
  sanitary engineering 628.364
  social services 363.728 4
  use as fertilizer 631.869
  see also Sewage treatment
Sewage treatment 363.728 4
  law 344.046 22
  military engineering 623.753
  rural 628.742
  social services 363.728 4
  technology 628.3
  see also Waste control
Seward County (Kan.) T2—781 735
Seward County (Neb.) T2—782 324
Seward Peninsula (Alaska) T2—798 6
Sewerage 628.2
Sewers 628.2
Sewing 646.2
  elementary education 372.54
  home economics 646.2
Sewing equipment 646.19
  home sewing 646.19
  manufacturing technology 681.767 7
Sewing machines
  home economics 646.204 4
  manufacturing technology 681.767 7
Sewing materials 646.1
  commercial technology 687.8
  home economics 646.1
Sex 306.7
  arts 700.453 8
    T3C—353 8
  customs 392.6
  evolution 576.855
  human physiology 612.6
  literature 808.803 538
    history and criticism 809.933 538
    specific literatures T3B—080 353 8
      history and criticism T3B—093 538
  psychology 155.3
    adolescents 155.53
    children 155.43
  religious worship 291.212
  sociology 306.7
  theological anthropology 291.22
    Christianity 233.5
    see also Humans—religion
Sex cells 571.845
Sex crimes 364.153
  law 345.025 3
  school problem 371.786
Sex differences 578.46
  animals 591.46
  physical anthropology 599.936
  psychology 155.33
Sex differentiation 571.882
Sex discrimination against men 305.32
Sex discrimination against women 305.42
  labor economics 331.413 3
    law 344.014 133
  law 342.087 8
Sex discrimination in education 379.26
  law 344.079 8
Sex education 613.907 1
  elementary level 372.372
Sex hormones 571.837 4
  biology 571.837 4
    animal reproduction 573.637 4
  chemistry 547.734 3
  human physiology 612.6
  pharmacology 615.366
  see also Genital system
Sex hygiene 613.95
  school programs 371.714
Sex instruction 613.907 1
  home child care 649.65
Sex manuals 613.96
Sex offenses 364.153
  law 345.025 3

Sex role 305.3
Sexadecimal system 513.57
Sexes
  evolution 576.855
  social aspects 305.3
  social theology 291.178 343
    Christianity 261.834 3
Sexism 305.3
Sexism in textbooks
  public control 379.156
Sext 264.15
  music 782.324
  see also Liturgy of the hours
Sextants
  astronomy 522.4
Sextets
  chamber music 785.16
  vocal music 783.16
Sexual abstinence
  health 613.9
Sexual abuse of children 362.76
  medicine 616.858 36
  school problem 371.786
  see also Child abuse
Sexual behavior (Animals) 591.562
Sexual deviation
  criminology 364.153 6
    criminal law 345.025 36
  medicine 616.858 3
  see also Mental illness
Sexual disorders
  gynecology 618.17
  medicine 616.69
  psychiatry 616.858 3
  see also Genital system; Mental illness
Sexual division of labor 306.361 5
Sexual ethics 176
  religion 291.566
  see also Sexual relations—ethics
Sexual factors in evolution 576.855
Sexual intercourse
  sociology 306.77
Sexual love 306.7
Sexual orientation 306.76
  arts 700.453
    T3C—353
  literature 808.803 53
    history and criticism 809.933 53
    specific literatures T3B—080 353
      history and literature T3B—093 53
  social groups T1—086 6
  sociology 306.76
Sexual practices 306.77
  public control 363.4
    public administration 353.37
  sociology 306.77
Sexual relations 306.7
  ethics 176
    religion 291.566
      Buddhism 294.356 6
      Christianity 241.66
      Hinduism 294.548 66
      Islam 297.566
      Judaism 296.366
        laws of family purity 296.742
  psychology 155.34
  social theology 291.178 357
    Christianity 261.835 7
  sociology 306.7
  technique 613.96
  see Manual at 306.7 vs. 155.34
Sexual reproduction 571.8
  animals 573.6
  microorganisms 571.845 29
  plants 575.6
  see also Genital system
Sexual selection (Animals) 591.562
Sexuality
  arts 700.453 8
    T3C—353 8
  literature 808.803 538
    history and criticism 809.933 538
    specific literatures T3B—080 353 8
      history and criticism T3B—093 538
Sexually abused children
  pediatrics 618.928 583 6
  social theology 291.178 327 2
    Christianity 261.832 72
  social welfare 362.76
  see also Child abuse
Sexually transmitted diseases
  incidence 614.547
  law 344.043 695 1
  medicine 616.951
  see also Communicable diseases (Human)
Seychelles 969.6
  T2—696
Seychellois T5—969 696
Seymour River (Columbia-Shuswap, B.C.) T2—711 68
Sgrafitto decoration 666.45
  arts 738.15
  technology 666.45

Shaanxi Sheng (China) T2—514 3
Shaba (Zaire) T2—675 18
Shabbat 296.41
Shabbat (Tractate) 296.123 2
  Babylonian Talmud 296.125 2
  Mishnah 296.123 2
  Palestinian Talmud 296.124 2
Shabuoth 296.438
  liturgy 296.453 8
Shackelford County (Tex.) T2—764 734
Shade plants
  floriculture 635.954 3
Shade-tolerant plants
  floriculture 635.954 3
Shade trees 635.977
Shades (Furnishings) 645.3
  household management 645.3
  manufacturing technology 684
Shadow boxes
  furniture arts 749.7
Shadow puppets 791.53
  see also Puppets
Shadow theaters 791.53
Shadows 535.4
  art 701.82
  drawing 742
  technical drawing 604.243
Shads 641.392
  cooking 641.692
  food 641.392
  zoology 597.45
Shafiites (Islamic sect) 297.812
Shaft currents (Electricity) 621.310 42
Shaft sinking 624.19
  mining 622.25
  underground construction 624.19
Shafts (Mechanisms) 621.823
  ship power plants 623.873
Shah Jahan, Emperor of India
  Indian history 954.025 7
Shahāda 297.34
Shahjahan, Emperor of India
  Indian history 954.025 7
Shaivism 294.551 3
Shaka, Zulu Chief
  Natal history 968.403 9
Shaka language 496.395
  T6—963 95
Shakers 289.8
  biography 289.809 2
  religious group T7—288
  see also Christian denominations
Shakes (Roofing) 695
Shakespeare, William 822.33
Shaktaism 294.551 4
Shakuhanchis 788.35
  see also Woodwind instruments
Shale oil
  processing 665.4
Shales
  petrology 552.5
Shallots 641.352 6
  botany 584.33
  cooking 641.652 6
  food 641.352 6
  garden crop 635.26
Shamāl Sīnā' (Egypt) T2—531
Shamālīyah (Sudan) T2—625
Shamanism 291.144
Shamans 200.92
  biography 200.92
  role and function 291.61
  see Manual at 200.92 and 291–299
Shambala languages 496.391
  T6—963 91
Shame 152.4
Shamisens 787.85
  see also Stringed instruments
Shamrocks (Clovers) 583.74
Shamrocks (Wood sorrel) 583.79
Shan T5—959 19
Shan language 495.919
  T6—959 19
Shan literature 895.919
Shandong Sheng (China) T2—511 4
Shang dynasty 931.02
Shanghai (China) T2—511 32
Shanghai dialect 495.17
  T6—951 7
Shankara (Philosophy) 181.482
Shanmukaism 294.551 6
Shannon County (Mo.) T2—778 873
Shannon County (S.D.) T2—783 66
Shannon River (Ireland) T2—417
Shansi Province (China) T2—511 7
Shantung Province (China) T2—511 4
Shanxi (China) T2—511 7
Shape
  animals 591.41
  biological organisms 578.41
  plants 581.41
Shape theory (Topology) 514.24
Shaped charges
  military engineering 623.454 5
Shapers (Tools) 621.912

Shaping metals
  decorative arts 739.14
  sculpture 731.41
Shar-Pei 636.72
Share renting
  agricultural land economics 333.335 563
  land economics 333.563
Sharecroppers 305.563
  T1—088 63
Sharecropping 306.365
  economics 333.335 563
Shared custody 306.89
Shareholders' meetings
  law 346.066 6
Shares (Corporate equity securities) 332.632 2
Sharia 340.59
  religious law 297.14
  secular law 340.59
Shāriqah (United Arab Emirates : Emirate) T2—535 7
Shārjah (United Arab Emirates : Emirate) T2—535 7
Sharkey County (Miss.) T2—762 414
Sharks 597.3
  commercial fishing 639.273
  cooking 641.692
  food 641.392
  paleozoology 567.3
  sports fishing 799.173
  zoology 597.3
Sharkskin fabrics 677.615
  see also Textiles
Sharp County (Ark.) T2—767 23
Sharp-tailed grouse 598.637 8
Sharpeville Massacre, 1960 968.058
Sharpshooters 356.162
Sharqīyah (Egypt) T2—621
Shasta County (Calif.) T2—794 24
Shastri, Lal Bahadur
  Indian history 954.043
Shavers
  manufacturing technology 688.5
Shaving 646.724
  customs 391.5
  personal care 646.724
Shavings
  wood 674.84
Shavuot 296.438
  liturgy 296.453 8
Shawano County (Wis.) T2—775 36
Shawls 391.44
  see also Accessories (Clothing)
Shawnee County (Kan.) T2—781 63
Shawnee Indians T5—973
Shawnigan Lake (B.C.) T2—711 2
Shawns 788.52
  see also Woodwind instruments
Shearing animals 636.083 3
Shearing stress
  effect on materials 620.112 45
Shearing textiles 677.028 25
Shears 621.93
Shearwaters 598.42
Sheaths (Nerve tissue) 573.852 5
  human histology 611.018 8
  see also Nervous system
Sheaths (Tendon) 573.753 56
  medicine 616.76
  see also Musculoskeletal system
Sheaves (Mathematics) 514.224
Sheboygan County (Wis.) T2—775 69
Sheehan's syndrome
  obstetrics 618.7
Sheep 636.3
  animal husbandry 636.3
  big game hunting 799.276 49
  zoology 599.649
Sheep dogs 636.737
Sheep's milk 641.371 7
  cooking 641.671 7
  food 641.371 7
  processing 637.17
Sheep's wool textiles 677.31
  arts 746.043 1
  see also Textiles
Sheet metal 671.823
Sheet music illustration 741.66
Sheeting
  rubber 678.36
Sheets 643.53
  arts 746.97
  home sewing 646.21
  household equipment 643.53
Sheffield (England : City) T2—428 21
Shefford (Quebec : County) T2—714 63
Shehitah 296.73
Shekalim 296.123 2
  Mishnah 296.123 2
  Palestinian Talmud 296.124 2
Shekhar, Chandra
  Indian history 954.052
Shelburne (N.S. : County) T2—716 25
Shelby County (Ala.) T2—761 79

Shelby County (Ill.) T2—773 798
Shelby County (Ind.) T2—772 59
Shelby County (Iowa) T2—777 484
Shelby County (Ky.) T2—769 435
Shelby County (Mo.) T2—778 323
Shelby County (Ohio) T2—771 45
Shelby County (Tenn.) T2—768 19
Shelby County (Tex.) T2—764 179
Sheldon, William Herbert
  personality theory 155.264
Shelf fungi 579.597
Shelf ice 551.342
Shelflisting
  library science 025.428
Shelikof Strait (Alaska) 551.466 34
  T2—164 34
Shell carving 736.6
Shell model (Nuclear physics) 539.743
Shell parakeets 636.686 4
Shellac 667.79
Shellfish 594
  conservation technology 639.974
  cooking 641.694
  culture 639.4
    economics 338.371 4
  fishing 639.4
  fishing industry 338.372 4
  food 641.394
    commercial processing 664.94
  resource economics 333.955
  sports fishing 799.254
  zoology 594
Shellfishing
  economics 338.372 4
    see Manual at 338.372
  sports 799.254
Shelling crops 631.56
Shells (Ammunition)
  artillery 623.451 3
  small arms
    military engineering 623.455
Shells (Animals) 591.477
  carving 736.6
  descriptive zoology 591.477
    mollusks 594.147 7
  handicrafts 745.55
  physiology 573.77
Shells (Structural elements) 624.177 62
  naval architecture 623.817 762
  structural engineering 624.177 62
    concrete 624.183 462
Shelter
  social welfare 361.05
Sheltered employment 362.042 5
  see also Employment services—social services
Shelving
  household management 645.4
  library collections
    maintenance 025.81
  library plant management 022.4
  manufacturing technology 684.16
Shemittah 296.439 1
Shenandoah County (Va.) T2—755 95
Shenandoah National Park (Va.) T2—755 9
Shenandoah River Valley (Va. and W. Va.) T2—755 9
Shengs 788.82
  see also Woodwind instruments
Shensi Province (China) T2—514 3
Shepherd's purse 583.64
Shepparton (Vic.) T2—945 4
Shepway (England : District) T2—422 395
Sherbet 641.863
  commercial processing 637.4
  home preparation 641.863
Sherbrooke (Quebec : County) T2—714 66
Sherbrooke (Quebec : Regional County Municipality) T2—714 66
Sherburne County (Minn.) T2—776 66
Sheridan County (Kan.) T2—781 145
Sheridan County (Mont.) T2—786 218
Sheridan County (N.D.) T2—784 76
Sheridan County (Neb.) T2—782 92
Sheridan County (Wyo.) T2—787 32
Sheriff Court (Scotland) 347.411 021
  criminal law 345.411 014
Sheriff-Principal (Scotland) 347.411 032
Sheriffs
  law 347.016
  police services 363.282
Sherman County (Kan.) T2—781 115
Sherman County (Neb.) T2—782 44
Sherman County (Or.) T2—795 64
Sherman County (Tex.) T2—764 813
Sherman's March to the Sea, 1864 973.737 8
Sherwood Forest (England) T2—425 24
Shetland (Scotland) T2—411 35
Shetland Islands (Scotland) T2—411 35
Shetland pony 636.16

Shevi'it 296.123 1
  Mishnah 296.123 1
  Palestinian Talmud 296.124 1
Shevu'ot 296.123 4
  Babylonian Talmud 296.125 4
  Mishnah 296.123 4
  Palestinian Talmud 296.124 4
Shewa (Ethiopia) T2—633
Sheyenne River (N.D.) T2—784 3
Shi language 496.394
  T6—963 94
Shia Islam 297.82
  doctrines 297.204 2
  Hadith 297.124 8
  relations with Sunni Islam 297.804 2
  worship 297.302
Shiawassee County (Mich.) T2—774 25
Shielding
  nuclear reactors 621.483 23
Shields (Armor) 623.441
  art metalwork 739.752
Shift work 331.257 2
  personnel management 658.312 1
Shifting cultivation
  agricultural technology 631.581 8
Shiga-ken (Japan) T2—521 85
Shigella 579.34
Shigella diseases
  incidence 614.516
  medicine 616.935 5
  see also Communicable diseases (Human)
Shih tzu (Dog) 636.76
Shikoku Island (Japan) T2—523
Shikoku Region (Japan) T2—523
Shilha language 493.3
  T6—933
Shilluk language 496.5
  T6—965
Shimane-ken (Japan) T2—521 96
Shin (Sect) 294.392 6
Shina language 491.499
  T6—914 99
Shina literature 891.499
Shinano River (Japan) T2—521 52
Shiners 597.482
Shingles (Disease)
  medicine 616.522
  see also Skin
Shingles (Roofing) 695
Shinto philosophy 181.095 61
Shinto temples and shrines 299.561 35
  architecture 726.195 61
Shintoism 299.561
  art representation 704.948 995 61
Shintoists
  biography 299.561 092
  religious group T7—299 56
Shinyanga Region (Tanzania) T2—678 28
Ship accidents 363.123
  see also Water transportation—safety
Ship canals 386.4
  engineering 627.137
  transportation services 386.4
    interoceanic 386.42
    noninteroceanic canals 386.47
  see also Canals
Ship canneries
  engineering 623.824 8
Ship fitting 623.843 3
Ship flags 929.92
Ship gear 623.862
Ship handling 623.881
Ship railroads 385.77
  engineering 625.39
  transportation services 385.77
Ship timber beetles 595.763
Ship-to-shore communication 384.53
  communications services 384.53
  port services 387.166
  see also Radiotelephony
Shipboard cooking 641.575 3
Shipboard health 613.68
Shipbuilding 623.82
Shipbuilding industry 338.476 238 2
  law 343.078 623 82
Shiplap 674.43
Shipment
  materials management 658.788
Shipping 387.5
  international law 341.756 6
  law 343.096
  materials management 658.788
  see also Inland water transportation; Ocean transportation
Shipping conferences (Business organizations) 387.506 5
Ships 387.2
  design 623.81
  engineering 623.82
  gear and rigging 623.862
  inland water 386.22
    transportation services 386.22
  international law 341.756 65

Ships (continued)
  law 343.096 5
  literature 808.803 56
    history and criticism 809.933 56
    specific literatures T3B—080 356
      history and criticism T3B—093 56
  naval equipment 359.83
  naval units 359.32
    see Manual at 359.32 vs. 359.83
  operation 387.540 44
    nautical engineering 623.881
    transportation services 387.540 44
      inland waterway 386.240 44
  ordnance 623.825 1
  sanitation services 363.729 3
    see also Waste control
  transportation services 387.2
  see Manual at 629.046 vs. 388
Ships in bottles 745.592 8
Shipworms 594.4
Shipwrecks 363.123
  adventure 910.452
  transportation safety 363.123
    see also Water transportation—safety
Shipwrights' work 623.844
Shipyards
  architecture 725.4
  production economics 338.476 238 3
  technology 623.83
Shira-Punu languages 496.396
  T6—963 96
Shire horse 636.15
Shires 320.83
  see also Counties
Shirts 391
  commercial technology 687.115
  customs 391
  home sewing 646.435
  see also Clothing
Shivaism 294.551 3
Shizuoka-ken (Japan) T2—521 65
Shoa (Ethiopia) T2—633
Shoah 940.531 8
  see also Holocaust, 1933–1945
Shoalhaven National Park (N.S.W.) T2—944 7
Shoalhaven River (N.S.W.) T2—944 7
Shock (Pathological)
  result of injury 617.21
  symptomatology 616.047
Shock absorbers
  automotive engineering 629.243
Shock resistance
  materials science 620.112 5
Shock-resistant construction 624.176
  buildings 693.85
Shock therapy
  psychiatry 616.891 2
  see also Mental illness
Shock tunnels
  aircraft 629.134 52
Shock waves 531.113 3
  fluid mechanics 532.059 3
  gas mechanics 533.293
  liquid mechanics 532.593
  solid mechanics 531.33
Shoe buckles 391.7
  customs 391.7
  making 739.278
  see also Jewelry
Shoe repairers 685.310 092
  occupational group T7—685 3
Shoemakers 685.310 092
  occupational group T7—685 3
Shoes 391.413
  commercial technology 685.31
  customs 391.413
  see also Clothing
Shogi 794.18
Shona (African people) T5—963 975
Shona language 496.397 5
  T6—963 975
Shona literature 896.397 5
Shooting game
  sports 799.21
    see also Sports
Shooting stars (Plants) 583.675
Shoots (Plants) 581.495
  descriptive botany 581.495
  physiology 575.4
Shop stewards 331.873 3
Shop technology 670.42
Shoplifting 364.162
  law 345.026 2
Shopping 381.1
  etiquette 395.53
  see also Commerce
Shopping centers 381.1
  architecture 725.21
  area planning 711.552 2
  management 658.87
  see also Commerce

Shopping malls 381.1
  architecture 725.21
  area planning 711.552 2
  institutional housekeeping 647.962 1
  management 658.87
  see also Commerce
Shops (Retail trade) 381.1
  architecture 725.21
  management 658.87
  see also Commerce
  see Manual at 381.1 vs. 381.4, 658.87
Shoran 621.384 893
  marine navigation 623.893 3
Shore, John, Baron Teignmouth
  Indian history 954.031 1
Shore biology 578.769 9
Shore birds 598.33
  sports hunting 799.248 33
Shore ecology 577.699
Shore flies 595.774
Shore protection 333.917 16
  engineering 627.58
  land economics 333.917 16
Shore reclamation 333.917 153
  engineering 627.58
  land economics 333.917 153
Shorebirds 598.33
  sports hunting 799.248 33
Shorelands 551.457
  T2—146
  see also Coasts
Shorelines 551.458
  T2—146
  geography 910.914 6
  geomorphology 551.458
  physical geography 910.021 46
Shoring
  foundation engineering 624.152
Short-haired cats 636.82
Short-necked lutes 787.8
  see also Stringed instruments
Short-order cooking 641.57
Short-range ballistic missiles 358.175 282
  engineering 623.451 952
  military equipment 358.175 282
Short-range weather forecasting 551.636 2
Short stories 808.831
  history and criticism 809.31
  specific literatures T3B—301
    individual authors T3A—3
Short takeoff and landing airplanes
  engineering 629.133 340 426
Short-term capital 332.041 2
  financial management 658.152 44
Short-term loans receivable
  financial management 658.152 44
Short-term securities
  public finance 336.32
Shortages
  agricultural industries 338.17
  natural resources 333.711
  production 338.02
  secondary industries 338.47
Shorthair cats 636.82
Shorthand 653
Shorthorn cattle 636.222
Shorts (Clothing) 391
  commercial technology 687.113
  customs 391
  home sewing 646.433
  see also Clothing
Shortwave electronics 621.381
  physics 537.534 3
Shortwave radio systems
  engineering 621.384 151
  military engineering 623.734 1
Shoshone County (Idaho) T2—796 91
Shoshonean languages 497.45
  T6—974 5
Shoshoni Indians T5—974 5
Shot peening 671.36
Shot-putting 796.435
  see also Sports
Shotguns 683.426
  manufacturing technology 683.426
  shooting game 799.213
  sports 799.202 834
  target shooting 799.31
  see also Guns (Small arms)
Shoulder muscles
  human anatomy 611.737
  see also Musculoskeletal system
Shoulders (Highways)
  maintenance
    engineering 625.761
Shoulders (Human) 612.97
  physiology 612.97
  regional medicine 617.572
  surgery 617.572 059
  see also Upper extremities (Human)
Show animals
  animal husbandry 636.081 1
Show jumping 798.250 79
  see also Sports

Shōwa period 952.033
Showboats 792.022
Showcase displays
  advertising 659.157
Showering
  personal care 646.71
Showing livestock 636.081 1
Shows 791
  advertising 659.152
  performances 791
Showtime (Cable television) 384.555 4
  see also Television
Shrapnel devices 623.451 4
Shreveport (La.) T2—763 99
Shrew opossums 599.27
Shrews 599.336
Shrewsbury and Atcham (England : Borough) T2—424 54
Shrike-vireos 598.878
Shrikes 598.862
Shrimp culture 639.68
Shrimping 639.58
  economics 338.372 538 8
Shrimps 595.388
  conservation technology 639.975 388
  cooking 641.695
  culture 639.68
  fishing 639.58
  fishing industry 338.372 538 8
  food 641.395
    commercial processing 664.94
  resource economics 333.955 58
  zoology 595.388
Shriners 366.16
  biography 366.160 92
  social group T7—366 1
Shrines 291.35
  architecture 726.1
    see Manual at 726.1
  Buddhist 294.343 5
  Christianity 263.042
  Hindu 294.535
  Islamic 297.35
  Jain 294.435
  Shinto 299.561 35
  Sikh 294.635
Shrinkage-controlled fabrics 677.688
  see also Textiles
Shropshire (England) T2—424 5
Shroud of Turin 232.966
Shrublands
  biology 578.738
  ecology 577.38
Shrubs 582.17
  floriculture 635.976
  landscape architecture 715.3
  see Manual at 635.9 vs. 582.1
Shuar Indians T5—983 72
Shuar language 498.372
  T6—983 72
Shuar literature 898.372
Shuara language 498.372
  T6—983 72
Shuara literature 898.372
Shuffleboard 796.2
  see also Sports
Shulḥan ʻarukh 296.182
Shumen, Bulgaria (Okrŭg) T2—499 4
Shumenski okrŭg (Bulgaria) T2—499 4
Shunts (Electrical instrument) 621.374 2
Shuswap Lake (B.C.) T2—711 68
Shuswap River (B.C.) T2—711 5
Shut-in persons 305.908 14
  T1—087 7
  T7—081 4
  health services 362.14
  home care 649.8
Shutters (Cameras) 771.36
Shuttle cars
  mining 622.66
Shyness 155.232
SI (Metric system) 530.812
  social aspects 389.15
Siam T2—593
Siam, Gulf of 551.465 72
  T2—164 72
Siamang 599.882
Siamese T5—959 11
Siamese cat 636.825
Siamese fighting fish 597.7
Siamese language 495.91
  T6—959 11
Siamese literature 895.91
Siassi Islands (Papua New Guinea) T2—957 1
Sibasa (South Africa : District) T2—682 91
Siberia (Russia) 957
  T2—57
Siberia, Eastern (Russia) T2—575
Siberia, Western (Russia) T2—573
Siberian husky 636.73
Siberian Yupik T5—971 4
Sibiu (Romania : Judeţ) T2—498 4
Sibley County (Minn.) T2—776 33

Siblings 306.875
T1—085 5
T7—045
child care handbooks 649.102 45
family relationships 306.875
home care 649.143
psychological influence 155.924
psychology 155.443
Sibyls
parapsychology 133.324 8
religion 291.61
Sichuan Sheng (China) T2—513 8
Sicilian dialect 457.8
T6—51
Sicilianas 793.3
music 784.188 3
Sicily T2—458
ancient T2—378
Sicily, Strait of 551.462 1
T2—163 81
Sick leave 331.257 62
economics 331.257 62
personnel management 658.312 2
Sick persons 305.908 14
T1—087 7
T7—081 4
architecture for 720.877
cooking for 641.563 1
devotional literature 291.432
Christianity 242.4
government programs (nonhealth) 353.539
guides to religious life 291.440 877
Christianity 248.861
health services 362.1
public administration 353.6
see also Health services
home care 649.8
pastoral care 291.61
Christianity 259.41
recreation 790.196
indoor 793.019 6
outdoor 796.087 7
religious rites 291.38
Christianity 265.82
social group 305.908 14
social theology 291.178 321
Christianity 261.832 1
social welfare 362.1
see also Health services
see Manual at 362.1–362.4 vs. 610: Biographies
Sickle cell anemia
medicine 616.152 7
see also Cardiovascular system
Sickness 362.1
medicine 616
see also Diseases (Human)
Sickness insurance 368.382
see also Insurance
Sidamo (African people) T5—935
Sīdamo Kifle Hāger (Ethiopia) T2—632
Sidamo languages 493.5
T6—935
Siddurim 296.45
Side arms
art metalwork 739.72
military engineering 623.44
Side-blown flutes 788.32
see also Woodwind instruments
Side chapels
architecture 726.595
Side dishes 641.81
Side drums 786.94
see also Percussion instruments
Side effects of drugs
pharmacodynamics 615.704 2
Side-sewing
bookbinding 686.35
Sideline markets 381.1
management 658.870 4
see also Commerce
Sideline stores 381.1
management 658.870 4
see also Commerce
Sidereal clocks
astronomy 522.5
Sidereal day 529.1
Sidereal month 523.33
Siderite
mineralogy 549.782
Sideshows 791.35
Sidewalks 388.411
road engineering 625.88
transportation services 388.411
Sidi Bel Abbès (Algeria : Province) T2—651
Sidi Kacem (Morocco : Province) T2—643
Sidings (Railroads) 625.163
Sidings (Walls)
buildings 698

Sidings (Walls) (continued)
  wood 674.43
Sidney (B.C.) T2—711 28
Sidon (Lebanon) T2—569 2
  ancient T2—394 4
Sidonian architecture 722.31
SIDS (Syndrome)
  pediatrics 618.92
Siedlce (Poland : Voivodeship) T2—438 4
Siege of Vicksburg, 1863 973.734 4
Siege warfare 355.44
Siemens process 669.142 2
Siena (Italy : Province) T2—455 8
Sieradz (Poland : Voivodeship) T2—438 4
Sierra (Ecuador) T2—866 1
Sierra County (Calif.) T2—794 36
Sierra County (N.M.) T2—789 67
Sierra Leone 966.4
  T2—664
Sierra Leoneans T5—966 4
Sierra Nevada Mountains (Calif. and Nev.) T2—794 4
Sierra Region (Ecuador) T2—866 1
Sieves (Mathematics) 512.72
Sifakas 599.83
Siftings
  cereal grains
    commercial processing 664.720 8
      wheat 664.722 8
Sight 573.88
  see also Vision
Sight method (Reading)
  elementary education 372.462
Sight-reading (Music) 781.423
  elementary education 372.873
Sighthounds 636.753 2
Sighting apparatus
  military engineering 623.46
Sigillography 929.9
  insignia 929.9
  numismatics 737.6
Sigmodon 599.357 2
Sigmoid colon
  human anatomy 611.347
  human physiology 612.36
  surgery 617.554 7
  see also Digestive system
Sigmoid flexure
  human anatomy 611.347
  human physiology 612.36
  surgery 617.554 7
  see also Digestive system
Sign language 419
  see Manual at 419 vs. 419.093–419.099
Sign painting 667.6
Signal corps 358.24
Signal generators
  electronics 621.381 548
Signal processing 621.382 2
Signal propagation
  communications engineering 621.382 4
Signal theory 003.54
  communications engineering 621.382 23
  systems 003.54
Signals 302.23
  communications engineering 621.382 2
  railroad transportation 385.316
    engineering 625.165
    law 343.095 2
    transportation services 385.316
  road transportation 388.312 2
    engineering 625.794
    law 343.094 6
    transportation services 388.312 2
  social psychology 302.23
  street transportation 388.413 122
    engineering 625.794
    law 343.098 2
    transportation services 388.413 122
  transportation 388.041
    engineering 629.040 289
    law 343.093
    transportation services 388.041
Signboards
  social psychology 302.23
Signets
  numismatics 737.6
Signs 302.23
  advertising 659.134
  law 346.045
  social psychology 302.23
  transportation 388.041
    engineering 629.040 289
    transportation services 388.041
  wooden 674.88
  see also Signals
Siirt İli (Turkey) T2—566 7
Sikh philosophy 181.046
Sikh temples and shrines 294.635
  architecture 726.146
Sikhism 294.6
  art representation 704.948 946
  Islamic polemics 297.294

Sikhism and Islam 294.617 2
  Islamic view 297.284 6
  Sikh view 294.617 2
Sikhs
  biography 294.609 2
  religious group T7—294 6
Sikkim (India) T2—541 67
Sikkimese T5—914 17
Sikoku Island (Japan) T2—523
Sikoku Region (Japan) T2—523
Siksika Indians T5—973
Siksika language 497.3
  T6—973
Silage 636.086 2
  forage crop 633.2
Silence
  musical element 781.236
Silencers (Automobile part) 629.252
Silesia T2—438 5
  Czech Republic T2—437 2
  Poland T2—438 5
Silhouettes 741.7
  animals 591.41
  cutting 736.984
  drawing 741.7
  plants 581.41
Silicates
  mineralogy 549.6
Silicon 553.6
  chemical engineering 661.068 3
  chemistry 546.683
  economic geology 553.6
  materials science 620.193
  organic chemistry 547.08
    aliphatic 547.48
    applied 661.88
  see also Chemicals
Silicon salts
  chemical engineering 661.43
Silicones 668.422 7
Silicosis
  medicine 616.244
  see also Respiratory system
Silistra (Bulgaria : Okrŭg) T2—499 3
Silistrenski okrŭg
    (Bulgaria) T2—499 3
Silk books 096.2
Silk cotton tree 583.68
Silk-screen printing 686.231 6
  graphic arts 764.8
  textile arts 746.62
Silk textiles 677.39
  arts 746.043 9
  see also Textiles
Silk tree 583.748
Silkworms 638.2
  culture 638.2
  zoology 595.78
Silky flycatchers 598.853
Silky terrier 636.76
Sillery (Quebec) T2—714 471
Sillimanite
  mineralogy 549.62
Sills (Geology) 551.88
Silo machinery
  manufacturing technology 681.763 1
Silos 633.208 68
Silphidae 595.764 2
Silt
  petrology 552.5
  reservoir engineering 627.86
  river engineering 627.122
Silurian period 551.732
  geology 551.732
  paleontology 560.173 2
Siluriformes 597.49
  paleozoology 567.49
Silver 669.23
  chemical engineering 661.065 4
  chemistry 546.654
  economic geology 553.421
  materials science 620.189 23
  metallography 669.952 3
  metallurgy 669.23
  metalworking 673.23
  mining 622.342 3
  physical metallurgy 669.962 3
  production economics 338.274 21
  see also Chemicals; Metals
Silver Bow County (Mont.) T2—786 68
Silver coins 332.404 2
  investment economics 332.63
  monetary economics 332.404 2
  numismatics 737.4
Silver processes
  photography 772.4
Silver standard 332.422 3
Silverfish (Insects) 595.723
Silverpoint drawing 741.25
Silversides 597.66
Silversmithing 739.23
Silverware
  arts 739.238 3
  table setting 642.7
Silviculture 634.95
Simaroubaceae 583.77
Simbu Province (Papua
    New Guinea) T2—956 7

Simcoe (Ont. : County) T2—713 17
Simdlangentsha (South Africa : District) T2—684 91
Simḥat Torah 296.433 9
liturgy 296.453 39
Similarity (Mathematics) 516.2
Simmering
home cooking 641.73
Simmond's disease
medicine 616.47
see also Endocrine system
Simonstown (South Africa : District) T2—687 35
Simple proteins 572.66
see also Proteins
Simples
pharmacognosy 615.321
Simplexes 514.223
Simpson County (Ky.) T2—769 735
Simpson County (Miss.) T2—762 585
Simpson Desert National Park (Qld.) T2—943 7
Simpson Peninsula (N.W.T.) T2—719 7
Simulation 003
T1—011
engineering 620.004 4
instructional use 371.397
management decision making 658.403 52
mathematics 511.8
Simuliidae 595.772
Simultaneous play (Chess) 794.17
Sin 291.22
Buddhism 294.342 2
Christianity 241.3
original sin 233.14
see Manual at 241.3–241.4 vs. 241.6
Hinduism 294.522
Islam 297.22
Judaism 296.32
moral theology 291.5
Buddhism 294.35
Christianity 241.3
see Manual at 241.3–241.4 vs. 241.6
Hinduism 294.548
Islam 297.5
Judaism 296.36
Sinai (Egypt) 953.1
T2—531
Sinai Campaign, 1956 956.044
Sinai Peninsula (Egypt) T2—531
ancient 939.48
T2—394 8
Sinaloa (Mexico : State) T2—723 2
Sind (Pakistan) T2—549 18
Sindhi T5—948
Sindhi language 491.41
T6—914 11
Sindhi literature 891.41
Sine-Saloum (Senegal) T2—663
Sinfonia concertantes 784.184 5
Sinfoniettas 784.184
musical form 784.184
orchestral music 784.218 4
Singapore 959.57
T2—595 7
Singapore Strait 551.465 72
T2—164 72
Singeing textiles 677.028 25
Singers 782.009 2
occupational group T7—782
Singh, Charan
Indian history 954.052
Singh, Vishwanath Pratap
Indian history 954.052
Singida Region (Tanzania) T2—678 26
Singing games 796.13
Single column tariffs 382.752
see also Customs (Tariff)
Single idiophones 786.88
see also Percussion instruments
Single-lens reflex cameras 771.32
Single-line outlets (Marketing) 381.14
management 658.876
see also Commerce
Single men 305.389 652
T1—086 52
psychology 155.642 2
social group 305.389 652
Single-parent family 306.856
social theology 291.178 358 56
Christianity 261.835 856
social welfare 362.829 4
see also Families—social welfare
Single parents 306.856
child care handbooks 649.102 43
Single persons 305.906 52
T1—086 52
psychology 155.642
social group 305.906 52

Single-photon emission-computed tomography 616.075 75
Single-piece processes
  production management 658.533
Single-reed bagpipes 788.49
  see also Woodwind instruments
Single-reed instruments 788.6
  see also Woodwind instruments
Single-shot pistols 683.432
  see also Pistols
Single-sideband radio systems 621.384 153
Single-stage programming 519.702
Single-story buildings 720.48
  architectural construction 721.042
  architecture 720.48
Single-story houses
  architecture 728.373
Single-tax school
  economics 330.155
Single-wicket cricket 796.358 8
Single wingback formation 796.332 22
Single women 305.489 652
  T1—086 52
  psychology 155.642 3
  social group 305.489 652
Singles (Tennis) 796.342 27
Singleton (N.S.W.) T2—944 2
Singspiels 782.13
  music 782.13
  stage presentation 792.5
    see also Theater
Sinhalese T5—914 8
Sinhalese language 491.48
  T6—914 8
Sinhalese literature 891.48
Sinhalese-Maldivian languages 491.48
  T6—914 8
Sinhalese-Maldivian literatures 891.48
Sink holes 551.447
  T2—144
  see also Caves
Sinkiang Uighur Autonomous Region (China) T2—516
Sinking 532.25
Sinking funds
  public finance 336.363
Sinn Fein Rebellion, 1916 941.508 21
Sino-Indian Border Dispute, 1957 954.042
Sino-Japanese Conflict, 1937–1945 940.53
  1937–1941 951.042
  1941–1945 940.53
Sino-Japanese War, 1894–1895 951.035
Sino-Tibetan languages 495
  T6—95
Sino-Tibetan literatures 895
Sinop İli (Turkey) T2—563
Sintering metals 671.373
Siouan Indians T5—975 2
Siouan languages 497.52
  T6—975 2
Sioux City (Iowa) T2—777 41
Sioux County (Iowa) T2—777 13
Sioux County (N.D.) T2—784 88
Sioux County (Neb.) T2—782 99
Sioux Falls (S.D.) T2—783 371
Sioux language 497.52
  T6—975 2
Sioux literature 897.52
Siphonales 579.835
Siphonaptera 595.775
Siphonocladales 579.83
Siphonophora 593.55
Siphunculata 595.756
Sipuncula 592.35
  paleozoology 562.35
Sirach (Bible) 229.4
Siracusa (Sicily : Province) T2—458 14
Sirenia 599.55
  paleozoology 569.5
Sirenidae 597.85
Sirens 621.389 2
  music 786.99
    see also Percussion instruments
  warning device 621.389 2
Sirens (Amphibians) 597.85
Sirionó language 498.38
  T6—983 8
Sisal
  botany 584.352
  fiber crop 633.577
Siskins 598.885
Siskiyou County (Calif.) T2—794 21
Sīstān and Balūchestān (Iran : Province) T2—558 3
Sisters 306.875
  T1—085 5
  T7—045
  see also Siblings
Sisters (Nurses) 610.730 92
  occupational group T7—613

Sisters (Nurses) (continued)
  role and function 610.730 69
  see also Nurses
Sisters (Women religious) 255.9
  biography 271.900 2
    see Manual at 230–280
  ecclesiology 262.24
  guides to Christian life 248.894 3
Sisters and brothers 306.875 3
  psychology 155.443
Sisters of Bon Secours 255.94
  church history 271.94
Sisters of Charity 255.91
  church history 271.91
Sisters of Mercy 255.92
  church history 271.92
Sistrums 786.885
  see also Percussion instruments
Siswati language 496.398 7
  T6—963 987
Siswati literature 896.398 7
Sit-down strikes 331.892 6
  see also Strikes (Work stoppages)
Sit-ins
  social conflict 303.61
Sitars 787.82
  see also Stringed instruments
Site planning
  architecture 720.28
Site selection
  home economics 643.12
  nuclear engineering 621.483 2
Sitka (Alaska) T2—798 2
Sittidae 598.82
Situation ethics 171.7
Situational influences
  psychology 155.93
Sivas İli (Turkey) T2—565
Siwa language 493.3
  T6—933
Siwi language 493.3
  T6—933
Six Days' War, 1967 956.046
Six-man football 796.332 8
Sixth-form colleges 378.154 3
  see also Higher education
Size 530.81
  animals 591.41
  biological organisms 578.41
  plants 581.41
Size of enterprise 338.64
  economics 338.64
Size of enterprise (continued)
  microeconomics 338.514 4
Size of farm
  economics 338.16
Size standards
  commerce 389.62
  production management 658.562
Sizing coal 662.623
Sizing ores 622.74
Sizing paper 676.234
Sizuoka-ken (Japan) T2—521 65
Sjælland (Denmark) T2—489 1
Sjögren's syndrome
  medicine 616.77
Skagerrak (Denmark and Norway) 551.461 36
  T2—163 36
Skagit County (Wash.) T2—797 72
Skamania County (Wash.) T2—797 84
Skaraborgs län (Sweden T2—486
Skateboarding 796.22
  see also Sports
Skateboards 796.22
  manufacturing technology 685.362
Skates (Fishes) 597.35
Skating (Ice) 796.91
  hockey 796.962 2
  see also Sports
Skating (Roller) 796.21
  see also Sports
Skeena Mountains (B.C.) T2—711 85
Skeena-Queen Charlotte (B.C.) T2—711 1
Skeena River (B.C.) T2—711 85
Skeet shooters 799.313 209 2
  sports group T7—799 3
Skeet shooting 799.313 2
  see also Sports
Skeletal muscle tissues
  human histology 611.018 6
  see also Musculoskeletal system
Skeletal system 573.76
  see also Bones
Skeleton 573.76
  see also Bones
Skepticism
  philosophy 149.73
    ancient 186
    epistemology 121.2
  philosophy of religion 211.7
Sketch books
  music 780
    treatises 780.262

Sketches T1—022 2
Sketches (Drama)
  literature 808.824 1
    history and criticism 809.241
    specific literatures T3B—204 1
      individual authors T3A—2
Skew bevel gears 621.833 2
Skhirate-Temara
    (Morocco : Prefecture) T2—643
Ski acrobatics 796.937
  see also Sports
Ski lifts 621.868
Ski troops 356.164
Skierniewice (Poland :
    Voivodeship) T2—438 4
Skiers 796.930 92
  sports group T7—796 9
Skiff beetles 595.762
Skiffle 781.64
Skiing 796.93
  equipment technology 688.769 3
    skis 685.364
  see also Sports
Skikda (Algeria : Province) T2—655
Skilled workers 331.794
  labor economics 331.794
  labor force 331.114 22
  personnel management 658.304 4
  unemployment 331.137 804
Skillets
  electric cooking 641.586
Skim milk 641.371 47
  cooking 641.671 47
  food 641.371 47
  processing 637.147
Skimmers (Birds) 598.338
Skin 573.5
  anesthesiology 617.967 477
  animal physiology 573.5
  anthropometry 599.945
  descriptive zoology 591.47
  geriatrics 618.976 5
  human anatomy 611.77
  human diseases 362.196 5
    incidence 614.595
    medicine 616.5
    social services 362.196 5
  human histology 611.018 977
  human physiology 612.79
  pediatrics 618.925
  personal care 646.726
  pharmacodynamics 615.778
  surgery 617.477
Skin beetles 595.763
Skin cancer 362.196 994 77
  incidence 614.599 947 7
  medicine 616.994 77
  social services 362.196 994 77
  see also Cancer (Human)
Skin diseases
  medicine 616.5
  see also Skin
Skin diving 797.23
  see also Sports
Skinner, B. F. (Burrhus
    Frederic)
  psychological system 150.194 34
Skipjack (Tuna) 597.783
Skipper flies 595.774
Skippers 595.788
Skips (Containers) 622.68
Skirmishing (Tactics) 355.422
Skirts 391
  commercial technology 687.117
  customs 391
  home economics 646.34
  home sewing 646.437
  see also Clothing
Skis 796.93
  manufacturing technology 685.364
Skuas 598.338
Skull
  anthropometry 599.948
  human anatomy 611.715
  human physiology 612.75
  medicine 616.71
  surgery 617.514
  see also Musculoskeletal
      system
Skull fractures
  medicine 617.155
Skunk cabbages 584.64
Skunks 599.768
Sky
  religious worship 291.212
Sky color 551.566
Sky marshals 363.287 6
Skydivers 797.560 92
  sports group T7—797 5
Skydiving 797.56
  see also Sports
Skye and Lochalsh
    (Scotland : District) T2—411 82
Skylights 721.5
  architecture 721.5
  construction 690.15
Skyros Island (Greece) T2—495 15
  ancient T2—391 1

Skyscrapers 720.483
  see also Tall buildings
Slabs
  structural engineering 624.177 2
    concrete 624.183 42
Slacks 391
  customs 391
  home sewing 646.433
  see also Clothing
Slag (Metallurgy) 669.84
Slalom skiing 796.935
  see also Sports
Slander 364.156
  ethics 177.3
  law 345.025 6
    criminal law 345.025 6
    torts 346.034
Slang 417.2
  specific languages T4—7
Slang dictionaries T1—03
Slash-and-burn agriculture
  technology 631.581 8
Slate 553.54
  building material 691.2
  economic geology 553.54
  petrology 552.4
  quarrying 622.354
Slaughterhouse residues
  use as fertilizer 631.843
Slaughterhouses
  meat processing 664.902 9
Slave kings
  Indian history 954.023 2
Slave labor 331.117 34
Slave River (Alta. and N.W.T.) T2—719 3
Slave trade
  commerce 380.144
  criminology 364.15
    criminal law 345.025
    international law 341.77
Slavery 306.362
  ethics 177.5
    see also Ethical problems
  labor economics 331.117 34
  law 342.087
  political science 326
Slaves 305.567
  T1—086 25
  customs 390.25
    dress 391.025
Slavic languages 491.8
  T6—918
Slavic literatures 891.8
Slavic people T5—918
Slavonia (Croatia) T2—497 2
Slavonic languages 491.8
  T6—918
Slavonic literatures 891.8
Slavs T5—918
Sled dog racing 798.83
Sled dogs 636.73
Sledding 796.95
  see also Sports
Sleep 154.6
  animal behavior 591.519
  animal physiology 573.868
  human physiology 612.821
  physical fitness 613.79
  psychology 154.6
  see also Nervous system
  see Manual at 612.821 vs. 154.6
Sleep disorders
  symptomatology
    neurological disease 616.849 8
  see also Nervous system
Sleeper services 388.042
  see also Passenger services
Sleepers (Ties) 625.143
Sleeping bags
  manufacturing technology 685.53
Sleeping cars 385.33
  engineering 625.23
  see also Rolling stock
Sleeping pills
  pharmacodynamics 615.782
Sleeping services 388.042
  see also Passenger services
Sleepwalking
  medicine 616.849 8
  psychology 154.64
  see also Nervous system
Slicers 621.93
Slide preparation 502.82
  biology 570.282 7
  botany 580.282 7
  zoology 590.282 7
Slide rules
  manufacturing technology 681.14
  mathematics 510.284
Slides (Photographs) 778.2
  bibliographies 011.37
  cataloging 025.347 3
  instructional use 371.335 22
  library treatment 025.177 3
Sliding bearings 621.822
Sligo (Ireland) T2—417 25

Sligo (Ireland : County) T2—417 2
Slime molds 579.52
Slings
  sports 799.202 82
Slip laws 348.01
  United States 348.731
Slip tracing 666.45
  arts 738.15
  technology 666.45
Slipcovers 645.4
  arts 746.95
  commercial technology 684.3
  home sewing 646.21
  household management 645.4
Slips (Plant propagation) 631.535
Sliven (Bulgaria : Okrŭg) T2—499 5
Slivenski okrŭg (Bulgaria) T2—499 5
Sloan shorthand system 653.425
Slocan Lake (B.C.) T2—711 62
Slope County (N.D.) T2—784 93
Slope failure 551.307
Slopes 551.43
  T2—143
  see also Mountains
Slot machines 795.27
  equipment technology 688.752
Sloth 179.8
  see also Vices
Sloths 599.313
Slotters 621.912
Slough (England) T2—422 97
Slovak language 491.87
  T6—918 7
Slovak literature 891.87
Slovakia 943.73
  T2—437 3
Slovaks T5—918 7
Slovene language 491.84
  T6—918 4
Slovenes T5—918 4
Slovenia T2—497 3
Slovenian language 491.84
  T6—918 4
Slovenian literature 891.84
Slovenians T5—918 4
Slow cooking 641.588
Slow learners 371.926
Sludge digestion 628.354
Slugs 594.3
Slugs (Land) 594.38
  agricultural pests 632.643 8
  control technology 628.964
  culture 639.483 8
Sluices
  canal engineering 627.135 2
  dam engineering 627.882
Slum clearance 307.344
Slums 307.336 4
  area planning 711.5
  social services to residents
    public administration 353.533 3
Słupsk (Poland :
    Voivodeship) T2—438 1
Small arms ammunition 683.406
  manufacturing technology 683.406
  military engineering 623.455
Small business 338.642
  accounting 657.904 2
  domestic investment in 332.672 2
  economics 338.642
  financial management 658.159 2
  government programs 354.279 9
  investment in 332.671 2
  law 343.07
    economic law 343.07
    income tax law 343.052 68
    private law 346.065 2
    tax law 343.068
  management 658.022
  personnel management 658.303
  tax economics 336.207
Small business loans 332.742
Small-claims courts 347.04
Small craft (Boats) 387.204 2
  design 623.812 042
  engineering 623.820 2
  handling 623.881 2
  transportation services 387.204 2
  see also Ships
Small craft canals 386.48
  engineering 627.138
  transportation services 386.48
  see also Canals
Small firearms 683.4
  see also Guns (Small arms)
Small forge work 682
Small fruits 581.464
  horticulture 634.7
  see also Berries
Small game hunting
  sports 799.25
    see also Sports
Small-group reading
  elementary education 372.416 2
Small groups 302.34
  pastoral work 253.7

Small industry 338.642
Small intestine 573.378
  biology 573.378
  human anatomy 611.341
  human physiology 612.33
  surgery 617.554 1
  see also Digestive system
Small-scale systems 003.7
Small states 321.06
  international role 327.101
Small towns 307.762
Smallmouth bass 597.738 8
Smallpox
  incidence 614.521
  medicine 616.912
  see also Communicable diseases (Human)
Smara (Morocco : Province) T2—648
Smart cards 332.76
  banking services 332.178
Smell 573.877
  animal physiology 573.877
  human physiology 612.86
Smell disorders
  medicine 616.87
  see also Nervous system
Smell perception
  psychology 152.166
Smelts 641.392
  cooking 641.692
  food 641.392
  zoology 597.5
Smilacaceae 584.356
Smilaxes (Cat briers) 584.356
Smilaxes (Ornamentals)
  botany 584.355
Smith, Adam
  economic school 330.153
Smith, Ian Douglas
  Zimbabwean history 968.910 4
Smith County (Kan.) T2—781 213
Smith County (Miss.) T2—762 582
Smith County (Tenn.) T2—768 52
Smith County (Tex.) T2—764 225
Smithers (B.C.) T2—711 82
Smithfield (South Africa : District) T2—685 6
Smithton (Tas.) T2—946 5
Smocking
  arts 746.44
Smog 363.739 2
  air pollution 363.739 2
  pollution technology 628.532
  see also Pollution
Smoke 541.345 15
  colloid chemistry 541.345 15
    applied 660.294 515
  pollution technology 628.532
Smoke bomb launchers 623.445
Smoke bombs 623.451 6
Smoke damage insurance 368.12
  see also Insurance
Smoke pollution 363.738 7
  see also Pollution
Smoke signals
  social psychology 302.222
Smoke trees (Anacardiaceae) 583.77
Smoke trees (Fabaceae) 583.74
Smoked foods
  cooking 641.616
Smokeless powder
  military engineering 623.452 6
Smokers' supplies 688.4
Smoking 394.14
  addiction 362.296
    medicine 616.865
    personal health 613.85
    social welfare 362.296
    see also Substance abuse
  customs 394.14
  law 344.054
  social problem 363.4
Smoking foods 664.028 6
  commercial preservation 664.028 6
  home preservation 641.46
Smolensk (Russia : Oblast) T2—472 7
Smolenskaia͡ oblast′ (Russia) T2—472 7
Smoli͡anski okrŭg (Bulgaria) T2—499 7
Smolyan (Bulgaria : Okrŭg) T2—499 7
Smooth muscle tissues
  human histology 611.018 6
  see also Musculoskeletal system
SMP (Insurance) 368.094
  see also Insurance
Smuggling 364.133
  law 345.023 3
Smut fungi 579.593
  agricultural diseases 632.493
Smuts 579.593
  agricultural diseases 632.493

Smuts, Jan Christiaan	
South African history	968.053
1919–1924	968.053
1939–1948	968.055
Smyrna (Extinct city)	T2—392 3
Smyth County (Va.)	T2—755 723
Snacks	642
commercial processing	664.6
cooking	641.53
Snail farming	639.483 8
Snails	594.3
Snails (Land)	594.38
agricultural pests	632.643 8
control technology	628.964
culture	639.483 8
food	641.394
commercial processing	664.95
cooking	641.694
home preservation	641.495
zoology	594.38
Snake eels	597.43
Snake flies	595.747
Snake plants	584.352
Snake River (Wyo.-Wash.)	T2—796 1
Idaho	T2—796 1
Oregon	T2—795 7
Washington	T2—797 4
Wyoming	T2—787 55
Snake venom	
human toxicology	615.942
Snakeflies	595.747
Snakeheads (Fishes)	597.64
Snakes	597.96
food	641.396
cooking	641.696
small game hunting	799.257 96
Snap beans	641.356 52
see also Kidney beans	
Snapdragons	635.933 95
botany	583.95
floriculture	635.933 95
Snappers (Fishes)	597.72
cooking	641.692
food	641.392
sports fishing	799.177 2
Snapping beetles	595.765
Snare drums	786.94
see also Percussion instruments	
Snares Islands (N.Z.)	T2—939 9
Snipe flies	595.773
Snipers	356.162
Snipes (Birds)	598.33
Snobbishness	
literature	808.803 53
history and criticism	809.933 53
specific literatures	T3B—080 353
history and criticism	T3B—093 53
Snohomish County (Wash.)	T2—797 71
Snooker	794.735
Snooks	597.72
sports fishing	799.177 2
Snorkeling	797.23
Snout beetles	595.768
Snow	551.578 4
building construction	693.91
meteorology	551.578 4
weather forecasting	551.647 84
weather modification	551.687 84
Snow camping	796.54
Snow carving	736.94
Snow-compacted roads	388.12
engineering	625.792
see also Roads	
Snow control	
airport engineering	629.136 37
road engineering	625.763
Snow cover	551.578 46
biology	578.758 6
ecology	577.586
see also Snow	
Snow drifts	551.578 47
Snow fences	
railroad engineering	625.13
road engineering	625.763
Snow goose	598.417 5
Snow leopard	599.755 5
conservation technology	639.979 755 5
resource economics	333.959 755 5
Snow monkey	599.864 4
Snow-on-the-mountain (Plant)	583.69
Snow removal	
airport engineering	629.136 37
road engineering	625.763
road transportation	388.312
Snow sports	796.9
equipment technology	688.769
see also Sports	
Snow surveys	551.579
Snowballs (Plants)	635.933 92
botany	583.92
floriculture	635.933 92
Snowboarding	796.9
see also Sports	
Snowdonia (Wales)	T2—429 25
Snowdrift (N.W.T.)	T2—719 3

Snowfall 551.578 4
  see also Snow
Snowmobiles 388.34
  driving 629.283 042
  engineering 629.220 42
  repair 629.287 042
  sports 796.94
    see also Sports
  transportation services 388.34
  see also Automotive vehicles
Snowplowing
  railroad engineering 625.100 288
  road engineering 625.763
Snowplows
  railroad engineering 625.22
Snowsheds 625.13
Snowshoeing 796.92
  see also Sports
Snowshoes
  manufacturing technology 685.363
Snowstorms 551.555
  social services 363.349 25
  see also Disasters
Snowy Mountains (N.S.W.) T2—944 7
Snuffboxes
  handicrafts 745.593 4
Snyder County (Pa.) T2—748 49
Soap carving 736.95
Soap operas 791.446
  radio programs 791.446
  television programs 791.456
Soapberries 583.78
Soapbox racing 796.6
  see also Sports
Soaps 668.12
Soapstone 553.55
  building material 691.2
  economic geology 553.55
  quarrying 622.355
Soaring
  aeronautics 629.132 31
  sports 797.55
    see also Sports
Sobhuza II, King of Swaziland
  Swazi history 968.870 3
Sobolev spaces 515.782
Soccer 796.334
  electronic games 794.863 34
  see also Sports
Soccer players 796.334 092
  sports group T7—796 33
Social acceptance 302.14
Social action 361.2
Social adjustment 302.14
Social anthropologists 306.092
  occupational group T7—309
Social anthropology 306
Social attitudes 303.38
Social behavior 302
  see Manual at 302–307 vs. 156
Social behavior (Animals) 591.56
Social breakdown 361.1
Social casework 361.32
Social causes of war 355.027 4
Social change 303.4
Social choice 302.13
Social classes 305.5
  T1—086 2
  T7—062
  civil rights 323.322
  customs 390.1–.4
  dress 391.01–.04
  dwellings 392.360 1–.360 4
  relations with government 323.322
  social theology 291.178 345
    Christianity 261.834 5
  see Manual at 305.9 vs. 305.5
Social clubs 367
Social conflict 303.6
  influence on crime 364.256
Social contract 320.11
Social control 303.33
Social credit money 332.56
Social Credit Party of Canada 324.271 05
Social customs 390
  armed forces 355.1
  see Manual at 390
Social dancing 793.3
  see Manual at 792.78 vs. 792.8, 793.3
Social decay 303.45
Social democracy 335.5
  economic system 335.5
  political ideology 320.531 5
Social democratic parties 324.217 2
  international organizations 324.172
Social deterioration 303.45
Social determinants
  individual psychology 155.234
Social dysfunction
  collective behavior 302.17
  individual interactions 302.542
  individual reactions 302.54
Social education 370.115

Social environment
  psychological influence 155.92
    see Manual at 302–307 vs. 155.92, 158.2
Social equality 305
  social theology 291.178 34
    Christianity 261.834
    Judaism 296.38
Social ethics 170
  sociology 303.372
  see also Ethical problems
  see Manual at 170 vs. 303.372
Social evolution 303.4
Social forecasts 303.49
Social gerontology 362.6
Social groups 305
  T1—08
  T7—02
  influence on crime 364.253
  see Manual at 305; *also at* 305 vs. 306, 909, 930–990
Social history 306.09
  Algerian Revolution 965.046 1
  Chaco War 989.207 161
  Civil War (England) 942.062 1
  Civil War (Spain) 946.081 1
  Civil War (United States) 973.71
  Crimean War 947.073 81
  Falkland Islands War 997.110 241
  Franco-German War 943.082 1
  Hundred Years' War 944.025 1
  Indo-Pakistan War, 1971 954.920 511
  Indochinese War 959.704 11
  Iraqi-Iranian Conflict 955.054 21
  Korean War 951.904 21
  Mexican War 973.621
  Napoleonic Wars 940.271
  Persian Gulf War, 1991 956.704 421
  South African War 968.048 1
  Spanish-American War 973.891
  Thirty Years' War 940.241
  United States Revolutionary War 973.31
  Vietnamese War 959.704 31
  War of 1812 973.521
  War of the Pacific 983.061 61
  World War I 940.31
  World War II 940.531
Social inequality 305
Social influence 303.34
  psychology 155.92
Social innovation 303.484
Social insects 595.79
  physiology of caste 571.882 157 9
Social insurance 368.4
  see also Government-sponsored insurance; Insurance
Social interaction 302
Social justice 303.372
Social justice school
  economics 330.155
Social law 344
  international law 341.76
Social learning 303.32
Social mobility 305.513
Social movements 303.484
Social norms 306
  social control 303.37
Social ownership of means of production
  Marxian theory 335.41
Social participation 302.14
Social pathology 361.1
  collective behavior 302.17
  individual interactions 302.542
  influence on crime 364.256
  see Manual at 301–307 vs. 361–365
Social perception 302.12
Social planning 361.25
Social policy 361.25
  governmental 361.61
Social prediction 303.49
Social pressure 303.3
  executive management 658.409 5
Social problems 361.1
  influence on crime 364.256
  social theology 291.178 3
    Buddhism 294.337 83
    Christianity 261.83
    Hinduism 294.517 83
    Islam 297.27
    Judaism 296.38
  welfare 362.042
  see Manual at 301–307 vs. 361–365; *also at* 301–307 vs. 361.1, 362.042; *also at* 361–365; *also at* 361–365 vs. 353.5; *also at* 361 vs. 362; *also at* 362–363: Add table; *also at* 362–363 vs. 364.1; *also at* 363 vs. 340, 353–354
Social processes 303
  see Manual at 302–307 vs. 320
Social progress 303.44

Social protest 303.6
Social psychology 302
  see Manual at 302–307 vs. 150, T1—019; *also at* 302–307 vs. 155.92, 158.2
Social reform 303.484
  see also Reform movements
Social reformers 303.484 092
  occupational group T7—309
  welfare 361.240 92
    occupational group T7—361
Social relations 302
  ethics 177
  see also Ethical problems
Social responsibility
  educational objective 370.115
  executive management 658.408
Social role 302.15
Social sciences 300
  elementary education 372.83
  information systems 025.063
  public administrative support 352.745
  see Manual at 300; *also at* 300 vs. 600
Social scientists 300.92
  occupational group T7—3
Social security 362
  government-sponsored insurance 368.4
    law 344.02
    old-age and survivors 368.43
      law 344.023
    public administration 353.54
    see Manual at 336.249 vs. 368.401, 368.4011
  international law 341.76
  public administration 353.5
  social welfare 362
    law 344.032
  United States 368.430 097 3
    law 344.730 23
  see also Insurance
  see Manual at 362 vs. 368.4: Social security
Social security tax 336.249
  accounting 657.46
  law 343.052 42
  public finance 336.249
  see Manual at 336.249 vs. 368.401, 368.4011
Social services 361
  see also Welfare services
Social skills
  personal living 646.7
  social psychology 302.14
Social stratification 305
  social classes 305.512
Social studies 300
  elementary education 372.83
Social survey methodology 300.723
Social teaching of the Church 261
Social themes
  arts 700.455
    T3C—355
  folklore 398.27
    history and criticism 398.355
  literature 808.803 55
    history and criticism 809.933 55
    specific literatures T3B—080 355
      history and criticism T3B—093 55
Social theology 291.17
  Buddhism 294.337
  Christianity 261
    see Manual at 241 vs. 261.8
  Hinduism 294.517
  Islam 297.27
  Judaism 296.38
Social understanding 302.12
Social values 303.372
Social welfare 361
  see also Welfare services
Social welfare reformers 361.240 92
  occupational group T7—361
Social work 361.3
Social workers 361.309 2
  occupational group T7—362
Socialism 335
  economics 335
  political ideology 320.531
  sociology 306.345
  see Manual at 335 vs. 306.345, 320.53
Socialist communities
  economics 335.9
    see Manual at 338.7 vs. 335.9
Socialist ethics 171.7
Socialist International 324.174
Socialist Labor Party 324.273 7
Socialist parties 324.217 4
  international organizations 324.174
Socialist Party (U.S.) 324.273 7
Socialist Workers Party 324.273 7
Socialists 335.009 2
  political group T7—335
Socialization 303.32

Socially disadvantaged children
  home care 649.156 7
  psychology 155.456 7
  see also Socially disadvantaged persons
Socially disadvantaged persons 305.906 94
  T1—086 94
  government programs 353.53
  social group 305.906 94
  social welfare 362
    public administration 353.53
Societies 060
  fraternal organizations 366
  see also Organizations
Society 301
Society Islands T2—962 1
Society of Friends 289.6
  church government 262.096
    parishes 254.096
  church law 262.989 6
  doctrines 230.96
    catechisms and creeds 238.96
  general councils 262.596
  guides to Christian life 248.489 6
  missions 266.96
  moral theology 241.049 6
  persecution of 272.8
  public worship 264.096
  religious associations 267.189 6
  religious education 268.896
  religious group T7—286
  seminaries 230.073 96
  theology 230.96
Society of Jesus 255.53
  church history 271.53
Society of the Cincinnati 369.13
Socinianism 289.1
Sociobiology 304.5
  animal behavior 591.56
  biological ecology 577.8
  ethical systems 171.7
  human behavior 304.5
  see Manual at 302–307 vs. 156
Socioeconomic classes 305.5
  T1—086 2
  T7—062
  see also Social classes
Socioeconomic problems 361.1
  influence on crime 364.256
  social theology 291.178
    Buddhism 294.337 8
    Christianity 261.8
    Hinduism 294.517 8
Socioeconomic problems
  social theology (continued)
    Islam 297.27
      see Manual at 297.26–297.27
    Judaism 296.38
Sociolinguistics 306.44
Sociological fiction 808.838 3
  history and criticism 809.383
  specific literatures T3B—308 3
    individual authors T3A—3
Sociological jurisprudence 340.115
Sociologists 301.092
  occupational group T7—309
Sociology 301
  see Manual at 301–307; *also at* 301–307 vs. 361–365; *also at* 302–307
Sociology and religion 291.175
  Christianity 261.5
  Islam 297.27
  Judaism 296.38
Sociometry 302.015 195
Sociopathic personality
  medicine 616.858 2
  see also Mental illness
Sockets
  electrical engineering 621.319 24
Socorro County (N.M.) T2—789 62
Socotrans T5—929
Socratic philosophy 183.2
Soda niter
  mineralogy 549.732
Soda process
  wood pulp 676.124
Sodalities 267
Sodas (Chemicals) 546.382 2
  chemical engineering 661.32
Södermanlands lan (Sweden) T2—487
Sodium
  applied nutrition 613.285
  biochemistry 572.523 82
    humans 612.015 24
  chemical engineering 661.038 2
  chemistry 546.382
  economic geology 553.499
  metabolism
    human physiology 612.392 4
  metallurgy 669.725
  organic chemistry
    applied 661.895
  see also Chemicals

Sodium bicarbonate 546.382 22
  chemical engineering 661.323
Sodium carbonate 546.382 24
  chemical engineering 661.324
Sodium chloride 553.632
  chemistry 546.382 24
  see also Salt (Sodium chloride)
Sodium-free salt
  food technology 664.4
Sodium hydroxide 546.382 22
  chemical engineering 661.322
Sodium nitrate 553.64
  economic geology 553.64
Sodium-vapor lighting 621.327 6
  see also Lighting
Sodomy 306.773
  criminology 364.153 6
    criminal law 345.025 36
  sociology 306.773
Soekarno
  Indonesian history 959.803 5
Sofala (Mozambique : Province) T2—679 4
Sofas 645.4
  manufacturing technology 684.12
  see also Furniture
Soferim 296.461 509 2
Soferim (Talmudic) 296.120 092
Sofia (Bulgaria) T2—499 9
Sofia (Bulgaria : Oblast) T2—499 8
Sofia (Bulgaria : Okrŭg) T2—499 8
Sof′i͡a Alekseevna, Regent of Russia
  Russian history 947.049
Sofiĭska (Bulgaria : Oblast) T2—499 8
Soft-fiber crops 633.5
Soft rock 781.66
Soft toys
  making 688.724
    handicrafts 745.592 4
    technology 688.724
  see also Toys
Soft-winged flower beetles 595.763
Softball 796.357 8
  see also Sports
Softening (Water treatment) 628.166 6
Software 005.3
  see Manual at 004 vs. 005
Software compatibility 005
Software documentation
  preparation 005.15
  text 005.3
  see Manual at 005.15 vs. 808.066005
Software engineering 005.1
Software maintenance 005.16
Software metrics 005.14
Software packages 005.3
Software portability 005
Software reliability 005
Softwoods
  forestry 634.975
  lumber 674.144
Sogdian language 491.53
  T6—915 3
Sogdian literature 891.53
Sogdiana T2—396
Sogn og Fjordane fylke (Norway) T2—483 8
Sohāg (Egypt : Province) T2—623
Soil 631.4
  see also Soils
Soil biochemistry
  soil science 631.417
Soil biology 578.757
  agriculture 631.46
Soil chemistry 631.41
Soil classification 631.44
Soil conditioners 631.82
  chemical engineering 668.64
Soil conservation 333.731 6
  agriculture 631.45
  land economics 333.731 6
  law 346.046 731 6
  public administration 354.343 4
Soil consolidation 624.151 362
Soil ecology 577.57
Soil erosion 551.302
  agriculture 631.45
  engineering 627.5
  geology 551.302
  see also Erosion
Soil factors
  floriculture 635.955
Soil fertility 631.422
Soil formation 551.305
  frost action 551.38
Soil mechanics 624.151 36
  agriculture 631.433
  engineering geology 624.151 36
  railroad engineering 625.122
  road engineering 625.732
Soil moisture 631.432

Soil physics
  soil science 631.43
Soil pollution 363.739 6
  law 344.046 34
  public administration 354.343 5
  social welfare 363.739 6
  technology 628.55
  see also Pollution
Soil science 631.4
Soil surveys 631.47
  agriculture 631.47
  engineering 624.151 7
  see Manual at 631.474–631.479 vs. 631.494–631.499
Soil temperature 631.436
Soil texture
  agriculture 631.433
  conditioners 631.826
Soil working 631.51
  equipment manufacturing technology 681.763 1
Soilless culture 631.585
Soils 631.4
  T2—148
  agriculture 631.4
  biology 578.757
  ecology 577.57
  engineering geology 624.151
  materials science 620.191
  petrology 552.5
  railroad engineering 625.122
  road engineering 625.732
Sojas 583.74
  see also Soybeans
Sōka Gakkai 294.392 8
Soko-Kele languages 496.396
  T6—963 96
Sokoto State (Nigeria) T2—669 62
Sokotrans T5—929
Sokotri language 492.9
  T6—929
Sokotri literature 892.9
Sokotri people T5—929
Solanaceae 583.952
Solano County (Calif.) T2—794 52
Solar batteries 621.312 44
Solar cells 621.312 44
Solar collectors 621.472
Solar day 529.1
Solar desalinization 628.167 25
Solar energy 333.792 3
  architectural consideration 720.472
  astronomy 523.72
Solar energy (continued)
  economics 333.792 3
  engineering 621.47
  law 343.092 8
  public administration 354.48
Solar energy-powered automobiles
  engineering 629.229 5
Solar engineers 621.470 92
  occupational group T7—621 4
Solar engines 621.473
  automotive 629.250 8
  ships 623.872 7
Solar flares 523.75
Solar furnaces 621.477
Solar granulation 523.74
Solar heating 621.47
  buildings 697.78
Solar houses 643.2
  architecture 728.370 472
  construction 690.837 047 2
  home economics 643.2
Solar interior 523.76
Solar prominences 523.75
Solar radiation 523.72
  meteorology 551.527 1
Solar system 523.2
  T2—99
Solar wind 523.58
Soldering 671.56
  decorative arts 739.14
  sculpture 731.41
Soldering equipment 621.977
Soldier beetles 595.764 4
Soldier flies 595.773
Soldierfishes 597.64
Soldierly qualities 355.13
Soldiers 355.009 2
  law 343.013
  law of war 341.67
  occupational group T7—355
Soldiers of fortune 355.354
Sole bargaining rights 331.889 2
Sole traders
  law 346.068
Solenodons 599.33
Solenogastres 594.2
Soles (Fishes) 597.69
  cooking 641.692
  food 641.392
Soleure (Switzerland : Canton) T2—494 35
Solicitor-General (Scotland) 345.411 01
Solid dynamics 531.3

Solid foams 541.345 13
 chemical engineering 660.294 513
Solid-gas interface 530.417
Solid geometry 516.06
 analytic 516.33
 Euclidean 516.23
Solid-liquid interface 530.417
Solid mechanics 531
 engineering 620.105
Solid particles 530.413
 classical mechanics 531.16
 solid-state physics 530.413
Solid propellants 662.26
 aircraft 629.134 351
 military engineering 623.452 6
 spacecraft 629.475 24
Solid solutions
 metallurgy 669.94
Solid-state chemistry 541.042 1
Solid-state lasers 621.366 1
Solid-state physics 530.41
 see Manual at 548 vs. 530.41
Solid wastes 363.728 5
 law 344.046 22
 social services 363.728 5
 technology 628.44
  rural 628.744
 see also Waste control
Solidification 536.42
 metallurgy 669.94
Solids
 chemical engineering 660.041
 expansion and contraction 536.414
 geometry 516.06
 heat transfer 536.23
 mechanics 531
 sound transmission 534.22
 specific heat 536.63
 state of matter 530.41
Solifugae 595.48
Solihull (England : District) T2—424 97
Solipsism
 epistemology 121.2
Solitaire 795.43
Solitary confinement 365.644
Solitude
 psychology 155.92
Solo instruments 786–788
 bands and orchestras 784
 chamber ensembles 785
Solo voices 783.2
Sololá (Guatemala : Dept.) T2—728 164
Solomon, King of Israel
 Biblical leader 222.530 92
 Palestinian history 933.02
Solomon Islands 995.93
 T2—959 3
Solomon River (Kan.) T2—781 2
Solomon Sea 551.465 76
 T2—164 76
Solothurn (Switzerland : Canton) T2—494 35
Solpugida 595.48
Solubility 541.342
 chemical engineering 660.294 2
Soluble soaps 668.124
Solutes 541.348 3
 chemical engineering 660.294 83
Solution chemistry 541.34
 applied 660.294
Solution mining 622.22
Solutions
 practical pharmacy 615.42
Solvent extraction
 chemical engineering 660.284 248
Solvents 541.348 2
 chemical engineering 660.294 82
  organic 661.807
Solway Firth (England and Scotland) 551.461 37
 T2—163 37
Somali (Ethnic group) T5—935
Somali (National group) T5—967 73
Somali Democratic Republic 967.73
 T2—677 3
 people T5—967 73
Somali-Ethiopian Conflict, 1977–1979 963.071
Somali-Ethiopian Conflict, 1979–1989 963.071
Somali language 493.54
 T6—935 4
Somali literature 893.54
Somalia 967.73
 T2—677 3
Somaliland 967.7
 T2—677
Somaschi 255.54
 church history 271.54
Somatization disorders
 medicine 616.852 4
 see also Mental illness
Somatoform disorders
 medicine 616.852 4
 see also Mental illness
Somatotypes 599.949

Somerset (England) T2—423 8
Somerset County (Md.) T2—752 23
Somerset County (Me.) T2—741 22
Somerset County (N.J.) T2—749 44
Somerset County (Pa.) T2—748 79
Somerset East (South Africa : District) T2—687 14
Somerset Island (N.W.T.) T2—719 5
Somerset West (South Africa : District) T2—687 3
Somervell County (Tex.) T2—764 521
Somme (France) T2—442 6
Somme, 1st Battle of the, 1916 940.427 2
Somnambulism
 medicine 616.849 8
 psychology 154.64
 see also Nervous system
Somogy Megye (Hungary) T2—439 7
Son of God (Christian doctrines) 231.2
Sonar 621.389 5
 marine navigation 623.893 8
Sonata form 784.183
Sonata-rondos 781.824
 instrumental 784.182 4
Sonatas 784.183
Sonatinas 784.183 2
Sønderjyllands amt (Denmark) T2—489 5
Sondrio (Italy : Province) T2—452 5
Song cycles 782.47
 choral and mixed voices 782.547
 single voices 783.094 7
Song of Solomon 223.9
Song of Songs 223.9
Song of the Three Children (Bible) 229.6
Songbirds 598.8
 animal husbandry 636.68
 see Manual at 598.824–598.88
Songe languages 496.393
 T6—963 93
Songhai (African people) T5—965
Songhai Empire 966.201 8
 T2—662
Songhai language 496.5
 T6—965
Songs 782.42
 choral and mixed voices 782.542
 folk literature 398.87
 single voices 783.094 2
Songs without words 784.189 6
Songwriting 782.421 3
Sonic booms
 aeronautics 629.132 304
Sonics
 engineering 620.2
Sonneratiaceae 583.763
Sonnets 808.814 2
 history and criticism 809.142
 specific literatures T3B—104 2
 individual authors T3A—1
Sonography
 diagnosis 616.075 43
Sonoma County (Calif.) T2—794 18
Sonora (Mexico : State) T2—721 7
Sonora Island (B.C.) T2—711 1
Sons 306.874
 T1—085 4
 T7—044 1
Sons of the American Revolution 369.13
Sonsonate (El Salvador : Dept.) T2—728 413
Sooke (B.C.) T2—711 28
Sooke Lake (B.C.) T2—711 28
Sophia, Regent of Russia
 Russian history 947.049
Sophistic philosophy 183.1
Sophonias (Biblical book) 224.96
Sopranino recorders 788.363
 see also Woodwind instruments
Soprano recorders 788.364
 see also Woodwind instruments
Soprano saxophones 788.72
 see also Woodwind instruments
Soprano voices 782.66
 children's 782.76
  choral and mixed voices 782.76
  single voices 783.76
 general works 782.66
  choral and mixed voices 782.66
  single voices 783.66
 women's 782.66
  choral and mixed voices 782.66
  single voices 783.66
Sør-Trøndelag fylke (Norway) T2—484 1
Sorbian language 491.88
 T6—918 8
Sorbian literature 891.88
Sorbs T5—918 8

Sorcerers (Religious leaders) 200.92
  biography 200.92
  role and function 291.61
  see Manual at 200.92 and 291–299
Sordariales 579.567
Sorex 599.336 2
Sorghum sugars 641.336 2
  agriculture 633.62
  commercial processing 664.133
  cooking 641.636 2
  food 641.336 2
  see also Sugar
Sorghum syrup 641.336 2
  agriculture 633.62
  commercial processing 664.133
  cooking 641.636 2
  food 641.336 2
  see also Sugar
Sorghums 584.92
  botany 584.92
  forage crop 633.257 4
  grain crop 633.174
  syrup crop 633.62
Sorgo 633.62
  forage crop 633.257 4
  syrup crop 633.62
Soria (Spain : Province) T2—463 55
Soriano (Uruguay : Dept.) T2—895 27
Soricidae 599.336
Sørlandet (Norway) T2—483 1
Sororities 366.008 2
  education 371.856
Sorosilicates
  mineralogy 549.63
Sorrel (Polygonaceae) 641.355 6
  botany 583.57
  cooking 641.655 6
  food 641.355 6
  garden crop 635.56
Sorrento (Vic.) T2—945 2
Sorrow 152.4
Sorsogon (Philippines : Province) T2—599 1
Sort algorithms 005.741
Sorting data 005.741
Sorting machines
  manufacturing technology 681.14
Soshanguve (South Africa : District) T2—682 3
Sotah 296.123 3
  Babylonian Talmud 296.125 3
  Mishnah 296.123 3
  Palestinian Talmud 296.124 3
Soteriology 291.22
  Christianity 234
  Islam 297.22
  Judaism 296.32
  see also Humans—religion
Sotho (African people) T5—963 977
Sotho-Tswana languages 496.397 7
  T6—963 977
Soto 294.392 7
Soufflés 641.82
Souk Ahras (Algeria : Province) T2—655
Soul 128.1
  philosophy 128.1
  religion 291.22
    Christianity 233.5
    Islam 297.225
    Judaism 296.32
    philosophy of religion 218
    see also Humans—religion
Soul food cooking 641.592 960 73
Soul music 781.644
  songs 782.421 644
Soulanges (Quebec : County) T2—714 26
Sound 534
  biophysics 571.444
    humans 612.014 453
  cinematography 778.534 4
  diagnosis 616.075 44
  engineering 620.2
  musical element 781.23
  physics 534
  video production 778.592
Sound, The (Denmark and Sweden) 551.461 34
  T2—163 34
Sound effects 792.024
  see also Special effects—dramatic performances
Sound engineering 620.2
Sound engineers 620.209 2
  occupational group T7—620 2
Sound-induced illness
  medicine 616.989 6
  see also Environmental diseases (Human)
Sound processing
  computer science 006.45
Sound-ranging devices 621.389 5
  communications engineering 621.389 5
  marine navigation 623.893 8
Sound recording systems 621.389 3

Sound recordings 384
  bibliographies 011.38
  cataloging 025.348 2
  communications services 384
  engineering 621.389 32
  instructional use 371.333 2
  library treatment 025.178 2
  music 780
    cover illustration 741.66
    treatises 780.266
    see Manual at 780.26
  reviews 028.138
Sound reproducing systems 621.389 3
Sound synchronization
  motion pictures 778.534 4
Sound synthesis
  computer science 006.5
    T1—028 565
    engineering 621.399
Sounding devices 621.389 5
  communications engineering 621.389 5
  marine navigation 623.893 8
Soundproofing 620.23
  aircraft 629.134 42
  buildings 693.834
Soupfin sharks 597.34
Soups 641.813
Sour gums (Plants) 583.84
Sour milk cheeses 641.373 56
  cooking 641.673 56
  food 641.373 56
  processing 637.356
Souris River T2—784 6
Sourwood 583.66
Sousaphones 788.98
  see also Brass instruments
South Africa 968
  T2—68
  see Manual at 968
South African Blacks T5—968
South African literature
  Afrikaans 839.36
  Bantu languages 896.39
  English 820
South African Republic 968.204 5
  T2—682
South African War, 1899–1902 968.048
South Africans
    (Afrikaners) T5—393 6
South Africans (British
    origin) T5—28
South Africans (National
    group) T5—968
South America 980
  T2—8
South American native
    languages 498
  T6—98
South American native
    literatures 898
South American native
    peoples T5—98
South Arabian languages 492.9
  T6—929
South Arabian literatures 892.9
South Arabic peoples T5—929
South Asia 954
  T2—54
South Asian ancestry T5—914
  see Manual at T5—9141
South Asians T5—914
South Atlantic Ocean 551.464
  T2—163 5
  see Manual at T2—1631 and
      T2—1635
South Atlantic States 975
  T2—75
South Australia T2—942 3
South Bedfordshire
    (England) T2—425 65
South Bend (Ind.) T2—772 89
South Boston (Va.) T2—755 662
South Bucks (England :
    District) T2—425 98
South Cambridgeshire
    (England) T2—426 57
South Carolina 975.7
  T2—757
South Caucasian languages 499.968
  T6—999 68
South China Sea 551.465 72
  T2—164 72
South Coast (South Africa) T2—684 5
South Cotabato
    (Philippines) T2—599 7
South Dakota 978.3
  T2—783
South Derbyshire
    (England : District) T2—425 19
South Dobruja T2—499 4
South Downs (England) T2—422 6
South Dravidian languages 494.81
  T6—948 1
South Dravidian literatures 894.81
South Dravidians T5—948 1
South-Eastern State
    (Nigeria) T2—669 44

South frigid zone T2—116
South Georgia and South Sandwich Islands T2—971 2
South Georgia Island T2—971 2
South Glamorgan (Wales) T2—429 86
South Hams (England) T2—423 592
South Herefordshire (England : District) T2—424 45
South Holland (England : District) T2—425 39
South Holland (Netherlands) T2—492 38
South Island (N.Z.) T2—937
South Kesteven (England) T2—425 38
South Korea 951.95
T2—519 5
South Lakeland (England : District) T2—427 83
South Ndebele (South Africa) T2—682 95
South Norfolk (England : District) T2—426 19
South Northamptonshire (England : District) T2—425 59
South Orange (N.J.) T2—749 33
South Orkney Islands T2—989
South Osset (Georgia) T2—475 8
South Oxfordshire (England) T2—425 79
South Pacific Ocean 551.465 8
T2—164 8
see Manual at T2—1644 and T2—1648, T2—1649
South Pembrokeshire (Wales) T2—429 63
South Platte River (Colo. and Neb.) T2—788 7
South Pole T2—989
South Ribble (England) T2—427 67
South Sandwich Islands T2—971 2
South Saskatchewan River (Atla. and Sask.) T2—712 42
South Semitic languages 492.8
T6—928
South Semitic literatures 892.8
South Shetland Islands T2—989
South Shropshire (England) T2—424 57
South Slavic languages 491.81
T6—918 1
South Slavic literatures 891.81
South Slavic peoples T5—918 1
South Slavs T5—918 1
South Somerset (England) T2—423 89
South Staffordshire (England : Borough) T2—424 66
South Taranaki District (N.Z.) T2—934 88
South temperate zone T2—126
South Thompson River (B.C.) T2—711 72
South Tyneside (England) T2—428 75
South Tyrol (Italy) T2—453 83
South Vietnam T2—597
South Waikato District (N.Z.) T2—933 63
South Wairarapa District (N.Z.) T2—936 6
South Wales T2—429 4
South-West Africa T2—688 1
South-Western Region (China) T2—513
South Wight (England : Borough) T2—422 85
South Yorkshire (England) T2—428 2
Southampton (England) T2—422 76
Southampton County (Va.) T2—755 552
Southampton Island (N.W.T.) T2—719 4
Southeast Asia 959
T2—59
Southeast Asian literatures 895
Southeast Asians T5—95
Southeast Pacific Ocean 551.466 1
T2—164 1
Southeastern Asia 959
T2—59
Southeastern Europe 949.6
T2—496
ancient 939.8
T2—398
Southeastern States 975
T2—75
Southend-on-Sea (England) T2—426 795
Southern Aegean (Greece) T2—495 85
Southern Africa 968
T2—68
see Manual at 968
Southern Alps (N.Z.) T2—937 1
Southern Bantu languages 496.397
T6—963 97
Southern Baptist Convention 286.132
see also Baptists
Southern Britain 942
T2—42
ancient 936.2
T2—362

Southern California	T2—794 9
Southern Cameroons	T2—671 1
Southern Darfur (Sudan : Province)	T2—627
Southern dynasties	
Chinese history	951.015
Southern Europe	940
	T2—4
ancient	938
	T2—38
Southern France	T2—448
Southern fur seals	599.797 38
Southern Hemisphere	T2—181 4
Southern Highlands Province (Papua New Guinea)	T2—956 1
Southern India	T2—548
Southern Italy	T2—457
ancient	T2—377
Southern Kordofan (Sudan)	T2—628
Southern Leyte (Philippines)	T2—599 5
Southern Low Countries	949.3
	T2—493
Southern Province (Zambia)	T2—689 4
Southern Rhodesia	968.910 2
	T2—689 1
Southern Sotho language	496.397 72
	T6—963 977 2
Southern Sotho literature	896.397 72
Southern Sporades (Greece)	T2—495 87
ancient	T2—391 6
Southern States	975
	T2—75
Southern Turkic languages	494.36
	T6—943 6
Southern Uplands (Scotland)	T2—413 7
Southern Yemen	953.35
	T2—533 5
Southern Yemenis	T5—927 533 5
Southland District (N.Z.)	T2—939 6
Southland Region (N.Z.)	T2—939 6
Southport (Qld.)	T2—943 2
Southwark (London, England)	T2—421 64
Southwest, New	979
	T2—79
Southwest, Old	976
	T2—76
Southwest jazz	781.653
Southwest Pacific Ocean	551.465 7
	T2—164 7
Southwest Turkic languages	494.36
	T6—943 6
Soutpansberg (South Africa : District)	T2—682 5
Sovereignty	320.15
international law	341.26
Sovereignty of God	212.7
Christianity	231.7
comparative religion	291.211 2
Judaism	296.311 2
philosophy of religion	212.7
Soviet Central Asia	958.4
	T2—584
Soviet communism	335.43
economics	335.43
political ideology	320.532 2
Soviet people	T5—917
Soviet Union	947.084
	T2—47
Asia	957
	T2—57
Soviets (People)	T5—917
Sow bugs	595.372
Soweto (South Africa)	T2—682 21
Soweto Uprising, 1976	968.062 7
Sowing	631.531
Soy oil	
food technology	664.368
Soyas	583.74
see also Soybeans	
Soybean flour	664.726
Soybean glue	668.33
Soybean meal	664.726
Soybean milk	
commercial processing	663.64
Soybeans	583.74
agricultural economics	338.173 34
botany	583.74
commercial processing	
economics	338.476 648 05655
technology	664.805 655
cooking	641.656 55
field crop	633.34
food	641.356 55
garden crop	635.655
Soyfoods	
commercial processing	
technology	664.805 655
Space	T2—19
astronomy	520
international law	341.47
philosophy	114

Space (continued)
  physics 530.1
  resource economics 333.94
    see Manual at 333.94 vs. 338.0919
  see Manual at T2—99 vs. T2—19; *also at* 520 vs. 500.5, 523.1, 530.1, 919.9
Space (Area)
  arts 701.8
    drawing 741.018
Space and time 530.11
  philosophy 115
  physics 530.11
Space art 709.040 79
  sculpture 735.230 479
Space artillery
  engineering 623.419
Space biology 571.091 9
Space colonies
  engineering 629.442
Space communications
  engineering 621.382 38
  radio engineering 621.384 197
Space engineering 620.419
Space exploration
  unmanned 629.435
Space facilities
  military engineering 623.69
Space flight 387.8
  engineering 629.41
  transportation services 387.8
  see Manual at 629.43, 629.45 vs. 919.904
Space forces (Military science) 358.8
Space forces personnel 358.809 2
  occupational group T7—358
Space hazards
  engineering 629.416
Space heaters 697.2
Space industrialization 338.091 9
  in extraterrestrial worlds 338.099 9
  see Manual at 333.94 vs. 338.0919
Space laboratories
  engineering 629.442
Space mail 383.144
  see also Postal service
Space medicine 616.980 214
Space perception
  psychology 153.752
    visual perception 152.142
Space photography 778.35
  military engineering 623.72
Space physiology 571.091 9
  humans 612.014 5
Space ports
  spacecraft 629.478
Space probes 629.435
Space psychology 155.966
Space rights
  sale and rental 333.339
  zoning 333.771 7
    law 346.045
Space sciences 500.5
  public administrative support 352.745
Space shuttle 387.8
  engineering 629.441
  transportation services 387.8
  see also Space transportation
Space stations 629.442
Space suits 629.477 2
Space surveying 526.982
Space telescopes 522.291 9
Space-time 530.11
  philosophy 115
  physics 530.11
Space transportation 387.8
  engineering 629.4
  international law 341.756 79
  law 343.097 9
  public administration 354.79
  transportation services 387.8
Space transportation safety 363.124
  see also Transportation safety
Space transportation workers 387.809 2
  occupational group T7—387 8
Space walks 629.458 4
Space warfare 358.8
Spacecraft
  engineering 629.47
  military engineering 623.749
  psychological influence 155.966
Spacecraft accidents 363.124
  see also Transportation safety
Spacecraft gunnery 623.556
Spacecraft rendezvous
  manned space flight 629.458 3
Spaces (Mathematics) 516
  combinatorial topology 514.224
  geometry 516
Spadefoots 597.86
Spaghetti 641.822
  commercial processing 664.755
  cooking 641.822

Spain 946
T2—46
ancient 936.6
T2—366
Spalacidae 599.35
Spalding County (Ga.) T2—758 443
Spaniards T5—61
Spaniels 636.752 4
Spanish (People) T5—61
Spanish America 980
T2—8
Spanish-American literature 860
Spanish-American War, 1898 973.89
Spanish Americans T5—68
Spanish Armada, 1588 942.055
Spanish folk music 781.626 1
Spanish folk songs 782.421 626 1
Spanish Guinea T2—671 8
Spanish language 460
T6—61
foreign language instruction
elementary education 372.656 1
Spanish literature 860
Spanish Merino sheep 636.366
Spanish-Moroccan War, 1859–1860 964.03
Spanish Morocco T2—642
Spanish moss 584.85
Spanish plums 641.344 4
botany 583.77
cooking 641.644 4
food 641.344 4
Spanish Sahara T2—648
Spanish Succession, War of the, 1701–1714 940.252 6
North American history 973.25
Spanish West Africa T2—648
Spar varnishes 667.79
Sparganiaceae 584.68
Sparganium 584.68
Sparidae 597.72
Spark control devices
automotive 629.258
Spark-ignition engines 621.434
automotive 629.250 4
ships 623.872 34
see Manual at 629.046 vs. 621.43
Sparkling wine 641.222 4
commercial processing 663.224
Sparrows 598.883
Sparrows (Fringillidae) 598.883
Sparrows (Passer) 598.887
Spars 623.862
Sparta (Greece) T2—495 22
ancient T2—389
Spartan supremacy 938.06
Spartanburg County (S.C.) T2—757 29
Spas
health 613.122
therapeutics 615.853
Spatial behavior
human ecology 304.23
Spatsizi River (B.C.) T2—711 85
Speaker recognition
computer science 006.454
engineering 621.399
Speakers (Communications devices) 621.382 84
Speaking
applied linguistics 418
specific languages T4—83
rhetoric 808.5
Speaking in tongues 234.132
Speaking voices 782.96
choral and mixed voices 782.96
single voices 783.96
Spearfishes 597.78
Spearfishing 799.14
Spears 623.441
art metalwork 739.72
sports 799.202 82
Special assessments
law 343.042
public administration 352.44
Special delivery 383.183
see also Postal service
Special districts 352.19
Special drawing rights 332.45
Special education 371.9
law 344.079 1
public administrative support 353.89
public support 379.119
Special effects 792.024
cinematography 778.534 5
dramatic performances 792.024
motion pictures 791.430 24
radio 791.440 24
stage 792.024
television 791.450 24
photography 778.8
video production 778.593
Special functions (Mathematics) 515.5
Special handling 383.183
see also Postal service
Special-interest groups
adult education 374.22

Special libraries 026
  architecture 727.83
  see Manual at 026–027
Special materials
  cataloging 025.34
  library acquisitions 025.28
  library treatment 025.17
Special multi-peril insurance 368.094
  see also Insurance
Special Olympics 796.087 4
  see also Sports
Special-purpose paints 667.69
Special-purpose railroads 385.5
  see also Railroad transportation
Special services (Armed forces) 355.346
Specialization
  economics 338.604 6
  international commerce 382.104 2
  social process 303.44
Specialty advertising 659.13
Specialty papers 676.284
Specialty plywoods 674.835
Specialty shops 381.14
  management 658.875
  see also Commerce
Speciation (Biology) 576.86
Species 578.012
Specific gravity 531.14
  gas mechanics 533.15
  liquid mechanics 532.4
  solid mechanics 531.54
Specific heat 536.6
Specifications T1—021 2
  production management 658.562
Specimen preservation
  biology 570.752
Speckled trout 597.554
SPECT (Tomography) 616.075 75
Spectral regions
  engineering 621.361
  light physics 535.01
Spectral theory 515.722 2
Spectral types (Stars) 523.87
Spectrochemical analysis 543.085 8
  qualitative 544.6
  quantitative 545.83
Spectrography 621.367
Spectroscopes
  manufacturing technology 681.414
Spectroscopic binaries 523.842
Spectroscopy 543.085 8
  analytical chemistry 543.085 8
    qualitative 544.6
    quantitative 545.83
  astronomy 522.67
  engineering 621.361
  interpretation of nuclear structure 539.744
  physics 535.84
  stars 523.87
Spectrum analysis 543.085 8
  physics 535.84
  qualitative 544.6
  quantitative 545.83
Speculation (Financial) 332.645
  guides 332.678
  stocks 332.632 28
Speculative psychology 150.19
Speech 302.224 2
  civil rights issues 323.443
  elementary education 372.622
  human physiology 612.78
  psychology 153.6
  social interaction 302.224 2
Speech disorders
  medicine 616.855
  special education 371.914 2
  see also Communicative disorders
Speech-impaired persons 305.908 164
  T1—087
  T7—081 64
  social group 305.908 164
  special education 371.914 2
Speech output devices 006.54
  engineering 621.399
Speech perception 401.9
Speech recognition
  computer science 006.454
    engineering 621.399
Speech synthesis
  computer science 006.54
    engineering 621.399
Speech therapy
  medicine 616.855 06
  special education 371.914 2
  see also Communicative disorders
Speeches 080
  literary criticism 809.5
    theory 808.5
  literary history 809.5

Speeches (continued)
  literature 808.85
    specific literatures T3B—5
      individual authors T3A—5
  rhetoric 808.5
  see Manual at 080
Speechwriting 808.5
Speed control devices 621.812
Speed drills and tests
  shorthand 653.15
  typing 652.307
Speed letters
  office use 651.75
Speed limits 388.314 4
  law 343.094 6
  urban 388.413 144
Speed reading 418.4
  elementary education 372.455
  specific languages T4—843 2
Speed skating 796.914
  see also Sports
Speedboats 387.231
  design 623.812 31
  engineering 623.823 1
  handling 623.882 31
  transportation services 387.231
  see also Ships
Speedways
  automobile racing 796.720 68
Speller-dividers 413.1
  specific languages T4—31
Spellers 418
  specific languages T4—81
Spelling 411
  applied linguistics 418
    specific languages T4—81
  elementary education 372.632
  linguistics 411
    specific languages T4—152
  standard language 410
Spelling reform 418
  specific languages T4—81
Spells (Occultism) 133.44
Spelthorne (England) T2—422 12
Spelunkers 796.525 092
  sports group T7—796 5
Spelunking 796.525
  see also Sports
Spence Bay (N.W.T.) T2—719 7
Spencer County (Ind.) T2—772 31
Spencer County (Ky.) T2—769 455
Spending 339.47
  see also Public expenditures
Sperm 571.845
Sperm banks 362.178 3
Sperm whale 599.547
Spermaceti
  chemical engineering 665.13
Spermatophyta 580
  see also Plants
Spermophilus 599.365
Sperrin Mountains
    (Northern Ireland) T2—416 2
Spey River (Scotland) T2—411 92
Spezia (Province) T2—451 83
Sphaeropsidales 579.55
Sphagnales 588.29
Sphalerite
  mineralogy 549.32
Sphecoidea 595.798
Sphenisciformes 598.47
  paleozoology 568.4
Sphenodontidae 597.945
Sphenophyllales 561.72
Sphenopsida 587.2
  paleobotany 561.72
Sphenopteris 561.597
Spheres 516.15
Spheres of influence 327.114
Spherical astronomy 522.7
Spherical harmonics 515.53
Spherical projection
  technical drawing 604.245
Spherical trigonometry 516.244
  analytic 516.34
Sphygmomanometry
  human physiology 612.140 28
  see also Cardiovascular
      system
Spices 641.338 3
  agriculture 633.83
  commercial processing 664.53
  cooking with 641.638 3
  economic botany 581.632
  food 641.338 3
Spider beetles 595.763
Spider fishes 597.61
Spider lilies 635.934 34
  botany 584.34
  floriculture 635.934 34
Spider monkeys 599.858
Spider venom
  human toxicology 615.942
Spiderfishes 597.61
Spiderflowers (Capparaceae) 583.64
Spiders 595.44
Spiderworts 584.86

Spies
  armed forces 355.343 209 2
  biography 327.120 92
Spike mosses 587.9
Spike rushes 584.84
Spillimacheen River (B.C.) T2—711 68
Spillways 627.883
Spin
  nuclear physics 539.725
  solid dynamics 531.34
Spin-fishing 799.126
Spina bifida
  medicine 616.83
    orthopedic aspects 616.73
  surgery 617.482
  see also Musculoskeletal system; Nervous system
Spinach 641.354 1
  botany 583.53
  commercial processing 664.805 41
  cooking 641.654 1
  food 641.354 1
  garden crop 635.41
Spinal anesthesia
  surgery 617.964
Spinal column
  fractures
    medicine 617.151
  human anatomy 611.711
  human physiology 612.75
  medicine 616.73
  surgery 617.471
  see also Musculoskeletal system
Spinal cord 573.869
  biology 573.869
  human anatomy 611.82
  human physiology 612.83
  medicine 616.83
  surgery 617.482
  see also Nervous system
Spinal deformities
  medicine 616.73
  see also Musculoskeletal system
Spinal dysraphism
  surgery 617.482
Spinal nerves
  human physiology 612.819
  medicine 616.87
  see also Nervous system
Spine
  medicine 616.73
  see also Musculoskeletal system
Spine fungi 579.6
Spinel
  mineralogy 549.526
Spinets 786.4
  instrument 786.419
  music 786.4
  see also Keyboard instruments
Spink County (S.D.) T2—783 217
Spinner dolphins 599.534
Spinning (Fishing) 799.126
Spinning machines
  textile technology 677.028 52
Spinning textiles 677.028 22
  arts 746.12
  manufacturing technology 677.028 22
Spinor algebras 512.57
Spinor analysis 515.63
Spinulosa 593.93
Spiny anteaters 599.29
Spiny eels 597.7
Spiny-headed worms 592.33
Spiny rats 599.359
Spiny-rayed fishes 597.64
Spiral gears 621.833 3
Spirals 516.15
Spireas 635.933 73
  botany 583.73
  floriculture 635.933 73
Spires 721.5
  architecture 721.5
  construction 690.15
Spirit leveling 526.36
Spirit photography 133.92
Spirit varnishes 667.79
Spirit writings 133.93
Spirits (Discarnate beings) 133.9
  apparitions 133.1
Spiritual beings 291.21
  Christianity 235
Spiritual direction 291.61
  Christianity 253.53
Spiritual exercises 291.43
  Christianity 248.3
Spiritual gifts
  Christian doctrines 234.13
Spiritual healing
  medicine 615.852
  religion 291.31
    African religions 299.64

Spiritual healing
  religion (continued)
    Christianity 234.131
      miracles 231.73
    miracles 291.211 7
    Native American religions 299.74
  see Manual at 615.852 vs. 291.31, 234.131
Spiritual life 291.44
  Buddhism 294.344 4
  Christianity 248.4
  Hinduism 294.544
  Islam 297.57
  Judaism 296.7
Spiritual renewal 291.3
  Christianity 269
  Islam 297.3
Spiritual world
  occultism 133.901 3
Spiritualism 133.9
  comparative religion 291.21
  literature 808.803 7
    history and criticism 809.933 7
    specific literatures T3B—080 37
      history and criticism T3B—093 7
  philosophy 141
Spiritualists 133.909 2
  occupational group T7—13
Spirituality 291.4
  Buddhism 294.344
  Christianity 248
  Hinduism 294.54
  Islam 297.57
  Judaism 296.7
Spirituals 782.253
  choral and mixed voices 782.525 3
  single voices 783.092 53
Spirochetes 579.32
Spitsbergen Island (Norway) T2—981
Spleen 573.155 5
  biology 573.155 5
  human anatomy 611.41
  human physiology 612.41
  medicine 616.41
  surgery 617.551
  see also Blood-forming system
Spleenworts 587.3
Splenic fever
  incidence 614.561
  medicine 616.956
  see also Communicable diseases (Human)
Splicing
  ropes and cables 623.888 2
Splines 511.42
Split-level houses
  architecture 728.373
Split T formation 796.332 22
Spodumene
  mineralogy 549.66
Spokane (Wash.) T2—797 37
Spokane County (Wash.) T2—797 37
Sponges 593.4
  paleozoology 563.4
Spongillidae 593.46
Spontaneous abortion
  obstetrics 618.392
Spontaneous generation 576.83
Spools
  wooden 674.88
Spoonbills (Birds) 598.34
Spoonworms 592.3
Sporades (Greece) T2—495 8
  ancient T2—391
Sporangia 575.6
Spores 571.847
  paleobotany 561.13
Sporoboleae 584.9
Sporozoa 579.47
Sport animals
  animal husbandry 636.088 8
Sporting dogs (United Kingdom) 636.75
Sporting dogs (United States) 636.752
Sporting goods
  manufacturing technology 688.76
Sports 796
  arts 700.455
    T3C—355
  child care 649.57
  ethics 175
    see also Ethical problems
  human physiology 612.044
  journalism 070.449 796
  law 344.099
  literature 808.803 55
    history and criticism 809.933 55
    specific literatures T3B—080 355
      history and criticism T3B—093 55
  physical fitness 613.711
  public administrative support 353.78
  safety 363.14
    public administration 353.97
    see also Safety
  sociology 306.483
  see Manual at 613.71 vs. 646.75, 796

Sports buttons
  numismatics 737.243
Sports cards 796.075
Sports cars 388.342 1
  driving 629.283
    recreation 796.77
  engineering 629.222 1
  repair 629.287 21
  transportation services 388.342 1
  see also Automobiles
Sports centers 796.068
  architecture 725.804 3
  construction 690.580 43
Sports clothes 391
  see also Clothing
Sports complexes 796.068
  architecture 725.804 3
  construction 690.580 43
Sports equipment
  manufacturing technology 688.76
Sports etiquette 395.5
Sports for disabled persons 796.087
Sports gymnastics 796.44
  see also Sports
Sports journalism 070.449 796
Sports medicine 617.102 7
Sports music 781.594
Sports pavilions 796.068
  architecture 725.804 3
  construction 690.580 43
Sports pins
  numismatics 737.243
Sportsmen 796.092
  sports group T7—796
  see Manual at 796: Sports personnel
Sporulation 571.847
Spot removal
  household sanitation 648.1
Spot tests
  microchemical analysis 543.081 34
Spot welding 671.521 3
Spotsylvania County (Va.) T2—755 365
Spotted bass 597.738 8
Spotted dolphins 599.534
Spotted fevers
  incidence 614.526 3
  medicine 616.922 3
  see also Communicable diseases (Human)
Spotted seal 599.792
Spouse abuse 362.829 2
  criminology 364.155 53
    criminal law 345.025 553
Spouse abuse (continued)
  family relationships 306.872
  psychiatry 616.858 22
  social welfare 362.829 2
  see also Family violence; Mental illness
Spouses 306.872
  see also Married persons
Spouses of alcoholics
  medicine 616.861 9
  social welfare 362.292 3
Spouses of substance abusers
  medicine 616.869
  social welfare 362.291 3
Sprains
  medicine 617.17
Sprang
  arts 746.422 4
Sprat 641.392
  cooking 641.692
  food 641.392
  zoology 597.452
Spray painting 667.6
Sprayed latex 678.538
Spraying
  agricultural pest control 632.94
  painting 667.6
Spraying plants
  manufacturing technology 681.763 1
Spread formation
  American football 796.332 22
Spread latex 678.538
Spread rubber 678.36
Spreading latex 678.527
Sprechgesang 782.97
  choral and mixed voices 782.97
  single voices 783.97
Spring 508.2
  music 781.524 2
  see also Seasons
Spring-flowering plants 581.43
  floriculture 635.953
Spring guns
  art metalwork 739.73
Springboard diving 797.24
  see also Sports
Springbok 599.646
Springfield (Ill.) T2—773 56
Springfield (Mass.) T2—744 26
Springhaas 599.359
Springs (Mechanisms) 621.824
  automotive engineering 629.243
  railroad engineering 625.21

Springs (South Africa : District) T2—682 2
Springs (Water) 551.498
  water supply engineering 628.112
Springtails 595.725
Sprinkler systems
  fire technology 628.925 2
Sprinters 796.422 092
  sports group T7—796 4
Sprints 796.422
Spruce budworm
  forest pest 634.975 267 8
Spruces 585.2
  forestry 634.975 2
  lumber 674.144
Spur gears 621.833 1
Spurge laurel 583.67
Spurges (Euphorbiaceae) 583.69
Spurious knowledge 001.9
Sputtering (Physics)
  solid-state physics 530.416
Spy stories 808.838 72
  history and criticism 809.387 2
  specific literatures T3B—308 72
    individual authors T3A—3
Spying 327.12
  see also Espionage
SQ3R technique
  elementary education
    reading 372.472
Squadrons (Air force units) 358.413 1
Squadrons (Naval air units) 359.943 4
Squadrons (Naval units) 359.31
Squads (Military units) 355.31
Squalidae 597.36
Squaloidei 597.36
Squamata 597.94
  paleozoology 567.94
Squamish (B.C.) T2—711 31
Squamish-Lillooet (B.C.) T2—711 31
Squamous epithelia
  human histology 611.018 7
Square books 099
Square dances 793.34
  music 784.188 7
Square root 513.23
Square-wave generators
  electronics 621.381 548
Squares (City planning) 711.55
Squares (Geometry) 516.15
Squaring the circle 516.204
Squash (Game) 796.343
  see also Sports
Squash players 796.343 092
  sports group T7—796 34
Squashes 641.356 2
  botany 583.63
  commercial processing 664.805 62
  cooking 641.656 2
  food 641.356 2
  garden crop 635.62
Squatter's right 346.043 2
Squawfishes 597.482
Squid 594.58
  cooking 641.694
  fishing 639.485 8
  food 641.394
    commercial processing 664.94
  zoology 594.58
Squirrel monkeys 599.852
Squirrelfishes 597.64
Squirrels 599.36
  agricultural pests 632.693 6
  small game hunting 799.259 36
Sranan language 427.988 3
  T6—217
Sranan Tongo 427.988 3
  T6—217
Sranantonga 427.988 3
  T6—217
Srê language 495.93
  T6—959 3
Sri Lanka 954.93
  T2—549 3
Sri Lankans T5—914 13
Śrīharṣa
  Indian history 934.07
St. John's (Nfld.) T2—718 1
St. Thomas (Ont.) T2—713 34
St. Thomas Christians 281.5
  see also Eastern churches
Stabiae (Extinct city) T2—377
Stabiles 731.55
Stability
  aeronautics 629.132 36
  foundation soils 624.151 363
Stability theory 515.35
Stabilization ponds
  sewage treatment 628.351
Stabilizers
  aircraft 629.134 33
Stable flies 595.774
Stable management 636.083
Stable waste
  animal husbandry 636.083 8
Stables 636.083 1

Stacks (Library)
  collections maintenance 025.81
  plant management 022.4
Stadiums 796.068
  architecture 725.827
Staff and line organization 658.402
  armed forces 355.330 4
  public administration 352.283
Staff development 370.113
  see also Vocational education
Staff notation 780.148
Staff trees 583.85
Staffing patterns 658.312 8
Stafford (England : Borough) T2—424 64
Stafford County (Kan.) T2—781 813
Stafford County (Va.) T2—755 26
Staffordshire (England) T2—424 6
Staffordshire Moorlands (England) T2—424 61
Stag beetles 595.764 9
Stage fright 792.028 019
  motion pictures 791.430 280 19
  radio 791.440 280 19
  stage 792.028 019
  television 791.450 280 19
Stage presentations 792
  see also Theater
Stagecoach transportation 388.322 8
Stagecoaches 388.341
  manufacturing technology 688.6
  transportation services 388.341
Stagflation 332.41
Staghorn ferns 587.3
Stags 599.65
  big game hunting 799.276 5
Stained glass
  arts 748.5
Staining (Microscopy) 502.82
  biology 570.282 7
Staining (Woodwork)
  buildings 698.32
Stairs 721.832
  architecture 721.832
  construction 690.183 2
Stalin, Joseph
  Russian history 947.084 2
Stalingrad, Battle of, 1942–1943 940.542 172 1
Stalk-eyed flies 595.774
Stamens 575.65
Stamford (Conn.) T2—746 9
Stammering
  medicine 616.855 4
  pediatrics 618.928 554
  see also Communicative disorders
Stamp Act, 1765–1766
  United States history 973.311 1
Stamp tax 336.272
  law 343.057
  public administration 352.44
  public finance 336.272
Stamping metals 671.334
  decorative arts 739.14
  sculpture 731.41
Stamping tools 621.984
Stamps (Postage) 383.23
  see also Postage stamps
Stamps (Seals)
  numismatics 737.6
Standard deviation 519.534
Standard-gage railroads 385
  see also Railroad transportation
Standard industrial classifications 338.020 12
Standard language
  applied linguistics 418
  description and analysis 411–415
  specific languages
    applied linguistics T4—8
    description and analysis T4—1–5
    see Manual at T4—1–T4—5 and T4—8 vs. T4—7
Standard money 332.420 42
Standard of living
  macroeconomics 339.47
Standard time 389.17
Standardbred horse 636.175
Standardization 389.6
  commerce 389.6
  international law 341.754
  law 343.075
  production management 658.562
  public administration 352.83
Standardized tests 371.262
  elementary education 372.126 2
    reading 372.482
  see Manual at 371.262 vs. 371.264
Standards T1—021 8
  executive management 658.401 3
    public administration 352.35

Standards (continued)
international law 341.754
law 343.075
production management 658.562
public administration 352.83
Standards (Flags) 929.92
armed forces 355.15
Standerton (South Africa : District) T2—682 7
Standing orders
library acquisitions 025.233
Stanger (South Africa) T2—684 4
Stanislaus County (Calif.) T2—794 57
Stanley (Tas.) T2—946 5
Stanley County (S.D.) T2—783 55
Stanley Cup 796.962 648
Stanly County (N.C.) T2—756 73
Stann Creek District (Belize) T2—728 23
Stanstead (Quebec : County) T2—714 67
Stanthorpe (Qld.) T2—943 3
Stanton County (Kan.) T2—781 712
Stanton County (Neb.) T2—782 535
Staphyleaceae 583.78
Staphylinidae 595.764 2
Staphylinoidea 595.764 2
Staphylococcal diseases
medicine 616.92
see also Communicable diseases (Human)
Staphylococcus 579.353
Star anise 641.338 2
botany 583.3
see also Flavorings
Star apples 583.674
floriculture 635.933 674
see also Sapotaceae
Star catalogs 523.802 16
Star clusters 523.85
Star formation 523.88
Star routes 383.143
see also Postal service
Star wars (Military science) 358.174
Stara Zagora (Bulgaria : Okrŭg) T2—499 6
Starch crops 633.68
Starch paste 668.33
Starches 572.566
applied nutrition 613.283
biochemistry 572.566
chemistry 547.782
food technology 664.2
Starches (continued)
metabolism
human physiology 612.396
see also Carbohydrates
Starfish 593.93
paleozoology 563.93
Stargazers (Fishes) 597.7
Stark County (Ill.) T2—773 513
Stark County (N.D.) T2—784 844
Stark County (Ohio) T2—771 62
Starke County (Ind.) T2—772 923
Starlings 598.863
Starozagorski okrŭg (Bulgaria) T2—499 6
Starr County (Tex.) T2—764 485
Stars 523.8
see Manual at 520 vs. 523.1, 523.112, 523.8
Starting devices
automotive 629.257
State (Political body) 320.1
see Manual at 320
State administration 352.13
see also States (Members of federations)—public administration
State aid
education 379.122
private schools 379.32
State bankruptcy 336.368
State banks 332.122 4
State colleges 378.053
see also Higher education
State courts (United States) 347.733
State flags 929.92
State governments 321.023
see also States (Members of federations)
State labor (Drafted workers) 331.117 32
State libraries 027.5
State-local relations 320.404 9
law 342.042
public administration 353.334
State of the Union messages 352.238 409 73
State planning
civic art 711.3
economics 338.9
State schools 371.01
State socialism 335
economics 335
political ideology 320.53
State succession
international law 341.26

State taxation 336.201 3
  law 343.043
  public administration 352.442 13
  public finance 336.201 3
State universities 378.053
  see also Higher education
State visits
  customs 394.4
Stateless persons 323.632
  international law 341.486
  law 342.083
Staten Island (New York, N.Y.) T2—747 26
States (Independent governments) 320.1
  governing systems 321
  international law 341.26
  public administration 351
States (Members of federations) 321.023
  law 342.042
  public administration 352.13
    grants-in-aid 352.734 3
    support and control 353.333
    see Manual at 351.3–351.9 vs. 352.13–352.19; *also at* 352.13 vs. 352.15
States of matter 530.4
  chemical engineering 660.04
States of the Church T2—456
States' Rights Party (U.S.) 324.273 3
Static determinacy 624.171 3
Static indeterminacy 624.171 3
Statically indeterminate structures 624.171 3
Statics 531.12
  air 533.61
    engineering 620.107 3
  engineering 620.103
  fluids 532.02
    engineering 620.106 3
  gases 533.12
    engineering 620.107 3
  liquids 532.2
    engineering 620.106 3
  solids 531.2
    engineering 620.105 3
Station posters
  transportation advertising 659.134 4
Station wagons
  driving 629.283
  engineering 629.222
  repair 629.287 2
  see also Automobiles
Stationary processes 519.232
Stationary steam engines 621.16
Stationary targets
  gun sports 799.312
Stationery 676.282 3
Stations of the Cross 232.96
  Roman Catholic liturgy 264.027 4
Statistical graphs T1—021
Statistical inference 519.54
Statistical mathematics 519.5
  see Manual at 519.5, T1—015195 vs. 001.422, T1—0727
Statistical mechanics 530.13
Statistical methods 001.422
  T1—072 7
  see Manual at 519.5, T1—015195 vs. 001.422, T1—0727
Statisticians 310.92
  collectors
    occupational group T7—31
  mathematicians
    occupational group T7—51
  occupational group T7—51
Statistics (Collections) 310
  T1—021
Statuary 731.7
Status (Law) 346.013
Status offenders 364.36
Statutes 348.022
Statutory actions 347.053
Statutory liability risks 368.08
Statutory rape 364.153
  law 345.025 3
Staunton (Va.) T2—755 911
Staurolite
  mineralogy 549.62
Stauromedusae 593.53
Stavropol′ (Russia : Kray) T2—475 2
Stavropol′skiĭ kraĭ (Russia) T2—475 2
Stawell (Vic.) T2—945 8
STD (Diseases)
  incidence 614.547
  medicine 616.951
  see also Communicable diseases (Human)
Stealing 364.162
  see also Theft
Steam cooking 641.587
Steam distilling oils and gases 665.028 2
Steam engineering 621.1
Steam engineers 621.109 2
  occupational group T7—621

Steam engines 621.1
automotive 629.250 1
ships 623.872 2
Steam fitting
buildings 696.3
Steam heating 621.1
buildings 697.5
Steam locomotives 385.361
engineering 625.261
transportation services 385.361
see also Rolling stock
Steam pipes 621.185
buildings
installation 696.3
Steam-powered automobiles
engineering 629.229 2
Steam-powered electric generation 621.312 132
Steam tractors
driving 629.284 92
engineering 629.229 2
repair 629.287 92
Steam turbines 621.165
Steaming
home cooking 641.73
Steamrollers
driving 629.284 92
engineering 629.229 2
repair 629.287 92
Steamships 387.204 4
engineering 623.820 4
transportation services 387.204 4
see also Ships
Stearns County (Minn.) T2—776 47
Steatite 553.55
Steel 669.142
building construction 693.71
building material 691.7
materials science 620.17
metallography 669.951 42
metallurgy 669.142
metalworking 672
physical metallurgy 669.961 42
production economics 338.476 691 42
ship design 623.818 21
shipbuilding 623.820 7
structural engineering 624.182 1
see also Metals
Steel drums 786.843
see also Percussion instruments
Steel workers 669.109 2
metallurgy 669.109 2
occupational group T7—669
Steel workers (continued)
metalworking 672.092
occupational group T7—672
occupational group T7—672
Steele County (Minn.) T2—776 193
Steele County (N.D.) T2—784 33
Steenrod algebras 512.55
Steeplechase races
horses 798.45
humans 796.426
see also Sports
Steeplechasing
equipment technology 688.78
Steeples
Christian church architecture 726.597
Steering gear
automotive engineering 629.247
ships 623.862
Stegosauria 567.915
Stegosaurus 567.915 3
Steiermark (Austria) T2—436 5
Stein algebras 512.55
Stellar evolution 523.88
Stellar magnitudes 523.822
Stellar radiation 523.82
Stellenbosch (South Africa : District) T2—687 3
Stelleroidea 593.93
paleozoology 563.93
Steller's sea cow 599.559 168
Stemonitales 579.52
Stems (Plants) 581.495
descriptive botany 581.495
physiology 575.4
Stenciling
decorative arts 745.73
Stencils
mechanical printing technique 686.231 6
office use 652.4
Stenella 599.534
Stenographers 651.374 109 2
office services 651.374 1
Stenographic machines
manufacturing technology 681.61
Stenography 653.14
Stenolaemata 594.67
Stepbrothers 306.875
T1—085 5
T7—045
see also Siblings
Stepchildren 306.874
T1—085 4
T7—044 1
Stephanotises 583.93

Stephen, King of England
  English history 942.024
Stephens County (Ga.) T2—758 132
Stephens County (Okla.) T2—766 53
Stephens County (Tex.) T2—764 546
Stephenson County (Ill.) T2—773 33
Stepparents 306.874
  T1—085
  T7—043 1
Steppes 333.74
  T2—145
  see also Prairies
Steps
  landscape architecture 717
Stepsisters 306.875
  T1—085 5
  T7—045
  see also Siblings
Stercorariidae 598.338
Sterculiaceae 583.68
Sterea Hellada (Greece) T2—495 15
Stereochemistry 547.122 3
  inorganic chemistry 541.223
  organic chemistry 547.122 3
Stereophonic sound systems
  engineering 621.389 334
Stereoscopic cinematography 778.534 1
Stereoscopic photography 778.4
Stereotypes
  sociology 303.385
Sterility
  gynecology 618.178
  medicine 616.692
  see also Genital system
Sterilization
  public health 614.48
  spacecraft 629.477 4
  surgery 617.910 1
Sterilization (Birth control)
  health 613.942
  social services 363.97
  surgery
    tubal ligation 618.120 59
    vasectomy 617.463
  see also Birth control
Sterkstroom (South Africa : District) T2—687 5
Sterling County (Tex.) T2—764 871
Sternoptychidae 597.5
Sternum
  human anatomy 611.713
  human physiology 612.75
  medicine 616.71
Sternum (continued)
  surgery 617.471
  see also Musculoskeletal system
Steroids 572.579
  biochemistry 572.579
    humans 612.015 73
  chemistry 547.73
Sterols 572.579 5
  biochemistry 572.579 5
  chemistry 547.731
Stethoscopes
  manufacturing technology 681.761
  use 616.075 402 8
Steuben County (Ind.) T2—772 78
Steuben County (N.Y.) T2—747 83
Stevenage (England) T2—425 82
Stevens County (Kan.) T2—781 725
Stevens County (Minn.) T2—776 42
Stevens County (Wash.) T2—797 23
Stewardship (Christian practice) 248.6
Stewart (B.C.) T2—711 85
Stewart County (Ga.) T2—758 922
Stewart County (Tenn.) T2—768 35
Stewart Island (N.Z.) T2—939 6
Stewartia 583.624
Stewartry (Scotland : District) T2—414 92
Stewing
  home cooking 641.73
Stews 641.823
Steynsburg (South Africa : District) T2—687 13
Steytlerville (South Africa : District) T2—687 14
Stick fighting 796.8
  see also Sports
Stick insects 595.729
  culture 638.572 9
Stick zithers 787.72
  see also Stringed instruments
Stickhandling
  ice hockey 796.962 2
Sticklebacks 597.672
Sticks
  music 786.82
    see also Rods (Musical instruments)
Stigmata 248.29
Stikine (B.C.) T2—711 85
Stikine River (B.C. and Alaska) T2—711 85
Stiletto flies 595.773
Still fishing 799.122

Still life
  art representation 704.943 5
  painting 758.4
Stillwater County (Mont.) T2—786 651
Stilts (Footwear)
  commercial technology 685.367
Stimulant abuse 362.299
  medicine 616.864
  personal health 613.84
  social welfare 362.299
  see also Substance abuse
Stimulants
  pharmacodynamics 615.785
Stinkhorns 579.599
Stipeae 584.9
Stipple engraving 765.5
Stirling (Scotland : District) T2—413 12
Stirling engines 621.42
Stirling Range (W.A.) T2—941 2
Stirling Range National Park (W.A.) T2—941 2
Stizostedion 597.758
Stoat 599.766 2
Stochastic integrals 519.2
Stochastic processes 519.23
Stochastic systems 003.76
  T1—011 76
Stock breeding 636.082
Stock control
  materials management 658.787
Stock exchange 332.642
  law 346.092 6
Stock exchange buildings
  architecture 725.25
Stock index futures 332.632 28
Stock issues
  capital management 658.152 24
Stock options 332.632 28
Stock ownership plans 331.216 4
  labor economics 331.216 4
  personnel management 658.322 5
Stock prices 332.632 22
Stock purchase plans 331.216 4
  labor economics 331.216 4
Stock rights 332.632 2
Stock savings banks 332.21
Stock tickers 384.14
  wireless 384.524
  see also Telegraphy
Stock warrants 332.632 2
Stockholders' meetings
  law 346.066 6
Stockholm (Sweden) T2—487 3
Stockholms län (Sweden) T2—487 3
Stockmen 636.009 2
  occupational group T7—636
Stockpiles
  secondary industries 338.47
Stockport (England : Metropolitan Borough) T2—427 34
Stocks 332.632 2
  accounting 657.76
  law 346.092 2
    corporate law 346.066 6
    income tax law 343.052 46
  see Manual at 332.6322 vs. 332.6323
Stocks (Matthiola) 583.64
Stockton-on-Tees (England : Borough) T2—428 51
Stockton Plateau (Tex.) T2—764 92
Stockyards
  animal husbandry 636.083 1
Stoddard County (Mo.) T2—778 95
Stoic ethics 171.2
Stoic philosophy 188
Stoichiometry 541.26
  applied chemistry 660.7
Stoke-on-Trent (England) T2—424 63
Stokes County (N.C.) T2—756 64
Stokes' integral 515.43
STOL airplanes
  engineering 629.133 340 426
Stoles 391
  commercial technology 687.147
    fur 685.24
  customs 391
  home sewing 646.457
  see also Clothing
Stolons 581.46
  see also Runners (Stolons)
Stomach 573.36
  biology 573.36
  human anatomy 611.33
  human physiology 612.32
  medicine 616.33
  surgery 617.553
  see also Digestive system
Stomatopoda 595.379 6
Stomiatoidei 597.5
Stone 553.5
  architectural construction 721.044 1
  architectural decoration 729.6
  building construction 693.1
  building materials 691.2
  economic geology 553.5
  materials science 620.132

Stone (continued)	
sculpture material	731.2
structural engineering	624.183 2
Stone Age	930.12
Stone carving	736.5
Stone County (Ark.)	T2—767 283
Stone County (Miss.)	T2—762 162
Stone County (Mo.)	T2—778 794
Stone flies	595.735
Stone lithography	763.22
Stone pavements	625.82
Stone plants	583.53
Stone sculpturing	731.463
Stonecrops	583.72
Stonewall County (Tex.)	T2—764 737
Stoneware	666.6
arts	738.3
technology	666.6
Stoneworts	579.839
Stopwatches	
technology	681.118
Storage	
coal technology	662.624
gas technology	665.742
home economics	648.8
museology	069.53
negatives and transparencies	771.45
petroleum technology	665.542
positives (photographs)	771.46
warehouse management	658.785
water supply engineering	628.13
Storage (Computer)	004.5
	T1—028 545
engineering	621.397
Storage (Mathematics)	519.83
Storage areas	
home economics	643.5
Storage batteries	621.312 424
Storage buildings	
architecture	725.35
Storage centers	
library role	021
Storage containers	
warehouse management	658.785
Storage elevators	
architecture	725.36
Storage of office records	651.53
Storage services	388.044
see also Freight services	
Storaxes	583.674
Store Bælt (Denmark)	551.461 34
	T2—163 34
Store detectives	363.289
Stores (Retail trade)	381.1
architecture	725.21
institutional housekeeping	647.962 1
management	658.87
see also Commerce	
see Manual at 381.1 vs. 381.4, 658.87	
Storey County (Nev.)	T2—793 56
Storing clothes	
home economics	646.6
Storing crops	631.568
Storing electric power	621.312 6
Storing food	
home use	641.48
Storing household goods	648.8
Storks	598.34
Storm insurance	368.122
see also Insurance	
Storm sewers	628.212
Storm surges	
oceanography	551.470 22
Stormberg Range (South Africa)	T2—687 6
Stormont (Ont.)	T2—713 75
Stormont, Dundas and Glengarry (Ont.)	T2—713 75
Storms	551.55
meteorology	551.55
social services	363.349 2
weather forecasting	551.645
weather modification	551.685
see also Disasters	
Storstrøms amt (Denmark)	T2—489 1
Story County (Iowa)	T2—777 546
Storytelling	808.543
child care	649.58
elementary education	372.677
library services	027.625 1
rhetoric	808.543
Stour River	T2—423 3
Stoves	
ceramic arts	738.8
heating buildings	697.22
household appliances	644.1
manufacturing technology	683.88
kitchen appliances	641.502 8
Strabane (Northern Ireland : District)	T2—416 41
Strabismus	
ophthalmology	617.762
see also Eyes	
Strafford County (N.H.)	T2—742 5
Straightening tools	621.983

Strain gauges
  materials science 620.112 302 87
Strains 531.381
  materials science 620.112 3
  naval architecture 623.817 6
  physics 531.381
  structural analysis 624.176
Strains (Injuries)
  medicine 617.17
Strait of Dover 551.461 36
  T2—163 36
Strait of Georgia (B.C.) 551.466 33
  T2—164 33
Strait of Gibraltar 551.462 1
  T2—163 81
Strait of Hormuz 551.467 35
  T2—165 35
Strait of Juan de Fuca (B.C. and Washington) 551.466 32
  T2—164 32
Strait of Magellan (Chile and Argentina) 551.469 4
  T2—167 4
Strait of Malacca 551.467 65
  T2—165 65
Strait of Mandab 551.467 32
  T2—165 32
Strait of Messina (Italy) 551.462 6
  T2—163 86
Strait of Sicily 551.462 1
  T2—163 81
Straits
  international law 341.446
Straits of Florida 551.464 63
  T2—163 63
Straits of Mackinac (Mich.) T2—774 923
Strand (South Africa : District) T2—687 3
Strange particles 539.721 6
Strangeness (Nuclear physics) 539.721 6
Strangers
  applied psychology 158.27
  psychological influence 155.927
Strangford Lough (Northern Ireland) T2—416 54
Strasbourg (France) T2—443 835 3
Strategic arms limitation 327.174 7
Strategic Defense Initiative 358.174
Strategic geography 355.47
Strategic management 658.401 2
  military administration 355.684
  public administration 352.34
Strategic materials 355.24
  land economics 333.8
  law 343.01
  military science 355.24
Strategic missile forces 358.17
  land 358.175 4
  navy 359.981 7
Strategic missiles 358.171 82
  engineering 623.451 9
  international law 341.738
  military equipment 358.171 82
Strategic planning (Management) 658.401 2
  military administration 355.684
  public administration 352.34
Strategic weapons 358.171 82
  engineering 623.451 9
  international law 341.738
  military equipment 358.171 82
Strategy 355.02
  Civil War (United States) 973.730 1
  military operations 355.4
  overall military objectives 355.02
  World War I 940.401
  World War II 940.540 1
  see also Military history
  see Manual at 355.02 vs. 355.4
Stratford District (N.Z.) T2—934 85
  Manawatu-Wanganui Region T2—935 3
  Taranaki Region T2—934 85
Stratford-on-Avon (England : District) T2—424 89
Strathclyde (Scotland) T2—414 1
Strathkelvin (Scotland) T2—414 36
Strathmore (Scotland) T2—412 5
Stratifications (Rock formations) 551.81
  economic geology 553.14
  specific areas 554–559
Stratigraphic paleontology 560.17
Stratigraphy 551.7
Stratiomyidae 595.773
Stratosphere 551.514 2
  T2—161 3
Straw pulp 676.14
Strawberries 641.347 5
  botany 583.73
  commercial processing 664.804 75
  cooking 641.647 5
  food 641.347 5
  horticulture 634.75

Stream of consciousness
  literature 808.802 5
    history and criticism 809.925
    specific literatures T3B—080 25
      history and criticism T3B—092 5
Streaming (Education) 371.254
Streams 551.483
  see also Rivers
Středočeský kraj (Czech Republic) T2—437 1
Středoslovenský kraj (Slovakia) T2—437 3
Street art (Murals) 751.73
Street cleaning 363.729 1
  public administration 353.94
  technology 628.46
  see also Waste control
Street cries 398.87
Street fighting (Military science) 355.426
Street furniture
  landscape architecture 717
Street markets 381.18
  management 658.87
  see also Commerce
Street music 781.532
Street noise 363.741
  see also Noise
Street patterns
  area planning 711.41
Street signals 388.413 122
  engineering 625.794
  law 343.098 2
  transportation services 388.413 122
Street signs 388.413 122
  see also Street signals
Street songs 398.87
Street theater 792.022
Street trees 635.977
Streetcars 388.46
  engineering 625.66
  transportation services 388.46
Streets 388.411
  engineering 625.7
  transportation services 388.411
  see also Roads
Strength
  crystals 548.842
  materials science 620.112
Strepsiptera 595.76
Streptochaeteae 584.9
Streptococcal diseases
  medicine 616.92
  see also Communicable diseases (Human)
Streptococcus 579.355
Streptomyces 579.378
Streptomycetes 579.378
Streptoneura 594.32
Stress
  child psychology 155.418
  medicine 616.98
  psychiatry 616.89
  psychology 155.904 2
  psychology of late adulthood 155.671 8
  see also Environmental diseases (Human)
Stress (Linguistics) 414.6
  specific languages T4—16
Stress-induced diseases
  medicine 616.98
  psychiatry 616.89
  see also Environmental diseases (Human)
Stresses (Physical forces) 531.381
  crystals 548.842
  naval architecture 623.817 6
  physics 531.381
  structural analysis 624.176
Striated muscle tissues
  human histology 611.018 6
  see also Musculoskeletal system
Strict liability 346.038
Stridulation 595.715 94
  insect communication 595.715 94
  physiology 573.927
Strigiformes 598.97
  paleozoology 568.9
Strijdom, Johannes Gerhardus
  South African history 968.057
Strike insurance 368.815
  see also Insurance
Strike requirements 331.898 2
Strike votes 331.892 1
Strikebreaking 331.894
Strikes (Geology) 551.85
Strikes (Work stoppages) 331.892
  economics 331.892
    government measures 331.898
    management measures 331.894
    public administration 354.97
  labor law 344.018 92
  personnel management 658.315 4
    public administration 352.68
  women workers 331.479 2
String art 746.047 1
String beans 641.356 52
  see also Kidney beans

String ensembles 785.7
String games 793.96
String orchestras 784.7
String quartets 785.719 4
String trios 785.719 3
Stringed instruments 787
  bands and orchestras 784
  chamber ensembles 785
    mixed 785.2–.5
    single type 785.7
  construction 787.192 3
    by hand 787.192 3
    by machine 681.87
  solo music 787
  see Manual at 784–788
Strings 677.71
Strip cropping (Soil conservation) 631.456
Strip-mined lands 333.765
  economics 333.765
  reclamation technology 631.64
Strip mining 622.292
  law 346.046 765
Striped bass 641.392
  cooking 641.692
  culture 639.377 32
  food 641.392
  sports fishing 799.177 32
  zoology 597.732
Striped dolphins 599.534
Striped polecat 599.766
Striped weasels 599.766 3
Striper (Striped bass) 641.392
  see also Striped bass
Stroboscopic photography 621.367
Stroke (Disorder)
  medicine 616.81
  see also Nervous system
Stromatoporoidea 563.58
Stromboli (Italy) T2—458 11
Strong interaction (Nuclear particles) 539.754 8
Strongboxes 683.34
Strontium 669.725
  chemical engineering 661.039 4
  chemistry 546.394
  metallurgy 669.725
  physical metallurgy 669.967 25
  see also Chemicals
Strophic form 781.823
  instrumental 784.182 3
Stroud (England : District) T2—424 19
Struck board zithers 787.74
  see also Stringed instruments
Struck drums 786.92
  see also Percussion instruments
Struck stringed instruments 787.7
  see also Stringed instruments
Structural analysis 624.171
  construction 690.21
  naval architecture 623.817 1
Structural chemistry 541.2
Structural clay products 666.73
  materials science 620.142
Structural crystallography 548.81
Structural decoration 729
  see Manual at 729
Structural design 624.177 1
  naval architecture 623.817 71
Structural elements
  architecture 721
  area planning 711.6
  construction 690.1
  see Manual at 721 vs. 690.1
Structural engineering 624.1
  see Manual at 624 vs. 624.1
Structural engineers 624.109 2
  occupational group T7—624
Structural foam products 668.493
Structural geology 551.8
Structural linguistics 410.18
  specific languages T4—018
Structural materials
  construction 691
Structural optimization 624.177 13
Structural polysaccharides 572.566 8
Structural proteins 572.67
Structural stone 553.5
  see also Stone
Structural theory 624.17
Structural unemployment 331.137 041
Structuralism
  fine arts 709.040 77
    sculpture 735.230 477
  philosophy 149.96
Structure (Philosophy) 117
Structure-activity relationships (Biochemistry) 572.4
Structured programming 005.113
Structures 720
  architecture 720
  interior decoration 747.8
  landscape architecture 717
Structures (Mathematics) 511.33
  combinatorial topology 514.224
  geometry 516
  topology 514

Struthioniformes 598.524
 paleozoology 568.5
Stuart, House of 941.06
 British history 941.06
 English history 942.06
 genealogy 929.72
 Irish history 941.506
Stuccowork 693.6
 architectural construction 721.044 6
Studbooks 636.082 2
Student activism 371.81
Student activities 371.8
Student adjustment 370.158
Student aid 371.22
 T1—079
 higher education 378.3
 law 344.079 5
Student assessment 371.26
Student clubs 371.83
Student competitions 371.89
Student councils 371.59
Student counseling 371.4
Student crime 371.782
Student discipline 371.5
 law 344.079 3
Student employment 371.225
 T1—079
 higher education 378.365
 see also Scholarships
Student exchanges 370.116 2
 higher education 378.016 2
 international law 341.767 3
 secondary education 373.011 62
Student expenditures
 higher education 378.38
Student experiments T1—078
Student expulsion 371.543
Student failure 371.285
Student government 371.59
Student guidance 371.4
Student health programs 371.71
Student housing 371.871
Student journalism 371.897
Student life 371.8
Student loans 371.224
 T1—079
 higher education 378.362
Student magazines
 journalism 371.897 5
Student mobility 371.291
 higher education 378.169 1
Student movements 371.81
Student newspapers
 journalism 371.897 4
Student organizations 371.83
 T1—06
Student participation in administration 371.59
Student periodicals
 journalism 371.897
Student personnel services 371.4
Student probation 371.543
Student projects T1—078
Student protest 371.81
Student rights
 law 344.079 3
Student service (Community service)
 higher education 378.103
 secondary education 373.119
Student services (Welfare) 371.7
 law 344.079 4
Student strikes 371.81
Student suspension 371.543
Student-teacher relations 371.102 3
Student teaching 370.71
Student transportation 371.872
Student unions
 architecture 727.38
Student unrest 371.81
Student welfare 371.7
 law 344.079 4
Students 371.8
 legal status 344.079
 occupational group T7—375
 see also entries beginning with School
Studies (Rooms) 643.58
 home economics 643.58
 residential interior decoration 747.73
Studies (Subject-oriented programs) T1—07
Studios
 broadcast engineering 621.384
 communications engineering 621.382 3
 photography 771.1
Study abroad 370.116
Study and teaching T1—071
Study clubs 367
Study collections
 museology 069.55
Study facilities 371.621
Study groups
 adult education 374.22
Study methods 371.302 81
Study scores 780
 treatises 780.265
Study skills 371.302 81

Stuffed toys
  making 688.724
    handicrafts 745.592 4
    technology 688.724
  see also Toys
Stunt animals
  animal husbandry 636.088 8
Stunt flyers 797.540 92
  sports group T7—797 5
Stunt flying 797.54
  see also Sports
Stuntmen 791.430 280 92
Stunts
  motion pictures 791.430 28
  television 791.450 28
Sturgeons 597.42
Sturnidae 598.863
Stutsman County (N.D.) T2—784 52
Stutterers 305.908 164
  T1—087
  T7—081 64
Stutterheim (South Africa : District) T2—687 5
Stuttering
  medicine 616.855 4
  pediatrics 618.928 554
  special education 371.914 2
  see also Communicative disorders
Stuttgart (Germany) T2—434 715
Stuttgart (Germany : Regierungsbezirk) T2—434 71
Stylasterina 593.55
Style
  fine arts 701.8
    drawing 741.018
  literary criticism 809
    specific literatures T3B—09
  rhetoric 808
Style manuals 808.027
  typing 652.3
Styles (Fine arts) 709
  see Manual at 704.9; *also at* 709.012–709.05 vs. 709.3–709.9; *also at* 753–758
Stylidiaceae 583.98
Stylommatophora 594.38
Styracaceae 583.674
Styrenes 668.423 3
Styria (Austria) T2—436 5
Sub-Saharan Africa 967
  T2—67
Subantarctic Islands (N.Z.) T2—939 9
Subatomic particles 539.72
Subconscious 154.2
  educational psychology 370.153
  philosophy 127
Subcontracting 346.022
  armed forces 355.621 2
Subcontracting fees
  labor economics 331.216 6
Subcultures 306.1
Subdivision of land 333.3
  law 346.043 77
  public administration 354.34
Subgroups 512.2
Subiya languages 496.399
  T6—963 99
Subject analysis
  information science 025.4
Subject and predicate (Grammar) 415
  specific languages T4—5
Subject bibliographies 016
  see Manual at 016 vs. 026, T1—07
Subject cataloging 025.47
Subject catalogs
  bibliography 017
Subject control
  information science 025.4
Subject headings 025.49
Subject indexing 025.48
Subject vocabularies 025.49
Subjective knowledge 121.4
Subjectivism 141
Subjectivity 126
  epistemology 121.4
Subjectless constructions 415
  specific languages T4—5
Sublanguage 418
  applied linguistics 418
    specific languages T4—8
Sublette County (Wyo.) T2—787 65
Sublimation 530.414
Sublimation (Psychology) 154.24
Subliminal perception
  psychology 153.736
Sublittoral biology 578.778
Sublittoral ecology 577.78
Submachine guns 355.824 24
  military engineering 623.442 4
  military equipment 355.824 24
Submanifolds 516.362
Submarine cable telegraphy 384.1
  see also Telegraphy
Submarine geology 551.460 8

Submarine geomorphology 551.460 84
Submarine medicine 616.980 22
  see also Environmental diseases (Human)
Submarine mining 622.295
Submarine physiology
  humans 612.014 415
Submarine sandwiches 641.84
Submarine swimming 627.72
  hydraulic engineering 627.72
  sports 797.23
Submarine warfare 359.93
  World War I 940.451
  World War II 940.545 1
Submarines 359.938 3
  design 623.812 57
  engineering 623.825 7
  environmental psychology 155.963
  naval equipment 359.938 3
  naval units 359.933
Submerged lands 551.41
  see also Wetlands
Submersible craft 387.204 5
  design 623.812 045
  engineering 623.820 5
  transportation services 387.204 5
  see also Ships
Submissiveness
  personality trait 155.232
Subordinate constructions (Grammar) 415
  specific languages T4—5
Subordinate levels of administration 352.14
  see Manual at 352
Subornation of perjury 364.134
  law 345.023 4
Subrings 512.4
Subscription books
  publishing 070.573
Subscription libraries 027.2
Subscription television 384.555 4
  see also Television
  see Manual at 384.555 vs. 384.5554
Subsidence 551.307
Subsidiary corporations 338.8
  see also Combinations (Enterprises)
Subsidies
  agricultural industries 338.18
  export trade 382.63
    see also Export trade
  law 343.074 2
Subsidies (continued)
  natural resources 333.715 8
  production economics 338.922
Subsidized housing 363.582
  see also Housing
Subsistence hunting 639.1
Subsistence theory of wages 331.210 1
Subsonic flow 533.273
  air mechanics 533.62
    aeronautics 629.132 303
Subsonic vibrations 534.52
  biophysics 571.443
    humans 612.014 452
  engineering 620.28
  physics 534.52
Substance (Philosophy) 111.1
Substance abuse 362.29
  criminology 364.177
  devotional literature 291.432
    Christianity 242.4
  ethics 178
  health insurance 368.382 5
    see also Insurance
  law 344.044 6
    criminal law 345.027 7
    social welfare law 344.044 6
  medicine 616.86
  pastoral theology 291.61
    Christianity 259.429
  personal health 613.8
  personnel management 658.382 2
    public administration 352.67
  religious guidance 291.442
    Christianity 248.862 9
  school problem 371.784
  social theology 291.178 322 9
    Christianity 261.832 29
  social welfare 362.29
    public administration 353.64
  transportation safety 363.120 1
    traffic accidents 363.125 14
  see Manual at 616.86 vs. 158.1, 248.8629, 291.442, 362.29: Recovery from addiction
Substance abusers T1—087 4
Substitute teaching 371.141 22
Substitution (Chemical reaction) 541.393
  chemical engineering 660.299 3
  organic chemistry 547.139 3
Subsurface mining 622.2

Subsurface resources
  land economics 333.8
    see Manual at 553 vs. 333.8, 338.2
  public administration 354.39
Subsurface water 553.79
  see also Groundwater
Subterranean land vehicles
  engineering 629.292
Subtraction 512.92
  algebra 512.92
  arithmetic 513.212
Subtractive processes
  color photography 778.66
Subtropical fruits
  cooking 641.646
  food 641.346
  orchard crops 634.6
Subud 299.933
Suburban areas 307.74
  T2—173 3
  see also Suburbs
Suburban families 306.853
Suburban sociology 307.74
Suburban transportation 388.4
Suburbs 307.74
  T2—173 3
  psychological influence 155.943
  public administration 352.169
    control by higher jurisdictions 353.336 9
  see also Cities
Subversion (Political) 327.12
  see also Subversive activities
Subversive activities 327.12
  armed forces 355.343 7
  criminology 364.131
    criminal law 345.023 1
  international politics 327.12
  political groups 322.42
  public administration of 353.17
Subversive groups 322.42
Subversive material
  postal handling 383.120 5
  see also Postal service
Subviral organisms 579.29
Subway stations 388.472
  architecture 725.31
  construction 690.531
  transportation services 388.472
Subway transportation 388.428
  see also Subways (Rail)
Subways (Pedestrian) 388.411
Subways (Rail) 388.428
  engineering 625.42
  law 343.098 3
  public administration 354.769
  transportation services 388.428
Success 646.7
  applied psychology 158
  business 650.1
  home economics 646.7
  literature 808.803 53
    history and criticism 809.933 53
    specific literatures T3B—080 353
      history and criticism T3B—093 53
  parapsychology 131
  public situations 650.1
  social psychology 302.14
Success in business 650.1
Success runs (Mathematics) 519.84
Successful living 646.7
Succession (Law) 346.052
Succubi 133.423
  see also Legendary beings
Succulent plants 581.754
  floriculture 635.952 5
Suceava (Romania : Judeţ) T2—498 1
Suchitepéquez (Guatemala) T2—728 165
Suckers (Fishes) 597.48
Suckers (Plants)
  agricultural propagation 631.533
Sucking lice 595.756
Sucre (Bolivia) T2—842 4
Sucre (Colombia : Dept.) T2—861 13
Sucre (Venezuela : State) T2—875 3
Sucrose 572.565
  biochemistry 572.565
  chemistry 547.781 5
  see also Carbohydrates
Suction lipectomy 617.95
Sucumbíos (Ecuador : Province) T2—866 412
Sud (Haiti) T2—729 462
Sud-Est (Haiti : Dept.) T2—729 456
Sud-Kivu (Zaire) T2—675 17
Sudan 962.4
  T2—624
Sudan grass 584.92
Sudanese T5—927 624
Sudanic languages (Chari-Nile) 496.5
  T6—965
Sudbury (Ont. : District) T2—713 133
Sudbury (Ont. : Regional municipality) T2—713 133
Sudden infant death syndrome
  pediatrics 618.92

Śuddhādvaita (Philosophy) 181.484 4
Sudetenland (Czech Republic) T2—437 1
Suede leather 675.25
Suez (Egypt : Province) T2—621 5
Suez, Gulf of 551.467 33
T2—165 33
Suez, Isthmus of T2—621 5
Suez Canal (Egypt) 386.43
T2—165 33
Suffering
consolatory devotions 291.432
Christinity 242.4
philosophy 128.4
religious guidance 291.442
Christianity 248.86
theodicy 291.211 8
Christianity 231.8
comparative religion 291.211 8
Islam 297.211 8
Judaism 296.311 8
philosophy of religion 214
see also Theodicy
theological anthropology 291.22
Christianity 233
comparative religion 291.22
Judaism 296.32
philosophy of religion 218
see also Humans—religion
Suffixes 415
specific languages T4—5
Suffolk (England) T2—426 4
Suffolk (Va.) T2—755 53
Suffolk Coastal (England) T2—426 46
Suffolk County (Mass.) T2—744 6
Suffolk County (N.Y.) T2—747 25
Suffolk horse 636.15
Suffrage 324.62
law 342.072
Suffrages (Liturgy) 264.13
music 782.292
Sufi orders 297.48
Sufis 297.409 2
Sufism 297.4
see Manual at 297.4
Sugar 641.336
biochemistry 572.565
chemistry 547.781 5
commercial processing 664.1
cooking with 641.636
food 641.336
see also Carbohydrates
Sugar beets 633.63
agriculture 633.63
botany 583.53
Sugar crops 633.6
Sugar maple 633.64
botany 583.78
syrup crop 633.64
Sugar substitutes
food technology 664.5
Sugarcane 633.61
agricultural economics 338.173 61
agriculture 633.61
botany 584.92
Sugars 572.565
applied nutrition 613.283
chemistry 547.781
metabolism
human physiology 612.396
see also Carbohydrates; Sugar
Suggestion therapy
medicine 615.851 2
Sūhāj (Egypt : Province) T2—623
Suhl (Germany : Bezirk) T2—432 26
Sui dynasty 951.016
Suicidal behavior 362.28
medicine 616.858 445
see also Suicide
Suicide 362.28
criminology 364.152 2
criminal law 345.025 22
customs 394.8
ethics 179.7
religion 291.569 7
Buddhism 294.356 97
Christianity 241.697
Hinduism 294.548 697
Judaism 296.369 7
medicine 616.858 445
pastoral care 259.428
social theology 291.178 322 8
Christianity 261.832 28
social welfare 362.28
see also Mental illness
Suidae 599.633
Suiformes 599.633
Suir River (Ireland) T2—419 1
Suitcases
manufacturing technology 685.51
Suites 784.185 8
Suits (Clothing) 391
commercial technology 687.113
customs 391
home sewing 646.433
see also Clothing

Suits (Law) 347.053
  procedure 347.050 4
Sukarno
  Indonesian history 959.803 5
Sukhothai (Kingdom) 959.302 2
Sukkah 296.123 2
  Babylonian Talmud 296.125 2
  Mishnah 296.123 2
  Palestinian Talmud 296.124 2
Sukkot 296.433
  liturgy 296.453 3
Suku (African people) T5—963 93
Suku language 496.393
  T6—963 93
Sukuma (African people) T5—963 94
Sukuma-Nyamwezi languages 496.394
  T6—963 94
Sukunka River (B.C.) T2—711 87
Sulawesi (Indonesia) T2—598 4
Sulawesi languages 499.22
  T6—992 2
Sulaymānīyah (Iraq : Province) T2—567 2
Sulfate process
  wood pulp 676.126
Sulfated hydrocarbons 668.14
Sulfated oils 668.14
Sulfates 546.723 24
  chemical engineering 661.63
  mineralogy 549.75
Sulfides 546.723 2
  chemical engineering 661.63
  mineralogy 549.32
Sulfinic acids 547.066
  chemical engineering 661.896
Sulfite process
  wood pulp 676.125
Sulfites 546.723 24
  chemical engineering 661.63
  organic chemistry 547.061
Sulfonation 547.27
  chemical engineering 660.284 47
Sulfones 547.065
  chemical engineering 661.896
Sulfonic acids 547.067
  chemical engineering 661.896
Sulfosalts
  mineralogy 549.35
Sulfoxides 547.065
  chemical engineering 661.896
Sulfur 553.668
  applied nutrition 613.285
  biochemistry 572.554
    humans 612.015 24
Sulfur (continued)
  chemical engineering 661.072 3
  chemistry 546.723
  economic geology 553.668
  metabolism
    human physiology 612.392 4
  mining 622.366 8
  organic chemistry 547.06
    aliphatic 547.46
    applied 661.896
    aromatic 547.66
  see also Chemicals
Sulfur bacteria 579.38
Sulfur dioxide
  gas technology 665.84
Sulfur salts
  chemical engineering 661.63
Sulfuric acid
  chemical engineering 661.22
Sulidae 598.43
Sullivan, Harry Stack
  psychological system 150.195 7
Sullivan County (Ind.) T2—772 41
Sullivan County (Mo.) T2—778 235
Sullivan County (N.H.) T2—742 75
Sullivan County (N.Y.) T2—747 35
Sullivan County (Pa.) T2—748 59
Sullivan County (Tenn.) T2—768 96
Sully County (S.D.) T2—783 284
Sulphur 553.668
  see also Sulfur
Sulpicians 255.75
  church history 271.75
Sultan Kudarat (Philippines) T2—599 7
Sulu (Philippines) T2—599 9
Sulu Archipelago (Philippines) T2—599 9
Sulu Sea 551.465 73
  T2—164 73
Sumacs 583.77
Sumatra (Indonesia) T2—598 1
Sumba Island (Indonesia) T2—598 6
Sumbawa (Indonesia) T2—598 6
Sumer T2—35
Sumerian language 499.95
  T6—999 5
Sumerian literature 899.95
Sumerian period 935.01
Sumerians T5—999 5
Sumie 751.425 2
Summability 515.243
Summaries
  rhetoric 808.062

Summation (Calculus) 515.43
Summation (Law) 347.075
Summer 508.2
  music 781.524 4
  see also Seasons
Summer air conditioning
  building systems 697.933 3
Summer-flowering plants 581.43
  floriculture 635.953
Summer school 371.232
Summer theater 792.022 4
Summers County (W. Va.) T2—754 76
Summit County (Colo.) T2—788 45
Summit County (Ohio) T2—771 36
Summit County (Utah) T2—792 14
Summons 347.072
  criminal law 345.072
Sumner County (Kan.) T2—781 87
Sumner County (Tenn.) T2—768 47
Sumner's method
  celestial navigation 527.3
Sumo 796.812 5
  see also Sports
Sumo Indians T5—978
Sumo language 497.8
  T6—978
Sums´ka oblast´ (Ukraine) T2—477 6
Sumter County (Ala.) T2—761 41
Sumter County (Fla.) T2—759 73
Sumter County (Ga.) T2—758 913
Sumter County (S.C.) T2—757 69
Sumu Indians T5—978
Sumy (Ukraine : Oblast) T2—477 6
Sun 523.7
  T2—994
  astrology 133.531
  astronomy 523.7
  religious worship 291.212
Sun bathing
  health 613.193
Sun-dried blocks
  architectural construction 721.044 22
  building construction 693.22
Sun spiders 595.48
Sun tables
  earth astronomy 525.38
Sunburn
  medicine 616.5
  see also Skin
Sunbury (N.B.) T2—715 43
Sunbury (Vic.) T2—945 2
Sunda Islands T2—598
Sunda Islands, Lesser
    (Indonesia) T2—598 6
Sundanese language 499.22
  T6—992 2
Sunday
  Christian observance 263.3
  music 781.522 2
Sunday school 268
  Jewish 296.680 83
Sunday school buildings
  administration 268.2
  architecture 726.4
Sunday work
  economics 331.257 4
Sunderland (England :
    Metropolitan Borough) T2—428 71
Sundews 583.75
Sundials
  technology 681.111 2
Sunfishes 597.738
Sunflower County (Miss.) T2—762 47
Sunflowers 583.99
  floriculture 635.933 99
Sung dynasty 951.024
Sunlight-favoring plants
  floriculture 635.954
Sunni Islam 297.81
  doctrines 297.204 1
  relations with Shia Islam 297.804 2
  worship 297.301
Sunshine Coast (B.C.) T2—711 31
Sunshine law 342.066 2
Sunspots 523.74
  geomagnetic effects 538.746
Sunwar language 495.49
  T6—954 9
Suomi language 494.541
  T6—945 41
Suomi literature 894.541
Super Bowl (Football) 796.332 648
Supercolliders 539.736
Supercomputers 004.11
  architecture 004.251
  communications 004.611
    programming 005.712 1
    programs 005.713 1
  engineering 621.391 1
  graphics programming 006.671
  graphics programs 006.681
  interfacing 004.611
    programming 005.712 1
    programs 005.713 1
  knowledge-based systems
    programming 006.337
  multimedia-systems
      programming 006.771

Supercomputers (continued)
  multimedia-systems programs 006.781
  operating systems 005.441
  performance evaluation 004.110 297
    for design and improvement 004.251
  peripherals 004.711
  programming 005.21
  programs 005.31
  systems analysis 004.251
  systems design 004.251
  see Manual at 004.11–004.16
Superconducting supercolliders 539.736
Superconductivity 537.623
  engineering 621.35
  materials science 620.112 973
Superconductor circuits 621.381 5
Superconductors 537.623
  engineering 621.35
Supercritical fluid
    chromatography 543.089 6
Supercritical gas
    chromatography 543.089 6
Superego 154.22
Superfluidity 530.42
Supergiant slalom skiing 796.935
  see also Sports
Supergravity 530.142 3
Superheaters
  nuclear reactors 621.483 4
  steam engineering 621.197
Superintendents of schools
  biography 371.200 92
  public control 379.157
  role and function 371.201 1
Superior (Wis.) T2—775 11
Superior, Lake T2—774 9
  Michigan T2—774 9
  Ontario T2—713 12
Superior courts 347.02
Superior intelligence 153.98
Supermarkets 381.148
  management 658.878
  see also Commerce
Supernatural
  occultism 133
Supernatural beings
  religious 291.211
    see also Gods and
      goddesses
  secular 398.21
    see also Legendary beings
Supernatural in arts 700.47
  T3C—37
Supernatural in literature 808.803 7
  history and criticism 809.933 7
  specific literatures T3B—080 37
    history and criticism T3B—093 7
Supernovas 523.844 65
Supersonic flow 533.275
  air mechanics 533.62
    aeronautics 629.132 305
Superstitions 001.96
  folklore 398.41
Superstring theory 539.725 8
Superstrings 539.725 8
Supersymmetry 539.725
Supertanker berthing areas 387.1
  engineering 627.22
  see also Ports
Supervised activities
  child care 649.5
Supervision of dramatic
    performances 792.023
  motion pictures 791.430 23
  radio 791.440 23
  stage 792.023
  television 791.450 23
Supervision of employees 658.302
  executive personnel 658.407
  library personnel 023.9
  military personnel 355.330 41
  public administration 352.66
Supervisors
  labor economics 331.794
  role and function 658.302
Supper 642
  cooking 641.53
  customs 394.15
Supplemental budgets (Public) 352.48
  see also Budgets (Public)
Supplies
  armed forces 355.8
  management 658.7
    armed forces 355.621
    public administration 352.55
    see Manual at 658.7 and
      T1—0687
  office services 651.29
Supply (Quantity)
  communications industry 384.041
  forecasts 338.02
    agricultural industries 338.17
    production economics 338.02
    secondary industries 338.47
  foreign exchange rate
      determination 332.456 2

Supply (Quantity) (continued)
  microeconomics 338.521 3
  natural resources 333.711
  transportation services 388.049
Supply and demand theory
  monetary economics 332.401
Supply depots (Armed forces) 355.75
Supply management 658.7
  armed forces 355.621
  public administration 352.55
  see Manual at 658.7 and T1—0687
Supply services (Armed forces) 355.621
  issuing units 355.341
Supply ships (Military) 359.985 83
  see also Military supply ships
Supply-side economics 330.15
Support (Domestic relations) 346.016 6
Supporting garments 391.42
  commercial technology 687.2
  customs 391.42
  home sewing 646.42
  see also Clothing
Suppressed books 098.1
Suppuration 571.937 9
Supranational states 321.04
Suprasegmental phonology 414.6
  specific languages T4—16
Supreme Court (U.S.) 347.732 6
Supreme court justices 347.035 092
  occupational group T7—342
Supreme Court of Judicature (Great Britain) 347.420 29
Supreme courts 347.035
Suras (Koran) 297.122 9
Surety bonds
  insurance 368.84
    see also Insurance
Suretyship 346.074
Surf riding 797.32
  see also Sports
Surface-active agents 668.1
Surface chemistry 541.33
  applied 660.293
Surface engineering 620.44
Surface finishing
  home woodworking 684.084
  wooden furniture 684.104 3
Surface integrals 515.43
Surface-mined lands 333.765
  economics 333.765
  reclamation technology 631.64
Surface mining 622.292
Surface-painted enamels
  ceramic arts 738.46
Surface physics 530.417
  liquids 530.427
  solids 530.417
Surface processes (Geology) 551.3
  see Manual at 551.302–551.307 vs. 551.35
Surface prospecting 622.12
Surface rail transit systems 388.46
  engineering 625.6
  public administration 354.769
  transportation services 388.46
Surface refinishing
  wooden furniture 684.104 43
Surface tension 541.33
  chemical engineering 660.293
  physics 530.427
Surface tillage 631.581
Surface-to-air guided missiles 358.174 82
  engineering 623.451 94
  military equipment 358.174 82
Surface-to-air missile forces 358.174
Surface-to-surface guided missiles 358.171 82
  engineering 623.451 95
  military equipment 358.171 82
Surface-to-underwater guided missiles 358.176 82
  engineering 623.451 96
  military equipment 358.176 82
Surface transportation 388
  mining 622.69
  see also Ground transportation
Surface treatment
  metals 671.7
Surface water 553.78
  T2—169
  economic geology 553.78
  hydrology 551.48
  resource economics 333.91
Surfaced lumber 674.42
Surfaces
  geometry
    algebraic 516.352
    configurations 516.15
    differential 516.36
    integral 516.362
Surfacing roads 625.8
  dirt roads 625.75
  paved roads 625.8
Surfactants 668.1

Surfers 797.320 92
sports group T7—797 3
Surfers Paradise (Qld.) T2—943 2
Surfing 797.32
see also Sports
Surgeons 617.092
law 344.041 2
malpractice 344.041 21
occupational group T7—617 1
role and function 617.023 2
Surgery 617
veterinary medicine 636.089 7
see Manual at 616 vs. 617.4; *also at* 617: Add table: 06; *also at* 617 vs. 616
Surgery (Topology) 514.72
Surgical abortion 363.46
medicine 618.88
see also Abortion
Surgical assistants
role and function 617.023 3
Surgical complications
medicine 617.01
Surgical dressings
use 617.93
Surgical gauzes 677.8
manufacturing technology 677.8
use 617.93
Surgical infections
medicine 617.01
Surgical insurance 368.382 2
see also Insurance
Surgical nursing
medicine 610.736 77
Surgical sequelae
medicine 617.01
Surgical shock
medicine 617.21
Surgical technicians
role and function 617.023 3
Surigao del Norte (Philippines) T2—599 7
Surigao del Sur (Philippines) T2—599 7
Surinam 988.3
T2—883
Suriname 988.3
Suriname (Surinam : District) T2—883 6
Surinamers T5—914 1
Surnames 929.42
Surpluses
agricultural industries 338.17
military supplies 355.621 37
Surpluses (continued)
natural resources 333.711
production 338.02
secondary industries 338.47
Surrealism
arts 700.411 63
T3C—116 3
fine arts 709.040 63
literature 808.801 163
history and criticism 809.911 63
specific literatures T3B—080 116 3
history and criticism T3B—091 163
painting 759.066 3
sculpture 735.230 463
Surrey (B.C.) T2—711 33
Surrey (England) T2—422 1
Surrey Heath (England) T2—422 13
Surrogate motherhood 306.874 3
ethics 176
religion 291.566
Christianity 241.66
see also Reproduction—ethics
law 346.017
Surry County (N.C.) T2—756 65
Surry County (Va.) T2—755 562
Surveillance
civil rights issue 323.448 2
engineering 621.389 28
law 345.052
law enforcement 363.232
Survey methodology 001.433
T1—072 3
Surveying 526.9
canal engineering 627.131
dam engineering 627.81
railroad engineering 625.11
road engineering 625.723
Surveying equipment
manufacturing technology 681.76
Surveyors 526.909 2
occupational group T7—526
Surveys
descriptive research 001.433
T1—072 3
marketing management 658.83
marketing reports 380.1
public administration of 352.75
see Manual at T1—07201–T1—07209 vs. T1—0722–T1—0724
Survival after accidents, disasters 613.69
Survival housekeeping 640.49

Survival training (Military training) 355.54
Survivors' insurance 368.3
  government-sponsored 368.43
  law 344.023
  see also Insurance
Sus 599.633 2
Susa (Extinct city) T2—35
Susanna (Deuterocanonical book) 229.6
Susliks 599.365
Suspended ceilings
  buildings 698
Suspended sentence 364.63
Suspense drama 792.27
  literature 808.825 27
    history and criticism 809.252 7
    specific literatures T3B—205 27
      individual authors T3A—2
  stage presentation 792.27
  see also Theater
Suspense stories 808.838 72
  history and criticism 809.387 2
  specific literatures T3B—308 72
    individual authors T3A—3
Suspension bridges 388
  construction 624.5
  see also Bridges
Suspension of rights 323.49
Suspensions (Chemistry) 541.34
  chemical engineering 660.294
Susquehanna County (Pa.) T2—748 34
Susquehanna River T2—748
  Maryland T2—752 74
  Pennsylvania T2—748
Susquehanna River, West Branch (Pa.) T2—748 5
Sussex (England) T2—422 5
Sussex cattle 636.222
Sussex County (Del.) T2—751 7
Sussex County (N.J.) T2—749 76
Sussex County (Va.) T2—755 565
Sustut River (B.C.) T2—711 85
Susu language 496.34
  T6—963 4
Sutherland (Scotland) T2—411 65
Sutherland (South Africa : District) T2—687 17
Sūtrapiṭaka 294.382 3
Suttapiṭaka 294.382 3
Suttee 393.9
  customs 393.9
  Hindu practice 294.538
Sutter County (Calif.) T2—794 34
Sutton (London, England) T2—421 92
Sutton County (Tex.) T2—764 879
Sutures
  surgical use 617.917 8
Suwałki (Poland : Voivodeship) T2—438 3
Suwannee County (Fla.) T2—759 82
Suwannee River (Ga. and Fla.) T2—759 8
Suwaydā' (Syria : Province) T2—569 14
Suways (Egypt : Province) T2—621 5
SV40 (Virus) 579.244 5
Svalbard (Norway) T2—981
Svan language 499.968
  T6—999 68
Svealand (Sweden) T2—487
Sverdlovsk (Russia : Oblast) T2—474 3
Sverdlovskaiâ oblast´ (Russia) T2—474 3
Svetambara (Jainism) 294.492
Swabia (Germany) T2—433 7
Swabian Alps (Germany) T2—434 73
Swabian dialect 437.37
  T6—33
Swabian Jura (Germany) T2—434 73
Swahili language 496.392
  T6—963 92
Swahili literature 896.392
Swahili-speaking peoples T5—963 92
Swain County (N.C.) T2—756 96
Swale (England) T2—422 33
Swale River (England) T2—428 48
Swallow-tanager 598.875
Swallowers (Fishes) 597.7
Swallows 598.826
Swamp eels 597.64
Swamp rats 599.35
Swamps 551.41
  see also Wetlands
Swan Hill (Vic.) T2—945 9
Swan River (W.A.) T2—941 2
Swans 598.418
  animal husbandry 636.681
Swansea (Wales) T2—429 82
Swanskin fabrics 677.624
  see also Textiles
Swarming of bees 595.799 156
  apiculture 638.146
Swartruggens (South Africa : District) T2—682 3
Swat (Pakistan) T2—549 122

Swati language 496.398 7
  T6—963 987
Swatow dialect 495.17
  T6—951 7
Swazi (Ethnic group) T5—963 987
Swazi (National group) T5—968 87
Swazi language 496.398 7
  T6—963 987
Swazi literature 896.398 7
Swaziland 968.87
  T2—688 7
Swearing
  customs 394
  ethics 179.5
Sweat glands 573.537 9
  biology 573.537 9
  human anatomy 611.77
  human physiology 612.792 1
  medicine 616.56
  see also Skin
Sweaters 391
  commercial technology 687.146
  customs 391
  home sewing 646.454
  see also Clothing
Sweden 948.5
  T2—485
  ancient 936.3
  T2—363
Swedenborgianism 289.4
  see also Christian denominations
Swedenborgians
  biography 289.409 2
  religious group T7—284
Swedes T5—397
Swedes (Plants) 641.351 26
  see also Rutabagas
Swedish language 439.7
  T6—397
Swedish literature 839.7
Swedish people T5—397
Swedish turnip 641.351 26
  see also Rutabagas
Sweep generators
  electronics 621.381 548
Sweeping
  housecleaning 648.5
Sweet bay 641.357
  botany 583.23
  see also Herbs
Sweet cider 641.341 1
  commercial processing 663.63
  cooking with 641.641 1
Sweet cider (continued)
  food 641.341 1
Sweet clovers 633.366
  botany 583.74
  forage crop 633.366
Sweet corn 641.356 72
  commercial processing 664.805 672
  cooking 641.656 72
  food 641.356 72
  garden crop 635.672
Sweet gale 583.43
Sweet Grass County (Mont.) T2—786 64
Sweet gums 583.44
  forestry 634.973 44
  ornamental arboriculture 635.977 344
Sweet herbs 641.357
  see also Herbs
Sweet peas (Flowers) 635.933 74
  botany 583.74
  floriculture 635.933 74
Sweet peppers 641.356 43
  botany 583.952
  commercial processing 664.805 643
  cooking 641.656 43
  food 641.356 43
  garden crop 635.643
Sweet potatoes 641.352 2
  agriculture 635.22
  botany 583.94
  commercial processing 664.805 22
  cooking 641.652 2
  food 641.352 2
Sweet sorghums 633.62
Sweetened condensed milk 641.371 424
  cooking 641.671 424
  food 641.371 424
  processing 637.142 4
Sweetleaf 583.674
Sweets (Candy) 641.853
  commercial processing 664.153
  home preparation 641.853
Sweets (Desserts and confections) 641.86
Sweetwater County (Wyo.) T2—787 85
Swellendam (South Africa : District) T2—687 3
Swells (Wind effects) 551.470 22
  lakes 551.482
Swift County (Minn.) T2—776 41
Swift Current (Sask.) T2—712 43
Swifts 598.762
Swimmers 797.210 92
  sports group T7—797 2

Swimming	797.21
physical fitness	613.716
see also Sports	
Swimming pools	797.2
architecture	725.74
domestic	643.55
architecture	728.962
construction	690.896 2
home economics	643.55
public	797.2
architecture	725.74
construction	690.574
sanitation services	363.729 2
see also Waste control	
Swine	636.4
see also Pigs	
Swing (Golf)	796.352 3
Swing (Music)	781.654
Swing bridges	388
construction	624.83
see also Bridges	
Swing drawbridges	388
construction	624.83
see also Bridges	
Swisher County (Tex.)	T2—764 838
Swiss	T5—35
Swiss cheese	641.373 54
cooking	641.673 54
food	641.373 54
processing	637.354
Swiss-German dialect	437.949 4
	T6—35
Swiss Germans	T5—35
Swiss literature	
French	840
German	830
Italian	850
Switchboard operators	
office services	651.374 3
Switchboards	
communications services	384.65
telephony	621.387
Switches	
electrical engineering	621.317
interior wiring	621.319 24
railroad engineering	625.163
telephony	621.387
Switching	
communications engineering	621.382 16
computer communications	004.66
engineering	621.398 1
computer engineering	621.395
telephone engineering	621.385 7
Switching circuits	
electronics	621.381 537
Switching equipment	
electrical engineering	621.317
Switching theory	
electronics	621.381 537 2
Switzerland	949.4
	T2—494
ancient	936.4
	T2—364
Switzerland County (Ind.)	T2—772 125
Swivel bridges	388
construction	624.83
see also Bridges	
Swivel embroidery	677.77
Sword dances	793.35
Sword fighting	796.86
see also Sports	
Sword lilies	635.934 38
botany	584.38
floriculture	635.934 38
Swordfish	597.78
Swordplay	796.86
see also Sports	
Swords	623.441
art metalwork	739.722
Swordtail (Fish)	597.667
Sycamores	583.44
forestry	634.973 44
ornamental arboriculture	635.977 344
Sydney (N.S.W.)	T2—944 1
Syenite	553.52
economic geology	553.52
petrology	552.3
quarrying	622.352
Syllabaries	411
specific languages	T4—11
Syllabi (Outlines)	T1—020 2
Syllogisms	166
Sylviidae	598.843
Sylvilagus	599.324
Sylvite	
mineralogy	549.4
Symbiosis	577.85
animals	591.785
factor in evolution	576.85
plants	581.785
Symbolic divination	133.33
Symbolic logic	511.3
computer programming	
languages	005.131
Symbolic programming	005.1
Symbolism	302.222 3
art representation	704.946

Symbolism (continued)
  arts 700.415
    T3C—15
  literature 808.801 5
    history and criticism 809.915
    specific literatures T3B—080 15
      history and criticism T3B—091 5
  of divinatory arts 133.3
  paintings 753.6
  religious significance 291.37
    Buddhism 294.343 7
    Christianity 246.55
    Hinduism 294.537
    Islam 297.3
    Judaism 296.46
  social psychology 302.222 3
Symbolism (Art style) 709.034 7
  painting 759.057
Symbolism in the Bible 220.64
Symbolism in the Talmud 296.120 64
Symbolism of numbers 133.335
Symbols 302.222 3
    T1—014 8
  cultural institutions 306.4
  linguistics 411
    specific languages T4—11
  social psychology 302.222 3
Symmetallic standards 332.424
Symmetric functions 515.22
Symmetry
  arts 701.8
Symmetry (Nuclear physics) 539.725
Sympathetic nervous system
  human physiology 612.89
  medicine 616.88
  see also Nervous system
Sympathetic strikes 331.892 3
Symphonic poems 784.184 3
  musical form 784.184 3
  orchestral music 784.218 43
Symphonies 784.184
  musical form 784.184
  orchestral music 784.218 4
Symphonions 786.65
  see also Mechanical musical instruments
Symphony orchestras 784.2
Symphyla 595.63
Symphyseotomy
  obstetrical surgery 618.85
Symphysodon 597.74
Symphyta 595.79
Symplocaceae 583.674
Symptomatology 616.047
Symptoms
  medicine 616.047
Synagogue dedication 296.446
  liturgy 296.454 6
Synagogues 296.65
  architecture 726.3
  history of specific congregations 296.09
  organization 296.65
  religious symbolism of buildings 296.46
Synapsida 567.93
Synbranchiformes 597.64
Syncarida 595.379
Synchro-cyclotrons 539.735
Synchronic linguistics 410
  see Manual at 410
Synchronized swimming 797.217
  see also Sports
Synchronous accelerators 539.735
Synchronous converters 621.313 5
Synchronous generators 621.313 4
Synchronous machinery 621.313 3
Synchronous transfer modes
  communications engineering 621.382 16
  computer communications 004.66
    engineering 621.398 1
Synchroscopes 621.374 9
Synchrotrons 539.735
Synclines 551.86
Syncretism
  philosophy 148
Syndetic structure 025.322 2
  name and title authorities 025.322 2
  subject authorities 025.49
Syndicalism 335.82
  economics 335.82
  political ideology 320.53
  sociology 306.347
Syndicated crime 364.106 8
Syndicates
  banking 332.16
  real estate investment 332.632 47
  unincorporated business enterprises 338.7
    see also Unincorporated business enterprises
Synecology 577.8
  animals 591.78
  microorganisms 579.178
  plants 581.78
Synesthesia
  psychology 152.189
Syngnathidae 597.679

Synod of Bishops 262.136
Synod of Evangelical Lutheran Churches 284.132 3
see also Lutheran church
Synodontidae 597.61
Synods
Christian ecclesiology 262.4
Synonym dictionaries 413.1
specific languages T4—31
specific subjects T1—03
Synopses T1—020 2
music 780
treatises 780.269
vocal music
treatises 782.002 69
Synoptic Gospels 226
Synoptic problem (Gospels) 226.066
Syntax 415
specific languages T4—5
Synthesis
chemical engineering 660.284 4
chemistry 541.39
organic chemistry 547.2
Synthesizers 786.74
instrument 786.741 9
music 786.74
see also Electrophones
Synthetic building materials 666.89
Synthetic chemicals
organic 661.805
Synthetic drugs
pharmacology 615.31
Synthetic drugs of abuse 362.299
personal health 613.8
social welfare 362.299
see also Substance abuse
Synthetic dyes 667.25
Synthetic fuels 662.66
Synthetic gems 666.88
Synthetic glue 668.31
Synthetic meat 664.64
Synthetic minerals 666.86
Synthetic petroleum 662.662
Synthetic textile fibers 677.4
Synthetism 709.034 7
painting 759.057
Syphilis
incidence 614.547 2
medicine 616.951 3
see also Communicable diseases (Human)
Syracuse (N.Y.) T2—747 66
Syracuse (Sicily) T2—458 14
ancient T2—378
Syracuse (Sicily : Province) T2—458 14
Syria 956.91
T2—569 1
ancient 939.43
T2—394 3
Syriac language 492.3
T6—923
Biblical texts 220.43
Syriac literature 892.3
Syrian Desert T2—569
Iraq T2—567 4
Jordan T2—569 59
Saudi Arabia T2—538
Syria T2—569 12
Syrian Orthodox Church 281.63
see also Eastern churches
Syrians T5—927 569 1
Syrians (Religious order) 255.18
church history 271.18
Syringas 583.72
Syro-Malabar Christians 281.5
see also Eastern churches
Syrphidae 595.774
Syrup crops 633.6
Syrups 641.336
commercial processing 664.1
cooking with 641.636
Syrups (Pharmaceuticals)
practical pharmacy 615.42
Systellommatophora 594.38
System administration (Computer science) 005.43
System identification 003.1
Systematic bibliography 010.44
Systematics (Biology) 578.012
Système international 530.812
social aspects 389.15
Systemic lupus erythematosus
medicine 616.77
see also Musculoskeletal system
Systems 003
T1—011
see Manual at 003.7; also at 510, T1—0151 vs. 003, T1—011
Systems analysis 003
computer science 004.21
T1—028 542 1
engineering 621.392
software 005.12
see Manual at 004.21 vs. 004.22, 621.392

Systems analysis (continued)
management 658.403 2
public administration 352.33
military administration 355.683
see Manual at 003; *also at* 003 vs. 004.21
Systems analysts 003.092
occupational group T7—090 3
Systems control 003.5
Systems design 003
computer science 004.21
engineering 621.392
software 005.12
see Manual at 004.21 vs. 004.22, 621.392
see Manual at 003 vs. 004.21
Systems engineering 620.001 171
Systems engineers 620.009 2
occupational group T7—62
Systems of government 321
Systems optimization 003
Systems programming 005.42
see Manual at 005.1–005.2 vs. 005.42
Systems programs 005.43
see Manual at 005.3 vs. 005.43–005.45
Systems stability 003.5
Systems theory 003
management 658.403 2
Szabolcs-Szatmár Megye (Hungary) T2—439 9
Szczecin (Poland : Voivodeship) T2—438 1
Szechwan Province (China) T2—513 8
Szolnok Megye (Hungary) T2—439 8
Szondi tests 155.284 3

T

T cells 571.966
human immunology 616.079 7
T formation 796.332 22
T lymphocytes 571.966
humans 616.079 7
Ta'anit (Tractate) 296.123 2
Babylonian Talmud 296.125 2
Mishnah 296.123 2
Palestinian Talmud 296.124 2
Tabanidae 595.773
Tabasaran language 499.964
T6—999 64
Tabasco (Mexico : State) T2—726 3
Tabby
building construction 693.22
Tabernacles
Christian church furniture 247.1
architecture 726.529 1
Judaism 296.49
Tabes dorsalis
medicine 616.838
see also Nervous system
Tablas 786.93
see also Percussion instruments
Tablature 780.148
Table decorations 642.8
Table furnishings 642.7
Table linens 642.7
arts 746.96
home sewing 646.21
table setting 642.7
Table manners 395.54
Table Mountain (Cape of Good Hope, South Africa) T2—687 355
Table salt
cooking with 641.6
see also Salt (Sodium chloride)
Table service 642.6
Table setting 642.6
Table tennis 796.346
see also Sports
Table tennis players 796.346 092
sports group T7—796 34
Table tipping (Spiritualism) 133.92
Tableaux 793.24
Tablecloths 642.7
arts 746.96
home sewing 646.21
table setting 642.7
Tables (Furniture) 645.4
decorative arts 749.3
manufacturing technology 684.13
outdoor 645.8
see also Outdoor furniture
see also Furniture
Tables (Lists) T1—021
Tabletop photography 778.8
Tablets
practical pharmacy 615.43
Tableware 642.7
earthenware 666.68
arts 738.38
technology 666.68

Tableware (continued)
glass
arts 748.83
gold
arts 739.228 3
handicrafts 745.593
ironwork
arts 739.48
porcelain 666.58
arts 738.28
technology 666.58
pottery 666.3
arts 738
technology 666.3
silver
arts 739.238 3
table setting 642.7
wood
arts 736.4
Taboos 390
Tabora Region (Tanzania) T2—678 28
Tabulated materials T1—021
Tacanan languages 498
T6—98
Taccaceae 584.35
Tachinid flies 595.774
Tachinidae 595.774
Táchira (Venezuela) T2—871 2
Tachometers
technology 681.118
Tachyglossidae 599.29
Tackles (Mechanisms) 621.863
Tackling
American football 796.332 26
Tacna (Peru : Dept.) T2—853 5
Tacoma (Wash.) T2—797 788
Tactical exercises (Military training) 355.54
Tactical geography 355.47
Tactical missile forces 358.175 2
Tactical rockets 355.825 43
engineering 623.454 3
military equipment 355.825 43
Tactics (Military science) 355.42
Tactile organs
human anatomy 611.88
human physiology 612.88
see also Nervous system
Tactile perception
psychology 152.182
Tacuarembó (Uruguay : Dept.) T2—895 32
Tadpole shrimps 595.32
Tadpoles 597.813 9
Tadzhik T5—915 7
Tadzhik language 491.57
T6—915 7
Tadzhik literature 891.57
Tadzhikistan 958.6
T2—586
Taeniodontia 569.31
Taeniopteris 561.597
Taff-Ely (Wales) T2—429 78
Ṭafīlah (Jordan : Province) T2—569 567
Taft, William H. (William Howard)
United States history 973.912
Tagalog language 499.211
T6—992 11
Tagalog literature 899.211
Tagus River (Spain and Portugal) T2—469 45
Portugal T2—469 45
Spain T2—462 8
Tahiti T2—962 11
Tahitian language 499.444
T6—994 44
Tahitian literature 899.444
Tahitians T5—994 44
Tahitic languages 499.44
T6—994 4
Tahoe, Lake (Calif. and Nev.) T2—794 38
California T2—794 38
Nevada T2—793 57
Tai chi 613.714 8
T'ai chi ch'üan 613.714 8
Tai languages 495.91
T6—959 1
Tai literatures 895.91
Tai peoples T5—959 1
Taigas
biology 578.737
ecology 577.37
Tailless whip scorpions 595.453 6
Tailoring 646.4
commercial technology 687.044
home sewing 646.4
Tailors 646.400 92
commercial 687.044 092
occupational group T7—687
occupational group T7—646 4
Taĭmyr (Russia : Okrug) T2—575
Taĭmyrskiĭ avtonomnyĭ okrug (Russia) T2—575
Taino Indians T5—979
Taiping Rebellion, 1850–1864 951.034
Taishō period 952.032

Taita language 496.395
T6—963 95
Taiwan 951.249
T2—512 49
Taiwan native peoples T5—992 5
Taiwan Strait 551.465 57
T2—164 57
Taiwanese dialect 495.17
T6—951 7
Tajik T5—915 7
Tajik language 491.57
T6—915 7
Tajik literature 891.57
Tajikistan 958.6
T2—586
Tajwīd 297.122 404 5
Tāk Sin, King of Siam
  Thai history 959.302 4
Takapuna (N.Z.) T2—932 2
Take-overs 338.83
  see also Mergers
Takeoff
  aeronautics 629.132 521 2
  manned space flight 629.452
  space flight 629.41
  unmanned space flight 629.432
Takeoff accidents 363.124 92
  see also Air safety
Taki-Taki 427.988 3
T6—217
Takla Lake (B.C.) T2—711 82
Talbot County (Ga.) T2—758 483
Talbot County (Md.) T2—752 32
Talc 553.676
  economic geology 553.676
  mineralogy 549.67
  mining 622.367 6
  technology 666.72
Talca (Chile : Province) T2—833 5
Talented persons 305.908 29
T1—087 9
T7—082 9
Taliaferro County (Ga.) T2—758 616
Talismans 133.44
  Islamic popular practices 297.39
  numismatics 737.23
  religious significance 291.37
    see also Symbolism—religious significance
Talk shows 791.446
  radio programs 791.446
  television programs 791.456
Talking books
  bibliographies 011.38
Tall buildings 720.483
  architectural construction 721.042
  architecture 720.483
  construction 690
  fire hazards 363.379
    see also Fire safety
Tall oil
  recovery from pulp 676.5
Talladega County (Ala.) T2—761 61
Tallahassee (Fla.) T2—759 88
Tallahatchie County (Miss.) T2—762 455
Tallapoosa County (Ala.) T2—761 53
Tallapoosa River (Ga. and Ala.) T2—761 5
Tallit 296.461
Tallow 665.2
Tallow tree 583.69
Talmud 296.12
Talmud Bavli 296.125
Talmud Yerushalmi 296.124
Talmudic literature 296.12
Talmudic period 956.940 2
Talpidae 599.335
Tama County (Iowa) T2—777 56
Tamang language 495.4
T6—954
Tamanrasset (Algeria : Province) T2—657
Tamar River (England) T2—423 5
Tamar River (Tas.) T2—946 5
Tamaracks 585.2
  see also Larches
Tamaricales 583.628
Tamarind 641.344 6
  botany 583.74
  cooking 641.644 6
  food 641.344 6
  orchard crop 634.46
Tamarins 599.84
  conservation technology 639.979 84
  resource economics 333.959 84
Tamarisk 583.628
Tamashek language 493.38
T6—933 8
Tamashek literature 893.38
Tamaulipas (Mexico) T2—721 2
Tamazight language 493.33
T6—933 3
Tamazight literature 893.33
Tambourines 786.95
  see also Percussion instruments
Tambov (Russia : Oblast) T2—473 5

Tambovskaia oblast′ (Russia) T2—473 5
Tamburas 787.82
  see also Stringed instruments
Tamerlane
  Asian history 950.2
Tameside (England) T2—427 35
Tamiasciurus 599.363
Tamid 296.123 5
  Mishnah 296.123 5
  Palestinian Talmud 296.124 5
Tamil T5—948 11
Tamil language 494.811
  T6—948 11
Tamil literature 894.811
Tamil Nadu (India) T2—548 2
Ta'mim (Iraq : Province) T2—567 4
Tampa (Fla.) T2—759 65
Tamworth (England) T2—424 69
Tamworth (N.S.W.) T2—944 4
Tan-Tan (Morocco : Province) T2—646
Tanagers 598.875
Tanaidacea 595.374
Tanakh 221
  see Manual at 221
Tandem bicycles
  engineering 629.227 6
  repair 629.287 76
  riding 629.284 76
Tandridge (England : District) T2—422 18
Taney County (Mo.) T2—778 797
T'ang dynasty 951.017
Tanga Region (Tanzania) T2—678 22
Tanganyika 967.82
  T2—678 2
Tanganyika, Lake T2—678 28
Tangible property risks 368.062
Tangier (Morocco : Province) T2—642
Tangipahoa Parish (La.) T2—763 13
Tangkhul language 495.4
  T6—954
Tangos 793.33
  music 784.188 85
Tank cars 385.34
  engineering 625.24
  see also Rolling stock
Tank warfare 358.18
Tankers (Ships) 387.245
  engineering 623.824 5
  petroleum technology 665.543
  see also Ships
Tanks (Containers)
  water supply engineering 628.13
Tanks (Vehicles) 358.188 3
  engineering 623.747 52
  military equipment 358.188 3
Tannaim 296.120 092
Tanners 675.230 92
  occupational group T7—675
Tanning leather 675.23
Tannins 572.567
  agricultural production 633.87
  biochemistry 572.567
  see also Carbohydrates
Tano languages 496.338 5
  T6—963 385
Tanoan languages 497.49
  T6—974 9
Tantalum 669.735
  chemical engineering 661.052 6
  chemistry 546.526
  economic geology 553.465
  materials science 620.189 35
  metallography 669.957 35
  metallurgy 669.735
  metalworking 673.735
  physical metallurgy 669.967 35
  see also Chemicals; Metals
Tantras
  Buddhist 294.385
  Hindu 294.595
Tantric Buddhism 294.392 5
Tantric Hinduism 294.551 4
Tanzania 967.8
  T2—678
Tanzanians T5—967 8
Taoism
  art representation 704.948 995 14
  arts T3C—382 995 14
  philosophy 181.114
  religion 299.514
Taoist holidays
  customs 394.265 951 4
  see also Holidays
Taoist philosophy 181.114
Taoists
  philosophy 181.114
  religion 299.514 092
  religious group T7—299 514
Taos County (N.M.) T2—789 53
Taos Indians T5—974 9
Taounate (Morocco : Province) T2—643
Tap dancing 792.78
  see also Theater

Tapas 641.812
Tape drives (Computer)
  computer science 004.56
  engineering 621.397 6
Tape players
  automobile 629.277
  sound reproduction 621.389 324
Tape recorders
  automobile 629.277
  sound reproduction 621.389 324
Tape recordings
  sound reproduction 621.389 324
Tapes (Adhesives) 668.38
Tapes (Computer)
  computer science 004.56
  engineering 621.397 6
Tapes (Recording devices) 621.382 34
Tapes (Sound) 384
  bibliographies 011.38
  see also Sound recordings
Tapes (Textiles) 677.76
Tapestries 677.64
  manufacturing technology 677.64
  textile arts 746.3
Tapestry makers 746.392
Tapestry-woven rugs
  arts 746.72
  see also Rugs
Tapestry yard goods 677.642
Tapeworm-caused diseases
  incidence 614.554
  medicine 616.964
  see also Communicable diseases (Human)
Tapeworms 592.46
Taphrinales 579.562
Tapia
  building construction 693.22
Tapioca 641.336 82
  cooking 641.636 82
  food 641.336 82
Tapiridae 599.66
Tapirs 599.66
Tapping tools 621.955
Taproom buildings
  architecture 725.72
Taps (Valves) 621.84
Tar
  materials science 620.196
Tar pavements 625.85
Tar sands 553.283
  economic geology 553.283
  mining 622.338 3
    law 343.077 2
Tar sands (continued)
  processing 665.4
Taraba State (Nigeria) T2—669 89
Tarahumara Indians T5—974 5
Taranaki (N.Z.) T2—934 8
Taranaki Region (N.Z.) T2—934 8
Taranto (Italy : Province) T2—457 55
Taranto, Gulf of (Italy) 551.462 6
  T2—163 86
Tarapacá (Chile : Region) T2—831 2
Tararua District (N.Z.) T2—935 7
  Manawatu-Wanganui Region T2—935 7
  Wellington Region T2—936 9
Tarascan Indians T5—97
Tarascan language 497
  T6—97
Tarasco Indians T5—97
Tarasco language 497
  T6—97
Tardigrada 592.72
Tardive dyskinesia
  medicine 616.83
  see also Nervous system
Taree (N.S.W.) T2—944 2
Tarf (Algeria : Province) T2—655
Target selection
  military gunnery 623.557
Target shooting 799.3
  see also Sports
Targets
  shooting sports 799.3
    manufacturing technology 688.793
Targums 221.42
Tariff 382.7
  see also Customs (Tariff)
Tarija (Bolivia : Dept.) T2—842 5
Tarka (South Africa : District) T2—687 14
Tarlac (Philippines : Province) T2—599 1
Tarn (France) T2—448 5
Tarn-et-Garonne (France) T2—447 5
Tarnobrzeg (Poland : Voivodeship) T2—438 4
Tarnów (Poland : Voivodeship) T2—438 6
Taro 641.336 8
  botany 584.64
  cooking 641.636 8
  food 641.336 8
  starch crop 633.68
Tarot 133.324 24

Taroudant (Morocco : Province) T2—646
Tarpons 597.43
 sports fishing 799.174 3
Tarraconensis T2—366
Tarragon 641.357
Tarragona (Spain : Province) T2—467 3
Tarrant County (Tex.) T2—764 531
Tarsals
 human anatomy 611.718
 see also Musculoskeletal system
Tarsiers 599.83
Tarsiidae 599.83
Tarsipedidae 599.23
Tartans
 heraldry 929.6
Tarts 641.865 2
 commercial processing 664.752 5
 home preparation 641.865 2
Ṭarṭūs (Syria : Province) T2—569 13
Taseko River (B.C.) T2—711 75
Task forces (Naval units) 359.31
Tasman District (N.Z.) T2—937 7
 Nelson-Marlborough Region T2—937 7
 West Coast Region T2—937 4
Tasman Peninsula (Tas.) T2—946 4
Tasman Sea 551.465 78
 T2—164 78
Tasmania T2—946
Tasmanian aborigines T5—991 5
Tasmanian cedar 585.5
Tasmanian devil 599.27
Tasmanian languages 499.15
 T6—991 5
Tasmanian tiger 599.27
Tasmanian wolf 599.27
Taste 573.878
 animal physiology 573.878
 human physiology 612.87
Taste (Aesthetics)
 music 781.17
Taste buds 573.878
Taste disorders
 medicine 616.87
 see also Nervous system
Taste perception
 psychology 152.167
Tata (Morocco : Province) T2—646
Tatar Empire 950.2
 T2—5
Tatar language 494.387
 T6—943 87
 Crimean 494.388
 T6—943 88
Tatar literature 894.387
 Crimean 894.388
Tatar Strait (Russia) 551.465 54
 T2—164 54
Tatar suzerainty
 Russian history 947.03
Tatars T5—943 87
 Crimean T5—943 88
Tatarstan (Russia) T2—474 5
Tate County (Miss.) T2—762 85
Tatted fabrics 677.663
 see also Textiles
Tatting
 arts 746.436
Tattnall County (Ga.) T2—758 775
Tattooing
 customs 391.65
Taung (South Africa : District) T2—682 94
Taunton Deane (England : District) T2—423 87
Taunus (Germany) T2—434 16
Taupo, Lake (N.Z.) T2—933 9
Taupo District (N.Z.) T2—933 9
 Bay of Plenty Region T2—934 24
 Hawke's Bay Region T2—934 63
 Manawatu-Wanganui Region T2—935 13
 Waikato Region T2—933 9
Tauranga District (N.Z.) T2—934 21
Taurus (Zodiac) 133.526 3
Taurus Mountains (Turkey) T2—564
Tautomerism 547.122 52
 inorganic chemistry 541.225 2
 organic chemistry 547.122 52
Tawhid 297.211 3
Tawi-Tawi (Philippines) T2—599 9
Tawitawi (Philippines) T2—599 9
Tax accounting 657.46
 law 343.042
  income tax 343.052 044
Tax administration 352.44
 law 343.04
 see Manual at 343.04 vs. 336.2, 352.44
Tax appeals
 law 343.042

Tax assessment 336.2
  law 343.042
    income tax 343.052 042
    property tax 343.054 2
  public administration 352.44
  public finance 336.2
Tax auditing
  law 343.04
Tax avoidance 336.206
  law 343.04
  public finance 336.206
Tax collection 352.44
  law 343.042
Tax credits 336.206
  income tax law 343.052 37
  public finance 336.206
Tax deductions 336.206
  income tax law 343.052 3
  public finance 336.206
Tax evasion 364.133
  law 345.023 3
Tax-exempt organizations
  law 343.066
Tax-exempt securities
  law 346.092 2
Tax exemption 336.206
  income tax law 343.052 3
  property tax law 343.054 3
  public finance 336.206
Tax expenditures 336.206
Tax incentives 336.206
  income tax law 343.052 304
  public finance 336.206
Tax incidence 336.294
Tax law 343.04
  see Manual at 343.04 vs.
    336.2, 352.44
Tax limitations
  law 343.034
Tax lists
  genealogy 929.3
Tax loopholes 336.206
Tax planning
  law 343.04
    income tax 343.052
Tax rebates 336.206
Tax reduction 336.206
  income tax law 343.052 3
  public finance 336.206
Tax reform 336.205
Tax returns
  income tax law 343.052 044
Tax shelters 336.206
  income tax law 343.052 38
Tax shelters (continued)
  investment economics 332.604 2
  public finance 336.206
Taxales 585.6
  paleobotany 561.56
Taxation 336.2
  see also Taxes
Taxes 336.2
  accounting 657.46
  financial management 658.153
  international law 341.484 4
  law 343.04
  macroeconomic policy 339.525
  public administration 352.44
    litigation 353.43
  public finance 336.2
  see Manual at 336.2009 vs.
    336.201; *also at* 343.04
    vs. 336.2, 352.44
Taxicab drivers 388.413 214 092
  occupational group T7—388
Taxicab service 388.413 214
  law 343.098 2
  public administration 354.765 3
  transportation services 388.413 214
Taxicabs 388.342 32
  driving 629.283 32
  engineering 629.222 32
  repair 629.287 232
  transportation services 388.342 32
  see also Automobiles
Taxidermy 590.752
Taxodiaceae 585.5
  paleobotany 561.55
Taxonomic nomenclature 578.014
  see Manual at 579–590
Taxonomy (Biology) 578.012
Tay River (Scotland) T2—412 8
Tay-Sachs disease
  medicine 616.858 845
  see also Mental retardation
Tayassuidae 599.634
Taylor, Zachary
  United States history 973.63
Taylor County (Fla.) T2—759 86
Taylor County (Ga.) T2—758 493
Taylor County (Iowa) T2—777 79
Taylor County (Ky.) T2—769 673
Taylor County (Tex.) T2—764 727
Taylor County (W. Va.) T2—754 55
Taylor County (Wis.) T2—775 26
Tayside (Scotland) T2—412 5
Taza (Morocco : Province) T2—643
Tazewell County (Ill.) T2—773 54

Tazewell County (Va.) T2—755 763
TCA cycle 572.475
Te Anau, Lake (N.Z.) T2—939 6
Tea 641.337 2
  agricultural economics 338.173 72
  agriculture 633.72
  botany 583.624
  commercial processing
    economics 338.476 639 4
    technology 663.94
  cooking with 641.637 2
  food 641.337 2
  home preparation 641.877
Tea (Meal) 642
  cooking 641.53
  customs 394.15
Tea Act, 1773
  United States history 973.311 5
Tea leaves
  divination 133.324 4
Teacher-administrator relations 371.106
Teacher aides 371.141 24
Teacher burnout 371.100 19
Teacher certification 371.12
Teacher-community relations 306.432
  education 371.19
  sociology 306.432
Teacher education 370.711
Teacher evaluation 371.144
Teacher exchanges 370.116 3
  international law 341.767 3
Teacher morale 371.100 19
Teacher-parent conferences 371.103
Teacher-parent relations 371.192
Teacher participation in
    administration 371.106
Teacher qualifications 371.12
  higher education 378.124
Teacher-staff relations 371.106
Teacher-student relations 371.102 3
Teacher training 370.711
  T1—071 1
Teacher turnover 371.14
Teachers 371.1
  biography 371.100 92
  higher education 378.12
  law 344.078
  occupational group T7—372
  public control 379.157
  religious educators 291.750 92
    Christian 268.092
      biography 268.092
        see Manual at 230–280
      role and function 268.3
Teachers
  religious educators (continued)
    Jewish 296.680 92
      biography 296.680 92
      role and function 296.68
  role in guidance 371.404 6
  workload 371.141 2
    higher education 378.122 12
Teachers' assistants 371.141 24
Teachers' colleges 370.711
Teaching 371.102
  T1—071
  educational psychology 370.15
  higher education 378.125
  law 344.078
  professional education 370.711
  special education 371.904 3
Teaching (Spiritual gift) 234.13
Teaching aids 371.33
  T1—078
Teaching load 371.141 2
  higher education 378.122 12
Teaching machines 371.334
  T1—078 5
  adult education 374.26
Teaching materials 371.33
  see also Instructional materials
Teaching methods 371.3
  elementary education 372.13
  personnel training 658.312 404
  religious education 291.75
    Christianity 268.6
  special education 371.904 3
Teaching office of the church 262.8
Teaching orders (Christianity) 255.03
  church history 271.03
  women 255.903
    church history 271.903
Teachings of Jesus Christ 232.954
Teak
  botany 583.96
  forestry 634.973 96
  lumber 674.144
Team management 658.402
  see also Work teams
Team teaching 371.148
Teamsters 388.324 092
Tear ducts
  human physiology 612.847
  see also Eyes
Tear gas
  military engineering 623.459 2
Tear-gas canister launchers 623.445
Teasels 583.92

Tébessa (Algeria :
  Province) T2—655
Technetium
  chemical engineering 661.054 3
  chemistry 546.543
  see also Chemicals
Technical assistance
  economics 338.91
  international law 341.759
  public finance 336.185
Technical chemistry 660
Technical drawing 604.2
  T1—022 1
Technical education T1—071
Technical high schools 373.246
  see also Secondary education
Technical libraries 026.6
Technical processing (Libraries) 025.02
Technical reports
  cataloging 025.343 6
  library treatment 025.173 6
  see Manual at 300 vs. 600:
    Technical reports
Technical training 607
  armed forces 355.56
Technical writing 808.066
Technological archaeology 609
Technological innovations
  agricultural industries 338.16
  cause of social change 303.483
    see Manual at 303.48 vs.
      306.4; *also at* 303.483
      vs. 306.45, 306.46
  economics 338.064
  mineral industries 338.26
Technological instruments
  manufacturing technology 681.76
Technological unemployment 331.137 042
Technologists 609.2
  occupational group T7—6
  works for T1—024 6
    see Manual at T1—015 vs.
      T1—0245–T1—0246
Technology 600
  art representation 704.949 6
  arts 700.456
  T3C—356
  elementary education 372.358
  folklore 398.2
    history and criticism 398.356
  law 344.095
Technology (continued)
  literature 808.803 56
    history and criticism 809.933 56
    specific literatures T3B—080 356
      history and criticism T3B—093 56
  production management 658.514
  public administrative support 352.745
  social effects 303.483
    see Manual at 303.48 vs.
      306.4; *also at* 303.483
      vs. 306.45, 306.46
  sociology 306.46
    see Manual at 303.48 vs.
      306.4; *also at* 303.483
      vs. 306.45, 306.46
  see Manual at 300 vs. 600;
    also at 500 vs. 600
Technology and religion 291.175
  Christianity 261.56
  Islam 297.266
  Judaism 296.376
  philosophy of religion 215
Technology assessment 303.483
  economic development 338.9
    public administration 354.27
  health services potential 362.104 2
  natural resources impact 333.714
    see also Environmental
      impact studies
  safety risk 363.1
  social change potential 303.483
Technology transfer 338.926
  economics 338.926
  international law 341.759
  law 343.074
Tecophilaeaceae 584.35
Tectibranchia 594.37
Tectonics 551.8
Tectosilicates
  mineralogy 549.68
Teddy bears
  making 688.724 3
    handicrafts 745.592 43
    technology 688.724 3
Teenage boys T1—083 51
Teenage fathers 306.874 2
Teenage girls T1—083 52
Teenage mothers 306.874 3
Teenage pregnancy
  obstetrics 618.200 835
Teenagers 305.235
  T1—083 5
  T7—055
  see also Adolescents

Tees River (England) T2—428 5
Teesdale (England : District) T2—428 61
Teesside (England) T2—428 5
Teeth 591.4
  animal physiology 573.356
  anthropometry 599.943
  descriptive zoology 591.4
  human anatomy 611.314
  human diseases
    dentistry 617.63
    incidence 614.599 6
  human physiology 612.311
  see also Dentistry
Tefillin 296.461 2
Tegucigalpa (Honduras) T2—728 371
Tehama County (Calif.) T2—794 27
Teheran (Iran) T2—552 5
Tehran (Iran) T2—552 5
Tehran (Iran : Province) T2—552 5
Tehuantepec, Gulf of (Mexico) 551.466 1
  T2—164 1
Tehuantepec Canal 386.447
Teichmüller spaces 515.94
Teignbridge (England : District) T2—423 55
Teignmouth, John Shore, Baron
  Indian history 954.031 1
Teke languages 496.396
  T6—963 96
Tekirdağ İli (Turkey) T2—496 1
Tekrur (Kingdom) 966.301
  T2—663
Tel Aviv (Israel : District) T2—569 48
Telangiectasis
  medicine 616.148
  see also Cardiovascular system
Telangitis
  medicine 616.148
  see also Cardiovascular system
Telecommunication 384
  accounting 657.84
  communications services 384
  engineering 621.382
  international law 341.757 7
  law 343.099 4
  public administration 354.75
Telecommunication workers 384.092
  occupational group T7—384
Telecommuting
  labor economics 331.25
  personnel management 658.312
Teleconferencing
  instructional use 371.358
Telecontrol
  engineering 620.46
  radio engineering 621.384 196
Telefacsimile 384.14
  engineering 621.382 35
  see also Facsimile transmission
Telefax 384.14
  engineering 621.382 35
  see also Facsimile transmission
Telegraphy 384.1
  communications services 384.1
  engineering 621.383
  international law 341.757 7
  law 343.099 42
  military engineering 623.732
  nautical engineering 623.856 2
  public administration 354.75
  sociology 302.235
Telegraphy stations
  communications industry 384.15
Telemark fylke (Norway) T2—482 8
Telemarketing 381.1
  management 658.84
  see also Commerce
Teleology 124
  philosophy 124
  philosophy of religion 210
Teleorman (Romania) T2—498 2
Teleostei 597
  see also Fishes
Telepathists 133.820 92
  occupational group T7—13
Telepathy 133.82
Telephone 384.6
  communications services 384.6
  engineering 621.385
  international law 341.757 7
  law 343.099 43
  military engineering 623.733
  public administration 354.75
  sociology 302.235
Telephone answering machines
  engineering 621.386 7
  office services 651.73
Telephone books 910.25
Telephone calls 384.64
  wireless 384.534
  see also Telephone
Telephone counseling 361.06

Telephone engineers 621.385 092
  occupational group T7—621 3
Telephone etiquette 395.59
Telephone lines
  communications services 384.65
Telephone-order houses 381.142
  management 658.872
  see also Commerce
Telephone selling 381.1
  management 658.84
  see also Commerce
Telephone services 384.64
  wire 384.64
  wireless 384.534
Telephone stations
  communications services 384.65
  wireless 384.535
Telephones 621.386
  automobile 629.277
  office services 651.73
Telephony 384.6
  see also Telephone
Telephotography 778.322
Telescopes 522.2
  astronomy 522.2
  manufacturing technology 681.412 3
Teletex 004.692
  communications services 384.34
    see Manual at 384.34 vs. 384.352
  see also Computer communications
Teletext 004.69
  communications services 384.352
    see Manual at 384.34 vs. 384.352
  see also Computer communications
Teletype 384.14
  wireless 384.524
  see also Telegraphy
Television 384.55
  accounting 657.84
  communications services 384.55
  engineering 621.388
  ethics 175
    religion 291.565
      Christianity 241.65
  influence on crime 364.254
  instructional use 371.335 8
    adult level 374.26
    T1—071 5
  international law 341.757 7
  journalism 070.195
Television (continued)
  law 343.099 46
  military engineering 623.735
  performing arts 791.45
    sociology 306.485
    see Manual at 384.54, 384.55, 384.8 vs. 791.4; *also at* 791.43, 791.45 vs. 778.5
  public administration 354.75
  religion 291.175
    Christianity 261.52
      evangelism 269.26
      preaching 251.07
      use by local Christian church 253.78
        administration 254.3
  sociology 302.234 5
Television advertising 659.143
Television broadcasting 384.55
  see also Television
  see Manual at 384.54, 384.55, 384.8 vs. 791.4
Television dinners
  commercial processing 664.65
  home serving 642.1
Television drama
  literature 808.822 5
    history and criticism 809.225
    specific literatures T3B—202 5
      individual authors T3A—2
  performing arts 791.457
  rhetoric 808.225
Television engineers 621.388 009 2
  occupational group T7—621 3
Television evangelism 269.26
Television genres 791.456
Television music 781.546
Television networks 384.550 65
  facilities 384.552 3
  organizations 384.550 65
  performing arts 791.45
  see Manual at 384.55065 vs. 384.5522, 384.5523
Television news 070.195
Television photography 778.59
Television plays
  literature 808.822 5
    history and criticism 809.225
    specific literatures T3B—202 5
      individual authors T3A—2
  performing arts 791.457

Television plays (continued)
  rhetoric 808.225
  see Manual at 791.437 and 791.447, 791.457, 792.9
Television programs 384.553 2
  broadcasting 384.553 2
  performing arts 791.45
Television public speaking 808.51
Television recorders
  photography 778.599 3
Television scripts
  rhetoric 808.066 791
Television selling 381.1
  management 658.84
  see also Commerce
Television selling organizations 381.142
  management 658.872
  see also Commerce
Television sets 621.388 8
  automobile 629.277
Television stations 384.552 2
  architecture 725.23
  engineering 621.388 6
  facilities 384.552 2
  organizations 384.550 65
  performing arts 791.45
  see Manual at 384.55065 vs. 384.5522, 384.5523
Television towers
  architecture 725.23
Television transmission
  engineering 621.388 1
Telex 384.14
  wireless 384.524
  see also Telegraphy
Telfair County (Ga.) T2—758 843
Telford pavements 625.86
Teller County (Colo.) T2—788 58
Tellurides
  mineralogy 549.32
Tellurium
  chemical engineering 661.072 6
  chemistry 546.726
  economic geology 553.499
  metallurgy 669.79
  see also Chemicals
Telopea 583.89
Telpherage 621.868
Telugu T5—948 27
Telugu language 494.827
  T6—948 27
Telugu literature 894.827
Tem (African people) T5—963 5
Tem language 496.35
  T6—963 5
Témiscamingue (Quebec) T2—714 13
Témiscouata (Quebec) T2—714 76
Témiscouata (Quebec : Regional County Municipality) T2—714 76
Temne (African people) T5—963 2
Temne language 496.32
  T6—963 2
Temotu (Solomon Islands) T2—959 39
Temouchent (Algeria : Province) T2—651
Tempera painting 751.43
Temperament (Musical instruments) 784.192 8
Temperament (Psychology) 155.262
Temperance 178
  see also Virtues
Temperate basses 597.73
Temperate zones T2—12
  diseases
    medicine 616.988 2
    see also Environmental diseases (Human)
Temperature 536.5
  biophysics 571.46
    humans 612.014 46
  health 613.1
  meteorology 551.525
  physics 536.5
  seawater 551.460 1
    meteorological effect 551.524 6
  weather forecasting 551.642 5
Temperature adaptation 578.42
  animals 591.42
  plants 581.42
Temperature changes
  effect on materials 620.112 15
  geologic work 551.39
  meteorology 551.525 3
Temperature control
  buildings 697.932 2
  mining 622.43
  ships 623.853
  spacecraft 629.477 5
Tempering glass 666.129
Tempering metals 671.36
Templars 255.791 3
  church history 271.791 3
Temples 291.35
  architecture 726.1
    see Manual at 726.1
  Buddhist 294.343 5

Temples (continued)
  Hindu 294.535
  Jain 294.435
  Jewish temple in Jerusalem 296.491
  Mormon 246.958 93
  Shinto 299.561 35
  Sikh 294.635
  see also Synagogues
Tempo (Music) 781.22
Temporal power of pope 262.132
Temporary deformation 531.382
  materials science 620.112 32
  see also Elasticity
Temporary housing
  social welfare 361.05
Temporomandibular joint dysfunction
  regional medicine 617.522
Temptation
  moral theology 291.5
    Christianity 241.3
Temptation of Jesus Christ 232.95
Temurah 296.123 5
  Babylonian Talmud 296.125 5
  Mishnah 296.123 5
Ten Commandments 222.16
  moral theology
    Christianity 241.52
    Judaism 296.36
Ten kingdoms (China) 951.018
Ten Thousand Islands (Fla.) T2—759 44
Tenancy
  land economics 333.53
  law 346.043 4
Tenant-landlord relations 333.54
  land economics 333.54
  law 346.043 4
Tenants' liability insurance 368.56
  see also Insurance
Tench 597.482
  sports fishing 799.174 82
Tenda (African people) T5—963 2
Tenda language 496.32
  T6—963 2
Tende-Yanzi languages 496.396
  T6—963 96
Tender offers (Securities) 332.632 2
  financial economics 332.632 2
  law 346.066 6
  mergers 338.83
    see also Mergers
Tenderizers
  food technology 664.4
Tendinitis
  medicine 616.75
  see also Musculoskeletal system
Tendon sheaths
  human anatomy 611.75
  human physiology 612.75
  medicine 616.76
  see also Musculoskeletal system
Tendons 573.753 56
  biology 573.753 56
  human anatomy 611.74
  human physiology 612.75
  medicine 616.75
  surgery 617.474
  see also Musculoskeletal system
Tendrils 581.48
Tendring (England : District) T2—426 725
Tenebrionidae 595.769
Tenedos Island (Turkey) T2—562
  ancient T2—391 1
Tenements 647.92
  architecture 728.314
  household management 647.92
  social provision 363.5
Tenericutes 579.328
Tennant Creek (N.T.) T2—942 95
Tennessee 976.8
  T2—768
Tennessee River T2—768
  Alabama T2—761 9
  Tennessee T2—768
Tennessee Valley T2—768
Tennessee walking horse 636.13
Tennis 796.342
  electronic games 794.863 42
  equipment technology 688.763 42
  see also Sports
Tennis courts 796.342 068
Tennis players 796.342 092
  sports group T7—796 34
Tenor horns 788.974
  see also Brass instruments
Tenor recorders 788.366
  see also Woodwind instruments
Tenor saxophones 788.74
  see also Woodwind instruments
Tenor viols 787.64
  see also Stringed instruments

Tenor voices 782.87
  choral and mixed voices 782.87
  single voices 783.87
Tenos Island (Greece) T2—495 85
Tenrecs 599.33
Tensas Parish (La.) T2—763 79
Tenses (Grammar) 415
  specific languages T4—5
Tension (Mechanical stress)
  effect on materials 620.112 41
Tension headaches
  symptomatology
    neurological diseases 616.849 1
  see also Nervous system
Tensor algebra 512.57
Tensor analysis 515.63
Tensor calculus 515.63
Tentaculata 593.8
Tenterfield (N.S.W.) T2—944 4
Tentering textiles 677.028 25
Tenth of Muḥarram 297.36
Tents 796.540 28
  manufacturing technology 685.53
Tenure 331.259 6
  labor economics 331.259 6
  personnel management 658.312
    teachers 371.104
      higher education 378.121
  public administration 354.98
Tepo language 496.33
  T6—963 3
Tequila 641.25
  commercial processing 663.5
Tequila (Plant) 584.352
Teramo (Italy : Province) T2—457 15
Teratogenic agents
  medicine 616.043
Teratology
  biology 571.976
  medicine 616.043
Terbium
  chemistry 546.416
  see also Rare earths
Terce 264.15
  music 782.324
  see also Liturgy of the hours
Terengganu T2—595 1
Term life insurance 368.323
  see also Insurance
Term limitation
  chief executives 352.23
  legislators 328.33
Terminal ballistics
  military engineering 623.516
Terminal care 362.175
  law 344.041 97
  medicine 616.029
  nursing 610.736 1
  pastoral theology 291.61
    Christianity 259.417 5
  social theology 291.178 321 75
    Christianity 261.832 175
  social welfare 362.175
  see also Health services
Terminals (Computer) 004.75
  engineering 621.398 5
  graphics 006.62
    engineering 621.399
Terminals (Transportation) 388
  see also Transportation facilities
Termination
  insurance 368.016
Terminology 401.4
  T1—014
  dictionaries 413
  specific languages T4—014
    dictionaries T4—3
    usage (Applied linguistics) T4—81
    see Manual at T4—3 vs. T4—81
  usage (Applied linguistics) 418
  see Manual at T1—014 vs. T1—03; *also at* T1—014 vs. T4—864
Termite damage prevention 691.14
Termite-resistant construction 693.842
Termites 595.736
  control technology 628.965 7
Ternary form 781.822 3
  instrumental 784.182 2
Ternary system (Numeration) 513.5
Terni (Italy : Province) T2—456 52
Ternopil′ (Ukraine : Oblast) T2—477 9
Ternopil′s′ka oblast′ (Ukraine) T2—477 9
Terns 598.338
Ternstroemiaceae 583.624
Terpenes
  chemistry 547.71
Terra-cotta
  architectural construction 721.044 3
  building construction 693.3
  building materials 691.4
  materials science 620.142
Terrace (B.C.) T2—711 85

Terraces
  landscape architecture 717
Terracing (Soil conservation) 631.455
Terrariums 578.073
  animals 590.73
  floriculture 635.982 4
  plants 580.73
Terrebonne (Quebec : County) T2—714 24
Terrebonne Parish (La.) T2—763 41
Terrell County (Ga.) T2—758 935
Terrell County (Tex.) T2—764 922
Terrestrial ecology 577
Terrestrial photogrammetry 526.982 5
Terrestrial radiation
  meteorology 551.527 2
Terriers 636.755
Terriers (Toy dogs) 636.76
Territorial property 320.12
  international law 341.42
Territorial waters
  international law 341.448
  law 342.041 3
Territoriality
  animal behavior 591.566
  human ecology 304.23
Territories (Local government units) 320.83
  see also Counties
Territories (State-level units) 321.023
  see also States (Members of federations)
Territories under international control 321
  law 341.29
  public administration 353.159
Territory of states 320.12
  international law 341.42
  law 342.041 3
Terrorism 303.625
  criminology 364.1
    criminal law 345.02
    international law 341.773
  international relations 327.117
  prevention
    management 658.473
    public safety 363.32
  social conflict 303.625
Terry cloth 677.617
Terry County (Tex.) T2—764 859
Tersinidae 598.875
Tertiary education 378
  see also Higher education
Tertiary period 551.78
  geology 551.78
  paleontology 560.178
Tertiary recovery
  oil extraction 622.338 2
Teruel (Spain : Province) T2—465 51
Terumot 296.123 1
  Mishnah 296.123 1
  Palestinian Talmud 296.124 1
Teso language 496.5
  T6—965
Tessin (Switzerland) T2—494 78
Test anxiety 371.260 19
Test bias
  education 371.260 13
  psychology 150.287
Test construction (Education) 371.261
  T1—076
  teacher-prepared tests 371.271
Test design (Education) 371.261
  teacher-prepared tests 371.271
Test reliability
  education 371.260 13
Test River (England) T2—422 732
Test-taking skills
  education 371.26
Test-tube babies
  ethics 176
    religion 291.566
      Christianity 241.66
    see also Reproduction—ethics
  gynecology 618.178 059
Test tubes 542.2
Test validity
  education 371.260 13
Test Valley (England : Borough) T2—422 732
Testaments
  pseudepigrapha 229.914
Testes 573.655
  biology 573.655
  human anatomy 611.63
  human physiology 612.61
  medicine 616.68
  see also Male genital system
Testicles 573.655
  see also Testes
Testing T1—028 7
  education 371.26
  T1—076
    teacher-prepared tests 371.271
  physics 530.8

Testing devices
  electronics 621.381 548
  manufacturing technology 681.2
  radio engineering 621.384 133
Tests T1—028 7
  education 371.26
    T1—076
    teacher-prepared tests 371.271
    see Manual at 371.262 vs. 371.264
  personnel selection 658.311 25
    public administration 352.65
Testudines 597.92
  paleozoology 567.92
Tetanus
  incidence 614.512 8
  medicine 616.931 8
  see also Communicable diseases (Human)
Tete (Mozambique : Province) T2—679 5
Tetela languages 496.396
  T6—963 96
Teton County (Idaho) T2—796 54
Teton County (Mont.) T2—786 55
Teton County (Wyo.) T2—787 55
Teton Indians T5—975 2
Teton Range (Wyo. and Idaho) T2—787 55
Tétouan (Morocco : Province) T2—642
Tetrahedrite
  mineralogy 549.35
Tetrao 598.634
Tetraodontiformes 597.64
Tetraonidae 598.63
Tetrapoda 596
  see also Vertebrates
Tetras 597.48
Teuthoidea 594.58
Teutoburg Forest (Germany) T2—435 65
Teutonic Knights 255.791 4
  church history 271.791 4
Teutonic languages 430
  T6—3
Teutonic literatures 830
Teutonic race T5—3
Tevul Yom 296.123 6
Tewa Indians T5—974 9
Tewkesbury (England) T2—424 12
Texada Island (B.C.) T2—711 31
Texas 976.4
  T2—764
Texas, East T2—764 14
Texas County (Mo.) T2—778 84
Texas County (Okla.) T2—766 135
Texas Panhandle (Tex.) T2—764 8
Texoma, Lake (Okla. and Tex.) T2—766 61
Text editors 652.5
  programming aids 005.13
  see Manual at 652.5
Text processing 005
  see Manual at 005: Text processing
Textbook bias 371.32
  public control 379.156
Textbooks 371.32
  bibliographies 011.7
  law 344.077
  public control 379.156
  teaching use 371.32
Textile arts 746
Textile chemicals 677.028 35
Textile handicrafters 746.092
  occupational group T7—746
Textile handicrafts 746
Textile industry 338.476 77
  law 343.078 677
Textile printing 667.38
Textile workers 677.009 2
  occupational group T7—677
Textiles 677
  equipment manufacturing technology 681.767 7
  field crops 633.5
  handicrafts 746
  home sewing 646.11
  manufacturing technology 677
  materials science 620.197
  product safety 363.19
    see also Product safety
  sculpture material 731.2
  ship design 623.818 97
  shipbuilding 623.820 7
Texts (Music) 780
  treatises 780.268
Textual criticism
  literature 809
    specific literatures T3B—09
    theory 801.959
  sacred books 291.82
    Bible 220.404 6
    Talmud 296.120 4
Texture
  materials science 620.112 92
Texture (Music) 781.28

Thabamoopo (South Africa : District) T2—682 93
Thabankulu (South Africa : District) T2—687 91
Thabazimbi (South Africa : District) T2—682 5
Thai T5—959 11
Thai language 495.91
T6—959 11
Thai literature 895.91
Thailand 959.3
T2—593
Thailand, Gulf of 551.465 72
T2—164 72
Thalamus
human anatomy 611.81
human physiology 612.826 2
see also Nervous system
Thalarctos 599.786
Thalassemia
medicine 616.152
see also Cardiovascular system
Thaliacea 596.2
Thallium 669.79
chemical engineering 661.067 8
chemistry 546.678
metallurgy 669.79
physical metallurgy 669.967 9
see also Chemicals
Thallobionta 579
Thallophyta 579
Thames Coromandel District (N.Z.) T2—933 23
Thames River (England) T2—422
Thamesdown (England) T2—423 13
Thanet (England) T2—422 357
Thanksgiving 394.264 9
Thao (Taiwan people) T5—992 5
Thar Desert (India and Pakistan) T2—544
Thasos Island (Greece) T2—495 7
ancient T2—391 1
Thatch grasses 584.92
Thayer County (Neb.) T2—782 335
The Pas (Man.) T2—712 72
Theales 583.624
Theater 792
accounting 657.84
elementary education 372.66
influence on crime 364.254
instructional use 371.399
performing arts 792
Theater (continued)
religious significance 291.37
Christianity 246.72
religious education 268.67
see also Arts—religious significance
sociology 306.484
Theater etiquette 395.53
Theater-in-the-round 792.022 8
Theater television 384.556
see also Television
Theaters (Buildings)
architecture 725.822
area planning 711.558
household management 647.968 22
music 781.538
Theatines 255.51
church history 271.51
Theatrical costumes 792.026
dramatic performances 792.026
home sewing 646.478
see also Costumes
Theatrical dancing 792.78
see Manual at 792.78 vs. 792.8, 793.3
Theatrical performers 792.028 092
occupational group T7—792
Theban supremacy 938.06
Thebes (Egypt : Extinct city) T2—32
Thebes (Greece) T2—384
Thecodontia 567.91
Thecosomata 594.34
Theft 364.162
law 345.026 2
prevention
household security 643.16
management 658.473
museology 069.54
Theft insurance 368.82
see also Insurance
Theism 211.3
Christianity 231
comparative religion 291.211
Islam 297.211
Judaism 296.311
philosophy of religion 211.3
Theistic religions 291.14
Thelephoraceae 579.6
Theligonales 583.5
Thelon Game Sanctuary (N.W.T.) T2—719 4
Thelon River (N.W.T.) T2—719 4

Thematic apperception tests 155.284 4
Thematic catalogs 780.216
Theme and variations 781.825
  instrumental 784.182 5
Theme parks 791.068
  see also Amusement parks
Themes
  arts T3C—3
    see Manual at T3C—353–T3C—358 vs. T3C—352
  literature 808.803
    history and criticism 809.933
    specific literatures T3B—080 3
      history and criticism T3B—093
    see Manual at T3B—102–T3B—108, T3B—205, T3B—308 vs. T3C—1, T3C—3
  musical element 781.248
Theocracy 321.5
  political ideology 320.55
  political system 321.5
  religion 291.177 3
    Christianity 261.73
Theodicy 291.211 8
  Buddhism 294.342 118
  Christianity 231.8
  comparative religion 291.211 8
  Hinduism 294.521 18
  Islam 297.211 8
  Judaism 296.311 8
  philosophy of religion 214
Theodore I, Czar of Russia
  Russian history 947.044
Theodore II, Negus of Ethiopia
  Ethiopian history 963.041
Theodore III, Czar of Russia
  Russian history 947.049
Theologians 291.209 2
  Christian 230.092
    see Manual at 230–280; *also at* 230.04 vs. 230.092, 230.1–230.9
  occupational group T7—2
Theological anthropology 291.22
  Christianity 233
  philosophy of religion 218
  see also Humans—religion
Theological seminaries
  Christianity 230.071 1
Theology 291.2
  Buddhism 294.342
  Christianity 230
Theology (continued)
  Hinduism 294.52
  Islam 297.2
    Sufi 297.41
  Judaism 296.3
Theophanies
  Christianity 231.74
Theophrastaceae 583.675
Theoretical biochemistry 572.33
  humans 612.015 82
Theoretical chemistry 541.2
  see Manual at 541 vs. 546
Theory T1—01
  see Manual at T1—01
Theosophists
  biography 299.934 092
  religious group T7—299 9
Theosophy 299.934
Thera Island (Greece) T2—495 85
  ancient T2—391 5
Therapeutic manipulations
  medicine 615.82
Therapeutic services 362.178
  see also Health services
Therapeutic spells and charms 133.446
Therapeutic systems 615.53
  see Manual at 615.53
Therapeutics 615.5
  veterinary medicine 636.089 55
  see Manual at 613 vs. 615.8; *also at* 615; *also at* 615.8
Therapists 615.509 2
  occupational group T7—615
Therapsida 567.93
Therapy 615.5
  see Manual at 617: Add table: 06
Theravada Buddhism 294.391
Theremins 786.73
  see also Electrophones
Thérèse-de-Blainville (Quebec) T2—714 24
Therevidae 595.773
Thermal analysis 543.086
  qualitative 544.2
Thermal capacity 536.6
Thermal conductivity 536.201 2
Thermal convective storms 551.554
Thermal cracking
  petroleum 665.533
Thermal diffusivity 536.201 4
Thermal dissociation 541.364
  chemical engineering 660.296 4
Thermal effects of electricity 537.624

Thermal engineering 621.402
Thermal expansion 536.41
Thermal forces
materials science 620.112 1
Thermal insulation 693.832
Thermal ocean power conversion 333.914
Thermal perception 152.182 2
Thermal pollution 363.739 4
ecological effect 577.627 26
social welfare 363.739 4
water supply engineering 628.168 31
see also Pollution
Thermal properties
materials science 620.112 96
Thermal waters 333.88
economics 333.88
geophysics 551.23
Thermal weapons 623.446
Thermionic converters 621.312 43
Thermionic tubes 621.381 51
Thermistors 621.381 548
Thermit welding 671.529
Thermobiology 572.436
biochemistry 572.436
body temperature 571.76
humans 612.014 46
Thermobiophysics 571.46
humans 612.014 46
Thermochemistry 541.36
biochemistry 572.436
chemical engineering 660.296
Thermocouples 536.52
Thermodynamics 536.7
biochemistry 572.436
chemical engineering 660.296 9
chemistry 541.369
engineering 621.402 1
meteorology 551.522
physics 536.7
Thermoelectric generation 621.312 43
Thermoelectricity 537.65
Thermography
medicine 616.075 4
Thermogravimetry 543.086
quantitative analysis 545.4
Thermoluminescence 535.356
Thermometry 536.502 87
Thermonuclear reaction 539.764
Thermonuclear reactors 621.484
Thermopenetration
therapeutics 615.832 3
Thermoplastic elastomers 678
Thermoplastic plastics 668.423
Thermosbaenacea 595.373
Thermosetting plastics 668.422
Thermostats
air conditioning buildings 697.932 2
heating buildings 697.07
Thermotherapy
medicine 615.832
Theropoda 567.912
Thesauri (Controlled vocabularies) 025.49
Thesauri (Synonym dictionaries) 413.1
specific languages T4—31
specific subject T1—03
Theses (Academic) 378.242
bibliographies 011.75
rhetoric 808.02
Thesprōtia (Greece) T2—495 3
Thessalia (Greece) T2—495 4
Thessalonians (Biblical books) 227.81
Thessalonikē (Greece : Nome) T2—495 65
Thessaly (Greece) T2—495 4
ancient T2—382
Theta function 515.984
Theunissen (South Africa : District) T2—685 3
Thiazoles 547.594
Thiès (Senegal : Region) T2—663
Thigh muscles
human anatomy 611.738
see also Musculoskeletal system
Thighs (Human) 612.98
physiology 612.98
regional medicine 617.582
surgery 617.582
see also Lower extremities (Human)
Thin-film circuits 621.381 5
Thin-film memory 004.53
engineering 621.397 32
Thin-film technology 621.381 52
Thin films 530.427 5
liquid-state physics 530.427 5
solid-state physics 530.417 5
Thin-layer chromatography 543.089 56
Things (Law) 346.04
Things (Philosophy) 111
Thinking 153.42
human physiology 612.82
psychology 153.42
Thinners
paint technology 667.624

Thioacids 547.064
  chemical engineering 661.896
Thioalcohols 547.063
  chemical engineering 661.896
Thioaldehydes 547.065
  chemical engineering 661.896
Thioethers 547.061
  chemical engineering 661.896
Thioketones 547.065
  chemical engineering 661.896
Thiophenes 547.594
Third-class mail 383.124
  see also Postal service
Third International 324.175
Third Order Regular of St. Francis 255.38
  church history 271.38
  women 255.973
    church history 271.973
Third orders
  religious orders 255.094
    church history 271.094
    women 255.909 4
      church history 271.909 4
Third parties (Law) 346.022
Third Reich 943.086
Third Republic (France) 944.081
Third stream jazz 781.657
Third World (Developing regions) T2—172 4
Third World (Unaligned blocs) T2—171 6
Thirst
  human physiology 612.391
  psychology 152.188 6
  see also Digestive system
Thirteen Articles of Faith (Judaism) 296.3
Thirty Years' War, 1618–1648 940.24
Thistles 583.99
Thlaping Tlaro (South Africa : District) T2—682 94
Thomas County (Ga.) T2—758 984
Thomas County (Kan.) T2—781 132
Thomas County (Neb.) T2—782 774
Thomist philosophy 189.4
  modern 149.91
Thompson (Man.) T2—712 71
Thompson, John S. D. (John Sparrow David), Sir
  Canadian history 971.055
Thompson-Nicola (B.C.) T2—711 72
Thompson River (B.C.) T2—711 72
Thonga (African people) T5—963 97
Thonga language 496.397
  T6—963 97
Thoracic surgery 617.540 59
Thoracica 595.35
Thorax 573.996
  biology 573.996
  human anatomy 611.94
  human physiology 612.94
  regional medicine 617.54
  surgery 617.540 59
Thorium
  chemistry 546.422
  economic geology 553.493
  metallurgy 669.292 2
  see also Chemicals; Metals
Thorndike, Edward L. (Edward Lee)
  psychological system 150.194 4
Thorns 581.47
  descriptive botany 581.47
  physiology 575.457
Thorough bass 781.47
Thoroughbred horse 636.132
Thothmes III, King of Egypt
  Egyptian history 932.014
Thought 153.42
  philosophy 128.3
  psychology 153.42
Thousand Islands (N.Y. and Ont.) T2—747 58
  New York T2—747 58
  Ontario T2—713 7
Thrace T2—495 7
  ancient T2—398
  Bulgaria T2—499 5
  Greece T2—495 7
Thrace, Eastern (Turkey) 949.61
  T2—496 1
  ancient 939.8
    T2—398
Thracian language 491.993
  T6—919 93
Thraco-Phrygian languages 491.993
  T6—919 93
Thrashers (Birds) 598.844
Thraupidae 598.875
Thread 677.028 62
Threatened species 578.68
  see also entries beginning with Rare
Threats
  international relations 327.117
  social control 303.36

Three-day event (Horsemanship) 798.24
  see also Sports
Three-dimensional chess 794.18
Three-dimensional graphics
  computer graphics 006.693
Three-quarter play
  rugby 796.333 25
Three Rivers (England) T2—425 88
Three-wheel vehicles
  engineering 629.220 4
Three wise men (Christian doctrines) 232.923
Three-year junior colleges 378.154 3
Thresholds (Psychology) 152.1
  quantitative studies 152.82
Threskiornithidae 598.34
Thrift industry 332.32
  law 346.082 32
  public administration 354.86
Thrift institutions 332.32
  law 346.082 32
  public administration 354.86
Thrifts (Plants) 635.933 5
  botany 583.5
  floriculture 635.933 5
Thrips 595.758
Throat
  human anatomy 611.32
  human physiology 612.31
  medicine 616.31
  regional medicine 617.531
  surgery 617.531 059
  see also Digestive system
Throckmorton County (Tex.) T2—764 735
Thrombin
  human physiology 612.115
  see also Cardiovascular system
Thrombocytes
  human histology 611.018 5
  see also Cardiovascular system
Thromboembolisms
  arteries
    medicine 616.135
  veins
    medicine 616.145
  see also Cardiovascular system
Thrombophlebitis
  medicine 616.142
  see also Cardiovascular system
Thromboses
  arteries
    medicine 616.135
  veins
    medicine 616.145
  see also Cardiovascular system
Throttles
  automotive 629.258
Throughways 388.122
  see also Roads
Thrushes 598.842
Thrust (Aeronautics) 629.132 33
Thulium
  chemistry 546.418
  see also Rare earths
Thumb pianos 786.85
  see also Percussion instruments
Thunder Bay (Ont. : District) T2—713 12
Thunderstorms 551.554
  social services 363.349 24
Thunnus 597.783
Thurgau (Switzerland) T2—494 59
Thüringen (Germany) T2—432 2
Thuringia (Germany) T2—432 2
Thuringian Forest T2—432 2
Thurniaceae 584.82
Thurrock (England) T2—426 78
Thurston County (Neb.) T2—782 227
Thurston County (Wash.) T2—797 79
Thutmose III, King of Egypt
  Egyptian history 932.014
Thylacine 599.27
Thymallus 597.559
Thyme 641.357
  botany 583.96
  see also Herbs
Thymelaeales 583.67
Thymus-derived lymphocytes 571.966
  humans 616.079 7
Thymus gland
  human anatomy 611.43
  human physiology 612.43
  medicine 616.43
  surgery 617.546
  see also Endocrine system
Thyristors 621.381 528 7
Thyroid extracts
  pharmacology 615.362
  see also Endocrine system

Thyroid gland 573.47
  biology 573.47
  human anatomy 611.44
  human physiology 612.44
  medicine 616.44
  surgery 617.539
  see also Endocrine system
Thyroxine
  chemistry 547.734 5
Thysanolaeneae 584.9
Thysanoptera 595.758
Thysanura 595.723
Tianjin Shih (China) T2—511 54
Tiaras 391.7
  customs 391.7
  making 739.278
  see also Jewelry
Tiaret (Algeria : Province) T2—651
Tibet (China) T2—515
Tibet Autonomous Region (China) T2—515
Tibetan Buddhism 294.392 3
Tibetan language 495.4
  T6—954 1
Tibetan literature 895.4
Tibetan spaniel 636.72
Tibetan terrier 636.72
Tibetans T5—954
Tibeto-Burman languages 495.4
  T6—954
Tibeto-Burman literatures 895.4
Tibias
  human anatomy 611.718
  see also Musculoskeletal system
Ticino (Switzerland) T2—494 78
Tick typhus
  incidence 614.526 3
  medicine 616.922 3
  see also Communicable diseases (Human)
Ticker tapes
  investment analysis 332.632 042
Ticks 595.429
  disease carriers 571.986
    medicine 614.433
Tidal currents 551.470 8
Tidal flats 551.457
  biology 578.769 9
  ecology 577.699
  see also Coasts
Tidal power plants 621.312 134
Tidal waves 551.470 24
Tide marshes
  biology 578.769
  ecology 577.69
  see also Wetlands
Tide pools
  biology 578.769 9
  ecology 577.699
Tide tables
  navigation aids 623.894 9
Tidelands (Shorelands) 551.457
  see also Coasts
Tidelands (Wetlands) 551.41
  see also Wetlands
Tides 551.470 8
Tidewater (Va. : Region) T2—755 1
Tie-dyeing
  textile arts 746.664
Tie plates 625.143
Tien Shan T2—516
  China T2—516
  Kyrgyzstan T2—584 3
Tientos 784.187 6
Tientsin (China) T2—511 54
Tierra del Fuego (Argentina) T2—827 6
Tierra del Fuego (Argentina and Chile) T2—827 6
Tierra del Fuego (Chile) T2—836 46
Ties (Neckwear) 391.41
  see also Accessories (Clothing)
Ties (Railroad) 625.143
Tift County (Ga.) T2—758 882
Tiger 599.756
  big game hunting 799.277 56
  conservation technology 639.979 756
  resource economics 333.959 756
Tiger beetles 595.762
Tiger fishes (Characidae) 597.48
Tiger shark 597.34
Tigerfishes (Characidae) 597.48
Tigerflowers
  botany 584.38
Tightrope walking
  circuses 791.34
  sports 796.46
    see also Sports
Tigray Kifle Hāger (Ethiopia) T2—634
Tigre (African people) T5—928
Tigré language 492.82
  T6—928 2
Tigré literature 892.82
Tigrinya (African people) T5—928

Tigrinya language 492.83
T6—928 3
Tigrinya literature 892.83
Tijānīyah 297.48
Tikar (African people) T5—963 6
Tikar language 496.36
T6—963 6
Tilapias 641.392
cooking 641.692
culture 639.377 4
food 641.392
zoology 597.74
Tile drains 666.733
Tile furniture 645.4
manufacturing technology 684.106
see also Furniture
Tile piping 666.733
Tiles
architectural construction 721.044 3
building construction 693.3
building materials 691.4
ceramic arts 738.6
floor coverings
building construction 698.9
materials science 620.142
rubber 678.34
structural engineering 624.183 6
Tiliaceae 583.68
Till (Geologic landforms) 551.315
Till (Geologic material) 551.314
Tillage 631.51
Tillamook County (Or.) T2—795 44
Tillman County (Okla.) T2—766 46
Tillodontia 569.31
Timaliidae 598.834
Timaru District (N.Z.) T2—938 7
Timber 338.174 98
agricultural economics 338.174 98
building material 691.1
see Manual at 338.1749 vs. 333.75; *also at* 583–585
Timber resources 333.75
see also Forest lands
see Manual at 338.1749 vs. 333.75
Timber wolf 599.773
Timbre (Sound)
musical element 781.234
Timbre perception
psychology 152.157
Time
arts 701.8
drawing 741.018
chronology 529
Time (continued)
literature 808.803 84
history and criticism 809.933 84
specific literatures T3B—080 384
history and criticism T3B—093 84
philosophy 115
sociology 304.23
Time (Music) 781.22
Time and date recorders
technology 681.118
Time clocks
technology 681.118
Time deposits 332.175 2
Time estimates
building construction 692.5
commercial T1—029 9
Time-invariant systems 003.8
Time-lapse cinematography 778.534 6
Time management
business 650.1
executives 658.409 3
home economics 640.43
sociology 304.23
Time of day
influence on crime 364.22
Time of Troubles, 1605–1613 947.045
Time payments (Wages) 331.216 2
personnel management 658.322 2
Time perception 153.753
Time series 519.232
Time-series analysis 519.55
Time-sharing (Computers)
computer hardware 004.3
systems programs 005.434
Time-sharing (Real estate) 333.323 4
economics 333.323 4
law 346.043 3
Time studies
production management 658.542 1
Time systems 389.17
Time-varying systems 003.8
Time wage rate 331.216 2
personnel management 658.322 2
Time zones 389.17
Timepieces
technology 681.11
Times
folklore 398.236
history and criticism 398.33
literature 808.803 3
history and criticism 809.933 3
specific literatures T3B—080 33
history and criticism T3B—093 3
music 781.52

Times (continued)
religious observance 291.36
Christianity 263
Islam 297.36
Judaism 296.43
Times Roman type 686.224 7
Timesaving cooking 641.555
Timework 331.216 2
personnel management 658.322 2
Timiş (Romania) T2—498 4
Timiskaming (Ont.) T2—713 144
Timor Island (Indonesia) T2—598 6
Timor Sea 551.467 74
T2—165 74
Timothy (Biblical books) 227.83
Timothy (Grass) 633.24
botany 584.9
forage crop 633.24
Timpani 786.93
see also Percussion instruments
Timur
Asian history 950.2
Tin 669.6
architectural construction 721.044 76
building construction 693.76
building material 691.86
chemical engineering 661.068 6
chemistry 546.686
decorative arts 739.532
economic geology 553.453
materials science 620.185
metallography 669.956
metallurgy 669.6
metalworking 673.6
mining 622.345 3
physical metallurgy 669.966
see also Chemicals; Metals
Tin soldiers
handicrafts 745.592 82
Tinamiformes 598.55
paleozoology 568.5
Tinamous 598.55
Tinctures
practical pharmacy 615.42
Tindouf (Algeria : Province) T2—657
Tineoidea 595.78
Tinian (Northern Mariana Islands) T2—967
Tinos Island (Greece) T2—495 85
Tinsel
textiles 677.76
see also Textiles
Tintype process 772.14
Tioga County (N.Y.) T2—747 77
Tioga County (Pa.) T2—748 56
Tipaza (Algeria : Province) T2—653
Tipiṭaka 294.382
Tippah County (Miss.) T2—762 923
Tippecanoe County (Ind.) T2—772 95
Tipperary (Ireland : County) T2—419 2
Tipping
economics 331.216 6
etiquette 395.5
Tipton County (Ind.) T2—772 555
Tipton County (Tenn.) T2—768 17
Tipulidae 595.772
Tires 678.32
automotive engineering 629.248 2
Tirmidhī, Muḥammad ibn ʻĪsá
Hadith 297.124 4
Tirol (Austria) T2—436 42
Tiryns (Extinct city) T2—388
Tishah b'Av 296.439
liturgy 296.453 9
Tishomingo County (Miss.) T2—762 995
Tissemsilt (Algeria : Province) T2—651
Tissue anatomy 571.533
humans 611.018
Tissue banks 362.178 3
see also Health services
Tissue biology 571.5
humans 611.018
Tissue culture 571.538
humans 612.028
Tissue degeneration 571.935
Tissue differentiation 571.835
Tissue grafting
surgery 617.95
Tissue morphology 571.533
humans 611.018
Tissue paper 676.284 2
handicrafts 745.54
Tissue regeneration 571.889 35
humans 611.018
Tissue respiration 572.47
human physiology 612.26
see also Respiratory system
Tissues 571.5
humans 611.018
Titanium 669.732 2
chemical engineering 661.051 2
chemistry 546.512
economic geology 553.462 3

Titanium (continued)
materials science 620.189 322
metallography 669.957 322
metallurgy 669.732 2
metalworking 673.732 2
physical metallurgy 669.967 322
see also Chemicals; Metals
Titanium group
chemical engineering 661.051
chemistry 546.51
Tithes
Christian practice 248.6
local church fund raising 254.8
Titicaca Lake (Peru and Bolivia) T2—841 2
Bolivia T2—841 2
Peru T2—853 6
Title (Property) 346.043 8
law 346.043 8
public administration 354.34
Title examinations 346.043 8
Title insurance 368.88
law 346.086 88
see also Insurance
Title manipulation
subject indexing 025.486
Title searching 346.043 8
Titles of honor
genealogy 929.7
Titling
cinematography 778.535
technical drawing 604.243
video production 778.593
Titmice 598.824
Tito, Josip Broz
Yugoslavian history 949.702 3
Titoism 335.434 4
economics 335.434 4
political ideology 320.532 309 497
Titration 545.2
Titus (Biblical book) 227.85
Titus County (Tex.) T2—764 215
Ti͡umenskai͡a oblastʹ (Russia) T2—573
Tiv (African people) T5—963 6
Tiv language 496.36
T6—963 6
Tivi (African people) T5—963 6
Tivi language 496.36
T6—963 6
Tizi Ouzou (Algeria : Province) T2—653
Tiznit (Morocco : Province) T2—646
Tlaxcala (Mexico : State) T2—724 7
Tlemcen (Algeria : Province) T2—651
Tlingit Indians T5—972
Tlingit language 497.2
T6—972
TMC (Television) 384.555 4
see also Television
TMJ dysfunction
regional medicine 617.522
TNT (Explosive) 662.27
military engineering 623.452 7
Toadfishes 597.62
Toads 597.87
Toadstools 579.6
Toamasina (Madagascar : Province) T2—691
Toasters
electric cooking 641.586
Toasting 394.1
see also Toasts
Toasts 394.1
customs 394.1
literature 808.851
history and criticism 809.51
specific literatures T3B—501
individual authors T3A—5
rhetoric 808.51
Tobacco
agriculture 633.71
botany 583.952
customs 394.14
ethics 178.7
see also Ethical problems
human toxicology 615.952 395 2
manufacturing technology 679.7
Tobacco abuse 362.296
medicine 616.865
personal health 613.85
social welfare 362.296
see also Substance abuse
Tobacco industry 338.173 71
agricultural economics 338.173 71
law 343.076 371
manufacturing 338.476 797
Tobacco industry workers 679.709 2
occupational group T7—679 7
Tobacco substitutes 688.4
Tobago 972.983
T2—729 83
Tobias (Deuterocanonical book) 229.22
Tobit (Deuterocanonical book) 229.22
Tobogganing 796.95
see also Sports

Tobote language 496.35
T6—963 5
Tocantins (Brazil) T2—811 7
Toccatas 784.189 47
Tocharian language 491.994
T6—919 94
Tocharish language 491.994
T6—919 94
Tochigi-ken (Japan) T2—521 32
Tocopilla (Chile : Province) T2—831 32
Toda (Dravidians) T5—948 1
Toda language 494.81
T6—948 1
Toda literature 894.81
Today's English Bible 220.520 82
Todd County (Ky.) T2—769 77
Todd County (Minn.) T2—776 88
Todd County (S.D.) T2—783 62
Tofu 641.356 55
  commercial processing 664.805 655
  cooking 641.656 55
  food 641.356 55
Togaviridae 579.256 2
Togo 966.81
T2—668 1
Togolanders T5—966 81
Togolese T5—966 81
Tōhoku Region (Japan) T2—521 1
Tohono O'Odham Indians T5—974 5
Tohono O'Odham language 497.45
T6—974 5
Tohorot (Order or tractate) 296.123 6
  Babylonian Talmud 296.125 6
  Mishnah 296.123 6
  Palestinian Talmud 296.124 6
Toilet paper 676.284 2
Toilet training 649.62
Tojiki language 491.57
T6—915 7
Tok Pisin 427.995 3
T6—217
Toka (African people) T5—963 91
Toka language 496.391
T6—963 91
Tokamaks 621.484
Tokat İli (Turkey) T2—565
Tokelau Islands 996.15
T2—961 5
Tokelau language 499.46
T6—994 6
Tokelauan dialect 499.46
T6—994 6
Tokelauans (New Zealand people) T5—994 6
Token coins 332.404 3
Tokens
  numismatics 737.3
Tokharian language 491.994
T6—919 94
Tokugawa period 952.025
Tokushima-ken (Japan) T2—523 4
Tokyo (Japan) T2—521 35
Tolbukhin (Bulgaria : Okrŭg) T2—499 4
Tolbukhinski okrŭg (Bulgaria) T2—499 4
Tolecraft 745.723
Toledo (Ohio) T2—771 13
Toledo (Spain : Province) T2—464 3
Toledo Bend Reservoir (La. and Tex.) T2—763 62
Toledo District (Belize) T2—728 24
Toleration 179.9
  moral theology 291.5
    Christianity 241.4
  social theology 291.177 2
    Christianity 261.72
    Judaism 296.382
    see also Politics and religion—social theology
  see also Virtues
Toliara (Madagascar : Province) T2—691
Tolima (Colombia : Dept.) T2—861 36
Tolland County (Conn.) T2—746 43
Tolls
  roads 388.114
  transportation services 388.049
Tollways 388.122
  see also Roads
Tolman, Edward Chace
  psychological system 150.194 34
Tolna Megye (Hungary) T2—439 7
Toltec empire 972.017
T2—72
Tom Green County (Tex.) T2—764 721
Tomahawks 623.441
Tomatoes 641.356 42
  botany 583.952
  commercial processing 664.805 642
  cooking 641.656 42
  food 641.356 42
  garden crop 635.642
Tombigbee River (Miss. and Ala.) T2—761 2

Tombs
  architecture 726.8
Tomography
  medicine 616.075 7
Tompkins County (N.Y.) T2—747 71
Tomsk (Russia : Oblast) T2—573
Tomskaîa oblast′ (Russia) T2—573
Tonal systems (Music) 781.26
Tonality 781.258
Tonbridge and Malling (England) T2—422 372
Tønder amt (Denmark) T2—489 5
Tone color
  musical element 781.234
  perception
    psychology 152.157
Tone River (Japan) T2—521 3
Tonga 996.12
  T2—961 2
Tonga (Mozambique and South African people) T5—963 97
Tonga (Zambian people) T5—963 91
Tonga language (Inhambane) 496.397
  T6—963 97
Tonga language (Nyasa) 496.391
  T6—963 91
Tonga language (Tonga Islands) 499.48
  T6—994 8
Tonga language (Zambesi) 496.391
  T6—963 91
Tongaat (South Africa) T2—684 4
Tongaland (South Africa) T2—684 91
Tongans T5—994 8
Tongariro National Park (N.Z.) T2—935 2
Tongic languages 499.48
  T6—994 8
Tongue 573.357
  biology 573.357
  human anatomy 611.313
  human physiology 612.312
    tasting 612.87
  surgery 617.522
  see also Digestive system
Tongue-and-groove products 674.43
Tongue twisters 398.8
Tongueless frogs 597.86
Tonguing (Music) 784.193 4
Tongwe languages 496.394
  T6—963 94
Tonic sol-fa 780.148
Toning solutions
  photography 771.54
Tonnage 387.2
  inland water 386.22
  ocean 387.2
Tonometry
  glaucoma treatment 617.741 075 4
  see also Eyes
Tonsillitis
  medicine 616.314
  see also Digestive system
Tonsils
  human anatomy 611.32
  human physiology 612.312
  medicine 616.314
  surgery 617.532
  see also Digestive system
Tonus
  muscles
    human physiology 612.741
    see also Musculoskeletal system
  skin
    human physiology 612.791
    see also Skin
Tooele County (Utah) T2—792 43
Tool engineers 621.900 92
  occupational group T7—621
Toole County (Mont.) T2—786 12
Tooling
  bookbinding 686.36
Tools 621.9
Toombs County (Ga.) T2—758 782
Tooth shells 594.29
Tooth sockets
  dentistry 617.632
  see also Dentistry
Tooth tissues
  dentistry 617.634
  see also Dentistry
Toothed whales 599.5
Toothpicks
  wooden 674.88
Toowoomba (Qld.) T2—943 3
Top-down programming 005.11
Top games 795.2
  equipment technology 688.752
Top management 658.42
  public administration 352.285
  see Manual at 658.4 vs. 658.42, 658.43
Topaz
  mineralogy 549.62
Topcoats 391
  commercial technology 687.144
  customs 391

Topcoats (continued)
  home sewing 646.452
  see also Clothing
Tope 597.34
Topectomy
  surgery 617.481
  see also Nervous system
Topeka (Kan.) T2—781 63
Topiary work 715.1
Topic and comment (Grammar) 415
  specific languages T4—5
Topminnows 597.66
Topographic surveying 526.98
Topographical anatomy
  humans 611.9
Topography 910
  city planning 711.42
  geographic description 910
  geomorphology 551.41
  influence on crime 364.22
  influence on precipitation 551.577 5
  mapping 526
  military engineering 623.71
  ocean floor 551.460 84
Topological algebras 512.55
Topological manifolds 514.3
Topological transformation groups 514
Topological vector spaces 515.73
Topology 514
Toposes 512.55
Tops (Clothing) 391
  commercial technology 687.115
  customs 391
  home sewing 646.435
  see also Clothing
Tops (Coverings)
  automobile 629.26
Toradja languages 499.22
  T6—992 2
Toradjas T5—992 2
Torah (Bible) 222.1
Torah scrolls 296.461 5
Toraja (Indonesian people) T5—992 2
Toraja languages 499.22
  T6—992 2
Toraja Sa'dan language 499.22
  T6—992 2
Torbay (England) T2—423 595
Torches 621.323
  see also Lighting
Torfaen (Wales) T2—429 97
Tories
  United States history 973.314
Torino (Italy : Province) T2—451 2
Tornadoes 551.553
  meteorology 551.553
  social services 363.349 23
  weather forecasting 551.645 3
  weather modification 551.685 3
  see also Disasters
Toronto (Ont.) T2—713 541
Torpedo boats 359.835 8
  design 623.812 58
  engineering 623.825 8
  naval equipment 359.835 8
  naval units 359.325 8
Torpedoes (Ammunition) 359.825 17
  engineering 623.451 7
  naval equipment 359.825 17
Torpedoes (Fishes) 597.35
Torquay (Vic.) T2—945 2
Torque 531.34
Torrance County (N.M.) T2—789 63
Torres Strait (Qld. and Papua New Guinea) 551.465 76
  T2—164 76
Torres Strait Islands (Qld.) T2—943 8
Torrid zone T2—13
  see also Tropics
Torridge (England) T2—423 51
Torsion
  effect on materials 620.112 43
Torsion (Mathematics) 516.36
Tort liability 346.03
Tortoises 597.92
  conservation technology 639.977 92
  resource economics 333.957 92
Tortola Island (V.I.) T2—729 725
Tortricoidea 595.78
Torts 346.03
  see Manual at 345.02 vs. 346.03
Tortuga Island (Haiti) T2—729 42
Torture
  war customs 399
Toruń (Poland : Voivodeship) T2—438 2
Tory Party (Great Britain) 324.241 02
Toscana (Italy) T2—455
Tosefta 296.126 2
Total derivatives 515.33
Total differentiation 515.33
Total productive maintenance 658.202
Total quality management 658.401 3
  production management 658.562
Total war 355.02
Totalitarian government 321.9

Totalitarianism 320.53
Totem poles
  religious significance 299.74
  sculpture 731.7
Totemic kinship 306.83
Totemism 291.211
Totonac language 497
  T6—97
Totonicapán (Guatemala : Dept.) T2—728 181
Tottori-ken (Japan) T2—521 93
Toucans 598.72
  animal husbandry 636.68
Touch 573.875
  animal physiology 573.875
  human physiology 612.88
  psychology 152.182
  see also Nervous system
Touch football
  American 796.332 8
  Canadian 796.335 8
  see also Sports
Touch-me-nots 583.79
Touch techniques
  music 784.193 68
Touchtone devices
  computer science 004.76
    engineering 621.398 6
Toulouse (France) T2—448 62
Touracos 598.74
Touraine (France) T2—445 4
Tourette syndrome
  medicine 616.83
  see also Nervous system
Tourism 338.479 1
  see also Tourist trade
Tourist exemptions
  customs duties 382.782
    see also Customs (Tariff)
Tourist trade 338.479 1
  air service 387.742
  boat service 387.542
    inland waterway 386.242
    ocean 387.542
  bus service 388.322 2
    urban 388.413 22
  economics 338.479 1
  international law 341.754
  law 343.078 91
  public administration 354.73
  railroad service 385.22
  transportation services 388.042
Tourmaline 553.87
  mineralogy 549.64
  see also Semiprecious stones
Tournaments
  customs 394.7
Tours (France) T2—445 45
Towada Lake (Japan) T2—521 12
Towboats 387.232
  design 623.812 32
  engineering 623.823 2
  see also Ships
Towed boats 387.29
  design 623.812 9
  engineering 623.829
  transportation services 387.29
  see also Ships
Toweling
  arts 746.98
Towels 643.52
  arts 746.98
  home economics 643.52
  home sewing 646.21
Tower Hamlets (London, England) T2—421 5
Towers (Structural elements) 721.5
  architecture 721.5
  Christian church architecture 726.597
  construction 690.15
Towers (Structures)
  architecture 725.97
Towhees 598.883
Towner County (N.D.) T2—784 38
Townhouses 643.1
  architecture 728.312
  home economics 643.1
Towns 307.76
  see also Cities
Towns County (Ga.) T2—758 282
Townshend Acts, 1767
  United States history 973.311 2
Townsville (Qld.) T2—943 6
Toxic chemicals 363.179 1
  hazardous materials
      technology 604.7
    chemical engineering 660.280 4
  pollution 363.738 4
    see also Pollution
  public safety 363.179 1
  see also Hazardous materials
Toxic drug reactions
  pharmacodynamics 615.704
Toxic materials 363.179
  see also Hazardous materials; Toxic chemicals

Toxic shock syndrome
  incidence 614.57
  medicine 616.92
  see also Communicable diseases (Human)
Toxic spills 363.728 7
  see also Waste control
Toxic torts 346.038
Toxic wastes 363.728 7
  technology 628.42
  see also Waste control
Toxicity testing 615.907
Toxicologists 615.900 92
  occupational group T7—615
Toxicology 571.95
  medicine 615.9
    see Manual at 615.7 vs. 615.9
  veterinary medicine 636.089 59
Toxin-antitoxins
  pharmacology 615.375
Toxins
  pharmacology 615.373
Toxoids
  pharmacology 615.373
Toy dogs 636.76
Toy instrument orchestras 784.46
Toy makers 688.720 92
  occupational group T7—688
Toy Manchester terrier 636.76
Toy soldiers
  handicrafts 745.592 82
Toy theaters 791.5
Toyama-ken (Japan) T2—521 53
Toys 790.133
  cataloging 025.349 6
  customs 394.3
  library treatment 025.179 6
  making 688.72
    handicrafts 745.592
    technology 688.72
  product safety 363.19
    law 344.042 35
    see also Product safety
  recreation 790.133
  use in child care 649.55
Toys (Dogs) 636.76
TPM (Maintenance management) 658.202
TQM (Management) 658.401 3
  production management 658.562
Trabzon İli (Turkey) T2—565
Trace elements 572.515
  applied nutrition 613.285
    animal husbandry 636.085 27
  biochemistry 572.515
    humans 612.015 24
  metabolism
    human physiology 612.392 4
Tracer testing
  materials science 620.112 73
Trachea 573.26
  biology 573.26
  human anatomy 611.23
  human physiology 612.2
  medicine 616.23
  surgery 617.533
  see also Respiratory system
Tracheitis
  medicine 616.23
  see also Respiratory system
Trachichthyidae 597.64
Trachoma
  incidence 614.599 7
  ophthalmology 617.772
  see also Eyes
Trachylina 593.55
Tracing
  materials management
    receiving operations 658.728
    shipping operations 658.788 6
Track (Sports) 796.42
  see also Sports
Track and field 796.42
  see also Sports
Track and field sportsmen 796.420 92
  sports group T7—796 4
Track laying 625.144
Tracking
  space flight 629.457
  unmanned space flight 629.437
Tracking hounds 636.753 6
Tracking systems
  spacecraft 629.474 3
  unmanned spacecraft 629.464 3
Tracks (Animals) 591.479
Tracks (Railroad) 385.312
  see also Railroad tracks
Tract (Music) 782.323 5
Traction systems
  electrical engineering 621.33
Tractor trailers 388.344
  engineering 629.224
  see also Trucks

Tractors 629.225 2
  agricultural use 631.372
  driving 629.284 52
  engineering 629.225 2
  repair 629.287 52
Trade 380.1
  see also Commerce
Trade acceptances 332.77
  exchange medium 332.55
  law 346.096
Trade advertising 659.131 5
Trade agreements 382.9
  international law 341.754 026
Trade associations 380.106
  law 346.064
Trade barriers 382.7
Trade bibliographies 015
Trade cards
  illustration 741.685
Trade catalogs T1—029 4
  see also Commercial catalogs
  see Manual at 338 vs. 060, 381, 382, 670.294, 910, T1—025, T1—0294, T1—0296
Trade promotion
  international banking 332.154
Trade secrets
  law 346.048
  management 658.472
Trade shows 381.1
  advertising 659.152
Trade unions 331.88
  see also Labor unions
Trade winds 551.518 3
Trademarks 929.95
  T1—027 5
  international law 341.758 8
  law 346.048 8
  products 602.75
  public administration 352.749
  sales promotion 658.827
Traders 380.109 2
  occupational group T7—38
Trading cards
  illustration 741.6
Trading stamps
  sales promotion 658.82
Tradition (Theology)
  Christianity 231.042
Traditionalism
  philosophy 148
  political ideology 320.52
Trafalgar, Battle of, 1805 940.274 5
Traffic accidents 363.125
  see also Highway safety; Transportation safety
Traffic circles
  area planning 711.7
  engineering 625.7
  transportation services 388.13
    urban 388.411
Traffic control 388.041
  air transportation 387.740 426
    see also Air traffic control
  inland waterway 386.240 42
  railroad transportation 385.204 2
    engineering 625.165
  road transportation 388.312
    engineering 625.794
    law 343.094 6
    police services 363.233 2
    public administration 354.772 8
    urban 388.413 12
      law 343.098 2
Traffic control failures 363.120 1
  air transportation 363.124 18
  railroad transportation 363.122 1
  see also Transportation safety
Traffic engineering (Urban) 388.413 12
  law 343.098
  public administration 354.772 8
Traffic flow (Road) 388.31
  urban 388.413 1
Traffic noise 363.741
  see also Noise
Traffic patterns
  highways 388.314 3
  streets 388.413 143
Traffic regulations 343.094 6
  urban transportation 343.098
Traffic safety 363.125
  see also Highway safety; Transportation safety
Traffic signals 388.312 2
  see also Traffic signs
Traffic signs 388.312 2
  engineering 625.794
  law 343.094 6
  transportation services 388.312 2
  urban 388.413 122
    law 343.098 2
Traffic surveys
  roads 388.314
    urban 388.413 14
Traffic violations 364.147
  law 345.024 7

Traffic volume
  highways 388.314 2
  streets 388.413 142
Trafficways
  engineering 629.047
  landscape architecture 713
Trafford (England) T2—427 31
Tragedies (Drama) 792.12
  literature 808.825 12
    history and criticism 809.251 2
    specific literatures T3B—205 12
      individual authors T3A—2
  stage presentation 792.12
    see also Theater
Tragedy
  arts T3C—162
  literature 808.801 62
    history and criticism 809.916 2
    specific literatures T3B—080 162
      history and criticism T3B—091 62
Tragelaphus 599.642 3
Tragicomedies (Drama)
  literature 808.825 23
    history and criticism 809.252 3
    specific literatures T3B—205 23
      individual authors T3A—2
Tragulidae 599.63
Trail (B.C.) T2—711 62
Trailer camps 647.94
  area planning 711.557
  household management 647.94
Trailer parks 647.92
  area planning 711.58
  household management 647.92
Trailers (Freight) 388.344
  engineering 629.224
  see also Trucks
Trailers (Passenger) 388.346
  architecture 728.79
  engineering 629.226
  pulling 629.284 6
  recreation 796.79
  repair 629.287 6
  see also Motor homes
Traill County (N.D.) T2—784 14
Train accidents 363.122
  see also Railroad safety
Trainers (Aircraft)
  military engineering 623.746 2
Training
  armed forces 355.5
  child care 649.6
Training (continued)
  employee education 370.113
    see also Vocational education
Training plants 631.546
Training programs
  personnel management 658.312 404
    public administration 352.669
  public administration 354.968
Training schools (Penology) 365.42
  see also Correctional institutions
Training teachers T1—071 1
Trains 385.37
  engineering 625.2
  sanitation services 363.729 3
    see also Waste control
  transportation services 385.37
  see also Rolling stock
Traits
  individual psychology 155.23
Trajectories
  military engineering 623.514
Tramp routes 387.523
Trampolining 796.47
  see also Sports
Tramps 305.568
  T1—086 942
Tramways 388.46
  engineering 625.6
  public transportation 354.769
  transportation services 388.46
Trance phenomena (Hypnotism) 154.772
Tranquilizer abuse 362.299
  medicine 616.86
  personal health 613.8
  social welfare 362.299
  see also Substance abuse
Tranquilizers
  pharmacodynamics 615.788 2
  see also Mental illness
Trans New Guinea languages 499.12
  T6—991 2
Trans-Uranian planets 523.48
Transaction tax 336.27
  see also Turnover tax
Transactional analysis
  applied psychology 158.2
    system 158.9
  psychiatry 616.891 45
    see also Mental illness
Transborder data flow 384.3
  computer communications services 384.3

Transborder data flow
(continued)
law 341.767 2
Transcarpathia (Ukraine : Oblast) T2—477 9
Transcaucasus 947.5
T2—475
Transcendence of God 212.7
see also Attributes of God
Transcendental functions 515.22
Transcendental meditation 158.125
system 158.9
Transcendental numbers 512.73
Transcendentalism
literature 808.803 84
history and criticism 809.933 84
specific literatures T3B—080 384
history and criticism T3B—093 84
philosophy 141.3
Transcription
linguistics 411
specific languages T4—11
shorthand notes 653.14
Transcription (Genetics) 572.884 5
Transcription (Music) 781.37
Transduction (Genetics) 571.964 8
Transepts
Christian church architecture 726.592
Transfection 571.964 8
Transfer (Law) 346.043 6
Transfer of employees
personnel management 658.312 8
public administration 352.66
Transfer of learning
psychology 153.154
Transfer painting
pottery 666.45
arts 738.15
technology 666.45
Transfer payments
macroeconomic policy 339.522
Transfer RNA 572.886
Transfer students 371.291 4
higher education 378.169 14
Transfer tax (Inheritance) 336.276
law 343.053 2
public finance 336.276
Transfer tax (Transactions) 336.27
law 343.055
public finance 336.27
Transferases 572.792
see also Enzymes
Transference (Psychology) 154.24
Transfiguration of Jesus Christ 232.956
Transfinite numbers 511.322
Transformation (Genetics) 571.964 8
Transformation of energy 531.68
Transformational grammar 415
specific languages T4—5
Transformations (Mathematics) 511.33
geometry 516.1
mathematical logic 511.33
number theory 512.72
Transformer substations 621.312 6
Transformers (Electrical equipment) 621.314
Transforms 515.723
Transient magnetism (Geomagnetism) 538.74
Transients (Electricity) 621.319 21
Transistors 621.381 528
television engineering 621.388 32
Transit insurance 368.2
see also Insurance
Transit tax 382.7
public finance 336.263
see also Customs (Tariff)
Transition metals
chemical engineering 661.06
chemistry 546.6
see also Chemicals
Transitional flow 532.052 6
gas mechanics 533.216
liquid mechanics 532.516
Transits 523.99
Mercury 523.91
Venus 523.92
Transkei (South Africa) T2—687 91
Translating
linguistics 418.02
specific languages T4—802
Translation (Genetics) 572.645
Translations
bibliographies 011.7
Translator stations 384.554
see also Television
Translators 418.020 92
specific languages T4—802 092
Translators (Computer science)
microprogramming languages 005.6
programming languages 005.45
Transliteration 411
specific languages T4—11
Translocation (Genetics) 572.877
Transmission devices
automotive engineering 629.244
Transmission facilities
communications engineering 621.382 3

Transmission media
  computer communications 004.64
    engineering 621.398 1
Transmission modes
  communications engineering 621.382 16
  computer communications 004.66
    engineering 621.398 1
Transmission of light 535.3
Transmission of sound 534.2
  see also Sound
Transmitters
  radio engineering 621.384 131
  television engineering 621.388 31
Transmitting electricity 621.319
Transmitting heat
  engineering 621.402 2
Transmitting steam 621.185
Transoceanic flights
  engineering 629.130 91
Transonic flow 533.274
  air mechanics 533.62
    aeronautics 629.132 304
Transpersonal psychology 150.198
Transpiration 575.8
  meteorology 551.572
Transplanting (Plant
    propagation) 631.536
Transplants (Medical) 362.197 95
  see also Organ transplants
Transport aircraft
  military engineering 623.746 5
Transport phenomena 530.475
  chemical engineering 660.284 2
  see also Mass transfer
Transport proteins 572.69
Transport theory (Statistical
    mechanics) 530.138
Transport workers 388.092
  occupational group T7—388
Transportation 388
  coal technology 662.624
  gas technology 665.743
  international law 341.756
  law 343.093
  military engineering 623.6
  mining 622.6
  museology 069.53
  petroleum technology 665.543
  public administration 354.76
  safety 363.12
    see also Transportation
      safety
  social effects 303.483 2
Transportation (continued)
  transportation services 388
  see Manual at 380
Transportation (Spiritualism) 133.92
Transportation accidents 363.12
  see also Transportation safety
Transportation advertising 659.134 4
Transportation diseases
  medicine 616.980 2
  see also Environmental
      diseases (Human)
Transportation engineering 629.04
Transportation equipment
  engineering 629.046
Transportation facilities 388
  architecture 725.3
  area planning 711.7
  construction 690.53
  military resources 355.27
Transportation for employees
  personnel management 658.383
Transportation injuries
  medicine 617.102 8
Transportation insurance 368.2
  see also Insurance
Transportation law 343.093
Transportation liability insurance 368.57
  see also Insurance
Transportation police 363.287
Transportation safety 363.12
  fire hazards 363.379
    see also Fire safety
  law 343.093 8
  public administration 353.98
  social services 363.12
  see Manual at 900: Historic
      events vs. nonhistoric
      events
Transportation workers 388.092
  occupational group T7—388
Transporter bridges 388
  construction 624.86
  see also Bridges
Transports (Ships) 359.985 83
  design 623.812 64
  engineering 623.826 4
  naval equipment 359.985 83
  naval units 359.985 3
Transposition (Music) 781.436
Transposons 572.869
Transsexuals 305.906 6
  T1—086 6
Transuranium elements 546.44
  see also Chemicals

Transvaal (Colony) 968.204 9
T2—682
Transvaal (South Africa) 968.2
T2—682
Transverse flutes 788.32
see also Woodwind instruments
Transvestism 306.77
Transylvania (Principality) T2—498 4
Transylvania Colony 976.902
T2—769
Transylvania County (N.C.) T2—756 93
Traoré, Moussa
Malian history 966.230 51
Trapaceae 583.76
Trapani (Sicily : Province) T2—458 24
Trapeze work
circuses 791.34
sports 796.46
see also Sports
Trappers 639.109 2
occupational group T7—639 1
Trapping 639.1
commercial 639.1
sports 799.2
Trappists 255.125
church history 271.125
Traps
military engineering 623.31
Traps Islands (N.Z.) T2—939 9
Trapshooters 799.313 209 2
sports group T7—799 3
Trapshooting 799.313 2
see also Sports
Traralgon (Vic.) T2—945 6
Trás-os-Montes (Portugal) T2—469 2
Trás-os-Montes e Alto Douro (Portugal) T2—469 2
Trash (Art style) 709.034 8
Trauma centers 362.18
Traumatic neuroses
medicine 616.852 1
see also Mental illness
Traumatic shock
medicine 617.21
Traumatology
medicine 617.1
Travel 910
literature 808.803 55
history and criticism 809.933 55
specific literatures T3B—080 355
history and criticism T3B—093 55
meal service 642.3
Travel (continued)
natural history 508
see Manual at 550 vs. 910; *also at* 900: Historic events vs. nonhistoric events; *also at* 909, 930–990 vs. 910; *also at* 913–919: Add table: 04
Travel by bicycle 796.64
Travel cooking 641.575
Travel diseases
medicine 616.980 2
see also Environmental diseases (Human)
Travel guides 910.202
Travel health 613.68
Travelers 910.92
social group T7—91
Traveling displays
transportation advertising 659.134 4
Traveling shows 791.1
Traveling-wave tubes 621.381 335
Traverse County (Minn.) T2—776 435
Traversing (Surveying) 526.33
Travertine 553.516
Travis County (Tex.) T2—764 31
Trawlers 387.28
design 623.812 8
engineering 623.828
see also Ships
Treason 364.131
law 345.023 1
Treasure County (Mont.) T2—786 313
Treasure hunting 622.19
Treasury bills 332.632 32
investment economics 332.632 32
public finance 336.32
Treasury departments (Public administration) 352.4
Treaties 341.37
texts 341.026
see Manual at 341.37
Treaty of Verdun, 843 943.02
Treaty powers (Legislative bodies) 328.346
Trebizond İli (Turkey) T2—565
Treble recorders 788.365
see also Woodwind instruments
Treble viols 787.63
see also Stringed instruments

Treble voices
  men's 782.86
    choral and mixed voices 782.86
    single voices 783.86
  women's 782.66
    see also Soprano voices
Tree crops 634
Tree frogs 597.87
Tree kangaroos 599.22
Tree lily 584.354
Tree of heaven 635.977 377
  botany 583.77
  ornamental arboriculture 635.977 377
Tree planting 634.956 5
  ornamental arboriculture 635.977
Tree shrews 599.338
Tree squirrels 599.362
Treenware 674.88
Trees 582.16
  art representation 704.943 4
  forestry 634.9
  landscape architecture 715.2
  literature 808.803 64
    history and criticism 809.933 64
    specific literatures T3B—080 364
      history and criticism T3B—093 64
  ornamental agriculture 635.977
  paleobotany 561.16
  religious worship 291.212
  see Manual at 633–635: Other crops; *also at* 635.9 vs. 582.1
Trees (Mathematics) 511.52
Trefoils 633.32
  botany 583.74
  forage crop 633.32
Trego County (Kan.) T2—781 165
Treinta y Tres (Uruguay : Dept.) T2—895 22
Trellises
  plant training 631.546
Trematoda 592.48
Trematode-caused diseases
  incidence 614.553
  medicine 616.963
  see also Communicable diseases (Human)
Tremellales 579.59
Trempealeau County (Wis.) T2—775 49
Trench fever
  incidence 614.526 6
  medicine 616.922 6
  see also Communicable diseases (Human)
Trench mouth
  medicine 616.312
  see also Digestive system
Trench warfare 355.44
Trengganu T2—595 1
Trent (Italy : Province) T2—453 85
Trent, River (England) T2—425
Trentino-Alto Adige (Italy) T2—453 8
Trento (Italy : Province) T2—453 85
Trenton (N.J.) T2—749 66
Trespass (Law) 346.036
Trestle bridges 388
  construction 624.32
  see also Bridges
Treutlen County (Ga.) T2—758 682
Treviño (Spain) T2—466 7
Treviso (Italy : Province) T2—453 6
Triakidae 597.36
Trial-and-error learning
  psychology 153.152 4
Trial of Jesus Christ 232.962
Trial practice 347.075
  criminal law 345.075
Trial procedure 347.075
Trials (Law) 347.07
  criminal law 345.07
Triangles 516.15
Triangles (Music) 786.884 2
  see also Percussion instruments
Triangulation 526.33
Triassic period 551.762
  geology 551.762
  paleontology 560.176 2
Triathlon 796.425 7
  see also Sports
Tribal communities 307.772
  government 321.1
Tribal fighting (Military tactics) 355.425
Tribal groups 306.08
Tribal land
  economics 333.2
Triboelectricity 537.21
Tribology 621.89
Tribulation (Christian doctrine) 236.9
Tribunals
  papal administration 262.136
Tricarboxylic acid cycle 572.475
Triceratops 567.915 8
Trichiales 579.52
Trichinosis
  incidence 614.562

Trichinosis (continued)
  medicine 616.965 4
  see also Communicable diseases (Human)
Trichiuridae 597.78
Trichoderma 579.567 7
Trichomycetes 579.53
Trichoptera 595.745
Trick games 793.5
Trick photography 778.8
  motion pictures 778.534 5
Trick skiing 796.937
  see also Sports
Tricks 793.8
  manufacturing technology 688.726
Tricuspid valve
  human anatomy 611.12
  human physiology 612.17
  medicine 616.125
  see also Cardiovascular system
Tricycles
  engineering 629.227 3
  repair 629.287 73
  riding 629.284 73
Trier (Germany) T2—434 313
Trier (Germany : Regierungsbezirk) T2—434 31
Trieste (Italy : Province) T2—453 93
Trifolium 633.32
  botany 583.74
  forage crop 633.32
Trigg County (Ky.) T2—769 79
Trigger circuits
  electronics 621.381 537
Triggerfishes 597.64
Trigonometric leveling 526.38
Trigonometry 516.24
Trihydroxy aromatics 547.633
Trikala (Greece : Nome) T2—495 4
Trilateration 526.33
Trilliums 584.32
  floriculture 635.934 32
Trills 781.247
Trilobita 565.39
Trimble County (Ky.) T2—769 375
Trimmers 621.93
Trimmings
  textiles 677.7
Trinidad 972.983
  T2—729 83
Trinidad and Tobago 972.983
  T2—729 83
Trinidadians T5—969 729 83
Trinitarians (Religious order) 255.42
  church history 271.42
Trinity 231.044
  art representation 704.948 52
Trinity County (Calif.) T2—794 14
Trinity County (Tex.) T2—764 172
Trinity River (Tex.) T2—764 14
Trinity Sunday 263.94
  devotional literature 242.38
  music 781.729 4
  sermons 252.64
Trios
  chamber music 785.13
  vocal music 783.13
Triphenylmethane dyes 667.254
Tripiṭaka 294.382
Triple Alliance, War of the, 1865–1870 989.205
Triple jump 796.432
  see also Sports
Triple points 530.474
  see also Phase transformations
Triplets 306.875
  psychology 155.444
  see also Siblings
Tripods (Cameras) 771.38
Tripoli (Libya) T2—612
Tripolis (Libya) 961.2
  T2—612
  ancient 939.74
  T2—397 4
Tripolitan War, 1801–1805 973.47
Tripp County (S.D.) T2—783 61
Tripura (India) T2—541 5
Triremes 387.21
  design 623.812 1
  engineering 623.821
  handling 623.882 1
  transportation services 387.21
  see also Ships
Trisecting an angle 516.204
Tristan da Cunha Islands T2—973
Tritium 546.213
  see also Chemicals
Trituberculata 569.2
Triumphs
  customs 394.4
Triuridales 584.37
tRNA 572.886
Troas T2—392 1
Trobriand Islands (Papua New Guinea) T2—954 1
Troches
  practical pharmacy 615.43

Trochili 598.764
Trochilidae 598.764
Trochodendrales 583.43
Troglodytidae 598.833
Trogoniformes 598.73
  paleozoology 568.7
Trogons 598.73
Trois-Rivières (Quebec) T2—714 451
Trois-Rivières (Quebec : Administrative Region) T2—714 45
Trojan horses (Computer security) 005.84
Trolleybus transportation 388.413 223
  engineering 625.6
  transportation services 388.413 223
Trolleys 388.413 223
  engineering 625.66
  transportation services 388.413 223
Trolling (Fishing) 799.128
Trombones 788.93
  instrument 788.931 9
  music 788.93
  see also Brass instruments
Trombonists 788.930 92
  occupational group T7—788
Trompsburg (South Africa : District) T2—685 7
Troms fylke (Norway) T2—484 5
Trøndelag (Norway) T2—484 1
Troop movements 355.411
Troop support 355.415
Troopships 359.985 83
  see also Transports (Ships)
Tropaeolaceae 583.79
Tropes (Music) 782.297
  choral and mixed voices 782.529 7
  single voices 783.092 97
Tropic birds 598.43
Tropical animals 591.709 13
Tropical biology 578.091 3
Tropical climate 551.691 3
  health 613.113
Tropical cooking 641.591 3
Tropical cyclones 551.552
  see also Hurricanes
Tropical diseases
  medicine 616.988 3
  see also Environmental diseases (Human)
Tropical ecology 577.091 3
Tropical forests
  biology 578.730 913
  ecology 577.309 13
Tropical fruits
  cooking 641.646
  food 641.346
  orchard crops 634.6
Tropical grasslands
  biology 578.748
  ecology 577.48
Tropical plants 581.709 13
  floriculture 635.952 3
Tropical rain forests
  biology 578.734
  ecology 577.34
Tropics T2—13
  biology 578.091 3
  ecology 577.091 3
Troposphere 551.513
  T2—161 2
Trotskyism 335.433
  economics 335.433
  political ideology 320.532 3
Trotskyist International 324.175
Trotters (Horses) 636.175
Troubadour poetry 808.814
  history and criticism 809.14
  specific literatures T3B—104
    individual authors T3A—1
Trough zithers 787.72
  see also Stringed instruments
Troughs
  music 786.82
    concussed 786.874
    friction 786.864
      set 786.864
      single 786.888
    percussed 786.844
      set 786.844
      single 786.884 4
    see also Percussion instruments
Troup County (Ga.) T2—758 463
Trousdale County (Tenn.) T2—768 482
Trousers 391
  commercial technology 687.113
  customs 391
  home sewing 646.433
  see also Clothing
Trout 641.392
  commercial fishing 639.275 7
  conservation technology 639.977 57
  cooking 641.692
  culture 639.375 7
    economics 338.371 375 7
  food 641.392
  resource economics 333.956 57

Trout (continued)
  sports fishing 799.175 7
  zoology 597.57
Trout-perches 597.62
Trover and conversion 346.036
Troy (Extinct city) T2—392 1
Truancy 371.295
  law 344.079 2
Truant officers 371.295
Trucial States T2—535 7
Truck accidents 363.125 9
  see also Highway safety
Truck cavalry 357.54
Truck farming 635
Truck terminals 388.33
  transportation services 388.33
    urban 388.473
Truck transportation 388.324
  international law 341.756 883
  law 343.094 83
  public administration 354.765 4
  transportation services 388.324
  urban 388.413 24
    law 343.098 2
Truckers 388.324 092
  occupational group T7—388
Trucks 388.344
  agricultural use 631.373
  driving 629.284 4
  engineering 629.224
  military engineering 623.747 4
  operation 388.324 044
    urban 388.413 24
  repair 629.287 4
  transportation services 388.344
  see also Automotive vehicles
Trudeau, Pierre Elliott
  Canadian history 971.064 4
    1968–1979 971.064 4
    1980–1984 971.064 6
True bugs 595.754
True lice 595.756
True seals 599.79
True wasps 595.798
True water beetles 595.762
Truffles 641.358
  agriculture 635.8
  biology 579.57
  commercial processing 664.805 8
  cooking 641.658
  food 641.358
Trujillo (Venezuela : State) T2—871 4
Trujillo Molina, Rafael Léonidas
  Dominican history 972.930 53
Truk (Micronesia) T2—966
Truman, Harry S.
  United States history 973.918
Trumbull County (Ohio) T2—771 38
Trumpet creepers 635.933 95
  botany 583.95
  floriculture 635.933 95
Trumpet fishes 597.67
Trumpeter swan 598.418 4
Trumpeters (Birds) 598.32
Trumpeters (Musicians) 788.920 92
  occupational group T7—788
Trumpets 788.92
  instrument 788.921 9
  music 788.92
  see also Brass instruments
Trunks (Luggage)
  manufacturing technology 685.51
Truro (N.S.) T2—716 12
Truss bridges 388
  construction 624.38
  see also Bridges
Trusses (Structural elements) 624.177 3
  naval architecture 623.817 73
Trust companies 332.26
Trust services 332.178
Trust territories 321.08
  see also Semisovereign states
Trust Territory of the Pacific
    Islands 996.5
  T2—965
Trustees
  executive management 658.422
  libraries 021.82
Trusts (Fiduciary) 346.059
  accounting 657.47
  income tax law 343.052 64
  tax law 343.064
Trusts (Organizations) 338.85
  see also Combinations
    (Enterprises)
Truth 121
Truth in lending 346.073
Truth tables 160
Truthfulness
  ethics 177.3
    see also Ethical problems
Trypanosomiasis
  incidence 614.533
  medicine 616.936 3
  see also Communicable
    diseases (Human)
Trypetidae 595.774
Tsafon (Israel : District) T2—569 45

Tsetse flies 595.774
Tsimshian Indians T5—974 1
Tsimshian language 497.41
T6—974 1
Tsin dynasty 931.04
Tsinghai Province (China) T2—514 7
Tsiranana, Philibert
Malagasy history 969.105 1
Tsitsikamma Forest and Coastal National Park (South Africa) T2—687 4
Tsogo languages 496.396
T6—963 96
Tsolo (South Africa : District) T2—687 91
Tsomo (South Africa : District) T2—687 91
Tsonga (African people) T5—963 978
Tsonga language 496.397 8
T6—963 978
Tsonga literature 896.397 8
Tsugaru Strait (Japan) 551.465 54
T2—164 54
Tsunami 551.470 24
Tsutsugamushi disease
incidence 614.526 4
medicine 616.922 4
see also Communicable diseases (Human)
Tswa-Ronga languages 496.397 8
T6—963 978
Tswana (African people) T5—963 977 5
Tswana language 496.397 75
T6—963 977 5
Tswana literature 896.397 75
Tuamotu Islands T2—963 2
Tuareg T5—933
Tuareg language 493.38
T6—933 8
Tuareg literature 893.38
Tuataras 597.945
Tubal pregnancy
obstetrics 618.31
Tubal sterilization
health 613.942
surgery 618.120 59
see also Birth control
Tubas 788.98
instrument 788.981 9
music 788.98
see also Brass instruments
Tube zithers 787.72
see also Stringed instruments
Tuberales 579.57
Tuberculosis 362.196 995
incidence 614.542
law 344.043 699 5
medicine 616.995
social services 362.196 995
see also Communicable diseases (Human)
Tubers 581.46
cooking 641.652
descriptive botany 581.46
food 641.352
food crops 635.2
nursery production 631.526
ornamental plants 635.915 26
physiology 575.498
planting 631.532
ornamental plants 635.915 32
Tubes
music 786.82
concussed 786.875
friction 786.865
set 786.865
single 786.888
percussed 786.845
set 786.845
single 786.884 5
see also Percussion instruments
Tübingen (Germany : Regierungsbezirk) T2—434 73
Tubuai Islands T2—962 2
Tubular bridges 388
construction 624.4
see also Bridges
Tubular drums 786.94
see also Percussion instruments
Tubulidentata 599.31
paleozoology 569.31
Tucano Indians T5—983 5
Tucano language 498.35
T6—983 5
Tucanoan languages 498.35
T6—983 5
Tucker County (W. Va.) T2—754 83
Tucson (Ariz.) T2—791 776
Tucumán (Argentina) T2—824 3
Tudor, House of 942.05
English history 942.05
genealogy 929.72
Irish history 941.505
Tufa 552.5
Tuff 552.23

Tug Fork T2—754 4
  Kentucky T2—769 2
  West Virginia T2—754 4
Tug services 387.166
  inland ports 386.866
  law 343.096 7
Tugboats 387.232
  design 623.812 32
  engineering 623.823 2
  see also Ships
Tugela (South Africa) T2—684 4
Tugela River (South Africa) T2—684
Tughluk dynasty 954.023 6
Tuition 371.206
  higher education 378.106
Tukano language 498.35
  T6—983 5
Tukanoan languages 498.35
  T6—983 5
Tuktoyaktuk (N.W.T.) T2—719 6
Tula (Russia : Oblast) T2—473 4
Tulameen River (B.C.) T2—711 5
Tulare County (Calif.) T2—794 86
Tularemia
  incidence 614.573 9
  medicine 616.923 9
  see also Communicable diseases (Human)
Tularosa Valley (N.M.) T2—789 65
Tulbagh (South Africa : District) T2—687 3
Tulcea (Romania : Judeţ) T2—498 3
Tulip tree 583.22
  forestry 634.973 22
Tulips 635.934 32
  botany 584.32
  floriculture 635.934 32
Tulles 677.654
  see also Textiles
Tulsa County (Okla.) T2—766 86
Tul´skaîa oblast´ (Russia) T2—473 4
Tulums 788.49
  see also Woodwind instruments
Tumbes (Peru : Dept.) T2—851 2
Tumble bugs 595.764 9
Tumbler Ridge (B.C.) T2—711 87
Tumbling 796.47
  see also Sports
Tumbling flower beetles 595.769
Tumboa plant 585.8
Tumbuka (African people) T5—963 91
Tumbuka language 496.391
  T6—963 91
Tumors (Biology) 571.978
Tumors (Human)
  incidence 614.599 9
  medicine 616.992
    see Manual at 616.994 vs. 616.992
  see also Diseases (Human)
Tunas 641.392
  commercial fishing 639.277 83
  conservation technology 639.977 783
  cooking 641.692
  food 641.392
  resource economics 333.956 783
  zoology 597.783
Tunas (Cuba : Province) T2—729 162
Tunbridge Wells (England : Borough) T2—422 38
Tunceli Ili (Turkey) T2—566 7
Tundras 551.453
  T2—145
  biology 578.758 6
  ecology 577.586
  geography 910.914 5
  geomorphology 551.453
  physical geography 910.021 45
Tung oil 665.333
Tung tree 583.69
Tungstates
  mineralogy 549.74
Tungsten 669.734
  chemical engineering 661.053 6
  chemistry 546.536
  economic geology 553.464 9
  materials science 620.189 34
  metallography 669.957 34
  metallurgy 669.734
  metalworking 673.734
  mining 622.346 49
  physical metallurgy 669.967 34
  see also Chemicals; Metals
Tungurahua (Ecuador) T2—866 15
Tungus T5—941
Tungus languages 494.1
  T6—941
Tungus-Manchu languages 494.1
  T6—941
Tungusic languages 494.1
  T6—941
Tungusic literatures 894.1
Tungusic peoples T5—941
Tunica County (Miss.) T2—762 86

Tunicata 596.2
  paleozoology 566
Tuning 784.192 8
Tunis (Tunisia) T2—611
Tunisia 961.1
  T2—611
Tunisians T5—927 611
Tunnel diodes 621.381 522
Tunnel engineers 624.193 092
  occupational group T7—624
Tunnel vaults 721.45
  architecture 721.45
  construction 690.145
Tunneling 624.193
  mining 622.26
Tunneling (Physics) 530.416
  semiconductors 537.622 6
Tunnels 388
  architecture 725.98
  construction 624.193
  military engineering 623.68
  mining 622.26
  psychological influence 155.964
  public administration 354.76
  transportation services 388
    railroads 385.312
    roads 388.13
Tuolumne County (Calif.) T2—794 45
Tupaiidae 599.338
  paleozoology 569.338
Tupelos 583.84
Tupí Indians T5—983 829
Tupí language 498.382 9
  T6—983 829
Tupí languages 498.38
  T6—983 8
Tupí literature 898.382 9
Tupian languages 498.38
  T6—983 8
Tupper, Charles, Sir
  Canadian history 971.055
Turacos 598.74
Turbellaria 592.42
Turbines 621.406
  hydraulic power 621.24
  steam engineering 621.165
Turbojet engines 621.435 2
  aircraft 629.134 353 3
Turbojet fuel 665.538 25
Turbomachines 621.406
Turboprop airplanes 387.733 43
  engineering 629.133 343
  transportation services 387.733 43
  see also Aircraft
Turboprop engines
  aircraft 629.134 353 2
Turboramjet engines
  aircraft 629.134 353 4
Turbots 597.69
Turbulent flow 532.052 7
  aeronautics 629.132 32
  air mechanics 533.62
  gas mechanics 533.217
  liquid mechanics 532.517
Turco-Tataric languages 494.3
  T6—943
Turcomans T5—943 64
Turdidae 598.842
Turf
  floriculture 635.964 2
Turfanish language 491.994
  T6—919 94
Tŭrgovishte (Bulgaria : Okrŭg) T2—499 3
Tŭrgovishtki okrŭg (Bulgaria) T2—499 3
Turin (Italy : Province) T2—451 2
Turing machines 511.3
Turkana (African people) T5—965
Turkana, Lake (Kenya and Ethiopia) T2—676 27
Turkana language 496.5
  T6—965
Turkestan 958.4
  T2—584
Turkey 956.1
  T2—561
  ancient 939.2
    T2—392
Turkey (Meat) 641.365 92
  commercial processing 664.93
  cooking 641.665 92
  food 641.365 92
Turkey in Europe 949.61
  T2—496 1
  ancient 939.8
    T2—398
Turkey vulture 598.92
Turkeys 636.592
  animal husbandry 636.592
  conservation technology 639.978 645
  resource economics 333.958 645
  sports hunting 799.246 45
  zoology 598.645
Turkic languages 494.3
  T6—943
Turkic literatures 894.3
Turkic peoples T5—943

Turkish baths
  personal care 646.75
Turkish language 494.35
  T6—943 5
Turkish literature 894.35
Turkish rugs
  arts 746.756 1
  see also Rugs
Turkish Thrace 949.61
  T2—496 1
  ancient 939.8
  T2—398
Turkish Van cat 636.83
Turkmen T5—943 64
Turkmen language 494.364
  T6—943 64
Turkmen literature 894.364
Turkmen rugs
  arts 746.758 4
  see also Rugs
Turkmenistan 958.5
  T2—585
Turko-Tatar languages 494.3
  T6—943
Turkoman language 494.364
  T6—943 64
Turkoman literature 894.364
Turkomans T5—943 64
Turks T5—943 5
  see Manual at T5—9435
Turks and Caicos Islands T2—729 61
Turku ja Pori (Finland : Lääni) T2—489 73
Turku-Pori (Finland : Lääni) T2—489 73
Turmeric 641.338 3
  botany 584.39
  see also Spices
Turn and bank indicators 629.135 2
Turner, John
  Canadian history 971.064 6
Turner County (Ga.) T2—758 885
Turner County (S.D.) T2—783 385
Turneraceae 583.626
Turnicidae 598.32
Turning
  home woodworking 684.083
Turning tools 621.94
Turnip celery 641.351 28
  see also Celeriac
Turnips 641.351 25
  botany 583.64
  commercial processing 664.805 125
  cooking 641.651 25
Turnips (continued)
  food 641.351 25
  garden crop 635.125
Turnouts
  railroad engineering 625.163
Turnover of employees
  personnel management 658.314
    public administration 352.66
Turnover tax 336.27
  law 343.055
  public administration 352.44
  public finance 336.27
Tŭrnovski okrŭg (Bulgaria) T2—499 2
Turnpikes 388.122
  see also Roads
Turnstones 598.33
Turpentine 665.332
  agriculture 633.895 9
  chemical technology 665.332
  recovery from pulp 676.5
Turquoise 553.87
  mineralogy 549.72
  see also Semiprecious stones
Turs 599.648
Tursiops 599.533
Turtle farming 639.392
Turtle grass 584.73
Turtles 597.92
  conservation technology 639.977 92
  farming 639.392
  food 641.396
    commercial processing 664.95
    cooking 641.696
    home preservation 641.495
  resource economics 333.957 92
  zoology 597.92
Turun ja Porin lääni (Finland) T2—489 73
Tuscaloosa County (Ala.) T2—761 84
Tuscany (Italy) T2—455
Tuscarawas County (Ohio) T2—771 66
Tuscola County (Mich.) T2—774 45
Tusk shells 594.29
Tusks 591.47
  descriptive zoology 591.47
  physiology 573.356
Tussah silk textiles 677.392
  see also Textiles
Tutankhamen, King of Egypt
  Egyptian history 932.014
Tutoring 371.394
Tutsi (African people) T5—963 946 1
Tuva (Russia) T2—575

Tuva-Altai languages 494.33
T6—943 3
Tuvalu 996.82
T2—968 2
Tuvalu language 499.46
T6—994 6
Tuvaluans T5—994 6
Tuvinian language 494.33
T6—943 3
TV 384.55
see also Television
TV dinners
commercial processing 664.65
home serving 642.1
Tver′ (Russia : Oblast) T2—472 8
Tverskaiā oblast′ (Russia) T2—472 8
Tweed River (Scotland and England) T2—413 7
Tweeddale (Scotland : District) T2—413 82
Tweedsmuir Provincial Park (B.C.) T2—711 82
Tweezers
manufacturing technology 688.5
Twelve patriarchs
pseudepigrapha 229.914
Twelve prophets (Bible) 224.9
Twelve step programs
devotional literature 291.432
Christianity 242.4
pastoral theology 291.61
Christianity 259.429
religious guidance 291.442
Christianity 248.862 9
social theology 291.178 322 9
Christianity 261.832 29
substance abuse
rehabilitation 616.860 3
therapy 616.860 6
see Manual at 616.86 vs. 158.1, 248.8629, 291.442, 362.29
Twelve-tone system 781.268
Twelve Tribes 933.02
Twelvers (Islamic sect) 297.821
Twentieth century 909.82
T1—090 4
Twenty-first century 909.83
T1—090 5
Twenty-one (Game) 795.423
Twi (Ghanaian people) T5—963 385
Twi language (Ghana) 496.338 5
T6—963 385
Twi literature (Ghana) 896.338 5
Twiggs County (Ga.) T2—758 545
Twilight 525.7
meteorology 551.566
Twill-woven rugs
arts 746.72
see also Rugs
Twin Cities Metropolitan Area (Minn.) T2—776 579
Twin Falls County (Idaho) T2—796 37
Twines 677.71
Twining
arts 746.42
Twins 306.875
obstetrics 618.25
psychology 155.444
see also Siblings
Twisters (Tornadoes) 551.553
see also Tornadoes
Twisting textiles 677.028 22
arts 746.12
manufacturing technology 677.028 22
Two Mountains (Quebec : County) T2—714 25
Two Mountains (Quebec : Regional County Municipality) T2—714 25
Two-way radios
automobile 629.277
Tyler, John
United States history 973.58
Tyler County (Tex.) T2—764 163
Tyler County (W. Va.) T2—754 19
Tympanic membranes
human anatomy 611.85
human physiology 612.854
otology 617.85
see also Ears
Tympanuchus 598.637
Tyndale Bible 220.520 1
Tyne and Wear (England) T2—428 7
Tyne River (England) T2—428 7
Tynedale (England) T2—428 81
Type ornaments 686.224
Typecasting 686.221
Typefaces 686.224
Typefounding 686.221
Typesetters 686.225 092
occupational group T7—686 2
Typesetting 686.225
Typewriter art 760
Typewriters 652.3
manufacturing technology 681.61
office practice 652.3
Typewriting 652.3

Typewriting analysis
  criminal investigation 363.256 5
Typha 584.68
Typhales 584.68
Typhoid fever
  incidence 614.511 2
  medicine 616.927 2
  see also Communicable diseases (Human)
Typhoons 551.552
  see also Hurricanes
Typhus
  incidence 614.526 2
  medicine 616.922 2
  see also Communicable diseases (Human)
Typing 652.3
Typists 651.374 109 2
  occupational group T7—651
  office services 651.374 1
Typographic masterpieces
  books 094.4
Typographical designs
  graphic arts 760
Typography 686.22
Typology
  Biblical interpretation 220.64
  Christian doctrines 232.1
  Talmudic interpretation 296.120 64
Typology (Linguistics) 410.1
  grammar 415.01
    specific languages T4—501
Typology (Psychology) 155.26
Tyrannidae 598.823
Tyrannosaurus 567.912 9
Tyrant flycatchers 598.823
Tyre (Lebanon) T2—569 2
  ancient T2—394 4
Tyrian architecture 722.31
Tyrol (Austria) T2—436 42
Tyrolean zithers 787.75
  see also Stringed instruments
Tyrone (Northern Ireland) T2—416 4
Tyrrell County (N.C.) T2—756 172
Tyrrhenian Sea 551.462 3
  T2—163 83
Tytonidae 598.97
Tyumen (Russia : Oblast) T2—573
Tzeltal Indians T5—974 15
Tzeltal language 497.415
  T6—974 15
Tzotzil Indians T5—974 15
Tzotzil language 497.415
  T6—974 15

U

Ubangi-Shari 967.410 3
  T2—674 1
Ubangian languages 496.361
  T6—963 61
Ubombo (South Africa : District) T2—684 91
Ubykh language 499.962
  T6—999 62
Ucayali (Peru) T2—854 3
Udine (Italy : Province) T2—453 91
Udmurt language 494.53
  T6—945 3
Udmurt literature 894.53
Udmurtia (Russia) T2—474 6
Udmurts T5—945 3
UFOs (Objects) 001.942
Uganda 967.61
  T2—676 1
Ugandans T5—967 61
Ugarit (Extinct city) T2—394 3
Ugaritic language 492.67
  T6—926 7
Ugaritic literature 892.67
Ugrians T5—945 1
Ugric languages 494.51
  T6—945 1
Ugric literatures 894.51
Ugric peoples T5—945 1
UHF radio systems 621.384 151
Uíge (Angola : Province) T2—673 2
Uighur T5—943 23
Uighur language 494.323
  T6—943 23
Uighur literature 894.323
Uigur T5—943 23
Uigur language 494.323
  T6—943 23
Uigur literature 894.323
Uillean pipes 788.49
  see also Woodwind instruments
Uinta County (Wyo.) T2—787 84
Uinta Mountains (Utah and Wyo.) T2—792 14
Uintah County (Utah) T2—792 21
Uitenhage (South Africa : District) T2—687 5
Ukaan-Akpes languages 496.33
  T6—963 3
Ukraine 947.7
  T2—477

Ukrainian language 491.79
T6—917 91
Ukrainian literature 891.79
Ukrainians T5—917 91
Ukuleles 787.89
instrument 787.891 9
music 787.89
see also Stringed instruments
Ukẓin 296.123 6
Ulama
role and function 297.61
Ulawa (Solomon Islands) T2—959 38
Ulcerations
skin
medicine 616.545
see also Skin
Ulcers
digestive system
medicine 616.343
see also Digestive system
Ulema
role and function 297.61
Ul′i͡anovskai͡a oblast′
(Russia) T2—474 6
Ulladulla (N.S.W.) T2—944 7
Ulmaceae 583.45
Ulnas
human anatomy 611.717
see also Musculoskeletal system
Ulster (Northern Ireland and Ireland) 941.6
T2—416
Ulster County (N.Y.) T2—747 34
Ultima Esperanza (Chile) T2—836 42
Ultimatums
international law 341.58
Ultrafiltration analysis 544.5
Ultrahigh-frequency electronics
physics 537.534 4
Ultrahigh frequency radio systems 621.384 151
Ultrahigh-speed photography 778.37
Ultralight airplanes 387.733 43
engineering 629.133 343
transportation services 387.733 43
see also Aircraft
Ultramicrobes
medical microbiology 616.019
Ultrasonic cardiography
medicine 616.120 754 3
see also Cardiovascular system
Ultrasonic diagnosis
medicine 616.075 43
Ultrasonic testing
materials science 620.112 74
Ultrasonic therapy
medicine 615.83
Ultrasonic vibrations 534.55
biophysics 571.445
humans 612.014 455
engineering 620.28
physics 534.55
Ultrasonic weapons 623.447
Ultrasonic welding 671.529
Ultrasonography
medicine 616.075 43
Ultraviolet photography
engineering 621.367 2
Ultraviolet radiation 535.014
biophysics 571.456
humans 612.014 484
chemical effect 541.353 4
chemical engineering 660.295 34
engineering 621.364
military engineering 623.042
physics 535.014
therapeutics 615.831 5
water supply treatment 628.166 2
Ultraviolet spectroscopes
manufacturing technology 681.414 4
Ultraviolet spectroscopy 543.085 85
analytical chemistry 543.085 85
engineering 621.361 4
physics 535.844
Ulundi (Kwazulu, South Africa) T2—684 91
Uluru (Ayers Rock)-Mt. Olga National Park (N.T.) T2—942 91
Ul′yanovsk (Russia : Oblast) T2—474 6
Umatilla County (Or.) T2—795 69
Umbanda 299.672
Umbelliferae 583.849
Umberto I, King of Italy
Italian history 945.084
Umbilical cord disorders
obstetrics 618.58
Umbrella liability insurance 368.5
see also Insurance
Umbrella plant (Cyperales) 584.84
Umbrellas
customs 391.44
Umbria (Italy) T2—456 5
ancient T2—374

Umbrian language 479.9
T6—799
Umbrians T5—79
Umbumbulu (South Africa : District) T2—684 91
Umbundu languages 496.399
T6—963 99
Umhlanga (South Africa) T2—684 4
Umhlanga Rocks (South Africa) T2—684 4
Umingmaktok (N.W.T.) T2—719 7
Umlazi (South Africa : District) T2—684 91
Umm al-Qaiwain (United Arab Emirates : Emirate) T2—535 7
Umm al-Qaywayn (United Arab Emirates : Emirate) T2—535 7
Umpiring (Recreation) 790.1
  American football 796.332 3
  baseball 796.357 3
  Canadian football 796.335 3
  cricket 796.358 3
  rugby 796.333 3
  soccer 796.334 3
  see also Sports
Umpqua River (Or.) T2—795 29
UMT (Military training) 355.225
Umtata (South Africa : District) T2—687 91
Umvoti (South Africa : District) T2—684 7
Umzimkulu (South Africa : District) T2—687 91
Umzinto (South Africa : District) T2—684 5
UN (United Nations) 341.23
  see also United Nations
Unaligned blocs T2—171 6
Unarmed combat 796.81
  military training 355.548
  sports 796.81
  see also Sports
Unauthorized strikes 331.892 4
  see also Strikes (Work stoppages)
Unclaimed estates 346.057
Uncles 306.87
T1—085
T7—046
Unconscious
  philosophy 127
Unconventional warfare 355.343
  Algerian Revolution 965.046 8
  Chaco War 989.207 168
  Civil War (England) 942.062 8
  Civil War (Spain) 946.081 8
  Civil War (United States) 973.785
  Crimean War 947.073 88
  Falkland Islands War 997.110 248
  Franco-German War 943.082 8
  Hundred Years' War 944.025 8
  Indo-Pakistan War, 1971 954.920 518
  Indochinese War 959.704 18
  Iraqi-Iranian Conflict 955.054 28
  Korean War 951.904 28
  Mexican War 973.628
  Napoleonic Wars 940.278
  Persian Gulf War, 1991 956.704 428
  South African War 968.048 8
  Spanish-American War 973.898
  Thirty Years' War 940.248
  United States Revolutionary War 973.385
  Vietnamese War 959.704 38
  War of 1812 973.528 5
  War of the Pacific 983.061 68
  World War I 940.485
  World War II 940.548 5
Undaria 579.887
Underachievers (Students) 371.28
  special education 371.9
Underberg District (South Africa) T2—684 7
Undercover police work 363.232
Underdeveloped areas T2—172 4
Underemployed 331.13
Underemployment 331.13
Underglaze painting 666.45
  arts 738.15
  technology 666.45
Underground architecture 720.473
Underground areas
  environmental psychology 155.964
Underground construction 624.19
Underground disposal 363.728
  sewage sludge disposal 628.366
  solid waste technology 628.445 66
  see also Waste control
Underground electrical lines 621.319 23
Underground mining 622.2
Underground movements
  World War II 940.533 6
Underground publications
  bibliographies 011.56

Underground railroad
  Civil War (United States)
      cause 973.711 5
Underground railroads 388.428
  see also Subways (Rail)
Underground shelters
  military engineering 623.38
Underground stems 581.46
  descriptive botany 581.46
  physiology 575.49
Underground transportation 388.428
  see also Subways (Rail)
Underground water 553.79
  see also Groundwater
Underpopulation 363.91
Undertaking (Mortuary) 363.75
  customs 393
  economics 338.473 637 5
  funerals 393.9
    see also Funerals
  law 344.045
  music 781.588
  social services 363.75
    public administration 353.6
  technology 614.6
  see also Death
Underwater acoustics
  engineering 620.25
Underwater archaeology 930.102 804
Underwater construction 627.702
Underwater demolition
  military engineering 623.27
Underwater demolition units
    (Navy) 359.984
Underwater engineering 627.7
Underwater guided missiles 359.981 782
  engineering 623.451 97
  military equipment 359.981 782
Underwater mining 622.295
Underwater photography 778.73
Underwater prospecting 622.17
Underwater reconnaissance
  military engineering 623.71
  naval operations 359.984
Underwater swimming
  sports 797.23
Underwater tunnels 388
  construction 624.194
  see also Tunnels
Underwater video production 778.596
Underwater welding 671.52
Underwear 391.42
  commercial technology 687.2
  customs 391.42
Underwear (continued)
  home sewing 646.42
  see also Clothing
Underweight persons
  cooking for 641.563 4
  weight-gaining diet 613.24
Underwriters 368.012 092
  occupational group T7—368
Underwriting 368.012
Undulant fever
  incidence 614.565
  medicine 616.957
  see also Communicable
      diseases (Human)
Unemployed persons 305.906 941
    T1—086 941
  labor economics 331.137
  social group 305.906 941
Unemployment 331.137
  economics 331.137
    see Manual at 331.1 vs.
        331.11, 331.12; *also at*
        331.12042 vs. 331.1377
  influence on crime 364.2
  sociology 306.361
  see Manual at 331.1372 vs.
      331.13704
Unemployment compensation 368.44
  see also Unemployment
      insurance
Unemployment insurance 368.44
  labor economics 331.255
  law 344.024
  public administration 353.54
  see also Insurance
Unesco 001.060 1
  law 341.767
  public administration 353.721 1
Unfair economic practices 338.604 8
  see also Restraint of trade
      (Competition)
Ungava Bay Region
    (Quebec and N.W.T.) T2—714 111
Ungraded schools 371.255
Ungulates 599.6
  conservation technology 639.979 6
  paleozoology 569.6
  resource economics 333.959 6
Unicameral legislatures 328.39
UNICEF (Children's Fund) 362.7
  law 341.76
  public administration 353.536 211
Unicoi County (Tenn.) T2—768 982
Unicorn fishes 597.64

Unicorn plants 635.933 95
  botany 583.95
  floriculture 635.933 95
Unicorns 398.245 4
  see also Legendary animals
Unidentified flying objects 001.942
Unification Church 289.96
  see also Christian denominations
Unified field theory 530.142
Uniflagellate molds 579.53
Uniform algebras 512.55
Uniform functions 515.223
Uniform spaces 516
  geometry 516
  topology 514.320 2
Uniform titles
  cataloging 025.322
Uniforms 391
  armed forces 355.14
    issue and use 355.81
    see Manual at 355.1409; *also at* 355.81 vs. 355.14
  commercial technology 687.15
  customs 391
  see also Clothing
Unincorporated banks 332.123
Unincorporated business enterprises 338.7
  law 346.068
  management 658.044
    initiation 658.114 4
    see Manual at 658.04 vs. 658.114, 658.402
  production economics 338.7
Unincorporated societies 060
  see also Nonprofit organizations
Unión (El Salvador : Dept.) T2—728 434
Union (Philippines) T2—599 1
Union-authorized strikes 331.892 2
  see also Strikes (Work stoppages)
Union catalogs 025.31
  bibliography 017
  library cooperation 021.642
  library science 025.31
Union County (Ark.) T2—767 61
Union County (Fla.) T2—759 14
Union County (Ga.) T2—758 285
Union County (Ill.) T2—773 995
Union County (Ind.) T2—772 625
Union County (Iowa) T2—777 853
Union County (Ky.) T2—769 885
Union County (Miss.) T2—762 925
Union County (N.C.) T2—756 755
Union County (N.J.) T2—749 36
Union County (N.M.) T2—789 23
Union County (Ohio) T2—771 532
Union County (Or.) T2—795 71
Union County (Pa.) T2—748 48
Union County (S.C.) T2—757 41
Union County (S.D.) T2—783 392
Union County (Tenn.) T2—768 935
Union dues checkoff 331.889 6
Union federations 331.872
  see also Labor unions
Union Islands 996.15
  T2—961 5
Union of Kalmar 948.03
  see also Kalmar Union
Union of Soviet Socialist Republics 947.084
  T2—47
Union organizing 331.891 2
Union Parish (La.) T2—763 89
Union Party (U.S. : 1854–) 324.273 4
Union pipes 788.49
  see also Woodwind instruments
Union racketeering 364.106 7
Union recognition 331.891 2
Union republics (Soviet Union) 321.023
  see also States (Members of federations)
Union security 331.889
Union shop 331.889 2
Uniondale (South Africa : District) T2—687 4
Unionidae 594.4
Unions 331.88
  see also Labor unions
Uniramia 595.7
  paleozoology 565.7
Unison voices 782.5
Unit method of teaching 371.36
Unit operations
  chemical engineering 660.284 2
Unit processes
  chemical engineering 660.284 4
Unit theory (Mathematics) 512.74
Unit trusts 332.632 7
Unitarian and Universalist churches 289.1
  church government 262.091
    parishes 254.091
  doctrines 230.91

Unitarian and Universalist churches (continued)
- guides to Christian life 248.489 1
- missions 266.91
- moral theology 241.049 1
- public worship 264.091
- religious associations 267.189 1
- religious education 268.891
- seminaries 230.073 91
- theology 230.91

Unitarian churches 289.133
- *see also* Unitarian and Universalist churches

Unitarian Universalist Association 289.132
- *see also* Unitarian and Universalist churches

Unitarianism 289.1

Unitarians
- biography 289.109 2
- religious group T7—281

Unitary spaces 515.73

Unitary state (System of government) 321.01

United Arab Emirates 953.57
- T2—535 7

United Arab Republic 962.053
- T2—62
- Egyptian history 962.053
- Syrian history 956.910 42

United Brethren in Christ 289.9
- *see also* Christian denominations

United charities 361.8

United Church of Canada 287.92
- *see also* Christian denominations

United Church of Christ 285.834
- *see also* Congregationalism

United Church of Religious Science 299.93

United Confederate Veterans 369.17

United Conference of Methodist Churches 287.532
- *see also* Methodist Church

United Daughters of the Confederacy 369.17

United Evangelical Lutheran Church 284.131 3
- *see also* Lutheran church

United givers funds 361.8

United Kingdom 941
- T2—41
- *see Manual at* 941

United Lutheran Church in America 284.133 5
- *see also* Lutheran church

United Methodist Church (Great Britain) 287.53
- *see also* Methodist Church

United Methodist Church (U.S.) 287.6
- *see also* Methodist Church

United Methodist Free Churches 287.53
- *see also* Methodist Church

United Nations 341.23
- armed forces 355.357
- finance 336.091 63
- international law 341.23
- public administration 352.113
  - law 341.233

United Nations. Charter 341.232

United Nations. General Assembly 341.232 2

United Nations. Security Council 341.232 3

United Nations (Military alliance)
- World War II 940.533 2

United Nations Children's Fund 362.7
- law 341.76
- public administration 353.536 211

United Nations Educational, Scientific, and Cultural Organization 001.060 1
- law 341.767
- public administration 353.721 1

United Nations International Children's Emergency Fund
- law 341.76
- public administration 353.536 211

United Nations philatelic issues 769.561

United Nations treaties series 341.026 2

United Pentecostal Church 289.94
- *see also* Christian denominations

United Presbyterian Church in the U.S.A. 285.131
- *see also* Presbyterian Church

United Presbyterian Church of North America 285.134
- *see also* Presbyterian Church

United Provinces of Central America 972.804
- T2—728
- Costa Rican history 972.860 42
- Guatemalan history 972.810 42
- Honduran history 972.830 4
- Nicaraguan history 972.850 42
- Salvadoran history 972.840 42

United Provinces of the
Netherlands 949.204
T2—492
United Reformed Church in the
United Kingdom 285.232
see also Presbyterian Church
United Society of Believers in
Christ's Second Appearing 289.8
see also Christian
denominations
United States 973
T2—73
see Manual at T2—73 vs.
T2—71
United States. Central
Intelligence Agency 327.127 3
United States. Continental
Congress
United States history 973.312
United States. Court of Customs
and Patent Appeals 347.732 8
United States. Navy. SEALs 359.984
United States. Supreme Court 347.732 6
reports 348.734 13
United States Code 348.732 3
United States customary
measurements 530.813
United States federal law
reporter system for the
Atlantic region 348.734 22
United States federal reporter
system for the Northeast
region 348.734 23
United States federal reporter
system for the Northwest
region 348.734 24
United States federal reporter
system for the Pacific region 348.734 28
United States federal reporter
system for the South region 348.734 27
United States federal reporter
system for the Southeast
region 348.734 25
United States federal reporter
system for the Southwest
region 348.734 26
United States national reporter
system 348.734 2
United States of Colombia 986.106 1
T2—861
Colombian history 986.106 1
Panamanian history 972.870 3
United States Pacific seawaters 551.466 32
T2—164 32
United States people
(National group) T5—13
United States Sanitary
Commission
Civil War (United States) 973.777
Uniting Church in Australia 287.93
see also Christian
denominations
Unitized cargo services 385.72
public administration 354.764
Units 530.81
Unity 111.82
Christian church 262.72
Unity School of Christianity 289.97
see also Christian
denominations
Universal algebra 512
Universal bibliographies 011.1
Universal Decimal Classification 025.432
Universal history 909
Universal joints 621.825
Universal languages 401.3
Universal life insurance 368.324
see also Insurance
Universal military training 355.225
law 343.012 2
Universal priesthood 234
Universal time 389.17
Universalism (Economic school) 330.155
Universalist churches 289.134
see also Unitarian and
Universalist churches
Universalists
biography 289.109 2
religious group T7—281
Universals (Philosophy) 111.2
Universe
astronomy 523.1
philosophy 113
see Manual at 520 vs. 523.1,
523.112, 523.8
Universities 378
T1—071 1
area planning 711.57
liability 344.075
see also Higher education;
entries beginning with
College
Universities without walls 378.03
see also Higher education
University extension 378.175

University graduates
  choice of vocation 331.702 35
  labor force 331.114 23
  social group 305.55
  unemployment 331.137 804
University libraries 027.7
  see also Academic libraries
University presses
  bibliographies of publications 011.54
  publishing 070.594
Unjust enrichment 346.029
Unlawful assembly 364.143
  law 345.024 3
Unloading operations
  materials management 658.788 5
  ships 623.888 1
Unmanned space flight
  engineering 629.43
  see Manual at 629.43, 629.45 vs. 919.904
Unmanned spacecraft
  engineering 629.46
  military engineering 623.749
Unmarried couples 306.735
  T1—086 5
  law 346.015
Unmarried fathers 306.874 2
Unmarried mothers 306.874 3
  T1—086 947
  family relationships 306.874 3
  government programs 353.533 1
  psychology 155.642 3
  social group 305.489 694 7
  social welfare 362.839 2
    public administration 353.533 1
Unofficial strikes 331.892 4
  see also Strikes (Work stoppages)
Unsized papers 676.286
Unskilled workers 331.798
  T1—086 24
  labor economics 331.798
  labor force 331.114 22
  personnel management 658.304 4
  unemployment 331.137 804
Unspecified keyboard instruments 786
  see also Keyboard instruments
Unspecified melody instrument 787
  see also Stringed instruments
Unterfranken (Germany) T2—433 3
Unterwalden (Switzerland : Canton) T2—494 76
Untouchables 305.568
  T1—086 94
  social theology 291.178 345 68
    Hinduism 294.517 834 568
Unwed parenthood 306.856
  ethics 173
  social theology 291.178 358 56
    Christianity 261.835 856
Upanishads 294.592 18
Upholstered furniture 645.4
  manufacturing technology 684.12
  see also Furniture
Upholstery 645.4
  arts 746.95
  home sewing 646.21
  household management 645.4
  interior decoration 747.5
Upholstery fabrics 677.616
  see also Textiles
Upholstery trimmings 677.76
Upland game birds 598.6
  conservation technology 639.978 6
  resource economics 333.958 6
  sports hunting 799.246
Upland rice
  food crop 633.179
Upper Arrow Lake (B.C.) T2—711 62
Upper atmosphere 551.514
  winds 551.518 7
Upper Austria (Austria) T2—436 2
Upper Avon River (England) T2—424 4
Upper Bavaria (Germany) T2—433 6
Upper Canada 971.03
  T2—71
  Ontario 971.302
    T2—713
Upper classes 305.52
  T1—086 21
Upper Egypt T2—623
Upper extremities (Human) 612.97
  anatomy 611.97
  bones 612.75
    anatomy 611.717
    medicine 616.71
    physiology 612.75
    surgery 617.471
  fractures
    medicine 617.157
  joints
    medicine 616.72
    surgery 617.57
  muscles
    anatomy 611.737

Upper extremities (Human) (continued)
  physiology 612.97
  regional medicine 617.57
  surgery 617.570 59
Upper Franconia (Germany) T2—433 1
Upper Guinea T2—665
Upper houses (Legislative bodies) 328.31
Upper Hutt City (N.Z.) T2—936 5
Upper Karoo (South Africa) T2—687 13
Upper Nile (Sudan : Province) T2—629 3
Upper Nile (Sudan : Region) T2—629 3
Upper Palatinate (Germany) T2—433 4
Upper Peninsula (Mich.) T2—774 9
Upper Volta 966.25
  T2—662 5
Upper Volta people T5—966 25
Uppsala län (Sweden) T2—487
Upshur County (Tex.) T2—764 222
Upshur County (W. Va.) T2—754 62
Upson County (Ga.) T2—758 486
Upton County (Tex.) T2—764 863
Ur (Extinct city) T2—35
Ur period 935.01
Urabá, Gulf of (Colombia) 551.463 5
  T2—163 65
Ural-Altaic languages 494
  T6—94
Ural-Altaic literatures 894
Ural Mountains (Russia) T2—474 3
Uralic languages 494.5
  T6—945
Uralic literatures 894.5
Uraninite
  mineralogy 549.528
Uranium 669.293 1
  chemical engineering 661.043 1
  chemistry 546.431
  economic geology 553.493 2
  human toxicology 615.925 431
  materials science 620.189 293 1
  metallography 669.952 931
  metallurgy 669.293 1
  mining 622.349 32
  physical metallurgy 669.962 931
  production economics 338.274 932
  prospecting 622.184 932
  see also Chemicals; Metals
Urantia 299
Uranus (Planet) 523.47
  T2—992 7
  astrology 133.538
Urban areas 307.76
  T2—173 2
  see also Cities
Urban biology 578.756
Urban communities 307.76
  see also Cities
Urban development 307.141 6
  law 344.06
  public administration 354.279 3
Urban dialects 417.209 173 2
  linguistics 417.209 173 2
    specific languages T4—7
  sociolinguistics 306.440 917 32
Urban ecology (Biology) 577.56
Urban economics 330.917 32
Urban education 370.917 32
Urban exodus 307.26
Urban families 306.854
Urban forestry 635.977
Urban government 320.85
Urban heat islands 551.525 091 732
Urban homesteading 363.583
  see also Housing
Urban lands 333.77
  economics 333.77
    sale and rental 333.337
  public administration 354.35
Urban mass transportation 388.4
  see also Urban transportation
Urban ministry 253.091 732
  church administration 254.22
Urban municipalities 320.85
Urban renewal 307.341 6
  civic art 711.4
Urban runoff 363.728 4
  sewer systems 628.21
  social services 363.728 4
  see also Waste control
Urban-rural migration 307.26
Urban schools 371.009 173 2
Urban sociology 307.76
Urban transportation 388.4
  law 343.098
  public administration 354.769
  safety 363.125
    public administration 353.98
    see also Transportation safety
  transportation services 388.4
Urban warfare 355.426

Urdu language 491.439
T6—914 39
Urdu literature 891.439
Ure River (England) T2—428 48
Urea fertilizers 631.841
  chemical engineering 668.624 1
Ureas 668.422 3
Uredinales 579.592
Uremia
  medicine 616.635
  see also Urinary system
Ureters 573.49
  biology 573.49
  human anatomy 611.61
  human physiology 612.467
  medicine 616.61
  surgery 617.461
  see also Urinary system
Urethra 573.49
  biology 573.49
  human anatomy 611.62
  human physiology 612.467
  medicine 616.62
    men 616.64
  surgery 617.462
  see also Urinary system
Urethritis
  medicine 616.624
  see also Urinary system
Urewera National Park
    (N.Z.) T2—934 25
Urfa İli (Turkey) T2—565
Uri (Switzerland) T2—494 77
Urinalysis
  diagnosis
    general disease 616.075 66
Urinary calculi
  medicine 616.622
  see also Urinary system
Urinary diseases
  medicine 616.63
  see also Urinary system
Urinary system 573.49
  anesthesiology 617.967 461
  biology 573.49
  geriatrics 618.976 6
  human anatomy 611.61
  human cancer 362.196 994 61
    incidence 614.599 946 1
    medicine 616.994 61
    social services 362.196 994 61
    see also Cancer (Human)
Urinary system (continued)
  human diseases 362.196 6
    incidence 614.596
    medicine 616.6
    social services 362.196 6
  human histology 611.018 961
  human physiology 612.46
  pediatrics 618.926
  pharmacodynamics 615.761
  surgery 617.461
  veterinary medicine 636.089 66
Urine
  human physiology 612.461
  see also Urinary system
Urochordata 596.2
  paleozoology 566
Urodela 597.85
  paleozoology 567.8
Urogenital organs 573.6
  see also Urogenital system
Urogenital system 573.6
  human physiology 612.46
  medicine 616.6
  pharmacodynamics 615.76
  surgery 617.46
  see also Genital system;
      Urinary system
Urology 616.6
  see also Urinary system
Uropygi 595.453 2
Ursidae 599.78
  paleozoology 569.78
Ursulines 255.974
  church history 271.974
Ursus 599.784
Urticales 583.45
Urticaria
  medicine 616.51
  see also Skin
Uru-Chipaya languages 498
T6—98
Uruguay 989.5
T2—895
Uruguay River T2—822
  Argentina T2—822
  Uruguay T2—895
Uruguayan literature 860
Uruguayans T5—688 95
Usability
  computer software 005
Usage (Applied linguistics) 418
  specific languages T4—8
Uşak İli (Turkey) T2—562

Use tax 336.271
  law 343.055
  public administration 352.44
  public finance 336.271
Useful animals 591.63
Useful organisms 578.63
  see Manual at 630 vs. 579–590, 641.3: Interdisciplinary numbers
Useful plants 581.63
User education
  libraries 025.56
User fees
  law 343.055
  library services 025.11
  public administration 352.44
  public finance 336.16
User interfaces
  graphics programming 006.678 4
  graphics programs 006.688 4
  knowledge-based systems
    programming 006.337
  multimedia-systems
    programming 006.778 4
  multimedia-systems programs 006.788 4
  systems programming 005.428
  systems programs 005.437
  see Manual at 005.269 and 005.284, 005.3684, 005.384
USSR 947.084
  T2—47
Ust-Orda Buriat (Russia : Okrug) T2—575
Ust-Orda Buriatskiĭ avtonomnyĭ okrug (Russia) T2—575
Ustilaginales 579.593
Usulután (El Salvador : Dept.) T2—728 431
Usury 332.83
  law 346.073
Utah 979.2
  T2—792
Utah County (Utah) T2—792 24
Ute Indians T5—974 5
Ute language 497.45
  T6—974 5
Utensils
  manufacturing technology 683.8
Uterine cervix
  gynecology 618.14
  human anatomy 611.66
  human physiology 612.62
Uterine cervix (continued)
  surgery 618.145
  see also Female genital system
Uterine hemorrhage
  obstetrics 618.54
Uterine infections
  gynecology 618.142
  see also Female genital system
Uterine malformations
  gynecology 618.144
  see also Female genital system
Uterus 573.667
  biology 573.667
  gynecology 618.14
  human anatomy 611.66
  human physiology 612.62
  surgery 618.145
  see also Female genital system
Utican architecture 722.32
Utilitarianism 144.6
  ethics 171.5
Utilities (Buildings facilities) 644
  construction 696
  household management 644
  museums 069.29
  plant management 658.26
    T1—068 2
    public administration 352.56
Utilities (Public services) 363.6
  see also Public utilities
Utility dogs (United Kingdom) 636.72
Utility programs 005.43
Uto-Aztecan languages 497.45
  T6—974 5
Utopian socialism 335.02
Utopian socialism (English) 335.12
Utopias 321.07
  arts T3C—372
  literature 808.803 72
    history and criticism 809.933 72
    specific literatures T3B—080 372
      history and criticism T3B—093 72
  political system 321.07
  socialism 335.02
Utrecht (Netherlands : Province) T2—492 32
Utrecht (South Africa : District) T2—684 1
Uttar Pradesh (India) T2—542
Uttlesford (England) T2—426 712
Uudenmaan lääni (Finland) T2—489 71
Uusimaa (Finland) T2—489 71
Uvalde County (Tex.) T2—764 432

Uveas
  human anatomy 611.84
  human diseases
    incidence 614.599 7
    ophthalmology 617.72
  human physiology 612.842
  see also Eyes
Uzbek T5—943 25
Uzbek language 494.325
  T6—943 25
Uzbek literature 894.325
Uzbekistan 958.7
  T2—587

V

Vaal River (South Africa) T2—682
Vaal Triangle (South Africa) T2—682 1
Vaasa (Finland : Lääni) T2—489 73
Vaasan Lääni (Finland) T2—489 73
Vacation homes 643.2
  architecture 728.72
  construction 690.872
  home economics 643.2
Vacation schools
  adult education 374.8
Vaccines
  pharmacology 615.372
Vacuoles 571.655
Vacuum deposition
  metal finishing 671.735
Vacuum electronics 537.53
Vacuum metallizing 671.735
Vacuum metallurgy 669.028 4
Vacuum pumps 621.55
Vacuum technology 621.55
Vacuum tubes
  electronics 621.381 512
  radio engineering 621.384 132
Vacuum ultraviolet spectroscopes
  manufacturing technology 681.414 5
Vacuum ultraviolet spectroscopy
  physics 535.845
Vacuums 533.5
  engineering 621.55
Vagala language 496.35
  T6—963 5
Vagina
  gynecology 618.15
  human anatomy 611.67
  human physiology 612.62
Vagina (continued)
  surgery 618.150 59
  see also Female genital system
Vaginal diaphragms
  health 613.943 5
  see also Birth control; Female genital system
Vaginiperineotomy
  obstetrical surgery 618.85
Vagrancy 364.148
  law 345.024 8
Vagrants 305.568
  T1—086 942
Vai (African people) T5—963 4
Vai language 496.34
  T6—963 4
Vaiśeṣika (Philosophy) 181.44
Vaisheshika (Philosophy) 181.44
Vaishnavism 294.551 2
Vaisnavism 294.551 2
Vajiravudh, King of Siam
  Thai history 959.304 1
Val-Bélair (Quebec) T2—714 471
Val-de-Marne (France) T2—443 63
Val-d'Oise (France) T2—443 67
Val-Saint-François (Quebec) T2—714 65
Val Verde County (Tex.) T2—764 881
Valais (Switzerland) T2—494 79
Valdivia (Chile : Province) T2—835 2
Vale of Glamorgan (Wales) T2—429 89
Vale of White Horse (England) T2—425 76
Vale Royal (England) T2—427 15
Valemount (B.C.) T2—711 82
Valences (Chemistry) 541.224
Valencia (Spain : Province) T2—467 63
Valencia (Spain : Region) T2—467 6
Valencia County (N.M.) T2—789 92
Valentine's Day 394.261 8
Valerianaceae 583.92
Valerians 583.92
Validation
  data 005.72
    file processing 005.74
  programming 005.14
Valises
  manufacturing technology 685.51
Vallabhācārya (Philosophy) 181.484 4
Valladolid (Spain : Province) T2—462 3
Valle (Honduras : Dept.) T2—728 352
Valle d'Aosta (Italy) T2—451 1

Valle del Cauca
(Colombia) T2—861 52
Vallée-de-la-Gatineau
(Quebec) T2—714 221
Vallée de l'Or (Quebec) T2—714 13
Vallée-du-Richelieu
(Quebec : Regional
County Municipality) T2—714 36
Valley County (Idaho) T2—796 76
Valley County (Mont.) T2—786 17
Valley County (Neb.) T2—782 48
Valley Forge
United States history 973.334 1
Valley of Mexico (Mexico) T2—725
Valley winds 551.518 5
Valleys 551.442
T2—144
geography 910.914 4
geomorphology 551.442
physical geography 910.021 44
Valois, House of 944.025
genealogy 929.74
Valparaíso (Chile :
Province) T2—832 55
Valparaíso (Chile : Region) T2—832 4
Valréas (France) T2—449 2
Valuation
businesses
financial management 658.15
law 346.065
investment economics 332.632 21
real property 333.332
law 346.043 7
Valuation of assets
accounting 657.73
Valuation theory 515.784
Value T1—013
labor theory
Marxian economics 335.412
microeconomics 338.521
Value-added networks 004.69
computer communications
services 384.33
see also Computer
communications
Value-added tax 336.271 4
law 343.055
public administration 352.44
public finance 336.271 4
Value analysis (Cost control) 658.155 2
Value cognition
psychology 153.45
Values T1—013
epistemology 121.8
social control 303.372
Valvatida 593.93
Valverde (Dominican
Republic : Province) T2—729 357
Valves 621.84
internal-combustion engines 621.437
Valvular activity
heart
human physiology 612.171
see also Cardiovascular
system
Valvular diseases
medicine 616.125
see also Cardiovascular
system
Vampire bats 599.45
Vampires 398.21
see also Legendary beings
Vampyromorpha 594.55
Van Allen radiation belts 538.766
Van Buren, Martin
United States history 973.57
Van Buren County (Ark.) T2—767 29
Van Buren County (Iowa) T2—777 98
Van Buren County (Mich.) T2—774 13
Van Buren County (Tenn.) T2—768 657
Van İli (Turkey) T2—566 2
Van pools 388.413 212
Van Wert County (Ohio) T2—771 413
Van Zandt County (Tex.) T2—764 276
Vanadates
mineralogy 549.72
Vanadium 669.732
chemical engineering 661.052 2
chemistry 546.522
economic geology 553.462 6
materials science 620.189 32
metallography 669.957 32
metallurgy 669.732
metalworking 673.732
organic chemistry
applied 661.895
physical metallurgy 669.967 32
see also Chemicals; Metals
Vanadium group
chemical engineering 661.052
chemistry 546.52
Vance County (N.C.) T2—756 532
Vancouver (B.C.) T2—711 33
Vancouver Island (B.C.) T2—711 2
Vandal language 439.9
T6—399

Vandalic language 439.9
T6—399
Vandalism 364.164
law 345.026 4
schools 371.782
Vandalism insurance 368.12
see also Insurance
Vandals (Germanic people) T5—39
Vanderbijlpark (South Africa : District) T2—682 1
Vanderburgh County (Ind.) T2—772 33
Vanderhoof (B.C.) T2—711 82
Vanga shrikes 598.8
Vanier (Quebec) T2—714 471
Vanillas 641.338 2
botany 584.4
see also Flavorings
Vanishing species 578.68
see also entries beginning with Rare
Vanrhynsdorp (South Africa : District) T2—687 2
Vans 388.343 4
driving 629.284 34
engineering 629.223 4
repair 629.287 34
transportation services 388.343 4
see also Trucks
Vanuatu 995.95
T2—959 5
Vapor lighting 621.327
see also Lighting
Vapor-phase deposition
metal finishing 671.735
Vapor plating
metal finishing 671.735
Vaporization 536.44
Var (France) T2—449 3
Varactors 621.381 522
Vardar Macedonia T2—497 6
Vardar River T2—497 6
Varese (Italy : Province) T2—452 2
Vargas, Getúlio
Brazilian history 981.061
Variable annuities
insurance 368.375
see also Insurance
Variable costs 338.514 2
financial management 658.155 3
Variable life insurance 368.325
see also Insurance
Variable rate securities 332.632 044
Variable stars 523.844
Variation (Biology) 576.54
humans 599.94
Variations (Mathematics) 515.64
Variations (Musical forms) 781.825
instrumental 784.182 5
Varicella
incidence 614.525
medicine 616.914
see also Communicable diseases (Human)
Varicose veins
medicine 616.143
see also Cardiovascular system
Varieties
agriculture 631.57
Variety drama
literature 808.825 7
history and criticism 809.257
specific literatures T3B—205 7
individual authors T3A—2
Variety shows 792.7
see also Theater
Variety stores 381.14
management 658.873
see also Commerce
Variola major
incidence 614.521
medicine 616.912
see also Communicable diseases (Human)
Variola minor
medicine 616.913
see also Communicable diseases (Human)
Variola vaccinia
incidence 614.521
medicine 616.913
see also Communicable diseases (Human)
Varix
medicine 616.143
see also Cardiovascular system
Varmints
small game hunting 799.25
Värmlands län (Sweden) T2—487
Varna (Bulgaria : Oblast) T2—499 4
Varna (Bulgaria : Okrŭg) T2—499 4
Varnenska oblast (Bulgaria) T2—499 4
Varnenski okrŭg (Bulgaria) T2—499 4
Varnish trees 583.77

Varnishing 667.79
technology 667.79
woodwork
buildings 698.34
Vas Megye (Hungary) T2—439 7
Vasa, House of 948.502
Vascongadas (Spain) T2—466
Vascular circulation 573.18
human physiology 612.13
see also Cardiovascular system
Vascular cryptogams 587
Vascular plants 580
see also Plants
Vascular seedless plants 587
Vascular surgery 617.413
see also Cardiovascular system
Vasectomy (Birth control)
health 613.942
surgery 617.463
see also Birth control; Male genital system
Vases
sculpture 731.72
Vaslui (Romania : Judeţ) T2—498 1
Vasoconstrictors (Drugs)
pharmacodynamics 615.71
see also Cardiovascular system
Vasoconstrictors (Nerves)
human physiology 612.18
see also Cardiovascular system
Vasodilators (Drugs)
pharmacodynamics 615.71
see also Cardiovascular system
Vasodilators (Nerves)
human physiology 612.18
see also Cardiovascular system
Vasomotors
human physiology 612.18
see also Cardiovascular system
Vasopressin
chemistry 547.734 5
human physiology 612.492
pharmacology 615.363
see also Endocrine system
Västerbottens län (Sweden) T2—488
Västernorrlands län (Sweden) T2—488
Västmanlands län (Sweden) T2—487
VAT (Tax) 336.271 4
see also Value-added tax
Vatican City 945.634
T2—456 34
Vaucluse (France : Dept.) T2—449 2
Vaud (Switzerland) T2—494 52
Vaudeville 792.7
see also Theater
Vaudreuil (Quebec : County) T2—714 26
Vaudreuil-Soulanges (Quebec) T2—714 26
Vaulting (Gymnastics) 796.44
see also Sports
Vaults 721.43
architecture 721.43
construction 690.143
Vaupés (Colombia) T2—861 65
VCR (Cassette recorders) 384.558
see also Video recorders
Veal 641.362
commercial processing 664.92
cooking 641.662
food 641.362
Vector algebra 512.5
Vector analysis 515.63
Vector calculus 515.63
Vector geometry 516.182
Vector processing 004.35
see also Processing modes—computer science
Vector processors 004.35
engineering 621.391
see also Processing modes—computer science
Vector quantities
mechanics 531.112
Vector spaces 512.52
Vector-valued functions 515.7
Vectorcardiography
medicine 616.120 754 7
see also Cardiovascular system
Vectors (Disease carriers) 571.986
biology 571.986
medicine 614.43
Vedanta (Philosophy) 181.48
Vedas 294.592 1
Vedic language 491.29
T6—912 9
Vedic literature 891.29
Vedic period 934.02

Vedic religion 294.509 013
Vega (Dominican Republic : Province) T2—729 369 7
Vegetable arrangements 745.924
Vegetable drugs
  pharmacology 615.32
Vegetable fats 665.3
  food technology 664.3
  industrial technology 665.3
Vegetable fibers
  textiles 677.54
    see also Textiles
Vegetable gardening 635
Vegetable glue 668.33
Vegetable juices 641.35
  commercial processing 663.63
  cooking with 641.65
  food 641.35
  home preparation 641.875
Vegetable manures
  agricultural use 631.87
Vegetable oils 665.3
  food technology 664.3
  industrial technology 665.3
Vegetable poisons
  human toxicology 615.952
Vegetable waxes 665.12
Vegetables 641.35
  commercial preservation 664.8
  commercial processing 664.8
  cooking 641.65
  food 641.35
  garden crop 635
  home preservation 641.4
Vegetarian cooking 641.563 6
Vegetarianism
  dietary regimen 613.262
  ethics 179.3
    religion 291.569 3
      Buddhism 294.356 93
      Christianity 241.693
      Hinduism 294.548 693
Vegetation and climate
  precipitation 551.577 5
Vegetation regions T2—15
Vegetative reproduction 571.89
  plants 575.49
  see Manual at 571.8 vs. 573.6, 575.6
Vegliote dialect 457.994 972
  T6—57
Vegliote literature 850
Vehicle failures 363.120 1
  air transportation 363.124 16
  see also Transportation safety
Vehicles 388
  engineering 629.046
  law 343.093
  military engineering 623.74
  military equipment 355.83
  transportation services 388
  see Manual at 629.046 vs. 388
Vehicular accidents 363.125
  see also Transportation safety
Vehicular safety 363.125
  see also Transportation safety
Vehicular transportation (Automotive) 388.3
  law 343.094
  public administration 354.765
  transportation services 388.3
  urban 388.41
Vei (African people) T5—963 4
Vei language 496.34
  T6—963 4
Veii (Extinct city) T2—376
Veinakh languages 499.964 1
  T6—999 641
Veins 573.186
  biology 573.186
  human anatomy 611.14
  human physiology 612.134
  medicine 616.14
  surgery 617.414
  see also Cardiovascular system
Veins (Geology) 553.19
  economic geology 553.19
  structural geology 551.88
Vejle amt (Denmark) T2—489 5
Veliko Tŭrnovo (Bulgaria : Okrŭg) T2—499 2
Velikotŭrnovski okrŭg (Bulgaria) T2—499 2
Velloziaceae 584.354
Vellum books 096.2
Velocity (Mechanics) 531.112
Velocity of flow
  air mechanics 533.62
  fluid mechanics 532.053 2
  gas mechanics 533.27
  liquid mechanics 532.57
Velocity of light 535.24
Velocity of sound 534.202
Velocity of stars 523.83

Velocity theory
  monetary economics 332.401
Velour 677.617
  see also Textiles
Velvet 677.617
  see also Textiles
Velveteen 677.617
  see also Textiles
Venango County (Pa.) T2—748 96
Venda (African people) T5—963 97
Venda (South Africa) T2—682 91
Venda language 496.397
  T6—963 97
Vendean War, 1793–1800 944.042
Vendée (France) T2—446 1
Vendettas
  influence on crime 364.256
Vending machines 629.82
Vendor selection
  library acquisitions 025.233
  materials management 658.722
Vendors and purchasers 346.043 63
Veneers 674.833
  architectural decoration 729.6
Venereal diseases
  incidence 614.547
  law 344.043 695 1
  medicine 616.951
  see also Communicable diseases (Human)
Venesection
  therapeutics 615.899
Venetia T2—373
Venetia (Italy : Region) T2—453
Venetic language 479.4
  T6—794
Veneto (Italy) T2—453
Venezia (Italy) T2—453 1
Venezia (Italy : Province) T2—453 1
Venezuela 987
  T2—87
Venezuela, Gulf of (Colombia and Venezuela) 551.463 5
  T2—163 65
Venezuelan literature 860
Venezuelans T5—688 7
Venial sin 241.31
Venice (Italy : Province) T2—453 1
Venice, Gulf of (Italy) 551.462 5
  T2—163 85
Venison 641.391
  commercial processing 664.92
  cooking 641.691
  food 641.391
Venoms
  human toxicology 615.942
Ventersburg (South Africa : District) T2—685 3
Ventersdorp (South Africa : District) T2—682 4
Venterstad (South Africa : District) T2—687 13
Ventilation
  aircraft 629.134 42
  automobile 629.277 2
  buildings 697.92
  household management 644.5
  library buildings 022.8
  mining 622.42
  museums 069.29
  plant management 658.25
  sewers 628.23
  underground construction 624.19
  vehicles 629.040 289
Ventilation engineers 697.920 92
  occupational group T7—697
Ventricles (Heart)
  human anatomy 611.12
  human physiology 612.17
  see also Cardiovascular system
Ventriloquism 793.89
Ventura County (Calif.) T2—794 92
Venus (Planet) 523.42
  T2—992 2
  astrology 133.534
  unmanned flights to 629.435 42
Venus's flytrap 583.75
Veps T5—945 4
Veps language 494.54
  T6—945 4
Veps literature 894.54
Veracruz (Mexico : State) T2—726 2
Veraguas (Panama : Province) T2—728 722
Verb phrases 415
  specific languages T4—5
Verb tables
  applied linguistics 418
    specific languages T4—82
Verbal communication 302.224
  psychology 153.6
Verbal intelligence tests 153.933 3
  individual 153.932 3
Verbenaceae 583.96
Verbenas 635.933 96
  botany 583.96
  floriculture 635.933 96

Verbs 415
  specific languages T4—5
Vercelli (Italy : Province) T2—451 7
Verchères (Quebec : County) T2—714 36
Verd antique marble 553.55
  economic geology 553.55
  quarrying 622.355
Verdefort (South Africa : District) T2—685 2
Verdicts 347.075
  criminal law 345.075
Verdun, Treaty of, 843 943.02
Vereeniging (South Africa : District) T2—682 1
Verification
  musical instruments 784.192 7
  programming 005.14
Vermicelli
  commercial processing 664.755
Vermicides 668.651
  agricultural use 632.951
  chemical engineering 668.651
Vermiculite 553.678
  economic geology 553.678
  mining 622.367 8
Vermiform appendix
  human anatomy 611.345
  human physiology 612.33
  medicine 616.34
  surgery 617.554 5
  see also Digestive system
Vermilion County (Ill.) T2—773 65
Vermilion Parish (La.) T2—763 51
Vermillion County (Ind.) T2—772 462
Vermont 974.3
  T2—743
Vernon (B.C.) T2—711 5
Vernon County (Mo.) T2—778 44
Vernon County (Wis.) T2—775 73
Vernon Parish (La.) T2—763 61
Verona (Italy : Province) T2—453 4
Verrucae
  medicine 616.544
  see also Skin
Versailles Treaty, 1783
  United States history 973.317
Versailles Treaty, 1919
  European history 940.314 1
Verse drama
  literature 808.82
    history and criticism 809.2
    specific literatures T3B—2
      individual authors T3A—2
Versification 808.1
Version
  obstetrical surgery 618.82
Vertebrate viruses 579.2
Vertebrates 596
  agricultural pests 632.66
  conservation technology 639.9
  paleozoology 566
  resource economics 333.954
  zoology 596
Vertical combinations (Enterprises) 338.804 2
  see also Combinations (Enterprises)
Vertical lift bridges 388
  construction 624.84
  see also Bridges
Vertical lift rotors
  aircraft 629.134 36
Vertical-speed indicators 629.135 2
Vertical takeoff and landing aircraft 387.733 5
  engineering 629.133 35
  military engineering 623.746 047
  transportation services 387.733 5
Vertigo
  symptomatology
    neurological diseases 616.841
  see also Nervous system
Vervains 635.933 96
  botany 583.96
  floriculture 635.933 96
Verwoerd, Hendrik Frensch
  South African history 968.058
Very-high-frequency radio systems 621.384 151
Very large scale integration 621.395
Very-low-frequency radio systems 621.384 153
Vesicles 571.655
Vesicular eruptions
  medicine 616.52
  see also Skin
Vespers 264.15
  Anglican 264.030 15
    texts 264.034
  music 782.324
  see also Liturgy of the hours
Vespertilionidae 599.47
Vespoidea 595.798

Vessel flutes 788.38
  see also Woodwind instruments
Vessels
  music 786.82
    concussed 786.876
    friction 786.866
      set 786.866
      single 786.888
    percussed 786.846
      set 786.846
      single 786.884 6
    see also Percussion instruments
Vessels (Nautical) 387.2
  see also Ships
Vest-Agder fylke (Norway) T2—483 2
Vested rights (Pensions) 331.252 2
  see also Pensions
Vesterålen (Norway) T2—484 4
Vestfold fylke (Norway) T2—482 7
Vestibular perception 152.188 2
Vestibules (Ears)
  human anatomy 611.85
  human physiology 612.858
  otology 617.882
  see also Ears
Vestinian language 479.7
  T6—797
Vestlandet (Norway) T2—483 3
Vestments 391
  commercial technology 687.15
  customs 391
  see also Clothing
Vestsjælland (Denmark) T2—489 1
Veszprém Megye (Hungary) T2—439 7
Vetches 633.35
  botany 583.74
  forage crop 633.35
Veterans 305.906 97
  T1—086 97
  education benefits 371.223
    college and university 378.32
  financial assistance
    social welfare 362.868 2
  government programs 353.538
  labor economics 331.52
  law 343.011
  social group 305.906 97
  social welfare 362.86
    law 343.011 5
    public administration 353.538
Veterans' homes 362.160 869 7
  architecture 725.594
Veterans' life insurance 368.364
  see also Insurance
Veterans of Foreign Wars of the United States 369.11
Veterans' pensions 331.252 913 55
  law 343.011 2
Veterans' preference 352.650 869 7
Veterinarians 636.089 092
  law 344.049
  occupational group T7—636
Veterinary epidemiology 636.089 44
Veterinary hospitals 636.083 2
  architecture 725.592
Veterinary hygiene 636.089 3
Veterinary law 344.049
Veterinary medicine 636.089
Veterinary public health 636.083 2
  law 344.049
Veterinary services
  armed forces 355.345
VFW (Veterans' organization) 369.11
VHF radio systems 621.384 151
Viana do Castelo (Portugal : District) T2—469 12
Viaticum 265.7
Viborg amt (Denmark) T2—489 5
Vibraphones 786.843
  see also Percussion instruments
Vibration perception
  psychology 152.182 3
Vibration prospecting 622.159 2
Vibration weapons 623.447
Vibrational spectra (Molecules) 539.6
Vibrations 620.3
  aeronautics 629.132 362
  biophysics 571.443
    humans 612.014 45
  effect on materials 620.112 48
  engineering 620.3
  fluid mechanics 532.05
  machinery 621.811
  solid-state physics 530.416
  solids 531.32
Vibrato 781.43
  instrumental technique 784.193 68
Viburnums 635.933 92
  botany 583.92
  floriculture 635.933 92
Vice-presidents 321
  democratic systems 321.804 2
  occupational group T7—351

Vice-presidents (continued)
  public administration 352.239
Vicenary system (Numeration) 513.5
Vicenza (Italy : Province) T2—453 5
Viceroys 321
  public administration 352.23
Vices 179.8
  literature 808.803 53
    history and criticism 809.933 53
    specific literatures T3B—080 353
      history and criticism T3B—093 53
  religion 291.5
    Buddhism 294.35
    Christianity 241.3
      see Manual at 241.3–241.4 vs. 241.6
    Hinduism 294.548
    Islam 297.5
    Judaism 296.369 8
Vichada (Colombia) T2—861 39
Vicksburg, Siege of, 1863 973.734 4
Victimology 362.88
Victims of crime 362.88
  T1—086 949
  insurance 368.82
    law 344.028
    see also Insurance
  school programs 371.782
  social welfare 362.88
    law 344.032 88
    public administration 353.533 7
Victims of oppression
  social welfare 362.87
    public administration 353.533 8
Victims of war 305.906 949
  see also War victims
Victor Emmanuel II, King of Italy
  Italian history 945.084
Victor Emmanuel III, King of Italy
  Italian history 945.091
Victor Harbour (S. Aust.) T2—942 32
Victoria T2—945
Victoria (B.C.) T2—711 28
Victoria (N.B. : County) T2—715 53
Victoria (N.S. : County) T2—716 93
Victoria (Ont. : County) T2—713 64
Victoria (Seychelles) T2—696
Victoria, Lake T2—678 27
Victoria, Queen of Great Britain
  British history 941.081
  English history 942.081
Victoria, Queen of Great Britain (continued)
  Scottish history 941.108 1
Victoria County (Tex.) T2—764 125
Victoria Falls T2—689 1
Victoria Island (Kitikmeot, N.W.T.) T2—719 7
Victoria swine 636.484
Victoria West (South Africa : District) T2—687 17
Victorian architecture 724.5
Victualing
  aircraft 387.736 4
  boats 387.168
  buses 388.33
  ships 387.168
  trains 385.26
  transportation services 388.041
Vicuña 599.636 7
  animal husbandry 636.296
Vicuña wool textiles 677.32
  see also Textiles
Video animation 778.593
Video art 700
  fine arts 702.81
Video cassette recorders 384.558
  see also Video recorders
Video cassettes 384.558
  see also Video recordings
Video disc players 384.558
  see also Video recorders
Video discs 384.558
  see also Video recordings
Video discs (Computer) 004.565
  engineering 621.397 6
Video display screens
  computer science 004.77
    engineering 621.398 7
Video games 794.8
Video photography 778.59
Video production 384.558
  communications services 384.558
  photography 778.59
    see Manual at 791.43, 791.45 vs. 778.5
Video recorders 384.558
  communications services 384.558
  engineering 621.388 33
  photography 778.599 3
  see also Television
Video recording 778.59
Video recordings 384.558
  bibliographies 011.37
  cataloging 025.347 3

Video recordings (continued)
communications services 384.558
engineering 621.388 332
instructional use 371.335 23
adult level 374.26
library treatment 025.177 3
music 780
treatises 780.267
see Manual at 780.26
performing arts 791.45
photography 778.599 2
see also Television
Video records 384.558
see also Video recordings
Video tape players 384.558
see also Video recorders
Video tapes 384.558
see also Video recordings
Videocassette players 384.558
see also Video recorders
Videocassettes 384.558
see also Video recordings
Videoconferencing
instructional use 371.335 8
Videodisc players 384.558
see also Video recorders
Videodiscs 384.558
see also Video recordings
Videodiscs (Computer) 004.565
engineering 621.397 6
Videography 778.59
Videorecordings 384.558
see also Video recordings
Videorecords 384.558
see also Video recordings
Videotape players 384.558
see also Video recorders
Videotapes 384.558
see also Video recordings
Videotex 004.696
communications services 384.35
see also Computer communications
Vidin (Bulgaria : Okrŭg) T2—499 1
Vidinski okrŭg (Bulgaria) T2—499 1
Vielles 787.69
instrument 787.691 9
music 787.69
see also Stringed instruments
Vienna (Austria) T2—436 13
Vienne (France : Dept.) T2—446 3
Vieques Island (P.R.) T2—729 59
Việt-Cộng (Vietnamese history) 959.704 332 2
Viet-Muong languages 495.92
T6—959 2
Viet-Muong literatures 895.92
Viet-Muong peoples T5—959 2
Vietcong (Vietnamese history) 959.704 332 2
Vietnam 959.7
T2—597
Vietnamese T5—959 2
Vietnamese language 495.922
T6—959 22
Vietnamese literature 895.922
Vietnamese War, 1961–1975 959.704 3
Viewdata 004.69
communications services 384.354
see also Computer communications
Viewer access
communications services 384.555 3
Viewfinders 771.37
Vige language 496.35
T6—963 5
Vigesimal system (Numeration) 513.5
Vigo County (Ind.) T2—772 45
Vihuelas 787.86
instrument 787.861 9
music 787.86
see also Stringed instruments
Vijnana Buddhism 294.392
Viking Mars Program 629.435 43
Viking period 948.022
Danish history 948.901 4
Norwegian history 948.101 4
Swedish history 948.501 4
Vikings T5—395
Vila Real (Portugal : District) T2—469 2
Vilas County (Wis.) T2—775 23
Vîlcea (Romania) T2—498 2
Viljoenskroon (South Africa : District) T2—685 2
Villa Clara (Cuba : Province) T2—729 142
Villages 307.762
T2—173 2
area planning 711.43
government 320.8
cities 320.85
see Manual at T2—4–T2—9: Cities, towns, villages
Villas
architecture 728.8
Villas (Cuba : Province) T2—729 14
Vinayapiṭaka 294.382 2

Vincentians 255.77
  church history 271.77
Vincent's angina
  medicine 616.312
  see also Digestive system
Vindelicia T2—363
Vinegar
  commercial processing 664.55
  cooking with 641.62
Vinegar flies 595.774
Vines 582.18
  floriculture 635.974
  landscape architecture 715.4
  see Manual at 635.9 vs. 582.1
Vinnytsa (Ukraine : Oblast) T2—477 8
Vinnyts′ka oblast′ (Ukraine) T2—477 8
Vinton County (Ohio) T2—771 837
Vinylidene chlorides 668.423 7
Vinyls 668.423 6
  textiles 677.474 4
    see also Textiles
Vinyons
  textiles 677.474 4
    see also Textiles
Viola concertos 784.273
Viola da gambas 787.65
  instrument 787.651 9
  music 787.65
  see also Stringed instruments
Viola d'amores 787.66
  instrument 787.661 9
  music 787.66
  see also Stringed instruments
Violales 583.625
Violas 787.3
  instrument 787.319
  music 787.3
  see also Stringed instruments
Violence 303.6
  arts 700.455
    T3C—355
  ethics 179.7
    religion 291.569 7
      Buddhism 294.356 97
      Christianity 241.697
      Hinduism 294.548 697
      Islam 297.569 7
      Judaism 296.369 7
  literature 808.803 55
    history and criticism 809.933 55
    specific literatures T3B—080 355
      history and criticism T3B—093 55
Violence (continued)
  public safety 363.32
  social conflict 303.6
Violent behavior
  medicine 616.858 2
  see also Mental illness
Violets 583.625
  floriculture 635.933 625
Violin concertos 784.272
Violin family 787.2
  see also Stringed instruments
Violin makers 787.219 092
Violinists 787.209 2
  occupational group T7—787
Violins 787.2
  instrument 787.219
  music 787.2
  see also Stringed instruments
Violoncellists 787.409 2
  occupational group T7—787
Violoncellos 787.4
  instrument 787.419
  music 787.4
  see also Stringed instruments
Viols 787.6
  instrument 787.619
  music 787.6
  see also Stringed instruments
Viperfishes 597.5
Viral diseases (Biology) 571.992
  agriculture 632.8
  plant crops 632.8
  veterinary medicine 636.089 692 5
Viral diseases (Human)
  incidence 614.575
  medicine 616.925
  see also Communicable diseases (Human)
Vireolaniidae 598.878
Vireonidae 598.878
Vireos 598.878
  conservation technology 639.978 878
  resource economics 333.958 878
Virgin birth of Jesus Christ 232.921
Virgin Gorda (V.I.) T2—729 725
Virgin Islanders T5—969 729 72
Virgin Islands 972.972
  T2—729 72
Virgin Islands (American) T2—729 722
Virgin Islands (Danish) T2—729 722
Virgin Islands, British T2—729 725
Virgin Islands National Park (Saint John, V.I.) T2—729 722

Virgin Islands of the
United States T2—729 722
Virginals 786.4
instrument 786.419
music 786.4
see also Keyboard instruments
Virginia 975.5
T2—755
Virginia (South Africa : District) T2—685 3
Virginia Beach (Va.) T2—755 51
Virginia City (Nev.) T2—793 56
Virginia cowslip 635.933 94
botany 583.94
floriculture 635.933 94
Virginia creeper 583.86
Virginia deer 599.652
conservation technology 639.979 652
resource economics 333.959 652
Virginia reels 793.34
Virginia willow 583.72
Virginity of Mary 232.913
Virgo (Zodiac) 133.526 7
Viroids 579.29
Virologists 579.209 2
Virology 579.2
medicine 616.019 4
Virtual memory 005.435
computer hardware 004.5
programming 005.425
programs 005.435
Virtual reality 006
Virtue 179.9
see also Virtues
Virtues 179.9
arts 700.453
T3C—353
literature 808.803 53
history and criticism 809.933 53
specific literatures T3B—080 353
history and criticism T3B—093 53
religion 291.5
Buddhism 294.35
Christianity 241.4
see Manual at 241.3–241.4 vs. 241.6
Hinduism 294.548
Islam 297.5
Judaism 296.369 9
Viruses 579.2
medical microbiology 616.019 4
see Manual at 579.24–579.25
Viruses (Computer security) 005.84
Visas 323.67
international law 341.484 2
law 342.082
political science 323.67
public administration 353.13
Visayan Islands (Philippines) T2—599 5
Viscaceae 583.88
Visceral leishmaniasis
medicine 616.936 4
see also Communicable diseases (Human)
Visceral perception
psychology 152.188 6
Viscose rayon 677.463
see also Textiles
Viscosity 531.113 4
fluid mechanics 532.053 3
gas mechanics 533.28
liquid mechanics 532.58
solid mechanics 531.4
Viscous flow 532.053 3
gas mechanics 533.28
liquid mechanics 532.58
Vises 621.992
Viseu (Portugal : District) T2—469 31
Vishnuism 294.551 2
Visibility
aeronautics 629.132 4
meteorology 551.568
Visible light 535
spectral region 535.013
see also Light
Visible light spectroscopes
manufacturing technology 681.414 3
Visigothic domination
Spanish history 946.01
Vision 573.88
artificial intelligence 006.37
arts 701.8
epistemology 121.35
human physiology 612.84
psychology 152.14
see also Eyes
Visions
religious experience 291.42
Christianity 248.29
Viśiṣṭādvaita (Philosophy) 181.483
Visitation rights (Domestic law) 346.017
Visitation Sisters 255.975
church history 271.975
Visiting housekeepers
social welfare 362.828 3

Visiting nurses 610.734 3
  medicine 610.734 3
  social welfare 362.14
    see also Health services
  see also Nurses
Visual-auditory memory 153.134
Visual binaries 523.841
Visual display units
  computer science 004.77
    engineering 621.398 7
Visual effects
  dramatic performances 792.024
    see also Special effects—dramatic performances
  video production 778.593
Visual memory 153.132
Visual novels 741.5
Visual perception
  psychology 152.14
Visual programming 005.118
Visual signaling
  communications services 384
  military engineering 623.731
  nautical engineering 623.856 1
Visualization (Psychology) 153.32
Visually-impaired persons 305.908 161
  T1—087 1
  T7—081 61
  library services 027.663
  social group 305.908 161
  social welfare 362.41
Vitaceae 583.86
Vitalism 147
Vitamin D treatment
  milk processing 637.141
Vitamin therapy 615.328
Vitamins 572.58
  applied nutrition 613.286
    animal husbandry 636.085 28
  biochemistry 572.58
    humans 612.399
  chemistry 547.74
  metabolism
    human physiology 612.399
  pharmacology 615.328
Vitebsk (Belarus : Voblasts) T2—478 4
Vitebskaīa voblasts′ (Belarus) T2—478 4
Viterbo (Italy : Province) T2—456 25
Viticulture 634.8
Vitiligo
  medicine 616.55
  see also Skin
Vitoria (Spain) T2—466 5
Vitreous bodies
  human anatomy 611.84
  human physiology 612.844
  ophthalmology 617.746
  see also Eyes
Viverridae 599.742
Vivisection
  ethics 179.4
    see also Animals—treatment of—ethics
Vizcaya (Spain) T2—466 3
Vizsla 636.752
Vladimir (Russia : Oblast) T2—473 3
Vladimirskaīa oblast′ (Russia) T2—473 3
VLF radio systems 621.384 153
VLSI (Computer circuits) 621.395
VMM insurance 368.12
  see also Insurance
Vocabulary 401.4
  dictionaries 413
  specific languages T4—014
    dictionaries T4—3
    usage (Applied linguistics) T4—81
    see Manual at T4—3 vs. T4—81
  usage (Applied linguistics) 418
Vocabulary development
  elementary education 372.44
Vocal communication
  animals 596.159 4
    physiology 573.92
Vocal cords 573.925
  biology 573.925
  medicine 616.22
  surgery 617.533
  see also Respiratory system
Vocal duets 783.12
Vocal expression
  psychology 152.384 2
Vocal forms 782
Vocal music 782
  diction 783.043
  see Manual at 782
Vocal quartets 783.14
Vocal trios 783.13
Vocalises 782.4
Vocalists 782.009 2
  occupational group T7—782
Vocalization
  animals 596.159 4
    physiology 573.92

Vocation
  applied psychology 158.6
Vocation (Ecclesiastical) 253.2
  ecclesiology 262.1
  guides to life 248.892
  monastic and religious orders 255
    men 255
      guides to life 248.894 22
    women 255.9
      guides to life 248.894 32
Vocational counseling 331.702
  see also Vocational guidance
Vocational education 370.113
  T1—071
  adult level 374.013
  on the job 331.259 2
    personnel management 658.312 4
  T1—068 3
      executives 658.407 124
      public administration 352.669
  secondary level 373.246
Vocational guidance 331.702
  T1—023
  economics 331.702
  education 371.425
  personnel management 658.385
  psychology 158.6
Vocational interest tests 153.94
  see Manual at 153.94
Vocational interests
  applied psychology 158.6
Vocational rehabilitation 362.042 5
  see also Employment services—social services
Vocational schools 370.113
  see also Vocational education
Vocational training 370.113
  T1—071 5
  see also Vocational education
Vochysiaceae 583.82
Vodka 641.25
  commercial processing 663.5
Vogul T5—945 1
Vogul language 494.51
  T6—945 1
Vogul literature 894.51
Voice
  human physiology 612.78
  music 783
    see Manual at 782
  preaching 251.03
  rhetoric of speech 808.5
Voice (Grammar) 415
  specific languages T4—5
Voice disguisers (Musical instruments) 783.99
Voice disorders
  medicine 616.855
  see also Communicative disorders
Voice input devices 006.454
  computer engineering 621.399
Voice instruments 783.99
Voice mail systems
  office services 651.73
Voice output devices 006.54
  computer engineering 621.399
Voice prints
  criminal investigation 363.258
Voice synthesis 006.54
  computer engineering 621.399
Voiōtia (Greece) T2—495 15
Voivodina (Serbia) T2—497 1
Volatiles (Volcanic gases) 551.23
Volatilization analysis 545.46
Volcanic ash 552.23
Volcanic gases 551.23
Volcanic rocks 552.2
Volcanoes 551.21
  disaster services 363.349 5
  see also Disasters
Voles 599.354
Volga languages, Middle 494.56
  T6—945 6
Volga literatures, Middle 894.56
Volga River (Russia) T2—474
Volgograd (Russia : Oblast) T2—474 7
Volgogradskaîa oblastʹ (Russia) T2—474 7
Volition 153.8
Volksrust (South Africa : District) T2—682 7
Volleyball 796.325
  see also Sports
Volleyball players 796.325 092
  sports group T7—796 32
Vologda (Russia : Oblast) T2—471 9
Vologodskaîa oblastʹ (Russia) T2—471 9
Volscian language 479.7
  T6—797
Volsinii (Orvieto, Italy) T2—374
Volsinii Novi (Bolsena, Italy) T2—376
Volt-ammeters 621.374 6
Volta-Comoe languages 496.338
  T6—963 38

Volta River (Ghana) T2—667
Voltage detectors 621.374 3
Voltaic languages 496.35
T6—963 5
Voltaic literatures 896.35
Voltameters 621.374 4
Voltans T5—966 25
Volterra equations 515.45
Voltmeters 621.374 3
Volume (Sound)
musical element 781.233
perception
psychology 152.154
Volumetric analysis 545.2
Voluntaries (Music) 784.189 3
musical form 784.189 3
organ music 786.518 93
Voluntarism 361.37
philosophy 141
public administrative support 352.78
social psychology 302.14
Voluntary association 302.3
Voluntary enlistment (Military) 355.223 62
Voluntary movement 573.7
psychology 152.35
see also Movement
Voluntary muscle tissues 573.753 5
human histology 611.018 6
see also Musculoskeletal system
Voluntary retail chains 381.12
management 658.870 3
see also Commerce
Voluntary service groups
international assistance 361.26
public administrative support 352.78
Volunteer social work 361.37
Volusia County (Fla.) T2—759 21
Volvocales 579.832
Volyn (Ukraine : Oblast) T2—477 9
Volyns´ka oblast´ (Ukraine) T2—477 9
Vombatidae 599.24
Von Mises, Ludwig
economic school 330.157
Von Neumann algebras 512.55
Von Willebrand's disease
medicine 616.157
see also Cardiovascular system
Voodooism 299.675
Vorarlberg (Austria) T2—436 45
Voreio Aigaio (Greece) T2—495 82
Voronezh (Russia : Oblast) T2—473 5
Voronezhskaîa oblast´ (Russia) T2—473 5
Voroshylovhrad (Ukraine : Oblast) T2—477 4
Voroshylovhrads´ka oblast´ (Ukraine) T2—477 4
Vorster, B. J. (Balthazar Johannes)
South African history 968.062
Vortex motion 532.059 5
fluid mechanics 532.059 5
gas mechanics 533.295
liquid mechanics 532.595
Vosges (France) T2—443 9
Vosges Mountains (France) T2—443 8
Vostok (Manned satellite) 629.454
Vote counting 324.65
Voter registration 324.64
law 342.075
Votic language 494.54
T6—945 4
Voting behavior 324.9
Voting machines 324.65
manufacturing technology 681.14
Voting offenses 364.132 4
law 345.023 24
Voting procedures 324.65
law 342.075
Voting qualifications 324.62
law 342.072
Voting rights 324.62
law 342.072
Votive offerings 291.37
Christianity 246.55
fine arts 704.948
Christianity 704.948 2
see also Symbolism—religious significance
Votyak T5—945 3
Votyak language 494.53
T6—945 3
Votyak literature 894.53
Voucher system (Education) 379.111
Voyageurs National Park (Minn.) T2—776 77
Vrachanski okrŭg (Bulgaria) T2—499 1
Vrancea (Romania) T2—498 1
Vrat͡sa (Bulgaria : Okrŭg) T2—499 1
Vrede (South Africa : District) T2—685 1
Vredenburg (South Africa : District) T2—687 3

Vredendal (South Africa : District) T2—687 2
Vryburg (South Africa : District) T2—687 11
Vryheid (South Africa : District) T2—684 2
VTOL aircraft 387.733 5
  engineering 629.133 35
  military engineering 623.746 047
  transportation services 387.733 5
Vulamehlo (South Africa : District) T2—684 91
Vulcanization 678.24
  latex 678.524
  rubber 678.24
Vulcanized papers 676.284 5
Vulcanized rubber 678.34
Vulgar Latin language 477
  T6—71
Vulgarisms 417.2
  specific languages T4—7
Vulgate Bible 220.47
Vulindlela (South Africa : District) T2—684 91
Vulpes 599.775
Vultures 598.92
Vultures (New World) 598.92
Vultures (Old World) 598.94
Vulva
  gynecology 618.16
  human anatomy 611.67
  human physiology 612.62
  surgery 618.160 59
  see also Female genital system
Vuwani (South Africa : District) T2—682 91
Východočeský kraj (Czech Republic) T2—437 1
Východoslovenský kraj (Slovakia) T2—437 3

W

W* algebras 512.55
Waadt (Switzerland) T2—494 52
Wabash County (Ill.) T2—773 78
Wabash County (Ind.) T2—772 83
Wabash River (Ind.) T2—772 4
Wabasha County (Minn.) T2—776 13
Wabaunsee County (Kan.) T2—781 61
Wadena County (Minn.) T2—776 87
Wādī al-Jadīd (Egypt) T2—622
Wading birds 598.3
Wafers (Electronics) 621.381 52
Waffle irons
  electric cooking 641.586
Waffle mixes 664.753
Waffles 641.815
Wage differentials 331.22
  see Manual at 331.29 vs. 331.22
Wage discrimination 331.215 3
Wage-price controls 332.415
Wage-price policy 331.21
  see Manual at 331.29 vs. 339.5
Wage scales 331.216
  personnel management 658.322 2
Wages 331.21
  economics 331.21
  international law 341.763 6
  law 344.012 1
  personnel management 658.32
    T1—068 3
    armed forces 355.64
    executives 658.407 2
    public administration 352.67
  public administration 354.98
  taxation 336.242 2
    law 343.052 42
    see also Income tax
  see Manual at 331.29 vs. 331.22
Wages fund theory 331.210 1
Wagga Wagga (N.S.W.) T2—944 8
Wagner tubas 788.98
  see also Brass instruments
Wagoner County (Okla.) T2—766 87
Wagons 388.341
  agricultural use 631.373
  manufacturing technology 688.6
Wagtails 598.854
Wahhābīyah (Islamic sect) 297.814
Wahkiakum County (Wash.) T2—797 91
Waiheke Island (N.Z.) T2—932 4
Waikato District (N.Z.) T2—933 3
Waikato Region (N.Z.) T2—933
Waimakariri District (N.Z.) T2—938 2
Waimate District (N.Z.) T2—938 93
Waipa District (N.Z.) T2—933 57
Wairarapa (N.Z.) T2—936 6
Wairoa District (N.Z.) T2—934 62
Waitakere City (N.Z.) T2—932 3
Waitaki District (N.Z.) T2—939 1
  Canterbury Region T2—938 97
  Otago Region T2—939 1

Waitomo District (N.Z.) T2—933 8
  Manawatu-Wanganui Region T2—935 17
  Waikato Region T2—933 8
Wakashan Indians T5—979
Wakashan languages 497.9
  T6—979
Wakatipu, Lake (N.Z.) T2—939 5
Wakayama-ken (Japan) T2—521 82
Wake County (N.C.) T2—756 55
Wake Island T2—965
Wakefield (England : City) T2—428 15
Wakes 393.9
  Christian rites 265.85
  music 781.588
Wakkerstroom (South Africa : District) T2—682 7
Wakool River (N.S.W.) T2—944 8
Wakulla County (Fla.) T2—759 89
Walachia T2—498 2
Walaga (Ethiopia) T2—633
Walbiri (Australian people) T5—991 5
Walbiri language 499.15
  T6—991 5
Wałbrzych (Poland : Voivodeship) T2—438 5
Waldenses
  biography 284.4
  religious group T7—244
Waldensian churches 284.4
  see also Christian denominations
Waldensianism 273.6
  denomination 284.4
    see also Christian denominations
  persecution of 272.3
Waldo County (Me.) T2—741 52
Waldorf method of education 371.39
Wales 942.9
  T2—429
  ancient 936.29
    T2—362 9
  see Manual at 941
Wales, North T2—429 1
Wales, South T2—429 4
Wales Island (N.W.T.) T2—719 5
Walgett (N.S.W.) T2—944 9
Walker County (Ala.) T2—761 76
Walker County (Ga.) T2—758 33
Walker County (Tex.) T2—764 169
Walkie-talkies 621.384 5
Walking
  animal physiology 573.79
Walking (continued)
  human physiology 612.044
  physical fitness 613.717 6
  sports 796.51
    equipment technology 688.765 1
    see also Sports
    see Manual at 913–919 vs. 796.51
Walkingsticks (Insects) 595.729
Wall coverings
  household management 645.2
Walla Walla County (Wash.) T2—797 48
Wallabies 599.22
Wallace County (Kan.) T2—781 123
Wallachia T2—498 2
Wallachia (Principality) 949.801 4
  T2—498 2
Wallaroos 599.222
Wallboards 676.183
Wallenpaupack, Lake (Pa.) T2—748 23
Waller County (Tex.) T2—764 249
Walleye 597.758
  conservation technology 639.977 758
  resource economics 333.956 758
  sports fishing 799.177 58
Walleyed pike 597.758
Wallflowers (Plants) 583.64
Wallis (Switzerland) T2—494 79
Wallis and Futuna Islands 996.16
  T2—961 6
Wallo (Ethiopia) T2—634
Wallonia (Belgium) T2—493 4
Walloons T5—42
Wallowa County (Or.) T2—795 73
Wallowa Mountains (Or.) T2—795 73
Wallpaper 676.284 8
  handicrafts 745.54
  household management 645.2
  interior decoration 747.3
Walls (Building element) 721.2
  architecture 721.2
  construction 690.12
  interior decoration 747.3
Walls (Structures)
  agricultural use 631.27
  architecture 725.96
Walnuts 641.345 1
  botany 583.49
  cooking 641.645 1
  food 641.345 1
  forestry 634.973 49
  nut crops 634.51
Walpiri (Australian people) T5—991 5

Walpiri language 499.15
T6—991 5
Walras, Léon
economic school 330.157
Walrus 599.799
Walsall (England) T2—424 92
Walsh County (N.D.) T2—784 18
Walthall County (Miss.) T2—762 22
Waltham Forest (London, England) T2—421 72
Walton County (Fla.) T2—759 97
Walton County (Ga.) T2—758 212
Waltzes 793.33
music 784.188 46
Walvis Bay (Namibia) T2—688 1
Walworth County (S.D.) T2—783 18
Walworth County (Wis.) T2—775 89
Wampanoag Indians T5—973
Wanaka, Lake (N.Z.) T2—939 5
Wandering Jews 584.86
Wandsworth (London, England) T2—421 66
Wanganui District (N.Z.) T2—935 4
Wangaratta (Vic.) T2—945 5
Wansbeck (England) T2—428 86
Wansdyke (England) T2—423 97
Wapello County (Iowa) T2—777 93
Wapiti 599.654 2
big game hunting 799.276 542
conservation technology 639.979 654 2
War 355.02
arts 700.458
T3C—358
effect on natural ecology 577.274
ethics 172.42
religion 291.562 42
Buddhism 294.356 242
Christianity 241.624 2
Hinduism 294.548 624 2
Islam 297.562 42
Judaism 296.362 42
law 341.6
literature 808.803 58
history and criticism 809.933 58
specific literatures T3B—080 358
history and criticism T3B—093 58
military science 355.02
social effects 303.485
social theology 291.178 73
Buddhism 294.337 873
Christianity 261.873
Hinduism 294.517 873
Islam 297.27
Judaism 296.382 7
War (continued)
sociology 303.66
War and emergency legislation 343.01
War and emergency powers
administrative law 342.062
constitutional law 342.041 2
War crime trials 341.69
War crimes 364.138
criminal law 345.023 8
international law 341.69
War customs 399
War dances 399
War games
military science 355.48
recreation 793.92
War loan interest 336.182
War memorials 725.94
see also Monuments
War neuroses
medicine 616.852 12
see also Mental illness
War news
journalism 070.433 3
War of 1812 973.52
War of nerves 327.14
War powers (Legislative bodies) 328.346
War relief 363.349 88
War risk insurance 368.14
see also Insurance
War risk life insurance 368.364
see also Insurance
War victims 305.906 949
T1—086 949
law of war 341.67
social group 305.906 949
social services 363.349 8
War with Algiers, 1815 973.53
Warao Indians T5—98
Warao language 498
T6—98
Warao literature 898
Waratahs 583.89
Warble flies 595.774
Warblers (Old World) 598.843
Ward (Law) 346.018
Ward County (N.D.) T2—784 63
Ward County (Tex.) T2—764 914
Ward management 362.173 068
medicine 610.733
Ware County (Ga.) T2—758 794
Warehouse management 658.785
military supplies 355.621 3
Warehouse receipts
law 346.096

Warehouses
  architecture 725.35
Warehousing 388.044
  commerce 380.1
  transportation services 388.044
  see also Freight services
Warfare 355.02
  see also War
Warlocks (Occultists) 133.430 92
  see also Legendary beings
Warm-blooded animals 599
  paleozoology 569
Warmbaths (South Africa : District) T2—682 3
Warning systems 363.35
  civil defense 363.35
  military engineering 623.737
  see also Civil defense
Warragul (Vic.) T2—945 6
Warrant officers 355.009 2
  role and function 355.332
Warrants (Law) 345.052
Warranty 343.08
Warren (N.S.W.) T2—944 9
Warren County (Ga.) T2—758 625
Warren County (Ill.) T2—773 415
Warren County (Ind.) T2—772 96
Warren County (Iowa) T2—777 82
Warren County (Ky.) T2—769 74
Warren County (Miss.) T2—762 29
Warren County (Mo.) T2—778 386
Warren County (N.C.) T2—756 52
Warren County (N.J.) T2—749 78
Warren County (N.Y.) T2—747 51
Warren County (Ohio) T2—771 763
Warren County (Pa.) T2—748 67
Warren County (Tenn.) T2—768 653
Warren County (Va.) T2—755 97
Warrenton (South Africa : District) T2—687 11
Warrick County (Ind.) T2—772 32
Warrington (England) T2—427 19
Warrnambool (Vic.) T2—945 7
Wars 355.02
  history 900
  military analysis 355.48
  military science 355.02
  social services 363.349 8
  see also Disasters
  see Manual at 900: Historic events vs. nonhistoric events; *also at* 930–990: Wars
Wars of the Roses, 1455–1485 942.04
Warsaw (Poland : Voivodeship) T2—438 4
Warsaw Pact 355.031 094 7
Warsaw Treaty Organization 355.031 094 7
Warships 359.83
  ancient and medieval 359.832
    design 623.812 1
    engineering 623.821
    handling 623.882 1
  naval equipment 359.83
  naval units 359.32
  power-driven 359.83
    design 623.812 5
    engineering 623.825
    naval equipment 359.83
  wind-driven 359.832
    design 623.812 25
    engineering 623.822 5
Warthog 599.633
Warts
  medicine 616.544
  see also Skin
Warwick (England : District) T2—424 87
Warwickshire (England) T2—424 8
Warwickshire Avon River (England) T2—424 4
Wasatch County (Utah) T2—792 23
Wasatch Range (Utah and Idaho) T2—792 2
  Idaho T2—796 44
  Utah T2—792 2
Wasco County (Or.) T2—795 62
Waseca County (Minn.) T2—776 195
Wash, The (England) T2—425 3
Washabaugh County (S.D.) T2—783 64
Washakie County (Wyo.) T2—787 34
Washboards
  music 786.886
    see also Percussion instruments
Washburn County (Wis.) T2—775 15
Washing clothes
  home economics 648.1
Washing coal 662.623
Washing fabrics
  home economics 648.1
Washing machines
  manufacturing technology 683.88
Washington 979.7
  T2—797
Washington (D.C.) 975.3
  T2—753

Washington (District) 976.803
T2—768
Washington, George
United States history 973.41
1789–1793 973.41
1793–1797 973.43
Washington County (Ala.) T2—761 243
Washington County (Ark.) T2—767 14
Washington County (Colo.) T2—788 79
Washington County (Fla.) T2—759 963
Washington County (Ga.) T2—758 672
Washington County (Idaho) T2—796 25
Washington County (Ill.) T2—773 88
Washington County (Ind.) T2—772 22
Washington County (Iowa) T2—777 923
Washington County (Kan.) T2—781 273
Washington County (Ky.) T2—769 493
Washington County (Md.) T2—752 91
Washington County (Me.) T2—741 42
Washington County (Minn.) T2—776 59
Washington County (Miss.) T2—762 42
Washington County (Mo.) T2—778 64
Washington County (N.C.) T2—756 165
Washington County (N.Y.) T2—747 49
Washington County (Neb.) T2—782 245
Washington County (Ohio) T2—771 98
Washington County (Okla.) T2—766 96
Washington County (Or.) T2—795 43
Washington County (Pa.) T2—748 82
Washington County (R.I.) T2—745 9
Washington County (Tenn.) T2—768 97
Washington County (Tex.) T2—764 245
Washington County (Utah) T2—792 48
Washington County (Va.) T2—755 725
Washington County (Vt.) T2—743 4
Washington County (Wis.) T2—775 91
Washington Parish (La.) T2—763 11
Washita County (Okla.) T2—766 42
Washita River (Tex. and Okla.) T2—766 5
Washo Indians T5—975 7
Washoe County (Nev.) T2—793 55
Washtenaw County (Mich.) T2—774 35
Wāsiṭ (Iraq) T2—567 5
Wasps 595.79
agricultural pests 632.79
Waste control 363.728
law 344.046 2
production management 658.567
public administration 353.93
rubber manufacturing 678.29
social services 363.728
spacecraft 629.477 4
technology 628.4
see also Waste control—technology
see also Wastes
Waste disposal 363.728
see also Waste control—technology; Waste control
Waste lands 333.731 37
Waste management 363.728
see also Waste control
Waste technology 628.4
T1—028 6
glassmaking 666.14
paper manufacturing 676.042
petroleum 665.538 9
plastics 668.419 2
rural 628.74
wood products 674.84
see also Waste control
Waste utilization
production management 658.567
Wastelands
public administration 354.34
Wastepaper pulp 676.142
Wastes 363.728
energy production
economics 333.793 8
fuel technology 662.87
law 344.046 2
pollution technology 628.5
social services 363.728
utilization
animal feed 636.085 56
production management 658.567
water pollution engineering 628.168
see also Waste control; Waste technology
Wastewater 363.728 4
see also Waste control
Watauga County (N.C.) T2—756 843
Watchdog agencies 352.88
Watchdogs 636.73
Watches 681.114
art metalwork 739.3
technology 681.114
Watchmakers 681.114 092
occupational group T7—681 1

Watchworks
  technology 681.112
Water 553.7
  biochemistry 572.539
    humans 612.015 22
      see Manual at 612.01522 vs. 612.3923, 616.3992
  chemical engineering 661.08
  chemistry 546.22
  dowsing 133.323 2
  economic geology 553.7
  folklore 398.26
    history and criticism 398.364
  geologic agent 551.35
    see Manual at 551.302–551.307 vs. 551.35
  health 613.287
  hydraulic engineering 627
  hydraulic-power technology 621.204 22
  law 346.046 91
  materials science 620.198
  metabolism
    human physiology 612.392 3
      see Manual at 612.01522 vs. 612.3923, 616.3992
  meteorology 551.57
  plant management 658.26
  prospecting 628.114
  public administration 354.36
  religious worship 291.212
  resource economics 333.91
  sanitary engineering 628.1
  supply services 363.61
  treatment engineering 628.162
Water absorption
  plants 575.76
Water-atmosphere interactions 551.524
  microclimatology 551.66
Water balance 551.48
Water bears 592.72
Water beetles 595.762
Water birds 598.176
  conservation technology 639.978 176
  paleozoology 568.4
  resource economics 333.958 28
Water bodies 551.46
  T2—16
  influence on precipitation 551.577 5
  physical geology 551.46
  public administration 354.36
Water buffalo 636.293
  animal husbandry 636.293
  zoology 599.642
Water chestnuts 583.765
Water clocks
  technology 681.111
Water clovers 587.3
Water collection systems
  engineering 628.142
Water conservation 333.911 6
  agriculture 631.7
  engineering 628.13
  law 346.046 911 6
  public administration 354.363 4
  resource economics 333.911 6
Water detention ponds 627.44
Water distribution systems 363.61
  engineering 628.144
  see also Water supply
Water diversion
  engineering 627.123
  flood control 627.45
Water drainage
  buildings 696.13
Water-electrolyte imbalances 571.937 5
  medicine 616.399 2
    see Manual at 612.01522 vs. 612.3923, 616.3992
  see also Digestive system
Water features
  landscape architecture 714
Water fixtures
  buildings 696.1
  see also Water supply
Water fleas 595.32
Water games 797.25
  see also Sports
Water gardens 635.967 4
Water gas 665.772
Water hammer
  engineering 620.106 4
Water heaters
  buildings 696.6
  manufacturing technology 683.88
Water hyacynths 584.72
Water ices (Desserts) 641.863
  commercial processing 637.4
  home preparation 641.863
Water impoundment
  flood control 627.44
Water lilies 635.933 29
  botany 583.29
  floriculture 635.933 29
Water mains 628.15

Water mills 621.21
Water ouzels 598.832
Water pageantry 797.203
Water plantains 584.72
Water pollution 363.739 4
ecological effect 577.627
international law 341.762 53
law 344.046 343
public administration 354.363 5
sanitary engineering 628.168
social welfare 363.739 4
toxicology 571.95
see also Pollution
Water polo 797.25
see also Sports
Water poppy 584.72
Water power 333.914
economics 333.914
electrical engineering 621.312 134
law 343.092 4
public administration 354.362 7
Water purification 628.162
Water-repellent fabrics 677.682
see also Textiles
Water resources 333.91
engineering 627
law 346.046 91
public administration 354.36
Water reuse 363.728 4
see also Waste control
Water rights
law 346.043 2
public control 346.046 91
sale and rental 333.339
Water safety 363.123
public administration 353.987
sports 797.200 289
see also Safety
Water scavenger beetles 595.763
Water skiers 797.350 92
sports group T7—797 3
Water skiing 797.35
see also Sports
Water softeners
buildings 696.12
hot-water supply 696.6
Water-soluble mediums
painting 751.42
Water-soluble paints 667.63
Water solutions 541.342 2
chemical engineering 660.294 22
Water spangles 587.3
Water sports 797
see also Sports
Water storage (Plant physiology) 575.78
Water striders 595.754
Water supply 363.61
economic geology 553.7
engineering 628.1
rural 628.72
household management 644.6
law 343.092 4
military engineering 623.751
plumbing 696.12
public administration 354.366
ships 623.854
social services 363.61
spacecraft 629.477 3
see Manual at 363.61
Water table 551.492
Water temperatures
meteorology 551.524
oceanography 551.460 1
Water towers 628.13
Water transportation 387
engineering 629.048
international law 341.756 6
law 343.096
military engineering 623.8
public administration 354.78
safety 363.123
international law 341.756 6
law 343.096
public administration 353.987
transportation services 387
Water treatment 628.162
Water turbines 621.24
Water voles 599.354
Water witching 133.323 2
Waterberg (South Africa : District) T2—682 5
Waterbuck 599.645
Waterclovers 587.3
Watercolor painting 751.422
Watercresses 641.355 6
botany 583.64
cooking 641.655 6
food 641.355 6
garden crop 635.56
Waterfalls T2—169 4
hydrology 551.484
Waterford (Ireland) T2—419 15
Waterford (Ireland : County) T2—419 1
Waterfowl 598.41
conservation technology 639.978 41
food 641.391
cooking 641.691

Waterfowl (continued)	
resource economics	333.958 41
sports hunting	799.244
zoology	598.41
Waterfowling	799.244
Waterleafs	583.94
Waterloo (Ont.)	T2—713 45
Waterloo (Ont. : Regional municipality)	T2—713 44
Waterloo, Battle of, 1815	940.274 2
Watermarks	676.280 27
Watermeals	584.64
Watermelons	641.356 15
botany	583.63
commercial processing	664.805 615
cooking	641.656 15
food	641.356 15
garden crop	635.615
Waterpower	333.914
see also Water power	
Waterproof construction	
buildings	693.892
Waterproof fabrics	677.682
see also Textiles	
Watersheds	
land economics	333.73
Waterspouts (Tornadoes)	551.553
see also Tornadoes	
Waterton-Glacier International Peace Park	T2—786 52
Alberta	T2—712 34
Montana	T2—786 52
Waterton Lakes National Park (Alta.)	T2—712 34
Waterval-Boven (South Africa : District)	T2—682 7
Waterways (Inland transportation)	386
see also Inland waterways	
Waterwheels	621.21
Watford (England)	T2—425 892
Watling Island (Bahamas)	T2—729 6
Watonwan County (Minn.)	T2—776 29
Watsonian behaviorism	150.194 32
Watt-hour meters	621.374 5
Wattled crows	598.8
Wattles (Trees)	583.748
forestry	634.973 748
ornamental arboriculture	635.977 374 8
Wattmeters	621.374 6
Waukesha County (Wis.)	T2—775 93
Waupaca County (Wis.)	T2—775 38
Waushara County (Wis.)	T2—775 57
Wave action	551.36
Wave guides	
microwave electronics	621.381 331
Wave mechanics	530.124
Wave propagation	
microwave electronics	621.381 31
radio engineering	621.384 11
Wave theories	530.14
electricity	537.12
light	535.13
modern physics	530.14
Wave transmission	
microwave electronics	621.381 31
radio engineering	621.384 11
Wavelets (Mathematics)	515.243 3
Wavell, Archibald Percival Wavell, Earl of	
Indian history	954.035 9
Waveney (England)	T2—426 41
Waveney River (England)	T2—426 19
Waverley (England : Borough)	T2—422 19
Waves	
air mechanics	533.62
fluid mechanics	532.059 3
gas mechanics	533.293
liquid mechanics	532.593
mechanics	531.113 3
oceanography	551.470 2
quantum theory	530.124
solid mechanics	531.33
Wax beans	641.356 52
see also Kidney beans	
Wax carving	736.93
Wax myrtles	583.43
Wax painting	751.46
Waxbills	598.886
Waxes	665.1
biochemistry	572.57
chemistry	547.77
sculpture material	731.2
Waxing	
woodwork	
buildings	698.33
Waxwings	598.852
Way of the Cross	232.96
Roman Catholic liturgy	264.027 4
Wayampi language	498.38
	T6—983 8
Wayãpi language	498.38
	T6—983 8
Wayne County (Ga.)	T2—758 756
Wayne County (Ill.)	T2—773 792
Wayne County (Ind.)	T2—772 63

Wayne County (Iowa) T2—777 88
Wayne County (Ky.) T2—769 64
Wayne County (Mich.) T2—774 33
Wayne County (Miss.) T2—762 573
Wayne County (Mo.) T2—778 92
Wayne County (N.C.) T2—756 395
Wayne County (N.Y.) T2—747 87
Wayne County (Neb.) T2—782 57
Wayne County (Ohio) T2—771 61
Wayne County (Pa.) T2—748 23
Wayne County (Tenn.) T2—768 39
Wayne County (Utah) T2—792 54
Wayne County (W. Va.) T2—754 47
Waynesboro (Va.) T2—755 912
Weak interaction (Nuclear particles) 539.754 4
Weakfish 597.725
Weakley County (Tenn.) T2—768 24
Weald of Kent (England) T2—422 5
Wealden (England) T2—422 51
Wealth 330.16
  economic theory 330.16
  ethics 178
    religion 291.568
      Buddhism 294.356 8
      Christianity 241.68
      Hinduism 294.548 68
  macroeconomics 339.3
    distribution 339.2
Wealthy classes 305.523 4
  T1—086 21
  customs 390.1
    dress 391.01
Weapons
  engineering 623.4
  military 355.8
    see also Arms (Military)
  small firearms 683.4
    see also Guns (Small arms)
Weapons industry 338.476 234
Weapons testing
  international law 341.733
Wear
  machine engineering 621.89
Wear resistance
  materials science 620.112 92
Wear River (England) T2—428 6
Wear Valley (England) T2—428 64
Weasel spiders 595.48
Weasels 599.766 2
Weather 551.6
  aeronautics 629.132 4
  crop damage 632.1
  earth sciences 551.6
Weather (continued)
  folklore 398.26
    history and criticism 398.363
  health 613.11
  influence on crime 364.22
  literature 808.803 6
    history and criticism 809.933 6
    specific literatures T3B—080 36
      history and criticism T3B—093 6
  public administration 354.37
  social effects 304.25
  transportation hazard 363.120 1
    air transportation 363.124 12
    see also Transportation safety
  see Manual at 551.5 vs. 551.6
Weather bureaus 354.37
Weather control 551.68
  international law 341.762
  see also Weather
Weather forecasting 551.63
  armed forces 355.343 2
  public administration 354.37
  see also Weather
Weather-induced illnesses
  medicine 616.988
  see also Environmental diseases (Human)
Weather lore 551.631
Weather modification 551.68
  international law 341.762
  see also Weather
Weather satellites
  use 551.635 4
Weather stripping 678.35
Weathering 551.302
  by water 551.352
  by wind 551.372
  materials science 620.112 23
  soil formation 551.305
Weatherization (Housing program) 363.583
Weaver finches 598.887
Weaver finches (Estrildidae) 598.886
Weaver finches (Ploceidae) 598.887
Weaverbirds 598.887
Weavers (Birds) 598.887
Weaving 677.028 242
  arts 746.14
    threads and yarns 746.14
    vegetable fibers 746.41
  elementary education 372.54
  manufacturing technology 677.028 242
Webb County (Tex.) T2—764 462

Weber County (Utah) T2—792 28
Webster County (Ga.) T2—758 916
Webster County (Iowa) T2—777 51
Webster County (Ky.) T2—769 883
Webster County (Miss.) T2—762 697
Webster County (Mo.) T2—778 823
Webster County (Neb.) T2—782 374
Webster County (W. Va.) T2—754 65
Webster Parish (La.) T2—763 96
Weddell Sea (Antarctic regions) 551.469 3
T2—167 3
Weddell seal 599.796
Wedding clothes 392.54
commercial technology 687.16
customs 392.54
home sewing 646.47
see also Clothing
Wedding music 781.587
Weddings
customs 392.5
dress 392.54
etiquette 395.22
flower arrangements 745.926
handicrafts 745.594 1
interior decoration 747.93
Weed killers 628.97
agriculture 632.5
chemical engineering 668.654
environmental engineering 628.97
Weeding (Library collections) 025.216
Weeds 632.5
control 363.78
agriculture 632.5
environmental engineering 628.97
social services 363.78
economic botany 581.652
Weeks 529.2
Weenen (South Africa : District) T2—684 7
Weevils 595.768
agricultural pests 632.768
Weight
biological organisms 578.41
plants 581.41
Weight-gaining diet
health 613.24
Weight lifters 796.410 92
sports group T7—796 4
Weight lifting 613.713
physical fitness 613.713
sports 796.41
see also Sports
Weight-losing programs
health 613.25
Weighting (Compensation)
labor economics 331.216 6
Weightlessness
space flight 629.418
Weights and measures 530.81
law 343.075
physics 530.81
public administration 352.83
social use 389.1
standardization 389.62
Weimar Republic 943.085
Weimaraner (Dog) 636.752
Weirs 627.883
Weld County (Colo.) T2—788 72
Welded joints 671.520 42
Welders 671.520 92
occupational group T7—671
Welding 671.52
decorative arts 739.14
sculpture 731.41
ship hulls 623.843 2
Welding equipment 621.977
Welding plastics 668.415
Welds 671.520 42
Welega Kifle Hāger (Ethiopia) T2—633
Welensky, Roy
Rhodesia and Nyasaland history 968.903
Welfare 361
see also Welfare services
Welfare economics school 330.155 6
Welfare fraud 364.163
law 345.026 3
Welfare law 344.03
Welfare liberalism
political ideology 320.513
Welfare power (Legislative bodies) 328.341 3
Welfare reform 361.68
Welfare rights 361.614
see Manual at 361.614 vs. 330
Welfare services 361
Algerian Revolution 965.046 7
Chaco War 989.207 167
Civil War (England) 942.062 7
Civil War (Spain) 946.081 7
Civil War (United States) 973.777
crime prevention 364.44
Crimean War 947.073 87
Falkland Islands War 997.110 247
Franco-German War 943.082 7
Hundred Years' War 944.025 7
Indo-Pakistan War, 1971 954.920 517

Welfare services (continued)
- Indochinese War 959.704 17
- international law 341.766
- Iraqi-Iranian Conflict 955.054 27
- Korean War 951.904 27
- law 344.03
- Mexican War 973.627
- Napoleonic Wars 940.277
- Persian Gulf War, 1991 956.704 427
- personnel management 658.38
- prisoner services 365.66
- public administration 353.5
- South African War 968.048 7
- Spanish-American War 973.897
- specific groups 362
  - law 344.032
- students 371.7
- Thirty Years' War 940.247
- United States Revolutionary War 973.37
- Vietnamese War 959.704 37
- War of 1812 973.527
- War of the Pacific 983.061 67
- World War I 940.477
- World War II 940.547 7
- *see Manual at* 301–307 vs. 361–365; *also at* 361–365; *also at* 361–365 vs. 353.5; *also at* 361 vs. 362; *also at* 362–363: Add table

Welfare state
- economics 330.126
- social welfare 361.65

Welfare workers 361.92
- occupational group T7—36

Welkom (South Africa : District) T2—685 35

Well-being
- applied psychology 158
- parapsychology 131

Well blowouts
- oil extraction 622.338 2

Well shrimps 595.378

Welland (Ont. : County) T2—713 38

Welland Canal (Ont.) T2—713 38

Welland River (England) T2—425 39

Wellesley, Richard Wellesley, Marquess
- Indian history 954.031 2

Wellingborough (England : Borough) T2—425 58

Wellington (N.S.W.) T2—944 5

Wellington (N.Z.) T2—936 3

Wellington (Ont. : County) T2—713 42

Wellington (South Africa : District) T2—687 3

Wellington City (N.Z.) T2—936 3

Wellington Province (N.Z.) T2—936

Wellington Region (N.Z.) T2—936

Wells (B.C.) T2—711 75

Wells (Water source)
- engineering 628.114
- hydrology 551.498

Wells County (Ind.) T2—772 72

Wells County (N.D.) T2—784 58

Wells Gray Provincial Park (B.C.) T2—711 72

Welo Kifle Hāger (Ethiopia) T2—634

Welsh T5—916 6

Welsh Calvinistic Methodist Church 285.235
- *see also* Presbyterian Church

Welsh corgis 636.737

Welsh language 491.66
- T6—916 6

Welsh literature
- English 820
- Welsh 891.66

Welsh Marches T2—424

Welsh pony 636.16

Welwitschiales 585.8

Welwyn Hatfield (England) T2—425 86

Wendish language 491.88
- T6—918 8

Wendish literature 891.88

Wendish people T5—918 8

Wends T5—918 8

Wens (Disorder)
- medicine 616.53
- *see also* Skin

Wentworth (Ont.) T2—713 52

Wepener (South Africa : District) T2—685 6

Werewolves 398.245 4
- *see also* Legendary animals

Werribee (Vic.) T2—945 2

Weser-Ems (Germany : Regierungsbezirk) T2—435 91

Wesleyan Conference 287.53
- *see also* Methodist Church

Wesleyan Methodist Church 287.1
- *see also* Methodist Church

Wesleyan Reform Union 287.534
- *see also* Methodist Church

Wesleyan Reformers 287.53
- *see also* Methodist Church

Wesselsbron (South Africa : District) T2—685 3
Wessex supremacy 942.016
West (U.S.) 978
T2—78
art representation 704.949 978
arts 700.427 8
T3C—327 8
literature 808.803 278
history and criticism 809.933 278
specific literatures T3B—080 327 8
history and criticism T3B—093 278 4
see also Westerns (Fiction)
West (Western world) 909.098 21
T2—182 1
West Africa 966
T2—66
West Atlantic languages (Africa) 496.32
T6—963 2
West Azerbaijan (Iran) T2—554
West Bank 956.953
T2—569 53
West Baton Rouge Parish (La.) T2—763 452
West Bengal (India) T2—541 4
West Berbice (Guyana : District) T2—881 6
West Berlin (Germany) T2—431 554
West Branch Susquehanna River (Pa.) T2—748 5
West Carroll Parish (La.) T2—763 83
West Coast Region (N.Z.) T2—937 1
West Demerara (Guyana : District) T2—881 4
West Devon (England : Borough) T2—423 53
West Dorset (England : District) T2—423 31
West Feliciana Parish (La.) T2—763 17
West Flanders (Belgium) T2—493 12
West Frisian Islands (Netherlands) T2—492 13
West Germanic languages 439
T6—39
West Germanic literatures 839
West Germany 943.087
T2—43
West Glamorgan (Wales) T2—429 81
West Indian boxwood 583.45
West Indian steel drums 786.843
see also Percussion instruments
West Indies 972.9
T2—729
West Indies, Dutch T2—729 86
West Indies, French T2—729 76
West Indies Associated States T2—729 73
West Iranian languages (Ancient) 491.51
T6—915 1
West Iranian literatures (Ancient) 891.51
West Irian T2—951
West Kettle River (B.C.) T2—711 62
West Lake Region (Tanzania) T2—678 27
West Lancashire (England) T2—427 612
West Lindsey (England : District) T2—425 31
West Lothian (Scotland) T2—413 3
West Malaysia T2—595 1
West Midlands (England) T2—424 9
West New Britain Province (Papua New Guinea) T2—958 7
West New Guinea T2—951
West Orange (N.J.) T2—749 33
West Oxfordshire (England : District) T2—425 71
West Pakistan (Pakistan) T2—549 1
West Prussia (Germany) T2—438 2
West Rand (South Africa) T2—682 2
West Redonda Island (B.C.) T2—711 1
West Riding of Yorkshire (England) T2—428 1
West Road River (B.C.) T2—711 75
West Scandinavian languages 439.6
T6—396
West Scandinavian literatures 839.6
West Scandinavians T5—396
West Semitic languages 492
T6—92
West Semitic literatures 892
West Semitic peoples T5—92
West Sepik Province (Papua New Guinea) T2—957 7
West Slavic languages 491.85
T6—918 5
West Slavic literatures 891.85
West Slavs T5—918 5
West Somerset (England : District) T2—423 85
West Suffolk (England) T2—426 44
West Sussex (England) T2—422 6
West Thurlow Island (B.C.) T2—711 1
West Vancouver (B.C.) T2—711 33

West Virginia 975.4
T2—754
West Wiltshire (England : District) T2—423 15
West Yorkshire (England) T2—428 1
Westchester County (N.Y.) T2—747 277
Westerlies 551.518 3
Western Aramaic languages 492.29
T6—922 9
Western Aramaic literatures 892.29
Western architecture 722–724
ancient 722.6
Western art music 781.68
Western Asian international organizations 341.247 7
Western Australia T2—941
Western Bay of Plenty District (N.Z.) T2—934 22
Western bloc T2—171 3
Western calendars 529.4
Western calligraphy 745.619 7
Western Canada T2—712
Western civilization 909.098 21
Western Desert (Egypt) T2—622
Western desert language 499.15
T6—991 5
Western Equatoria (Sudan : Province) T2—629 5
Western Europe 940
T2—4
ancient 936
T2—36
Western folk music modes 781.263
Western front
World War I 940.414 4
Western Greece (Greece) T2—495 27
Western Hemisphere T2—181 2
see Manual at T2—7 vs. T2—1812
Western Hemisphere international organizations 341.245
Western Highlands (Papua New Guinea) T2—956 5
Western Hindi languages 491.43
T6—914 3
Western Hindi literatures 891.43
Western Isles (Scotland) T2—411 4
Western Macedonia (Greece) T2—495 62
Western Mediterranean Sea 551.462 1
T2—163 81
Western philosophy 190
see Manual at 140 vs. 180–190
Western popular music 781.64
country and western 781.642
songs 782.421 642
songs 782.421 64
Western Province (Kenya) T2—676 28
Western Province (Papua New Guinea) T2—954 9
Western Province (Solomon Islands) T2—959 31
Western Province (South Africa) T2—687 3
Western Province (Zambia) T2—689 4
Western Region (Nigeria) T2—669 2
Western Sahara 964.8
T2—648
Western Samar (Philippines) T2—599 5
Western Samoa 996.14
T2—961 4
Western Samoans T5—994 62
Western Siberia (Russia) T2—573
Western State (Nigeria) T2—669 2
Western States (U.S.) 978
T2—78
Western stories 808.838 74
history and criticism 809.387 4
specific literatures T3B—308 74
individual authors T3A—3
Western Turkic languages 494.38
T6—943 8
Western world 909.098 21
T2—182 1
Westerns
motion pictures 791.436 278
radio programs 791.446 278
television programs 791.456 278
Westerns (Fiction) 808.838 74
history and criticism 809.387 4
specific literatures T3B—308 74
individual authors T3A—3
Westland District (N.Z.) T2—937 1
Westland National Park (N.Z.) T2—937 1
Westland Province (N.Z.) T2—937 1
Westmeath (Ireland) T2—418 15
Westminster (London, England) T2—421 32
Westmoreland County (Pa.) T2—748 81
Westmoreland County (Va.) T2—755 24
Westmorland (England) T2—427 8

Westmorland (N.B. : County) T2—715 23
Weston County (Wyo.) T2—787 14
Westonaria (South Africa : District) T2—682 2
Westphalia (Germany) T2—435 6
Wet-collodion process 772.14
Wet-weather photography 778.75
Wetlands 551.41
  biology 578.768
    resource economics 333.952 88
      animals 333.954 88
  ecology 577.68
  geomorphology 551.41
  law 346.046 918
  public administration 354.34
  resource economics 333.918
Wetting agents 668.14
Wetzel County (W. Va.) T2—754 18
Wexford (Ireland) T2—418 856
Wexford (Ireland : County) T2—418 85
Wexford County (Mich.) T2—774 67
Weymouth and Portland (England) T2—423 35
Whakatane District (N.Z.) T2—934 25
Whale fishes 597.64
Whale lice 595.378
Whale oil 665.2
Whalers 639.280 92
  occupational group T7—639 2
Whales 599.5
  conservation technology 639.979 5
  hunting 639.28
  paleozoology 569.5
  resource economics 333.959 5
    law 346.046 959 5
  zoology 599.5
Whaling
  international law 341.762 2
  production economics 338.372 95
  products 338.372 95
    commerce 380.143 95
  technology 639.28
Whaling industry 338.372 95
Whaling ships
  engineering 623.824 8
Whanganui National Park (N.Z.) T2—935 2
Whangarei District (N.Z.) T2—931 6
Wharton County (Tex.) T2—764 133
Wharves
  engineering 627.31
Whatcom County (Wash.) T2—797 73
Wheat 641.331 1
  botany 584.9
  commercial processing 664.722
  cooking 641.631 1
  food 641.331 1
  food crop 633.11
  forage crop 633.251
Wheatland County (Mont.) T2—786 63
Wheel games 795.2
  equipment technology 688.752
Wheelbarrows
  manufacturing technology 688.6
Wheelchair basketball 796.323 8
Wheelchair sports 796.045 6
  see also Sports
Wheeler County (Ga.) T2—758 835
Wheeler County (Neb.) T2—782 762
Wheeler County (Or.) T2—795 81
Wheeler County (Tex.) T2—764 828
Wheeler Lake (Ala.) T2—761 98
Wheeling (W. Va.) T2—754 14
Wheels
  automotive engineering 629.248
  railroad engineering 625.21
Whelks 594.32
Whey 641.373
  cooking 641.673
  food 641.373
  processing 637.3
Whig Party (Great Britain) 324.241 02
Whig Party (U.S.) 324.273 23
Whip scorpions 595.453 2
Whippet (Dog) 636.753 2
Whippoorwill 598.99
Whips
  music 786.99
    see also Percussion instruments
Whirligig beetles 595.762
Whisk ferns 587.4
Whiskey 641.252
  commercial processing 663.52
Whist 795.413
Whistle (Voices) 782.98
  choral and mixed voices 782.98
  single voices 783.98
Whistle blowing
  law 342.068
  public administration 353.46
Whistler (B.C.) T2—711 31
White bass 597.732
White blood cells 571.96
  human immunology 616.079

White collar crime 364.168
  law 345.026 8
White collar workers 331.792
  T1—086 22
  labor economics 331.792
    labor force 331.119 042
    labor market 331.129 042
  labor unions 331.880 41
  personnel management 658.304 4
  social class 305.556
White corpuscles 571.96
  human histology 611.018 5
  human immunology 616.079
  human physiology 612.112
  see also Cardiovascular system
White County (Ark.) T2—767 76
White County (Ga.) T2—758 277
White County (Ill.) T2—773 96
White County (Ind.) T2—772 93
White County (Tenn.) T2—768 66
White dwarfs 523.887
White-footed mice 599.355
White-fronted goose 598.417 3
White Horse, Vale of (England) T2—425 76
White-listing (Labor) 331.894
White mangrove 583.763
White Mountains (N.H. and Me.) T2—742 2
White Nile (Sudan : Province) T2—626 4
White Nile River T2—629 3
White perch 597.732
White Pine County (Nev.) T2—793 15
White race T5—034
White River (Ark. and Mo.) T2—767 2
White River (Ind.) T2—772 3
White River (South Africa : District) T2—682 6
White Rock (B.C.) T2—711 33
White Sands National Monument (N.M.) T2—789 65
White Sea (Russia) 551.468 4
  T2—163 24
White shark 597.33
White slave traffic 364.153 4
  law 345.025 34
White-tailed deer 599.652
  big game hunting 799.276 52
  conservation technology 639.979 652
  resource economics 333.959 652
White whale 599.542
White wine 641.222 2
  commercial processing 663.222
  sparkling 641.222 4
    commercial processing 663.224
Whitefish Bay (Mich. and Ont.) T2—774 91
Whitefishes 597.55
Whiteflies 595.752
Whitehorse (Yukon) T2—719 1
Whiteshell Provincial Park (Man.) T2—712 74
Whiteside County (Ill.) T2—773 35
Whitetip shark 597.34
Whitewash 667.63
Whitewashing
  buildings 698.2
Whitfield County (Ga.) T2—758 324
Whiting (Kingfish) 597.725
Whitings (Cods) 597.633
Whitings (Whitefishes) 597.55
Whitley County (Ind.) T2—772 75
Whitley County (Ky.) T2—769 132
Whitman County (Wash.) T2—797 39
Whitney, Mount (Calif.) T2—794 86
Whitsunday 263.94
  devotional literature 242.38
  music 781.729 3
  sermons 252.64
Whitsunday Group (Qld.) T2—943 6
Whitsunday Island National Park (Qld.) T2—943 6
Whittling 736.4
Whole-class reading
  elementary education 372.416 4
Whole-language approach
  elementary education 372.62
    language arts 372.62
    reading 372.475
Whole life insurance 368.326
  see also Insurance
Whole tonality 781.266
Whole-word method (Reading)
  elementary education 372.462
Wholesale marketing 381.2
  management 658.86
  see also Commerce
Wholesale trade 381.2
  accounting 657.839
  law 343.088 8
  marketing management 658.86
  see also Commerce
Whooping cough
  incidence 614.543
  medicine 616.204

Whooping cough (continued)
  pediatrics 618.922 04
  see also Respiratory system
Whyalla (S. Aust.) T2—942 38
Wibaux County (Mont.) T2—786 34
Wichita (Kan.) T2—781 86
Wichita County (Kan.) T2—781 423
Wichita County (Tex.) T2—764 745
Wickerwork plants
  agriculture 633.58
Wicketkeeping 796.358 24
Wicklow (Ireland : County) T2—418 4
Wicomico County (Md.) T2—752 25
Wide-area networks 004.67
  see also Computer communications
Widgeon grass 584.74
Widowed persons 305.906 54
  T1—086 54
  family relationships 306.88
  psychology 155.644
  social group 305.906 54
Widowers 305.389 654
  T1—086 54
  family relationships 306.88
  psychology 155.644 2
  social group 305.389 654
Widows 305.489 654
  T1—086 54
  family relationships 306.88
  psychology 155.644 3
  social group 305.489 654
Wieringermeer (Netherlands) T2—492 35
Wiesbaden (Germany) T2—434 165
Wieser, Friedrich, Freiherr von
  economic school 330.157
Wife abuse 362.829 2
  criminology 364.155 53
    criminal law 345.025 553
  social welfare 362.829 2
  see also Family violence
Wife and husband 306.872
  law 346.016 3
Wigan (England) T2—427 36
Wight, Isle of (England) T2—422 8
Wigs 646.724 8
  customs 391.5
  manufacturing technology 679
  personal care 646.724 8
Wigtown (Scotland : District) T2—414 95
Wilbarger County (Tex.) T2—764 746
Wilcox County (Ala.) T2—761 38
Wilcox County (Ga.) T2—758 845
Wild and scenic rivers 333.784 5
  law 346.046 784 5
  natural resources 333.784 5
Wild boars 599.633 2
  agricultural pests 632.696 33
  big game hunting 799.276 332
  conservation technology 639.979 633 2
  resource economics 333.959 633 2
Wild children 155.456 7
Wild edible plants 641.303
  economic botany 581.632
  food 641.303
Wild flowers 582.13
  floriculture 635.967 6
  see also Flowers
Wild horse 599.665 5
  conservation technology 639.979 665 5
  resource economics 333.959 665 5
Wild mango (Dika) 583.79
Wild rice 584.9
  cooking 641.631 78
  food 641.331 78
  food crop 633.178
Wild sarsaparilla 583.84
Wild silk textiles 677.392
  see also Textiles
Wild turkeys 598.645
  conservation technology 639.978 645
  resource economics 333.958 645
  sports hunting 799.246 45
Wild West shows 791.84
Wildcat (Felis silvestris) 599.752 6
Wildcat (Lynx rufus) 599.753 6
Wildcat strikes 331.892 4
  see also Strikes (Work stoppages)
Wildebeests 599.645 9
Wilderness (South Africa) T2—687 4
Wilderness areas
  law 346.046 782
  natural resources 333.782
Wildfowl 598.163
  conservation technology 639.978 163
  economic zoology 598.163
  food 641.391
    cooking 641.691
  resource economics 333.958 29
  sports hunting 799.24
Wildfowl (Waterfowl) 598.41
  see also Waterfowl
Wildfowling 799.24
Wildfowling (Waterfowling) 799.244

Wildlife 590
resource economics 333.954
see also Animals
Wildlife conservation 333.954 16
law 346.046 951 6
technology 639.9
Wildlife management 333.954
technology 639.9
Wildlife refuges 333.954 16
see also Wildlife reserves
Wildlife reserves 333.954 16
conservation technology 639.95
economics 333.954 16
landscape architecture 719.36
law 346.046 951 6
Wilhelmina, Queen of the Netherlands
Dutch history 949.207 1
Wilhelmshaven (Germany) T2—435 917
Wilkes County (Ga.) T2—758 172
Wilkes County (N.C.) T2—756 82
Wilkin County (Minn.) T2—776 91
Wilkinson County (Ga.) T2—758 543
Wilkinson County (Miss.) T2—762 25
Will 153.8
philosophy 128.3
freedom of will 123.5
Will County (Ill.) T2—773 25
Willacy County (Tex.) T2—764 493
Willamette River (Or.) T2—795 3
Willem Pretorius Game Reserve (South Africa) T2—685 3
William I, German Emperor
German history 943.083
William I, King of England
English history 942.021
William II, German Emperor
German history 943.084
William II, King of England
English history 942.022
William III, King of England
British history 941.068
English history 942.068
Scottish history 941.106 8
William IV, King of Great Britain
British history 941.075
English history 942.075
Scottish history 941.107 5
Williams County (N.D.) T2—784 73
Williams County (Ohio) T2—771 113
Williams Lake (B.C.) T2—711 75
Williamsburg (Va.) T2—755 425 2
Williamsburg County (S.C.) T2—757 83
Williamson County (Ill.) T2—773 993
Williamson County (Tenn.) T2—768 56
Williamson County (Tex.) T2—764 289
Williamsoniaceae 561.592
Willingdon, Freedman Freedman-Thomas, Marquess of
Indian history 954.035 8
Williston (South Africa : District) T2—687 17
Williston Lake (B.C.) T2—711 87
Willmore Wilderness Provincial Park (Alta.) T2—712 332
Willowmore (South Africa : District) T2—687 15
Willows 583.65
ornamental arboriculture 635.977 365
Willowvale (South Africa : District) T2—687 91
Wills 346.054
genealogy 929.3
Willy-willies (Hurricanes) 551.552
see also Hurricanes
Wilmington (Del.) T2—751 2
Wilmington (N.C.) T2—756 27
Wilmot Proviso, 1847 973.61
Civil War (United States)
cause 973.711 3
Wilson, Woodrow
United States history 973.913
Wilson cloud chambers
nuclear physics 539.777
Wilson County (Kan.) T2—781 925
Wilson County (N.C.) T2—756 43
Wilson County (Tenn.) T2—768 54
Wilson County (Tex.) T2—764 445
Wilsons Promontory National Park (Vic.) T2—945 6
Wiltshire (England) T2—423 1
Wimmera (Vic. : District) T2—945 8
Wimmera River (Vic.) T2—945 9
Winburg (South Africa : District) T2—685 3
Winches 621.864
Winchester (England : District) T2—422 735
Winchester (Va.) T2—755 991
Wind 551.518
crop damage 632.16
geologic agent 551.37
Wind bands 784.8

Wind Cave National Park
(S.D.) T2—783 95
Wind chimes 786.872
see also Percussion instruments
Wind-driven ships 387.204 3
design 623.812 043
engineering 623.820 3
modern 387.22
design 623.812 2
engineering 623.822
handling 623.882 2
transportation services 387.22
transportation services 387.204 3
see also Ships
Wind energy 333.92
Wind engines 621.45
Wind ensembles 785.43
Wind erosion 551.372
Wind instruments 788
bands and orchestras 784
chamber ensembles 785
construction 788.192 3
by hand 788.192 3
by machine 681.88
solo music 788
see Manual at 784–788
Wind loads 624.175
Wind-powered electric generation 621.312 136
Wind propulsion 621.45
Wind River Range (Wyo.) T2—787 6
Wind scorpions 595.48
Wind tunnels
aircraft 629.134 52
Wind waves
oceanography 551.470 22
Windham County (Conn.) T2—746 45
Windham County (Vt.) T2—743 9
Windhoek (Namibia) T2—688 1
Windlasses 621.864
Windmills 621.453
Window-box gardens 635.967 8
Window displays
advertising 659.157
Window furnishings 645.3
home sewing 646.21
household management 645.3
manufacturing technology 684
Window gardening 635.967 8
Window glass 666.152
Window insurance 368.6
see also Insurance
Window managers (Systems programs) 005.437
Windowing programs 005.437
Windows
automobile 629.266
buildings 721.823
architecture 721.823
construction 690.182 3
interior decoration 747.3
Windshield wipers 678.35
automobile 629.276
Windshields
automobile 629.266
Windsor (N.S.) T2—716 35
Windsor (Ont.) T2—713 32
Windsor, Edward, Duke of
British history 941.084
English history 942.084
Scottish history 941.108 4
Windsor, House of 941.08
British history 941.08
English history 942.08
genealogy 929.72
Scottish history 941.108
Windsor and Maidenhead (England) T2—422 96
Windsor County (Vt.) T2—743 65
Windsor Tableland National Park (Qld.) T2—943 6
Windstorm insurance 368.122
see also Insurance
Windsurfing 797.33
see also Sports
Windward Islands 972.984
T2—729 84
Wine 641.22
commercial processing 663.2
cooking with 641.622
home preparation 641.872
Wings (Air force units) 358.413 1
Wings (Airplanes)
engineering 629.134 32
Wings (Animals) 591.479
descriptive zoology 591.479
birds 598.147 9
insects 595.714 78
physiology 573.798
Wings (Naval air units) 359.943 4
Winkler County (Tex.) T2—764 913
Winn Parish (La.) T2—763 66
Winnebago, Lake T2—775 64
Winnebago County (Ill.) T2—773 31
Winnebago County (Iowa) T2—777 22
Winnebago County (Wis.) T2—775 64

Winneshiek County (Iowa) T2—777 32
Winnipeg (Man.) T2—712 743
Winnipeg, Lake (Man.) T2—712 72
Winnipegosis, Lake (Man.) T2—712 72
Winnipesaukee, Lake (N.H.) T2—742 4
Winona County (Minn.) T2—776 12
Winooski River (Vt.) T2—743 17
Winston County (Ala.) T2—761 74
Winston County (Miss.) T2—762 692
Winter 508.2
  music 781.524 8
  see also Seasons
Winter air conditioning
  building systems 697.933 2
Winter flounder 597.694
Winter-flowering plants 581.43
  floriculture 635.953
Winter Olympic Games 796.98
  see also Sports
Winteraceae 583.22
Wintergreens 583.66
  flavorings 641.338 2
    see also Flavorings
Winter's bark 583.22
Wire communication systems 384.6
  see also Telephone
Wire services
  journalism 070.435
Wire-stitching
  bookbinding 686.35
Wire walking
  sports 796.46
    see also Sports
Wirehaired pointing griffon 636.752
Wireless communication 384.5
  communications services 384.5
  international law 341.757 7
  law 343.099 45
  public administration 354.75
Wires
  electrical circuits 621.319 33
  metal 671.842
  power transmission 621.854
  sculpture material 731.2
  structural engineering 624.177 4
Wiretapping
  criminal investigation 363.252
  electronic engineering 621.389 28
  law 345.052
Wireworms 595.765
  agricultural pests 632.765
Wirral (England) T2—427 51
Wirt County (W. Va.) T2—754 26
Wisconsin 977.5
  T2—775
Wisconsin Evangelical Lutheran Synod 284.134
  see also Lutheran church
Wisconsin River (Wis.) T2—775
Wisdom literature (Bible) 223
  Apocrypha 229.3
  Old Testament 223
  pseudepigrapha 229.912
Wisdom of God 212.7
  Christianity 231.6
  comparative religion 291.211 2
  Judaism 296.311 2
  philosophy of religion 212.7
Wisdom of Solomon (Bible) 229.3
Wise County (Tex.) T2—764 532
Wise County (Va.) T2—755 743
Wise men (Christian doctrines) 232.923
Wisent 599.643
Wisterias 635.933 74
  botany 583.74
  floriculture 635.933 74
Wit and humor 152.43
  see also Humor
Witbank (South Africa : District) T2—682 7
Witch hazels (Plants) 583.44
Witchcraft 133.43
  arts 700.47
    T3C—37
  literature 808.803 7
    history and criticism 809.933 7
    specific literatures T3B—080 37
      history and criticism T3B—093 7
  religious practice 291.33
    African religions 299.64
    modern revivals 299
    Native American religions 299.74
Witches (Occultists) 133.430 92
  persecution by Church 272.8
  social group T7—13
  see also Legendary beings
Witches (Religious leaders) 200.92
  biography 200.92
  modern revivals of old religions 299
  role and function 291.61
  see Manual at 200.92 and 291–299
Witham River (England) T2—425 3
Withholding tax 336.242 2
  law 343.052 424
  public finance 336.242 2

Withlacoochee River (Fla.) T2—759 7
Witness bearing 248.5
Witnesses 347.066
  police interrogation 363.254
  trial procedure 347.075
Witoto Indians T5—98
Witotoan languages 498
  T6—98
Witsieshoek (South Africa : District) T2—685 91
Wittmund (Germany : Landkreis) T2—435 917
Wives 306.872
  T1—086 55
  Christian devotional literature 242.643 5
  family relationships 306.872
  guides to Christian life 248.843 5
Wives of alcoholics
  medicine 616.861 9
  social welfare 362.292 3
Wives of clergymen
  biography 270.092
    specific denominations 280
      see Manual at 280
    see Manual at 230–280
  pastoral theology 253.22
Wives of substance abusers
  medicine 616.869
  social welfare 362.291 3
Wiyot language 497.3
  T6—973
Wizardry 133.43
  religious practice 291.33
Wizards (Occultists) 133.430 92
  see also Legendary beings
Wizards (Religious leaders) 200.92
  biography 200.92
  role and function 291.61
  see Manual at 200.92 and 291–299
Włocławek (Poland : Voivodeship) T2—438 2
Wobblies 331.886
Wodehouse (South Africa : District) T2—687 6
Wodonga (Vic.) T2—945 5
Wok cooking 641.589
Woking (England) T2—422 142
Wokingham (England : District) T2—422 94
Wolds, The (England) T2—428 3
Wolf children 155.456 7
Wolf-Rayet stars 523.88
Wolfe (Quebec : County) T2—714 573
Wolfe County (Ky.) T2—769 213
Wolfhounds 636.753 5
Wolfram 669.734
  see also Tungsten
Wolframite
  mineralogy 549.74
Wolfsbanes 583.34
Wolfville (N.S.) T2—716 34
Wollastonite
  mineralogy 549.66
Wollongong (N.S.W.) T2—944 6
Wolmaransstad (South Africa : District) T2—682 4
Wolof (African people) T5—963 214
Wolof language 496.321 4
  T6—963 214
Wolof literature 896.321 4
Wolverhampton (England) T2—424 91
Wolverine 599.766
Wolves 599.773
  animal husbandry 636.977 3
  conservation technology 639.979 773
  predator control technology 636.083 9
    conservation technology 639.966
  resource economics 333.959 773
  zoology 599.773
Wombats 599.24
Women 305.4
  T1—082
  T7—042
  art representation 704.942 4
  arts 700.452 042
  T3C—352 042
  biography 920.72
  civil rights 323.34
  criminal offenders 364.374
  drawing 743.44
  education 371.822
  etiquette 395.144
  government programs 353.535
  grooming 646.704 2
  health 613.042 44
  journalism for 070.483 47
  legal status 346.013 4
    constitutional law 342.087 8
    private law 346.013 4
  literature 808.803 520 42
    history and criticism 809.933 520 42
    specific literatures T3B—080 352 042
      history and criticism T3B—093 520 42
  painting 757.4
  physical fitness 613.704 5
  political organizations 324.3
  psychology 155.633

Women (continued)
recreation 790.194
indoor 793.019 4
outdoor 796.082
relations with government 323.34
religion 200.82
Christianity 270.082
devotional literature 242.643
guides to Christian life 248.843
social theology 261.834 4
guides to life 291.440 82
Islam 297.082
guides to life 297.570 82
Judaism 296.082
guides to life 296.708 2
social theology 291.178 344
sex hygiene 613.954
social aspects 305.4
social welfare 362.83
public administration 353.535
suffrage 324.623
see Manual at T1—081 and T1—082, T1—08351, T1—08352, T1—08421, T1—08422
Women and religion 200.82
see also Women—religion
Women authors (Literature) 809.892 87
specific literatures T3B—099 287
Women clergy 200.92
biography 200.92
Christian 270.092
biography 270.092
specific denominations 280
see Manual at 230–280
ecclesiology 262.1
ordination 262.14
pastoral theology 253.082
see also Clergy—Christian
Judaism 296.092
see also Women rabbis
ordination 291.610 82
role and function 291.610 82
see Manual at 200.92 and 291–299
Women in combat 355.408 2
Women in education 370.82
secondary level 373.082
Women in the Bible 220.830 54
Women of the Bible 220.920 82
Women rabbis 296.092
biography 296.092
specific denominations 296.8
ordination 296.610 82
Women rabbis (continued)
role and function 296.610 82
Women workers 331.4
economics 331.4
public administration 354.908 2
Women's baseball 796.357 8
Women's basketball 796.323 8
Women's clothing 391.2
commercial technology 687.082
customs 391.2
home economics 646.34
home sewing 646.404
see also Clothing
Women's football 796.332 8
Women's liberation movement 305.42
Women's political organizations 324.3
Women's prisons 365.43
see also Correctional institutions
Women's suffrage 324.623
Women's units (Armed forces) 355.348
Women's voices 782.6
choral and mixed voices 782.6
single voices 783.6
Wonderboom (South Africa : District) T2—682 35
Wood 575.46
architectural construction 721.044 8
architectural decoration 729.6
biology 575.46
building material 691.1
fuel 333.953 97
chemical technology 662.65
resource economics 333.953 97
handicrafts 745.51
lumber technology 674
materials science 620.12
sculpture material 731.2
ship design 623.818 4
shipbuilding 623.820 7
structural engineering 624.184
Wood boring beetles 595.764 8
Wood briquettes 662.65
Wood Buffalo National Park (Alta.) T2—712 32
Wood carving 736.4
Wood construction 694
Wood County (Ohio) T2—771 16
Wood County (Tex.) T2—764 223
Wood County (W. Va.) T2—754 22
Wood County (Wis.) T2—775 52
Wood duck 598.412 3
conservation technology 639.978 412 3
resource economics 333.958 412 3

Wood engraving		761.2
Wood flour		674.84
Wood laminates		674.835
Wood lice		595.372
Wood mice (Apodemus)		599.358 5
Wood oil		665.33
Wood pavements		625.83
Wood products		674.8
Wood products workers		674.809 2
occupational group	T7—674	
Wood pulp		676.12
Wood rats		599.357 3
Wood sculpturing		731.462
Wood shavings		674.84
Wood shrews		599.332
Wood shrikes		598.8
Wood sorrels		583.79
Wood-stove cooking		641.58
Wood swallows		598.8
Wood technology		
equipment manufacturing technology		681.767 6
Wood-using technologies		674.8
Wood warblers		598.872
Woodbury County (Iowa)	T2—777 41	
Woodchuck		599.366
small game hunting		799.259 366
Woodcocks		598.33
sports hunting		799.248 33
Woodcraft		
camp activity		796.545
Woodcreepers		598.822
Wooden furniture		645.4
manufacturing technology		684.104
see also Furniture		
Wooden ships		
construction		623.820 7
Wooden shoes		391.413
commercial technology		685.32
customs		391.413
see also Clothing		
Woodend (Vic.)	T2—945 3	
Woodenware		674.88
Woodford County (Ill.)	T2—773 53	
Woodford County (Ky.)	T2—769 465	
Woodland Indians	T5—97	
Woodlands		333.75
	T2—152	
see also Forest lands		
Woodlark Island (Papua New Guinea)	T2—954 1	
Woodlots		
agroforestry		634.99
Woodpeckers		598.72

Woodruff County (Ark.)	T2—767 92	
Woods (Golf equipment)		796.352 32
Woods, Lake of the	T2—776 81	
Canada	T2—713 11	
Minnesota	T2—776 81	
Woods County (Okla.)	T2—766 21	
Woodson County (Kan.)	T2—781 923	
Woodspring (England : District)	T2—423 96	
Woodward County (Okla.)	T2—766 19	
Woodwind bands		784.89
Woodwind instruments		788.2
bands and orchestras		784
chamber ensembles		785
mixed		785.2–.5
single type		785.8
construction		788.219 23
by hand		788.219 23
by machine		681.882
solo music		788.2
see Manual at 784–788		
Woodwork		
interior decoration		747.3
Woodworking		684.08
carpentry		694
home workshops		684.08
lumber technology		674
Woody plants		582.16
landscape architecture		715
Wool growing		636.314 5
Wool textiles		677.31
see also Textiles		
Wool wax		665.13
Woolly monkeys		599.858
Woolsorters' disease		
incidence		614.561
medicine		616.956
see also Communicable diseases (Human)		
Worcester (England)	T2—424 48	
Worcester (South Africa : District)	T2—687 3	
Worcester County (Mass.)	T2—744 3	
Worcester County (Md.)	T2—752 21	
Word-attack skills (Reading)		
elementary education		372.46
Word dividers (Dictionaries)		413.1
specific languages	T4—31	
Word formation		415
specific languages	T4—5	
Word games		793.734
Word of God		
Bible		220.13
Jesus Christ		232.2

Word order 415
  specific languages T4—5
Word origins 412
  specific languages T4—2
Word processing 652.5
Word-recognition method
  elementary education 372.462
Word study
  elementary education 372.61
Word usage
  rhetoric 808
Words 401.4
  T1—014
  dictionaries 413
  music 780
    treatises 780.268
  specific languages T4—014
    dictionaries T4—3
    usage (Applied linguistics) T4—81
    see Manual at T4—3 vs. T4—81
  usage (Applied linguistics) 418
Work 331
  see also Labor
Work (Mechanics) 531.6
Work (Physiological exertion) 573.79
  human physiology 612.042
Work animals 636.088 6
Work areas
  home economics 643.58
Work associates
  applied psychology 158.26
  psychological influence 155.926
Work camps (Penology) 365.34
  see also Correctional institutions
Work cars 385.32
  engineering 625.22
  transportation services 385.32
  see also Rolling stock
Work day 331.257 23
  economics 331.257 23
  personnel management 658.312 1
Work environment 331.25
  economics 331.25
  engineering 620.8
  personnel management 658.38
    public administration 352.67
  public administration 354.98
  safety 363.11
    public administration 353.96
    see also Industrial safety
Work environment (continued)
  sanitation 363.729 5
    public administration 353.94
Work ethic 306.361 3
Work furloughs
  penology 365.65
Work groups 658.402
  see also Work teams
Work load
  production management 658.54
Work music 781.593
Work periods 331.257
  economics 331.257
  personnel management 658.312 1
    public administration 352.67
  public administration 354.98
Work places 331.25
  see also Work environment
Work pressures
  executive management 658.409 5
Work productivity
  personnel management
    public administration 352.66
  promotion of
    personnel management 658.314
Work release
  penology 365.65
Work sharing 331.257 2
Work songs 782.421 593
Work studies
  production management 658.54
Work-study plan 371.227
  higher education 378.37
  secondary education 373.28
Work-study programs 371.225
  higher education 378.365
Work teams 658.402
  group decision making 658.403 6
  internal organization 658.402
  personnel utilization 658.312 8
    public administration 352.66
  production management
    quality control 658.562
Work training 370.113
  see also Vocational education
Work vehicles
  automotive engineering 629.225
  driving 629.284 5
  repair 629.287 5
Work week 331.257 22
  economics 331.257 22
  personnel management 658.312 1
Workaholism
  personality trait 155.232

Workbooks T1—076
Worker control of industry 338.6
  production economics 338.6
  theory of union role 331.880 1
Worker parties 324.217
  international organizations 324.17
Worker security 331.259 6
  law 344.012 596
  public administration 354.98
Worker self-management 338.6
  personnel management 658.315 2
  see also Worker control of industry
Workers 331.11
  economics 331.11
  occupational group T7—331 7
  public administration 354.9
  social class 305.562
  see Manual at 331.1 vs. 331.11, 331.12
Workers' compensation insurance 368.41
  employers' liability 368.56
  government-sponsored 368.41
  law 344.021
  personnel management 658.325 4
  public administration 353.69
  see also Insurance
Workforce diversity 331.114 3
  personnel management 658.300 8
Workhouses (Penology) 365.34
  see also Correctional institutions
Working capital 332.041 2
  financial management 658.152 44
Working-class parties 324.217
  international organizations 324.17
Working classes 305.562
  T1—086 23
  see also Laboring classes
Working conditions (Physical) 331.25
  see also Work environment
Working dogs 636.73
Working environment 331.25
  see also Work environment
Working mothers
  economics 331.44
Working ships 387.2
  engineering 623.82
  power-driven 387.248
    engineering 623.824
    transportation services 387.248
Working ships (continued)
  small craft 387.204 26
    engineering 623.820 26
    transportation services 387.204 26
  transportation services 387.2
  wind-driven 387.226
    engineering 623.822 6
    transportation services 387.226
  see also Ships
Workmen's compensation insurance 368.41
  see also Workers' compensation insurance
Workplace environment 331.25
  see also Work environment
Workplaces 331.25
  see also Work environment
Workshops (Adult education) T1—071 5
Workshops (Workrooms)
  agriculture 631.304
World Bank 332.153 2
  law 341.751 153 2
World-circling travel 910.41
World community
  international law 341.2
World Community of al-Islam in the West 297.87
World Court 341.552
World Cup competition
  soccer 796.334 668
World fairs 907.4
  see also Exhibitions
World government 321.04
  law 341.21
World Party of Socialist Revolution 324.175
World politics and religion
  social theology 291.177
    Christianity 261.7
    see also Politics and religion—social theology
World series (Baseball) 796.357 646
World Trade Organization 382.92
World views 140
  see Manual at 140
World War I, 1914–1918 940.3
World War II, 1939–1945 940.53
Worm-caused diseases (Biology) 571.999
  agriculture 632.623
  plant crops 632.623
  veterinary medicine 636.089 696 2

Worm-caused diseases (Human)
  incidence 614.552
  medicine 616.962
  see also Communicable diseases (Human)
Worm culture 639.75
WORM discs 004.565
Worm farming 639.75
Worm gears 621.833 3
Worms 592.3
  agricultural pests 632.623
  culture 639.75
  paleozoology 562.3
  plant crop pests 632.623
  veterinary medicine 636.089 696 2
Worms (Computer security) 005.84
Worms (Germany) T2—434 352
Wormwood 641.338 2
  botany 583.99
  see also Flavorings; Herbs
Wororan languages 499.15
  T6—991 5
Worry 152.46
Worship 291.43
  Buddhism 294.344 3
  Christianity 248.3
  Hinduism 294.543
  Islam 297.3
    Sufi 297.43
  Judaism 296.45
  see also Public worship
Worth
  epistemology 121.8
Worth County (Ga.) T2—758 945
Worth County (Iowa) T2—777 232
Worth County (Mo.) T2—778 143
Worthing (England) T2—422 68
Wounds
  medicine 617.14
Woven felt 677.62
  see also Textiles
Wrangel Island (Russia) T2—577
Wrangell-Saint Elias National Park and Preserve (Alaska) T2—798 3
Wrapping paper 676.287
Wraps (Clothing) 391
  customs 391
  home sewing 646.45
  see also Clothing
Wrasses 597.7
Wreaths 745.926
Wreckage studies
  aeronautics 629.132 55
Wreckage studies (continued)
  automotive 629.282 6
  naval architecture 623.817 6
  seamanship 623.888 5
  structural analysis 624.176
  see Manual at 363.1065 vs. 620.86: Accident investigation
Wrecking bars 621.93
Wrecking buildings 690.26
Wrekin, The (England : District) T2—424 56
Wren-tit 598.834
Wrenches 621.972
Wrens 598.833
Wrestlers 796.812 092
  sports group T7—796 8
Wrestling 796.812
  see also Sports
Wrexham Maelor (Wales) T2—429 39
Wright County (Iowa) T2—777 274
Wright County (Minn.) T2—776 51
Wright County (Mo.) T2—778 825
Wrigley (N.W.T.) T2—719 3
Wrinkle-resistant fabrics 677.681
  see also Textiles
Wrist techniques
  music 784.193 64
Wrists (Human) 612.97
  physiology 612.97
  regional medicine 617.574
  surgery 617.574
  see also Upper extremities (Human)
Write once read many discs 004.565
Write once read many drives 004.565
Writing (Manual skill) 652.1
Writing instruments
  manufacturing technology 681.6
Writing skills
  elementary education 372.623
Writing systems (Linguistics) 411
  specific languages T4—11
Writings (Bible) 223
Written communication 302.224 4
  elementary education 372.623
  management use 658.453
  office services 651.74
  rhetoric 808
  sociology 302.224 4
Written language disorders
  medicine 616.855 3
  see also Communicative disorders

Wrocław (Poland : Voivodeship) T2—438 5
Wrongful death 346.032 3
Wrongful entry 346.036
Wrought iron 669.141 4
WTO (World Trade Organization) 382.92
Wú dialect 495.17
T6—951 7
Wuchereriasis
incidence 614.555 2
medicine 616.965 2
see also Communicable diseases (Human)
Wujs 787.94
see also Stringed instruments
Wuppertal (Germany) T2—435 532
Württemberg (Germany) T2—434 7
Würtz-Fittig reaction 547.21
chemical engineering 660.284 41
Würzburg (Germany) T2—433 39
Wyandot County (Ohio) T2—771 26
Wyandot Indians T5—975 5
Wyandotte chicken 636.583
Wyandotte County (Kan.) T2—781 39
Wychavon (England : District) T2—424 49
Wycliffe Bible 220.520 1
Wycliffites 284.3
Wycombe (England : District) T2—425 95
Wye, River (Wales and England) T2—429 5
Wynberg (South Africa : District) T2—687 35
Wyndham (W.A.) T2—941 4
Wynyard (Tas.) T2—946 5
Wyoming 978.7
T2—787
Wyoming County (N.Y.) T2—747 93
Wyoming County (Pa.) T2—748 35
Wyoming County (W. Va.) T2—754 45
Wyperfeld National Park (Vic.) T2—945 9
Wyre (England) T2—427 682
Wyre Forest (England) T2—424 41
Wythe County (Va.) T2—755 773

X

X-linked mental retardation
medicine 616.858 8
see also Mental retardation
X-ray astronomy 522.686 3
X-ray electronics 537.535
X-ray equipment
manufacturing technology 681.753
public safety 363.189
X-ray examination
medicine 616.075 72
see Manual at 616.0757 vs. 616.0754, 616.07572
X-ray metallography 669.950 283
X-ray photography
engineering 621.367 3
X-ray spectroscopes
manufacturing technology 681.414 8
X-ray spectroscopy 543.085 86
analytical chemistry 543.085 86
engineering 621.361 6
physics 537.535 2
X-ray testing
materials science 620.112 72
X-ray therapy
medicine 615.842 2
X rays 539.722 2
biophysics 571.457
humans 612.014 485
Xanthē (Greece : Nome) T2—495 7
Xanthophyta 579.82
Xanthorrhoeaceae 584.35
Xavante language 498.4
T6—984
Xenarthra 599.31
Xenon
chemistry 546.755
gas technology 665.822
see also Chemicals
Xenungulata 569.62
Xeroderma
medicine 616.544
see also Skin
Xerography 686.442
equipment manufacturing technology 681.65
office use 652.4
technology 686.442
Xhosa (African people) T5—963 985
Xhosa language 496.398 5
T6—963 985
Xhosa literature 896.398 5
Xiāng dialect 495.17
T6—951 7
Xinjiang Weiwuer Zizhiqu (China) T2—516
Xiphiidae 597.78

Xiphosura 595.492
paleozoology 565.492
Xizang Zizhiqu (China) T2—515
Xoloizuintli 636.76
Xosa language 496.398 5
T6—963 985
Xosa literature 896.398 5
Xylariales 579.567
Xylem 575.46
Xylophones 786.843
see also Percussion instruments
Xyridaceae 584.86

Y

Yacht basins
engineering 627.38
Yacht racing 797.14
see also Sports
Yachting 797.124 6
see also Sports
Yachts 387.204 23
engineering 623.820 23
handling 623.881 23
power-driven 387.231 4
engineering 623.823 14
transportation services 387.231 4
sailing
design 623.812 23
transportation services 387.204 23
wind-driven 387.223
engineering 623.822 3
transportation services 387.223
see also Ships
Yad ha-ḥazaḳah 296.181 2
Yadayim 296.123 6
Yadkin County (N.C.) T2—756 66
Yadkin River (N.C.) T2—756 68
Yahuna language 498.35
T6—983 5
Yahya Khan, Aga Muhammad
Pakistani history 954.904 6
Yajurveda 294.592 14
Yak 599.642 2
Yaka (African people) T5—963 93
Yakima County (Wash.) T2—797 55
Yakima Indians T5—974 1
Yakima River (Wash.) T2—797 55
Yakut T5—943 32
Yakut language 494.332
T6—943 32
Yakut literature 894.332
Yakutia (Russia) T2—575
Yalobusha County (Miss.) T2—762 82
Yamagata-ken (Japan) T2—521 16
Yamaguchi-ken (Japan) T2—521 97
Yamal-Nenets (Russia) T2—573
Yamal-Nenetskiĭ avtonomnyĭ okrug (Russia) T2—573
Yamanashi-ken (Japan) T2—521 64
Yamaska (Quebec : County) T2—714 54
Yambol (Bulgaria : Okrŭg) T2—499 5
Yamhill County (Or.) T2—795 39
Yami (Taiwan people) T5—992 5
Yamoussoukro (Ivory Coast) T2—666 8
Yams (Dioscorea) 641.352 3
agriculture 635.23
botany 584.357
commercial processing 664.805 23
cooking 641.652 3
food 641.352 3
Yams (Sweet potatoes) 641.352 2
botany 583.94
see also Sweet potatoes
Yancey County (N.C.) T2—756 873
Yang ch'ins 787.74
see also Stringed instruments
Yangtze River (China) T2—512
Yankton County (S.D.) T2—783 394
Yanomam languages 498
T6—98
Yanomamo Indians T5—98
Yanomamo language 498
T6—98
Yanzi language 496.396
T6—963 96
Yao (African people) T5—963 97
Yao (Southeast Asian people) T5—959 4
Yao language (Southeastern Asia) 495.97
T6—959 7
Yao languages (Africa) 496.397
T6—963 97
Yaoundé (Cameroon) T2—671 1
Yap (Micronesia) T2—966
Yaqui Indians T5—974 5
Yaracuy (Venezuela) T2—872 6
Yard goods 677.632
Yard sales 381.195
management 658.87
see also Commerce

Yards
  landscape architecture 712.6
Yare River (England) T2—426 1
Yarmouth (N.S. : County) T2—716 31
Yarn 677.028 62
Yaroslavl′ (Russia :
    Oblast) T2—473 2
Yarra River (Vic.) T2—945 2
Yaruro language 498
  T6—98
Yass (N.S.W.) T2—944 7
Yates County (N.Y.) T2—747 82
Yaunde-Fang languages 496.396
  T6—963 96
Yavapai County (Ariz.) T2—791 57
Yaw (Aeronautics) 629.132 364
Yaws
  medicine 616.57
  see also Skin
Yazd (Iran : Province) T2—559 5
Yazoo County (Miss.) T2—762 49
Yazoo Mississippi Delta
    (Miss. : Region) T2—762 4
Yazoo River (Miss.) T2—762 4
Year-round school 371.236
Year-round systems
  air conditioning 697.933 4
Yearbooks 050
  T1—05
  encyclopedia 030
  publishing 070.572
Yearly Conference of People
    Called Methodists 287.53
  see also Methodist Church
Years 529.2
Yeasts 579.562
Yeasts (Basidiomycetes) 579.59
Yeasts (Common yeasts) 579.563
  leaven 664.68
Yeasts (Saccharomycetaceae) 579.562
Yell County (Ark.) T2—767 38
Yellow-dog contracts 331.894
Yellow-eyed grass 584.86
Yellow fever
  incidence 614.541
  medicine 616.928
  see also Communicable
      diseases (Human)
Yellow-green algae 579.82
Yellow Medicine County
    (Minn.) T2—776 37
Yellow pages (Directories) T1—029 4
  see Manual at 338 vs. 060,
      381, 382, 670.294, 910,
      T1—025, T1—0294,
      T1—0296
Yellow poplar 583.22
  forestry 634.973 22
Yellow River (China) T2—511
Yellow Sea 551.465 56
  T2—164 56
Yellowknife (N.W.T.) T2—719 3
Yellowstone County
    (Mont.) T2—786 39
Yellowstone National Park T2—787 52
Yellowstone River T2—786 3
Yellowwoods 585.3
Yemen 953.3
  T2—533
Yemen (People's Democratic
    Republic) 953.350 5
  T2—533 5
Yemen (Republic of Yemen) 953.305 3
  T2—533
Yemen (Yemen Arab Republic) 953.320 5
  T2—533 2
Yemen Arab Republic 953.320 5
  T2—533 2
Yemenis T5—927 533
  Northern T5—927 533 2
  Southern T5—927 533 5
Yenisei-Ostyak language 494.6
  T6—946
Yenisei Samoyed language 494.4
  T6—944
Yeppoon (Qld.) T2—943 5
Yersinia 579.34
Yeshivot 296.071 1
Yevamot 296.123 3
  Babylonian Talmud 296.125 3
  Mishnah 296.123 3
  Palestinian Talmud 296.124 3
Yevrey Autonomous
    Region (Russia) T2—577
Yews 585.6
Yeye language 496.399
  T6—963 99
Yezidis
  religion 299.159
Yi dynasty 951.902
Yiddish language 439.1
  T6—391
Yiddish literature 839.1
Yield point (Mechanics) 531.381

Yields
  crop production 631.558
Yin dynasty 931.02
Yindjibarndi language 499.15
  T6—991 5
YMCA (Association) 267.3
Ynys Môn (Wales) T2—429 21
Yo-Yos® 796.2
  see also Sports
Yoakum County (Tex.) T2—764 849
Yobe State (Nigeria) T2—669 87
Yodo River (Japan) T2—521 83
Yoga 181.45
  Buddhism 294.344 36
  comparative religion 291.436
  health 613.704 6
  Hinduism 294.543 6
  philosophy 181.45
Yogacara Buddhism 294.392
Yogurt 641.371 476
  cooking 641.671 476
  food 641.371 476
  processing 637.147 6
Yoho National Park (B.C.) T2—711 68
Yokohama-shi (Japan) T2—521 364
Yolo County (Calif.) T2—794 51
Yom Kippur 296.432
  liturgy 296.453 2
Yom Kippur War, 1973 956.048
Yoma 296.123 2
  Babylonian Talmud 296.125 2
  Mishnah 296.123 2
  Palestinian Talmud 296.124 2
Yonne (France) T2—444 1
York (England) T2—428 43
York (N.B.) T2—715 51
York (Ont.) T2—713 541
York (Ont. : County) T2—713 54
York (Ont. : Regional municipality) T2—713 547
York, House of 942.04
  English history 942.04
  Irish history 941.504
York County (Me.) T2—741 95
York County (Neb.) T2—782 345
York County (Pa.) T2—748 41
York County (S.C.) T2—757 43
York County (Va.) T2—755 423
Yorke Peninsula (S. Aust.) T2—942 35
Yorkshire (England) T2—428 1
Yorkshire Dales (England) T2—428 4
Yorkshire terrier 636.76
Yorkshire Wolds (England) T2—428 3
Yorkton (Sask.) T2—712 42
Yoro (Honduras : Dept.) T2—728 314
Yoruba (African people) T5—963 33
Yoruba language 496.333
  T6—963 33
Yoruba literature 896.333
Yosemite National Park (Calif.) T2—794 47
Young adult literature 808.899 283
  history and criticism 809.892 83
  specific literatures T3B—080 928 3
    history and criticism T3B—099 283
Young adults 305.242
  T1—084 2
  T7—056 2
  civil rights 323.353
  etiquette 395.123
  journalism for 070.483 3
  labor economics 331.34
  legal status 346.013 5
    constitutional law 342.087
    private law 346.013 5
  physiology 612.661
  political organizations 324.3
  psychology 155.65
  publications for
    bibliographies 011.625
  recreation 790.192
    indoor 793.019 2
    outdoor 796.083 5
  relations with government 323.353
  religion 200.842
    Christianity 270.084 2
      devotional literature 242.64
      guides to Christian life 248.84
      pastoral care of 259.25
      religious associations 267.6
      religious education 268.434
      social theology 261.834 242
    social theology 291.178 342 42
  social aspects 305.242
  social welfare 362
  under eighteen
    social welfare 362.708 3
      law 344.032 708 3
      see Manual at 362.7083
  under twenty-one 305.235
  T1—083 5
  T7—055
    see also Adolescents
Young animals 591.39
  domestic animals 636.07
  mammals 599.139
Young County (Tex.) T2—764 545

Young men 305.242
T1—084 21
T7—056 2
  etiquette 395.123 2
  grooming 646.704 4
  journalism for 070.483 36
  publications for
    bibliographies 011.624 1
  social aspects 305.242
  social welfare 362
  under eighteen
    social welfare 362.708 3
  under twenty-one 305.235
T1—083 51
    health 613.042 33
    psychology 155.532
    sex hygiene 613.953
    social aspects 305.235
  see Manual at T1—081 and T1—082, T1—08351, T1—08352, T1—08421, T1—08422
Young Men's Christian Association camps 796.542 2
Young Men's Christian Associations 267.3
Young people 305.23
T1—083
T7—054
  civil rights 323.352
  government programs 353.536
  legal status 346.013 5
    constitutional law 342.087
    private law 346.013 5
  publications for
    bibliographies 011.62
    reviews 028.162
  reading
    library science 028.534
  relation to government 323.352
  religion 200.83
    Christianity 270.083
      devotional literature 242.62
      guides to Christian life 248.82
      pastoral care of 259.2
      religious education 268.432
      social theology 261.834 23
    guides to life 291.440 83
    Judaism 296.083
      guides to life 296.708 3
      religious education 296.680 83
    social theology 291.178 342 3
  sex hygiene 613.951
  social aspects 305.23
Young people (continued)
  social welfare 362.7
    public administration 353.536
Young people's books
  bibliographies 011.62
Young people's societies 369.4
  biography 369.409 2
  social group T7—369 4
Young women 305.242
T1—084 22
T7—056 2
  etiquette 395.123 3
  grooming 646.704 2
  journalism for 070.483 37
  publications for
    bibliographies 011.624 2
  social aspects 305.242
  social welfare 362
  under eighteen
    social welfare 362.708 3
  under twenty-one 305.235
T1—083 52
    health 613.042 43
    psychology 155.533
    sex hygiene 613.955
    social aspects 305.235
  see Manual at T1—081 and T1—082, T1—08351, T1—08352, T1—08421, T1—08422
Young Women's Christian Associations 267.5
Young workers 331.34
Youngstown (Ohio) T2—771 39
Youth 305.235
T1—083 5
T7—055
  over twenty 305.242
T1—084 2
T7—056 2
  see also Adolescents
Yozgat Ili (Turkey) T2—563
Ytterbium
  chemistry 546.419
  see also Rare earths
Yttrium 669.290 3
  chemical engineering 661.040 3
  chemistry 546.403
  metallurgy 669.290 3
  physical metallurgy 669.962 903
  see also Chemicals
Yttrium-group metals
  economic geology 553.494 7
  see also Metals

Yüan dynasty 951.025
Yuat River (Papua New Guinea) T2—957 5
Yuba County (Calif.) T2—794 35
Yucatán (Mexico : State) T2—726 5
Yucatán Channel 551.463 4
T2—163 64
Yucatec Maya language 497.415 2
T6—974 152
Yucatecan language 497.415 2
T6—974 152
Yucatecan literature 897.415 2
Yuccas 584.352
Yuchi language 497.9
T6—979
Yuchian languages 497.9
T6—979
Yuè dialect 495.17
T6—951 7
Yuëh dialect 495.17
T6—951 7
Yugoslav Banat T2—497 1
Yugoslav communism 335.434 4
  economics 335.434 4
  political ideology 320.532 309 497
Yugoslavia 949.710 3
T2—497 1
  ancient 939.8
T2—398
Yugoslavia (1918–1991) 949.702
T2—497
  ancient 939.8
T2—398
Yugoslavs T5—918 2
Yui language 499.12
T6—991 2
Yuit T5—971 4
Yuit language 497.14
T6—971 4
Yukaghir language 494.6
T6—946
Yukaghir literature 894.6
Yuki Indians T5—975
Yuki language 497.5
T6—975
Yukian Indians T5—975
Yukian languages 497.5
T6—975
Yukon T2—719 1
Yukon-Koyokuk Borough (Alaska) T2—798 6
Yukon River (Yukon and Alaska) T2—798 6
  Alaska T2—798 6
  Yukon T2—719 1
Yuma County (Ariz.) T2—791 71
Yuma County (Colo.) T2—788 78
Yuman Indians T5—975 7
Yuman languages 497.57
T6—975 7
Yunnan Province (China) T2—513 5
Yupik T5—971 4
Yupik languages 497.14
T6—971 4
Yupik literatures 897.14
Yurak Samoyed language 494.4
T6—944
Yurok Indians T5—973
Yurok language 497.3
T6—973
Yvelines (France) T2—443 66
YWCA (Association) 267.5

Z

Z transform 515.723
Zacapa (Guatemala : Dept.) T2—728 132
Zacatecas (Mexico : State) T2—724 3
Zaire 967.51
T2—675 1
Zaire (Angola) T2—673 2
Zaire River T2—675 1
Zairians T5—967 51
Zakarpats´ka oblast´ (Ukraine) T2—477 9
Zakat 297.54
Zakynthos (Greece) T2—495 5
Zala Megye (Hungary) T2—439 7
Zambales (Philippines) T2—599 1
Zambezi River T2—679
Zambézia (Mozambique) T2—679 6
Zambia 968.94
T2—689 4
Zambians T5—968 94
Zamboanga del Norte (Philippines : Province) T2—599 7
Zamboanga del Sur (Philippines) T2—599 7
Zamora (Spain : Province) T2—462 4
Zamora-Chinchipe (Ecuador) T2—866 44
Zamość (Poland : Voivodeship) T2—438 4

Zande (African people) T5—963 61
Zande language 496.361
 T6—963 61
Zander 597.758
Zanichelliaceae 584.74
Zanjān (Iran) T2—551
Zante (Greece) T2—495 5
Zanzibar 967.81
 T2—678 1
Zanzibar Central/South (Tanzania) T2—678 1
Zanzibar North (Tanzania) T2—678 1
Zanzibar Urban/West Tanzania) T2—678 1
Západočeský kraj (Czech Republic) T2—437 1
Západoslovenský kraj (Slovakia) T2—437 3
Zapata County (Tex.) T2—764 483
Zaporizhzhya (Ukraine : Oblast) T2—477 3
Zaporiz´ka oblast´ (Ukraine) T2—477 3
Zapotec Indians T5—976
Zapotec language 497.6
 T6—976
Zapotec literature 897.6
Zaragoza (Spain : Province) T2—465 53
Zaramo language 496.391
 T6—963 91
Zarma (African people) T5—965
Zarma language 496.5
 T6—965
Zarqā' (Jordan : Province) T2—569 593
Zastron (South Africa : District) T2—685 6
Zavala County (Tex.) T2—764 437
Zavim 296.123 6
Zaydites (Islamic sect) 297.824
Zealand (Denmark) T2—489 1
Zealots (Judaism) 296.81
Zebra fishes (Freshwater) 597.482
 culture 639.374 82
Zebra fishes (Scorpaenidae) 597.68
Zebra plant 635.934 39
 botany 584.39
 floriculture 635.934 39
Zebras 599.665 7
 animal husbandry 636.18
Zebus 636.291
Zechariah (Biblical book) 224.98
Zedillo Ponce de León, Ernesto
 Mexican history 972.083 6
Zeeland (Netherlands : Province) T2—492 42
Zeewolde (Netherlands) T2—492 2
Zeiformes 597.64
Zelaya (Nicaragua : Dept.) T2—728 532
Zen Buddhism 294.392 7
Zener diodes 621.381 522
Zenith telescopes 522.4
Zeolite
 mineralogy 549.68
Zephaniah (Biblical book) 224.96
Zera'im 296.123 1
 Babylonian Talmud 296.125 1
 Mishnah 296.123 1
 Palestinian Talmud 296.124 1
Zero-base budgeting 658.154
 public administration 352.48
 see also Budgets (Public)
Zero-memory systems 003.8
Zeta function 515.56
Zevaḥim 296.123 5
 Babylonian Talmud 296.125 5
 Mishnah 296.123 5
Zhejiang Sheng (China) T2—512 42
Zhytomyr (Ukraine : Oblast) T2—477 8
Žhytomyrs´ka oblast´ (Ukraine) T2—477 8
Ziebach County (S.D.) T2—783 53
Zielona Góra (Poland : Voivodeship) T2—438 1
Zigula-Zaramo languages 496.391
 T6—963 91
Zimbabwe 968.91
 T2—689 1
Zimbabwe Rhodesia T2—689 1
Zimbabweans T5—968 91
Zimbabweans (British origin) T5—210 689 1
Zinc 669.52
 building construction 693.752
 building material 691.852
 chemical engineering 661.066 1
 chemistry 546.661
 decorative arts 739.55
 economic geology 553.452
 materials science 620.184 2
 metallography 669.955 2
 metallurgy 669.52
 metalworking 673.52
 mining 622.345 2
 organic chemistry
 applied 661.895

Zinc (continued)
  physical metallurgy 669.965 2
  see also Chemicals; Metals
Zinc lithography 763.24
Zincite
  mineralogy 549.522
Zingiberales 584.39
Zinnias 635.933 99
  botany 583.99
  floriculture 635.933 99
Zion National Park (Utah) T2—792 48
Zionism 320.540 956 94
  see Manual at 322.1 vs. 296.382, 320.54095694
Zip code 383.145 5
  see also Postal service
Ziphiidae 599.545
Zircon
  mineralogy 549.62
Zirconia
  technology 666.72
Zirconium 669.735
  chemical engineering 661.051 3
  chemistry 546.513
  economic geology 553.465
  materials science 620.189 352
  metallography 669.957 35
  metallurgy 669.735
  metalworking 673.735
  physical metallurgy 669.967 35
  see also Chemicals; Metals
Zithers 787.7
  instrument 787.719
  music 787.7
  see also Stringed instruments
Ziwa Magharibi Region (Tanzania) T2—678 27
Zoantharia 593.6
Zoarcidae 597.63
Zodiac
  astrology 133.52
  astronomy 523
  folklore 398.26
    history and criticism 398.362
Zodiacal light 523.59
Zohar 296.162
Zombiism
  African religions 299.64
Zonal regions T2—1
Zone time 389.17
Zones of latitude
  astronomical geography 525.5
Zonguldak İli (Turkey) T2—563
Zoning 333.731 7
  area planning 711
    urban 711.4
  land use 333.731 7
    urban 333.771 7
  law 346.045
  public administration 354.333
    urban 354.353
Zoo animals
  animal husbandry 636.088 9
Zooflagellates 579.42
Zoological gardens 590.73
  see also Zoos
Zoological specimens
  preservation 590.752
Zoologists 590.92
  occupational group T7—59
Zoology 590
Zoomastigophorea 579.42
  paleozoology 561.992
Zoonoses (Biology) 571.98
  veterinary medicine 636.089 695 9
Zoonoses (Human)
  incidence 614.56
  medicine 616.959
  see also Communicable diseases (Human)
Zooplankton 592.177 6
  freshwater 592.176
Zoos 590.73
  animal care 636.088 9
  architecture 727.659
  landscape architecture 712.5
Zoque Indians T5—974 1
Zoraptera 595.738
Zorilla 599.766
Zoroastrianism 295
  philosophy 181.05
Zoroastrians
  biography 295.092
  religious group T7—295
Zosteraceae 584.74
Zoug (Switzerland : Canton) T2—494 756
Zoysieae 584.9
Zug (Switzerland : Canton) T2—494 756
Zuid-Holland (Netherlands) T2—492 38
Zuidelijke IJsselmeerpolders (Netherlands) T2—492 2
Zuider Zee (Netherlands) T2—492 2
Zulia (Venezuela) T2—872 3
Zulu (African people) T5—963 986

Zulu language	496.398 6
	T6—963 986
Zulu literature	896.398 6
Zulu War, 1879	968.404 5
Zululand (South Africa)	968.404
	T2—684 91
Zuni Indians	T5—979
Zurich (Switzerland : Canton)	T2—494 57
Zuzus	787.92
see also Stringed instruments	
Zwelitsha (South Africa : District)	T2—687 92
Zygnematales	579.837
Zygomycetes	579.53
Zygophyllaceae	583.79
Zygotes	571.864
Zymases	572.791
see also Enzymes	
Zyrian	T5—945 3
Zyrian language	494.53
	T6—945 3
Zyrian literature	894.53

Manual

Use of the Manual

Full instructions on the use of the Manual are found in section 10 of the Introduction to the Dewey Decimal Classification in volume 1.

The Manual contains three kinds of notes:

(A) Notes on problems common to more than one number (the notes for numbers linked by "–" or "and," e.g., 583–585 or 380.1 and 381, 382).

(B) Notes on problems involving only one number (or a single number and its subdivisions).

(C) Notes on differentiating numbers (the notes linked by "vs.," e.g., 500 vs. 600).

The Manual is arranged in the numerical order of the tables and schedules. For classes with more than one note, the notes are usually arranged in the order listed above. Within each sequence, the broader span comes before the narrower span (e.g., 583–585 precedes 583–584); however, a note for a single number ending in 0 always comes first in the sequence. A "vs." note always appears last (e.g., 362–363 vs. 364.1 follows 362–363).

The numbers are accompanied by their corresponding captions from the tables and schedules. The captions are listed in boldface type on the line following the numbers. Additional terms are added in square brackets to provide context. If the note is narrower than the caption would suggest, a subheading is included (centered in boldface type). Subheadings are also used to divide lengthy notes into sections. In several places, sections in notes are divided into subsections. The headings for subsections appear centered in italics.

There are lengthy notes explaining 351 Public administration and 560–590 Life sciences (two major revisions introduced in this edition). A special optional arrangement for books of the Bible as arranged in Tanakh (222)–(224) appears as a subsection of the Manual note for 221.

See-Manual references in the schedules, tables, and Relative Index refer the classifier to the entries in the Manual. In addition, there are several see-also references within the Manual.

The appendix to the Manual describes the policies and procedures of the Decimal Classification Division of the Library of Congress with respect to segmentation in centrally cataloged records, alternate DDC notation in LC bibliographic records, and the classification of children's books in the Decimal Classification Division.

Notes on Table Numbers

Table 1. Standard Subdivisions

1. Use whether or not supplied in the schedules

Standard subdivisions may be used anywhere in the schedules unless there are instructions to the contrary. They are not normally printed in the schedules except where needed to fill out three-digit numbers under the main classes, e.g., 605 Serial publications in technology (applied sciences), and in a few other instances. Standard subdivisions may be printed when the subdivisions have special meanings, when extended notation is required for the topic in question, or when notes are required. The rest of the standard subdivisions (those not printed in the schedules) are to be used with their normal meanings as given in Table 1.

An example of a special meaning is found under 540.11, where the number means "Ancient and medieval theories," not systems. Right below it, 540.28 is printed in brackets to show that the standard subdivision is not used, but that 542 is used instead for auxiliary techniques and procedures, apparatus, equipment, materials.

Whenever the base digits of a normal standard subdivision are supplied, all further subdivisions found in Table 1 are implied. For example, the regular heading of notation 07 from Table 1 Education, research, related topics is supplied at 507. That entry is followed immediately by 507.2 Statistical methods and research, and 507.8 Use of apparatus and equipment in study and teaching, each with the regular heading found in Table 1. These three entries are supplied for technical reasons only: 507 to fill out the three-digit number; 507.2 to supply a reference to 001.4, 001.42, and a Manual note; and 507.8 to supply a note on science fair projects. The presence of these three entries does not limit the use of other standard subdivisions found under T1—07 in Table 1, e.g., 507.24 Experimental research, 507.6 Review and exercise.

2. Kinds of standard subdivisions

There are are several kinds of standard subdivisions:

A. Subdivisions which bring the methods of other disciplines to bear on the subject, e.g., auxiliary techniques, education, research, management, philosophy and theory

B. Subdivisions which relate the subject to its users, e.g., the subject as a profession, the subject for persons in specific occupations

C. Subdivisions which identify a specific kind of information about the subject, e.g., directories, product lists, identification marks, statistics, illustrations

D. Subdivisions which treat the whole subject but in a restricted situation, e.g., by kinds of persons, areas, historical periods

E. Subdivisions which indicate the bibliographic forms that the information may take, e.g., encyclopedias, periodicals

F. Miscellaneous subdivisions, e.g., biography, formulas and specifications, humorous treatment

3. Use standard subdivisions with caution

The common feature of standard subdivisions is that they identify limited treatment of the subject. This feature leads to the first general rule in applying them: in doubtful cases, do not use standard subdivisions, since they serve to segregate specialized material from works of general interest. For example, avoid using the most recent period subdivision in T1—0904 for "state of the art" works on a subject because most users will expect to find such works in the main number.

Some standard subdivisions used in doubtful situations may be annoying as well as superfluous. For example, many works in social sciences refer mostly to well-developed countries or to the subject in the West but do not intentionally exclude other areas. Use T1—091722 or T1—091821 sparingly for such works, since it will help few users to double the length of the number in order to segregate the material according to aspects that the authors do not emphasize.

In some cases the standard subdivision may be redundant, or nearly so. For example, T1—024694 indicates the subject for carpenters. It is never used with 694 Carpentry, since works on a subject are written primarily for its practitioners. One need not (until the 21st century) use 004.0904 for computers in the 20th century, since the computer is a 20th-century phenomenon. In certain cases a standard subdivision would simply redefine the base discipline, e.g., T1—01 in its overall meaning of "philosophy and theory" in most of the subdivisions in 100 Philosophy. (*See also discussion at T1—01.*)

4. Approximating the whole

(The principles explained here apply equally to the use of recurring subdivisions indicated by footnotes.)

Standard subdivisions should be added only when the work in hand covers the whole, or approximately the whole, of the subject of the number. For example, there is no number for black widow spiders under 595.44, the number for spiders. Do not, therefore, assume that black widows are "just another spider," and start using 595.440972 for an account on black widow spiders in Mexico. Stop at 595.44, where works on black widow spiders have standing room pending further development of the schedule.

When two or more topics are listed in a heading, assume that none of the topics approximates the whole unless there is a note saying that standard subdivisions are added for certain topics or combination of topics. For example, under 417.22 (Pidgins and creoles) the note reads "Standard subdivisions are added for either or both topics in heading." (The note will lack the word "Standard," and read merely "Subdivisions are added . . ." where there are add instructions providing special as well as standard subdivisions.)

In certain places, there are specific instructions overriding the approximate-the-whole restriction. These instructions are supplied when the nature of the subject or the usefulness of a secondary arrangement (e.g., geographic subarrangement) makes further topical subdivision undesirable. The instructions may take the form of a standard-subdivisions-are-added (or subdivisions-are-added) note, or class-here note. For example, the instructions in the entry for 599.367 Cynomys (Prairie dogs) allow subdivisions to be added for the genus as a whole and for individual species of prairie dogs, even though individual species do not approximate the whole of the genus. (*See also section 5, Class-here notes and approximating the whole.*)

When a number is subdivided, the normal rule for determining what topic or combination of topics spelled out in the subdivisions approximates the whole subject of the larger number is that a work covering three subdivisions approximates the whole. If there are only three subdivisions, then normally two subdivisions approximate the whole. However, if a subject consists of a large number of distinct subclasses, e.g., species in biology or kinds of minerals in economic geology, a work on representatives of three or more distinct subdivisions is counted as approximating the whole. For example, a work on coal, gold, and diamond resources in South Africa will be classed in 553.0968, that is, as representative mineral resources (553) of South Africa (T1—0968).

5. Class-here notes and approximating the whole

The class-here note, that is, the instruction note beginning with the words "Class here," indicates that standard subdivisions may be added to the notation for the term or terms listed. While some terms will refer to subjects larger than the one indicated by the heading, any term in a class-here note for a concept smaller than the subject for the heading is regarded as approximating the whole for purposes of classification.

6. Table of preference

The table of preference at the beginning of Table 1 yields to two other citation order rules: First, the rule of application (paragraph 5.7 in the Introduction to DDC) remains basic to sound classification. Therefore teaching financial management in hospital administration is classed in 362.110681, not 362.11071, even though T1—07 is above T1—068 in the table of preference. Second, when standard subdivisions are displaced to nonzero positions, the rule of zero (paragraph 5.7 in the Introduction to DDC) overrides the table of preference here, e.g., management of prisons in Great Britain 365.941068, not 365.068 as would be the case if prisons in Great Britain were classed in 365.0941. (*See also section 8, Multiple standard subdivisions.*)

7. Subdivision of displaced standard subdivisions

A displaced standard subdivision is one that has been moved from its normal position, e.g., under 362 standard subdivision T1—09 has been displaced from 362.09 to 362.9 for historical, geographic, persons treatment of social welfare problems and services. A displaced standard subdivision is subdivided as shown in Table 1, except for units that have been given a changed or extended meaning. However, whenever one is displaced, add instructions are supplied to make clear that standard notation may be used. For example, at 362.9, the first note reads "Add to base number 362.9 notation 01–9 from Table 2, e.g., social welfare in France 362.944."

8. Multiple standard subdivisions

Do not add one standard subdivision to another standard subdivision unless specifically instructed. In the following cases, addition of a second standard subdivisions is allowed:

A. With standard subdivision T1—04 (a special topic subdivision available to permit introduction of a new development when there is no suitable vacant notation in direct 1–9 subdivisions).

B. With standard subdivisions that have changed or extended meanings, e.g., encyclopedias on educational psychology 370.1503, on pyrometallurgy 669.028203, on political situations and conditions 320.9003. (In contrast, the encyclopedia subdivision is not added to the true standard subdivisions nearby, e.g., not to psychological principles of political science 320.019, or metallurgical patents 669.0272.)

C. Under standard subdivision T1—08 and T1—09, certain other standard subdivisions are specifically provided, notably for statistics (T1—021); illustrations (T1—022); and museums, collections, exhibits (T1—074). (In the case of T1—074 when used in T1—09, it is not redundant to add a second area number that is more specific than the area notation to which T1—074 is applied, e.g., to use T1—09810748161 for collections of Brazilian objects in São Paulo.)

D. With standard subdivision concepts displaced to nonzero numbers (usually for geographic treatment), the full range of standard subdivisions is available, e.g., management of penal institutions in Great Britain 365.941068. In contrast, management of hospitals in Great Britain is classed in 362.11068. For encyclopedias on British penal institutions and hospitals the numbers are 365.94103 and 362.110941, respectively, since encyclopedias yield preference to place under the latter number. Many of the displaced standard subdivisions date from early editions of the Dewey Decimal Classification, and reflect aspects of unusual importance in particular subjects. Therefore there is often a larger and more diverse literature on these displaced concepts than is normal for the regular standard subdivisions.

9. Standard subdivisions applied to built numbers

Take care in using a standard subdivision when the number to which it is to be attached is the result of number building. The standard subdivision applies to the entire number that has been synthesized, not to any of its elements. Take the number building for trade in specific products as an example. 380.145 means trade in products of secondary industries and services. 687 means manufacturing of clothing, a number which is used for products, i.e., clothing. Add 687 to 380.145 and the result is 380.145687 trade in clothing. When T1—05 is added to 687 the number means 687.05 periodicals on clothing. Do not then add 687.05 as a unit to the trade number, since the resultant number would mean trade in clothing periodicals, an unlikely subject. Rather, take 380.145687 as a unit and add T1—05 to create a number for periodicals on the clothing trade.

The only exception to the foregoing rule is 016 Bibliography. When a built number is added to 016, bibliography is logically like a standard-subdivision concept in that it applies to the whole of the built number plus any attached standard subdivisions. Thus 016.38014568705 is used only for bibliographies of periodicals of the clothing trade; it is not used for a periodical bibliography of the clothing trade. There is no standard subdivision notation to show periodical bibliographies, since T1—05 must be reserved here for the material covered by the bibliography.

10. Number of zeros

If there is no indication to the contrary, use one zero for standard subdivisions, e.g., history of radiobroadcasting 384.5409. The following kinds of instructions indicate when a different number of zeros must be used:

A. Notation in the number column, e.g., 321.001–.008 for standard subdivisions of Systems of governments and states, 620.009 for history of engineering.

B. Footnotes leading to an add table where subdivisions are supplied, e.g., to the add table under 616.1–.9 where 001–009 are for standard subdivisions. At 616.1 the heading *Diseases of cardiovascular system is governed by a footnote that says add as instructed under 616.1–.9. Thus we get 616.1009 for the history of diagnosis and treatment of cardiovascular diseases.

C. Footnotes from the add instruction itself stipulating the use of extra zeros, e.g., the footnote to the add note under 327.3–.9 which gives us 327.41009 for the history of foreign policy of the United Kingdom. This footnote cites instructions at the beginning of Table 1 which govern in any case: standard subdivisions must have enough zeros to avoid any possible conflict with a number supplied in the schedules.

When building numbers according to add instructions, use the same number of zeros in the segment that is added as are found in the schedule from which it is taken. For example, under 372.11–.18 one is instructed to add to 372.1 the numbers following 371 in 371.1–.8, e.g., administration of elementary schools 372.12 (372.1 for organization and activities in elementary education plus 2 from 371.2 for school administration). The double zeros for standard subdivisions under 371.2 must be carried over to 372.12, e.g., study and teaching of elementary school administration 372.120071. As in most cases where two zeros are used for standard subdivisions, the single zero subdivisions at 371.2 are used for specific topics that might be needed when the 2 is used in elementary education. For example, notation 207 from 371.207 can be used in 372.1207 for works on executive management of elementary schools.

T1—01

Philosophy and theory

While most subdivisions of T1—01 are easy to understand and apply, T1—01 by itself can cause problems. The term "philosophy and theory" is a unitary one, covering the general or abstract principles applied to a field of activity or thought, such as science or art. However, it should not be used where theory constitutes the bulk of the subject matter of a field, e.g., nuclear physics. In philosophy subdivisions of 100, T1—01 is seldom used without subdivisions, and then only in the sense of theory and method of the topic.

A work discussing the discipline itself as a discipline, rather than the subject matter of the discipline, is a likely candidate for use of T1—01. Aspects of a discipline that are likely to be indicated by T1—01 include:

1. The boundaries and limits of a field of study; its nature as an art or science.

2. Schools of thought within a discipline. However, if there is a heavy literature on schools or systems of thought, there may be special provisions, e.g., 150.19 for psychological schools and 330.1 for economic systems and theories. Numbers for theories found in certain disciplines are often an extension of the work of such schools of thought, e.g., political theories 320.5, physical theories 530.1.

3. The ideal state of a discipline, and how far it can be expected to reach its goal, e.g., how close science can come to absolute truth.

4. Techniques and principles of criticism of a discipline. However, the criticism itself is classed in the same number as the subject of the criticism, e.g., criticism of Browning's poetry 821.8, of Frank Lloyd Wright's architecture 720.92, of Italian cooking 641.5945.

Historical, geographic, and persons treatment of a discipline, however, is classed in T1—09.

T1—014 vs. T1—03

Language and communication vs. Dictionaries, encyclopedias, concordances

Use T1—014 for discourses on terminology; T1—03 for works systematically arranged for ready reference, e.g., alphabetical and picture dictionaries, thesauri in classified order. However, use T1—0142 for etymological dictionaries and T1—0148 for lists of abbreviations and symbols. If in doubt, prefer T1—014.

T1—014 vs. T4—864

[Table 1 notation for] Languages and communication vs. [Table 4 notation for] Readers for those whose native language is different

Class in T4—864, plus notation 024 from Table 1, readers for nonnative speakers intended to instill a knowledge of the special vocabulary of a specific subject or discipline, e.g., science readers (in a language other than Spanish) for Spanish-speaking people T4—864610245, German-language science readers for Spanish-speaking people 438.64610245. Class works on the vocabulary of a specific subject or discipline without regard to the language status of the user with the subject or discipline, plus notation 014 from Table 1, e.g., 501.4 science vocabulary. If in doubt, prefer T1—014.

T1—015 vs. T1—0245–0246

Scientific principles vs. [The subject for persons in scientific and technological occupations]

Use the organization of the table of contents as a guide to distinguish between the scientific principles of a technology (e.g., mathematical principles of engineering) and the corresponding science written for technologists and engineers (e.g., mathematics for engineers). If the table of contents is developed in terms of concepts found in subdivisions of the science (or in the tables of contents of common treatises on the science), class with the science plus notation 024 from Table 1. Conversely, if the table of contents is developed in terms of concepts found in subdivisions of the technology (or in the tables of contents of common treatises on the technology), class with the technology plus notation 015 from Table 1. If in doubt between science and technology, prefer the technology number.

When not to use either subdivision

Do not use T1—015 and T1—024 in 500 and 600 when there is a direct relationship between a science and a corresponding technology, e.g., do not use 540.2466 for chemistry for chemical engineers, or 660.0154 for chemical principles in chemical engineering.

Do not use T1—0246 in 500 for all the applications of a science, since such a work is not for specific occupations. Although T1—015 may be used in 600 for all the sciences applied in a technology, use it with caution, since the distinction between the principles of a technology and the principles of science used in a technology is not often observed in practice.

T1—019

Psychological principles

Counseling

Because counseling in a specific subject usually encompasses the entire subject and not just the psychological aspect, be cautious about using T1—019 for counseling in a specific subject, e.g., investment counseling 332.6, not

332.6019. Counseling in welfare is classed in 361.06 and that counseling and guidance often have specific numbers in 362–363 through use of notation 86 from the table at 362–363, e.g., counseling and guidance of poor people 362.586. Guidance and counseling in education are classed in 371.4 and cognate numbers for specific levels of education.

T1—0207 vs. T3B—7, T3A—8 + 02, T3B—802, T3B—8 + 02, T3A—8 + 07, T3B—807, T3B—8 + 07

Humorous treatment vs. Humor and satire vs. Anecdotes, epigrams, graffiti, jokes, quotations vs. Works without identifiable literary form

Jokes are classed in T3B—802 (or T3A—8 + 02 or T3B—8 + 02), humorous literary works without identifiable literary form in T3B—807 (or T3A—8 + 07 or T3B—8 + 07). In T3B—7 are classed *only* collections of humor or satire in more than one literary form, including both verse and prose. (Works in a particular form, e.g., drama or fiction, are classed with the form; works in prose are classed with prose.)

Any subject may be dealt with in a humorous or satirical manner. Works dealing with a subject in such a manner fall in one of the following categories:

1. The humor involved is entirely incidental to the serious treatment of the subject, e.g., a joke injected in a lecture to provide respite from a serious mood;

2. The author's intent is serious—to inform, to persuade, to criticize—but humor or satire is the method, e.g., political satire grounded in genuine political criticism;

3. The subject merely provides the occasion for humor, the author's primary concern being to amuse, e.g., a collection of jokes about cats.

Only works falling in the third category are classed in literature, usually at T3B—802 (or T3A—8 + 02 or T3B—8 + 02). Works in the second category are classed with the subject plus notation 0207 from Table 1. Works in the first category are classed with the subject without T1—0207. If in doubt between literature and the subject, prefer the subject. If in doubt whether to use T1—0207, prefer the subject without it.

T1—0222 vs. T1—0223

Pictures and related material vs. Maps, plans, diagrams

The basic concept in T1—0222 is *picture*, i.e., a naturalistic representation of a subject. It may be sketchy, impressionistic, or detailed, but it is intended to represent what will be seen. In contrast, the basic concept in T1—0223 is *plan*, i.e., a two-dimensional representation such as a ground or floor layout, or a vertical plane representation. The word "diagram" adds to T1—0223 the concept of a graphic design which explains, rather than represents. It shows arrangements and relations among the parts, and need not be limited to a single plane.

Unfortunately, the classifier must work with a number of words which blur the basic distinction of picture vs. plan, e.g., charts, designs, atlases. Use T1—0222 for charts that are basically pictures of things, T1—0223 for charts that are basically maps or diagrams. Use T1—0222 for designs which give a visual impression of what something does or will look like, e.g., architectural drawings; T1—0223 for designs that show details on horizontal or vertical planes (often as a preliminary to construction), or the arrangement and relations of parts showing how something works. Atlases are usually compilations of maps, plans, or diagrams (T1—0223), but be alert for atlases that are simply compilations of pictorial material. Anatomical atlases are so picture-like that they are classed in T1—0222. Also be alert for atlases that are simply heavily illustrated texts on a subject. These are classed in 001–999 without adding either standard subdivision.

Class comprehensive works in T1—0222, e.g., architectural drawings and plans, 720.222. If in doubt, use T1—0222.

T1—024

The subject for persons in specific occupations

Do not use T1—024 when it is redundant, that is, when it is directed towards persons who would normally be expected to study the subject, e.g., engineering for engineers, students, beginners 620 (*not* 620.002462, 620.0024375, or 620.00240909, respectively).

Use T1—024 with caution for works that effectively cover the subject for the general reader but simply draw examples from one broad discipline or for one kind of professional user. For example, a work on cardiology for nurses is often just as suitable for patients, relatives, or social workers as for nurses. Therefore, prefer 616.12 over 616.120024613 unless the work emphasizes special instructions for nurses that general readers would not find useful.

T1—025 vs. T1—0601–0609

Directories of persons and organizations vs. Organizations

Certain works covering several or many organizations are directories, even if not so called, i.e., works that supply addresses, key officers or contact people, phone numbers, and brief statements of purpose. There may be directory information about component parts of individual organizations, and/or a limited amount of general information on structure and component parts. These works are classed in T1—025. However, if there is significant information (more than a page) per organization, consider T1—06. The chief thrust of material intended for T1—0601–0609 is indicated by the terms in the class-here note: history, charters, regulations, membership lists, and administrative reports; but the span also includes conference programs and organizational handbooks.

Normally a combined organizational handbook and membership directory is classed in T1—06, even if the membership part predominates. However, if the organizational part consists of only a few preliminary pages followed by an extensive directory of members, then the work may be more useful classed as a directory of the organization in T1—025, plus the Table 2 notation for the area that the organization serves.

A membership list that includes addresses is counted as a directory, and is classed in T1—025.

If in doubt, prefer T1—025.

T1—028

Auxiliary techniques and procedures; apparatus, equipment, materials

Unless specific instructions are given, do not use T1—028 for the techniques and procedures that are basic to a subject. For example, use 640 (*not* 640.28) for the basic techniques of home economics, 264 (*not* 264.0028) for the conduct of public worship. The subdivision is not normally used for the technology of subjects in 600; however, 610.28 is used for medical technology since "medical technology" does not refer to the basic arts or techniques of medicine, but to the specialized apparatus, equipment, and materials of medicine and their use.

There are several schedule numbers ending in 028 that once were standard subdivisions, but have been expanded for a variety of techniques specific to the subject. They often contain subdivisions for apparatus, equipment, and materials, that is, for displaced standard subdivision concepts. These special numbers can be identified by the fact that the headings lack the word "Auxiliary," e.g., 677.028 (Techniques, procedures, apparatus, equipment, products). They usually have references to standard subdivision T1—028 in the double zero position, e.g., from 677.028 to 677.0028 for auxiliary techniques and procedures.

T1—0285

Data processing Computer applications

Do not use T1—02854 by itself, since the digit 4 simply repeats the meaning of notation 0285. If the applied concept is one for which 004 is the interdisciplinary number, simply stop at T1—0285, e.g., digital computers T1—0285. However, it is not redundant to add 4 plus additional digits to T1—0285, e.g., digital microcomputers T1—0285416.

It is similarly redundant to add only the digit 4 to numbers divided like 004–006 when the base number is limited to data processing and computer concepts, e.g., 651.8, 658.05.

Machine-readable materials and programs

Do not use T1—0285 to indicate that a work is in machine-readable form, e.g., for census data stored on machine-readable tapes use 310 (*not* 310.285). T1—028 (Auxiliary techniques and procedures; apparatus, equipment, materials) is not used as a form subdivision. A program, however, may be regarded as a kind of apparatus, that is, a device to make a computer work properly or to accomplish a particular task, and works about programs typically discuss techniques and procedures. Hence T1—028553 should be used for programs themselves and for works about programs, regardless of form (e.g., programs in machine-readable form, such as disk or tape, and printed program listings bound into books).

Do not use T1—028553 for items that include both programs and data files, unless the data files are clearly of minor importance, e.g., small files intended merely to help beginners learn to use the programs.

If in doubt, do not use T1—028553.

T1—0285 vs. T1—0113

Data processing Computer applications vs. [Computer modeling and simulation]

Use T1—0285 for general works on use of computers, programs, etc., by persons working with a subject. However, use T1—0113 for attempts to represent the subject and to predict outcomes under various hypothetical conditions. In the absence of a specific design number, T1—0113 is also used for computer modeling in design. For example (using microcomputer numbers in each case), ordinary programs for lathe operators 621.9420285536, programs for chemical process simulation in ceramics 666.0113536, programs for research modeling of nuclear structure 539.740113536. If in doubt, prefer T1—0285.

See also discussion at 510, T1—0151 vs. 003, T1—011.

T1—0285 vs. T1—068

Data processing Computer applications vs. Management

Class management of applied data processing with the application, plus notation 0285 from Table 1. It is more common, however, for books to treat data processing applied to management of a subject, in which case T1—068 is used, e.g., data processing applied to the management of hospitals 362.11068. If in doubt, prefer T1—0285.

T1—0601–0609

Organizations

Organization subdivisions in T1—0601–0609 are used primarily for membership organizations and associations, but they are also used for a selection of nonmembership institutions, foundations, and agencies that do not belong to the categories listed in class-elsewhere notes under T1—0601–0609. However, before using T1—06 for nonmembership organizations, determine that "organization" is not inherent in the subject. For example, except as indicated below, do not use T1—06 for most subdivisions in 250–280 Christian church or for many subdivisions in 360 for social services. Under such numbers, use T1—09 for the basic organizations in specific areas, and for specific basic organizations, e.g., hospitals in China 362.110951. However, use T1—06 for associations that include the basic organizations and their staffs as members, e.g., hospital associations in China 362.1106051.

T1—06 is also used for administrative (in contrast to service) histories of institutions, e.g., administrative histories of hospitals (362.1106) or police agencies (363.206). These histories are not to be confused with how-to works on management, which are classed in T1—068.

Do not use T1—06 for membership organizations where "membership organization" is inherent in the subject, e.g., in 366 Association or 061–068 General organizations. Because of the ambiguity of membership organization in religion, T1—06 is not used with numbers for a religion. For example, 296.06 is bracketed, and a reference leads to 296.67 where "membership" is inherent in the organization number.

Selection of area number

For membership organizations, use the area that is the chief focus of the membership, e.g., American Medical Association 610.6073. For local affiliated associations or chapters that have their own name, use the area number of the local organization, e.g., Massachusetts Medical Association 610.60744. For offices and chapters that take the name of the parent body, use the number of the parent organization, e.g., the Washington office of the American Medical Association 610.6073 (*not* 610.60753).

For nonmembership organizations, institutions, foundations, and conferences use the area number of the headquarters. Also use the number of the headquarters for membership organizations whose area cannot be determined.

T1—068 vs. 353–354

[Table 1 notation for] Management vs. [Specific fields of public administration]

In the Dewey Decimal Classification "public administration" refers primarily to running government agencies that regulate and exercise control of various fields, while "management" refers to running organizations, public or private, that directly perform the work within their scope. In several fields traditionally dominated by public agencies, this operational management is called administration, as in library, hospital, or school administration.

In some of the fields dominated by public agencies special provisions for administration were made in the Dewey Decimal Classification before notation 068 in Table 1 was developed, e.g., library administration 025.1, military administration 355.6, educational administration 371.2. In each case, however, "administration" refers to running an agency or system in direct contact with its clients, i.e., an agency providing books, teaching students, or controlling the activities and lives of soldiers, not one telling other agencies or persons how to do so.

The word "system" is often an indicator pointing to the use of a number outside public administration, because in normal usage it refers to an agency operating (rather than regulating) a number of units. In this sense, a system is usually analogous to a company operating a number of plants. Managing the company or system as well as the individual plants or units is normally classed in the subject of the operations, plus notation 068 from Table 1, e.g., managing a prison system 365.068.

Other indicators pointing outside public administration are emphasis on subordinate decision makers; on internal policy formulation; on delegated activities; on routine financial, personnel, and property administration; or on how the reader should exercise control in person. For example, class a work on how to manage the nationalized railways of the United Kingdom in 385.068, on financial management of railways in the United Kingdom in 385.0681.

Public hearings are *not* an indicator of public administration. Class hearings on a subject like any other work on the subject. For example, hearings on the performance of a regulatory agency are classed in public administration, but hearings on public policy or on management of an agency delivering services are normally classed outside public administration. Nomination hearings, however, are classed in 352–354 regardless of how much public policy is discussed. (*See also discussion at 300, 320.6 vs. 352–354: Nomination hearings.*)

Foreign affairs are among the few major activities for which administration of an actual operation is classed in 353–354, since it is hard to think of "managing" foreign relations in the usual sense. Use 353.13, not 327.068 or cognate numbers in 327.4–.9. Similarly, foreign intelligence management is classed in 353.17, not 327.12. The administration of activities specific to government such as licensing, taxing, and gathering census information (that is, activities found in 352 that are not also found in 658) are likewise classed in 353–354 when applied to specific fields of public administration.

There is a small handful of large "bureaucratic" organizations based on either a nationwide monopoly or coercive laws for which the organization and management aspects of the national department or agency (sometimes called a "service") are classed in public administration. The two most common examples are agencies running government-sponsored insurance, e.g., the United States Social Security Administration (353.540973), and agencies running postal or other communications services, e.g., the United States Post Office and the United States Postal Service (both 354.7590973). However, the management of specific activities of postal and other communications services is classed in 383–384, e.g., management of parcel post 383.125068, of radio broadcasting facilities 384.545068. (*See also discussion at 380: Add table: 09 vs. 065.*)

Nevertheless, size is not a factor in differentiating between public administration and management. Running a one-person bureau licensing commercial establishments is classed in public administration (354.73284), while running a transcontinental nationalized railroad is classed in railroad transportation plus notation 068 for management (385.068).

Often a field has both public administration and management aspects. For example, managing railroads is classed in 385.068, while running agencies that regulate railroads is found in 354.76728; administering a public library system is classed in 025.1974, while administering agencies that support public libraries is found in 353.73.

If in doubt, prefer the number outside public administration.

See also discussion at note in schedule under 353.3–.9.

T1—072 vs. T1—0601–0609

Research; statistical methods vs. Organizations

Use T1—072 for organizations that conduct research, e.g., agricultural research stations in the United States 630.72073, but T1—06 for membership organizations which primarily promote research, e.g., the American Association for the Advancement of Science 506.073. If in doubt, class in T1—072.

See also discussion at T1—07201–07209 vs. T1—0722–0724.

T1—07201–07209 vs. T1—0722–0724

Geographic treatment of research and statistical methods together, of research alone vs. Specific kinds of research

Most works on research in specific areas consist of general descriptions of research projects, and normally do not emphasize the kind of research. Furthermore, when kind (that is, descriptive, experimental, or historical research) is emphasized, it is usually redundant, e.g., historical research in history, or experimental research in an experimental science such as chemistry. Hence, it is usually more useful to class works on research in progress or being planned in the geographic treatment span than in a number for a specific kind that might be mentioned.

It is also generally more useful to class research organizations in the area span, even if they have names like agricultural experiment stations. While the names may allude to specific kinds of research, they perform or sponsor all or most of the research in their fields, regardless of kind.

Exceptions to this rule of thumb are surveys and data collection projects that concentrate on specific areas. These differ from the normal "research in progress" work mentioned above in that the individual works usually concentrate on a single survey rather than on a number of projects. In fact, there is often a series of monographs on different parts of a single large survey. In such cases, class in T1—0723.

If in doubt, prefer T1—07201–07209.

T1—074 vs. T1—0294

Museums, collections, exhibits vs. Trade catalogs and directories

While most catalogs of products for sale are classed in T1—0294, catalogs of collections are an exception. The distinction is based upon primary purpose: use T1—074 for catalogs whose primary purpose is to promote knowledge or art, use T1—0294 for catalogs whose primary purpose is to promote sale or distribution of products. The meaning of T1—074 is extended to cover catalogs of replicas, duplicates, and minor items when offered for sale in museum- or exhibit-like settings by noncommercial institutions. Also use T1—074 for auction catalogs (e.g., in art), and for catalogs of temporary exhibits of groups of artists, even if a succession of such exhibits provides most of the artists with their primary source of income. If in doubt, prefer T1—074.

T1—08

History and description with respect to kinds of persons

Be alert for provisions for certain age and sex groups or groups with disabilities which were assigned numbers before T1—08 was developed for kinds of persons. In these cases, follow the references from bracketed T1—08 subdivisions to the correct numbers, e.g., to 613.04 for age and sex groups, and to 646.31–.36 and cognate numbers in 646.4–.7 for persons with disabilities and for men, women, and children.

T1—081 and T1—082, T1—08351, T1—08352, T1—08421, T1—08422

Men [and] Women [and] Males twelve to twenty [and] Females twelve to twenty [and] Young men [and] Young women

Subdivisions for men and women should be used only for works explicitly emphasizing the sex of the people treated. For example, do not use 363.37081 for men as a group in respect to fire fighting unless the work makes clear that fire*men* are being contrasted with fire*women*, or 364.3608351 for juvenile delinquents (a term often implying young men under eighteen) unless *male* delinquents are being contrasted to *female* delinquents.

T1—088 vs. T1—024

[History and description with respect to] Occupational and religious groups vs. The subject for persons in specific occupations

Notation 024 from Table 1 refers to the treatment of a discipline for the instruction of members of an occupation other than the primary students and practitioners of the discipline, e.g., mathematics for engineers 510.2462. Subdivisions from Table 7 are used under T1—024 only when they refer to occupations, that is, the subject for clergymen T1—0242.

In contrast, T1—088 covers all other relations of occupational and religious groups to a subject, e.g., farmers as elected politicians 324.208863. (*See discussion at T1—0882 and 200 for use of the religious groups number.*)

If in doubt, prefer T1—088.

T1—0882 and 200

[Table 1 notation for History and description with respect to religious groups and] Religion

Subdivisions of T1—0882 taken from notation 21–29 in Table 7 are used in 200 to represent official or semi-official positions of denominations and sects, e.g., Catholic teachings on socioeconomic problems 261.808822. (These subdivisions will be useful in 200 mostly for Christianity, since only one denomination [the Black Muslim movement] is developed under notation 29 of Table 7.)

T1—0882 is not used for works of an individual except in the rare cases in which an individual's view has become an official statement of a group. That is, use 261.8 (*not* 261.80882) for writings of persons who happen to be Catholic on Christian attitudes toward socioeconomic problems.

T1—0882 vs. T1—09

[Religious groups] vs. Historical, geographic, persons treatment

Treatment of a religious group is classed in T1—0882 even if the group is limited to an area in which it is predominant, e.g., Roman Catholics of Spain T1—08822, not T1—0946, even though Catholics predominate in Spain.

T1—09

Historical, geographic, persons treatment

Be alert for distinctions occasionally made between the historical and geographic treatment of a subject and the historical and geographic treatment of the discipline within which the subject is treated. For example, 364.9 is provided for historical and geographic treatment of crime and its alleviation, while 364.09 is provided for comparable treatment of criminology. Use 364.9 for area treatment of offenses, offenders, causes, prevention, and treatment (when all are considered together). Use 364.09 for area treatment of criminology and of the principles and methods used in analyzing causes and remedies of crime. Where the distinction is not made between the subject and the discipline, use T1—09 for either or both aspects.

T1—09 vs. T1—089

Historical, geographic, persons treatment vs. Racial, ethnic, national groups

Prefer T1—089 over T1—09 except for groups which predominate in an area, e.g., French people in Australia T1—08941094, but French people in Paris T1—0944361; Caucasoids in Europe T1—094, but Caucasoids in Africa T1—08903406; Arabs generally T1—089927, Arabs in Egypt T1—0962, Arabs in France T1—089927044.

T1—09174 (regions where specific ethnic groups predominate) is not used for groups of persons treatment since such use would practically duplicate the group treatment numbers. For example, Arabs living in all areas where Arabs predominate constitute the overwhelming majority of all Arabs; therefore, use T1—089927 for treatment of Arabs as a group, and limit T1—09174927 to works about the area where they live, and works about styles prevailing in areas where they live.

Use T1—09 to identify distinguishing characteristics of a subject in an area where a specific group of people lives rather than T1—089, e.g., Arab architecture 720.9174927, not 720.89927; French desserts 641.860944, not 641.8608941.

If in doubt, prefer T1—09.

T1—0901–0905

Historical periods

Do not use historical periods for subjects that have no significant history outside the period indicated, e.g., the history of railroads 385.09 (*not* 385.0903), but the history of railroads during the 19th century 385.09034. If in doubt, do not use periods, e.g., use 629.1309, not 629.130904, for 20th-century aviation, since aviation hardly existed before the 20th century.

Avoid using the most recent period subdivision in T1—0904 for works on current practice or the state of the art of a subject. Most users will expect to find these works in the base number. However, when the nature of the subject requires attention to the changing situation, the latest period number must be used, e.g., 320.9049 for world political conditions in 1990.

Use earlier historical periods only for retrospective works, not for contemporary works. For example, class a current work on music theory of the baroque in 781.09032; but a reprint of a treatise on music theory written in 1620 (when baroque music was in style) in 781.

T1—092

Persons

These instructions apply also to notation 2 from Table 2 when numbers from Table 2 are added directly without the interposition of T1—09.

In the notes below, the word "biography" is used for stylistic convenience; however, the instructions apply fully to description and critical appraisal as well as other "persons" aspects.

Do not use T1—092 for the actual works of a person except where so instructed at certain numbers in 700–770.

See also discussion at 913–919: Add table: 04: Biography; also at 930–990: Wars: Personal narratives; also at 930–990: Biography.

Comprehensive biography

Class a comprehensive biography of a person with the subject of the person's most noted contribution. If the person made approximately equal contributions to a number of fields, class in the subject which provides the best common denominator, giving some extra consideration to the person's occupational commitment. For example, a physicist who became a science teacher, then head of a school of science, but went on to become a university president would be classed in the university's area number under 378. The biography of a person who made significant contributions in political science, in university education, and the study of administrative and economic aspects of utility regulation will be classed in 300.92, since that number provides the best common denominator for his work. However, a famous woman doctor who also served as a feminist leader, wrote minor novels, and often served as a delegate to political conventions will normally be classed in 610.92 unless there is an obvious emphasis on her avocations. Give weight to designations listed first in biographical dictionaries, but make allowances for the tendency to list occupation first even when a career transcends occupation.

If in doubt between a number for a discipline and a number for a specific subject within the discipline, prefer the number for the discipline, e.g., a mechanical engineer who also did important work in transportation and construction engineering 620.0092 rather than 621.092.

Public figures

Biographies of public figures frequently present difficulties because the figures may have filled several positions which are given varying emphasis by different authors, or may have filled one position which had many facets. For persons who held such positions, prefer history numbers in 930–990 for comprehensive works. However, for biographies that emphasize one position or interest of a person's career, prefer a number reflecting that position or interest, e.g., a biography emphasizing Wayne Morse's promotion of the National Institutes of Health 362.1092, even though he was a U.S. senator. (*See also Partial biography, below.*)

There are a number of offices a public figure may hold that afford an opportunity to exert a wide-ranging impact upon the history of the jurisdiction served. For example, Daniel Webster is most famous as a U.S. senator, although he served twice as secretary of state. In both positions, as well as in his position as lawyer and orator, he influenced the history of his time; thus the best number for his biography is 973.5092, not 328.73092 for his senatorial service, 327.730092 for his foreign relations service, or 349.73092 for his legal activities. However, if a person in a high office of general responsibility concentrated on a single important field, consider a number which identifies that field. For example, Claude Pepper's chief interest while serving in the U.S. Congress, both as senator, and later as representative, was the promotion of services to older people. Thus the suitable number for his comprehensive biography would be 362.6092 for his services to the elderly rather than 973.92092 for his impact on the general history of his period or 328.73092 for his legislative work.

For public figures who served in several capacities, give greatest weight to the highest office reached, normally the one in the highest category in the following table. When there is no clear reason to the contrary, use the following table of preference:

1. 930–990 for monarchs, presidents, other heads of state, prime ministers, vice presidents, and regents, using the number for the period during which they held office. Also class here public figures of any position or combination of positions who had a significant impact upon general history, including the king makers and the powers behind the throne, using the period numbers which best approximate their period of influence. Candidates of major parties for the highest office of a country are also assigned history numbers, generally using the number for the period during which they ran for office, e.g., 973.68092 for Stephen Douglas, who ran against Lincoln in 1860. Sometimes a candidate defeated for party nomination made enough difference in the outcome to warrant a history number for his comprehensive biography, e.g., 973.923092 for Eugene McCarthy who ran unsuccessfully for the Democratic presidential nomination in 1968.

2. The number for the field of service for cabinet members, e.g., a foreign minister of France 327.440092, a secretary of the treasury 336.092.

3. 327.3–.9 for ambassadors and pre-World War II ministers plenipotentiary.

4. 328.4–.9 for legislators not warranting a specific subject number, e.g., a floor leader, whip, or member noted for promoting legislative work. Consider, however, that biographers tend to concentrate upon legislators who left their mark on general history; therefore, always weigh the number in 900 for the area the legislature served before assigning another. Only occasionally will a work focus on a legislator's own constituency.

5. 327.3–.9 for diplomats below the level of ambassador or pre-World War II minister plenipotentiary; if associated with notable events, then with the events.

6. The number for field of service for public administrators not holding cabinet positions, if their contribution to the service was significant, e.g., J. Edgar Hoover, director of the U.S. Federal Bureau of Investigation 363.25092; otherwise 352–354.

Give comparable preference to public figures of state, provincial, and local jurisdictions. Normally national office takes preference over other levels, but the weight of contributions must be considered. For example, DeWitt Clinton, the famous governor of New York, was briefly U.S. senator, and was a minor party candidate for president, but his comprehensive biography should be classed in 974.703092 for the state history of his time. Fiorello La Guardia served fourteen years as U.S. representative, and briefly as chief of the U.S. Office of Civilian Defense and as director of the United Nations Relief and Rehabilitation Administration; but he is more noted as mayor of New York City, and should be classed in 974.71042092.

Systems and laws named after persons

Do not use T1—092 for a system or law named after a single individual, but *do* use it for treatment of the individual emphasizing biography, e.g., a work on Freudianism 150.1952, a biography of Freud 150.1952092.

When more than one individual is named in a heading or notes, treat the system according to the normal rules for topics, but be liberal about adding notation 092 from Table 1 for treatment emphasizing the individual. For example, 576.52 (Laws of genetics) gives laws of Galton and Weismann in an including note, and Mendel's laws in a class here note. Any subdivision may be added for Mendel's laws (because they are given in a class-here note), but standard subdivisions are not added for laws of Galton or Weismann (because they are given in an including note). However, notation 092 may be used for strictly persons treatment of any one of the three, e.g., a biography emphasizing Weismann's work on laws of genetics 576.52092. (*See also Division policies, below.*)

Families and close associates of the famous

Class a history of the immediate or extended family of a famous person with the biography of that person if the work strongly emphasizes the famous person. The same rule applies to the biography of a single relative or close associate of a famous person. However, if the relative or associate is important in his or her own right, or if the famous person is not strongly featured, class the life of the relative in the subject warranted by his or her own work, e.g., a biography of evangelist Ruth Carter Stapleton, sister of President Jimmy Carter, that treats the president only incidentally in 269.2092. If in doubt, do not use the number assigned to a famous person for a relative or close friend; prefer a number warranted by the biographee's own activities. Class a general family history in 929.2.

Partial biography

Each partial biography featuring a specific contribution of a person is classed with the contribution. However, a biography of the portions of a person's life that preceded the activity with which he is chiefly associated is classed in his comprehensive biography number when there is no significant alternative subject emphasis. For example, Justice Byron White's earlier life as an All-American football player 796.332092; but the childhood of Indira Gandhi 954.045092, the number for her period as prime minister of India.

Division policies

It is the policy of the Decimal Classification Division to add T1—092 even in cases when a person's work may not approximate the whole of the most specific available number. Conversely, T1—092 is not added to extremely minute subjects, e.g., ball players are classed in the game they played, not in subordinate numbers for specific positions on the field, even if a player filled only one position.

It is also Division policy for individual biography, when a work is not clearly associated with any subject but is clearly associated with a place, to class the biography in the number most nearly covering the history and civilization of the place and time of the activity emphasized, e.g., the diary of a resident of San Francisco during the Gold Rush 979.46104092.

T1—0922

Collected persons treatment

Treat as collected biography a work on two people collaborating in the same field, e.g., the Wright brothers 629.1300922, Pierre and Marie Curie 530.0922. However, when the focus is strongly on one of the two, use T1—092.

Do not use area subdivisions for collected biography of groups that have a strong collective personal identity, even though all the members are known to have come from one particular area, e.g., the Beatles 782.421660922 (*not* 782.42166092242 or 782.42166092242753).

T1—0922 vs. T1—093–099

Collected persons treatment vs. [Geographic] Treatment by specific continents, countries, localities; extraterrestrial worlds

Persons treatment covers "description and critical appraisal of work," and geographic treatment covers "description by place, by specific instance of the subject." For material limited by persons yet emphasizing area aspects, prefer persons treatment over geographic treatment. However, when the intent of the author or compiler is to describe works of art characteristic of an area, or simply to describe such works in an area (even though the works may be listed under their producers), the material should be classed in T1—093–099. When the title and front matter does not reveal the intent, any discussion of style is an important indicator. A discussion focusing on the character and style of the individual producers indicates persons treatment; one focusing on the characteristics of the place and times indicates geographic treatment. For example, a book on the style and character of sculptures by Cellini, Donatello, and Michelangelo is classed in 730.92245, but a book illustrating Italian Renaissance sculpture by describing the work of these same men is classed in 730.94509024. If in doubt, prefer T1—0922.

If the text is largely confined to concise descriptions of works of technology or art (or to identifications and illustrations of them), class in the area number, even if persons are indicated in the title, e.g., descriptions of the works of six famous Italian sculptors 730.945.

However, for individual persons use T1—092 without further subdivision for all description and critical appraisal of works they have produced.

T1—093–099 and T2—3–9

[Table 1 notation for] Treatment by specific continents, countries, localities; extraterrestrial worlds [and Table 2 notation for] Specific continents, countries, localities; extraterrestrial worlds

Change of preference when area notation is added directly

When area notation from Table 2 is added directly in the schedules rather than through notation 09 from Table 1, and all or most of the other subdivisions are in their regular positions, the rule of zero (paragraph 5.7 of Introduction to the DDC) changes the preference for areas with respect to other standard subdivisions. The table of preference at the beginning of Table 1 shows areas almost in the middle. Areas move to the top when there is no zero. As a result, all standard subdivisions (including persons notation 092 if persons has not been moved to the same span as areas) can be added. For example, management of prisons in Great Britain is classed in 365.941068 (*not* 365.068 as it would be if prisons in Great Britain were 365.0941).

The change of preference takes place whenever the number of zeros differs, e.g., when areas remain in T1—09 but other subdivisions are displaced to 001–009.

Differences in standard subdivisions added to area notation

While normally one standard subdivision is not added to another standard subdivision, a limited number may be added in T1—09. Special tables in T1—09 show which of the subdivisions falling below T1—09 subdivisions in the table of preference may be used in area and history period subdivisions. The special table under T1—093–099 also allows T1—09 to be used to add historical periods and to add area notation to area notation in certain cases.

When the area notation is added directly, standard subdivisions T1—01–091 can be added without restrictions, e.g., periodicals about penal institutions in France 365.94405. Notation 092 for persons can be used, but only when the area notation is added directly while the persons notation remains in its standard subdivision position. For example, if all of T1—09 is vacated, as when 365.09 is moved to 365.9, all biography regardless of area is classed in 365.92, e.g., persons associated with penal institutions in France 365.92244. But if only some of T1—09 is vacated, as when treatment by specific continents, countries, and localities is moved from 373.093–.099 to 373.3–.9, then notation 092 is added to area notation, e.g. secondary educators in Europe 373.40922. Notation 093–099 can also be used when the base area notation specifies origin or style, while the added notation identifies the area in which the subject is found or practiced, e.g., French cooking 641.5944, a work on the popularity of French cooking in America 641.59440973.

T1—0940902 vs. T1—0902

[Medieval period in European history] vs. 6th–15th centuries, 500-1499

The Middle Ages and the Medieval period often refer to European history. However, the medieval record of many subjects outside Europe is poorly documented, so a work attempting worldwide coverage may in fact be predominantly about the subject in Europe. Therefore, one must distinguish carefully between T1—0940902 for works that are clearly focused on Europe, and T1—0902 for works that attempt to cover the whole world during the period. If in doubt, prefer T1—0940902.

Table 2. Areas, Periods, Persons

T2—1

Areas, regions, places in general

Subdivisions of T2—1 are used only for areas, regions, and places that overlap more than one continent (considering Oceania as a continent), e.g., urban regions of the United States, Europe, and Japan T2—1732. Such regions within one continent are classed in T2—4–9. (*See also discussion at T2—4–9.*)

T2—162

Oceans and seas

Parts of oceans and non-inland seas limited by either country or locality are classed in T2—163–168, not in T2—3–9. For example, Chesapeake Bay, an arm of the Atlantic Ocean that is almost surrounded by Maryland and Virginia, is classed in T2—16347, not in either T2—752 or T2—7551. Be alert that estuaries are sometimes named rivers. Estuaries that are parts of oceans and non-inland seas are classed in T2—16. For example, the York River, an estuary of the Chesapeake Bay, is classed in T2—16347 (*not* T2—7553).

Comprehensive works on the coastal waters of a country are classed in T2—163–168 with the number which includes the majority of the waters, e.g., coastal waters of Russia T2—1632 (*not* T2—16334 or T2—16451), of the United States T2—1634 (*not* T2—16364 or T2—1643). If the areas are approximately equal in size, class in the number coming first, e.g., coastal waters of Spain T2—16338 (*not* T2—16381), of Panama T2—16365 (*not* T2—1641).

See also discussion at T2—163, T2—164, T2—165 vs. T2—182.

T2—163 and T2—164, T2—165

Atlantic Ocean [and] Pacific Ocean [and] Indian Ocean

This table follows the latest thinking of geographers in dividing the world ocean in three parts—Atlantic, Indian, and Pacific Oceans. The "Arctic Ocean" is considered a sea of the Atlantic. There is no Antarctic Ocean, but provision in made in T2—167 for the extreme southern portions of the three oceans.

Divisions between the oceans are considered to be as follows:

Atlantic-Pacific: north, Bering Strait; south, a line drawn southeasterly from Cape Horn to the northern tip of Palmer Peninsula, Antarctica

Pacific-Indian: north, a line from Melville Island to Timor, thence through the islands of Indonesia to Singapore Strait; south, a line drawn south from Cape Howe, Victoria, Australia, on the 150° east meridian

Indian-Atlantic: north, Suez Canal; south, a line drawn south from Cape Agulhas, South Africa, on the 20° east meridian

Notes and references throughout show where to class connecting bodies of water, e.g., Bering Strait T2—16451, not T2—16325 or T2—16327.

See also discussion at T2—1631 and T2—1635; also at T2—1644 and T2—1648, T2—1649.

T2—163, T2—164, T2—165 vs. T2—182

Atlantic Ocean [and] Pacific Ocean [and] Indian Ocean vs. Ocean and sea basins

T2—163, T2—164, and T2—165 deal with the oceans and seas themselves, i.e., their waters. Specific lands are classed in T2—3–9, while the total lands around an ocean or sea or surrounded by an ocean or sea are classed in the appropriate subdivision of T2—182. Class works on both the land and water of an ocean basin in T2—182. If in doubt, class in T2—163, T2—164, or T2—165.

T2—1631 and T2—1635

North Atlantic Ocean [and] South Atlantic Ocean

In this table, the division of the North Atlantic Ocean from the South Atlantic Ocean occurs along a line drawn from the Strait of Gibraltar to the Straits of Florida.

Notes and references throughout show where to class connecting bodies of water, e.g., Straits of Florida T2—16363, not T2—16348.

T2—1644 and T2—1648, T2—1649

North Pacific Ocean [and] South Pacific Ocean [and] Central Pacific Ocean

In this table, the Pacific Ocean is divided into the North Pacific Ocean, the South Pacific Ocean, and the Central Pacific Ocean according to the following definitions:

North Pacific Ocean: the American and Asian coastal waters located in an arc from the Mexico-United States boundary to the southern tip of the Philippines, excluding the South China Sea and the inner seas of the Philippines

South Pacific Ocean: the American coastal waters from the Mexico-United States boundary to the Strait of Magellan; the coastal water of Antarctica, New Zealand, Australia, and New Guinea; the waters of Melanesia; and the coastal waters west and south of the Philippines, including the South China Sea and the inner seas of the Philippines

Central Pacific Ocean: the American and Asian non-coastal waters and the waters of Polynesia and isolated islands of the Pacific, such as Wake and Easter Island

Notes and references throughout show where to class connecting bodies of water, e.g., Formosa Strait T2—16474, not T2—16472.

T2—3 vs. T2—4–9

The ancient world vs. The modern world; extraterrestrial worlds

Under T2—3 "The ancient world" are gathered those parts of the world more or less known to classical antiquity, and considered only during the period of "ancient history." The same areas in later times, as well as other areas such as America in both ancient and later times, are classed in T2—4–9. Examples: ancient China T2—31, later China T2—51; ancient Palestine T2—33, later Palestine T2—5694; ancient Gaul T2—364, France T2—44; Yucatán, both ancient and later, T2—7265. The date of demarcation between "ancient" and "later" varies from place to place and may be determined by examination of the terminal dates in classes 931–939, e.g., 931 China to 420, 933 Palestine to 70, 936.4 Celtic regions to 486.

T2—4–9

The modern world; extraterrestrial worlds

Physiographic features and regions

Class a specific feature or region not named in the area table and that is wholly or almost wholly contained within a political or administrative unit with the unit, e.g., Mount Washington, New Hampshire T2—7421; Lake Moultrie, South Carolina T2—75793. Class a river with the unit where its mouth is located, e.g., Escanaba River, Michigan T2—77494. However, if the upper part of the stream is more important politically, economically, or culturally, class the river with that part, e.g., Tigris and Euphrates Rivers T2—5674 rather than T2—5675.

Class general treatment of a specific kind of feature or region limited to a specific continent with the continent, country, or locality plus notation 091 from the table under T1—093–099 in Table 1, e.g., rivers of Europe T2—4091693, rivers of England T2—42091693. However, do not add notation 091 for individual features or regions, e.g., Nile River of Egypt T2—62 (*not* T2—62091693). Class treatment of a specific kind of feature or region not limited to a specific continent in T2—1, e.g., rivers T2—1693.

Cities, towns, villages

Class cities, towns, and villages not given in Table 2 with the narrowest political or administrative unit that contains them. With certain exceptions, cities are not named in Table 2. The exceptions include:

1. The capital and largest city of each state of the United States, e.g., Pierre and Sioux Falls, South Dakota, at T2—78329 and T2—783371 respectively

2. Major world cities, usually with their own numbers, e.g., Athens at T2—49512 and Mecca included at T2—538

3. Smaller cities given their own numbers early in the development of the DDC, e.g., Guelph, Ontario T2—71343

4. Independent cities, e.g., Alexandria, Virginia T2—755296

5. United States cities coextensive with their counties (or parishes), e.g., Philadelphia T2—74811, San Francisco T2—79461

6. Cities, towns, and villages named to indicate the boundaries when not readily available in reference works, e.g., throughout Australia T2—94 and the western provinces of Canada T2—711–712

The foregoing explains why many large cities are not named, while many smaller and less important ones are.

Class a metropolitan area with the central city, e.g., the metropolitan area of Chicago T2—77311. Standard subdivisions may be applied as needed.

Class general treatment of urban regions limited to a specific continent with the continent, country, or locality plus notation 091732 (derived from notation 091 from the table under T1—093–099), e.g., urban regions of Europe T2—4091732, urban regions of England T2—42091732. Class treatment of urban regions not limited to a specific continent in T2—1732.

See also discussion at T2—41 and T2—42; also at T2—93.

Order within notes

When more than one kind of geographic area or feature are given in either an including or class-here note, the kinds are separated by semicolons and are given in the following order:

1. Large jurisdictions, e.g., districts
2. Small jurisdictions, e.g., towns
3. Other units with man-made boundaries
    a. Parks
    b. Reserves
4. Physiographic regions or entities, e.g., islands
5. Physiographic features
    a. Mountains
    b. Rivers
    c. Lakes

For example, at T2—71187 Peace River-Liard Regional District is the following note:

> Including Dawson Creek, Fort Nelson, Fort St. John, Tumbler Ridge; Finlay, Fort Nelson, Ingenika, Mesilika, Murray, Pine, Sukunka Rivers; *Williston Lake

Dawson Creek, Fort St. John, and Tumbler Ridge are towns. The first Fort Nelson is a town, while the second Fort Nelson is a river.

Changes in geographic concepts

Some geographic concepts of an earlier day have been divided by whims of history. Many such concepts are given special notes to show where comprehensive works are to be classed, e.g., Armenia as a whole and Turkish Armenia at T2—5662, country of Armenia at T2—4756.

However, in many cases adjustments have been made between recent editions of the DDC to conform to historical changes. For example, Finland, which before World War I was part of the Russian empire, was placed by Melvil Dewey in T2—471, as the first subdivision of Russia. It was not until recently that the DDC relocated works on Finland to T2—4897, thus removing the block of material that had separated comprehensive works on Russia in T2—47 from works on its various parts in T2—472–474.

On the other hand, Hawaii, which is not part of North America, is classed in T2—969 under Oceania, separated from the rest of the United States in T2—73–79; and the Asian parts of Russia are classed in T2—57, quite apart from the European portion of Russia in T2—472–474.

T2—41 and T2—42

British Isles [and] England and Wales

In the United Kingdom, the jurisdiction directly below the County is referred to as either District, Borough, or City. The term "City" does not refer to urban localities. The Districts, Boroughs, and Cities are usually named after an urban locality either within or coextensive with the jurisdiction. If the urban locality is coextensive with the jurisdiction, the locality is given in a class-here note. For example, City of Bristol, the jurisdiction, and Bristol, the urban locality, are coextensive; thus, the table entry:

T2—423 93 City of Bristol

Class here Bristol

If the urban locality is not coextensive with the jurisdiction, only the jurisdiction is given. The classifier can assume that if the locality were to be given, the locality would be in an including note. For example, City of Canterbury, the jurisdiction, and Canterbury, the urban locality, are not coextensive; thus, the table entry:

T2—422 34 City of Canterbury

See also discussion at T2—4–9: Cities, towns, villages.

T2—7 vs. T2—1812

North America vs. Western Hemisphere

Use T2—1812 for the Western Hemisphere, i.e., the portion of the world between 20° west longitude and 160° east longitude. The Western Hemisphere includes not only North and South America but also most of the North Atlantic Ocean (excluding the northeastern portion), Southwest Atlantic Ocean, Northeast Pacific Ocean, and most of the South Pacific Ocean (excluding the southwestern portion). Use T2—7 for the comprehensive works on North and South America, including neighboring islands. When the work includes not only the land portion but also the waters of the Western Hemisphere, use T2—1812, e.g., weather patterns of the Americas and Atlantic and Pacific Oceans 551.651812. When the work deals primarily with only the land portion, use T2—7, e.g., reptiles of the Western Hemisphere 597.9097. (Most reptiles are land or freshwater animals.) If in doubt, prefer T2—7.

T2—7193–7197

Specific regions of Northwest Territories

Although there seems to be agreement on which communities are situated in which region, the boundaries drawn on available maps do not always agree. The Decimal Classification Division uses the following to define each region:

Fort Smith Region: Area north of 60° N, west of 106° W, south of 65° N (from 106° W to 123° W), and south of 64° N (123° W to the Yukon boundary); and the eastern part of Great Bear Lake and its immediate environs

Keewatin Region: Mainland between 60° N and 66° N, and east of 106° W; land surrounding Repulse Bay; and Southampton and Coats Island

Baffin Region: Baffin, Bylot, Mansel, Nottingham, Salisbury, Somerset, and Wales Islands; all other islands north of M'Clure Strait and Viscount Melville and Lancaster Sounds; all islands in Hudson, James, and Ungava Bays and Hudson Strait; and Melville Peninsula

Inuvik Region: Area between the Yukon boundary and 123° W, and north of 64° N; and Banks Island

Kitikmeot Region: Victoria, King William, and Prince of Wales Islands; mainland north of 66° N (from 87° W to 106° W) and north of 65° N (from 106° W to 123° W); and excluding Great Bear Lake and its immediate environs

T2—73 vs. T2—71

United States vs. Canada

Books about the United States and Canada are often predominately about the United States and are classed in T2—73. Books are classed in T2—71 when Canada receives fuller treatment or the United States and Canada are given equal treatment. Even though Canada and the United States are assigned most of the numbers in T2—7, i.e., T2—71 and T2—73–79, T2—7 is used only when the work also discusses areas in T2—72.

T2—93

New Zealand

In New Zealand, the jurisdiction directly below the Region is referred to as either District or City. The term "City" does not necessarily refer to an urban locality. A District or City can be named after an urban locality within the jurisdiction. If the urban locality is approximately the same as the jurisdiction, the locality is given in a class-here note. For example, Auckland City, the jurisdiction, and Auckland, the urban locality, are approximately the same; thus, the table entry:

T2—932 4 Auckland City

Class here Auckland

If the urban locality is not approximately the same as the jurisdiction, only the jurisdiction is given. The classifier can assume that if the locality were to be given, the locality would be in an including note. For example, Dunedin City, the jurisdiction, and Dunedin, the urban locality, are not approximately the same; thus, the table entry:

T2—939 2 Dunedin City

See also discussion at T2—4–9: Cities, towns, villages.

T2—99 vs. T2—19

Extraterrestrial worlds vs. Space

Class in T2—19 only space itself. The various bodies of the universe moving through space are classed in T2—99, e.g., moon rocks 552.09991. Limited use of T2—19 is anticipated.

Table 3. Subdivisions for the Arts, for Individual Literatures, for Specific Literary Forms

Number building

Here are examples of basic number building for works in an individual language by or about individual authors (with use of Table 3–A) and by or about more than one author (with use of Table 3–B). The following elements are used to build the numbers: base number; form; period; kind, scope, or medium; notation 08 Collections or notation 09 Criticism (plus additional 0s in some cases); subform; additional notation from Table 3–C and other tables. Detailed instructions for building the numbers appear in Tables 3–A and 3–B.

Note: in the following discussion, "T3" refers to both Table 3–A (individual authors) and Table 3–B (more than one author).

More than one form

1. Works by or about more than one author: not restricted by period or form (Table 3–B)

Base no. + notation 08 or 09

81 + 08 = 810.8 (an anthology of American literature)

2. Works by or about more than one author: restricted to a specific period but not to a specific form (Table 3–B)

Base no. + notation 08 or 09 + period

83 + 08 + 006 = 830.8006 (a collection of 18th-century German literature)

Forms T3—1–7

1. Works by or about an individual author: restricted to a specific form and period (Table 3–A)

Base no. + form + period

82 + 1 + 3 = 821.3 (Spenser's *Faerie Queene*)

2. Works by or about more than one author: restricted to a specific form, to a specific kind, scope, or medium, and to a specific period (Table 3–B)

Base no. + form + kind, scope, or medium + notation 08 or 09 + period

84 + 3 + 01 + 08 + 07 = 843.010807 (a collection of 19th-century French short stories)

3. Works by or about more than one author: restricted to a specific form but not to a specific kind, scope, or medium; restricted to a specific period (Table 3–B)

Base no. + form + period + notation 08 or 09

83 + 2 + 914 + 09 = 832.91409 (criticism of German drama of the second half of the 20th century)

Form T3—8 Miscellaneous writings

1. Works by or about an individual author: restricted to a specific form, period, and subform (T3A—8)

Base no. + form + period + subform

81 + 8 + 4 + 02 = 818.402 (a collection of quotations of an individual American author of the later 19th century)

2. Works by or about more than one author: restricted to a specific form, period, and subform (T3B—8)

Base no. + form + period + subform + notation 08 or 09

84 + 8 + 914 + 02 + 08 = 848.9140208 (a collection of quotations of several French authors of the later 20th century)

Affiliated literatures for which period numbers are not used

1. Works by or about an individual author or more than one author: restricted to a specific form and a specific period (Table 3–A or 3–B)

Base no. + form

86 + 1 = 861 (may represent a collection of Spanish-language poetry by an individual Argentine author or criticism of Spanish-language poetry of several Mexican authors)

2. Works by or about more than one author: restricted to a specific form but not to a specific period (Table 3–B)

Base no. + form + notation 008 or 009

82 + 4 + 008 = 824.008 (a collection of essays in English by several Australian authors of several periods)

3. Works by or about more than one author: restricted to a specific form and to a specific kind, scope, or medium; regardless of period (Table 3–B)

Base no. + form + kind, scope, or medium + notation 08 or 09

84 + 2 + 041 + 09 = 842.04109 (criticism of French-Canadian one-act plays)

4. Works by or about more than one author: restricted to a specific period but not to a specific form (Table 3–B)

Base no. + notation 08 or 09

82 + 08 = 820.8 (an anthology of post-World War II Australian literature in several forms)

5. Works by or about more than one author: not restricted by form or period; place of authorship emphasized (Table 3–B)

Base no. + notation 080 or 09 + 9 from Table 3–C + area notation from Table 2

(a) 869 + 080 + 9 + 81 = 869.080981 (an anthology of literature in Portuguese in several forms by Brazilian authors)

(b) 81 + 09 + 9 + 7292 = 810.997292 (criticism of literature in English in several forms by Jamaican authors)

Table 3–A. Subdivisions for Works by or about Individual Authors

To determine the comprehensive number for collected works, critical evaluation, or biography of an author, follow the criteria given below on language, form, and literary period.

Language

Class an author with the language in which the author writes.

For an author who continues to write in the same language, but who changes place of residence or national affiliation to a country with a different language, use the language in which the author writes. For example, class a novel in Russian by Solzhenitsyn in 891.7344, even if the novel was written while he was living in the United States.

For an author who changes national affiliation to a country with the same language as that in which the author has been writing, use the literature number for the country of which the author is now a citizen. Thus, T. S. Eliot is classed as a British author. All works of such an author, including individual works written before the change of citizenship, are classed with the same national literature.

For an author who changes place of residence, but not national affiliation, to another country with the same language as that in which the author has been writing, continue to use the literature number of the author's original country. Thus, a New Zealand author living in London, but still retaining New Zealand citizenship, is classed as a New Zealand author.

If information about an author's national affiliation is not readily available in the work being classed or in standard reference books, use the literature number of the author's country of origin, if known; or the literature number of the country in which the author's earlier works were published.

Class an author who writes in more than one language with the language that the author used last, e.g., Samuel Beckett 848.91409. However, if another language is predominant, class with that language. (Individual works of such an author are classed with the language in which they were originally written.)

Literary form

Use the form with which an author is chiefly identified, e.g., Jane Austen 823.7. If the author is not chiefly identified with one form, use T3A—8 Miscellaneous writings plus literary period plus notation 09 from the table at T3A—81–89. Thus, class a late-20th-century English author who is equally famous as a novelist, dramatist, and poet in 828.91409. (An individual work of such an author, of course, is classed with the form exemplified by the work.)

Literary periods

Only one literary period is used for an author and all of the author's works, including works that may have been published earlier or later than the literary period. The literary period is determined in accordance with scholarly consensus about when an author flourished. Thus an author commonly regarded as an early 19th-century writer is classed as such, even if the author published literary works at the end of the 18th century. If the period when an author flourished cannot be determined, use the date of the author's earliest known separate literary publication, disregarding magazine contributions, isolated student works, and juvenilia.

For an author who begins writing in one country, then changes residence or national affiliation but continues to write in the same language, use or do not use a literary period as appropriate for the literature with which the author is being classed. Thus the Russian literary period continues to be used for Solzhenitsyn even when he is writing in the United States. No literary period is used for a New Zealand author retaining New Zealand citizenship even when the author is living in London. (*See also 800: Literary period.*)

Biography

Do not use notation 092 from Table 1 for biography. Class literary reminiscences in T3A—8 plus period subdivision plus subdivision 03, e.g., Hemingway's *A Moveable Feast* 818.5203.

Number building

Examples of number building are given in the *Manual* at the beginning of Table 3. The following flow chart is offered as an aid to building numbers and as a supplement to the detailed instructions at Table 3–A.

Flow chart A: Works by or about an individual author

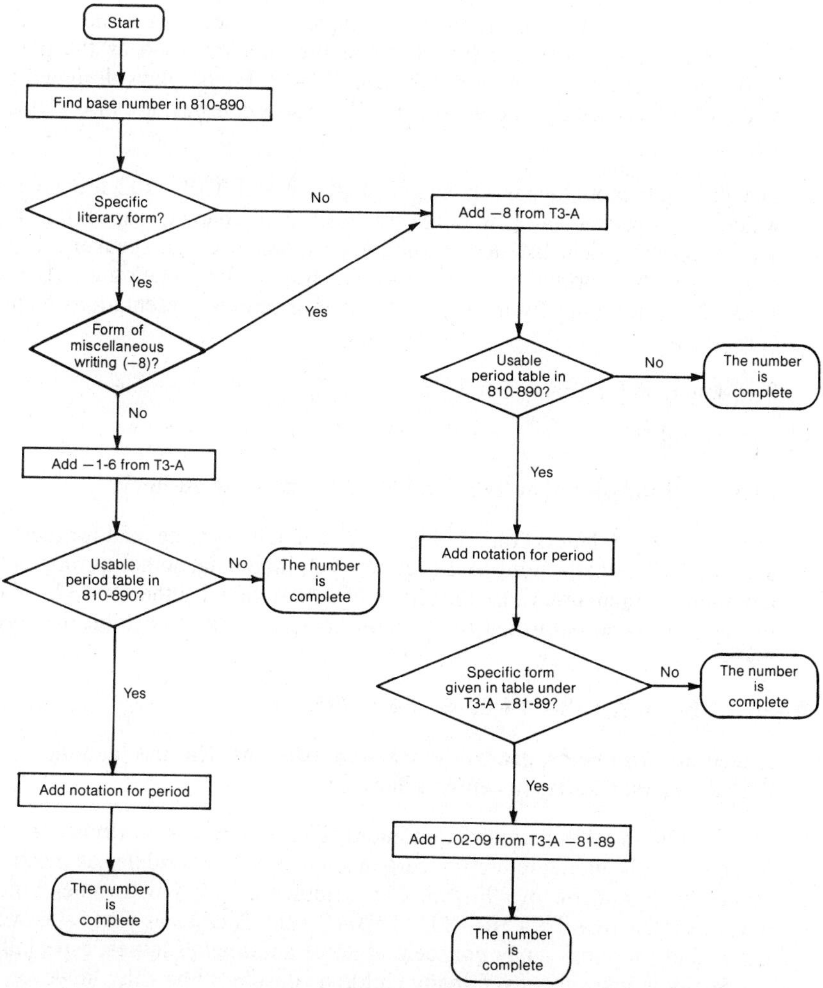

T3A—2, T3B—2 vs. T3A—1, T3B—102

Drama vs. Dramatic poetry

Dramatic poetry in T3A—1 and T3B—102 is poetry that employs dramatic form or some element of dramatic technique as a means of achieving poetic ends. Poetic plays intended for theatrical presentation, such as the plays of Shakespeare and Marlowe, are classed in T3—2. Poetic plays designed to be read rather than acted, such as Milton's *Samson Agonistes*, are also classed in T3—2.

The dramatic monologues classed in T3A—1 and T3B—102 are poems in which the speaker is a fictional or historical character speaking to an identifiable but silent listener at a dramatic moment in the speaker's life, for example, Robert Browning's "My Last Duchess." The monologues classed in T3B—2045 are typically intended for use in theatrical presentations featuring only one actor.

If in doubt, prefer T3A—2 or T3B—2.

T3A—6 and T3B—6

Letters [of individual authors and of more than one author]

Class in T3B—6 letters compiled from several authors to be read for their literary value. Class collections of the letters of an individual author as biography if biographical in nature. Class the letters of an individual author in T3A—6 only if they have been published for a literary purpose, e.g., to exhibit the style of the writer.

T3A—8 + 02, T3B—802, T3B—8 + 02 vs. 398.6, 793.735

Anecdotes, epigrams, graffiti, jokes, quotations vs. Riddles [as folk literature] vs. Riddles [as entertainment]

Class riddles as folk literature and interdisciplinary works on riddles in 398.6. Riddles as folk literature are typically anonymous. Class riddles as puzzles for indoor entertainment in 793.735. Class riddles as jokes with other kinds of jokes in T3A—8 + 02, T3B—802, T3B—8 + 02. Riddles as jokes—as well as other kinds of jokes—may not seem at home amid belles lettres, especially juvenile riddle jokes that even many children consider to be silly; however, they are classed as miscellaneous writings in T3—8.

If in doubt between 398.6 and 793.735, prefer 398.6. If in doubt between either 398.6 or 793.735 and riddles as jokes in T3A—8 + 02, T3B—802, T3B—8 + 02, prefer riddles as jokes.

T3A—8 + 03 and T3B—803, T3B—8 + 03

Diaries, journals, notebooks, reminiscences [of individual authors and of more than one author]

Class in T3A—8 + 03, T3B—803, and T3B—8 + 03 diaries of literary authors not identified with a specific form of literature, in which the life of the author or authors as such is of key interest. If the author or authors are identified with a specific form, class the diary or diaries with that form. However, class the diaries of literary authors that emphasize some other subject besides the general life of the author with the subject emphasized. For example, class the diary of an author compiled while in a prisoner-of-war camp during World War II in 940.5472.

Table 3–B. Subdivisions for Works by or about More than One Author

Preference order

The preference order in case of conflict between literary forms is spelled out at the beginning of the 800 schedule and in Table 3–B under T3B—1–8. In addition, there are preference orders in case of conflict among other aspects. The four aspects expressed by means of Table 3–C are used in accordance with the following table of preference:

Themes and subjects	T3C—3
Elements	T3C—2
Qualities	T3C—1
Persons	T3C—8–9

Thus, for example, a general anthology of poetry about war written by American women poets is classed in 811.0080358, not 811.00809287.

The preference given to literary period in relation to the four aspects expressed by means of Table 3–C varies: for works treating more than two literatures or more than one form in one literature, literary periods have a lower priority than the aspects from Table 3–C; for works treating a specific form in an individual literature, literary periods have a higher priority than the aspects from Table 3–C.

Specific kinds, scopes, media consistently have preference over both period and the aspects from Table 3–C. The preference given to scope in relation to kind, however, varies: for drama, scope has a higher preference; but for fiction, kind has higher preference.

Here, for example, are complete priority listings for fiction:

More than two literatures

1. Specific kinds
2. Specific scopes
3. Specific themes and subjects
4. Specific elements
5. Specific qualities
6. Period

One or two literatures

1. Specific kinds
2. Specific scopes
3. Period
4. Specific themes and subjects
5. Specific elements
6. Specific qualities
7. Works for and by specific kinds of persons

In all cases, the preference orders are the same for collections of literary texts and criticism of the texts.

Sometimes elements low in the priority listings can be added to a number after the higher priority elements. For example, a critical appraisal of later-20th-century American fiction about the sea is classed in 813.540932162: 813 (American fiction) + 54 (period: later 20th century) + 09 (critical appraisal) + 32162 (theme: the sea). The period is given first because it has higher priority than the theme; but the theme can also be expressed. The same preference order is used for these additional elements, e.g., for critical appraisal of later-20th-century American fiction about the sea by women, the theme of the sea would be expressed by means of Table 3–C and the authorship by a specific kind of person would not, because themes appear higher in the priority listing.

Sometimes aspects low in the priority listings can be expressed only by means of standard subdivision notation from Table 1. In the example of a critical appraisal of American fiction of the later 20th century about the sea by women, notation 082 from Table 1 could be used to bring out the aspect of women: 813.540932162082. For another example, a collection of 19th-century fiction of several literatures about urban life is classed in 808.83932173209034: 808.839 (collection of fiction from more than two literatures displaying specific features) + 321732 (theme: urban life) + 09034 (standard subdivision for the historical period of the 19th century). In the priority listing, theme comes before period; and once the theme has been expressed, there is no way to express the period except by use of the standard subdivision.

See also discussion at 808.8, T3B—08–09, and specific forms in Table 3–B for additional priority listings.

Number building

Examples of number building are given in the *Manual* at the beginning of Table 3. The following flow charts are offered as an aid to building numbers and as a supplement to the detailed directions at Table 3–B.

Flow chart B: Works by or about more than one author

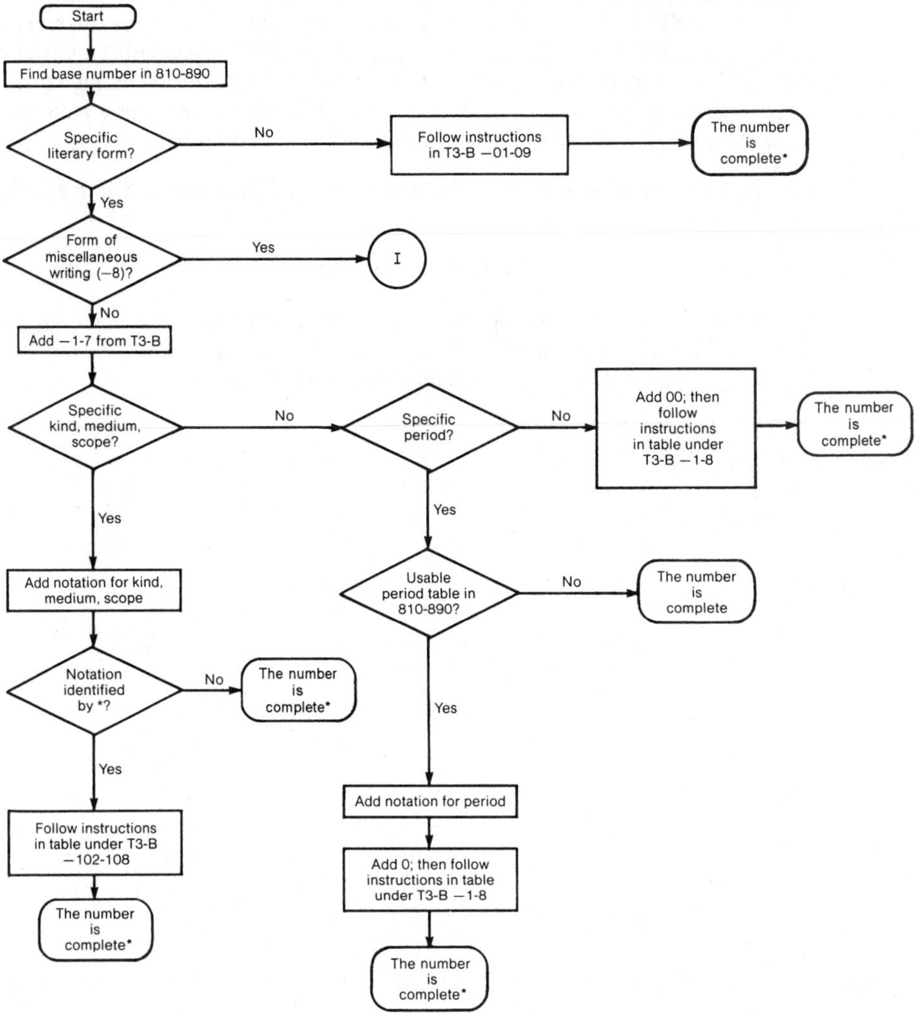

*If appropriate, standard subdivisions may be added

Flow chart B for notation 8 Miscellaneous writings

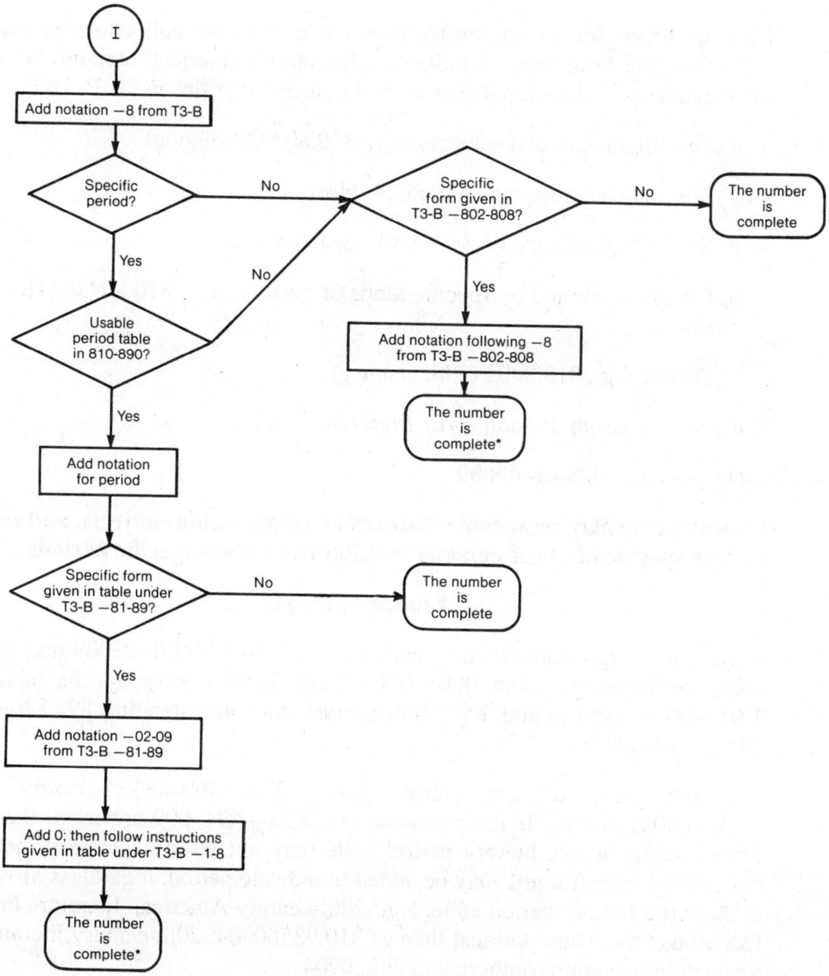

*If appropriate, standard subdivisions may be added

T3B—08 and T3B—09

Collections of literary texts in more than one form [and] History, description, critical appraisal of works in more than one form

Preference order

Here are examples illustrating the preference order for collections of texts in more than one form from an individual literature (American literature used for the examples). The preference order is the same for criticism (T3B—09).

1. Specific themes and subjects, e.g., 810.80382 (religion)
2. Specific elements, e.g., 810.8024 (plot)
3. Specific qualities, e.g., 810.8013 (idealism)
4. Literature for and by specific kinds of persons, e.g., 810.809282 (for children)
5. Period, e.g., 810.8003 (19th century)

See also discussion at Table 3–B: Preference order.

T3B—091–099 vs. T3B—09001–09009

Literature displaying specific features or emphasizing subjects, and for and by specific kinds of persons vs. Literature from specific periods

Literary periods

If there is no applicable literary period table, T3B—09001–09009 may not be used; moreover, notation 0901–0905 from Table 1 may not be added to T3B—09 to show period, e.g., 20th-century Amharic literature 892.8709 (*not* 892.8709000904).

However, the rule of zeros gives T3B—091–099 priority over T3B—09001–09009. If the provisions of T3B—091–099 are used, then any otherwise applicable literary period table may not be used. Instead, notation 0901–0905 from Table 1 may be added to indicate period, regardless of whether there is a literary period table, e.g., 20th-century American literature in English on historical and political themes 810.93580904, 20th-century literature in Spanish by Argentine authors 860.99820904.

T3B—1

Poetry

Preference order

Here are examples illustrating the preference order for poetry (A) from more than two literatures and (B) from one or two literatures. The preference order is the same for collections and criticism.

A. Poetry from more than two literatures

(Collections used as example)

1. Specific kinds, e.g., 808.8142 (sonnets)
2. Specific themes and subjects, e.g., 808.819353 (friendship)
3. Specific elements, e.g., 808.81922 (description)
4. Specific qualities, e.g., 808.819145 (romanticism)
5. Period, e.g., 808.81033 (18th century)

B. Poetry from one or two literatures

(Criticism of American poetry used as example)

1. Specific kinds, e.g., 811.032 (epic)
2. Period, e.g., 811.5409 (later 20th century)
3. Specific themes and subjects, e.g., 811.009353 (friendship)
4. Specific elements, e.g., 811.00922 (description)
5. Specific qualities, e.g., 811.00914 (romanticism)
6. Works for and by specific kinds of persons, e.g., 811.0098924 (by Jews)

See also discussion at Table 3–B: Preference order.

T3B—102–108, T3B—205, T3B—308 vs. T3C—1, T3C—3

[Specific kinds of poetry, drama, fiction] vs. [Arts and literature displaying specific qualities of style, mood, viewpoint or dealing with specific themes and subjects]

The numbers for specific kinds of poetry, drama, and fiction are for works belonging to specific literary genres, e.g., the genres of historical drama T3B—20514 and realistic fiction T3B—3083. Often the themes and other characteristics that mark specific genres can also be expressed by means of notation 1 or 3 from Table 3–C, e.g., works about historical themes T3C—358, works displaying realism T3C—12. For literary works belonging to a specific genre, always prefer the genre number over the number derived from Table 3–C; for example, a collection of historical drama is classed in T3B—2051408, not T3B—20080358; criticism of realistic novels in T3B—308309, not T3B—300912. Notation 1 or 3 from Table 3–C may be added to the genre number if it is not redundant. For example, T3C—358 is added for a discussion of historical themes in tragedy (T3B—2051209358), but not for a discussion of historical themes in historical drama.

Notation 1 or 3 from Table 3–C may be used for literary works that display specific features and are not limited to a specific genre, e.g., a discussion of historical themes in serious and comic drama not limited by period

T3B—2009358, a discussion of realistic elements in fiction of various kinds not limited by period T3B—300912. Notation 1 or 3 from Table 3–C may also be used for literary works displaying specific features that might be regarded as marking a genre but where no such genre is named for the relevant literary form in Table 3–B. For example, under T3B—205 Specific kinds of drama, there is no mention of western drama; thus it is possible to use T3B—20093278 for a discussion of western drama not limited by period. For western fiction, however, use genre notation 30874 from Table 3–B (*not* T3B—30093278).

If in doubt between T3B—102–108, T3B—205, or T3B—308 and T3C—1 or T3C—3 for a literary work, prefer the notation from Table 3–B.

Notation from Table 3–B is used only for literature (belles lettres); it is never used for the arts, for films, for radio or television programs. Therefore, notation 1 and 3 from Table 3–C are used to express genre for the arts, films, radio and television programs. For example, use T3C—15 for science fiction in the arts, in film, in radio and television programs; but use T3B—30876 for science fiction as a genre of fiction. Use T3C—11 for experimental works in the arts, for experimental films, for experimental radio and television programs; however, use T3B—807 for experimental literary works without identifiable literary form.

T3B—2

Drama

Preference order

Here are examples illustrating the preference order for drama (A) from more than two literatures and (B) from one or two literatures. The preference order is the same for collections and criticism.

A. Drama from more than two literatures

(Criticism used as example)

1. Specific media, e.g., 809.225 (television)
2. Specific scopes, e.g., 809.241 (one-act plays)
3. Specific kinds, e.g., 809.2512 (tragedy)
4. Specific themes or subjects, e.g., 809.29351 (Faust)
5. Specific elements, e.g., 809.2925 (stream of consciousness)
6. Specific qualities, e.g., 809.29145 (romanticism)
7. Period, e.g., 809.204 (20th century)

B. Drama from one or two literatures
(Collections of American drama used as example)

1. Specific media, e.g., 812.025083548 (television plays on death)

2. Specific scopes, e.g., 812.04108 (one-act plays)

3. Specific kinds, e.g., 812.051208 (tragedy)

4. Period, e.g., 812.5408 (collection of later 20th century, no focus), 812.540809287 (20th century, by women)

5. Specific themes and subjects, e.g., 812.008036 (weather)

6. Specific elements, e.g., 812.008027 (characters)

7. Specific qualities, e.g., 812.008015 (symbolism)

8. Works for and by specific kinds of persons, e.g., 812.008092827 (for girls)

See also discussion at Table 3–B: Preference order.

T3B—3

Fiction

Preference order

Here are examples illustrating the preference order for fiction (A) from more than two literatures and (B) from one or two literatures. The preference order is the same for collections and criticism.

A. Fiction from more than two literatures
(Collections used as example)

1. Specific kinds, e.g., 808.8383 (sociological)

2. Specific scopes, e.g., 808.831 (short stories)

3. Specific themes and subjects, e.g., 808.839362 (animals)

4. Specific elements, e.g., 808.83922 (description)

5. Specific qualities, e.g., 808.83913 (idealism)

6. Period, e.g., 808.83034 (19th century)

B. Fiction from one or two literatures
(Criticism of American fiction used as example)

1. Specific kinds, e.g., 813.0876209 (science fiction)

2. Specific scopes, e.g., 813.0109358 (short stories about war)

3. Period, e.g., 813.5409 (later 20th century), 813.540932162 (later 20th century, about the sea)

4. Specific themes and subjects, e.g., 813.009351 (about King Arthur)

5. Specific elements, e.g., 813.00927 (characters)

6. Specific qualities, e.g., 813.00912 (naturalism)

7. Works for and by specific kinds of persons, e.g., 813.009896073 (fiction by African Americans)

See also discussion at Table 3–B: Preference order.

T3B—308729 vs. T3B—3085

Gothic fiction vs. Love and romance

Some modern fiction is called Gothic romance even when it does not contain most of the traditional elements of 18th- and 19th-century Gothic fiction, such as the supernatural and the isolated, picturesque setting. This modern romance is classed in T3B—3085. The traditional Gothic romance, however, is classed in T3B—308729. If in doubt, prefer T3B—308729.

T3B—7 vs. T3C—17

Humor and satire vs. Comedy

Class in T3C—17 textbooks and teaching collections showing the development of manifestations of comedy in literature of various forms. Class collections of humor in various forms to be read for pleasure in T3B—7008. If in doubt, prefer T3B—7008.

Table 3–C. Additional Notation for Arts and Literature

T3C—353–358 vs. T3C—352

Specific human, social, scientific, technical, artistic, literary, historical, political themes vs. Specific kinds of persons

Class in T3C—352 works on specific kinds of persons that treat no particular theme other than the person as a person, e.g., a work on women with no particular theme other than women T3C—352042. Also class in T3C—352 works on specific kinds of persons that treat multiple types of themes associated with the person, e.g., a work on many types of themes associated with heroes T3C—352. Class in T3C—353–358 a specific theme or specific type of theme associated with a specific kind of person unless there is emphasis on the person as a person. For example, class a work about the theme of war associated with soldiers in T3C—358 rather than T3C—352355 unless there is strong emphasis on the soldiers as persons. If in doubt, prefer T3C—353–358.

T3C—37 vs. T3C—15

The supernatural, mythological, legendary vs. Symbolism, allegory, fantasy, myth

Class in T3C—15 abstract myths not tied to specific mythologies of the past, e.g., the myth of a search for lost innocence. Class in T3C—37 mythological themes closely tied to specific mythologies of the past, e.g., Roman mythology in Renaissance poetry. If in doubt, prefer T3C—37.

Class specific mythological persons in T3C—351, specific kinds of mythological persons in T3C—352, mythology as a religious theme in T3C—3829113.

T3C—93-99, T3C—9174 vs. T3C—8

Literature for and by persons resident in specific continents, countries, localities [and Literature for and by persons resident in regions where specific racial, ethnic, national groups predominate] vs. Literature for and by persons of racial, ethnic, national groups

Prefer T3C—8 over T3C—93–99 with two exceptions. The first exception is for groups that predominate in an area, e.g., a collection of English literature by persons of Irish ancestry in Australia 820.8089162094, but a collection of English literature by persons of Irish ancestry in Ireland 820.809415; a collection of Spanish literature by Mexican-Americans 860.8086872073, but a collection of Spanish literature by Mexicans 860.80972; a collection of French literature by Arabs in France 840.808927044, but a collection of French literature by Arabs in North Africa 840.80961. The second exception is for the ethnic or national group so closely associated with the language that specifying the group would be redundant, e.g., a collection of Arabic literature by Arabs 892.708 (*not* 892.70808927); thus a collection of Arabic literature by Arabs residing in France would be 892.7080944 (*not* 892.70808927044).

Do not use T3C—9174 for groups-of-persons treatment because such use would practically duplicate the group treatment numbers; for example, Arabs who are residents of all areas where they predominate taken together constitute the overwhelming majority of all Arabs, so that T3C—8927 would be used for them rather than T3C—9174927. In most cases, however, use of T3C—8 would be redundant; for example, most books about literature by Arabs from all areas where they predominate are about literature in Arabic, so that expressing the ethnic group Arabs with either T3C—9174 or T3C—8 would be redundant.

If in doubt, prefer T3C—93–99.

T3C—93–99

Literature for and by persons resident in specific continents, countries, localities

Notation 93–99 from Table 3–C is used primarily for the following:

1. Literature in a language by persons from a certain area within a country, e.g., a collection of American literature by residents of Illinois 810.809773.

2. Literature in a language by persons in a country other than the traditional homeland of the dominant literature of the language, e.g., a collection of Spanish literature by Chilean authors 860.80983. The persons in a country other than the traditional homeland may be either native or nonnative residents of the country, e.g., a collection of English literature by non-Japanese residents of Japan 820.80952.

3. Literature in a language by residents of several countries on the same continent from more than one period (only for works in which the literature of one country does not predominate), e.g., French literature by residents of France, Switzerland, Belgium 840.8094; French literature by residents of Africa 840.8096.

Do not use T3C—93–99 for literature in a language by persons in the traditional homeland of the dominant literature of the language except for persons in only part of the country, e.g., a collection of Spanish literature by residents of Spain 860.8, but a collection of Spanish literature by residents of Madrid 860.8094641.

It is the practice of the Decimal Classification Division not to use T3C—943 for German literature by residents of the Federal Republic of Germany, but to use T3C—9436 for German literature by residents of Austria.

It is the practice of the Decimal Classification Division not to use T3C—973 for literature in English by residents of the United States, but to use T3C—971 for literature in English by residents of Canada.

Table 4. Subdivisions of Individual Languages and Language Families

T4—1-5 and T4—8 vs. **T4—7**

Description and analysis of the standard form of the language [and] Standard usage of the language (Prescriptive linguistics) Applied linguistics vs. Historical and geographic variations, modern nongeographic variations

Remember that a language may have multiple standard forms. A work on standard Australian English pronunciation, for example, is classed in 421.52, not 427.994. A work on Australian English pronunciation is classed in 427.994 only if it stresses the distinctive characteristics that make Australian pronunciation different from British or American pronunciation. If in doubt, prefer T4—1-5 and T4—8.

T4—3 vs. **T4—81**

Dictionaries of the standard form of the language vs. [Standard usage of] Words

Works classed in T4—3 are intended for ready-reference use. While specialized dictionaries may be arranged in other ways besides alphabetically (e.g., picture dictionaries in subject order, thesauri in classified order), the order must be appropriate for ready reference.

Works classed in T4—81 are intended to be read or studied in full in order to learn vocabulary. They may be informal and entertaining, e.g., narratives for small children, or they may be formally organized into lessons with quizzes.

If in doubt, prefer T4—3.

T4—32-39

Bilingual dictionaries

The Decimal Classification Division classes a bilingual dictionary with entry words in both languages with the language coming later in the sequence 420–490.

T4—7

Historical and geographic variations, modern nongeographic variations

A specific pidgin or creole is classed as a variation of the source language from which more of its vocabulary comes than from its other source language(s). A pidgin or creole is customarily associated with a specific geographic area and is therefore classed in T4—709 plus the area number from Table 2 or in one of the subdivisions of T4—7 for geographic variations where they are provided in 420–490, e.g., the Krio language of Sierra Leone 427.9664.

T4—862

Readers for new literates

Works intended to serve as readers to help newly literate adults improve their reading skills are classed in T4—862, even if they focus on a specific subject or discipline. Readers for newly literate adults usually indicate the work's intended use somewhere in the prefatory material. The works may contain questions to check reading comprehension and glosses to help with difficult words. If in doubt, prefer T4—862 over subject or discipline.

Table 5. Racial, Ethnic, National Groups

Table 5 and Table 6 Languages are similar, both based on the traditional sequence of languages in 420–490. Two tables have been developed, however, because language and nationality do not always match. For example, there are Canadian people (T5—11 in Table 5), but no Canadian language; there is a Yiddish language (T6—391 in Table 6) but no Yiddish people.

The citation order given at some specific numbers in Table 5 differs from the generally preferred citation order of ethnic group over nationality. For example, for Canadians of French and British origin, the prescribed citation order is nationality first (T5—11 Canadians), then ethnic group: T5—112 for Canadians of British origin, T5—114 for Canadians of French origin. The numbers T5—21071 (T5—21 people of British Isles + [notation from Table 2] T2—71 Canada) and T5—41071 (T5—41 French + T2—71 Canada) are used only for persons of British and French origin in Canada who are not Canadian citizens. In the absence of specific instructions to the contrary, however, use the citation order given at the beginning of the table, e.g., Canadians of Ukrainian descent T5—91791071 (*not* T5—11). The same number is used for both Canadians of Ukrainian descent and persons of Ukrainian descent who are in Canada but not Canadian citizens. This lumping together of citizens and noncitizens is typical for Table 5 because of the low priority normally given to nationality; the developments for Canadians of British and French descent are atypical.

Normally the same number is used for both the majority ethnic group of a nation and the total population viewed as a national group, e.g., T5—94541 for both ethnic Finns and all citizens of Finland viewed as a national group. In such cases the question of priority between ethnic and national affiliation arises only for minority ethnic groups. Finnish citizens who are ethnic Swedes, a minority ethnic group, are classed in T5—39704897 (T5—397 Swedes + [notation from Table 2] T2—4897 Finland) because their ethnic group takes priority over their nationality. If Finnish citizens who are ethnic Finns move to the United States, their number in Table 5 is T5—94541073 (T5—94541 Finns + [notation from Table 2] T2—73 United States); but if Finnish citizens who are ethnic Swedes move to the United States, their number is T5—397073 (Swedes + United States), the same number for all persons of Swedish descent in the United States. The Finnish national origin is not expressed because of the low priority given to nationality. The exception to this rule occurs when the present location of the group is defined by the class number to which Table 5 notation is added, so that it is possible to express both present and past specific location of the group, e.g., ethnic Swedes from Finland in United States history 973.0439704897.

Special developments that allow expression of both ethnic and national affiliation are typically made only for the majority ethnic group in a nation, under the rubric "national group." Thus T5—6887 expresses both Spanish American ethnicity and Venezuelan nationality, while T5—9697292 expresses both African ancestry and Jamaican nationality. There is no special development to express both African ancestry and Venezuelan nationality because Blacks are a minority in Venezuela and cannot be called a "national group." The number for Black Venezuelans in England (T5—96042) is the same as the number for Blacks in general in England; the link to Venezuela is not expressed (except when it is possible to express both present and past location, e.g., Blacks from Venezuela in English history 942.00496087). The Table 5 numbers for Venezuelans of Spanish origin in England (T5—6887042) and Black Jamaicans in England (T5—9697292042), by contrast, always express the national origins.

An atypical development for United States Blacks (T5—96073) gives extra emphasis to nationality for a minority group, while still preserving the usual citation order of ethnic group before nationality. The full Table 5 number for Black U.S. citizens in New York is T5—960730747, but for Black noncitizens in New York T5—960747. For most ethnic groups in the United States, there are no such special developments; thus, for example, T5—510747 specifies persons of Italian descent in New York regardless of whether they are U.S. citizens. The Table 5 number for United States Blacks in England (T5—96073042) always expresses the U.S. national origin, but the number for Italian Americans in England (T5—51042) is the same as for Italians in England (with the usual exception for history, e.g., Italian Americans in English history 942.00451073).

In some cases, special developments for national groups lead to the number for a national group being clearly different from the number for the majority ethnic group of the country. For example, the number for the Bhutanese as a national group is T5—91418; but the Bhutia, the majority ethnic group, speak Tibetan dialects and are classed as an ethnic group with the Tibetans in T5—954. In some other cases, the national-group number for a country may be seen as expressing or not expressing the ethnicity of the majority of the population, depending on how one defines that ethnicity. For example, the national-group numbers for all the modern nations of Latin America where Spanish is at least one of the official languages express Spanish-American ethnicity, though the majority of the population in some countries is of native American origin. In Guatemala, 55% of the population is of Mayan origin; but a majority of the people, including some of the Maya, speak Spanish and follow Spanish-American customs. Class works that discuss all the people of a nation in the national-group number specified in the table. Class works that focus on a specific ethnic group with the ethnic group. If the national-group number expresses the appropriate ethnicity, use it for a work that focuses on a specific ethnic group. For example, class in T5—687281 works that discuss all the people of Guatemala and works that focus on the Guatemalans who speak Spanish and follow Spanish-American customs; but class in T5—97415207281 works that focus on the Maya of Guatemala.

T5—1

North Americans

Use this number and its subdivisions for (a) comprehensive works on all the peoples of North America, (b) the people of Canada (T5—11) and the United States (T5—13) as national groups, (c) North Americans of British origin, and (d) Canadians of French origin (T5—114). Works focusing on other national or ethnic groups in North America are all classed elsewhere in Table 5, e.g., people of French origin in the United States T5—41073, Mexicans as a national group T5—6872, the Inuit T5—9712.

T5—112, T5—114 vs. T5—2, T5—41

Canadians of British origin [and] Canadians of French origin vs. British, English, Anglo-Saxons [and] French

Use T5—112 for Canadian citizens of British origin and T5—114 for Canadian citizens of French origin, even with numbers that already specify Canada, e.g., 971.004112 for Canadian citizens of British ancestry in Canadian history. Use T5—112 or T5—114 for accounts of persons of British or French ancestry becoming Canadian citizens. Also use T5—112 and T5—114 for persons of British or French origin living in the territory that later became the nation Canada if they are regarded as among the precursors of British or French Canadians or founders of the nation, e.g., the French in Canada 1600–1867 971.004114.

Use T5—2 and T5—41 for persons of British or French ancestry who were not and never became Canadian citizens, even though they may have resided in Canada or in the territory that later became Canada. The inhabitants of the French colony Acadia in what is now Nova Scotia who were expelled in 1755 and became the Cajuns of today's Louisiana were never Canadian citizens; hence the correct notation for Louisiana Cajuns is T5—410763, not T5—1140763.

If in doubt, prefer T5—112 or T5—114.

T5—13 vs. T5—2073, T5—21073

People of United States ("Americans") vs. [British, English, Anglo-Saxons in United States] and [People of British Isles in United States]

Use T5—13 rather than T5—2073 or T5—21073 for U.S. citizens of British ancestry, even with a number that already means United States, e.g., British Americans in U.S. history 973.0413. Use T5—13 for comprehensive works on both U.S. citizens and non-U.S. citizens of British ancestry in the United States. Use T5—13 for accounts of persons of British ancestry becoming U.S citizens. Use T5—2073 or T5—21073 for non-U.S. citizens of British ancestry in the United States. (If T5—2 or T5—21 is used with a number that already means United States, then notation 073 is dropped as redundant, e.g., all non-citizens of British ancestry in U.S. history 973.042.) If in doubt, prefer T5—13.

T5—201–209 vs. T5—2101–2109

[British English Anglo-Saxons by area] vs. [People of British Isles by area]

Use T5—2101–2109 for persons of British ancestry in an area when they are or have most recently been citizens of the United Kingdom, e.g., persons from the United Kingdom in the Third World T5—2101724. Use T5—201–209 for persons of British ancestry in an area when many of them are or have most recently been citizens of the United States, Canada, Australia, and New Zealand, e.g., persons from the United Kingdom, the United States, Canada, and Australia in the Third World T5—201724. If in doubt, prefer T5—201–209.

T5—9141

National groups [of South Asians]

As specified in the see reference at T5—9141, Trinidadians and Fijians of South Asian origin are classed according to their nationality rather than their ethnic origins. Other South Asians, however, are classed according to the normal citation order for Table 5, which gives precedence to ethnic origins. For example, South Africans of South Asian descent are classed in T5—914068 (*not* T5—968).

T5—9435

[Turks]

Class here (a) the people of Turkey as a national group; (b) people who speak, or whose ancestors spoke, Turkish (Osmanli Turks and their descendants), including those who are not Turkish nationals, e.g., Turkish Cypriots T5—943505693.

T5—948 vs. T5—914

Dravidians and Scytho-Dravidians vs. South Asians

Speakers of Marathi (notation 9146 in Table 6) and Sindhi (notation 91411 in Table 6) are classed as Scytho-Dravidians in T5—948. If in doubt, prefer T5—948.

T5—96073

African Americans (United States Blacks)

In Table 5 notation 96073 for African Americans, the 073 signifies U.S. nationality rather than location; it is never dropped even where it would be redundant if it simply signified location, e.g., 973.0496073 African Americans in U.S. history (as distinct from 973.0496 for noncitizens of African ancestry in U.S. history), 305.8960730747 sociology of African Americans in New York (as distinct from 305.8960747 sociology of non-U.S. citizens of African ancestry in New York). This notation for African Americans is atypical; usually 073 added to a Table 5 number simply signifies location, and it is dropped whenever it is redundant, e.g., 973.046872 Mexican Americans in U.S. history (*not* 973.046872073), 305.8968720747 sociology of Mexican Americans in New York (*not* 305.8968720730747).

Table 6. Languages

T6—926

Canaanite languages

Minoan Linear A

It is not known what language is represented by the Minoan Linear A script. At one time the language was thought to be a West Semitic language, and works on the script have been classed in T6—926 Canaanite languages for many years. If the script is deciphered and the language identified as a non-Canaanite language, then Minoan Linear A will be moved to the appropriate place.

T6—9639

Bantu languages

The subdivisions of Bantu languages are adapted from the Voegelins' arrangement of Guthrie's Bantu language zones. See Charles F. and Florence M. Voegelin, *Classification and Index of the World's Languages* (New York: Elsevier, 1977), and Malcolm Guthrie, *Comparative Bantu; an Introduction to the Comparative Linguistics and Prehistory of the Bantu languages* (Farnborough: Gregg, 1967–1971).

Notes on Schedule Numbers

000

Generalities

Two categories of works fall within the Generalities class:

(1) Works in "umbrella" or "tool" disciplines, that is, disciplines relating to or applied to many other disciplines, e.g., systems analysis and computer science (003–006), bibliography (010 and 090), library and information sciences (020), museology (069), journalism and publishing (070). In some cases the links between these disciplines and other disciplines may be shown by attachment of a number from the 001–999 span, e.g., 016.54 bibliographies of chemistry, 026.61 medical libraries. In other cases the links may be shown by the use of standard subdivisions notation from Table 1, e.g., systems analysis in civil engineering 624.011, computer applications in business 650.0285.

(2) Multidisciplinary works, e.g., general encyclopedias (030), general periodicals (050), works on general organizations (060), general collections (080). There is parallel standard subdivisions notation in Table 1 for three of these types of works, so that they may be shown in connection with specific subjects:

030 General encyclopedic works

T1—03 Dictionaries, encyclopedias, concordances

050 General serial publications

T1—05 Serial publications

060 General organizations . . .

T1—06 Organizations . . .

001.9 and 130

Controversial knowledge [and] Paranormal phenomena

001.9 and 130 both pertain to topics in the twilight realms of half-knowledge, topics that refuse either to be disproved or to be brought into the realm of certain and verifiable knowledge. Certain characteristics of a work are good indicators that they belong in either 001.9 or 130:

1. A claim of access to secret or occult sources;

2. A rejection of established authority;

3. A pronounced reverence for iconoclasts, for laymen-become-experts;

4. An uncritical acceptance of lay observation of striking phenomena;

5. A fixation on the unexplained, the enigmatic, the mysterious;

6. A confidence verging on certainty in the existence of conspiracies and the working of malevolent forces;

7. An acknowledgment of the powers of extraterrestrial beings or intelligences (other than religious beings).

Phenomena classed in 130 are closely linked to human beings—the human mind, human capabilities and powers, human happiness. Phenomena classed in 001.9 are not closely linked to humans. In case of doubt, and for interdisciplinary works, prefer 001.9.

003

Systems

Despite having names that make them sound quite different, systems analysis and operations research often deal with the same problems using the same techniques, especially mathematical models of systems. They are classed in the same numbers because there is not enough difference to justify separate numbers.

Class works treating systems in related disciplines in the appropriate broad number for those disciplines, using notation 011 from Table 1, e.g., systems in medicine, engineering, management, and manufacturing 601.1. To be classed in 003 a work must be applicable to at least three main classes (e.g., 300, 500, 600).

Class use of systems analysis and operations research in management in 658.4032. Be especially careful with works on operations research, because they often appear at first glance to be general, but in fact emphasize management applications.

See also discussion at 003 vs. 004.21.

003 vs. 004.21

Systems vs. Systems analysis and design

In addition to the analysis and design of computer-based systems, class in 004.21 systems analysis of a user's problem in order to design a computer-based system to solve it. Class a work on systems analysis and design that is not concerned primarily with computer-based systems in 003 or with the specific system. If in doubt, prefer 003.

003.2

Forecasting and forecasts

Most works on forecasting and forecasts treat primarily social forecasting; such works are classed in 303.49. Works classed in 003 treat forecasting as applied in a variety of social and nonsocial disciplines. Such works typically focus on methods of forecasting. Interdisciplinary works that stress forecasting in a particular kind of system are classed with the system in 003.7–.8, e.g., forecasting in stochastic systems 003.760112.

003.5 vs. 629.8

Theory of communication and control vs. Automatic control engineering

Class interdisciplinary works on control of living and nonliving systems in 003.5 or with various specific kinds of systems in 003.7–.8. Class automatic control of man-made physical systems in 629.8. If in doubt, prefer 003.5.

003.7

Kinds of systems

Many kinds of systems are defined in terms of the equations used to model them, e.g., distributed-parameter systems are defined as systems governed by partial differential equations. Other equations may be used to model the behavior of the same real-world system. Class a work about a specific kind of system according to the way the work describes the system, e.g., a work that discusses applying the mathematics of stochastic (random) processes to systems 003.76.

004–006

[Data processing Computer science]

Here are key questions to guide in classifying works about computer science, with sample titles and references to relevant Manual notes.

004–006 vs. other disciplines

1. Is the work (A) computer science per se (004–006), or (B) an application of computers to another discipline (T1—0285)?

A. Understanding parallel processing computers and technology 004.35

B. Parallel computational fluid dynamics: implementations and results using parallel computers 532.050285435
532.05 ([Fluid] Dynamics) + T1—0285 (Data processing Computer applications) + 435 (from 004.35 Multiprocessing)

See also discussion at T1—0285.

2. If the work gives broad coverage to computers, is it (A) predominantly about computer science (004), or (B) predominantly about the role of computers in society (300), e.g., computers and the right of privacy (323.448)? Works that are predominantly about computer science often have a chapter about the role of computers in society; such works should still be classed in 004.

A. Introduction to computers 004

B. Computers and social change 303.4834

See also discussion at 303.483 vs. 306.45, 306.46.

3. If the work covers hardware topics, is it about (A) computer engineering (621.39), or (B) use of computer hardware (004), or hardware and software combined (004)?

A. Build your own PC clone and save a bundle 621.3916
Discusses hardware only; says nothing about software.

B. Upgrade your PC: hardware and software to give your PC a new lease on life 004.165

See also discussion at 004–006 vs. 621.39.

4. If the work is highly mathematical, is it (A) mathematics (510), or (B) mathematics applied to computer science (004–006 + T1—0151)?

A. Introduction to the theory of Turing machines 511.3

B. The role of mathematical logic in computer science 004.015113
004 (Data processing Computer science) + T1—015 (Scientific principles) + 113 (from 511.3 Mathematical logic)

See also discussion at 005.1 vs. 510; also at 005.101; also at 510, T1—0151 vs. 004–006, T1—0285.

5. If the work is about databases or information systems, is it (A) computer science (005.74–.75) or (B) information science (025.04–.06)?

A. Full-text database management systems: data structures and database design 005.759

B. User's guide to searching full-text databases online 025.04

See also discussion at 005.74.

6. If the work is about computer communications, is it about (A) computer science aspects (004–005) or (B) economic and related aspects (384.3)?

A. The Internet: what it is and how it works 004.678

B. Directory of Internet access providers 384.33

See also discussion at 004.6 vs. 384.3; also at 004.678 vs. 025.04, 384.33.

Within 004–006

Once you have determined that the work belongs in 004–006 rather than in one of the alternative class numbers discussed above, you must decide whether the work is about a special computer method only (006); programming, programs, and data only (005); hardware only (004); or hardware plus programming, programs, data (004). For special computer methods, both software (programming, programs, data) and hardware aspects are classed in 006.

Here is a summary to show the overall structure of 004–006.

004	Data processing Computer science
004.1	General works on specific types of computers
004.2	Systems analysis and design, computer architecture, performance evaluation
004.3	Processing modes
004.5	Storage
004.6	Interfacing and communications
004.7	Peripherals
004.9	Nonelectronic data processing
005	Computer programming, programs, data
005.1	Programming
005.2	Programming for specific types of computers, for specific operating systems, for specific user interfaces
005.3	Programs
005.4	Systems programming and programs
005.6	Microprogramming and microprograms
005.7	Data in computer systems
005.8	Data security
006	Special computer methods
006.3	Artificial intelligence
006.4	Computer pattern recognition
006.5	Computer sound synthesis
006.6	Computer graphics
006.7	Multimedia systems

The best way to approach the computer science schedule is to start at the end (006.78) and work backward toward 004. At 004, 005, and 006 there are instructions to class complex subjects with aspects in two or more subdivisions in the subdivision coming last in the schedule. Many works in computer science treat complex subjects to which these preference notes apply. The questions are:

1. Is the work limited to a special computer method (006)?

   A. Yes: Go to Key question: 006.

   B. No: Go to question 2.

2. Does the work cover 005 concepts only (programming, programs, data)?

   A. Yes: Go to Key question: 005.

   B. No: Go to question 3.

3. Does the work cover both hardware (004) and computer programming, programs, data (005)?

   A. Yes: Go to Key question: 004–005

   B. No: Go to Key questions: 004.

Key questions: 004

These key questions apply only to works limited to 004 concepts.

1. Does the work cover more than one 004 concept?

A. Yes: Are all the 004 concepts aspects of a single complex subject?

i. Yes: Class with the last number for a covered topic (following second note at 004).

Standards and protocols for local-area networks 004.68 (*not* 004.62)

ii. No: Unless there are notes to the contrary, follow the first-of-two rule.

Advances in distributed and parallel computing 004.35 (*not* 004.36)

B. No: Class in the appropriate subdivision of 004.

Computer tape cartridges: care and handling 004.56

See also discussion at 004 vs. 004.33; also at 004.1; also at 004.1 vs. 004.3; also at 004.11–.16; also at 004.24; also at 004.6.

Key question: 004–005

This key question applies only to works that cover concepts expressed in both 004 (computer hardware) and 005 (computer programming, programs, data).

1. What is the relationship between the 004 concept(s) and the 005 concept(s)?

A. The 004 and 005 concepts together constitute a single system. Class in 004 or a subdivision of 004.

Local-area networking with Novell Netware 004.68 (*not* 005.4476)
005.4476, the number for operating systems for distributed computer systems, is not used because the work covers hardware aspects of local-area networks as well as the networking software Novell Netware.

B. The information on the 004 concept is a brief supplement or background for the 005 concept. Class in 005 or a subdivision of 005.

Using microcomputers: core concepts and applications 005.36 (*not* 004.16)
004.16 is not used because only a small portion of the work treats microcomputer hardware; the work focuses on how to use microcomputer software.

C. The 005 concept is applied to the 004 concept. Class in 005 or a subdivision of 005.

Data security in client-server computer systems 005.8 (*not* 004.36)

D. The 004 concept is applied to the 005 concept. Class in 005 or a subdivision of 005. If the topic of the work approximates the whole of the class number, add T1—0285.

The Clipper chip: a microprocessor for data encryption 005.8202854165 (*not* 004.165)
005.82 (Data encryption) + T1—0285 (Data processing Computer applications) + 4165 (from 004.165 Specific digital microcomputers)

See also discussion at 004 vs. 005; also at 004.6 vs. 005.71.

Key question: 005

This key question applies only to works limited to 005 concepts (computer programming, programs, data).

1. Are all the 005 concepts aspects of a single complex subject?

A. Yes: Class with the last number in the schedule for a covered aspect, following the second note at 005.

Structured programming using Think Pascal on the Macintosh 005.265 (*not* 005.133 or 005.113)
The number for programming for specific microcomputers (005.265) comes later in the schedule than the numbers for specific programming languages (005.133) and structured programming (005.113).

B. No: Unless there are notes to the contrary, follow the first-of-two rule.

Advanced operating systems for parallel and distributed computing 005.4475 (*not* 005.4476)
005.44 (Operating systems for specific types of computers) + 75 (from 005.375 Programs for multiprocessor computers)
At 004.35 Multiprocessing is the note: Class here parallel processing.

See also discussion at 004 vs. 005; also at 004.6 vs. 005.71; also at 005: Examples from 005; also at 005.1–.2 vs. 005.42; also at 005.1 vs. 005.3; also at 005.3; also at 005.3 vs. 005.43–.45; also at 005.362.

Key question: 006

This question applies only to works limited to special computer methods.

1. Does the topic in 006 have subdivisions for hardware, programming, and programs?

A. Yes: In choosing between subdivisions for hardware, programming, and programs in 006, the same distinctions are made as between 004 and 005 concepts; hence the questions about 004 and 005 are relevant to choosing between hardware and software subdivisions of 006.

Reference guide to Harvard Graphics 006.6869
006.68 ([Computer graphics] Programs) + 69 (from 005.369 Specific [microcomputer] programs)

Harvard Graphics is a specific computer graphics program for microcomputers.

B. No: Class in the appropriate topical subdivision.

Macintosh animation software 006.696

004–006 vs. 621.39

[Data processing Computer science] vs. [Engineering of] Computers

Works classed in 004–006 treat (a) computer hardware from the user's viewpoint and/or (b) software or firmware. Works classed in 621.39 (a) treat computer hardware solely from the viewpoint of engineering, manufacturing, or repair and (b) do not treat software or the program aspect of firmware. Works limited to assembling the physical components of a computer system—the kind of activity that requires screwdrivers and a wrist grounding wire—are classed in 621.39. Comprehensive works on assembling the physical components and installing the software of a computer system are classed in 004. A work treating the physical processes of manufacturing firmware chips, not discussing the programs embodied in those chips, would be classed in 621.39. Comprehensive works on the computer science and computer engineering aspects of a computer topic are classed in 004–006. If in doubt, prefer 004–006.

Works treating 004–006 concepts may be classed in 621.39 only if the 004–006 concepts are applied to 621.39 concepts, as in computer graphics programs to assist in design of computer circuitry 621.3950285668.

621.39 parallels 004 in structure, except for 621.399, which is analogous to 006. Because certain numbers in 621.39 were skipped to minimize reuse of numbers, the parallel to 004 is not as close as it would otherwise be.

Computers in general; comprehensive works on digital computers	004	621.39
Digital supercomputers	004.11	621.3911
Digital mainframe computers	004.12	621.3912
Digital minicomputers	004.14	621.3914
Digital microcomputers	004.16	621.3916
Hybrid and analog computers	004.19	621.3919
Systems analysis and design, computer architecture, performance evaluation	004.2	621.392
Storage	004.5	621.397
Interfacing and communications	004.6	621.3981
Peripherals	004.7	621.3984
Special computer methods	006	621.399

There is no analogue for 004.3 Processing modes in 621.39 because most works focusing on processing modes include treatment of software or the program aspect of firmware and thus are not classed in 621.39. Class general works on the engineering of computers, processors (central processing units), computer systems distinguished by their processing modes in 621.391; class specific aspects of such machinery with the aspect, e.g., engineering design of multiprocessors 621.392.

Most works on computer architecture and computer performance evaluation include treatment of software or the program aspect of firmware; hence there are separate subdivisions of 004.2–.3 for these topics (004.22 Computer architecture, 004.24 Performance evaluation, and cognate subdivisions of 004.3), but no such separate subdivisions of 621.392. Works on these topics that truly are limited to computer engineering, however, are classed at 621.392.

Engineering of devices for the special computer methods named in 006 is classed in 621.399, whether the devices or methods are named there or not.

There is no analogue in 004 for 621.395 Circuitry because circuitry is strictly an engineering aspect of computers, not something that the computer user needs to understand.

Computer engineering is not part of notation 0285 in Table 1. It is, however, subject to the same rule that applies to electronic engineering in general: a specific application is classed with the application, e.g., electronic engineering of computers in robots 629.892.

004 vs. 004.33

Data processing Computer science vs. Real-time processing

When most data processing was batch processing, interactive, online, and real-time processing were close to synonymous. As the speed of data processing systems increased, real-time processing acquired the more restricted meaning of data processing systems that must meet constraints of timing and predictability in performing one or more tasks. Typical examples of real-time systems in this narrower sense include control systems, robotics, image processing, computer vision, and stock market tracking systems. Use 004.33 only for works on real-time processing in this narrower sense. Class works on interactive, online, and real-time processing in the sense of non-batch processing in 004. Class a specific application of real-time processing with the application, e.g., real-time computerized process control 629.895433. If in doubt, prefer 004.

004 vs. 005

Data processing Computer science vs. Computer programming, programs, data

Class in 004 works on computer hardware and works treating both computer hardware and the "soft" aspects of computer systems—programs, programming, and data. Class works treating only these "soft" aspects in 005. Be alert to words that can refer to either hardware or software: architecture, processing, communication, interfacing, system analysis, system design. Like other "system" phrases, system development and system specification can refer to hardware or to hardware plus software; however, they usually refer to software. Be alert for topics like multiprogramming and virtual memory, which technically have hardware aspects but in books are almost always discussed in terms of programming or programs, e.g., process management programs for multiprogramming (005.434), memory management programs for virtual memory (005.435).

Exception to the general rule that works treating both hardware and software are classed in 004: Class hardware applied to topics named in 005 with the topic using notation 0285 from Table 1, e.g., parallel architectures for database machines 005.740285435. Exception to the exception: Class hardware for interfacing and data communications in 004.6 (*not* 005.71).

If in doubt, prefer 004.

See also discussion at 004.6 vs. 005.71.

004.1

General works on specific types of computers

In this number, its subdivisions, and analogous numbers elsewhere in 004–006 and 621.39, computers and processors (central processing units) are treated for classification purposes as if they were the same. In fact they are not, but few works about processors can avoid discussing the other parts of the computer with which the processor must interact; hence works about specific types of computers and processors are typically not different enough to justify separate numbers.

Programmable calculators are classed in 510.28541 rather than 004.1 because they are limited-function computers, capable of working only with numbers, not alphabetic data.

004.1 vs. 004.3

General works on specific types of computers vs. Processing modes

Many computers, processors, and computer systems can be classified either by type of computer as defined in 004.1 or by processing mode. Use 004.3 and its subdivisions only for works that emphasize the processing mode. For example, the Intel Pentium® processor is a microprocessor that supports multiprogramming, interactive processing, and multiprocessing. Use 004.165 for works discussing the Pentium in general, but class Pentium-based multiprocessing computers in 004.357. If in doubt, prefer 004.1 and its subdivisions.

004.11–.16

Digital computers

Use these numbers and the analogous engineering numbers (621.3911–.3916) with caution: use them only for works that emphasize the specific type of computer, not for works that may refer most of the time to a particular type as an illustration of what computers in general do. For example, use 004, not 004.12, for a general introduction to computers written at a time when the only computers were mainframes. If in doubt, prefer 004 or 621.39 without subdivision.

Supercomputers are the largest, fastest, most powerful, most expensive computers; mainframe computers are next; minicomputers are midrange computers; finally microcomputers are the smallest, slowest, least powerful and least expensive computers. Specific distinctions among these types of computers have been made in terms of performance or cost; but the distinctions vary from authority to authority, manufacturer to manufacturer, and especially over time. Both low-end mainframe computers and high-end microcomputers overlap minicomputers in performance and cost. Class a particular computer according to the way it is presented in the first work about it that a library acquires (unless it is known that that work presents an atypical view of the computer).

Do not class a work treating more than one computer or processor in a number for specific computers in 004–006 unless:

1. The work treats a single series of very closely related computers or processors (e.g., the IBM 390® series of mainframe computers 004.125 or the Intel 80x86® microprocessors 004.165); or

2. The work treats primarily one specific computer or processor but adds that it is also applicable to other similar machines (e.g., a work about programming the IBM PC® that says it can also be used as a guide to programming "IBM-compatible" computers 005.265).

Note: A work that discusses a computer and its processor is in effect a work about the computer and should be treated as such (e.g., a work about the Macintosh® computer and the Motorola 68000® series of microprocessors 004.165).

In case of doubt, do not use a number for specific computers.

004.21 vs. 004.22, 621.392

Systems analysis and design vs. Computer architecture vs. Systems analysis and design, computer architecture [in computer engineering]

In 004.21 systems analysis and design of a computer-based system involves a computer, application programs, and procedures, usually also other hardware, often a database and communications network, all working together to accomplish a task for the user.

In 004.22 computer architecture focuses on the design and structure of the computer itself and on the computer in relation to its peripheral devices. Most works on computer architecture treat software or the program aspect of firmware as well as hardware; but in the discussion of programs, the focus is on system programs, which make the computer function properly, rather than on application programs, which accomplish user tasks.

In 621.392 are classed works that treat computer hardware but do not treat software or firmware.

004.24

Performance evaluation

Class here only specialized works treating performance measurement and evaluation as an aid in designing or improving the performance of a computer system. Class general evaluations of computers in the appropriate general works number, e.g., general evaluations of microcomputers 004.16, of the Amiga 3000® 004.165. If in doubt, prefer the general works number. Add notation 0297 from Table 1 to the general works number if the emphasis is on evaluation as a consideration in purchasing, e.g., evaluation and purchasing manuals for microcomputers 004.160297.

004.6

Interfacing and communications

It is impossible to make a distinction useful for classification between computer interfacing and computer communications. For example, there are many similarities between (a) the interfacing techniques that link a computer and a printer located next to it and (b) the communications techniques that link a computer and a physically remote printer, terminal, or other computer. The schedule is designed so that the classifier need not distinguish computer interfacing from computer communications. In 004.6, 005.71, and 621.3981, computer interfacing and computer communications are classed in the same numbers.

See also discussion at 004.6 vs. 384.3.

004.6 vs. 005.71

Interfacing and communications vs. Data communications

These two numbers are parallel: interfacing is classed in both, and *computer communications* and *data communications* are synonyms. Class in 004.6 selection and use of computer interfacing and communications equipment—"hard" aspects. Class in 005.71 comprehensive works on "soft" aspects—programming, programs, and data in interfacing and communications. (Class specific data aspects of interfacing and communications with the aspect in 005.7–.8, e.g., error-correcting codes 005.72, data compression 005.746, data encryption 005.82.) Class comprehensive works on both the "hard" and "soft" aspects of computer interfacing and communications in 004.6.

004.6 vs. 384.3

Interfacing and communications vs. Computer communication

Class economic and related aspects of providing computer communication services to the public in 384.3. Works focusing on services and service providers, on broad issues of public good in relation to computer communication are classed in 384.3. Class computer communication and its hardware in office and private use, computer science applied to the technological aspects of computer communication, and interdisciplinary works in 004.6. Practical works explaining how to use the hardware and software involved in computer communications are classed in 004.6. If in doubt, prefer 004.6.

004.6 vs. 621.382, 621.3981

Interfacing and communications [in computer science] vs. Communications engineering vs. [Computer] Interfacing and communications devices

Digital communications

Exercise caution in classifying works on digital communications. If they emphasize engineering, they may be either computer data communications (621.3981), digital telecommunications (621.382), or digital aspects of both telecommunications and data communications (also 621.382). If in doubt between 621.382 or 621.3981, prefer 621.382.

However, in works that do not emphasize engineering, "digital communications" is apt to refer to communications in computer science 004.6. This number is used for works dealing with telecommunications and data communications engineering plus interfacing and communications in computer science. For the other choices for works not emphasizing engineering, see 004.6 vs. 005.71; 384.3 vs. 004.6.

If in doubt between 004.6 and 621.382 or 621.3981, prefer 004.6.

004.678 vs. 025.04, 384.33

Internet vs. Information storage and retrieval systems vs. [Computer communication] Activities and services

Internet

Class interdisciplinary works about the Internet in 004.678 if they contain a substantial amount of computer science material and at least some information about computer hardware. If an interdisciplinary work about the Internet does not contain enough computer science material to be classified in 004.678, the first alternate number to consider is 025.04.

Class computer science works about the Internet that are wholly or predominantly about communications software in 005.713, e.g., works emphasizing software packages for connecting to the Internet or emphasizing the commands needed for electronic mail, FTP, and telnet.

Class in 025.04 interdisciplinary works about the Internet that do not contain enough computer science material to be classified in 004.678, but that do contain some information science material. Class in 025.04 information science works that emphasize search and retrieval, including use of front-end systems and interfaces such as Gopher and Netscape® to facilitate search and retrieval on the Internet. Also class in 025.04 works that describe information resources available on the Internet.

Class in 384.33 works on Internet access providers and works on economic and public policy issues concerning the Internet.

If in doubt, prefer 004.678. If in doubt between 025.04 and 384.3, prefer 025.04.

005

Computer programming, programs, data

Text processing

Text processing as classed here is broader than word processing; it includes all computer processing of information coded as characters or sequences of characters (as contrasted with information coded as numbers), e.g., counting word frequency, making concordances, storing and retrieving text, sorting lists alphabetically. Class specific applications of text processing with the application, e.g., alphabetic sorting 005.741, word processing 652.5.

Examples from 005

Structured programming in Macintosh® assembly language 005.265
005.265 (Programming for specific [microcomputers])

Application programming for Windows NT® 005.268
005.268 (Programming for specific operating systems [for microcomputers])
Windows NT®, unlike Windows®, is an operating system.

Easy object programming for Windows® using Visual C++ 005.269
005.269 (Programming for specific user interfaces [for microcomputers])

Guide to parallel programming on Sequent® computer systems 005.2755
005.275 (Programming for multiprocessor computers) + 5 (from 005.265 Programming for specific computers)

Client/server programming with OS/2® 2.1 005.2768
005.276 (Programming for distributed computer systems) + 8 (from 005.268 Programming for specific operating systems)

A guide to the hottest Mac software 005.365
005.365 (Programs for specific [microcomputers])

Using microcomputer applications for DOS®: WordPerfect®, Lotus 1–2–3®, dBase IV® 005.3682
005.3682 (Programs for specific [microcomputer] operating systems

Learning to use Windows® applications: Microsoft Word® for Windows®, Microsoft Excel® for Windows®, Paradox® for Windows® 005.3684
005.3684 (Programs for specific user interfaces [for microcomputers])

Mastering Quattro Pro® for Windows® 005.369
005.369 (Specific programs [for microcomputers])

Developing utilities in Microsoft C® for the IBM PC® 005.42262
005.422 (Systems programming for specific types of computers, for specific operating systems, for specific user interfaces) + 62 (from 005.262 Programming [for microcomputers] in specific programming languages)

Unix® system programming 005.42282
005.422 (Systems programming for specific types of computers, for specific operating systems, for specific user interfaces) + 82 (from 005.282 Programming for specific operating systems [*not* limited by type of computer])

GUI development with C++®: creating interfaces portable to many types of computers 005.428
005.428 (Programming of user interfaces)

Symantec learning tools for the Norton Utilities® 005.43
005.43 (Systems programs Operating systems)

Unix® system administration guide 005.432
005.432 (Specific operating systems [*not* limited by type of computer])

Multitasking DOS® with DESQview/386® 005.43469
005.434 (Process management programs) + 69 (from 005.369 Specific programs [for microcomputers])

DOS 6® memory management 005.435682
005.435 (Memory management programs) + 682 (from 005.3682 Programs for specific [microcomputer] operating systems)

Hard disk management in DOS® 005.436682
005.436 (File system management programs) + 682 (from 005.3682 Programs for specific operating systems [for microcomputers])

Intermediate user's guide to Microsoft Windows® 3.1 005.43769
005.437 (User interfaces) + 69 (from 005.369 Specific programs [for microcomputers])

System 7.5® book: getting the most from your Macintosh operating system 005.4469
005.44 (Operating systems for specific types of computers) + 69 (from 005.369 Specific programs [for microcomputers])

Writing 0S/2® device drivers 005.71282
005.712 ([Data communications] Programming for specific types of computers, for specific operating systems, for specific user interfaces) + 82 (from 005.282 Programming for specific operating systems)

Paradox® for Windows®: self-instruction guide 005.7565
005.7565 (Specific relational database management systems)

Understanding HyperCard 005.7598
005.7598 (Specific full-text database management systems)

How to back up your PC® 005.86
005.86 (Data backup and recovery)

See also discussion at 004 vs. 005.

005.1–.2 vs. 005.42

[Programming] vs. Systems programming

Class in 005.42 works about writing systems programs, e.g., writing operating systems 005.42, writing user interfaces 005.428. Class in 005.1–.2 works on writing application programs and comprehensive works about writing both application and systems programs. Class in 005.1–.2 works about writing application programs that run on specific operating systems or user interfaces, e.g., writing application programs that run on the microcomputer operating system MS-DOS 005.268, writing application programs that run on the microcomputer graphical user interface Microsoft Windows 005.269. The key distinction is, What kind of programs are being written, systems programs or application programs? If in doubt, prefer 005.1–.2.

See also discussion at 005.3 vs. 005.43–.45 for the distinction between systems programs and application programs.

005.1 vs. 005.3

Programming vs. Programs

Class in 005.1 and other programming numbers works on writing programs, on software engineering, on modifying existing programs in ways that are typically done by computer programmers. Class in 005.3 and other numbers for programs works on using programs that have already been created by others, including works on writing macros of the kind that are typically written by end users of software packages.

Class in 005.1 and other programming numbers works on programming to achieve reliability, compatibility, portability, and other ideal qualities. Class in 005.3 and other numbers for programs works that discuss whether existing programs actually have these qualities.

Class in 005.10218 and 005.150218 standards for programs and program documentation that are aimed at programmers and documentation writers, to ensure that they produce good programs and documentation. Class in 005.30218 and other numbers for programs works that discuss standards to help users in selecting from among existing programs and documentation.

Class in 005.14 testing and measurement as part of program development. Class in 005.30287 and other numbers for programs works that discuss ways for users to test or measure programs as an aid in selection.

Class a work devoted equally to programming and programs in 005.1 Programming or 005.2 Programming for specific types of computers.

005.1 vs. 510

[Computer] Programming vs. Mathematics

Certain terms may be used for both a computer science concept and a mathematics concept. *Algorithm*, for example, may be used for processes to solve mathematical problems—with or without the aid of a computer. General works on algorithms in this sense are classed in 511.8. *Algorithm* may also be used in the context of computer programming for processes to solve many different kinds of problems—information-retrieval and word-processing problems, for example, as well as mathematical problems. General works on algorithms in this sense are classed 005.1.

Programming may refer to a branch of applied mathematics that has no necessary connection with computers, though computations necessary for this branch are commonly accomplished with the aid of a computer. For example, *linear programming* refers to the study of maximizing or minimizing a linear function $f(x_1, \ldots, x_n)$ subject to given constraints which are linear inequalities involving the variables of x_i. *Nonlinear programming* refers to the study of maximizing or minimizing a function of several variables, when the variables are constrained to yield values of other functions lying in a certain range, and either the function to be maximized or minimized, or at least one of the functions whose value is constrained, is nonlinear. Works on programming as a branch of applied mathematics are classed in 519.7. *Programming* may also refer to writing instructions to direct the operation of a computer or its peripheral equipment. Programming in this sense is classed in 005.1.

005.101

Philosophy and theory [of programming]

Notation 01 from Table 1 is not used here or with subdivisions of 005.1–.2 for general discussions of logic in programming because logic is inherent in programming and is discussed in nearly every work about programming. Notation 01 from Table 1 may be used for specialized works with an unusually intense focus on logical analysis. Typically such works treat not logic in general but rather symbolic (mathematical) logic, for which notation 015113 is used.

005.11

Special programming techniques

Here are classed special programming techniques as applied to the multiple phases of programming, e.g., works on functional programming that treat program design, coding, and testing 005.114. Special programming techniques applied to only one phase of programming are classed with the phase, e.g., works on functional program design 005.12, on how to create a programming language that facilitates functional programming 005.13, on functional programming with a specific programming language 005.133.

005.15 vs. 808.066005

Preparation of program documentation vs. [Composition of works about programs]

Class in 005.15 comprehensive works on how to prepare program documentation; works on how to prepare the technical documentation needed by the personnel who will maintain, modify, and enhance the program (including such things as program source listings, program comments, flow charts, decision logic tables, file specifications, program function descriptions, program test history records, modification logs); works on how to prepare program users' manuals that focus on content rather than form; works on policies for program documentation.

Class in 808.066005 works that emphasize effective technical writing—that is, works that emphasize such things as organizing for clarity, writing appropriately for the intended audience, using good paragraph structure, preferring the active voice, using consistent terminology. Typically such works are concerned only with users' manuals.

005.268 vs. 005.265, 005.269

Programming for specific operating systems vs. Programming for specific computers vs. Programming for specific user interfaces

The distinctions among 005.268, 005.265 and 005.269 are the same as the distinctions among 005.3682 Programs for specific operating systems, 005.365 Programs for specific computers, and 005.3684 Programs for specific user interfaces. *(See discussion at 005.3682 vs. 005.365, 005.3684.)*

005.269 and 005.284, 005.3684, 005.384

Programming for specific user interfaces [limited to microcomputers and not limited by type of computer] and Programs for specific user interfaces [limited to microcomputers and not limited by type of computer]

The native interface of an operating system is the user interface bundled inseparably with the operating system. For example, the native interface for DOS® is a command-driven interface. Graphical user interfaces that run on DOS®, such as Microsoft Windows®, are add-on programs.

005.3

Programs

Class a program or programs designed to run on two types of computers with the predominant type if there is one, e.g., a program that runs on five mainframe computers and one minicomputer 005.329. If neither of two types is predominant, class with the smaller type, e.g., a program for minicomputers and microcomputers 005.369.

Class programs for a specific application in computer science with the application in 005–006, but never in 004. Among the numbers most frequently used for software besides 005.3 and its subdivisions are 005.43 for systems software and operating systems, 005.713 for interfacing and data communications programs, 005.74 for database management systems, and 006.68 for computer graphics programs.

Programs applied to a particular subject or discipline are classed with the subject or discipline, plus notation 028553 from Table 1, e.g., programs for tax accounting 657.46028553.

See also discussion at T1—0285; also at 005.1 vs. 005.3.

005.3 vs. 005.43–.45

Programs vs. [Systems programs]

Class in 005.43–.45 systems programs and works about them. Systems programs are programs that enable computers to function properly; in effect, they provide life support and housekeeping for computers. Systems programs accomplish little that interests users except to make it possible for application programs to run. Examples of systems programs are operating systems, utilities packages, user interfaces, and programming language translators.

Class application programs and comprehensive works on application programs and systems programs in 005.3. Application programs are programs that do things users want done, for example, electronic spreadsheets, statistical packages, computer games, word processing programs, desktop publishing programs, educational programs, tax preparation programs, inventory control programs. A specific type of application program is classed with the type, e.g., computer games 794.8. General-purpose application programs and works on many types of applications programs are classed in 005.3.

Works about application programs that run on specific systems programs are classed in appropriate subdivisions of 005.3, e.g., application programs that run on a specific microcomputer operating system such as DOS 005.3682, application programs that run on a specific microcomputer graphical user interface such as Microsoft Windows® 005.3684. Works about the specific systems programs themselves, as distinct from works about the application programs that run on them, are of course classed in 005.43–.45.

If in doubt, prefer 005.3 and its subdivisions.

See also discussion at 005.3682 vs. 005.365, 005.3684.

005.362

Programs in specific programming languages

Class here (and in cognate numbers for other types of computers) programs and works about programs only if the material being classified emphasizes the programming language. For much off-the-shelf software, the user does not need to know in what programming language it was written; such software is classed in subdivisions of 005.3 not devoted to specific programming languages.

005.3682 vs. 005.365, 005.3684

Programs for specific operating systems vs. Programs for specific computers vs. Programs for specific user interfaces

Class in 005.365 (and cognate numbers for other types of computers) application programs that run on specific computers, and comprehensive works on application and systems programs that run on specific computers. Class in 005.3682 (and cognate numbers for other types of computers) application programs that run on specific operating systems, and comprehensive works on application and systems programs that run on specific operating systems. Class in 005.3684 (and cognate numbers for other types of computers) application programs that run on specific user interfaces other than the native interface of the operating system, and comprehensive works on application and systems programs that run on specific user interfaces other than the native interface of the operating system. Programs that run on the native interface of an operating system are classed in 005.3682 as programs that run on specific operating systems. (*See also discussion at 005.269 and 005.284, 005.3684, 005.384.*)

If two or three of these numbers are applicable to the same work, follow the preference note at 005 and class with number coming last in the schedule (with the exception specified below). For example, if a work treats application programs that run on a specific computer (IBM PC®), on a specific operating system (MS-DOS®), and on a specific add-on user interface (Microsoft Windows®), prefer 005.3684. Exception: If a specific computer has only one operating system, so that all programs that run on that computer also run on the operating system, e.g., the Macintosh® and System 7®, class programs that run on that computer and operating system with the computer in 005.365. Earlier and later versions of the same operating system (e.g., Macintosh System 6 and Macintosh System 7) count as one operating system, even though the differences between the earliest and the latest versions may be great.

If in doubt, prefer 005.3682 and cognate numbers for operating systems over both 005.3684 and 005.365. If in doubt between 005.3684 and 005.365, prefer 005.3684.

See also discussion at 005.3 vs. 005.43–.45.

005.369

Specific programs

Class here (and in cognate numbers for other types of computers) programs having interdisciplinary applications, such as electronic spreadsheets (which can be used in research, business, personal finance, indeed any time a matrix format is useful) and statistics packages that are used more widely than just in research and that have report formatting or other features beyond statistical capabilities. If a work discussing how to use such a program is a guide that would be helpful to users applying the program in many fields, class it in 005.369 and cognate numbers even if most of the examples come from one field. If a work truly focuses on how to use such a program in a particular field, however, class it with that field, using notation 02855369 from Table 1 and cognate numbers, e.g., use of a particular electronic spreadsheet in financial administration 658.1502855369. If in doubt, the work's table of contents may serve as a guide: if the table of contents is organized by functions and features of the computer program, prefer 005.369 and cognate numbers. If the table of contents is organized by topics in the field of application (e.g., topics found in DDC subdivisions in the field or in tables of contents of works in the field), class with the field of application. If in doubt, prefer 005.369 and cognate numbers.

005.6

Microprogramming and microprograms

Microprogramming does not mean programming for microcomputers, nor does *microprogram* mean a program for a microcomputer. *Microprogramming* means writing programs in which each instruction specifies a minute operation of the computer. Such programs are microprograms. Class programming for microcomputers in 005.26, programs for microcomputers in 005.36.

See also discussion at 004 vs. 005; also at 004–006 vs. 621.39.

005.713

[Data communications] Programs

An example of a program for data communications is one that enables a user with a microcomputer and a modem to transmit and receive data and possibly also to store and manipulate data. The program may also prepare a computer to handle different forms of data, change transmission speeds to suit the hardware, store phone numbers and provide automatic routines so that the user need not repeat the connect process, etc.

005.74

Data files and databases

Although there are technical differences between data files and databases, they are treated as the same for classification.

Class in 005.74 computer science aspects of databases—that is, the narrowly technical issues of designing, programming, and installing databases and database management systems—the kinds of things that system designers and programmers need to know but that users generally do not need to know unless they are installing a database on their own computer. Class the subject content of databases (and works discussing that content) as if the databases were books, e.g., encyclopedic databases 030, bibliographic databases 010, nonbibliographic chemistry databases 540. Do not use notation 0285574 from Table 1 except for works that focus on the computer science aspects of the databases rather than the subject content. Class in 025.04 the information science aspects of the automated storage and retrieval systems that make databases available—the kinds of things that users need to know about the systems in order to benefit fully from them. Class in 025.06 the information science aspects of the automated systems that make databases on specific subjects available to users. Class interdisciplinary works on databases in 025.04.

See also discussion at 011.3 vs. 011.77, 005.30296.

005.74 vs. 005.436

Data files and databases vs. File system management programs

A file manager in the sense of software that manages data files provides the ability to create, enter, change, query and produce reports on a data file or data files; file managers of this type are classed in 005.74 or 005.75. A file manager in the sense of software used to manage files on a disk provides the ability to delete, copy, move, rename and view files as well as create and manage directories. A file manager in this sense may be part of an operating system or a separate utility program. File managers of this type are classed in 005.436.

File organization may refer to the structure of data within a single file that permits access to the data; file organization in this sense is classed in 005.741. File organization may refer to the way that multiple files are organized on a disk; file organization in that sense is classed in 005.436.

Class comprehensive works on both 005.436 and 005.74 in 005.436. If in doubt, prefer 005.74.

006.37 vs. 006.42, 621.367, 621.391, 621.399

Computer vision vs. Optical pattern recognition vs. Technological photography and photo-optics vs. General works on [engineering of] specific types of computers vs. Devices for special computer methods

Computer vision and optical pattern recognition both involve recognition of forms, shapes, or other optical patterns for the purpose of classification, grouping, or identification; but computer vision makes extensive use of artificial intelligence for the complex interpretation of visual information, whereas optical pattern recognition involves only simple interpretation.

Most works on computer vision and optical pattern recognition give substantial treatment to the computer programs needed to interpret optical patterns; such works are classed in 006.37 and 006.42, as are also works treating computer-vision and optical-pattern-recognition devices from the user's point of view. Class at 621.399 works on designing and manufacturing the hardware for computer vision and optical pattern recognition.

Class in 621.367 works on devices that record and process optical signals while doing virtually no interpreting (either because interpretation is not needed or because interpretation is left to others—computers or humans), e.g., devices for image enhancement.

At 621.391 *optical computer* refers to general-purpose computers in which the central data processing mechanism is based on light (e.g., lasers). Sometimes *optical computer* is used for special-purpose computers designed to process optical data, regardless of the type of central data processing mechanism. Works on such computers are classed in 006.37, 006.42, or 621.399.

011.3 vs. 005.30296, 011.77

General bibliographies of works published in specific forms vs. Buyers' guides and consumer reports [about computer programs] vs. [General bibliographies of] Computer programs

Class general bibliographies of machine-readable works *not limited to software* in 011.3. A general list of *software only*, however, is a list of works with a special content, not merely a special form; yet it is not a list on a specific subject in the 016 sense. Class a general list of software in 011.77. Class annotated lists in 011.77 if the annotations are relatively brief; but class lists with lengthy reviews as buyers' guides in 005.30296, e.g., a collection of reviews of microcomputer software 005.360296. If in doubt, class in 011.3.

See also discussion at 005.74.

016 vs. 026, T1—07

Bibliographies and catalogs of works on specific subjects or in specific disciplines vs. Libraries, archives, information centers devoted to specific subjects and disciplines vs. [Table 1 notation for] Education, research, related topics

Notation 07 from Table 1 is used for comprehensive works on resources for education, research, and related topics. Many of the resources are encompassed by subdivisions of T1—07, e.g., schools and laboratories, collections of objects (such as botanical collections), and financial support. Books, manuscripts, recordings, and the like are also resources, but works that describe such resources will normally be classed in 016 or 026 unless the work (a) also describes kinds of resources not found in libraries and archives or (b) emphasizes how to use the library or archival resources for study, teaching, and research. If in doubt, prefer 016 or 026.

To be classed in 016, a work about resources in a field must describe individual works, such as books and articles. A work about kinds of material not traditionally described in detail, however, is classed in 016 if small units are described, e.g., five shelf feet of correspondence of a particular person on a particular subject. Inventories and calendars of archives are typically classed in 016. Works about resources in a field that give broad descriptions of whole collections held by libraries, archives, and other information organizations are classed in 026. Such works often include directory information about the institutions and organizations. If in doubt, prefer 016.

Notation 07 from Table 1 may be used in 016 if the resources being described treat education and research, e.g., a bibliography of material on education and research in mathematics 016.5107.

020

Library and information sciences

The preference order in the schedule for library and information science is complex. The following table shows preference among 022, 023, 025, 026, and 027:

025 Operations, such as technical services, e.g., acquisitions, cataloging; readers' services, e.g., reference, circulation
  Exceptions: (a) Prefer other operations over 025.1 Administration (see below). (b) Readers' services for special groups and organizations are classed with libraries for special groups and organizations in 027.6, not in 025.5. (c) Comprehensive works on operations in a specific kind of institution are classed with the kind of institution in 026–027, not in 025.

022, 023, 025.1 Administration

026 Institutions devoted to specific disciplines and subjects

027 General institutions

Examples follow:

Administration of cataloging 025.3068
  025.3 (Cataloging) + T1—068 (Management)

Administration of law libraries 025.19634
  025.19 (Administration of specific types of institutions) + 6 (from 026 Libraries . . . devoted to specific subjects and disciplines) + 34 (from 340 Law)

Personnel administration in university libraries 023
  The type of institution cannot be indicated in the number.

Book selection in public libraries 025.21874
  025.218 (Collection development in specific types of institutions) + 74 (from 027.4 Public libraries)

Reference services in the corporate library 027.69
  The usual facet order of operation + institution is reversed here because of the exception listed above under 025. Note also that the operation (reference services) cannot be indicated in the number.

In two contexts in 020, materials by subject or discipline (e.g., chemistry) are preferred over materials by format or special bibliographic characteristics (e.g., sound recordings, serials). Institutions devoted to specific disciplines and subjects (026) are preferred over institutions devoted to materials in special formats or with special bibliographic characteristics (027); selection and acquisition of materials on specific disciplines and subjects (025.27) are preferred over selection and acquisition of materials in special forms (025.28). In the context of bibliographic control, however, materials in special formats or with special bibliographic characteristics (025.34) are preferred over materials in specific disciplines and subjects (025.46 classification, 025.49 controlled subject vocabularies).

Examples follow:

Selection and acquisition of chemistry serials for university libraries 025.2754

025.27 (Acquisition of and collection development for materials on specific disciplines and subjects) + 54 (from 540 Chemistry)

The format of material (serial) and type of institution (university library) cannot be indicated in this number. If notation 05 from Table 1 were added to form 025.275405, the number would mean serials on selection and acquisition of chemistry materials, not selection and acquisition of chemistry serials.

Classifying sound recordings of music 025.3482

The subject of material (music) cannot be indicated in this number.

025.3

Bibliographic analysis and control

Most works on bibliographic analysis and control treat some form of standard (e.g., standard cataloging codes, standard lists of subject headings) because standards are inherent in control. For this reason, do not use notation 0218 from Table 1 here or in any subdivision of 025.3–.4.

026–027

Specific kinds of institutions

A specific operation in a specific kind of institution is classed with the operation, e.g., collection development in patients' libraries 025.2187662; however, services to special groups and organizations are classed in 027.6, e.g., reader services in patients' libraries 027.662.

Libraries, archives, information centers devoted to specific kinds of special materials are classed in 026–027. Those limited to a specific subject or discipline are classed in 026, e.g., libraries devoted to music scores 026.78026, to maps 026.912.

A general library (1) devoted to a kind of special material and (2) not serving special groups and organizations may be loosely regarded as devoted to a subject and classed in 026 plus the number in 001–999 for the kind of material, e.g., a rare book library 026.09. If, however, a library devoted to a kind of special material is limited to what may be properly called a specific subject or discipline, it is classed with the subject or discipline, e.g., a rare book library devoted to literature 026.8. A general library devoted to a kind of special material and serving special groups and organizations is classed in 027.6, e.g., a braille library 027.663.

027

General libraries, archives, information centers

Few archives are sufficiently general to be classed here; most are classed in 026 because they contain primarily material on specific disciplines and subjects, e.g., archives of religious organizations 026.2 (*not* 027.67).

027.5

Government libraries

General government archives for a specific jurisdiction usually contain primarily material reflecting the history and civilization of the place; works on such archives are classed in 026 plus the history number for the jurisdiction, e.g., United States National Archives 026.973.

070.433

Reporting local, foreign, war news

General reporting on a specific area is treated as reporting on the history and civilization of the area and is classed in 070.449 plus the history number for the area from notation 909.09 or 940–990, e.g., reporting the local news of London 070.4499421, foreign correspondents reporting on South Africa 070.449968.

080

General collections

To be classed here a work must contain a collection of writings, statements, or quotations on a variety of topics. Examples: selected articles of a general nature from one or more periodicals, such as highlights from *The Atlantic*; a collection of quotations by Winston Churchill on various topics.

080 vs. 800

General collections vs. Literature (Belles-lettres) and rhetoric

Class a collection of quotations in 800 if all or nearly all the quotations come from works of poetry, drama, or fiction. Otherwise, class a collection of essays or quotations in 800 only if the intent of the collection, as revealed in prefatory matter, is clearly literary, e.g., to exhibit literary style. Usually essays and quotations are collected for nonliterary purposes, e.g., quotations collected to answer reference questions about who said something familiar; such collections belong in 080. If in doubt, prefer 080.

081–089

General collections in specific languages and language families

Collections originally written in one language or language family are classed with that language or language family. Collections originally written in two or more languages or language families are classed with the preponderant language or language family if there is one. If no original language or language family is preponderant, but the work appears in one language as a result of translation, class it with the language in which it appears. Class in 080 collections in which the material appears in multiple languages with none preponderant, even if accompanied by translations into the language of the intended audience.

133 vs. 130

Parapsychology and occultism vs. Paranormal phenomena

130 by itself is seldom used; most general works on paranormal phenomena in fact focus on parapsychology and occultism and thus are classed in 133, not 130.

133 vs. 200

Parapsychology and occultism vs. Religion

If the author of a work about parapsychological or occult phenomena describes them as religious, or the believers and practitioners consider them to be religious, the work is classed in 200. If parapsychological and occult phenomena are not presented as religious, or if in doubt as to whether they have been so presented, prefer 133.

Class knowledge reputedly derived from secret and ancient religious texts but not applied for religious purposes in 133; however, class editions of the texts in 200, even if annotated from an occultist viewpoint, e.g., discussion of occult traditions derived from the Zohar 135.47, but the text of the Zohar 296.162.

133.109 vs. 133.129

[Historical, geographic, persons treatment of apparitions (ghosts)] vs. Specific haunted places

Use 133.129 only for works that treat one single haunted place, e.g., old Monterey's Hotel del Monte 133.12979476. Use 133.109 for works that treat two or more haunted places during a specific historical period or in a specific geographic area, e.g., haunted places in Cornwall 133.1094237. If in doubt, prefer 133.109.

133.9013 vs. 129

Personal survival, nature of spiritual world and life after death vs. Origin and destiny of individual souls

Class in 133.9013 accounts of life after death from personal sources or from within the occult tradition. Class in 129 philosophical discussions of personal survival and life after death. If in doubt, prefer 133.9013.

140

Specific philosophical schools and viewpoints

Viewpoints or schools of philosophy are sets of attitudes or presuppositions that a given philosopher or group of philosophers brings to the study of various topics. Topics are the questions studied by philosophy, such as the self 126. Only general works that discuss how a viewpoint or school treats a wide variety of topics are classed in 140, e.g., existentialism 142.78, but existentialist views of the self 126.

140 vs. 180–190

Specific philosophical schools and viewpoints vs. Historical, geographic, persons treatment of philosophy

Unless other instructions are given, class in 140 specific modern western schools and viewpoints and comprehensive works on specific schools and viewpoints, but class in 180 ancient, medieval, and Oriental schools and viewpoints, e.g., modern western idealism, comprehensive works on ancient and modern idealism or on Indian and western idealism 141, but Indian idealism 181.4. Class in 190 historical and geographic treatment of modern western philosophy not limited to a specific viewpoint, but class a specific school or viewpoint with the school or viewpoint regardless of time or place, e.g., French philosophy 194, but existentialism in France 142.780944.

Class collected works of an individual philosopher and criticism of the philosopher's work as a whole in 180–190, even if the philosopher's work falls entirely within one philosophical viewpoint or serves as the foundation of a school, e.g., the works of Immanuel Kant 193, but Kantianism as a viewpoint espoused by philosophers 142.3.

152–158 vs. 150.19

Specific topics in psychology vs. [Psychological] Systems, schools, viewpoints

Certain schools and systems draw their fundamental principles from a few selected psychological topics. When such topics are used to illustrate a system, class with the system in 150.19, e.g., the subconscious, fantasies, and dreams used to illustrate psychoanalytic principles 150.195 (*not* 154). If in doubt, prefer the specific topic in 152–158.

153 vs. 006.3

Conscious mental processes and intelligence vs. Artificial intelligence

Cognitive science

Class cognitive science (interdisciplinary study of the mind and computers as information processing systems) in 153 if the goal is to understand better how the human mind works. Class cognitive science in 006.3 if the goal is to produce computer systems with better artificial intelligence. If in doubt, prefer 153.

153 vs. 153.4

Conscious mental processes and intelligence vs. Thought, thinking, reasoning, intuition, value, judgment

The terminology in this field is used in a variety of overlapping senses. Many works that claim to be about thought and thinking or reasoning also cover such subjects as memory, communication, perception, motivation, and intelligence. These broader works are classed in 153, not 153.4. A book about "cognitive psychology" is more apt to belong at 153 than 153.4. Use 153.4 only for works that focus narrowly on thought and thinking, reasoning, intuition, value, judgment. If in doubt, prefer 153.

153.15 vs. 370.15

[Psychology of] Learning vs. Educational psychology

Be careful to distinguish between studies that use students as subjects for research into the fundamental processes of learning, which are classed in 153.15 and related numbers, and studies on the application of learning psychology to education, which are classed in 370.15 and related numbers. If in doubt, prefer 153.15.

153.43 vs. 160

Reasoning vs. Logic

Class the psychology of reasoning and problem solving in 153.43. Class the science of reasoning and problem solving, that is, the logical processes considered apart from internal mental operations, in 160. If in doubt, prefer 153.43.

153.69 vs. 152.384

Nonverbal communication vs. Expressive movements

Use of 152.384 is limited to noncognitive aspects of expressive movements, e.g., habituation, emotional content. Class the meaning of movements (as in body language) and the cognitive processes involved in interpreting movements in 153.69. If in doubt, prefer 153.69.

153.7 vs. 152.1

Perceptual processes vs. Sensory perception

Class in 153.7 comprehensive works on sensory perception and perceptual processes in general, and works that focus on the active, interpretative mental processes associated with perception in general. Also class in 153.7 types of perception that involve more than one sense, e.g., space perception that involves vision and touch 153.752. Class in 152.1 works that focus on the receptive aspects of sensory perception and comprehensive works on perception by a specific sense, e.g., visual perception 152.14. If in doubt, prefer 153.7.

153.94

Aptitude tests

153.94 has priority over other psychology numbers, as shown in the table of preference at 150. Class in 153.94001–.94999 tests to determine aptitude in specific fields even if drawn from other branches of psychology, e.g., color matching tests for interior decorators 153.94747 (*not* 152.145), personality tests for social workers 153.943613 (*not* 155.28). Also class in 153.94 aptitude and vocational interest tests and testing limited to categories of persons defined in 155.3–.6, e.g., vocational interest tests for young people twelve to twenty 153.94000835 (*not* 155.51394).

155

Differential and developmental psychology

Some works on the psychology of sensory perception, movement, emotions, physiological drives (152) and conscious mental processes (153) analyze research based on persons belonging to one or several differential categories or subject to one or several environmental influences that are provided for in 155.3–.9. If there is clearly little or no interest in the distinctiveness of the category or influence, class the work in 152–153. This guideline is particularly applicable to ethnic and national groups (155.8), adults (155.6), and social environment (155.92) where the researcher has simply reached out for convenient samples.

Similarly, a study on sex psychology, drawing almost exclusively upon adult middle-class whites, but showing only marginal interest in the class, age, or race of the respondents, is classed in 155.3. Discussion of the class, national, or ethnic bias of such research is classed with the research in 155.3 since the interest is in the validity of the findings about sex psychology.

155.4–.6 vs. 153.15

Psychology of specific ages vs. [Psychology of] Learning

Class a work on the learning psychology of people of a specific age bracket in 155.4–.6 when age is actually the focus of the work. If the reference to age is vague or incidental, class the work in 153.15. If in doubt, prefer 155.4–.6.

155.89 vs. 155.84

National psychology vs. [Psychology of] Specific racial and ethnic groups

Class in 155.89 the psychology of nations taken as a whole, and the psychology of racial and ethnic groups that are predominant in an area constituting an independent nation. Class in 155.84 the psychology of racial and ethnic groups taken as a whole and the psychology of racial, ethnic, and national groups in areas where they are not predominant. For example, class the national psychology of Malaysia or the psychology of Malays in Malaysia in 155.89595; but class the psychology of Malays taken as a whole in 155.849928, of Malays in Thailand in 155.8499280593. If in doubt, class in 155.89.

158 vs. 155.2

Applied psychology vs. Individual psychology

Works of applied psychology that treat topics named under 155.2 in a loose or vaguely defined way are classed in 158 or subdivisions of 158, most commonly in 158.1 Personal improvement and analysis. Such topics include the self, character, identity, individuality, and personality (named at 155.2), adaptability and adjustment (named at 155.24), character and personality (named at 155.25). Only analytical and explanatory works on these topics are classed under 155.2, e.g., how character develops. The above also holds true of vague topics not named, e.g., self-actualization, self-esteem.

In contrast, both works of applied psychology and analytical and explanatory works that treat specific, clearly defined topics of individual psychology are classed in subdivisions of 155.2. For example, works of applied psychology on specific character traits, such as perfectionism and aggressiveness, are classed in 155.232, on typology are classed in 155.26, and on appraisals and tests are classed in 155.28.

If in doubt, prefer 158.

170

Ethics (Moral philosophy)

Ethics is an exception to the rule that the philosophy of a discipline or subject is classed with the discipline or subject. Class the ethics of a discipline or subject in 172–179. Class ethics within or based on a religious tradition with the religion in 200. For example, class philosophy and theory of international relations in 327.101; the ethics of relations between states in 172.4; the ethics of those relations treated as part of Christian moral theology in 241.624.

170 vs. 303.372

Ethics (Moral philosophy) vs. Belief systems and customs

Social ethics may be a subject either in moral philosophy or in methods of social control. Social ethics in 170 refers to the rightness or wrongness of conduct as it affects individuals or society. Social ethics in 303.372 refers to beliefs and system of beliefs influencing the way society and its institutions operate. 303.372 is descriptive, while 170 is prescriptive. If in doubt, prefer 170.

170.92 vs. 171

Persons [associated with ethics] vs. Ethical systems

Class collected works, biography, and critical appraisal of the work of an individual moral philosopher in 171, if the ethical system represented can be determined (e.g., critical appraisal of the ethics of Jeremy Bentham 171.5092). Otherwise, class such works in 170.92.

174.1

[Occupational ethics of] Clergy

Class in 174.1 a discussion of occupational ethics for clergy from a secular or philosophical viewpoint. If the subject is treated as part of the moral theology or ethics of a particular religion, class it with the religion, e.g., a discussion of the occupational ethics of clergy as part of Christian morality 241.641.

180–190

Historical, geographic, persons treatment of philosophy

Class single works by individual philosophers with the topic in philosophy. If there is no focus on a specific topic, class a work expressing primarily the philosopher's own viewpoint with the collected works of the philosopher in 180–190. For example, a general work by Hegel, such as *Phenomenology of Spirit*, is classed in 193.

Class a work by an individual philosopher that is primarily a discussion of other philosophers' writings with the other philosophers' writings. For example, a work by a western philosopher that is mostly a criticism of contemporary philosophers would be classed in 190.

Class a work by an individual that takes a broad look at many questions in philosophy and does not seek to argue for the individual's own viewpoint in 100.

190 vs. 100, 109

Modern western and other non-Oriental philosophy vs. Philosophy, paranormal phenomena, psychology [and] Historical and collected persons treatment of philosophy

190 is the comprehensive number for (a) Christian philosophy; (b) western philosophy from ancient Greece to the present; (c) modern philosophy, even when both modern western and modern Oriental philosophies are treated; and (d) European philosophy. For this reason, 190 is used more often than 100 or 109 for what appear to be general works on philosophy.

To be classed in 100 or 109, works must include (a) discussion of the discipline of philosophy itself or several of philosophy's major questions and branches, as is common in introductory works; or (b) discussion of philosophy broad enough to include nonwestern and ancient or medieval as well as modern western philosophy. If in doubt, prefer 190.

200 vs. 100

Religion vs. Philosophy, paranormal phenomena, psychology

Both philosophy and religion deal with the ultimate nature of existence and relationships, but religion treats them within the context of revelation, deity, worship. Philosophy of religion (210) does not involve revelation or worship but does examine questions within the context of deity.

Any work that emphasizes revelation, deity, or worship is classed in 200, even if it uses philosophical methods, e.g., a philosophical proof of the existence of God 212.1. Sometimes the thought of a religious tradition is used to examine the questions of philosophy without reference to deity or religious topics, e.g., Jewish philosophy 181.06, Christian philosophy 190. However, class ethics based on a religion in 200. If in doubt, prefer 200.

200.9 vs. 294, 299.5

Historical, geographic, persons treatment [of religion] vs. Religions of Indic origin [and] Religions of East and Southeast Asian origin

294 and 299.5 refer to religions that originated in particular geographic areas. Most of these religions have spread beyond the area where they originated. The areas also have adherents of religions that originated elsewhere, e.g., Buddhism (which originated in India) is present in China. If a work covers various religious traditions in an area, not just the religions that originated there, class it in 200.9. For example, class the religions of India (including Christianity and Islam) in 200.954, of China (including Christianity and Buddhism) in 200.951.

200.92 and 291–299

Persons [associated with religion] and Comparative religion, Religions other than Christianity

Persons associated with the religions in 292–299 are often identified with a number of religious functions and activities. A Hindu guru, for example, may be thought of as a theologian, a teacher, a missionary, or a clergyman. If a religious leader cannot be identified primarily with one function, activity, or sect, class his biography in the base number for the religion and add notation 092 from Table 1. Class collected biography of persons from many religions who are not identified with one function or activity in 200.922. For persons associated with a specific religion, use a number that corresponds to the number given in the table below, e.g., a Buddhist member of a religious order 294.365 (corresponds to 291.65 in the table below). For comprehensive biographies of persons primarily identified with one function, activity, or sect, use the following table of preference:

Founders of religions	291.63
Founders of sects	291.9
Founders of religious orders	291.65
Religious leaders (high ranking officials)	200.92
Of specific sects	291.9
Theologians	291.2092
Moral theologians	291.5092
Missionaries	291.72092
Martyrs, heretics, saints	200.92
Of specific sects	291.9
Teachers	291.75092
Members of religious orders	291.65
Clergy	200.92
Of specific sects	291.9

Except for founders of religions (291.63) and founders of religious orders (291.65), the subdivisions of 291.6 are not used for biography, but for the nature, role, and function of religious leaders.

Works dealing with only one aspect of a person's career are classed with the aspect, e.g., Muḥammad as a moral theologian 297.5092 (*not* 297.63).

220

Bible

Biblical theology

Biblical theology usually means using the Bible for the basis of Christian or Jewish doctrine and is classed as directed at 220. But if a book on Biblical theology does no more than interpret the text of the Bible, it is classed in 220.6 and cognate numbers in 221–229. The key difference is whether the author adheres to the Biblical text and its meaning, or whether the author uses the Biblical text as a springboard to the interpretation of theological concepts.

220.92

Collected persons [in Bible]

Class a comprehensive biography of a Biblical character with the book or books with which the character is most closely associated. In many cases this is the historical part of the Bible in which persons' lives are narrated, e.g., Solomon, King of Israel, in 1st Kings 222.53092. Solomon's association with 223 Poetic books is weaker. However, some Biblical characters are more closely associated with nonhistorical books. For example, class Isaiah and Timothy with the books that bear their names, 224.1092 and 227.83092, respectively. They appear briefly in historical narratives, but their lives are not narrated in full there. Class the apostles John, Peter, and Paul at 225.92 since each is associated with a number of books in the New Testament, but class the rest of the original Apostles, associated primarily with Gospels and Acts, in 226.092.

See also discussion at 230–280: Biography.

221

Old Testament (Tanakh)

Optional numbers for books of Tanakh

Alphabetical index

Each of the books of the Old Testament (Tanakh) and the combination of them can have one of three different numbers depending on whether one chooses the preferred arrangement at 222–224 or one of the two optional arrangements. Optional numbers showing the books in the order found in Jewish Bibles appear as the second half of this entry (Option A) and at 296.11 (Option B). The following alphabetical listing gives the three numbers for each book or combination of books:

Book	Preferred	Option A	Option B
Amos	224.8	223.63	296.1143
Canticle of Canticles	223.9	224.41	296.11641
Chronicles	222.6	224.8	296.1168
Chronicles 1	222.63	224.81	296.11681
Chronicles 2	222.64	224.82	296.11682
Daniel	224.5	224.5	296.1165
Deuteronomy	222.15	222.5	296.1125
Ecclesiastes	223.8	224.44	296.11644
Exodus	222.12	222.2	296.1122
Esther	222.9	224.45	296.11645
Ezekiel	224.4	223.5	296.1139
Ezra	222.7	224.6	296.1166
Five scrolls	221.044	224.4	296.1164

Former Prophets	222	223.1	296.1131
Genesis	222.11	222.1	296.1121
Habakkuk	224.95	223.68	296.1148
Haggai	224.97	223.72	296.1152
Hosea	224.6	223.61	296.1141
Isaiah	224.1	223.3	296.1137
Jeremiah	224.2	223.4	296.1138
Job	223.1	224.3	296.1163
Joel	224.7	223.62	296.1142
Jonah	224.92	223.65	296.1145
Joshua	222.2	223.11	296.1132
Judges	222.32	223.12	296.1133
Ketuvim	223	224	296.116
Kings	222.5	223.14	296.1135
Kings 1	222.53	223.141	296.11351
Kings 2	222.54	223.142	296.11352
Kohelet	223.8	224.44	296.11644
Lamentations	224.3	224.43	296.11643
Later Prophets	224	223.2	296.1136
Leviticus	222.13	222.3	296.1123
Malachi	224.99	223.74	296.1154
Megillot	221.044	224.4	296.1164
Micah	224.93	223.66	296.1146
Minor Prophets	224.9	223.6	296.114
Nahum	224.94	223.67	296.1147
Nehemiah	222.8	224.7	296.1167
Nevi'im	224	223	296.113
Numbers	222.14	222.4	296.1124
Obadiah	224.91	223.64	296.1144
Pentateuch	222.1	222	296.112
Prophetic books	224	223	296.113
Proverbs	223.7	224.2	296.1162
Pslams	223.2	224.1	296.1161
Qohelet	223.8	224.44	296.11644
Ruth	222.35	224.42	296.11642
Samuel	222.4	223.13	296.1134
Samuel 1	222.43	223.131	296.11341
Samuel 2	222.44	223.132	296.11342
Song of Solomon	223.9	224.41	296.11641
Song of Songs	223.9	224.41	296.11641
Torah	222.1	222	296.112
Writings	223	224	296.116
Zechariah	224.98	223.73	296.1153
Zephaniah	224.96	223.71	296.1151

Optional numbers for books of Bible as arranged in Tanakh (Jewish Bible, Hebrew Bible) (Option A)

The following schedule is an optional arrangement for books of the Bible as found in Jewish Bibles. The preferred arrangement is at 222–224 in the regular schedule. Option B is given at 296.11 in the regular schedule. The see references and footnote instructions in this optional arrangement refer to numbers in the schedules, not to other numbers found in the Manual entries.

> (222–224) Optional numbers for books of Bible as arranged in Tanakh (Jewish Bible, Hebrew Bible)

Class comprehensive works in 221

For Apocrypha, pseudepigrapha, see 229

See Manual at 221: Optional numbers for books of Bible

(222) *Torah (Pentateuch)

(Optional number; prefer standard 222.1)

(.1) *Genesis

(Optional number; prefer standard 222.11)

(.2) *Exodus

(Optional number; prefer standard 222.12)

For Ten Commandments, see 222.6

(.3) *Leviticus

(Optional number; prefer standard 222.13)

(.4) *Numbers

(Optional number; prefer standard 222.14)

(.5) *Deuteronomy

(Optional number; prefer standard 222.15)

For Ten Commandments, see 222.6

(.6) *Ten Commandments (Decalogue)

(Optional number; prefer standard 222.16)

*Add as instructed under 221–229

Optional numbers for books of Bible as arranged in Tanakh (Jewish Bible, Hebrew Bible) (Option A)

(223) *Prophetic books (Nevi'im)

(Optional number; prefer standard 224)

(.1) *Former Prophets (Nevi'im rishonim)

(Optional number; prefer standard 222)

(.11) *Joshua

(Optional number; prefer standard 222.2)

(.12) *Judges

(Optional number; prefer standard 222.32)

(.13) *Samuel

(Optional number; prefer standard 222.4)

(.131) *Samuel 1

(Optional number; prefer standard 222.43)

(.132) *Samuel 2

(Optional number; prefer standard 222.44)

(.14) *Kings

(Optional number; prefer standard 222.5)

(.141) *Kings 1

(Optional number; prefer standard 222.53)

(.142) *Kings 2

(Optional number; prefer standard 222.54)

(.2) *Later Prophets (Nevi'im aḥaronim)

(Optional number; prefer standard 224)

For Isaiah, see 223.3; for Jeremiah, see 223.4; for Ezekiel, see 223.5; for Minor Prophets, see 223.6

(.3) *Isaiah

(Optional number; prefer standard 224.1)

(.4) *Jeremiah

(Optional number; prefer standard 224.2)

(.5) *Ezekiel

(Optional number; prefer standard 224.4)

*Add as instructed under 221–229

Optional numbers for books of Bible as arranged in Tanakh (Jewish Bible, Hebrew Bible) (Option A)

(.6) *Minor prophets

(Optional number; prefer standard 224.9)

For Zephaniah, Haggai, Zechariah, Malachi, see 223.7

(.61) *Hosea

(Optional number; prefer standard 224.6)

(.62) *Joel

(Optional number; prefer standard 224.7)

(.63) *Amos

(Optional number; prefer standard 224.8)

(.64) *Obadiah

(Optional number; prefer standard 224.91)

(.65) *Jonah

(Optional number; prefer standard 224.92)

(.66) *Micah

(Optional number; prefer standard 224.93)

(.67) *Nahum

(Optional number; prefer standard 224.94)

(.68) *Habakkuk

(Optional number; prefer standard 224.95)

(.7) *Zephaniah, Haggai, Zechariah, Malachi

(Optional number; prefer standard 224.9)

(.71) *Zephaniah

(Optional number; prefer standard 224.96)

(.72) *Haggai

(Optional number; prefer standard 224.97)

(.73) *Zechariah

(Optional number; prefer standard 224.98)

(.74) *Malachi

(Optional number; prefer standard 224.99)

*Add as instructed under 221–229

Optional numbers for books of Bible as arranged in Tanakh
(Jewish Bible, Hebrew Bible) (Option A)

(224) *Writings (Ketuvim)

(Optional number; prefer standard 223)

(.1) *Psalms

(Optional number; prefer standard 223.2)

(.2) *Proverbs

(Optional number; prefer standard 223.7)

(.3) *Job

(Optional number; prefer standard 223.1)

(.4) *Megillot (Five scrolls)

(Optional number; prefer standard 221.044)

(.41) *Song of Solomon (Canticle of Canticles, Song of Songs)

(Optional number; prefer standard 223.9)

(.42) *Ruth

(Optional number; prefer standard 222.35)

(.43) *Lamentations

(Optional number; prefer standard 224.3)

(.44) *Ecclesiastes (Kohelet, Qohelet)

(Optional number; prefer standard 223.8)

(.45) *Esther

(Optional number; prefer standard 222.9)

(.5) *Daniel

(Optional number; prefer standard 224.5)

(.6) *Ezra

(Optional number; prefer standard 222.7)

(.7) *Nehemiah

(Optional number; prefer standard 222.8)

*Add as instructed under 221–229

Optional numbers for books of Bible as arranged in Tanakh
(Jewish Bible, Hebrew Bible) (Option A)

(.8) *Chronicles

(Optional number; prefer standard 222.6)

(.81) *Chronicles 1

(Optional number; prefer standard 222.63)

(.82) *Chronicles 2

(Optional number; prefer standard 222.64)

*Add as instructed under 221-229

230–280

Christianity

Biography

Use the following table of preference for comprehensive biographies:

Jesus Christ, Mary, Joseph, Joachim, Anne, John the Baptist	232.9
Other persons in the Bible	220
Founders of denominations	280
Founders of religious orders	271
Higher clergy (e.g., popes, metropolitans, archbishops, bishops) prior to 1054	270.1–.3
Higher clergy subsequent to 1054	280
Theologians	230
Moral theologians	241
Missionaries	266
Evangelists	269.2
Persons noted for participation in associations for religious work	267
Martyrs	272
Heretics	273
Saints	270
Saints prior to 1054	270.1–.3
Saints subsequent to 1054	280
Mystics	248.22
Hymn writers	264.23
Religious educators	268
Members of religious orders	271
Clergy prior to 1054	270.1–.3
Clergy subsequent to 1054	280
Members of the early church to 1054	270.1–.3
Members of denominations	280
Christian biography of persons who fall in none of the above categories	270

Class in 270 biographies of persons known not to be members of any church or for whom it has not been possible to determine whether there is church membership or not. Use the historical period that most closely matches the individual's life span or the time period of his greatest prominence, e.g., biography of a twentieth century Christian 270.82092. Class in 280 without subdivision church members whose affiliation is not known and members of nondenominational and interdenominational churches.

Do not use 248.2 Religious experience or its subdivisions except 248.22 for comprehensive biographies, e.g., a biography of Teresa of Avila's religious life 282.092, not 248.2092. However, biographical accounts written for devotional purposes, not as comprehensive accounts of a person's life, may be classed in 248.2, e.g., the story of one's conversion 248.246092.

253, 255, and 262.1 are not used for biographies of the kinds of persons listed above in the table of preference.

Certain numbers in the range 220–269 other than those listed in the table of preference above may be used for comprehensive biographies of persons with specialized religious careers, but are more commonly used for books treating only one aspect of a person's life and work, e.g., 220.092 for a Biblical scholar.

Examples:

270.0922	(Collected biography of saints)
225.92	(New Testament biography) Paul the Apostle
230.2092	(Catholic theology) Saint Thomas Aquinas
232.94	(John the Baptist) John the Baptist
266.2092	(Catholic missions) Saint Francis Xavier
269.2092	(Evangelism) Billy Graham
271.12502	(Trappist order in church history) Thomas Merton
270.2092	(Church history, 325–787) Pope Gregory the Great
283.092	(Anglican churches) Thomas Cranmer
287.092	(Methodist churches) John Wesley

See also discussion at 220.92; also at 230.04 vs. 230.092, 230.1–.9; also at 232; also at 280: Biography.

230

Christianity Christian theology

Contextual theology

Contextual theology refers to the study of the doctrines of Christian theology within the context of an area or of a group of people. Usually, specific examples are classed with theology using standard subdivisions T1—08 or T1—09. For example, feminist theology, 230.082; black theology 230.08996; theology in the Asian context 230.095.

The relation of a group of people to Christianity, the church, or to church history is classed in 270.08, e.g., women in Christianity through the centuries 270.082, in the 20th century 270.82082.

230.04 vs. 230.092, 230.1–.9

Specific types of Christian theology vs. [Persons treatment of theology] vs. Doctrines of specific denominations and sects

Use these subdivisions with notation 092 from Table 1 for biography and criticism of individual theologians, e.g., criticism of a United Methodist theologian 230.76092. Class Protestant theologians who are not connected with a specific denomination or who are important and influential enough to transcend their own denominations in 230.044092, e.g., Karl Barth 230.044092. Class theologians not connected with any specific type of theology in 230.092. If in doubt, prefer 230.092. Class critical appraisal of an individual theologian's thought on a specific topic with the topic, e.g., on justification 234.7092.

230.15–.2

[Doctrines of Eastern churches, of Roman Catholic Church]

Class here theology of Eastern and Roman Catholic churches after 1054; for earlier theology, use 230.11–.14.

231.7652 vs. 213, 500, 576.8

Relation of scientific and Christian viewpoints of origin of universe vs. Creation [in philosophy of religion] vs. Natural sciences and mathematics vs. Evolution

Evolution versus creation

Most works on creation science or creationism are classed in 231.7652 because they are written by Christians who assume that the Bible provides a chronology of natural history and who rely upon religious premises in responding to theories from the natural sciences. On the other hand, works by creationist authors that attempt to refute evolution theory by examining the writings, hypotheses, and findings of scientists are classed in 500 with the branch of science criticized. Similarly, works that attempt to refute creation science are usually classed in 231.7652, unless they take the writings of creationists as a starting point from which to demonstrate the case for evolution.

The difficulty stems from the fact that on the question of evolution the *pro* and *con* positions differ so radically that they normally belong in different disciplines, science and religion, respectively. However, when a religious author is trying to enlighten scientists on a specific scientific matter, class the work with science, while if a scientist is trying to enlighten the religious on a specific religious matter, class the work with religion. The place in the classification is determined by the intent of the author, and the interest of the readers that the author is seeking to reach, not by the truth, falsity, or validity of interpretations and premises.

Class comprehensive works including both religion and science in 231.7652.

Among the works that belong in 500, the most common focus of interest is on biological evolution. Class these works in 576.8. If the emphasis of a work is mainly on stellar evolution, class in 523.88; if on basic physical principles, in 530; if on historical geology, in 551.7; and if on paleontology, in 560. If there is no clear emphasis on a specific branch of science, then class in the broad number, 500.

Works that consider the relation between divine creation and evolution as a philosophical problem, without appealing to a particular religion or scripture, are classed in 213. If in doubt between 213 and 231.7652, prefer 231.7652.

232

Jesus Christ and his family Christology

Class doctrine and theories about Jesus Christ in 232.1–.8, events in the life of Jesus in 232.9, e.g., the doctrine of the resurrection 232.5, historicity and narration of events surrounding the resurrection 232.97.

Use notation 092 from Table 1 for criticism, biography of Christologists (232.092) and Mariologists (232.91092). Class biography of Jesus, Mary, Joseph, Joachim, Anne, and John the Baptist in 232.9, without use of notation 092 from Table 1.

241 vs. 261.8

[Christian] Moral theology vs. Christianity and socioeconomic problems

Some topics are covered in both moral and social theology, e.g., family relationships (241.63, 261.83587). Works classed in 241 focus on what conduct is right or wrong. Works classed in 261.8 may discuss right and wrong, but they treat the topic in a broader context as a problem in society and discuss Christian attitudes toward and influence on the problem. Class in 241 works that emphasize what is right and wrong, or what the individual should do. Class in 261.8 works that stress what the church's stance should be, what response the church or Christian community should make to alleviate the problem, or the church's view on problems transcending individual conduct. If in doubt, prefer 241.

241.3–.4 vs. 241.6

[Sin, vices, virtues] vs. Specific moral issues

Class in 241.3–.4 works about sin, about vices and virtues in general, and about specific vices and virtues. Class in 241.6 works treating specific moral issues in such a way that the works cannot be viewed as being about specific vices or virtues. Vices and virtues are habits, e.g., gluttony, temperance. Works on specific moral issues discuss the morality or immorality of specific actions, e.g., whether it is right to eat meat 241.693. In case of doubt, prefer 241.3–.4.

260 vs. 251–254, 259

Christian social and ecclesiastical theology vs. Local church [and] Pastoral care of specific kinds of persons

The local church is the group in which individual believers can meet regularly face to face for worship, fellowship, and church activities—for example, a congregation, a college church group.

Among the more recent forms of the local church are the small groups called basic Christian communities or basic ecclesial communities. These are smaller than parishes or congregations, but, like other forms of the local church, are organized for the general religious welfare of their members, not just for special projects or functions. They are classed in the same way as parishes, i.e., comprehensive works are classed in 250 (or in 262.26 when treated as part of ecclesiology) and specific aspects are classed with the aspect in the subdivisions of 250.

Activities undertaken by the church may be classed in 250 or 260, depending on the context. Most of the works in 250 are intended for the individual practitioner in the local setting. The local setting may be as small as a parish youth group or as large as a counseling program that serves a metropolitan area. Class the church's attitude to cultural and social problems, and its activities regarding them in 261 unless the context is limited to the local church, e.g., a practical work for the prison chaplain 259.5, but the church's attitude to the treatment of criminals 261.8336. If in doubt, prefer 260.

Some activities that can be conducted by the local church are classed in 260, e.g., public worship (264–265), religious education (268), spiritual renewal and evangelism (269). The context of works on these subjects is often broader than that of the local church.

Class church organization in 262, unless the scope is limited to administration of the local church (254).

261.5

Christianity and secular disciplines

Class here personal Christian views and church teachings about secular disciplines as a whole, their value, how seriously a Christian should take them, how far the disciplines should affect faith. Class Christian philosophy of a secular discipline or Christian theories within a discipline with the discipline, e.g., a Christian philosophy of psychology 150.1. Be alert for specific uses of secular disciplines for religious purposes, e.g., use of drama 246.72. If in doubt, class with the secular discipline.

261.5 vs. 231–239

Christianity and secular disciplines vs. Christian doctrinal theology

Class in 261.5 works treating generally antagonism between and reconciliation of Christian belief and another discipline. Class antagonism of a specific Christian doctrine and another discipline with the doctrine in 231–239. For example, class the relation between Christian doctrines in general and science in 261.55; but class the relation between Christian doctrine on the soul and modern biology in 233.5.

263.9, 291.36 vs. 394.265–.267

Church year and other days and times [of Christian religious observance] and Sacred times [among religions] vs. [Religious holidays]

Class in 263.9, 291.36, and cognate numbers in 290 the religious customs associated with religious holidays, e.g., sunrise Easter services 263.93. Class in 394.265–.267 the secular customs associated with religious holidays, e.g.,

Easter egg hunts 394.266. If in doubt, prefer 263.9, 291.36, and cognate numbers in 290.

268 vs. 230.071

[Christian] Religious education vs. Education in Christianity, in Christian theology

Class education in and teaching of Christianity as an academic subject in 230.071, e.g., a course on Christianity in secular secondary schools 230.0712. Class in 268 religious education as a ministry of the church for the purpose of confirming believers in Christian faith and life, and religious education programs sponsored by the local church. If in doubt, prefer 268.

Higher education in Christianity and Christian theology usually takes place in divinity schools, theological seminaries, and graduate departments of theology or ministry in universities. Students and scholars in such institutions may be preparing for the ordained ministry or they may be following a course of studies in the academic discipline of theology, or they may be doing both simultaneously. Such institutions are usually engaged both in religious education as a ministry of the church and in the academic study of Christianity and Christian theology. Class all such institutions with higher education in theology, i.e., in 230.0711, rather than in 268. Education or training of the clergy for specialized work is classed with the specialty, e.g., courses in Biblical studies 220.0711, programs in pastoral counseling 253.50711.

Christian religious education of adults, other than in the setting of formal higher education, is provided for at 268.434. Examples of works to be classed in 268.434 are works about adult education in parish religious education programs or Sunday schools.

Study and teaching with regard to any specific topic in Christianity are classed as follows:

> For religious education of children of elementary-school age, class a work on teaching a specific topic with works on religious education of children in general in 268.432.
>
> For religious education of persons of secondary-school age and older, class a work on teaching a specific topic with the topic, plus notation 071 from Table 1, e.g., study and teaching of church history 270.071.

See also discussion at 291.75 vs. 200.71.

280

Denominations and sects of Christian church

Biography

The kinds of biographies to be classed here are shown in the table of preference for biographies under 230–280: Biography.

The Decimal Classification Division classifies biographies with the main branch of the denomination rather than with the most specific organization or area, e.g., a biography of a clergyman of the Lutheran Church in America 284.1092, not 284.133092; of the African Methodist Episcopal Church 287.8092, not 287.83; of a Russian clergyman of the Eastern Orthodox Church 281.9092, not 281.947092; collected biography of Catholics in the United States 282.092273.

280.042 vs. 262.0011

Relations between denominations vs. Ecumenism

Class the ecumenical movement and interdenominational cooperation in 280.042. Also class in 280.042 relations between two or more specific denominations having notation that differs in the first three digits, e.g., relations between Roman Catholics (282) and Lutherans (284.1). Class works about relations among denominations having the same notation in the first three digits in the most specific number that includes them all, e.g., relations among the various Baptist denominations, between Baptists and Disciples of Christ 286. Class works about relations between one denomination and several others with the denomination emphasized, e.g., relations of Baptists with other denominations 286. Class theoretical works on ecumenism at 262.0011. Class discussions among denominations with respect to a specific subject with the subject, e.g., the Eucharist 234.163. If in doubt, class in 280.042.

281.1–.4

Early church

The early church is considered to be undivided by denominations until the schism of 1054. Therefore, the history of the Church prior to 1054 is classed in 270.1–.3, not here. The history of specific churches prior to 1054 is classed in 274–279.

The early history of the Eastern and Roman Catholic churches is also classed in 270. The history of these churches before 1054 is classed in 270.1–.3 or 274–279. Works on later history or works that cover both the early and later history are classed in 281.5–.9 or 282.

283–289

Protestant and other denominations

Notation for specific denominations is provided under the general name of some denominations, e.g., Presbyterian churches of United States origin 285.1, specific denominations 285.13. A specific denomination here means a named church body uniting a number of individual local churches, e.g., the Presbyterian Church (U.S.A.) 285.137, the Associate Presbyterian Church of North America 285.13 (the latter denomination is not listed in the schedule). In these cases, there is a special span for treatment of the denomination by continent, country, or locality, e.g., 285.14–.19. Class specific denominations in the notation provided for them (under the heading "specific denominations") if they are treated with regard to all or nearly all the geographic area they cover. Class works on a specific denomination covering a smaller area in the span for treatment by continent, country, or locality. For example, the Southern Baptist Convention is classed in 286.132, but a state association of Southern Baptist churches in Tennessee is classed in 286.1768 (286.1 plus notation 768 for Tennessee from Table 2). Class individual local churches in the special area span, regardless of the specific denomination to which they belong. Also class a work about several specific denominations in one country by area, e.g., a work describing the various Presbyterian denominations in the United States 285.173, not 285.13.

In several cases, the notation for specific denominations is limited to churches centered in the United States or the United Kingdom, e.g., the numbers following 284.1, 285.1, 285.2 and 287.5. In these cases, specific denominations in other countries are classed by dividing by area. For example, the Evangelical Lutheran Church in America is classed in 284.135, but the Lutheran Church of Sweden is classed in 284.1485 (284.1 plus notation 485 for Sweden from Table 2).

Churches which are centered in the United States or the United Kingdom may have branches in other countries; thus, there are usually instructions to add any area from Table 2, e.g., at 285.14–.19.

284.143

Lutheran church in Germany

Class here Evangelische Kirche in Deutschland, even though some non-Lutheran churches have joined with it.

290

Comparative religion and religions other than Christianity

290 by itself will never be used, since 291 has been designated as the number for comprehensive works on the non-Christian religions, on Christian and non-Christian religions, and for works on comparative religion.

291

Comparative religion

Except for 296 Judaism and 297 Islam, the subdivisions of the various religions in 292–299 are based on the subdivisions of 291. The order is sometimes different, but all topics in 291 are provided for either explicitly, by synthesis, or by implication under the separate religions included in 292–299. What is said about 291, therefore, will also be true of 292–299.

A comparison of the topics in 291 with the subdivisions of Christianity can sometimes be helpful in determining what goes where. A comparative list follows:

Social theologies	291.17	261
Doctrinal theologies	291.2	230
Public worship	291.3	246–247, 263–265
Religious experience, life, practice	291.4	242, 248
Moral theology	291.5	241
Leaders and organizations	291.6	250, 262, 267
Pastoral theology and work	291.61	253
Missions, religious education	291.7	266, 268
Sources	291.8	220
Denominations, sects, reform movements	291.9	280

A comparison of 291.211 (God, gods, goddesses, divinities and deities) with 231 (God) shows that 291.211 includes the topics listed at 231 that are not limited to Christianity: ways of knowing God, general concepts of God, attributes, providence, love and wisdom, relation to human experience, justice, and goodness.

Denominations and sects

In some cases, there is disagreement as to whether a specific sect should be listed under a religion or whether it should be considered a separate religion. The majority or mainstream members of the religion may not consider it a part of their religion. The criterion used in the Classification is that a denomination or sect is listed in the schedule with the religion to which its members say it belongs.

Treat the early history of a specific religion before its division into sects as general history of the religion, but class a comprehensive survey of the various sects in the number for the sects of the religion, e.g., the sects and reform movements of Buddhism 294.39. A work dealing with both early history and sects is classed in the general number for history of the religion.

Class the history of a specific congregation in the number for the sect to which it belongs, if this can be determined. ("Congregation" here refers to organizations in other religions analogous to the local church in Christianity.) If the sect cannot be determined, class the work in the broadest number for the sects of the religion.

Class religious orders in 291.65 and cognate numbers in 292–299, and not with any sect within the religion to which they may belong.

Common terms

Some terms that have their origin in a particular religion have become commonly used in other religions. Such terms as "karma" and "yoga" originated in Hinduism or other religions of Indic origin. These terms appear in the schedule under 291, because they may be discussed from a point of view not limited to the religion of origin. However, a work on yoga from a Hindu point of view should be classed with Hinduism in 294.5436 rather than in 291.436.

291.75 vs. 200.71

Religious education vs. Education [in religion]

Class in 200.71 education in and teaching of comparative religion, the religions of the world, and religion as an academic subject. 291.75 is meant for discussion of how various religions educate their members (especially young members) to be good followers of their own religions. Such education stresses knowledge of the faith and living as a member of a religion. It is meant to instill the values of a particular religion, not to study it in a detached manner. This type of education is usually termed "religious education" in contrast to the study of religion or "religious studies". In case of doubt as to which type of education is being treated, prefer 291.75.

At the level of higher education, students may be studying their own religion as an academic subject or they may be studying in order to become members of the clergy or they may be doing both at the same time. Religious education at the level of higher education is classed in 200.711 rather than in 291.75. Works about the education of the clergy are also classed with higher education in 200.711.

With regard to any specific topic in comparative religion or the specific religions in 292–299, study and teaching are classed as follows:

For religious education of children of elementary-school age, class a work on teaching a specific topic with works on religious education of children in general, e.g., Jewish religious education courses on the Tanakh (scriptures) for children 296.68.

For religious education of persons of secondary-school age and older, class a work on teaching a specific topic with the topic using notation 071 from Table 1, e.g., study of the Tanakh in Jewish colleges and universities 221.0711.

See also discussion at 268 vs. 230.071.

296.12–.14

Talmudic literature and Midrash

Add table

07

Modern commentaries since 1500

Most editions of the Talmud include the commentaries of ancient and medieval commentators along with the text. Use 07 only for works where the focus is on a commentary written by a modern author. Do not use 07 for works where there are some notes by a modern author but where the focus is on the original text or a translation of the text.

296.18 vs. 340.58

Halakhah (Legal literature) vs. Oriental law

Jewish law concerns itself with most of the issues of life, but its basis is religious. Also, it has rarely been the law of the land of any country. When it addresses secular matters, it is often from a religious perspective, because it is not the civil or criminal law of the land. For these reasons, comprehensive works on Jewish law are classed in 296.18. Class in 340.58 only works proposing or treating Jewish law as the law of a country, or comparing Jewish and other Oriental systems of law.

Class Jewish law on a specific religious topic with the topic elsewhere in 296, e.g., laws of marriage 296.444. Most works on this topic emphasize religious obligations, since they do not discuss the marriage law of a country.

If the law of a country is discussed, class the work with the law in 340, e.g., marriage law of Israel 346.5694016.

297.092

Persons

If a Muslim cannot be identified primarily with one function, activity, or sect, class his biography in 297.092.

For comprehensive biographies of persons of an identifiable function, activity, or sect, use the following table of preference:

Muḥammad the Prophet	297.63
Muḥammad's family	297.64
Muḥammad's companions	297.648
Prophets prior to Muḥammad	297.246092
Other persons in Koran	297.122092
Founders of sects and reform movements	297.8
Founders of Sufi orders	297.48
Higher non-Sufi religious leaders	297.092
Of specific sects and movements	297.8
Theologians	297.2092
Moral theologians	297.5092
Da‘wah workers	297.74
Leaders and members of Sufi orders	297.48
Other Sufis (mystics)	297.4
Religious educators	297.77092
Mosque officers	297.092
Of specific sects and movements	297.8
Members of sects and movements	297.8

Use 297.61 Leaders and their work for the role, function, and duties of religious leaders, not for biography of religious leaders.

Works dealing with only one specialized aspect of a person's career or religious experience are classed with the aspect, e.g., an account of conversion to Islam 297.574092.

297.26–.27

[Islam and secular disciplines]

Class in 297.26–.27 works that focus on theological issues in relation to secular disciplines. Class with the secular discipline works that focus on issues of importance to practitioners of the discipline, works that describe achievements of Muslims working within the discipline. For example, class in 297.267 Islamic attitudes toward the arts, e.g., what kinds of music and visual arts are consistent with Islamic belief. Class works describing achievements of Islamic arts with art. Class a work on Islam and politics that emphasizes Islamic religious issues in 297.272, but class a work on Islam and politics that emphasizes issues primarily of concern to political scientists in 320.917671 (political situation and conditions in the Islamic world) or another subdivision of 320. Class a general theological discussion about what kind of economic system is appropriate for an Islamic country in 297.273, but class a discussion of how to run an interest-free bank that would be of practical interest to a banker in 332.1. If in doubt, prefer a number outside 297.

297.4

Sufism (Islamic mysticism)

All works on Sufism are classed in 297.4 or one of its subdivisions, e.g., Sufi concepts of God 297.4111, Sufi worship 297.43, Sufi religious life and practice 297.44, Sufi orders 297.48. Comprehensive and non-Sufi works on Islam are classed in 297 and its subdivisions other than 297.4, e.g., comprehensive works on Sufi and non-Sufi Islamic views of God 297.211.

If in doubt, prefer a number outside 297.4.

299.93

Religions of eclectic and syncretistic origin

New Age religions

The "New Age" is a term that can be used to describe a great variety of works. There are New Age perspectives on health and medicine, environmentalism, gardening, and other activities and areas of knowledge. Class such works with the subject and discipline under discussion, even if the discussion rejects some of the main tenets of the discipline, e.g., using mental energy to cure illness 615.851.

Some New Age literature is mostly concerned with psychic and paranormal phenomena and is classed in 130 and its subdivisions.

Much of the New Age literature is religious. If a work is concerned with several New Age religions, class it in 299.93, unless it includes sects of the more established religions, e.g., sects of Buddhism, Hinduism, Native American religion, etc. In that case, class the work in 291, with other works on comparative religion.

In some cases, a writer will address some aspect of religion from a New Age perspective without attempting to speak for a particular known religion or to establish a new religion or sect. Class such works in 291, e.g., a New Age perspective on spirituality 291.4.

Class comprehensive works on the New Age as a whole or as a movement in 299.93.

300

Social sciences

Sociology 301–307 is the study of the processes, interactions, groups, culture, and cultural institutions that give form and purpose to every society. Part of the subject matter of sociology is found in 390 Customs, etiquette, folklore.

Some of the raw data for the study of human society is found in 310 Statistics, which constitutes a displacement of a standard subdivision concept from 300.21. Statistics on specific social subjects, however, are scattered throughout

300, plus notation 021 from Table 1, e.g., demographic statistics 304.6021.

In order to maintain internal peace and safety from external threat, societies devise political processes and institutions such as the state and government. These are dealt with in 320 Political science and in 351–354, the latter span of numbers dealing with the executive branch of government and public administration. The legislative branch is classed in 328, the judicial branch in 347. The military arm of government is found in 355–359.

The production, distribution, and consumption of the goods and services needed to maintain society are dealt with in 330 Economics. The part of economics that deals with commerce and trade is found in 380–382. Also found in the 380s are two of the major auxiliaries to commerce: communication 383–384 and transportation 385–388.

Law 340 treats the codified social, political, and economic rules that society requires and by which its members agree to live.

No social structure, however good, is perfect. Social problems are inevitable. The nature of these problems and the services society performs to overcome them are classed in the 360s.

Education 370 is one of the means through which society attempts to socialize the young and to prepare them for a useful role in the life of the society.

300, 320.6 vs. 352–354

Social sciences [and] Policy formulation vs. Specific topics of public administration

Public policy

Public policy in specific fields of social concern is normally classed with the field in the social sciences, regardless of whether the policy is formulated by legislation, administrative decision, or informal public consensus. For example, economic development and growth policies are classed in 338.9; welfare policies in 361.61. Public policy in matters outside the social sciences is normally classed in public administration, e.g., art policy 353.77, not 700. However, a policy with civil rights implications will be classed with civil rights in 323, e.g., religious policy 323.442, not 200 or 353.7. Be alert for exceptions given elsewhere in the schedules, e.g., public policy for libraries 021.8.

Certain policies have names that suggest one discipline but actually concern another. For example, technology policy, technology transfer policy, research and development (R&D) policy, and even science policy are usually formulated in terms of promoting economic growth and development. In each of these case, where the policies are metaphors for growth policies, they should be classed in 338.926.

For policy formulation, there is a choice between the interdisciplinary number 320.6 and the public administration number 352.34. The former covers how society as a whole makes up its mind; the latter concerns details of how an executive decides upon policies and gets them carried out. Governments usually, but not always, make up the leading parties in policy formulation, e.g., presidents, governors, courts, and legislatures at various levels. Hence the distinction must be made between policy formulation led or mediated by agencies in two or more branches of government (320.6) and that conducted by executive agencies (352.34). Policy formulation in a specific field by "the government" or society is classed with the policy as explained above, but policy formulation by executive agencies in specific fields is classed in 352–354, plus notation 234 derived from 352.34.

For example, class a work about what civil rights policies are or should be, and on how society as a whole decides what they should be, in 323; a work on how to administer civil rights policies in 353.485; and a work on how a civil rights agency resolves policy issues in 353.48234. Similarly, class a work on economic development in 338.9, report on an economic development agency in 354.27, and a work on policy making in an economic development agency in 354.27234.

Nomination hearings

One exception to the rule on hearings on public policy is nomination hearings. Because it is difficult to determine whether emphasis is on matters like personal qualifications and administrative issues or on the policies that the agency should carry out, all nominations for executive officers are classed in 352–354. Class nominations for the head of an agency in the field that the agency administers, using notation 2293 from the table under 352–354, e.g., nomination hearing for an attorney general 353.42293.

If in doubt about a work other than a nomination hearing, prefer the number outside public administration.

See also discussion at T1—068 vs. 353–354.

300 vs. 600

Social sciences vs. Technology

Many topics can be discussed from either a technological or a social point of view. If a work discusses how to make, operate, maintain, or repair something, it is normally classed in technology. If, on the other hand, it discusses the social implications of a technological operation, it falls in the social sciences, e.g., the economic importance of lumbering 338.17498, not 634.98.

Class the social utilization, the social control, and the social effect of technology in 300. The distinction between social science and technology is especially difficult for works on technology and its use or control, works that fall somewhere along the continuum from technology at one end to social science at the other. This is particularly true of regulatory control and popular works.

The following criteria will be useful in determining what material should be classed in 300 rather than 600:

1. When the emphasis in on the social use of the topic rather than on operating or processing it, e.g., tea drinking in England 394.12, not 641.33720942 or 641.63720942.

2. When the emphasis is on the overall perspective, e.g., the shift from coal to oil in American industry 333.82130973, not 621.4023.

3. When the emphasis is on social control as opposed to the control exercised during the manufacturing process, e.g., standards of drug quality imposed by a government agency or a trade association 363.1946, not 615.19.

4. When the raw statistics are cited, e.g., crop production, acreage, fertilizer consumption, farm size, use 338.1, not 630.

Technical reports

Many technical and research reports actually emphasize procedural technicalities and may refer to economic, legal, administrative, or regulatory complexities. Such reports should be classed in the social sciences. In determining the classification of a report series, and of individual reports in a series, consider the purpose of the writer and the mission of the agency authorizing the reports. If the emphasis is on the exercise of social control over a process, the report is classed in 300, not with the process in technology which is being controlled. For example, water quality monitoring systems are more likely to be classed in 363.739463 than 628.161.

It cannot be stressed too strongly that most of the social sciences are involved in technological processes, but are quite distinct from them. The classifier must go behind the technological vocabulary that often dominates title pages and tables of contents and analyze what is being described. If a book describes how railroads serve Argentina, it is classed in 385.0982, not 625.100982; a report on fertilizer and rice studying production efficiency in developing countries is classed in 338.162, not 633.1889.

Interdisciplinary works

Generally speaking, the 300 number is the interdisciplinary number for a phenomenon of social significance; it is used as the place of last resort for general works on a subject lacking disciplinary focus, e.g., a work on industrial archaeology not emphasizing how things were made 338.47609, not 609. However, works that emphasize descriptions of products or structures, such as clocks, locomotives, windmills, are classed in technology.

Biography and company history

Works on artisans, engineers, and inventors are normally classed in technology. Works on artisans, engineers, and inventors who are of more interest as entrepreneurs are classed in 338.7, e.g., Henry Ford 338.76292092.

Many works on products concentrate on the products of specific companies, e.g., Seth Thomas clocks or Ferrari automobiles. So long as these works emphasize the description and design of the products, class them in technology (or art 700 if the interest is artistic). But as soon as the organization or history of the company receives significant attention, class the works in 338.7, e.g., Seth Thomas clocks 681.113097461, but the Seth Thomas Clock Company and its clocks 338.7681113097461.

301–307

[Sociology and anthropology]

Sociology is the description and analysis of social phenomena. A work on social phenomena is classed in 301–307 even if it is being studied in a special context, e.g., in a political or economic institution. For instance, a descriptive work on family patterns of members of the executive branch of government is classed at 306.87; on the social role of political institutions in Korea at 306.209519; on the use of power among committee chairmen of a national legislature at 306.23.

See also discussion at 305 vs. 306, 909, 930–990 for aspects of anthropology.

301–307 vs. 361–365

[Sociology and anthropology] vs. Social problems and services

To be classed in 301–307 works on social phenomena must deal exclusively, or almost exclusively, with the phenomenon in its pure state, i.e., its social background, its role in the social structure, its effects on society, its innate characteristics and inner structure.

Consideration of social pathology apart from remedial measures is often found in 301–307, but is more likely to be considered in connection with actual and potential remedies found in the 361–365 span. The family as a social phenomenon is classed in 306.85. The dissolution of the family can be classed in either 306.88 or 362.82 depending on the focus of the work. A work discussing the effect of the changing social role of women in bringing about family dissolution is classed at 306.88. When the work discusses the actual and potential remedies for the topic, then the work is classed in 362.82, e.g., what can or should be done to prevent family dissolution 362.827. If in doubt, prefer 301–307.

Criminal anthropology (criminal sociology) is found in 364.2.

301–307 vs. 361.1, 362.042

[Sociology and anthropology] vs. Social problems vs. Social [welfare] problems

301 is used for social problems primarily when they are discussed as social phenomena, rather than as matters that society should take action to solve. 361.1 comprises social problems as a background to social action. 361.1 encompasses any and all kinds of social problems from providing child care to supplying water. Social problems at 362.042 should be thought of as social welfare problems, a narrower concept than 361.1. Usually the emphasis in works on social problems is clearly towards actual or potential remedies and

thus indicates 361.1. If the emphasis is not clear or if in doubt between 301 and 361.1 or 362.042, prefer 301.

302–307

Specific topics in sociology and anthropology

Topics in sociology and anthropology are arranged in a sequence that moves from the general to the specific. The most general topics and those most applied to other topics come first, followed in order by the less general and less applied, ending with the ones most often subject to analysis by the preceding topics. Social interaction, covering the basic forms of behavior in groups and between groups is found in 302; social processes that must be maintained so that society can continue, in 303; consideration of environment and population that affects development of all societies, in 304; the social groups, classes, and kinds of persons that make society possible, in 305; the culture and institutions that are the framework within which groups carry on the processes, in 306; and geographically restricted communities studied in various ways but always considered as whole communities, in 307.

302–307 vs. 150, T1—019

Specific topics in sociology and anthropology vs. Psychology [and] Psychological principles

Class in 150 works that focus on the individual, including those that discuss the influence of group behavior on the individual. Class in 302–307 works that focus on group behavior, including those that discuss the role of the individual in group behavior. If in doubt, prefer 302–307.

While application of psychology to any subject is classed with the subject plus notation 019 from Table 1, application of social psychology to a subject is classed in the social sciences (most often in 302–307) without adding notation 019. For example, class individual psychology of religion in 200.19, social psychology of religion in 306.6. If in doubt, prefer 302–307.

302–307 vs. 155.92, 158.2

Specific topics in sociology and anthropology vs. Influence of social environment [on psychology of individual] vs. [Applied psychology of] Interpersonal relations

Class in 155.92 the influence of family, friends, and other people upon the individual. Class in 158.2 the art of getting along with people. Class in 302–307 social interaction regarded as group behavior. If in doubt, prefer 302–307.

When a work treats both the psychology of social influences (155.92 or 155.94) and social interaction (302–307), prefer 302–307, e.g., the influence of a rural community on individuals and interactions within a rural community 307.72 (*not* 155.944).

302–307 vs. 156

Specific topics in sociology and anthropology vs. Comparative psychology

Class in 156 comparative social psychology when used to shed light on the behavior of the individual. Class in 302–307 works considering the social behavior of animals as a background to human social behavior. If in doubt, prefer 302–307.

302–307 vs. 320

Specific topics in sociology and anthropology vs. Political science (Politics and government)

Some works on major social institutions, processes, and phenomena may have a decidedly political cast, but if they emphasize how the social topics are related to and manifested in political ones, they are classed in 302–307. For example, a work on the relation between the feminist movement and the enfranchisement of women is classed in 305.42, not 324.623. If in doubt, class in 302–307.

302.2308

History and description [of media (means of communication)] with respect to kinds of persons

For the effects of mass media upon social groups, the rule that the effect of one subject on another is classed with the subject affected is reversed, since discussion of the social processes of mass media cannot be separated from their effects on society and on the various groups that constitute society. Thus, a work about the effect of television on young people is primarily about the role of television in society (and often about the issues involved in altering the impact of that role), and only secondarily about the effect on young people. This principle holds true for all groups and all media, e.g., the effect of radio on the life style of the middle class 302.234408622.

302.35 vs. 658, T1—068

Social interaction in complex groups vs. General management [and Table 1 notation for] Management [in specific fields]

Class in 658 and T1—068 works that emphasize how to manage. Class in 302.35 works that analyze and describe the social dynamics of how people behave and work in organizations. If in doubt, prefer 302.35.

303.48 vs. 306.4

Causes of change vs. Specific aspects of culture

Social effects of science and technology

Class in 303.48 the effects of scientific discoveries and technological innovations upon society, e.g., a work on the transformation of religious, economic, and leisure institutions stemming from the development of electronic media

303.4833. Class in 306.4 the patterns of behavior of the individuals and groups engaged in scientific or technical endeavors, e.g., a description of the milieu that seems to be conducive to technological innovation 306.4. If in doubt, prefer 303.48.

303.483 vs. 306.45, 306.46

Development of science and technology [as causes of social change] vs. Science [and] Technology [as cultural institutions]

Class in 303.483 the effects of scientific discoveries and technological innovations upon society, e.g., a work on the transformation of religious, economic, and leisure institutions stemming from the development of electronic media 303.4833. Class in 306.45 or 306.46 the patterns of behavior of the individuals and groups engaged in scientific or technical endeavors, e.g., a description of the milieu which seems to be conducive to technological innovation 306.46. If in doubt, prefer 303.483.

305

Social groups

It is the policy of the Decimal Classification Division not to add notation 08 from Table 1 to numbers in 305 unless otherwise instructed.

305 vs. 306, 909, 930–990

Social groups vs. Culture and institutions vs. World history [and] History of ancient world, of specific continents, countries, localities; of extraterrestrial worlds

305 is the comprehensive number for social groups interacting more or less freely with the rest of society. The role of social groups in specific institutions of society, however, is classed with the institution in 306, plus notation 08 from Table 1, e.g., women as a social category 305.4, but women in the family 306.85082; the status of serfs in society 305.563, but serfs in agricultural systems of labor 306.365 (where addition of T1—08625 is redundant); improvement of the status of gays in society 305.90664, but sexual institutions and orientation of gays 306.766 (where addition of T1—08664 is redundant). The role of social groups in history is classed in 909 and 930–990. The history of specific social groups, particularly that part of their history which is called their civilization, is more troublesome. Class in 909 and 930–990 only accounts of the major events shaping the history and civilization of a group. Normally, "history" is written only about racial, ethnic, and national groups, while "civilization" of all social groups tends to equate more with their culture (broadly conceived) than with the major events of their history. But be alert for exceptions: histories of major events, and description of nonanthropological civilization can be written for any group. If in doubt between 305 and 909, 930–990, prefer 305; if in doubt between 305 and 306, prefer 306.

The following table indicates the general relation among these numbers and other related ones:

Anthropology	301
Cultural and social anthropology	306
Of specific groups	305
Unassimilated indigenous ethnic groups	306.08
Physical anthropology	599.9
Criminal anthropology	364.2
Ethnology, cultural ethnology	305.8
Of unassimilated indigenous ethnic groups	306.08
History of specific ethnic groups	909.04
In specific countries	930–990
Social situation and conditions	306
In specific areas	306.09
Of specific groups	305
Specific unassimilated indigenous ethnic groups	306.08

305.8 vs. 306.089

Racial, ethnic, national groups [as social groups] vs. [Culture and institutions of] Indigenous racial, ethnic, national groups

Use 305.8 as the comprehensive number for specific racial, ethnic, national groups which interact more or less freely (whether in a dominant, nondominant, or intermediate position) with the rest of society. Use 306.089 only for indigenous groups living in distinct communities or "tribal areas" not fully integrated into the economic and social life of the nation in which they are (often involuntarily) incorporated. Such groups are normally perceived as culturally autonomous societies with their own distinctive cultures and institutions. If in doubt, prefer 305.8.

305.9 vs. 305.5

Occupational and miscellaneous groups vs. Social classes

Social classes take precedence over occupational and miscellaneous groups. Therefore, whenever a group found in 305.9 is considered in terms of its specific social status, 305.5 must be used. Use 305.9 for works on its component groups when either

1. There is little or no emphasis on class,

2. The group is well represented in two or more distinct classes, or

3. The group has an indefinite or transitional status.

If in doubt, prefer 305.9.

306.7 vs. 155.34

Institutions pertaining to relations of the sexes vs. [Individual psychology of] Sexual relations

Most works on the psychology of sexual relations treat social psychological aspects—the interaction between the partners. Such works are classed in 306.7. Only an occasional work emphasizes the psychology of the individual and is therefore classed in 155.34, e.g., a work that focuses on the anxieties of the individual with regard to sexual relations. In case of doubt, prefer 306.7.

307

Communities

This section includes works on the community in a relatively restricted area as a social phenomenon and works on community planning, development, and redevelopment. These terms are used here in their ordinary meaning to imply the planning for and development of the community as a whole. When specific subjects of community interest are addressed, the work is classed elsewhere in 300, e.g., economic development of the community 338.93–.99, developing hospitals for the community 362.11, planning community housing 363.5525, planning the city water supply 363.61, planning the education system 379.4–.9.

307.12 vs. 711

[Community] Planning vs. Area planning (Civic art)

Works that focus on the presentation and analysis of the physical plans, even if some historical and social material is included, are classed in 711. Works that focus on the historical or social aspects are classed in 307.12. If in doubt, class in 307.12.

320

Political science (Politics and government)

The state and government

The concepts of "the state" and "government" are emphasized in varying proportions in the subdivisions in 320–323. The state refers to the politically organized body of people occupying a more or less definite territory, while government (in the sense relevant here) is the organization through which the state exercises its authority and functions. The state may be considered an abstraction, the government its concrete embodiment. Comprehensive works on the abstraction are classed in 320.1; specific kinds of states in 321; and the relation of the state to people (and *vice versa*) in 322–323, e.g., political rights 323.5.

In contrast to "the state," the concept of "government" is more central to political science, and the word is often used loosely as an approximate equivalent of political science; therefore it has no separate number. However, specific aspects do have separate numbers, notably comparative government in 320.3, structure and functions of government in 320.4, and systems of government in

321.3–.9.

Most political theories transcend the distinction between the state and government, and are classed in 320.011 or with ideologies in 320.5.

See also discussion at 320.011 vs. 320.5; also at 320.9, 320.4 vs. 351.

Politics of specific subjects

Political activities relating to specific problems, issues, and organizations are classed with the subject in social science, e.g., the politics of immigration 325.1, of the banking system 332.1, of welfare policy 361.61. The politics of an administrative agency is classed with the subject that it administers, not with the subject in public administration (unless there is no alternative), e.g., politics of the U.S. Federal Highway Administration 388.10973 (*not* 354.770973), but politics of the U.S. Bureau of the Census 352.750973.

320 vs. 306.2

Political science (Politics and government) vs. [Sociology of] Political institutions

Be alert for works that discuss not politics and government but the social dynamics of political institutions. The basic thrust of 306.2 is to find out the social sources (e.g., race, class, family) and the social processes of political institutions, or the impact of these institutions and their activity upon the social environment. In addition, it is used for works dealing with political institutions and processes as models for social institutions and processes. In contrast, the objective in 320 is the descriptive, comparative, historical, and theoretical study of political institutions and processes. In these political studies, the social environment is considered only as a background. If in doubt, prefer 320.

320.011 vs. 320.5

General [political] theory; systems vs. Political ideologies

The distinction between general theory and political ideologies is more straightforward than might appear, since in most cases authors define their frame of reference. Class in 320.5 the schools of thought that are more or less prescriptive, and that, at least potentially, provide the rallying themes of political movements seeking to organize or reorganize the state and government in characteristic ways. Class in 320.011 theory that is more analytical, or that attempts to define the purposes of government rather than to recommend how to achieve these purposes. If in doubt between the two for a theory that is not named in 320.5, prefer 320.011.

320.55 vs. 297.09, 322.1

Religiously oriented [political] theories and ideologies vs. Historical, geographic, persons treatment [of Islam] vs. [Relation of the state to] Religious organizations and groups

Islamic fundamentalism

Class in 297.09 and other subdivisions of 297 only works that emphasize religious aspects of Islamic fundamentalism, such as a concern to maintain and hand down a pure version of the Islamic faith, a mindfulness to follow the strict letter of the Koran and Hadith, an attempt to generate a religious reawakening through preaching, teaching, and other forms of religious communication. Class in 297.272 Islam and politics only works that treat politics from the religious point of view.

Many works about Islamic fundamentalism, however, emphasize political aspects from a secular viewpoint; such works are classed in political science. Works emphasizing the religiously oriented political ideologies of Islamic fundamentalism are classed in 320.55. Works emphasizing the political role of Islamic fundamentalist organizations and groups in relation to the state are classed in 322.1.

If in doubt between a political science number and a subdivision of 297, prefer a political science number. If in doubt between 320.55 and 322.1, prefer 320.55.

320.9, 320.4 vs. 351

Political situation and conditions [and] Structure and functions of government vs. Public administration

The terms "government" and "public administration" can be easily confused and are sometimes used interchangeably. In the Dewey Decimal Classification, however, they are kept quite distinct. Government is limited to top-level considerations: the nature, role, goals, structure of states; their political direction and control; and the critical matter of forms by which central controls are exercised and balanced against each other. Public administration concentrates on executive agencies and the procedures used to carry out their goals, policies, and actions in various fields.

Of the several numbers in 320 concerning different aspects of government, 320.4 is the one most often confused with public administration. It includes works on the overall structure of governments, emphasizing their chief legislative, judicial, and executive organs. It may be used for works that discuss typical activities of the different branches, e.g., regulating safety as an illustration of the police function. It is also used for comprehensive works on government and public administration of specific areas. However, it should not be used for works emphasizing the work of carrying out goals and policies. Interdisciplinary works on government and public administration not limited to specific areas are classed in 320.

Some works that seem to cover the activities of government are simply discussing the habitual conduct and methods of people in high office, and should be classed in 320.9.

Most works that should be classed in 351 will clearly emphasize agencies of the executive branch, or the usual components of administration: planning, organizing, staffing, financing, and equipping agencies to do a job.

If in doubt, prefer 320.4 or 320.9 over 351, and 320.9 over 320.4.

322.1 vs. 261.7, 291.177

[Relation of the state to] Religious organizations and groups vs. Christianity and political affairs [and] Religions and political affairs

261.7, 291.177 and related numbers in 292–299 are in social theology, and are used for works on the position that religious people and organizations take or should take toward political affairs (including the state). 322.1 is used for works with a secular perspective, discussing the relationships between religious organizations or movements and states or governments. If in doubt, class in 322.1.

322.1 vs. 296.382, 320.54095694

[Relation of state to] Religious organizations and groups vs. Judaism and politics vs. [Nationalism in] Palestine Israel

Class in 296.382 works concerning politics and the state from the point of view of the religion of Judaism, e.g., whether it is a religious duty to support civil rights, whether Judaism encourages political freedom. Class political ideologies which are inspired by Judaism with Zionism in 320.54095694. Class the relation of religious groups to the state from a secular viewpoint in 322.1, e.g., religion and the state in Israel 322.1095694.

If in doubt between 296.382 and a political science number, prefer a political science number. If in doubt between 320.54095694 and 322.1, prefer 322.1.

324 vs. 320

The political process vs. Political science (Politics and government)

In the subheading "Politics and government" at 320, the word "politics" adds to "government" the concepts of adjusting relationships among individuals and groups in a political community, guiding and influencing the policy of government, and winning and holding control of society. More of the subdivisions of 320 are used for politics in the broad sense than are used for government. While the number 320 is used for comprehensive works on politics, most works use the word in the sense of party politics, and fall in 324. If in doubt, prefer 324.

See also discussion at 909, 930–990 vs. 320.

324 vs. 320.5, 320.9

The political process vs. Political ideologies vs. Political situation and conditions

Political movements

The word "movement" is used in various different senses in each of these numbers, and a given ideological movement may be treated in subdivisions of any one of them, depending upon the emphasis of the work. Use 320.5 for works concerning the thought and internal history or dynamics of such movements, 324 for their attempts to achieve power by nonviolent means and their ventures into electoral politics (even as splinter parties with scant chance of success), and 320.9 for the impact of movements upon the political system and their interaction with other political forces. Class comprehensive works on specific ideological movements in 320.5, but if in doubt, give preference first to 324, then to 320.9. However, also consider history numbers for movements which come to power or directly affect the major events of history.

See also discussion at 909, 930–990 vs. 320.

324.2 vs. 324.1

Political parties vs. International party organizations, auxiliaries, activities

For international treatment of parties, a distinction is made between collected accounts of national parties (324.2) and the organizations which parties and their activists create to promote party activities and influence on an international scale (324.1). The material which belongs in 324.1 is usually quite distinctive, since it concentrates on international organizations and their goals and influence, while generally considering specific national parties only in passing. Comprehensive works on national parties and international party organizations are classed in 324.2. If in doubt, prefer 324.2.

324.2094–.2099 and 324.24–.29

Treatment [of political parties] in specific continents, countries, localities in modern world [and] Parties in specific countries in modern world

For political parties, the three kinds of areas that are usually treated in a single span (continents, countries, and localities) are treated in three different ways. They are differentiated because the country (nation) is the main effective unit of political activity, and thus of party life and power. In most countries the local party is a branch of the national party, or, at least, a local organization of persons who regard themselves as members of a national party. The subordination of local party organization is achieved by using a separate span 324.24–.29, where country (nation) has first preference, followed by topic (party), and finally locality.

Treatment by continent and by region larger than a specific country is classed in 324.209 (or in 324.21 for specific kind of party). Treatment by country is classed in 324.24–.29, using area notation for country taken directly from Table 2. Treatment by locality within a country is classed in the country number, plus notation 09 from Table 1 at the appropriate point. In Canada, the United States, and Australia, each of which have strong traditions of autonomy for state and provincial parties, the states and provinces are treated like "countries" rather than like "localities."

For example, parties in any part of the United Kingdom are found under 324.241 and its zero subdivisions. The Conservative Party is classed in 324.24104, the Conservative Party in Wales in 324.2410409429 (*not* 324.242904). Sectionalist and separatist parties are classed by the same rule, e.g., a separatist party in Wales 324.241098409429 (*not* 324.24290984). Comprehensive works on parties of a specific part of a nation are classed in the national number, plus modified standard subdivision 009, e.g., parties of Wales 324.241009429, of Catalonia 324.246009467.

In the three countries provided with state and provincial spans, regions and localities are subordinated to national or state and provincial numbers, e.g., the Democratic Party in the Midwest 324.27360977, in New York City 324.274706097471.

Even though parties for specific countries and localities are never classed in 324.2094–.2099, the words "countries" and "localities" nevertheless are retained in the heading for the span because notation for countries and smaller areas is sometimes needed for history of the discipline, e.g., for a work on studies of political parties around the world conducted by German scholars 324.20943.

324.24–.29

Parties in specific countries in modern world

Parties in right-to-left spectrum vs. Other parties

If in doubt between parties identified primarily by position on the right-to-left spectrum (03–07 from the add table) and other recent parties (08 from the add table), prefer 08.

330 vs. 650

Economics vs. Management and auxiliary services

Works about business can be classed in several places. Most often the choice is between 330 and 650. Use 330 if the work presents general information, economic conditions, financial information (such as interest rates), and reports on what certain companies are doing. Use 650 when the work presents only practical managerial information that covers 651 Office services as well as 658 General management. If the work is limited to general management, use 658. Class comprehensive works on 330 and 650 in 330. If in doubt, prefer 330.

331 vs. 331.8

Labor economics vs. Labor unions (Trade unions), labor-management (collective) bargaining and disputes

Industrial relations in the broad sense of all relations between management and individual employees or employee groups is classed in 331. Industrial relations in the narrow sense of relations between management and labor unions is classed in 331.8. If in doubt, prefer 331.

331 vs. 658.3

Labor economics vs. Personnel management

Many of the topics in 658.3 are paralleled in 331. Class in 658.3 works written from the viewpoint of management, in 331 works written from the viewpoint of the employee (the worker). Also class in 331 works written from a neutral standpoint, simply describing the phenomena, and comprehensive works including both management and employee views. If in doubt, prefer 331.

331.1 vs. 331.11, 331.12

Labor force and market vs. Labor force vs. Labor market

Class comprehensive works on labor force and labor market in 331.1. Class works that discuss the labor force only in relation to the demand for labor in 331.12. Class employment and the part of the labor force that is actively employed in 331.125. If in doubt, prefer 331.1.

Class comprehensive works on employment and unemployment in 331.1; however, class works that merely give the number and characteristics of employed and unemployed workers without discussing the labor market in 331.11. If in doubt, prefer 331.1.

331.12042 vs. 331.1377

Government policy on the labor market vs. Prevention and relief of unemployment

Class in 331.12042 government labor policies and programs discussed in terms of broader purposes than just combating unemployment, e.g., public service employment as a countercyclical measure to provide both jobs for the unemployed and assistance to distressed areas and state and local governments. Class in 331.1377 works about government labor policies and programs that discuss them solely in terms of prevention and relief of unemployment. If in doubt, prefer 331.12042.

331.1372 vs. 331.13704

Causes of unemployment vs. Kinds of unemployment

Kinds of unemployment are frequently defined in terms of their causes. Class a specific cause that defines a kind of unemployment with the kind, e.g., structural causes of unemployment 331.137041 (*not* 331.1372). Class comprehensive works on causes of unemployment in 331.1372. If in doubt, prefer 331.1372.

331.2 vs. 331.89

Conditions of employment vs. Labor-management (Collective) bargaining and disputes

Class the process of collective bargaining on compensation and other conditions of employment in 331.89. Class the compensation and other conditions that result in 331.2. Class comprehensive works in 331.2.

331.29 vs. 331.22

Historical, geographic, persons treatment of compensation vs. Compensation differentials

General surveys of compensation in an area are classed in 331.29, but surveys that emphasize the differences in compensation among industries, occupations, and regions are classed in 331.22. If in doubt, prefer 331.29.

331.29 vs. 339.5

Historical, geographic, persons treatment of compensation vs. Macroeconomic policy

Wage-price policies of specific jurisdictions are classed in 331.29; but if the policies are discussed in relation to stabilizing the economy, they are classed in 339.5. If in doubt, prefer 331.29.

332, 336 vs. 339

Financial economics [and] Public finance vs. Macroeconomics and related topics

Macroeconomics is the study of the economy as a whole, especially with reference to its general level of output and income and the interrelationships among sectors of the economy. Some topics appearing in 332 and 336 are considered in macroeconomics (339). These topics, however, will be classed in 339 only when they are clearly discussed in relation to the total economic picture of a country or region. For example, monetary activities of central banks, normally 332.112, are classed in 339.53 when undertaken primarily to carry out macroeconomic policy. If in doubt, prefer 332 and 336.

332 vs. 338, 658.15

Financial economics vs. Production vs. Financial management

The choice among 332, 338, and 658.15 depends upon the point of view from which the topics are treated. Class in 332 works treating financial topics from the viewpoint of people or organizations with money to invest and those who serve them—investors, bankers, stockbrokers, and the like. Class in 338 works that treat financial topics from the viewpoint of people concerned with the production of goods and services, people who are interested in capital because it is necessary for production. For example, class in 332.6722 (domestic investment in specific types of enterprise) a work discussing whether mining is a safe and profitable field of investment for the general public; but class in 338.23 (financial aspects of extraction of minerals) a work discussing whether the mining industry will attract enough investment to expand production. Class in 658.15 (or with the subject, plus notation 0681 from Table 1) works that treat financial topics from the viewpoint of an executive responsible for the financial management of an organization, works that focus narrowly on managerial concerns. If in doubt, prefer 332.

332.024 vs. 640.42

Personal finance vs. [Personal] Management of money

Class in 640.42 works that deal only with everyday household finance, e.g., how to control day-to-day expenditures, how to budget for rent and groceries. Class in 332.024 works that are broader in scope, e.g., how to plan for one's financial future, including such topics as insurance and IRAs (individual retirement accounts). Class interdisciplinary works in 332.024.

332.632044 vs. 332.6323

General types of securities vs. Bonds

Gilt-edged securities

In American usage the term "gilt-edged securities" may refer to any security of exceptionally high quality, or it may refer primarily to high-quality bonds. Works on all types of gilt-edged securities are classed in 332.632044, works on bonds in 332.6323. In British usage the term "gilt-edged securities" refers to government bonds. Works on that topic are classed in 332.63232. If in doubt, prefer 332.632044.

332.6322 vs. 332.6323

Stocks (Shares) vs. Bonds

In British usage the term "stocks" usually refers to bonds rather than shares, but in American usage the term always refers to shares. Class stocks in the sense of shares in 332.6322, stocks in the sense of bonds in 332.6323. If in doubt, prefer 332.6322.

332.7 vs. 332.1

Credit vs. Banks

At 332.7 credit is divided by the type of credit, e.g., agricultural credit, home finance, personal loans, credit cards. At 332.1 (including 332.2 and 332.3, which are logically subordinate to 332.1), credit is divided by the type of financial institution offering it as a service, e.g., commercial banks, savings and loan associations, consumer finance institutions, insurance companies. Comprehensive works on a particular type of credit are classed in 332.7, e.g., a work discussing home mortgages as issued by commercial banks, mutual savings banks, savings and loan associations, and insurance companies 332.722. Comprehensive works on the credit offered by a particular type of institution and works discussing only one type of credit offered by a particular type of institution are both classed with the institution in 332.1–.3. For example, a work discussing all the kinds of loans and debit cards available from savings and loan associations and a work discussing the home mortgages available from savings and loan associations are both classed in 332.32. Similarly, comprehensive works on credit cards offered by commercial banks, department stores, oil companies, and travel agencies are classed in 332.765, but works about credit cards issued by commercial banks are classed in 332.178. If in doubt, prefer 332.7.

333.7–.9

[Natural resources and energy]

Consumption, development, and control of usage of natural resources are classed in 333.7–.9, with notation from the add table under 333.7. Consequently, some works discussing natural resources that are no longer in their natural state are properly classed in 333.7–.9, e.g., works about the economics of uses of urban lands 333.77.

333.7–.9 vs. 333

[Natural resources and energy] vs. Economics of land and energy

Use 333 for comprehensive works on natural resources only if the works contain substantial discussion of ownership. Use 333.7–.9 for comprehensive works on natural resources that treat predominantly nonownership aspects. If in doubt, prefer 333.7–.9.

It is more common for comprehensive works on land than for comprehensive works on other natural resources to be classed in 333 because it is more common for comprehensive works on land to contain substantial discussion of ownership.

See also discussion at 333.73–.78 vs. 333, 333.1–.5.

333.7–.9 vs. 363.1, 363.73, 577

[Natural resources and energy] vs. Public safety programs vs. Pollution vs. Ecology

Social aspects of ecology

Many works on ecology and specific natural environments are more about public policy and resource economics than biology. Terms that indicate a possible emphasis on economic and social problems are biodiversity, conservation, development, environmental impacts and monitoring, natural resource management, and risk assessment. Specific numbers to consider for these terms are:

1. For biodiversity: 333.95 (especially for works emphasizing its value or importance).

2. For conservation: 333.72 or the number for the specific resource plus notation 16 from the table under 333.7, e.g., conservation of biodiversity 333.9516.

3. For development: 333.715 or the number for the specific resource plus notation 15 from the table under 333.7, e.g., hydroelectric power development 333.91415.

4. For environmental impacts and monitoring:

A. The resource situation in general: 333.7 or the number for the specific resource (without adding any further subdivisions), e.g., monitoring biodiversity 333.95;

B. Environmental impacts: 333.714 or the number for the specific resource plus notation 14 from the table under 333.7, e.g., monitoring the impact of reclamation projects on wetlands 333.91814;

C. Potential environmental impacts: Class with the development whose impact is being studied, e.g., the potential impact of an oil pipeline on tundra ecology 388.55;

D. Pollution levels: 363.7363 or the number for the specific kind of pollutant or environment plus notation 63 from table under 362–363, e.g. monitoring oil pollution 363.738263. (The *impact* of pollution, however, is classed in 333.7–.9 as instructed under 4.B above, e.g., monitoring the impact of oil pollution on wetlands 333.91814.)

5. For natural resource management: 333.7 or the number for the specific resource, e.g., management of wetlands 333.918. (Management and control is represented by the span 15–17 in the add table under 333.7. Resource management is considered to approximate the whole of 333.7 or of the numbers for specific resources.)

6. For risk assessment:

A. Generalized risks to the environment: Treat as an impact study and class in 333.714 or the number for the specific resource plus notation 14 from the table under 333.7, e.g., contemporary risks to wetlands of America 333.918140973;

B. Risks of specific developments: Treat as a study of potential impacts, and class with the specific development, e.g., assessing the risk of tourism to biodiversity in East Africa 916.7604;

C. Safety risks: Use the subdivision for the specific threat in 363.1 plus notation 72 from the table under 362–363, e.g., assessing the risk to humans of pesticides in food 363.19272.

If in doubt, prefer 333.7–.9, 363.1, and 363.73, in that order.

See also discussion at 363.73 vs. 571.95, 577.27.

333.7–.9 vs. 363.6

[Natural resources and energy] vs. Public utilities and related services

Use care in distinguishing between the resources and energy (333.7–.9) and the utilities delivering the resources to customers (363.6). For instance, class in 333.7–.9 comprehensive works on resources, projection of needs and supplies, development, conservation, protection of resources. Class in 363.6 problems and services related to distributing the resources to users. A useful device in distinguishing the two is to consider that "supply" as a noun is classed in 333.7–.9, while "supply" as a verb is classed in 363.6. If in doubt, class in 333.7–.9.

An exception is made for electrical power companies. Works about these utilities almost always emphasize the problems of developing the "supply" as a noun, saying little about the problems of distributing the electricity to customers, and seldom discuss prices without reference to production costs. A work about electrical power utilities focusing on distribution should be classed in 333.7932 with the bulk of works about electrical power companies.

Class the rationing of natural resources still in their natural state at 333.717 and cognate numbers in 333.7–.9, but of final products in 363, e.g., wellhead allocation of natural gas for companies or jurisdictions 333.823317, but rationing of natural gas among consumers or classes of consumers at the other end of the line 363.63. If in doubt, prefer 333.717 and cognate numbers in 333.7–.9.

333.7–.9 vs. 508, 913–919, 930–990

[Natural resources and energy] vs. Natural history vs. Geography of and travel in ancient world and specific continents, countries, localities in modern world; extraterrestrial worlds vs. History of ancient world; of specific continents, countries, localities; of extraterrestrial worlds

National parks and monuments

Class general guidebooks to all the national parks of an area in 913–919, plus notation 04 from the add table at 913–919 followed by notation for the historic period when the guidebook was written, e.g., a 1989 general guidebook to the national parks of South America 918.0438.

Class general works about historical monuments with the events commemorated. For example, class a battlefield national park with the battle, e.g., Gettysburg National Military Park 973.7349. Class a park associated with the life of an individual in the biography number for that individual, e.g., Lyndon B. Johnson National Historical Park 973.923092, George Washington Carver National Monument 630.92.

For works on national parks where the main attraction is nature, use 333.7–.9 if the emphasis is on conservation and protection of natural resources, e.g., forest parks 333.784, game reserves 333.954916. If the emphasis is on description of and guides to natural phenomena, use 508 or related number in the 500s, e.g., a comprehensive guide to the natural history of Yellowstone National Park 508.78752, a guide to the geology of Yellowstone 557.8752.

If in doubt, prefer 333.7–.9 over 508 and related numbers or 900; prefer 508 and related numbers over 900; prefer 930–990 over 913–919.

See also discussion at 913–919: Historic sites and buildings; also at 913–919: Add table: 04: Guidebooks; also at 930–990: Wars; also at 930–990: Historic preservation.

333.714

[Environmental impact studies]

Class impacts on specific environments or resources with the impact, e.g., economic impact on Rome of a major new waste treatment facility 330.945632, impact of the same treatment plant on the waters of the Tiber River 333.916214094562. Class projected impacts with the program or development that is being studied, e.g., projected impact of proposed standards for water pollution 363.739462.

333.72 vs. 304.28, 363.7

Conservation and protection [of natural resources and the environment] vs. Environmental abuse [in human ecology] vs. Environmental problems and services

"Environmentalism" refers to two different sets of issues. Use 363.7 when the issues are preserving and restoring the quality of the social living space, i.e., taking care of wastes, pollution, noise, the dead, and pests. Use 333.72 for the broader concept of preserving and protecting the supply as well as the quality of natural resources. Works about the environmental movement that focus on the concerns it shares with the long established conservation movement are classed in 333.72. Use 304.28 for works that emphasize the effect upon society of overuse, misuse, or pollution of the environment. If in doubt between 333.72 and either 363.7 or 304.28, prefer 333.72. If in doubt between 304.28 and 363.7, prefer 304.28.

333.73–.78 vs. 333, 333.1–.5

[Land] vs. Economics of land and energy vs. Ownership of land

Land as property is classed in 333.1–.5, where the central issues are the right to possession and use, and the right to transfer possession and use. The only control of land that belongs in 333.1–.5 is the control that stems from ownership.

Land as a natural resource, as a source of economic goods (chiefly agricultural and mineral), is classed in 333.73–.78. The usage of the land and its resources is classed there, as distinct from the right to use that is classed in 333.1–.5. The controls of usage that hold regardless of who owns the land are classed in 333.73–.78, with notation 17 from the add table under 333.7. Price control and zoning are among the controls covered by notation 17. Comprehensive works on land policy are classed in 333.73.

Land inventories often focus on land as a resource and land usage; such inventories are classed in 333.73–.78.

Comprehensive works on both 333.1–.5 and 333.73–.78 concepts are classed in 333 only if they contain substantial discussion of ownership. If in doubt, prefer 333.73–.78.

See also discussion at 333.7–.9 vs. 333.

333.76 vs. 333.73

Rural lands Agricultural lands vs. Land

Class rural lands of a specific physical condition, if not devoted to a specific use, in 333.73. For example, class rural semiarid lands in general in 333.736; however, class semiarid lands devoted to agriculture in 333.76, semiarid lands devoted to grazing in 333.74. If in doubt, prefer 333.76.

333.94 vs. 338.0919

Space [as a natural resource] vs. [Economics of production in space]

Class in 333.94 works that discuss space as a scarce resource analogous to land or air, for example, because there are a limited number of good positions for geostationary satellites, because we cannot afford to fill the space around the earth with orbiting garbage. Class in 338.0919 comprehensive works on the industrialization of space, e.g., works that discuss transportation and manufacturing in space. If in doubt, prefer 333.94.

333.955–.959 vs. 639.97

[Resource economics of] Specific taxonomic groups of animals vs. [Conservation technology of] Specific kinds of animals

Conservation and management

When determining whether works on specific kinds of animals should be classed in economics (333.955–.959) or technology (639.97), one should bear in mind that conservation and resource management are primarily economic concepts. Discussion of public policy and programs; estimates or statistics of populations, abundance, harvest, catches, and kills; appeals for resource management; and calls to protect an animal or save it from extinction are all signs that a work belongs in economics.

A few terms used in conservation work are troublesome because they may refer to either economics or technology. Class works on rescue, reintroduction, management, and habitat improvement in technology only if they are focused on hands-on activities where the animals are living. Class the works in economics if they are focused on programs and the rationale behind the activities.

If in doubt, class in 333.955–.959.

335 vs. 306.345, 320.53

Socialism and related systems [of economics] vs. [Sociology of] Socialism [as an economic system] vs. Collectivism and fascism [as political ideologies]

Since socialism and related systems are based upon theories of how the economy does or should work, interdisciplinary works and works on their philosophic foundations are classed in 335. The number is also used for wide-ranging works that do not fit within normal disciplinary boundaries but are clearly about socialism and related systems. Other numbers are used only for works clearly limited to a specific discipline.

Use 320.53 for works that emphasize how political movements intend to introduce socialism and what political forces they expect to harness to attain and keep power, or that discuss political movements and forces without in-depth discussion of the economic dynamics or theory. Works on political ideology often discuss questions such as the class bias or motivation of political forces, the dependability of political allies of different economic background, and progress (or lack of it) toward economic goals, but do not usually get into economics *per se*.

In contrast to 306.345, both the other numbers may include material that is prescriptive, that says how society, the economy, or the political system ought to be organized. 306.345 is intended for sociological studies of how socialist economic systems work out in practice. It should be limited to such studies. Works discussing how another economic system should be reorganized into a socialist system must be classed in 335.

335.4 vs. 335.401, 335.411

Marxian systems vs. Philosophy [of Marxian systems] vs. Philosophic foundations [of Marxian systems]

General works on theory of Marxian systems are classed in 335.4. Works that emphasize the philosophic foundations of Marxian systems are classed in 335.411. 335.401 should seldom be used, except for its subdivisions, e.g., 335.4014 for Marxist terminology. If in doubt, prefer 335.4.

335.4112 vs. 146.32

Dialectical materialism [as a philosophic foundation of Marxian systems] vs. Dialectical materialism [as a philosophic viewpoint]

Class in 335.4112 dialectical materialism applied to the economic and political aspects of Marxian systems. Class in 146.32 dialectical materialism as a philosophical viewpoint either not applied to topics outside philosophy or else applied to many different disciplines. If in doubt, prefer 335.4112.

336 vs. 352.4

Public finance vs. Financial administration and budgets

Class in 352.4 works focusing on the practical aspects and details of financial management and accounting in the public sector. For example, class financial control, debt management, and government budgets in subdivisions of 352.4. Class in 336 works on the economics of public finance, e.g., economic analyses of government spending policy 336.39. Class works treating both public finance and public financial administration in 336.

336.093, 336.4–.9 vs. 336.01

[Public finance in] The ancient world [and] Public finance of specific continents, countries, localities in modern world vs. Public finance by governmental level

Class works about multiple jurisdictions at the same level in 336.01, e.g., public finance at the state level in the United States 336.01373. Class works about a single jurisdiction in 336.093 or 336.4–.9, e.g., public finance at the national level in the United States 336.73 (*not* 336.01273). If in doubt, prefer 336.093 and 336.4–.9 over 336.01.

336.2009 vs. 336.201

Historical, geographic, persons treatment [of taxes and taxation] vs. Taxes by governmental level

Class works about multiple jurisdictions at the same level in 336.201, e.g., state taxes in the United States 336.201373. Class works about a single jurisdiction in 336.2009, e.g., federal taxes in the United States 336.200973 (*not* 336.201273). If in doubt, prefer 336.2009.

336.249 vs. 368.401, 368.4011

Social security taxes [in public finance] vs. [General principles of social security] and [Rates for social security]

Class broad economic, public finance, tax policy aspects of social security taxes in 336.249. Class actuarial and administrative aspects of finance for social security in 368.401, of rates and rate making for social security in 368.4011. If in doubt, prefer 336.249.

336.3409 vs. 336.343

Historical, geographic, persons treatment [of public debt] vs. Public debt by governmental level

Class works about multiple jurisdictions at the same level in 336.343 and its subdivisions, e.g., public borrowing and public debt at the state level in the United States 336.343273, international debt in Latin America 336.3435098. Class works about a single jurisdiction in 336.3409, e.g., borrowing and debt at the national level in the United States 336.340973 (*not* 336.343373).

337.3–.9 vs. 337.1

Foreign economic policies and relations of specific jurisdictions and groups of jurisdictions vs. Multilateral economic cooperation

Class cooperative relations among the states of multistate groups in 337.1, e.g., cooperation within the European Union in 337.142; but class relations between a cooperative group treated as a whole and other countries or groups in 337.3–.9, e.g., economic relations of the European Union with Japan 337.4052 (*not* 337.142), economic relations of the European Union with the rest of the world 337.4 (*not* 337.142). If in doubt, prefer 337.3–.9.

338 vs. 060, 381, 382, 670.294, 910, T1—025, T1—0294, T1—0296

Production vs. General organizations and museology vs. Internal commerce (Domestic trade) vs. International commerce (Foreign trade) vs. Trade catalogs and directories [of manufacturers] vs. Geography and travel vs. [Table 1 notation for] Directories of persons and organizations vs. [Table 1 notation for] Trade catalogs and directories vs. [Table 1 notation for] Buyers' guides and consumer reports

1. Directories

Business directories should be classed in business numbers, usually 338 or 381–382, while nonbusiness directories should be classed in nonbusiness numbers in 001–999. There are many qualifications about what constitutes business directories; thus, the following guidelines need to be considered.

2. Directories of products and services

Directories of products and services may be either of products and services *produced* by people active in the field, or of products and services *used* by people active in a field, and (unless other instruction is given below) should be classed with the producers or users, respectively. If the directories cover a narrow range of products and/or services from one or two kinds of producers intended for one kind of user, class with the producers, e.g., a directory of library equipment and furniture 681, not 022.90294. When there are three or more kinds of producers serving one kind of user, then stay with the user number, e.g., publishers, binders, and furniture makers serving libraries 020.294.

Product directories

Class comprehensive directories of manufacturers that emphasize the products for sale and give little information about the companies beyond address and phone number (the basic information needed to help the buyer obtain and use the product) in 670.294. Such works may be arranged by product category, or by company with a products index. If the works concentrate on a specific line of products, class them with the line of products, plus notation 0294 from Table 1.

Class "yellow pages" directories that emphasize products (often called industrial yellow pages) as instructed for product directories of manufacturers in the previous paragraph. (*See the next paragraph for "yellow pages" directories that include a wide range of services, and the second paragraph of section 4 [Directories of persons and organizations] for yellow pages that are published in connection with telephone or city directories.*)

Directories listing services

Class directories that include a wide range of services as well as products in 338 or 338.4, depending upon coverage, even though they are aimed at end users and give little information about the companies beyond that needed to help buyers obtain goods and services. Use 338.00294 if the directories list unprocessed products of agriculture or mining; otherwise, use 338.47000294 for comprehensive directories of services, for comprehensive directories covering services along with products of secondary industries. Class directories of specific services with the service in 001–999. (*See section 3 [Buyers' guides] on the choice between standard subdivisions T1—0294 and T1—0296, and section 4 [Directories of persons and organizations] on the choice between standard subdivisions T1—0294 and T1—025.*)

Directories including economic or organizational information

Class in 338.7 directories of manufacturers and/or other enterprises that in addition to information about products and services give an approximately equal amount of economic and/or organizational information about individual enterprises (that is, information intended for people who might want to invest in the companies, go into joint ventures with them, hire them as subcontractors, or serve as sales representatives for them). Directories that give information about the ownership of companies, approximate worth of companies, names of companies' bankers, for example, as well as the product information, belong to this category. Use 338.70294 for directories that give that kind of information about providers of a wide range of services as well as goods (or 338.740294 if the providers are explicitly identified as corporations); use 338.761000294 for directories that give that kind of information about services alone; and use subdivisions of 338.76 plus notation 0294 from Table 1 for directories giving that kind of information for specific lines of goods and/or services. (*See section 5 [Directories of products and services vs. Directories of organizations] on the choice between standard subdivision T1—0294 and T1—025 when one or the other kind of information predominates.*)

Directories of importers and exporters

Class product directories of importers and exporters (which are usually aimed at establishing trade relationships between importers in one country and exporters in another) in 382, plus notation 0294 from Table 1. However, directories of foreign chambers of commerce are usually classed in 382.025 or 382.06, since they seldom get specific about products. An example would be a directory of the American Chamber of Commerce in Rome 382.02545632. Directories of domestic chambers of commerce should be classed in 380.1 if there is significant material about importers, exporters, or foreign markets; otherwise, class in 381. (*See also T1—0601–0609 vs. T1—025.*)

Retail directories

Class retail directories (often called commercial directories or industrial buyers' guides) in 381.1 or 381.4. Directories *for* retailers, that is, for persons expecting to resell what they buy, are usually product and service directories, and will normally be classed in numbers ending with notation 0294, while directories *of* retailers will normally be classed in numbers ending with notation 025 from Table 1. Use 381.1 with the appropriate standard subdivision for comprehensive retail directories of an area if farm and mining products are listed; otherwise, use 381.45 with the appropriate standard subdivision for comprehensive retail directories of secondary industries and services, and 381.45 without standard subdivision for retail service directories. Class retail directories for a specific line of goods or services in the appropriate subdivision of 381.4.

3. Buyers' guides

Buyers' guides in the sense intended in T1—0296 refer only to works evaluating products and/or services. When there is no evaluation, as is usually the case in the industrial buyers' guides mentioned in the preceding paragraph, use T1—0294.

If a directory or other listing, either of persons and organizations or of products and services, gives major attention to evaluation of products and services, use T1—0296. That is, consider the work to be a buyers' guide regardless of whether it is organized by product and service, or by organization and person, and regardless of what related directory-type information there is on where or how to get the products and services. For example, class evaluative industrial buyers' guides in T1—0296 rather than T1—0294.

4. Directories of persons and organizations

Class directories that give details of the internal organization of, or list the directors of, business enterprises in 338.7, 338.8, or 334 or their subdivisions, plus notation 025 from Table 1, regardless of the field of operation of the enterprises. However, class comprehensive directories on all types of organizations, comprehensive directories on nonbusiness organizations, and directories of specific general noncommercial organizations in 060. Class directories of *nonbusiness* organizations limited to a specific subject with the subject, plus notation 025 from Table 1.

Class local telephone and city directories in 914–919, plus notation 025 from Table 1; and international telephone directories not limited to one continent in 910.25. Class yellow pages published in connection with city or telephone directories with the city or telephone directory. (*See the first two subsections of section 2 [Directories of products and services] for separately published yellow pages.*)

Class all other directories of persons with the subject in 001–999, plus notation 025 from Table 1.

5. Directories of products and services vs. Directories of organizations

If a directory combines information on products and services with economic and organizational information on business enterprises in roughly equal proportion, class it in 338.70294 (if general); in 338.740294 (if general, but explicitly limited to corporations); or in subdivisions of 338.76, plus notation 0294 from Table 1 if limited to specific lines of goods and/or services. However, relatively few directories do combine the two kinds of information in roughly equal proportion, so be alert for predominance. If the organizational and economic information predominates, and the product and service information serves mostly to describe where the enterprise puts its money and effort, class the directory in 338.7025, 338.74025, or in subdivisions of 338.76, plus notation 025 from Table 1. If the product information clearly predominates, and the organizational information does not extend far beyond listing contacts for ordering the product, class the directory in 670.294 or the specific technology number, plus notation 0294 from Table 1.

Extensive yellow page sections are a good indicator for use of T1—0294 for product directories. Most of them will be classed as instructed in the first two subsections of section 2 (Directories of products and services). However, see the second paragraph of section 4 (Directories of persons and organizations) for yellow pages of telephone and city directories.

See subsection "Retail directories" of section 2 (Directories of products and services) for the choice between T1—0294 and T1—025 with retail directories.

6. Directories of noncommercial organizations

Directories (even of services and miscellaneous products) of noncommercial organizations, are seldom classed in 338: they seldom give economic information (other than prices when the products or services are not free); and the interdisciplinary number for organizational information on noncommercial organizations is 060. Even interdisciplinary directories of services of noncommercial organizations (that is, directories of services covering a broader scope than what could reasonably be classed in 360) should be classed in 060 (*not* in 338), plus notation 0294 from Table 1, e.g., a directory of services provided by French societies for the sciences and humanities 064.0294. Only directories of nonprofit organizations that compete in fields normally served by business organizations are classed in economic numbers, e.g., organizational directories of publicly run utility companies 338.7613636025, directories of products and services provided by cooperatives in all fields 334.0294.

338.09 vs. 332.67309, 338.6042, 346.07, 658.11, T1—0681, 658.21, T1—0682

Historical, geographic, persons treatment of production vs. Historical, geographic, persons treatment [of international investment] vs. Location [of production] vs. Commercial law vs. [Management of] Initiation of business enterprises [and Table 1 notation for] Organization and financial management vs. [Management of plant] Location [and Table 1 notation for] Plant management

Class in 338.09 works showing where industry is in fact located. Class in 338.6042 the rationale for and the process of locating business organizations. A useful device in distinguishing the two is to consider location in 338.09 to be a condition, in 338.6042 an action.

Class in 332.67309 works describing the advantages and disadvantages of making international investments, including establishing international enterprises, in particular areas.

If in doubt among the economics numbers 338.09, 338.6042, and 332.67309, prefer 338.09.

Class in 346.07 laws and regulations for governing investment in and initiation of businesses. If in doubt between an 346.07 and 338.09, 338.6042, or 332.67309, prefer the economics number.

Class in 658.11 or with the subject, plus notation 0681 from Table 1 works on managerial techniques for locating a new business that treat multiple issues, e.g., tax and labor laws in various jurisdictions, location of markets, location of sources of raw materials and skilled labor. Class in 658.21 or with the subject, plus notation 0682 from Table 1 works limited to managerial techniques for locating the physical plant itself, with emphasis on a location that will facilitate good plant management, e.g., one with adequate level ground for possible future expansion. If in doubt between 658.11 and 658.21, prefer 658.11. If in doubt between a management number and an economics number, prefer the economics number.

338.092

[Business biography]

Class a biography of an entrepreneur or business leader associated with a specific business enterprise in 338.76, e.g., the founder of a cosmetics manufacturing company 338.766855092. Class biographies of business leaders not limited to a specific enterprise but limited to a specific field in 338.1–.4, e.g., business leaders in the automotive manufacturing industry 338.4762920922. Class biographies of people associated with the development and operation of specific types of enterprises but not confined to a specific industry or group of industries in 338.6–.8, e.g., small-business owners 338.6420922, persons associated with trusts 338.850922. Class company directors on the boards of companies in several industries or groups of industries in 338.70922.

Class collected biography of entrepreneurs in many fields in 338.040922. Class collected biography of businessmen in many fields in 338.0922.

338.1 vs. 631.558

[Economics of] Agriculture vs. [Crop] Yields

Usually works on crop yields are compilations giving the total production of an area, and are classed in 338.1. Works on yields per unit of area are classed in 338.16 if they are taken as indicators of production efficiency, either of agricultural systems using various methods (e.g., crop rotation) or of agricultural systems prevailing in various areas. If yield studies per unit of area are used in technical tests of varieties or specific production techniques, they are classed with the subject in agriculture, e.g., yield tests of fertilizer use 631.80287. Use of 631.558 is limited to works that have little or no economic or testing implications, e.g., lists of record yields of various crops. If in doubt, class in 338.1.

338.1749 vs. 333.75

Products of forestry vs. Forest lands

Several of the concepts provided at 333.75 by virtue of the add table under 333.7 potentially conflict with concepts provided at 338.1749. The general distinction is that works classed in 333.75 are primarily concerned with forest land and uncut timber as present and future resources, whereas works classed in 338.1749 are primarily concerned with cut timber as a product to be sold. Class comprehensive works in 338.1749.

Use of add table under 333.7

11

Reserves (Stock, Supply)

Class in 333.7511 the supply of forest land and uncut timber, in 338.17498 the supply of cut timber.

12

Requirements (Need, Demand)

Class in 333.7512 the demand for timber discussed in terms of its effect on the supply of forest land and uncut timber. Class in 338.17498 the demand for timber discussed in terms of how much timber will have to be cut in order to meet the demand.

13

Consumption (Utilization)

Class in 333.7513 use and abuse discussed in terms of the effect it has on the future supply of uncut timber. Class in 338.17498 utilization of forests to provide products for sale.

15

Development

Class in 333.7515 measures to increase the supply of forests as a long-term resource, e.g., reforestation 333.75153. Class in 338.174956 reforestation viewed as a way to produce crops that can be harvested and sold.

338.37 vs. 333.954

Products [derived from other extractive industries] vs. Animals [as resources]

Several of the concepts provided at 333.954 (and 333.955–.959) by virtue of the add table under 333.7 potentially conflict with concepts provided at 338.37. To distinguish between the two numbers, apply the same general criteria as explained at 338.1749 vs. 333.75. For example, class the supply of uncaught animals in 333.95411 (333.954 plus notation 11 Reserves [Stock, Supply]). Class the supply of caught animals in 338.37. Works classed in 333.95411 may, however, use statistics of catches as an aid in estimating the population of uncaught animals. Class comprehensive works in 338.37.

Class measures to increase the supply of animals in nature as a long-term resource in 333.954 or 333.955–.959, plus notation 15 Development, e.g., stocking mountain streams with fish 333.95615. Class the culture of nondomesticated animals viewed as a way to produce crops that can be harvested and sold in 338.371. Do not use 338.372 (Products of fishing, whaling, hunting, trapping) for measures to increase the supply of animals.

If in doubt, prefer 338.37.

338.372

Products of fishing, whaling, hunting, trapping

Class finfishing and comprehensive works on finfishing and shellfishing in 338.3727. Class fishing for mollusks and comprehensive works on shellfishing (mollusks and crustaceans) in 338.3724, fishing for crustaceans in 338.37253. Class hunting for mammals and comprehensive works on hunting in 338.3729.

For geographic treatment of a fishing industry, use the area number for the industry's home base, not the place where the fish or other animals are caught. Thus a fleet based at Los Angeles is classed in 338.37270979494, even though the fish are caught off Lower California. It is not classed in either 338.372709722 Lower California or 338.3727091641 Southeast Pacific Ocean.

338.4 vs. 338.47

Secondary industries and services vs. Goods and services

For works covering many industries, class in 338.47 works that focus on products or services themselves. Class in 338.4 broader works that consider such topics as financial aspects and productions efficiency in industries as well as discussing the products or services. If in doubt, prefer 338.4.

For works that treat a specific industry or service, use 338.47 both for works that focus on the product or service and for broader works that consider financial aspects and production efficiency as well as the the product or service.

338.7 vs. 335.9

Business enterprises and their structure vs. Voluntary socialist and anarchist communities

Use 335.9 only for truly voluntary communities. Use 338.7 for communes or collectives imposed by force, if discussed as organizations of production, e.g., nonvoluntary agricultural communes 338.763. If in doubt, prefer 338.7.

338.888–.889

[Foreign-owned enterprises]

Enterprises classed here include those with mixed ownership in which some of the owners are local, but the principal owners are foreign.

338.926 vs. 352.745, 500

Information policy vs. Promoting general fields of knowledge vs. Natural sciences and mathematics

"Science policy" generally focuses on what society should do to promote the utilization of science and the growth of industries and activities based on science. Thus, it generally should be regarded as a policy or program to promote economic development and growth (338.926 and cognate numbers in 338.93–.99). Class works on public administration of science policy in 352.745 and cognate numbers in 352–354. If there is an emphasis on administration of economic development use 354.274. In the absence of a focus on the social sciences, use 509 for natural science policy in an area. If in doubt, prefer 338.926.

339.32 vs. 339.22

Other kinds of national accounts and accounting vs. Personal distribution of income and wealth

Personal income as a measure of national income is classed in 339.32. Personal income in relation to distribution of the national income is classed in 339.22. If in doubt, prefer 339.32.

339.41, 339.42 vs. 332.41

Income and its relation to consumption [and] Cost of living (Prices) vs. Value of money

Class in 332.41 works on purchasing power that focus on the value of money as measured by the goods and services it can buy. Class in 339.41–.42 works on purchasing power that focus on the ability of consumers to buy. If in doubt, prefer 339.41–.42.

340

Law

Law, one of the chief instruments of social control, consists of the whole body of customs, practices, and rules that are recognized in a society as binding, and are promulgated or enforced by a central authority.

Forms of legal literature

Three general forms of literature may be distinguished in this field:

1. The laws themselves as promulgated by a body officially authorized to do so

2. Decisions of the courts or other adjudicative bodies on matters of dispute that arise under these laws

3. Treatises written on various aspects of the laws

The first two of these, laws and decisions, are considered to be original materials. Treatises are derivative in nature and are considered to be secondary. A special section (348) has been provided for original materials and guides to them when such materials are not limited to any specific branch or subject in law. Original materials that are limited to a specific branch or subject are to be classed with that branch or subject, plus special subdivision 026 and its subdivisions. (This subdivision is given in detail in the schedule under 342–347. There is a similar development of 026 under 341 International law.) Treatises have no special place or designation, but are classed in 349 if dealing with the whole law of a jurisdiction, or in the number for the specific branch or subject without further indication.

Law and aboriginal groups

Certain groups, such as the aborigines of Australia and the native peoples of the United States, had legal systems of their own prior to their incorporation into the national systems of other groups. Such laws are classed in 340.52 Law of traditional societies, e.g., laws of North American native tribes before becoming a part of the United States 340.5273. Class laws of such groups on a specific subject with the subject in 342–347, plus notation 089 from Table 1, e.g., family law of North American native peoples 346.01508997.

Class in international law the relations between aboriginal groups and a nation established in their territory before their incorporation into the nation, e.g., treaties between the United States and native American peoples on territorial matters 341.42026673008997.

Relations between an aboriginal group and a nation established in its territory after its incorporation into the nation are classed in the regular numbers for the law of the jurisdiction, e.g., law regulating nursing services for Australian aborigines 344.9404140899915.

Terminology and notation used

To avoid cumbersome repetition, the phrase "the law of" is frequently omitted. Unless otherwise stated, law is understood. If, for example, the phrase "taxes are classed in 343.04" is used, it means that the law of taxes is classed in 343.04. Similarly, in references to the law of specific subjects in 342–348 the number is given as it appears in the schedule, e.g., the law of taxes 343.04. It is to be understood that in most instances, to use the same example, the number will actually be 343 plus notation from Table 2 plus 04.

340 vs. 808.06634

Law vs. [Legal writing]

Legal writing

Class works on the composition of legal briefs, law reports, and other documents at 808.06634; however, if the work emphasizes how to make the document comply with the law, class it with the subject in law, e.g., how to draw up a legal contract 346.022. If in doubt, class in 340.

340.02–.09 vs. 349

Standard subdivisions [of law] vs. Law of specific jurisdictions, areas, socioeconomic regions

Geographic treatment

The presence of a geographic concept does not automatically mean that the work must be classed in 349 instead of 340.02–.09. To be classed in 349, the book must emphasize that the law is limited to a specific jurisdiction. For example, even though the majority of the cases cited in *Black's Law Dictionary* are from the United States, it is classed in 340.03, general law dictionaries, instead of 349.7303, dictionaries of American law. A directory of Maryland lawyers may be classed either in 340.025752 (for a directory of lawyers who can practice law not only in Maryland but in other parts of the United States but whose place of residence is in Maryland) or in 349.752025 (for a directory of lawyers who can practice in Maryland but whose place of residence need not be in Maryland). If in doubt, prefer in 340.02–.09.

340.023 vs. 347.0504

Law as a profession, occupation, hobby vs. Practice [of law]

Class in 340.023 such topics as what it is like to be a lawyer, professional relationships, specialties available in the profession, career opportunities, and the like. Class in 347.0504 the technicalities of conducting a lawsuit. If in doubt, prefer 340.023.

340.56 vs. 342–347

Civil law systems vs. Branches of law

Civil law has two meanings that must be carefully distinguished. In one sense it is the name of a system of law (340.56) derived from Roman law and in use to a greater or lesser extent in most countries in the modern world, e.g., Germany, France, Japan, Brazil, and even in some subordinate jurisdictions of countries that otherwise use another system, e.g., the province of Québec in Canada and the state of Louisiana in the United States. It is frequently used in contrast to other great systems of law, e.g., the common law (340.57), which is derived from the customs and laws of ancient and medieval England and is used in the United Kingdom, the United States, and most countries belonging to the British Commonwealth, e.g., Canada, Australia, New Zealand.

The more common meaning of civil law is all law that is not international law or criminal law (342–344, 346–347). It is normally used in stated or implied contrast to criminal law.

340.57 vs. 342–347

Common law systems vs. Branches of law

The phrase "common law" is used in several ways: (1) Law that is not the result of legislation but rather of custom and judicial decision; (2) The branch of English law that derives from the old English courts of common law as opposed to the branch of law known as equity that grew up in the Court of Chancery; (3) The system of law of England and other countries, such as the United States, whose law is derived from English law. Common law in the first sense is found in 340.57. Common law in the second and third senses gives form and structure to 342–347.

340.59 vs. 297.14

Islamic law vs. [Islamic] Religious and ceremonial laws and decisions

Class in 297.14 comprehensive works on Islamic law concerning religious matters, such as ritual purification, ritual prayer, fasting, zakat, the hajj, sacred places. Class Islamic law on a specific religious topic with the topic, e.g., fasting 297.53. Class Islamic law on religious topics in religion even if the laws are being enforced by the state rather than just by religious organizations.

Class in 340.59 comprehensive works on Islamic law concerning secular matters, such as contract law, criminal law, social welfare law, law of inheritance.

Class Islamic law on a specific secular topic with the topic in 342–347, e.g., law of inheritance in Saudi Arabia 346.538052.

Class in 340.59 interdisciplinary works about Islamic law covering both religious and secular topics. If in doubt, prefer 340.59.

Some topics, such as family and marriage, have both religious and secular aspects. Works on the Islamic law of such topics are rarely limited to the religious aspects and thus rarely classed in religion. In particular, always class in 340 works about laws on such topics if the laws under discussion are enforced by the state. For example, class family law of Pakistan in 346.549015, marriage law of Pakistan in 346.549016.

340.9

Conflict of laws

This topic is usually called private international law, which is something of a misnomer, since it is not the law governing the interrelationships of nations, but is the law governing the conflicts and disputes between private citizens of different nations. Its matter is drawn from private law. The chief point at issue is usually which jurisdiction's laws are to govern the case, hence the term conflict of laws. For example, whose laws will govern in the case of a Canadian citizen married in France to a citizen of Germany and later divorced in Mexico when a dispute arises as to the disposition of jointly owned personal property?

341 vs. 327

International law vs. International relations

Works on international relations will discuss what is actually transpiring (including the theory as to why things happen as they do), and the effects of what has happened. Works on international law will discuss those standards and principles which it is commonly felt should govern international relations, and will also discuss concrete events from the standpoint of the problems that they pose to this system of order. Included in international law, of course, will also be works on treaties and cases of international courts. If in doubt, prefer 341.

341.22–.24

International governmental organizations

Interdisciplinary works on international governmental organizations and works dealing with the structure and overall functions of such organizations are classed in 341.22–.24, even when no substantial discussion of the organic law establishing such organizations appears in the work under consideration, e.g., interdisciplinary works on the European Union 341.2422. A specific aspect of one of these organizations is classed with the subject outside of law, e.g., the economic aspects of the European Union 337.142.

However, interdisciplinary works on a specialized international governmental organization are classed with the subject with which the organization deals, plus notation 0601 from Table 1, e.g., Interpol, an international police organization, 363.20601. The legal aspects of the organization are classed with the subject with which it deals in 341.2–.7, e.g., Interpol 341.77.

341.37

Treaties

Class the approval of a treaty by a nation in international law. However, class legislation to enforce the provisions of a treaty within national boundaries with the law of that nation. For example, a work on a treaty between the United States and Canada with respect to fish and wildlife conservation is classed in 341.762, but a work on a fish and game law passed by the United States Congress to enforce the provisions of such a treaty on the citizens of the United States is classed in 346.73046954.

342–349

Branches of law; laws (statutes), regulations, cases; law of specific jurisdictions, areas, socioeconomic regions

Law limited by geographic treatment is classed as follows:

1. Law limited to a specific jurisdiction is classed in 349 or 342.3–.9 and parallel numbers plus the area number for that jurisdiction, e.g., law of Germany 349.43, railroad law of Germany 343.43095.

2. The laws of specific local jurisdictions (cities, counties, subprovincial jurisdictions) are classed in 349 or 342.3–.9 and parallel numbers plus the area number for that jurisdiction; but for the laws of all the localities of a given area, use the area number for the jurisdiction that contains them: tax laws of Bayreuth, Bavaria 343.4331504; by-laws relating to public parks in Sheffield, England 346.42821046783; but, tax laws of the cities of Bavaria 343.43304, of the cities of Germany 343.4304, laws relating to the public parks of cities in the United Kingdom 346.41046783.

The principle of approximating the whole is relaxed for jurisdictions for which there is no specific area number, i.e., subdivisions may be added for a jurisdiction not having its own number, e.g., Flint, Michigan's ordinance governing mental health services to the addicted 344.77437044. Flint is in an including note, which normally means subdivisions may not be added for it. Even if the jurisdiction is not mentioned in a note, subdivisions may be added to it, e.g., a similar ordinance for Mt. Morris, Michigan, a suburb of Flint 344.77437044.

3. The application of law of a specific jurisdiction to a limited area within the jurisdiction is classed with the law of the jurisdiction plus notation 09 from the table under 342–347, e.g., German law as practiced in Bavaria 349.4309433, application of German railroad law in Bavaria 343.4309509433.

4. The laws of more than one jurisdiction are classed as follows:

A collection of laws from various jurisdictions located in a particular area is classed in 349 or 342.3–.9 and parallel numbers plus the area number for that area, e.g., law of Germany, France, Italy 349.4, railroad laws of Germany, France, Italy 343.4095.

Laws that affect more than one jurisdiction are classed in 341, e.g., treaties among Germany, France, Italy 341.02644, international laws regulating railroads in Germany, France, Italy 341.7565094.

See also discussion at 340.02–.09 vs. 349.

Law of countries with federal governments

In federally organized countries, e.g., the United States, Australia, Federal Republic of Germany, there are two sets of laws: those of the central jurisdiction (national laws) and those of subordinate jurisdictions (laws of the provinces or states). Laws of an individual state or province are classed using the area number for the jurisdiction in question, e.g., criminal law of Virginia 345.755, of New South Wales 345.944. However, laws of the states or provinces taken as a whole are classed in the same numbers as the laws of the federal jurisdiction, e.g., criminal laws of the states of the United States 345.73, of the states of Australia 345.94. Normally the discussion of state and provincial laws of a region are classed in the same manner, e.g., provincial criminal law of western Canada 345.712.

Use of area number for capital districts

Use notation 753 from Table 2 for laws of Washington, D.C., even though some of these laws are passed by the United States Congress. These are, in effect, local laws even though passed by the national legislature. The same situation may occur in other countries.

Jurisdiction in time

Laws of an area that was at some point not an independent jurisdiction are classed as follows:

1. If the law is still operative in the now-independent jurisdiction, class with the jurisdiction in question, e.g., class the Limitation Act of 1908 (which was enacted before Pakistan became independent but is the currently operating law for Pakistan) in 347.5491052.

2. If the law is no longer operative in the now-independent jurisdiction, class with the laws of the jurisdiction that was previously dominant, e.g., a law of 1908 no longer operative in Pakistan is classed with the law of India, plus notation 54 from Table 2.

342.06

Executive branch of government

Administrative law

Administrative law involves the exercise by the executive branch of certain judicial functions, e.g., settling disputes, imposing fines, specifying certain remedies. When a work deals with such functions, it is classed here. Class administrative law on a specific subject with the subject in 342–347, e.g., the role of the U.S. Federal Aviation Administration in settling a dispute with air traffic controllers 343.730976. Standards set by an agency in connection with a specific subject are classed with the subject outside of law, e.g., standards for safety in health care facilities 363.1562.

342.07 vs. 324.6

Election law vs. Election systems and procedures

Use 324.6 for manuals outlining procedures for the conduct of elections. However, if laws or administrative regulations for elections, or legal discussions of them, are discussed to any significant extent, use 342.07. If in doubt, prefer 342.07.

343.04 vs. 336.2, 352.44

Tax law vs. Taxes and taxation vs. Revenue administration

Most works on taxes, especially popular works, are classed in law, because they explain what the law allows and prohibits. For example, a work for taxpayers about U.S. income tax deductions is classed in 343.730523. Tax administration, which includes especially the administration of assessment and collection, is classed in 352.44. Works on the economics of taxes and interdisciplinary works on taxes are classed in 336.2, e.g., an economic and political analysis of U.S. tax policy 336.200973. If in doubt, class in 343.04.

343.078 vs. 343.08

[Regulation of] Secondary industries and services vs. Regulation of trade (commerce)

In sorting out industrial versus trade regulations, the following may help. When production quotas, quality of the material produced, sizes of products specified, and the like are treated, industrial regulations are involved. When truth-in-labeling, advertising practices, and other aspects of marketing are treated, trade regulations are involved. For instance, what services hotels are permitted to provide, how they are to provide them, what activities are permitted in them, and what rates they may charge are classed in industrial regulation 343.07864794. How hotels may advertise is classed in 343.085564794. If in doubt, prefer 343.078.

345

Criminal law

Criminal law deals with actions of so damaging a nature that the interests of society are considered to be directly at stake. For this reason cases in criminal law are always between the state in its capacity as the body politic and the individual charged with a crime. A dispute between two private persons (natural or corporate) becomes a civil law case. Penal action is a possible result of a criminal case. In a civil case damages are awarded or some other remedy is found. It should be noted that the state can also bring a suit at civil law, acting in this case as a juristic person rather than as the body politic.

345.02 vs. 346.03

Crimes (Offenses) vs. Torts (Delicts)

Certain acts listed as criminal offenses here are also to be found in 346.03 as torts (a part of civil law). Works on these acts should be classed according to the point of view taken in the work or the type of legal action being brought. Thus libel and slander considered from the standpoint of criminal law are classed in 345.0256, considered as a tort in 346.034. Whether a particular act is regarded as a crime or as a tort or as neither will often depend on the jurisdiction in which it is regarded. For example, adultery may be regarded as a crime for which the offender may be prosecuted, a tort for which the offender may be sued, or merely as a fact to be adduced in evidence in a divorce case. If in doubt, prefer 345.02.

346.02

Contracts and agency

Contracts

A contract is an agreement, implicit or explicit, between two or more parties. The contract itself is not law, but is enforceable as law. The following aspects of contracts are classed in law: their legality and enforceability, disputes concerning them, breach of contract, how to draft contracts so that they will be legal.

346.043 vs. 333.1–.5

[Law of] Real property vs. Ownership and control of land and natural resources

Class economic aspects of the various forms of ownership and transfer of land in 333.1–.5; the legal aspects in 346.043. If in doubt, prefer 346.043.

347

Civil procedure and courts

Jurisdiction

Care must be taken in determining the jurisdiction involved in procedure and courts. The location of the court does not necessarily determine this. For example, procedure in a court in Boston, Massachusetts, would be classed in 347.744 if a state court, in 347.73 if a United States district court.

350 vs. 342–347

Public administration and military science vs. Branches of law

Preliminary materials on laws and appropriations

Preliminary materials are documents relating to proposed legislation. Even after passage of the legislation these documents continue to be relevant in law as showing the mind and intention of the legislators responsible for turning the bill into law.

The main forms are:

Bills (the proposed laws themselves)

Hearings on the bills

Statements of witnesses

Executive messages with respect to bills

Reports on the hearings

Class in 342–347:

Bills, including authorizations and appropriation bills that establish government agencies. These last-named bills are classed in law with the subject with which the agency deals, e.g., a bill to establish an education department 344.070262

Hearings, reports, and resolutions relating to bills for ordinary laws. (*See below for appropriations bills and bills setting public policy.*)

Hearings on the proposed appointments of judges

These are classed in 345 or 347, e.g., a hearing on the proposed appointment of a justice to the United States Supreme Court 347.732634

Class in 351–354:

Routine hearings on authorizations and appropriations (that is, hearings that do not emphasize public policy and the needs of society

Class routine hearings on authorizations and appropriations (other than those for military services) in 352.49, plus notation 023 from the table under 352.493–.499, e.g., hearings on appropriations in Germany 352.4943023. Class routine hearings on authorizations and appropriations for a specific agency with the agency in 352–354, plus notation 249 from the table under 352–354, e.g., hearings on appropriations to support health facilities 353.68249, to support health care facilities in Germany 353.6824943023. (*See below for hearings on authorizations and appropriations that emphasize policy issues and social needs.*)

Oversight hearings focusing on agency performance

These are not usually hearings on a bill, but are examinations into the effectiveness with which an agency is doing its job. Class them with the agency number in public administration, e.g., an oversight hearing on the U.S. Bureau of Indian Affairs 353.53497073. (*See below for more general oversight hearings.*)

Class in 355–359:

Military appropriation and authorization bills and the hearings and reports pertaining to them

Class elsewhere in the schedules (usually in the social sciences) general hearings and reports on them, reports on legislative investigations not related to proposed legislation, e.g., United States congressional investigations into the sale of arms to Iran and the subsequent transfer of the proceeds of the sales to Nicaraguan rebels 364.131. Also class elsewhere hearings on public policy, and oversight hearings that focus on whether present appropriations, laws and public policies are meeting the needs of society.

Reports of hearings are classed with the hearings to which they pertain. Materials containing such statements as "under authority of" or "pursuant to" are not usually classed in law.

If in doubt, prefer 350 over 342–347, prefer numbers outside law and public administration over 350 or 342–347.

See also discussion at 300, 320.6 vs. 352–354: Nomination hearings.

351

Public administration

A new emphasis on subject over jurisdiction

The new *completely revised schedule* for public administration places the emphasis upon classifying by subject rather than by jurisdiction as was done in earlier editions. Two adjustments have been made, however, to recognize the importance of jurisdiction. First, for comprehensive works on public administration in a specific area, area notation 3–9 is added directly to 351, saving two digits when compared with the use of standard subdivision notation 09. For example, public administration in or of Germany is classed in 351.43.

The second adjustment is indirect, the result of a liberal use of class-here and subdivisions-are-added notes. These notes are signals that differences among jurisdictions are considered more important than the differences among the particular topics named in the notes. When public administration topics are named in these two kinds of notes, standard subdivisions and notation from the table under 352–354 may be added freely.

For example, price supports and price controls are distinct, if overlapping concepts. The supports naturally fall under financial assistance in 352.73, while the controls naturally fall under general forms of control in 352.8. However, it is hard to get into one activity without getting into the other, and any specific program might shift its emphasis over time, so both concepts are treated as integral parts of 352.85. This number is under "general forms of control" (covering regulation), and has the heading price and cost controls; price supports is given in a class-here note. Hence works on administration of either price controls *or* price supports in Germany are classed in 352.850943.

Similarly, grants-in-aid to subordinate jurisdictions are combined with grants to private parties in the number for financial support (352.73), since the methods of dispensing public grants varies in unpredictable ways among jurisdictions, and varies in a single jurisdiction over time. Hence, administration of grants to either public bodies *or* to private individuals in Germany is classed in 352.730943.

Number building

The new schedule allows considerable synthesis of numbers to bring out the various aspects (facets) of public administration. For example, area is one of the important aspects, and "in Germany" in the earlier examples is a facet represented by notation 43 (under 351) or T1—0943 (under 352–354). The general rule in number building in the new schedule is to start with the aspect coming last in the schedule, and work forward. Thus the aspect that defines the basic subject of the work (which is placed last in the schedule) comes first in the number.

The facets are found in or derived from the two main units of the public administration schedule (352 and 353–354), and from Table 1. Since field of activity comes last, the 353–354 numbers are used in their entirety. They are not represented in the notation from the add table under 352–354. In contrast, notation for general considerations of public administration found in 352 is represented in notation 2 from the add table under 352–354, and can thus be added to other public administration numbers. In fact, notation from one part of 352 can be added to other parts of 352 through notation 2.

There are three categories of facets in public administration (apart from public administration itself, represented by the 35 with which all numbers begin):

Facet	Schedule number	Add table notation
Field of activity	353–354	
General consideration	352	21–28
Standard subdivision	01–09	

There will be many works treating only one facet of public administration, e.g., social welfare 353.5, budgeting 352.48, public administration in Germany 351.43, a periodical on public administration 351.05. To illustrate the fundamentals of how the number building works, the examples used in the next three paragraphs will, when possible, be formed by combining the whole or the underscored parts of the numbers just given. Area as a facet is added directly in 351, but is added as part of the standard subdivision facet in 352–354. Sometimes the standard subdivision facet is used twice, e.g., first for area, then for periodicals. (The pluses inserted when more than one segment is added are not a part of the numbers to be used on books.)

Works with two facets will be more common, e.g., public welfare administration in Germany 353.50943, budgeting social welfare programs 353.5248, a periodical on public welfare in Germany 351.4305.

Works delimited by three facets will be less common, but by no means rare, e.g., budgeting welfare programs in Germany 353.5248+0943, periodicals on budget administration in Germany 352.480943+05.

Occasionally a work will be delimited by four or more facets, e.g. a periodical on budgeting welfare programs in Germany 353.5248+0943+05.

Number building with 352 subdivisions

The subdivisions of 352 represent a wide range of topics that are not mutually exclusive. In fact, the topics found in "general considerations of public administration" are often studied in relation to each other. Hence, many works will have numbers built by combining one or more segments derived from 352 notation. The following summary of 352 illustrates the range of topics:

Summary of 352

352.1	Jurisdictional levels of administration
352.2	Organization of administration
352.3	Executive management
352.4	Financial administration and budgets
352.5	Property administration and related topics
352.6	Personnel (Human resource) administration
352.7	Administration of general forms of assistance
352.8	Administration of general forms of control

Typical topics found in subdivisions of these numbers (showing the segment used when facets are combined):

Topic	Schedule number	Add table notation
State and provincial administration	352.13	213
Chief executives	352.23	223
Information management	352.38	238
Specific budgets	352.49	249
Procurement	352.53	253
Job description	352.64	264
Advisory bodies	352.743	2743
Licensing	352.84	284
Price controls and supports	352.85	285

Examples

In the explanation of examples below, notation 2 is identified simply as a facet indicator. It comes from the table under 352–354 and is used to introduce any subdivision of 352 General considerations of administration.

When area is shown via a combination of notation 09 from Table 1 and the appropriate notation from Table 2, only the name of the area is given in the number building explanation. Information identifying the United States as the country is not explicitly given when "federal" or "state" is used in the title.

Provincial administration in Canada 352.130971
352.13 (State and provincial administration) + T1—0971 (Canada)
Canadian provinces constitute major administrative units.

Provincial administration in Chile 352.150983
352.15 (Intermediate levels of local administration) + T1—0983 (Chile)
Chilean provinces are small units that can be described as intermediate units of local administration, in contrast to the much larger Canadian provinces above.

The Chancellor of the Exchequer 352.422930941
352.4 (Financial administration) + 2 (facet indicator) + 293 (from 352.293 Heads of departments) + T1—0941 (Great Britain)

Procurement of supplies 352.553
352.55 (Equipment and supplies) + 3 (Contracts and procurement, from table under 352.55–.57)

Role and functions of state personnel offices 352.62130973
352.6 (Personnel [Human Resource] administration) + 2 (facet indicator) + 13 (from 352.13 State and provincial administration) + T1—0973 United States)
Notation 213 is used because the work explicitly discusses the branch of administration at the state level, and is not limited to any one state.

Commission to reform human resources management in Minnesota state government 352.6237509776

352.6 (Personnel [Human resource] administration) + 2 (facet indicator) + 375 (from 352.375 Promotion of efficiency) + T1—09776 (Minnesota)

Notation 225 (derived from 352.25 Governing boards and commissions) is not used for administration of a specific agency that just happens to be a commission.

The federal government's use of private attorneys 352.652538088344

352.65 (Recruiting and selection [of personnel]) + 2 (facet indicator) + 538 (from 352.538 Contracting for services) + T1—088 (Occupational groups) + T7—344 (Lawyers)

The general number for contracts and procurement is 352.53, and notation 253 derived from it may be used for either contracting or procurement in any part of public administration. Area notation cannot be added to subdivisions of T1—088.

Advisory commissions on price control in India 352.8527430954

352.85 (Price and cost controls) + 2 (facet indicator) + 743 (from 352.743 Fact-finding and advisory bodies) + T1—0954 (India)

Notes at both 352.85 and 352.743 indicate that subdivisions are added for either or both topics in the headings. Notes like these, as well as numerous class-here notes, encourage the expectation that subdivisions will be added freely to numbers for broad categories in public administration. The scope of agencies vary widely from time to time, and from country to country, and it is advisable to avoid scattering agencies that have the same core responsibility.

Ministry of the Interior of France 353.30944

353.3 (Administration of services related to domestic order) + T1—0944 (France)

The class-here note at 353.3 lists home departments and ministries, and European style interior ministries. Compare with "The United States Department of the Interior," four titles below.

Procurement in welfare departments 353.5253

353.5 (Administration of social welfare) + 2 (facet indicator) + 53 (from 352.53 Procurement)

Cost control in health administration 353.6285

353.6 (Administration of health services) + 2 (facet indicator) + 85 (from 352.85 Price and cost controls)

Annual report of educational activities of the United States Bureau of Indian Affairs 353.808997073

353.8 (Administration of agencies supporting and controlling education) + T1—089 (Racial, ethnic, national groups) + T5—97 (North American native peoples) + 0 (facet indicator from second note at beginning of Table 5) + T2—73 (United States)

Notation 05 from Table 1 for annual reports cannot be added to area notation following ethnic group notation from Table 5.

The United States Department of the Interior 354.30973

354.3 (Administration of environment and natural resources) + T1—0973 (United States)

Unlike European interior departments, the American department concentrates on natural resources matters rather than matters of domestic order. Compare with "Ministry of the Interior in France," four titles above.

Public administration and the conservation of water 354.3634

354.36 (Water) + 3 (Special forms of protection and control, from table under 354.34–.37) + 4 (from 354.334 Conservation)

Administration of international organizations concerned with climate change 354.37211

354.37 (Air and atmospheric phenomena) + 2 (facet indicator) + 11 (from 352.11 International administration)

The class-here note at 354.37 mentions weather bureaus. It is unlikely that there will be a consistent distinction in public administration between climate and weather, when popular works on meteorology blur the terms. Therefore, further subdivisions may be added.

Administrative initiatives to encourage the development of oil in Latin America 354.4527098

354.45 (Oil) + 2 (facet indicator) + 7 (from 352.7 Administration of general forms of assistance) + T1—098 (Latin America)

Notation 27 derived from 352.7 is widely used in 354 for administration of development.

Administrative control of gas utilities 354.4628

354.46 (Gas) + 2 (facet indicator) + 8 (from 352.8 Administration of general forms of control)

Notation 28 derived from 352.8 (the number for regulatory agencies) is widely used in 354 for the control of public utilities.

Licensing commercial establishments 354.73284

354.73 (Commerce) + 2 (facet indicator) + 84 (from 352.84 Licensing)

Projected highway budget for California 354.7724979401

354.77 (Road transportation) + 2 (facet indicator) + 49 (from 352.49 Budgets for specific jurisdictions) + T2—794 (California) + 01 (Proposed budgets, from table under 352.493–.499)

Federal support and control of employment services in the building trades 354.9649

354.96 (Employment services) + 4 (Specific extractive, manufacturing, construction occupations, from table under 354.96–.98) + 9 (from 690 Buildings)

Optional use of 351

As explained above, most of 351 is used for area treatment of public administration. Subdivisions 351.01–.09 are used for a modified set of standard subdivisions, but 351.1 is used for areas, regions, places in general, and 351.3–.9 is used for treatment in specific continents, countries, localities.

Because some libraries serve subject specialists who are more interested in the administration of specific jurisdictions than they are in specific topics in public administration, options A and B have been provided to allow for classification of specific topics under the area subdivisions of 351. These options use an add table like the standard table under 352–354, except that a 0 is needed before the first added facet.

Under option A, 352–354 continues to be used as given in the schedule except when a specific continent, country, or locality is an aspect of the work. Similarly, all subdivisions in 351 continue to be used as given except that standard subdivisions added without an intervening facet must have an extra 0. For example, of the twenty number-building examples supplied earlier, only the five for a given topic in Germany and the one for a periodical in Germany are affected by the option. It is likely, however, that in libraries considering the option, a high proportion of the public administration material will be classed in 351. To illustrate how the option affects classification, let us consider five of the German examples just mentioned:

The topic or s.s. in Germany	Standard	Option
Periodical on public administration	351.4305	351.43005
Periodical on budget administration	352.48094305	351.43024805
Social welfare administration	353.50943	351.43035
Budgeting social welfare programs	353.52480943	351.43035248
Public administration of the economy	354.0943	351.4304

Option B is provided for libraries that want to use 352–354 for material relevant to their areas, but prefer to keep material that is limited to outside jurisdictions separated from material of local interest. Such libraries may also achieve shorter notation by leaving off notation 09 from Table 1 for the material of local interest they class in 352–354. The material that they class in 351, however, will be handled in exactly the same way as under option A.

351.3–.9 vs. 352.13–.19

Administration in specific continents, countries, localities vs. Administration of subordinate jurisdictions

Administration in and of specific subordinate jurisdictions

The distinction between material on subordinate jurisdictions that is classed in 351.3–.9 and material that is classed in 352.13–.19 plus notation 09 from Table 1 separates the practical works on individual jurisdictions (351.3–.9) from the theoretical works on state and provincial or local administration (352.13–.19). Use the latter only for general treatises on subordinate jurisdictions or on specific kinds of subordinate jurisdictions, e.g., provincial administration in Canada 352.130971, county administration in Illinois 352.1509773, rural administration in United Kingdom 352.170941. Use 351.3–.9 for administrative activity in any specific subordinate jurisdiction, e.g., administration of the government of Ontario 351.713, of Cook County (Illinois) 351.7731, of Ross and Cromarty (Scotland) 351.41172.

This distinction insures consistent classification of works on administration of specific subordinate jurisdictions, since a classifier does not need to decide to which category a specific government belongs, e.g., whether Cook County is urban, or Ross and Cromarty is rural. The answer would be easy in these two cases, but often it is not.

The distinction is carried over under specific topics of public administration through notation from the add table under 352–354. Area notation 093–099 from this add table brings together reports and practical works on the administration of a specific activity in a given region. In contrast, notation 213–219 from the add table brings together theoretical works on how state (provincial) and local administration of a subject has been or should be conducted.

If in doubt, prefer 351.3–.9.

352–354

Specific topics of public administration

Agencies and their divisions

No distinction is made between the administration of a function and the administration of an agency designated to perform that function. For example, public administration of agriculture in the United States and administration of the United States Department of Agriculture are both classed in 354.50973. Administrative reports of specific agencies are also classed in the same numbers as independent studies of the functions that the agencies perform. For example, the Annual Report of the United States Department of Agriculture and an independent journal on agricultural administration in the United States are both classed in 354.5097305.

Specific agencies must be classed according to "best fit," since they tend to have a range of responsibilities that do not fit the definitions devised to cover the common patterns. Furthermore, in any specific jurisdiction, the responsibilities tend to shift with time, as agencies are enlarged, reduced, divided, or merged. For example, a general services agency may have a wide range of miscellaneous functions, but if the predominant duty concerns property administration (as is often the case), class it in 352.5, even if it has sections on archives and personnel training.

Works on component parts of an agency are classed in numbers fitting the components. For example, class a procurement section in the general services agency mentioned above in 352.53, a personnel training section in the agency in 352.669, and an archives section of the agency in either 352.744 (if it is promoting archival activity) or in 026.93–.99 (if it is maintaining general archives of the jurisdiction).

In some cases, the schedule will give a specific name of a generalized type of agency in a class-here note at a given number. It must be understood that the note refers to the typical agency so named, and care must be taken to be sure that the agency one is classifying does in fact have a function fitting its name. Only when there is a conspicuous difference in the usage of different countries will the notes explain the difference. For example, at 353.3 one note reads "Class here home departments and ministries, European style interior ministries;" another note reads "See also 354.30973 for United States Department of the Interior."

When two agencies independently cover the same field, they are classed in the same number. However, one of the agencies may have a different relation to the subject that can be brought out by notation from the table under 352–354. For example, the United States Department of Transportation is classed in 354.760973, while the United States Interstate Commerce Commission (the ICC, which regulates transportation, not commerce) is classed in 354.76280973. The base number for administration of transportation (354.76) and the final notation for area (notation 0973) are the same in both cases, but notation 28 for regulation (and here, as indicated by the second note under 354.728, for administration of public utilities in the field) is interposed between them for the ICC.

Nominal subordination of an agency to a nonexecutive branch of government does not affect classification. For example, the United States General Accounting Office is officially part of the legislative branch, but it performs a classical executive function of reviewing accounts and judging the effectiveness of expenditures throughout the government. It is, therefore, classed in 352.430973.

A representative list of departments and agencies of the United States government is given below with the recommended public administration numbers in the middle column. The list provides a useful guide to classifying comparable agencies of any jurisdiction, since the final notation 0973 can easily be replaced by notation specifying any other area. Also, by studying the list, classifiers can find clues to the use of notation beginning with 2 derived from 352 for certain types of agencies. For example, notation 28 is used (as shown above) for the ICC (354.76280973) to define it as a regulatory agency, while notation 28 is not used with the Department of Transportation (354.760973), because it covers a variety of administrative activities relating to transportation. On the other hand, the Food and Drug Administration, another regulatory agency, is classed in 353.9970973 without notation 28 because virtually all agencies in the field of safety are regulatory, and the 28 would be redundant. (*The list includes a few agencies and institutions with administrative numbers outside 352–354 that are nevertheless listed in the "352–354 number" column.*)

The numbers in the rightmost column are the ones that are most likely to fit typical works on the fields that the agencies administer. This column serves as a reminder that many works that conspicuously identify a given agency may discuss either public policy or the situation and conditions in the field rather than public administration. The numbers are for guidance only; always classify according to the emphasis of the work in hand. (*When there is no single appropriate non-352–354 number, the 352–354 number is repeated in this column.*) (*See also discussion at 300, 320.6 vs. 353–354: Public policy.*)

Representative list of United States government agencies

Agency name	352–354 number	Non-352–354 number
ACTION	352.780973	361.370973
Agency for International Development	353.132730973	338.9173
Bureau of Indian Affairs	353.53497073	305.897073
Bureau of Mines	354.390973	338.20973
Bureau of the Census	352.750973	317.3
Central Intelligence Agency	353.170973	327.1273
Council of Economic Advisors	354.27430973	330.973
Department of Agriculture	354.50973	338.10973
Department of Commerce	354.730973	380.10973
Department of Defense	355.60973	355.00973
Department of Education	353.80973	370.973
Department of Energy	354.40973	333.790973
Department of Health and Human Services	353.60973	362.10973
Department of Housing and Urban Development	353.550973	363.50973
Department of Justice	353.40973	349.73
Department of Labor	354.90973	331.0973
Department of State	353.130973	327.73
Department of the Air Force	358.4160973	358.400973
Department of the Army	355.60973	355.00973
Department of the Interior	354.30973	333.70973
Department of the Navy	359.60973	359.00973
Department of the Treasury	352.40973	336.73
Department of Transportation	354.760973	388.0973
Department of Veterans Affairs	353.5380973	362.860973
Environmental Protection Agency	354.3280973	363.70973
Equal Employment Opportunity Commission	354.9080973	331.1330973
Executive Office of the President	352.2370973	352.2370973
Federal Bureau of Investigation	363.25068	363.250973
Federal Communications Commission	354.75280973	384.0973
Federal Emergency Management Agency	353.950973	363.340973
Federal Highway Administration	354.770973	388.10973
Federal Trade Commission	354.73280973	381.0973
Food and Drug Administration	353.9970973	363.1920973
General Accounting Office	352.430973	352.430973
General Services Administration	352.50973	352.50973
Government Printing Office	070.509753	070.509753
Information Agency	353.132740973	327.11

Internal Revenue Service	352.44	336.240973
International Trade Commission	354.742740973	382.0973
Interstate Commerce Commission	354.76280973	388.0973
Library of Congress	025.197573	027.573
Merit System Protection Board	352.630973	352.630973
National Aeronautics and Space Administration	354.79	629.40973
National Archives and Records Administration	025.196973	026.973
National Foundation on the Arts and the Humanities	353.772730973	001.30973
National Labor Relations Board	354.970973	331.80973
National Oceanic and Atmospheric Administration	354.3690973	333.9164
National Park Service	353.78	363.680973
National Security Council	353.12240973	355.033073
National Transportation Safety Board	353.980973	363.1200973
National Weather Service	354.370973	551.6573
Nuclear Regulatory Commission	354.47280973	333.79240973
Occupational Safety and Health Administration	353.960973	363.1100973
Office of Personnel Management	352.60973	352.60973
Office of the Comptroller of the Currency	354.860973	332.10973
Post Office Department	354.7590973	383.4973
Postal Service	354.7590973	383.4973
Rural Electrification Administration	354.4927360973	333.7932
Securities and Exchange Commission	354.880973	332.64273
Small Business Administration	354.27990973	338.6420973
Social Security Administration	353.540973	368.4300973
Veterans Administration	353.5380973	362.860973

See also discussion at T1—068 vs. 353–354 for the choice between management and public administration for agencies providing the actual services.

Terminology of administration and management

To avoid cumbersome repetition, the phrase "public administration" is used only in headings and notes referring to three-digit numbers, and the word "administration" is normally limited to headings and notes referring to four-digit numbers. Elsewhere the word "administration" is used only if needed to make a heading complete e.g., 352.14 Local administration, or to avoid confusion, e.g., under 353.17 Intelligence and counterintelligence, where the note reads "Limited to administration of operations primarily conducted abroad."

An important feature of public administration is the application of principles and concepts of management to public agencies. Normally the phrases used in management (that is, in 658) are carried over to 352–354 without qualification, except that phrases ending in the word "management" end in the word "administration." For example, financial management in public administration is called financial administration. ("Executive management," however, remains executive management in 352.3.)

The interdisciplinary numbers for specific topics in management, as well as for management as a whole, are found in 658. The indexing of management terms reflects the fact that management in public administration is a part of management by listing the public administration numbers in subheadings under the management terms. For example:

Financial management	658.3
public administration	352.6

See also discussion at 352.

Add table

27–28

Administration of supporting and controlling functions of government

Do not use notation 27 and 28 when it is redundant or nearly so. That is, do not use notation 27 in fields where the primary role of government is supportive, and do not use notation 28 in fields where the primary role of government is regulation and control. For example, class agencies supporting public libraries in 353.73 (*not* 353.7327) because government action concerning libraries is usually supportive, and class agencies regulating safety in 353.9 (*not* 353.928) because the main thrust of most safety agencies is to make sure that people act in a way to reduce hazards. (On the other hand, for the less common works on these fields, use notation 27 and 28, e.g., class works on regulating libraries in 353.7328, on promoting safety programs in 353.927.)

In contrast, notation 27 and 28 are both extensively used in fields where the government sometimes promotes and sometimes regulates activities. Throughout 354, notation 27 is used in a special sense of administering development, or research and development, as explained under 354.27 in the schedule. Likewise, in much of 354, notation 28 is used in a special sense of controlling public utilities, as explained under 354.728 and 354.428 in the schedule.

352

General considerations of public administration

It is important to bear in mind that numbers in 352 are used primarily for comprehensive and general works. Whenever the topics are treated in terms of specific fields of administration or specific agencies, they are classed in 353–354, plus notation derived from 352. For example, financial administration is found in 352.4, but financial administration of a specific agency is found in the field the agency administers plus notation 24 derived from 352.4. Since an agricultural department is classed in 354.5, financial administration of a department of agriculture is classed in 354.524.

Notation derived from numbers coming early in 352 can be added to numbers coming later, especially numbers from 352.1 for international administration and administration of subordinate levels of government. For example, notation 214 for local government is derived from 352.14, and may be added to 352.4 to obtain 352.4214 for financial administration in local government.

Some numbers in 352 may have little use in 352, yet notation derived from them may be quite significant in 353–354. For example, 352.7 and 352.8 emphasize the supporting and the regulatory roles of government, respectively. From them are derived notation 27 to indicate agencies that concentrate on promoting a field, and notation 28 to indicate agencies that regulate the field, e.g, 354.327 for agencies that develop the environment, and 354.328 for environmental protection agencies.

Notation 27 and 28 are prime examples of numbers derived from 352 that should not be used when redundant. *See discussion under 352–354: Add table: 27–28.*

For a few subjects, especially where there are scatter references such as are found under 352.77 Public works, the number will scarcely ever be used for the specific topic, e.g., for a specific public work, since the administration of specific ones should all be classed in some specific field of public administration.

See also discussion at 351: Examples; also at 352–354: Terminology of administration and management.

352.13 vs. 352.15

State and provincial administration vs. Intermediate units of local administration

Territorial subdivisions with an extent that places them distinctly above "local administration" go by a variety of names. Unfortunately, the names used for very large units in some countries are often used in other countries for very small units. The Decimal Classification Division of the Library of Congress considers the major territorial units of the countries in the list given below to constitute states or provinces in the meaning intended for 352.13. It considers comparably named units in other countries to belong in 352.15.

The degree of autonomy is not the deciding factor in classification, especially since it changes over time. The list includes some "regions" that have been superimposed over long established and still important districts, departments, or provinces. These regions may not have been given fully developed administrative functions. Similar units that may be created in the future will also be considered to belong in 352.13.

Argentina (provinces)
Australia (states)

Brazil (federal units)
Canada (provinces)
China (provinces, autonomous regions)
Czechoslovakia (regions)
France (regions)
Germany (states)
India (states)
Indonesia (provinces)
Italy (regions)
Japan (regions
Korea (regions)
Mexico (states)
Nigeria (states)
Pakistan (provinces)
Philippines (regions)
Russia (provinces, territories, autonomous republics)
South Africa (provinces)
(former) Soviet Union (union republics, autonomous republics)
Spain (autonomous communities)
Sudan (regions)
United States (states)
(former) Yugoslavia (republics, autonomous provinces)

Class "territories" in the sense of areas on the road to statehood in 352.13, but general treatment of special urban units coordinate with states and provinces in 352.16. For example, class historic treatment of administration in territories of the United States 352.13097309, administration of nationally controlled municipalities in China 352.160951.

352.29

Organization and structure of departments and agencies

Use 352.29 and notation 22 from the add table under 352–354 only for works emphasizing the organizational aspects of departments and agencies, never for general descriptions of the agencies and their work. The latter are classed in 351 if they cover a representative sample of the agencies of a jurisdiction, e.g., a work on the ministries of the Indian government 351.54. General works on specific agencies are classed in the number for the field that it administers, without use of notation 22, e.g., a work describing the Indian Home Ministry 353.30954.

352.293

Heads and deputy heads of departments and agencies

Do not use 352.293 or notation 2293 derived from 352.293 through use of add table under 352–354 for departments (usually quite small ones) named for their heads, e.g., inspectors general, ombudsmen, or secretaries of state of states in United States; rather, class them in the subject which most nearly approximates their duties.

Reports for such agencies are often written as if by the officer for which they are named, e.g., report of the inspector general. When such reports concern the work the officer is charged with handling, class accordingly, e.g., reports of inspectors general and ombudsmen 352.88, of ombudsmen in personnel agencies 352.6288.

Secretaries of state

There are three quite different uses of the term "secretary of state." In the United Kingdom and countries in the Commonwealth of Nations it is a generic term for heads of executive departments, often of cabinet level. Class the term used in such a sense here in 352.293.

In the United States there are two quite distinct specific uses of the term. The Secretary of State of the United States is what is called the foreign minister or minister of foreign affairs in most other countries, and is therefore classed in 353.132293.

It is the secretaries of state in the states of the United States that are the most problematic, because they have different duties in different states. Their central duty, however, seems to be the authentication and preservation of the most important state papers, and they usually maintain other records as well, including records of appointments. Their offices often compile organization manuals of the state government. Therefore, the span of numbers suggested in the schedule (352.3870974–.0979) refers to the record-management function in American states. This span is recommended simply as one that will generally fit most works on the offices of state secretaries of state, and should be used with caution. The office of a specific secretary of state having a range of duties that does not fit into this span should be classed in a number that covers a majority the duties reported.

353.53 vs. 351.08

Programs directed to kinds of persons vs. History and description with respect to kinds of persons

Comprehensive works on administration of programs directed to kinds of persons are found in 353.53, where families and the kinds of persons who are most often the target of government assistance are emphasized.

351.08 is limited to other relationships between the group and public administration, e.g., contributions of Blacks to public administration 351.08996, the success of women in public administration 351.082. Neither provision should be used for works involving basic policy matters, which should be classed outside public administration, e.g., lobbying for government programs for African Americans 362.8496073 (*not* 353.53496073).

Elsewhere in public administration, the distinction is not made. Administration of specific kinds of services directed to kinds of persons is classed with the kind of service, plus notation 08 from Table 1, e.g., poor people T1—086942, veterans T1—08697.

The convenience of 353.53 is first, that it allows notation for general considerations of administration to be added for comprehensive numbers for each kind of persons; and second, that it provides relatively short notation for some groups, e.g., for poor people 353.5332 (three digits shorter than 353.5086942), veterans 353.538 (three digits shorter than 353.508697 and two digits shorter than 351.08697), as well as for families 353.5331 (that are not provided for in notation 08 from Table 1).

353.53 vs. 352.1

Programs directed to kinds of persons vs. Jurisdictional levels of administration

Use of table notation for kinds of persons

Caution must be observed in using notation 08 from Table 1 in 352.1, because programs directed to kinds of persons by international, state and provincial, or local bodies should be classed in 353.53, not 352.1. These programs are not covered by the instructions in the class-elsewhere note at 353.53 that the administration of programs directing that *a specific kind of service* to kinds of persons be classed with the kind of service, plus notation 08 from Table 1. For example, class comprehensive works on Canadian provincial programs for minorities in 353.532130971, not in 352.13080971. Notation 21 from the table under 352–354 is likewise used with asterisked subdivisions of 353.53, e.g., administration of Canadian provincial programs for veterans 353.5382130971, not in 352.13086970971.

353.5339 and 353.534

[Programs for] Racial, ethnic, national groups in general [and Programs for] Specific racial, ethnic, national groups

There are two numbers for ethnic minorities. The number for comprehensive works precedes the one for specific minorities so that notation for standard subdivisions (e.g., for areas) and general considerations of administration (e.g., state and local programs) can be given for ethnic minorities in general without excluding numbers for certain ethnic groups. For example, programs for mixed races in South Africa are classed in 353.534044068, for ethnic minorities in Germany in 353.53390943. Notation specifying these two concepts could not both be added to the same base number.

355 vs. 623

Military science vs. Military and nautical engineering

Use 623 for physical description, design, manufacture, operation, and repair of ordnance; use 355–359 for procurement and deployment, and also for the units and services that use the ordnance. Histories of the development of weapons emphasizing the interplay of human and social factors are regarded as procurement history, and are classed in 355.8 and related numbers in 356–359. If in doubt, prefer 355–359.

355.00711

Higher education

In designating the area number for an official service academy, use notation for the country it serves, e.g., the Royal Military Academy (Sandhurst, England) 355.0071141, the U.S. Naval Academy (Annapolis, Maryland) 359.0071173.

355.02 vs. 355.4

War and warfare vs. Military operations

Strategy

Use 355.02 for works on strategy that consider the overall problems and objectives of national policy; use 355.4 for works on strategy that emphasize military operations. If in doubt, prefer 355.02.

355.134092

Persons

Class here biographies of awardees, e.g., of recipients of the Croix de Guerre 355.1342092. However, do not class a comprehensive biography of an awardee here if the person's life embraces other significant activities; class with the subject for which the person is otherwise famous, e.g., Audie Murphy 791.43028092, not 355.134092.

355.1409

Historical, geographic, persons treatment

Class uniforms of several participants in a particular war in the area number corresponding to the one used for the war in general history, e.g., uniforms of the Peninsular War (part of the Napoleonic Wars classed in 940.27) 355.14094, not 355.140946.

Class uniforms of a specific branch of the armed services with the branch, e.g., uniforms of the Royal Air Force 358.41140941.

355.81 vs. 355.14

Clothing, food, camp equipment, office supplies vs. Uniforms

Use 355.14 for military clothing if the emphasis is on cut, style, or color of uniforms; on insignia, identification of units or branches of service; or on the history of uniforms. Use 355.81 if the emphasis is on the function of various articles of clothing, or on supply administration (from development through issue and disposition). If in doubt, prefer 355.81.

359.32 vs. 359.83

Ships as naval units vs. [Ships as] Transportation equipment and supplies

Naval ships may be written about either as units of organization or as items of equipment. When a work on ships focuses on matters normally covered by analogous works on regiments and other military units, class it in 359.32 or cognate numbers in 359.9. Such a work will normally emphasize the crew and its organization, duties, effectiveness, and history. When, in contrast, the work focuses on development, procurement, operation, and actual or potential combat effectiveness of the hardware, class it in 359.83 or cognate numbers in 359.9. Whatever discussion of personnel or personalities such a work has will usually concern persons responsible for development and procurement of ships, e.g., Admiral Rickover's work in developing nuclear submarines 359.93834092. Works about a specific ship will most often consider the ship as a naval unit (unless there is only one ship of a class). Class comprehensive works in 359.83, but if in doubt, prefer 359.32.

Use country numbers in notation 09 from Table 1 for either specific ships, or a number of ships of a specific class employed by a specific nation.

361–365

Social problems and services

Problems and services in this section of the schedules are often linked terms, and, where one is spelled out, the other is implied. Thus, addictions at 362.29 implies services to the addicted, while services of extended care facilities at 362.16 implies the problems that require such services.

See also discussion at 300 vs. 600.

Political, economic, and legal considerations

Many publications give considerable emphasis to the political and legal considerations related to social services. If the focus is on the problem or the service, class such publications here. For example, class a discussion of political obstacles to effective poverty programs in 362.5, a discussion of the political maneuvering behind the adoption of an act of the United States Congress spelling out a new housing program in 363.580973.

361–365 vs. 353.5

Social problems and services vs. [Public] Administration of social welfare

Much of the material on social problems and services consists of government reports. Reports about welfare programs and institutions are classed in 361–365. Reports concentrating on the administrative activities of agencies supporting and regulating the programs and institutions are classed in 353.5. If in doubt, class in 361–365; however, prefer 353.5 for administrative annual reports of government agencies.

361 vs. 362

Social problems and social welfare in general vs. Social welfare problems and services

361 is used for two kinds of material: comprehensive works on the whole range of problems and services found in 362–363, and works on principles and methods of assessing and solving the problems. The second kind of material normally does not address specific problems but may refer to welfare problems, usually found in 362. Material on the principles and methods of welfare work in general is classed in 361. Application of the principles and methods to a specific problem is classed with the problem, plus notation 5 from the table under 362–363.

A helpful guide in deciding between 361 and 362 is the table of contents. If it reads like a summary of the subdivisions of 362, class in 362; if like a summary of the subdivisions of 361, class in 361. In the absence of a table of contents or summary, the coverage of topics is a useful guide. If topics in both 361 and 362 are covered, class in 361. If in doubt, class in 361.

361.6 vs. 361.7, 361.8

Governmental action vs. Private action vs. Community action

Organizations are classed in 361.6, 361.7, and 361.8 depending upon who has financial control. For example, the Peace Corps, a governmentally funded organization of overseas volunteers, is classed in 361.6; Canadian University Service Overseas, a privately funded organization of overseas volunteers, is classed in 361.763.

The scope of the membership, not the area served, determines whether the organization is national or international. For example, the International Red Cross is classed in 361.77, but the United States Red Cross, a national organization which provides service worldwide, is classed in 361.76340973.

361.614 vs. 330

Welfare and human rights vs. Economics

Use 330 for welfare rights when the term refers to economic rights such as equal opportunity for employment; use 361.614 when the term refers to rights to welfare services. If in doubt, prefer 361.614.

362–363

Specific social problems and services

Add table

These digits are to be added to numbers bearing an asterisk (*) in 362–363. Topics are not usually marked with an asterisk when the concepts in this table have already been provided for in another manner. In some cases these concepts have been provided for in another location altogether.

362.1 is a good example. In general, causes of disease are medical in nature and are classed in 616.1–.9. Strictly social causes are classed in 362.1042, e.g., changes in social attitudes leading to an increase in various diseases. Incidence of disease is ordinarily classed in 614.42, social effects at 362.10422. Control of disease is classed in 614.43 and 614.5, prevention in 614.44–.48 and 614.5. The chief remedial measures are hospital and related services, classed in 362.11–.19 (or direct medical treatment, classed in 616–618). Subdivision 81 Rescue operations is not applicable with respect to diseases. Its closest relative, emergency services, is classed in 362.18. Financial assistance to the sick is classed in 362.104252. (However, class medical insurance in 368.3822 and 368.42.) Subdivisions 83–85 are not applicable here. Counseling and guidance are provided for at 362.104256.

When certain subdivisions are not applicable under numbers marked with an asterisk, they will be listed with an instruction that they are not to be used. Subdivisions with altered meanings are also listed. For example, at 362.86, the entry for subdivision 82 Financial assistance has been included to carry additional information not found in the table. The listing of only one subdivision does not mean that other subdivisions may not be used. Thus residential care for veterans is classed in 362.8685.

362–363 vs. 364.1

Specific social problems and services vs. Criminal offenses

Some human activities can be considered either as social problems or as crimes. An activity as a social problem is classed in 362–363. The activity treated as a crime is classed in 364.1. For example, drug addiction as a social problem is classed in 362.29, but illegal use of drugs is classed in 364.177. Suicide as a social problem is classed in 362.28, but suicide treated as a crime is classed in 364.1522. If in doubt, prefer 362–363.

362 vs. 368.4

Social welfare problems and services vs. Government-sponsored insurance

Social security

Social security as a government-sponsored insurance scheme is classed in 368.4 and cognate numbers, e.g., social security in the United States 368.4300973. Social security that is not insurance classes in 362, e.g., social security in the United Kingdom 362.941. If in doubt, prefer 362.

362.1–.4 vs. 610

Problems of and services to persons with illnesses and disabilities vs. Medical sciences   Medicine

Class health services from the social viewpoint in 362.1–.4, from the technological viewpoint in 610. For example, class social measures for the provision of dental care through clinics in 362.1976, but how dentists actually use their skill in 617.6. Class works treating both the medical sciences and the medical social services in 362.1–.4. If in doubt, prefer 362.1–.4.

Biographies

Class in 362.1–.4, plus notation 092 from Table 1, biographies and memoirs of the dying and persons with illnesses and disabilities that lack any other disciplinary focus. The rationale behind this rule is that these biographies illustrate the way society addresses itself to fundamental health problems and their solution. Be alert, however, for significant disciplinary emphasis, e.g., a work offering guidance in the Christian life with respect to health misfortunes is classed in 248.86, Christian meditations in 242.4. Class studies of individual cases designed for the use of researchers, practitioners, and students in the field in the number for the field, without adding notation 092 from Table 1. Class in 616–618 studies of patients describing their illnesses in medical terms rather than their lives in social terms, plus notation 09 from the table under 616.1–.9, e.g., case studies of heart disease 616.1209. If in doubt, prefer 362; however, prefer 616.8909 and related numbers for psychiatric disorders, since the consideration of external circumstances is generally subordinated to the discussion of the state of mind of the patient.

While most personal and biographical treatment of medical personnel is classed in 610, works on public health doctors or nurses emphasizing their influences on public health services and awareness are classed in 362, e.g., a biography of a doctor noted chiefly for promoting nursing homes 362.16092.

362.1042 vs. 368.382

Social aspects [of health services] vs. Health insurance

Works on health insurance plans that focus on their insurance features are classed in 368.382, e.g., a work on the need to raise prepaid health care rates in California 368.38201109794. Works that focus on the health services features of insurance plans are classed in 362.1042, e.g., a work on the adequacy of managed care plans in California 362.10425809794. If in doubt, prefer 362.1042.

362.7083

[Problems of and services to] Young people twelve to seventeen

Since the majority of the books on the problems of and services to young people are about children, it is redundant to add notation 083 from Table 1 to 362.7 except for works limited to the problems of and services to young people twelve to seventeen.

363

Other social problems and services

Several subdivisions involve the control of technology, particularly under safety (363.1) and environment (363.7). Class in 363 works addressing what must be done, regulating how it is to be done, inspecting to see whether or not it has been done, and investigating when it was not done. Only works dealing with the technological procedures for carrying out a given operation are classed in technology. Finding out what broke is 600; finding out who let it break is 363. Machinery breakdown is 600; institutional breakdown is 363.

A useful clue in choosing the appropriate discipline is the perspective of the author or publishing agency. If the author is interested in social service and social need, the work is classed in 363; in economics, 333.7; in human ecology, 304.2; in how to make things, 620–690; in how organisms survive, 570–590; in how crops survive, 632–635; in physical techniques for controlling pollution, 628.5. In general, commercial publishers and environmental or safety advocacy groups tend to produce works that are classed in the social sciences, e.g., 304.2, 333.7, or 363.

To summarize: class comprehensive works and works oriented toward problems and their solution in 363, resource-oriented material in 333.7, works giving significant consideration to the social dynamics of the problem in 302–307, works emphasizing technology in 600.

See also discussion at 300 vs. 600; also at 301–307 vs. 361–365.

363 vs. 340, 353–354

Other social problems and services vs. Law vs. [Specific fields of public administration]

Class the work of agencies by which the government carries out the detailed intent of the law in matters of population, safety, the environment, and provision of basic necessities in 363. Class the internal administration of agencies concerned with these fields, including their administrative annual reports, in 353–354. The law itself, draft laws, and enforcement of the law in courts are classed in 341–346. Most of the discussion of policy and most detailed procedures for enforcing law, policy, or regulation are classed in 363. If in doubt, prefer 363.

Law enforcement

Law enforcement is not necessarily a police matter, although it may be. Any government agency may enforce the law. A department of education, for instance, is enforcing the law when it sees that the requirements of the law are being met by the schools. Enforcement of law in this sense is classed with the government agency outside of law. A work about the law enforcement activities of the department of education mentioned above would be classed in 353.8. Law enforcement by the police is classed in 363.23. It should be noted, however, that laws governing how such enforcement should be carried out are classed in law, e.g., the law governing what measures police may use in enforcing the law 344.0523 (or 345.052 if it pertains to matters of criminal investigation). If in doubt, prefer 363.23.

Enforcement of the law through the courts is always classed in law, plus law subdivision 0269 where appropriate, e.g., court procedure that promotes the enforcement of tax law 343.040269.

363.1

Public safety programs

All headings in this section, however worded, include the conditions or potential conditions that pose a threat to safety, the measures of prevention and control contemplated or adopted, disasters resulting from the failure or lack of such measures, and the measures of relief and rehabilitation initiated.

The word "safety" is used loosely and equivocally in many instances. It may be so broad as to cover most of the social services. In this case the work is classed at 363, or even at 361 if sufficient 362 material is included. On the other hand, it may be so narrow as to comprise only the work of the police and fire departments, in which case the work is classed at 363.2.

Safety regulations

Class safety regulations that spell out operating and construction techniques in explicit detail with the technology involved even if they are in the form of an officially promulgated regulation by a safety authority. On the other hand, manuals written by or for safety agencies may discuss, among other things, various technical details useful as background for regulation and inspection of various operations while still focusing primarily on safety services. These are classed in 363.1 and its subdivisions as appropriate, often with numbers using subdivision 6 from the table under 362–363.

Priority of safety

Class those aspects of safety that society must deal with through investigations and programs (e.g., the topics in the add table at 362–363) in 363.1 or 363.3 rather than with the subject elsewhere in the social sciences, e.g., railroad safety 363.122, not 385.0289. However, the public administration of safety is classed in 353.9.

363.1065 vs. 620.86

Investigation of specific incidents vs. Safety engineering

Accident investigation

Prefer 363.1065 and cognate numbers in 363 to numbers in 620.86 and cognate numbers in 600 for accident investigations when the investigation implicates large, impersonal agencies (companies or governments) that should have prevented the accident by proper supervision, inspection, or regulation. For example, class a technical description of what went wrong at Three Mile Island in

621.48350974818, but an investigation of why it took so long to find out what went wrong in 363.1799650974818.

363.11 vs. 613.62

Occupational and industrial hazards vs. Industrial and occupational health

Use 613.62 for works that emphasize technical measures to be taken for promotion of industrial and occupational health. Use 363.11 for works that emphasize social and institutional arrangements. In case of doubt, prefer 363.11.

363.17

Hazardous materials

Many works on hazardous materials are not classed in 363. The material as an environmental factor affecting the natural ecology is classed in 577.275, as a cause of disease or injury in an organism in 571.95, and as a cause of injury to persons in 615.9 (for chemicals) and 616.9897 (for radiation hazards).

363.176 vs. 604.7

Control [of hazardous materials] vs. Hazardous materials technology

While the technology of handling hazardous materials is classed in 604.7, works on "handling" that are addressed to those responsible for monitoring or inspecting the handling, and that may be devoid of engineering considerations are classed in 363.176. If in doubt, prefer 363.176.

363.31 vs. 303.376, 791.4

Censorship [as an aspect of public safety] vs. Censorship [as social control] vs. Motion pictures, radio, television

Class in 303.376 theories of censorship and sociological studies of censorship of movies, radio, and television. Class in 363.31 censorship of movies and programs after being released or aired. Class in 791.4 censorship of films and programs as they are being produced, e.g., censorship through editing. If in doubt, prefer 363.31.

363.5, 363.6, 363.8 vs. 338

Housing [and] Public utilities and related services [and] Food supply vs. Production

363.5, 363.6, and 363.8 deal with the problems of providing the basic necessities of life. Each has economic implications; thus, a careful distinction must be made between these numbers and the economics of industries under 338. If the work deals with the effect of these topics on the economic aspects of society, or the impact of economic conditions on the availability of housing, water, fuel, or food, class it in 338. If it deals with broader social factors affecting these commodities, or with social measures to insure an adequate supply, class it in 363.5, 363.6, or 363.8. For example, class a study of the effect of a drop in farm prices on the food supply in 338.19, a study of the mismatch between the expected growth of the food supply and of the population in 363.81. If in doubt, prefer 363.5, 363.6, or 363.8.

363.5 vs. 307.336, 307.34

Housing [problems and services] vs. Residential use vs. [Community] Redevelopment

Class in 307.336 the descriptive analysis of housing patterns that touches upon problems only in the larger context of the sociology of communities. Class in 363.5 works on housing problems and solutions addressed specifically to housing. However, class in 307.34 works addressing housing problems in the context of restructuring whole communities. If in doubt, prefer 363.5 over the other two numbers, and 307.34 over 307.336.

363.5 vs. 643.1

Housing [in social services] vs. Housing [in home economics]

A distinction is often made between "housing" and "houses." The term "housing" normally refers to the provision of shelter considered in the abstract, while the term "houses" normally refers to the buildings considered as physical objects. 643.1 is used for the home economics aspects of either housing or houses. It is also the number for interdisciplinary works on *houses* and their use. However, since works on housing often treat the social aspects of shelter, interdisciplinary works on *housing* are classed in 363.5.

363.61

Water supply

Water reports

Water supply reports concentrating on the supply of water on hand are classed in 553.7; on water used, or needed in the future, in 333.91; on the problem of treating and delivering water to consumers in 363.61; on assuring that wastewaters are properly treated in 363.7284; on protection of natural waters in 363.739472. Interdisciplinary reports on water supply are classed in 363.61.

Water quality monitoring reports serve several purposes. As tools for assuring compliance with water supply standards they are classed in 363.61, for assuring compliance with wastewater pollution standards in 363.739463, for determining plant loads and technical difficulties in water treatment in 628.16, and for checking the effectiveness of sewage treatment works in 628.3. Those reporting the present chemical and biological status of available water, but not focusing on a specific objective, are classed as economic geology in 553.7, plus notation 1–9 from Table 2 where appropriate, e.g., a base-line study of the quality of French surface waters 553.780944. The most general works on monitoring "to protect water quality" are classed in 333.9116, e.g., an environmentalist's alert "we must monitor our water supply."

363.73 vs. 571.95, 577.27

Pollution vs. Toxicology vs. Effects of humankind on ecology

In using 571.95 and 577.27 for studies of the effect of pollution and other deleterious agents, keep in mind that the former is part of pathology (571.9) while the latter is part of ecology (577). Therefore, use 571.95 for the pathological conditions caused by pollution and other agents in tissues of organisms. Use 577.27 or the number for the specific ecological environment (biome) in 577.3–.7 plus notation 27 derived from instructions under 577.3–.6 and 577.76–.79 for the more generalized effects of substances upon the community of organisms, e.g., the reduction of species counts (biodiversity) and the general health and vigor of surviving species.

Use biology numbers with caution, however, for pollution studies, because the growth and decline of indicator species are often used to measure the extent and kind of pollution, and are interpreted to suggest the need for, or sufficiency of, remedial measures. Such studies are classed in 363.7363 or in the number for the specific pollutant or environment in 363.738–.739, plus notation 63 from the table under 362–363, e.g., acid rain monitoring by use of indicator species 363.738663.

If in doubt between 363.73, 571.95 or 577.27, prefer 363.73; if in doubt between 571.95 and 577.27, prefer 571.95.

See also discussion at 333.7–.9 vs. 363.1, 363.73, 577.

363.8 vs. 338.19

[Social problems and services relating to] Food supply vs. [Economics of] Food supply

363.8 encompasses the whole problem of supplying food to society, while 338.19 concerns the routine economic aspects. Economic problems like poverty and maldistribution are at the root of most food supply and nutrition problems, but most works concerning such problems focus on the resulting social problems and on the social services needed to overcome them, and therefore are classed in 363.8. Requirements of specific segments of the population are also classed in 363.8. For example, total economic demand for food in Nigeria is classed in 338.19669, food requirements of the urban poor in Nigeria in 363.82086942, normal food trade in Nigeria in 381.41, distribution of food during a famine in Nigeria in 363.88309669. If in doubt, prefer 363.8.

363.8 vs. 613.2, 641.3

Food supply vs. Dietetics vs. Food

Class comprehensive works on personal aspects of nutrition in 613.2. However, class interdisciplinary works on food in 641.3, on nutrition in 363.8. The essential thrust of 613.2 is to help individuals meet dietary requirements and maintain optimal balanced intake without gaining or losing weight. Also included is material for dietitians in planning diets for individuals. In contrast, the emphasis in 641.3 is on the food itself, and in 363.8 it is on meeting and maintaining the needs of society in general and of various social groups. If in doubt between 363.8, 613.2, or 641.3, prefer 363.8; if in doubt between 613.2 and 641.3, prefer 641.3.

363.82 vs. 614.5939

Incidence, extent, severity [of food supply problems] vs. [Incidence of and public measures to prevent nutritional diseases]

Class nutrition surveys in 363.82. These surveys sometimes mention prevalence of malnutrition as an indicator of nutrition levels. Only if the emphasis is on the malnutrition problem *per se* should a survey be classed in 614.5939.

363.9 vs. 304.66

Population problems vs. Demographic effects of population control efforts

Class in 304.66 the effects upon society of control efforts by its members, regardless of whether or not society sanctions the effort. But class in 363.9 programs or policies that are discussed as population control efforts. If in doubt, prefer 363.9.

368 vs. 658.155

Insurance vs. Management of income and expense

Risk management

Be alert to works that call themselves "risk management." Some are about insurance and belong in 368. Others treat a variety of management techniques to reduce loss or possible loss, with a goal of economic benefit to the organization; these works belong in 658.155. In the management context, risk management can include safety problems and their solutions, employee health programs, and all aspects of business security; specific topics are classed with the topic in management, e.g., safety management 658.408. If in doubt, prefer 368.

368.12

Allied fire insurance lines and extended coverage endorsement

Allied fire insurance lines are those miscellaneous lines which have evolved from fire insurance. One example of this is sprinkler leakage insurance; another is crop insurance (368.121), a line that historically evolved from a seemingly unrelated type of insurance.

370

Education

Scope of the extensive revision

The *extensively revised schedule* for education retains the basic outline of earlier editions. The new schedule includes expansions for new topics, updated and international terminology, and revision of some subdivisions. The great majority of changes listed in the comparative and equivalence tables for 370 Education in volume 4 (except the major revisions explained below) are either technical ones, or involve very little shelf material. They rectify irregular standard subdivisions, dual provisions, and separation of similar topics in different numbers, all of which invited errors even by careful classifiers.

The basic emphasis of earlier editions on levels of education is continued in this one. (*See also discussion at 371 vs. 372–374, 378.)*

The major revisions

1. Educational sociology has been relocated from 370.19 to 306.43, where it takes its place among the sociologies of other major disciplines.

2. The standard subdivision notation for education, research, and related topics applied to education has been regularized. The price of regularization is the immediate reuse of some of the irregular numbers: 370.72 had been used for teachers' centers and other adult education concepts; it is now the regular number for research and statistical methods. 370.78 had been used for research; it is now the regular number for use of apparatus and equipment in study and teaching *of education.* (The interdisciplinary number for use of apparatus and equipment as teaching aids has been shifted from 371.3078 to 371.33.)

3. The education of women has been relocated from 376 to 371.822, where it takes its place with education of other specific kinds of students in 371.82. In a related revision, two groups were relocated from special education (371.9) to other subdivisions of 371.82: students distinguished by racial, ethnic, and national origin (from 371.97 to 371.829); and students distinguished by social class (from 371.96 to 371.8262). The meaning of 371.82 has been expanded from simply "specific kinds of students" to include education of and schools for specific kinds of students.

4. Religious schools have been relocated from 377 to 371.07, where they take their place next to other kinds of schools. Likewise, the place of religion in public education has been relocated from 377.1 to 379.28, where it takes its place with other public policy issues in education.

Expansion for reading and language arts

The new schedule includes a significant expansion for reading and language arts in elementary education (372.4 and 372.6). While there are some relocations, most of the provisions in 372.4 (Reading) and 372.67 (oral presentations other than drama and public speaking) are for subjects not represented in earlier editions.

371 vs. 353.8, 371.2, 379

Schools and their activities; special education vs. Administration of agencies supporting and controlling education vs. School administration; administration of student academic activities vs. Public policy issues in education

The basic numbers for operations and activities of schools and school systems are found in 371. Most specific topics in administration are concentrated in 371.201–.207, and 371.2 is the comprehensive number for school (or school-system) administration. Public administration in 353.8 is limited to the administration of national and state or provincial departments of education that regulate and support local school systems. In 379 are found the policy and debate on major policy issues in education. This number includes discussion of the role of government and the public in regulation and support of public and private school systems.

Subdivisions are provided in 379 only for general works on support and control of public education, and for a limited selection of major, controversial issues in education. Public policy and debate concerning all other issues (that is, all issues not specifically named in 379) are classed in 370–378.

Each of the numbers is comprehensive in its own domain, but there are many works that do not quite fit in one or the other. Class works covering 371.2 and 353.8 in 371.2; and works covering both 371 and 379 in 370. If in doubt among the specific numbers, prefer them in the following order: 371, 371.2, 379, and 353.8.

371 vs. 372–374, 378

Schools and their activities; special education vs. Specific levels of education [and] Higher education

The one overriding principle of arrangement in the education schedule is that level of education is preferred over specific topics in 371.01–.8. For the most part, the final digits of the 371 numbers are used in the notation for the topics under specific level. Therefore, when looking up a topic in 371.01–.8, be sure to ask, "Does this topic apply to a specific level?" If so, make note of the number, but then check under the specific level to find the base number to which to add the final digits of the 371 number.

The prevailing pattern is for notation following the decimal in 371.1–.8 to be added directly to the 1 subdivision under specific level, e.g., to 372.1 and 373.1. However, there are a few exceptions in each case, and there is an entirely exceptional pattern in 378.1. Yet even in 378.1, most of the subdivisions (other than 378.11–.12) are in the same order as in 371. That order is obtained in 378.1 through three different add instructions, using 378.16, 378.17, and 378.19 as base numbers. In summary, expect a lot of parallelism, but check carefully to find out just how it is obtained, and where the exceptions are.

The specific kinds of schools found in 371.01–.07 are handled differently under each level. For the elementary level, notation following 371.0 is added directly to 372.1042. For the secondary level, there is a special development for public and private schools in 373.22, but the other kinds are found in 373.21 using notation parallel to that found in 371.03–.07. The specific kinds are not spelled out under adult education, but should be classed in 374.8. The one subdivision here is for folk high schools in 374.83. For higher education there is a special development in 378.03–.07.

371.262 vs. 371.264

Standardized tests vs. Academic prognosis and placement

Prognosis and placement, and standardized tests are (in part) opposite sides of the same coin. Many works will clearly emphasize one or the other, but works relating the two sides remain a problem. Class general discussion of the use of results of standardized tests in prognosis and placement in 371.264, but class works that focus on particular tests and their use in 371.262. (Works giving substantial treatment to both subjects are classed in 371.26.) If in doubt, prefer 371.262.

372.24 and 373.23

Specific levels of elementary education [and] Specific levels of secondary education

There are many different ways of dividing the levels of elementary and secondary education. The Decimal Classification Division assigns individual grades (when they are treated separately) according to the 3-3-3-3 plan shown in the first table below. The other tables after the first show how the Division classifies the most common American pattern of levels.

Names often used for the specific levels, and numbers in which they are classed follow:

Grades	Number
1–3 (Primary grades)	372.241
4–6 (Intermediate grades)	372.242
7–9 (Junior high school)	373.236
10–12 (Senior high school)	373.238

The 6-6 pattern:

Grades	Number
1–6 (Elementary school)	372
7–12 (High school)	373

The six-year elementary school is often called grammar school in the United States, and primary school in the United Kingdom.

The 8-4 pattern:

Grades	Number
1–8 (Elementary school)	372
9–12 (High school)	373

The 4-4-4 pattern:

Grades	Number
1–4 (Elementary school)	372
5–8 (Middle school)	373.236
9–12 (High school)	373

Other combinations are classed with the higher level, e.g., a K–2 infant school in 372.241, unless the majority of the grades are at a lower level. Schools extending from first to ninth grade or beyond are classed in 371.

These guidelines apply only to discussion of sublevels in general, e.g., junior high schools in the United States 373.2360973. The situation in specific schools, however, tends to change so much over time that specific schools are classed in the geographic span under the general number for elementary or secondary education, or in 371.009. For example, a specific junior high school in Atlanta, Georgia, is classed in 373.758231.

378 vs. 355.00711

Higher education vs. Higher education [in military science]

Military schools

College level military schools that are not official training academies, that is, those whose students (except in wartime) normally enter civilian occupations, are treated like other higher educational institutions and classed in 378 plus notation for the area where they are located, e.g., Virginia Military Institute (Lexington, Virginia) 378.755853, The Citadel (Charleston, South Carolina) 378.757915.

380

Commerce, communications, transportation

Commerce deals with the distribution of goods and services, and is a part of the discipline of economics. So too is transportation, an activity that adds to the value of the goods moved. Both communication and transportation developed primarily in response to commercial needs and practices, i.e., to trade, banking, accounting; therefore, they have been placed in 380 with commerce. The technical aspects of commerce, transportation, and communication are classed in 600.

In order of preference of subjects under 330 in the Manual, commerce and transportation take the same position as production. Therefore, a work on the labor force in transportation would be classed in 331.1251388, but production economics of transportation 388.049.

Add table

09 vs. 065

Historical and geographic treatment vs. Business organizations

Use notation 065 when the work discusses the corporate history of the organization, e.g., the corporate history of the Union Pacific Railroad 385.06578. For international companies use the area number for the country which is its home base, e.g., Pan American World Airways 387.706573.

Use notation 09 when the work discusses the system (facilities, activities, services) maintained by the company in a specific area, e.g., railroad transportation provided by the Union Pacific Railroad 385.0978, air transportation provided by Pan American World Airways 387.7.

If in doubt, prefer 09.

380.1 and 381, 382

Commerce (Trade) [and] Internal commerce (Domestic trade) [and] International commerce (Foreign trade)

Commercial miscellany

In most cases, notation 029 from Table 1 is not to be used with the subdivisions of these numbers. Commercial miscellany of specific products or groups of products is classed with the product, plus notation 029 from Table 1, e.g., offers to sell tools 621.900294. Commercial miscellany of a broad range of products, however, is classed here, e.g., offers to sell products of secondary industries 380.145000294, department store catalogs 381.1410294, agricultural export directories 382.410294. A noncurrent offer for sale of a broad range of products that is used primarily to illustrate customs of an earlier period is classed in 909 or 930–990.

See also discussion at 338 vs. 060, 381, 382, 670.294, 910, T1—025, T1—0294, T1—0296.

380.1 vs. 658.8

Commerce (Trade) vs. Management of distribution (Marketing)

Class in 380.1 the economic aspects of trading and selling goods, what is traded and in what amounts. Class managerial techniques for disposing successfully of the products and services of enterprises in 658.8. If in doubt, prefer 380.1.

381.1 vs. 381.4, 658.87

Retail trade vs. Specific products and services and specific groups of products and services vs. Marketing through retail channels

The choice of base number for management of retail stores is complex. For management of a particular kind of retail store, use a subdivision of 658.87 if there is no emphasis on a specific kind of product. For example, class management of retail chain stores in 658.8702, not 381.12068, since chain stores are a form of management organization. Use 658.87 also for a specific aspect of managing retail stores, e.g., financial management of chain stores 658.87020681. However, class management of retail stores marketing a specific product in 381.4 plus notation for the product, e.g., management of book stores 381.45002068, financial management of bookstores 381.450020681. The same holds true for the other subdivisions of 658.87, e.g., management of franchise businesses selling cars 381.45629222068. If in doubt whether a management work focuses on marketing a specific product, prefer 658.87.

When there is no emphasis on a specific kind of product, use 381.1 for economic aspects of retail stores and for interdisciplinary works on economics and management of retail stores. If in doubt whether a work is limited to management or is an interdisciplinary work with both economics and management, prefer 381.1.

383–388

Communications and transportation

Offers for sale vs. Economic aspects

Notation 0294 from Table 1 is added throughout 384–388 to designate offers for sale made by organizations producing various kinds of services. Provisions for "economic aspects" of the various services listed are given throughout 384–388 (usually in .1 under a given topic, but sometimes in standing room in the general number). In distinguishing between these two concepts the following may be helpful:

1. Class in the "economic aspects" number schedules of rates and fares published by an agency other than the one offering the service, since these are not offers to sell. A listing of railroad fares put out by a government regulatory agency is an example of this, and is classed in 385.1.

2. Class a list of rates and fares published by the agency offering the service in the "economic aspects" number when such a list is no more than a list of charges for various services, even though this is, in a sense, an offer to sell. For example, class in 387.51 a list emanating from a shipping company that gives only destinations and prices.

3. Class in the number for the appropriate activity or service, plus notation 0294 from Table 1, a publication containing a more or less full description of the services being offered as well as the information about rates and

fares. Thus, if the shipping company were running a passenger liner and put out a brochure describing the various classes of accommodations offered, the kinds of staterooms, the dining facilities, the garage accommodations, and the medical facilities aboard, such a publication would be classed at 387.5420294, not 387.51, even though fares are given.

384.34 vs. 384.352

Electronic mail vs. Broadcast videotex (Teletext)

Teletex vs. Teletext

Teletex is not the same as teletext. Teletex is an electronic-mail system linking telex terminals, word processors, and computer terminals. Teletext is a system for transmitting computer-based information in coded form within the standard television signal for display on visual display units or television sets. Teletex is classed in 384.34, teletext in 384.352.

384.54, 384.55, 384.8 vs. 791.4

Radiobroadcasting [and] Television [and] Motion pictures vs. [Performing arts aspects of] Motion pictures, radio, television

Class works combining aspects of 384 and 791.4 in 384.

Class in 791.4 the various aspects of producing an individual program, e.g., arranging the various acts of a television variety show 791.450232. Class in 384.54, 384.55, and 384.8 the various aspects of presenting the finished program to the general public, e.g., selecting the correct day and time to broadcast a television variety show 384.5531.

The history of a radio, television, or motion picture company is classed using the following criteria:

1. Class in 384, plus notation 09 from Table 1, a general history of the organization, e.g., a history of NBC (National Broadcasting Company) Television Network 384.5540973, and the history of the system (facilities, activities, services) maintained by the organization, e.g., stations broadcasting NBC television programs 384.554530973.

2. Class in 384, plus notation 065 from the add table under 380, the corporate history of the organization, e.g., the corporate history of the NBC Television Network 384.55406573.

3. Class in 791.4, plus notation 09 from Table 1, the history and critical appraisal of the products of the organization, e.g., the history of the television programs provided by NBC 791.450973.

384.54065 vs. 384.5453, 384.5455

Business organizations vs. Stations [and] Networks

The terms "station" and "network" can refer either to the facility used to broadcast the program or the organization in general. Class in 384.5453 and 384.5455 stations and networks as facilities. Class in 384.54065 stations and networks as business organizations. If in doubt, prefer 384.54065.

384.55065 vs. 384.5522, 384.5523

Business organizations vs. Stations [and] Networks

The terms "station" and "network" can refer either to the facility used to broadcast the program or to the business organization. Class in 384.5522 and 384.5523 stations and networks as facilities. Class in 384.55065 stations and networks as business organizations. If in doubt, prefer 384.55065.

See also discussion at 384.54, 384.55, 384.8 vs. 791.4.

384.555 vs. 384.5554

Pay television vs. Premium (Subscription) television

In this schedule, "cable television" and "pay television" are treated as the same thing, i.e., systems that provide television signals to customers for a fee, and are classed in 384.555. If "pay-cable" is used to mean premium (or subscription television), i.e., the provision of scrambled signals that are decoded for a fee, it is classed in 384.5554. If in doubt, class in 384.555.

386.8 vs. 387.1

[Inland] Ports vs. Ports

The choice between 387.1 and 386.8 for a specific port is based on whether the port is on tidal waters (387.1) or on nontidal waters (386.8), not upon either distance from the sea or the ability to handle oceangoing ships. For example, class the port of New Orleans (110 miles from the mouth of the Mississippi River but on tidal waters) in 387.10976335, the port of Chicago (which can handle oceangoing vessels but is on nontidal waters) in 386.80977311.

390

Customs, etiquette, folklore

Customs, etiquette, and folklore are among the raw material of the social sciences, particularly of anthropology and sociology—the descriptive and analytical aspects of the study of the behavior of mankind in general social groups. Melvil Dewey considered customs to be the culmination of social activity and classed them in 390, just before language, the last of the social sciences and a main class requiring a whole digit (4) to itself.

391 vs. 646.3, 746.92

Costume and personal appearance vs. Clothing and accessories vs. [Artistic aspects of] Costume

Costume, clothing, and fashion can be treated in terms of customs, home economics, or art. Customs, such as what was worn, what is fashionable, national costumes, are classed in 391, e.g., Edwardian fashion 391.0094109041, Lithuanian national costumes 391.0094793. Home economics aspects, such as how to dress on a limited budget, select the best quality clothing, dress correctly for the business world, are classed in 646.3. Artistic aspects, such as clothing considered as a product of the textile arts, fashion design, are classed in 746.92. If in doubt between 391 and 646.3 or 746.92, prefer 391; between 646.3 and 746.92, prefer 746.92.

394.5 vs. 791.6

Pageants, processions, parades vs. Pageantry

Class in 394.5 works that discuss traditions of pageants, processions, or parades and works that describe the event. Class in 791.6 works that discuss planning, promoting, and staging the event, including such topics as publicity and float construction. If in doubt, prefer 394.5.

395

Etiquette (Manners)

Etiquette includes prescriptive works on rules of conduct designed to make life pleasanter and more seemly and to eliminate causes of friction in the numerous minor opportunities for conflict or offense in daily life. More important matters of conduct are classed in 170 Ethics.

398.2

Folk literature

There is no notation available for folk literature in 398.2 to distinguish literary forms or collections as there is for general literature in 800. In each case, disregard these aspects in classifying, and use the most specific number available.

Notation 09 from Table 1 is used to distinguish literary criticism of collections of tales and lore, e.g., criticism of ghost stories 398.2509, criticism of French ghost stories 398.209440509. However, do not add notation 09 for individual tales or lore, e.g., a ghost story from France 398.2094405.

Standard subdivisions may be added to subdivisions of this number for any topic even if the subject of the work does not approximate the whole, e.g., 18th century folktales about elves 398.2109033.

Secondary characters do not affect the classification. For example, the presence of Morgan le Fay, a fairy, in the tales of King Arthur does not prevent the tales from being classed at 398.22, even though "fairies" is given as a type under

398.21. However, tales about Morgan le Fay would be classed in 398.21.

398.2 vs. 291.13

Folk literature vs. Mythology and mythological foundations [of religions]

Works on the mythology of a people or on mythologies from around the world are usually concerned with the most basic beliefs of people and with religious beliefs and practices. Such works are predominantly concerned with religion and are classed in 291.13. But mythology may refer also to beliefs and stories that can be referred to as superstitions, legends, fairy tales, etc., where the religious content or interest is not apparent. Class in 398.2 mythology having a nonreligious basis. Interdisciplinary works on mythology are classed in 398.2, since this number includes folk narratives with a broader focus than religion alone. If in doubt, prefer 398.2.

Religious myths are classed either in 398.2 or 291.13 according to content, mode of presentation, or author's or editor's intention. Mythology presented from a strictly theological point of view or presented as an embodiment of the religion of a people is classed in 291.13. However, myths or mythology presented in terms of cultural entertainment or, especially, as representatives of the early literary expression of a society are classed in 398.2, even if they are populated by gods and goddesses. Often the literary or religious focus is clear. For example, almost all Greco-Roman myths retold for a juvenile audience are classed in 398.2; but Jataka tales are usually classed in 294.382325 because they illustrate the character of the Buddha.

Specific myths and legends presented as examples of a people's religion are classed with the subject in religion, e.g., legends of Jesus' coming to Britain 232.9.

398.2 vs. 398.3–.4

Folk literature vs. History and criticism of specific subjects of folklore

Class the folk tale on a specific subject and literary criticism of the tale in 398.2. Class comprehensive works on the history and criticism of the tale in 398.3–.4. For example, tales of witches and wizards are classed in 398.21, a treatise on why in the tales witches are usually evil and wizards are usually good is classed in 398.45. If in doubt, prefer 398.2.

398.2093–.2099

Treatment by specific continents, countries, localities

Standard subdivisions may be added for a tale or tales on a specific topic even if the topic does not approximate the whole, e.g., 18th-century English folktales about fairies 398.209420109033.

See also discussion at 398.2.

398.27, 398.353 vs. 615.882

Tales and lore or everyday human life [and History and criticism of folklore about] Human body, mind, personality, qualities, activities vs. Folk medicine

Medical folk literature

Class a work of medical folk literature in 398.27 if the emphasis is on the story told or literary criticism of the lore; a work on the history and criticism of medical folklore in 398.353. Class in 615.882 only if the emphasis is on the medical practice. If in doubt, class in either 398.27 or 398.353.

400 vs. 800

Language vs. Literature (Belles-lettres) and rhetoric

Many works treating both language and literature are predominantly about literature; such works are classed in 800. Comprehensive works on language and literature, giving equal attention to both, are classed in 400. If in doubt, prefer 400.

401 vs. 121.68, 149.94, 410.1

Philosophy and theory [of language] vs. Meaning, interpretation, hermeneutics [in philosophy] vs. Linguistic philosophies vs. Philosophy and theory [of linguistics]

Language can be a topic of study for linguists, philologists, or philosophers. Semantics and semiotics are among the traditional topics studied by linguists, along with such topics as phonetics and syntax. Linguists study semantics and semiotics to answer traditional questions about natural languages. Such works are classed in 401.41 Semiotics or 401.43 Semantics. When linguists reflect on their discipline and its methods, such reflection is classed in 410.1. (*See also discussion at 401.43 vs. 306.44, 401.9, 412, 415.*)

Philologists may have broader concerns, especially studying literature as well as linguistics; or studying language, literature, and various other cultural issues, but with an emphasis on language. When philologists with broader concerns than linguists reflect on their discipline and its methods, such reflection is classed in 401. Also, broad works on philosophy and theory of language and languages written by linguists and philologists are classed in 401.

If in doubt between 410.1 and 401, prefer 401.

Philosophy of language

Philosophy of language, as a branch of philosophy, is conducted by philosophers to investigate some traditional concerns of philosophy; for example, meaning, reference, truth, predication. When philosophers study meaning, they are not asking what a word means in a particular language, but such questions as, "What conditions must an expression meet to be meaningful or true? How can we make meaningful statements about things other than the evidence of sense experience? Do names refer to objects or to our ideas of objects?" Philosophers also study language as a human attribute; for example, what does the use of language tell us about the mental and social life of human beings? Most of the philosophical writing on language has been done in the 20th century, and the literature constantly quotes philosophers more than linguists. Works of this type are classed in 121.68.

Some 20th-century philosophers claim that by reflecting on language, some of the problems of philosophy can be solved, some can be shown to be not real problems, and others can be better understood or addressed with new methods. Viewpoints or schools of philosophy that put study of language at the center and use its methods to study multiple questions in philosophy, such as metaphysics, aesthetics, logic, or ethics, are called "linguistic philosophies" and are classed in 149.94.

If in doubt between 121.68 and 149.94, prefer 149.94. If in doubt between 401 or 410.1 and either 121.68 or 149.94, prefer 401 or 410.1.

401.43 vs. 306.44, 401.9, 412, 415

Semantics vs. [Sociology of] Language vs. Psychological principles [of language] vs. Etymology vs. Grammar

Meaning

Semantics at 401.43 is the branch of linguistics that deals with meaning in language. In trying to answer the question of what meaning is, semantics deals with such subtopics as synonymy, ambiguity, semantic truth (metalinguistic truth), and entailment. Closely linked with philosophy, semantics is particularly concerned with the underlying logical structure of natural language, i.e., what elements are necessary beyond correct grammar for statements to make sense.

Etymology at 412 has only a narrow interest in meaning; it studies the history of the meanings of individual words.

Grammar at 415 also has only a narrow interest in meaning; it is concerned with meaning only in relation to morphology and syntax.

The sociology of language at 306.44 is concerned with meaning as affected by sociocultural context. Most works on linguistic pragmatics deal with language in its sociocultural context and are classed in 306.44. The exception is works on pragmatics that focus on the individual psychological context; such works are classed in 401.9 psycholinguistics.

If in doubt about where to class a work on meaning in language, prefer 401.43.

407.1, T1—071 vs. 401.93, 410.71, 418.0071, T4—80071

Education [in language] and [Table 1 notation for] Education vs. [Psychological principles of] Language acquisition vs. [Education in linguistics] vs. [Education in standard usage of language] and [Table 4 notation for education in standard usage of individual languages]

The basic distinction between prescriptive and nonprescriptive linguistics is explained in the Manual note at 410. Class in 418.0071 works on how to study or teach language using a prescriptive approach.

Class in 407.1 broad works on language education not limited to the prescriptive approach and comprehensive works on the study and teaching of both language and literature.

Class in 410.71 works on the study and teaching of linguistics.

If in doubt about 407.1, 410.71, and 418.0071, prefer 407.1.

Class in notation 80071 from Table 4 works on how to study or teach a specific language using a prescriptive approach, e.g., how to teach basic French 448.0071. In Table 4 there is no analogue to 410.71. Class with the specific language, plus notation 071 from Table 1 (which is incorporated in Table 4), works on studying and teaching the linguistics of the language, broad works on studying and teaching the language that are not limited to the prescriptive approach, and comprehensive works on studying and teaching both the language and its literature. If in doubt between using T4—80071 and T1—071, prefer T1—071.

Class in 401.93 works on the psychology of learning language, including both the psychology of learning language informally, as a child learns from its parents, and the psychology of formal study and teaching of language.

410

Linguistics

Prescriptive linguistics is concerned with promoting standard or correct usage of language. Anyone trying to learn to speak or write like educated native users of a standard form of a language is involved with prescriptive linguistics. The various nonprescriptive approaches to linguistics (e.g., descriptive, theoretical, comparative linguistics) are concerned with describing or explaining language usage as it does or did exist, without regard to an ideal of correct usage. Most works of prescriptive linguistics are classed in 418 or with the specific language, using notation 8 from Table 4; works of nonprescriptive linguistics are classed elsewhere in 410–490. For example, descriptive works about grammar are classed in 415 and with the specific language, using notation 5 from Table 4; but prescriptive works about grammar are classed in 418 or with the specific language, using notation 8 from Table 4. Dictionaries, however, are classed in 413 or with the specific language, using notation 3 from Table 4, regardless of whether they are prescriptive or descriptive.

Comprehensive works containing both nonprescriptive and prescriptive linguistics are classed in the number for nonprescriptive approaches; for example, a collection containing both descriptive and prescriptive papers about grammar in general or the grammar of many different languages is classed in 415. If in doubt, prefer the number for nonprescriptive approaches.

A work of contrastive linguistics may be a work of applied linguistics that focuses on finding ways to prevent errors caused by interference or negative transfers from a first language in learning a second language or in translating into a second language; such a work belongs in 418 or with a specific language plus notation 8 from Table 4. Alternatively, a work of contrastive linguistics may be a work of purely descriptive or theoretical linguistics, or a combination of applied and nonapplied linguistics, and thus belong in 410 or other numbers not limited to applied linguistics. If in doubt, prefer the number not limited to applied linguistics.

General historical (diachronic) linguistics is classed in 417.7. No comparable provision exists for individual languages, although under some languages, subdivisions of notation 7 from Table 4 are provided for works that focus on the distinctive characteristics of specific early forms of the language, e.g., 427.02 Middle English. For general historical linguistics of a specific language, or for historical linguistics of a specific topic, use notation 09 from Table 1 if the work gives a history, but not if the work merely discusses the processes of change in a general way. For example, class a general discussion of grammatical change in 415, a history of grammatical changes in the English language in 425.09, a history of all kinds of changes in the English language in 420.9.

Class a comparison of two languages with the language requiring local emphasis (usually the language that is less common in the particular setting). For example, a work comparing English and Japanese is classed in 495.6 in English-speaking countries, but in 420 in Japan. If no emphasis is required, class the work with the language coming later in Table 6.

Class a comparison of three or more languages in the most specific number that will contain them all; e.g., class a comparison of Dutch, German, and English in 430 since all are Germanic languages; class a comparison of Gaelic, Welsh, and Breton in 491.6 since all are Celtic languages.

If there is no number that will contain them all (e.g., a comparison of French, Hebrew, and Japanese), class the work in 410.

For comparisons of just one feature of various languages, apply the criteria given above, except do not add notation from Table 4 to the number for language families unless there are special instructions to do so. A comparison of English and Japanese grammar is classed in 495.65 in English-speaking countries, in 425 in Japan; a comparison of French, Hebrew, and Russian grammar is classed in 415; a comparison of Dutch, German, and English grammar is classed in 430.045 (because at 430.04 there are instructions to add); but a comparison of Gaelic, Welsh, and Breton grammar is classed in 491.6.

See also discussion at 407.1, T1—071 vs. 401.93, 410.71, 418.0071, T4—80071.

410.285 vs. 006.35

Data processing Computer applications [in linguistics] vs. Natural language processing

Class in 006.35 computer processing of natural human language used for computer science purposes, e.g., to allow people to communicate with computers in ordinary English instead of formalized commands. Class in 410.285635 and elsewhere in 400 computer processing of natural language used for linguistics purposes, e.g., for machine translation 418.0285635. If in doubt, prefer 410.285.

411–418 and T4—1–8

[Specific elements of linguistics] and [Table 4 notation for specific elements of individual languages and language families]

Most of the topics in 411–418 correspond to the topics listed in Table 4 notation 1–8, although there is not a complete correspondence in the extent to which the notation is developed or applied. For example, a general bibliographic guide to foreign-language texts is classed in 016.418, but a bibliographic guide to English texts for non-English-speaking students is classed in 016.42824.

419 vs. 419.093–.099

Structured verbal language other than spoken and written vs. Treatment [of structured verbal language other than spoken and written] by specific continents, countries, localities; extraterrestrial worlds

Do not use 419.093–.099 for a specific sign language; class in 419.

Use 419.093–.099 for works discussing various sign languages in an area, e.g., a work discussing use of American Sign Language, Canadian Sign Language, and French Canadian Sign Language in Canada 419.0971.

If in doubt, prefer 419.

420–490

Specific languages

The citation order of 420–490 is straightforward: Language + language subdivision from Table 4 + standard subdivision from Table 1.

Grammar of the Hungarian language 494.5115
494.511 + T4—5

History of the Korean language 495.709
495.7 + T1—09

Dictionary of foreign words in the Portuguese language 496.2403
469 + T4—24 + T1—03

For languages with short numbers, three-digit numbers appear in the schedule that have been built with a Table 4 number added to a two-digit base number, e.g., 425 (42 + T4—5) Grammar of standard English.

Dialects

It frequently happens that one source calls a particular tongue a language, and another calls it a dialect. Consequently, it is common for a tongue to be treated as a dialect in the Dewey Decimal Classification and as a language in the work being classified, or vice versa.

Language vs. subject

Class examples and collections of "text" whose purpose is to display and study a language with the language, even if limited to a specific subject, e.g., a grammar of scientific English 425. Language analysis of a specific work is criticism and is classed with the work. If in doubt, prefer the specific subject or work.

See also discussion at T1—014 vs. T4—864; also at T4—862.

471–475, 478 vs. 477

[Description and analysis of classical Latin] and Classical Latin usage (Prescriptive linguistics) Applied linguistics vs. Old (Preclassical), Postclassical, Vulgar Latin

The dates of the Classical Age of Latin are 80 B.C. to 130 A.D. (the Ciceronian Age 80 B.C. to 43 B.C., the Golden Age of Augustan literature 43 B.C. to 18 A.D., the Silver Age 18 A.D. to 130 A.D.). The formal or literary Latin written at any time thereafter that conforms to the standards of that age is classed in 471–475 and 478. However, works on Vulgar Latin, on Old Latin (80 B.C. or earlier), or on Postclassical Latin are classed in 477. The phrase "Postclassical Latin" refers to the nonclassical or vulgarized Latin used from the death of Juvenal (140 A.D.) until the period of renewed interest in the "pure" Latin of the Classical Age in the eleventh and twelfth centuries, and from the fourteenth century onward. Classical Latin did not die out during the interim, however; and a linguistic study written on, say, Latin manuscripts of the monks of Iona is properly classed with Classical Latin. If in doubt, prefer 471–475 and 478.

500 vs. 001

Natural sciences and mathematics vs. Knowledge

Be careful about equating the word "science" with the natural sciences and mathematics in 500. Quite often the word is used to cover the social sciences and the analytical aspects of other disciplines. Class a work in 001 when "science" is used without implying emphasis on "natural science," in 001.2 Scholarship and learning when it is used to cover disciplines outside 500, and in 500 only when it is clearly used to imply emphasis on the natural sciences. Works on scientific method and scientific research are apt to belong in 001.4 Research rather than 507.2. According to literary warrant, however, "history of science" more often than not relates to the natural sciences and mathematics and is classed in 509. If in doubt, class in 500.

500 vs. 600

Natural sciences and mathematics vs. Technology (Applied sciences)

The natural sciences (500) describe and attempt to explain the world we live in, while technology (600) consists of utilizing these sciences to manipulate the natural world and its resources for the benefit of humankind. Be alert, however, for certain subdivisions of 500 that consist largely of technology, e.g., surveying and cartography in 526 and celestial navigation in 527 (all of which would fit better in 620 Engineering); and certain subdivisions of 600 which consist largely of natural science, e.g., human anatomy and physiology in 611–612 (which clearly are parts of internal biological processes and structures of animals [571–573]).

Class in 500 interdisciplinary works on any science and its applications in technology. For example, a work on space science (500.5), engineering in space (620.419), and astronautics (629.4) is classed in 500.5.

510

Mathematics

The type of mathematics presently taught in elementary and secondary schools of the United States is not usually classed in 510. The following is a list of the school subjects and their numbers:

Arithmetic	513
Algebra	512.9
Geometry	516.2
Trigonometry	516.24

Use caution, however, when classifying books with "precalculus" in the title. Depending on the topics addressed, such works may be classed in 510, 512, or 515.

Combination of topics

Use the following instructions when classing in 512.1 Algebra combined with other branches of mathematics, 513.1 Arithmetic combined with other branches of mathematics, and 515.1 Analysis and calculus combined with other branches of mathematics and when using "Class here linear algebra combined with analytic geometry" at 512.5 Linear, multilinear, multidimensional algebras:

1. These sections are designed for works that deal basically with one subject but have some information on another subject either added at the end of the work or interspersed throughout it. For example, class a textbook with ten chapters on algebra and two on Euclidean geometry in 512.12 Algebra and

Euclidean geometry.

2. The work must be predominately about the branch first named. For example, the work must be about algebra with some trigonometry added to be classed in 512.13 Algebra and trigonometry. If it is about trigonometry with some algebra added, it is classed in 516.24 Trigonometry.

510, T1—0151 vs. 003, T1—011

Mathematics [and Table 1 notation for mathematical principles] vs. Systems [and Table 1 notation for] Systems

Many works properly classed in 003 are highly mathematical. What distinguishes them from works properly classed in 510 is that the mathematics is applied to real-world systems.

Some works about systems treat purely mathematical systems, e.g., systems of equations. Such works are classed in 510. Beware: the same or similar terms may be applied to both mathematical systems and mathematical descriptions of real-world systems; for example, a work on dynamical systems may discuss either mathematics (515.352) or real-world systems (003.85).

Half a work on systems in the 003 sense may be organized according to mathematical concepts, but typically the introduction makes clear that the mathematics is intended as background for systems theory. The systems part of such a work will typically be organized according to specific applications, types of systems, or systems concepts such as control, stability, input-output, feedback, observability, or state estimation.

If in doubt whether or not mathematics is applied to real-world systems, prefer 510.

The distinction between the standard subdivisions for systems and mathematics is more difficult than that between 003 and 510 because works classed with the subject plus notation 0151 from Table 1 usually involve mathematics applied to the real world. Use T1—011 for works that clearly stress systems, modeling, forecasting, or other topics named in 003. For works lacking such stress, and in case of doubt, prefer T1—0151.

See also discussion at 519.5, T1—015195 vs. 001.422, T1—072.

510, T1—0151 vs. 004–006, T1—0285

Mathematics [and Table 1 notation for mathematical principles] vs. [Data processing Computer science] and [Table 1 notation for] Data Processing Computer applications

Mathematics is frequently applied to data processing, and data processing is heavily used in mathematics. In each case, class a work with the discipline to which the other discipline is applied, e.g., recursive functions (511.35) used to explain how computers work 004.0151135, computer programs (005.3) used to solve differential equations 515.35028553.

If the application is in a third discipline, the choice between the two standard subdivisions is governed by the same rule of application. However, normally the distinction between the use of computers in a subject heavily dependent on mathematics, and the use of computers in the mathematics of the subject is not made, so the computer standard subdivision is used. For example, a computer program for solving astronomical calculations will normally be found in 522.8553 (522.8 being the irregular notation for standard subdivision T1—028 in astronomy).

519.5, T1—015195 vs. 001.422, T1—0727

Statistical mathematics [and Table 1 notation for statistical mathematics] vs. Statistical methods [and Table 1 notation for] statistical methods

The subject of statistics can be divided into three parts:

1. How to obtain and arrange statistical data
2. How to manipulate the data by mathematical means to produce information regarding the topic being examined
3. How to interpret the statistical results

When a work gives equal treatment to 1, 2, and 3, or contains information about only 1 or 3 or both 1 and 3, class it with statistical methods in 001.422 or with the subject, plus notation 0727 from Table 1. When it contains only 2 or 2 with 1 or 3 or both as incidental information, class the work as statistical mathematics in 519.5 or with the subject, plus notation 015195 from Table 1.

In many disciplines a word derived from the discipline name combined with -metrics or -statistics is used for statistical work, e.g., sociometrics, econometrics, biometrics, biostatistics. Commonly works on these subjects concentrate on 2 from the above list, with secondary treatment of 3 or 1 or both. Therefore, they usually require notation 015195 from Table 1. However, note that works of broader treatment, emphasizing 1 or 3 or both 1 and 3, require notation 0727 from Table 1.

If in doubt, prefer 519.5 or T1—015195.

See also discussion at 003, T1—011 vs. 510, T1—0151.

520 vs. 500.5, 523.1, 530.1, 919.9

Astronomy and allied sciences vs. Space sciences vs. The universe, galaxies, quasars vs. Theories and mathematical physics vs. [Geography of and travel in extraterrestrial worlds]

Outer space

The terms "space" and "outer space" are widely used in popular works on astronomy, but almost never refer to empty space devoid of matter and energy. Class works that use such terms while discussing the various interesting astronomical bodies and phenomena of the universe in 520, and works that use the terms as synonymous with the universe treated as a single unit in 523.1.

Works on exploring space or outer space may refer to either astronomical or geographic exploration. When the emphasis is on astronomical findings, class in 520 (or a specific number in 523 if the work is limited to specific bodies, e.g., the solar system 523.2). When the works refer to geographic exploration, that is, live humans going out on real or imaginary visits to the planets or stars, class in 919.9 plus notation 04 from the table under 913–919.

If a work having no particular reference to astronomical bodies refers to space sciences in general, class it in 500.5; if it refers simply to space with nothing in it, class it in 530.1, where an including note mentions space.

If in doubt, prefer a science number over 919.9, a specific space science number over 500.5, an astronomy number over 530.1, and 520 over 523.1.

520 vs. 523.1, 523.112, 523.8

Astronomy and allied sciences vs. The universe, galaxies, quasars vs. Galaxies vs. Stars

Use 520 for works describing the universe in its several distinct components, e.g., as individual planets, stars, galaxies. Use 523.1 for works treating the universe as a single unit. If in doubt, prefer 520.

Stars and galaxies

When a work treats only stars and galaxies, two more specific numbers must be considered. Use 523.8 for comprehensive works on stars and galaxies when they are treated as individual astronomical bodies. However, use 523.112 when stars are considered primarily as components of galaxies. If the galaxies and stars are considered primarily in the context of cosmological theories, however, prefer 523.1. Usually in works belonging in the universe number (523.1) there is little discussion of individual stars or galaxies. When works discuss other astronomical bodies, e.g., planets and comets, as well as stars and galaxies, use 520.

When the choice is between 523.8 and 523.112, prefer 523.8.

530 vs. 500.2

Physics vs. Physical sciences

Physics deals with the ultimate nature and behavior of matter and energy. As originally formulated in what is now called classical physics (exemplified by most of the span 531–538), it deals largely with matter and energy on a visible or palpable scale. Thus, it was logically located between astronomy (520) which deals with matter and energy on an extremely large scale, and chemistry (540) which deals with matter and energy on an extremely small scale. In this classical view the atoms of chemistry were the smallest particles of matter. The three disciplines together constituted the physical sciences, and co-opted mathematics, which had not yet been recognized as a universal tool valid far beyond the domain of the natural sciences.

Over time, chemistry has continued its focus on atoms and their interactions and combinations with each other to form the molecules of solids, liquids, and gases. However, modern physics has outflanked chemistry by developing physical theories about the even smaller components of atoms. Chemists have borrowed the part of this new physics that explains the behavior of atoms and molecules in chemical reactions and in the fascinating pathways of these reactions in both the inorganic world and the phenomena of life. They have for the most part left all other physical relationships and reactions to the physicists. Physics, however, has grown to a point where it can be fairly said that chemistry is but a part of physics.

The resulting expansion of physics has created anomalies in the Dewey Decimal Classification schedule. Not only does physics in 530 conceptually outflank chemistry at both the macro and micro levels, but also modern physics, dealing with the smallest of components, appears at the two ends of the 530s, in 530.1–.4 and 539, leaving the classical physics of large scale phenomena in the middle. The classical and modern approaches to sound, light, heat, and electromagnetic phenomena are often combined in 534–538. While 539 is the comprehensive number for modern (quantum) physics, the subject is more often written about either in its parts or in conjunction with classical physics, so the number 539 itself is relatively unused.

The upshot is that 530 and its standard subdivisions are used for comprehensive works on classical physics, on classical and modern physics, and on physics and chemistry. If mathematics *per se* or astronomy, or both, are added to the mix, the result is classed in 500.2 Physical sciences. If in doubt, class in 530.

530 vs. 540

Physics vs. Chemistry and allied sciences

Class works on specific topics common to both physics and chemistry with chemistry when they relate to chemical composition, or to reactions affecting the combination of atoms in chemical processes. Class other works with physics. Clues more useful here than in most disciplines are the occupations of the authors or the fields of the sponsoring organizations; the presumption being that chemists are writing and publishing about chemistry and physicists, about physics. If in doubt, class in 530.

530 vs. 621

Physics vs. Applied physics

When the heading of an applied physics subdivision corresponds to one in physics, use the 621 number when the focus is on technology, even though much of the work is scientific background; use the 530 number when the focus is equally on science and technology. If in doubt, prefer 530.

530.12 vs. 531

Quantum mechanics (Quantum theory) vs. Classical mechanics Solid mechanics

Quantum mechanics (530.12) is the concept that energy exists in small separate units (quanta) and is not continuous. It is contrasted with continuum or classical mechanics (531), which applies to the large scale phenomena of the solids, liquids, and gases of everyday observation. Since the two mechanics have practically nothing in common, and are fundamental to modern (sometimes called quantum) and classical physics respectively, class works covering both in 530. The word mechanics by itself is often used when only classical mechanics is being referred to; therefore, check the contents of a work on mechanics to make sure that both 530.12 and 531 are covered before placing it in 530.

530.416 vs. 539.75

Responsive behavior and energy phenomena vs. Nuclear activities and interactions

Many of the topics in responsive behavior and energy phenomena of the solid state overlap similar topics in nuclear reactions and interactions. Some of the examples listed under each topic may be found treated in the other. Class the topics in 530.416 if studied in the context of the condensed (solid and liquid) state, i.e., in answer to the question, what is taking place in condensed matter that makes it behave the way it does. Class them in 539.75 if they are studied in the abstract, or in the context of nuclear structure, i.e., in answer to the question, what makes the atom and its particles behave the way they do. If in doubt, prefer 530.416.

530.475 vs. 530.12, 531.16

Diffusion and mass transfer vs. Quantum mechanics (Quantum theory) vs. Particle mechanics

Brownian motion and particle mechanics

Particle mechanics is a subject which exists in both quantum and classical physics, but is far more basic to the study of quantum physics, where the quanta for which it is named can be considered particles. Particles are particularly important in the study of diffusion and mass transfer, where the basic mechanism is random oscillation or Brownian motion of particles. Use 530.12 for comprehensive works on particle mechanics, but prefer 530.475 or cognate numbers in 530.4 for treatment of particles in diffusion within various states of matter. Also consider other appropriate numbers in modern physics, e.g., 539.725 for orbits of subatomic particles. Use 531.16 only if it is clear that the emphasis is on classical mechanics. If in doubt between 530.475 and either 531.16 or 530.12, prefer 530.475.

Brownian motion usually refers to the random motion of microscopic particles. However, the concept is extended by analogy to a variety of similar random movements, e.g., of prices, of biological populations, of instrumental recordings. Use 530.475 for interdisciplinary works on the concept, and class specific analogies with the subject.

Many works on Brownian motion have an unstated emphasis on such motion in fluids, and should be classed in 530.425.

536.4 vs. 530.474

Effects of heat on matter vs. Phase transformations

The difference between studies of expansion, melting, vaporization, etc., in 536.4 and in 530.474 is essentially that between classical physics and modern or quantum physics. Class in 536.4 the effects of heat that can be readily observed or measured with simple instruments for determining temperature, expansion, viscosity, etc. Class in 530.474 the analysis of what is happening to matter at the molecular and submolecular level. If in doubt, prefer 536.4.

541 vs. 546

Physical and theoretical chemistry vs. Inorganic chemistry

The rule that physical and theoretical chemistry of specific elements or compounds is classed in 546 does not apply when one or two examples drawn from large groupings like metals (546.3) or nonmetals (546.7) are used primarily to study or explain a specific topic in physical or theoretical chemistry. In such cases, use the number in 541, e.g., hydrogen-ion concentration 541.3728, not 546.2.

If in doubt, prefer 541.

543 vs. 544–545

Analytical chemistry vs. [Qualitative and quantitative analysis]

The distinction between qualitative and quantitative analysis has been rendered largely obsolete by the growing sophistication of techniques. Therefore, prefer numbers in 543.08 over those in 544 or 545 for specific techniques unless qualitative or quantitative use is specifically emphasized.

548 vs. 530.41

Crystallography vs. Solid-state physics

Use 530.41 for works on crystallography and the crystalline state in their broad senses, that is, when the terms are used to cover atomic arrangement in metals, ceramics, amorphous materials, polymers, or liquids. Use 548 for works on crystals and crystallography when the terms are used to refer to discrete objects and abstract lattice patterns. While 530.41 is the comprehensive number, use 548 if in doubt between the two numbers for works clearly emphasizing ordinary crystals.

549 vs. 546

Mineralogy vs. Inorganic chemistry

Chemistry and mineralogy are considered to be coordinate subjects. As a result, many topics of physical and theoretical chemistry pertaining to the structure and behavior of homogeneous crystalline solids will not be classed in 546. Use 546 numbers for comprehensive works on the chemistry and mineralogy of specific chemical types, but if in doubt, prefer 549.

549 vs. 548

Mineralogy vs. Crystallography

The relation between crystallography and mineralogy is approximately the same as between physical and theoretical chemistry (541) and inorganic chemistry (546). The crystallography of specific minerals is classed in 549 unless used to study or explain a topic in 548, e.g., quartz, feldspar, and related crystals 549.68, but a study of isomorphism using quartz, feldspar, and related crystals 548.3. If in doubt, prefer 549.

549.1

Determinative mineralogy

Topics spelled out in subdivisions of 549.1 (other than meteorites in 549.112 and physical mineralogy in 549.12) should be interpreted narrowly, within the context of techniques of identifying and characterizing minerals. If in doubt between 549.1 and a comprehensive number elsewhere in 540 and 550, prefer the comprehensive number, e.g., minerals in sedimentary rocks 552.5 (*not* 549.1145).

550 vs. 910

Earth sciences vs. Geography and travel

Geophysics (550) is the analysis of the structure of the earth and the forces shaping it; physical geography (910.02) is the description of the resulting landscape. Descriptions of the results of a specific force or process are classed with the force or process in 551; the operation of all forces and processes which combined to create a specific topographic land form is classed with the land form in 551.41–.45; the operation of all the forces and processes taken as a whole in a specific area, especially if emphasizing solid geology, is classed with the area in 554–559. However, when a work treats the geographic landscape with only minor consideration of geophysical processes, it is classed in 910.02 or under the specific area number in 913–919, plus notation 02 from the table at 913–919. For example, graphical description of surface features in Myanmar 915.9102, geophysical processes operating in Myanmar or the geology of Myanmar 555.91, earthquakes in Myanmar 551.2209591, mountains in Myanmar 551.43209591. If in doubt, prefer 550.

Descriptions of surface features for travelers, which usually cover resort accommodations and the ambience as well as geographic features are also classed in 910, plus notation 04 from the table under 913–919 as appropriate, e.g., contemporary tourist beaches in Myanmar 915.91045.

551.302–.307 vs. 551.35

Erosion and weathering, sediments and sedimentation, soil formation, mass movement vs. Geologic work of water

Since water is by far the most important agent in the erosion, transport, and deposit of geologic materials, the normal rule of preference does not apply in choosing between 551.302–.304 and 551.352–.354. Use the latter numbers only for works limited to the work of water or to materials transported by water; prefer 551.302–.304 when the treatment gives due coverage to the work of wind, glaciers, or frost, even if agents other than water take up a small part of the text.

Water is also the most important agent in soil formation (551.305) and mass movement (551.307). However, it almost always acts in conjunction with other agents to produce soil or mass movement, e.g., action of dissolved chemicals, temperature changes, or earthquake vibrations. Therefore, the work of water in these two phenomena is brought together with that of other agents in 551.305 and 551.307.

551.5 vs. 551.6

Meteorology vs. Climatology and weather

Meteorology analyzes and describes the properties and phenomena of the atmosphere, and thus explains climate and weather. Meteorology is also the comprehensive subject, encompassing consideration of climatology and weather. Unfortunately, however, some works on the larger subject (meteorology) may be called "climatology," "climate and weather," or simply "climate" or "weather," but must be classed in 551.5 in spite of the words used in the titles. Books so titled are classed in 551.6 only when the words are limited to four senses:

1. The description of phenomena of the atmosphere taken as a whole, weather usually being the short-range description, and climate the long-range description

2. The prediction of weather, climate, or specific meteorological phenomena, that is, weather forecasting and forecasts (551.63–.65)

3. The study of climate or meteorology in small areas, that is, microclimatology or micrometeorology (551.66)

4. The attempt to modify weather or any specific meteorological phenomena (551.68), which is actually a technology

All other aspects, including description (weather reports) of specific phenomena, remain in 551.5, regardless of the terms used in the work in hand. For example, reports of rainfall are classed in 551.577, forecasts of rainfall in 551.6477, a forecast of a rainy day in Singapore in 551.655957, a description of climate types of Asia in 551.62095, a discussion of the factors that produce weather 551.5.

If in doubt, prefer 551.5.

551.7

Historical geology

It is not anticipated that the periods and epochs presently given in 551.72–.79 will be further subdivided; therefore, standard subdivisions may be added for specific epochs, stages, or formations, e.g., Albian stage (of Lower Cretaceous) in France 551.770944. However, the Precambrian eras (551.71) may be further divided; therefore, standard subdivisions are used only for works approximating the whole of the given eras.

551.7 vs. 560

Historical geology vs. Paleontology Paleozoology

Paleontology is the study of life in former geological ages through the interpretation of fossils. It utilizes the same material as historical geology (that is, the geologic record), but only as a record of life and the environment in which life evolved. Historical geology emphasizes the rocks and their strata, using paleontological facts to help date and interpret deposition, movement, and erosion. If in doubt, prefer 551.7.

552 vs. 549

Petrology vs. Mineralogy

Rocks can be defined as aggregates of minerals, the minerals being homogeneous, usually crystalline grains (large and small) that give rocks their texture. Petrology encompasses the study of rocks and minerals, or of rocks alone. The homogeneous minerals studied by themselves are classed in 549. If in doubt, prefer 552.

553

Economic geology

Works classed in 553 may include either scientific analysis or economic evaluation or both, and may range from very technical to very superficial. Deposits may be defined in terms of volume, monetary value, years' supply; or simply as good, rich, or promising.

While 553 is the interdisciplinary number for specific nonmetallic materials, be alert for works that emphasize economics of the materials as a whole (*not* just reserves, stocks, supplies), e.g., a work on the importance of water, not giving much consideration to scientific or other aspects, 333.91 (*not* 553.7).

Also be alert for works having a heavy but unstated emphasis on metallic deposits: these are classed in 553.4.

See also discussion at 553 vs. 333.8, 338.2.

553 vs. 333.8, 338.2

Economic geology vs. Subsurface resources vs. Extraction of minerals

For subsurface resources, class reserves in nature in appropriate subdivisions of 553, e.g., reserves of oil that have never been pumped out of the ground 553.282. Use notation 11 Reserves (Stock, Supply) from the add table at 333.7 with subdivisions of 333.8 only for reserves in storage, e.g., crude oil stored in salt caves as a strategic reserve and crude oil in tanks awaiting refinement both 333.823211. Class works treating equally reserves in nature and in storage in 553. Do not class any sort of reserves in 338.2.

Class requirements (need, demand) for subsurface resources in 333.8, plus notation 12 from the add table at 333.7. Do not class demand in 338.2 or 553.

Do not use notation 15 Development from the add table under 333.7 with subdivisions of 333.8, because there is no development of subsurface resources comparable to that possible with other types of resources. New coal mines cannot be grown. What is often referred to as development is almost always some form of extraction, which is classed in 338.2.

Class interdisciplinary works on subsurface resources that include reserves in nature, requirements, and development in 553.

559.9

[Earth sciences in extraterrestrial worlds]

Use 559.9 and notation 0999 from Table 1 in 551–553 for phenomena of celestial bodies directly comparable to terrestrial phenomena. Generally the analogy with earth holds only if the bodies have distinct lithospheres; otherwise hydrosphere and meteorology are moot concepts. For example, class the atmosphere of Mars (which has a lithosphere) in 551.5099923, but the atmosphere of stars (which do not) in 523.86, the red spot of Jupiter (a planet without a distinct lithosphere) in 523.45.

560–590

Life sciences

Summary of major units of the new schedule

The schedule for the life sciences presented in this edition has received a major overhaul. Some units have been more drastically revised than others. Parts of the old schedule that did not need to be changed have been retained. The basic outline of 560 and 580–590 remains intact. Even where revision is complete, a deliberate effort was made to avoid unnecessary reuse of numbers. In most cases, the most heavily used old numbers were sidestepped without compromising the logic of the new schedule.

560 Paleontology

While 560 is listed as extensively revised, the changes mainly reflect revisions in the taxonomic part of 580–590. Dinosaurs have also been revised in 567.9 and 567.91.

570 Life sciences Biology

570 becomes the comprehensive number for biology as well as life sciences.

571–575 Internal biological processes and structures

The completely revised span for biological processes is the core of the new schedule. Biological processes in microorganisms, plants, and animals are now classed in this span, not with the specific organisms as in Edition 20. The reversal of preference from organism to process is the most significant change of the revision. The processes include physiology, pathology, biochemistry, and related subjects. Anatomy and structure are placed in this sequence because they are basic to an understanding of how all internal biological processes work.

576–578 General and external biological phenomena

Biological subjects other than internal processes and structures are developed in this unit: genetics and evolution, ecology, and natural history of organisms. When these subjects refer to microorganisms, plants, or animals, they are classed with the organisms in 579–590. For these subjects, the preference in favor of organisms continues as in earlier editions. Because behavior refers only to animals, it is developed under animals in 591.5.

579–590 Natural history of specific kinds of organisms

The schedule for specific kinds of organisms retains the basic outline of earlier editions, except that microorganisms, fungi, and algae have all been brought together in 579. Plants remain in 580, animals in 590, and no three-digit number in 580–590 has changed its essential meaning. Dicotyledons have been completely revised in 583, and worms have been relocated from 595.1 to 592.3–.7, while 597 and 599 have been extensively revised to provide greater detail and shorter numbers for fishes and mammals.

The two biologies

While preference between organism and process was reversed for internal biological processes and structures developed in 571–575, preference for organism was retained in other subjects in biology. The distinction is based upon the recognition of fundamental differences between the literature on the biology of processes and the literature on biology of whole organisms. The distinction between the two biologies is not absolute, but there are a number of basic differences enumerated below:

1. The first requires study of parts of the organisms to find out how the various processes work; the second requires study of whole organisms or taxonomic groups and their relationships to each other and the environment.

2. The first is studied primarily in laboratories, where it usually involves experimental research; the second is studied primarily in the field, where it usually involves descriptive research. (Either kind of research, however, can be used in either biology.)

3. In the first, the process studied in one organism is usually seen as typical of all living organisms (or as typical of a large class of organisms such as animals, vertebrates, or mammals), e.g., cell division, blood circulation, immune reactions. In the second, topics are usually seen as typical only of the specific type of organism being studied, e.g., snail shells, reproductive behavior of sticklebacks, weaverbird nests.

4. Physiology is at the core of the first, and approximates the whole of internal processes; natural history is at the core of the second, and approximates the whole of it.

5. Most of the literature in the first biology is written by specialists named after the processes and structures they study, e.g., biochemists and cytologists, while much of the literature on the second biology is written by specialists named after kinds of organisms, e.g., ornithologists and ichthiologists. The biggest exception is ecology, (a study of processes involving whole organisms, counted here in the second biology), where the specialists tend to concentrate on the ecology of different kinds of environments.

6. Finally, the first is collected much more heavily in academic and research libraries, while the second dominates the shelves on the great majority of general and small libraries.

For the most part, the biology of processes needed the most fundamental revision. The outline of the part of the old schedule devoted to the biology of whole organisms remains recognizable in the new.

Recasting of 570

570 was completely revised for two reasons: *First*, the preference previously given to specific kind of organism over biological process resulted in scattering of material that should be kept together under process. Internal biological processes and structures have been developed in 571–575, and the plant and animal materials on these subjects have been relocated from 580–590 (particularly from 581 and 591) to the new span.

Now, for example, biochemistry is classed in 572 regardless of the plant or animal in which it is studied, and the digestive system is classed in 573.3 regardless of the animal in which it is studied. Where biochemistry of a specific plant or animal is emphasized, notation for the plant or animal can be added; where digestion of a specific animal is emphasized, notation for the animal can be added.

Second, the old 570 schedule was very unbalanced, with about 80% of the material found in two subdivisions (70% in 574, and 10% in 575). Many subdivisions (especially at the four-digit and five-digit level) were left unused or scarcely used at all. Many important subjects were in six-digit to eight-digit numbers, e.g., biochemistry, marine ecology.

The imbalance of useful notation in the old schedule makes it possible to limit the reuse of numbers in the new one. In order to help libraries implement the new schedule without requiring them to reclassify the bulk of their collections immediately, 574 and 575 through 575.2 have been left vacant.

Major changes in 579–590

The term "natural history" in the heading of this unit (Natural history of specific kinds of organisms) is shorthand for topics found in 576–578 General and external biological phenomena.

579 Microorganisms, fungi, and algae

The three minor kingdoms of organisms have been brought together in 579 by relocations from 576, 589, and 593.1. In the process, viruses and bacteria have been changed from obsolete classifications to modern ones. 579 was one of the least used subdivisions of 570 in earlier editions.

583 Magnoliopsida (Dicotyledons)

Dicotyledons have been completely revised because the old schedule was an illogical mix of two obsolete classification schemes, that of Engler Prantl and that of Hutchinson. Here again it was possible to avoid the worst reuse of old numbers by leaving vacant the five-digit numbers which collectively contain about half of the material classified according to the old schedule. Also, only about half the new material will be classed in five-digit numbers that were used for different kinds of dicotyledons in earlier editions.

584 Liliopsida (Monocotyledons)

Monocotyledons have also been revised from the same obsolete scheme that had been used for dicotyledons. Fortunately, the outline of the old schedule could be kept. Reuse of old numbers is marginal, even though 584.4 is reused for orchids. In earlier editions, subdivisions of 584.4 covered plants that are seldom written about, while 584.4 itself was hardly used at all.

592 Invertebrates

Worms and related animals have been relocated from 595.1 to 592.3–.7, thus utilizing most of the previously unused subdivisions of this number. 595 is now limited to arthropods, the largest and most important group of invertebrates.

597 Cold-blooded vertebrates Pisces (Fishes)

Bony fishes in 597 have been completely revised and greatly expanded in 597.4–.7, partly by utilizing the relatively unused numbers 597.6–.7, formerly dedicated to amphibians. While the four-digit numbers 597.5, 597.6, and 597.7 are reused with different meanings, it is anticipated that less than 1% of the new material will be classed in five-digit subdivisions of these numbers that were used for unrelated kinds of vertebrates in earlier editions. Comprehensive works on bony fishes are now classed in 597 instead of 597.5.

599 Mammalia (Mammals)

Mammals were revised and expanded to provide specific and shorter numbers for important genera and species. Rodents, carnivores, and hoofed mammals were relocated to nearby vacant numbers. Less that 1% of the new material will be classed in numbers that were used for different kinds of mammals in earlier editions.

Regular use of notation 1 in 579–590

In addition to revisions of these major units, one systematic revision in 580–590 required relocation of almost all all taxonomic numbers ending in 1 to subdivisions ending in 2–9. In the new schedule, notation 1 is reserved for general topics of natural history of plants and animals. In earlier editions, notation 04, 01–09, and 2 (in 598.2) were used for general topics.

581 and 591 have been retained with much narrower meanings and simpler notation. For the most part, subdivisions vacated when internal biological processes and structures in plants and animals were relocated to 571–575 were not reused. 581.4 and 591.4 are exceptions; the old morphology numbers have been redefined to serve for physical adaptations. 581.7 and 591.7 now replace both the former ecology subdivisions (581.5 and 591.5) and the former subdivisions for biology of areas, regions, places in general (581.909–.92 and 591.909–92). Subdivisions of 581.7 and 591.7 parallel those in the new ecology number in 577. While the old plant ecology (581.5) number is not reused, 591.5 retains the behavior meaning from former editions as well as several of the behavior subdivisions.

Notation developed in 581 and 591 for plants and animals in general can be used with numbers for each kind of plant or animal having its own number as specified by the instructions at 583–588 and 592–599. For example, notation 17 (derived from 591.7) is added to the mammal number (599) to produce 599.17 for ecology of mammals. Similar notation developed in 579.1 for microorganisms, fungi, and algae is added to numbers in 579.2–.8 in the same manner to produce numbers like 579.617 for ecology of mushrooms.

See also discussion at 570–590: Number building.

560

Paleontology Paleozoology

Specific plants and animals

The development in paleontology for groups of plants and animals that have surviving relatives parallels that found in 580 and 590. Numbers found in 583–588 are reflected in subdivisions of 561.3–.8, and numbers found in 592–599 are reflected in subdivisions of 562–569. The schedule is sometimes not as fully developed for organisms that have left few if any fossils.

Most of the parallel notation is provided by instructions to add numbers found in 580 or 590. Even when numbers are printed in 560 to match numbers in 580 or 590, the including notes are generally limited to extinct groups not found in 580 or 590. The paleontology numbers for groups with abundant fossils are usually indexed, even if the number is derived from an add instruction.

When a botany or zoology number is given in the index without a corresponding 560 number for the kind of organism, the paleontology number can easily be derived. If the corresponding span of numbers in 560 is covered by an add instruction, simply add the numbers following 58 to 561, and the numbers following 59 to 56, e.g., for fossil pines, 585.2 becomes 561.52, and for oysters, 594.4 becomes 564.4. If the corresponding number is not covered by an add instruction, use the fullest number given in 560, e.g., class fossil magnolia in 561.3 because there is no instruction to add the last two digits from 583.22.

570–590

Biology

Number building

The main point to remember in classifying works that treat both a specific biological subject and a specific kind of organism is that the subject takes precedence in 571–575 (the span devoted to internal processes and structures), while the organism takes precedence in the rest of biology. Comprehensive works on subjects other than internal processes and structures are classed in 576–578, while works on these other subjects limited to specific kinds of organisms are classed with the kind of organism in 579–590.

Notation for specific kinds of organisms in 571–575

Because there are many occasions where there is a specific interest in the kind of microorganism, plant, or animal in which a process is being studied, it is desirable to have notation available that identifies the organism.

Notation 1 represents animals throughout 571–573. Specific animals are shown by adding the numbers following 59 in 591–599, e.g., mammals 19 (notation 1 + 9 from 59<u>9</u>). There is no need to use notation 1 in topics limited to animals (except for comparative treatment). Likewise, there is often no need to show specific kind of animal under numbers for organs found in only one kind of animal, e.g., for general works on the uterus of mammals (573.667).

Notation 2 is used for plants and microorganisms in 571–572, but only for specific plants (embryophytes) in 575. Specific plants are shown by adding notation following 58 in 581–588, e.g., monocotyledons 24 (notation 2 + 4 from 58<u>4</u>). Microorganisms, fungi, and algae are placed in notation 29, where specific organisms are shown by adding the numbers following 579 in 579.1–.8, e.g., protozoa 294 (notation 29 + 4 from 579.<u>4</u>). As with notation 1, there are a few numbers where notation 2 may not be needed, e.g., for general works on photosynthesis (572.46).

The following table shows how notation 1, 2, and 29 work for representative subjects:

Subject (number)	In animals	In plants	In microbes
Physiology (571)	571.1	571.2	571.29
Biophysics (571.4)	571.41	571.42	571.429
Cytology (571.6)	571.61	571.62	571.629
Diseases (571.9)	571.91	571.92	571.929
Biochemistry (572)	572.1	572.2	572.29

Since 575 is reserved for specific parts and processes in plants, neither notation 1 for animals nor notation 29 for microorganisms is needed (or available) there. Likewise, 573 is reserved for specific physiological systems in animals, and notation 2 is not needed there for plants or microorganisms. An alternative use for notation 2 in 573 is explained below.

See also discussion at 571–575: Processes limited to kinds of organisms.

Add instructions in 571–575

Within 571–575 Internal biological processes and structures, there are footnotes leading to six different add instructions, four of which have add tables. All the instructions are built upon a similar plan:

A. They all use facet indicators, that is, digits from 0 to 4 showing that there is a switch in aspect of the subject being treated.

B. With two exceptions, a given indicator has a constant value in any of the six instructions in which it appears. The first exception is that notation 2 (normally used to represent plants and microorganisms wherever plants and microorganisms are part of the subject) is used for something else in 573, a number devoted exclusively to topics in animals. The second exception is that notation 3 and 4 are used for special topics in biochemistry in 572 since their regular use is not applicable to biochemistry.

The first three facet indicators are usually combined in one instruction to save space, e.g., (from 571–572) "Add to each subdivision identified by * the numbers following 571 in 571.01–.2." Notation 0 is always used for a regular or modified standard subdivisions, notation 1 is always used for animals, and 2 (when given in the same line with 0 and 1) is always used for plants and microorganisms.

The five facet indicators are used in the following ways:

0 Always used for standard subdivisions

Instructions at 571.01–.09 introduce notation 01–09 from Table 1 as modified under 570.1–.9. The instructions mentioned above to add the numbers following 571 in 571.01–.2 allow the modifications such as notation 0282 for microscopy and 0752 for preserving biological specimens to be used under every number with a footnote in 571–575.

1 Always used for animals or specific animals

Instructions at 571.1 introduce the numbers following 59 in 590.1–599 for specific animals. Because the span being added starts from 590.1, modified standard subdivisions for microscopy and preservation, and numbers for nontaxonomic kinds of animals provided for in 591 become a part of notation 1, and can be added under every number with a footnote. For example, notation 177 for marine animals (derived from 591.77) may be added to the number for respiratory systems to give 573.3177 for respiration in marine animals.

2 Used for plants and microorganisms except except in 573

Instructions at 571.201–.28 similarly introduce the numbers following 58 in 580.1–588 for specific plants. This instruction forms the basis of notation 2 that allows numbers for modified standard subdivisions and both nontaxonomic and taxonomic kinds of plants to be added as needed in 571–575.

Instructions at 571.29 likewise introduce the numbers following 579 in 579.01–.8 in order that specific numbers for microorganisms, fungi, and algae can be added through notation 29.

2 Used for special topics in animal physiology in 573

There is no need for notation designating plants and microorganisms in a class devoted to specific physiological systems in animals. Thus notation 2 is available for certain situations where one physiological system is studied within another, e.g., circulation in muscles. The table under 573 spells out these situations: notation 21 for circulation, 25 for integument or enveloping membranes of an organ, 27 for muscles of a system, and 28 for innervation of the system. The notation is parallel to the corresponding subdivisions of 573, e.g., 21 is parallel to 573.1, the number for circulatory systems.

3 Used when one topic in physiology is studied in another, except under biochemistry in 572

Instructions in add tables under 571.5–.9, 573, and 575 provide notation 3 with the numbers following 571 in 571.3–.9 for the anatomy, biophysics, tissue and cell biology, biological control, and pathology of a subject, e.g., 34 for biophysics, 39 for pathology.

This notation is used with the understanding that the number building is retroactive, that is, that numbers are always built by adding notation from the number coming first in the schedule to the number coming last, unless there is specific instruction to the contrary, e.g., anatomy of cell walls 571.6833 (571.68 cell walls + 33 anatomy [derived from notation 3 plus the 3 from 571.3]).

4 Used for biochemistry of specific physiological systems in animals (573) and plants (575.6–.9)

Instructions in the two add tables provide notation 4 with the numbers following 572 in 572.01–.8, e.g., proteins in the system 46. There are a few places in 571 where it is useful to use notation 4 for biochemistry, but they are so uncommon that they are spelled out in the schedule instead of an add table, e.g., 571.94 for pathochemistry. The add instruction here allows notation 46 (that is, 571.946) to be used in a parallel sense, e.g., for protein deficiency.

3–4 Used for biochemical topics of specific chemicals in 572.5–.8

Since the topics for which notation 3–4 is used elsewhere are not needed for biochemistry of specific elements, notation 3–4 in 572.5–.8 derives its meaning from numbers in 572.3–.4, e.g., structure of specific chemicals 33 (from 572.33), metabolism of a specific chemical 4 (from 572.4).

See also discussion at 571–575.

Add instructions in 576–590

Number-building instructions for the rest of biology consist of variations on three somewhat overlapping themes. First, there are provisions for use of modified standard subdivisions throughout the whole of 576–590. Second, there are provisions for certain regional and environmental concepts in 577 Ecology and related numbers. Some of these provisions replace certain standard subdivision notation for regions; others are carried over in notation representing the final theme. The final theme is the regular use of notation 1 for general topics in natural history relating to specific kinds of organisms in 579–590.

1. Modified standard subdivisions for bioparks, botanical gardens, and zoos

   The modified standard subdivisions for microscopy (0282) and preserving biological specimens (0752) are used throughout 570–590. A third modified subdivision is also provided in most of 578–590: 073 for collections of live plants and animals, that is, for bioparks, botanical gardens, and zoos.

2. Provisions for regional and environmental concepts in 577–590

   The development of 577.3–.7 for ecology of specific environments eliminates most need for standard subdivision notation 0914–0919 from Table 1. Therefore this notation covering areas, regions, places in general is bracketed (that is, made unavailable for use) under 577. It is also made unavailable for use by a special provision in 578 (natural history of organisms) and add instructions in most of 579–590 (specific organisms). The bracketed notation is replaced by 578.7 under 578, and by part of notation 1 (explained below) in 579–590.

3. Notation 1 in 579–590

   There are three distinct but quite parallel sources for notation 1. The notation 1 used in 579.2–.8 for microorganisms, fungi, and algae carries the subdivisions developed under 579.1; the 1 used in 583–588 for plants carries the subdivisions developed under 581; and the 1 used in 592–599 carries the subdivisions developed under 591.

The main subdivisions of 579.1, 581, and 591 are parallel to those found in 578. For example, 578.7 (mentioned above) provides for organisms characteristic of specific kinds of environments. 591.7 covers ecology of animals as well as animals characteristic of specific environments. Notation 17 (derived from 591.7) can be added to any number with a footnote in 592–599, e.g., ecology of mammals 599.17.

The numbers ending in 7 indicated above are all subdivided like the numbers in 577.3–.7 for specific environments. The subdivisions of 577 thus have wide use. For example, 591.74 for grassland animals is derived from 577.4 for grasslands, and 591.77 for marine animals is derived from 577.7 for marine environments.

Examples

571–575 Internal biological processes

Physiology of trees 571.2216
571.2 ([Physiology of] Plants) + 216 (from 582.16 Trees)

Physiology of biodegrading microorganisms 571.29163
571.29 ([Physiology of] Microorganisms) + 163 (from 579.163 Beneficial [micro]organisms)

Anatomy of flowering plants 571.32
571.3 (Anatomy) + 2 (from 571.2 Plants, in accordance with instructions under 571–572)

Effects of light on mammalian tissues 571.45519
571.455 (Light) + 1 (from 571.1 Animals, in accordance with instructions under 571–572) + 9 (from 599 Mammals)
A note at 571.5 (Tissue biology) leads to 571.4 (Biophysics) for biophysics of tissues in general.

Electron microscopy in tissue biology 571.502825
571.5 (Tissue biology) + 2825 (from 570.2825 Electron microscopes, in accordance with instructions under 571–572)
Add instructions allow notation derived from special subdivisions for microscopy (570.282) and preservation of biological specimens (570.752) to be added to numbers for most specific subjects and organisms in 570–590. (Similarly, instructions allow notation derived from 578.073 Collections of living organisms to be added to numbers for specific kinds of organisms in 579–590.)

Regulation of cell division 571.84437
571.844 (Cell division) + 3 (Anatomy and application of processes to other processes, from table under 571.5–.9) + 7 (from 571.7 Biological control)
Regulation is the same as biological control.

Mouse histopathology 571.93519353
571.93 (Generalities of disease) + 5 (from 571.5 Tissue biology) + 1 (from 571.1 Animals, in accordance with instructions under 571.5–.9) + 9353

(from 599.353 Common mice)

Genetic aspects of plant mineral nutrition 572.5142
572.51 (Bioinorganic chemistry) + 4 (from 572.4 Metabolism) + 2 (from 571.2 Plants, in accordance with instructions under 571–572)
A note at 576.5 (Genetics) leads to 572.8 (Biochemical genetics); a note at 572.8 leads to 571.5–572.7 for genetic aspects of specific biochemicals other than nucleic acids. Nutrition is given in the class-here note at 572.4.

Biochemistry of rare earths 572.5241
572.52 (Bioinorganic chemistry of metals other than calcium, iron, copper) + 41 (from 546.41 Rare earth elements)

Translation of proteins 572.645
572.6 (Proteins) + 45 (from 572.45 Biosynthesis)
572.645 is printed in the schedule even though it is built according to instructions under 572.5–.8 in order to call attention to the fact that "translation" is a technical term for genetic aspects of protein synthesis.

Physiology of fish circulation 573.117
573.1 (Circulatory system) + 1 (from 571.1 Animals, in accordance with instructions at 01–1 in table under 573) + 7 (from 597 Fishes)

Diseases of teeth in animals 573.35639
573.356 (Teeth) + 3 (Anatomy and general biological processes of the system, from table under 573) + 9 (from 571.9 Diseases)

Physiology of feathers 573.597
Notation 18 (derived from 598 Birds) is not needed with the number for feathers since no other animals have feathers.

Locomotor neural mechanisms in arthropods and vertebrates 573.79281
573.79 (Locomotion and related activities) + 28 (Inervation of the system, from table under 573) + 1 (from 571.1 Animals, in accordance with instructions at 28 in table under 573)
In this case, notation 1 is used in the sense of "comparative physiology."

The rat brain 573.8619352
573.86 (Central nervous system) + 1 (from 571.1 Animals, in accordance with instructions at 01–1 in table under 573) + 9352 (from 599.352 Common rats)
The class-here note at 573.86 tells one that the brain approximates the whole of the central nervous system.

Atlas of the developing rat brain 573.863833193520222
573.86 (Central nervous system) + 3 (Anatomy and general biological processes of the system, from table under 573) + 8 (from 571.8 Reproduction, development, growth) + 3 (Anatomy and application of processes to other processes, from table under 571.5–.9) + 3 (from 571.3 Anatomy) + 1 (from 571.1 Animals, in accordance with instructions under 571–572) + 9352 (from 599.352 Common rats) + T1—0222 (Pictures and related illustrations)

The number building is tricky here because facet indicator 3 is used twice, once to add a facet for a general biological process or structure, and then again to add a facet for anatomy. With practice, a classifier will learn that notation 38 is code for reproduction, development, and growth of the process or structure, and notation 33 is code for anatomy of a structure. Unless there is instruction to the contrary, the lower number is added to the higher number, in this case, 33 is added to 38.

The note at 571.8 (Subdivisions are added for any or all topics in heading) means that number building can continue after notation 38 is added, even though the title is limited to development.

Standard subdivision T1—0222 is normally used for anatomical atlases because they are more like pictures than maps and diagrams. (*See also discussion at T1—0222 vs. T1—0223.*)

Facial and cranial growth in the rhesus monkey 573.99538198643

573.995 (Head) + 3 (Anatomy and biological processes of the system or region, from table under 573) + 8 (from 571.8 Reproduction, development, growth) + 1 (from 571.1 Animals, in accordance with instructions under 571.5–.9) + 98643 (from 599.8643 Rhesus monkey)

576–590 General and external phenomena

Pond life 578.7636

578.7 (Organisms characteristic of specific kinds of environment) + 636 (from 577.636 Pond ecology)

This title illustrates how notation for ecology of specific environments in 577 is converted into notation for biology of specific environments when it is added to 578.7 in accordance with the first note under 578.7, "Class here biology of specific environments."

Marine algae 579.8177

579.8 (Algae) + 17 (from 579.17 Organisms characteristic of specific kinds of environment, ecology, in accordance with instructions under 579.2–.8) + 7 (from the final 7 in 577.7 Marine ecology)

Whereas notation 1 is used for animals, specific animals, or comparative physiology in the examples that illustrated the add instructions in 571–575, notation 1 in 579–590 (Natural history of specific kinds of organisms) is reserved for specific topics in natural history of the organisms.

Notation 17 is used with the numbers throughout 579–590 to bring out either biology or ecology of the organisms in specific environments, or (as with marine algae) kinds of organisms characteristic of specific environments.

Coastal plant communities of Latin America 581.751098

581.7 (Plants characteristic of specific environments, plant ecology) + 51 (from 577.51 Coastal ecology) + T1—09 (Historical, geographic, persons treatment) + T2—8 (South America)

A search in the Index under plant communities leads to 581.7<u>82</u> (derived from 577.<u>82</u> Ecological communities). A note under 577.82, however, instructs one to class plant associations characteristic of specific environments in 577.3–.7.

British plant communities 581.7820941

581.78 (Synecology and population biology) + 2 (from 577.82 Ecological communities) + T1—09 (Historical, geographic, persons treatment) + T2—41 (Great Britain)

Pocket guide to seashells 594.1477

594 (Mollusca and Molluscoidea) + 1 (General topics of natural history of animals, from table under 592–599) + 477 (from 591.477 Protective covering)

The class-here note at 591.477 shows that the number is used for exoskeletons, shells, or armored animals.

Acoustic behavior of insects 595.71594

595.7 (Insects) + 1 (General topics of natural history of animals, from table under 592–599) + 594 (from 591.594 Acoustical communication)

Fish evolution 597.138

597 (Fishes) + 1 (General topics of natural history of animals, from table under 592–599) + 38 (from 591.38 Evolution)

Human evolution 599.938

There is a special development for physical anthropology under 599.9 Hominidae Homo sapiens. Notation 38 in 599.938 [Human] Evolution, however, is parallel to notation 38 used in the previous sample.

See also discussion at 560–590: Summary of major units of the new schedule.

571–575

Internal biological processes and structures

Reversal of preference between organism and process

The major change in the new biology schedule is the reversal of preference between organism and process or structure for internal biological processes and structures. The schedule in 571–575 now gives preference to the process or structure, and provides notation to bring out the specific kind of organism when the kind of organism is emphasized by the author.

See also discussion at 570–590: Notation for specific kinds of organisms in 571–575.

Definition and arrangement of internal biological processes

The internal biological processes encompass physiology in its broadest sense. They include biophysics; tissue biology; cell biology; biological control and secretions; reproduction, development and growth; diseases and pathology; biochemistry; and physiological systems.

The summary in the schedule at the beginning of 570 gives a simple outline of the subdivisions in 571–575. An explanation of the rationale for the arrangement follows.

The specific biological processes are preceded by anatomy and morphology, and are arranged in 571–575 in the order given above. The basic order is to place first the subjects needed to explain or help one understand subjects that come later. Thus anatomy and morphology come first in 571.3 because they are considered basic to an understanding of how all biological processes work. Biophysics comes next in 571.4 because it is basic to all the other processes. The progression continues from relatively simple subjects to complex subjects that are fully explained only through the application of the subjects placed earlier in the schedule.

Three biological subjects, however, differ in their relative scale rather than in their application to each other: tissue biology, cell biology, and biochemistry. These three might be best placed together and arranged according to scale, from the visible level through the microscopic to the submicroscopic level. The first two have been so arranged, tissue biology in 571.5, followed by cell biology in 571.6.

Logically, biochemistry follows cell biology, especially since all cellular processes are basically chemical, e.g., cell digestion and cell respiration. Because of the amount of literature on the subject, however, biochemistry has a three-digit number to itself in 572, following all the other general processes in 571.

Returning to 571, biological control and secretions follow in 571.7. Next are reproduction, development, and growth in 571.8, subjects in which all the previously mentioned processes come together to produce living organisms. The last general processes, diseases and pathology (in which all the aforementioned processes unravel), come in 571.9.

Specific physiological systems follow biochemistry, those of animals in 573 and those of plants in 575. (574 is left vacant because over 70% of the 570 material classed under earlier editions fell in that single main subdivision.) The arrangement of physiological systems in 573 for animals is generally parallel to that found in medicine under 616.1–.8, e.g., respiratory system in 573.2 and 616.2. At the end of the parallel span, 573.9 is used for miscellaneous systems and topics specific to animals: physiology of communication, bioelectric organs, and regional physiology and histology.

There are relatively few parallels between 573 (for animal systems) and 575 (for plant parts and systems) because the structures and the principles upon which plants and animals work are so different. The subdivisions of 575 begin with parts and move into physiological systems. Stems are found in 575.4, roots and leaves in 575.5, and flowers in 575.6. 575.6 (Reproductive organs Flowers) is the only subdivisions that parallel the corresponding subdivisions for animals (573.6 Reproductive system). Here the fundamental similarity between male and female organs in plants and animals is striking. (*For the relation between reproductive systems and organs [573.6 and 575.6] and reproduction, development, and growth in general, see discussion at 571.8 vs. 573.6, 575.6.*)

The final three subdivisions of 575 are devoted to physiological systems in plants that are only vaguely similar to systems found in animals. Plant circulation (575.7) is driven by the forces of physical chemistry, not muscular action as in animals; therefore, there is no occasion for notational parallelism with animal circulation. Transpiration follows in 575.8. The last subdivision, 575.9, covers animal-like processes in plants: movement, sensitivity, and the physiological activity of carnivorous plants.

Processes limited to kinds of organisms

Most of the span 571–572 is devoted to internal processes that are common to plants and animals, but some of the subdivisions are used for processes that are more fully developed in animals than in other organisms, e.g., 571.96 Immunity. All organisms must have defenses against diseases, but the elaborate immune system in higher vertebrates requires subdivisions for topics like B cells and T cells that are relevant only for some animals. Similarly, photosynthesis, a biochemical process limited to plants and certain organisms, is developed in 572.46, not in 575. (*See also discussion at 570–590: Notation for specific kinds of organisms.*)

Since microorganisms, fungi, and algae do not have the unique organ systems and specialized structures that require the special developments found in 573 and 575, all internal processes and structures related to them will be found in appropriate subdivisions of 571–572. For example, respiration in microorganisms is the cellular respiration found in biochemistry at 572.47, and notation 29 for microorganisms is added to that number to give 572.4729 for respiration in microorganisms.

571–575 vs. 630

Internal biological processes and structures vs. Agriculture and related disciplines

The classification of physiology and anatomy differs between agricultural plants and agricultural animals. Physiology and anatomy of agricultural plants are classed in biology (571.2 and 571.32 and cognate numbers in 571.5–.9 and 575); physiology and anatomy of agricultural animals, in agriculture (636.0891–.0892 and related numbers in 636.1–.8).

The classification of pathology and diseases is the same for agricultural plants and animals; both are classed in agriculture. The number for pathology and diseases of agricultural plants (and for comprehensive works on pathology and diseases of agricultural plants and animals) is 632. The number for pathology and diseases of agricultural animals is 636.0896.

When internal biological processes or structures of a specific kind of plant or animal are classed in 630, they are classed with the number for the agriculture of the plant or animal with the appropriate subdivision for the process. For example, the notation for diseases of specific agricultural plants is 9 from the table under 633–635, yielding diseases of cotton in 633.519 (633.51 cotton + 9 diseases).

The rules given above do not apply to experimental work on basic biology that uses domestic plants and animals as models. Class such work in 571–575.

If in doubt, prefer 571–575.

See also discussion at 571–573 vs. 610.

571–573 vs. 610

[Internal processes and structures in animals] vs. Medical sciences Medicine

Class results of anatomical and physiological research with animal models in 571–573, but results of pharmacological, therapeutic, and pathological research in 615–618 if the medical relevance for humans is either stated or implied. If in doubt, prefer 571–573.

571.629 vs. 571.29

[Cell biology of] Microorganisms, fungi, algae vs. [Physiology and related subjects of] Microorganisms, fungi, algae

There is a significant overlap between the general physiology of microorganisms and their cell biology. Class in 571.29 works that are either limited to generalities, or discuss cell reproduction of microorganisms (571.8429) as well as their general cell biology. Class in 571.629 works that go into details of internal structures, e.g., membranes and organelles, without also discussing details of reproduction. If in doubt, prefer 571.629.

571.8 vs. 573.6, 575.6

Reproduction, development, growth vs. Reproductive system [in animals and] Reproductive organs [in plants] Flowers

Reproduction has a place in both parts of the schedule for internal biological processes and structures. In the part concerned with general processes (571–572), it is found in 571.8 linked with development and growth as a general process affecting the whole body of all kinds of organisms. In the part concerned with organ systems and specialized structures unique to either plants or animals (573–575), it is found in 573.6 (reproductive system in animals) and 575.6 (reproductive organs or flowers of plants).

The distinction between general processes in one unit of biology and unique organs and structures in another unit is a useful ordering device for most biological processes, but it does not work well for the literature on reproduction and reproductive systems. While a distinction could be made between works on animal reproduction in general and the animal reproductive system, it would not be practical for the ordinary classifier or library patron. Therefore, the distinction is not made. Instead, instructions are given to class both reproduction and the reproductive system of animals in 573.6, and both reproduction and reproductive organs of plants in 575.6.

In summary:

Subject	Number
Comprehensive works on reproduction, development, growth	571.8
In animals	571.81
In plants	571.82
Comprehensive works on reproduction, or on reproductive systems	571.8
In animals	573.6
In plants	575.6

Reproduction in other organisms

All reproduction of fungi and algae is found in 571.829, that is, in 571.8 plus notation 29 for fungi and algae. Although some fungi and algae have reproductive organs, e.g., mushrooms and seaweeds, most do not, and the organs are poorly developed at best. This branch of physiology of the fungi and algae is kept together in 571.8.

The reproduction of unicellular microorganisms is not found in 571.829 since the number for cell reproduction is 571.84, and the reproduction of cells in all specific organisms is provided for in 571.841–.842. Thus reproduction of unicellular organisms is classed in 571.8429.

Vegetative reproduction

While vegetative reproduction of animals is found in 571.891 (571.89 Vegetative reproduction + notation 1 for animals) and the vegetative reproduction of microorganisms is found in 571.829 (571.8 Reproduction + notation 29 for microorganisms), the vegetative reproduction of plants is found in 575.49, the number for stems modified for reproduction.

572.8

Biochemical genetics

The terminology of biochemical genetics is unusually confusing because certain terms for one part or aspect of the subject are often used as symbols of the whole. In the schedule, such terms are listed in (and indexed to) the subdivisions that fit their literal meaning. A classifier, however, must always consider the possibility that titles containing terms like chromosomes, DNA, double helix, genes, and genome may, in fact, cover the whole subject of biochemical genetics. If the terms in a title are used in a symbolic sense, class the work in 572.8, not in the subdivision where the symbolic terms are mentioned.

On the other hand, a term like molecular biology that appears to have a much broader meaning, has in professional usage been treated as virtual synonym of molecular genetics, which, in turn, is another way of speaking of biochemical genetics.

573.44 vs. 571.74

Biochemistry [of Endocrine and excretory systems] vs. Biochemistry of control

Hormones

571.74 is the comprehensive number for hormones, but the hormones of the endocrine system of animals are much more elaborately developed than the hormones of plants and microorganisms. Most of the literature on hormones emphasizes hormones in animals. Hence, one should use 571.74 only for the truly comprehensive works that give balanced treatment of hormones in plants and microorganisms. Use 573.44 for works that emphasize endocrine hormones while giving relatively limited treatment to hormones outside the animal kingdom. If in doubt, prefer 573.44.

576.5 vs. 572.8

Genetics vs. Biochemical genetics

The big division in genetics is between those topics that held the attention of scientists before the discovery of the double helix structure of DNA and those that emerged after the discovery. Once the basic chemical structure of genetic material was understood, a set of topics emerged that are basically biochemical, e.g., the study of crossing over and errors in transcription. These are classed in 572.8. Although chromosomes and genes were known long before the structure of DNA, their operation and function cannot be explained except by studying the chemistry of the DNA they contain. Thus they are also classed in 572.8. Class comprehensive works on genetics, and discussion of topics that do not emphasize chemicals like DNA, RNA, and their components in 576.5; class those topics in which an understanding of the structure of DNA is central in 572.8. If in doubt, prefer 576.5.

576.8 vs. 560

Evolution vs. Paleontology Paleozoology

Paleontology provides a major part of the evidence for evolution, and many works cover both fields. Class in 576.8 works that emphasize how paleontological findings are evidence for evolution and works that include significant nonpaleontological evidence. Class in 560 works on the evolution of extinct organisms and works on the history of life that emphasize the description of extinct organisms and ancient environments. If in doubt, prefer 576.8.

577 vs. 578.7

Ecology vs. Organisms characteristic of specific kinds of environment

The kinds of environments treated in ecology (577) all have counterparts under the number for organisms in specific kinds of environments (578.7). Class in 578.7 descriptive accounts of organisms found in a specific kind of area; class in 577 works emphasizing the interrelationships among various elements in a specific kind of area. 578.7 is the comprehensive number for biology of specific kinds of areas, e.g., marine biology 578.77. As soon as discussion begins to emphasize interrelationships among organisms, however, consider 577. If in doubt about the emphasis, prefer 577 (even though 578.7 is the comprehensive number).

577.26 vs. 579–590

Autecology vs. Natural history of specific kinds of organisms

Autecology

Use notation for autecology in 579–590 (notation 17 from the add tables in 579–590) with caution for works on dominant organisms (usually plants) of a specific ecological environment (biome). For example, class the role of grass in grasslands in 577.4 (*not* 584.917 [584.9, the number for grasses, plus notation 17 built from from 581.7 as instructed in the add table at 583–588]). Similarly, class the ecology of specific forest associations in the number for the specific biome, e.g., ecology of coniferous forest associations in Canada 577.30971 (*not* 585.0971 or 585.170971).

The same principle applies for ecosystems named after animals, e.g., fishpond ecosystems. Unless the emphasis is really on the fishes in the fishpond, class in 577.636 (*not* 597.17636).

In summary, to be classed in 579–590, a work must emphasize the kind of organism, not the biome which takes its name from a kind of organism, e.g., it must emphasize grasses rather than grasslands in general. If in doubt, prefer 577.

578 vs. 304.2, 508, 910

Natural history of organisms vs. Human ecology vs. Natural history vs. Geography and travel

Use 508 if a work on nature has significant emphasis on earth sciences phenomena, e.g., weather, water features, and mountains; but use 578 if the work concentrates on various living things and their settings. If the work covers the description of human settlement as well as natural phenomena, class it in 910. If the emphasis is on the relationship between natural phenomena and human institutions, class it in 304.2. If in doubt between 304.2 and 910, prefer 910. If in doubt between science (508 and 578) and nonscience (304.2 and 910) numbers, prefer 508 and 578. If in doubt between 508 and 578, prefer 578.

578.76–.77 vs. 551.46

Aquatic environments vs. Hydrosphere Oceanography

While 551.46 is the number for comprehensive treatment of the hydrosphere and biology of water bodies, works on aquatic biology and marine biology may include significant consideration of land and sea waters as part of the lives of aquatic organisms. If in doubt, prefer 578.76–.77.

579–590

Natural history of specific kinds of organisms

Nomenclature

The notes below mention several of the commonly recognized taxonomic levels used in classifying organisms. The broadest is kingdom, followed (in order of increasing specificity) by phylum or division, class, order, family, genus, species.

Scientific terms are preferred in headings for taxonomic numbers below the kingdom level. If there is an alternative scientific name still in current use, it is given in parentheses following the preferred term. If there are more than two scientific alternative names in current use, they are given in a variant name note. For example, Mycetozoa, Myxomycetes, Myxomycophyta, Myxomycota are given as variant names for Myxomycotina (slime molds) at 579.52. Most obsolete names have been dropped. If a common name is well established in the literature but does not have a clear-cut corresponding scientific term (or terms), the common names may be used alone, e.g., 598.412–.415 Ducks.

A scientific name given in a class-here note is usually that of a subordinate taxon that comprises all or most of the members of the group in the heading. For example, under 583.99 Asterales, the class here note gives Asteraceae (Compositae), the only family in the order.

Common names are linked to scientific names by parentheses when they are generally understood to be exact equivalents. When two common names are linked to a scientific name, a comma between them means that they are alternative common names, e.g. "(doves, pigeons)" after Columbidae in the class here note at 598.65. An "and" means that the two groups with common names together comprise the scientific group, e.g., "(Pipits and wagtails)" after Motacillidae in the heading at 598.854. Common names that simply refer to well-known members of a scientific class, however, are listed alphabetically in an including note.

With plants (and occasionally with animals) the familiar name for families consists of the name of a typical member or members plus the word "family," e.g., Ranunculaceae (buttercup family) at 583.34. The typical member may be a single species or a large genus with hundreds of species, but seldom approximates the whole of the family. Classifiers must not assume that if the family approximates the whole of an order, the typical members do also.

An illustration of two terminology problems appears at 583.23 Laurales. The main family of this order is Lauraceae, the laurel family, which encompasses over 85% of the species of the order. The family is therefore given in a class here note, signifying that subdivisions can be added to the number for works on the family because it approximates the whole of the order.

Only a few species of the laurel family, however, are individually known as laurels, while several plants of other orders are also called laurels. Since it is useful to know where to class comprehensive works on laurels, the including note reads, in part: "Including . . . comprehensive works on laurels." Being listed in an including note means that laurels (even in its broadest sense encompassing all plants called laurels) do not approximate the whole of the 2800 species in the order Laurales.

The use of two including notes under some large classes of organisms is for reader convenience. The first one lists the scientific names of families or higher taxa and their corresponding common names, the second the common names that do not correspond with the given scientific names. Genera are listed with the common names because so many have become common names.

Sources of taxonomic information

In the course of this revision, primary reliance was placed upon reference works that cover all organisms, give both scientific and common names in detail, and are normally available even in relatively small libraries. Schedules that were significantly revised or expanded usually follow the arrangement accepted in *The New Encyclopaedia Britannica,* 1989. Other works that often proved helpful were *Synopsis and Classification of Living Organisms* edited by Sybil P. Parker (McGraw-Hill, 1982), and *Webster's Third New International Dictionary.*

See also discussion at 579.24–.25, 579.3, and 599 for sources used to revise viruses, bacteria, and mammals, respectively.

When subdivisions are added for individual species

Now that taxonomic schedules have been expanded to provide specific numbers for individual genera, it is not likely that further subdivision for individual species will serve users in most libraries. It is likely, however, that standard subdivisions or subdivisions from the add tables at 579.2–.8, 583–588, and 592–599 will be useful for libraries requiring close classification.

These genera and similar groups are indicated in the schedules by special wording of the "subdivisions" note, e.g., "Subdivisions are added for the genus as a whole and for individual species." This note tells the classifier that the genus or group is very unlikely to be divided in future editions, and subdivisions may be used now, e.g., genetics of Strepticoccus equi 579.35515, nesting behavior of the three-spined stickleback 597.6721564.

There are certain small groups of animals comparable to genera in which the individual species are quite similar and share the same common name, e.g., salmon (597.56), sticklebacks (597.672), zebra (599.6657) For these groups, regular subdivisions will also be more useful than species numbers that might not be warranted for a long time.

There are, of course, exceptions where the individual species are very different and are well known. For these, subdivisions have often been provided, e.g., for the lions, tigers, and other great cats in 599.755.

579.165 vs. 616.01

Harmful organisms vs. Medical microbiology

Class in 579.165 the biology of pathogenic microorganisms. Class in 616.01 the study of the microorganisms in relation to human diseases. If in doubt, prefer 579.165.

579.24–.25

Specific kinds of viruses

Subdivisions for specific kinds of viruses in 579.24–.25 are based upon *Classification and Nomenclature of Viruses* by the International Committee on Taxonomy and Viruses, 1982.

579.3

Prokaryotes (Bacteria)

Subdivisions for specific kinds of bacteria in 579.3 are based upon sections of *Bergey's Manual of Systematic Bacteriology*, 1984–1988. This work rejects taxonomic hierarchy above the level of its 33 "sections." In most cases the sections have what are called "trivial" names, which are English phrases defining exactly what the section contains, e.g., Anaerobic Gram-Negative Straight, Curved and Helical Rods. (These are placed in 579.325 and follow DDC rules on capitalization and commas.)

Bergey's does use some traditional Latin or Greek names. In one case where it is clear that *Bergey's* trivial name corresponds to traditional names, the traditional ones are preferred in the heading. At 579.39, "Cyanobacteria and Prochlorales" is used rather than *Bergey's* "Oxygenic photosynthetic bacteria;" the latter name is given as a definition.

The Actinomycetes are a special case. (*See discussion at 579.37.*)

579.32

Minor kinds of bacteria

This number includes the bacteria described in sections 1–3, 6–11, 20–25, and 33 of *Bergey's Manual of Systematic Bacteriology*, 1984–88.

579.37

Actinomycetes and related orders

This number includes the bacteria described in sections 14–17 and 26–32 of *Bergey's Manual of Systematic Bacteriology*, 1984–1988. In the previous (1974) edition of *Bergey's*, these sections were in one unit, Part 17, "Actinomycetes and Related Organisms." They are kept together here because they are a recognizable natural group.

580 vs. 582.13

Plants vs. Plants noted for their flowers

The difference between flower books and books on flowering plants is analogous to the difference between a flower garden and a vegetable garden. Everything normally planted in a vegetable garden is a "flowering plant," yet a vegetable garden is rarely confused with a flower garden. Likewise, one should not confuse general works on flowering plants that cover anything from magnolias to grass with works that emphasize flowers. Class the former in 580, and the latter in 582.13. If in doubt, prefer 580.

583–585

Spermatophyta (Seed plants)

Interdisciplinary works

Many common terms for plants are listed in the schedule to help librarians understand what the scientific terms mean. A large number of the plants named, however, are primarily of agricultural interest. Furthermore, many of the names of plants are also names of products, especially food, but also textiles and lumber. Most works for such plants or products will be classed in technology numbers.

Interdisciplinary works on most plants important for food or other economic interest are likewise classed in technology numbers. The general rule is to prefer numbers in which a thing is used for interdisciplinary works on the thing. Therefore, prefer numbers in 641.33–35 for food plants, e.g., apples 641.3411 (*not* 583.73); in 635.9 for ornamental plants, e.g., roses 635.933734 (*not* 583.734); and in 677 for textile plants, e.g., cotton 677.21 (*not* 583.685).

The choice is easy for common useful plants. But when the use is less important, or when there are many wild species, take care to determine the focus of a work.

For example, for a work on peppers a classifier must determine whether the basic interest is on cayenne, red, and sweet peppers (and perhaps black pepper), which would point to a food number; or on all the species of Capsicum and other genera that are called peppers, which would point to 583.952 (the comprehensive number for botany of peppers).

Works on minor flowers and other ornamental plants in particular must be examined. For example, buttercups may refer to a relatively few cultivated flowers, or to a large representation of the 250 species of the genus Ranunculus. Class works emphasizing cultivated buttercups in 635.93334, but those emphasizing the 250 species in 583.34. The word "family" in the title or front matter almost invariably points to a 580 number, that is, 583.34 for the buttercup family.

When there are two or more uses in technology, or one big use offset by an obvious botanical interest, the interdisciplinary number remains in botany. For example, the interdisciplinary number for oaks is 583.46, because oaks are useful as ornamental trees as well as lumber trees. Laurels are well known as ornamentals, but the interdisciplinary number, 583.23, reflects the many wild species of interest to botanists.

If in doubt, class interdisciplinary works on a plant of minor economic interest in 583–585.

583–584

Angiospermae (Flowering plants)

Subdivisions for specific kinds of Magnoliopsida (dicotyledons) in 583 are based upon the arrangement developed in the article on Angiosperms in *The New Encyclopedia Britannica*, 1989, volume 13, pages 627–835. The changes in taxonomic thinking during the past century have been so drastic that 583 has been completely revised.

The arrangement of Liliopsida (monocotyledons) in 584 has also been revised by reference to the same article in *The New Encyclopaedia Britannica*, but the basic outline of the old schedule has been kept in place. Therefore, 584 has received an extensive revision rather than a complete one, and many of the old numbers have been retained. The new numbers in 584 do not, for the most part, conflict with old ones that were used for many books.

Exercise caution in identifying orders and families of flowering plants by common names; many such names are used for plants in several unrelated taxonomic groups. Notes in the schedule linking the common names are not exhaustive.

598.824–.88

Oscines (Passeres, Songbirds)

Not all oscine families are provided for in 598.824–.88. Use 598.8 for those not listed. Exercise caution in identifying families of oscine birds by common names; many such names are used for birds of several different families. Cautionary notes in the schedule are not exhaustive.

599

Mammalia (Mammals)

Sources of taxonomic information

In addition to the general sources of taxonomic information used throughout 579–590, *Walker's Mammals of the World*, 1991, was particularly helpful for genera and families. The most used general source was *The New Encyclopaedia Britannica*, 1989, supplemented by *Synopsis and Classification of Living Organisms* edited by Sybil P. Parker (McGraw-Hill, 1982) and *Webster's Third New International Dictionary*.

599.94 vs. 611

Anthropometry vs. Human anatomy, cytology (cell biology), histology (tissue biology)

Anthropometry is concerned with measuring human beings to determine variation and presumed evolutionary development. The emphasis is generally on external variation and bone structure, in contrast to anatomy (611), which is more concerned with norms of structure, internal as well as external. Prefer 599.94 for external features and shapes, and gross bone structure (e.g., the comparison of heavy-boned and thin-boned people, indexes of length and breadth of skeletal features); 611 for all other features. If in doubt, prefer 599.94.

604.7 vs. 660.2804

Hazardous materials technology vs. Safety technology [in chemical engineering]

Use 660.2804 for consideration of hazardous chemicals during chemical engineering; prefer 604.7 for comprehensive consideration of hazardous chemicals that includes handling, transporting, and utilization outside the chemical industry.

However, for specific hazardous chemicals, the comprehensive technology number is usually found in 660, e.g., processing, transportation, utilization of natural gas 665.73.

If in doubt, prefer 604.7.

608 vs. 609

Inventions and patents vs. Historical, geographic, persons treatment [of technology]

Use 608 for works on inventions that are primarily descriptive (and usually arranged topically); 609 for works that emphasize historic factors that led to inventions, or that arrange inventions chronologically. If in doubt, prefer 608.

610 vs. 362.17

Medical sciences Medicine vs. Specific [medical] services

Services at 362.17 refer to societal arrangements to make sure that specific kinds of medical work are provided, e.g., services of nurses 362.173. The work actually performed is classed in 610, e.g., the work of nurses 610.73. Interdisciplinary works covering both societal arrangements for medical work and the work itself are classed in 362.17. If in doubt, prefer 610.

610 vs. 616

Medical sciences Medicine vs. Diseases

Class in 616 comprehensive works on the diseases listed in 616–618. However, if a work contains separate treatment of health, pharmacology, and therapeutics, as well as of diseases, class it in 610.

When the whole of medicine is brought to bear on the concept of diseases in a single treatise that discusses group after group of diseases, class the work in 616. The table of contents usually offers guidance. If it reads like a summary of topics in 610.73–619.98, class the work in 610; if it reads like a summary of topics in 616.01–.99 or in 616–618, class the work in 616.

If in doubt, prefer 610.

Standard subdivisions

Use notation from Table 1 with caution under 616 except for internal medicine or works clearly limited to the concept of diseases. Prefer 610.3 for medical dictionaries, 610.711 for medical schools, 610.92 for doctors not having a distinct specialty.

610.69

Medical personnel

Be careful not to confuse the nature of the duties performed by the personnel with the technology of the operations used to discharge the duties, e.g., the technology of the services of medical technicians 610.737, not 610.6953; of surgeons 617, not 617.0232.

610.73

Nursing and services of medical technicians and assistants

Class here only works that emphasize what the nurse does. As the nursing profession continues to expand its responsibilities and gain recognition for those it already performs, more and more works by and for nurses are about the subjects of medical science in a larger context than intended here. Class such works in other medical numbers, e.g., a survey of medical sciences for nurses 610, not 610.73; a work treating the problems and techniques of surgery written to help nurses understand the context of their duties 617, not 610.73677, even if called surgical nursing. If the broader works contain many special instructions for nurses that general readers would not find useful, add notation 024613 from Table 1 (the subject for nurses), e.g., a general work about surgery that contains many special instructions for nurses 617.0024613.

See also discussion at T1—024.

610.9

Historical, geographic, persons treatment [of medical sciences, of medicine]

Class in 610.9 the history of three or more medical sciences. Class the history of a particular medical science with the science, e.g., the history of nursing 610.7309, of surgery 617.09, of internal medicine 616.009. Class histories of major diseases and their distribution in 614.42, and histories of medical service and the resulting medical welfare of people in 362.109. (*See also discussion at 362.1–.4 vs. 610.*)

Class works on former medical practices emphasizing therapy in 615.88 Empirical and historical remedies, 615.882 Folk medicine, or 615.899 Ancient and medieval remedies.

612 vs. 611

Human physiology vs. Human anatomy, cytology (cell biology), histology (tissue biology)

Anatomy concerns the form and structure of organs in contrast to their physiology, which deals with how they work. Sometimes works bearing the names of organs emphasize their physiology or treat physiology as well as anatomy; class these works in 612, unless they are limited to the cytological and histological level. Class treatment of anatomy, physiology, and pathology at the cytological and histological level in 611.018. If in doubt, prefer 612.

612.01522 vs. 612.3923, 616.3992

[Biochemistry of] Fluids vs. [Metabolism of] Water vs. Body fluid disorders

Only water may be considered at 612.3923. Class fluid metabolism in the sense of all the biochemical and metabolic processes taking place in cellular and interstitial fluids in 612.01522. Also class fluid balance and electrolytic balance in 612.01522. If in doubt, prefer 612.01522.

Class body fluid disorders, water-electrolyte imbalance in 616.3992. For comprehensive works on water-electrolyte balance and imbalance, on fluid balance and imbalance, and if in doubt, prefer 612.01522.

612.1–.8

Specific functions, systems, organs

Here is found the basic division of the human body into physiological systems. Parallel subdivisions 1–8 appear elsewhere in shortened or slightly altered form: under human anatomy in 611.1–.8; under pharmacodynamics in 615.71–.78; under diseases in 616.1–.8; under surgery by system in 617.41–.48.

If in doubt where to class an organ or function not provided for in one of the parallel arrays, use 612.1–.8 as a guide. For example, use 615.74 Drugs affecting lymphatic and glandular systems for pharmacodynamics of the pituitary gland. This is comparable to 612.4 Secretion, excretion, related functions, where this gland is named at 612.492. In the same manner use 615.73 Drugs affecting digestive system and metabolism for pharmacodynamics of the pancreas. This is comparable to 612.3 Digestion, where the pancreas is named at 612.34. However, class pharmacodynamics of the kidneys in 615.761, where the urinary system is provided for, even though kidney physiology is at 612.463 under secretions.

612.8 vs. 152

[Physiology of] Nervous functions Sensory functions vs. [Psychology of] Sensory perception, movement, emotions, physiological drives

Class in 152 works that emphasize awareness, sensation, intentions, meanings, and actions as experienced by the individual or observed and described without reference to the physics or chemistry of the nervous system, e.g., seeing colors, feeling anger. Class in 612.8 works that emphasize the physical and chemical mechanisms and pathways of sensations, emotions, movements, e.g., studies using electrodes to determine what parts of the brain process different kinds of stimuli. Class comprehensive works in 152. If in doubt, prefer 612.8.

612.821 vs. 154.6

[Physiology of] Sleep phenomena vs. [Psychology of] Sleep phenomena

Class sleep phenomena in 154.6 if the emphasis is on the overall state of sleep, on the effect of sleep on other psychological activity, or on dreams as phenomena that have meaning in themselves or in the life of the dreamer. Class sleep phenomena in 612.821 if the emphasis is on the chain of bodily activities or on other physiological activity accompanying sleep or dreams, e.g., eye movements, breathing, brain waves. If in doubt, prefer 612.821.

613 vs. 615.8

Promotion of health vs. Specific therapies and kinds of therapies

Many of the topics in 613 appear also in 615.8, e.g., breathing 613.192 and 615.836, diet 613.2 and 615.854, exercise 613.71 and 615.82. In each case the 613 number refers to the preventive or "staying healthy" aspects, while the 615.8 number refers to the therapeutic or "regaining health" aspects. Class comprehensive works in 613.

613.71 vs. 646.75, 796

Exercise and sports activities [for fitness] vs. [Grooming for] Physique and form vs. Athletic and outdoor sports and games [as recreation]

Exercise and sports activities as means of improving physical fitness are classed in 613.71, as means of improving the appearance of the body in 646.75, as recreation in 796. For example, lifting weights for physical fitness is classed in 613.713, bodybuilding contests in 646.75079, weight lifting as a sport (i.e., contests to determine who can lift the most weight) in 796.41. If in doubt among 613.71, 646.75, and 796, prefer 613.71.

614.4–.5 vs. 362.1–.4

[Incidence of and public measures to prevent disease] vs. Problems of and services to persons with illnesses and disabilities

Studies of epidemics and of the incidence of physical disease (including mental retardation and physical disabilities) are classed in 614 when treated solely from the medical standpoint. Works emphasizing diseases as social problems are classed in 362.1. If in doubt, prefer 614.4–.5.

Works on the social provision of services to the persons with physical illness are classed in 362.1. Works on preventive measures, however, are classed in 614.4–.5, regardless of whether the emphasis is medical or social. Thus works on social provision of immunization services are classed in 614.47, as are works on the medical aspects of immunization. Note that the public measures classed in 614.4–.5 are strictly limited to preventive ones. For example, class fluoridation and programs advising people how to avoid cavities in 614.5996, but class programs to identify and treat people with cavities in 362.19767. If in doubt, prefer 362.1.

Works about the incidence and prevention of mental illness, mental illness as a social problem, and social provision of services to persons with mentally illness, are all classed in 362.2.

614.4

Incidence of and public measures to prevent disease

The term "epidemiology" sometimes refers to a research technique with application outside 614, e.g., in determining etiologies, such as smoking as a cause of cancer 616.994071; in determining the dimensions of social service requirements, such as the boundaries of the mental retardation problem 362.32; in exploring the possible effectiveness of proposed preventive measures, such as in reducing traffic accidents 363.1257.

614.5

Incidence of and public measures to prevent specific diseases and kinds of diseases

When adding notation from Table 1 to numbers built by use of the add notes in 614.526–.598 directing addition of digits from 616, two zeros are required for most diseases—those that have an asterisk in 616—while one zero is required for diseases and groups of diseases not marked by an asterisk.

615

Pharmacology and therapeutics

615 is seldom used by itself because pharmacology (615.1) and therapeutics (615.5) are usually treated separately or with a preponderance of one or the other.

615.1 vs. 615.2–.3

Drugs (Materia medica) vs. Specific drugs and groups of drugs

Most drugs are organic (615.3). Class comprehensive works on drugs in 615.1 even if there is a strong predominance of organic drugs so long as coverage of inorganic drugs is in proportion to their importance. However, class in 615.321 comprehensive works on crude drugs and simples (products that serve as drugs with minimal processing, e.g., medicinal teas, baking soda, royal jelly). If in doubt, prefer 615.1.

615.1 vs. 615.4

Drugs (Materia medica) vs. Practical pharmacy

Practical pharmacy at 615.4 covers only a limited aspect of pharmacy: putting drugs into forms that can be used by human beings. Class works on the larger meaning of pharmacy in 615.1, e.g., managing a pharmacy 615.1068. Follow the same procedure when adding 615 numbers in other disciplines, e.g., economics of the pharmacy industry 338.476151. If in doubt, prefer 615.1.

615.1 vs. 615.7

Drugs (Materia medica) vs. Pharmacodynamics

"Pharmacology" is often used in the titles of works mainly limited to pharmacodynamics. If the table of contents is arranged by physiological systems (as 615.7 is), the chances are good that the work emphasizes the physiological and therapeutic action of drugs, making 615.7 the appropriate number. If in doubt, prefer 615.1.

615.2–.3 vs. 615.7

Specific drugs and groups of drugs vs. Pharmacodynamics

The note in the schedule at 615.2–.3 saying to class a specific drug or group of drugs affecting a specific system in 615.7 means that the numbers 615.2–.3 are not used for drugs known primarily for their effect on a single system. For example, digitalis is classed in 615.711 Heart stimulants (or 616.129061 drug therapy for heart failure), not in 615.32395 drugs derived from Scrophulariales; alcohol in 615.7828, not 615.32. If in doubt, prefer 615.2–.3.

615.53

General therapeutic systems

Use this number and its subdivisions only when the discussion is historical or theoretical, e.g., a discussion of the theory of naturopathy 615.535. When these systems are discussed in their application to therapy, class them in a therapy number, e.g., the application of chiropractic 615.82. When the therapies are applied to specific conditions, class in 616–618, e.g., chiropractic in musculoskeletal diseases 616.7062.

Be careful about biography. Founders of systems are usually classed with the respective systems, e.g., a biography of Andrew Taylor Still, the founder of osteopathy, 615.533092. Other practitioners of a specific system are usually classed in 610.92. (*See also 615.534 for chiropractic.*)

615.534

Chiropractic

Many chiropractors limit their practice to therapeutic manipulation (615.82) or to manipulation for diseases of the musculoskeletal system (616.7062). For these people, the best biography number is one that emphasizes their special therapeutic system—615.534092. For chiropractors who do not limit their practice, use 610.92 for biographies.

615.7 vs. 615.9

Pharmacodynamics vs. Toxicology

Class toxic effects and interactions of drugs primarily of pharmacodynamic interest in 615.704 or with the system affected in 615.71–.78. However, a drug primarily of pharmacodynamic interest may be considered a poison if it is so toxic that a single inadvertent ingestion would cause serious complications or death, e.g., the pharmacodynamics of atropine (belladonna) 615.7 (*not* in any specific subdivision because it affects several systems), but the toxicology of belladonna 615.9523952. If in doubt, prefer 615.7.

615.8

Specific therapies and kinds of therapies

Several therapies listed in 615.8 are usually applied only to certain specific types of disorders, and works on the therapies take such application for granted without highlighting it in the title. Note the unstated emphasis and class accordingly, e.g., radiotherapy emphasizing cancer treatment 616.9940642, not 615.842; music therapy emphasizing psychiatric uses 616.891654, not 615.85154.

615.852 vs. 291.31, 234.131

Religious and psychic therapy vs. Religious healing [and the Christian gift of] healing

In many cultures, medicine and healing involve rites and ceremonies and religious beliefs, as well as physical practices. Class a work on healing and medicine in 615.852 if it focuses on religious practices as a part of the medical practice.

Also class in 615.852 works on the use of psychic and paranormal powers in healing that do not mention a religious context.

Class in 291.31 or 234.131 healing as a religious practice, including such topics as religious beliefs about illness, rituals and prayers for healing, miraculous cures by charismatic leaders or saints. Often, works on this topic are also concerned with emotional or spiritual healing as well as physical healing, or in place of physical healing.

If in doubt, prefer 615.852.

Other numbers used for works concerning illness or medicine and religion should be kept in mind:

Religion and health and illness and the social questions and programs concerning them	291.178321
Christianity	261.8321
Religion and the art and science of medicine	291.175
Christianity	261.561
Discussion of whether cures are miracles	291.2117
Christianity	231.73
Philosophy of religion	212

615.854

Diet therapy

Use with caution; when a single food element is heavily emphasized, diet therapy may amount to drug therapy, e.g., a diet distinctive largely by its use of enzymes 615.35, by its use of royal jelly 615.36.

615.8809

Historical, geographic, persons treatment of empirical and historical remedies

This number is limited to therapy. If pathological or etiological beliefs are also emphasized, e.g., the theory of the four humors or the influence of bad airs, the work must be classed in 610.9.

Class here discussions of old remedies of a specific geographic area that are not limited by the terms of Folk medicine 615.882 or Ancient and medieval remedies 615.899. If in doubt whether to class geographic treatment in

615.8809 or either 615.88209 or 615.89909, prefer 615.8809.

615.882

Folk medicine

615.882 is under therapy. If a work gives more than token consideration to folk theories on the causes of disease, it must be classed in 610, e.g., folk etiologies and therapies of India 610.954 (or 616.00954 when the material is arranged by class of disease as in 616.1–.9).

See also discussion at 615.8809.

616–618 vs. 615.7

[Diseases, surgery, other branches of medicine] vs. Pharmacodynamics

Class in 615.7 only general works on the pharmacodynamic action of drugs and their effects on the human body. Class the use of a drug in treatment in 616–618, adding notation 061 from the various tables under these numbers. If in doubt, prefer 616–618.

616 vs. 612

Diseases vs. Human physiology

Class in 612 comprehensive works on physiology (612) and pathological physiology (616.07). Class in 616 comprehensive works on diseases that move from a discussion of physiology to a more general consideration of causes of disease, complications, prevention, and therapy. For example, class the normal and pathological conditions of the circulatory system in 612.1, but the physiology, pathology, and therapeutics of the circulatory system in 616.1. If in doubt, prefer 616.

616 vs. 616.07

Diseases vs. Pathology

Use 616.07 and notation 07 from the table under 616.1–.9 for detailed descriptions of diseased conditions, mechanisms and processes of disease, causes and manifestations, diagnostic techniques. For more general works about disease that include prevention and treatment as well as pathology, use 616 or the number for a specific disease or kind of disease without adding from the table under 616.1–.9. If in doubt, prefer 616 or the number for a specific disease or kind of disease.

616 vs. 616.075

Diseases vs. Diagnosis and prognosis

"Clinical medicine" has two meanings. In one sense it approximates the whole of 616, i.e., the application of all branches of medicine to treatment of various diseases. However, just as often it is shorthand for the work of a clinical diagnostic laboratory, and is properly classed at 616.075. If in doubt, prefer 616.

616 vs. 617.4

Diseases vs. Surgery by systems

617.4 is primarily limited to operative surgery of systems. Nonoperative therapies are usually classed in 616, e.g., therapeutic manipulations of muscles 616.74062, not 617.473062. Nonoperative therapies are classed in 617.4 only if they have some connection with operative surgery, e.g., electrotherapy by heart pacer 617.4120645, since the pacer must be surgically implanted (617.412059). If in doubt, prefer 616.

616 vs. 618.92

Diseases vs. Pediatrics

Use caution in classing in 618.92 certain diseases that are most often treated in children, but that remain lifetime problems or threats, e.g., congenital diseases, mumps. Class these in 616 unless the work in hand is actually limited to their occurrence in children.

616.0757 vs. 616.0754, 616.07572

Radiological diagnosis vs. Physical diagnosis vs. Radiography (Roentgenology, X-ray examination)

Diagnosticians use the term "radiology" with meanings of differing scope, with the result that three different works on diagnostic radiology may be classed in three different places. Class a work limited to the use of X-rays in 616.07572; a work about the use of X-rays, radioactive materials, other ionizing radiations in 616.0757; and a work about the use of all kinds of radiation, both ionizing and non-ionizing, in 616.0754. If in doubt, prefer 616.0757.

616.079 vs. 571.96

Immunity [in medical sciences] vs. Immunity

Class in 616.079 and cognate numbers in 616–618 works emphasizing immunology in relation to diseases and problems in human beings. Class in 571.96 works emphasizing immunology in relation to diseases in general and in animals. If in doubt, prefer 616.079.

616.1–.9

Specific diseases

Add table

071 vs. 01

Etiology vs. Microbiology

When the etiological agent for a specific disease is known to be a single type of microorganism, use notation 01 for the work without further subdivision, unless predisposing and contributing factors are emphasized, e.g., Treponema pallidum causing syphilis 616.951301, predisposing factors leading to severity of syphilis 616.9513071.

When the cause of a disease is complex and not yet fully understood, use notation 01 or one of its subdivisions if the emphasis of a study is on microorganisms or a specific type of microorganism, e.g., oncogenic viruses 616.9940194. When a work considers multiple possible causes for a disease, use notation 071, e.g., genetic factors, environmental factors, and viruses as causes of cancer 616.994071.

If in doubt, prefer notation 071.

616.1–.8

Diseases of specific systems and organs

When a disease of one system affects another system so strongly that it is the second system that must be the focus of concern and treatment, class the work with the affected system, e.g., retinal complications of diabetes 617.73 (*not* 616.462).

616.1–.8 vs. 616.9

Diseases of specific systems and organs vs. Other diseases

Communicable diseases

Communicable diseases that affect primarily one organ or system are most often classed with the system or organ in 616.1–.8, but there are many exceptions. For example, comprehensive works on diarrhea are classed in 616.3427, but Asiatic cholera is classed in 616.932. Check the index to see where a specific communicable disease should be classed. If in doubt, prefer 616.1–.8 over 616.9 for a communicable disease affecting primarily one organ or system.

616.8583

Sexual disorders

Homosexuality

Only works in which the author treats homosexuality as a medical disorder—or focuses on arguing against the views of those who consider homosexuality to be a medical disorder—should be classed in 616.8583. Works about gay men and lesbians in relation to other topics in medicine should be classed with the topic plus notation 08664 from Table 1, e.g., advice to gay men and lesbians about finding psychotherapy for a variety of psychiatric problems 616.891408664. Most works about gay men and lesbians are classed outside medicine, e.g., Christian social theology about homosexuality 261.835766, gay liberation movement 305.90664, interdisciplinary works on homosexuality 306.766, gay men and lesbians in armed forces 355.008664. If in doubt, prefer a number other than 616.8583.

616.86 vs. 158.1, 248.8629, 291.442, 362.29

[Medical aspects of] Substance abuse (Drug abuse) vs. [Applied psychology aspects of] Personal improvement and analysis vs. [Guides to Christian life for persons experiencing substance abuse and Religious life for] Persons experiencing illness, trouble, addiction, bereavement vs. Substance abuse [as a social problem]

Recovery from addiction

Class in 616.86 self-help programs for individuals recovering from substance abuse and interdisciplinary works about recovery programs that focus on the individual's life with addiction, covering the individual's experience with both social and medical aspects. Class in 362.29 the organization providing the program, including administration of the program, and interdisciplinary works that cover both organizational and therapeutic aspects of recovery programs. Class in 248.8629, 291.442, and related numbers in 290 religious guides and inspirational works for the recovering addict. If in doubt, class in 616.86.

As a kind of medical service, recovery programs for persons recovering from a specific kind of substance abuse are classed with the substance, plus notation 03 Rehabilitation or notation 06 Therapy from the add table under 616.1–.9. No distinction is made between programs run by professionals, such as psychiatrists or clinical psychologists, and self-help programs run by laypersons; both kinds of recovery programs are classed as therapy for or rehabilitation from a medical problem. Notation 06 is used for programs, such as twelve step programs, to stop or cure the illness. Notation 03 is used for programs to help the individual remain cured. If in doubt, prefer notation 06.

As a kind of social service, recovery programs for those recovering from a specific kind of substance abuse are classed with the substance in 362.29, plus notation 86 Counseling and guidance from the add table under 362–363. Works classed in 362.29 typically emphasize the organizational or institutional aspects of the program.

For example, interdisciplinary works on life as a recovering alcoholic are classed in 616.86103. The twelve step Alcoholics Anonymous program is classed in 616.86106. Comprehensive works on Alcoholics Anonymous, the organization which provides the program and places for individuals in the program to meet, are classed in 362.29286. A general guide to a recovering alcoholic on how to live a religious life is classed in 291.442; a Christian life, 248.86292.

Works on recovery from addiction are not classed in 158.1 Personal improvement and analysis in applied psychology because psychology applied to a medical problem is classed with the medical problem, not in 150.

616.89 vs. 150.195

Mental disorders vs. Psychoanalytic systems

The psychoanalytic systems classed in 150.195 are the foundation of much of the writing on psychiatric disorders (616.89), and are also the bases of several schools of psychology. Most of the founders of psychoanalytic systems were physicians, so material from psychiatry is heavily used to illustrate the principles of the various psychoanalytic systems. Class comprehensive works on a system or its founder in 150.195. Class applications of a system to specific topics or branches of normal psychology or of both normal and abnormal psychology in the appropriate subdivision of 150. Class applications of a system to psychiatry in 616.89 and related numbers, e.g., psychoanalytic treatment of mental illness 616.8917. If in doubt, prefer 616.89.

616.9 vs. 616.01

Other diseases vs. Medical microbiology

Communicable diseases

Do not confuse medical microbiology with the classes of communicable disease in 616.91–.96 caused by various types of microorganisms. The emphasis in 616.01 is on the organism, usually as the cause of disease, while in 616.9 it is on the whole disease and its course, cure, and prevention. Each is comprehensive in its own way, 616.01 as the interdisciplinary number for pathogenic organisms affecting humans and domestic animals, and 616.9 for the resulting diseases. If in doubt, prefer 616.9.

616.932 vs. 616.33

Cholera vs. Diseases of stomach

"Cholera" was formerly a nonspecific term for a variety of gastrointestinal disturbances. Cholera morbus and other choleras using the former meaning of "cholera" are classed in 616.33. Today, "cholera" is limited to the type of viral disease formerly called Asiatic cholera and is classed in 616.932. If in doubt, prefer 616.932.

616.994 vs. 616.992

Cancers vs. Tumors

Many works about neoplasms, tumors, and oncology discuss only or predominantly cancer (616.994). Therefore, before using 616.992, check to be sure that benign tumors (616.993) are significantly represented. If in doubt, prefer 616.994.

617

Miscellaneous branches of medicine Surgery

Add table

06

Therapy

Do not use notation 06 by itself under numbers whose meaning is limited to surgery, since surgery is a therapy. Subdivisions of 06 are added to surgery numbers for specific physical therapies used in preparation for or rehabilitation from operative surgery, or for branches of surgery not limited to operative surgery, e.g., drug therapy in treatment of burns 617.11061. Notation 06 is used freely under numbers not limited to surgery, e.g., ophthalmological therapy 617.706.

617 vs. 616

Miscellaneous branches of medicine Surgery vs. Diseases

617 contains a mixed set of nonsurgical and surgical specialties. If there is a provision in both 616 and 617 for an organ that defines a specialty, use the 617 number only for surgery. *(See also discussion at 617.5.)*

Class comprehensive works on medical treatment of persons with disabilities in 617 unless the term is clearly used to cover all disabling diseases, in which case, class in 616. If in doubt whether to class a work on persons with disabilities in 616 or 617, prefer 617.

617.5

Regional medicine Regional surgery

Two quite different concepts are brought together here: (1) regions, which incorporate parts of several physiological systems, e.g., the abdominal region 617.55; and (2) organs, which are parts of single systems, e.g., the stomach 617.553. Since the numbers for regions are used for regional medicine as well as regional surgery, notation 059 from the add table under 617 must be used for regional surgery, e.g., abdominal surgery 617.55059. However, since the nonsurgical treatment of specific organs is provided for with the system in 616.1–.8, the numbers for specific organs in 617.5 are used only for surgery, and notation 059 by itself is not used except for surgery utilizing specific instruments or techniques, e.g., endoscopic surgery of stomach 617.553059, but stomach surgery 617.553. Notation 0592 remains valid with organ numbers for plastic surgery, transplantation of tissue and organs, implantation of artificial organs, e.g., liver transplantation 617.55620592. In the case of regions, resolve doubts in favor of 617.5 numbers. In the case of organs, resolve doubts in favor of 616 numbers or numbers in 617.6–.8 for teeth, eyes, and ears.

617.605 vs. 617.522

[Dental] Surgery vs. [Surgery of] Oral region

"Oral surgery" is a term much used in the dental profession. Do not class a work so identified in 617.522 unless it covers substantially more than procedures for which one could go to a dentist (617.605). Class a specific kind of dental surgery with the kind in 617.6, e.g., root canal surgery in 617.6342059, tooth extraction in 617.66, cavity preparation and treatment in 617.672.

618.92097 vs. 617

Regional medicine, ophthalmology, otology, audiology [in pediatrics] vs. Miscellaneous branches of medicine Surgery

Class in 618.92097 nonsurgical specialties provided for in 617.5 and 617.7–.8 when applied to children (regional medicine, ophthalmology, otology, audiology). Class surgical specialties applied to children in 617—comprehensive works in 617.98, surgery of a specific organ, system, disorder with the subject. For example, class medicine of the back for children in 618.9209756, but surgery of the back in 617.560083.

Class both nonsurgical and surgical aspects of topics provided for in 617.1–.2 in 617 when applied to children, e.g., pediatric sports medicine 617.1027083. Class both medical and surgical aspects of dentistry for children in 617.6—comprehensive works in 617.645, diseases of the teeth and gums in 617.630083, dental surgery in 617.605083.

618.977 vs. 617

Special branches of geriatric medicine vs. Miscellaneous branches of medicine Surgery

Class in 618.9775–.9778 nonsurgical specialties provided for in 617.5–.8 when applied to persons in late adulthood (regional medicine, dentistry, ophthalmology, otology, audiology). Class surgical specialties applied to persons in late adulthood in 617—comprehensive works in 617.97, surgery of a specific organ, system, disorder with the subject. For example, class medicine of the back for persons in late adulthood in 618.97756, but surgery of the back in 617.5600846; class diseases of the teeth and gums in 618.97763, but dental surgery in 617.6050846.

Class both nonsurgical and surgical aspects of topics provided for in 617.1–.2 in 617 when applied to persons in late adulthood, e.g., injuries in late adulthood 617.100846.

621.36 vs. 621.381045, 621.3827

Applied optics and paraphotic technology vs. Optoelectronics [and] Optical communications

Two major applications of engineering optics (specifically of lasers in 621.366 and fiber optics in 621.3692) are optoelectronics and optical communications. On the other hand, an important application of electronics, especially of optoelectronics, is in optics, e.g., in remote sensing technology (621.3678). It is sometimes difficult to determine if a focus on a specific application is intended by an author. In the absence of a clear emphasis upon a specific kind of application, class a specific topic found in 621.36 in 621.36, and of a specific topic found in 621.38 in 621.38. However, if a process or device of engineering optics is considered as an integral link in an electronics processing system, class the process or device with the system in 621.38, e.g., optical fibers in communication 621.38275.

If electronics or communications is emphasized, class in 621.38. If in doubt, prefer 621.36.

621.38416 vs. 621.38454

Amateur (Ham) radio vs. Citizens band radio

Both ham and citizens band radio are two-way systems for nonprofessionals involving reserved bandwidths not available to commercial stations. However, the word "amateur" has by tradition been reserved for long-distance (usually shortwave) communication regulated by international treaties, with stiff licensing requirements for operators. In contrast, citizens band is local (ca. 10 miles or 15 kilometers), with easier or no licensing requirements. If in doubt, prefer 621.38416.

621.3845 vs. 621.38782

Radiotelephony vs. Long distance systems [in telephone transmission]

Radiotelephony in 621.3845 refers to the use of terminals which both receive and send messages by radio. The use of radio relays (either ground-based or satellite-based) as integral parts of what appear to users to be a wire-based telephone system is classed with telephone transmission systems in 621.38782. If in doubt, prefer 621.3845.

622.22, 622.7 vs. 662.6, 669

In-situ processing [and] Ore dressing vs. [Chemical engineering of] Fuels [and] Metallurgy

In-situ processing involves using chemical techniques to get the target materials (or compounds containing the target materials) out of the ground. It is usually considered as mining, and is classed in 622.22 or with the specific material in 622.3, e.g., solution mining of uranium 622.34932. However, in-situ processing of a fossil fuel usually transforms the fuel into another form. When there is such a transformation, class the processing in the chemical engineering number for the material produced, e.g., coal gasification 665.772.

Ore dressing, which refers to physical means of separating more usable ore from the low-grade materials that are dug out of the ground, is classed in 622.7. When physical means that effect substantial chemical change are applied, the process normally becomes chemical engineering (usually metallurgy, 669). For example, magnetic separation of iron ore is classed in 622.77, but electrodeposition of iron from ores is classed in 669.14.

Since use of high temperatures causes drastic chemical changes, it is counted as chemical engineering, e.g., pyrometallurgy 669.0282.

If in doubt, prefer 622.22 or 622.7.

624 vs. 624.1

Civil engineering vs. Structural engineering and underground construction

Structural engineering may be considered the "general topics" heading for civil engineering. It comprises the specific subdisciplines of civil engineering that have general applicability to all kinds of structures. Since a civil engineer is normally trained in all branches of structural engineering, basic texts on civil engineering emphasize the subject. Use 624.1 only for works that take a narrow view of structural engineering, that is, that do not discuss the various types of structures to which the engineering is applied. If in doubt, prefer 624.

624 vs. 690

Civil engineering vs. Buildings

To be classed in 690, the work must limit its discussion to habitable structures (buildings). If other structures are discussed, the work is classed in 624. Works about "building" in the sense of constructing all types of structures are classed in 624, not 690. If in doubt, prefer 624.

The word "construction" in the title usually implies that a work covers more than habitable structures. However, it is sometimes used loosely for construction of the type of buildings found in 690.

628.7

Sanitary engineering for rural and sparsely populated areas

Prefer 628.7 over 628.1–.4. While the goals of operations in rural and sparsely populated areas are the same as in other areas, the population served is so scattered that special methods other than those developed for urban settings must normally be used.

629.046 vs. 388

Transportation equipment vs. Transportation Ground transportation

The following guidelines help to distinguish between the vehicle numbers in 385–388 and those in 623.74, 623.82, 625.2, 629, and 688.6.

Class in 385–388:

1. Services provided by the vehicle, e.g., transportation of passengers by trains 385.22.

2. Operation (general) of the vehicle, e.g., duties of the ship's captain 387.54044.

3. Economic and social aspects of the vehicle, e.g., a register of the airplanes owned by a company 387.73340216.

Class in 629.046 and related numbers in the 600s:

1. Description of the vehicle, e.g., steam locomotives of the 1930s 625.26109043.

2. Technology of the vehicle, e.g., design tests for ships 623.810287.

3. Operation (technical) of the vehicle, e.g., piloting spacecraft 629.4582.

4. Maintenance and repair of the vehicle, e.g., repairing motorcycles 629.28775.

Interdisciplinary works are classed in 385–388. If in doubt, prefer 629.046 and related numbers in the 600s.

629.046 vs. 621.43

Transportation equipment vs. Internal-combustion engines

Several specific internal-combustion engines and propulsion systems have their greatest development as engines for a single type of transportation, e.g., spark-ignition engines in passenger automobiles, jet engines in aircraft, and rocket propulsion engines or booster rockets in space vehicles. Although 621.43 is the comprehensive number of each specific kind of engine, most works will emphasize the engine in the specific type of transportation. Therefore, if in doubt between 621.43 and a number in 629, prefer the number in 629.

A work on rocket engines that discusses both missile rockets 623.451 and space transportation rockets 629.475 is classed in 621.4356, the comprehensive works number for rocket engines.

629.1366 vs. 387.740426

Air traffic control systems vs. Air traffic control

Class in 629.1366 works on the equipment needed, e.g., radar devices, and the duties of the air traffic controllers. Class in 387.740426 works on general operational aspects, such as, determining how many controllers are needed per airport; and on economic and social aspects, such as the radio call letters of the control tower. Interdisciplinary works are classed in 387.740426; however, if in doubt, class in 629.1366.

629.43, 629.45 vs. 919.904

Unmanned space flight [and] Manned space flight vs. Geography of and travel in extraterrestrial worlds

Class in 629.43 and 629.45 works about getting to an extraterrestrial world and exploring it from space, e.g., Viking Mars Program 629.43543. Class in 919.904 works about exploring the world once the vehicle has landed. Currently, works that class in 919.9 are projected accounts, e.g., astronautics on Mars 919.92304. If in doubt, class in 629.43 and 629.45.

Most discoveries of extraterrestrial worlds concern the "earth sciences" of the world and are classed in 550, e.g., volcanic activity of Mars 551.21099923.

630 vs. 579–590, 641.3

Agriculture and related technologies vs. Natural history of specific kinds of organisms vs. Food

Interdisciplinary numbers

Numbers from 579–590 are used for interdisciplinary works on plants and animals in general, but not for domestic plants and animals, or species known almost exclusively in agriculture. Discussion of varieties not known in nature is a good indicator that the interdisciplinary number for a species is in agriculture.

The interdisciplinary numbers for species harvested in the wild, e.g., mushrooms, trees, and fishes, are usually found in 579–590 unless the species is best known for a single product, e.g., teak for lumber 674.144 (*not* 583.96). Class works that have material on where to find species in the wild but concentrate on how to grow them in 630, e.g., finding and growing wild flowers 635.9676 (*not* 582.13), where aquarium fish are found and how to raise them 639.34 (*not* 597).

A complicating consideration is that the interdisciplinary number for food is 641.3. Thus works that discuss the utilization and food value as well as the agriculture and biology of edible plants and animals are classed in 641.3, not in 579–590 or 630.

If in doubt, prefer 600 numbers over 579–590, and prefer 630 over 641.3.

631.474–.479 vs. 631.494–.499

[Soil and land-use surveys by specific continents, countries, localities in modern world] vs. Soil science by specific continents, countries, localities in modern world

Soil surveys usually involve small areas (the size of a United States county or less), are quite detailed, and are accompanied by numerous detailed maps. Geographic studies of soils normally cover much larger areas and are not so detailed. If in doubt, use 631.47 for small areas, 631.49 for large areas.

632.2–.8

Specific diseases and pests

Most subdivisions in this span are either "diseases" caused by microorganisms and funguses or "pests" in the sense of multicellular organisms other than fungus that crowd, consume, poison, or parasitize crops. However, the sequence is scrambled. First come galls in 632.2, which are a little bit of both, in that they might be called diseases that are usually caused by pests. Then come most diseases in 632.3–.4, followed by the rest of the pests (that is, those not causing galls) in 632.5–.7. Finally, the viral and rickettsial diseases come at the end in 632.8.

Diseases caused by pollution are found outside the span, in 632.19. Any other disease caused by inanimate agencies (e.g., radiation) is in standing room in 632.3.

See also discussion at 632.95 vs. 632.2–.8

632.95 vs. 632.2–.8

Pesticides vs. Specific diseases and pests

Pesticides are an exception to the general rule that control of specific pests and diseases is classed with the disease or pest. That is, if a work concentrates on a pesticide, it is classed in 632.95, even if the pesticide is used on only a single kind of pest or disease. Such works may discuss the mechanism of action, the on-farm environmental effects, or the safety aspects.

Once the emphasis is off the pesticide and its toxicity, and turns to control of the pest or disease in crops, then the work is classed with the pest or disease. For example, class a work on how a rodenticide kills rats, or how it is a danger to local wildlife that eats poisoned rats in 632.951, the safety hazards of herbicides in 632.9540289, but control of rats by laying out rodenticides in 632.69352, weed control by spraying herbicides 632.5. If in doubt, prefer 632.95.

The mention of on-farm environmental effect in the first paragraph is intended to limit the discussion to technical aspects of the effects. Class interdisciplinary works on environmental effects of pesticides in 363.7384.

633–635

Specific plant crops

Certain plants are important for two or more quite different crops, and may have different numbers assigned to each. Some of the more important distinctions are:

Cereals versus cereal grasses (633.1 vs. 633.25)

Class in 633.1 if grown for grain (even if the fodder is an important by-product), in 633.25 if the whole plant is to be consumed by livestock (even if the grain is allowed to ripen).

Legumes (633.3 vs. 635.65)

Class in 633.3 if grown for either the ripened seed or forage, in 635.65 if the pod is to be picked green or unripened for human consumption.

Other crops

For crops which are listed in only one number, use that number if the difference in production techniques and the appearance of the crop produced by the farmer is minor. For example, potatoes grown for food, feed, or starch are all grown in the same manner and look alike; therefore, they are all classed in 635.21. However, a hemlock grown for lumber is grown in a quite different manner (and looks quite different when shipped) from a hemlock grown for landscaping. The first is classed in 634.9753, the second in 635.97752. If the crop described in a work does not fit existing numbers where the plant is named, class the work in the closest suitable number, e.g., a legume grown for hard fibers 633.58. If in doubt, prefer the existing number coming first in the schedule.

635.3 and 635.4, 635.5

Edible leaves, flowers, stems [and] Cooking greens and rhubarb [and] Salad greens

The distinctions which set off cooking greens and salad greens from each other and from edible leaves in general are not rigidly maintained. Class all works on growing a leafy vegetable named in 635.3–.5 in the number where it is named, regardless of any emphasis on its use, e.g., growing kale for cooking 635.347 (*not* 635.4).

635.9 vs. 582.1

Flowers and ornamental plants [in agriculture] vs. Herbaceous and woody plants, plants notable for their flowers

The groupings of plants in 582.1 are similar to some groupings found in floriculture. Class in 635.9 (often in 635.97 Other groupings of ornamental plants) if the emphasis is on plants to be cultivated or appreciated in human-made settings, in 582.1 if the emphasis is on the plants in nature or on their biology. If in doubt, prefer 635.9.

See also discussion at 630 vs. 579–590, 641.3.

636.1–.8 vs. 636.088

Specific kinds of domestic animals vs. Animals for specific purposes

Several of the terms used in subdivisions of 636.088 apply primarily to one or a few kinds of animals provided for in 636.1–.8. Such terms are listed in 636.088 primarily for number-building purposes. For example, the numbers for raising cows for milk and raising poultry for eggs are both derived in part from the eggs and milk number 636.08842. Notation 42 is added to 636.21 (cattle for specific purposes) giving 636.2142 for dairy farming; to 636.51 (poultry for specific purposes) giving 636.5142 for egg production. Since there are few works on producing both milk and eggs or on producing milk from several kinds of animals, and since producing eggs from several kinds of birds is classed in the poultry number, 636.08842 will seldom be used. If in doubt between a subdivision of 636.088 and a derived subdivision under a specific kind of animal, prefer the latter.

636.72–.75

Specific breeds and groups of dogs

The main groupings used are those recognized by the American Kennel Club (AKC) in *The Complete Dog Book,* 1992. The roughly corresponding groupings of the Kennel Club of England (KCE) are given in class-here notes when the names differ materially. Most, but not all, of the breeds listed in the schedule are those recognized by the AKC. Class other breeds having pedigrees recognized in other nations that fit within the AKC or KCE groupings with the groupings, e.g., European gundogs 636.752.

If in doubt about a breed not named in the schedule, class it in 636.7 (*not* 636.71).

Hounds

Help in separating scenthounds from sight hounds may be found in *Encyclopedia Americana.* It lists the Norwegian elkhound (which is counted as a hound by AKC) as a Northland-type dog.

636.82–.83

Specific breeds and kinds of domestic cats

Help in determining where a specific breed of cats should be classed may be found in David Taylor's *The Ultimate Cat Book,* 1989.

643.2, 690.879, 728.79 vs. 629.226

Special kinds of housing [and Construction of mobile homes] and [Architecture of] Mobile homes vs. Campers, motor homes, trailers (caravans)

Use 629.226 (which is listed under types of motor land vehicles) for what are essentially either automobiles with living accommodations, collapsible living accommodations to be used with trucks or trailers, or trailers with such limited living accommodations that they would not (even when hooked up) serve as permanent homes. Do not use 629.226 for mobile homes that must be towed and are meant to stay in one location for a long time. Use the housing numbers if in doubt, and use 643.2 for interdisciplinary works on movable homes.

647 vs. 647.068, 658.2, T1—0682

Institutional housekeeping vs. Management [of institutional housekeeping] vs. Plant management [and Table 1 notation for] Plant management

Use the management notation from Table 1 with caution in 647.068 and in subdivisions of 647.9, because the term "management" often refers to the basic techniques of operating an establishment, i.e., to the topics found in 642–646 and 648 taken as a whole, when they apply to public facilities. Use 647.068 (or 647.94068, 647.95068, etc.) only when the reference is to the kind of management topics found in 658.1–.2 and 658.4–.8, e.g., financial management and marketing. Personnel management is not a part of T1—068 in 647.

Plant management covers some of the same topics as institutional housekeeping, e.g. utilities, equipment, maintenance. The emphasis in 647 (or in other 640 numbers for specific aspects) is on doing the actual work, while the emphasis in 658.2 is on making sure that the work is done. For example, class a how-to work on running utilities for restaurants in 644, on hospital housecleaning in 648.5; but class a work on managing restaurant utilities in 647.950682, on managing hospital housecleaning services in 362.110682.

649.33 vs. 613.269

Breast feeding vs. Human breast milk diet

Class in 649.33 interdisciplinary works on breast feeding and practical mothers' guides to breast feeding. Works classed in 649.33 may cover a range of topics, including mother-infant bonding and the joy of breast feeding, how to position the baby to avoid nipple soreness, how to cope with an over-abundant milk supply, expressing and storing breast milk, breast feeding for working mothers. Nutrition and personal health are likely to be among the topics covered in a work that belongs in 649.33, but they are not the focus. Class works about breast feeding that focus on nutrition and personal health in 613.269, e.g., works emphasizing the effect of a mother's diet on the composition and volume of her breast milk, the nutritional values of human breast milk, changes in the composition of breast milk during lactation. Also classed in 613.269 are comprehensive works on medical aspects of breast feeding. If in doubt, prefer 649.33.

652.5

Word processing

Text editors

Although there are technical differences between a type of utility program called a text editor and a word processing program, they are both classed in 652.5. However, text editors specially designed to assist with coding computer programs, e.g., by catching errors in program grammar and punctuation, are classed with coding of computer programs in 005.13 Programming languages.

657 vs. 658.1511, 658.1512

Accounting vs. Managerial accounting [and] Use of reports

How to do accounting is classed in 657, use of accounting information by management in 658.1511. How to prepare a financial statement is classed in 657.32, use of a financial statement by management to improve business performance in 658.1512. Design of accounting systems in general and for outside reporting is classed in 657.1. Design of accounting systems with specific emphasis on increasing the internal flow of information to management is classed in 658.1511. If in doubt, prefer 657.

658 and T1—068

General management [and Table 1 notation for] Management [in specific fields]

Management comprises the conduct of all types of enterprises except government agencies that do not themselves provide direct services. *(See discussion at T1—068 vs. 353–354.)* Management is not confined to "business enterprises."

Organizations to be managed may be divided in three ways. First is division by size or scope of the enterprise, which is classed in 658.02. Second is division by the legal form of the enterprise, e.g., corporations, partnerships, etc., which is classed in 658.04. Third, and most important, is division by the kind of work the organization does: selling books, manufacturing light bulbs, carrying freight, caring for the sick, etc. Management of enterprises doing specific kinds of work is classed with the kind of work being done, plus notation 068 from Table 1. 658 and its subdivisions are reserved for discussions of management applicable to any type of enterprise. Comprehensive works on management of public enterprises are classed in 352.266.

For an enterprise's field of work, select if possible a straightforward number for making a product or performing a service. For example, class works on the management of automobile manufacturing in 629.222068, not 338.7629222068, because 338.7629222 is for the economics of automobile manufacturing.

Specific fields of management are also brought out in the same way as general management of a particular kind of enterprise, e.g., financial management of automobile manufacturing 629.2220681.

The subdivisions of T1—068 parallel the subdivisions of 658; hence 658 may be used as a guide to selecting the correct subdivision of T1—068. For example, information management is classed in 658.4038, and information management applied to automobile manufacturing is classed in 629.2220684.

See also discussion at 302.35 vs. 658, T1—068; also at 363.1; also at 381.1, 381.4 vs. 658.87.

658.04 vs. 658.114, 658.402

Management of enterprises of specific forms vs. Initiation of business enterprises by form of ownership organization vs. Internal organization

Class organization by legal and ownership forms (e.g., corporations, partnerships) in 658.04 and 658.114. Class in 658.04 comprehensive works on management of enterprises of specific legal or ownership forms. Class in 658.114 works that focus on initiating a particular form of organization—either starting a new business or converting an existing business to a new form, e.g., starting up a new individual proprietorship (658.1141) or converting an individual proprietorship to a corporation (658.1145). If in doubt between 658.04 and 658.114, prefer 658.04.

In 658.402 "organization" means the internal managerial organization of an enterprise, not the legal or ownership organization classed in 658.04 or 658.114. Internal organization is concerned with the way that authority and responsibility are apportioned. For example, in a line organization a single manager exercises final authority, either directly over production workers or over several supervisors who in turn supervise workers. If in doubt between 658.04 or 658.114 and 658.402, prefer 658.04 or 658.114.

658.15 and T1—0681

Financial management [and Table 1 notation for] Organization and financial management [in specific fields]

Financial management deals with money: how to raise funds to initiate or expand an organization, how to invest capital in capital goods or in the securities of other organizations, how to allocate funds to various operations (budgeting), and how to control expenses and costs. These aspects of financial management do not vary greatly from enterprise to enterprise, except with respect to sources of funds. Examples follow:

Financial management of airlines 387.70681

Financial management of commercial banks 332.120681

A bank's *work* is finance. Notation 0681 from Table 1 can apply only to its internal finance: raising money to start the bank; using money to finance its internal operations, such as paying the employees and the light bills; keeping down costs of operation. The financial services that the bank renders to the public are part of production management, which is discussed at 658.5 and T1—0685.

Financial management of hotels: 647.940681

Financial management of schools 371.206

Financial management of libraries 025.11

It should be noted that 658.15 and T1—0681 do not include bookkeeping or accounting for specific types of organizations. Class works on these subjects in 657.8.

658.2 and T1—0682

Plant management [and Table 1 notation for] Plant management [in specific fields]

Plant management deals with the physical environment and tools necessary for the performance of the organization's work. It includes land, buildings, utilities (light, heat, etc.), and the specific equipment (such as vehicles, machinery, furnishings) necessary to do the work. Acquisition of grounds, buildings, and major equipment is classed in 658.15242, since these are considered to be capital goods. Their maintenance is classed with plant management, as is the use of land, buildings, and utilities. Use of production equipment is classed with production management. Examples follow:

Plant management for airlines 387.73068
Since 387.73 already implies the plant (as will be clear from an examination of the subdivisions), the notation from Table 1 is T1—068, the 2 being redundant.

Plant management for commercial banks 332.120682

Plant management for hotels 647.940682

Plant management for schools 371.6

Plant management for libraries 022

See also discussion at 647 vs. 647.068, 658.2, T1—0682.

658.3 and T1—0683

Personnel management (Human resource management) [and Table 1 notation for] Personnel management (Human resource management) [in specific fields]

Personnel management deals with people: how to recruit, select, place, train, develop, and motivate them in performing the work of the organization. It also includes pay, hours, leave, retirement, and pensions, as well as subjects like discipline and discharge. Examples follow:

Personnel management in airlines 387.70683

Personnel management in commercial banks 332.120683

Personnel management in hotels 647.2

Personnel management in schools 371.201

Personnel management in libraries 023.9

658.4 and T1—0684

Executive management [and Table 1 notation for] Executive management

Executive management concerns the work of top and middle management. Because top and middle managers deal with all aspects of management, however, many aspects of executive management are classed in other management numbers besides 658.4 and T1—0684. The numbers 658.4 and T1—0684 are limited to works that focus on the role, function, powers, or position of top and middle management; or to works that treat the topics enumerated under 658.4, e.g., planning, internal organization, decision making, information management, project management, conflict management, safety management, communication as a managerial technique, use of consultants, business intelligence and security. Broader works are classed in 658 and T1—068. The table of contents can be a useful guide: if the chapter headings read like the subdivisions of 658.4, class in 658.4; but if they read like the principal subdivisions of 658 (e.g., separate chapters on finance, personnel, production, and marketing), class in 658. Works on executive management applied to another branch of management are classed with the branch, e.g., executive management of marketing 658.8 and T1—0688. Examples follow:

Executive management of airlines 387.70684

Executive management of commercial banks 332.120684

Executive management of hotels 647.940684

Executive management of schools 371.207

Executive management of libraries 025.1

658.4 vs. 658.42, 658.43

Executive management vs. Top management [and] Middle management

Class works in 658.42 and 658.43 only if they make a real point of being about top or middle management as opposed to executive management in general. If in doubt, prefer 658.4.

658.4038 vs. 658.455

Information management vs. [Management of] Informational programs

Class communication of information by management in order to maintain control of people and processes in 658.455. Class gathering of information by management and its use in decision making in 658.4038. If in doubt, prefer 658.4038.

658.45 vs. 651.7, 808.06665

Communication [in management] vs. Communication Creation and transmission of records [as an office service] vs. [Business writing]

Class in 651.7 such topics as the use of the telephone, techniques of dictation, how to use microcomputer software for form letters, mail-handling techniques—in short, the mechanics of communication. Do not class in 651.7 works that emphasize effective business writing style.

Class in 808.06665 style manuals for business writing and works on how to do effective business writing, whether aimed at secretaries or executives. Class in 808.066651 works on how to write a specific type of communication (e.g., business letters) and model collections of a specific type intended to illustrate good writing style. If in doubt between 651.7 and 808.06665, prefer 808.06665.

Class in 658.45 works that focus on use of communication to achieve management goals. Often these works emphasize the personal relations aspects of management communication. If in doubt between 651.7 and 658.45, prefer 658.45. If in doubt between 808.06665 and 658.45, prefer 658.45.

658.5 and T1—0685

Management of production [and Table 1 notation for] Management of production [in specific fields]

Production management is the management of the work that the organization exists to perform. It concerns itself with the organization of the work flow and the methods to be used in performing individual operations. It also deals with insuring the quality and accuracy of the operations and of their results. It is related to, but not the same as, the technology involved in the operations. It differs radically from one organization to another. Examples follow:

Management of factory production 658.5

This is the organization and direction of the processes by which raw materials, parts, and subassemblies are combined and processed through the operation of people and machines to produce such concrete objects as automobiles, bread, toys, etc. This is also known as logistics.

658.5 fits the nature of factory operations better than production management of other kinds of enterprises because it reflects an earlier state of the management art when books of management were chiefly concerned with industrial management. Accordingly, 658.5 is used for production management in factories in general rather than 670.

Production management for airlines 387.70685
There are elements of production management in subdivisions of 387.7, e.g., planning airline routes 387.72; assigning airplanes to routes and scheduling them 387.740420685; planning, organizing and supervising meal services, baggage services, and reservation services 387.7420685.

Production management for book stores 381.450020685

Production management for commercial banks 332.120685
This includes planning, organizing, and supervising customer services, maintenance of checking and savings accounts, vault services, trust services, etc.

Production management for hotels 647.940685
This consists of managing the operations directly involved in providing food, entertainment, and clean and attractive rooms and facilities for guests.

Production management for schools 371.2
This is the management of the activities involved in imparting knowledge and attitudes to students, and includes such things as scheduling of classes and grouping students for instruction.

Production management for libraries 025.1

658.7 and T1—0687

Management of materials [and Table 1 notation for] Management of materials [in specific fields]

Management of materials involves the raw materials, parts, and subassemblies used in creating the final product or service; the supplies necessary for conducting the business, e.g., ink, pens, paper; and other small pieces of equipment, e.g., typewriters, filing cabinets.

The activities dealing with these materials fall into three distinct categories: acquisition, internal management, and physical distribution.

Acquisition, or procurement, involves contracts and their negotiation, vendor selection, order work, receiving and unloading shipments, and expediting and tracing when done by the purchaser.

Internal management involves storage and the maintenance of inventory, checking materials out of inventory for use in the work process, their movement from work station to work station, checking them into storage and storing them prior to sale, and maintaining the inventory at this point. In service organizations, where there is no sale of a final product, the process is complete when materials and supplies are issued for and used in the work process.

Physical distribution involves processing orders received, matching the orders to items in inventory, checking the items out of inventory, packing them, loading them, selecting carrier and routing, and expediting and tracing when done by the shipper. Physical distribution is not a factor in most service organizations.

Major equipment is considered to be capital, and its acquisition is classed in 658.15242 and T1—0681. Once major equipment is in use, its management is classed in 658.27 and T1—0682 as part of plant management.

Examples follow:

Materials management for airlines 387.70687

Materials management in banks 332.120687

Materials management in hotels 647.940687

Materials management in schools 371.6

Materials management in libraries 025.1
However, class management of the acquisition of books and other information media at 025.2068, their internal management in 025.8, their circulation (analogous to physical distribution) in 025.6.

658.8 and T1—0688

Management of distribution (Marketing) [and Table 1 notation for] Management of distribution (Marketing) [in specific fields]

Marketing management deals with the sale of the product or service of the organization. This concept also includes credit management. Examples follow:

Marketing management for airlines 387.70688
This number is used chiefly for sales promotion and credit management. Most sales effort for such an organization is concentrated in advertising, which is classed in 659.1.

Marketing management for commercial banks: chiefly advertising, which is classed in 659.1

Marketing management for hotels 647.940688
This is usually credit management and other limited applications, e.g., sale of facilities for conventions.

Marketing management for schools: not applicable
Private schools do some advertising and public relations but these are classed in 659.

Marketing management for libraries: class public relations of libraries in 021.7

658.8, T1—0688 vs. 659

Management of distribution (Marketing) [and Table 1 notation for] Management of distribution (Marketing) [in specific fields] vs. Advertising and public relations

Marketing (658.8) is the broader concept; it includes sales management, marketing research, channels of distribution, and customer credit management, which are classed in 658.8; it also includes the advertising and public relations that have been drawn off to 659. What belongs in 659 is the publicity used by an organization to present itself and its goods and services to the public. Research focused on advertising or public relations is the only kind of marketing research classed in 659; broader research is classed in 658.83. If in doubt, prefer 658.8.

669

Metallurgy

Alloys

Class comprehensive works on alloys of a variety of metals in 669; comprehensive works on a specific alloy, on the alloys of a specific metal in 669.1–.7; the physical and chemical metallurgy of alloys, the process of forming alloys in 669.9.

Class an alloy not listed in 669 with the chief constituent metal if readily ascertainable, e.g., Monel®, a nickel alloy of about 67 percent nickel and 30 percent copper 669.7332, not 669.3. If the chief constituent is not readily ascertainable, class with the metal coming first in the schedule, except class all alloys of steel in 669.142.

670.427 vs. 670.285

Mechanization and automation of factory operations vs. Data processing Computer applications [in manufacturing]

Flexible manufacturing systems

Works on flexible manufacturing systems are classed in 670.427 if limited to computer-aided manufacture; in 670.285 if including also other computer applications in manufacturing, such as computer-aided design or computer applications in management of manufacturing. If in doubt, prefer 670.427.

671–679 vs. 680

Manufacture of products from specific materials vs. Manufacture of products for specific uses

The distinction between 671–679 and 680 cannot be drawn consistently because some manufacture of products by materials appears in 680, e.g., leather and fur goods 685; and some products for specific uses appear in 671–679, e.g., paper plates and cups 676.34. In general 671–679 has primary products in contrast to the final products from a given material in 680, e.g., textiles 677, clothing 687; but that distinction is not relevant in many specific cases, e.g., brushes 679.6, combs 688.5. If in doubt, prefer 671–679.

The order of the subdivisions of 680 is drawn from that of 670; the 680 numbers usually represent a type of final product related in some general way to the material in the comparable 670 number:

672	682	Ferrous metals [vs.] Small forge work
673	683	Nonferrous metals [vs.] Hardware and household appliances
674	684	Lumber, cork, wood [vs.] Furnishings and home workshops
675	685	Leather and fur [vs.] Leather and fur goods
676	686	Pulp and paper [vs.] Printing
677	687	Textiles [vs.] Clothing

680 vs. 745.5

Manufacture of products for specific uses vs. [Artistic] Handicrafts

Handicraft when limited to artistic work is classed in 745.5. In general usage the term "crafts" may be used for country crafts, and cottage industries and trades, such as those of the farrier, the cooper, and the thatcher. Crafts in this sense and handicrafts as the routine way of manufacturing secondary and final products are classed in 680. If in doubt, prefer 680.

690 vs. 643.7

[Construction of] Buildings vs. Renovation, improvement, remodeling [in home economics]

The scope note at 643 reading "works for owner-occupants and renters covering activities by members of household" indicates that 643.7 and other numbers in 643 are used for a broad range of material intended for the do-it-yourself enthusiast. Works on home renovation and remodeling for professional builders are classed in 690.80286 or other numbers in 690. (The special standard subdivision notation 0286 for remodeling is used in 690 only with numbers drawn from 725–728; elsewhere in 690 no standard subdivision is used.) If in doubt, prefer 690.

700

The arts Fine and decorative arts

Generally the word "arts," used without a qualifier, is a signal that the area covered is broader than the fine and decorative arts. Literature, music, and the performing arts are the other kinds of arts most often included. A quick check each time that "art" or "arts" is used should establish the area covered.

"Computer art" usually refers to two different uses of computers in the arts. The computer can be a device employed in creating the final art work, as when the computer serves as an aid in composing music to be played on traditional instruments or as an aid in designing or engraving the plates for otherwise traditional prints. Alternatively, the computer can serve as the instrument on which music is performed, as in computer music, or as the display medium for visual art, as when computer graphics works are intended for display on a computer monitor. The computer as a device is classed with other devices using either notation 0285 from Table 1 or specific provisions in the schedule, e.g., computers and the arts 700.285, computers in the graphic arts 760.0285, computer composition of music 781.34. The computer as an instrument or display medium is classed with the type of art, e.g., history of computer art 709.04, computer graphic art 760, computer music 786.76.

700.92

Persons [in the arts]

The instructions at each major area for the classification of artists vary. Even within one division, the 730s, the treatment varies: 730.92 for a sculptor, 739.2272 for a goldsmith, 730.092 for a sculptor who has also worked in one or more of the other plastic arts.

Works of an artist or artists are designated in one of two ways, either by notation 092 from Table 1 as in sculpture, or by notation for period or place as in drawing 741.92–.99.

704.9

Iconography

Prefer iconography over historical and geographic treatment, e.g., a general work on Romanesque art 709.0216, Romanesque art of Normandy 709.44209021, but the Virgin Mary and Child in Romanesque art of Normandy 704.948550944209021. However, care should be taken in classifying schools and styles that usually are limited in subject matter, such as early Christian, Byzantine, and Romanesque schools, which usually treat religious themes. Class in 704.9 only if a point is made that iconography or one of its aspects is the focus of the work.

Use of standard subdivisions

Generally, standard subdivisions are added to iconography numbers even if the topic does not approximate the whole of the heading. There are three exceptions: 704.9428 Pornography, 704.9434 Plants, and notation from Table 2. For instance, if a work covers only roses in art, a standard subdivision should not be added.

Notation 09 from Table 1 plus notation 3–9 from Table 2 is added to show the nationality or locality of the artists rather than the location of the subject, e.g., Canadian portraits of British royal children 704.94250971. Do not add notation 074 from the table under T1—093–099 in Table 1 unless the area covered by the work being classed approximates the whole of the area indicated by the notation from Table 2.

709.012–.05 vs. 709.3–.9

Periods of development [of fine and decorative arts] vs. Treatment by specific continents, countries, localities [of fine and decorative arts]

Class the works produced by an artistic school or in a particular style as follows:

1. From the same locality, with the locality in 709.3–.9

2. From various localities within a specific country, with the country in 709.3–.9

3. From two countries, with the country coming first in Table 2 in 709.3–.9

4. From three or more European countries, with the period when the school or style flourished in 709.012–.05

5. From three or more non-European countries within the same continent, with the continent in 709.3–.9

6. From three or more countries not within the same continent, with the period when the school or style flourished in 709.012–.05

If in doubt between classing with country or locality, prefer country; if between 709.012–.05 or 709.3–.9, prefer 709.012–.05.

709.2 vs. 380.1457092

Persons [associated with fine and decorative arts] vs. [Persons associated with the trade of art]

Works about art dealers that focus on the economics of trading in art are classed in 380.1457092. Works that focus on the dealers as a part of the art world, e.g., the artists the dealers knew and works of art they handled, are classed in 709.2. If in doubt, class in 709.2.

721

Architectural structure

The note "Class here interdisciplinary works on design and construction" is not meant to broaden the scope of 721 to include all aspects of architecture. Works that are classed here are concerned with the elements included in 721.04 and 721.1–.8. Works about the architecture of buildings as a whole are classed in 720.

721 vs. 690.1

Architectural structure vs. Structural elements [of buildings]

Descriptive details of buildings erected in the past or planned for the future are classed in 721. Principles of engineering design and construction or actual instruction (e.g., for the builder) on how to put structural elements, shapes, and materials together are classed in 690.1. If in doubt, prefer 721.

726.1

[Architecture of] Temples and shrines

In number building, be as specific as the information supplied allows, e.g., a Theravada Buddhist temple in Thailand 726.1439109593. If the branch or sect is not given, add the religion number from 292–299, then add notation from Table 1, e.g., Buddhist temples in Java (sect not specified) 726.143095982; temple forms in southern India (specific Indic religion not identified) 726.1409548.

729

Design and decoration of structures and accessories

More material is taken out of 729 by notes than is left in. Class in 729 only those general works in which the focus is specifically architectural design. Design and construction treated together are classed in 721. Construction alone is classed in 690. Decoration is classed in 729 only when the subject is being treated as an aspect of architectural decoration rather than as an art object in itself. For example, comprehensive works on murals are classed in 751.73; however, the use of murals as architectural decoration is classed in 729.4.

731–735 vs. 736–739

Sculpture vs. Other plastic arts

The products and techniques of the plastic arts in 736–739 are often difficult to separate from those of sculpture; if in doubt, prefer 731–735. For example, bronze figures are classed in sculpture, but a bronze figure is classed in 739.512 if it was a part (such as a finial or handle) of a larger decorative work.

741.6 vs. 800

Graphic design, illustration, commercial art vs. Literature (Belles-lettres) and rhetoric

Class illustration in general in 741.6. Class a specific type of illustration with the art form represented if the type is emphasized, e.g., etchings. If the illustrations merely accompany or enhance the literary text, class with the text in literature. If in doubt, class in 741.6.

745.1

Antiques

Class a specific type of antique with the subject in art if a number is provided, e.g., gold coins 737.43, antique New England furniture 749.214.

If there is no available number in 700–799, use the appropriate number in 600–699, e.g., antique passenger automobiles 629.222. If there is a separate technology number for the use of the object in question as opposed to the number for the manufacture of the object, prefer the use number, e.g., thimbles 646.19 rather than 687.8.

If antiques and collectibles fit in neither the art nor the technology numbers, class with the subject with which they are most closely associated, e.g., Shirley Temple collectibles 791.43028092.

745.5928

[Handcrafted] Models and miniatures

Class handcrafted miniatures and models as follows:

Class in 700:

1. If there is a specific number for the model, e.g., paper airplanes 745.592.

2. If there is a specific number for the subject illustrated by the model, e.g., handcrafted miniature furniture 749.0228. (Note: notation 0228 from Table 1 is used to indicate the model or miniature.)

3. If there is no number for the model or the subject illustrated in 600. In this case the most specific number possible is chosen.

Class in 600 if there is no specific number in 700–779 *and* either of the following conditions is met:

1. If there is a specific number in 600–699 for the model, e.g., handcrafted model airplanes 629.133134.

2. If there is a specific number for the subject illustrated by the model, e.g., handcrafted miniature reciprocating steam engines 621.1640228. (Note: notation 0228 from Table 1 is used to indicate the model or miniature.)

753–758

Iconography

Prefer iconography over historical and geographic treatment, e.g., a general work on Romanesque painting 759.0216, Romanesque painting of Normandy 759.4209021, but the Virgin Mary and Child in Romanesque painting of Normandy 755.550944209021. However, care should be taken in classifying schools and styles that usually are limited in subject matter, such as early Christian, Byzantine, and Romanesque schools, which usually treat religious themes. Class in 753–758 only if a point is made that iconography or one of its aspects is the focus of the work.

Use of standard subdivisions

Generally, standard subdivisions are added to iconography numbers even if the topic does not approximate the whole of the heading. There are four exceptions: 757.8 Pornography, 758.3 Animals, 758.5 Plants, and notation from Table 2. For instance, if a work covers only dogs in painting, a standard subdivision should not be added.

Notation 09 from Table 1 plus notation 3–9 from Table 2 is added to show the nationality or locality of the artists rather than the location of the subject, e.g., Canadian portraits of British royal children 757.50971. Do not add notation 074 from the table under T1—093–099 in Table 1 unless the area covered by the work being classed approximates the whole of the area indicated by the notation from Table 2.

769.92

Persons

Both the printmakers who copy other artists and the artists being copied (if only prints are being discussed) are classed here, e.g., prints after Gainsborough 769.92. Prints produced by a print workshop or a studio are classed in 769.93–.99.

778.3 vs. 621.367

Special kinds of photography vs. Technological photography and photo-optics

The techniques of producing the photograph as an end unto itself are classed in 778.3. The engineering technology underlying the photography and the scientific applications are classed in 621.367. Applications to a specific field of science are classed with the field, e.g., to astronomy 522.63. If in doubt, prefer 778.3.

779

Photographs

Notation 092 from Table 1 can be added to 779 and its subdivisions for collections of works by individuals. Class biographies and critical appraisals, which may also contain some photographs, in 770.92. For collections of photographs by several artists from the same area, add notation 09 from Table 1 and notation 1–9 from Table 2 to show the area where the photographers originated.

780

Music

Citation order

The citation order is:

Voices and instruments	782–788
Musical forms	781.8
Sacred music	781.7
Traditions of music	781.6
Kinds of music	781.5
Techniques of music	781.4
Composition	781.3
Elements of music	781.2
Basic principles of music	781.1
Standard subdivisions	780.1–.9

A major facet, the composer, is not indicated in the class number (unless the option at 789 is used for literature about music). *(For a fuller discussion on composers, see discussion at 780.92: Composers.)*

Building numbers

Building a number for a work that is classed in the 780s is a four-step process: 1) Determine the various facets of the work, 2) Arrange the facets in the proper order, 3) Determine whether or not the topics belonging to the facets can be indicated, and 4) Follow the add instructions. For example, in building the number for a work entitled *Harmony in Beethoven's piano sonatas*, one takes the following steps:

1) *Determine the various facets of the works*: For the work being classed, there are four facets, or aspects: a general musical topic, harmony; the composer, Beethoven; the instrument, piano; and a musical form, sonata.

2) *Arrange the facets in proper order*: The usual arrangement is the executant (the voice or instrument that produces the music), here the piano at 786.2; the music form, here the sonata at 784.183; general principles, here harmony at 781.25; standard subdivisions, here a person associated with the music at 780.92 (in this case Beethoven). This arrangement obeys the general instruction at 780 which states: unless other instructions are given, class subjects with aspects in two or more subdivisions of 780 in the one coming last. The major exception to executant before form occurs when classing vocal music (*see 782 for complete details*). If you decided to follow the option of classing all works related to a composer in 789, the arrangement would then be composer, the executant, the musical form, general principles, other standard subdivisions.

3) *Determine whether or not the topics belonging to the facets can be indicated*: If the topic is given in a class-here note or is the same or approximately the same as a number's heading, a topic from another facet can be indicated. If the topic is given in an including note, topics in other facets cannot be indicated.

Since the topics, piano, sonata, and harmony, are the headings at 786.2, 784.183, and 781.255, respectively, further topics can be indicated. (For *Harmony in Chopin's mazurkas for piano*, the topics harmony and Chopin cannot be indicated because mazurka is a part of the including note at 784.1884.)

4) *Follow the add instructions*: At 786.2 *Pianos, the * refers to the footnote, which instructs one to add as instructed in the add table under the centered entry at 784–788. The add instruction in the add table says that musical forms and instruments are shown by adding 1, then the numbers following 784.1 in 784.18–.19. Thus, facet indicator 1 plus 83 from 784.183 !Sonata form and sonatas added to 786.2 produces 786.2183 Piano sonatas. At 784.183, the ! refers to the footnote, which instructs one to add as instructed in the add table under the centered entry at 781.2–.8, which says that in order to show general principles add 1 and then the numbers following 781 in 781.1–.7. The result of adding 1 and then 25 from 781.25 *Harmony is 786.2183125 harmony in piano sonatas. Even though the * at 781.25 indicates that further additions are possible, i.e., adding 092 to indicate Beethoven, the general add instruction at 780 forbids using 0 or 1 (alone or in combination) more than twice. (An option does allow further additions.) Thus, the class number for *Harmony in Beethoven's piano sonatas* is 786.2183125.

Examples

Works about music

New music vocabulary: a guide to notational signs	780.148
Music notation	780.148
Sound structure in music	781.234
Timbre	781.234
New life in country music	781.642
Western popular music	
Country	781.642
Wagner as man and artist	782.1092
Opera	782.1
General biography and criticism	092 (from Table 1)
Voice production in choral technique	782.5143
Choral music	782.5
Facet indicator	1
Performance technique	43 (from 781.43)
Bartok orchestral music [criticism]	782.2092
Orchestra	784.2
Composer	092 (from Table 1)

Bartok. Concerto for orchestra [criticism]	784.2186
Orchestra	784.2
Facet indicator	1
Concerto form	86 (from 784.186)
Scoring for brass band	784.9138
Brass band	784.9
Facet indicator	1
Arrangement	38 (from 781.38)
Beethoven string quartets [criticism]	785.7194092
Chamber group—strings	785.7
Size of ensemble	19
Quartet	4 (from 785.14)
Composer	092 (from Table 1)
The fugue in piano music	786.21872
Piano	786.2
Facet indicator	1
Fugue	872 (from 784.1872)
Scientific piano tuning and servicing	786.21928
Piano	786.2
Facet indicator	1
Tuning	928 (from 784.1928)
The origins of bowing	787.1936909
Bowed stringed instruments	787
Facet indicator	1
Bowing	9369 (from 784.19369)
History	09 (from Table 1)
Pablo Casals; a biography	787.4092
Cello	787.4
Performers	092 (from Table 1)
Discography of zither music	016.78770266
Subject bibliography	016
Zither	787.7
Recordings	0266 (from 780.266)
The organs of London	786.519421
Organ	786.5
Facet indicator	19
London	421 (from Table 2)
The Story of "Silent Night"	782.281723
Carols	782.28
Facet indicator	1
Christmas music	723 (from 781.723)

Scores

Hymns for choirs, arranged for mixed voices and organ by David Willocks	782.527
Choral music for mixed voices	782.5
Hymns	27 (from 782.27)
Lees. Breathe on me, breath of God; anthem for 3–part female voice choir unaccompanied	782.6265
Choral music—women's voices	782.6
Anthems	265 (from 782.265)
Schubert song cycles	783.247
Solo voice	783.2
Song cycle	47 (from 782.47)
Brahms. Variations on the St. Anthony Chorale	784.21825
Orchestra	784.2
Facet indicator	1
Variations	825 (from 784.1825)
Berlioz. Romeo and Juliet; a dramatic symphony	784.22184
Orchestra with vocal parts	784.22
Facet indicator	1
Symphony form	84 (from 784.184)
Schuller. Trio: oboe, horn, viola	785.42193
Ensembles of woodwind, brass, strings	785.42
Size of ensemble	19
Trios	3 (from 785.13)
Chopin. Mazurka, piano	786.21884
Piano	786.2
Facet indicator	1
Mazurka form	884 (from 784.1884)

780.079 vs. 790.2

[Music and the performing arts] vs. The performing arts in general

780.079 is used for works focusing on music in relation to the other performing arts, while 790.2 is used for works on the performing arts as a whole. If in doubt, prefer 780.079.

780.26

Treatises on music scores, recordings, texts

The meaning of 026 is different when used within 780–788 than when used with 780–788 numbers added elsewhere in the schedules. Within 780, 026 is used only for treatises about scores and recordings in order to shelve them apart from the treatises about the music. Because the formats of scores and recordings differ from that of treatises, they are normally shelved separately, and the Classification does not distinguish among them. A library that wishes to distinguish them has to apply either the optional provision or some other notational device. However, when 780–788 numbers are added elsewhere in the schedules, 026 is used for scores and recordings, as well as for treatises about them. The notation is added because the material outside 780 that concerns scores and recordings are usually bibliographic in nature and would interfile with the treatises on the shelf unless the notation distinguished them. For example:

Number	Used for
787.2	A treatise on violin music
787.2	Violin scores
787.2	Recordings of violin music
787.2026	A treatise on violin scores
787.20266	A treatise on recordings of violin music
016.7872	A bibliography of treatises on violin music
016.7872026	A bibliography of violin scores
016.7872026	A bibliography of treatises on violin scores
016.78720266	A discography of recordings of violin music
016.78720266	A bibliography of treatises on recordings of violin music.

See also discussion at 780.92.

780.92

Persons associated with music

Musicians

Comprehensive works on musicians are classed in the most specific number that describe their careers. 780.92 is used only for musicians who are equally known for both their vocal and instrumental work, e.g., Ludwig van Beethoven 780.92. Musicians known primarily for vocal music are classed in 782–783, e.g., Richard Wagner, an opera composer, 782.1092; Elvis Presley, a rock singer, 782.42166092. Musicians known primarily for instrumental music are classed in 784–788, e.g., Sir Thomas Beecham, a conductor, 784.2092; Nicolò Paganini, a violinist, 787.2092. (*See also 781.6 for discussion on musicians associated with traditions of music other than classical.*)

Composers

Notation 092 from Table 1 is used to indicate a biography, a general criticism of the composer, an analysis of a composer's contribution to the development of some aspect of music (such as Haydn's role in the development of the concerto form), critical works on the body of a composer's work (such as a critique of the piano music of Ravel), and a collection of analyses of the individual pieces of music. Criticism of an individual work by a composer does not receive notation 092 in order that a piece of music and criticism of it will fall at the same class number.

The citation order for music requires that general criticism of a composer's works in a specific form and criticism of a single aspect of the works be separated because the aspect is shown by adding from 781. For example, general criticism of Brahms' symphonies is classed in 784.2184092, while criticism of harmony in Brahms' symphonies is classed in 784.2184125. However, if a library wishes to keep all criticism of a composer's works in the same number, it is optional not to add from 781, e.g., criticism of Brahms' symphonies and of harmony in Brahms' symphonies both 784.2184092.

781.382–.388

Original voice, instrument, ensemble of the arrangements

Use these numbers only for building other numbers; never use them by themselves. These numbers are added to the number for the voice, instrument, or ensemble for which the music was arranged in order to indicate the original voice, instrument, or ensemble. For example, an arrangement of violin music for piano would be classed in 786.213872, 786.2 (piano music) plus 13872 (arrangements of violin music). Arrangements in general either of or for a voice, instrument, or ensemble are classed in 782–788. For example, class in 787.2138 both violin music arranged for various instruments and music of several instruments arranged for the violin.

781.47

Accompaniment

When 147 accompaniment (from 781.47) is added to treatises, it indicates how to accompany the work, e.g., how to accompany violin music 787.2147.

(Option: With scores, add 147 to indicate the presence of accompaniment, e.g., accompanied violin music 787.2147, unaccompanied violin music 787.2.)

781.6

Traditions of music

Musicians

Comprehensive works on musicians are classed in the most specific number that describe their careers. 781.62–.66 and 781.69 is used only for musicians that are equally known for both their vocal and instrumental work, e.g., Louis

Armstrong, a jazz trumpeter, singer, and band leader, 781.65092. Musicians known primarily for vocal music are classed in 782–783, e.g., Ella Fitzgerald, a jazz singer, 782.42165092. Musicians known primarily for instrumental music are classed in 784–788, e.g., John Coltrane, a jazz tenor-saxophonist, 788.74092.

The tradition of musicians who are not in the nonwestern art (classical) tradition is shown by classing the musicians either in 781.62–.66 or 781.69 or by adding traditions-of-music notation to the number for the vocal or instrumental music for which they are best known.

781.62 vs. 780.89

Folk music vs. Music with respect to specific racial, ethnic, national groups

Works discussing a racial, ethnic, or national group in relation to music in general are classed in 780.89, e.g., a work about African American composers, opera singers, jazz conductors is classed in 780.8996073. Works discussing music indigenous to the group is classed in 781.62, e.g., African American music 781.6296073. If in doubt, class in 781.62.

782

Vocal music

The primary characteristic of arrangement is that of *character*. Vocal music is either dramatic (782.1) or nondramatic (782.2–.4); nondramatic is either sacred (782.2–.3) or secular (782.4). (Staging dramatic music is classed in 792.5.)

For nondramatic vocal music (782.2–783) classification is determined by whether an item is a treatise or a recording, on the one hand, or a score, on the other. A person interested in reading about or listening to a singer or a piece of music will usually not know the singer's vocal range or the vocal requirements of that piece of music. In contrast, a person interested in scores will know the type of voice or voices involved, e.g., a song cycle sung by a soprano, or a mass sung by a tenor and male chorus. Therefore, treatises about and recordings of singers and nondramatic vocal forms are classed in 782.2–.4, while scores and texts are classed in 782.5–783.9.

The following flow chart will help users select the correct section of vocal music.

Flow chart for vocal music

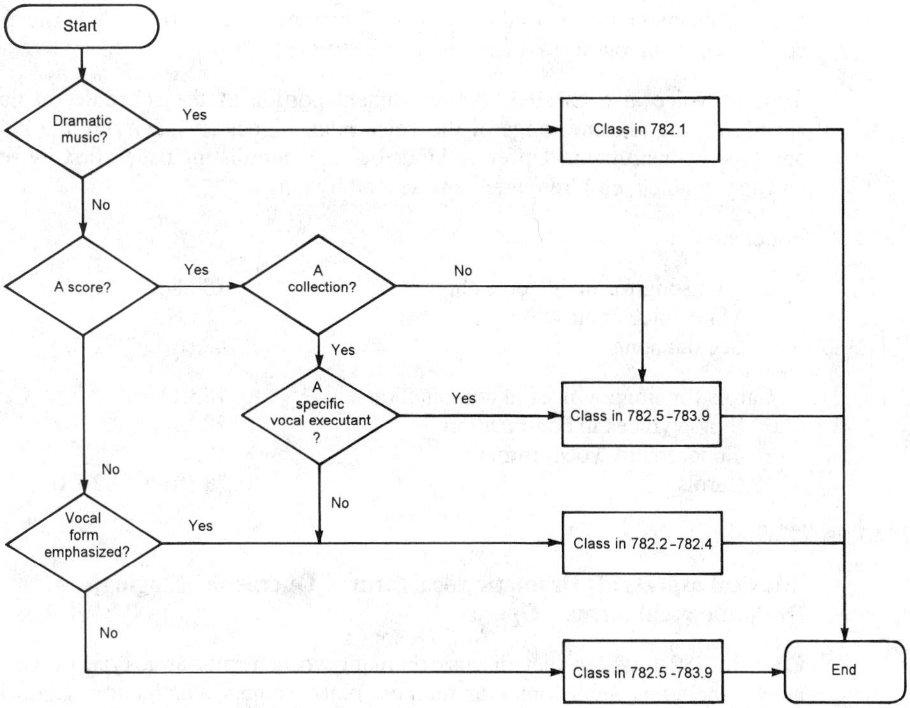

Examples (from applying the flow chart):

Soprano arias from opera [scores]	782.1
Soprano airs not from opera [scores]	783.66
Sacred songs by sopranos [recordings]	782.25
Women's soprano voice [treatise]	783.66

Vocal scores

When dealing with scores, kind of voice and size of vocal ensemble must be considered. The distinction between 782.5–.9 and 783 is based upon the number of voices per part. Class in 782.5–.9 works that treat music having several voices per part (what is usually meant by choral music). Class in 783 works that treat music having one voice per part (part songs and solos). Observe the following preference order for scores and parts of nondramatic vocal music:

Size of vocal ensemble (including solos)
Type of voice, e.g., male, high, soprano, child's
Vocal forms

Size of vocal ensemble parallels the primary division in the instrument portion of the schedule. Choral music is analogous to orchestral music (more than one voice/instrument per part in some parts); single voices in combination is analogous to chamber music (only one voice/instrument per part); and music for solo voice is analogous to music for solo instrument.

Type of voice also parallels the instrument portion of the schedule, in that specifying the sex and range of the voice is analogous to specifying the kind and type of instrument. Different kinds of voice are distinguished first by sex and age (women, children, men) and second by range.

For example:

Secular song for male voice choir	782.842
Male voice choir	782.8
Secular song	42 (from 782.42)
Carols for single voices in combination	783.11928
Single voices in combination	783.1
Nondramatic vocal forms	19
Carols	28 (from 782.28)

782.1 vs. 792.5

[Musical aspects of] Dramatic vocal forms Operas vs. [Staging] Dramatic vocal forms Operas

Class in 782.1 works that discuss dramatic vocal forms as a type of vocal music, including such topics as tempos, plots, singers, conducting. Class in 792.5 and related numbers works that discuss dramatic vocal forms as a type of stage presentation, including such topics as costumes, sets, direction. For example, operas as vocal music are classed in 782.1, staging of operas in 792.5; musical plays as vocal music in 782.14, staging of musical plays in 792.6. Works about an opera house and its productions are classed in 792.509, e.g., a history of La Scala, Milan 792.5094521. If in doubt, class in 782.1.

784–788

Instruments and their music

Instruments and their music are allotted the span 784–788, which to a substantial degree maintains a large to small arrangement that proceeds from orchestral ensembles (more than one instrument to a part) through chamber music (only one instrument per part) to single instruments.

Although most instruments named or given as examples in the schedule are familiar to Westerners, the classification is applicable to all instruments from whatever culture, since it is based on the acoustical arrangement found in the "Systematik der Musikinstrumente; ein Versuch" of E. M. von Hornbostel and C. Sachs, first published in *Zeitschrift für Ethnologie* 4–5, 1914. (The arrangement was consulted in the translation by A. Baines and K. P. Wachsmann in

Galpin Society Journal 14:3–29, 1961.) Many nonwestern instruments are found in the Relative Index, e.g., gaitas, hichirikis, santirs, surunais, and tulums.

The 780 schedule reconciles the Sachs-Hornbostel four divisions with the traditional western divisions with which they are broadly synonymous: percussion (idiophones and membranophones), strings (chordophones), and wind (aerophones). In addition, the schedule provides for the functional divisions necessitated by the application of western technology to musical instruments, by treating keyboard and mechanical instruments (however the sound is produced) as primary classes, and by adding a fifth acoustical category of electrophones to the instrumental classification. The order in the schedule is as follows:

Functional categories of instruments	
Instruments in combination (orchestral and chamber music)	784.2–785
Keyboard instruments	786.2–.5
Mechanical and aeolian instruments	786.6
Acoustical categories of instruments	
Electrophones (electrical sound producers)	786.7
Idiophones (sonorous solids) [Percussion]	786.8
Membranophones (drums) [Percussion]	786.9
Chordophones (stringed instruments)	787
Aerophones (wind instruments)	788

The two main characteristics within instrumental music are the number of instruments per part (the size), e.g., full symphony orchestra, chamber groups, and solo instruments; and instrumental grouping, e.g., orchestra with solo instrument, woodwind ensembles. The two characteristics are enumerated in the schedule, in most cases without the need for building a number. However, where particular instruments are involved in the ensemble, it may be necessary to specify them by building numbers with segments from other parts of the schedule (*see also 780: Building numbers*). For example,

785.832 Flute ensembles (from 788.32)

785.962 Clarinet ensembles (from 788.62)

The subdivisions of 784.1 will be heavily used because the numbers for providing for specific musical forms for specific instruments, for performance upon specific instruments, and for the instrument itself are given there. For example:

Breathing techniques in playing the clarinet	788.621932
Clarinet	788.62
Facet indicator	1
Breath technique	932 (from 784.1932)
Organ fugues	786.51872
Organ	786.5
Facet indicator	1
Fugues	872 (from 784.1872)

Add table

092

[Persons associated with instruments and their music]

For persons associated with an instrument and its music and for persons associated with the music for the instrument, add notation 092 from Table 1 directly to the number for the instrument and its music, e.g., Nicolò Paganini (a violinist and composer) and Isaac Stern (a violinist) 787.2092. However, for persons interested only in the instrument, add the the instrument notation 19 (derived from 784.19) before adding notation 092 from Table 1, e.g., Antonio Stradivari (a violin maker) 787.219092.

For persons associated with a specific tradition of music other than western art music, add traditions-of-music notation (derived from 781.62–.66 and 781.68) before adding notation 092 from Table 1, e.g., a country music violinist 787.21642092. If the person is associated with more than one tradition, do not add to show the tradition.

790

Recreational and performing arts

The original heading for 790 was Amusements. There are two ways of being amused: One can be entertained by others (791 and 792) or one can amuse oneself (793–799). The settings for amusements are indoors (793–795) and outdoors (796–799). As Dewey made the first number of each span the general number for the activity (i.e., 791, 793, 796), the classifier can usually expect to find in these numbers a broader spectrum of forms of entertainment or amusement.

During the past century participatory amusements have become entertainments as well. Where once golfers were accompanied by only a few individuals who wished to witness this novel recreation, now millions watch them in person or on television. The same is true of most sports. And some outdoor amusements, such as American football, are now played indoors occasionally. Consequently, technology and social values have so altered over the past century that while the location of a subject within the 790s is predictable and reasonable with respect to the original structure of the class, it is neither predictable nor reasonable in the light of modern practices and concepts.

791.092

Persons [associated with public performances]

Class the biography of a performer with the activity which the person's career is chiefly identified, e.g., the biography of an opera singer 782.1092. If the person's career involves more than one kind of public performance with no particular predominance, class the biography with the activity that comes first in the following table of preference:

Music	780
Dancing	792.8
Stage	792
Motion pictures	791.43
Television	791.45
Radio	791.44

For example, class the biography of a stage actor who has also done considerable work in television in 792.028092. Give preference to activities listed in the table above over all other activities listed in 791.

791.43, 791.45 vs. 778.5

Motion pictures [and] Television vs. Cinematography, video production, related activities

Works on the technical aspects of making motion pictures and videos are classed in 778.5. Works on motion pictures and television as art forms and comprehensive works on producing them are classed in 791.43 and 791.45. For example, a work on determining what kind of lighting apparatus to use while filming in bright sunlight is classed in 778.5343. A work on the use of lighting techniques to enhance the mood of the scene and a comprehensive work on lighting are classed in 791.43025. If in doubt, prefer 791.43 and 791.45.

791.437 and 791.447, 791.457, 792.9

Films [and] Radio programs [and] Television programs [and] Stage productions

The text of a play is classed in the appropriate number in literature, e.g., the text of Thornton Wilder's *Our Town* 812.52. A production script is classed in either 791 or 792, e.g., the production script for a staged production of *Our Town* 792.92. A production script is distinguished from a literary text in that it contains a variety of directions, e.g., where the furniture is to be placed, where the actors are to stand.

A production recorded in a different medium than the original production is classed with the recording, not with the production. For example, a staged opera recorded for television is classed with television in 791.4572, not with staged opera in 792.542.

792.78 vs. 792.8, 793.3

Theatrical dancing vs. Ballet and modern dance vs. Social, folk, national dancing

A social, folk, or national dance can be given in the theater, just as a theatrical dance can become a social dance. In addition, either kind can be a part of a ballet. A dance is classed in 792.78, 792.8, or 793.3 depending upon the focus of the work. For example, the waltz is usually treated as a ballroom dance and is classed in 793.33; but waltzes as an integral part of Balanchine's *Vienna Waltzes,* a ballet, are classed in 792.842.

793.932 vs. 794.822

Computer adventure games   Computer fantasy games vs. Arcade games

Computer adventure games present the player with a situation and a goal (or goals). These goals may involve solving a mystery or problems and accumulating points. The player must think as opposed to making reflex actions, and is projected into an interactive story. Examples of this type are *Witness*® and *King's Quest*®. Class this type of game in 793.932.

Computer fantasy role-playing games also involve reaching a goal by solving intellectual problems. However, reflex actions are necessary because of the fighting or athletic action. Outcomes are decided by the computer. Examples of this type are *Exodus: Ultima II*® and *Wizardry: Proving Grounds of the Mad Overlord*®. Also class this type of game in 793.932.

Arcade games refer to a type of game, not just those games played in video arcades. They emphasize quick reflexes, as opposed to intellectual decisions. Among the types of these games are fighting, space flight, shooting, pinball, mazes, space shootouts, and strategy. Examples are *Robo Cop*® and *Pac-Man*®. Class this type of game in 794.822.

If in doubt, prefer 793.932.

795.015192 vs. 519.2

Probabilities [applied to games of chance] vs. Probabilities

"Games of chance" in the recreational sense are any games in which chance, not skill, is the most important factor in determining the outcome, e.g., craps, poker, solitaire. Works discussing the probabilities, or "odds," of winning these games are classed in 795.015192. In the mathematical sense, "games of chance" are limited to games played by a single player to determine the optimal policy or strategy of winning the games. Because these games are a part of the theory of controlled probabilities, they are classed in 519.2. If in doubt, prefer 795.015192.

796

Athletic and outdoor sports and games

Facilities

Notation 068 is sometimes used under 796–798 for the description of the playing field, court, or similar facility. The use of the facility is classed with the use. For example, the description of the greens of a golf course is classed in 796.352068; however, how the slope of the greens affects putting is classed in 796.35235.

Sports personnel

It is the practice of the Decimal Classification Division to class the biography of sports personnel in the general number for the specific sport regardless of position played or type of game. For example, a quarterback in American professional football is classed by the Division in 796.332092, not 796.33225092 or 796.33264092.

796.08 vs. 796.04

History and description of sports and games with respect to kinds of persons vs. General kinds of sports and games

If the sports or games are not modified to allow participation of a specific kind of persons, class with the kind either in 796.08 or with the specific sport or game with use of notation 08 from Table 1. If the sports or games have been modified, class either in 796.04 or with the modified version. (The modified versions of a sport are usually given in the "specific types" or "variants" subdivisions of the sport, e.g., baseball 796.357, Little League baseball 796.35762, indoor baseball 796.3578. If these subdivisions are not provided, class in the number for the type of sport as a whole.) If in doubt, class in 796.08 or in the number for the specific sport or game with use of notation 08 from Table 1. For example, a person who has lost a leg can usually play golf without a major change to the rules of golf. Thus, works for that person on how to golf would class in 796.3520873. However, in order to participate in other sports, the person who has lost a leg usually requires a wheelchair. Comprehensive works on wheelchair sports are classed in 796.0456. The wheelchair version of a specific sport is classed with variants of the sport, e.g., wheelchair basketball 796.3238.

The name of a variant of the sport may give the impression that it is for only one class of person when any type can play it. For example, women's basketball before 1971 was a variant of basketball in which there are six players per team and the three forwards played in the forecourt. This variant can be played by either men or women and is classed in 796.3238, not 796.323082.

Some sports and games have similar sounding names but the rules are so different as to create separate, though related, sports and games. For example, American football, Canadian football, and Australian-rules football are similar sports but they each have their own separate rules and are classed in 796.332, 796.335, and 796.336, respectively.

796.15 vs. 629.0460228

Play with remote-control models, kites, similar devices vs. Models and miniatures [of transportation equipment]

Class in 629.0460228 and related numbers in the 620s the design and construction of model vehicles, e.g., building model airplanes 629.133134. Class in 796.15 both play with and interdisciplinary works on remote-control vehicles, e.g., flying and building remote-control airplanes 796.154. If in doubt, class in 796.15.

Because most play with model railroads and trains does not involve remote-control vehicles, play with all types of model railroads and trains is classed in 790.133.

798.2

Horsemanship

The cross reference at 798.2 "*For horse racing, see 798.4*" means that horse racing is considered a part of 798.2. Therefore, only works that discuss both riding and racing are classed here. Many works having "horsemanship" in their titles do not cover racing; they are classed in 798.23.

800

Literature (Belles-lettres) and rhetoric

In the following discussion, whenever application of principles to various literatures is being discussed, notation from Table 3 is mentioned. For example, "T3—1" is used to discuss poetry in specific literatures rather than "811, 841, etc." The number "T3—1" refers to both 1 from Table 3–A (individual authors) and 1 from Table 3–B (more than one author). Difficulties arise with the notation for T3—8 Miscellaneous writings because the literary period intervenes between T3—8 and its various subdivisions. When reference is made to this form, it is expressed as T3—8 + the notation for the subdivision, e.g., diaries T3—8 + 03.

Choice between literature and nonliterary subject

The aims of literature, according to Horace, are twofold: to teach and delight. The Dewey Decimal Classification holds to this precept. Works of the imagination intended to delight are classed in 800, but works that are essentially informational are classed according to subject in other parts of the schedule. The discipline of literature is restricted to: (1) works of the imagination that are written in the various literary forms, e.g., fiction, poetry; (2) literary criticism and description; (3) literary history and biography. The exclusion of informational works from the realm of belles-lettres holds regardless of the literary form of a work. Jonathan Swift's *The Drapier's Letters*, therefore, is not classed as a collection of the author's letters, rather as a work on monetary policy in 332.49415.

Essays, speeches, letters, and diaries are commonly used for nonliterary purposes. If in doubt whether a work in one of these forms should be classed as literature in 800 or with a subject elsewhere in the schedule, class with the subject.

The nonfiction novel is a problem for classifiers. This kind of novel uses the techniques of fiction writing to tell the story of actual people and actual events. Class an account of a true event or series of events using the names of the people involved, not inventing characters or distorting facts to enhance an intended artistic effect, not going beyond the information available to the author from investigation and interviews, in the discipline appropriate to the facts described. Truman Capote's *In Cold Blood*, a true account of a multiple murder, has not been assigned a fiction number, but is classed in 364.1523, the criminology number for murder. If, however, the author goes beyond what is learned from investigation and interviews in describing conversations, feelings, thoughts, or states of mind of the people depicted in the book, then the author is treating them as fictional persons, and the work should be classed as fiction, e.g., Norman Mailer's *The Executioner's Song* 813.54. In case of doubt, class as fiction.

Other kinds of fiction, and poetry and drama, are sometimes used as vehicles for conveying factual information. Biographies have been written in verse, and fiction has been employed to teach the fundamentals of mathematics. Prefer 800 for poetry, drama, and fiction unless the form is purely incidental to the explanation of a specific subject, e.g., Harvey's *Circulation of the Blood* (written in Latin verse) 612.13, not 871.04.

An exception to the general rule is made for certain ancient works that have long been classed as literature regardless of the content of the work. For example, Hesiod's *Works and Days* is classed in 881.01, not 630, even though it deals with practical agriculture. These ancient works continue to be classed as literature, but new works whose major purpose is to inform are classed with the subject treated.

Class a collection of literary texts or excerpts from literary texts that is meant to serve as a model for studying another discipline with the discipline illustrated. For instance, class in 307 a collection meant to explain what a community is.

Class a literary study of nonliterary works in 809.935, e.g., the Bible as literature 809.93522.

Language

Literature always involves the use of language, and language is the basic facet for building numbers in 800.

Class literary works by language, not by country of origin. A major exception to this rule is that works in English originating in countries of the Western Hemisphere are classed in 810, not in 820 with English literature from the Eastern Hemisphere and comprehensive works on English literature. (*In certain other instances, country of origin can be indicated through the use of*

Table 3–C. See T3C—93–99.)

Class literary works in the language in which they were originally written. An English translation of a work originally written in Spanish is classed with Spanish literature in 860, not with English literature in 820.

Literature of two or more languages

Works treating literature of two or more languages are usually collections or works of criticism. If two languages are involved, class the work in the number coming first in 820–890, except where there are different instructions; for example, class English and Spanish in 820 (*not* 860), but class Greek and Latin in 880 (*not* 870). If more than two languages are involved, but the languages all belong to a particular language family, class the work in the most specific number that will contain all the languages. For instance, class a work including English, German, and Dutch in 830 since these are all Germanic languages. Do not class in 820–890 such a broad grouping as Indo-European literature; for example, class a work involving English, French, and Russian (all Indo-European languages) in 808 for collections, 809 for criticism, 800 for a combination of collections and criticism. Similarly, class in 800, 808, or 809 a work about literature in more than two languages when the languages are unrelated except that they belong to a broad grouping such as nonwestern or Asian languages; for example, class a collection of Arabic, Persian, and Turkish literary texts in 808, not 890. If any one language is predominant, class with that language.

Literary form

The second facet to be applied in literature is form. In literature there are two basic modes of expression: poetry and prose. Drama, whether in poetry or prose, is classed with drama in T3—2. The epigram is classed with miscellaneous writings in T3—8 + 02, regardless of mode. Works in other forms are classed with poetry in T3—1 if written in verse. Prose works are classed in T3—3 Fiction, T3—4 Essays, T3—5 Speeches, T3—6 Letters, and T3—8 Miscellaneous writings. The subdivision for prose literature, T3—8 + 08, is used only for prose works in more than one literary form; prose works in a specific form are classed with the form.

Though humor and satire have the number T3B—7 in the span for specific forms, they are neither form nor mode; rather, they are categories of writing marked in the case of humor by a manner of expression that makes a point amusingly, in the case of satire by ridicule and derision. Literary works in a particular form (T3—1–6 and T3—8) exhibiting humor and satire are classed with the form. Table 3–A for individual authors has no notation parallel to T3B—7; a collection of works by an individual author in more than one form exhibiting humor and satire is classed in T3A—8 + 09.

Kinds, scopes, media

For works by more than one author, the major forms can be subdivided. Poetry, drama, fiction, and speeches can be divided by kind, e.g., lyric and narrative poetry, science fiction and historical fiction. Drama and fiction can also be divided by scope, e.g., one-act plays and short stories. Drama can be divided by medium, e.g., plays written for television.

Literary period

The third facet in literature is literary period. Period tables are supplied under the literature of every language where their use is recommended. They are used for the literature of the language from throughout the world and for the literature from the traditional homeland of the language. For instance, French-language poetry of the later 19th century from throughout the world and French-language poetry of the later 19th century from France are both 841.8. The same periods are used for affiliated literatures (literatures in the same language, but from countries other than the traditional homeland) if the affiliated literature emanates from the same continent. Thus Swiss and Belgian French-language poems of the later 19th century are also classed in 841.8. The periods of Great Britain are used for English-language literature of Ireland, the U.S. periods for English-language literature of Puerto Rico. For English-language literature of Canada, however, the Canadian periods are used, not U.S. periods. Period is usually omitted if the literature emanates from a country on another continent, e.g., French-language poetry of the 19th century from Canada 841. (Optional periods are sometimes provided for use with such a country if some special device is used to set such literature apart from the literature in general. The options are described at 810–890 in the schedule.) *(In certain cases, for affiliated literatures both in and outside the continent of origin, country of origin can be shown through the use of Table 3–C. See T3C—93–99.)*

In literary period tables, a particular century is specified in a note only if the heading for the relevant number covers fewer than 75 years of the century. Thus in the period table for English literature at 820.1–828, a class-here note for the 19th century appears under notation 8 Victorian period, 1837–1900, but no class-here note for the 20th century appears under notation 91 1900–1999.

Other elements

For works by or about more than one author, two key elements are commonly added from Table 3–B: T3B—08 and cognate numbers for collections, T3B—09 and cognate numbers for history, description, and critical appraisal. This notation also serves as a link to Table 3–C, the table that allows for expression of additional features. These features are literary themes or subjects, literary elements (e.g., dialogue), literary qualities (e.g., romanticism), and specific kinds of persons for whom or by whom the literature is written.

Literary criticism

The chief rule to be observed in classing criticism is that it is always classed with the literature being criticized.

Criticism of a specific work is classed with the work, e.g., a critical analysis of Hemingway's *For Whom the Bell Tolls* is classed in 813.52, the same number as the work itself. Criticism of the work of an author in general is classed in the comprehensive number for the author in question, e.g., criticism of Hemingway 813.52.

809 and notation 09 from Table 3–B and cognate numbers under specific forms of literature are used for criticism of all kinds of literature except the works of individual authors. Criticism of several literatures as a whole is classed in 809, criticism of fiction from several literatures in 809.3. Criticism of the English-language literature of the United States in general is classed in 810.9, criticism of English-language fiction of the United States in general in 813.009, criticism of early 20th-century American fiction in English in 813.5209.

Class criticism of literature in a specific form from more than two literatures in 809.1–.7. Class in 808.1–.7 critical works in which the emphasis is on the various forms of literature as such, not on the various authors and literatures that may be used as examples. If in doubt between 808.1–.7 and 809.1–.7, prefer 809.1–.7.

Class in 801.95 the theory and technique of literary criticism. Class the theory and technique of criticism of specific literary forms in 808.1–.7. If in doubt between 801.95 and 808.1–.7, prefer 801.95.

Appreciation of literature is classed in the same manner as other criticism.

Textual criticism of literature is classed in the same manner as other criticism except that the theory and technique of textual criticism of specific literary forms is classed in 801.959, not in 808.1–.7.

Criticism of criticism is classed with the criticism being criticized and hence with the original subject of criticism. Criticism of Hemingway is classed in 813.52. If a third person writes a criticism of the criticism of Hemingway, this also is classed in 813.52.

Works about critics are treated in the same manner as works about other authors, i.e., critics are classed with the kind of literature that they chiefly criticize. Thus, a man who devoted the major part of his life to criticizing the works of Hemingway is classed in 813.52. A critic of Spanish literature is classed in 860.9.

It should be noted that criticism and critics are classed with the language of the literature they are criticizing, not with the language in which the criticism is written. For example, a French critic writing in French but criticizing American literature is classed in 810.9.

Adaptations

An adaptation may alter the form of a work or modify the content to such an extent in language, scope, or level of presentation that it can no longer be considered a version of the original. An adaptation is classed in the number appropriate to the adaptation, e.g., Lamb's *Tales from Shakespeare* 823.7. (*For translations, see 800: Language.*)

Note, however, that a prose translation of poetry (which is merely a change in mode) is not treated as an adaptation, e.g., Dante's *Divine Comedy* translated into German prose 851.1.

Excerpts

Treat a collection of excerpts from different literary works as a collection.

800 vs. 398.2

Literature (Belles-lettres) and rhetoric vs. Folk literature

Folk literature consists of brief works in the oral tradition and is classed in 398.2. Whatever literary individuality the folk literature may once have had has been lost to the anonymity that the passage of time brings. Anonymous classics, however, are not considered to be folk literature. Despite the fact that their authorship is unknown, such works have a recognized literary merit, are almost always lengthy, and form a part of the literary canon. Therefore, they are classed in 800, e.g., *Chanson de Roland* 841.1, *Cantar de mio Cid* 861.1, *Kalevala* 894.54111.

Some legendary or historical events or themes, such as the search for the Holy Grail or the battle of Roland with the Saracens, appear as the basis for original works in many literatures, periods, and forms, the medieval works involving them often being anonymous. Although the theme rather than the literature is the binding thread, what is read is a literary work. Consequently, class each retelling of the event or theme with the literature, form, and period in which it was written, e.g., Mary Stewart's Merlin trilogy 823.914. Class works about a specific theme treated in several literatures in 809.933.

If in doubt, prefer 800.

800 vs. 398.245, 590, 636

Literature (Belles-lettres) and rhetoric vs. [Folk literature of] Animals vs. Animals vs. Animal husbandry

Works about animals intended to contribute to some discipline other than literature are classed in the relevant discipline. Class animal stories in which the author's emphasis is on the habits and behavior of the animal in 590, on the care and training of the animal in 636. Class folk literature of animals in 398.245.

Literary accounts of animals are classed with the appropriate form in literature, e.g., poetry. Such accounts may be either fictional or true. A book about animals is certainly fiction if it contains conversations or thoughts of animals. Literary accounts of actual animals are often in the form of anecdotes or personal reminiscences. Such accounts are usually accommodated in T3—8 Miscellaneous writings. They are to be classed, as appropriate, at T3—8 + 02 for anecdotes, at T3—8 + 03 for reminiscences, diaries, journals; or at T3—8 + 07 for works without identifiable literary form.

If in doubt, prefer 800.

808.001–.7 vs. 070.52

Rhetoric vs. [Publishers'] Relations with authors

Three elements combine to produce the finished piece of writing: composition, preparation of the manuscript, and publishing:

1. Composition

General 808

How to write for newspapers 808.06607

How to write about law 808.06634

How to write plays 808.2

2. Preparation of the manuscript

General 808.02

For newspapers 808.06607

For works about law 808.06634

For plays 808.2

3. Publishing 070.52

Class in 070.52 works limited to securing agents, submitting manuscripts, the relations of authors and publishers.

Works combining (2) and (3) are classed in the numbers for preparation of the manuscript (808.02, etc.) unless heavily weighted toward the publishing end:

How to make money in free-lance writing 808.02

Where to market your manuscript 070.52

If in doubt, prefer 808.001–.7.

808.0427

Study of rhetoric through critical reading

Readers used in the study of composition are classed here. Readers limited to a particular literary form are classed in the rhetoric number for the form, e.g., short stories 808.31. Academic readers in a subject are classed with the subject.

808.1 vs. 414.6

Rhetoric of poetry vs. Suprasegmental features [in linguistics]

Because many studies of prosody are concerned with how to write poetry, general studies of literary prosody are classed in 808.1. However, works on the prosody of a specific literature are classed as criticism of the literature, e.g., a study of the use of language by American poets 811.009, a study of the prose rhythms of a later-19th-century French essayist 844.8.

Prosodic studies of a particular language as a whole from the linguist's viewpoint are classed with intonation for the specific language, plus notation 16 from Table 4, e.g., 451.6 for prosodic studies of the Italian language. Linguistic studies of prosody across several languages and from the linguist's viewpoint are classed in 414.6.

If in doubt, prefer 808.1.

808.8

Collections of literary texts from more than two literatures

Here are examples illustrating the preference order for collections of texts in more than one form from more than two literatures. The preference order is the same for criticism (809).

1. Specific themes and subjects, e.g., 808.80382 (religion)
2. Specific elements, e.g., 808.8024 (plot)
3. Specific qualities, e.g., 808.8013 (idealism)
4. For and by specific kinds of persons, e.g., 808.899282 (children)
5. Period, e.g., 808.80033 (18th century)

See also discussion at Table 3–B: Preference order.

900

Geography, history, and auxiliary disciplines

History is a record of events, their causes and effects, and of the contemporary conditions that clarify and enrich these events. When a work is the story of events that have transpired or an account of the conditions that have prevailed in a particular place or region, it is classed in 900. When it is the history of a specific subject, it is classed in the appropriate discipline, e.g., a history of political developments (such as internal developments in government) without respect to their effect upon the larger society and place where they occur 320.9; of economic events in France 330.944; of warfare 355.0209; of clocks 681.11309.

Political history is a strong component of history because it affects the whole of a particular society. But the history of political developments as they affect the internal activity of parties or other political groups is classed in 320.9 or in the 324 numbers for parties, campaigns, and election history.

History includes the present (situation and conditions), but not the future (projected events). Class projected events at 303.49.

Position on the map rather than political affiliation usually determines the number assigned to the history or the geography of a particular place, for while political affiliation may change, position on the earth's surface does not.

Citation order

The citation order in the 900s is straightforward:

History: 9 + place + period + standard subdivision, e.g., a periodical of the history of Jalisco state (Mexico) during the 20th century 972.350805.

Geography and travel: 91 + place + physical geography, travel, or regional geography + standard subdivision, e.g., an encyclopedia of travel in Italy today 914.50492903, a periodical about mountains in Italy 914.5094305.

Historic events vs. nonhistoric events

Depending upon their impact, specific events are classed either in 900 or in specific disciplines in 001–899. Events that are important enough to affect the general social life and history of the place are classed with the history of the place regardless of any discipline involved. For example, the sinking of the Lusitania is classed in 940.4514, the assassination of Abraham Lincoln in 973.7092, the San Francisco earthquake of 1906 in 979.461051.

Other specific events are classed with the history of the discipline to which they relate. For example, the history of a crime is classed in 364, e.g., the Whitechapel murders committed by Jack the Ripper 364.1523. A sporting accident is classed in 796–799, e.g., a fatal accident during an automobile race 796.72.

In applying the above, the classifier should take into account the author's purpose or point of view. For instance, a work about the assassination of John F. Kennedy that is focused on the modus operandi of the crime, the detective work involved in solving it, or both, is classed at 364.1524092, not at 973.922092.

Works about events are more apt to emphasize social aspects than technological aspects and are usually classed in 300 rather than 600. If safety factors are stressed, the work is classed in 363, not with any other discipline involved. For example, a study of the wreck of the Andrea Doria to determine what the causes of the accident were, what preventive measures might be mandated as a result of the incident, is classed at 363.12365.

Collected accounts of events are treated in the same manner, provided that they all pertain to one discipline, e.g., scientific travel 508. Class collected events without such focus in 904.

909, 930–990 vs. 320

World history [and] History of ancient world; of specific continents, countries, localities; of extraterrestrial worlds vs. Political science (Politics and government)

Political history

Political history with an emphasis on major political events typified by the "battles, kings, and dates" school of history is clearly 900. Political history with an emphasis on the mechanics of give and take of political forces and movements and on their internal development is usually classed in 320.9, but if the forces and movements come to power or bring about major changes in society, their successes or failures become general history, and should be classed in 900.

Political activities

The sum total of political activity of a specific period or place is also considered general history, and is classed in 909 and 930–990. Various subdivisions of 320 include material on important political activities when considered in terms of the discipline "political science," but whenever an activity is discussed in a manner which highlights its influence on general events 900 must be considered. The general rule is: Important events and leaders with wide-ranging responsibilities are classed in general history, unless considered primarily in the context of a specific subject. The chief problems concern three numbers: 320.9, 324, and 328.

320.9: Under political situation and conditions there can be works on habitual activities and styles of leading political figures as a group, and on the activities reflecting the adjustment of political forces or the status of political parties and movements. But when the activities are analyzed in terms of their effect on general events, use 900.

324: Party histories are classed in 324.2; and histories of nomination and election campaigns, in 324.5 and 324.9, respectively, but only when they concern largely internal events of the parties and campaigns, or report winners, losers, and votes. A history of how a party or candidate came to power (or almost did), or a discussion of how party and campaign events move nations (or other areas) in certain directions is classed in 900.

328: Histories of specific legislative bodies are classed in 328.4–.9, but only when they are largely limited to what happened within or to the bodies, without significant consideration of what the legislative body did for the political unit it served. The accomplishments of a given legislative session are normally a matter of general history and are classed in 900, but if a work concentrates on the body's internal history it is classed in 328. While the report of proceedings of a legislature (i.e., its motions, debates, actions) may constitute the raw material of history, it is not in itself general history, and remains in 328.

909, 930–990 vs. 320.4, 321, 321.09

World history [and] History of ancient world; of specific continents, countries, localities; of extraterrestrial worlds vs. Structure and function of government vs. Systems of governments and states vs. Change in system of government

Change of government

The number for changes in systems of government (321.09) is used primarily for studies of *the process* of change, rather than for works on particular changes. Prefer other numbers in 321 or subdivisions of 320.4 for works on particular systems or kinds of systems, and 900 numbers for the history of changes in government or particular coups and revolutions in specific areas.

For example, class general political treatment of a specific system of government preceding or following changes in 321 (e.g., 321.86 for new republics); class political treatment of systems of government that precede or follow changes in a specific country in 320.4 (e.g., the government of the Soviet Union after the 1917 revolution 320.4470904); and class general history of changes of government in specific areas and works on specific coups in 909 or 930–999 (e.g., revolutions in the 20th century 909.82, the Russian Revolution 947.0841).

If in doubt, give preference in order of the numbers in the heading, that is, prefer 909 or 930–990 over 320.4 or 321, 320.4 over 321, and all other subdivisions of 321 over 321.09.

909, 930–990 vs. 400

World history [and] History of ancient world; of specific continents, countries, localities; of extraterrestrial worlds vs. Language

Class in 400 studies that emphasize language and literature, even though some material on culture and history is included; but class in 900 studies in history and culture that include but do not emphasize language and literature. If in doubt, prefer 900.

909, 930–990 vs. 910

World history [and] History of ancient world; of specific continents, countries, localities vs. Geography and travel

If a work deals with geography and civilization or travel and civilization, class it in 909 or 930–990; however, if the treatment of geography or travel is predominant, class the work in 910. If in doubt, prefer 909 or 930–990.

If the work deals with the description of the physical earth only, class it in 910.02 or in 913–919, plus notation 02 from table under 913–919.

912 vs. T1—0223

Graphic representations of surface of the world and of extraterrestrial worlds vs. [Table 1 notation for] Maps, plans, diagrams

Geographic atlases and maps, i.e., atlases and maps which either do not emphasize a subject, or are devoted to any subject in 910 (general geography and travel) are classed in 912. Road atlases and maps, being primarily intended for travelers, are also classed in 912, but railroad atlases will normally be devoted to transportation, thus will fall in 385.0223 or in 385.09 with notation 022 from the add tables found under T1—093–099, e.g., railroad atlases in Brazil 385.0981022. If in doubt, class in 912.

913–919

Geography of and travel in ancient world and specific continents, countries, localities in modern world; extraterrestrial worlds

Historic sites and buildings

Works describing historic sites and buildings should be classed with the discipline that is emphasized.

If a building has or had a specific purpose, class the work about it with the purpose of the building unless some other discipline is emphasized, e.g., a work about a Benedictine monastery in Lower Austria that emphasizes the history of the religious order in that place 271.1043612, a guide to the New York Stock Exchange building 332.64273. Works about buildings that are associated with the life of an individual are classed with the biography number for that person, e.g., the home of Thomas Wolfe in Asheville, North Carolina 813.52. Works about a site that is famous for an historic event are classed with the history of the event, e.g., Gettysburg National Military Park 973.7349.

A work on a building or buildings in an area that focuses on the architecture of the building or buildings is classed in 720.9 or 725–728. Works on religious buildings often fall in this category. For example, a work on a church in Paris that emphasizes architectural history is classed in 726.50944361. Also class in 725–728 the art history of a building and its contents, including the architecture of the building and the art works it contains.

If a work describing the buildings in an area is written for the purpose of suggesting historic preservation projects to be undertaken, see the discussion at *930–990: Historic preservation.* A work that describes the buildings in an area for the purpose of illustrating the history of the area is classed in 930–990.

If no specific purpose or discipline is evident, class the work in 913–919. For guidebooks, see the discussion below under 04 Travel on *Guidebooks*.

See also discussion at 333.7–.9 vs. 508, 913–919, 930–990.

Add table

The following flow chart is offered as an aid to building numbers and as a supplement to the detailed directions at 913–919.

Flow chart for geography and travel

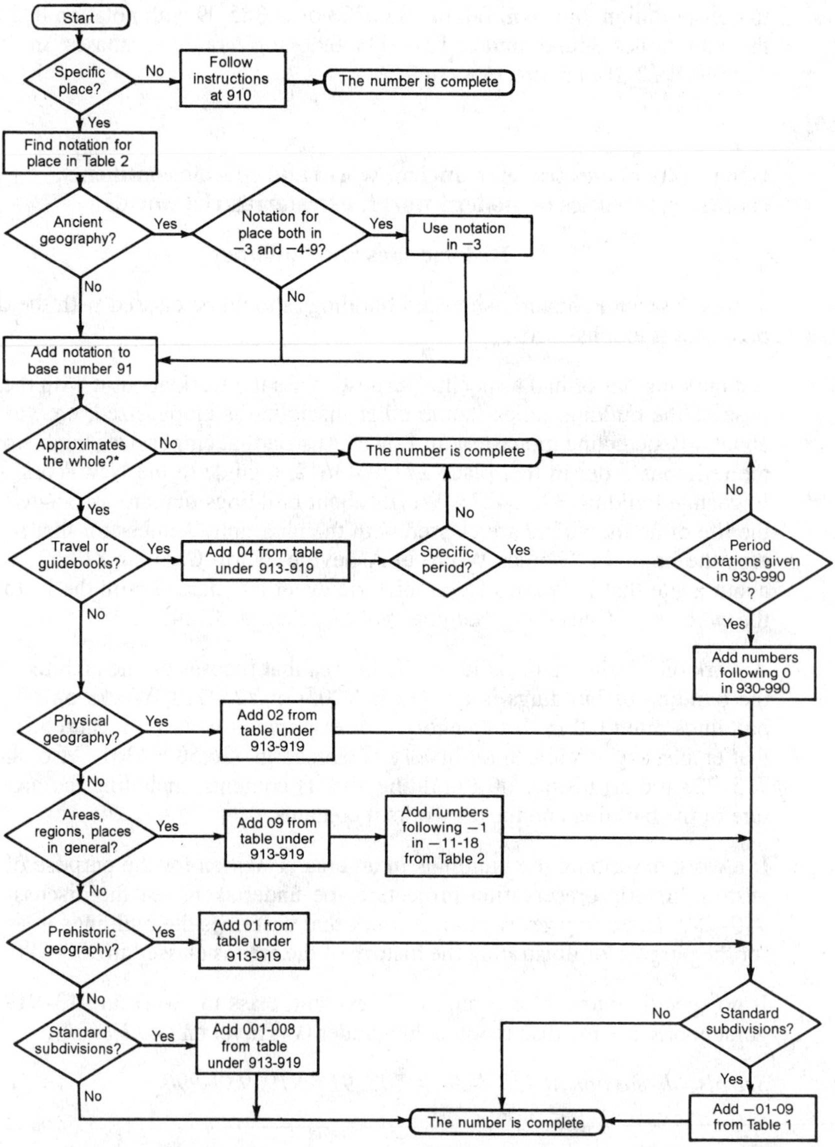

*See also "Approximates the whole" section of Manual notes on Table 1

04

Travel

Use this subdivision for accounts of travel. Such accounts should emphasize events of the trip, places stopped at, accommodations, modes of transportation. If the work is purely a description of the area visited, with none, or very few, of these accompaniments, use subdivision 02 for physical geography, or class the work in 930–990 for civilization and social conditions of the place visited, as the case may be. Works of a person who has lived for several years in the area described are usually classed in 930–990.

Travel does not normally cover the whole of any given area. Class accounts according to the widest span covered. For example, travel from New York to San Francisco 917.304, from Marseilles to Paris 914.404, from New York City in 1981 to Buffalo, New York 917.470443. Standard subdivisions may be added to such numbers.

Discovery and exploration

Use 04 for works describing excursions into previously unknown or little known areas, e.g., the Lewis and Clark expedition 917.8042, Byrd's expedition to the South Pole 919.8904. However, if the initial exploration of a place forms an important part of its early history, class the work in 930–990, e.g., early exploration of North America 970.01.

Class accounts of archaeological expeditions in 930.1.

Guidebooks

A guidebook can be either a residential guidebook, i.e., a guide for either the permanent resident and long-term visitor of an area, or a tourist guidebook, ie., a guide for the short-term visitor. The residential guidebook covers not only the tourist attractions but also the other parts of the area, such as banks, churches, grocery stores, real estate agencies, and residential neighborhoods. These guidebooks normally give a snapshot view of the history of the area and are classed in 940–990, plus the period notation for when it was written, e.g., a residential guidebook to Washington, D.C., written in 1995 975.3041. Tourist guidebooks provide detailed information about the area through which the tourists travel, telling them what to see, where to stay, and where to dine. These guidebooks are classed following the instructions in the following paragraphs. If in doubt whether the book is a residential or a tourist guidebook, class it as a tourist guidebook.

Tourist guidebooks are usually classed in 913–919, plus notation 04 from the table at 913–919, e.g., guidebooks to the United States 917.304. For individual guidebooks the notation for the historical period during which the book was written is added, e.g., a tourist guidebook to Washington, D.C., written in 1995 917.530441. Guidebooks written before ca. 499 are classed in 913, e.g., Pausanias' guide to Attica written ca. 130 913.85049. Class modern guidebooks to ancient areas in the corresponding modern area numbers in 914–919, e.g., a 1995 guide to the ruins of Rome 914.563204929.

A guidebook that is limited to an aspect of the trip is classed with that aspect, e.g., a guide to London's underground rail system 388.42809421, lodgings for tourists in London 647.94421, bed and breakfast establishments of London 647.9442103, restaurants of Hawaii 647.95969. In addition, guidebooks emphasizing a specific subject are classed with the subject, e.g., a guidebook to holy places in Spain 263.04246, a skiing guide to Aspen, Colorado 796.930978843. (*For guidebooks to historic sites and buildings, see the discussion in the section above, Historic sites and buildings.*)

A guidebook to a locality that is usually visited for only one type of attraction is classed with that attraction. For example, most people go to Orlando, Florida, in order to visit its theme parks: Walt Disney World, Sea World of Florida, and Universal Studios Florida. Thus, both guidebooks to the theme parks and to Orlando in general are classed with theme parks in 791.06875924. However, a guidebook that covers more than one locality is usually classed in 913–919, plus notation 04 from the table at 913–919, e.g., a guide to central Florida which covers not only Orlando but also Cape Canaveral, Daytona Beach, and Tampa 917.59204.

See also discussion at 333.7–.9 vs. 508, 913–919, 930–990; also at 913–919 vs. 796.51.

Biography

Notation 092 from Table 1 is added to subdivisions 041–049 for biographies of discoverers, explorers, and travelers, but not for general geographers nor for first-person accounts of travel. Class biographies of general geographers in the base number for the area without further subdivision. Use subdivisions 041–049 for first-person accounts of travel, but do not add notation 092.

913–919 vs. 796.51

Geography of and travel in ancient world and specific continents, countries, localities in modern world; extraterrestrial worlds vs. Walking

Walkers' guides

Walkers' guides can be written for either the hiker or the tourist. Both types of guides give detail instructions on how to get from point A to point B, e.g., at the fork turn left, and a general description of the route in order for the walker to choose one route over another, such as distance, what can be seen. Guides for the tourist also give detail description of things en route, e.g., the type of rock outcropping, the history of the wayside shrine. Guides for the hiker are classed in 796.51, while those for the tourist in 913–919, plus notation 04 from the table at 913–919. Walking guides to an urban area are classed in 913–919, plus notation 04 from the table at 913–919, e.g., walking guides to San Francisco 917.946104. If in doubt, class in 913–919.

A guide limited to one topic is classed with that topic, e.g., a walker's guide to the geology of Yosemite National Park 557.9447, a walking tour of the skyscrapers of San Francisco 720.4830979461.

929.1

Genealogy

This is the comprehensive number for works providing information about genealogy itself: what it is, where to go to find genealogical records, what to look for, what sources to use, how to obtain these sources, how to trace family trees. The sources themselves are classed in 929.3.

929.2

Family histories

Inasmuch as families disperse from their place of origin, the area number selected for a family history should not be too specific. The Decimal Classification Division adds area numbers only for the country in which the family lives, not for the state, province, or smaller area. (For the purpose of classification, England, Scotland, Wales, and Northern Ireland are to be considered separate countries.) For example, the Division classes the history of a Florida family in 929.20973, not 929.209759.

Class a family history with the country in which the family presently lives, not with the country from which the family's ancestors came. For example, class the Duponts, a United States family of French origin, in 929.20973, not 929.20944.

Family histories that give historical information about the area in which the family is located are classed with the history of the area, e.g., prominent families in New York City 974.71.

929.2 vs. 929.7

Family histories vs. Royal houses, peerage, gentry, orders of knighthood

Family histories of the nobility and gentry are usually classed in 929.2. Family histories that emphasize lineage or descent of the peerage or gentry are classed in 929.7, e.g., *Burke's Peerage* 929.72, *Virginians of Gentle Birth* 929.709755. If in doubt, prefer 929.2.

930–990

History of ancient world; of specific continents, countries, localities; of extraterrestrial worlds

Wars

In most instances, the history of a war is classed with the history of the country or region in which most of the fighting took place, e.g., the Vietnam War 959.7043, the Napoleonic wars 940.27, the Falkland Islands War (1982) 997.11024. However, some wars are arbitrarily assigned to either the history of one of the principal participants or to the region where the war began. For example, the Spanish-American War is classed with United States history in 973.89. World War II is classed in European history (the area where the war began) at 940.53, and not in world history at 909.824. In addition, when a war is fought within a limited portion of a country, it is classed with the history of the country as a whole, e.g., the Second Seminole War, which was fought against the Seminole Indians in Florida, is classed in 973.57, not 975.904.

Regardless of the area to which a war is assigned, specific battles or actions of a war are classed in the number for the war, not with the number of the place where the action occurred. For example, a battle occurring in the Philippines during the Spanish-American War is classed in 973.8937, not 959.9031; air raids on Tokyo in World War II 940.5425, not 952.135033.

There are two kinds of wartime history that are not classed in the war numbers (unless the area covered coincides with the area used for the war). Routine history of the everyday events of an area, even if during wartime, is classed with the numbers for the area, not with the war, e.g., the history of Maryland during the Civil War 975.203, not 973.709752. The effect of military action on the everyday life and civilization of a place is classed with the history of the place, e.g., the effect of Civil War military actions on Maryland 975.203, not 973.709752. These two kinds of history must be carefully distinguished from the participation of an area in the war because the area's participation in the war is classed with the war, e.g., Maryland's participation in the Civil War 973.709752, not 975.203. Usually, national histories covering a time of war will emphasize the country's participation and will be classed with the war; if there is no such emphasis, the history will be classed in the appropriate national history number. For example, British participation in World War II 940.5341, history of Britain during George VI's reign 941.084.

See also discussion at 333.7–.9 vs. 508, 913–919, 930–990; also at 930–990 vs. 355.009.

Wars: Occupied countries

The history of the occupation of a country during time of war is classed with the war, e.g., occupation of countries in World War II 940.5336. Military administration of the government of an occupied country during or following the war is classed in 355.49. International law with respect to occupation is classed in 341.66.

Wars: Military units

The history of specific military units in a war is classed with the numbers for military units under history of the particular war, e.g., military units in World War I 940.412–.413. If there is no specific number for military units, a work on military units is classed in the number for military operations, e.g., military units in the Vietnam War 959.70434.

Class comprehensive works on specific military units and military units in peacetime in 355.3 or cognate numbers in 355–359.

Wars: Personal narratives

The personal narratives of participants in a war are classed in the appropriate subdivision of the history numbers for the specific war, e.g., personal narratives of American soldiers in World War II 940.548173. Narratives that focus on a specific campaign, battle, or other subject are classed with the subject, e.g., a personal account of the Battle of Berlin 940.5421092, of Axis intelligence operations in World War II 940.548743092.

The narrative of a person's experiences during time of war, if it does not focus on the war as such, is classed as biography and not in the number for the war. For example, an actor's personal experiences of performing in Scotland during 1940–1942 are classed in 792.092, not 940.5315792092.

See also discussion at 930–990: Biography; also at 930–990 vs. 355.009.

Historic preservation

Class comprehensive works on historic preservation and lists of preservation projects to be undertaken in 363.69. However, if such a list is primarily devoted to inventorying or describing the sites, class the list in the appropriate number in 930–990, or, if primarily a description of buildings at the site, class in 720.

Class administrative annual reports of agencies promoting the preservation of historical sites in 353.77.

Class historic preservation in an architectural context in 720.288 and cognate numbers in 721–729.

See also discussion at 333.7–.9 vs. 508, 913–919, 930–990.

Biography

Notation 092 from Table 1 is added to subdivisions 01–09 for biographies of persons who lived during the historical period and of historians and historiographers of that period, e.g., biographies of Abraham Lincoln and of Bruce Catton, Civil War historian, 973.7092. Even if the life span of the person or the time during which the person impacted upon the history of the country or locality does not approximate the whole of the period, notation 092 can be added, e.g., biography of Rajiv Gandhi 954.052092. Subdivision 0099 (which is limited to collected treatment) is used *only* for works not limited to a specific period, e.g., biographies of the kings and queens of Great Britain 941.0099. If subdivisions 01–09 for historical periods are not given in the schedule, do not add subdivision 0099 either for collected biographies limited to a specific period or for individual biographies, e.g., biographies of the 20th-century princes and princesses of Monaco and a biography of Grace, Princess of Monaco 944.949, not 944.9490099. Subdivision 0099 is added, however, for collected biographies *not* limited to a specific period, e.g., biographies of the princes and princesses of Monaco 944.9490099. Subdivision 007202 is used for biographies of historians and historiographers whose works are not limited to a specific period, e.g., biographies of historians of British history 941.007202.

Add table

The following flow chart is offered as an aid to building numbers and as a supplement to the detailed instructions at 930–990.

Flow chart for history

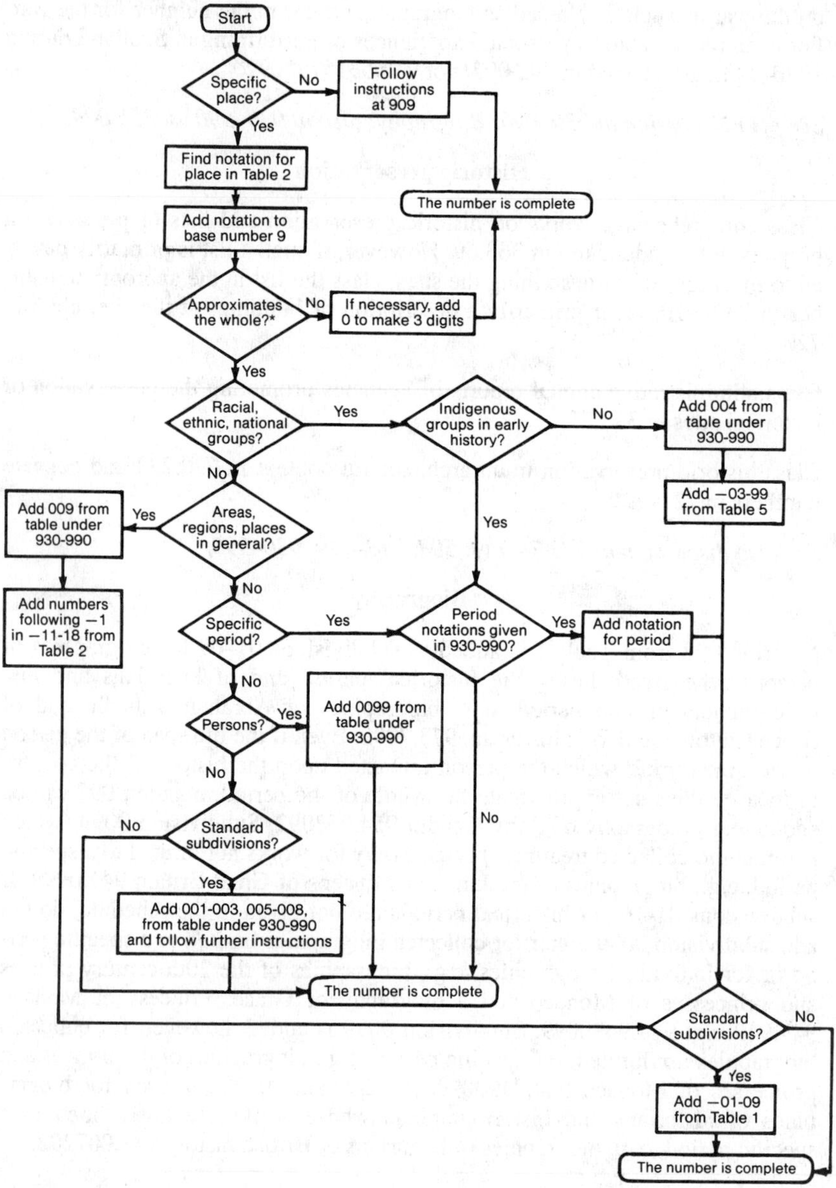

*See also "Approximates the whole" section of Manual notes on Table 1

01–09

Historical periods

The history of the area is usually subdivided into periods defined by the events that affected the area. The events, whether stated or implied in the heading, rarely occurred on either January 1 or December 31. Thus, the year during which the event occurred will normally be given at two different numbers. For example, 1861, the year when Kansas became a state, appears at both 978.102 Territorial period, 1803–1861 and 978.103 Statehood period, 1861–. In like manner, 1945, the year when World War II ended, appears at both 978.1032 1918–1945 and 978.1033 1945–.

The history of the area can also be subdivided by periods of time, such as centuries or decades. Since they start on January 1 and end on December 31, the year either beginning or ending the period will appear in only one notation. For example, in the development for the history of the Western United States, 978.02 1800–1899 and 978.03 1900–. (The DDC uses the convention that a century begins with the year 0 and ends with the year 99.) The name for a particular century is given only if the span of years in the heading is less than 75 years. For example, the 15th century in German history is given in a class-here note at 943.028 Reigns of Albert II and Frederick III, 1438–1493. The 17th century in German history is not given at 943.04 1618–1705.

When adding standard subdivisions to the historical periods, use notation 01–09 from Table 1, not 001–009 from the table under 930–990. However, T1—089 and T1—091 are not used since the provisions for them given at 004 and 0091–0098 in the table under 930–990 take precedence over provisions for historical periods.

930–990 vs. 355.009

History of ancient world; of specific continents, countries, localities; of extraterrestrial worlds vs. Historical, geographic, persons treatment [of military science]

Military topics and war

Use the historical treatment standard subdivisions in 355–359 for works emphasizing military history or topics without consideration of the general course of a war, e.g., changes in tank tactics during the course of World War II 358.18409044. Use numbers in 900 for works on the military history of wars that deal with the outcome of significant events, e.g., the use of tanks on the Eastern Front and how the use affected various battles 940.54217. If in doubt between 355–359 and 930–990, prefer 930–990.

Persons

Use 930–990 for comprehensive works on soldiers chiefly associated with the history of a specific war, e.g., William Tecumseh Sherman 973.73092; use 355.0092 for comprehensive works on soldiers associated with more than one war, or who had long and varied careers, e.g., Douglas MacArthur. If in doubt, prefer 930–990.

See also discussion at 930–990: Wars.

941

[History of the] British Isles

Class here works on the United Kingdom (England, Wales, Scotland, and Northern Ireland), a political entity, and on Great Britain (England, Wales, and Scotland), a geographic entity. Class in 942 only works dealing with England alone, or with England and Wales. Histories of the period since 1603 (or including this period) will seldom deal with England or England and Wales alone. Histories of the period before 1603 may deal with England or England and Wales alone. Books on the civilization of this area may deal with any combination. The following combinations of two areas will be classed in 941: England and Scotland, England and Ireland, Ireland and Wales.

968

Southern Africa Republic of South Africa

Period notation for a country or region is added to each geographic subdivision of the country not provided with its own periods, regardless of considerations of sovereignty. Thus, the historical periods of the provinces of Republic of South Africa also apply to the homelands in the area of each province. For example, the historical periods of Natal apply also to KwaZulu, e.g., history of KwaZulu during the reign of Shaka 968.491039, during the prime ministership of P. W. Botha 968.491063.

970.004

[General history of North American] Racial, ethnic, national groups

The principal fact to keep in mind in assigning class numbers to works of the various native American peoples is that they have moved in the course of time from place to place and that these places are often widely scattered.

Therefore, in general, a work on specific peoples is classed in 970.00497, no attempt being made to assign a more specific location. For example, general works on Cherokees class in 970.004975.

If, however, the focus of the work is clearly on the native peoples in a specific place, use the number for the place plus notation 00497 from the table under 930–990. For example, native races of Canada, 971.00497, Cherokees in North Carolina 975.6004975.

Appendix

Policies and Procedures of the Library of Congress Decimal Classification Division

Segmentation

One aid to reduction of the full DDC number is the segmentation provided in Dewey for Windows and in DDC numbers assigned by such centralized cataloging services as the Decimal Classification Division of the Library of Congress and the National Library of Canada. The segmentation is indicated by a prime mark (′), a slash mark (/), or other comparable indicators.

The segmentation provided by the Decimal Classification Division is applied according to two different principles. A segmentation mark can indicate the end of an abridged number (as found in the abridged edition of the DDC), or the beginning of a standard subdivision. Thus, a DDC number can consist of one, two, or three segments. For example:

155.6′6	The psychology of midlife
155.6	Psychology of adults (the number found in the abridged edition)
6	Persons in middle adulthood (the remainder of the number found in the schedules in the unabridged edition)
324.6′ 23′092	A biography of Susan B. Anthony
324.6	Election systems and procedures; suffrage (the number found in the abridged edition)
23	Women's suffrage (the remainder of the number found in the schedules of the unabridged edition)
092	Persons (from unabridged Table 1)
323′.025′73	Directory of civil rights leaders and organizations in the United States
323	Civil and political rights (the number found in the abridged edition)
.025	Directories of persons and organizations (applicable standard subdivision from abridged Table 1)
73	United States (area notation from Table 2 that can be added to the directories number [025] from unabridged Table 1)

Alternate DDC Notation in LC Bibliographic Records

Libraries using cataloging data provided by the Library of Congress will notice that there are sometimes two or more DDC numbers or non-numeric notation in the DDC field. The following examples (omitting segmentation marks described above) explain the practices of the Decimal Classification Division with respect to alternate DDC notation.

Nonjuvenile Works

A. For works belonging to a monographic series classed as a set but analyzed in full or in part according to the decisions of the Library of Congress, the Decimal Classification Division assigns two numbers:

081 s	the number for the item if the series is kept together at one class number
[327.7]	the number for the specific item in the series

B. For biography and works primarily biographical, the Division assigns a number and the letter [B]:

780.92	the number for the item if added to the classified collection
[B]	the letter for the item if added to a biography collection

C. Alternate notation for a monograph in a series and for biography may be present:

780.92 s	the number for the series
[787.66092] [B]	the number and the letter for a monograph in a series

D. For law, the Division in recent years made the only exception to its practice of eschewing optional numbers. It supplied both the preferred number and the Option B number:

345.7308	the preferred number
[347.3058]	the Option B number

E. When works on law belonged to analyzed monographic sets, four numbers were supplied:

343.41052 s	[343.410523]
344.10352 s	[344.103523]

The policy of providing Option B numbers for law materials will be discontinued with the implementation of Edition 21.

Juvenile Works

For juvenile works, alternative numbers and alphabetical codes (other than [B]) are assigned by the Children's Literature Team of the Library's History and Literature Cataloging Division.

A. Easy books

1. Easy fiction, in English or in a foreign language, intended for children through grade 2 or age 8 is assigned [E].

2. Alphabet books with or without a topical orientation and counting books with or without a topical orientation are assigned [E].

B. Fiction, in English or in a foreign language, intended for children beyond grade 2 or age 8 and for young adults is assigned [Fic]. Adult fiction that has been deemed appropriate for young adults and children's literature that has a continuing adult audience may be assigned [Fic] as well as a class number, e.g., *Treasure Island* 823.8 [Fic].

C. Folk literature (tales, sagas, myths, legends, fairy tales, etc.) may be assigned [398.2]. Picture song books, which are primarily illustrated texts, may be assigned [782.42].

The Decimal Classification Division classifies most children's literature processed by the Children's Literature Team, and it sometimes adjusts or adds to the above notation. Works that are designated by [Fic] or [E] are normally sent on without further classification.

Copy Cataloging

In common with other cataloging units at the Library of Congress, the Decimal Classification Division is increasingly seeking processing efficiencies through the use of copy cataloging. The Division aims to capitalize on Dewey numbers already present in MARC bibliographic records that reach classifiers with the items being processed. While our aim remains the provision of standard, complete Dewey numbers that include segmentation marks, reliance on numbers supplied by others may result in numbers at variance with those that would be assigned under the Division's policies and procedures. By monitoring the copy cataloging process and through liaison with our cataloging/classifying partners, we hope to keep these instances to a minimum.

The copy cataloging procedures in place at the time of publication of Edition 21 follow. If a bibliographic record imported into the Library of Congress cataloging stream from an outside library source has a Dewey Decimal Classification number with a valid edition number in subfield 2, the Dewey number is copied into the USMARC 082 field (Dewey Decimal Classification number) and the second indicator (Source of call number) is set to 4 (Assigned by agency other than LC). The record is sent to the Decimal Classification Division for review if it is within the regular language and material scope of the Division; otherwise, it is distributed without Decimal Classification Division review. If the Division reviews the record, the second indicator in the 082 field is set to 0 (Assigned by LC) and the edition number in subfield 2 is verified. If the record is distributed without Decimal Classification review, the second indicator remains at 4 (Assigned by agency other than LC), and the first indicator (Type of edition) is left at the value in the original record.

The 21st edition of the Dewey Decimal Classification was designed by Lisa Hanifan of Albany, New York. Edition 21 was generated from an online database. Database design, technical support, and programming for this edition were provided by John Finni and Kurt Lanza from Inforonics, Inc. of Littleton, Massachusetts. Composition was done in Times Roman and Helvetica under the supervision of Inforonics, Inc. and Word Management, Inc. of Albany, New York. The book was printed and bound by Hamilton Printing Company of Rensselaer, New York.